McDougal Littell

THE LANGUAGE OF
LITERATURE

McDougal Littell

THE LANGUAGE OF
LITERATURE

Arthur N. Applebee

Andrea B. Bermúdez

Sheridan Blau

Rebekah Caplan

Franchelle Dorn

Peter Elbow

Susan Hynds

Judith A. Langer

James Marshall

McDougal Littell
A HOUGHTON MIFFLIN COMPANY

Evanston, Illinois ▪ Boston ▪ Dallas

Acknowledgments

Unit One

Susan Bergholz Literary Services: "Three Wise Guys" by Sandra Cisneros; Copyright © 1990 by Sandra Cisneros. First published by *Vista Magazine*, December 23, 1990. By permission of Susan Bergholz Literary Services, New York.

Miriam Altshuler: "The Treasure of Lemon Brown" by Walter Dean Myers, from *Boys' Life Magazine,* March 1983; Copyright © 1983 by Walter Dean Myers. By permission of Miriam Altshuler Literary Agency on behalf of Walter Dean Myers.

Delacorte Press/Seymour Lawrence: "The Lie," from *Welcome to the Monkey House* by Kurt Vonnegut, Jr.; Copyright © 1962 by Kurt Vonnegut, Jr. By permission of Delacorte Press/Seymour Lawrence, a division of Bantam Doubleday Dell Publishing Group, Inc.

Doubleday Books: "Country Boys," from *Reflections on the Civil War* by Bruce Catton; Copyright © 1981 by Gerald Dickler as the executor of the estate of Bruce Catton and John Leckley. By permission of Doubleday Books, a division of Bantam Doubleday Dell Publishing Group, Inc.

Elizabeth Barnett, literary executor: "Dirge Without Music" from *Collected Poems,* by Edna St. Vincent Millay, published by HarperCollins. Copyright 1928, 1955 by Edna St. Vincent Millay and Norma Millay Ellis. By permission of Elizabeth Barnett, literary executor.

Continued on page 918

Cover Art

Background photo: Atlanta skyline, Copyright © Phyllis Picadi / Uniphoto Stock Agency. **Village scene:** *Old Houses in Lindau* (1928), Rudolf Wacker. Statliche Kunstsammulunger, Dresden, Germany, Photo © Erick Lessing / Art Resource, New York. **Soldier:** Reproduced from the Collections of the Library of Congress. **Bugle:** Courtesy Steve and Patricia Mullinaz Collection; Photo by J. Stoll. **Horse:** *Whistlejacket* (1762), George Stubbs. Kenwood House, Hampstead, London / Bridgeman Art Library, London / Superstock. **Book:** Photo by Alan Shortall. **Frame:** Photo by Sharon Hoogstraten.

ISBN 0-395-73703-6

6 7 8 9 – RRD – 01 00 99 98

Senior Consultants

The senior consultants guided the conceptual development for *The Language of Literature* series. They participated actively in shaping prototype materials for major components, and they reviewed completed prototypes and/or completed units to ensure consistency with current research and the philosophy of the series.

Arthur N. Applebee Professor of Education, State University of New York at Albany; Director, Center for the Learning and Teaching of Literature; Senior Fellow, Center for Writing and Literacy

Andrea B. Bermúdez Professor of Studies in Language and Culture; Director, Research Center for Language and Culture; Chair, Foundations and Professional Studies, University of Houston-Clear Lake

Sheridan Blau Senior Lecturer in English and Education and former Director of Composition, University of California at Santa Barbara; Director, South Coast Writing Project; Director, Literature Institute for Teachers; Vice President, National Council of Teachers of English

Rebekah Caplan Coordinator, English Language Arts K-12, Oakland Unified School District, Oakland, California; Teacher-Consultant, Bay Area Writing Project, University of California at Berkeley; served on the California State English Assessment Development Team for Language Arts

Franchelle Dorn Professor of Drama, Howard University, Washington, D.C.; Adjunct Professor, Graduate School of Opera, University of Maryland, College Park, Maryland; Co-founder of The Shakespeare Acting Conservatory, Washington, D.C.

Peter Elbow Professor of English, University of Massachusetts at Amherst; Fellow, Bard Center for Writing and Thinking

Susan Hynds Professor and Director of English Education, Syracuse University, Syracuse, New York

Judith A. Langer Professor of Education, State University of New York at Albany; Co-director, Center for the Learning and Teaching of Literature; Senior Fellow, Center for Writing and Literacy

James Marshall Professor of English and English Education, University of Iowa, Iowa City

Contributing Consultants

Tommy Boley Associate Professor of English, University of Texas at El Paso

Jeffrey N. Golub Assistant Professor of English Education, University of South Florida, Tampa

William L. McBride Reading and Curriculum Specialist; former middle and high school English instructor

Multicultural Advisory Board

The multicultural advisors reviewed literature selections for appropriate content and made suggestions for teaching lessons in a multicultural classroom.

Dr. Joyce M. Bell, Chairperson, English Department, Townview Magnet Center, Dallas, Texas

Dr. Eugenia W. Collier, author; lecturer; Chairperson, Department of English and Language Arts; teacher of Creative Writing and American Literature, Morgan State University, Maryland

Kathleen S. Fowler, President, Palm Beach County Council of Teachers of English, Boca Raton Middle School, Boca Raton, Florida

Noreen M. Rodriguez, Trainer for Hillsborough County School District's Staff Development Division, independent consultant, Gaither High School, Tampa, Florida

Michelle Dixon Thompson, Seabreeze High School, Daytona Beach, Florida

Teacher Review Panels

The following educators provided ongoing review during the development of the tables of contents, lesson design, and key components of the program.

CALIFORNIA
Steve Bass, 8th Grade Team Leader, Meadowbrook Middle School, Ponway Unified School District

Cynthia Brickey, 8th Grade Academic Block Teacher, Kastner Intermediate School, Clovis Unified School District

Karen Buxton, English Department Chairperson, Winston Churchill Middle School, San Juan School District

continued on page 928

Manuscript Reviewers

The following educators reviewed prototype lessons and tables of contents during the development of *The Language of Literature* program.

William A. Battaglia, Herman Intermediate School, San Jose, California

Hugh Delle Broadway, McCullough High School, The Woodlands, Texas

Robert M. Bucan, National Mine Middle School, Ishpeming, Michigan

Ann E. Clayton, Department Chair for Language Arts, Rockway Middle School, Miami, Florida

Linda C. Dahl, National Mine Middle School, Ishpeming, Michigan

Shirley Herzog, Reading Department Coordinator, Fairfield Middle School, Fairfield, Ohio

continued on page 929

Student Board

The student board members read and evaluated selections to assess their appeal for eighth-grade students.

Iruma Bello, Henry H. Filer Middle School, Hialeah, Florida

Leslie M. Blaha, Walnut Springs Middle School, Westerville, Ohio

Osvelia Cantoran, Chester W. Nimitz Middle School, Huntington Park, California

Elizabeth Donaldson, Bettendorf Middle School, Bettendorf, Iowa

Patricia Ernst, East Aurora Middle School, East Aurora, New York

Theresa Ernst, East Aurora Middle School, East Aurora, New York

Aaron Fitzstephens, Fairfield Middle School, Fairfield, Ohio

Stephen Tremayne Johnson, Lincoln College Prep School, Kansas City, Missouri

John Paul Marshall, RAA Middle School, Tallahassee, Florida

Meghan McGuire, St. John of the Cross School, Western Springs, Illinois

Jaret Heath Radford, Fondren Middle School, Houston, Texas

Erick Strauss, Cobb Middle School, Tallahassee, Florida

Christine Warner, Keith Valley Middle School, Horsham, Pennsylvania

THE LANGUAGE OF LITERATURE
Overview

Literature Connections

Each book in the Literature Connections series combines a novel or play with related readings—poems, stories, plays, essays, articles—that provide new perspectives on the theme or subject matter of the longer work. For example, Jack London's *The Call of the Wild* is combined with the following readings, which focus on such topics as dog behavior, relationships between humans and animals, and animal survival.

Marie de France	**The Wolf and the Dog**
Elizabeth Marshall Thomas	*from* **The Hidden Life of Dogs**
A. G. Rochelle	**The Wolf Said to Francis**
Julius Lester	**The Man Who Was a Horse**
Sally Carrighar	**Unsentimental Mother**
Robert Murphy	**Long Duel**

*A Spanish version is also available.
†SourceBook only.

Part 2   Fooled by Appearances

WRITING FROM EXPERIENCE   **Firsthand and Expressive Writing**

ACROSS TIME AND PLACE: The Oral Tradition

For more stories related to the unit theme,
see page 700.

Part 1 Twinges of Conscience

WRITING ABOUT LITERATURE   Interpretation

Part 2 Unexpected Developments

WRITING FROM EXPERIENCE **Narrative and Literary Writing**

Guided Assignment: Write a Short Story 272
Prewriting: Working Out Your Ideas
Drafting: Telling the Story
Revising and Publishing: Polishing Your Story
SKILLBUILDERS: Ordering Events, Planning the Climax, Using Precise Verbs

ACROSS TIME AND PLACE: The Oral Tradition

For more stories related to the unit theme, see page 716.

Part 1 Struggling for Survival

Part 2 Going to Extremes

WHAT DO YOU THINK? Reflecting on Theme   368

✏️ WRITING FROM EXPERIENCE | Informative Exposition |

Guided Assignment: Write a Problem-Solution Essay 412
Prewriting: Exploring Solutions
Drafting: Writing Your Ideas
Revising and Publishing: Finishing Your Essay
   SKILLBUILDERS: Conducting Group Discussions,
                  Elaborating on Ideas, Using Direct Objects

UNIT REVIEW: REFLECT & ASSESS 420

ACROSS TIME AND PLACE: The Oral Tradition

For more stories related to the unit theme,
see page 732.

Part 1 So Much at Stake

WRITING ABOUT LITERATURE   **Direct Response**

Part 2 Unlikely Heroes

WRITING FROM EXPERIENCE   **Informative Exposition**

ACROSS TIME AND PLACE: The Oral Tradition

For more stories related to the unit theme,
see page 760.

Part 1 Finding Your Place

Part 2 Vital Connections

WRITING FROM EXPERIENCE   Persuasion

Guided Assignment: Write a Persuasive Essay 684
Prewriting: Building Your Case
Drafting: Making Your Point
Revising and Publishing: Finishing Your Essay
SKILLBUILDERS: Evaluating Sources, Avoiding Loaded Language, Avoiding Double Negatives

ACROSS TIME AND PLACE: The Oral Tradition

For more stories related to the unit theme, see page 784.

WRITING ABOUT LITERATURE | **Creative Response**

WRITING FROM EXPERIENCE | **Report**

Guided Assignment: Write a Research Report 798
Prewriting: Researching Folklore
Drafting: Reporting the Facts
Revising and Publishing: Finishing Your Report
SKILLBUILDERS: Taking Notes, Crediting Sources, Capitalizing Titles
of Created Works

UNIT REVIEW: REFLECT AND ASSESS 806

Selections by Genre, Writing Workshops

The Oral Tradition
Myths, Legends, Folk Tales, and Fables

Writing About Literature

Writing From Experience

Reading the World: Visual Literacy

Möbius II, M. C. Escher. Copyright © M. C. Escher/Cordon Art, Baarn, Holland,
all rights reserved.

Where Are They Going?

Nine ants are busily walking along this oddly shaped figure. How many ants are on each side? Before you try to answer that question, look at the activity below.

LOOK AGAIN

A German mathematician discovered the figure at the left during the 1800s. The Möbius strip can turn your thoughts inside out.

1. Make your own Möbius strip. Cut out a rectangular strip of paper about 17 inches long and 1 inch wide. How many sides does the strip of paper have?

2. Turn over one end of the strip, twisting it 180 degrees, and join the ends with a staple or tape.

3. Examine your strip. Now how many sides do you think it has?

4. Draw a line down the middle of the strip. Stop when you've made a continuous line running all the way around your Möbius strip. What have you learned?

5. What happens when you cut the Möbius strip in two along the line that you have drawn? What do these exercises tell you about the Möbius strip? Do you know anything you didn't know before?

6. Tell your friends how many sides the Möbius strip has and explain why you think this is the right number.

CONNECT TO LITERATURE

Did your examination of the Möbius strip confirm your expectation, or did you discover something new? Like a Möbius strip, literature can have many twists and turns that surprise and challenge you. The next pages will show you how to follow literature's lead to eye-opening destinations.

Where Can Literature Take You?

Everyday life can sometimes be routine. When you enter the world of literature, put your expectations aside. Literature can turn you inside out, flip you upside down, and zip you around the world. Are you ready to go?

ON A FAR JOURNEY

Reading is like entering a kind of cosmic internet—you can move backward and forward in time and worlds away in space. With a little help from your imagination, you can experience almost anything. The **literature selections** in this book will take you to a planet in the future, to the United States during World War II, and to the English countryside with a veterinarian. So get ready! The journey is about to begin.

INTO YOURSELF

Thinking about what you read casts a spotlight on your own personality. Most selections in this book begin with a **Previewing** page. This page taps into what you already know about a subject and gives you background information. For example, on page 149 you'll explore the subject of extended families before reading "The Horned Toad," a story about a boy learning how to understand his family. The **Responding** pages help you develop your ideas after you've read a selection. For a look at some responding activities, see page 159.

Literature opens many doorways, introducing you to new people and other ways of life. The **Writing About Literature** workshops help you share your discoveries. For example, in the workshop on page 490 you'll explore the special message one story brings to you. The **Writing from Experience** workshops help you connect unit themes to your life. In Unit Three for example, you will see how some people triumph over their problems. In the workshop on page 412, you will write an essay tackling a problem important to you.

TOWARD A NEW OUTLOOK

As you read literature, you may find yourself questioning things you have never questioned before, which can lead you to see the world and yourself in a new way. As you will see in the **Reading the World** features, the knowledge you gain while studying literature can help you develop a better understanding of the world you live in. For example, the lesson on page 80 helps you see why an event, idea, or object can be interpreted in many different ways.

How Do You Get There from Here?

Your pencils are sharp and so is your mind. You are almost ready to enter the world of literature. In this world your unique personality can help you find rewards that are all your own.

MULTIPLE PATHWAYS

Do you learn better when working alone or with a friend? Do your strengths lie in writing, speaking, acting, or art? This book contains a wide variety of learning options. You can choose the activities that suit you best. In addition, you will be given opportunities to collaborate with classmates to share ideas, improve your writing, and make connections to other subject areas. Perhaps you will use technological tools such as the LaserLinks and the Writing Coach software program to further customize your learning.

PORTFOLIO

Artists, photographers, designers, and writers often keep samples of their work in a portfolio that they show to others. This year you also will be collecting samples of your work in a portfolio—writing samples, records of activities, artwork. You probably won't put all your work in your portfolio, just carefully chosen pieces. Discuss with your teacher portfolio options for this year. Suggestions for using your portfolio occur throughout this book.

Notebook

"Three Wise Guys: Un Cuento de Navidad/ A Christmas Tale" by Sandra Cisneros

I know all about waiting for Dia de los Reyes! When I was younger, I used to get jealous because my friends got to open their presents on Christmas Day. Some of them even got to open theirs on Christmas Eve! For the whole week before Christmas, I would beg Mama to let me open my presents on Christmas Day. But she never gave in.

understood, I ... was Clifford Slick again with pe... ink dribbling from his mouth. He wasn't imitating ... time. He was putting on another of his stupid comic rou- tines, disturbing students who were trying to work. I rushed back to Clifford to get him out of my classroom before he completely ruined the lesson. However, when I grabbed his hair to propel him down to the office, my fin- gers slid through the greasiest slime.

Teachers always send bad students to the office. It's just the normal thing to do. When you think about it, though, you have to ask yourself what happens to a kid in the office. Sure, they probably get yelled at or made to stay

NOTEBOOK

Choose any type of notebook and dedicate it to your study of literature. Divide the notebook into three sections. Use the first section to jot down ideas, describe personal experiences, take notes, and express your thoughts before, while, and after you read a selection. Also include any charts, diagrams, and drawings that help you connect your reading to your life. The second section is for your reading log, which is described below. Use the third section as a writer's notebook to record ideas and inspira- tions that you might use later in your writing.

READING LOG

In your reading log you will record a special kind of response to literature—your direct comments as you read a selection. The reading strategies detailed at the right will help you think about what you read. Experiment with recording your own comments in your reading log as you read. Specific opportunities to use your reading log appear throughout this book.

Reading Log

"Three Wise Guys: Un Cuento de Navidad/ A Christmas Tale" by Sandra Cisneros

The mother introduced in the first paragraph reminds me of my mother. I wonder if I'll be able to relate to the rest of the story so well.

Strategies for Reading

When you get involved in reading, literature will take you far. How can you get involved? Simply get into the habit of thinking about what you read. The strategies below describe some of the ways that active readers think as they read.

QUESTION

Question what's happening while you read. Searching for reasons behind events and charac- ters' feelings can help you feel more involved in what you're reading. Make notes about confus- ing words or statements, but don't worry if you don't understand everything. As you read further, you will probably begin to see things more clearly.

CONNECT

Connect personally with what you're reading. Think of similarities between the descriptions in the selection and what you have personally experienced, heard about, or read about.

PREDICT

Try to figure out what will happen next and how the selection might end. Then read on to see if you made good guesses.

CLARIFY

Stop occasionally to review what you understand so far, and expect to have your understanding change and develop as you read on. Also, watch for answers to questions you had earlier.

EVALUATE

Form opinions about what you read, both while you're reading and after you've finished. Try to visualize characters and develop your ideas about events.

Now turn the page to see how two student readers put these strategies to work.

Alongside "Three Wise Guys: *Un Cuento de Navidad /* A Christmas Story" are comments made by Philip Colas and Lindsay Iversen, two eighth-grade students, as they read the story for the first time. Their comments show how different readers made use of active reading strategies while reading this story. (A label after each comment identifies the strategy the comment reflects.) To benefit most from the students' comments, read the story first, using the strategies of active reading yourself. Then review Philip's and Lindsay's comments, comparing their responses with your own.

three wise guys

UN CUENTO DE NAVIDAD ❦ A CHRISTMAS TALE

BY SANDRA CISNEROS

Three Kings (about 1950), unknown Puerto Rican artist. Museum of New Mexico Collections, Museum of International Folk Art, Santa Fe. Photo by Blair Clark.

The big box came marked DO NOT OPEN TILL XMAS, but the mama said not until the Day of the Three Kings. Not until *Día de los Reyes,* the 6th of January, do you hear. That is what the mama said exactly, only she said it all in Spanish. Because in Mexico where she was raised it is the custom for boys and girls to receive their presents on January 6th, and not Christmas, even though they were living on the Texas side of the river now. Not until the 6th of January.

Yesterday the mama had risen in the dark same as always to reheat the coffee in a tin saucepan and warm the breakfast tortillas. The papa had gotten up coughing and spitting up the night, complaining how the evening before the buzzing of the *chicharras* had kept him from sleeping. By the time the mama had the house smelling of oatmeal and cinnamon the papa would be gone to the fields, the sun already tangled in the trees and the urracas screeching their rubber-screech cry. The boy Rubén and the girl Rosalinda would have to be shaken awake for school. The mama would give the baby Gilberto his bottle, and then she would go back to sleep before getting up again to the chores that were always waiting. That is how the world had been.

But today the big box had arrived. When the boy Rubén and the girl Rosalinda came home from school, it was already sitting in the living room in front of the television set that no longer worked. Who had put it there? Where had it come from? A box covered with red paper with green Christmas trees and a card on top that said: Merry Christmas to the González Family. Frank, Earl, and Dwight Travis. P.S. DO NOT OPEN TILL XMAS. That's all.

Two times the mama was made to come into the living room, first to explain to the children and later to their father how the brothers Travis had arrived in the blue pickup, and how it had taken all three of those big men to lift the box off the back of the truck and bring it inside, and how she had had to nod and say thank-you thank-you thank-you over and over because those were the only words she knew in English. Then the brothers Travis had nodded as well the way they always did when they came and brought the boxes of clothes, or the turkey each November, or the canned ham on Easter ever since the children had begun to earn high grades at the school where Dwight Travis was the principal.

But this year the Christmas box was bigger than usual. What could be in a box so big? The boy Rubén and the girl Rosalinda begged all afternoon to be allowed to open it, and that is when the

Philip: This story reminds me of a story I heard in storytelling club.
CONNECTING

Lindsay: The mama seems like a 1950s housewife.
EVALUATING

Lindsay: Why did they keep a TV set that didn't work?
QUESTIONING

Philip: The suspense is building: "Don't open till Christmas." I wonder what's going to be in the box.
QUESTIONING, PREDICTING

Lindsay: Maybe it's a box full of food.
PREDICTING

mama had said the 6th of January, the Day of the Three Kings. Not a day sooner.

It seemed the weeks stretched themselves wider and wider since the arrival of the big box. The mama got used to sweeping around it because it was too heavy for her to push into a corner, but since the television no longer worked ever since the afternoon the children had poured iced tea through the little grates in the back, it really didn't matter if it obstructed the view. Visitors who came inside the house were told and told again the story of how the box had arrived, and then each was made to guess what was inside.

It was the *comadre* Elodia who suggested over coffee one afternoon that the big box held a portable washing machine that could be rolled away when not in use, the kind she had seen in her Sears Roebuck catalogue. The mama said she hoped so because the wringer washer she had used for the last ten years had finally gotten tired and quit. These past few weeks she had had to boil all the clothes in the big pot she used for cooking the Christmas tamales. Yes. She hoped the big box was a portable washing machine. A washing machine, even a portable one, would be good.

But the neighbor man Cayetano said, What foolishness, *comadre*. Can't you see the box is too small to hold a washing machine, even a portable one? Most likely God has heard your prayers and sent a new color TV. With a good antenna you could catch all the Mexican soap operas, the neighbor man said. You could distract yourself with the complicated troubles of the rich and then give thanks to God for the blessed simplicity of your poverty. A new TV would surely be the end to all your miseries.

Each night when the papa came home from the fields he would spread newspapers on the cot in the living room where the boy Rubén and the girl Rosalinda slept, and sit facing the big box in the center of the room. Each night he imagined the box held something different. The day before yesterday he guessed a new record player. Yesterday an ice chest filled with beer. Today the papa sat with his bottle of beer, fanning himself with a magazine, and said in a voice as much a plea as a prophecy: air conditioner.

But the boy Rubén and the girl Rosalinda were sure the big box was filled with toys. They had even punctured a hole in one corner with a pencil when their mother was busy cooking, although they could see nothing inside but blackness.

Only the baby Gilberto remained uninterested in the contents of the big box and seemed each day more fascinated with the exterior of the box rather than the interior. One afternoon he tore off a fistful of paper which he was chewing when his mother swooped him up with one arm, rushed him to the kitchen sink, and forced him to swallow handfuls of lukewarm water in case the red dye of the wrapping paper might be poisonous.

When Christmas Eve finally came, the family González put on their good clothes and went to midnight mass. They came home to a house that smelled of tamales and atole, and everyone was allowed to open one present before going to sleep, but the big box was to remain untouched until the 6th of January.

On New Year's Eve the little house was filled with people, some related, some not, coming in and out. The friends of the papa came with bottles, and the mama set out a bowl of grapes to count off the New Year. That night the children did not sleep on the living room cot as they usually did because the living room was crowded with big-fannied ladies and fat-stomached men sashaying to the accordion music of the midget twins from McAllen. Instead, the children fell asleep on a lump of handbags and crumpled suit jackets on top of the mama and the papa's bed, dreaming of the contents of the big box.

Lindsay: What do grapes have to do with the new year?
QUESTIONING

Finally the 5th of January. And the boy Rubén and the girl Rosalinda could hardly sleep. All night they whispered last-minute wishes. The boy thought perhaps if the big box held a bicycle, he would be the first to ride it since he was the oldest. This made his sister cry until the mama had to yell from her bedroom on the other side of the plastic curtains, Be quiet or I'm going to give you each the stick, which sounds worse in Spanish than it does in English. Then no one said anything. After a very long time, long after they heard the mama's wheezed breathing and the papa's piped snoring, the children closed their eyes and remembered nothing.

Philip: That's like my family. If your little sister wants something and starts crying, your parents get mad—I know how the boy is feeling.
CONNECTING

The papa was already in the bathroom coughing up the night before from his throat when the *urracas* began their clownish chirping. The boy Rubén awoke and shook his sister. The mama frying the potatoes and beans for breakfast nodded permission for the box to be opened.

Lindsay: The father is coughing again. Is he sick?
QUESTIONING

With a kitchen knife the boy Rubén cut a careful edge along the top. The girl Rosalinda tore the Christmas wrapping with her fingernails. The papa and the mama lifted the cardboard flaps, and everyone peered inside to see what it was the brothers Travis had brought them on the Day of the Three Kings.

There were layers of balled newspaper packed on top. When these had been cleared away, the boy Rubén looked inside. The

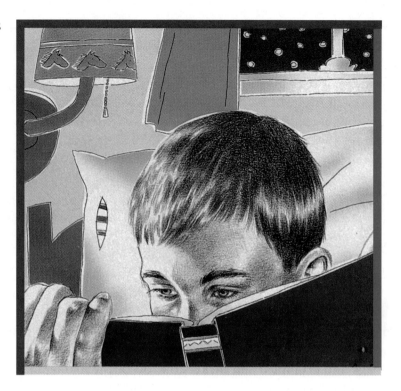

Philip: *Strange that it's* Encyclo-paedia Britannica. *I thought it would be something they wanted. Now everyone's disappointed.*
EVALUATING, CLARIFYING

Lindsay: *A set of encyclopedias isn't a good gift for a family who can't speak English.*
EVALUATING

Lindsay: *They're not going to read the encyclopedias. They're going to sit on them!*
CLARIFYING, EVALUATING

girl Rosalinda looked inside. The papa and the mama looked.

This is what they saw: the complete Encyclopaedia Britannica Junior, 24 volumes in red imitation leather with gold-embossed letters beginning with Volume I, Aar-Bel, and ending with Volume XXIV, Yel-Zyn. The girl Rosalinda let out a sad cry as if her hair was going to be cut again. The boy Rubén pulled out Volume IV, Ded-Fem. There were many pictures and many words, but there were more words than pictures. The papa flipped through Volume XXII, but because he could not read English words, simply put the book back and grunted, What can we do with this? No one said anything, and shortly after, the screen door slammed.

Only the mama knew what to do with the contents of the big box. She withdrew Volumes VI, VII, and VIII, marched off to the dinette set in the kitchen, placed two on Rosalinda's chair so she could better reach the table and put one underneath the plant stand that danced.

When the boy and the girl returned from school that day, they found the books stacked into squat pillars against one living room wall and a board placed on top. On this were arranged several plastic doilies and framed family photographs. The rest of the volumes the baby Gilberto was playing with, and he was already rubbing his sore gums along the corners of Volume XIV.

The girl Rosalinda also grew interested in the books. She took out her colored pencils and painted blue on the eyelids of all the illustrations of women, and with a red pencil dipped in spit she painted their lips and fingernails red-red. After a couple of days when all the pictures of women had been colored in this manner, she began to cut out some of the prettier pictures and paste them on loose-leaf paper.

One volume suffered from being exposed to the rain when the papa improvised a hat during a sudden shower. He forgot it on the hood of the car when he drove off. When the children came home from school, they set it on the porch to dry. But the pages puffed up and became so fat, the book was impossible to close.

Only the boy Rubén refused to touch the books. For several days he avoided the principal because he didn't know what to say in case Mr. Travis were to ask how they were enjoying the Christmas present.

On the Saturday after New Year's the mama and the papa went into town for groceries and left the boy in charge of watching his sister and baby brother. The girl Rosalinda was stacking books into spiral staircases and making her paper dolls descend them in a fancy manner.

Perhaps the boy Rubén would not have bothered to open the volume left on the kitchen table if he had not seen his mother wedge her name-day corsage in its pages. On the page where the mama's carnation lay pressed between two pieces of Kleenex was a picture of a dog in a spaceship. FIRST DOG IN SPACE the caption said. The boy turned to another page and read where cashews came from. And then about the man who invented the guillotine. And then about Bengal tigers. And about clouds. All afternoon the boy read, even after the mama and the papa came home. Even after the sun set, until the mama said time to sleep, and put the light out.

In their bed on the other side of the plastic curtain the mama and the papa slept. Across from them in the crib slept the baby Gilberto. The girl Rosalinda slept on her end of the cot. But the boy Rubén watched the night sky turn from violet. To blue. To grey. And then from grey. To blue. To violet once again. ❖

Philip: They think they have no use for the books. Mother is using them like a household utensil. They really don't know what to do with them and really don't care for them.
CLARIFYING

Philip: They cared for books so little that they left one on top of the car when it was raining, and now it's so wet they can't even close it.
CLARIFYING, EVALUATING

Philip: The boy is starting to show interest in reading the book, and he's learning things too.
CLARIFYING

Lindsay: I guess at least the boy will use the encyclopedias.
EVALUATING, PREDICTING

Changing Perceptions

Things don't pass for what they are, but for what they seem. Most things are judged by their jackets.

Baltasar Gracián
17th-century Spanish writer

TAUGHT BY EXPERIENCE

WHAT DO Y?u THINK?

REFLECTING ON THEME

Has someone or something ever caused you to change completely the way you view things? Use the activities on this page to begin exploring ways in which experience can be one of the greatest teachers. Keep a record of your impressions, ideas, or results. Later you can compare them with the lessons the characters in this unit learn.

Whom would you picture?

Think of people who have caused you to change your attitudes and your perception of the world. They could be people you know or people whom you admire, such as writers or world leaders. Create a collage of photos or drawings featuring these people. Be sure to identify the people in the collage.

Were you surprised?

Have you ever learned something about a person that surprised you and caused you to revise completely your opinion of that individual? Write a letter addressed to that person, telling her or him what surprised you.

How would you handle this?

Imagine you really want to spend the night at a friend's house. The friend's parents are away, and so your parents say no. What would you say? Role-play the situation with a partner. After a few minutes, switch roles and continue the role play. Discuss whether the role play gave you a better understanding of the other side of the argument.

Who knows you?

Do people really know what you're about? As a class, play hangman or a game of charades in which you reveal a skill or an interest people may not know you have.

FOCUS ON FICTION

A story is a work of fiction. **Fiction** is writing that comes from an author's imagination—whether the author made the whole idea up or based it on real events.

Depending on its length, a work of fiction may be classified as a short story or as a novel. A **short story** usually revolves around a single idea and is short enough to be read at one sitting. The fiction selections that you will read in this book are short stories. A **novel** is much longer and more complex.

Fiction writing contains four main elements: **character, setting, plot,** and **theme.**

CHARACTER Characters are the people, animals, or imaginary creatures that take part in the action of a story. Usually, a short story centers on events in the life of one person, animal, or creature. This is the story's **main character.**

Generally, there are also one or more **minor characters** in the story. Minor characters interact with the main character and with one another, sometimes providing part of the background for the story. Their words and actions help to move the plot along.

SETTING A story's setting is the time and place in which the action of the story happens. The time may be in the past, the present, or the future; in daytime or in the night; at any season. The story may be set in a small town or a large city, in outer space, in a desert, or in an empty room.

PLOT The sequence of events in a story is called the story's plot. The plot is the writer's plan for what happens, when it happens, and to whom it happens. One event causes another, which causes another, and so on until the end of the story.

Generally, a plot is built around a **conflict**—a problem or struggle involving two or more opposing forces. A conflict can be as serious as a boy's attempt to cope with a lie he told or as frivolous as a boy's game of marbles with aliens.

Although the development of each plot is different, traditional works of fiction generally follow a pattern that includes the following stages:

Exposition Exposition sets the stage for a story. Characters are introduced, the setting is described, and the conflict begins to unfold.

Complications As the story continues, the plot becomes more complex. While the characters struggle to find solutions to the conflict, suspense and a feeling of excitement and energy build.

Climax The climax is the point of greatest interest or suspense in the story. It is the turning point, when the action reaches a peak and the outcome of the conflict is decided. The climax may occur because of a decision the characters reach or because of a discovery or an event that changes the situation. The climax usually results in a change in the characters or a solution to the conflict.

Resolution The resolution occurs at the conclusion of the story. Loose ends are tied up, and the story comes to a close.

THEME The theme of a story is the main message the writer conveys to the reader. This message might be a lesson about life or a belief about people and their actions. In most cases, the theme is not stated directly; it is like a hidden message that the reader must decode. As you discuss literature, however, you will find that different readers can discover different themes in the same story. The following suggestions will help you unlock a theme:

- Review what happened to the main character. Did he or she change during the story? What did he or she learn about life?

- Skim the story for key phrases and sentences—statements that go beyond the action of the story to say something important about life or people.

- Think about the story's title. Does it have a special meaning that could lead you to the main idea of the work?

STRATEGIES FOR READING FICTION

To really "get inside" a story, try the following strategies:

- **Preview the story.** Before you read, look at the title and the pictures. Perhaps even skim through the pages and read some words here and there.

- **Visualize the setting and the characters.** Can you picture a similar place in your mind? Can you "see" the action and the characters?

- **Make connections.** Do any of the characters have thoughts or experiences that you have had? Does any character remind you of someone you know? Does the story remind you of an event you've heard of or read about?

- **Question as you read.** Ask questions about the events, characters, and ideas in the story. "Why isn't she able to tell the truth?" "Why is he so angry?" Asking good questions is at the heart of good reading.

- **Make predictions.** During your reading, stop occasionally to predict what might happen next and how the story will end.

- **Clarify your understanding.** As you read, build on what you learn about the characters and events in the story, and let your thoughts change and grow as you learn more.

- **Evaluate the story.** Think about your feelings about the characters and their actions. Also consider how well the author is telling his or her story.

- **Discuss the story.** When you have finished reading, talk about the story with someone else.

Remember, a story never tells you everything; it leaves room for your own ideas. After you read a story, you are left with first impressions, but you need to be able to elaborate and explain them on the basis of the story itself, your own experiences, and other stories you have read.

FICTION

The Treasure of Lemon Brown
Walter Dean Myers

PERSONAL CONNECTION

"Every man got a treasure," claims Lemon Brown in the story you are about to read. With your classmates, discuss what kinds of things people treasure. Then, in a chart like the one shown, list five of your treasures and have a parent or another adult list five of his or hers. In the third column, write ways in which your treasures and the other person's are similar or different.

My Treasures	Other Person's Treasures	Ways They Are Similar or Different

SOCIAL STUDIES CONNECTION

This story deals with the treasure of a character named Lemon Brown—a homeless person living in an abandoned, decaying tenement in New York City. Tenements are buildings designed to house low-income families in small, usually poorly maintained apartments.

Today, many homeless people like Lemon Brown live in abandoned tenements. Others live on the streets or in emergency shelters. Estimates of the number of homeless people in the United States range from 250,000 to 3,000,000. With few possessions to their name, what do you suppose homeless people might keep and treasure?

READING CONNECTION

Appreciating Dialogue One way writers help readers get to know characters is through dialogue, or conversation between two or more characters. When Lemon Brown says, "You ain't one of them bad boys looking for my treasure, is you?" (page 21), we learn that he is suspicious and not highly educated. As you read, notice what other things Lemon Brown's words reveal about his personality and about what he treasures.

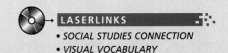

The Treasure of Lemon Brown

by Walter Dean Myers

Study of Williams (1976), Hubert Shuptrine. Copyright © 1976 Hubert Shuptrine.
All rights reserved, used with permission of the S. Hill Corporation.

The dark sky, filled with angry, swirling clouds, reflected Greg Ridley's mood as he sat on the stoop[1] of his building. His father's voice came to him again, first reading the letter the principal had sent to the house, then lecturing endlessly about his poor efforts in math.

"I had to leave school when I was thirteen," his father had said. "That's a year younger than you are now. If I'd had half the chances that you have, I'd . . ."

Greg had sat in the small, pale green kitchen listening, knowing the lecture would end with his father saying he couldn't play ball with the Scorpions. He had asked his father the week before, and his father had said it depended on his next report card. It wasn't often the Scorpions took on new players, especially 14-year-olds, and this was a chance of a lifetime for Greg. He hadn't been allowed to play high school ball, which he had really wanted to do, but playing for the community center team was the next best thing. Report cards were due in a week, and Greg had been hoping for the best. But the principal had ended the suspense early when she sent that letter saying Greg would probably fail math if he didn't spend more time studying.

"And you want to play *basketball?*" His father's brows knitted over deep brown eyes. "That must be some kind of a joke. Now you just get into your room and hit those books."

That had been two nights before. His father's words, like the distant thunder that now echoed through the streets of Harlem,[2] still rumbled softly in his ears.

It was beginning to cool. Gusts of wind made bits of paper dance between the parked cars. There was a flash of nearby lightning, and soon large drops of rain splashed onto his jeans. He stood to go upstairs, thought of the lecture that probably awaited him if he did anything except shut himself in his room with his math book, and started walking down the street instead. Down the block there was an old tenement that had been abandoned for some months. Some of the guys had held an impromptu checker tournament there the week before, and Greg had noticed that the door, once boarded over, had been slightly ajar.

Pulling his collar up as high as he could, he checked for traffic and made a dash across the street. He reached the house just as another flash of lightning changed the night to day for an instant, then returned the graffiti-scarred building to the grim shadows. He vaulted over the outer stairs and pushed tentatively on the door. It was open, and he let himself in.

The inside of the building was dark except for the dim light that filtered through the dirty windows from the street lamps. There was a room a few feet from the door, and from where he stood at the entrance, Greg could see a squarish patch of light on the floor. He entered the room, frowning at the musty smell. It was a large room that might have been someone's parlor at one time. Squinting, Greg could see an old table on its side against one wall, what looked like a pile of rags or a torn mattress in the corner, and a couch, with one side broken, in front of the window.

---

1. **stoop:** a small porch or staircase at the entrance of a building.
2. **Harlem:** a section of New York City; since about 1910, it has been one of the largest African-American communities in the United States.

WORDS TO KNOW

impromptu (ĭm-prŏmp'tōō) *adj.* done on the spur of the moment; unplanned
ajar (ə-jär') *adj.* partially open
vault (vôlt) *v.* to jump or leap
tentatively (tĕn'tə-tĭv-lē) *adv.* with uncertainty or hesitation

19

He went to the couch. The side that wasn't broken was comfortable enough, though a little creaky. From this spot he could see the blinking neon sign over the bodega[3] on the corner. He sat awhile, watching the sign blink first green, then red, allowing his mind to drift to the Scorpions, then to his father. His father had been a postal worker for all Greg's life and was proud of it, often telling Greg how hard he had worked to pass the test. Greg had heard the story too many times to be interested now.

For a moment Greg thought he heard something that sounded like a scraping against the wall. He listened carefully, but it was gone.

Outside, the wind had picked up, sending the rain against the window with a force that shook the glass in its frame. A car passed, its tires hissing over the wet street and its red taillights glowing in the darkness.

Greg thought he heard the noise again. His stomach tightened as he held himself still and listened intently. There weren't any more scraping noises, but he was sure he had heard something in the darkness—something breathing!

He tried to figure out just where the breathing was coming from; he knew it was in the room with him. Slowly he stood, tensing. As he turned, a flash of lightning lit up the room, frightening him with its sudden brilliance. He saw nothing, just the overturned table, the pile of rags, and an old newspaper on the floor. Could he have been imagining the sounds? He continued listening but heard nothing and thought that it might have just been rats. Still, he thought, as soon as the rain let up he would leave. He went to the window and was about to look out when he heard a voice behind him.

"Don't try nothin' 'cause I got a razor here sharp enough to cut a week into nine days!"

Greg, except for an involuntary tremor in his knees, stood stock-still. The voice was high and brittle, like dry twigs being broken, surely not one he had ever heard before. There was a shuffling sound as the person who had been speaking moved a step closer. Greg turned, holding his breath, his eyes straining to see in the dark room.

The upper part of the figure before him was still in darkness. The lower half was in the dim rectangle of light that fell unevenly from the window. There were two feet, in cracked, dirty shoes from which rose legs that were wrapped in rags.

"Don't try nothin' 'cause I got a razor here sharp enough to cut a week into nine days!"

"Who are you?" Greg hardly recognized his own voice.

"I'm Lemon Brown," came the answer. "Who're you?"

"Greg Ridley."

"What you doing here?" The figure shuffled forward again, and Greg took a small step backward.

"It's raining," Greg said.

"I can see that," the figure said.

The person who called himself Lemon Brown peered forward, and Greg could see him clearly. He was an old man. His black, heavily wrinkled face was surrounded by a halo of crinkly white hair and whiskers that seemed to separate his head from the layers of dirty coats piled on his smallish frame. His pants were bagged to the knee, where they were met with rags that went down to the old shoes. The rags were held on with strings, and

---

3. **bodega** (bō-dā′gə): a small grocery store.

there was a rope around his middle. Greg relaxed. He had seen the man before, picking through the trash on the corner and pulling clothes out of a Salvation Army box. There was no sign of the razor that could "cut a week into nine days."

"What are you doing here?" Greg asked.

"This is where I'm staying," Lemon Brown said. "What you here for?"

"Told you it was raining out," Greg said, leaning against the back of the couch until he felt it give slightly.

"Ain't you got no home?"

"I got a home," Greg answered.

"You ain't one of them bad boys looking for my treasure, is you?" Lemon Brown cocked his head to one side and squinted one eye. "Because I told you I got me a razor."

"I'm not looking for your treasure," Greg answered, smiling. "*If* you have one."

"What you mean, *if* I have one," Lemon Brown said. "Every man got a treasure. You don't know that, you must be a fool!"

"Sure," Greg said as he sat on the sofa and put one leg over the back. "What do you have, gold coins?"

"Don't worry none about what I got," Lemon Brown said. "You know who I am?"

"You told me your name was orange or lemon or something like that."

"Lemon Brown," the old man said, pulling back his shoulders as he did so. "They used to call me Sweet Lemon Brown."

"Sweet Lemon?" Greg asked.

"Yessir. Sweet Lemon Brown. They used to say I sung the blues so sweet that if I sang at a funeral, the dead would <u>commence</u> to rocking with the beat. Used to travel all over Mississippi and as far as Monroe, Louisiana, and east on over to Macon, Georgia. You mean you ain't never heard of Sweet Lemon Brown?"

"Afraid not," Greg said. "What . . . what happened to you?"

"Hard times, boy. Hard times always after a poor man. One day I got tired, sat down to rest a spell, and felt a tap on my shoulder. Hard times caught up with me."

"Sorry about that."

"What you doing here? How come you didn't go on home when the rain come? Rain don't bother you young folks none."

"Just didn't." Greg looked away.

"I used to have a knotty-headed boy just like you." Lemon Brown had half walked, half shuffled back to the corner and sat down against the wall. "Had them big eyes like you got. I used to call them moon eyes. Look into them moon eyes and see anything you want."

"How come you gave up singing the blues?" Greg asked.

"Didn't give it up," Lemon Brown said. "You don't give up the blues; they give you up. After a while you do good for yourself, and it ain't nothing but foolishness singing about how hard you got it. Ain't that right?"

"I guess so."

"What's that noise?" Lemon Brown asked, suddenly sitting upright.

Greg listened, and he heard a noise outside. He looked at Lemon Brown and saw the old man was pointing toward the window.

Greg went to the window and saw three men, neighborhood thugs, on the stoop. One was carrying a length of pipe. Greg looked back toward Lemon Brown, who moved quietly across the room to the window. The old man looked out, then beckoned frantically for Greg to follow him. For a moment Greg couldn't move. Then he found himself following Lemon Brown into the hallway and up darkened stairs. Greg followed as closely as he could. They reached the top of the stairs, and Greg felt Lemon Brown's hand, first lying on his shoulder, then probing down his arm until he finally took Greg's hand into his own as they crouched in the darkness.

"One day I got tired, sat down to rest a spell. . . . Hard times caught up with me."

"They's bad men," Lemon Brown whispered. His breath was warm against Greg's skin.

"Hey! Rag man!" a voice called. "We know you in here. What you got up under them rags? You got any money?"

Silence.

"We don't want to have to come in and hurt you, old man, but we don't mind if we have to."

Lemon Brown squeezed Greg's hand in his own hard, gnarled fist.

There was a banging downstairs and a light as the men entered. They banged around noisily, calling for the rag man.

"We heard you talking about your treasure." The voice was slurred. "We just want to see it, that's all."

"You sure he's here?" One voice seemed to come from the room with the sofa.

"Yeah, he stays here every night."

"There's another room over there; I'm going to take a look. You got that flashlight?"

"Yeah, here, take the pipe too."

Greg opened his mouth to quiet the sound of his breath as he sucked it in uneasily. A beam of light hit the wall a few feet opposite him, then went out.

"Ain't nobody in that room," a voice said. "You think he gone or something?"

"I don't know," came the answer. "All I know is that I heard him talking about some kind of treasure. You know they found that shopping-bag lady with that money in her bags."

"Yeah. You think he's upstairs?"

"HEY, OLD MAN, ARE YOU UP THERE?" Silence.

"Watch my back. I'm going up."

There was a footstep on the stairs, and the beam from the flashlight danced crazily along the peeling wallpaper. Greg held his breath. There was another step and a loud crashing noise as the man banged the pipe against the wooden banister. Greg could feel his temples throb as the man slowly neared them. Greg thought about the pipe, wondering what he would do when the man reached them—what he *could* do.

Then Lemon Brown released his hand and moved toward the top of the stairs. Greg looked around and saw stairs going up to the next floor. He tried waving to Lemon Brown, hoping the old man would see him in the dim light and follow him to the next floor. Maybe, Greg thought, the man wouldn't follow them up there. Suddenly, though, Lemon Brown stood at the top of the stairs, both arms raised high above his head.

"There he is!" a voice cried from below.

"Throw down your money, old man, so I won't have to bash your head in!"

Lemon Brown didn't move. Greg felt himself near panic. The steps came closer, and still Lemon Brown didn't move. He was an eerie sight, a bundle of rags standing at the top of the stairs, his shadow on the wall looming over him. Maybe, the thought came to Greg, the scene could be even eerier.

Greg wet his lips, put his hands to his mouth, and tried to make a sound. Nothing came out. He swallowed hard, wet his lips once more, and howled as evenly as he could.

"What's that?"

As Greg howled, the light moved away from Lemon Brown, but not before Greg saw him hurl his body down the stairs at the men who had come to take his treasure. There was a crashing noise and then footsteps. A rush of warm air came in as the downstairs door opened, then there was only an <u>ominous</u> silence.

Greg stood on the landing. He listened, and after a while there was another sound on the staircase.

"Mr. Brown?" he called.

"Yeah, it's me," came the answer. "I got their flashlight."

Greg exhaled in relief as Lemon Brown made his way slowly back up the stairs.

"You O.K.?"

"Few bumps and bruises," Lemon Brown said.

"I think I'd better be going," Greg said, his breath returning to normal. "You'd better leave, too, before they come back."

"They may hang around outside for a while," Lemon Brown said, "but they ain't getting their nerve up to come in here again. Not with crazy old rag men and howling spooks. Best you stay awhile till the coast is clear. I'm heading out west tomorrow, out to East St. Louis."[4]

"They were talking about treasures," Greg said. "You *really* have a treasure?"

"What I tell you? Didn't I tell you every

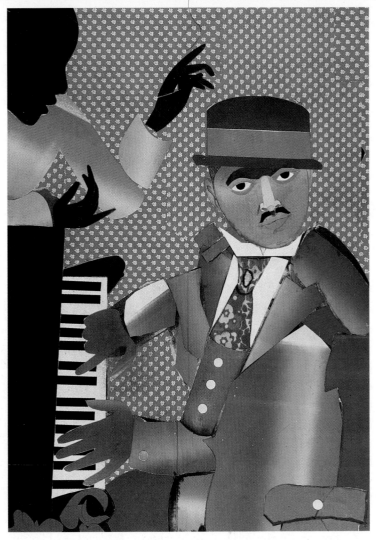

Sitting In at Baron's (1980), Romare Bearden. Courtesy of the Estate of Romare Bearden.

man got a treasure?" Lemon Brown said. "You want to see mine?"

"If you want to show it to me," Greg shrugged.

"Let's look out the window first, see what them scoundrels be doing," Lemon Brown said.

They followed the oval beam of the flashlight into one of the rooms and looked out the window. They saw the men who had tried to take the treasure sitting on the curb near the

---

4. **East St. Louis:** a city in southwestern Illinois, across the Mississippi River from St. Louis, Missouri.

corner. One of them had his pants leg up, looking at his knee.

"You sure you're not hurt?" Greg asked Lemon Brown.

"Nothing that ain't been hurt before," Lemon Brown said. "When you get as old as me, all you say when something hurts is 'Howdy, Mr. Pain, sees you back again.' Then when Mr. Pain see he can't worry you none, he go on mess with somebody else."

Greg smiled.

"Here, you hold this." Lemon Brown gave Greg the flashlight.

He sat on the floor near Greg and carefully untied the strings that held the rags on his right leg. When he took the rags away, Greg saw a piece of plastic. The old man carefully took off the plastic and unfolded it. He revealed some yellowed newspaper clippings and a battered harmonica.

"There it be," he said, nodding his head. "There it be."

Greg looked at the old man, saw the distant look in his eye, then turned to the clippings. They told of Sweet Lemon Brown, a blues singer and harmonica player who was appearing at different theaters in the South. One of the clippings said he had been the hit of the show, although not the headliner. All of the clippings were reviews of shows Lemon Brown had been in more than 50 years ago. Greg looked at the harmonica. It was dented badly on one side, with the reed holes on one end nearly closed.

"I used to travel around and make money for to feed my wife and Jesse—that's my boy's name. Used to feed them good, too. Then his mama died, and he stayed with his mama's sister. He growed up to be a man, and when the war come, he saw fit to go off and fight in it. I didn't have nothing to give him except these things that told him who I was and what he come from. If you know your pappy did something, you know you can do something too.

"Anyway, he went off to war, and I went off still playing and singing. 'Course by then I wasn't as much as I used to be, not without

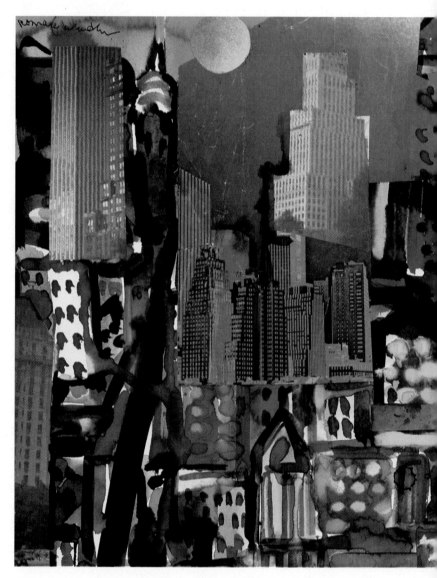

Midtown Sunset (1981), Romare Bearden. Courtesy of the Estate of Romare Bearden.

somebody to make it worth the while. You know what I mean?"

"Yeah," Greg nodded, not quite really knowing.

"I traveled around, and one time I come home, and there was this letter saying Jesse got killed in the war. Broke my heart, it truly did.

"They sent back what he had with him over there, and what it was is this old mouth fiddle and these clippings. Him carrying it around with him like that told me it meant something

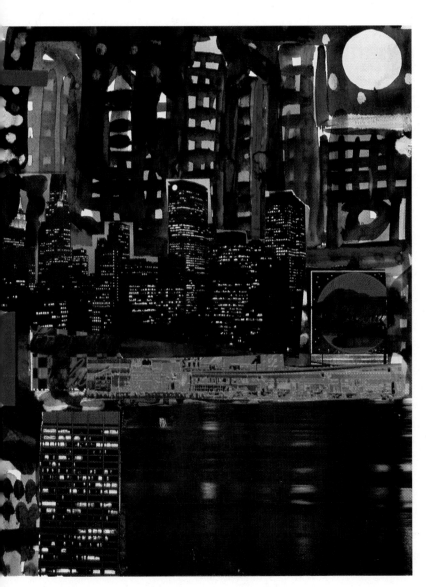

to him. That was my treasure, and when I give it to him, he treated it just like that, a treasure. Ain't that something?"

"Yeah, I guess so," Greg said.

"You *guess* so?" Lemon Brown's voice rose an octave as he started to put his treasure back into the plastic. "Well, you got to guess 'cause you sure don't know nothing. Don't know enough to get home when it's raining."

"I guess . . . I mean, you're right."

"You O.K. for a youngster," the old man said as he tied the strings around his leg, "better than those scalawags what come here looking for my treasure. That's for sure."

"You really think that treasure of yours was worth fighting for?" Greg asked. "Against a pipe?"

"What else a man got 'cepting what he can pass on to his son, or his daughter if she be his oldest?" Lemon Brown said. "For a big-headed boy you sure do ask the foolishest questions."

Lemon Brown got up after patting his rags in place and looked out the window again.

"Looks like they're gone. You get on out of here and get yourself home. I'll be watching from the window so you'll be all right."

Lemon Brown went down the stairs behind Greg. When they reached the front door, the old man looked out first, saw the street was clear, and told Greg to scoot on home.

"You sure you'll be O.K.?" Greg asked.

"Now didn't I tell you I was going to East St. Louis in the morning?" Lemon Brown asked. "Don't that sound O.K. to you?"

"Sure it does," Greg said. "Sure it does. And you take care of that treasure of yours."

"That I'll do," Lemon said, the wrinkles about his eyes suggesting a smile. "That I'll do."

The night had warmed, and the rain had stopped, leaving puddles at the curbs. Greg didn't even want to think how late it was. He thought ahead of what his father would say and wondered if he should tell him about Lemon Brown. He thought about it until he reached his stoop, and decided against it. Lemon Brown would be O.K., Greg thought, with his memories and his treasure.

Greg pushed the button over the bell marked Ridley, thought of the lecture he knew his father would give him, and smiled. ❖

BLUES MUSIC

In "The Treasure of Lemon Brown," Lemon Brown tells Greg, "I sung the blues so sweet that if I sang at a funeral, the dead would commence to rocking with the beat." Blues music had its origins in West African musical traditions brought to the United States by slaves. Blues songs were first sung in the late 1800s by African Americans living in the Mississippi Delta. These recently freed slaves, many of whom worked on cotton plantations, had no economic or political power. The misery of their daily lives was reflected in the lyrics of their songs. Their distinctive music featured "blue," or flattened, notes and a beat that seemed to conflict with the melody. In time, instrumental accompaniment—at first a banjo and later a guitar—was added to the songs.

In the early 1900s, as African Americans migrated from the country to the cities, the blues became more widely known. By the 1920s, blues music had become a craze, and orchestras were playing versions of it in many popular nightclubs. In later years, blues influenced the development of jazz, rock, and country music.

In the 1920s, one famous blues singer, Blind Lemon Jefferson, became widely known throughout the South. He recorded 81 songs but spent nearly all of his earnings and died poor at the age of 32. The last stanza of one of his songs, "Tin Cup Blues," illustrates the sad and tragic tone of the blues:

Now gather 'round me people and let
   me tell you a true fact
Now gather 'round me people and let
   me tell you a true fact
That tough luck has sunk me and the
   rats is getting in my hat.

RESPONDING
O P T I O N S

FROM PERSONAL RESPONSE TO CRITICAL ANALYSIS

REFLECT

1. What are your impressions of Lemon Brown? Jot down your thoughts in your notebook.

RETHINK

2. Why does Greg smile at the end of the story?

   Consider
   - what he has learned from Lemon Brown
   - how his perception of his father may have changed

3. Why do you think Lemon Brown decides to show his treasure to Greg?

RELATE

4. In your opinion, does society have a responsibility to protect homeless people? If so, what should be done?

ANOTHER PATHWAY
Cooperative Learning

Most blues songs have slow, emphatic rhythms and express sad thoughts. In small groups, try creating the lyrics of a blues song about Lemon Brown's life and his treasure. You might include his encounter with Greg. Share your group's lyrics with other groups.

LITERARY CONCEPTS

The techniques that writers use to bring characters to life are known as **characterization.** The basic methods of characterization are physical description of a character; the character's speech, thoughts, or actions; the dialogue, thoughts, or actions of other characters; and the writer's direct comments about the character's personality. Make a chart like the one below, adding at least one more example of each of the three methods used to make Lemon Brown seem real.

QUICKWRITES

1. Write a **dialogue** that might take place between Greg and his father during their next encounter. Remember what concerns Greg's father has about him and how Greg's perceptions may have changed.

2. Look at the chart you made for the Literary Concepts activity. Use your entries in the chart to help you write a **character sketch** of Lemon Brown.

PORTFOLIO Save your writing. You may want to use it later as a springboard to a piece for your portfolio.

Physical Description of Lemon Brown	His Own Speech, Thoughts, and Actions	Other Characters' Dialogue, Thoughts, and Actions
African American; wrinkled face	moved quietly across room to window	Greg relaxed; he had seen man before

ALTERNATIVE ACTIVITIES

Cooperative Learning With a group of classmates, create a **radio play** version of this story. Keep in mind that a radio play relies on dialogue more than narration. Perform the play for your class.

ACROSS THE CURRICULUM

Geography Lemon Brown says that he is going to East St. Louis. On a map, locate New York City, where the story takes place, and East St. Louis. Then use the map's distance scale to calculate how far Lemon will travel.

WORDS TO KNOW

Review the Words to Know at the bottom of the selection pages. On your paper, write the word that is most clearly related to each description below. Some words will be used twice.

1. mountain goats leaping from rock to rock
2. an open refrigerator
3. how to enter a tiger's den
4. an unrehearsed show
5. an oncoming storm with heavy clouds and high winds
6. the arthritic hands of an old person
7. a nervous amateur singing a solo
8. the only way to get going
9. the bark of an old, twisted tree
10. a stranger approaching in a dark alley

WALTER DEAN MYERS

Walter Dean Myers was born into a large, poor family in Martinsburg, West Virginia. After the death of his mother, he was raised by the Deans, friends of his family, with whom he moved to Harlem, where most of his stories take place. "Compared to Martinsburg," he says, "I found Harlem a marvel, an exotic land with an inexhaustible supply of delights and surprises."

1937–

Myers began to write fiction on a regular basis when he was only 10 or 11, but he did not imagine that writing might become his career. "I was from a family of laborers . . . Writing had no practical value for a Black child."

Nevertheless, Myers wrote stories throughout his high school years, during his three years in the army, and after his discharge. Finally, several of his stories were published, and in the late 1960s he won a contest with his text for a children's picture book. Since 1975, Myers has written more than 20 novels and many short stories, most of them for young adults. He has won two Newbery Awards and four Coretta Scott King Awards.

OTHER WORKS *Malcolm X: By Any Means Necessary, The Glory Field, Brown Angels*

LASERLINKS
• *MUSIC CONNECTION*

FICTION

The Lie

Kurt Vonnegut, Jr.

PERSONAL CONNECTION

Teenagers often feel pressure to meet their parents' expectations. The pressure is usually created by the parents' desire to see their children succeed, whether in simply cleaning their rooms or in earning college scholarships.

With your classmates, discuss the most common expectations parents have. Of these expectations, which do you think result in the most pressure on teenagers? On the chalkboard, rank the expectations on a diagram like the one shown.

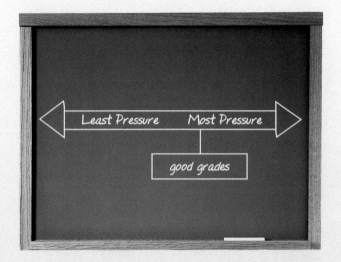

SOCIAL STUDIES CONNECTION

In this story, Eli Remenzel is faced with the expectations of his parents. They pressure him to attend the preparatory school that many generations of Remenzels have attended.

Prep schools are expensive private high schools that prepare students for college. Many provide a high-quality education with a great deal of individual attention. Because of the high cost of a prep school education, and because admission to these schools usually involves passing difficult entrance examinations, most of their students are bright children from wealthy families. Families develop strong loyalties to prep schools, sometimes donating large sums of money to the schools.

WRITING CONNECTION

Think about the discussion you had about parental expectations and pressure. In your notebook, jot down your ideas about how teenagers react to those pressures. Then, as you read, evaluate Eli's way of reacting to the pressure he faces.

- Some teenagers might get mad.
- The pressure could make others want to succeed.

LASERLINKS
• EDUCATIONAL CONNECTION

The
LIE

It was early springtime. Weak sunshine lay cold on old gray frost. Willow twigs against the sky showed the golden haze of fat catkins about to bloom. A black Rolls-Royce streaked up the Connecticut Turnpike from New York City. At the wheel was Ben Barkley, a colored chauffeur.

"Keep it under the speed limit, Ben," said Doctor Remenzel. "I don't care how ridiculous any speed limit seems; stay under it. No reason to rush—we have plenty of time."

Ben eased off on the throttle. "Seems like in the springtime she wants to get up and go," he said.

"Do what you can to keep her down—O.K.?" said the doctor.

"Yes, sir!" said Ben. He spoke in a lower voice to the thirteen-year-old boy who was riding beside him, to Eli Remenzel, the doctor's son. "Ain't just people and animals feel good in the springtime," he said to Eli. "Motors feel good too."

"Um," said Eli.

"Everything feels good," said Ben. "Don't you feel good?"

"Sure, sure I feel good," said Eli emptily.

"Should feel good—going to that wonderful school," said Ben.

The wonderful school was the

Copyright © Fred Lynch.

by
Kurt Vonnegut, Jr.

Whitehill School for Boys, a private preparatory school in North Marston, Massachusetts. That was where the Rolls-Royce was bound. The plan was that Eli would enroll for the fall semester while his father, a member of the class of 1939, attended a meeting of the board of overseers of the school.

"Don't believe this boy's feeling so good, doctor," said Ben. He wasn't particularly serious about it. It was more genial springtime blather.

"What's the matter, Eli?" said the doctor absently. He was studying blueprints, plans for a thirty-room addition to the Eli Remenzel Memorial Dormitory—a building named in honor of his great-great-grandfather. Doctor Remenzel had the plans draped over a walnut table that folded out of the back of the front seat. He was a massive, dignified man, a physician, a healer for healing's sake, since he had been born as rich as the Shah of Iran.[1] "Worried about something?" he asked Eli without looking up from the plans.

"Nope," said Eli.

Eli's lovely mother, Sylvia, sat next to the doctor, reading the catalogue of the Whitehill School.

"If I were you," she said to Eli, "I'd be so excited I could hardly stand it. The best four years of your whole life are just about to begin."

"Sure," said Eli. He didn't show her his face. He gave her only the back of his head, a pinwheel of coarse brown hair above a stiff white collar, to talk to.

"I wonder how many Remenzels have gone to Whitehill," said Sylvia.

"That's like asking how many people are dead in a cemetery," said the doctor. He gave the answer to the old joke, and to Sylvia's question too. "All of 'em."

"If all the Remenzels who went to Whitehill were numbered, what number would Eli be?" said Sylvia. "That's what I'm getting at."

The question annoyed Doctor Remenzel a little. It didn't seem in very good taste. "It isn't the sort of thing you keep score on," he said.

"Guess," said his wife.

"Oh," he said, "you'd have to go back through all the records, all the way back to the end of the eighteenth century, even, to make any kind of a guess. And you'd have to decide whether to count the Schofields and

---

1. **Shah of Iran:** one of the wealthy former monarchs of Iran.

the Haleys and the MacLellans as Remenzels."

"Please make a guess—" said Sylvia, "just people whose last names were Remenzel."

"Oh—" The doctor shrugged, rattled the plans. "Thirty maybe."

"So Eli is number thirty-one!" said Sylvia, delighted with the number. "You're number thirty-one, dear," she said to the back of Eli's head.

Doctor Remenzel rattled the plans again. "I don't want him going around saying something asinine, like he's number thirty-one," he said.

"Eli knows better than that," said Sylvia. She was a game, ambitious woman, with no money of her own at all. She had been married for sixteen years but was still openly curious and enthusiastic about the ways of families that had been rich for many generations.

"Just for my own curiosity—not so Eli can go around saying what number he is," said Sylvia, "I'm going to go wherever they keep the records and find out what number he is. That's what I'll do while you're at the meeting and Eli's doing whatever he has to do at the admissions office."

"All right," said Doctor Remenzel, "you go ahead and *do* that."

"I will," said Sylvia. "I think things like that are interesting, even if you don't." She waited for a rise[2] on that but didn't get one. Sylvia enjoyed arguing with her husband about her lack of <u>reserve</u> and his <u>excess</u> of it, enjoyed saying, toward the end of arguments like that, "Well, I guess I'm just a simple-minded country girl at heart, and that's all I'll ever be, and I'm afraid you're going to have to get used to it."

But Doctor Remenzel didn't want to play that game. He found the dormitory plans more interesting.

"Will the new rooms have fireplaces?" said Sylvia. In the oldest part of the dormitory, several of the rooms had handsome fireplaces.

"That would practically double the cost of construction," said the doctor.

"I want Eli to have a room with a fireplace, if that's possible," said Sylvia.

"Those rooms are for seniors."

"I thought maybe through some fluke—"[3] said Sylvia.

"What kind of fluke do you have in mind?" said the doctor. "You mean I should demand that Eli be given a room with a fireplace?"

"Not *demand*—" said Sylvia.

"Request firmly?" said the doctor.

"Maybe I'm just a simple-minded country girl at heart," said Sylvia, "but I look through this catalogue, and I see all the buildings named after Remenzels, look through the

back and see all the hundreds of thousands of dollars given by Remenzels for scholarships, and I just can't help thinking people named Remenzel are entitled to ask for a little something extra."

"Let me tell you in no uncertain terms," said Doctor Remenzel, "that you are not to ask for anything special for Eli—not anything."

"Of course I won't," said Sylvia. "Why do you always think I'm going to embarrass you?"

"I don't," he said.

"But I can still think what I think, can't I?" she said.

---

2. **rise:** an angry reaction to teasing or provoking.

3. **fluke:** a stroke of luck.

"If you have to," he said.

"I have to," she said cheerfully, utterly unrepentant. She leaned over the plans. "You think those people will like those rooms?"

"What people?" he said.

"The Africans," she said. She was talking about thirty Africans who, at the request of the State Department, were being admitted to Whitehill in the coming semester. It was because of them that the dormitory was being expanded.

"The rooms aren't for them," he said. "They aren't going to be segregated."

"Oh," said Sylvia. She thought about this awhile, and then she said, "Is there a chance Eli will have one of them for a roommate?"

"Freshmen draw lots[4] for roommates," said the doctor. "That piece of information's in the catalogue too."

"Eli?" said Sylvia.

"H'm?" said Eli.

"How would you feel about it if you had to room with one of those Africans?"

Eli shrugged listlessly.

"That's all right?" said Sylvia.

Eli shrugged again.

"I guess it's all right," said Sylvia.

"It had better be," said the doctor.

The Rolls-Royce pulled abreast of an old Chevrolet, a car in such bad repair that its back door was lashed shut with clothesline. Doctor Remenzel glanced casually at the driver, and then, with sudden excitement and pleasure, he told Ben Barkley to stay abreast of the car.

The doctor leaned across Sylvia, rolled down his window, yelled to the driver of the old Chevrolet, "Tom! Tom!"

The man was a Whitehill classmate of the doctor. He wore a Whitehill necktie, which he waved at Doctor Remenzel in gay recognition. And then he pointed to the fine young son who

Jerry (1955, repainted 1975), Fairfield Porter. Private collection.

sat beside him, conveyed with proud smiles and nods that the boy was bound for Whitehill.

Doctor Remenzel pointed to the chaos of

---

4. **draw lots:** pick numbers or names from a container to assure a random outcome.

WORDS TO KNOW

unrepentant (ŭn'rĭ-pĕn'tənt) *adj.* feeling or showing no regret the back of Eli's head, beamed that his news was the same. In the wind blustering between the two cars they made a lunch date at the Holly House in North Marston, at the inn whose principal business was serving visitors to Whitehill.

"All right," said Doctor Remenzel to Ben Barkley, "drive on."

"You know," said Sylvia, "somebody really ought to write an article—" And she turned to look through the back window at the old car now shuddering far behind. "Somebody really ought to."

"What about?" said the doctor. He noticed that Eli had slumped way down in the front seat. "Eli!" he said sharply. "Sit up straight!" He returned his attention to Sylvia.

"Most people think prep schools are such snobbish things, just for people with money," said Sylvia, "but that isn't true." She leafed through the catalogue and found the quotation she was after.

"*The Whitehill School operates on the assumption,*" she read, "*that no boy should be* <u>*deterred*</u> *from applying for admission because his family is unable to pay the full cost of a Whitehill education. With this in mind, the Admissions Committee selects each year from approximately 3,000 candidates the 150 most promising and deserving boys, regardless of their parents' ability to pay the full $2,200* <u>*tuition*</u>. *And those in need of financial aid are given it to the full extent of their need. In certain instances, the school will even pay for the clothing and transportation of a boy.*"

Sylvia shook her head. "I think that's perfectly amazing. It's something most people don't realize at all. A truck driver's son can come to Whitehill."

"If he's smart enough," he said.

"Thanks to the Remenzels," said Sylvia with pride.

"And a lot of other people too," said the doctor.

Sylvia read out loud again: "*In 1799, Eli Remenzel laid the foundation for the present Scholarship Fund by donating to the school forty acres in Boston. The school still owns twelve of those acres, their current evaluation being $3,000,000.*"

"Eli!" said the doctor. "Sit up! What's the matter with you?"

Eli sat up again but began to slump almost immediately, like a snowman in hell. Eli had good reason for slumping, for actually hoping to die or disappear. He could not bring himself to say what the reason was. He slumped because he knew he had been denied admission to Whitehill. He had failed the entrance examinations. Eli's parents did not know this, because Eli had found the awful notice in the mail and had torn it up.

Doctor Remenzel and his wife had no doubts whatsoever about their son's getting into Whitehill. It was inconceivable to them that Eli could not go there, so they had no curiosity as to how Eli had done on the examinations, were not puzzled when no report ever came.

PREDICT

What is going to happen when Eli's parents find out the truth?

"What all will Eli have to do to enroll?" said Sylvia as the black Rolls-Royce crossed the Rhode Island border.

"I don't know," said the doctor. "I suppose they've got it all complicated now with forms to be filled out in quadruplicate and punch-

---

WORDS TO KNOW

deter (dǐ-tûr') *v.* to discourage; prevent from acting

tuition (tōō-ǐsh'ən) *n.* the fee charged for instruction at a college or private school

inconceivable (ǐn'kən-sē'və-bəl) *adj.* impossible to understand; unbelievable card machines and <u>bureaucrats</u>. This business of entrance examinations is all new too. In my day a boy simply had an interview with the headmaster. The headmaster would look him over, ask him a few questions, and then say, 'There's a Whitehill boy.'"

"Did he ever say, 'There isn't a Whitehill boy'?" said Sylvia.

"Oh, sure," said Doctor Remenzel, "if a boy was impossibly stupid or something. There have to be standards. There have always been standards. The African boys have to meet the standards, just like anybody else. They aren't getting in just because the State Department wants to make friends. We made that clear. Those boys had to meet the standards."

"And they did?" said Sylvia.

"I suppose," said Doctor Remenzel. "I heard they're all in, and they all took the same examination Eli did."

"Was it a hard examination, dear?" Sylvia asked Eli. It was the first time she'd thought to ask.

"H'm," said Eli.

"What?" she said.

"Yes," said Eli.

"I'm glad they've got high standards," she said, and then she realized that this was a fairly silly statement. "Of course they've got high standards," she said. "That's why it's such a famous school. That's why people who go there do so well in later life."

Sylvia resumed her reading of the catalogue again, opened out a folding map of the Sward, as the campus of Whitehill was traditionally called. She read off the names of features that memorialized Remenzels—the Sanford Remenzel Bird Sanctuary, the George MacLellan Remenzel Skating Rink, the Eli Remenzel Memorial Dormitory—and then she read out loud a quatrain[5] printed on one corner of the map:

When night falleth gently
  Upon the green Sward,
It's Whitehill, dear Whitehill,
  Our thoughts all turn toward.

"You know," said Sylvia, "school songs are so corny when you just read them. But when I hear the Glee Club sing those words, they sound like the most beautiful words ever written, and I want to cry."

"Um," said Doctor Remenzel.

"Did a Remenzel write them?"

"I don't think so," said Doctor Remenzel. And then he said, "No—wait. That's the *new* song. A Remenzel didn't write it. Tom Hilyer wrote it."

"The man in that old car we passed?"

"Sure," said Doctor Remenzel. "Tom wrote it. I remember when he wrote it."

"A scholarship boy wrote it?" said Sylvia. "I think that's awfully nice. He *was* a scholarship boy, wasn't he?"

"His father was an ordinary automobile mechanic in North Marston."

"You hear what a democratic school you're going to, Eli?" said Sylvia.

Half an hour later Ben Barkley brought the limousine to a stop before the Holly House, a rambling country inn twenty years older than the Republic. The inn was on the edge of the Whitehill Sward, glimpsing the school's rooftops and spires over the innocent wilderness of the Sanford Remenzel Bird Sanctuary.

Ben Barkley was sent away with the car for an hour and a half. Doctor Remenzel shepherded

---

5. **quatrain** (kwŏt′rān′): a four-line poem or stanza.

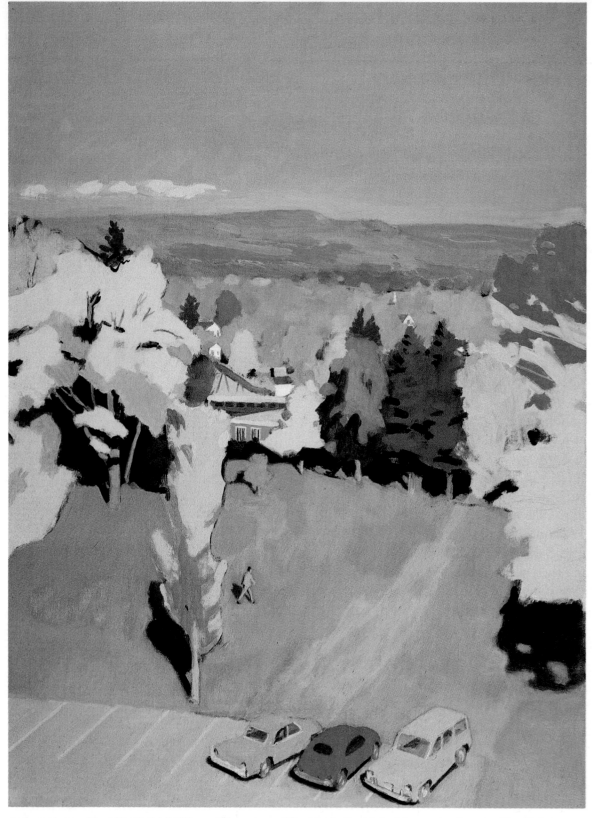

Amherst Campus No. 1 (1969), Fairfield Porter. Oil on canvas, 62″ × 46″, The Parrish Art Museum, Southampton, New York, gift of the Estate of Fairfield Porter. Photo by Jim Strong.

Sylvia and Eli into a familiar, low-ceilinged world of pewter,[6] clocks, lovely old woods, agreeable servants, elegant food and drink.

Eli, clumsy with horror of what was surely to come, banged a grandmother clock with his elbow as he passed, made the clock cry.

Sylvia excused herself. Doctor Remenzel and Eli went to the threshold of the dining room, where a hostess welcomed them both by name. They were given a table beneath an oil portrait of one of the three Whitehill boys who had gone on to become president of the United States.

The dining room was filling quickly with families. What every family had was at least one boy about Eli's age. Most of the boys wore Whitehill blazers[7]—black, with pale blue piping, with Whitehill seals on their breast pockets. A few, like Eli, were not yet entitled to wear blazers, were simply hoping to get in.

The doctor ordered a martini, then turned to his son and said, "Your mother has the idea that you're entitled to special privileges around here. I hope you don't have that idea too."

"No, sir," said Eli.

"It would be a source of the greatest embarrassment to me," said Doctor Remenzel with considerable grandeur, "if I were ever to hear that you had used the name Remenzel as though you thought Remenzels were something special."

"I know," said Eli wretchedly.

"That settles it," said the doctor. He had nothing more to say about it. He gave abbreviated salutes to several people he knew in the room, speculated as to what sort of party had reserved a long banquet table that was set up along one wall. He decided that it was for a visiting athletic team. Sylvia arrived, and Eli had to be told in a sharp whisper to stand when a woman came to a table.

Sylvia was full of news. The long table, she related, was for the thirty boys from Africa. "I'll bet that's more colored people than have eaten here since this place was founded," she said softly. "How fast things change these days!"

"You're right about how fast things change," said Doctor Remenzel. "You're wrong about the colored people who've eaten here. This used to be a busy part of the Underground Railroad."[8]

"Really?" said Sylvia. "How exciting." She looked all about herself in a birdlike way. "I think everything's exciting here. I only wish Eli had a blazer on."

Doctor Remenzel reddened. "He isn't entitled to one," he said.

"I know that," said Sylvia.

"I thought you were going to ask somebody for permission to put a blazer on Eli right away," said the doctor.

"I wouldn't do that," said Sylvia, a little offended now. "Why are you always afraid I'll embarrass you?"

"Never mind. Excuse me. Forget it," said Doctor Remenzel.

Sylvia brightened again, put her hand on Eli's arm, and looked radiantly at a man in the dining-room doorway. "There's my favorite person in all the world, next to my son and husband," she said. She meant Dr. Donald Warren, headmaster of the Whitehill School. A thin gentleman in his early sixties, Doctor Warren was in the doorway with the manager of the inn, looking over the arrangements for the Africans.

It was then that Eli got up abruptly, fled the dining room, fled as much of the nightmare as

---

6. **pewter** (py$\overline{oo}$'tər): a metal—consisting mainly of tin—formerly used for the making of fine kitchen utensils and tableware.

7. **blazers:** lightweight single-breasted jackets, often used as part of school uniforms.

8. **Underground Railroad:** a secret system, created by antislavery forces before the Civil War, to help slaves escape to free states or Canada.

he could possibly leave behind. He brushed past Doctor Warren rudely, though he knew him well, though Doctor Warren spoke his name. Doctor Warren looked after him sadly.

"I'll be damned," said Doctor Remenzel. "What brought that on?"

"Maybe he really *is* sick," said Sylvia.

The Remenzels had no time to react more elaborately, because Doctor Warren spotted them and crossed quickly to their table. He greeted them, some of his perplexity about Eli showing in his greeting. He asked if he might sit down.

"Certainly, of course," said Doctor Remenzel expansively. "We'd be honored if you did. Heavens."

"Not to eat," said Doctor Warren. "I'll be eating at the long table with the new boys. I would like to talk, though." He saw that there were five places set at the table. "You're expecting someone?"

"We passed Tom Hilyer and his boy on the way," said Doctor Remenzel. "They'll be along in a minute."

"Good, good," said Doctor Warren absently. He fidgeted, looked again in the direction in which Eli had disappeared.

"Tom's boy will be going to Whitehill in the fall?" said Doctor Remenzel.

"H'm?" said Doctor Warren. "Oh—yes, yes. Yes, he will."

"Is he a scholarship boy, like his father?" said Sylvia.

"That's not a polite question," said Doctor Remenzel severely.

"I beg your pardon," said Sylvia.

"No, no—that's a perfectly proper question these days," said Doctor Warren. "We don't keep that sort of information very secret any more. We're proud of our scholarship boys, and they have every reason to be proud of themselves. Tom's boy got the highest score anyone's ever got on the entrance examinations. We feel privileged to have him."

"We never *did* find out Eli's score," said Doctor Remenzel. He said it with good-humored resignation, without expectation that Eli had done especially well.

"A good strong medium, I imagine," said Sylvia. She said this on the basis of Eli's grades in primary school, which had ranged from medium to terrible.

The headmaster looked surprised. "I didn't tell you his scores?" he said.

"We haven't seen you since he took the examinations," said Doctor Remenzel.

CLARIFY

What do Eli and Dr. Warren know that Dr. and Mrs. Remenzel don't know?

"The letter I wrote you—" said Doctor Warren.

"What letter?" said Doctor Remenzel. "Did we get a letter?"

"A letter from me," said Doctor Warren, with growing incredulity. "The hardest letter I ever had to write."

Sylvia shook her head. "We never got any letter from you."

Doctor Warren sat back, looking very ill. "I mailed it myself," he said. "It was definitely mailed—two weeks ago."

Doctor Remenzel shrugged. "The U.S. mails don't lose much," he said, "but I guess that now and then something gets misplaced."

Doctor Warren cradled his head in his hands. "Oh, dear—oh, my, oh, Lord," he said. "I was surprised to see Eli here. I wondered that he would want to come along with you."

"He didn't come along just to see the scenery,"

WORDS TO KNOW   **resignation** (rĕz′ĭg-nā′shən) *n.* an unresisting acceptance of what seems unavoidable

incredulity (ĭn′krĭ-do͞o′lĭ-tē) *n.* an unwillingness to accept what is offered as true; disbelief said Doctor Remenzel. "He came to enroll."

"I want to know what was in the letter," said Sylvia.

Doctor Warren raised his head, folded his hands. "What the letter said was this, and no other words could be more difficult for me to say: *'On the basis of his work in primary school and his scores on the entrance examinations, I must tell you that your son and my good friend Eli cannot possibly do the work required of boys at Whitehill.'*" Doctor Warren's voice steadied, and so did his gaze. *"To admit Eli to Whitehill, to expect him to do Whitehill work,"* he said, *"would be both unrealistic and cruel."*

The chaos that followed this statement was not only emotional. It was real as well. Thirty African boys, escorted by several faculty members, State Department men, and diplomats from their own countries, filed into the dining room.

And Tom Hilyer and his boy, having no idea that something had just gone awfully wrong for the Remenzels, came in, too, and said hello to the Remenzels and Doctor Warren gaily, as though life couldn't possibly be better.

"I'll talk to you more about this later, if you like," Doctor Warren said to the Remenzels, rising. "I have to go now, but later on—" He left quickly.

"My mind's a blank," said Sylvia. "My mind's a perfect blank."

Tom Hilyer and his boy sat down. Hilyer looked at the menu before him, clapped his hands, and said, "What's good? I'm hungry." And then he said, "Say—where's your boy?"

"He stepped out for a moment," said Doctor Remenzel evenly.

"We've got to find him," said Sylvia to her husband.

"In time, in due time," said Doctor Remenzel.

"That letter," said Sylvia; "Eli knew about it. He found it and tore it up. Of course he did!"

She started to cry, thinking of the hideous trap Eli had caught himself in.

"I'm not interested right now in what Eli's done," said Doctor Remenzel. "Right now I'm a lot more interested in what some other people are going to do."

"What do you mean?" said Sylvia.

Doctor Remenzel stood impressively, angry and determined. "I mean," he said, "I'm going to see how quickly people can change their minds around here."

"Please," said Sylvia, trying to hold him, trying to calm him, "we've got to find Eli. That's the first thing."

"The first thing," said Doctor Remenzel quite loudly, "is to get Eli admitted to Whitehill. After that we'll find him, and we'll bring him back."

"But darling—" said Sylvia.

"No 'but' about it," said Doctor Remenzel. "There's a majority of the board of overseers in this room at this very moment. Every one of them is a close friend of mine, or a close friend of my father. If they tell Doctor Warren Eli's in, that's it—Eli's in. If there's room for all these other people," he said, "there's damn well room for Eli too."

He strode quickly to a table nearby, sat down heavily, and began to talk to a fierce-looking and splendid old gentleman who was eating there. The old gentleman was chairman of the board.

Sylvia apologized to the baffled Hilyers and then went in search of Eli.

Asking this person and that person, Sylvia found him. He was outside—all alone on a bench in a bower of lilacs that had just begun to bud.

Eli heard his mother's coming on the gravel path, stayed where he was, resigned. "Did you find out," he said, "or do I still have to tell you?"

"About you?" she said gently. "About not getting in? Doctor Warren told us."

"I tore his letter up," said Eli.

"I can understand that," she said. "Your father and I have always made you feel that you had to go to Whitehill, that nothing else would do."

"I feel better," said Eli. He tried to smile, found he could do it easily. "I feel so much better now that it's over. I tried to tell you a couple of times—but I just couldn't. I didn't know how."

"That's my fault, not yours," she said.

"What's Father doing?" said Eli.

Sylvia was so intent on comforting Eli that she'd put out of her mind what her husband was up to. Now she realized that Doctor Remenzel was making a ghastly mistake. She didn't want Eli admitted to Whitehill, could see what a cruel thing that would be.

She couldn't bring herself to tell the boy what his father was doing, so she said, "He'll be along in a minute, dear. He understands." And then she said, "You wait here, and I'll go get him and come right back."

But she didn't have to go to Doctor Remenzel. At that moment the big man came out of the inn and caught sight of his wife and son. He came to her and to Eli. He looked dazed.

"Well?" she said.

"They—they all said no," said Doctor Remenzel, very subdued.

"That's for the best," said Sylvia. "I'm relieved. I really am."

"Who said no?" said Eli. "Who said no to what?"

"The members of the board," said Doctor Remenzel, not looking anyone in the eye. "I asked them to make an exception in your case—to reverse their decision and let you in."

Eli stood, his face filled with incredulity and shame that were instant. "You what?" he said, and there was no childishness in the way he said it. Next came anger. "You shouldn't have done that!" he said to his father.

Doctor Remenzel nodded. "So I've already been told."

"That isn't done!" said Eli. "How awful! You shouldn't have."

"You're right," said Doctor Remenzel, accepting the scolding lamely.

"Now I *am* ashamed," said Eli, and he showed that he was.

Doctor Remenzel, in his wretchedness, could find no strong words to say. "I apologize to you both," he said at last. "It was a very bad thing to try."

"Now a Remenzel *has* asked for something," said Eli.

"I don't suppose Ben's back yet with the car?" said Doctor Remenzel. It was obvious that Ben wasn't. "We'll wait out here for him," he said. "I don't want to go back in there now."

"A Remenzel asked for something—as though a Remenzel were something special," said Eli.

"I don't suppose—" said Doctor Remenzel, and he left the sentence unfinished, dangling in the air.

"You don't suppose what?" said his wife, her face puzzled.

"I don't suppose," said Doctor Remenzel, "that we'll ever be coming here anymore." ❖

RESPONDING
O P T I O N S

FROM PERSONAL RESPONSE *TO* CRITICAL ANALYSIS

REFLECT 1. What were your reactions to Eli? Record your thoughts in your notebook. Share your reactions with a partner.

RETHINK 2. Who do you think deserves blame for the lie? Explain your answer.

3. Which characters feel pressure in this story? What kinds of pressure do they feel? Give reasons to support your answer.

4. What do you think of Dr. and Mrs. Remenzel?
Consider
 • their expectations of Eli
 • their remarks about the African students
 • how they respond when they discover the lie
 • their reactions at the end of the story

5. Do you sympathize with any of the characters in the story? Why or why not?

RELATE 6. Compare and contrast the way teenagers facing today's pressures react to them with the way Eli reacts. Do you consider his reaction normal? Explain your opinion.

ANOTHER PATHWAY
Cooperative Learning
The members of the Remenzel family have trouble communicating with one another. Plan and conduct a panel discussion in which you and other students analyze the Remenzels' problems and offer suggestions to help them.

QUICKWRITES

1. Write a **personal narrative** about a time when you disappointed someone else or when you were disappointed by someone. Try to judge whether anyone's expectations were too high.

2. Compose a **quatrain** that could be the start of a song about your school, or add four lines to the one about Whitehill on page 35.

3. What different way of handling his situation might you suggest to Eli? Write a **letter of advice** to him.

📁 *PORTFOLIO Save your writing. You may want to use it later as a springboard to a piece for your portfolio.*

LITERARY CONCEPTS

An author must decide from whose perspective a story will be told. A story told from the **third-person point of view** is narrated by a person outside the story, who uses pronouns such as *he, she,* and *it.* Why do you think Kurt Vonnegut chose to tell "The Lie" from the third-person point of view? How would the story be different if Eli narrated it?

A contrast between what is expected and what actually happens in a story is called **irony.** For example, the Remenzels' snobbish attitude about the school's high standards makes it ironic that their own son can't meet them. What do you think is ironic about Dr. Remenzel's actions at the end of the story?

THE LIE **41**

ALTERNATIVE ACTIVITIES

1. **Cooperative Learning** With a small group of classmates, look up and discuss the definition of the term *stereotype*. Then **list** stereotypes of rich people that you've heard. Finally, look through the story to locate behaviors that seem stereotypical of the rich.

2. With other students, **dramatize** the conversation that might take place between the Remenzels and Ben Barkley, the chauffeur, when the family returns to the car.

WORDS TO KNOW

EXERCISE A Answer the questions on your paper.

1. Would you be more likely to find a **bureaucrat** in an office or on a playground? Why?

2. If you fight a school policy, are you acting with **resignation?** Why or why not?

3. Who or what receives **tuition?**

4. Do principals want their teachers to act with **reserve?** Why or why not?

5. If a teacher looked at you with **incredulity,** how would you feel? Explain.

EXERCISE B Copy the following items on your paper. Label each word that follows a boldfaced word as a synonym or antonym of the boldfaced word, as in the example.

Example: **large**   big *synonym*   small *antonym*

1. **excess**   surplus   shortage
2. **inconceivable**   unimaginable   understandable
3. **subdued**   intense   excited
4. **unrepentant**   sorry   remorseful
5. **deter**   prevent   encourage

KURT VONNEGUT, JR.

The Great Depression of the 1930s made a lasting impression on Kurt Vonnegut and strongly influenced his writing. During that period, his architect father faced ten years of unemployment, while his mother unsuccessfully tried writing fiction. Although Vonnegut's parents had attended private schools, they could not afford to send their son to a private school.

After college, Vonnegut served in the U.S. infantry during World War II and was awarded a Purple Heart. Captured by the Germans, he was sheltered in an underground meat locker in

1922–

Dresden during the Allied firebombing of that city, in which 135,000 people died. Afterward, he was set to work digging corpses from the ruins. Twenty-three years passed before he could write about what he had seen.

Vonnegut's books, with their strongly antiwar, antitechnology, and antiscience themes, have sold in the millions. There are no heroes and villains in his stories, but he says, "I have always rigged my stories so as to include myself."

OTHER WORKS "The Kid Nobody Could Handle," "Long Walk to Forever," "Harrison Bergeron"

LASERLINKS
• AUTHOR BACKGROUND

FOCUS ON NONFICTION

hat many readers enjoy reading most is **nonfiction**—writing about real people, places, and events. Nonfiction falls into two broad categories. One category, called **informative nonfiction,** is mainly written to provide factual information. Nonfiction of this type includes history and science books, encyclopedias, pamphlets, and most of the articles in magazines and newspapers. An example of informative nonfiction that you will read in this book is the Historical Insight on page 119, which gives information about developments in space exploration.

The other category of nonfiction is called **literary nonfiction** because it is written to be read and experienced in much the same way as fiction. However, literary nonfiction differs from fiction in that it deals with real people rather than fictional characters and with settings and plots that are not imagined but are actual places and true events.

The selections of literary nonfiction you will read in this book include **autobiographies, biographies,** and **essays.**

AUTOBIOGRAPHY An autobiography is the true story of a person's life, told by that person. It is almost always written from the first-person point of view. In this book, you will read an excerpt from an autobiography by Clifton L. Taulbert, in which Taulbert describes an influential person in his life.

An autobiography is usually book length because it covers a long period of the writer's life. However, there are shorter types of autobiographical writing, such as **journals, diaries,** and **memoirs.**

BIOGRAPHY A biography is the true story of a person's life, told by someone else. The writer, or **biographer,** interviews the subject if possible and also researches the subject's life by reading letters, books, diaries, and any other information he or she can find. In this book, you will read an excerpt from a biography of Harriet Tubman, a famous runaway slave who helped other slaves escape from the United States to Canada.

As you will see, biographies and autobiographies often contain many elements that fiction contains, such as character, setting, and plot.

ESSAY An essay is a short piece of nonfiction that deals with one subject. Essays are often found in newspapers and magazines. The writer might share an opinion, try to entertain or persuade the reader, or simply describe an incident that has special significance. Essays that explain how the author feels about a subject are called **informal essays** or **personal essays.** In this book, the selection "The Power of the Powerless" is an example of an informal essay. **Formal essays** are scholarly and serious and are rarely found in literature textbooks.

STRATEGIES FOR READING NONFICTION

Nonfiction can be read as literature or as a source of information. The nonfiction selections in this book will provide you with opportunities both to learn new information and to enjoy the true stories and opinions the authors have to share.

Use the following strategies when you read nonfiction:

- **Preview the selection.** Before you read a selection, look at the title, the pictures or diagrams, and any subtitles or terms in boldface or italic type. All of these will give you an idea of what the selection is about.

- **Figure out the organization.** If the work is a biography, an autobiography, or a historical selection, the organization is probably chronological—that is, events are told in the order they happened. Other selections may be organized around ideas the author wants to discuss.

- **Separate facts and opinions.** Facts are statements that can be proved, such as "The letter written by Frederick Douglass is the shortest nonfiction selection in this book." Opinions are statements that cannot be proved. They simply express a person's beliefs, such as "'The Clown' is the funniest nonfiction selection in this book." Writers sometimes present opinions as if they were facts. Be sure you can recognize the difference.

- **Question as you read.** "Why did things happen the way they did?" "Who or what caused this event?" "How did people feel?" "What is the writer's opinion?" Try to decide whether you share the writer's opinion or have different ideas on the subject.

- **Make predictions.** During your reading, stop now and then and try to predict what will come next. Sometimes you will be surprised by what happens or by what an author has to say about an issue.

- **Clarify your understanding.** As you read, add new information to what you have already learned, and see if your ideas and opinions change.

- **Continually evaluate what you read.** Form opinions about the people, events, and ideas that are presented. Decide whether you like the way the piece was written.

Finally, it is important to recognize that your understanding of a selection does not end when you stop reading. As you think more about what you have read and discuss it with others, you will find that your understanding continues to grow.

PREVIEWING

NONFICTION

from Reflections on the Civil War
Bruce Catton

PERSONAL CONNECTION

This selection tells about young soldiers during the Civil War. What do you already know about Civil War soldiers? What do you want to know? With your classmates, make a chart like the one shown here and fill in the first two columns. You will complete the third column after you read the selection.

What We Know About Civil War Soldiers	What We Want to Know About Them	What We Learned About Them

HISTORICAL CONNECTION

Confederate cap worn during the Battle of Gettysburg.

During the American Civil War (1861–1865), the Northern states, called the Union, and the Southern states, called the Confederacy, fought each other in the bloodiest war in U.S. history. More than 600,000 American soldiers died, nearly as many as have been killed in all our nation's other wars combined.

A young man who joined the army during the Civil War had a hard life. He was issued a poorly made uniform, ill-fitting shoes, and unappetizing food rations. His only weapon was a musket, a gun that required reloading after each shot. As part of a regiment—a large unit of soldiers—he experienced a daily life quite different from anything he may have known or imagined before.

READING CONNECTION

Finding the Main Idea Authors of nonfiction often organize each paragraph around a main idea. The main idea is often stated in a **topic sentence** at the beginning of the paragraph, although it may be stated anywhere in the paragraph. Other sentences in the paragraph give details about the main idea. Look for topic sentences as you read this selection to help you understand the organization of Catton's thoughts about young soldiers and the lives they led during the Civil War.

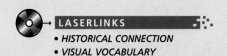

LASERLINKS
• *HISTORICAL CONNECTION*
• *VISUAL VOCABULARY*

from
Reflections
on the Civil War

by BRUCE CATTON

In the Civil War, the common soldiers of both sides were the same sort of people: untrained and untaught young men, mostly from the country. There weren't many cities then, and they weren't very large, so the average soldier generally came either from a farm or from some very small town or rural area. He had never been anywhere; he was completely unsophisticated. He joined up because he wanted to, because his patriotism had been aroused. The bands were playing, the recruiting officers were making speeches, so he got stirred up and enlisted. Sometimes, he was not altogether dry behind the ears.

When the boy joined the army, he would, of course, be issued clothing. He would get his uniform—pants, coat, shoes, and underwear. In the frontier regions, the quartermasters discovered that quite a lot of these young men picked up the underwear and looked at it and said, "What is this?" They had never seen any before. They hadn't worn it back home. Well, they caught on. They were fresh out of the backwoods, most of them.

The boys from the country and the very small towns seemed to have made better soldiers than the boys from the cities. In the North, for instance, the boys from the rural areas, and especially from the Middle West, which they then called the Northwest, were a little tougher than the boys from the big cities. They could stand more; they were more self-reliant; perhaps they were more used to handling weapons. In any case, they made very good soldiers. On the Southern side, the same was true—even more so. A larger percentage of the men came from rural areas because there were fewer cities in the South. A number of them didn't even bother with shoes, but they were very, very bad boys to get into a fight with.

The war was greeted in its first few weeks almost as a festival. Everybody seemed relieved. People went out and celebrated, both in the North and in the South. There were parades, bands playing, flags flying; people seemed almost happy. Large numbers of troops were enlisted; as a matter of fact, again in both the North and the South, more men offered themselves than could be handled. Neither the Union nor the Confederate government had the weapons, uniforms, or anything else to equip all of the men who tried to enlist.

Both armies contained a number of very ardent teenagers who had lied about their age in order to get into the army in the first place. Legal age, of course, was eighteen. It turned out that, in the North at least, a very common little gag had been developed. A boy who was under eighteen and wanted to enlist would take a piece of paper and scribble the figure eighteen on it. Then he would take off his shoe, placing the piece of paper into the sole of his shoe, put it back on and tie it up. He would go to the recruiting station, and since he would obviously be looking rather young, sooner or later the recruiting officer would look at him and say, "How old are you, son?" Then the boy, in perfect honesty, could say, "I am over eighteen."

The point about that is not so much that young men were lying about their age in order to get into the army but that they would go to the trouble of working out a gag like that. A man simply wouldn't dream of taking an oath that he was eighteen when he wasn't. Lying to the government was a little beyond him, but he would work out a thing like this and could say honestly, "I'm over eighteen," and that made it quite all right.

A set of statistics were compiled about the average Northern soldier that are rather interesting. They apply pretty much to the South as well. An average soldier was 5 feet 8¼ inches tall; he weighed just over 143 pounds. Forty-eight percent were farmers, 24 percent were mechanics, 15 percent were laborers, 5 percent were businessmen, and 3 percent were professional men. That was really a kind of cross-section of the population of the United States at that time: about one-half farmers, about 40 percent working men, and 10 percent businessmen or professionals.

When a man joined the Union army, he was given shoes that must have been a little bit of a trial to wear. In a great many cases, army

ardent (är′dnt) *adj.* enthusiastic; devoted

contractors simply made the right and left shoes identical. They were squared off at the toe, and it didn't matter which one you put on which foot; they were supposed to work either way. They must have been very uncomfortable, and I imagine they account for a great many of the cases of footsore soldiers who fell out on the march and stumbled into camp long after everybody else had gone to bed.

The Civil War soldier, on the Northern side at least, got a great deal to eat; the trouble was that most of it was not very good. The Union army enlisted no cooks or bakers during the entire war. Originally, each man was supposed to cook for himself. It happened, of course, practically immediately that company kitchens were established. Men were detailed from the ranks to act as cooks; some of them cooked fairly well, and some of them, of course, cooked abominably. But whatever they cooked, the boys ate.

The basic ration for the Civil War soldier, particularly on the march, where it was not possible to carry along vegetables, was salt pork or bacon and hardtack. The hardtack was a big soda cracker, quite thick and, as the name implies, very tough—made tough so that it wouldn't fall into pieces while it was joggling about in a man's haversack.[1] When the hardtack was fresh, it was apparently quite good to eat. The trouble is that it was very

rarely fresh. Boxes of hardtack would sit on railroad platforms or sidetracked in front of warehouses for weeks and months at a time, and by the time the soldier got them, they were often infested and not very good.

Every soldier carried some sort of a tin can in which he could boil coffee. Coffee was issued in the whole bean, for when the government issued ground coffee, they could never quite trust the contractors not to adulterate it. When the soldier made coffee, he would put a handful of beans in a bucket and grind them with the butt of his musket. In the morning, in camp, you could tell when the boys were getting up by the rhythmic clinking, grinding noise that came up from in front of every tent.

The soldier also had sugar to go with his coffee, and he would boil his coffee in his little tin can and then dump in some sugar. He would usually have a skillet in which to fry his bacon. Sometimes he would crumble up hardtack and drop the crumbs in the sizzling bacon fat and make a rather indescribable mess—I guess a healthy young man who got a good deal of exercise could digest it without too much difficulty.

In the Civil War, which lasted four years, about 600,000 young Americans, North and

---

1. **haversack:** a bag carried over one shoulder and used to carry supplies or personal belongings.

49

South together, lost their lives. That is not the total casualty list; it is the number that actually went under the sod.[2] The wounded, the missing, the prisoners, were in another list. Six hundred thousand is the number of lives that were actually lost.

If you want to understand what a terrible drain that was on the country, reflect that the total population in the United States in the 1860s was about an eighth or a ninth of what it is today. The number of men killed in that war, if you interpret it in today's terms, would come to something between four and four and one-half million. In other words, a perfectly frightful toll of American lives was taken.

There are a good many reasons why the toll was so high. More than *one-half* of the men who died were not killed in action; they simply died of camp diseases: typhoid fever, pneumonia, dysentery, and childhood diseases like measles and chicken pox.

To begin with, medical science then was woefully inadequate. Doctors simply did not know what caused such devastating camp diseases as typhoid fever, which accounted for about one-fourth of all deaths in army hospitals. Malaria, a plague of the Virginia swamp country, was attributed to "miasmic vapors" arising from stagnant waters and not to the pestiferous mosquitoes bred therein. (The vapors were also largely blamed for typhoid and dysentery.) Nothing was known about how and why wounds became infected, and so nothing much was done to prevent infection; surgeons talked soberly about "laudable pus" which was expected to appear a few days after an operation or a gunshot wound, its laudable character arising because it showed that the body was discharging poisons.

The number of men who simply got sick and died, or who got a minor scratch or cut and then could do nothing to check the infection, was appalling. Just to be in the army in the 1860s was much more dangerous than anything we know about today, even though many a man in the army never got into action. It was a very common thing—in fact, almost the rule—for a Civil War regiment on either side to lose about half of its strength in men who either became sick and died or became so ill they had to get medical discharges before the regiment ever saw action. Whereas a Civil War regiment, on paper, contained about one thousand men, in actual fact, a regiment that went into battle with as many as five hundred men was quite fortunate.

2. **went under the sod:** died and were buried—literally, "went beneath the grass."

WORDS TO KNOW

devastating (dĕv′ə-stā′tĭng) *adj.* causing great destruction **devastate** *v.*
soberly (sō′bər-lē) *adv.* in a serious or solemn way
laudable (lô′də-bəl) *adj.* deserving approval; praiseworthy
appalling (ə-pô′lĭng) *adj.* causing horror or dismay; frightful

Not long after the war began, whenever a Northern army and a Southern army were camped fairly close to each other, the men on the picket lines[3] would get acquainted with one another and would call little informal truces.[4] The Northern soldiers would bring in coffee to trade. Along the Rappahannock River, they made quite a thing of constructing little toy boats out of planks. A boat would be maybe two feet long, with a mast and a sail. Loaded with coffee, it would be sent out into the stream, pointed south, and when it would get across the river, the Confederate soldiers would unload the coffee, stock it with tobacco, and send it back.

This led to some rather odd happenings, since men who are stopping to trade with each other are <u>apt</u> to get a little friendly along the way. There was one rather famous occasion, again along the Rappahannock River, when in a building not far behind the Confederate lines back of the outposts,[5] there was going to be a dance one evening, and the Confederate pickets invited their Yankee friends to come over and go to the dance.

Half a dozen Yankee soldiers, leaving their guns behind them, crossed the river in the darkness, went to the dance, and had a very good time—until a Confederate officer appeared just when festivities were at their height. He was, of course, horrified and ordered the Yankee soldiers arrested and thrown into prison, at which point the Confederates begged him not to do this. They said they had given the Yankees their word that everything would be all right if they came to the dance, and asked that the officer let them go.

Well, the officer saw some point to that appeal. He couldn't violate or cause his men to violate their honor, so after giving all hands a don't-let-it-happen-again lecture, he released the Yankee prisoners, and they went home, with a good dance under their belts.

Along the Rapidan River during the winter of 1863 and 1864, the armies for a number of miles had outposts that were drawn up very close to each other. In fact, in one or two places, they actually overlapped. The Yankees had a way of advancing their picket lines in the night and pulling them back in the daytime. The Confederates did it just the other way around; their picket lines were a little farther forward by day than by night. Pretty soon it turned out that there was a picket post, with a log cabin and a fireplace, that was used at night by the Yankees and in the daytime by the Confederates. The boys worked out a deal: each party would leave a stack of firewood on hand and be sure to get out before the other one got there. They kept on that way quite pleasantly for some months.

At the great Battle of Fredericksburg, down at the far end of the line where the fighting was not very heavy, there was a woodland stretch held by the Confederates on one side and the Yankees on the other. The pickets, again, were quite close together, and the skirmish lines[6] not much farther apart. The men got to catcalling and jeering at each other and making insulting remarks. This went on for quite a while in much the same way that a couple of high school football cheering

---

3. **picket lines:** lines of soldiers posted around encampments to guard against surprise attack.

4. **truces:** agreements to temporarily stop fighting.

5. **outposts:** places where troops are stationed away from a main force.

6. **skirmish lines:** lines of opposing troops attacking each other.

sections might yell back and forth at each other. Finally, a couple of soldiers, a Confederate and a Yankee, got really angry. They got so angry that they had to have a fight. So all along the line in this particular section of the woodland, the soldiers called an informal truce, and the riled-up Yankee and Southerner got out and had a very fine, soul-satisfying fistfight. I don't know who came out on top, but at last the fight ended, as all such fights do, and the men went to a nearby stream and washed the blood off their faces and shook hands. Then both sides went back, picked up their weapons, and started shooting at each other again.

I t was that kind of war—rather informal, and fought between men who, when left alone, got along together beautifully. You've often heard it spoken of as the War Between Brothers. Actually, it really was that.

The siege[7] of Vicksburg was another case where the picket lines were so close together that on one occasion the Southerners and the Northerners had a little meeting and came to an agreement as to just where the picket lines ought to go, so they wouldn't trespass on each other's territory.

During this siege, one of the Confederates out on the picket line asked if there were any Missouri regiments in the army immediately opposing his section. He was a Missourian himself and was looking for his brother. The Yankees made inquiry, and pretty soon they came forward with the Confederate soldier's brother—both boys from Missouri, one of them in Confederate gray and the other in Federal blue. The Confederate had a roll of bills in his hand and gave them to his brother to send to their mother, who was peaceably at home in Missouri. He couldn't get things out from Vicksburg through the Union lines,

Vicksburg being completely surrounded, so he asked his brother to send them to her, and the brother did. There was no shooting while these arrangements were made, then the brothers shook hands and retired to their individual lines, and the shooting started up again.

During the fighting at Crampton's Gap in Maryland in the fall of 1862, the Confederates were slowly withdrawing. They were fighting a rear-guard action rather than a regular battle. One Yankee soldier got a little too far forward, slipped, and accidentally slid down the side of the steep hill on which he had been posted, winding up at the bottom of the hill in a thicket. There he confronted a Confederate soldier who wasn't ready to retreat yet. The two men grabbed their guns. But eventually they figured there was no point in shooting each other here, off in a quiet corner where there wasn't much going on, so they laid down their weapons and made an agreement. They would stay where they were with no shooting. At the end of the day if the Confederates had advanced, the Yankee would be the Confederate soldier's prisoner. If the Yankees had advanced, then the Confederate would be the Yankee's prisoner. Meanwhile, there wasn't any sense in getting shot. The Confederates eventually withdrew, and the Yankee soldier found he had taken a prisoner.

One of the most touching stories I know involving this acquaintanceship—friendship, really—between the rival soldiers took place at Fredericksburg, Virginia, along the Rappahannock, a couple of months after the big battle there. The Rappahannock River is not very wide, and the men on the northern bank could easily talk with the men on the southern bank if they raised their voices a little. One winter afternoon when nothing much was going on, a

---

7. **siege** (sēj): the blockading of a city or fort by a hostile surrounding army.

number of the Federal army bands were massed on the hillside overlooking the river valley to give a little informal concert. They played all of the Northern patriotic songs, and the Northern soldiers crowded around to listen. On the opposite shore, the Confederate soldiers gathered to enjoy the concert.

After a while, the band had pretty well run through its <u>repertoire</u>, and there was a pause, whereupon some of the Confederates shouted, "Now play some of ours." So the band began to play Southern tunes. They played "Dixie" and "Bonnie Blue Flag" and "Yellow Rose of Texas" and I don't know what all. They played Southern tunes while the Southern and Northern armies sat in the quiet and listened.

It was getting on toward dusk by this time, so the band, to signal the end of the concert, went into "Home, Sweet Home." Both armies together tried to sing it, and it was rather a sentimental occasion. After all, these boys were a long way from home. They knew perfectly well that a great many of them were never going to see home again; as soon as the warm weather came, they would be fighting each other. The song got to be a little too much for them, and pretty soon they choked up and couldn't sing, and the band finished the music all by itself.

A couple of months later, the troops faced each other in the terrible Battle of Chancellorsville. ❖

Dirge Without Music

BY EDNA ST. VINCENT MILLAY

I am not resigned to the shutting away of
   loving hearts in the hard ground.
So it is, and so it will be, for so it has been,
   time out of mind:
Into the darkness they go, the wise and the
   lovely. Crowned
With lilies and with laurel they go; but I am
   not resigned.

Lovers and thinkers, into the earth with
   you.
Be one with the dull, the indiscriminate
   dust.
A fragment of what you felt, of what you
   knew,
A formula, a phrase remains,—but the best
   is lost.

The answers quick and keen, the honest
   look, the laughter, the love,—
They are gone. They are gone to feed the
   roses. Elegant and curled
Is the blossom. Fragrant is the blossom. I
   know. But I do not approve.
More precious was the light in your eyes
   than all the roses of the world.

Down, down, down into the darkness of
   the grave
Gently they go, the beautiful, the tender, the
   kind;
Quietly they go, the intelligent, the witty,
   the brave.
I know. But I do not approve. And I am not
   resigned.

WORDS TO KNOW

repertoire (rĕp′ər-twär′) *n.* the stock of songs, plays, or other pieces that a person or group is prepared to perform

RESPONDING OPTIONS

FROM PERSONAL RESPONSE TO CRITICAL ANALYSIS

REFLECT

1. What surprised you about Civil War soldiers? Jot down the most surprising facts in your notebook.

RETHINK

2. How might the perceptions of a soldier who was eager to enlist have changed once he was in the army?

3. Do you think you would be as eager to enlist in a war as the young men Catton describes? Give reasons for your answer.

4. What title would you give this selection to indicate the kinds of facts it contains?

5. Do you think Catton would agree with the sentiments expressed in Edna St. Vincent Millay's "Dirge Without Music" (page 53)? Why or why not?

   Consider
   - the feelings about war that "Dirge Without Music" conveys
   - how you think Catton feels about war

RELATE

6. Compare and contrast what you have learned about the life of Civil War soldiers with what you envision as the life of a soldier today. Share your thoughts with your class.

ANOTHER PATHWAY

Cooperative Learning

Look at the chart you created for the Personal Connection on page 45. With your classmates, discuss what you learned about Civil War soldiers from this selection. Write those facts in the third column of your chart.

QUICKWRITES

1. Imagine that you are a common soldier in the Civil War, and write a **letter** about your experiences to your family or girlfriend back home.

2. Rewrite an **anecdote** in this selection from the point of view of a soldier involved in the incident.

3. Imagine that you are a newspaper reporter given the assignment of observing firsthand a day in the life of a Confederate or Union soldier. Write an **article** that presents the events of the day.

📁 *PORTFOLIO Save your writing. You may want to use it later as a springboard to a piece for your portfolio.*

LITERARY CONCEPTS

An **anecdote** is a brief story told to entertain or to make a point. What point do you think Catton makes by means of the anecdotes he tells about encounters between Union and Confederate soldiers? What else do the anecdotes add to the presentation of factual information?

ALTERNATIVE ACTIVITIES

1. *Cooperative Learning* Research the tunes and lyrics of some Confederate and Union songs and of "Home, Sweet Home." With a small group of classmates, organize a **concert** in which half the class sings Confederate songs, half sings Union songs, and all sing "Home, Sweet Home."

2. Create a Confederate or Union army **recruitment poster** that includes a full-length portrait of a soldier in uniform with a haversack and a musket. Research the details of his outfit.

3. Find out what food today's soldiers carry. List some of the foods and their nutritional value. Design and fill in a **comparison chart** that shows the nutritional value of these foods alongside the nutritional value of soda crackers and bacon, the foods mentioned in the selection.

ACROSS THE CURRICULUM

Mathematics Make a **circle graph** that shows, in percentages, the kinds of jobs the soldiers held before they enlisted. Keep in mind that the percentages given in the selection add up to 95, rather than 100. Once you have completed your circle graph, design another type of graph to display the same data.

Social Studies Some women disguised themselves as men in order to fight in the Civil War. Find out about some of these women and share what you learn with the class in an **oral report.**

Cooperative Learning Catton mentions the battles of Fredericksburg, Vicksburg, and Chancellorsville. With a small group of classmates, research one of these battles, then write a short **report** about it. Include pictures or illustrations if possible.

THE WRITER'S STYLE

By his use of colloquial expressions—like "not altogether dry behind the ears," meaning "young and inexperienced," in the first paragraph of the selection—Catton creates an informal style. Find another such expression that Catton uses, and explain its relationship to the soldiers' experiences.

The Battle of Fredericksburg. The Bettmann Archive.

On your paper, write the letter of the best answer.

1. Which person would be *least* likely to speak **soberly?**
   a. a victorious general   **b.** an injured soldier   **c.** a surgeon

2. An officer whose soldiers behaved **abominably** would feel
   a. relieved.   **b.** proud.   **c.** angry.

3. At which of these places would you most likely hear a **repertoire?**
   a. a concert hall   **b.** an army hospital   **c.** a battlefield

4. Which one of these behaviors is most **appalling?**
   a. tripping on steps   **b.** abandoning a baby   **c.** singing

5. Food that has been **infested** may be
   a. full of bugs.   **b.** undercooked.   **c.** cooked to perfection.

6. Which one of these people could *not* be described as **ardent?**
   a. a bored student   **b.** a heroic soldier   **c.** an avid sports fan

7. A person who is **apt** to enlist in the army is
   a. likely to enlist.   **b.** not likely to enlist.   **c.** refusing to enlist.

8. A soldier who performed a **laudable** act would most likely be
   a. ridiculed.   **b.** arrested.   **c.** praised.

9. If someone made a **devastating** remark to you, you would probably feel
   a. elated.   **b.** upset.   **c.** confident.

10. Something that is **adulterated** is
    a. purified.   **b.** contaminated.   **c.** used only by adults.

BRUCE CATTON

With the publication of 13 books in the last third of his life, Bruce Catton became the Civil War's most famous chronicler. His historical narratives, highly respected for their accuracy, have been credited with starting a renewed interest in the Civil War in the 1950s. Written from the enlisted man's point of view, they are dramatic, personal, and realistic. His most famous book, *A Stillness at Appomattox,* won a Pulitzer Prize in 1954 and became an overnight bestseller.

1899–1978

Catton's interest in the Civil War began in the small northern Michigan town of Benzonia, where he was raised. "All the old men," he explained,

"were Civil War veterans. We boys used to sit around and listen to their yarns." As a result of that experience, Catton became a master of storytelling.

The Civil War was Catton's lifelong interest, but it wasn't until the age of 50 that he began writing about the war. When he was not writing, Catton enjoyed studying Central American archaeology, whittling wooden soldiers, fishing, and walking in the northern Michigan woods.

OTHER WORKS *This Hallowed Ground* (young readers' edition), *Glory Road*

PREVIEWING

NONFICTION

The Clown
Patrick F. McManus

PERSONAL CONNECTION

Have you ever turned blue in the face or almost passed out trying to keep from laughing in class? Think back to the crazy moments you have had in the classroom during your school career. Share any comical stories that come to mind. If you remember a class clown, tell how your teacher and your classmates reacted to this student. Did he or she cause you to burst out laughing or simply to roll your eyes? Use your notebook to jot down what you recall.

- My friend Tommy made the teacher laugh by . . .
- We never had a class clown but . . .

BIOGRAPHICAL CONNECTION

Like many of us, the humorist Patrick McManus enjoys reminiscing about his life experiences. Most of his stories are based on actual incidents, with exaggeration added for humorous effect. McManus explains, "If I stick to the unembellished truth for too long at a stretch, I tend to tense up, get a headache."

This kind of humorous writing is usually categorized as nonfiction, which, as you recall, tells about real people, places, and events. In this account, McManus starts with a true incident in his own classroom experience and then magnifies it somewhat. He confides, "Although I may base a story on an actual experience I've had, I usually will use characters who will produce the best comic effect."

READING CONNECTION

Exaggeration As you have learned, humorists use exaggeration to make readers laugh. An exaggeration is a statement that something is much more than it actually is. For example, in "The Clown," the narrator claims Miss Bindle, his teacher, has "an eighty-year-old face and twenty-year-old red hair." If you saw her, it is doubtful that you would find this to be true. As you read McManus's account, look for and enjoy his exaggeration of the truth.

THE Clown

by Patrick F. McManus

I admit it: my sense of humor is a bit weird. It's caused me some trouble over the years. For example, the only time I ever got sent to the principal's office at Delmore Blight Junior High was because I laughed in the wrong place at the wrong time—Miss Bindle's math class.

They don't make teachers like Miss Bindle anymore. At least, I hope they don't. She was tiny, scrawny, and fierce, with an eighty-year-old face and twenty-year-old red hair. Her wrinkles were permanently fused into a frown beneath the glowing halo of frizzy hair. Miss Bindle was the Jesse James of sarcasm: she could quick-draw a sarcastic remark and drill you between the eyes with it at thirty paces. She once hit Mort Simmons with a slug of sarcasm that spun him around half out of his desk. Then she walked over and coolly finished him off with two shots to the head. Mort recovered, but he was never the same afterward. His was a sad case.

Mort had always been dumb. The reason Miss Bindle drilled him was that he had been sneaking a look at one of my answers during a test; that's how dumb he was, or so Miss Bindle remarked, catching me with a ricochet from her shot at Mort. She never coddled us dumb kids, as did some of the kinder, more merciful teachers. She made us learn the same stuff as the smart kids. A few teachers took pity on us and let us relax in the cozy vacuum of our dumbness, but Miss Bindle forced us to learn everything the smart kids did, even though it took us three times as long. Everybody hated her for it, even the smart kids, who were cheated out of the satisfaction of knowing more than the dumb ones. Anybody could see that wasn't fair.

But I started to tell about Mort. He couldn't do arithmetic without counting on his fingers.

WORDS TO KNOW

sarcasm (sär′kăz′əm) *n.* humor intended to hurt, criticize, or ridicule a person
ricochet (rĭk′ə-shā′) *n.* a rebound, as from a surface

Miss Bindle said she didn't care what parts of his anatomy he had to count on, he was going to learn just as much math as anybody else. Mort did, too, but it was a terrible strain on him, dumb as he was. When we got to multiplying and dividing fractions, his fingers moved so fast he had to keep a glass of ice water on his desk to cool them off. It was a good thing we didn't do algebra in seventh grade, because somebody would have had to stand next to Mort with a fire extinguisher.

It is my understanding that modern educational theory dismisses the use of fear as a means of <u>inducing</u> learning in adolescents. Educators now take a more civilized approach and try to make learning an enjoyable experience. I agree with that. I know that all my children enjoyed school much more than I did. On the other hand, none of them knows how to multiply and divide fractions. I suppose that's part of the trade-off.

Fear was Miss Bindle's one and only <u>motivator</u>. It was as though she had done her teacher training at Marine boot camp. She would stick her face an inch from yours and, snarling and snapping, rearrange the molecules of your brain to suit her fancy. It was clearly evident to the person whose brain molecules were being rearranged that breath mints either hadn't been invented or hadn't come in a flavor pleasing to Miss Bindle. The oral hygiene of an executioner, however, is scarcely a matter of great concern to the potential victim.

Miss Bindle preferred psychological violence—whipping your <u>psyche</u> into a pink froth—to physical violence. Physical violence was direct and straightforward, something all of us youngsters thoroughly understood. There was no mystery to it. Given a choice, we would have taken the teacher's physical violence, which consisted of snatching the culprit by the hair and dragging him off to the principal's office. As I say, Miss Bindle was extremely short, only about half the size of some of the larger boys. When Miss Bindle grabbed them by the hair and took off for the office, they had to trail along behind her in a bent-over posture, which didn't do a lot for the macho image of some of the guys, particularly if they were saying, "Ow ow ow," as they went out the door. On the other hand, if they had stood erect, in order to depart from the room in a dignified fashion, Miss Bindle would have dangled from their hair, her feet swinging a good six inches off the floor. It was a no-win situation, and wisdom dictated the less painful of the two modes of being escorted to the office. In contrast to Miss Bindle, other teachers merely pointed toward the door and ordered, "Go to the office!" This method allowed the typical louts, some of whom were near voting age, to leave the room swaggering and sneering. No lout ever left Miss Bindle's room swaggering and sneering.

I was a fairly timid fellow and took great care never to attract the wrath of Miss Bindle. I studied ways to make myself invisible in her class, with such success that a couple of times she marked me absent when I was there. Pitiful victims were snatched from their desks on all sides of me, but month after month I escaped unsnatched, making myself increasingly invisible, until finally there were only a few weeks left of my seventh-grade sentence. I thought I was going to make it safely through to the end of the school year, but I hadn't taken into

WORDS
TO
KNOW

inducing (ĭn-dōō′sĭng) *n.* bringing about the occurrence of **induce** *v.*
motivator (mō′tə-vā′tər) *n.* a spur to action
psyche (sī′kē) *n.* a mind or soul

account my weird sense of humor—or my friend Slick.

Clifford Slick was the class clown. Ol' Slick felt his purpose in life was to make people laugh, and he was pretty good at it. Everybody liked Slick. We would gather around him during lunch hour to watch his routines and laugh ourselves sick. He did a wonderful impression of Miss Bindle snatching a kid by the hair and dragging him off. He did both parts alternately, the kid and Miss Bindle, and it was hilarious. One of the reasons Slick got the routine down so well was that he got snatched about once a week. It was as though he had researched the act. He knew every little nuance of a snatching, and how to exaggerate it just enough to turn the horror into humor. It was a gift.

One day before school, I made the mistake of bragging to Slick that I was going to make it all the way through the year without getting snatched by Miss Bindle. Slick was concentrating on combing his hair into a weird shape. His father had shot a bear, and Slick had come into a quantity of bear grease. He slathered a copious amount of bear grease on his hair and was delighted to see that he could now comb it into any shape he wanted. He combed it flat down against his skull, so that it looked as though he were wearing a shiny, tight leather helmet.

"How's that look?" he asked me. "Funny?"

I grinned. "Yeah, pretty funny, Cliff. I like the one best, though, where you comb it straight out from your forehead. It looks like a duck bill. Ha!"

"Okay, good," he said. "I'll go with that. Should get some laughs. Now what was that you were saying?"

"I said I've never been snatched by Miss

Bindle. I'm going to make it all the way through the year without getting snatched."

Slick turned a malevolent smile on me. "No you ain't. Today you're going to bust out laughing right in old Bindle's class!"

"Not a chance!" The mere thought of bursting out laughing in Miss Bindle's class would totally paralyze my entire laughing apparatus. It was like having a fail-safe mechanism.

"You'll laugh," Slick said. "I'll make you laugh."

I shook my head. "No way."

In the whole hundred or so years that Miss Bindle had taught, I was reasonably sure that not so much as a snicker had ever been heard in her class, let alone a laugh. It was absolutely insane for Slick to think that I, a profoundly fearful and insecure person, would achieve fame as the one kid ever to burst out laughing within snatching range of Miss Bindle.

As soon as Miss Bindle's back was turned to scratch some fractions on the blackboard, Slick went into his routine. He took a dainty sip from his ink bottle and then made a terrible face. His greasy duck-bill hair contributed considerably to the comedy. I felt a laugh coming on but easily strangled it. Slick looked disappointed. Then he stuck two yellow pencils up his nose, his impression of a walrus. I felt a major laugh inflating inside me. Slick next imitated a walrus taking a dainty sip of tea. That almost got me, but the laugh exploded deep in my interior with a muffled *whump!* Suspicious, Olga Bonemarrow, in the next row, glared at me. Feeling as though I had suffered major internal injuries, I wiped some tears from my eyes. Slick took this as an encouraging sign and pulled out all the stops. He was doing his duck-bill walrus daintily sipping tea while wiggling its ears when Miss Bindle turned to face the class.

He was doing his duck-bill walrus daintily sipping tea while wiggling its ears.

"Clifford!" she roared, hurtling down the aisle like a tiny, ancient, redheaded dreadnought.[1] Slick's ears ceased to wiggle; the pencils in his nose quivered; a bit of inky drool dribbled from his gaping mouth. He clenched his eyes in preparation for a major-league snatching. Miss Bindle grabbed at his hair and headed off down the aisle, obviously expecting Slick to be firmly in tow. But Slick was still seated at his desk, eyes clenched, pencils up nose. Miss Bindle rushed back and made another pass at his hair, but again her hand slipped off. She snatched again and again, with even less effect. Apparently, it was the first time she had ever encountered bear-greased hair on one of her snatchees.

All the while, Slick sat there numbly, the yellow pencils poking out of his nose and a terrible expression on his face. Maybe it was Slick's expression that got to me, or maybe it was the way the teacher stared down at her greasy palms, her eyes full of rage and disgust and incomprehension. Whatever the trigger, it bypassed the fail-safe mechanism. My wild, booming laugh detonated like a bomb in the frozen silence of the room. I could scarcely believe it was my own laugh. I hoped it might be Mort's: only he might possibly be stupid enough to laugh in Miss Bindle's math class. But no, the laugh, now diminishing from a roar into a sort of breathless squealing, was none other than my own. I had been betrayed by my weird sense of humor! By Clifford Slick and his bear grease! And yes, even by Miss Bindle! As I writhed in an agony of mirth, half hilarity and half terror, I could feel Miss Bindle's stiletto[2] eyes piercing my living—for the moment—flesh. My stunned classmates failed to find my laughter infectious. He who laughed in Miss Bindle's class laughed alone.

And then it happened. "Clifford! Pat!" snarled Miss Bindle. "Go to the office!" She pointed the way with a finger shiny with bear grease.

I left the classroom erect and dignified. Cliff went out the door sideways, doing his comical little vaudeville[3] dance. It didn't get a laugh.

After the principal, Mr. Wiggens, gave us his bored lecture on the importance of discipline in a learning environment, he ordered us back to class. As I was passing the entrance of the cloakroom, I heard strange sounds emanating from the far end. A quick glance revealed that it was Miss Bindle. At first I thought she was crying, possibly over the disappointment of failing to snatch Cliff's and my hair. But no! She was laughing! Cackling, actually, quietly and to herself. It struck me that Miss Bindle had a weird sense of humor, too. ❖

---

1. **dreadnought** (drĕd′nôt′): a heavily armed battleship.
2. **stiletto**: a small dagger with a slender blade.
3. **vaudeville** (vôd′vĭl′): a stage performance made up of song-and-dance numbers and slapstick comedy.

RESPONDING OPTIONS

FROM PERSONAL RESPONSE TO CRITICAL ANALYSIS

REFLECT 1. Did you find this selection funny? Why or why not?

RETHINK 2. What is the narrator's opinion of Miss Bindle? Give evidence to support your answer.

Consider
- the two teaching methods he mentions
- his own behavior
- whether his perceptions of Miss Bindle have changed by the end of the selection

3. Use details from the selection to evaluate Miss Bindle as a teacher.

4. What do you think of Slick's behavior? Use pantomime to show what you think his behavior is like.

5. Could the events described in this selection occur in your classroom? Why or why not?

RELATE 6. The narrator seems to believe that modern teaching methods are more enjoyable but result in inferior learning. Do you agree with him? Do you feel that harsher discipline would improve students' performance? Explain your opinion.

ANOTHER PATHWAY

With another student, choose a section of "The Clown" that you would enjoy telling from Miss Bindle's point of view. Then rewrite that section in Miss Bindle's words. Don't forget about her "weird sense of humor," and feel free to exaggerate as McManus did. Tell your story to the class.

LITERARY CONCEPTS

McManus uses several methods to create **humor,** or make his writing funny. How does he use repetition in the third paragraph? What comical actions does he describe? What names of people and places add humor? What examples of exaggeration did you notice as you read?

CONCEPT REVIEW: Irony As you know, irony is a contrast between what is expected and what actually happens. Explain how the end of this selection is ironic and why the irony is amusing.

QUICKWRITES

1. Pretend that you are Miss Bindle and create an amusing rhyming **poem** about Clifford Slick.

2. Imagine other antics that Clifford Slick might perform in class. Write a brief **narrative** of new trouble he gets into. You may wish to include other characters, like Olga Bonemarrow.

📁 **PORTFOLIO** *Save your writing. You may want to use it later as a springboard to a piece for your portfolio.*

ALTERNATIVE ACTIVITIES

A caricature is a drawing of a person in which certain physical characteristics and mannerisms are exaggerated for the sake of humor. Using the descriptions in the selection, draw a **caricature** of Miss Bindle or Clifford Slick. If you have an art program on your computer, here is a chance to use it.

ACROSS THE CURRICULUM

Media Watch a situation comedy or a standup comedian on television. Compare the ways in which humor is created on the television show with the techniques that McManus uses in "The Clown." Which methods work more easily in visual media, and which seem more appropriate for speaking or writing? Discuss your findings with the class.

WORDS TO KNOW

Review the Words to Know at the bottom of the selection pages. Decide which word is described in each riddle below, and write the answer on your paper.

1. Bullets, balls, and smart remarks can do this and come back at you!
2. I am a lot—maybe more than you need, like a great deal of homework.
3. Sticks and stones can break your bones, but I can hurt your feelings.
4. I can be money, praise, or a spanking; I'll make you do what I want!
5. Just a shade of me can make all the difference!
6. I'm more than naughty; I'm evil, and I wish you harm!
7. I'm what you might do if you laugh really hard or feel terrible pain.
8. Belly laughs, chuckles, howls, guffaws—these are all signs of me.
9. A girl in mythology is named for me; she really knew her own mind!
10. I'm making things happen.

PATRICK F. MCMANUS

The humor and practical jokes that sustained the young Patrick McManus and his family through tragedy and hardship resurface in his humorous stories. McManus's father and stepfather died when he was young, and his family lost their first home to fire.

He claims that his entire family had a weird sense of humor. For example, his mother told him that after his birth in Sandpoint, Idaho, she paid the attending doctor in homemade preserves and canned vegetables.

When McManus was in the first grade, his mother taught in a rundown, one-room schoolhouse, and the family slept on beds in the back of

1933–

the classroom. McManus attended the school where his mother taught until the eighth grade. He says that she flunked him in second grade. If it had not been for his love of reading about such heroes as Huck Finn and Tom Sawyer, the author claims, "I might have run totally wild."

McManus began his writing career while attending college. He published his first book of humorous stories in 1978 and later was an editor for *Field and Stream* and *Outdoor Life* magazines.

OTHER WORKS *Real Ponies Don't Go Oink!; Kid Camping from Aaaaiii! to Zip*

The Garden Road (1962), Fairfield Porter. Oil on canvas, 62″ × 48″, collection of the Whitney Museum of American Art, New York, gift of the Greylock Foundation (62.55). Copyright © 1995 Whitney Museum of American Art. Photo by Geoffrey Clements, New York.

The Apprentice

BY DOROTHY CANFIELD FISHER

The day had been one of the unbearable ones, when every sound had set her teeth on edge like chalk creaking on a blackboard, when every word her father or mother said to her or did not say to her seemed an intentional injustice. And of course it would happen, as the fitting end to such a day, that just as the sun went down back of the mountain and the long twilight began, she noticed that Rollie was not around.

Tense with exasperation[1] at what her mother would say, she began to call him in a carefully casual tone—she would simply explode if mother got going: "Here Rollie! He-ere boy! Want to go for a walk, Rollie?" Whistling to him cheerfully, her heart full of wrath at the way the world treated her, she made the rounds of his haunts: the corner of the woodshed, where he liked to curl up on the wool of father's discarded old sweater; the

hay barn, the cow barn, the sunny spot on the side porch. No Rollie.

Perhaps he had sneaked upstairs to lie on her bed, where he was not supposed to go—not that *she* would have minded! That rule was part of mother's fussiness, part, too, of mother's bossiness. It was *her* bed, wasn't it? But was she allowed the say-so about it? Not on your life. They *said* she could have things the way she wanted in her own room, now she was in her teens, but—her heart burned at unfairness as she took the stairs stormily, two steps at a time, her pigtails flopping up and down on her back. If Rollie was there, she was just going to let him stay there, and mother could say what she wanted to.

But he was not there. The bedspread and pillow were crumpled, but that was where she

---

1. **exasperation** (ĭg-zăs´pə-rā´shən): frustrated annoyance.

had flung herself down to cry that afternoon. Every nerve in her had been twanging discordantly, but she couldn't cry. She could only lie there, her hands doubled up hard, furious that she had nothing to cry about. Not really. She was too big to cry just over father's having said to her, severely, "I told you if I let you take the chess set, you were to put it away when you got through with it. One of the pawns was on the floor of our bedroom this morning. I stepped on it. If I'd had my shoes on I'd have broken it."

Well, he *had* told her that. And he hadn't said she mustn't ever take the set again. No, the instant she thought about that, she knew she couldn't cry about it. She could be, and was, in a rage about the way father kept on talking, long after she'd got his point: "It's not that I care so much about the chess set. It's because if you don't learn how to take care of things, you yourself will suffer for it. You'll forget or neglect something that will be really important, for *you*. We *have* to try to teach you to be responsible for what you've said you'll take care of. If we—" on and on.

She stood there, dry eyed, by the bed that Rollie had not crumpled and thought, *I hope mother sees the spread and says something about Rollie—I just hope she does.*

She heard her mother coming down the hall, and hastily shut her door. She had a right to shut the door to her own room, hadn't she? She had *some* rights, she supposed, even if she was only thirteen and the youngest child. If her mother opened it to say, "What are you doing in here that you don't want me to see?" she'd say—she'd just say—

But her mother did not open the door. Her feet went steadily on along the hall, and then,

carefully, slowly, down the stairs. She probably had an armful of winter things she was bringing down from the attic. She was probably thinking that a tall, thirteen-year-old daughter was big enough to help with a chore like that. But she wouldn't *say* anything. She would just get out that insulting look of a grownup silently putting up with a crazy unreasonable kid. She had worn that expression all day; it was too much to be endured.

Up in her bedroom behind her closed door the thirteen-year-old stamped her foot in a gust of uncontrollable rage, nonetheless savage and heart-shaking because it was mysterious to her.

But she had not located Rollie. She would be cut into little pieces before she would let her father and mother know she had lost sight of him, forgotten about him. They would not scold her, she knew. They would do worse; they would look at her. And in their silence she would hear, droning on reproachfully, what they had said when she had been begging to keep for her own the sweet, woolly collie puppy in her arms.

How warm he had felt! Astonishing how warm and alive a puppy was compared with a doll! She had never liked her dolls much after she had held Rollie, feeling him warm against her breast, warm and wriggling, bursting with life, reaching up to lick her face. He had loved her from that first instant. As he felt her arms around him his liquid, beautiful eyes had melted in trusting sweetness. And they did now, whenever he looked at her. Her dog was the only creature in the world who *really* loved her, she thought passionately.

And back then, at the very minute when, as a darling baby dog, he was beginning to love her, her father and mother were saying, so cold, so reasonable—gosh, how she *hated* reasonableness!— "Now, Peg, remember that, living where we do, with sheep on the farms around us, it is a serious responsibility to have a collie dog. If you keep him, you've got to be the one to take care of him. You'll have to be the one to train him to stay at home. We're too busy with you children to start bringing up a puppy too."

Rollie, nestling in her arms, let one hind leg drop awkwardly. It must be uncomfortable. She looked down at him tenderly, tucked his leg up under him and gave him a hug. He laughed up in her face—he really did laugh, his mouth stretched wide in a cheerful grin. Now he was snug in a warm little ball.

Her parents were saying, "If you want him, you can have him. But you must be responsible for him. If he gets to running sheep, he'll just have to be shot, you know that."

They had not said, aloud, "Like the Wilsons' collie." They never mentioned that awfulness—her racing unsuspectingly down across the fields just at the horrible moment when Mr. Wilson shot their collie, caught in the very act of killing sheep. They probably thought that if they never spoke about it, she would forget it—*forget* the crack of that rifle, and the collapse of the great beautiful dog! Forget the red red blood spurting from the hole in his head. She hadn't forgotten. She never would. She knew as well as they did how important it was to train a collie puppy about sheep. They didn't have to rub it in like that. They always rubbed everything in. She had told them, fervently, indignantly, that of *course* she would take care of him, be responsible for him, teach him to stay at home. Of course. Of course. *She* understood!

"If he gets to running sheep, he'll just have to be shot, you know that."

And now, when he was six months old, tall, rangy,[2] powerful, standing up far above her knee, nearly to her waist, she didn't know where he was. But of course he must be somewhere around. He always was. She composed her face to look natural and went downstairs to search the house. He was probably asleep somewhere. She looked every room over carefully. Her mother was nowhere visible. It was safe to call him again, to give the special piercing whistle which always brought him racing to her, the white-feathered plume of his tail waving in elation that she wanted him.

But he did not answer. She stood still on the front porch to think.

Could he have gone up to their special place in the edge of the field where the three young pines, their branches growing close to the ground, made a triangular, walled-in space, completely hidden from the world? Sometimes he went up there with her, and when she lay down on the dried grass to dream he, too, lay down quietly, his head on his paws, his beautiful eyes fixed adoringly on her. He entered into her every mood. If she wanted to be quiet, all right, he did too. It didn't seem as though he would have gone alone there. Still—she loped up the steep slope of the field rather fast, beginning to be anxious.

No, he was not there. She stood irresolutely[3] in the roofless, green-walled triangular hide-out, wondering what to do next.

Then, before she knew what thought had come into her mind, its emotional impact knocked her down. At least her knees

---

2. **rangy** (rān'jē): slender and long-limbed.

3. **irresolutely** (ĭ-rĕz'ə-lōōt'lē): in an undecided way.

crumpled under her. The Wilsons had, last Wednesday, brought their sheep down from the far upper pasture, to the home farm. They were—she herself had seen them on her way to school, and like an idiot had not thought of Rollie—on the river meadow.

She was off like a racer at the crack of the starting pistol, her long, strong legs stretched in great leaps, her pigtails flying. She took the short cut, regardless of the brambles. Their thorn-spiked, wiry stems tore at her flesh, but she did not care. She welcomed the pain. It was something she was doing for Rollie, for her Rollie.

She was in the pine woods now, rushing down the steep, stony path, tripping over roots, half falling, catching herself just in time, not slackening her speed. She burst out on the open knoll above the river meadow, calling wildly, "Rollie, here Rollie, here, boy! Here! Here!" She tried to whistle, but she was crying too hard to pucker her lips.

There was nobody to see or hear her. Twilight was falling over the bare, grassy knoll. The sunless evening wind slid down the mountain like an invisible river, engulfing her in cold. Her teeth began to chatter. "Here, Rollie, here, boy, here!" She strained her eyes to look down into the meadow to see if the sheep were there. She could not be sure. She stopped calling him as she would a dog, and called out his name despairingly, as if he were her child, "Rollie! Oh, *Rollie,* where are you?"

The tears ran down her cheeks in streams. She sobbed loudly, terribly; she did not try to control herself, since there was no one to hear. "Hou! Hou! Hou!" she sobbed, her face contorted grotesquely. "Oh, Rollie! Rollie! Rollie!" She had wanted something to cry about. Oh, how terribly now she had something to cry about.

She saw him as clearly as if he were there beside her, his muzzle and gaping mouth all smeared with the betraying blood (like the Wilsons' collie). "But he didn't *know* it was wrong!" she screamed like a wild creature. "Nobody *told* him it was wrong. It was my fault. I should have taken better care of him. I will now. I will!"

But no matter how she screamed, she could not make herself heard. In the cold gathering darkness, she saw him stand, poor, guiltless victim of his ignorance, who should have been protected from his own nature, his beautiful soft eyes looking at her with love, his splendid plumed tail waving gently. "It was my fault. I promised I would bring him up. I should have *made* him stay at home. I was responsible for him. It was my fault."

But she could not make his executioners hear her. The shot rang out, Rollie sank down, his beautiful liquid eyes glazed, the blood spurting from the hole in his head—like the Wilsons' collie. She gave a wild shriek, long, soul-satisfying, frantic. It was the scream at sudden, unendurable tragedy of a mature, full-blooded woman. It drained dry the girl of thirteen. She came to herself. She was standing on the knoll, trembling and quaking with cold, the darkness closing in on her.

Her breath had given out. For once in her life she had wept all the tears there were in her body. Her hands were so stiff with cold she could scarcely close them. How her nose was running, simply streaming down her upper lip! And she had no handkerchief. She lifted her skirt, fumbled for her slip, stooped, blew her nose on it, wiped her eyes, drew a long quavering breath—and heard something! Far off in the distance, a faint sound, like a dog's muffled bark.

She whirled on her heels and bent her head to

Lizzie and Bruno (1970), Fairfield Porter. Collection of Dr. and Mrs. Joseph Del Gaudio. Photo by Affiliated Photographic Services, Inc.

listen. The sound did not come from the meadow below the knoll. It came from back of her, from the Wilsons' maple grove higher up. She held her breath. Yes, it came from there. She began to run again, but now she was not sobbing. She was silent, absorbed in her effort to cover ground. If she could only live to get there, to see if it really were Rollie. She ran steadily till she came to the fence, and went over this in a great plunge. Her skirt caught on a nail. She impatiently pulled at it, not hearing or not heeding the long sibilant tear as it came loose. She was in the dusky maple woods, stumbling over the rocks as she ran. As she tore on up the slope she knew it was Rollie's bark.

She stopped short and leaned weakly against a tree, sick with the breathlessness of her straining lungs, sick in the reaction of relief, sick with anger at Rollie, who had been here having a wonderful time while she had been dying, just dying in terror about him.

For she could now not only hear that it was Rollie's bark; she could hear, in the dog language she knew as well as he, what he was saying in those excited yips: that he had run a woodchuck into a hole in the tumbled stone wall, that he almost had him, that the intoxicating wild animal smell was as close to him—almost—as if he had his jaws on his quarry. Yip! Woof! Yip! Yip!

The wild, joyful quality of the dog talk enraged the girl. She was trembling in exhaustion, in indignation. So that was where he had been, when she was killing herself trying to take care of him. Plenty near enough to hear her calling and whistling to him, if he had paid attention. Just so set on having his foolish good time, he never thought to listen for her call.

She stooped to pick up a stout stick. She would teach him! It was time he had something to make him remember to listen. She started forward.

But she stopped, stood thinking. One of the things to remember about collies—everybody knew that—was their sensitiveness. A collie who had been beaten was never "right" again. His spirit was broken. "Anything but a broken-spirited collie," the farmers often said. They were no good after that.

She threw down her stick. Anyhow, she thought, he was too young to know, really, that he had done wrong. He was still only a puppy. Like all puppies, he got perfectly crazy over wild-animal smells. Probably he really and truly hadn't heard her calling and whistling.

All the same, all the same— she stared intently into the twilight—he couldn't be let to grow up just as he wanted to. She would have to make him understand that he mustn't go off this way by himself. He must be trained to know how to do what a good dog does— not because *she* wanted him to, but for his own sake.

She walked on now, steady, purposeful, gathering her inner strength together, Olympian[4] in her understanding of the full meaning of the event.

When he heard his own special young god approaching, he turned delightedly and ran to meet her, panting, his tongue hanging out. His eyes shone. He jumped up on her in an ecstasy of welcome and licked her face.

But she pushed him away. Her face and voice were grave. "No, Rollie, *no!*" she said severely. "You're *bad*. You know you're not to go off in the woods without me! You are—a—*bad—dog.*"

He was horrified, stricken into misery. He stood facing her, frozen, the gladness going out of his eyes, the erect waving plume of his tail slowly lowered to slinking, guilty dejection.

"I know you were all wrapped up in that woodchuck. But that's no excuse. You *could* have heard me, calling you, whistling for you, if you'd paid attention," she went on. "You've got to learn, and I've got to teach you."

With a shudder of misery he lay down, his tail stretched out limp on the ground, his head flat on his paws, his ears drooping—ears ringing with the doomsday awfulness of the voice he so loved and revered.[5] He must have been utterly wicked. He trembled, and turned his head away from her august look of blame, groveling in remorse[6] for whatever mysterious sin he had committed.

She sat down by him, as miserable as he. "I don't *want* to scold you. But I have to! I have to bring you up right, or you'll get shot, Rollie. You *mustn't* go away from the house without me, do you hear, *never!*"

Catching, with his sharp ears yearning for her approval, a faint overtone of relenting affection in her voice, he lifted his eyes to her, humbly, soft in imploring[7] fondness.

"Oh, Rollie!" she said, stooping low over him. "I *do* love you. I do. But I *have* to bring you up. I'm responsible for you, don't you see?"

He did not see. Hearing sternness, or

He was horrified, stricken into misery.

_____

4. **Olympian:** godlike; from the name of Mount Olympus, the dwelling place of the gods in Greek mythology.

5. **revered** (rĭ-vîrd′): regarded with awe and devotion.

6. **groveling in remorse:** lying submissively as a sign of guilt or regret.

7. **imploring:** begging; appealing.

something else he did not recognize, in the beloved voice, he shut his eyes tight in sorrow, and made a little whimpering lament in his throat.

She had never heard him cry before. It was too much. She sat down by him and drew his head to her, rocking him in her arms, soothing him with inarticulate small murmurs.

He leaped in her arms and wriggled happily as he had when he was a baby; he reached up to lick her face as he had then. But he was no baby now. He was half as big as she, a great, warm, pulsing, living armful of love. She clasped him closely. Her heart was brimming full, but calmed, quiet. The blood flowed in equable gentleness all over her body. She was deliciously warm. Her nose was still running a little. She sniffed and wiped it on her sleeve.

It was almost dark now. "We'll be late to supper, Rollie," she said responsibly. Pushing him gently off, she stood up. "Home, Rollie, home!"

Here was a command he could understand. At once he trotted along the path toward home. His plumed tail, held high, waved cheerfully. His short dog memory had dropped into oblivion the suffering just back of him.

Her human memory was longer. His prancing gait was as carefree as a young child's. Plodding heavily like a serious adult, she trod behind him. Her very shoulders seemed bowed by what she had lived through. She felt, she thought, like an old, old woman of thirty. But it was all right now. She knew she had made an impression on him.

When they came out into the open pasture, Rollie ran back to get her to play with him. He leaped around her in circles, barking in cheerful yawps, jumping up on her, inviting her to run a race with him, to throw him a stick, to come alive.

His high spirits were ridiculous but infectious. She gave one little leap to match his. Rollie pretended that this was a threat to him, planted his forepaws low and barked loudly at her, laughing between yips. He was so funny, she thought, when he grinned that way. She laughed back, and gave another mock-threatening leap at him. Radiant that his sky was once more clear, he sprang high on his steel-spring muscles in an explosion of happiness, and bounded in circles around her.

Following him, not noting in the dusk where she was going, she felt the grassy slope drop steeply. Oh, yes, she knew where she was. They had come to the rolling-down hill just back of the house. All the kids rolled down there, even the little ones, because it was soft grass without a stone. She had rolled down that slope a million times—years and years ago, when she was a kid herself. It was fun. She remembered well the whirling dizziness of the descent, all the world turning over and over crazily. And the delicious giddy staggering when you first stood up, the earth still spinning under your feet.

"All right, Rollie, let's go," she cried, and flung herself down in the rolling position, her arms straight up over her head.

Rollie had never seen this skylarking before. It threw him into almost hysterical amusement. He capered around the rapidly rolling figure, half scared, mystified, enchanted.

His wild frolicsome barking might have come from her own throat, so accurately did it sound the way she felt—crazy, foolish, like a little kid, no more than five years old, the age she had been when she had last rolled down that hill.

At the bottom she sprang up, on muscles as steel-strong as Rollie's. She staggered a little, and laughed aloud.

The living room windows were just before

Hilltop—Farmhouse (1929), Marie Atkinson Hull. Oil on canvas board, 24″ × 20″, Lauren Rogers Museum of Art, Laurel, Mississippi, Lauren Rogers Museum Purchase, 1984 (84.3).

them. How yellow lighted windows looked when you were in the darkness going home. How nice and yellow. Maybe mother had waffles for supper. She was a swell cook, mother was, and she certainly gave her family all the breaks, when it came to meals.

"Home, Rollie, home!" She burst open the door to the living room. "Hi, mom, what you got for supper?"

From the kitchen her mother announced coolly, "I hate to break the news to you, but it's waffles."

"Oh, *mom!*" she shouted in ecstasy.

Her mother could not see her. She did not need to. "For goodness' sakes, go and wash," she called.

In the long mirror across the room she saw herself, her hair hanging wild, her long bare legs scratched, her broadly smiling face dirt-streaked, her torn skirt dangling, her dog laughing up at her. Gosh, was it a relief to feel your own age, just exactly thirteen years old! ❖

DOROTHY CANFIELD FISHER

1879–1958

Dorothy Canfield Fisher's novels and short stories, both those for children and those for adults, were inspired by the ordinary events and human problems she saw around her. Major elements of "The Apprentice" were part of her life: her collie, her daughter Sally, and her country home.

Fisher was born in Lawrence, Kansas. Her father taught at a college, and her mother was an artist. She attended Ohio State University, planning to be a violinist or a language teacher. Soon after receiving her doctorate from Columbia University, with her stories selling, she decided on a writing career.

During World War I, Fisher took her children to France while her husband served with an ambulance unit there. She wrote stories that were translated into Braille for blinded soldiers and started a fund to aid French children affected by the war. Later, in 1940, she started the Children's Crusade for Children, in which American children donated pennies to help refugee children.

A member of the first Book-of-the-Month Club selection panel, and the only woman on the panel, Fisher read and critiqued more than 4,000 books over 25 years before failing eyesight forced her to resign.

So popular were Fisher's compassionate stories and her nonfiction about children, parenting, and education that she received many awards and honorary degrees. The Dorothy Canfield Fisher Children's Book Award was established in her honor, and a group of Indiana women named their literary club after her. Eleanor Roosevelt placed Fisher among the ten American women who had had the most influence on women's lives.

WRITING ABOUT LITERATURE

EXPLORING PERSPECTIVES

In literature, as in life, looking at an event from another point of view can change your understanding. For example, if Miss Bindle narrated "The Clown" or if Greg narrated "The Treasure of Lemon Brown," imagine how the stories would change! In the following pages you will

- look at how authors use point of view in stories
- explore how changing a story element affects a story
- notice how people react differently to an experience

The Writer's Style: Point of View In literature, point of view refers to the perspective from which the story is told. Two common types of point of view are first person and third person. In first-person point of view, the narrator is a character in the story. In third-person, the narrator describes the action but doesn't take part in it.

BEAR GREASE

Read the Literature

Notice the point of view in each of the following excerpts.

Literature Models

First-Person Point of View
What does the point of view allow you to learn about the narrator? How does it affect your view of Miss Bindle?

> I was a fairly timid fellow and took great care never to attract the wrath of Miss Bindle. I studied ways to make myself invisible in her class, with such success that a couple of times she marked me absent when I was there. Pitiful victims were snatched from their desks on all sides of me, but month after month I escaped unsnatched, making myself increasingly invisible . . .
>
> Patrick F. McManus, from "The Clown"

Third-Person Point of View
Is the narrator part of this story? What kind of information did you get in the first model that you do not get here?

> Greg went to the window and saw three men, neighborhood thugs, on the stoop. One was carrying a length of pipe. Greg looked back toward Lemon Brown, who moved quietly across the room to the window. The old man looked out, then beckoned frantically for Greg to follow him. For a moment Greg couldn't move.
>
> Walter Dean Myers, from "The Treasure of Lemon Brown"

Connect to Life

Newspaper, magazine, television, and radio writers and reporters use both first-person and third-person point of view. When might a reporter want to write in the first person? When might third person be better?

Magazine Article

I'm a mediator, and I carry what I learn into the street. One time, there was something going on, and I told the guys, "Look, you're not talking, you're arguing. You're not listening, all you're doing is yelling. You don't get along. Just forget about it. You go your way, you go yours. Because, whatcha gonna do? You're gonna fight. *Boom!* . . . and it never ends. Just let it be."

Janet Gonzales, 19, New York City
from "Fresh Voices"
Parade, January 8, 1995

First-Person Point of View
Would this paragraph be more or less interesting written in the third person? Why do you think so?

Try Your Hand: Understanding Point of View

1. **Use Point of View** Use first-person or third-person point of view to develop one of these ideas into a paragraph.

   - A teenager attends a concert.
   - A child finds a stray pet.

2. **Revise a QuickWrite** Look through your QuickWrites to find a story idea that you can develop by using the point of view of one of the characters. Visualize one event as this person would experience it. Think about how this character would feel and how he or she would express these feelings. Then write a scene based on your idea.

3. **Rewrite a Scene** Choose a paragraph from one of the selections you have read so far in this unit and rewrite it, changing its point of view. Consider what information you will need to add or leave out depending on the point of view you are using.

Using Pronouns
The pronouns you use in a story will depend on the point of view you're telling the story from. Notice how authors Patrick F. McManus and Walter Dean Myers use pronouns to show the story's point of view.

I thought I was going to make it safely through to the end of the school year. (first-person point of view: I)

He hadn't been allowed to play high school ball, which he had really wanted to do. (third-person point of view: he)

APPLYING WHAT YOU'VE LEARNED
Rewrite the following sentences so that the speaker's point of view changes.

1. Greg knew he would fail math if he didn't study.
2. When I saw Miss Bindle laughing, I realized that she had a sense of humor, too.
3. Lemon Brown untied the strings around his leg and revealed his treasure.

For more information on pronouns, see page 872 in the Grammar Handbook.

Creative Response

One way to explore how the elements of a story work together is to change one element, such as the point of view. Then watch what happens to the story.

GUIDED ASSIGNMENT
Changing a Story Element In this assignment you will rewrite a scene from a story by changing the point of view or by changing another story element, such as the story's setting, characters, or plot.

1 Prewrite and Explore

Reexamine the stories you have read in Unit One. Examine the role of the elements in each one. Which story might be the most interesting to experiment with?

CHOOSING A SCENE AND A NEW STORY ELEMENT

Choose a story that you think would be fun to rework. Consider these questions:

- What scene in the story would be interesting to change?
- If you changed the story's setting (either the time period or the place), how would that affect the characters and what they do?
- If a key event didn't happen, how would that affect the plot?
- How would the scene change with a new narrator or different point of view?

Decision Point Now that you have thought about it, which scene would you like to retell? Which story element change would have the most impact?

**Student's
Prewriting Chart**

"The Clown"	Event: Pat Laughs in Class	
Point of View	First Person Pat	First Person Miss Bindle
Feelings	Mirth, Terror	Frustration
Thoughts	I can't believe I'm laughing	I'll never get through this lesson
Observations	Miss Bindle's stiletto eyes glaring	Pat's flushed face

GATHERING INFORMATION

Think about how changing one story element would affect the scene you've selected. For example, suppose you had Miss Bindle narrate "The Clown." How would her view of characters and events differ from Pat's? What new information would Miss Bindle give the reader? What details would her point of view *not* include? Jot down your ideas.

➋ Try a Draft

Before you write, visualize the scene. Then begin drafting new descriptions, dialogue, and events. If you're rewriting the story's opening, the SkillBuilder on writing introductions may help you. When you've finished, ask yourself a few questions:

- Does this scene reveal a change in a story element?
- Have I stuck with this new element throughout?
- What dialogue and descriptions can I add?

Student's Draft

Once I caught Mort looking at Pat's paper. I thought Pat, at least, knew better. I guess I lost my temper, and I said something sarcastic about Pat being a poor source for answers. Maybe I also wanted to get some response from Pat. He'd improved in spelling and arithmetic, but he was so quiet that I worried about him.

Introduction: Tell what Miss B. thinks of Pat. Make it sound like a teacher talking.

Describe what Clifford was doing and how he looked. Add more details about the scene.

I was used to Clifford's antics, but the bear grease was a surprise. At first I was furious. But when Pat started laughing, I saw how funny it was. And Pat was finally acting like a normal boy. I controlled myself until the boys left. Then I went into the cloakroom and laughed.

➌ Share Your Work

After you have completed your draft, use these questions to help a classmate give you feedback.

 PEER RESPONSE

- What story element have I changed? How could you tell?
- What are some ideas I might include?
- How can I make my introduction better?

SkillBuilder

 WRITER'S CRAFT

Writing Introductions

As you draft, keep in mind that your introduction should capture your audience's attention and should present the change in a story element.

- You might begin with a vivid description of the setting, the characters, or the events of your scene.
- You could start with a question to get your readers thinking about the change in the story element.
- You might begin with an interesting or humorous incident to draw your readers into your scene.
- You could begin with dialogue between characters in your scene.

APPLYING WHAT YOU'VE LEARNED
Look at the introduction to the scene you're retelling and answer these questions:

- How does the introduction engage the attention of my readers?
- What information about the change of setting, point of view, characters, or events is provided?
- What effect will the introduction have on readers?

 WRITING HANDBOOK

For more information on introductions, see page 826 in the Writing Handbook.

④ Revise and Edit

Use the information from Grammar in Context on the opposite page along with your peer comments as you revise and edit your draft. Reflect on how your change of a story element affects the scene you chose. Think about how you might share your final draft with the class.

The Quiet One

Pat sat in the back of my seventh grade classroom. He was a nice-looking boy, but he never said anything. No matter what subject the class was working on, he never volunteered to answer a question. He did his homework and never made any trouble. If I called on him, he usually had the right answer, so I knew he wasn't stupid.

How does this paragraph introduce the change of a story element (in this case, Miss Bindle as the narrator)?

I was explaining a problem and writing on the chalkboard. When I turned around to make sure the students understood, I saw something that made my blood boil. It was Clifford Slick again with pencils stuck in his nose and ink dribbling from his mouth. He wasn't imitating me this time. He was putting on another of his stupid comic routines, disturbing students who were trying to work. I rushed back to Clifford to get him out of my classroom before he completely ruined the lesson.

What information does the writer add here that could only come through the point of view of the teacher?

Standards for Evaluation

A creative response
- retells one scene from a story by changing a story element: point of view, setting, character, or plot
- keeps the new element the same throughout the scene
- changes other story elements and adds or removes information to make sense with the new element
- begins with an introduction that catches readers' attention and makes clear what element has changed

Grammar in Context

Sentence Fragments and Run-on Sentences As you turn your rough notes into a story, pay particular attention to correcting sentence fragments or run-ons.

A **sentence fragment** is a group of words that does not express a complete thought. A sentence fragment can be corrected by adding the missing subject or predicate or by combining the incomplete thought with another sentence.

A **run-on sentence** is two or more sentences incorrectly written as one. Sometimes a run-on sentence can be corrected by separating the two complete thoughts with an end mark or with a conjunction and a comma.

Clifford was my problem student. Because his only interest was in making others laugh. Clifford would do anything to disrupt my class, he never was concerned about hurting my feelings or making me angry. He Delighted in making me look like an ogre. When I would have to take him to the principal's office.

In the example above, the sentence fragments and run-on sentence are corrected.

Try Your Hand: Writing Correct Sentences

Revise the following paragraph by correcting any sentence fragments or run-on sentences.

> The year was almost over. When I learned that Pat actually had a sense of humor. I was anxious to cover the last chapter of the arithmetic text that morning. (Every student had learned to multiply and divide fractions some of them still needed to work on word problems.) I wasn't thinking. When I turned my back on Clifford.

SkillBuilder

G → GRAMMAR FROM WRITING

Avoiding Fragments
Sentence fragments can often be eliminated in your writing by combining them with another sentence.

If I called on him, he usually had the right answer.

Be careful, however, that you are not putting two simple sentences together with a comma and creating a run-on sentence. Two simple sentences can correctly be combined with a comma and conjunction such as *and, but,* or *or.*

I was used to Clifford's antics, but the bear grease was a surprise.

Sometimes two simple sentences can be joined with a semicolon if they are very closely related.

He wasn't imitating me this time; he was putting on a comic routine.

APPLYING WHAT YOU'VE LEARNED
Combine the fragments below into complete sentences.

When Pat started laughing. I saw how funny it was. And how Pat was finally acting like a normal boy. I controlled myself. Until the boys left.

 GRAMMAR HANDBOOK

For more information about writing complete sentences, see page 860 of the Grammar Handbook.

CLOSE-UP ON PERSPECTIVE

Like characters you read about in literature, people that you see every day have different ways of looking at the same experience. Look at the faces of the people in this situation and think about each person's response.

View In your journal, describe what you think is happening here and how people are reacting.

Interpret Using the observations in your journal, continue writing about the scene. Why do you think the riders' reactions are different? How would you interpret what they are feeling, based on their expressions?

Discuss Discuss this situation in a small group. Say why you think the riders' reactions are different. Imagine each of these people retelling the event later. How might their versions differ? Now use the SkillBuilder on the opposite page for help in evaluating perspectives.

CRITICAL THINKING

Analyzing Perspective

Perspective refers to the way we look at events and people around us. Because we have different likes and dislikes and because we come from different backgrounds, our perspectives are often different. Conflicts can occur when we don't take the time to think about what the other person sees. For example, you may think the new student is stuck-up. If you look at the situation through her eyes, however, you may see that she is shy and unsure of herself.

Point of view also affects the information you receive from others. What does this tell you about how you might judge news stories, political speeches, and other kinds of information you receive? Be sure you consider any event, idea, or person from different perspectives.

APPLYING WHAT YOU'VE LEARNED
In a small group, discuss one or more of the following.

- List situations in which seeing someone else's perspective would be important.
- What problems can occur when someone insists that his or her perspective is more important than someone else's?
- Can you think of a time when considering someone else's point of view helped you solve a problem?

FOOLED BY APPEARANCES

WHAT DO YOU THINK?

REFLECTING ON THEME

Looks can be deceiving. Have you ever read a terrific book that had a dull and uninteresting cover? The activities on this page will help you to begin investigating how things may not always be as they first appear. Keep a record of your impressions, ideas, and results.

How would you handle this?

Things aren't always what they seem. You start talking to someone you think is a new kid in your school. In fact, he or she is a student teacher, who looks much younger than he or she really is. With a partner, develop a skit about the confusions that might arise.

What would you do?

Is a white lie, or deception, ever justified? Would you tell the truth in these situations?

A Your boyfriend or girlfriend has a new hairstyle, which you think is awful.

B A friend has written a song, which you absolutely hate! Working in groups, think of three other situations in which some people might avoid telling the truth. Survey your classmates to see how they would react in each situation.

Situation A
definitely
probably
possibly
definitely not

What do you see in nature?

We can be fooled by changing appearances in nature. Sometimes the sky is calm and clear, at other times gloomy and threatening. Brainstorm elements of nature that can have more than one aspect or face. Then choose one element and create a work of art that shows several of its faces.

Looking back

At the beginning of this unit, you thought about ways in which people or events have caused you to change your perceptions. Did your ideas change as you read the selections in Part 1? Test this by choosing one of the selections and considering the ways in which it connects to events and people in your life. In what ways is it different from your life? Convey your thoughts in a diagram or picture.

REFLECT & ASSESS

NONFICTION

from All Things Bright and Beautiful
James Herriot

PERSONAL CONNECTION

This selection was written by British country veterinarian and author James Herriot, known for his accounts of his funny and often unusual dealings with a wide variety of animals and their owners. Have you ever had a comical, unusual, or even dangerous experience with an animal? Share with the class any interesting encounters you can remember.

SCIENCE CONNECTION

As a veterinarian, Herriot treated all kinds of animals with much less knowledge and technology than is available today. Today's veterinarians use new drugs and new technologies and techniques that are nearly as advanced as those used in medicine for humans. These days, veterinarians are more specialized: country vets chiefly treat farm animals, while city vets care mainly for pets. Some vets treat zoo animals, and others conduct research on diseases and new drugs.

READING CONNECTION

Word	Clues	Probable Meaning
pelt		
flank		

Context Clues As Herriot discusses the animals he treats and their human owners, he may use terms unfamiliar to you. You can infer the general meaning of a word by using context clues, which are hints in the words or sentences around the word. For example, on page 84, you can infer the meaning of the word *calipers* from the way they are used on the animal, the number that Herriot calls out, and the statement about the animal's size. Calipers must be an instrument used to measure thickness.

As you read, keep track of unfamiliar words on a chart like the one shown.

LASERLINKS
• *SCIENCE CONNECTION*
• *GEOGRAPHICAL CONNECTION*

from All Things Bright & Beautiful

by James Herriot

"Move over, Bill!" Mr. Dacre cried some time later as he tweaked the big bull's tail.

Nearly every farmer kept a bull in those days and they were all called Billy or Bill. I suppose it was because this was a very mature animal that he received the adult version. Being a <u>docile</u> beast he responded to the touch on his tail by shuffling his great bulk to one side, leaving me enough space to push in between him and the wooden partition against which he was tied by a chain.

I was reading a tuberculin test and all I wanted to do was to measure the intradermal[1] reaction. I had to open my calipers very wide to take in the thickness of the skin on the enormous neck.

"Thirty," I called out to the farmer.

He wrote the figure down on the testing book and laughed.

"By heck, he's got some pelt on 'im."

"Yes," I said, beginning to squeeze my way out. "But he's a big fellow, isn't he?"

Just how big he was was brought home to me immediately because the bull suddenly swung round, pinning me against the partition. Cows did this regularly and I moved them by bracing my back against whatever was behind me and pushing them away. But it was different with Bill.

Gasping, I pushed with all my strength against the rolls of fat which covered the vast roan-colored flank, but I might as well have tried to shift a house.

The farmer dropped his book and seized the tail again but this time the bull showed no response. There was no <u>malice</u> in his behavior—he was simply having a comfortable lean

---

1. **intradermal** (ĭn′trə-dûr′məl): inside the layers of skin.

against the boards and I don't suppose he even noticed the morsel of puny humanity wriggling frantically against his rib cage.

Still, whether he meant it or not, the end result was the same; I was having the life crushed out of me. Popeyed, groaning, scarcely able to breathe, I struggled with everything I had, but I couldn't move an inch. And just when I thought things couldn't get any worse, Bill started to rub himself up and down against the partition. So that was what he had come round for; he had an itch and he just wanted to scratch it.

The effect on me was <u>catastrophic</u>. I was certain my internal organs were being steadily ground to pulp and as I thrashed about in complete panic the huge animal leaned even more heavily.

I don't like to think what would have happened if the wood behind me had not been old and rotten, but just as I felt my senses leaving me there was a cracking and splintering and I fell through into the next stall. Lying there like a stranded fish on a bed of shattered timbers I looked up at Mr. Dacre, waiting till my lungs started to work again.

The farmer, having gotten over his first alarm, was rubbing his upper lip vigorously in a polite attempt to stop himself laughing. His little girl who had watched the whole thing from her vantage point in one of the hayracks had no such inhibitions. Screaming with delight, she pointed at me.

"Ooo, Dad, Dad, look at that man! Did you see him, Dad, did you see him? Ooo what a funny man!" She went into helpless convulsions.[2] She was only about five but I had a feeling she would remember my performance all her life.

At length I picked myself up and managed to brush the matter off lightly, but after I had driven a mile or so from the farm I stopped the car and looked myself over. My ribs ached pretty uniformly as though a light road roller had passed over them and there was a tender area on my left buttock where I had landed on my calipers but otherwise I seemed to have escaped damage. I removed a few spicules of wood from my trousers, got back into the car and consulted my list of visits.

And when I read my next call a gentle smile of relief spread over my face. "Mrs. Tompkin, 14, Jasmine Terrace. Clip budgie's[3] beak."

Thank heaven for the infinite variety of veterinary practice. After that bull I needed something small and weak and harmless and really you can't ask for much better in that line than a budgie.

Number 14 was one of a row of small mean houses built of the cheap bricks so beloved of the jerrybuilders[4] after the first world war. I armed myself with a pair of clippers and stepped on to the narrow strip of pavement which separated the door from the road. A pleasant looking red-haired woman answered my knock.

"I'm Mrs. Dodds from next door," she said. "I keep an eye on t'old lady. She's over eighty and lives alone. I've just been out gettin' her pension[5] for her."

She led me into the cramped little room. "Here y'are, love," she said to the old woman who sat in a corner. She put the pension book and money on the mantelpiece. "And here's Mr. Herriot come to see Peter for you."

Mrs. Tompkin nodded and smiled. "Oh that's good. Poor little feller can't hardly eat with 'is long beak and I'm worried about him. He's me

---

2. **convulsions:** violent fits of laughter.

3. **budgie:** shortened form of *budgerigar,* an Australian parakeet.

4. **jerrybuilders:** builders who make poorly constructed, cheap houses.

5. **pension:** money paid regularly by a company or government to a retired person.

only companion, you know."

"Yes, I understand, Mrs. Tompkin." I looked at the cage by the window with the green budgie perched inside. "These little birds can be wonderful company when they start chattering."

She laughed. "Aye, but it's a funny thing. Peter never has said owt much. I think he's lazy! But I just like havin' him with me."

"Of course you do," I said. "But he certainly needs attention now."

The beak was greatly overgrown, curving away down till it touched the feathers of the breast. I would be able to revolutionize his life with one quick snip from my clippers. The way I was feeling this job was right up my street.

I opened the cage door and slowly inserted my hand.

"Come on, Peter," I wheedled as the bird fluttered away from me. And I soon cornered him and enclosed him gently in my fingers. As I lifted him out I felt in my pocket with the other hand for the clippers, but as I poised them I stopped.

The tiny head was no longer poking cheekily[6] from my fingers but had fallen loosely to one side. The eyes were closed. I stared at the bird uncomprehendingly for a moment then opened my hand. He lay quite motionless on my palm. He was dead.

Dry mouthed, I continued to stare; at the beautiful iridescence[7] of the plumage,[8] the long beak which I didn't have to cut now, but mostly at the head dropping down over my forefinger. I hadn't squeezed him or been rough with him in any way, but he was dead. It must have been sheer fright.

Mrs. Dodds and I looked at each other in horror and I hardly dared turn my head toward Mrs. Tompkin. When I did, I was surprised to see that she was still nodding and smiling.

I drew her neighbor to one side. "Mrs. Dodds, how much does she see?"

"Oh she's very shortsighted but she's right vain despite her age. Never would wear glasses. She's hard of hearin', too."

"Well look," I said. My heart was still pounding. "I just don't know what to do. If I tell her about this the shock will be terrible. Anything could happen."

Mrs. Dodds nodded, stricken faced. "Aye, you're right. She's that attached to the little thing."

"I can only think of one alternative," I whispered. "Do you know where I can get another budgie?"

Mrs. Dodds thought for a moment. "You could try Jack Almond at t'town end. I think he keeps birds."

I cleared my throat but even then my voice came out in a dry croak. "Mrs. Tompkin, I'm just going to take Peter along to the surgery to do this job. I won't be long."

I left her still nodding and smiling and, cage in hand, fled into the street. I was at the town end and knocking at Jack Almond's door within three minutes.

"Mr. Almond?" I asked of the stout, shirt-sleeved man who answered.

"That's right, young man." He gave me a slow, placid smile.

"Do you keep birds?"

He drew himself up with dignity. "I do, and I'm t'president of the Darrowby and Houlton Cage Bird Society."

"Fine," I said breathlessly. "Have you got a green budgie?"

"Ah've got canaries, budgies, parrots, parakeets. Cockatoos . . ."

---

6. **cheekily:** without respect.

7. **iridescence** (ĭr´ĭ-dĕs´əns): shifting, rainbowlike colors.

8. **plumage** (plōō´mĭj): feathers.

"I just want a budgie."

"Well ah've got albinos, blue-greens, barreds, Lutinos . . ."

"I just want a green one."

A slightly pained expression flitted across the man's face as though he found my attitude of haste somewhat unseemly.

"Aye . . . well, we'll go and have a look," he said.

I followed him as he paced unhurriedly through the house into the back yard which was largely given over to a long shed containing a bewildering variety of birds.

Mr. Almond gazed at them with gentle pride and his mouth opened as though he was about to launch into a dissertation[9] then he seemed to remember that he had an impatient chap to deal with and dragged himself back to the job in hand.

"There's a nice little green 'un here. But he's a bit older than t'others. Matter of fact I've got 'im talkin'."

"All the better, just the thing. How much do you want for him?"

"But . . . there's some nice 'uns along here. Just let me show you . . ."

I put a hand on his arm. "I want that one. How much?"

He pursed his lips in frustration then shrugged his shoulders.

"Ten bob."[10]

"Right. Bung[11] him in this cage."

As I sped back up the road I looked in the driving mirror and could see the poor man regarding me sadly from his doorway.

Mrs. Dodds was waiting for me back at Jasmine Terrace.

"Do you think I'm doing the right thing?" I asked her in a whisper.

"I'm sure you are," she replied. "Poor awd[12] thing, she hasn't much to think about and I'm sure she'd fret over Peter."

"That's what I thought." I made my way into the living room.

Mrs. Tompkin smiled at me as I went in. "That wasn't a long job, Mr. Herriot."

"No," I said, hanging the cage with the new bird up in its place by the window. "I think you'll find all is well now."

It was months before I had the courage to put my hand into a budgie's cage again. In fact to this day I prefer it if the owners will lift the birds out for me. People look at me strangely when I ask them to do this; I believe they think I am scared the little things might bite me.

It was a long time, too, before I dared go back to Mrs. Tompkin's but I was driving down Jasmine Terrace one day and on an impulse I stopped outside Number 14.

The old lady herself came to the door.

"How . . .," I said, "How is . . . er . . .?"

She peered at me closely for a moment then laughed. "Oh I see who it is now. You mean Peter, don't you, Mr. Herriot. Oh 'e's just grand. Come in and see 'im."

In the little room the cage still hung by the window and Peter the Second took a quick look at me then put on a little act for my benefit; he hopped around the bars of the cage, ran up and down his ladder and rang his little bell a couple of times before returning to his perch.

His mistress reached up, tapped the metal and looked lovingly at him.

"You know, you wouldn't believe it," she said. "He's like a different bird."

I swallowed. "Is that so? In what way?"

"Well he's so active now. Lively as can be. You know 'e chatters to me all day long. It's wonderful what cuttin' a beak can do." ❖

---

9. **dissertation** (dĭs′ər-tā′shən): a long speech.

10. **bob:** slang for *shilling*, a silver British coin no longer minted.

11. **bung:** to toss.

12. **awd:** *dialect*, old.

RESPONDING
O P T I O N S

FROM **PERSONAL RESPONSE** TO **CRITICAL ANALYSIS**

REFLECT 1. What is your impression of James Herriot? Jot down any phrases that come to mind.

RETHINK 2. When Mrs. Tompkin's budgie dies, Herriot fools her by buying one similar in appearance. Do you agree or disagree with his action? Explain.

3. Judging from the incidents he reports and the way he relates them, how would you describe Herriot's attitude toward himself and others?

Consider
   • his response in the bull's stall
   • his reaction to the incident at Mrs. Tompkin's
   • his feelings toward the animals he cares for

RELATE 4. Would you want Herriot to be your animal's veterinarian? Why or why not?

5. Based on your reading of this selection, why do you think Herriot's books are so popular?

ANOTHER PATHWAY

How important do you think Herriot's "bedside manner" toward the animals' owners is? Write a paragraph in which you evaluate his behavior toward the humans in this selection. Then discuss your evaluation with a partner.

LITERARY CONCEPTS

The particular way in which an author uses words and sentences is known as **style.** Style refers to *how* something is said, rather than *what* is said. Herriot's style is lighthearted, down-to-earth, and engaging. Find examples of humor, descriptive detail, dialect, and choice of words that illustrate his style.

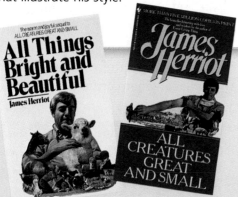

QUICKWRITES

1. Reread the passage in which the budgie dies in Herriot's hand. How might the outcome have been different if Herriot had admitted what happened? Rewrite the **ending** from this point on.

2. Based on this selection and your experiences with animals, would you want to be a veterinarian? Write a **personal essay** explaining why or why not.

   📁 *PORTFOLIO Save your writing. You may want to use it later as a springboard to a piece for your portfolio.*

ALTERNATIVE ACTIVITIES

1. The scene in which the bull pins Herriot against the wall is vivid with description. Use this detail to draw a **picture** of the scene.

2. Research the four-year program a student must complete to become a veterinarian, and the two-year program required for veterinary technology. What schools offer each kind of training? What courses does one take? If you have access to an encyclopedia program or an on-line service, use your computer to start your research. Share your information in an **oral report** to the class.

WORDS TO KNOW

Create a word map for each of the five Words to Know and three of the unfamiliar words that you identified in the Reading Connection on page 83. Include a synonym, an antonym, and an example of the word. A sample map, using the word *aggressive,* is provided.

```
                    ( Aggressive )
                   /      |       \
          ( pushy )  ( an aggressive lion )  ( passive )
           synonym        example            antonym
```

JAMES HERRIOT

1916–1995

For most of his career, James Herriot had talked to his wife about writing a book concerning his veterinary experiences in Yorkshire, England. Herriot explained, "One day, when I was fifty, she said: 'Who are you kidding? Vets of fifty don't write first books.' Well, that did it. I stormed out and bought some paper and taught myself to type."

Because of the British veterinary system's ban on advertising, Herriot changed the names of people and communities in his books and wrote under a pseudonym, or pen name. James Alfred Wight was the author's real name.

Herriot wrote more than a dozen books, including his bestsellers—*All Creatures Great and Small, All Things Bright and Beautiful, All Things Wise and Wonderful,* and *The Lord God Made Them All.*

Several of his works were adapted for film and television. The author received many awards and honors, including the James Herriot Award established by the Humane Society of America.

Said Herriot, "The life of a country vet was dirty, uncomfortable, sometimes dangerous. It was terribly hard work and I loved it." He continued to see patients, but his veterinarian son eventually took over his practice. He convinced his daughter, Rosemary, who he said was "mad keen to be a country vet," to be a doctor of humans, "which," he added, "is the next best thing."

OTHER WORKS *James Herriot's Cat Stories, It Shouldn't Happen to a Vet, James Herriot's Yorkshire, Every Living Thing*

PREVIEWING

FICTION

The Inn of Lost Time
Lensey Namioka (nä′mē-ō′kə)

PERSONAL CONNECTION

What does the saying "Things aren't always what they appear to be" mean to you? For example, have you ever formed an impression of someone, only to change it after you got to know the person better? Perhaps you attended an event that turned out to be different than you expected. With your classmates, discuss situations you have experienced in which things or people did not turn out to be what you expected.

HISTORICAL CONNECTION

Japan in the 1570s was a time of turmoil in which the military class ran the country. Powerful landowners, called feudal lords, ruled over thousands of peasants. The lords and their estates were protected by samurai warriors.

When the lords waged war with one another, some were forced to dismiss both workers and warriors. The unemployed samurai, or *ronin,* roamed the countryside looking for adventure and work. Contrary to the code of honor of the samurai, some ronin preyed upon defenseless farmers.

READING CONNECTION

Frame Story A frame story is a story that contains one or more other stories. In the selection two stories are told within the structure of the frame story. The first is the tale of Urashima Taro. The second is the tale of Zenta and Tokubei. To keep the stories straight, ask questions as you read: Who tells each story? Why is it told? What does the story reveal? Jot down your answers in a chart like the one shown.

	Frame Story	Tale of Urashima Taro	Tale of Zenta and Tokubei
Who tells it?			
Why is it told?			
What does it reveal?			

LASERLINKS
• *VISUAL VOCABULARY*

The Inn of Lost Time

BY
LENSEY NAMIOKA

Detail of *Portrait of Sato Issai*
(1824), Watanabe Kazan. Ink and
color on silk, Japan, Edo Period,
Nanga School, 113.0 cm × 51.5 cm,
courtesy of the Freer Gallery of Art,
Smithsonian Institution, Washington,
D.C. (68.66).

"ill you promise to sleep if I tell you a story?" said the father. He pretended to put on a stern expression.

"Yes! Yes!" the three little boys chanted in unison. It sounded like a nightly routine.

The two guests smiled as they listened to the exchange. They were wandering ronin, or unemployed samurai, and they enjoyed watching this cozy family scene.

The father gave the guests a helpless look. "What can I do? I have to tell them a story, or these little rascals will give us no peace." Clearing his throat, he turned to the boys. "All right. The story tonight is about Urashima Taro."

Instantly the three boys became still. Sitting with their legs tucked under them, the three little boys, aged five, four, and three, looked like a descending row of stone statuettes. Matsuzo, the younger of the two ronin, was reminded of the wayside half-body statues of Jizo, the god of travelers and protector of children.

Behind the boys the farmer's wife took up a pair of iron chopsticks and stirred the ashes of the fire in the charcoal brazier.[1] A momentary glow brightened the room. The lean faces of the two ronin, lit by the fire, suddenly looked fierce and hungry.

The farmer knew that the two ronin were supposed to use their arms in defense of the weak. But in these troubled times, with the country torn apart by civil wars, the samurai didn't always live up to their honorable code.

Then the fire died down again, and the subdued red light softened the features of the two ronin. The farmer relaxed and began his story.

The tale of Urashima Taro is familiar to every Japanese. No doubt the three little boys had heard their father tell it before—and more than once. But they listened with <u>rapt</u> attention.

Urashima Taro, a fisherman, rescued a turtle from some boys who were battering it with stones. The grateful turtle rewarded Taro by carrying him on his back to the bottom of the sea, where he lived happily with the princess of the undersea. But Taro soon became home-sick for his native village and asked to go back on land. The princess gave him a box to take with him but warned him not to peek inside.

When Taro went back to his village, he found the place quite changed. In his home he found his parents gone, and living there was another old couple. He was stunned to learn that the aged husband was his own son, whom he had last seen as a baby! Taro thought he had spent only a pleasant week or two under-sea with the princess. On land, seventy-two years had passed! His parents and most of his old friends had long since died.

<u>Desolate</u>, Taro decided to open the box given him by the princess. As soon as he looked inside, he changed in an instant from a young man to a <u>decrepit</u> old man of more than ninety.

At the end of the story the boys were close to tears. Even Matsuzo found himself deeply touched. He wondered why the farmer had told his sons such a <u>poignant</u> bedtime story. Wouldn't they worry all evening instead of going to sleep?

But the boys recovered quickly. They were soon laughing and jostling each other, and they made no objections when their mother shooed them toward bed. Standing in order of age,

---

1. **brazier** (brā′zhər): a metal pan holding burning charcoal or coals for cooking.

WORDS
TO
KNOW

rapt (răpt) *adj.* deeply interested
desolate (dĕs′ə-lĭt) *adj.* miserable; very unhappy
decrepit (dĭ-krĕp′ĭt) *adj.* weakened by old age
poignant (poin′yənt) *adj.* very touching or moving; painful

they bowed politely to the guests and then lay down on the mattresses spread out for them on the floor. Within minutes the sound of their regular breathing told the guests that they were asleep.

Zenta, the older of the two ronin, sighed as he glanced at the peaceful young faces. "I wish I could fall asleep so quickly. The story of Urashima Taro is one of the saddest that I know among our folk tales."

The farmer looked proudly at his sleeping sons. "They're stout lads. Nothing bothers them much."

The farmer's wife poured tea for the guests and apologized. "I'm sorry this is only poor tea made from coarse leaves."

Zenta hastened to reassure her. "It's warm and heartening on a chilly autumn evening."

"You know what I think is the saddest part of the Urashima Taro story?" said Matsuzo, picking up his cup and sipping the tea. "It's that Taro lost not only his family and friends but a big piece of his life as well. He had lost the most precious thing of all: time."

The farmer nodded agreement. "I wouldn't sell even one year of my life for money. As for losing seventy-two years, no amount of gold will make up for that!"

Zenta put his cup down on the floor and looked curiously at the farmer. "It's interesting that you should say that. I had an opportunity once to observe exactly how much gold a person was willing to pay for some lost years of his life." He smiled grimly. "In this case the man went as far as one gold piece for each year he lost."

"That's bizarre!" said Matsuzo. "You never told me about it."

"It happened long before I met you," said Zenta. He drank some tea and smiled ruefully. "Besides, I'm not particularly proud of the part I played in that strange affair."

"Let's hear the story!" urged Matsuzo. "You've made us all curious."

The farmer waited expectantly. His wife sat down quietly behind her husband and folded her hands. Her eyes looked intently at Zenta.

"Very well, then," said Zenta. "Actually, my story bears some resemblance to that of Urashima Taro. . . ."

It happened about seven years ago, when I was a green, inexperienced youngster not quite eighteen years old. But I had had a good training in arms, and I was able to get a job as a bodyguard for a wealthy merchant from Sakai.

As you know, wealthy merchants are relatively new in our country. Traditionally the rich have been noblemen, landowners, and warlords with thousands of followers. Merchants, considered as parasites in our society, are a despised class. But our civil wars have made people unusually mobile and stimulated trade between various parts of the country. The merchants have taken advantage of this to conduct businesses on a scale our fathers could not imagine. Some of them have become more wealthy than a warlord with thousands of samurai under his command.

The man I was escorting, Tokubei, was one of this new breed of wealthy merchants. He was trading not only with outlying provinces but even with the Portuguese[2] from across the sea. On this particular journey he was not carrying much gold with him. If he had, I'm sure he would have hired an older and more experienced bodyguard. But if the need should arise, he could always write a message to his clerks at home and have money forwarded to him. It's important to remember this.

---

2. **Portuguese:** here, merchants from Portugal; the first Europeans to reach Japan.

The actor Onoe Baikō VII as Mokuzume in Tamamo no Mae Kumoi no Hareginu (1984), Tsuruya Kokei. Color woodblock print, 39.8 cm × 27.5 cm. Copyright © British Museum.

The second day of our journey was a particularly grueling one, with several steep hills to climb. As the day was drawing to its close, we began to consider where we should spend the night. I knew that within an hour's walking was a hot-spring resort known to have several attractive inns.

But Tokubei, my employer, said he was already very tired and wanted to stop. He had heard of the resort and knew the inns there were expensive. Wealthy as he was, he did not want to spend more money than he had to.

While we stood talking, a smell reached our noses, a wonderful smell of freshly cooked rice. Suddenly I felt ravenous. From the way Tokubei swallowed, I knew he was feeling just as hungry.

We looked around eagerly, but the area was forested, and we could not see very far in any direction. The tantalizing smell seemed to grow, and I could feel the saliva filling my mouth.

"There's an inn around here, somewhere," muttered Tokubei. "I'm sure of it."

We followed our noses.

94

We had to leave the well-traveled highway and take a narrow, winding footpath. But the mouth-watering smell of the rice and the vision of fluffy, freshly aired cotton quilts drew us on.

The sun was just beginning to set. We passed a bamboo grove,[3] and in the low evening light the thin leaves turned into little golden knives. I saw a gilded clump of bamboo shoots. The sight made me think of the delicious dish they would make when boiled in soy sauce.

We hurried forward. To our delight we soon came to a clearing with a thatched house standing in the middle. The fragrant smell of rice was now so strong that we were certain a meal was being prepared inside.

Standing in front of the house was a pretty girl beaming at us with a welcoming smile. "Please honor us with your presence," she said, beckoning.

There was something a little unusual about one of her hands, but being hungry and eager to enter the house, I did not stop to observe closely.

You will say, of course, that it was my duty as a bodyguard to be suspicious and to look out for danger. Youth and inexperience should not have prevented me from wondering why an inn should be found hidden away from the highway. As it was, my stomach growled, and I didn't even hesitate but followed Tokubei to the house.

Before stepping up to enter, we were given basins of water to wash our feet. As the girl handed us towels for drying, I saw what was unusual about her left hand: she had six fingers.

PREDICT

What do you think might happen at the inn?

Tokubei had noticed it as well. When the girl turned away to empty the basins, he nudged me. "Did you see her left hand? She had—" He broke off in confusion as the girl turned around, but she didn't seem to have heard.

The inn was peaceful and quiet, and we soon discovered the reason why. We were the only guests. Again, I should have been suspicious. I told you that I'm not proud of the part I played.

Tokubei turned to me and grinned. "It seems that there are no other guests. We should be able to get extra service for the same amount of money."

The girl led us to a spacious room which was like the principal chamber of a private residence. Cushions were set out for us on the floor, and we began to shed our traveling gear to make ourselves comfortable.

The door opened, and a grizzled-haired man entered. Despite his vigorous-looking face his back was a little bent, and I guessed his age to be about fifty. After bowing and greeting us he apologized in advance for the service. "We have not always been innkeepers here," he said, "and you may find the accommodations lacking. Our good intentions must make up for our inexperience. However, to compensate for our inadequacies, we will charge a lower fee than that of an inn with an established reputation."

Tokubei nodded graciously, highly pleased by the words of our host, and the evening began well. It continued well when the girl came back with some flasks of wine, cups, and dishes of salty snacks.

---

3. **bamboo grove:** a group of tall, tropical grasses with woody stems.

WORDS TO KNOW   **gilded** (gĭl′dĭd) *adj.* as if covered with a thin layer of gold **gild** *v.*
compensate (kŏm′pən-sāt) *v.* to make up for

95

While the girl served the wine, the host looked with interest at my swords. From the few remarks he made, I gathered that he was a former samurai, forced by circumstances to turn his house into an inn.

Having become a bodyguard to a tight-fisted merchant, I was in no position to feel superior to a ronin turned innkeeper. Socially, therefore, we were more or less equal.

We exchanged polite remarks with our host while we drank and tasted the salty snacks. I looked around at the pleasant room. It showed excellent taste, and I especially admired a vase standing in the alcove.

y host caught my eyes on it. "We still have a few good things that we didn't have to sell," he said. His voice held a trace of bitterness. "Please look at the panels of these doors. They were painted by a fine artist."

Tokubei and I looked at the pair of sliding doors. Each panel contained a landscape painting, the right panel depicting a winter scene and the left one the same scene in late summer. Our host's words were no idle boast. The pictures were indeed beautiful.

Tokubei rose and approached the screens for a closer look. When he sat down again, his eyes were calculating. No doubt he was trying to estimate what price the paintings would fetch.

After my third drink I began to feel very tired. Perhaps it was the result of drinking on an empty stomach. I was glad when the girl brought in two dinner trays and a lacquered container of rice. Uncovering the rice container, she began filling our bowls.

Again I noticed her strange left hand with its six fingers. Any other girl would have tried to keep that hand hidden, but this girl made no effort to do so. If anything, she seemed to use that hand more than her other one when she served us. The extra little finger always stuck out from the hand, as if inviting comment.

The hand fascinated me so much that I kept my eyes on it and soon forgot to eat. After a while the hand looked blurry. And then everything else began to look blurry. The last thing I remembered was the sight of Tokubei shaking his head, as if trying to clear it.

When I opened my eyes again, I knew that time had passed, but not how much time. My next thought was that it was cold. It was not only extremely cold but damp.

I rolled over and sat up. I reached immediately for my swords and found them safe on the ground beside me. *On the ground? What was I doing on the ground?* My last memory was of staying at an inn with a merchant called Tokubei.

The thought of Tokubei put me into a panic. I was his bodyguard, and instead of watching over him, I had fallen asleep and had awakened in a strange place.

I looked around frantically and saw that he was lying on the ground not far from where I was. Had he been killed?

I got up shakily, and when I stood up, my head was swimming. But my sense of urgency gave some strength to my legs. I stumbled over to my employer and to my great relief found him breathing—breathing heavily, in fact.

When I shook his shoulder, he grunted and finally opened his eyes. "Where am I?" he asked thickly.

It was a reasonable question. I looked around and saw that we had been lying in a bamboo grove. By the light I guessed that it was early morning, and the reason I felt cold and damp was because my clothes were wet with dew.

"It's cold!" said Tokubei, shivering and

> **QUESTION**
>
> What do you think has happened to them?

climbing unsteadily to his feet. He looked around slowly, and his eyes became wide with disbelief. "What happened? I thought we were staying at an inn!"

His words came as a relief. One of the possibilities I had considered was that I had gone mad and that the whole episode with the inn was something I had imagined. Now I knew that Tokubei had the same memory of the inn. I had not imagined it.

But why were we out here on the cold ground, instead of on comfortable mattresses in the inn?

"They must have drugged us and robbed us," said Tokubei. He turned and looked at me furiously. "A fine bodyguard you are!"

There was nothing I could say to that. But at least we were both alive and unharmed. "Did they take all your money?" I asked.

Tokubei had already taken his wallet out of his sash and was peering inside. "That's funny! My money is still here!"

This was certainly unexpected. What did the innkeeper and his strange daughter intend to do by drugging us and moving us outside?

At least things were not as bad as we had feared. We had not lost anything except a comfortable night's sleep, although from the heaviness in my head I had certainly slept deeply enough—and long enough too. Exactly how much time had elapsed since we drank wine with our host?

All we had to do now was find the highway again and continue our journey. Tokubei suddenly chuckled. "I didn't even have to pay for our night's lodging!"

As we walked from the bamboo grove, I saw the familiar clump of bamboo shoots, and we found ourselves standing in the same clearing again. Before our eyes was the thatched house. Only it was somehow different. Perhaps things looked different in the daylight than at dusk.

But the difference was more than a change of light. As we approached the house slowly, like sleepwalkers, we saw that the thatching was much darker. On the previous evening the thatching had looked fresh and new. Now it was dark with age. Daylight should make things appear brighter, not darker. The plastering of the walls also looked more dingy.

Tokubei and I stopped to look at each other before we went closer. He was pale, and I knew that I looked no less frightened. Something was terribly wrong. I loosened my sword in its scabbard.[4]

e finally gathered the courage to go up to the house. Since Tokubei seemed unable to find his voice, I spoke out. "Is anyone there?"

After a moment we heard shuffling footsteps, and the front door slid open. The face of an old woman appeared. "Yes?" she inquired. Her voice was creaky with age.

What set my heart pounding with panic, however, was not her voice. It was the sight of her left hand holding on to the frame of the door. The hand was wrinkled and crooked with the arthritis[5] of old age—and it had six fingers.

I heard a gasp beside me and knew that Tokubei had noticed the hand as well.

The door opened wider, and a man appeared beside the old woman. At first I thought it was our host of the previous night. But this man was much younger, although the resemblance was strong. He carried himself straighter, and his hair was black, while the innkeeper had been grizzled and slightly bent with age.

---

4. **scabbard** (scăb′ərd): a sheath or case for a sword.

5. **arthritis**: an inflammation of joints resulting in pain and swelling.

Detail of mountain landscape (15th–16th century), Sesshū Tōyō. Six-fold screen, ink and color on paper, Japan, Muromachi Period, 161.0 cm × 351.2 cm, courtesy of the Freer Gallery of Art, Smithsonian Institution, Washington, D.C. (58.5).

"Please excuse my mother," said the man. "Her hearing is not good. Can we help you in some way?"

Tokubei finally found his voice. "Isn't this the inn where we stayed last night?"

The man stared. "Inn? We are not innkeepers here!"

"Yes, you are!" insisted Tokubei. "Your daughter invited us in and served us with wine. You must have put something in the wine!"

The man frowned. "You are serious? Are you sure you didn't drink too much at your inn and wander off?"

"No, I didn't drink too much!" said Tokubei, almost shouting. "I hardly drank at all! Your daughter, the one with six fingers in her hand, started to pour me a second cup of wine . . ." His voice trailed off, and he stared again at the left hand of the old woman.

"I don't have a daughter," said the man slowly. "My mother here is the one who has six fingers in her left hand, although I hardly think it polite of you to mention it."

"I'm getting dizzy," muttered Tokubei and began to totter.

"I think you'd better come in and rest a bit," the man said to him gruffly. He glanced at me. "Perhaps you wish to join your friend. You don't share his <u>delusion</u> about the inn, I hope?"

"I wouldn't presume to contradict my elders," I said carefully. Since both Tokubei and the owner of the house were my elders, I wasn't committing myself. In truth I didn't know what to believe, but I did want a look at the inside of the house.

The inside was almost the same as it was before, but the differences were there when I looked closely. We entered the same room with the alcove and the pair of painted doors. The vase I had admired was no longer there, but the doors showed the same landscapes painted by a master. I peered closely at the pictures and saw that the colors looked faded. What was more, the left panel, the one depicting a winter scene, had a long tear in one corner. It had been painstakingly mended, but the damage was impossible to hide completely.

Tokubei saw what I was staring at, and he became even paler. At this stage we had both considered the possibility that a hoax of some sort had been played on us. The torn screen convinced Tokubei that our host had not played a joke: the owner of a valuable painting would never vandalize it for a trivial reason.

As for me, I was far more disturbed by the sight of the sixth finger on the old woman's hand. Could the young girl have disguised herself as an old crone?[6] She could put rice powder in her hair to whiten it, but she could not transform her pretty straight fingers into old fingers twisted with arthritis. The woman here with us now was genuinely old, at least fifty years older than the girl.

It was this same old woman who finally gave us our greatest shock. "It's interesting that you should mention an inn, gentlemen," she croaked. "My father used to operate an inn. After he died, my husband and I turned this back into a private residence. We didn't need the income, you see."

"Your . . . your . . . f-father?" stammered Tokubei.

"Yes," replied the old woman. "He was a ronin, forced to go into innkeeping when he lost his position. But he never liked the work. Besides, our inn had begun to acquire an unfortunate reputation. Some of our guests disappeared, you see."

Even before she finished speaking, a horrible suspicion had begun to dawn on me. Her *father* had been an innkeeper, she said, her father who used to be a ronin. The man who

---

6. **crone:** an ugly, withered old woman.

had been our host was a ronin turned inn-keeper. Could this mean that this old woman was actually the same person as the young girl we had seen?

I sat stunned while I tried to absorb the implications. What had happened to us? Was it possible that Tokubei and I had slept while this young girl grew into a mature woman, got married, and bore a son, a son who was now an adult? If that was the case, then we had slept for fifty years!

QUESTION

How could they have slept for 50 years?

The old woman's next words confirmed my fears. "I recognize you now! You are two of the lost guests from our inn! The other lost ones I don't remember so well, but I remember *you* because your disappearance made me so sad. Such a handsome youth, I thought, what a pity that he should have gone the way of the others!"

A high wail came from Tokubei, who began to keen[7] and rock himself back and forth. "I've lost fifty years! Fifty years of my life went by while I slept at this accursed inn!"

The inn was indeed accursed. Was the fate of the other guests similar to ours? "Did anyone else return as we did, fifty years later?" I asked.

The old woman looked uncertain and turned to her son. He frowned thoughtfully. "From time to time wild-looking people have come to us with stories similar to yours. Some of them went mad with the shock."

Tokubei wailed again. "I've lost my business! I've lost my wife, my young and beautiful wife! We had been married only a couple of months!"

A gruesome chuckle came from the old woman. "You may not have lost your wife. It's just that she's become an old hag like me!"

That did not console Tokubei, whose keening became louder. Although my relationship with my employer had not been characterized by much respect on either side, I did begin to feel very sorry for him. He was right: he had lost his world.

As for me, the loss was less traumatic. I had left home under extremely painful circumstances and had spent the next three years wandering. I had no friends and no one I could call a relation. The only thing I had was my duty to my employer. Somehow, some way, I had to help him.

"Did no one find an explanation for these disappearances?" I asked. "Perhaps if we knew the reason why, we might find some way to reverse the process."

The old woman began to nod eagerly. "The priestess! Tell them about the shrine priestess!"

"Well," said the man, "I'm not sure if it would work in your case. . . ."

"What? What would work?" demanded Tokubei. His eyes were feverish.

"There was a case of one returning guest who consulted the priestess at our local shrine," said the man. "She went into a trance and revealed that there was an evil spirit dwelling in the bamboo grove here. This spirit would put unwary travelers into a long, unnatural sleep. They would wake up twenty, thirty, or even fifty years later."

"Yes, but you said something worked in his case," said Tokubei.

The man seemed reluctant to go on. "I don't like to see you cheated, so I'm not sure I should be telling you this."

---

7. **keen:** to wail or cry out loudly.

WORDS TO KNOW

implication (ĭm'plĭ-kā'shən) *n.* a possible meaning or significance
traumatic (trou-măt'ĭk) *adj.* emotionally shocking
unwary (ŭn-wâr'ē) *adj.* not alert or cautious
reluctant (rĭ-lŭk'tənt) *adj.* unwilling

100

"Tell me! Tell me!" demanded Tokubei. The host's reluctance only made him more impatient.

"The priestess promised to make a spell that would undo the work of the evil spirit," said the man. "But she demanded a large sum of money, for she said that she had to burn some very rare and costly incense before she could begin the spell."

At the mention of money Tokubei sat back. The hectic flush died down on his face, and his eyes narrowed. "How much money?" he asked.

The host shook his head. "In my opinion the priestess is a fraud and makes outrageous claims about her powers. We try to have as little to do with her as possible."

"Yes, but did her spell work?" asked Tokubei. "If it worked, she's no fraud!"

"At least the stranger disappeared again," cackled the old woman. "Maybe he went back to his own time. Maybe he walked into a river."

Tokubei's eyes narrowed further. "How much money did the priestess demand?" he asked again.

"I think it was one gold piece for every year lost," said the host. He hurriedly added, "Mind you, I still wouldn't trust the priestess."

"Then it would cost me fifty gold pieces to get back to my own time," muttered Tokubei. He looked up. "I don't carry that much money with me."

"No, you don't," agreed the host.

Something alerted me about the way he said that. It was as if the host knew already that Tokubei did not carry much money on him.

Meanwhile Tokubei sighed. He had come to a decision. "I do have the means to obtain more money, however. I can send a message to my chief clerk, and he will <u>remit</u> the money when he sees my seal."

"Your chief clerk may be dead by now," I reminded him.

"You're right!" moaned Tokubei. "My business will be under a new management, and nobody will even remember my name!"

"And your wife will have remarried," said the old woman, with one of her chuckles. I found it hard to believe that the gentle young girl who had served us wine could turn into this dreadful harridan.[8]

"Sending the message may be a waste of time," agreed the host.

"What waste of time!" cried Tokubei. "Why shouldn't I waste time? I've wasted fifty years already! Anyway, I've made up my mind. I'm sending that message."

"I still think you shouldn't trust the priestess," said the host.

That only made Tokubei all the more determined to send for the money. However, he was not quite resigned to the amount. "Fifty gold pieces is a large sum. Surely the priestess can buy incense for less than that amount?"

"Why don't you try giving her thirty gold pieces?" cackled the old woman. "Then the priestess will send you back thirty years, and your wife will only be middle-aged."

While Tokubei was still arguing with himself about the exact sum to send for, I decided to have a look at the bamboo grove. "I'm going for a walk," I announced, rising and picking up my sword from the floor beside me.

The host turned sharply to look at me. For an instant a faint, rueful smile appeared on his lips. Then he looked away.

---

8. **harridan** (hăr′ĭ-dn): a scolding, vicious woman.

Outside, I went straight to the clump of shoots in the bamboo grove. On the previous night—or what I perceived as the previous night—I had noticed that clump of bamboo shoots particularly, because I had been so hungry that I pictured them being cut up and boiled.

The clump of bamboo shoots was still in the same place. That in itself proved nothing, since bamboo could spring up anywhere, including the place where a clump had existed fifty years earlier. But what settled the matter in my mind was that the clump looked almost exactly the way it did when I had seen it before, except that every shoot was about an inch taller. That was a reasonable amount for bamboo shoots to grow overnight.

vernight. Tokubei and I had slept on the ground here overnight. We had not slept here for a period of fifty years.

Once I knew that, I was able to see another inconsistency: the door panels with the painted landscapes. The painting with the winter scene had been on the *right* last night, and it was on the *left* this morning. It wasn't simply a case of the panels changing places, because the depressions in the panel for the handholds had been reversed. In other words, what I saw just now was not a pair of paintings faded and torn by age. They were an entirely different pair of paintings.

But how did the pretty young girl change into an old woman? The answer was that if the screens could be different ones, so could the women. I had seen one woman, a young girl, last night. This morning I saw a different woman, an old hag.

The darkening of the thatched roof? Simply blow ashes over the roof. The grizzled-haired host of last night could be the same man who claimed to be his grandson today. It would be a simple matter for a young man to put gray in his hair and assume a stoop.

And the purpose of the hoax? To make Tokubei send for fifty pieces of gold, of course. It was clever of the man to accuse the shrine priestess of fraud and pretend reluctance to let Tokubei send his message.

I couldn't even feel angry toward the man and his daughter—or mother, sister, wife, whatever. He could have killed me and taken my swords, which he clearly admired. Perhaps he was really a ronin and felt sympathetic toward another one.

When I returned to the house, Tokubei was looking resigned. "I've decided to send for the whole fifty gold pieces." He sighed.

"Don't bother," I said. "In fact we should be leaving as soon as possible. We shouldn't even stop here for a drink, especially not of wine."

Tokubei stared. "What do you mean? If I go back home, I'll find everything changed!"

"Nothing will be changed," I told him. "Your wife will be as young and beautiful as ever."

"I don't understand," he said. "Fifty years . . ."

"It's a joke," I said. "The people here have a peculiar sense of humor, and they've played a joke on us."

Tokubei's mouth hung open. Finally he closed it with a snap. He stared at the host, and his face became first red and then purple. "You— you were trying to swindle me!" He turned furiously to me. "And you let them do this!"

"I'm not letting them," I pointed out. "That's why we're leaving right now."

"Are you going to let them get away with this?" demanded Tokubei. "They might try to swindle someone else!"

"They only went to this much trouble when they heard of the arrival of a fine fat fish like you," I said. I looked deliberately at the host.

WORDS TO KNOW **inconsistency** (ĭn′kən-sĭs′tən-sē) *n.* something that is not in agreement or harmony

"I'm sure they won't be tempted to try the same trick again."

nd that's the end of your story?" asked Matsuzo. "You and Tokubei just went away? How did you know the so-called innkeeper wouldn't try the trick on some other luckless traveler?"

Zenta shook his head. "I didn't know. I merely guessed that once the trick was exposed, they wouldn't take the chance of trying it again. Of course I thought about revisiting the place to check if the people there were leading an honest life."

"Why didn't you?" asked Matsuzo. "Maybe we could go together. You've made me curious about that family now."

"Then you can satisfy your curiosity," said Zenta, smiling. He held his cup out for more tea, and the farmer's wife came forward to pour.

Only now she used both hands to hold the pot, and for the first time Matsuzo saw her left hand. He gasped. The hand had six fingers.

"Who was the old woman?" Zenta asked the farmer's wife.

"She was my grandmother," she replied. "Having six fingers is something that runs in my family."

At last Matsuzo found his voice. "You mean this is the very house you visited? This is the inn where time was lost?"

"Where we *thought* we lost fifty years," said Zenta. "Perhaps I should have warned you first. But I was almost certain that we'd be safe this time. And I see that I was right."

He turned to the woman again. "You and your husband are farmers now, aren't you? What happened to the man who was the host?"

"He's dead," she said quietly. "He was my brother, and he was telling you the truth when he said that he was a ronin. Two years ago he found work with another warlord, but he was killed in battle only a month later."

Matsuzo was peering at the pair of sliding doors, which he hadn't noticed before. "I see that you've put up the faded set of paintings. The winter scene is on the left side."

The woman nodded. "We sold the newer pair of doors. My husband said that we're farmers now and that people in our position don't need valuable paintings. We used the money to buy some new farm implements."

She took up the teapot again. "Would you like another cup of tea?" she asked Matsuzo.

Staring at her left hand, Matsuzo had a sudden qualm. "I—I don't think I want any more."

Everybody laughed. ❖

RESPONDING OPTIONS

FROM PERSONAL RESPONSE TO CRITICAL ANALYSIS

REFLECT **1.** What are your thoughts about Zenta's story of the hoax? Write your reactions in your notebook. Share your thoughts with a partner.

RETHINK **2.** Why do you think the hoax worked on other people, but not on Zenta?
Consider
- the nature of Zenta's profession
- his relationship with Tokubei
- why Zenta questioned appearances

3. If you had been Zenta or Tokubei, would you have punished the innkeepers? Why or why not?

4. Why do you think Zenta told the story to the farmer's family?

5. Tokubei thought that he had lost several years of his life. How realistic was his reaction to this loss? Explain your opinion.

RELATE **6.** Suppose both Tokubei and Zenta lived in our country today. What professions would each have? How might the problems they had in the story be similar to or different from what they would encounter today?

ANOTHER PATHWAY
Cooperative Learning
In small groups, using the chart you made on page 90, try to figure out the **theme** of this story—or the author's message about life. Summarize your group's finding in a statement. Then compare and discuss the theme statements that each group decided on.

QUICKWRITES

1. The Urashima Taro folktale could be adapted to any setting. Write a contemporary or futuristic version of this **tale,** placing it in the setting of your choice.

2. Imagine that Zenta and Tokubei really did age 50 years. How might their story be different? Rewrite the **story ending** as if the men actually had grown older.

3. The farmer's wife appeared calm as she sat listening to Zenta. Do you think she was really calm, or was her appearance deceiving? With another student, write an **interior monologue** that shows what she might have been thinking and feeling.

📁 *PORTFOLIO Save your writing. You may want to use it later as a springboard to a piece for your portfolio.*

LITERARY CONCEPTS

Setting is the time and place of the action of a story. A setting may be real or imaginary. In some stories, such as "Collecting Team" on page 107, the setting has a major influence on the story. Is the setting of "The Inn of Lost Time" real or imaginary? In what ways is the setting important to the story?

ALTERNATIVE ACTIVITIES

1. Imagine that you are Zenta and that you are looking for a new job. Design a **classified ad** in which you describe the job you want and your qualifications for it. Consider your training and experience. Also think about including various graphic elements for grabbing the reader.

2. During the time of this story, Japanese screen painting was popular. Artists used bold colors, gold leaf, and details to depict scenes such as samurai at war. Find examples of 16th-century Japanese **screen painting** and share them with the class.

3. Rent and watch the **videos** of the Japanese classic *Seven Samurai* and the American classic *The Magnificent Seven*. What differences and what similarities between the two cultures do you notice? How are the movies' heroes alike, and how are they different? With other viewers, compare and contrast the two movies.

Yul Brynner and Steve McQueen in *The Magnificent Seven*. Archive Photos.

ART CONNECTION

Look again at the painting on page 94. Does the painting match the image you had of the female character in the story? What details add or detract from your own mental picture of the character?

Detail of *The actor Onoe Baikō VII as Mokuzume* in Tamamo no Mae Kumoi no Hareginu (1984), Tsuruya Kokei. Color woodblock print, 39.8 cm × 27.5 cm. Copyright © British Museum.

ACROSS THE CURRICULUM

History Investigate Japan's history during the late 1500s, including the role of the samurai during this period. Create a time line that highlights major events. Use pictures or your own drawings to illustrate the key dates on your time line.

EXERCISE A Review the Words to Know at the bottom of the selection pages. Then, on your paper, write the word that fills each blank below. Use each word once.

The children listened with ___1___ attention as the samurai began the moving, ___2___ story of the crippled, ___3___ old feudal lord.

"The fearful old man, living in poverty, was ___4___ to leave his home because he knew that poor and hungry ronin would set upon any ___5___ travelers and take their belongings. To ___6___ for his fear and to avoid any ___7___ or upsetting experiences with robbers, the man wanted to hire me as a bodyguard. He offered to ___8___ payment in the form of a special kimono covered with shimmering gold threads, his only valuable possession.

"Even though the ___9___ kimono was ___10___ to me, I suddenly felt an unusual ___11___ about this assignment. I sensed an unexplained ___12___ in such a poor man's owning such a splendid garment. I started to wonder if I was suffering from some sort of ___13___.

"However, the ___14___ of this situation soon became clear to me. The old man looked so ___15___ that I knew there was more to this than met the eye. The lord then revealed that he was a shogun who was disguised to protect himself from ruthless ronin. The lord's desperation made me want to help him, so I became the best dressed bodyguard in all of Japan in my splendid new kimono!"

EXERCISE B Select six of the Words to Know in this selection. Draw pictures to illustrate or represent each one. Have a partner guess the words.

LENSEY NAMIOKA

1929–

Lensey Namioka was born in Beijing, China, and spent most of her childhood there. It wasn't until she was a teenager that she and her parents came to the United States.

Namioka began writing professionally during the 1960s. At that time, China was beginning its Cultural Revolution, and the Communist government attempted to eliminate counterrevolutionaries. Because of this situation, Namioka was afraid to write about China. "I had relatives who could have been harmed," she says. Therefore, she chose her husband's country, Japan, as the setting of her stories—specifically, late 16th-century Japan because it was "rich ground for conflict."

After the Cultural Revolution, when Namioka felt "safe," she wrote about the Chinese-American immigrant experience in *Yang the Youngest and His Terrible Ear,* which is based on her own childhood experience. Namioka's latest book, set in Japan, is her seventh book about the two samurai Zenta and Matsuzo. She has received awards for several of these books.

OTHER WORKS *White Serpent Castle, Valley of the Broken Cherry Trees, Phantom of Tiger Mountain, Who's Hu?*

LASERLINKS
• *ART GALLERY*

PREVIEWING

Collecting Team
Robert Silverberg

PERSONAL CONNECTION

The story you are about to read involves travel to distant planets and suggests the idea of life beyond our solar system. Some people believe there is life elsewhere in the universe. What do you think? Discuss your thoughts with the class.

LITERARY CONNECTION

On Halloween Eve in 1938, thousands of people panicked when a radio broadcast announced a Martian invasion of New Jersey. One woman nearly committed suicide when she learned of the alien attack. Rather than a news report, however, listeners had actually heard a science fiction radio play produced by Orson Welles and based on H.G. Wells's novel *The War of the Worlds*.

Modern **science fiction**—stories about real or imagined scientific developments—emerged during the late 1800s with the works of H. G. Wells and Jules Verne. At this time, advancements in science and technology were occurring rapidly and having a significant effect on the development of science fiction. Verne's novel *From the Earth to the Moon*, written in 1863, describes a moon launch with surprising scientific accuracy. He was one of the first writers to draw attention to science fiction as a distinct branch of literature.

WRITING CONNECTION

Suppose that there were living creatures on other planets. How frightening would they be? Use your imagination to write a brief description of such a creature in your notebook. Add a sketch of the creature and share it with classmates if you wish. Then read to see how Silverberg's tale of alien life compares to your mental image.

Orson Welles performs in one of his radio productions during the 1930s. Archive Photos.

COLLECTING TEAM

by Robert Silverberg

Return from the Stars, Gregory Manchess. Copyright © Gregory Manchess.

From fifty thousand miles up, the situation looked promising. It was a middle-sized, brown-and-green, inviting-looking planet, with no sign of cities or any other such complications. Just a pleasant sort of place, the very sort we were looking for to redeem what had been a pretty <u>futile</u> expedition.

I turned to Clyde Holdreth, who was staring reflectively at the thermocouple.

"Well? What do you think?"

"Looks fine to me. Temperature's about seventy down there—nice and warm, and plenty of air. I think it's worth a try."

Lee Davison came strolling out from the storage hold, smelling of animals, as usual. He was holding one of the blue monkeys we picked up on Alpheraz, and the little beast was crawling up his arm. "Have we found something, gentlemen?"

"We've found a planet," I said. "How's the storage space in the hold?"

"Don't worry about that. We've got room for a whole zooful more before we get filled up. It hasn't been a very fruitful trip."

"No," I agreed. "It hasn't. Well? Shall we go down and see what's to be seen?"

"Might as well," Holdreth said. "We can't go back to Earth with just a couple of blue monkeys and some anteaters, you know."

"I'm in favor of a landing too," said Davison. "You?"

I nodded. "I'll set up the charts, and you get your animals comfortable for deceleration."

Davison disappeared back into the storage hold, while Holdreth scribbled furiously in the logbook, writing down the coordinates of the planet below, its general description, and so forth. Aside from being a collecting team for the zoological department of the Bureau of Interstellar Affairs, we also double as a survey ship, and the planet down below was listed as *unexplored* on our charts.

I glanced out at the mottled brown-and-green ball spinning slowly in the view port and felt the warning twinge of gloom that came to me every time we made a landing on a new and strange world. <u>Repressing</u> it, I started to figure out a landing orbit. From behind me came the furious chatter of the blue monkeys as Davison strapped them into their acceleration cradles, and under that the deep, unmusical honking of the Rigelian anteaters, noisily bleating their displeasure.

The planet was inhabited, all right. We hadn't had the ship on the ground more than a minute before the local fauna[1] began to congregate. We stood at the view port and looked out in wonder.

"This is one of those things you dream about," Davison said, stroking his little beard nervously. "Look at them! There must be a thousand different species out there."

"I've never seen anything like it," said Holdreth.

I computed how much storage space we had left and how many of the thronging creatures outside we would be able to bring back with us. "How are we going to decide what to take and what to leave behind?"

"Does it matter?" Holdreth said gaily. "This is what you call an embarrassment of riches, I guess. We just grab the dozen most bizarre creatures and blast off—and save the rest for another trip. It's too bad we wasted all that time wandering around near Rigel."

"We *did* get the anteaters," Davison pointed

---

1. **fauna** (fô′nə): animals of a particular region.

out. They were his find, and he was proud of them.

I smiled sourly. "Yeah. We got the anteaters there." The anteaters honked at that moment, loud and clear. "You know, that's one set of beasts I think I could do without."

"Bad attitude," Holdreth said. "Unprofessional."

"Whoever said I was a zoologist, anyway? I'm just a spaceship pilot, remember. And if I don't like the way those anteaters talk—and smell—I see no reason why I—"

"Say, look at that one," Davison said suddenly.

I glanced out the view port and saw a new beast emerging from the thick-packed vegetation in the background. I've seen some fairly strange creatures since I was assigned to the zoological department, but this one took the grand prize.

It was about the size of a giraffe, moving on long, wobbly legs and with a tiny head up at the end of a <u>preposterous</u> neck. Only it had six legs and a bunch of writhing snakelike tentacles as well, and its eyes, great violet globes, stood out nakedly on the ends of two thick stalks. It must have been twenty feet high. It moved with exaggerated grace through the swarm of beasts surrounding our ship, pushed its way smoothly toward the vessel, and peered gravely in at the view port. One purple eye stared directly at me, the other at Davison. Oddly, it seemed to me as if it were trying to tell us something.

"Big one, isn't it?" Davison said finally. "I'll bet you'd like to bring one back, too."

"Maybe we can fit a young one aboard," Davison said. "If we can find a young one." He turned to Holdreth. "How's that air analysis coming? I'd like to get out there and start collecting. God, that's a crazy-looking beast!"

The animal outside had apparently finished its inspection of us, for it pulled its head away and, gathering its legs under itself, squatted near the ship. A small doglike creature with stiff spines running along its back began to bark at the big creature, which took no notice. The other animals, which came in all shapes and sizes, continued to mill around the ship, evidently very curious about the newcomer to their world. I could see Davison's eyes thirsty with the desire to take the whole kit and caboodle back to Earth with him. I knew what was running through his mind. He was dreaming of the umpteen thousand species of extraterrestrial wildlife roaming around out there, and to each one he was attaching a neat little tag: *Something-or-other davisoni.*

"The air's fine," Holdreth announced abruptly, looking up from his test tubes. "Get your butterfly nets, and let's see what we can catch."

There was something I didn't like about the place. It was just too good to be true, and I learned long ago that nothing ever is. There's always a catch someplace.

Only this seemed to be on the level. The planet was a <u>bonanza</u> for zoologists, and Davison and Holdreth were having the time

WORDS TO KNOW

preposterous (prĭ-pŏs'tər-əs) *adj.* contrary to nature; absurd
bonanza (bə-năn'zə) *n.* source of great wealth

of their lives, hip deep in obliging specimens.

"I've never seen anything like it," Davison said for at least the fiftieth time as he scooped up a small purplish squirrel-like creature and examined it curiously. The squirrel stared back, examining Davison just as curiously.

"Let's take some of these," Davison said. "I like them."

"Carry 'em on in, then," I said, shrugging. I didn't care which specimens they chose, so long as they filled up the storage hold quickly and let me blast off on schedule. I watched as Davison grabbed a pair of the squirrels and brought them into the ship.

Holdreth came over to me. He was carrying a sort of dog with insect-faceted[2] eyes and gleaming furless skin. "How's this one, Gus?"

THE PLANET WAS TOO FLATLY INCREDIBLE FOR ME TO ACCEPT AT FACE VALUE.

"Fine," I said bleakly. "Wonderful."

He put the animal down—it didn't scamper away, just sat there smiling at us—and looked at me. He ran a hand through his fast-vanishing hair. "Listen, Gus, you've been gloomy all day. What's eating you?"

"I don't like this place," I said.

"Why? Just on general principles?"

"It's too *easy*, Clyde. Much too easy. These animals just flock around here waiting to be picked up."

Holdreth chuckled. "And you're used to a struggle, aren't you? You're just angry at us because we have it so simple here!"

"When I think of the trouble we went through just to get a pair of miserable vile-smelling anteaters, and—"

"Come off it, Gus. We'll load up in a hurry if you like. But this place is a zoological gold mine!"

I shook my head. "I don't like it, Clyde. Not at all."

Holdreth laughed again and picked up his faceted-eyed dog. "Say, know where I can find another of these, Gus?"

"Right over there," I said, pointing. "By that tree. With its tongue hanging out. It's just waiting to be carried away."

Holdreth looked and smiled. "What do you know about that!" He snared his specimen and carried both of them inside.

I walked away to survey the grounds. The planet was too flatly incredible for me to accept at face value, without at least a look-see, despite the <u>blithe</u> way my two companions were snapping up specimens.

For one thing, animals just don't exist this way—in big miscellaneous quantities, living all together happily. I hadn't noticed more than a few of each kind, and there must have been five hundred different species, each one stranger looking than the next. Nature doesn't work that way.

For another, they all seemed to be on friendly terms with one another, though they acknowledged the unofficial leadership of the giraffelike creature. Nature doesn't work *that* way, either. I hadn't seen one quarrel between the animals yet. That argued that they were all herbivores,[3] which didn't make sense <u>ecologically</u>.

I shrugged my shoulders and walked on.

---

2. **insect-faceted:** having eyes like insects, with many simple eyes functioning together.

3. **herbivores** (hŭr′bə-vôrz): grass-eating and plant-eating animals.

| WORDS TO KNOW | **blithe** (blīth) *adj.* showing a lack of concern; casual |
| | **ecologically** (ĕk′ə-lŏj′ĭ-kə-lē) *adv.* having to do with the biological relationships between organisms and their environment |

Half an hour later, I knew a little more about the geography of our bonanza. We were on either an immense island or a peninsula of some sort, because I could see a huge body of water bordering the land some ten miles off. Our vicinity was fairly flat, except for a good-sized hill from which I could see the terrain.

There was a thick, heavily wooded jungle not too far from the ship. The forest spread out all the way toward the water in one direction but ended abruptly in the other. We had brought the ship down right at the edge of the clearing. Apparently most of the animals we saw lived in the jungle.

On the other side of our clearing was a low, broad plain that seemed to trail away into a desert in the distance; I could see an uninviting stretch of barren sand that contrasted strangely with the fertile jungle to my left. There was a small lake to the side. It was, I saw, the sort of country likely to attract a varied fauna, since there seemed to be every sort of habitat within a small area.

And the fauna! Although I'm a zoologist only by osmosis,[4] picking up both my interest and my knowledge secondhand from Holdreth and Davison, I couldn't help but be astonished by the wealth of strange animals. They came in all different shapes and sizes, colors and odors, and the only thing they all had in common was their friendliness. During the course of my afternoon's wanderings a hundred animals must have come marching boldly right up to me, given me the once-over, and walked away. This included half a dozen kinds that I hadn't seen before, plus one of the eye-stalked, intelligent-looking giraffes and a furless dog. Again, I had the feeling that the giraffe seemed to be trying to communicate.

I didn't like it. I didn't like it at all.

I returned to our clearing and saw Holdreth and Davison still buzzing madly around, trying to cram as many animals as they could into our hold.

"How's it going?" I asked.

"Hold's all full," Davison said. "We're busy making our alternate selections now." I saw him carrying out Holdreth's two furless dogs and picking up instead a pair of eight-legged penguinish things that uncomplainingly allowed themselves to be carried in. Holdreth was frowning unhappily.

"What do you want *those* for, Lee? Those doglike ones seem much more interesting, don't you think?"

"No," Davison said, "I'd rather bring along these two. They're curious beasts, aren't they? Look at the muscular network that connects the—"

"Hold it, fellows," I said. I peered at the animal in Davison's hands and glanced up. "This *is* a curious beast," I said. "It's got eight legs."

"You becoming a zoologist?" Holdreth asked, amused.

---

4. **osmosis** (ŏz-mō′sĭs): a gradual process of absorption.

"No—but I am getting puzzled. Why should this one have eight legs, some of the others here six, and some of the others only four?"

They looked at me blankly, with the scorn of professionals.

"I mean, there ought to be some sort of logic to evolution here, shouldn't there? On Earth we've developed a four-legged pattern of animal life; on Venus, they usually run to six legs. But have you ever seen an evolutionary hodgepodge like this place before?"

"There are stranger setups," Holdreth said. "The symbiotes[5] on Sirius Three, the burrowers of Mizar—but you're right, Gus. This *is* a peculiar evolutionary dispersal.[6] I think we ought to stay and investigate it fully."

Instantly I knew from the bright expression on Davison's face that I had blundered, had made things worse than ever. I decided to take a new tack.

"I don't agree," I said. "I think we ought to leave with what we've got and come back with a larger expedition later."

Davison chuckled. "Come on, Gus, don't be silly! This is a chance of a lifetime for us— why should we call in the whole zoological department on it?"

I didn't want to tell them I was afraid of staying longer. I crossed my arms. "Lee, I'm the pilot of this ship, and you'll have to listen to me. The schedule calls for a brief stopover here, and we have to leave. Don't tell me I'm being silly."

"But you are, man! You're standing blindly in the path of scientific investigation, of—"

"Listen to me, Lee. Our food is calculated on a pretty narrow margin, to allow you fellows more room for storage. And this is strictly a collecting team. There's no provision for extended stays on any one planet. Unless you want to wind up eating your own specimens, I suggest you allow us to get out of here."

hey were silent for a moment. Then Holdreth said, "I guess we can't argue with that, Lee. Let's listen to Gus and go back now. There's plenty of time to investigate this place later, when we can take longer."

"But—oh, all right," Davison said reluctantly. He picked up the eight-legged penguins. "Let me stash these things in the hold, and we can leave." He looked strangely at me, as if I had done something criminal.

As he started into the ship, I called to him.

"What is it, Gus?"

"Look here, Lee. I don't *want* to pull you away from here. It's simply a matter of food," I lied, masking my nebulous suspicions.

"I know how it is, Gus." He turned and entered the ship.

I stood there thinking about nothing at all for a moment, then went inside myself to begin setting up the blastoff orbit.

I got as far as calculating the fuel expenditure when I noticed something. Feed wires were dangling crazily down from the control cabinet. Somebody had wrecked our drive mechanism, but thoroughly.

For a long moment, I stared stiffly at the sabotaged drive. Then I turned and headed into the storage hold.

"Davison?"

"What is it, Gus?"

"Come out here a second, will you?"

---

5. **symbiotes** (sĭm′bē-ōts): organisms that live very close together and depend on one another for survival.

6. **evolutionary dispersal:** distribution or pattern according to the laws of evolution.

| WORDS TO KNOW | **hodgepodge** (hŏj′pŏj) *n.* a mixture of unlike ingredients; a jumble
nebulous (nĕb′yə-ləs) *adj.* not clear or definite; vague
sabotaged (săb′ə-täzhd′) *adj.* harmed with the purpose of producing failure or damage **sabotage** *v.* |

I waited, and a few minutes later he appeared, frowning impatiently. "What do you want, Gus? I'm busy and I—" His mouth dropped open. *Look at the drive!*

"You look at it," I snapped. "I'm sick. Go get Holdreth, on the double."

While he was gone, I tinkered with the shattered mechanism. Once I had the cabinet panel off and could see the inside, I felt a little better; the drive wasn't damaged beyond repair, though it had been pretty well scrambled. Three or four days of hard work with a screwdriver and solder beam[7] might get the ship back into functioning order.

But that didn't make me any less angry. I heard Holdreth and Davison entering behind me, and I whirled to face them.

"All right, you idiots. Which one of you did this?"

They opened their mouths in protesting squawks at the same instant. I listened to them for a while, then said, "One at a time!"

"If you're implying that one of us deliberately sabotaged the ship," Holdreth said, "I want you to know—"

"I'm not implying anything. But the way it looks to me, you two decided you'd like to stay here a while longer to continue your investigations and figured the easiest way of getting me to agree was to wreck the drive." I glared hotly at them. "Well, I've got news for you. I can fix this, and I can fix it in a couple of days. So go on—get about your business! Get all the zoologizing you can in, while you still have time. I—"

Davison laid a hand gently on my arm. "Gus," he said quietly, *"we didn't do it.* Neither of us."

Suddenly all the anger drained out of me and was replaced by raw fear. I could see that Davison meant it.

"If you didn't do it, and Holdreth didn't do it, and *I* didn't do it—then who did?"

Davison shrugged.

"Maybe it's one of us who doesn't know he's doing it," I suggested. "Maybe—" I stopped. "Oh, that's nonsense. Hand me that tool kit, will you, Lee?"

They left to tend to the animals, and I set to work on the repair job, dismissing all further speculations and suspicions from my mind, concentrating solely on joining Lead A to Input A and Transistor F to Potentiometer K, as indicated. It was slow, nerve-harrowing work, and by mealtime I had accomplished only the barest <u>preliminaries</u>. My fingers were starting to quiver from the strain of small-scale work, and I decided to give up the job for the day and get back to it tomorrow.

I slept uneasily, my nightmares punctuated by the moaning of the accursed anteaters and the occasional squeals, chuckles, bleats, and hisses of the various other creatures in the hold. It must have been four in the morning before I dropped off into a really sound sleep, and what was left of the night passed swiftly. The next thing I knew, hands were shaking me, and I was looking up into the pale, tense faces of Holdreth and Davison.

I pushed my sleep-stuck eyes open and blinked. "Huh? What's going on?"

Holdreth leaned down and shook me savagely. "Get up, Gus!"

I struggled to my feet slowly. "Hell of a thing to do, wake a fellow up in the middle of the—"

I found myself being propelled from my cabin and led down the corridor to the control room. Blearily, I followed where Holdreth pointed, and then I woke up in a hurry.

---

7. **solder** (sŏd′ər) **beam**: an imaginary device used to repair wiring.

The drive was battered again. Someone—or *something*—had completely undone my repair job of the night before.

If there had been bickering among us, it stopped. This was past the category of a joke now; it couldn't be laughed off, and we found ourselves working together as a tight unit again, trying desperately to solve the puzzle before it was too late.

"Let's review the situation," Holdreth said, pacing nervously up and down the control cabin. "The drive has been sabotaged twice. None of us knows who did it, and on a conscious level each of us is convinced *he* didn't do it."

He paused. "That leaves us with two possibilities. Either, as Gus suggested, one of us is doing it unaware of it even himself, or someone else is doing it while we're not looking. Neither possibility is a very cheerful one."

"We can stay on guard, though," I said. "Here's what I propose: first, have one of us awake at all times—sleep in shifts, that is, with somebody guarding the drive until I get it fixed. Two—jettison[8] all the animals aboard ship."

"*What?*"

"He's right," Davison said. "We don't know what we may have brought aboard. They don't seem to be intelligent, but we can't be sure. That purple-eyed baby giraffe, for instance—suppose he's been hypnotizing us into damaging the drive ourselves. How can we tell?"

"Oh, but—" Holdreth started to protest, then stopped and frowned soberly. "I suppose we'll have to admit the possibility," he said, obviously unhappy about the prospect of freeing our captives. "We'll empty out the hold, and you see if you can get the drive fixed. Maybe later we'll recapture them all if nothing further develops."

We agreed to that, and Holdreth and Davison cleared the ship of its animal cargo while I set to work determinedly at the drive

mechanism. By nightfall, I had managed to accomplish as much as I had the day before.

THE EXPEDITION HAD TURNED INTO A NIGHTMARE.

I sat up as watch the first shift, aboard the strangely quiet ship. I paced around the drive cabin, fighting the great temptation to doze off, and managed to last through until the time Holdreth arrived to relieve me.

Only—when he showed up, he gasped and pointed at the drive. It had been ripped apart a third time.

Now we had no excuse, no explanation. The expedition had turned into a nightmare.

I could only protest that I had remained awake my entire spell on duty and that I had seen no one and no thing approach the drive panel. But that was hardly a satisfactory explanation, since it either cast guilt on me as the saboteur or implied that some unseen external power was repeatedly wrecking the drive. Neither hypothesis made sense, at least to me.

By now we had spent four days on the planet, and food was getting to be a major problem. My carefully budgeted flight schedule called for us to be two days out on our return journey to Earth by now. But we still were no closer to departure than we had been four days ago.

The animals continued to wander around outside, nosing up against the ship, examining it, almost fondling it, with those damned pseudo-giraffes[9] staring soulfully at us always. The beasts were as friendly as ever, little

---

8. **jettison:** to cast overboard or off.

9. **pseudo-giraffes** (so͞o′dō): false giraffes in the sense that they look something like, but are not, the giraffes found on Earth.

knowing how the tension was growing within the hull. The three of us walked around like zombies, eyes bright and lips clamped. We were scared—all of us.

Something was keeping us from fixing the drive.

Something didn't want us to leave this planet.

I looked at the bland face of the purple-eyed giraffe staring through the view port, and it stared mildly back at me. Around it was grouped the rest of the local fauna, the same incredible hodgepodge of improbable genera[10] and species.

That night, the three of us stood guard in the control room together. The drive was smashed anyway. The wires were soldered in so many places by now that the control panel was a mass of shining alloy, and I knew that a few more such sabotagings and it would be impossible to patch it together anymore—if it wasn't so already.

The next night, I just didn't knock off. I continued soldering right on after dinner (and a pretty skimpy dinner it was, now that we were on close rations) and far on into the night.

By morning, it was as if I hadn't done a thing.

"I give up," I announced, surveying the damage. "I don't see any sense in ruining my nerves trying to fix a thing that won't stay fixed."

Holdreth nodded. He looked terribly pale. "We'll have to find some new approach."

"Yeah. Some new approach."

I yanked open the food closet and examined our stock. Even figuring in the synthetics[11] we would have fed to the animals if we hadn't released them, we were low on food. We had overstayed even the safety margin. It would be a hungry trip back—if we ever did get back.

I clambered through the hatch and sprawled down on a big rock near the ship. One of the furless dogs came over and nuzzled in my shirt. Davison stepped to the hatch and called down to me.

"What are you doing out there, Gus?"

"Just getting a little fresh air. I'm sick of living aboard that ship." I scratched the dog behind his pointed ears and looked around.

The animals had lost most of their curiosity about us and didn't congregate the way they used to. They were meandering all over the plain, nibbling at little deposits of a white doughy substance. It precipitated every night. Manna,[12] we called it. All the animals seemed to live on it.

I folded my arms and leaned back.

We were getting to look awfully lean by the eighth day. I wasn't even trying to fix the ship anymore; the hunger was starting to get me. But I saw Davison puttering around with my solder beam.

"What are you doing?"

"I'm going to repair the drive," he said. "You don't want to, but we can't just sit around, you know." His nose was deep in my repair guide, and he was fumbling with the release on the solder beam.

I shrugged. "Go ahead if you want to." I didn't care what he did. All I cared about was the gaping emptiness in my stomach, and about the dimly grasped fact that somehow we were stuck here for good.

"Gus?"

"Yeah?"

"I think it's time I told you something. I've

---

10. **genera:** plural of *genus;* categories of living organisms that are made up of groups of species with similar traits.

11. **synthetics:** artificial food produced by chemical means.

12. **manna:** in the Bible, the food miraculously provided for the Israelites in the wilderness during their flight from Egypt.

been eating the manna for four days. It's good. It's nourishing stuff."

"You've been eating—the manna? Something that grows on an alien world? You crazy?"

"What else can we do? Starve?"

I smiled feebly, admitting that he was right. From somewhere in the back of the ship came the sounds of Holdreth moving around. Holdreth had taken this thing worse than any of us. He had a family back on Earth, and he was beginning to realize that he wasn't ever going to see them again.

"Why don't you get Holdreth?" Davison suggested. "Go out there and stuff yourselves with the manna. You've got to eat something."

"Yeah. What can I lose?" Moving like a mechanical man, I headed toward Holdreth's cabin. We would go out and eat the manna and cease being hungry, one way or another.

"Clyde?" I called. "Clyde?"

I entered his cabin. He was sitting at his desk, shaking convulsively, staring at the two streams of blood that trickled in red spurts from his slashed wrists.

"*Clyde!*"

He made no protest as I dragged him toward the infirmary cabin and got tourniquets around his arms, cutting off the bleeding. He just stared dully ahead, sobbing.

I slapped him, and he came around. He shook his head dizzily, as if he didn't know where he was.

"I—I—"

"Easy, Clyde. Everything's all right."

"It's *not* all right," he said hollowly. "I'm still alive. Why didn't you let me die? Why didn't you—"

Davison entered the cabin. "What's been happening, Gus?"

"It's Clyde. The pressure's getting him. He tried to kill himself, but I think he's all right now. Get him something to eat, will you?"

We had Holdreth straightened around by evening. Davison gathered as much of the manna as he could find, and we held a feast.

"I wish we had nerve enough to kill some of the local fauna," Davison said. "Then we'd have a feast—steaks and everything!"

"The bacteria," Holdreth pointed out quietly. "We don't dare."

"I know. But it's a thought."

"No more thoughts," I said sharply. "Tomorrow morning we start work on the drive panel again. Maybe with some food in our bellies we'll be able to keep awake and see what's happening here."

Holdreth smiled. "Good. I can't wait to get out of this ship and back to a normal existence. God, I just can't wait!"

"Let's get some sleep," I said. "Tomorrow we'll give it another try. We'll get back," I said with a confidence I didn't feel.

The following morning I rose early and got my tool kit. My head was clear, and I was trying to put the pieces together without much luck. I started toward the control cabin.

And stopped.

And looked out the view port.

I went back and awoke Holdreth and Davison. "Take a look out the port," I said hoarsely.

They looked. They gaped.

"It looks just like my house," Holdreth said. "My house on Earth."

"With all the comforts of home inside, I'll bet." I walked forward uneasily and lowered myself through the hatch. "Let's go look at it."

We approached it, while the animals frolicked around us. The big giraffe came near and shook its head gravely. The house stood in the middle of the clearing, small and neat and freshly painted.

I saw it now. During the night, invisible hands had put it there. Had assembled and built a cozy little Earth-type house and dropped it next to our ship for us to live in.

"Just like my house," Holdreth repeated in wonderment.

"It should be," I said. "They grabbed the model from your mind, as soon as they found out we couldn't live on the ship indefinitely."

Holdreth and Davison asked as one, "What do you mean?"

"You mean you haven't figured this place out yet?" I licked my lips, getting myself used to the fact that I was going to spend the rest of my life here. "You mean you don't realize what this house is intended to be?"

They shook their heads, baffled. I glanced around, from the house to the useless ship to the jungle to the plain to the little pond. It all made sense now.

"They want to keep us happy," I said. "They knew we weren't thriving aboard the ship, so they—they built us something a little more like home."

"*They?* The giraffes?"

"Forget the giraffes. They tried to warn us, but it's too late. They're intelligent beings, but they're prisoners just like us. I'm talking about the ones who run this place. The super-aliens who make us sabotage our own ship and not even know we're doing it, who stand someplace up there and gape at us. The ones who dredged together this motley assortment of beasts from all over the galaxy. Now we've been collected too. This whole damned place is just a zoo—a zoo for aliens so far ahead of us we don't dare dream what they're like."

I looked up at the shimmering blue-green sky, where invisible bars seemed to restrain us, and sank down dismally on the porch of our new home. I was resigned. There wasn't any sense in struggling against *them*.

I could see the neat little placard now:

EARTHMEN. Native Habitat, Sol III. ❖

SPACE EXPLORATION

"Collecting Team" was published just one year before the space age began. It was on October 4, 1957, that space exploration took off, and the line between science fiction and science fact started to blur. The former Soviet Union launched *Sputnik*, the first artificial satellite to orbit the earth, forever changing the relationship between human beings and outer space. This impressive show of scientific might spurred the United States on to launch its first two satellites, *Explorer 1* and *Vanguard 1*, in 1958.

These necessary first steps in the quest for space would eventually lead to the launching of human beings into orbit. Yuri A. Gagarin, a Soviet cosmonaut, was the first human being in space. Gagarin orbited the earth on April 12, 1961. Following him, in 1962, John H. Glenn, Jr., was hailed as the first American to orbit the earth. Then, beginning with Neil A. Armstrong's historic first "small step," U.S. Apollo astronauts explored the surface of the moon six times between 1969 and 1972.

During the 1970s, astronauts and cosmonauts developed technology for living in space aboard the Skylab and Salyut space stations. Between 1983 and 1992, the National Aeronautics and Space Administration (NASA) achieved a number of firsts in the sending of astronauts into space: Sally K. Ride became the first U.S. woman in space; Guion S. Bluford, Jr., the first African American; Marc Garneau, the first Canadian; and Mae C. Jemison, the first African-American woman in space.

The crew of the space shuttle Endeavor on an 8-day mission in 1992. Mae Jemison is on the right.

Researchers are now investigating ways to manufacture products in space, studying the possibility of identifying other intelligent life in the universe, and planning bases to be set up on the moon and Mars. Some scientists are even looking to a time when people might be born, live, and die on space colonies.

RESPONDING OPTIONS

FROM **PERSONAL RESPONSE** *TO* **CRITICAL ANALYSIS**

REFLECT 1. What is your reaction to the ending of the story?

RETHINK 2. How does the narrator, Gus, explain what has happened? Do you agree with him? Why or why not?

3. Why do you think Gus, rather than Davison or Holdreth, realizes that they have been fooled by appearances?

   Consider
   - his role in the expedition
   - how Gus feels as they land on a new planet
   - what he observes while the others collect specimens

4. If you were with the men, what would you do next? Draw a picture that shows what you would do.

5. In your opinion, how frightening is this tale?

   Consider
   - what events and details are believable
   - how your concept of life on other planets compares with that shown in the story

6. What is ironic about the title of the story?

RELATE 7. Just as the team does in this story, people on earth remove animals from their natural habitats for scientific study and for placement in zoos. Do you think both reasons justify the removal of animals? Explain your answer.

ANOTHER PATHWAY

Carefully reread "Collecting Team" and gather clues that hint at how the story ends. Combine your listed clues with those of your classmates to compile a complete list.

QUICKWRITES

1. Gus seems resigned to living in his new home. How do you think Holdreth and Davison feel? What might they do? Write the next **episode** of the story.

2. As the spaceship approaches the planet, Holdreth scribbles what he sees in the ship's logbook, the daily record of data and events. Write a series of **log entries** that reflect highlights of the story.

3. Imagine that you are one of the "super-aliens" who collect the space travelers. Write observations of your specimens in the form of a **science journal entry**.

   📁 *PORTFOLIO Save your writing. You may want to use it later as a springboard to a piece for your portfolio.*

LITERARY CONCEPTS

The **climax** of a story is the moment at which the action is at a peak, the readers are most interested, and the conflict is resolved. The climax may involve a change, a decision, or a new understanding. At what point do you think the climax of "Collecting Team" occurs? Explain your answer.

ALTERNATIVE ACTIVITIES

1. Make a **diorama** of the planet in the story. Use Gus's descriptions of the geography and animals to create the three-dimensional scene.

2. If this story were made into a movie, what music would you choose as background for the drama? Make an **audiotape** to accompany an oral reading of the story by taping a combination of sound bites from music you select. Have someone read parts of the story aloud as you share your music with the class.

3. The narrator guesses that there are 500 species on the planet. Skim the selection and count how many are referred to. Count the species, not the number of individual animals, and be careful not to include the animals already on the ship. What percentage of the narrator's estimate is this sample? Write an **equation** to show how you arrived at the results.

WRITER'S STYLE

On page 110, Silverberg uses an idiom in the expression "whole kit and caboodle," which means *the entire collection.* An idiom is a phrase or an expression that has a meaning different from what the words usually suggest. Use of such idioms enables Silverberg to create an informal style. Find a couple of other examples of idioms in the story. Then, for these idiomatic phrases, think of other idioms with roughly the same meaning, or invent your own. For example, "the whole shootin' match" has a meaning similar to "whole kit and caboodle."

CRITIC'S CORNER

One student board reviewer, Iruma Bello, said this about the ending of this story: "It would have been better if they could have returned to their home on Earth and gone back with their families." Do you agree with this statement? Give reasons for your opinion.

ACROSS THE CURRICULUM

Science The story tells us that many different animal species would never live together in a real ecosystem. Research ecosystems on the earth to find out exactly what they are and how they function. Then look more closely at the ecological facts in "Collecting Team," and explain what does and does not make sense, considering how ecosystems actually work.

whole
kit and
the entire collection
caboodle

Review the Words to Know at the bottom of the selection pages. Identify the word that is most closely related to the situation described in each sentence below. The boxed letters will spell the name of one of the animals in the story.

1. Gus tried again and again to repair the spaceship before giving up. ☐ _ _ _ _ _

2. The space travelers must have looked as silly to the super-aliens as the animals looked to the men.
_ _ _ _ _ _ _ _ _ _ ☐ _

3. With food low and the spaceship damaged, Gus could no longer ignore his anxiety.
☐ _ _ _ _ _ _

4. Davison and Holdreth seemed unconcerned about their safety. _ ☐ _ _ _ _

5. The many preparations needed to repair the spaceship took a long time.
_ _ ☐ _ _ _ _ _ _ _ _ _

6. Gus suspected that the damage was not accidental but was done on purpose.
☐ _ _ _ _ _ _ _ _

7. Gus did not fully understand his uneasy feelings about the planet.
_ _ _ _ _ _ ☐

8. The odd mixture of animals was unnatural.
_ _ ☐ _ _ _ _ _ _ _ _

9. The zoologists never expected to find this rich source of animals all in one place.
_ ☐ _ _ _ _ _

10. The animal life did not fit Gus's knowledge of how animals live in their environment.
_ _ _ _ _ ☐ _ _ _ _ _

ROBERT SILVERBERG

1935–

For over 40 years, Robert Silverberg has produced a great body of varied work, ranging from science fiction to diverse nonfiction topics. Silverberg started preparing for this impressive career at age 6, when he began writing stories in addition to editing his school newspaper. He loved science fiction and wrote his first science fiction tale when he was 12 years old. Silverberg explains, "We worked on it in class, I recall, whispering details of the plot to each other despite our teacher's scowls."

Silverberg has won science fiction's Nebula and Hugo awards and has received more award nominations for his work than any other writer in the field. Silverberg says he writes science fiction stories because "I couldn't not write them. There are plenty of other things I'd rather be doing—tidying up the garden, taking a trip, or just sitting in the sunshine and giggling quietly to myself. But story first, sunshine afterward. I won't allow it to be any other way. I can't."

OTHER WORKS *Nightwings, Lost Race of Mars, Lord Valentine's Castle*

FOCUS ON POETRY

Almost everyone, young or old, knows at least one poem. Poetry is the most compact form of literature, and often the most memorable. A poem packs all kinds of ideas, feelings, and sounds into a few carefully chosen words. The words, the sounds—even the form of a poem—all work together to create a total effect.

FORM The way a poem looks—or its arrangement on the page—is its form. Poetry is written in lines, which may or may not be sentences. Sometimes the lines are combined into groups called **stanzas.** Poets deliberately choose the arrangements of words and lines. Some poets even plan the spaces between words and letters to create the form, as in "Mixed Singles" on page 125.

SOUND Poems are meant to be read aloud. Therefore, poets choose and arrange words to create the sounds they want the listener to hear. There are many techniques poets can use to achieve different sounds. Three of these techniques are described below.

Rhyme Words that end with the same sound rhyme. In Western cultures, traditional poems, such as "Sea Lullaby" on page 131, often contain rhyming words at the ends of the lines.

> The old moon is tarnished
> With smoke of the flood,
> The dead leaves are varnished
> With color like blood,

Rhythm A poem's rhythm is sometimes called its beat. The rhythm is the pattern of stressed and unstressed syllables in a line of poetry. Stressed syllables are those word parts that are read with more emphasis; they can be indicated with a ′ mark. Unstressed syllables are those word parts that are read with less emphasis; they can be indicated with a ˘ mark. In these lines from "Paul Revere's Ride," listen for the beat that makes the lines sound like the pounding of horses' hooves.

> Ĭn thĕ hoúr ŏf dárknĕss ănd pérĭl ănd neéd,
> Thĕ peóplĕ wĭll wákĕn ănd lístĕn tŏ heár
> Thĕ húrrÿĭng hoóf-beáts ŏf thăt steéd,
> Ănd thĕ mídnĭght méssăge ŏf Paúl Rĕvére.

Poems that do not have a regular rhythm and that sound more like conversation are called **free verse.** The poem "Lost" on page 267 is written in free verse.

Repetition Poets often choose to repeat sounds, words, phrases, or whole lines in a poem.

Repetition helps the poet emphasize an idea or convey a certain feeling.

IMAGERY Imagery refers to words and phrases that appeal to the five senses. Poets use imagery to create a picture in the reader's mind or to remind the reader of a familiar sensation. Notice how these lines from "Simile: Willow and Ginkgo" on page 132 give you a visual picture as well as appealing to your sense of touch:

> The willow is sleek as a velvet-nosed calf;
> The ginkgo is leathery as an old bull.

FIGURATIVE LANGUAGE Poets use figurative language when they choose words and phrases that help the reader to picture ordinary things in new ways. The following are three kinds of these special descriptions, called **figures of speech.**

Simile A comparison that uses the word *like* or *as* is called a simile. This simile from "Simile: Willow and Ginkgo" compares the willow tree to a nymph:

> The willow is like a nymph with streaming
>   hair;

Metaphor A comparison that does not use the word *like* or *as* is called a metaphor. To what does the speaker compare herself in these lines from "I Belong" on page 622?

> I am the mountain, to stand
>   with pride, strength, and faith.

Personification When a poet describes an animal or an object as if it were human or had human qualities, he or she is using personification. In these lines from "Sea Lullaby," the poet gives human characteristics to the sea:

> Her bright locks were tangled,
> She shouted for joy,
> With one hand she strangled
> A strong little boy.

THEME All the poetic elements you have read about help the poet establish the theme. Just as in fiction, the message about life that the poem conveys is its theme.

STRATEGIES FOR READING POETRY

- **Preview the poem.** Notice the poem's form: its shape, its length, the length of the lines, and whether or not it has stanzas.

- **Read the poem aloud.** Pause at the ends of complete thoughts, not necessarily at the ends of lines. Look for end punctuation to help you find the end of a complete thought. As you read, listen for rhyme and listen for rhythm as well as the overall sound of the words in the poem.

- **Visualize the images.** In your mind's eye, picture the images and comparisons in the poem. Do the images remind you of feelings or experiences you have had?

- **Think about the words and phrases.** Allow yourself to wonder about any words or phrases that seem to stand out. Think about what that choice of words adds to the poem.

- **Try to figure out the theme.** Ask yourself, What's the point of the poem? What message is the poet trying to send or help me understand?

- **Let your understanding grow.** When you finish reading, you are left with first impressions of the poem. Reread the poem; each time you read it, you will find new meanings that add to your understanding and appreciation of the poem.

- **Allow yourself to enjoy poetry.** Remember that poetry is about feelings. You may connect with a particular poem because it expresses feelings that you have felt.

PREVIEWING

Moco Limping
David Nava Monreal

Mixed Singles
Arnold Adoff

PERSONAL CONNECTION

Have you ever made a surprising discovery about someone familiar to you? For example, you might suddenly realize that your brother has an annoying habit you overlooked before or that your friend has a talent you never noticed. In your notebook, jot down something you have learned recently about someone whom you've known a long time.

- I just recently noticed that my sister Kathleen cracks her knuckles—she's driving me crazy!
- I didn't know my friend Ricardo could play the cello. He even performs on stage.

LITERARY CONNECTION

Poems often enable readers to picture familiar things in new ways. Sometimes poets even use the spacing of words and lines to help the reader visualize the idea. In the two poems you are about to read, the spacing of words and lines reflects the subject matter of the poem. Before you read each poem, look at its shape on the page. As you read "Moco Limping," think about why the lines are short and irregular. As you read "Mixed Singles," think about how the lines reflect what is happening in the poem.

READING CONNECTION

Speaker In poetry, the voice that "talks" to the reader is called the speaker. The speaker is like a narrator in a work of fiction. In some poems, the speaker expresses the feelings of the poet. In other poems, the speaker and the poet are not the same.

In "Moco Limping" and "Mixed Singles," look for clues to the personality of the speaker, the qualities the speaker notices in his subject, and the speaker's reactions to the subject. Record your findings in a chart like the one below.

Poem	Speaker's Personality	Subject's Qualities	Speaker's Reactions
"Moco Limping"			
"Mixed Singles"			

MoCo
LiMPiNg

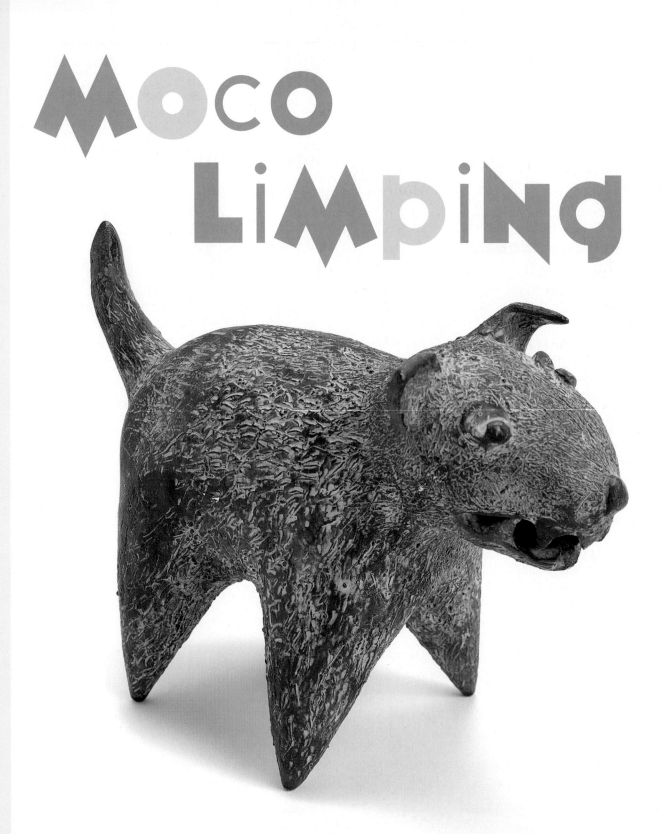

by david Nava Monreal

My dog hobbles
with a stick
of a leg that
he drags behind
5 him as he moves.
And I was a man
that wanted a
beautiful, noble
animal as a pet.
10 I wanted him
to be strong and
capture all the
attention by
the savage grace
15 of his gait.
I wanted him to
be the first
dog howling in
the pack.

20 The leader,
the brutal hunter
that broke through
the woods with
thunder.
25 But, instead he's
this rickety
little canine
that leaves trails
in the dirt
30 with his club foot.
He's the stumbler
that trips while
chasing lethargic
bees and butterflies.
35 It hurts me to
see him so
abnormal,
so clumsy and
stupid.

40 My vain heart weeps
knowing he
is mine.
But then he turns
my way and
45 looks at me with
eyes that cry out
with life.
He jumps at me with
his feeble paws,
50 I feel his warm fur
and his imperfection is
      forgotten.

FROM PERSONAL RESPONSE TO CRITICAL ANALYSIS

REFLECT 1. In this poem, did you react more strongly to the speaker or to the dog? Why? Jot down your thoughts in your notebook.

RETHINK 2. Could you identify with the speaker's thoughts and feelings in this poem? Explain your answer.
   Consider
   • how Moco's appearance contrasted with the speaker's expectations
   • the speaker's opinion of himself
   • how you would feel if Moco were your dog

   3. Did your ideas about the speaker change as you read the poem? Give reasons for your answer.

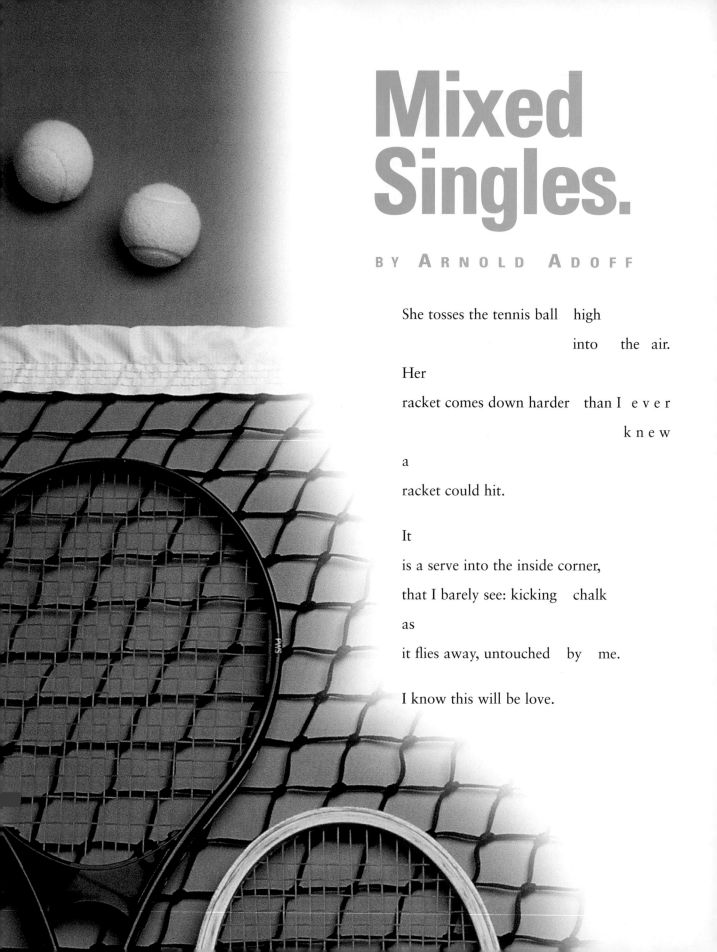

Mixed Singles.

BY ARNOLD ADOFF

She tosses the tennis ball   high
                              into   the   air.
Her
racket comes down harder   than I e v e r
                                         k n e w
a
racket could hit.

It
is a serve into the inside corner,
that I barely see: kicking   chalk
as
it flies away, untouched   by   me.

I know this will be love.

RESPONDING
O P T I O N S

FROM PERSONAL RESPONSE TO CRITICAL ANALYSIS

REFLECT
1. What was your first thought when you finished reading "Mixed Singles"?

RETHINK
2. What is the speaker's opinion of his opponent? Give reasons to support your answer.

   Consider
   - the speaker's description of her tennis playing
   - the meaning of the title and of the last line of the poem

3. What outcome(s) does the speaker expect from the tennis match?

4. What do the speakers in the two poems have in common?

RELATE
5. Look back at the chart you made for the Reading Connection on page 125. Compare and contrast how the speakers reacted to the subjects in the poems. Did their perceptions of the subjects change? Explain your answer.

ANOTHER PATHWAY

Cooperative Learning

Practice reading one of the two poems aloud. Then make an audiotape of your reading. The class can critique the presentations of each poem, noticing the varied interpretations that different readers give the same poem.

LITERARY CONCEPTS

The **form** of a poem is the way it looks, or its arrangement on the page. A poet chooses this arrangement deliberately. How do you think the forms the poets chose for "Moco Limping" and "Mixed Singles" reflect the subject matter and what is happening in those poems? Use a chart like the one shown to organize your thoughts.

Form	
"Moco Limping"	**"Mixed Singles"**

QUICKWRITES

1. Try your hand at writing a **poem** about someone or something very familiar to you, such as your best friend, your favorite sport, or a pet. Create a form for your poem that reflects its meaning.

2. Imagine that you are a sportswriter who attended the tennis match described in "Mixed Singles." Write an **article** for your newspaper in which you tell how the rest of the match was played.

   📁 *PORTFOLIO Save your writing. You may want to use it later as a springboard to a piece for your portfolio.*

ALTERNATIVE ACTIVITIES

1. Create a pair of **illustrations** of Moco, first showing the dog the speaker wanted and then showing Moco as he is.

2. Look for other poems whose unusual shape or form reflects their meaning. Copy the poems and compile a **booklet** of them to share in class.

DAVID NAVA MONREAL

David Nava Monreal (1935–) wrote about his own dog in "Moco Limping," a poem that was part of his 55-piece poetry collection appearing in *Sighs and Songs of Aztlan,* a collection of Chicano literature published in 1975. That same year, he won a nationwide contest sponsored by the Chicano Cultural Center of Bakersfield College for his works.

Monreal's poetry is personal, expressing his deep feelings about nature, peasants, love, jealousy, and poverty. Without bitterness, he writes poems of protest against injustice. Monreal's idea of peace is rolling fields under a warm sun, an April shower, or a duck floating like a leaf.

A California native, Monreal has worked on the staff of a public library and as a group supervisor in a county probation department.

ARNOLD ADOFF

Arnold Adoff was born in New York City, in the East Bronx. As a youngster, he enjoyed exploring both his neighborhood and the rest of the city. After attending City College and Columbia University, he taught in Harlem for 12 years. While teaching his African-American students, Adoff, a poet himself, realized how hard it was to find books of African-American poetry to share with them. He decided to do something about it. Adoff gathered African-American poetry into an anthology and published it under the title *I Am the Darker Brother.* The book won an American Library Association Notable Book Award in 1968.

1935–

Besides compiling several more anthologies of African-American poetry, Adoff has continued to write his own poetry. He married the writer Virginia Hamilton in 1960, and they later had two children. Many of his poems for young people celebrate the joys of loving families like his own. Adoff has long championed the need for relevant and exciting poetry for children. Besides writing and teaching, he lectures and is part of a multicultural center that promotes the writing of poetry by young people.

OTHER WORKS *Slow Dance Heartbreak Blues, All the Colors of the Race, Sports Pages, Chocolate Dreams*

PREVIEWING

POETRY

Simile: Willow and Ginkgo
Eve Merriam

Sea Lullaby
Elinor Wylie

PERSONAL CONNECTION

You are probably aware that the weather has an effect on your mood, but have you ever noticed how objects in nature influence you? For example, how do you feel when you look at a lake or the ocean? How do you feel when you see a desolate landscape, a huge tree, a tiny flower, or a rocky cliff? Sketch or describe one or two scenes or objects from nature that have affected you the most.

SCIENCE CONNECTION

The poems you are about to read describe objects in nature—two kinds of trees and the sea. The willow is a graceful tree with slender, drooping branches and narrow, pointed leaves. Willow trees generally grow near water, and their network of roots prevents soil erosion. Many of the 300 species of willow are planted for their beauty.

The ginkgo tree, on the other hand, is a relic from the past—the only survivor of a species of prehistoric plants. Its squat shape and fan-shaped leaves make it look quite different from the willow. The female tree yields a nasty-smelling nut that fouls the air around it.

READING CONNECTION

Comparisons in Poetry In these poems, the poets make comparisons to help you picture objects or scenes from nature using two literary devices: **simile** and **personification.** A simile is a comparison that usually uses the word *like* or *as.* "The willow is *like* an etching" is a simile from "Simile: Willow and Ginkgo." Using personification, a poet gives human qualities to an object, animal, or idea. In "Sea Lullaby," the words *smiler* and *teeth* make the sea seem human.

As you read the poems, record other comparisons, using a web like the one shown. Label each comparison with a tree or a wave to show which poem it came from.

- Comparisons in Poetry
  - Simile
  - Personification

SIMILE: WILLOW AND GINKGO/SEA LULLABY **131**

Simile:
Willow and Ginkgo

by Eve Merriam

The willow is like an etching,
Fine-lined against the sky.
The ginkgo is like a crude sketch,
Hardly worthy to be signed.

5 The willow's music is like a soprano
Delicate and thin.
The ginkgo's tune is like a chorus
With everyone joining in.

The willow is sleek as a velvet-nosed calf;
10 The ginkgo is leathery as an old bull.
The willow's branches are like silken thread;
The ginkgo's like stubby rough wool.

The willow is like a nymph with streaming hair;
Wherever it grows, there is green and gold and fair.
15 The willow dips to the water,
Protected and precious, like the king's favorite daughter.

The ginkgo forces its way through gray concrete:
Like a city child, it grows up in the street.
Thrust against the metal sky,
20 Somehow it survives and even thrives.

My eyes feast upon the willow,
But my heart goes to the ginkgo.

FROM **PERSONAL RESPONSE** *TO* **CRITICAL ANALYSIS**

REFLECT   **1.** What images came to mind as you read this poem?

RETHINK   **2.** Why does the speaker's heart go to the ginkgo? Would yours? Explain.

3. How does the poet appeal to the reader's senses? Give examples.

Sea Lullaby

by Elinor Wylie

The old moon is tarnished
With smoke of the flood,
The dead leaves are varnished
With color like blood,

5 A treacherous smiler
With teeth white as milk,
A savage beguiler
In sheathings of silk,

The sea creeps to pillage,
10 She leaps on her prey;
A child of the village
Was murdered today.

She came up to meet him
In a smooth golden cloak,
15 She choked him and beat him
To death, for a joke.

Her bright locks were tangled,
She shouted for joy,
With one hand she strangled
20 A strong little boy.

Now in silence she lingers
Beside him all night
To wash her long fingers
In silvery light

RESPONDING
O P T I O N S

FROM PERSONAL RESPONSE *TO* CRITICAL ANALYSIS

REFLECT   **1.** How did this poem affect you? Jot down your reactions in your notebook. Share your thoughts with a partner.

RETHINK   **2.** How is the portrayal of the sea different from what you expected? Explain your answer.

3. As you have learned, the sea is personified in this poem. If the sea in the poem were actually a woman, how would you describe her personality? To support your answer, include relevant phrases from the web you made for the Reading Connection on page 131.

4. Why do you think the poet chose the title she did?

RELATE   **5.** Compare and contrast how the two poems make you feel. Use words and phrases from each in your comparison.

6. Which poem do you like better? Why?

ANOTHER PATHWAY
Cooperative Learning

In a paragraph, explain how "Simile: Willow and Ginkgo" and "Sea Lullaby" fit the theme, "Fooled by Appearances." Look for examples of figurative language in each poem that fit the theme.

LITERARY CONCEPTS

In contrast to "Moco Limping" and "Mixed Singles," Merriam's and Wylie's poems use rhyme and rhythm. **Rhyme** involves the repetition of the same or similar sounds, with matching sounds often falling at the ends of lines.

Rhythm, sometimes called the "beat" of the poem, is the pattern of stressed and unstressed syllables. Stressed syllables are read with more emphasis, unstressed syllables with less emphasis.

Read both poems aloud. Which poem has a more consistent end-rhyme pattern? Which one has a stronger, more even rhythm? How does that regularity reflect the subject of the poem?

QUICKWRITES

1. In the Personal Connection on page 131, you described or sketched a scene or an object from nature. Now write a list of **similes** that compare that scene or object to other things familiar to readers.

2. "Sea Lullaby" reminds us that nature can seem cruel. Choose another natural killer, such as a hurricane, and write a **poem** about it. Include comparisons in your poem.

📁 *PORTFOLIO Save your writing. You may want to use it later as a springboard to a piece for your portfolio.*

EVE MERRIAM

1916–1992

The daughter of Russian immigrants, Eve Merriam grew up in small Pennsylvania towns. As a child, she enjoyed reading poetry, and she began writing her own poems when she was seven or eight. She went on to become one of the most respected poets in the United States, publishing more than 25 volumes of adult's and children's poetry.

Merriam won the Yale Younger Poets Prize in 1946, and the National Council of Teachers of English honored her poetry for children in 1981. One of her volumes of poetry, *The Inner City Mother Goose*, published in 1969, became contro-versial when law enforcement officials claimed it glamorized crime. It was later adapted into an award-winning play.

About her craft, Merriam said, "There is a special magic about rhyme, the chime that rings in time. It's like the little bell at the end of the typewriter line." It was not unusual for her to have "spent weeks looking for precisely the right word. It's like having a tiny marble in your pocket; you can just feel it."

OTHER WORKS *It Doesn't Always Have to Rhyme, Out Loud, Fresh Paint: New Poems*

ELINOR WYLIE

1885–1928

Free-spirited Elinor Wylie chose to ignore the social conventions of her day. As a teenager, she was an outstanding student, but chose to enjoy the social life of Washington, D.C., rather than attend college. In 1905, she married Philip Hichborn. However, the marriage soon fell apart over Hichborn's violent fits of jealousy. They had one child together before Elinor left him and began a romantic relationship with Horace Wylie.

The scandal surrounding Elinor and Horace's behavior forced them to move to England, where Elinor published her first collection of poems. In response to the loss of her second baby, Elinor went blind for a number of weeks. Meanwhile, back in the United States, Hichborn committed suicide, and Horace Wylie's wife agreed to a divorce. Elinor and Horace returned to the United States in 1916 and were finally married in 1917. Soon after, Elinor joined a New York literary group that included William Rose Benét and Sinclair Lewis. Nine years after publication of her first book, she published her second collection of poems, *Nets to Catch the Wind,* which she considered her first significant work.

In 1923, William Rose Benét became her third husband. During the next five years, until her death, Wylie published four novels, three volumes of poetry, and short stories.

OTHER WORKS *Incidental Numbers, Black Armour*

WRITING A FIRSTHAND NARRATIVE

How do you view your parents or guardians and other relatives? What do you know about them? What were they like when they were your age? We may think we know everything about the people in our families. Often our perceptions change as we learn more about one another, as you discovered in Unit One, "Changing Perceptions."

GUIDED ASSIGNMENT

Write Your Family History Exploring family history can help you understand your background and maybe where some of your beliefs and attitudes come from. It might also change your perceptions about yourself and the people you live with. The next few pages will help you find ways to write about your family history.

Souvenir

Letter

① Find the Clues

To learn about what sorts of materials can be clues to your family history, take a look at the letter and the other family items on these pages.

Examine the Items What story do they tell? Suppose these items were in your family. What clues do you see that could help you make connections from one item to another? Write your ideas.

> I wonder how Preston and Susie met.

December 5, 1975

177-20 105th Street
Jamaica, NY 11433

Preston Washington
651 Riverside Drive
Pontiac, Michigan 48058

Dear Preston,

Mama is thrilled that we're getting married. (You were always her favorite.) Daddy didn't say anything about our wedding, the last time I saw him. Now that he and Mama are divorced, I hardly ever see him. When we have children, I'd hate for them not to know their grandfather.

I miss you. I'm glad we'll be getting married soon, now that your tour of duty is over.

Love always,
Susie

Family Tree

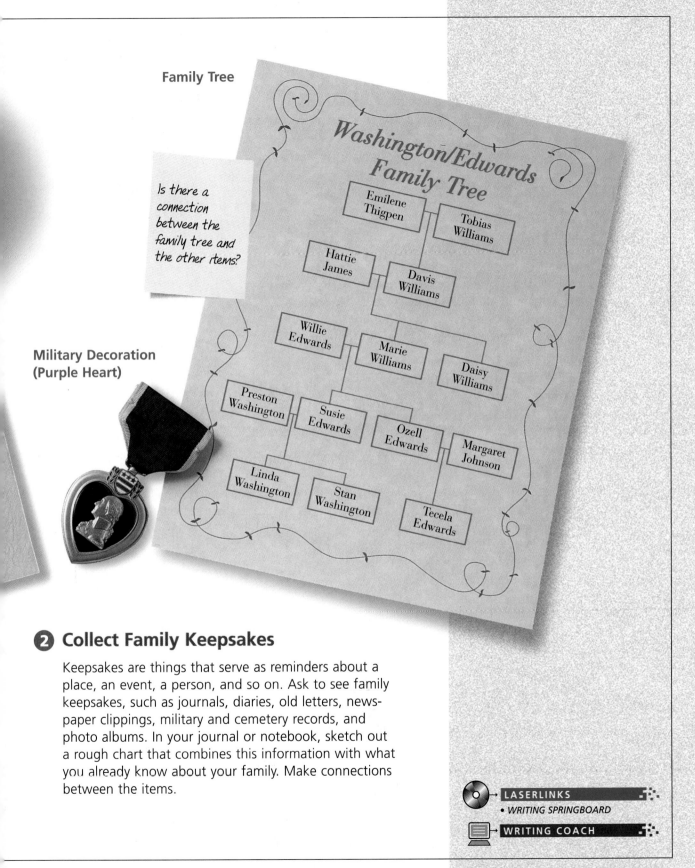

Is there a connection between the family tree and the other items?

Washington/Edwards Family Tree

- Emilene Thigpen
- Tobias Williams
- Hattie James
- Davis Williams
- Willie Edwards
- Marie Williams
- Daisy Williams
- Preston Washington
- Susie Edwards
- Ozell Edwards
- Margaret Johnson
- Linda Washington
- Stan Washington
- Tecela Edwards

Military Decoration (Purple Heart)

❷ Collect Family Keepsakes

Keepsakes are things that serve as reminders about a place, an event, a person, and so on. Ask to see family keepsakes, such as journals, diaries, old letters, newspaper clippings, military and cemetery records, and photo albums. In your journal or notebook, sketch out a rough chart that combines this information with what you already know about your family. Make connections between the items.

LASERLINKS
• *WRITING SPRINGBOARD*

WRITING COACH

Exploring the Past

Researching Your Family When it comes to researching the history of a family, there are a lot of people and events to consider. You'll need to go to many different sources for the information you need. As you begin to discover more about your family, you may be surprised by what you learn.

dma Edwards

Linda and Stan at Ozell's wedding

❶ Gather Oral Histories

The best way to start gathering information is to talk to your family. Here are some possible resources for gathering oral histories— the stories that have been handed down by word of mouth from generation to generation.

Talk to Older Relatives Older relatives can be a rich source of information on family history. Take time to talk to your parents or guardians, grandparents, aunts, uncles, and other family members about their lives. Use the phone to talk to relatives who live far away.

Record What Relatives Say The SkillBuilder on the following page can help you develop good questions. Taking notes on your conversations will help you remember key events and the people involved in them. You might want to tape-record your interviews so that later you can check your memory or clarify a point. If you can, make a duplicate copy to share with other members of your family.

❷ Use a Variety of Resources

There are many ways to go about finding information to use in your family history.

Community Resources Your local library has books and pamphlets that can help you trace your family history. Other sources include courthouse records, military records, adoption records, and state records of births, marriages, and land titles.

On-line Services The Census Bureau has genealogy services records on Internet. Other on-line services are as follows:

- The International Genealogical Index of the Latter Day Saints Family History Library at Salt Lake City, Utah
- The National Archives in Washington, D.C., which has Ante-Bellum Plantation Records and the Freedmen's Bureau records

Use the Multimedia Handbook for tips on conducting computerized searches.

❸ Organize Your Research

Keep Track of Your Facts Consider using one of these organizing methods to help you keep track of the information you collect through research.

- Record your information on numbered note cards.
- Store family keepsakes in labeled boxes.
- List dates and other important information about a person or event. Make a time line of events, showing the order in which they occurred.

Decision Point What will you focus on? What details do you want to stress? Will you write about one person, time period, or event? You might consider focusing on an event or a person about which you have a strong feeling.

Family Time Line

SkillBuilder

 SPEAKING & LISTENING

Asking Questions

The tips below will help you develop effective questions to use as you collect oral histories.

- Avoid questions that can be answered yes or no. Try to ask more open-ended questions—for example: "What did you think about Dad when the two of you first met?"
- Ask questions that can be answered with details that appeal to the senses—for example: "What did you see when you stepped out your front door?"
- Ask follow-up questions to aid your understanding of a point. ("And then what happened?")

APPLYING WHAT YOU'VE LEARNED
With a partner, brainstorm a list of questions to ask relatives. Share your questions with another set of partners. Which of their questions might you use in your interviews?

THINK & PLAN

Reflecting on Your Ideas

1. What other information do you need? Where might you look for what you need?
2. Has something you learned changed the way you look at family members? How will you describe your discoveries in your report?

Shaping Your History

Getting It All Down Once you have organized your notes and decided on a focus, begin getting your ideas on paper. The steps on these two pages will help you develop a draft of your family history.

1 Write a Rough Draft

Try not to edit yourself while you write. Just concentrate on getting the facts down in a way that makes sense. The Writing Coach can give you drafting ideas. Afterward, read your draft out loud. What do you like about what you've written? What do you need to change?

Student's Rough Draft

My Family

My Rough Draft	My Comments My Rough Draft
I always liked going to see Grandma in her home in Lake Providence, Louisiana. Lake Providence was once labeled the poorest place in America by Time magazine in 1994. Yet that's where both of my parents were raised.	Maybe I should move the first sentence. It doesn't seem as interesting as the fact about Lake Providence being the poorest place in America.
My grandparents were sharecroppers. They didn't have much money. So they got up at 3 a.m. to work in fields that belonged to other people. My grandparents had fifteen children. Two died before they were ten years old. My mom is the oldest in her family. She was born on January 8, 1952. I was born 30 years later.	I need to mention that my mom and her brothers and sisters also had to work.
My dad's family lived just thirty miles away from my mom's family in a place called Sonheimer. You can't find it on a map, it's so small. My mom and dad have known each other since they were in elementary school. My mom was really popular in school. My dad had a hard time in school. He had to repeat the eighth grade twice!	
I used to think I had it hard. Compared to how my grandmother lived, I'm rich! Now when my parents tell me I have it easy, maybe I'll believe them!	Maybe I should add that Dad went back to school and got a master's degree.

2 Rework Your Draft

The following guidelines can help you develop a more formal draft.

Strengthen the Shape of Your Story These points can help you develop a smooth flow of ideas:

- As you write your draft, you might need to refer to your time line to check the order of events. One way you can order events is through the use of words that show the passing of time. Some transitional words that show time order are *later, meanwhile, first, then, soon,* and *immediately*—for example: "My mom is the oldest in her family. She was born on January 8, 1952. I was born 30 years *later.*"
- Most effective narratives have an attention-grabbing beginning. If you don't grab your readers at the beginning, they may not stick around for the end. The middle of the narrative should develop the thought you expressed at the beginning and lead to a conclusion or concluding thought.

Create Vivid Images The SkillBuilder at the right and the techniques below can help you create vivid images for your readers.

- Use descriptions to enliven dry facts. What did the person you are writing about see, hear, taste, smell, or feel?
- Dialogue can help readers understand the excitement and significance of an event. Include remembered conversations whenever possible.

 PEER RESPONSE

When you are ready to share what you have written with others, ask a peer reviewer for feedback. You can ask questions such as the following to get the kind of feedback you need to revise your draft.

- What was the most memorable point for you?
- Were you able to understand the sequence of events? If not, where did you become confused?

Finishing Your Narrative

Making It Final Make any changes you think are necessary based on your readers' responses. Pay special attention to any suggestions made by family members who are mentioned in your narrative. Make sure you've presented them fairly and accurately. As you revise, though, don't lose sight of the focus of your family history.

1 Revise and Edit Your Draft

Use the following guidelines as you revise your draft:

- Refer to the comments made by your peer reviewers.
- Use the Standards for Evaluation and the Editing Checklist on page 143 to be sure that you've presented events of your family history in the correct order.
- This model will help you see how one student revised her draft. How did she make use of the notes she wrote to herself during the drafting stage?

Which words or phrases indicate a sense of time order?

What does the last paragraph tell you about what the student learned from her family?

Student's Final Draft

My Family

According to an August 1994 issue of *Time* magazine, Lake Providence, Louisiana, is one of the poorest places in America. Yet this is where both of my parents grew up.

My mother's parents were sharecroppers. They didn't have much money. They had to get up at 3 A.M. to go to work in fields they didn't own.

Fifteen children were born into my mom's family. My mom is the oldest. Two of her siblings died before they reached the age of ten. The kids who survived also had to work in the fields to get the crops ready for harvest.

My parents have known each other since they were in elementary school. My mom was popular in school and did well. Dad had a harder time in school. He had to repeat the eighth grade twice! Later he went to college and received a master's degree.

I used to think I had it hard. Compared to how my parents lived, I'm rich! Now when my parents tell me I have it easy, maybe I'll believe them.

Storyboard

Start with shot of my photo album.

Next, show footage of Grandma.

Making a video is one way to share your family history with others.

❷ Share Your Work

The format your writing takes may be determined by your reason for writing your family history. Below are some possible formats you can use for your family history. What do you like best about each format?

PUBLISHING IDEAS

- Make a family video, with narration. A storyboard like the one above can help you plan each scene.
- Use family photos in a photo essay with captions.
- Collect family recipes passed down from generation to generation, and include them with your history.

Standards for Evaluation

The firsthand narrative
- shows the writer's strong personal interest in the topic
- presents events in a clear order
- includes vivid imagery to give the reader a clear impression of the events
- concludes with the writer's personal reactions and observations

REFLECT & ASSESS

UNIT ONE: CHANGING PERCEPTIONS

In this unit, many of the characters experience situations and encounters that change the way they view things. As you read the selections, did your own perceptions change in any way? Did any of the selections lead you to think that things may not be as you once believed? Explore these questions by completing one or more of the options in each of the following sections.

REFLECTING ON THEME

OPTION 1 **Reading from Within** The characters in Unit One, "Changing Perceptions," learn important lessons as a result of their experiences. Which character do you think learns the most valuable lesson? Whose life will change the most as a result of what he or she has learned? Pretend that you are that character and write a letter to a friend, explaining how your perceptions have changed and what you plan to do from now on.

OPTION 2 **Connecting to Experience** Which situation or encounter in this unit's selections reminds you the most of an event in your own life? Write a few paragraphs, stating the similarities and telling whether your views changed as a result of your experience.

OPTION 3 **Discussion** With a small group of class-mates, discuss the different ways in which people learn that things are not as they once believed. Use examples from your own experiences and from the selections. You might consider the following factors:

- friends
- society
- family
- parents
- human nature
- the natural world

REFLECT & ASSESS *Self-Assessment: What new ways of looking at things have you developed as a result of reading the selections in Unit One? Jot down your thoughts in a chart like the one shown, naming the selection that influenced your thinking.*

What I Thought	What I Think Now
My parents were too strict about homework.	They have my best interests at heart. ("The Treasure of Lemon Brown")

REVIEWING LITERARY CONCEPTS

OPTION 1 **Looking at Characterization** Which characters in Unit One do you think you came to know best? What methods of characterization did the writers use to make those characters so memorable? Create a chart like the one shown. For each character you chose, fill in details from the story that show how the writer developed the character.

Character	Physical Description	Own Speech, Thoughts, and Actions	Others' Speech, Thoughts, and Actions	Direct Comments About Character
Dr. Remenzel ("The Lie")	a large man	". . . you are not to ask for anything special for Eli—not anything."	Mrs. Remenzel: "Why do you always think I'm going to embarrass you?"	dignified, wealthy

OPTION 2 **Thinking About Climax** As you know, the climax of a plot is the moment when the reader's interest is at its highest point. Look back over the short stories you have read, and summarize the climax of each in a single sentence. Discuss your summaries with a classmate. See if you agree on exactly where each climax occurs. If you don't, try to persuade your partner to adopt your views.

"The Inn of Lost Time"

Climax: Zenta realizes that the innkeeper is trying to trick them.

Self-Assessment: *On a sheet of paper, copy this list of other literary terms that were introduced in this unit. Next to each term, indicate whether you feel you understand it well, somewhat, or not at all. Review the terms you are not sure about by looking them up in* The Handbook of Reading Terms and Literary Concepts *(page 812).*

irony	*frame story*	*form*
anecdote	*setting*	*simile*
humor	*third-person*	*personification*
style	*point of view*	*rhyme*
	speaker	*rhythm*

PORTFOLIO BUILDING

- **QuickWrites** Several of the QuickWrites in this unit asked you to write continuations of stories, new endings for stories, and narratives involving characters from stories. Choose the piece of writing in which you think you most successfully portrayed characters, wrote in an appropriate style, and reflected the theme of the unit. In a cover note, explain why you think you were successful. Add the piece and the cover note to your portfolio.

- **Writing About Literature** In this unit, you responded to a story by changing one of its elements. Look back at the scene you rewrote. Think about your changes and the way they affected the story. Before you add the scene to your portfolio, write a letter to the story's author, briefly describing what changes you made and why you made them. Tell whether you think you were successful, giving reasons for your opinion. Ask the author to read and respond to your scene.

- **Writing from Experience** Reread the family history that you prepared, and begin to list some of its highlights on a sheet of paper. Who was the most interesting person you wrote about? What do you think was the most interesting period in your family's history? What was the most interesting thing that you discovered about your family?

Add any other highlights that you wish to include, then attach your list to your family history.

- **Personal Choice** Look back through your records and evaluations of the activities you completed in this unit. Also look at any activities and writing you have done on your own. Are there any activities you would do differently in the light of what you have learned since doing them? Write a brief paragraph outlining the changes you would make, attach it to the evaluation or writing, and add both to your portfolio.

Self-Assessment: *At this point, you are just beginning your portfolio. Do you think the pieces of writing that you have included are the ones you'll keep, or do you think you will be replacing them as the year goes on?*

SETTING GOALS

As you completed the reading and writing activities in this section, you probably identified certain skills on which you need work. Look back through your writing folder, worksheets, and notebook. Create a list of skills or concepts you'd like to work on in the next unit.

Critical
Adjustments

There are two ways

of meeting difficulties.

You alter the difficulties

or you alter yourself to

meet them.

Phyllis Bottome
British novelist and short story writer

Zwei Köpfe [Two heads] (1932), Paul Klee. Encaustic on canvas, 31 ⅞″ × 33 ⅞″, Norton Simon Museum, Pasadena, California, The Blue Four Galka Scheyer Collection, 1953.

TWINGES OF CONSCIENCE

WHAT DO Y?u THINK?

REFLECTING ON THEME

What causes people to change their behavior? The following activities will help you to think about the critical adjustments that people make in their lives. Keep a record of your impressions and ideas. As you read this part of Unit Two, you can compare them with the characters' shifts in behavior.

What can you do?

Mother Earth's health weighs on many consciences. Name three things you could do to help save the environment. Then gather into a booklet all of the class's ideas. Create illustrations and a cover design for your notebook.

How do you view your changing relationships?

Think about your relationships with your parents or grandparents. How have these relationships changed since you were younger? Pinpoint two or three critical changes you can identify. For example, perhaps you've only recently begun to enjoy thoughtful conversations with your grandfather. Make a series of drawings to convey the changes. In other drawings, predict what the relationships might be like ten years from now.

How would you react?

Sudden wealth requires a number of adjustments—and not all of them are happy ones. Imagine you've just won a million dollars! Your new-found wealth is, however, making you miserable. Stage a mock talk show in which the host interviews you about the negative side of becoming a millionaire.

What would you say now?

Have you ever felt guilty about something you did or said to someone, wishing you could make up for it? Think of a particularly memorable example. Then write the letter of apology that you never sent but wish you had.

FICTION

The Horned Toad
Gerald Haslam

PERSONAL CONNECTION

This story is about an extended family—a boy, his parents, and relatives from several generations. Talk about some of the people in your extended family. What are their ethnic backgrounds? Are any of them recent immigrants? In a word map like the one shown here, jot down what you know about these relatives.

Aunt B, Irish

Extended Family

CULTURAL CONNECTION

Gerald Haslam's great-great-grandparents immigrated to California from Mexico in the 1850s, just after California became the 31st state of the United States. A great many Hispanics immigrated to the United States at that time. They brought with them a heritage that emphasizes the importance of the extended family and the community in daily life.

Despite the changes that modern living and marriage to members of other ethnic groups have brought, many Hispanic families still manage to maintain intense feelings of loyalty and cooperation among their members.

Mexican family crossing the international bridge at the border between Brownsville, Texas, and Mexico. UPI/Bettmann.

READING CONNECTION

Connecting One way to become a better reader is by consciously connecting your personal experiences with what you read. Reading is much more enjoyable when you make associations between what you are reading and what you already know.

Try connecting to a key aspect of "The Horned Toad" by considering how your life might change if an older relative came to stay with you. What would be good and bad about such a situation? Share your thoughts with the class. Then, as you read this story, look for other connections you have with the characters. You might jot them down in your notebook.

LASERLINKS
• *GEOGRAPHICAL CONNECTION*

THE HORNED TOAD

BY GERALD HASLAM

"Expectoran su sangre!"[1] exclaimed Great-grandma when I showed her the small horned toad I had removed from my breast pocket. I turned toward my mother, who translated: "They spit blood."

"De los ojos,"[2] Grandma added. "From their eyes," mother explained, herself uncomfortable in the presence of the small beast.

I grinned, "Awwwwww."

But my great-grandmother did not smile. *"Son muy toxicos,"*[3] she nodded with finality. Mother moved back an involuntary step, her hands suddenly busy at her breast. "Put that thing down," she ordered.

"His name's John," I said.

"Put John down and not in your pocket, either," my mother nearly shouted. "Those things are very poisonous. Didn't you understand what Grandma said?"

I shook my head.

"Well . . ." mother looked from one of us to the other—spanning four generations of California, standing three feet apart—and said, "of course you didn't. Please take him back where you got him, and be careful. We'll all feel better when you do." The tone of her voice told me that the discussion had ended, so I released the little reptile where I'd captured him.

During those years in Oildale, the mid-1940s, I needed only to walk across the street to find a patch of virgin desert. Neighborhood kids called it simply "the vacant lot," less than an acre without houses or sidewalks. Not that we were desperate for desert then, since we could walk into its scorched skin a mere half-mile west, north, and east. To the south, <u>incongruously</u>, flowed the icy Kern River, fresh from the Sierras and surrounded by riparian forest.[4]

Ours was rich soil formed by that same Kern River as it ground Sierra granite and turned it into coarse sand, then carried it down into the valley and deposited it over <u>millennia</u> along its many changes of channels. The ants that built miniature volcanoes on the vacant lot left piles of tiny stones with telltale markings of black on white. Deeper than ants could dig were pools of petroleum that led to many fortunes and lured men like my father from Texas. The dry hills to the east and north sprouted forests of wooden derricks.

Despite the abundance of open land, plus the constant lure of the river where desolation and <u>verdancy</u> met, most kids relied on the vacant lot as their primary playground. Even with its bullheads and stinging insects, we played everything from football to kick-the-can on it. The lot actually resembled my father's head, bare in the middle but full of growth around the edges: weeds, stickers, cactuses, and a few bushes. We played our games on its sandy center, and conducted such sports as ant fights and lizard hunts on its brushy <u>periphery</u>.

That spring, when I discovered the lone horned toad near the back of the lot, had been rough on my family. Earlier, there had been quiet, unpleasant tension between Mom and Daddy. He was a silent man, little given to emotional displays. It was difficult for him to

---

1. *Expectoran su sangre* (ĕs-pĕk-tô′rän sōō säng′grĕ) *Spanish.*

2. *de los ojos* (dĕ lôs ô′hôs) *Spanish.*

3. *Son muy toxicos* (sôn mwē tôk′sē-kôs) *Spanish:* They are very poisonous.

4. **riparian** (rĭ-pâr′ē-ən) **forest:** a forest along the banks of a river.

WORDS TO KNOW	**incongruously** (ĭn-kŏng′grōō-əs-lē) *adv.* in a way that is not appropriate or fitting
	millennium (mə-lĕn′ē-əm) *n.* a period of 1000 years; *plural—* **millennia** (mə-lĕn′ē-ə)
	verdancy (vûr′dn-sē) *n.* the greenness of vegetation
	periphery (pə-rĭf′ə-rē) *n.* a region on an outer boundary; outskirts

show affection and I guess the openness of Mom's family made him uneasy. Daddy had no kin[5] in California and rarely mentioned any in Texas. He couldn't understand my mother's large, intimate family, their constant noisy concern for one another, and I think he was a little jealous of the time she gave everyone, maybe even me.

I heard her talking on the phone to my various aunts and uncles, usually in Spanish. Even though I couldn't understand—Daddy had warned her not to teach me that foreign tongue because it would hurt me in school—I could sense the stress. I had been afraid they were going to divorce, since she only used Spanish to hide things from me. I'd confronted her with my suspicion, but she comforted me, saying, no, that was not the problem. They were merely deciding when it would be our turn to care for Grandma. I didn't really understand, although I was relieved.

I later learned that my great-grandmother—whom we simply called "Grandma"—had been moving from house to house within the family, trying to find a place she'd accept. She hated the city, and most of my aunts and uncles lived in Los Angeles. Our house in Oildale was much closer to the open country where she'd dwelled all her life. She had wanted to come to our place right away because she had raised my mother from a baby when my own grandmother died. But the old lady seemed unimpressed with Daddy, whom she called "ese gringo."[6]

In truth, we had more room, and my dad made good money in the oil patch. Since my mother was the closest to Grandma, our place was the logical one for her, but Ese Gringo didn't see it that way, I guess, at least not at first. Finally, after much debate, he relented.

In any case, one windy afternoon, my Uncle Manuel and Aunt Toni drove up and deposited four-and-a-half feet of bewigged, bejeweled Spanish spitfire: a square, pale face topped by a tightly curled black wig that hid a bald head—her hair having been lost to typhoid[7] nearly sixty years before—her small white hands veined with rivers of blue. She walked with a prancing bounce that made her appear half her age, and she barked orders in Spanish from the moment she emerged from Manuel and Toni's car. Later, just before they left, I heard Uncle Manuel tell my father, "Good luck, Charlie. That old lady's dynamite."

Daddy only grunted.

She had been with us only two days when I tried to impress her with my horned toad. In fact, nothing I did seemed to impress her, and she referred to me as *el malcriado*,[8] causing my mother to shake her head. Mom explained to me that Grandma was just old and lonely for Grandpa and uncomfortable in town. Mom told me that Grandma had lived over half a century in the country, away from the noise, away from clutter, away from people. She would not accompany my mother on shopping trips, or anywhere else. She even refused to climb into a

> four-and-a-half feet of bewigged, bejeweled Spanish spitfire

---

5. **kin:** relatives; family.

6. *ese gringo* (ě′sě grēng′gô) *Spanish:* that Yankee; that American.

7. **typhoid:** typhoid fever—a very serious disease that is transmitted by contaminated food or water.

8. *el malcriado* (ěl mäl-kryä′dô) *Spanish:* the rude fellow.

Nito Herrera in Springtime (1960), Peter Hurd. Denver Art Museum (1961.24).

car, and I wondered how Uncle Manuel had managed to load her up in order to bring her to us.

She disliked sidewalks and roads, dancing across them when she had to, then appearing to wipe her feet on earth or grass. Things too civilized simply did not please her. A brother of hers had been killed in the great San Francisco earthquake and that had been the end of her tolerance of cities. Until my great-grandfather died, they lived on a small rancho near Arroyo Cantua, north of Coalinga. Grandpa, who had come north from Sonora as a youth to work as a *vaquero*,[9] had bred horses and cattle, and cowboyed for other

ranchers, scraping together enough of a living to raise eleven children.

He had been, until the time of his death, a dark-skinned man with wide shoulders, a large nose, and a sweeping handlebar mustache that was white when I knew him. His Indian blood darkened all his progeny[10] so that not even I was as fair-skinned as my great-grandmother, Ese Gringo for a father or not.

As it turned out, I didn't really understand very much about Grandma at all. She was old, of course, yet in many ways my parents treated

---

9. *vaquero* (vä-kě′rô) *Spanish:* cowboy.
10. **progeny:** children and other descendants.

her as though she were younger than me, walking her to the bathroom at night and bringing her presents from the store. In other ways—drinking wine at dinner, for example—she was granted adult privileges. Even Daddy didn't drink wine except on special occasions. After Grandma moved in, though, he began to occasionally join her for a glass, sometimes even sitting with her on the porch for a premeal sip.

She held court[11] on our front porch, often gazing toward the desert hills east of us or across the street at kids playing on the lot. Occasionally, she would rise, cross the yard and sidewalk and street, skip over them, sometimes stumbling on the curb, and wipe her feet on the lot's sandy soil, then she would slowly circle the boundary between the open middle and the brushy sides, searching for something, it appeared. I never figured out what.

One afternoon I returned from school and saw Grandma perched on the porch as usual, so I started to walk around the house to avoid her sharp, mostly incomprehensible tongue. She had already spotted me. *"Venga aqui!"*[12] she ordered, and I understood.

I approached the porch and noticed that Grandma was vigorously chewing something. She held a small paper bag in one hand. Saying *"Qué deseas tomar?"*[13] she withdrew a large orange gumdrop from the bag and began slowly chewing it in her toothless mouth, smacking loudly as she did so. I stood below her for a moment trying to remember the word for candy. Then it came to me: *"Dulce,"* I said.

Still chewing, Grandma replied, *"Mande?"*[14]

Knowing she wanted a complete sentence, I again struggled, then came up with *"Deseo dulce."*[15]

She measured me for a moment, before answering in nearly perfect English, "Oh, so you wan' some candy. Go to the store an' buy some."

I don't know if it was the shock of hearing her speak English for the first time, or the way she had denied me a piece of candy, but I suddenly felt tears warm my cheeks and I sprinted into the house and found Mom, who stood at the kitchen sink. "Grandma just talked English," I burst between light sobs.

"What's wrong?" she asked as she reached out to stroke my head.

"Grandma can talk English," I repeated.

"Of course she can," Mom answered. "What's wrong?"

I wasn't sure what was wrong, but after considering, I told Mom that Grandma had teased me. No sooner had I said that than the old woman appeared at the door and hiked her skirt. Attached to one of her petticoats by safety pins were several small tobacco sacks, the white cloth kind that closed with yellow drawstrings. She carefully unhooked one and opened it, withdrawing a dollar, then handed the money to me. *"Para su dulce,"*[16] she said. Then, to my mother, she asked, "Why does he bawl like a motherless calf?"

"It's nothing," Mother replied.

"Do not weep, little one," the old lady comforted me, "Jesus and the Virgin love you." She smiled and patted my head. To my mother she said as though just realizing it, "Your baby?"

Somehow that day changed everything. I wasn't afraid of my great-grandmother any longer and, once I began spending time with

---

11. **held court:** sat as the center of attention, like a ruler on a throne.

12. *Venga aqui!* (vĕng′gä ä-kē′) *Spanish:* Come here!

13. *Qué deseas tomar?* (kĕ dĕ-sĕ′äs tô-mär′) *Spanish:* What would you like to have?

14. *Mande?* (män′dĕ) *Spanish:* What did you say?

15. *Deseo dulce* (dĕ-sĕ′ô dōōl′sĕ) *Spanish:* I want candy.

16. *para su dulce* (pä′rä sōō dōōl′sĕ) *Spanish:* for your candy.

her on the porch, I realized that my father had also begun directing increased attention to the old woman. Almost every evening Ese Gringo was sharing wine with Grandma. They talked out there, but I never did hear a real two-way conversation between them. Usually Grandma rattled on and Daddy nodded. She'd chuckle and pat his hand and he might grin, even grunt a word or two, before she'd begin talking again. Once I saw my mother standing by the front window watching them together, a smile playing across her face.

No more did I sneak around the house to avoid Grandma after school. Instead, she waited for me and discussed my efforts in class gravely, telling mother that I was *muy inteligente*,"[17] and that I should be sent to the nuns who would train me. I would make a fine priest. When Ese Gringo heard that, he smiled and said, "He'd make a fair-to-middlin' Holy Roller preacher,[18] too." Even Mom had to chuckle, and my great-grandmother shook her finger at Ese Gringo. "Oh you debil, Sharlie!" she cackled.

Frequently, I would accompany Grandma to the lot where she would explain that no fodder[19] could grow there. Poor pasture or not, the lot was at least unpaved, and Grandma greeted even the tiniest new cactus or flowering weed with joy. "Look how beautiful," she would croon. "In all this ugliness, it lives." Oildale was my home and it didn't look especially ugly to me, so I could only grin and wonder.

Because she liked the lot and things that grew there, I showed her the horned toad when I captured it a second time. I was determined to keep it, although I did not discuss my plans with anyone. I also wanted

"Give him his freedom, my son."

to hear more about the bloody eyes, so I thrust the small animal nearly into her face one afternoon. She did not flinch. "*Ola señor sangre de ojos,*"[20] she said with a mischievous grin. "*Qué tal?*"[21] It took me a moment to catch on.

"You were kidding before," I accused.

"Of course," she acknowledged, still grinning.

"But why?"

"Because the little beast belongs with his own kind in his own place, not in your pocket. Give him his freedom, my son."

I had other plans for the horned toad, but I was clever enough not to cross Grandma. "Yes, Ma'am," I replied. That night I placed the reptile in a flower bed cornered by a brick wall Ese Gringo had built the previous summer. It was a spot rich with insects for the toad to eat, and the little wall, only a foot high, must have seemed massive to so squat an animal.

Nonetheless, the next morning when I searched for the horned toad it was gone. I had no time to explore the yard for it, so I trudged off to school, my belly troubled. How could it have escaped? Classes meant little to me that day. I thought only of my lost pet—I had changed his name to Juan, the same as my great-grandfather—and where I might find him.

I shortened my conversation with Grandma

17. *muy inteligente* (mwē ēn-tĕ-lē-hĕn'tĕ) *Spanish:* very intelligent.

18. **Holy Roller preacher:** a preacher who leads services that include shouting, singing, and movement.

19. **fodder:** plants grown as food for livestock.

20. *Ola señor sangre de ojos* (ô'lä sĕ-nyôr' säng'grĕ dĕ ô'hôs) *Spanish:* Hi, Mr. Bloody Eyes.

21. *Qué tal?* (kĕ täl) *Spanish:* How are you?

that afternoon so I could search for Juan. "What do you seek?" the old woman asked me as I poked through flower beds beneath the porch. "Praying mantises,"[22] I improvised, and she merely nodded, surveying me. But I had eyes only for my lost pet, and I continued pushing through branches and brushing aside leaves. No luck.

Finally, I gave in and turned toward the lot. I found my horned toad nearly across the street, crushed. It had been heading for the miniature desert and had almost made it when an automobile's tire had run over it. One notion immediately swept me: If I had left it on its lot, it would still be alive. I stood rooted there in the street, tears slicking my cheeks, and a car honked its horn as it passed, the driver shouting at me.

Grandma joined me, and stroked my back. "The poor little beast," was all she said, then she bent slowly and scooped up what remained of the horned toad and led me out of the street. "We must return him to his own place," she explained, and we trooped, my eyes still clouded, toward the back of the vacant lot. Carefully, I dug a hole with a piece of wood. Grandma placed Juan in it and covered him. We said an Our Father and a Hail Mary,[23] then Grandma walked me back to the house. "Your little Juan is safe with God, my

A Medio Día/Pedacito de mi Corazón [At high noon/A little piece of my heart] (1986), Carmen Lomas Garza. Gouache on cotton rag paper, 28″ × 20″. Copyright © 1986 Carmen Lomas Garza. Photo by Wolfgang Dietze.

son," she comforted. We kept the horned toad's death a secret, and we visited his small grave frequently.

Grandma fell just before school ended and summer vacation began. As was her habit, she had walked alone to the vacant lot but this time, on her way back, she tripped over the curb and broke her hip. That following week, when Daddy brought her home from the hospital, she seemed to have shrunken. She sat hunched in a wheelchair on the porch, gazing with faded eyes toward the hills or at the lot, speaking rarely. She still sipped wine every evening with Daddy and even I could tell how concerned he was about her. It got to where he'd look in on her before leaving for work every morning and again at night before turning in. And if Daddy was home, Grandma always wanted him to push her chair when she needed moving, calling, "Sharlie!" until he arrived.

---

22. **praying mantises:** long, slender insects that feed on other insects and, when at rest, hold their front legs as if praying.

23. **an Our Father and a Hail Mary:** the Lord's Prayer and a prayer to the Virgin Mary.

I was tugged from sleep on the night she died by voices drumming through the walls into darkness. I couldn't understand them but was immediately frightened by the uncommon sounds of words in the night. I struggled from bed and walked into the living room just as Daddy closed the front door and a car pulled away.

Mom was sobbing softly on the couch and Daddy walked to her, stroked her head, then noticed me. "Come here, son," he gently ordered.

I walked to him and, uncharacteristically, he put an arm around me.

"What's wrong?" I asked, near tears myself. Mom looked up, but before she could speak, Daddy said, "Grandma died." Then he sighed heavily and stood there with his arms around his weeping wife and son.

The next day my Uncle Manuel and Uncle Arnulfo, plus Aunt Chinta, arrived and over food they discussed with my mother where Grandma should be interred. They argued that it would be too expensive to transport her body home and, besides, they could more easily visit her grave if she was buried in Bakersfield. "They have such a nice, manicured grounds at Green-lawn," Aunt Chinta pointed out. Just when it seemed they had agreed, I could remain silent no longer: "But Grandma has to go home," I burst. "She has to! It's the only thing she really wanted. We can't leave her in the city."

Uncle Arnulfo, who was on the edge, snapped to Mother that I belonged with the other children, not interrupting adult conversation. Mom quietly agreed, but I refused. My father walked into the room then. "What's wrong?" he asked.

"They're going to bury Grandma in Bakersfield, Daddy. Don't let 'em, please."

"Well, son . . ."

"When my horny toad got killed and she helped me to bury it, she said we had to return him to his place."

"Your horny toad?" Mother asked.

"He got squished and me and Grandma buried him in the lot. She said we had to take him back to his place. Honest she did."

No one spoke for a moment, then my father, Ese Gringo, who stood against the sink, responded: "That's right . . ." he paused, then added, "We'll bury her." I saw a weary smile cross my mother's face. "If she wanted to go back to the ranch then that's where we have to take her," Daddy said.

I hugged him and he, right in front of every-one, hugged back.

No one argued. It seemed, suddenly, as though they had all wanted to do exactly what I had begged for. Grownups baffled me. Late that week the entire family, hundreds it seemed, gathered at the little Catholic church in Coalinga for Mass, then drove out to Arroyo Cantua and buried Grandma next to Grandpa. She rests there today.

My mother, father, and I drove back to Oildale that afternoon across the scorching westside desert, through sand and tumble-weeds and heat shivers. Quiet and sad, we knew we had done our best. Mom, who usually sat next to the door in the front seat, snuggled close to Daddy, and I heard her whisper to him, "Thank you, Charlie," as she kissed his cheek.

Daddy squeezed her, hesitated as if to clear his throat, then answered, "When you're family, you take care of your own." ❖

IN A NEIGHBORHOOD IN LOS ANGELES

BY FRANCISCO X. ALARCÓN

I learned
Spanish
from my grandma

mijito[1]
don't cry
she'd tell me

on the mornings
my parents
would leave

to work
at the fish
canneries

my grandma
would chat
with chairs

sing them
old
songs

dance
waltzes with them
in the kitchen

when she'd say
niño barrigón[2]
she'd laugh

with my grandma
I learned
to count clouds

to point out
in flowerpots
mint leaves

my grandma
wore moons
on her dress

Mexico's mountains
deserts
ocean

in her eyes
I'd see them
in her braids

I'd touch them
in her voice
smell them

one day
I was told:
she went far away

but still
I feel her
with me

whispering
in my ear
mijito

---

1. *mijito* (mē-hē′tô): a contraction of Spanish *mi hijito*, "my little child."

2. *niño barrigón* (nē′nyô bä-rē-gôn′) *Spanish*: big-bellied baby.

RESPONDING
O P T I O N S

FROM PERSONAL RESPONSE TO CRITICAL ANALYSIS

REFLECT 1. What is your impression of the grandmother in this story? Write your reactions in your notebook.

RETHINK 2. Why is the horned toad important?
Consider
- the boy's treatment of the animal, and its escape
- the grandmother's feelings about her new home, and the circumstances surrounding her death
- the significance of the vacant lot to the boy, the grandmother, and the horned toad

3. How does the boy's relationship with his grandmother change?

4. How do the father and the grandmother adjust to each other?

RELATE 5. Consider the Insight poem on page 158 and "The Horned Toad" together. What do you think older relatives bring to a family? Share your ideas with the class.

ANOTHER PATHWAY

Cooperative Learning

Grandma's personality has many facets. In small groups, find and list her personality traits, supported with examples from the story. Then find a picture that captures her personality.

LITERARY CONCEPTS

A story told from the **first-person point of view** is told by a narrator who is one of the characters. In "The Horned Toad," the first-person narrator is the boy. He tells everything that happens in his own words, using such pronouns as *I* and *we*. How might his mother's account of what happens differ from his own account?

QUICKWRITES

1. An epitaph is a brief statement inscribed on a tombstone to honor the memory of the person buried there. Write an **epitaph** for the grandmother in this story. Before writing, think about what was important to her in life.

2. Suppose the grandmother were describing her family to a friend. Write a **letter** that describes her impression of "Ese Gringo" and her grandson after she has lived with them awhile.

📁 *PORTFOLIO Save your writing. You may want to use it later as a springboard to a piece for your portfolio.*

ALTERNATIVE ACTIVITIES

Cooperative Learning As you have learned, the Spanish word for a cowboy is *vaquero*. Use an English-Spanish dictionary to find the Spanish equivalents of some of the key English nouns in this story. Then create a **Spanish match game.** On a sheet of poster board, display a list of the Spanish words, along with magazine pictures of the things they name. Have classmates try to match each word with the appropriate picture.

ACROSS THE CURRICULUM

Science Using the library or a computer data base, find out what you can about horned toads. Present your findings in the form of a poster display or in any other inventive form that comes to mind.

THE WRITER'S STYLE

Haslam sprinkles this story with Spanish words and phrases. Why do you think he uses Spanish in an English-language story? What does his use of Spanish add to the story?

WORDS TO KNOW

Review the Words to Know at the bottom of the selection pages. Then, on your paper, write the vocabulary word that is related to each rhyming phrase below.

1. put to rest in her best
2. a lizard caught in a blizzard
3. all around the lot's vacant ground
4. a scene lush and green
5. hundreds of years make the climb with this measure of time

GERALD HASLAM

Gerald Haslam (1937–) was born and raised in California's San Joaquin Valley. He describes it as a richly varied environment, where "oral tale-telling was a fine art." About his mixed Anglo-Hispanic heritage, Haslam has written, "I am more openly and proudly Hispanic than my pale skin and fair hair might suggest (I am three-quarters Anglo and equally pleased with that). At home, however, Spanish was our secret language, Catholicism our church, *la familia* our real religion. I tell my children (who add Cree, French, Polish, and German to the mix) that we are what America is becoming."

Before beginning his writing and teaching career, Haslam was a jack-of-all-trades. He worked as a roustabout (a person who performs odd jobs in oil fields); he picked, plowed, irrigated, and packed crops in the San Joaquin Valley; he worked in banks and stores. Haslam graduated from San Francisco State College in 1963.

Haslam has published six collections of stories, including his most recent, the award-winning *That Constant Coyote*. He has also written essays, other nonfiction, and a novel and has compiled anthologies. He has said, "It is a continuing source of both wonder and satisfaction to me that I have evolved into a storyteller."

OTHER WORKS *Okies: Selected Stories, The Man Who Cultivated Fire, Voices of a Place*

LASERLINKS
• *AUTHOR BACKGROUND*

FICTION

The Splendid Outcast

Beryl Markham

PERSONAL CONNECTION

The narrator of this story travels from Africa to England to purchase a special racehorse for breeding purposes. Have you ever wanted something so much that you went to extraordinary lengths to get it? What did you do to get what you wanted? Did you succeed? Write about the experience in your notebook.

CULTURAL CONNECTION

Raising racehorses is big business in many countries. Stallions (male horses) and mares (female horses) are carefully selected for mating in the hope of producing champion racers. Breeders take into account the horses' racing records, ancestry, and physical traits. A champion racing stallion can earn millions of dollars in stud fees—money paid to the stallion's owner when it sires foals.

In England, the setting of this story, records of horses' ancestry have been kept since the early 17th century. Rigel, the Thoroughbred stallion that the narrator is so keen to purchase, is a known winner with an outstanding ancestry. His sire (father) was unbeaten, and his dam (mother) was a superior steeplechaser, or runner of obstacle races.

READING CONNECTION

Challenging Vocabulary Remember that you do not need to understand every word to enjoy the story. The footnotes and the definitions of the Words to Know will help you with the meanings of the difficult words and phrases that are most important for your understanding.

To help you keep track of the plot, questions have been inserted at various points in the story for you to answer in your reading log. After you finish the story, you can go back and enrich your vocabulary by using organizers like the one shown here to analyze unfamiliar words.

Apprehensive

anxious or fearful
Dictionary Definition

uneasy
Synonyms

nervousness before a dentist appointment
Examples the Word Brings to Mind

Whistlejacket (1762), George Stubbs. Kenwood House, Hampstead, London/Bridgeman Art Library, London/Superstock.

THE SPLENDID OUTCAST

by

BERYL MARKHAM

The stallion was named after a star, and when he fell from his particular heaven, it was easy enough for people to say that he had been named too well. People like to see stars fall, but in the case of Rigel, it was of greater importance to me. To me and to one other—to a little man with shabby cuffs and a wilted cap that rested over eyes made mild by something other than time.

It was at Newmarket, in England, where, since Charles I instituted the first cup race, a kind of court has been held for the royalty of the turf.[1] Men of all classes come to New-market for the races and for the December sales.[2] They come from everywhere—some to bet, some to buy or sell, and some merely to offer <u>homage</u> to the resplendent peers of the Stud Book,[3] for the sport of kings[4] may, after all, be the pleasure of every man.

December can be bitterly cold in England, and this December was. There was frozen sleet on buildings and on trees, and I remember that the huge Newmarket track lay on the downs below the village like a noose of diamonds on

a tarnished mat. There was a festive spirit everywhere, but it was somehow lost on me. I had come to buy new blood for my stable in Kenya, and since my stable was my living, I came as serious buyers do, with figures in my mind and caution in my heart. Horses are hard to judge at best, and the thought of putting your hoarded pounds[5] behind that judgment makes it harder still.

I sat close on the edge of the auction ring and held my breath from time to time as the bidding soared. I held it because the casual mention of ten thousand guineas in payment for a horse or for anything else seemed to me

---

1. **turf:** the grass track on which horses race.
2. **December sales:** end-of-year auctions of horses.
3. **resplendent peers of the Stud Book:** outstanding racehorses whose family trees are carefully preserved like those of the nobility.
4. **sport of kings:** horseracing, so called because many British monarchs and noblemen have owned racehorses.
5. **pounds:** British units of money. At the time of this story, one pound (£1) was equivalent to $5.00 in U.S. currency; today a pound is worth considerably less than this.

WORDS
TO
KNOW

homage (hŏm′ĭj) *n.* an expression of honor or respect

163

wildly beyond the realm of probable things. For myself, I had five hundred pounds to spend and, as I waited for Rigel to be shown, I remember that I felt uncommonly maternal about each pound. I waited for Rigel because I had come six thousand miles to buy him, nor was I apprehensive lest anyone should take him from me; he was an outcast.

Rigel had a pedigree that looked backward and beyond the pedigrees of many Englishmen—and Rigel had a brilliant record. By all odds, he should have brought ten thousand guineas[6] at the sale, but I knew he wouldn't, for he had killed a man.

He had killed a man—not fallen upon him, nor thrown him in a playful moment from the saddle, but killed him dead with his hooves and with his teeth in a stable. And that was not all, though it was the greatest thing. Rigel had crippled other men and, so the story went, would cripple or kill still more, so long as he lived. He was savage, people said, and while he could not be hanged for his crimes, like a man, he could be shunned as criminals are. He could be offered for sale. And yet, under the implacable rules of racing, he had been warned off the turf for life—so who would buy?

Well, I for one—and I had supposed there would not be two. I would buy if the price were low enough, because I had youth then, and a corresponding contempt for failure. It seemed probable that in time and with luck and with skill, the stallion might be made manageable again, if only for breeding—especially for breeding. He could be gentled, I thought. But I found it hard to believe what I saw that day. I had not known that the mere touch of a hand could, in an instant, extinguish the long-burning anger of an angry heart.

I first noticed the little man when the sale was already well on its way, and he caught my attention at once, because he was incongruous there. He sat a few benches from me and held his lean, interwoven fingers upon his knees. He started down upon the arena as each horse was led into it, and he listened to the dignified encomiums[7] of the auctioneer with the humble attention of a parishioner at mass. He never moved. He was surrounded by men and women, who, by their <u>impeccable</u> clothes and by their somewhat bored familiarity with pounds and guineas, made him conspicuous. He was like a stone of granite in a jeweler's window, motionless and grey against the glitter.

You could see in his face that he loved horses—just as you could see, in some of the faces of those around him, that they loved the idea of horses. They were the cultists, he the votary,[8] and there were, in fact, about his grey eyes and his slender lips, the deep, tense lines so often etched in the faces of <u>zealots</u> and of lonely men. It was the cast of his shoulders, I think, the devotion of his manner that told me he had once been a jockey.

A yearling came into the ring and was bought, and then another, while the pages of catalogues were quietly turned. The auctioneer's voice, clear but scarcely lifted, intoned the virtues of his magnificent merchandise as other voices, responding to this magic, spoke

---

6. **ten thousand guineas** (gǐn′ēz): a sum of money equivalent to $52,500 at the time the story was written. A guinea, a British monetary unit no longer in use, was equal to £1.05.

7. **encomiums** (ĕn-kō′mē-əmz): expressions of enthusiastic praise.

8. **cultists . . . votary:** Here, *cultists* refers to people attracted to something because it is fashionable, in contrast to the votary, who is intensely devoted to something for its own sake.

reservedly of figures: "A thousand guineas . . . two thousand . . . three . . . four! . . ."

The scene at the auction comes to me clearly now, as if once again it were happening before my eyes.

"Five, perhaps?" The auctioneer scans the audience expectantly as a groom[9] parades a dancing colt around the arena. There is a moment of near silence, a burly voice calls, "Five!" and the colt is sold while a murmur of polite approval swells and dies.

And so they go, one after another, until the list is small; the audience thins, and my finger traces the name, Rigel, on the last page of the catalogue. I straighten on my bench and hold my breath a little, forgetting the crowd, the little man, and a part of myself. I know this horse. I know he is by Hurry On out of Bounty[10]—the sire unbeaten, the dam a great steeplechaser—and there is no better blood than that. Killer or not, Rigel has won races and won them clean. If God and Barclays Bank stay with me, he will return to Africa when I do.

And there, at last, he stands. In the broad entrance to the ring, two powerful men appear with the stallion between them. The men are not grooms of ordinary size; they have been picked for strength, and in the clenched fist of each is the end of a chain. Between the chain and the bit there is on the near side a short rod of steel, close to the stallion's mouth—a rod of steel, easy to grasp, easy to use. Clenched around the great girth of the horse, and fitted with metal rings, there is a strap of thick leather that brings to mind the restraining harness of a madman.

Together, the two men edge the stallion forward. Tall as they are, they move like midgets beside his massive shoulders. He is the biggest thoroughbred I have ever seen. He is the most beautiful. His coat is chestnut, flecked with white, and his mane and tail are close to gold. There is a blaze on his face—wide and straight and forthright, as if by this marking he proclaims that he is none other than Rigel, for all his sins, for all the hush that falls over the crowd.

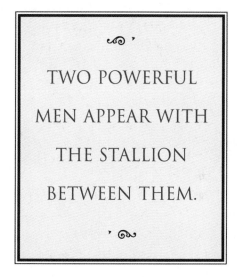

TWO POWERFUL MEN APPEAR WITH THE STALLION BETWEEN THEM.

He is Rigel, and he looks upon the men who hold his chains as a captured king may look upon his captors. He is not tamed. Nothing about him promises that he will be tamed. Stiffly, on reluctant hooves, he enters the ring and flares his crimson nostrils at the crowd, and the crowd is still. The crowd whose pleasure is the docile beast of pretty paddocks,[11] the gainly horse of cherished prints that hang upon the finest walls, the willing winner of the race—upon the rebel this crowd stares, and the rebel stares back.

His eyes are lit with anger or with hate. His head is held <u>disdainfully</u> and high, his neck an

---

9. **groom:** a man or boy whose job it is to care for horses.

10. **he is by Hurry On out of Bounty:** Hurry On was his father, and Bounty was his mother.

11. **paddocks:** fenced-in areas where horses are saddled before they race.

WORDS TO KNOW	**disdainfully** (dĭs-dān′fə-lē) *adv.* in a manner showing contempt or aloofness; scornfully

Detail of *Portrait of Mrs. Whelan* (about 1911), Harold Gilman. Courtesy of the Fine Art Society, London.

crimes. Who will buy the outcast? The auctioneer shakes his head as if to say that this is a trick beyond his magic. But he will try. He is an <u>imposing</u> man, an experienced man, and now he clears his throat and confronts the crowd, a kind of pleading in his face.

"This splendid animal—" he begins—and does not finish. He cannot finish.

Rigel has scanned the silent audience and smelled the unmoving air, and he—a creature of the wind—knows the indignity of this skyless temple. He seems aware at last of the chains that hold him, of the men who cling forlornly to the heavy reins. He rears from the tanbark, higher and higher still, until his golden mane is lifted like a flag unfurled and defiant. He beats the air. He trembles in his rising anger, and the crowd leans forward.

CLARIFY

What is Rigel doing?

A groom clings like a monkey to the tightened chain. He is swept from his feet while his partner, a less tenacious man, sprawls ignobly below, and men—a dozen men—rush to the ring, some shouting, some waving their arms. They run and swear in lowered voices; they grasp reins, chains, rings, and swarm upon their towering Gulliver.[12] And he subsides.

With something like contempt for this hysteria, Rigel touches his forehooves to the tanbark once more. He has killed no one, but they are jabbing at his mouth now, they are surrounding him, adding fuel to his fiery reputation, and the auctioneer is a wilted man.

He sighs, and you can almost hear it. He raises both arms and foregoes his speech.

arc of arrogance. He prances now—impatience in the thudding of his hooves upon the tanbark, defiance in his manner—and the chains jerk tight. The long stallion reins are tightly held— apprehensively held—and the men who hold them glance at the auctioneer, an urgent question in their eyes.

The auctioneer raises his arm for silence, but there is silence. No one speaks. The story of Rigel is known—his breeding, his brilliant victories, and finally his insurgence and his

---

12. **Gulliver:** the first-person narrator of Jonathan Swift's satire *Gulliver's Travels*. One of the places Gulliver visits is the island of Lilliput, where he is a giant among the six-inch-tall Lilliputians.

WORDS TO KNOW   **imposing** (ĭm-pō′zĭng) *adj.* impressive in size or strength

"What," he asks with weariness, "am I offered?" And there is a ripple of laughter from the crowd. Smug in its wisdom, it offers nothing.

But I do, and my voice is like an echo in a cave. Still there is triumph in it. I will have what I have come so far to get—I will have Rigel.

> SUDDENLY I AM AWARE THAT I HAVE A COMPETITOR, AND I AM CAUTIOUS.

"A hundred guineas!" I stand as I call my price, and the auctioneer is plainly shocked—not by the meagerness of the offer, but by the offer itself. He stares upward from the ring, incredulity in his eyes.

He lifts a hand and slowly repeats the price. "I am offered," he says, "one hundred guineas."

There is a hush, and I feel the eyes of the crowd and watch the hand of the auctioneer. When it goes down, the stallion will be mine.

But it does not go down. It is still poised in midair, white, expectant, compelling, when the soft voice, the gently challenging voice is lifted. "Two hundred!" the voice says, and I do not have to turn to know that the little jockey has bid against me. But I do turn.

He has not risen from the bench, and he does not look at me. In his hand he holds a sheaf of bank notes. I can tell by their color that they are of small denomination, by their rumpled condition that they have been hoarded long. People near him are staring—horrified, I think—at the vulgar spectacle of cash at a Newmarket auction.

I am not horrified, nor sympathetic. Suddenly I am aware that I have a competitor, and I am cautious. I am here for a purpose that has little to do with sentiment, and I will not be beaten. I think of my stable in Kenya, of the feed bills to come, of the syces[13] to be paid, of the races that are yet to be won if I am to survive in this unpredictable business. No, I cannot now yield an inch. I have little money, but so has he. No more, I think, but perhaps as much.

I hesitate a moment and glance at the little man, and he returns my glance. We are like two gamblers bidding against the other's unseen cards. Our eyes meet for a sharp instant—a cold instant.

I straighten, and my catalogue is crumpled in my hand. I moisten my lips and call, "Three hundred!" I call it firmly, steadily, hoping to undo my opponent at a stroke. It is a wishful thought.

He looks directly at me now but does not smile. He looks at me as a man might look at one who bears false witness against him, then soundlessly he counts his money and bids again, "Three fifty!"

The interest of the crowd is suddenly aroused. All these people are at once conscious of being witnesses, not only before an auction, but before a contest, a rivalry of wills. They shift in their seats and stare as they might stare at a pair of duelists, rapiers in hand.[14]

---

13. **syces** (sī′səz): stablemen or grooms.
14. **duelists, rapiers** (rā′pē-ərz) **in hand:** two people fighting with swords.

But money is the weapon, Rigel the prize. And prize enough, I think, as does my adversary.

I ponder and think hard, then decide to bid a hundred more. Not twenty, not fifty, but a hundred. Perhaps by that I can take him in my stride. He need not know there is little more to follow. He may assume that I am one of the casual ones, impatient of small figures. He may hesitate, he may withdraw. He may be cowed.

Still standing, I utter, as indifferently as I can, the words, "Four fifty!" and the auctioneer, at ease in his element of contention, brightens visibly.

I am aware that the gathered people are now fascinated by this battle of pounds and shillings over a stallion that not one of them would care to own. I only hope that in the heat of it some third person does not begin to bid. But I need not worry; Rigel takes care of that.

The little jockey has listened to my last offer, and I can see that he is already beaten—or almost, at least. He has counted his money a dozen times, but now he counts it again, swiftly, with agile fingers, as if hoping his previous counts had been wrong.

I feel a momentary surge of sympathy, then smother it. Horse training is not my hobby. It is my living. I wait for what I am sure will be his last bid, and it comes. For the first time, he rises from his bench. He is small and alone in spirit, for the glances of the well-dressed people about him lend him nothing. He does not care. His eyes are on the stallion, and I can see that there is a kind of passion in them. I have seen that expression before—in the eyes of sailors appraising a comely ship, in the eyes of pilots sweeping the clean, sweet contours of a plane. There is reverence in it, desire—and even hope.

The little man turns slightly to face the expectant auctioneer, then clears his throat and makes his bid. "Four eighty!" he calls, and the slight note of desperation in his voice is unmistakable, but I force myself to ignore it.

Now, at last, I tell myself, the prize is mine.

The auctioneer receives the bid and looks at me, as do a hundred people. Some of them, no doubt, think I am quite mad or wholly inexperienced, but they watch while the words "Five hundred" form upon my lips. They are never uttered.

Throughout the bidding for Rigel, Rigel has been ignored. He has stood quietly enough after his first brief effort at freedom; he has scarcely moved. But now, at the climax of the sale, his impatience overflows, his spirit flares like fire, his anger bursts through the circle of men who guard him. Suddenly, there are cries, shouts of warning, the ringing of chains and the cracking of leather, and the crowd leaps to its feet. Rigel is loose. Rigel has hurled his captors from him, and he stands alone.

It is a beautiful thing to see, but there is terror in it. A thoroughbred stallion with anger in his eyes is not a sight to entrance anyone but a novice. If you are aware of the power and the speed and the intelligence in that towering symmetrical body, you will hold your breath as you watch it. You will know that the teeth of a horse can crush a bone, that hooves can crush a man. And Rigel's hooves have crushed a man.

He stands alone, his neck curved, his golden tail a battle plume, and he turns, slowly, deliberately, and faces the men he has flung away. They are not without courage, but they

WORDS TO KNOW

adversary (ăd′vər-sĕr′ē) *n.* an opponent
cow (kou) *v.* to frighten by a show of force
novice (nŏv′ĭs) *n.* a person new to an activity; beginner

are without resource. Horses are not tamed by whips or by blows. The strength of ten men is not so strong as a single stroke of a hoof; the experience of ten men is not enough, for this is the unexpected, the unpredictable. No one is prepared. No one is ready.

> ## HE STANDS ALONE, HIS NECK CURVED, HIS GOLDEN TAIL A BATTLE PLUME.

The words "Five hundred" die upon my lips as I watch, as I listen. For the stallion is not voiceless now. His challenging scream is shrill as the cry of winter wind. It is bleak and heartless. His forehooves stir the tanbark. The auction is forgotten.

A man stands before him—a man braver than most. He holds nothing in his hands save an exercise bat; it looks a feeble thing, and is. It is a thin stick bound with leather—enough only to enrage Rigel, for he has seen such things in men's hands before. He knows their meaning. Such a thing as this bat, slight as it is, enrages him because it is a symbol that stands for other things. It stands, perhaps, for the confining walls of a darkened stable, for the bit of steel, foreign, but almost everpresent in his mouth, for the tightened girth, the command to gallop, to walk, to stop, to parade before the swelling crowds of gathered people, to accept the measured food gleaned from forbidden fields. It stands for life no closer to the earth than the sterile smell of satin on a jockey's back or the dead wreath hung upon a winner. It stands for servitude. And Rigel has broken with his overlords.

He lunges quickly, and the man with a bat is not so quick. He lifts the pathetic stick and waves it in desperation. He cries out, and the voice of the crowd drowns his cry. Rigel's neck is outstretched and straight as a saber.[15] There is dust and the shouting of men and the screaming of women, for the stallion's teeth have closed on the shoulder of his forlorn enemy.

The man struggles and drops his bat, and his eyes are sharp with terror, perhaps with pain. Blood leaves the flesh of his face, and it is a face grey and pleading, as must be the faces of those to whom retribution is unexpected and swift. He beats against the golden head while the excitement of the crowd mounts against the fury of Rigel. Then reason vanishes. Clubs, whips, and chains appear like magic in the ring, and a regiment of men advance upon the stallion. They are angry men, brave in their anger, righteous and justified in it. They advance, and the stallion drops the man he has attacked, and the man runs for cover, clutching his shoulder.

I am standing, as is everyone. It is a strange and unreal thing to see this trapped and frustrated creature, magnificent and alone, away from his kind, remote from the things he understands, face the punishment of his minuscule masters. He is, of course, terrified, and the terror is a mounting madness. If he could run, he would leave this place, abandoning his fear and his hatred to do it. But he cannot run. The

---

15. **saber** (sā′bər): a dueling or fencing sword.

walls of the arena are high. The doors are shut, and the trap makes him blind with anger. He will fight, and the blows will fall with heaviness upon his spirit, for his body is a rock before these petty weapons.

The men edge closer, ropes and chains and whips in determined hands. The whips are lifted,

CLARIFY

Why does Rigel fight back?

the chains are ready; the battle line is formed, and Rigel does not retreat. He comes forward, the whites of his eyes exposed and rimmed with carnelian fire, his nostrils crimson.

There is a breathless silence, and the little jockey slips like a ghost into the ring. His eyes are fixed on the embattled stallion. He begins to run across the tanbark and breaks through the circle of advancing men and does not stop. Someone clutches at his coat, but he breaks loose without turning, then slows to an almost casual walk and approaches Rigel alone. The men do not follow him. He waves them back. He goes forward, steadily, easily and happily, without caution, without fear, and Rigel whirls angrily to face him.

Rigel stands close to the wall of the arena. He cannot retreat. He does not propose to. Now he can focus his fury on this insignificant David[16] who has come to meet him, and he does. He lunges at once as only a stallion can—swiftly, invincibly, as if escape and freedom can be found only in the destruction of all that is human, all that smells human, and all that humans have made.

He lunges and the jockey stops. He does not turn or lift a hand or otherwise move. He stops, he stands, and there is silence every-where. No one speaks; no one seems to breathe. Only Rigel is motion. No special

hypnotic power emanates from the jockey's eyes; he has no magic. The stallion's teeth are bared and close, his hooves are a swelling sound when the jockey turns. Like a matador of nerveless skill and studied <u>insolence</u>, the

---

16. **David:** the shepherd boy who, according to the Bible, killed the giant warrior Goliath with only a slingshot.

WORDS
TO
KNOW

insolence (ĭn′sə-ləns) *n.* arrogance; disrespect

does not know—a man who neither
cringes in fear nor threatens with
whips or chains. It is a thing beyond
his memory perhaps—as far beyond
it as the understanding of the mare
that bore him.

Rigel is suddenly motionless, rigid,
suspicious. He waits, and the grey-
eyed jockey turns to face him. The
little man is calm and smiling. We
hear him speak, but cannot understand his words. They are low and
they are lost to us—an incantation.
But the stallion seems to understand
at least the spirit if not the sense of
them. He snorts but does not move.
And now the jockey's hand goes
forward to the golden mane—neither
hurriedly nor with hesitance, but
unconcernedly, as if it had rested
there a thousand times. And there
it stays.

There is a murmur from the crowd,
then silence. People look at one
another and stir in their seats a
strange self-consciousness in their
stirring, for people are uneasy before
the proved worth of their inferiors, unbelieving
of the virtue of simplicity. They watch with open
mouths as the giant
Rigel, the killer Rigel,
with no harness save a
head collar, follows his
Lilliputian master, his
new friend, across the ring.

All has happened in so little time—in
moments. The audience begins to stand, to

jockey turns his back on Rigel and does not
walk away, and the stallion pauses.

Rigel rears high at the back of the little
man, screaming his defiant scream, but he does
not strike. His hooves are close to the jockey's
head but do not touch him. His teeth are
sheathed. He hesitates, trembles, roars wind
from his massive lungs. He shakes his head,
his golden mane, and beats the ground. It is
frustration—but of a new kind. It is a thing he

> **CLARIFY**
>
> How does the jockey
> gain control of Rigel?

leave. But they pause at the lift of the auctioneer's hand. He waves it and they pause. It is all very well, his gestures say, but business is, after all, business, and Rigel has not been sold. He looks up at me, knowing that I have a bid to make—the last bid. And I look down into the ring at the stallion I have come so far to buy. His head is low and close to the shoulder of the man who would take him from me. He is not prancing now, not moving. For this hour, at least, he is changed.

I straighten and then shake my head. I need only say "Five hundred," but the words won't come. I can't get them out. I am angry with myself—a sentimental fool—and I am disappointed. But I cannot bid. It is too easy—twenty pounds too little, and yet too great an advantage.

No. I shake my head again, the auctioneer shrugs and turns to seal his bargain with the jockey.

On the way out, an old friend jostles me. "You didn't really want him then," he says.

"Want him? No. No, I didn't really want him."

"It was wise," he says. "What good is a horse that's warned off every course in the Empire? You wouldn't want a horse like that."

"That's right, I wouldn't want a horse like that."

We move to the exit, and when we are out in the bright cold air of Newmarket, I turn to my friend and mention the little jockey. "But he wanted Rigel," I say.

And my old friend laughs. "He would," he says. "That man has himself been barred from racing for fifteen years. Why, I can't remember. But it's two of a kind, you see—Rigel and Sparrow. Outlaws, both. He loves and knows horses as no man does, but that's what we call him around the tracks—the Fallen Sparrow."

RESPONDING
OPTIONS

FROM PERSONAL RESPONSE *TO* CRITICAL ANALYSIS

REFLECT   **1.** What is your reaction to the narrator's decision at the end? Share your thoughts with a partner.

RETHINK   **2.** After being so intent on purchasing Rigel, why does the narrator give up her chance?

3. Do you think the narrator makes the right decision? Why or why not?
   Consider
   • Rigel's reputation and his behavior at the auction
   • Rigel's reaction to the jockey
   • the narrator's financial situation

4. Compare Rigel, the jockey, and the narrator. What characteristics do they share?

5. How does this story relate to the Unit Two theme, "Critical Adjustments," and the theme of this part of the unit, "Twinges of Conscience"?

RELATE   **6.** Even though Rigel's actions have made him an outcast, the narrator considers him valuable. What kinds of actions make a human being an outcast? What human outcasts do you consider valuable? Explain your answers.

ANOTHER PATHWAY
Cooperative Learning
A dramatic series of events leads up to the climax of this story. With a group of classmates, decide at what point the climax of the story occurs. Then work with the group to create a graph that shows the main events leading up to the climax.

QUICKWRITES

1. Compose a series of **newspaper headlines** that relate events in the lives of Rigel and the jockey before the story begins.

2. Write a **poem** about Rigel. Take into account the subject matter and mood of the story as you decide whether to use rhyme and a regular rhythm.

3. Write a short **paragraph,** including at least two allusions, about a time when you felt like an outcast. You may wish to review the Literary Concepts for this selection before you start.

📁 *PORTFOLIO Save your writing. You may want to use it later as a springboard to a piece for your portfolio.*

LITERARY CONCEPTS

Markham includes **allusions,** or references to famous people, places, and works of literature. Understanding the allusions can help a reader better appreciate the story. For example, when the narrator calls the jockey Lilliputian, she is alluding to a nation of tiny people in the book *Gulliver's Travels.* Find two other allusions to fictional or historical people in the story. What idea does each allusion add?

CONCEPT REVIEW: Setting The setting of a story involves not only the time and place of the action but also the customs, manners, and attitudes of that time and place. In this story, what attitudes and manners are characteristic of the majority of people who come to Newmarket to buy horses?

ALTERNATIVE ACTIVITIES

1. Select a passage from this story and give a **dramatic reading** of it for the class. You may wish to include a brief introduction and conclusion to clarify the context of your passage in the story.

2. Create a **drawing, painting,** or **sculpture** of Rigel in his most defiant moment. Refer to the narrator's vivid descriptions of Rigel's size, appearance, and behavior before you begin.

BERYL MARKHAM

Markham's fictitious Rigel is similar to a real horse she owned and tamed. Messenger Boy, a stallion with an excellent pedigree, had killed a groom and attacked another man before Markham bought the horse and trained him to become one of the best racers in Kenya.

Born in England, Beryl Markham moved to East Africa with her father when she was three years old. There she

1902–1986

learned African languages and customs as she watched her father turn wilderness into a working farm. As a girl, she suffered a leg injury from a lion attack, remembering "an immense roar that encompassed the world and dissolved me in it."

Before turning to the training and breeding of horses, which she learned from her father, Markham became the first woman to obtain a com-

mercial pilot's license in East Africa. Flying a flimsy, fabric-covered plane with no radio, she spotted game for safari parties and carried passengers, mail, and supplies to remote areas. She spent most of her later life training racehorses. Eight of her horses were winners of the prestigious Kenya Derby.

Markham was famous for being the first person to fly solo across the Atlantic Ocean from east to west. Her 1936 flight, which took 21 hours 25 minutes, ended in Canada, where she ran out of fuel and crash-landed. Although her plane was severely damaged, she walked away with only minor injuries.

OTHER WORKS *West with the Night,* "Something I Remember"

LASERLINKS
• *ART GALLERY*

PREVIEWING

We Alone
Alice Walker

Hard Questions
Margaret Tsuda

oil crisis
Naoshi Koriyama

PERSONAL CONNECTION

Imagine that you and your family are moving to a remote cabin to live close to nature. You cannot take much with you, and you will not be able to use anything that runs on electricity. What do you think will be the advantages and the disadvantages of your new life? Jot down your ideas in a web like the one shown.

Advantages — Living Close to Nature — Disadvantages

SCIENCE CONNECTION

You may find it difficult to imagine life without things like televisions, VCRs, and cars. However, there is a high price to pay for such luxuries. Increased industrialization is eliminating more and more of our natural environment, draining the earth's supply of mineral resources, and polluting our air and water.

The debate rages between those who want to use the earth's resources to provide jobs, thus improving or maintaining people's standard of living, and those who say we have to cut back our use of natural resources no matter what the effect on our lifestyles.

Settlers clearing rainforest in northern Guatemala. Copyright © David Hiser / Tony Stone Images.

WRITING CONNECTION

The writers of the three poems you are about to read feel that we should value and take care of our natural environment. What do you think is the greatest environmental problem facing our world today? Write your thoughts in a few sentences. Then read to discover the environmental problems the poets point out.

We Alone

by Alice Walker

We alone can devalue gold
by not caring
if it falls or rises
in the marketplace.
5   Wherever there is gold
there is a chain, you know,
and if your chain
is gold
so much the worse
10 for you.

Feathers, shells
and sea-shaped stones
are all as rare.

This could be our revolution:
15 To love what is plentiful
as much as
what is scarce.

Copyright © Roxana Villa/SIS.

FROM PERSONAL RESPONSE TO CRITICAL ANALYSIS

REFLECT   1. What were your thoughts as you read this poem? Record them in your notebook.

RETHINK   2. What problems does the speaker associate with gold?
   Consider
   • how the price of gold is influenced by buyers and sellers
   • the double meaning of *chain* in the poem
   • why a gold chain might be a problem

3. What is the speaker's solution to the problems associated with the value of gold?

4. What is your opinion of the speaker's solution? Explain your answer.

Hard Questions

by Margaret Tsuda

Why not mark out the land
into neat rectangles
squares and clover leafs?

Put on them cubes of
5   varying sizes
according to use—
dwellings
        singles/multiples
complexes
10   commercial/industrial.

Bale them together with
bands of roads.

What if a child shall cry
"I have never known spring!
15 I have never seen autumn!"

What if a man shall say
"I have never heard
silence fraught with living as
in swamp or forest!"
20 What if the eye shall never see
marsh birds and muskrats?

Does not the heart need
wildness?
Does not the thought need
25 something
to rest upon
not self-made by man,
a bosom
not his own?

FROM **PERSONAL RESPONSE** *TO* **CRITICAL ANALYSIS**

REFLECT   **1.** What does this poem mean to you? Write your thoughts in your notebook.

RETHINK   **2.** Summarize the hard questions asked by the speaker in lines 13–21. Why does the speaker ask these questions?

3. How do the questions in lines 22–29 serve as the speaker's answer to the hard questions?

4. Do you agree or disagree with the speaker's answer? Why?

oil crisis

by Naoshi Koriyama

when our last drop
of oil
has been used up
and all our cars
5 come to a stop
and all our planes
begin to rust
on the runway
in the rain
10 and the lights
go out

from the soaring sky-
        scrapers
we will walk
to the hill
15 to pick
raspberries wild
and steal
dappled eggs
from quails' nests
20 and then
we will walk

down to a stream
and catch eels
and by night
25 we will sit
by the river's bank
looking up
into the clear silent sky
reading poetry
30 in the stars

HISTORICAL INSIGHT

The Oil Crisis of the 1970s

The oil crisis Koriyama writes about struck the world in 1973. Arab countries of the Middle East, in protest against certain countries' support for Israel, reduced or stopped oil exports to Japan and some Western countries, including the United States. Heightening the crisis, the main association of oil-producing countries began to raise oil prices, which increased from less than $3 a barrel in 1973 to $30 a barrel in 1980. These events caused serious problems for the United States. Even though the United States was a major oil producer, in the early 1970s the cost of producing oil was greater than the cost of importing it. The United States was importing nearly half of the oil it needed and was therefore dependent on Middle Eastern oil.

The oil crisis led to fuel shortages and increases in fuel prices, which in turn caused some U.S. businesses and schools to close or lay off workers, to lower thermostats, and to dim lights. Drivers formed long lines to buy expensive gasoline, gas stations were closed on Sundays, and speed limits were lowered. Industrial production decreased, and the stock market fell.

In response to the crisis, Congress worked to boost domestic oil production, reduce the demand for imported oil, and control domestic oil prices, while oil companies searched for new sources of oil and cheaper and better ways to recover and refine it.

Today, because of the depletion of the earth's supply of fossil fuels and the air and water pollution caused by the production, transfer, and use of these fuels, many people have come to advocate the use of alternative sources of energy, such as synthetic fuels, solar energy, and nuclear power.

RESPONDING
OPTIONS

FROM *PERSONAL RESPONSE* TO CRITICAL ANALYSIS

REFLECT

1. What feeling were you left with at the end of "oil crisis"? What caused you to have that feeling? Jot down your thoughts in your notebook.

RETHINK

2. The speaker assumes that the world's oil will eventually be used up. Does the speaker see this outcome as a crisis? Use evidence from the poem to support your answer.

3. Do the activities the speaker describes in lines 13–30 appeal to you? Why or why not?

4. Do you think that most people would react to an oil crisis as the speaker does? Explain.

RELATE

5. Compare and contrast the speakers' attitudes toward our natural resources in the poems.

6. Which of the three poems do you think gives the strongest advice about humanity's relationship with the earth? Present your choice to a partner in the form of pantomime.

ANOTHER PATHWAY

Note the contrast in each poem between human-made objects and natural objects or scenes. Choose one of the poems and illustrate the contrast by drawing or using magazine pictures.

QUICKWRITES

1. These poets have strong feelings about nature. Write a **poem** in which you give advice on the subject of using natural resources.

2. Imagine that there is a severe oil crisis. Write a **description** of a day in your life without oil or oil products. Before writing, brainstorm with a classmate or a parent to think of some of the many ways in which oil affects your daily life.

PORTFOLIO Save your writing. You may want to use it later as a springboard to a piece for your portfolio.

LITERARY CONCEPTS

A poem's **theme** is a message about life that the poem conveys to a reader. For example, "Moco Limping" (page 125) might be said to have the theme "It's what's inside that counts." Since themes are not directly stated and must be inferred by readers, different readers may discover different themes in a poem. What do you think is the theme of each of these three poems? How does each theme relate to the unit theme, "Critical Adjustments"?

ALICE WALKER

1944–

"To me, writing really is magic, and I want people to feel rather than just know," says Alice Walker—a novelist, short story writer, poet, and essayist. Her writings about family relationships, poverty, women's issues, and civil rights have touched the hearts and minds of her readers.

Walker was born in Eatonton, Georgia, to share-cropper parents who did not go to school beyond fifth grade. She has said, "Sometimes I thought I'd gotten into the family by mistake. I always seemed to need more peace and quiet than anybody else."

At the age of eight, Walker was blinded in her right eye after being shot accidentally with a BB gun. She began to express her thoughts and feelings in poetry that she recorded in a personal notebook. However, she says, "I think the poetry that I actually *call* poetry didn't start coming until I was a teenager."

One of Walker's best-known novels is *The Color Purple,* a story about growing up in the South. It won a Pulitzer Prize and an American Book Award and was made into a movie.

OTHER WORKS *Horses Make a Landscape Look More Beautiful; Langston Hughes, American Poet; Once: Poems; Five Poems; Revolutionary Petunias and Other Poems; Goodnight, Willie Lee, I'll See You in the Morning*

MARGARET TSUDA

Margaret Tsuda (1921–) is a poet and artist whose poems have been translated into eight languages, including Hindi. She drew the illustrations for her books *Cry Love Aloud* and *Urban River,* using a bamboo pen. Her poems have been published in many anthologies and in the *Christian Science Monitor,* the *Sentinel,* and the magazines *Living Wilderness* and *Bodhi.* Tsuda graduated from Hunter College in New York City and lives in Newark, New Jersey.

NAOSHI KORIYAMA

1926–

Naoshi Koriyama studied English in Japan before coming to the United States to complete his college education. Since 1967 he has been a professor of English, teaching American poetry, at Toyo University in Tokyo.

Koriyama says that he writes about "any subject that may happen to interest me in the course of my daily life." He has published eight volumes of poetry in English, including his latest collection, *Eternal Grandeur and Other Poems.* His poems have appeared in high school textbooks in the United States, Canada, and Australia.

Koriyama also made translations into English of Japanese poetry and of folk songs from the Amami Islands in southern Japan, where he was born and raised.

OTHER WORKS *We Wrote These Poems* (trans.), *Coral Reefs, Songs from Sagamihara, Plum Tree in Japan and Other Poems, By the Lakeshore and Other Poems*

LASERLINKS
• *SCIENCE CONNECTION*

FOCUS ON DRAMA

Have you watched any good movies lately? If you have, you are already familiar with drama. A **drama,** or **play,** is a work of literature that is performed for an audience, either on stage or before a camera. People see dramas on television, in movies, and on stage. Occasionally people listen to dramas in the form of radio plays, which were a very popular form of entertainment before the coming of television.

The elements of drama are similar to the elements of fiction. Like a work of fiction, a drama usually tells a story with characters, a plot, and a setting. Unlike fiction, drama is written to be performed for an audience. For this reason, drama is written in a special form called a **script,** in which lines are written out for the characters to speak. The various parts of a script are described below.

CAST OF CHARACTERS A script usually begins with a list of the characters in the play, presented in the order of their appearance. Often a short description appears next to each character's name.

DIALOGUE Most plays consist almost entirely of dialogue—conversation between the characters. Both the plot of the play and the characters' personalities are revealed through the dialogue. The words spoken by each character are preceded by the character's name, as in this example from *The Million-Pound Bank Note* (page 185):

>   **Henry.** I'd like to discuss the matter.
>
>   **Gordon.** There is nothing to discuss at the
>   moment.

>   **Henry.** Is this a joke?
>
>   **Abel.** Not at all. And now good day.
>
>   **Gordon.** And good luck.

STAGE DIRECTIONS In addition to dialogue, a play almost always includes instructions for the director, the performers, and the stage crew. These are called stage directions and are printed in italics in this book; often they are also enclosed in parentheses. Many stage directions tell actors how to speak or move. Others describe **sound effects,** which are especially important in radio plays, since the success of such plays depends entirely on dialogue and sound. Notice how the stage directions in this excerpt from *The Hitchhiker* (page 337) describe sound effects and tell how the actors should speak:

Voice (*closer*). Going to California?

(*Sound: starter starting ... gears jamming*)

Adams (*as though sweating blood*). No. Not today. The other way. Going to New York. Sorry ... sorry ...

(*Sound: Car starts with squeal of wheels on dirt ... into auto hum.*)

Stage directions are also used to describe the **scenery**—stage decorations that represent the setting. Some stage directions describe **props**— the objects used by the actors.

ACTS AND SCENES The action of a play is sometimes divided into scenes. A new scene begins whenever the setting—time, place, or both time and place—changes. Sometimes scenes are grouped into acts, especially in long plays. *Survival,* on pages 459–479, is an example of a three-act play.

STRATEGIES FOR READING DRAMA

- **Read the play silently.** Before you try to read a play aloud, read it to yourself. You need to know the entire plot and understand the characters before you can perform a part in the play.

- **Figure out what is happening.** When you watch a movie, it usually takes you a while to understand exactly what the movie is about. The same is true when you read a play. Since the plot and the characters are revealed through dialogue, you will need to read several pages to understand what is happening.

- **Read the stage directions carefully.** If you were watching a drama on stage or on television, you would see the action and the scenery. When you read a drama, you have to imagine both. The stage directions tell where and when each scene is happening and help you visualize the action. If you skip the stage directions, you will miss important information.

- **Get to know the characters.** Drama does not usually contain descriptions of characters' personalities. You get to know the characters through their actions and through the dialogue— both what the characters say themselves and

what others say to and about them. Analyze each character's words carefully and try to discover the feelings behind them, just as if you were reading fiction.

- **Keep track of the plot.** As in fiction, the plot of a drama usually centers on a main conflict. Look for the conflict and let yourself become involved in the story. Watch for the action to build to a climax, and evaluate the way in which the conflict is resolved.

- **Read the play aloud with others.** When drama is performed, it takes on a whole new aspect; it becomes almost like real life. When you read the part of a character, you become an actor. Your reading of the part will be different from anyone else's because you will bring your own interpretation to the role. Let yourself "get into" the part and become that character for a while. React to what other characters say and do. Be ready with your character's lines, and read only the words your character says; do not read the stage directions aloud. You may find that you really enjoy playing the part of someone different from yourself.

PREVIEWING

DRAMA

The Million-Pound Bank Note

Mark Twain

Dramatized by Walter Hackett

PERSONAL CONNECTION

Imagine a man dressed in a designer suit and driving a $50,000 sports car. Then picture a bag lady getting on a city bus. What different assumptions would you make about these people? In other words, how much does the appearance of wealth affect your judgment of people? Discuss your thoughts with your classmates.

CULTURAL CONNECTION

Most of this play is set in England in the late 1800s. Then as now, the pound was the main British monetary unit, similar to our dollar. In 1893, when Mark Twain published the story on which this play is based, the million-pound bank note was worth 5 million U.S. dollars. Today, however, the British pound is worth less than two dollars in U.S. currency.

Respectability guided the lives of the British upper and middle classes; the keeping up of appearances was extremely important. Fine clothes, polished manners, an attractive home, financial success, and influential friends were common goals.

READING CONNECTION

Setting Changes This selection is a rewriting of Mark Twain's original story as a radio play. The setting changes are described in very little detail, making them somewhat difficult to spot. The play opens in a restaurant in San Francisco and then moves to a London street. While you read about the changing fortunes of the American in London, note the changes of setting on a setting tracker like the one started here.

Setting Tracker: Restaurant in Frisco → London Street

The Million-Pound Bank Note

by Mark Twain

Dramatized by
Walter Hackett

Going to the City, Hansom Cab
(1879), James J. Tissot. Private
collection, Bridgeman Art
Library, London/Superstock.

CAST OF CHARACTERS

Henry Adams	Servant	Second Man
Lloyd Hastings	Tod	Woman
First Cockney	Mr. Smedley	Third Man
Gordon Featherstone	Hotel Manager	Butler
Abel Featherstone	Second Cockney	Portia Langham
Albert Hawkins	First Man	Sir Alfred

Henry. When I was twenty-seven years old, I was a mining broker's[1] clerk in San Francisco. I was alone in the world and had nothing to depend upon but my wits and a clean reputation. These were setting my feet in the road to eventual fortune, and I was content with the prospect. During my spare time, I did outside work. One of my part-time employers was Lloyd Hastings, a mining broker. During this period I was helping Hastings to verify the Gould and Curry Extension papers, covering what seemed to be a highly valuable gold mine. One morning at two, after six hard hours of work on these papers, Lloyd Hastings and I went to the What Cheer restaurant in Frisco.[2] As we lingered over our coffee, he offered me a proposition.

Hastings. Henry, how would you like to go to London?

Henry. Thank you, no.

Hastings. Listen to me. I'm thinking of taking a month's option on the Gould and Curry Extension for the locators.

Henry. And—?

Hastings. They want one million dollars for it.

Henry. Not too much—if the claim works out the way it appears it may.

Hastings. I'm going to try to sell it to London interests, which means a trip there, and I want you to go with me, because you know more about these papers than I.

Henry. No, thanks.

Hastings. I'll make it well worth your while. I'll

---

1. **mining broker's:** relating to a person who acts as an agent in the buying or selling of mineral rights.
2. **Frisco:** short for "San Francisco."

pay all your expenses and give you something over if I make the sale.

Henry. I have a job.

Hastings. I'll arrange for you to get a leave of absence. What do you say?

Henry. No.

Hastings. Why?

Henry. If I go to London, I'll get out of touch with my work and with mining conditions here, and that means months getting the hang of things again.

Hastings. That's a pretty slim excuse, Henry.

Henry. More important, perhaps, I think you're doomed to failure.

Hastings. But you just said the claim is valuable.

Henry. It may well turn out that way, but right now its real value can't be proved. And even so, a month's option may leave you too little time to sell it; unless you sell it within the option time, you'll go stone broke.

Hastings. I'm willing to gamble.

Henry. Well, I'm not.

Hastings. Think—a free trip to London.

Henry. I've no desire to go to London. I'll remain right here in Frisco.

Hastings (*fading*). Very well, but I know you're making a mistake, Henry.

Henry. One of my few <u>diversions</u> was sailing in the bay. One day I ventured too far and was carried out to sea. Late that night, I was picked up by a freighter which was bound for London. It was a long voyage, and the captain made me work my passage without pay, as a common sailor. When I stepped ashore at

London, my clothes were ragged and shabby, and I had only a dollar in my pocket. This money fed and sheltered me for twenty-four hours. During the next twenty-four I went without food and shelter. I tried to get a job, doing manual labor. But the reply was always the same.

First Cockney. I'm not sure you'd do. You ain't the sort. (*suspiciously*) Look, 'ere, you're a Yank, ain't you?

Henry. The next morning, seedy and hungry, I was dragging myself along Portland Place when my desiring eye fell on a tempting treasure lying in the gutter. It was a luscious big pear—minus one bite. My mouth watered for it. But every time I made a move to get it, some passing eye detected my purpose. I was just getting desperate enough to brave all the shame when a window behind me was raised.

Gordon (*away*). I say, you there, will you step in here, please?

Henry. It was a very sumptuous house and an equally sumptuous room into which I was ushered by a servant. A couple of elderly gentlemen were sitting by the window. At that moment if I had known what they had in mind, undoubtedly I would have bolted for the door. They looked me over very thoroughly.

Gordon. He looks poor enough, don't you think, Brother?

Abel. Very. Er, young man, you are poor?

Henry. Extremely!

Abel. Good! And honest, too?

Henry. Honesty is about all I have left; that and character.

WORDS TO KNOW
diversion (dĭ-vûr′zhən) *n.* a distraction, entertainment, or relaxation

186

Abel. Splendid!

Gordon. If my brother and I are judges of people, we'd say you are just the man for whom we have been searching. By the way, you are also intelligent, I would say.

Henry. Yes, sir, I am. But what do you mean by saying that I appear to be just the man for whom you have been searching?

Gordon. And we don't know you. You're a perfect stranger. And better still, an American.

Henry. It's very kind of you gentlemen to call me into your home, but I'm a bit puzzled. Could you tell me what you have in mind?

Abel. Might we inquire into your background?

Henry. Pretty soon they had my full story. Their questions were complete and searching, and I gave them straightforward answers. Finally one said:

Gordon. Oh, yes, we're certain you will do, eh, Brother?

Abel. Definitely! He is elected.

Henry. To what am I elected, please?

Gordon. This envelope will explain everything. Here, take it. (*hastily*) No, don't open it now. Take it to your lodgings and look it over carefully.

Abel. Being sure not to be rash or hasty.

Henry. I'd like to discuss the matter.

Gordon. There is nothing to discuss at the moment.

Henry. Is this a joke?

Abel. Not at all. And now good day.

Gordon. And good luck.

Abel. Cheerio!

Henry. As soon as I was out of sight of the house, I opened my envelope and saw it contained money. I lost not a moment but shoved note and money into my pocket and broke for the nearest cheap eating house. How I did eat! Finished, I took out my money and unfolded it. I took one glimpse and nearly fainted. It was a single million-pound bank note. Five millions of dollars! It made my head swim. The next thing I noticed was the owner of the eating house. His eyes were on the note, and he was petrified. He couldn't stir hand or foot. I tossed the note toward him in careless fashion.

Hawkins. I-is it real, sir? A million-pound note?

Henry (*casually*). Certainly. Let me have my change, please.

Hawkins. Oh, I'm very sorry, sir, but I can't break the bill.

Henry. Look here—

Hawkins. Hawkins is the name, Albert Hawkins, proprietor. It's only a matter of two shillings[3] you owe, a trifling sum. Please owe it to me.

Henry. I may not be in this neighborhood again for a good time.

Hawkins. It's of no consequence, sir. And you can have anything you want, any time you choose, and let the account run as long as you please. I'm not afraid to trust as rich a gentleman as you just because you choose to play larks[4] by dressing as a tramp.

---

3. **shillings:** former British coins; a shilling was equal to a twentieth of a pound.

4. **play larks:** joke around; engage in harmless pranks.

WORDS
TO
KNOW   **consequence** (kŏn'sĭ-kwĕns') *n.* importance

187

Henry. Well, thank you. I shall take advantage of your kindness.

Hawkins. Not at all, sir, (*fading*) and please, sir, enter my humble restaurant place any time you wish. I shall be honored to receive you.

Henry. I was frightened, afraid that the police might pick me up. I was afraid of the two brothers' reaction when they discovered they had given me a million-pound note instead of what they must have intended giving—a one-pound note. I hurried to their house and rang the bell. The same servant appeared. I asked for the brothers.

Servant. They are gone.

Henry. Gone! Where?

Servant. On a journey.

Henry. But whereabouts?

Servant. To the Continent,[5] I think.

Henry. The Continent?

Servant. Yes, sir.

Henry. Which way—by what route?

Servant. I can't say, sir.

Henry. When will they be back?

Servant. In a month, they said.

Henry. A month! This is awful! Tell me how to get word to them. It's of great importance.

Servant. I can't, indeed. I've no idea where they've gone, sir.

Henry. Then I must see some member of the family.

Servant. Family's been away too; been abroad months—in Egypt and India, I think.

Henry. There's been an immense mistake made. They'll be back before night. Tell them I've been here, and that I'll keep coming till it's all made right, and they needn't worry.

Servant. I'll tell them, if they come back, but I'm not expecting them. They said you'd be here in an hour to make inquiries, but I must tell you it's all right, they'll be here on time to meet you. (*fading*) And that's all they said.

Henry (*slowly*). I had to give it up and go away. What a riddle it all was! They would be here "on time." What could that mean? Then I thought of the letter. I got it out and read it. It said: "You are an intelligent and honest man, as one can see by your face. We conceive you to be poor and a stranger. Enclosed you will find a sum of money. It is lent to you for thirty days, without interest. Report to this house at the end of that time. I have a bet on you. If I win it, you shall have any situation that is in my gift, any, that is, that you shall be able to prove yourself familiar with and <u>competent</u> to fill." That was all. No signature, no address, no date. I hadn't the least idea what the game was, nor whether harm was meant me or kindness. The letter said there was a bet on me. What kind of a bet? Was the bet that I would abscond with the million-pound bank note? Which brother was betting on my honesty? I reasoned this way: if I ask the Bank of England to deposit it to the credit of the man it belongs to, they'll ask me how I came by it, and if I tell the truth, they'll put me in the asylum; on the other hand, if I lie, they'll put me in jail. The same result would follow if I try to bank it anywhere or borrow money on it. Therefore, I have to carry this burden around until those

---

5. **the Continent:** mainland Europe.

| WORDS TO KNOW | **competent** (kŏm′pǐ-tənt) *adj.* qualified; capable |

Liverpool Quay by Moonlight (1887), John Atkinson Grimshaw. Tate Gallery, London/Art Resource, New York.

men come back. A month's suffering without wages or profit—unless I help win that bet, whatever it may be. If I do, I will get the situation I am promised. My hopes began to rise high. Then I looked at my rags. Could I afford a new suit? No, for I had nothing in the world but a million pounds. Finally I gave in and entered a fashionable tailor shop. The clerk looked at me very arrogantly.

Tod (*icily*). No chores to be done here. Get out!

Henry. Perhaps you have a misfit suit.

Tod. We don't give away suits, even misfits.

Henry. I can pay for it.

Tod. Follow me.

Henry. He took me into a back room and over-hauled a pile of rejected suits. He tossed the rattiest-looking one at me. I put it on. It didn't fit. It wasn't in any way attractive.

Tod. You may have that for four pounds, cash.

Henry. It would be an <u>accommodation</u> to me if you could wait some days for the money. I haven't any small change about me.

Tod (*sarcastically*). Oh, you haven't? Well, of course, I didn't expect it. I'd only expect gentlemen like you to carry large change.

Henry (*nettled*[6]). My friend, you shouldn't judge

---

6. **nettled:** irritated; annoyed.

a stranger always by the clothes he wears. I am quite able to pay for this suit.

Tod. Hah!

Henry. I simply don't wish to put you to the trouble of changing a large note.

Tod. As long as <u>rebukes</u> are going around, I might say that it wasn't quite your affair to infer that we couldn't change any note that you might happen to be carrying around. On the contrary, we can.

Henry. Oh, very well. I apologize. Here you are.

Tod. Thank you. (*A complete change. He stutters and fumbles.*) Ah—it's—ah—that is—we—ah—you see— It's— (*quickly*) Take it back, please. (*raising voice*) Mr. Smedley! Mr. Smedley! Help! Oh, Mr. Smedley.

Smedley (*coming in; a fussy man*). What is it, Tod, what is it? Stop shouting!

Tod. Oh, but Mr. Smedley, I can't control myself.

Smedley. What's up? What's the trouble? What's wanting? Who's this?

Henry. I am a customer, and I am waiting for my change.

Smedley. Change, change! Tod, give him his change. Get it for him.

Tod. Get him his change! It's easy for you to say that, Mr. Smedley, but look at the bill yourself.

Smedley. Bill, bill! Let me see it! (*pause*) Tod, you ass, selling an <u>eccentric</u> millionaire such an unspeakable suit as that. Tod, you're a fool—a born fool! Drives every millionaire away from this place, because he can't tell a millionaire from a tramp. Here, sir, are some suits more in keeping with your position.

Henry. Thank you, but this one will do.

Smedley. Of course it won't do! I shall burn it. Tod, burn this suit at once.

Tod. Yes, Mr. Smedley.

Smedley. We shall be honored to outfit you completely, sir . . . morning clothes, evening dress, sack suits, tweeds, shetlands[7]—everything you need. Come, Tod, book and pen. Now—length of leg, 32 inches; sleeve—

Henry. But look here. I can't give you an order for suits unless you can wait indefinitely or change this bill.

Smedley. Indefinitely, sir. It's a weak word, a weak word. *Eternally, that's* the word, sir. Tod, rush these things through. Let the minor customers wait. Set down the gentleman's address and—

Henry. I'm changing my quarters. I'll drop in and leave the new address.

Smedley. Quite right, sir, quite right. One moment—allow me to show you out, sir. And don't worry about paying us. (*fading*) Your credit is the highest. Good day, sir, good day. You honor us greatly, sir.

Henry (*as though sighing*). Well, don't you see what was bound to happen? I drifted naturally into whatever I wanted. Take my hotel, for example. I merely showed the resident manager my million-pound note, and he said:

Manager. We are honored to have you as a guest, sir. Now, I have just the suite for you. It con-

---

7. **morning clothes ... sack suits ... shetlands:** men's garments—formal daytime dress, business suits with loose-fitting jackets, and suits made of wool from the Shetland Islands.

WORDS TO KNOW

rebuke (rĭ-byōōk′) *n.* a sharp scolding or criticism
eccentric (ĭk-sĕn′trĭk) *adj.* very unusual in behavior; odd

sists of a bedroom, a sitting room, a dressing room, a dining room, two baths, and—

Henry. I'll pay you a month in advance with this.

Manager (*laughing*). You honor our simple hotel, sir. Pray, don't worry about the bill.

Henry. But it may be several months before I can pay you.

Manager. We're not worried, Mr.—er—

Henry. Henry Adams.

Manager. Mr. Adams, you are a most distinguished guest. (*fading*) Anything you desire, please name it, and we shall procure it for you immediately. Thank you, sir.

Henry. And there I was, sumptuously housed in an expensive hotel in Hanover Square. I took my dinners there, but for breakfast I stuck by Hawkins's humble feeding-house, where I had got my first meal on my million-pound bank note. I was the making of Hawkins.

(*Rattle of dishes and silver. Customers' voices ad-libbing in background.*)

Hawkins. Business is brisk, sir, very brisk, indeed, and has been ever since you and your million-pound bank note became patrons of my humble establishment. I've had to hire extra help, put in additional tables. Look for yourself, sir. There's a long queue[8] waiting to get in. Why, I'm famous and fair on my way to becoming wealthy.

Second Cockney. Pardon me, Guv'ner, but aren't you the gentleman what owns the million-pound bank note?

Hawkins. Look here, you, go away and stop bothering Mr.—Mr.—

Henry. Adams.

Hawkins. Mr. Adams.

Second Cockney. I was just anxious to get a look at him.

Hawkins. Who? Mr. Adams?

Second Cockney. No. The bank note.

Henry. Glad to oblige. There you are.

Second Cockney. By george, it *is* real. (*fading*) Now I can go home and tell me old lady I've seen it with me own eyes. I hopes she believes me, but she won't.

Hawkins. Mr. Adams, I wonder if I couldn't force upon you a small loan—even a large one.

Henry. Oh, no.

Hawkins. Please allow me, sir.

Henry (*relenting*). Well, as a matter of fact, I haven't gotten around to changing this note.

Hawkins. Fifty pounds might help tide you over. You know, a little spending money?

Henry. It would help, a bit.

Hawkins. I consider it a great honor. (*fading*) Indeed, a very great honor. Here you are, Mr. Adams, fifty pounds it is. (*fading*) And don't worry about repaying me.

Henry. I was in, now, and must sink or swim. I walked on air. And it was natural, for I had become one of the notorieties[9] of London. It turned my head, not just a little, but a great deal. The newspapers referred to me as the Vest-Pocket Millionaire. Then came the climaxing stroke: *Punch*[10] caricatured me!

---

8. **queue** (kyōō): a line of people.

9. **notorieties** (nō´tə-rī´ĭ-tēz): famous people; celebrities.

10. *Punch*: An English humor magazine, known for its cartoons poking fun at famous people.

WORDS TO KNOW	**ad-libbing** (ăd-lĭb´ĭng) *adj.* speaking spontaneously, without preparation **ad-lib** *v.*

Lord Ribblesdale (1902), John Singer Sargent. Tate Gallery, London/A.K.G., Berlin/Superstock.

Wherever I went, people cried:

First Man. There he goes!

Second Man. That's him!

Woman. Morning, Guv'ner.

Third Man. He's a bit of all right, he is.

Henry. Why, I just swam in glory all day long. About the tenth day of my fame I fulfilled my duty to my country by calling upon the American ambassador. He received me with enthusiasm and insisted that I attend a dinner party he was giving the following night. Two important things happened at that dinner. I met two people who were to play important roles in the little drama I was living. Among the guests was a lovely English girl, named Portia Langham, whom I fell in love with in two minutes, and she with me; I could see it without glasses. And just before dinner, the butler announced:

(*Guests ad-libbing in background, very politely.*)

Butler (*calling out*). Mr. Lloyd Hastings.

Henry. I stared at Hastings, and he at me, his mouth open in surprise.

Hastings. I, er—pardon me, but are you?—no, of course you can't be.

Henry (*chuckling*). But I am, Lloyd.

Hastings. Henry, I'm speechless. (*suddenly*) Don't tell me that you're also the Vest-Pocket Millionaire?

Henry. Correct!

Hastings. I've seen your own name coupled with the nickname, but it never occurred to me you were *the* Henry Adams. Why, it isn't six months since you were clerking in Frisco and sitting up nights helping me verify the Gould and Curry Extension papers. The idea of your being in London, and a vast millionaire, and a colossal celebrity! It's out of the *Arabian Nights!*

Henry. I can't realize it myself.

Hastings. It was just three months ago that we were eating together and I tried to persuade you to come to London with me. You turned me down, and now here you are. How did you happen to come, and what gave you this incredible start?

Henry. I'll tell you all about it, but not now.

Hastings. When?

Henry. The end of this month.

Hastings. Make it a week.

Henry. I can't. How's your business venture coming along?

Hastings (*sighing*). You were a true prophet, Henry. I wish I hadn't come.

Henry. Stop with me, when we leave here, and tell me all about it. I want to hear the whole story.

Hastings. You'll hear it, every last dismal word. (*fading a bit*) I'm so grateful to find a willing and sympathetic ear.

(*Background ad-libbing out. A pause, then piano playing semiclassical tune in background.*)

Henry. After dinner there was coffee and an informal piano recital and dear Miss Langham—lovely Portia Langham, the English girl. I eased her away from the music and the guests to the library, where we talked.

(*Piano out.*)

Portia. I'm really quite excited, Mr. Adams, meeting you like this. A millionaire!

Henry. But I'm not one.

Portia. B-but of course you are.

Henry. You're wrong.

Portia. I don't understand.

Henry. You will! You will, that is, if you allow me to see you tomorrow.

Portia (*as though smiling*). Well, Mr. Adams—

Henry. Henry.

Portia. Henry, then. I will give the invitation serious thought.

Henry. Tomorrow is going to be a sunny day, just right for a picnic in the country. Yes?

Portia. Yes.

Henry. I'll tell you the whole story then.

Portia. Do you think you should?

Henry. Certainly! After all, we're going to be married.

Portia (*amazed*). We—we're—going to—marry!

Henry. Absolutely! I'll call for you at noon. Where?

Portia. Meet me here.

Henry. You're a guest here?

Portia. N—no, but it will be more convenient.

Henry. Do you like me?

Portia. Yes, Henry. (*fading*) You're a very unusual young man, even if you are a millionaire, and even if you claim you aren't.

Henry. All the way home I was in the clouds, Hastings talking and I not hearing a word. When we reached my suite, he said to me:

Hastings. This luxury makes me realize how poor, how defeated I am. Even the drippings of your daily income would seem like a tremendous fortune to me.

Henry. Unreel your story, Lloyd.

Hastings. I told you the whole story on the way over here.

Henry. You did?

Hastings. Yes.

Henry. I'll be hanged if I heard a word of it.

Hastings. Are you well?

Henry. Yes. I'm in love.

Hastings. That English girl you were speaking to?

Henry. Yes. I'm going to marry her.

Hastings. Small wonder you didn't hear a word I said.

Henry. Now I'm all attention.

Hastings. I came here with what I thought was a grand opportunity. I have an option to sell the Gould and Curry Mine and keep all I can get over a million dollars.

Henry. Sounds like a good proposition.

Hastings. Yes, it's a fine claim.

Henry. Well?

Hastings. The parties here whom I tried to interest have backed down. And so here I am, trying to peddle a gold mine but with nary a[11] buyer in sight. In addition, I am almost penniless.

Henry. Surely you'll find a buyer.

Hastings. My option on the mine expires in a matter of days—in fact, at the end of this month.

Henry. You *are* in a fix.

Hastings. Henry, you can save me. Will you do it?

Henry. I? How?

Hastings. Give me a million dollars and my passage home for my option.

Henry. I can't.

Hastings. But you're wealthy.

Henry. I—I—not really.

Hastings. You have a million pounds—five millions of dollars. Buy the mine and you'll double, maybe triple, your investment.

Henry. I'd like to help, but I can't.

Hastings. You know the value of this mine as well as I do.

Henry (*tired*). Oh, Lloyd, I wish I could explain, but I can't. What you ask is impossible.

Hastings. That's quite all right. I'm sorry to have bothered you, Henry. (*fading*) You must have a good reason in turning me down, I'm sure.

Henry. It hurt me to have to refuse Lloyd, but it made me comprehend my delicate and <u>precarious</u> position. Here I was, deep in debt, not a cent in the world, in love with a lovely girl, and nothing in front of me but a promise of a position if, *if,* I won the bet for the nameless brother. Nothing could save me. The next day, Portia and I went on our picnic in the country. I told her the whole story, down to the last detail. Her reaction wasn't exactly what I thought it would be.

(*Sound of bird singing in background, weaving in and out of this scene.*)

Portia (*laughs*). Oh, Henry, that's priceless.

Henry (*a bit stiffly*). I fail to see the humor.

Portia. But I do, more than you can imagine.

---

11. **nary a:** not one.

precarious (prĭ-kâr′ē-əs) *adj.* not secure; risky

Henry. Here I am, mixed up in a bet between two eccentric old men, and for all they care I might well be in jail.

Portia (*still laughing*). Wonderful, the funniest thing I've ever heard.

Henry. Pardon me if I don't laugh.

Portia (*stops laughing*). Sorry, but it is both funny and pathetic. But you say that one of the men is going to offer you a position?

Henry. If I win the bet.

Portia. Which one is he?

Henry. I don't know. But I have one solution. If I win, I get the position. Now, I've kept very careful track of every cent I either owe or have borrowed, and I'm going to pay it back from my salary. If the position pays me six hundred pounds a year, I'll—I'll—

Portia. You'll what?

Henry. I'll— (*He whistles.*) To date I owe exactly six hundred pounds, my whole year's salary.

Portia. And the month isn't ended.

Henry. If I'm careful, my second year's salary may carry me through. Oh, dear, that is going to make it difficult for us to get married immediately, isn't it?

Portia (*dreamily*). Yes, it is. (*suddenly*) Henry, what are you talking about? Marriage! You don't know me.

Henry. I know your name, your nationality, your age, and most important, I know that I love you. I also know that you love me.

Portia. Please be sensible.

Henry. I can't. I'm in love.

Portia. All this sounds like a play.

Henry. It is—a wonderful one. I'll admit my

owing my first two years' pay is going to pose a problem insofar as our getting married is concerned. (*suddenly*) I have it! The day I confront those two old gentlemen, I'll take you with me.

Portia. Oh, no. It wouldn't be proper.

Henry. But so much depends upon that meeting. With you there, I can get the old boys to raise my salary—say, to a thousand pounds a year. Perhaps fifteen hundred. Say you'll go with me.

Portia. I'll go.

Henry. In that case, I'll demand two thousand a year, so we can get married immediately.

Portia. Henry.

Henry. Yes?

Portia. Keep your expenses down for the balance of the month. Don't dip into your third year's salary.

Henry. And that is how matters stood at that point. Thoughts raced through my mind. What if I lost the bet for my nameless benefactor?[12] What if he failed to give me a position? Then the answer came to me like a flash of lightning. I roused Lloyd Hastings from bed. He was a bit bewildered.

Hastings. I don't understand you. What are you getting at?

Henry. Lloyd, I'm going to save you. Save you— understand?

Hastings. No.

Henry. I'll save you, but not in the way you ask, for that wouldn't be fair after your hard work and the risks you've run. Now, I don't need to buy a mine. I can keep my capital

---

12. **benefactor:** a person who provides money or help.

moving without that; it's what I'm doing all the time. I know all about your mine; I know its immense value and can swear to it if anybody wishes it. You shall sell it inside of the fortnight[13] for three million cash.

Hastings. Three million!

Henry. Right!

Hastings. But how?

Henry. By using my name freely—and right now my name is on the tip of everybody's tongue. We'll divide the profits, share and share alike.

Hastings (*overjoyed*). I may use your name! Your name—think of it! Man, they'll flock in droves,[14] these rich English. They'll fight for that stock. I'm a made man, a made man forever. (*fading*) I'll never forget you as long as I live . . . never, never . . .

Henry. In less than twenty-four hours, London was abuzz! I hadn't anything to do, day after day, but sit home and wait for calls.

Sir Alfred. Then I may assume, Mr. Adams, that you consider this mining property a sound investment?

Henry. A very sound investment, Sir Alfred.

Sir Alfred. And what of this American chap, Hastings?

Henry. I know him very well, and he is as sound as the mine.

Sir Alfred. Then I think I shall invest in this property. Your recommendation does it.

(*Sound of telephone bell.*)

Henry. Excuse me, Sir Alfred.

(*Sound of receiver lifted from hook.*)

Henry (*into phone*). Yes, this is Henry Adams.

Who? Sir John Hardcastle. Yes, Sir John. The Gould and Curry Extension? Yes, I know a great deal about it. I certainly would recommend it as a shrewd investment. The mine is worth far more than the asking price. Yes, Mr. Hastings is very well known in the States. Honest as the day is long, as they say. Yes, I suggest you contact Mr. Hastings. Thank you. Not at all. Good day, Sir John.

(*Sound of receiver replaced onto hook.*)

Sir Alfred. That clinches it. If Sir John is in, so am I. Do you suppose that your Mr. Hastings would mind if I brought in a few <u>discreet</u> friends on this venture?

Henry. Er, no, in fact I'm sure he wouldn't. Mr. Hastings is a very democratic chap.

Sir Alfred. Directly I shall go and call upon Mr. Hastings. By the way, exactly where is this mine?

Henry. California.

Sir Alfred. Is that near Washington, D.C.?

Henry. Not exactly.

Sir Alfred. A pity, for I had thought of asking the British ambassador to look at it. (*fading*) Well, I'm off. Thank you for your advice. Good day, Mr. Adams.

Henry. And that's the way it went—a steady stream of wealthy Londoners asking my advice, which, of course, I gave freely. Meanwhile I said not a word to Portia about the possible sale of the mine. I wanted to save it as a surprise; and then there always was the

---

13. **fortnight:** two weeks.
14. **droves:** mobs; crowds.

possibility the sale might fall through. The day the month was up, she and I, dressed in our best, went to the house on Portland Place. As we waited for the two old gentlemen to enter, we talked excitedly.

Portia. You're certain you have the bank note with you?

Henry. Right here. Portia, dearest, the way you look it's a crime to ask for a salary a single penny under three thousand a year.

Portia. You'll ruin us.

Henry. Just trust in me. It'll come out all right.

Portia (*worried*). Please remember, if we ask for too much, we may get no salary at all; and then what will become of us, with no way in the world to earn our living? (*fading*) Please handle this delicately, Henry.

Henry. When the two old gentlemen entered, of course they were surprised to see Portia with me. I asked them to introduce themselves, which they did.

Gordon. I am Gordon Featherstone.

Abel. And I am Abel Featherstone.

Henry. Gentlemen, I am ready to report, but first may I ask which of you bet on me?

Gordon. It was I. Have you the million-pound note?

Henry. Here it is, sir.

Gordon. Ah! I've won. *Now* what do you say, Abel?

Abel. I say he did survive, and I've lost twenty thousand pounds. I never would have believed it.

Henry. Perhaps you might enlighten me as to the terms of the bet.

Les adieux [The good-bye] (1871), James J. Tissot. City of Bristol Museum and Art Gallery, England/Bridgeman Art Library, London/Superstock.

Gordon. Gladly! The Bank of England once issued two notes of a million pounds each. Only one of these had been used and canceled; the other lay in the vaults. Well, Abel and I got to wondering what would happen to a perfectly honest and intelligent stranger turned adrift in London without a friend and with no money in the world but the million-pound bank note. Abel said he would starve to death, and I claimed he wouldn't. My brother said he would be arrested if he offered the note at a bank. Well, we went on arguing until I bet him twenty thousand pounds that the man would live thirty days, *anyway,* on that million, and keep out of jail, too.

Abel. And I took him up.

Henry. How did you know I was the right choice?

Abel. After talking with you, we decided you had all the qualifications.

Gordon. And that pear incident—if you had picked it up very boldly, it would have proved to us you were nothing but a tramp.

Henry. You don't know how tempted I was to do just that.

Gordon. And so you shall receive your reward— a choice of any position you can fill.

Henry. First I ask that you look at this scrap of paper, all of you. You, too, Portia.

Gordon. A certificate of deposit in the London and County Bank—

Abel. In the sum of—

Gordon. Two hundred thousand pounds.

Portia. Henry, is it yours?

Henry. It is. It represents my share of the sale of a mining property in California, sold by my friend Lloyd Hastings—a sort of commission, as it were. It all came about by thirty days' judicious use of that little loan you gentlemen let me have. And the only use I made of it was to buy trifles and offer the bill in change.

Abel. Come, this is astonishing.

Gordon. It's incredible.

Henry (*laughing*). I can prove it.

Portia. Henry, is that really your money? Have you been fibbing to me?

Henry. I have, indeed. But you'll forgive me, I know.

Portia (*half smiling*). Don't you be so sure.

Henry. Oh, you'll get over it. Come, let's be going.

Gordon. Wait! I promised to give you a situation, you know.

Henry. Thank you, but I really don't want one.

Portia. Henry, I'm ashamed of you. You don't even thank the good gentleman. May I do it for you?

Henry. If you can improve upon it.

Portia. I shall. Uncle Abel, first, thank you for making this possible. And, dear Father—

Henry. Hold on. You're her uncle?

Abel. I am.

Henry. And you—

Gordon. Yes, I'm her stepfather.

Portia. And the dearest one that ever was. You understand now, don't you, Henry, why I was able to laugh when you told me the story of the bet with the two nameless gentlemen. Of course I couldn't miss knowing that it was this house and that the two men were Father and Uncle Abel.

Henry. Sir, you *have* got a situation open that I want.

Gordon. Name it.

Henry. Son-in-law.

Gordon. Well, well, well! But if you haven't ever served in that capacity, you of course can't furnish satisfactory recommendations to satisfy the conditions of the contract.

Henry. Only just try me for thirty or forty years.

Gordon. What do you think, Abel?

Abel. Well, he does look to be a satisfactory sort.

Gordon. And you, Portia?

Portia. I agree—heartily.

Gordon. Very well. Take her along. If you hurry, you can reach the license bureau before it closes. (*fading*) Hop to it now.

Henry. Happy, we two? Indeed, yes! And when London got the whole history of my adventure for a month, how it did talk. My Portia's father took the million-pound bank note to the Bank of England, cashed it, had it canceled; and he gave it to us at our wedding. Framed, it now hangs in our home. It gave me my Portia; but for it I could not have remained in London, would not have appeared at the American ambassador's, never should have met her. And so I always say: Yes, it's a million-pounder, but it made but one purchase in its life and then got the article for only about a tenth part of its value. ❖

RESPONDING OPTIONS

FROM PERSONAL RESPONSE *TO* CRITICAL ANALYSIS

REFLECT
1. What are your impressions of Henry? Jot down your thoughts in your notebook. Draw a series of sketches showing how Henry makes use of the bank note.

RETHINK
2. How does having the million-pound note affect Henry? What adjustments does he make?

3. Why do you think people's attitudes toward Henry change when he appears rich?

4. How would you evaluate Henry as a person?

   Consider
   - why he declines to go to London with Hastings
   - how he responds initially to receiving the bank note, and how he uses it
   - his response to Portia

5. What is your opinion of the scheme devised by the two brothers? Explain your answer.

RELATE
6. Like Henry, people who win big lottery jackpots suddenly become fabulously wealthy, forcing them to make critical adjustments in their lives. How do you imagine winning a lottery might affect a person's life? What might be the good and the bad effects of instant wealth?

ANOTHER PATHWAY
Cooperative Learning

With your classmates, present a full-scale stage production of this play. To make your production authentic, research the setting and the costumes of late 19th-century England. Divide tasks among the members of the class, assigning one to videotape the production.

QUICKWRITES

1. The Vest-Pocket Millionaire is big news in London. Write a **script** for a TV-news-show feature about this lucky young man's experiences.

2. The biggest social event in London is the wedding of the Vest-Pocket Millionaire to his English bride. Write a **society-page report** of the event for a San Francisco newspaper.

3. Put yourself in the shoes of one of the characters who encounters the Vest-Pocket Millionaire in the play. Write a **character sketch** of Henry from that character's point of view.

📁 *PORTFOLIO Save your writing. You may want to use it later as a springboard to a piece for your portfolio.*

LITERARY CONCEPTS

As in fiction, the climax or turning point of a drama is usually followed by a **resolution** that shows how the conflict or conflicts are resolved and how the story ends. This is the time when loose ends are tied up and the story comes to a close. Summarize what happens in the resolution of this play.

ALTERNATIVE ACTIVITIES

1. ***Cooperative Learning*** With other students, research the political leaders and the royalty of Great Britain in the 1890s using the library or an on-line service. Find out how British society was changing during this time and what caused the changes. Present your findings in an **oral report.**

2. Suppose Henry regularly donates a portion of his earnings to special causes or to individuals in need. Write a **letter** to Henry, telling him why your cause or need deserves his help. The class can read its letters aloud and vote to select the three special causes or needs to which Henry should donate money.

3. Take a **survey** or **poll** to find out what each of your classmates would do with a million dollars. Plot the responses on a chart or graph.

ACROSS THE CURRICULUM

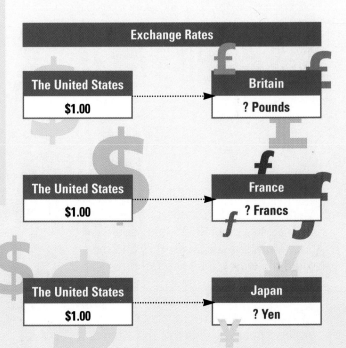

Mathematics Exchange rates are ratios used to compare the values of different currencies. These rates change daily. Find out how exchange rates are determined and what a U.S. dollar is worth in the currencies listed below. What is the current dollar equivalent of 1 million British pounds?

Exchange Rates

The United States	Britain
$1.00	? Pounds

The United States	France
$1.00	? Francs

The United States	Japan
$1.00	? Yen

ART CONNECTION

Examine all of the artwork in the selection. What can you say about the use of color and the style of painting across these four works? Evaluate their effectiveness in grabbing the reader's attention and conveying time and place.

LITERARY LINKS

Using a Venn diagram like the one below, compare and contrast Kurt Vonnegut's attitude toward the wealthy in "The Lie" with the attitude shown in this play.

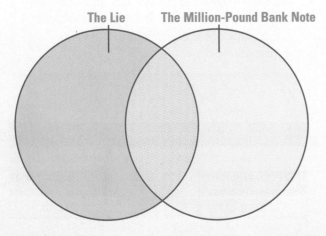

The Lie   The Million-Pound Bank Note

Review the Words to Know at the bottom of the selection pages. Then decide whether the words in each pair below are synonyms or antonyms. On your paper, write S for *Synonyms* or A for *Antonyms.*

1. judicious—foolish
2. rebuke—compliment
3. competent—unfit
4. accommodation—favor
5. precarious—secure
6. consequence—importance
7. diversion—amusement
8. discreet—guarded
9. eccentric—strange
10. ad-lib—recite

SAMUEL CLEMENS (MARK TWAIN)

Samuel Clemens took his pen name, Mark Twain, from a cry used by boatmen on the Mississippi River. They would call out "Mark twain!" when they had measured the water to be two fathoms deep —deep enough for travel. Traveling the Mississippi River in makeshift rafts as a child and piloting riverboats as an adult inspired Twain to write his most famous books, *The Adventures of Tom Sawyer,* *The Adventures of Huckleberry Finn,* and *Life on the Mississippi.*

1835–1910

Twain grew up in Hannibal, Missouri, during the mid-1800s. As an adult, he headed west, mining for gold and silver and eventually working for newspapers in San Francisco. Like the character Hastings in this play, he also invested in mines, but these ventures failed.

Twain's courtship was perhaps even more romantic than Henry and Portia's. In 1867, he fell in love with a picture of Olivia Langdon. When he finally met "Livy," he was determined to marry her, but his busy lecture schedule kept them apart. In one year, Twain wrote her well over 100 love letters. They were finally married in 1870.

In the 1890s, Twain and his family were plagued with tragedy. One daughter died after contracting meningitis, a disease of the brain and spine. Her daughter's death resulted in emotional and physical problems for Livy, who died soon afterward. Four years later, another daughter drowned in the bath during an epileptic seizure. A third daughter suffered a nervous collapse.

Although Twain grew increasingly bitter and mean-spirited during the final decade of his life, he is remembered for his love of fun, his frontier spirit, and his commitment to democracy.

OTHER WORKS *The Prince and the Pauper,* "The Celebrated Jumping Frog of Calaveras County," "The $30,000 Bequest," *A Connecticut Yankee in King Arthur's Court*

> LASERLINKS
> • AUTHOR BACKGROUND

Mother & Daughter

by GARY SOTO

Yollie's mother, Mrs. Moreno, was a large woman who wore a muu-muu[1] and butterfly-shaped glasses. She liked to water her lawn in the evening and wave at low-riders, who would stare at her behind their smoky sunglasses and laugh. Now and then a low-rider from Belmont Avenue would make his car jump and shout *"Mamacita!"* But most of the time they just stared and wondered how she got so large.

Mrs. Moreno had a strange sense of humor. Once, Yollie and her mother were watching a late-night movie called *They Came to Look*. It was about creatures from the underworld who had climbed through molten lava to walk the earth. But Yollie, who had played soccer all day with the kids next door, was too tired to be scared. Her eyes closed but sprang open when her mother screamed, "Look, Yollie! Oh, you missed a scary part. The guy's face was all ugly!"

But Yollie couldn't keep her eyes open. They fell shut again and stayed shut, even when her mother screamed and slammed a heavy palm on the arm of her chair.

"Mom, wake me up when the movie's over so I can go to bed," mumbled Yollie.

"OK, Yollie, I wake you," said her mother through a mouthful of popcorn.

But after the movie ended, instead of waking her daughter, Mrs. Moreno laughed under her breath, turned the TV and lights off, and tiptoed to bed. Yollie woke up in the middle of the night and didn't know where she was. For a moment she thought she was dead. Maybe something from the underworld had lifted her from her house and carried

---

1. **muu-muu** (mo͞o′mo͞o′): a long, loose dress, often brightly colored.

her into the earth's belly. She blinked her sleepy eyes, looked around at the darkness, and called, "Mom? Mom, where are you?" But there was no answer, just the throbbing hum of the refrigerator.

Finally, Yollie's grogginess cleared, and she realized her mother had gone to bed, leaving her on the couch. Another of her little jokes.

But Yollie wasn't laughing. She tiptoed into her mother's bedroom with a glass of water and set it on the night stand next to the alarm clock. The next morning, Yollie woke to screams. When her mother reached to turn off the alarm, she had overturned the glass of water.

Yollie burned her mother's morning toast and gloated. "Ha! Ha! I got you back. Why did you leave me on the couch when I told you to wake me up?"

Despite their jokes, mother and daughter usually got along. They watched bargain matinees together and played croquet[2] in the summer and checkers in the winter. Mrs. Moreno encouraged Yollie to study hard because she wanted her daughter to be a doctor. She bought Yollie a desk, a typewriter, and a lamp that cut glare so her eyes would not grow tired from hours of studying.

Yollie was slender as a tulip, pretty, and one of the smartest kids at Saint Theresa's. She was captain of crossing guards, an altar girl, and a whiz in the school's monthly spelling bees.

"Tienes que estudiar mucho,"[3] Mrs. Moreno said every time she propped her work-weary feet on the hassock. "You have to study a lot, then you can get a good job and take care of me."

"Yes, Mama," Yollie would respond, her face buried in a book. If she gave her mother any sympathy, she would begin her stories about how she had come with her family from Mexico with nothing on her back but a sack with three skirts, all of which were too large by the time she crossed the border because

she had lost weight from not having enough to eat.

Everyone thought Yollie's mother was a riot. Even the nuns laughed at her antics. Her brother Raul, a nightclub owner, thought she was funny enough to go into show business.

But there was nothing funny about Yollie needing a new outfit for the eighth-grade fall dance. They couldn't afford one. It was late October, with Christmas around the corner, and their dented Chevy Nova had gobbled up almost one hundred dollars in repairs.

Everyone thought Yollie's mother was a riot.

"We don't have the money," said her mother, genuinely sad because they couldn't buy the outfit, even though there was a little money stashed away for college. Mrs. Moreno remembered her teenage years and her hard-working parents, who picked grapes and oranges and chopped beets and cotton for meager pay around Kerman. Those were the days when "new clothes" meant limp and out-of-style dresses from Saint Vincent de Paul.[4]

The best Mrs. Moreno could do was buy Yollie a pair of black shoes with velvet bows and fabric dye to color her white summer dress black.

---

2. **croquet** (krō-kā′): an outdoor game in which players use mallets to hit wooden balls through a series of wire arches.

3. *Tienes que estudiar mucho* (tyĕ′nĕs kĕ ĕs-tōō-dyär′ mōō′chô) *Spanish.*

4. **Saint Vincent de Paul:** a reference to the Society of Saint Vincent de Paul, a Roman Catholic organization that operates stores where donated goods are sold cheaply.

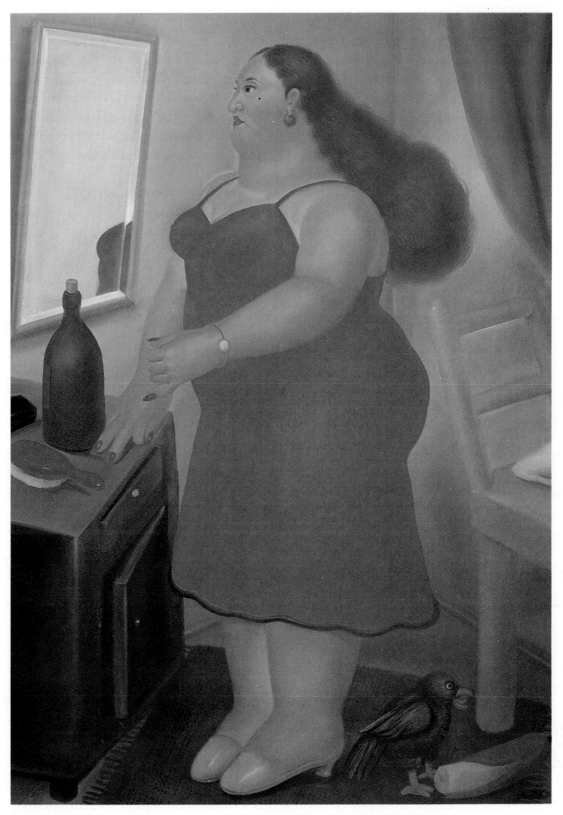

Colombiane (1978), Fernando Botero. Copyright ©1995 Fernando Botero/Licensed by VAGA, New York.

"We can color your dress so it will look brand-new," her mother said brightly, shaking the bottle of dye as she ran hot water into a plastic dish tub. She poured the black liquid into the tub and stirred it with a pencil. Then, slowly and carefully, she lowered the dress into the tub.

Yollie couldn't stand to watch. She *knew* it wouldn't work. It would be like the time her mother stirred up a batch of molasses for candy apples on Yollie's birthday. She'd dipped the apples into the goo and swirled them and seemed to taunt Yollie by singing *"Las Mañanitas"* to her. When she was through,

she set the apples on wax paper. They were hard as rocks and hurt the kids' teeth. Finally they had a contest to see who could break the apples open by throwing them against the side of the house. The apples shattered like grenades, sending the kids scurrying for cover, and in an odd way the birthday party turned out to be a success. At least everyone went home happy.

To Yollie's surprise, the dress came out shiny black. It looked brand-new and sophisticated, like what people in New York wear. She beamed at her mother, who hugged Yollie and said, "See, what did I tell you?"

Yucateca Sentada (1979), Alfredo Zalce. Acrylic on wood, 60 cm × 80 cm, courtesy of the Mexico Fine Arts Center Museum, Chicago.

The dance was important to Yollie because she was in love with Ernie Castillo, the third-best speller in the class. She bathed, dressed, did her hair and nails, and primped until her mother yelled, "All right already." Yollie sprayed her neck and wrists with Mrs. Moreno's Avon perfume and bounced into the car.

Mrs. Moreno let Yollie out in front of the school. She waved and told her to have a good time but behave herself, then roared off, blue smoke trailing from the tail pipe of the old Nova.

Yollie ran into her best friend, Janice. They didn't say it, but each thought the other was the most beautiful girl at the dance; the boys would fall over themselves asking them to dance.

The evening was warm but thick with clouds. Gusts of wind picked up the paper lanterns hanging in the trees and swung them, blurring the night with reds and yellows. The lanterns made the evening seem romantic, like a scene from a movie. Everyone danced, sipped punch, and stood in knots of threes and fours, talking. Sister Kelly got up and jitterbugged[5] with some kid's father. When the record ended, students broke into applause.

Janice had her eye on Frankie Ledesma, and Yollie, who kept smoothing her dress down when the wind picked up, had her eye on Ernie. It turned out that Ernie had his mind on Yollie, too. He ate a handful of cookies nervously, then asked her for a dance.

"Sure," she said, nearly throwing herself into his arms.

They danced two fast ones before they got a slow one. As they circled under the lanterns, rain began falling, lightly at first. Yollie loved the sound of the raindrops ticking against the leaves. She leaned her head on Ernie's shoulder, though his sweater was scratchy. He felt warm and tender. Yollie could tell that he was in love, and with her, of course. The dance continued successfully, romantically, until it began to pour.

"Everyone, let's go inside—and, boys, carry in the table and the record player," Sister Kelly commanded.

The girls and boys raced into the cafeteria. Inside, the girls, drenched to the bone, hurried to the restrooms to brush their hair and dry themselves. One girl cried because her velvet dress was ruined. Yollie felt sorry for her and helped her dry the dress off with paper towels, but it was no use. The dress was ruined.

Yollie went to a mirror. She looked a little gray now that her mother's makeup had washed away but not as bad as some of the other girls. She combed her damp hair, careful not to pull too hard. She couldn't wait to get back to Ernie.

> Drip, black drip. Drip, black drip. The dye was falling from her dress like black tears.

Yollie bent over to pick up a bobby pin, and shame spread across her face. A black puddle was forming at her feet. Drip, black drip. Drip, black drip. The dye was falling from her dress like black tears. Yollie stood up. Her dress was now the color of ash. She looked around the room. The other girls, unaware of Yollie's problem, were busy grooming themselves. What could she do? Everyone would laugh. They would know she dyed an old dress because she couldn't afford a new one. She hurried from the restroom with her head down, across the

---

5. **jitterbugged:** danced in a lively, acrobatic style popular in the early 1940s.

cafeteria floor and out the door. She raced through the storm, crying as the rain mixed with her tears and ran into twig-choked gutters.

When she arrived home, her mother was on the couch eating cookies and watching TV.

"How was the dance, *m'ija?*[6] Come watch the show with me. It's really good."

Yollie stomped, head down, to her bedroom. She undressed and threw the dress on the floor.

Her mother came into the room. "What's going on? What's all this racket, baby?"

"The dress. It's cheap! It's no good!" Yollie kicked the dress at her mother and watched it land in her hands. Mrs. Moreno studied it closely but couldn't see what was wrong. "What's the matter? It's just little bit wet."

"The dye came out, that's what."

Mrs. Moreno looked at her hands and saw the grayish dye puddling in the shallow lines of her palms. Poor baby, she thought, her brow darkening as she made a sad face. She wanted to tell her daughter how sorry she was, but she knew it wouldn't help. She walked back to the living room and cried.

The next morning, mother and daughter stayed away from each other. Yollie sat in her room turning the pages of an old *Seventeen,* while her mother watered her plants with a Pepsi bottle.

"Drink, my children," she said loud enough for Yollie to hear. She let the water slurp into pots of coleus and cacti. "Water is all you need. My daughter needs clothes, but I don't have no money."

Yollie tossed her *Seventeen* on her bed. She was embarrassed at last night's tirade. It wasn't her mother's fault that they were poor.

When they sat down together for lunch, they felt awkward about the night before. But Mrs. Moreno had made a fresh stack of tortillas and cooked up a pan of *chile verde,*

and that broke the ice. She licked her thumb and smacked her lips.

"You know, honey, we gotta figure a way to make money," Yollie's mother said. "You and me. We don't have to be poor. Remember the Garcias. They made this stupid little tool that fixes cars. They moved away because they're rich. That's why we don't see them no more."

> "Water is all you need. My daughter needs clothes, but I don't have no money."

"What can we make?" asked Yollie. She took another tortilla and tore it in half.

"Maybe a screwdriver that works on both ends? Something like that." The mother looked around the room for ideas but then shrugged. "Let's forget it. It's better to get an education. If you get a good job and have spare time, then maybe you can invent something." She rolled her tongue over her lips and cleared her throat. "The county fair hires people. We can get a job there. It will be here next week."

Yollie hated the idea. What would Ernie say if he saw her pitching hay at the cows? How could she go to school smelling like an armful of chickens? "No, they wouldn't hire us," she said.

The phone rang. Yollie lurched from her chair to answer it, thinking it would be Janice wanting to know why she had left. But it was Ernie wondering the same thing. When he

---

6. **m'ija** (me' hä) *Spanish:* a shortened version of *mi hija,* meaning "my daughter."

found out she wasn't mad at him, he asked if she would like to go to a movie.

"I'll ask," Yollie said, smiling. She covered the phone with her hand and counted to ten. She uncovered the receiver and said, "My mom says it's OK. What are we going to see?"

After Yollie hung up, her mother climbed, grunting, onto a chair to reach the top shelf in the hall closet. She wondered why she hadn't done it earlier. She reached behind a stack of towels and pushed her chubby hand into the cigar box where she kept her secret stash of money.

"I've been saving a little every month," said Mrs. Moreno. "For you, *m'ija.*" Her mother held up five twenties, a blossom of green that smelled sweeter than flowers on that Saturday. They drove to Macy's and bought a blouse, shoes, and a skirt that would not bleed in rain or any other kind of weather. ❖

GARY SOTO

A native of Fresno, California, Gary Soto writes about the experiences of Mexican Americans. As a child, Soto worked as a field laborer, but he dreamed of becoming a priest, a hobo, and a paleontologist. Once in college, he planned to study geography until he discovered poetry. "I don't think I had any literary aspirations when I was a kid," says Soto. "In fact, we were pretty much an illiterate family. We didn't have books, and no one encouraged us to read. So my wanting to write poetry was a sort of fluke." He graduated with high honors from California State University, Fresno.

Since college, Soto has been writing novels, short stories, and essays in addition to poetry. His first book of poems, *The Elements of San Joaquin,* won the United States Award of the International

1952–

Poetry Forum. In 1985, his collection of autobiographical pieces *Living up the Street* won the American Book Award of the Before Columbus Foundation.

Among young readers, Soto is best known for his short story collections. However, he has also written a one-act play, *Novio Boy*, that is frequently staged in high schools and has produced three films for Spanish-speaking children. Soto currently teaches English and Chicano studies at the University of California, Berkeley.

OTHER WORKS *The Skirt, Local News, The Pool Party, Crazy Weekend, Neighborhood Odes, Baseball in April and Other Stories, A Summer Life, The Tale of Sunlight, Where Sparrows Work Hard, Black Hair*

WRITING ABOUT LITERATURE

FINDING THE MESSAGE

What was *The Million-Pound Bank Note* really about? What made "The Splendid Outcast" splendid? Stories have messages, and uncovering them can help you under-stand and appreciate the stories. To find a story's message, notice the ways the writer emphasizes, or draws attention to, his or her ideas. On the next few pages, you will

- discover how writers emphasize a message
- write an interpretive essay on a story's message
- take a closer look at the messages around you

The Writer's Style: Creating Emphasis Writers emphasize their ideas in several ways—by using place-ment, vivid language, and repetition.

Read the Literature

Notice how these authors create emphasis.

Literature Models

Emphasis Through Placement
An important message may appear at the beginning of a work or at the end, as it does in this example.

Henry. Happy, we two? Indeed yes! And when London got the whole history of my adventure for a month, how it did talk. My Portia's father took the million-pound bank note to the Bank of England, cashed it, had it cancelled; and he gave it to us at our wedding. Framed, it now hangs in our home. It gave me my Portia; but for it I could not have remained in London, would not have appeared at the American ambassador's, never should have met her. And so I always say: Yes, it's a million-pounder, but it made but one purchase in its life and then got the article for only about a tenth part of its value.

Mark Twain, from *The Million-Pound Bank Note*

Emphasis Through Vivid Language
What examples of word choice make this scene vivid? What effect does the language have?

But now, at the climax of the sale, his impatience overflows, his spirit flares like fire, his anger bursts through the circle of men who guard him. Suddenly, there are cries, shouts of warning, the ringing of chains and the cracking of leather, and the crowd leaps to its feet.

Beryl Markham, from "The Splendid Outcast"

Connect to Music

Do you have favorite song lyrics that you know by heart? What is it about them that draws you to them? In the lyrics to a popular song below, the writers use repetition to get across a key idea.

Song Lyrics

I see trees of green, red roses too,
I see them bloom for me and you,
and I think to myself
What a wonderful world.

I see skies of blue and clouds of
    white,
the bright blessed day, the dark
    sacred night,
and I think to myself
What a wonderful world.

> recorded by Louis Armstrong
> from "What a Wonderful World"
> written by George David Weiss
> and Bob Thiele

Emphasis Through Repetition
What words are repeated in this passage? What main idea does the repetition emphasize?

Try Your Hand: Creating Emphasis

1. **Describe a Scene** Write a paragraph describing a scene based on one of these situations: a race, a surprise party, a friend moving away. Emphasize the mood with vivid language.

2. **Write New Lyrics** Use the lyrics for "What a Wonderful World" above as a model. Think of a simple, short message you could repeat as a refrain. Then write song lyrics that emphasize your song's message.

3. **Revise a QuickWrite** Choose one of your QuickWrites or another piece of writing in which you tried to make a point or get across an important idea. Revise the piece, using placement, vivid language, or repetition for emphasis.

Using Interjections

An **interjection** is a word or group of words that can add emphasis to a sentence by expressing a feeling or emotion. An interjection that expresses strong emotion is followed by an exclamation point. One that expresses mild emotion is usually followed by a comma. Notice how this sentence changes when interjections are added.

I'm going to change my vote.

Wow! No way! Well, I'm going to change my vote.

Find the interjections in these lines from *The Million-Pound Bank Note* by Mark Twain. What emotional changes in the character are expressed by the interjections?

Tod. Thank you. (*A complete change. He stutters and fumbles.*) Ah—it's—ah—that is—we—ah—you see—It's— (*quickly*) Take it back, please. (*raising voice*) Mr. Smedley! Mr. Smedley! Help! Oh, Mr. Smedley.

APPLYING WHAT YOU'VE LEARNED
Rewrite these sentences. Use interjections to add emphasis.

1. I'm drowning.
2. I won't help you.
3. Where are you going?
4. I was only joking.

Interpretation

You've studied some of the techniques writers use to create emphasis. Now you can use your knowledge of those techniques to uncover key ideas and meanings in literature.

GUIDED ASSIGNMENT

Interpret a Selection's Meaning For this assignment, you'll choose one selection and look for its message or meaning. You'll write your interpretation of the message and support it with details and examples from the selection.

Student's Prewriting Chart

Scenes from the Selection	My Interpretation or Thoughts
Two men give Henry a million-pound note.	The two men are betting on how people will react to the note.
Restaurant, clothing store, and hotel all give Henry credit.	Henry gets treated better just because he appears rich.
Henry helps Hastings sell his mine.	People trust Henry because he's rich and famous.
Gordon says if Henry had picked up the pear, they wouldn't have trusted him.	Is this a fair judgment?

① Prewrite and Explore

Which selection in this unit did you think about long after you finished reading it? Which led to the most interesting discussions with your friends or classmates? These may be clues as to which story carried the most powerful message for you. Choose a selection you would like to explore more deeply.

EXPLORING THE SELECTION

Reread the selection carefully, taking notes about your questions, your thoughts, and your interpretation of what is happening. You might use a chart like the one here to keep track of your thinking. Consider the following questions as you reread:

- What makes this selection intriguing?
- What parts of the selection are puzzling or unclear?
- What does the author seem to be emphasizing through placement, vivid language, or repetition?

Discuss your impressions and findings with others who chose the same selection. Keep in mind that your interpretation may differ from someone else's. You may need to reread all or parts of the selection to answer questions or to understand someone else's impressions.

❷ Write and Analyze a Discovery Draft

Once you have reread and discussed the selection, write a discovery draft to help sort through your ideas. Explore these questions as you write.

- Which parts of the selection seem to tell me something?
- Which details or events still puzzle me? How important are these puzzling parts?

Student's Discovery Draft

> I wonder if the gentlemen judged Henry fairly when they chose him.

> The gentlemen say they picked Henry because he seemed intelligent and honest. Why did they think so? One of the men says it's because he didn't pick the pear up boldly. But Henry was just about to do that.

> One thing that keeps happening is that Henry gets stuff free when he waves that bank note around. The clothing store salesman is rude to him until he sees the note. Then the store gives him a whole wardrobe for free. Also, the hotel gives him a luxury room, and the restaurant feeds him. Everyone says he shouldn't worry about paying them back.

> Maybe the story's message is something about the way people treat the rich and the poor.

❸ Draft and Share

Remember that the message you discovered may not be the same as someone else's. Look back through your notes for supporting details to use as you write your draft. See the SkillBuilder at the right for help in organizing your essay. Then use these questions to get feedback from other students.

 PEER RESPONSE

- Restate what you think my interpretation is.
- What other details would support my ideas?

SkillBuilder

 WRITER'S CRAFT

Organizing Your Interpretive Essay
A well-organized interpretive essay will make it easy for readers to understand your thinking. Your interpretive essay should include the following sections:

- An introduction that gives the author and title and familiarizes your reader with the selection. You don't need to tell the whole story. Just give a brief summary of the work.
- A body that states your interpretation of the message supported with details from the selection.
- A conclusion that summarizes your interpretation and the reasons for it.

APPLYING WHAT YOU'VE LEARNED
Evaluate your draft against the guidelines above. Make sure you have an introduction, a body, and a conclusion and that your writing is clear and easy to follow.

 WRITING HANDBOOK

For help in writing introductions and conclusions, see pages 826; 834–835 of the Writing Handbook.

4 Revise and Edit

Before revising, reflect on your draft. Have you explained the selection's meaning clearly? Have you supported your ideas with enough details and examples? Use your peer comments and the Standards for Evaluation below as you finalize your draft.

Student's Final Draft

The Million-Pound Bank Note by Mark Twain tells the story of a young broker's clerk named Henry. Henry finds himself in London without money or friends. Two elderly gentlemen bet on whether he can survive a month with nothing but a million-pound bank note. Henry finds out that trying to cash the note would land him in prison. Instead, he uses the note just to make people think he is rich. In this story, Twain shows how the way people treat someone depends on whether the person appears to be rich or poor.

What information makes the essay topic clear? What main point will the essay make?

What evidence supports the statement made in the first sentence of this paragraph?

Henry is treated much differently as a poor man than he is as a rich one. When he enters a clothing store in rags, the clerk speaks to him rudely. "We don't give away suits, even misfits," says the clerk. When Henry displays the million-pound note, the salesmen suddenly fall all over themselves trying to please him. While they wouldn't give away a useless suit to a ragged man, they offer a millionaire a complete wardrobe for nothing.

Standards for Evaluation

An interpretive essay
- has an introduction that gives the author, title, and a brief summary of the selection
- has a logical organization and a clear focus
- summarizes the interpretation in its conclusion
- supports its interpretation with reasons, examples, quotations, or other evidence

Grammar in Context

Subject-Verb Agreement Whenever you interpret literature, you are likely to be discussing several characters and events. As you write, keep in mind the rules of subject-verb agreement. The subject and the verb in a sentence must agree in number. If the subject is singular, the verb should be singular. If the subject is plural, the verb should be plural as well.

> Sir Alfred, as well as many other wealthy men, ~~trust~~ *trusts*
>
> Henry's opinion of the mine because he thinks he is rich.
>
> One of the men ~~invite~~ *invites* his friends to invest. Henry and
>
> Hastings ~~becomes~~ *become* rich.

As in the example above, be careful that the verb agrees with its subject, not with the nearest noun. The verb and its subject may be separated by other words or phrases.

Try Your Hand: Subject-Verb Agreement

Imagine that the following article appeared in the local newspaper. Read the article, and then use a separate sheet of paper to correct any subject-verb agreement problems.

Vest-Pocket Millionaire Takes London by Storm

London's Miss Portia Langham and Henry Adams, better known as the Vest-Pocket Millionaire, is happily married. They met after Miss Langham's stepfather, Gordon Featherstone, and his younger brother, Abel, chose Adams for a now-famous experiment. The elder of the brothers are quick to praise Adams's cleverness. He says that both he and his brother is impressed by the 200,000 pounds Adams raised without ever cashing the million-pound bank note.

Miss Portia Langham, granddaughter of the Cambridge Langhams, agree with her stepfather, Gordon. "My family and I am so proud of Henry," she says.

Using Inverted Sentences

In most sentences, the subject comes before the verb. In sentences with inverted order, the verb comes before the subject. The rules of subject-verb agreement still apply, however. For example:

In the park were two trees.

First, look for the verb. (*were*) Ask yourself who or what goes with the verb. What was in the park? (*two trees*) Then put the sentence in its natural order to check the subject-verb agreement. (*Two trees were in the park.*)

APPLYING WHAT YOU'VE LEARNED
Copy the sentences below in your journal or on a sheet of paper. Be sure the subject and verb in each sentence agree. Then check the subject-verb agreement in your draft.

1. Abel said, "There is several honest men in London."
2. Through Henry's recommendation comes investors for the gold mine.
3. In Portia's lovely hands rest Henry's future.

 GRAMMAR HANDBOOK

For more information on inverted sentences and subject-verb agreement, see pages 863, 866–869 of the Grammar Handbook.

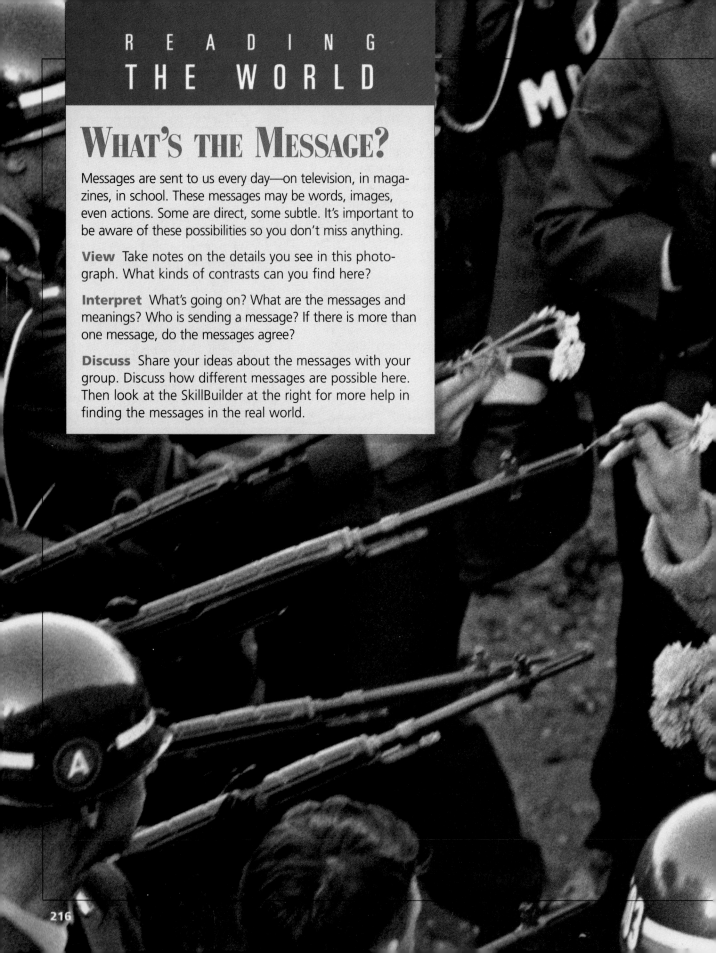

WHAT'S THE MESSAGE?

Messages are sent to us every day—on television, in magazines, in school. These messages may be words, images, even actions. Some are direct, some subtle. It's important to be aware of these possibilities so you don't miss anything.

View Take notes on the details you see in this photograph. What kinds of contrasts can you find here?

Interpret What's going on? What are the messages and meanings? Who is sending a message? If there is more than one message, do the messages agree?

Discuss Share your ideas about the messages with your group. Discuss how different messages are possible here. Then look at the SkillBuilder at the right for more help in finding the messages in the real world.

CRITICAL THINKING

Analyzing for Meaning

When you analyze something, you can begin by identifying separate elements. In this picture, the separate elements include the military police, their guns, the young man in the sweater, the people with him, the flowers, and his gesture of placing a flower in a gun.

Once you've identified what you feel are the most important elements, you can begin to analyze each element for meaning. Start listing words and phrases you associate with each element. For the military police, you might list *combat, uniform, defend,* and so on. When you have a similar list for each element, review each list for meanings and messages. As you look over all your lists, look for an overall meaning or message. You may find that your analysis has led you to new insights.

APPLYING WHAT YOU'VE LEARNED
With a small group, discuss one of the following items.

- Find and discuss an ad that sends both visual and verbal messages. Explain how the messages are alike or different from each other.
- Where else can you use what you've learned here about interpreting messages?

UNEXPECTED DEVELOPMENTS

WHAT DO Y?u THINK?

REFLECTING ON THEME

Life is unpredictable—people are often faced with unexpected developments. Use the activities on this page to help you examine how unexpected developments push human beings to make critical changes in their lives. Keep a record of your impressions, ideas, and results in your notebook.

What would you do?

War demands that people make swift adjustments in their lives. If war broke out, how would you feel? Try to imagine what might go on around you in a war. Present your response in a series of diary entries.

What would you argue?

Strong feelings about a cause can inspire people to make critical changes in their lives. Is there any cause you feel especially enthusiastic about, like saving endangered species or improving the quality of television? Write a newspaper editorial that argues the important points of your case.

Looking Back

At the beginning of this unit, you thought about ways in which people make critical adjustments in their lives. After reading the selections in Part 1, do you have a better sense of the kinds of choices people make when their circumstances change? Recall the characters' twinges of conscience. For each major character in Part 1, think of one word that best describes what troubles his or her conscience.

What if . . .

Life is full of twists and turns. Think back to an important turning point in your life. Imagine how things might have been different if that event had not happened. Design a flow chart like the one at left, showing what really occurred and what might have been.

Born in New Jersey

Early childhood in New York

Actual Path   What-If Path

Move to California   Stay in New York

218

FICTION

A Mother in Mannville
Marjorie Kinnan Rawlings

PERSONAL CONNECTION

The main characters in this story are a lonely orphan boy and a writer who seeks time alone. What do you think is the difference between being lonely and being alone? Using examples from your own life and the lives of people you know, discuss the differences in meaning with your classmates. Use a chart like the one shown to help you organize your thoughts.

Being Lonely	Being Alone

HISTORICAL CONNECTION

This story takes place in the North Carolina mountains, near an orphanage. An orphanage is an institution for the care of children who are alone because their parents have died, have abandoned them, or can no longer care for them. Orphanages for large groups of children were more prevalent in the past than they are today. Nowadays, orphaned children are often cared for by foster families until permanent adoptive families are found. When neither foster nor adoptive parents are available, children are placed in group homes, where small numbers of children are cared for by professionals.

READING CONNECTION

Visualizing You can enjoy a story more when you picture its characters, setting, and events. When you use descriptive details to form a picture in your mind as you read, you are visualizing. "A Mother in Mannville" contains vivid description of the isolated setting. As you read, visualize the details of the surroundings. Think about why the narrator, a writer, might have chosen such a setting in which to work. You might sketch a few of your mental pictures in your notebook.

An orphan boy at a New York mission repairs toys for the young, December, 1948. UPI/Bettmann.

A Mother in Mannville

by Marjorie Kinnan Rawlings

The orphanage is high in the Carolina mountains. Sometimes in winter the snowdrifts are so deep that the institution is cut off from the village below, from all the world. Fog hides the mountain peaks, the snow swirls down the valleys, and a wind blows so bitterly that the orphanage boys who take the milk twice daily to the baby cottage reach the door with fingers stiff in an agony of numbness.

"Or when we carry trays from the cook house for the ones that are sick," Jerry said, "we get our faces frostbit, because we can't put our hands over them. I have gloves," he added. "Some of the boys don't have any."

He liked the late spring, he said. The rhododendron was in bloom, a carpet of color, across the mountainsides, soft as the May winds that stirred the hemlocks. He called it laurel.

"It's pretty when the laurel blooms," he said. "Some of it's pink and some of it's white."

I was there in the autumn. I wanted quiet, isolation, to do some troublesome writing. I wanted mountain air to blow out the malaria from too long a time in the subtropics. I was homesick, too, for the flaming of maples in October, and for corn shocks and pumpkins and black-walnut trees and the lift of hills. I found them all, living in a cabin that belonged to the orphanage, half a mile beyond the orphanage farm. When I took the cabin, I asked for a boy or man to come and chop wood for the fireplace. The first few days were warm, I found what wood I needed about the cabin, no one came, and I forgot the order.

I looked up from my typewriter one late afternoon, a little startled. A boy stood at the door, and my pointer dog, my companion, was at his side and had not barked to warn me. The boy was probably twelve years old, but undersized. He wore overalls and a torn shirt, and was barefooted.

He said, "I can chop some wood today."

I said, "But I have a boy coming from the orphanage."

"I'm the boy."

"You? But you're small."

"Size don't matter, chopping wood," he said. "Some of the big boys don't chop good. I've been chopping wood at the orphanage a long time."

I visualized mangled and inadequate branches for my fires. I was well into my work and not inclined to conversation. I was a little blunt.

"Very well. There's the ax. Go ahead and see what you can do."

I went back to work, closing the door. At first, the sound of the boy dragging brush annoyed me. Then he began to chop. The blows were rhythmic and steady, and shortly I had forgotten him, the sound no more of an interruption than a consistent rain. I suppose an hour and a half passed, for when I stopped and stretched, and heard the boy's steps on the cabin stoop, the sun was dropping behind the farthest mountain, and the valleys were purple with something deeper than the asters.

The boy said, "I have to go to supper now. I can come again tomorrow evening."

I said, "I'll pay you now for what you've done," thinking I should probably have to insist on an older boy. "Ten cents an hour?"

"Anything is all right."

We went together back of the cabin. An astonishing amount of solid wood had been cut. There were cherry logs and heavy roots of rhododendron, and blocks from the waste pine and oak left from the building of the cabin.

"But you've done as much as a man," I said. "This is a splendid pile."

I looked at him, actually, for the first time. His hair was the color of the corn shocks, and his eyes, very direct, were like the mountain sky when rain is pending—gray, with a shadowing of that miraculous blue. As I spoke, a light came over him, as though the setting sun had touched him with the same suffused glory with which it touched the mountains. I gave him a quarter.

"You may come tomorrow," I said, "and thank you very much."

He looked at me, and at the coin, and seemed to want to speak, but could not, and turned away.

"I'll split kindling tomorrow," he said over his thin ragged shoulder. "You'll need kindling and medium wood and logs and backlogs."

At daylight I was half wakened by the sound of chopping. Again it was so even in texture that I went back to sleep. When I left my bed in the cool morning, the boy had come and gone, and a stack of kindling was neat against the cabin wall. He came again after school in the afternoon and worked until time to return to the orphanage. His name was Jerry; he was twelve years old, and he had been at the orphanage since he was four. I could picture him at four, with the same grave gray-blue eyes and the same—independence? No, the word that comes to me is "integrity."

The word means something very special to me, and the quality for which I use it is a rare one. My father had it—there is another of whom I am almost sure—but almost no man of my acquaintance possesses it with the clarity, the purity, the simplicity of a mountain stream. But the boy Jerry had it. It is bedded on courage, but it is more than brave. It is honest, but it is more than honesty. The ax handle broke one day. Jerry said the wood shop at the orphanage would repair it. I brought money to pay for the job, and he refused it.

"I'll pay for it," he said. "I broke it. I brought the ax down careless."

"But no one hits accurately every time," I told him. "The fault was in the wood of the handle. I'll see the man from whom I bought it."

It was only then that he would take the money. He was standing back of his own carelessness. He was a free-will agent, and he

---

WORDS
TO
KNOW

inadequate (ĭn-ăd′ĭ-kwĭt) *adj.* not good enough for what is needed
blunt (blŭnt) *adj.* abrupt; rudely straightforward or honest
kindling (kĭnd′lĭng) *n.* pieces of dry wood or other material that can be easily lighted to start a fire; tinder
clarity (klăr′ĭ-tē) *n.* the quality of being easily seen; clearness

Autumn Leaves (1873), Winslow Homer. Cooper-Hewitt, National Design Museum, Smithsonian Institution/Art Resource, New York.

over the bank. I found that when I tried to return his thoughtfulness with such things as candy and apples, he was wordless. "Thank you" was, perhaps, an expression for which he had had no use, for his courtesy was instinctive. He only looked at the gift and at me, and a curtain lifted, so that I saw deep into the clear well of his eyes, and gratitude was there, and affection, soft over the firm granite of his character.

He made simple excuses to come and sit with me. I could no more have turned him away than if he had been physically hungry. I suggested once that the best time for us to visit was just before supper, when I left off my writing. After that, he waited always until my typewriter had been some time quiet. One day I worked until nearly dark. I went outside the cabin, having forgotten him. I saw him going up over the hill in the twilight toward the orphanage. When I sat down on my stoop, a place was warm from his body where he had been sitting.

He became intimate, of course, with my pointer, Pat. There is a strange communion between a boy and a dog. Perhaps they possess the same singleness of spirit, the same kind of wisdom. It is difficult to explain, but it exists. When I went across the state for a weekend, I left the dog in Jerry's charge. I gave him the dog whistle and the key to the cabin and left sufficient food. He was to come two or three times a day and let out the dog and feed and exercise him. I should return Sunday night, and Jerry would take out the dog for the last time Sunday afternoon and then leave the key under an agreed hiding place.

My return was belated, and fog filled the mountain passes so treacherously that I dared

chose to do careful work, and if he failed, he took the responsibility without subterfuge.[1]

And he did for me the unnecessary thing, the gracious thing, that we find done only by the great of heart. Things no training can teach, for they are done on the instant, with no predicated experience. He found a cubbyhole beside the fireplace that I had not noticed. There, of his own accord, he put kindling and "medium" wood, so that I might always have dry fire material ready in case of sudden wet weather. A stone was loose in the rough walk to the cabin. He dug a deeper hole and steadied it, although he came, himself, by a shortcut

---

1. **subterfuge** (sŭb′tər-fyo͞oj′): anything used to hide one's true purpose or avoid a difficult situation.

WORDS TO KNOW

instinctive (ĭn-stĭngk′tĭv) *adj.* having a natural tendency; spontaneous
communion (kə-myo͞on′yən) *n.* close relationship in which deep feelings are shared; intimacy

222

not drive at night. The fog held the next morning, and it was Monday noon before I reached the cabin. The dog had been fed and cared for that morning. Jerry came early in the afternoon, anxious.

"The superintendent said nobody would drive in the fog," he said. "I came just before bedtime last night and you hadn't come. So I brought Pat some of my breakfast this morning. I wouldn't have let anything happen to him."

"I was sure of that. I didn't worry."

"When I heard about the fog, I thought you'd know."

He was needed for work at the orphanage, and he had to return at once. I gave him a dollar in payment, and he looked at it and went away. But that night he came in the darkness and knocked at the door.

"Come in, Jerry," I said, "if you're allowed to be away this late."

"I told maybe a story," he said. "I told them I thought you would want to see me."

"That's true," I assured him, and I saw his relief. "I want to hear about how you managed with the dog."

He sat by the fire with me, with no other light, and told me of their two days together. The dog lay close to him and found a comfort there that I did not have for him. And it seemed to me that being with my dog, and caring for him, had brought the boy and me, too, together, so that he felt that he belonged to me as well as to the animal.

"He stayed right with me," he told me, "except when he ran in the laurel. He likes the laurel. I took him up over the hill and we both ran fast. There was a place where the grass was high, and I lay down in it and hid. I could hear Pat hunting for me. He found my trail and he barked. When he found me, he acted crazy, and he ran around and around me, in circles."

We watched the flames.

"That's an apple log," he said. "It burns the prettiest of any wood."

We were very close.

He was suddenly <u>impelled</u> to speak of things he had not spoken of before, nor had I cared to ask him.

"You look a little bit like my mother," he said. "Especially in the dark, by the fire."

"But you were only four, Jerry, when you came here. You have remembered how she looked, all these years?"

"My mother lives in Mannville," he said.

For a moment, finding that he had a mother shocked me as greatly as anything in my life has ever done, and I did not know why it disturbed me. Then I understood my distress. I was filled with a passionate resentment that any woman should go away and leave her son. A fresh anger added itself. A son like this one— The orphanage was a wholesome place, the executives were kind, good people, the food was more than adequate, the boys were healthy, a ragged shirt was no hardship, nor the doing of clean labor. Granted, perhaps, that the boy felt no lack, what blood fed the bowels of a woman who did not yearn over this child's lean body that had come in parturition out of her own? At four he would have looked the same as now. Nothing, I thought, nothing in life could change those eyes. His quality must be apparent to an idiot, a fool. I burned with questions I could not ask. In any, I was afraid, there would be pain.

"Have you seen her, Jerry—lately?"

"I see her every summer. She sends for me."

I wanted to cry out, "Why are you not with her? How can she let you go away again?"

He said, "She comes up here from Mannville whenever she can. She doesn't have a job now."

His face shone in the firelight.

"She wanted to give me a puppy, but they can't let any one boy keep a puppy. You remember the suit I had on last Sunday?" He was plainly proud. "She sent me that for Christmas. The Christmas before that"—he drew a long breath, savoring the memory— "she sent me a pair of skates."

"Roller skates?"

My mind was busy, making pictures of her, trying to understand her. She had not, then, entirely deserted or forgotten him. But why, then— I thought, "I must not condemn her without knowing."

"Roller skates. I let the other boys use them. They're always borrowing them. But they're careful of them."

What circumstance other than poverty—

"I'm going to take the dollar you gave me for taking care of Pat," he said, "and buy her a pair of gloves."

I could only say, "That will be nice. Do you know her size?"

"I think it's 8½," he said. He looked at my hands.

"Do you wear 8½?" he asked.

"No. I wear a smaller size, a 6."

"Oh! Then I guess her hands are bigger than yours."

I hated her. Poverty or no, there was other food than bread, and the soul could starve as quickly as the body. He was taking his dollar to buy gloves for her big stupid hands, and she lived away from him, in Mannville, and contented herself with sending him skates.

"She likes white gloves," he said. "Do you think I can get them for a dollar?"

"I think so," I said.

After the Chase (1965), Andrew Wyeth. Wichita (Kansas) Art Museum.

I decided that I should not leave the mountains without seeing her and knowing for myself why she had done this thing.

The human mind scatters its interests as though made of thistledown, and every wind stirs and moves it. I finished my work. It did not please me, and I gave my thoughts to another field. I should need some Mexican material.

I made arrangements to close my Florida place. Mexico immediately, and doing the writing there, if conditions were favorable. Then, Alaska with my brother. After that, heaven knew what or where.

I did not take time to go to Mannville to see Jerry's mother, nor even to talk with the orphanage officials about her. I was a trifle abstracted about the boy, because of my work and plans. And after my first fury at her— we did not speak of her again—his having a mother, any sort at all, not far away, in Mannville, relieved me of the ache I had had about him. He did not question the anomalous[2] relation. He was not lonely. It was none of my concern.

He came every day and cut my wood and did small helpful favors and stayed to talk. The days had become cold, and often I let him come inside the cabin. He would lie on the floor in front of the fire, with one arm across

---

2. **anomalous** (ə-nŏm′ə-ləs): differing from the general rule; abnormal.

the pointer, and they would both doze and wait quietly for me. Other days they ran with a common ecstasy through the laurel, and since the asters were now gone, he brought me back vermilion maple leaves, and chestnut boughs dripping with imperial yellow. I was ready to go.

I said to him, "You have been my good friend, Jerry. I shall often think of you and miss you. Pat will miss you too. I am leaving tomorrow."

He did not answer. When he went away, I remember that a new moon hung over the mountains, and I watched him go in silence up the hill. I expected him the next day, but he did not come. The details of packing my personal belongings, loading my car, arranging the bed over the seat, where the dog would ride, occupied me until late in the day. I closed the cabin and started the car, noticing that the sun was in the west and I should do well to be out of the mountains by nightfall. I stopped by the orphanage and left the cabin key and money for my light bill with Miss Clark.

"And will you call Jerry for me to say goodbye to him?"

"I don't know where he is," she said. "I'm afraid he's not well. He didn't eat his dinner this noon. One of the other boys saw him going over the hill into the laurel. He was supposed to fire the boiler this afternoon. It's not like him; he's unusually reliable."

I was almost relieved, for I knew I should never see him again, and it would be easier not to say goodbye to him.

I said, "I wanted to talk with you about his mother—why he's here—but I'm in more of a hurry than I expected to be. It's out of the question for me to see her now too. But here's some money I'd like to leave with you to buy things for him at Christmas and on his birthday. It will be better than for me to try to send him things. I could so easily duplicate— skates, for instance."

She blinked her honest spinster's eyes.

"There's not much use for skates here," she said.

Her stupidity annoyed me.

"What I mean," I said, "is that I don't want to duplicate things his mother sends him. I might have chosen skates if I didn't know she had already given them to him."

She stared at me.

"I don't understand," she said. "He has no mother. He has no skates." ❖

The World Is Not a Pleasant Place to Be
by Nikki Giovanni

the world is not a pleasant place
to be without
someone to hold and be held by

a river would stop
its flow if only
a stream were there
to receive it

an ocean would never laugh
if clouds weren't there
to kiss her tears

the world is not
a pleasant place to be without
someone

WORDS TO KNOW   **ecstasy** (ĕk′stə-sē) *n.* intense joy or delight; bliss

RESPONDING
OPTIONS

FROM **PERSONAL RESPONSE** TO **CRITICAL ANALYSIS**

REFLECT
1. What was your reaction to learning the truth behind Jerry's story?

RETHINK
2. In your opinion, why does Jerry make up the story about his mother?

3. Why do you think the narrator believes Jerry?

4. The narrator and Jerry seem to have very different needs. How do their needs differ? Explain.

   Consider
   - Jerry's life in an orphanage
   - Jerry's response to the narrator and her dog
   - why the narrator comes to the cabin and then leaves
   - what the narrator says about Jerry

RELATE
5. Which character, the narrator or Jerry, might agree more with the view expressed in the poem "The World Is Not a Pleasant Place to Be"? Does the poem relate more to being lonely or to being alone?

ANOTHER PATHWAY

Cooperative Learning

In a small group, discuss what the narrator means by *integrity* as she defines it on page 221. Then decide if either Jerry or the narrator behaves with integrity.

QUICKWRITES

1. Use clues in the story to compose a **personal ad** Jerry might write to find a new mother.

2. Write an **epilogue,** or closing section, for the story that tells what the narrator says and does after she learns that Jerry has no mother.

3. Write a **poem** Jerry might send to the narrator as a memento of their friendship.

   📁 *PORTFOLIO Save your writing. You may want to use it later as a springboard to a piece for your portfolio.*

LITERARY CONCEPTS

The plot of a story almost always revolves around a **conflict** between opposing forces. An **external conflict** involves a character's struggle against an outside person or force. An **internal conflict** occurs when a struggle is within a character. In the story, Jerry struggles internally with the loneliness he feels. What is the narrator's internal conflict? Are these conflicts ever resolved?

CONCEPT REVIEW: Setting In Rawlings's story, what role does the setting play in bringing the narrator to the cabin? How does the setting affect the narrator's general view of Jerry?

ALTERNATIVE ACTIVITIES

1. A montage is an image created from a series of overlapping pictures. Use pictures and drawings to create a **montage** that suggests the mood of the story's setting.

2. With a partner, practice playing the role of Jerry and then record each other for a **videotape** that an adoption agency might show to adoptive parents.

WORDS TO KNOW

EXERCISE A On your paper, write the letter of the word that is closest in meaning to the boldfaced Word to Know.

1. It appears that the attention the narrator paid Jerry was **inadequate.**
   a. insufficient   b. unhappy   c. effective
   d. forceful

2. The narrator was **impelled** to seek isolation.
   a. moved   b. uninspired   c. driven
   d. expected

3. Jerry did not notice the **blunt** way she spoke.
   a. delicate   b. short   c. curious   d. abrupt

4. The dog's bonding was **instinctive**.
   a. intentional   b. abnormal   c. natural
   d. healthy

5. The narrator saw the scenery with more **clarity** than she saw Jerry.
   a. intelligence   b. integrity   c. clearness
   d. understanding

EXERCISE B Draw a picture to portray the meaning of each Word to Know listed below.

kindling   clarity   communion   ecstasy   impel

MARJORIE KINNAN RAWLINGS

A boy whom Marjorie Kinnan Rawlings met in North Carolina was the model for Jerry in "A Mother in Mannville." This story and others she wrote about farmers, trappers, and fishermen were collected in a book titled *When the Whippoorwill—*.

As a child growing up in Washington, D.C., Rawlings entertained neighborhood children with stories, and at age 11 she won her first award for writing. After graduating from the University of Wisconsin, Rawlings

1896–1953

worked as a newspaper reporter in Kentucky and New York while writing stories at night.

Like the narrator in "A Mother in Mannville," Rawlings eventually felt the need for a quiet place in which to write.

Rawlings is considered one of America's outstanding regional writers, one who carefully portrays nature, dialect, and local culture. Her most famous novel, *The Yearling,* won a Pulitzer Prize in 1939.

OTHER WORKS *Mountain Prelude, Cross Creek*

FICTION

White Mice
Rubén Sálaz-Márquez

PERSONAL CONNECTION

Most of us have ancestors who were born in another country. From them, we have inherited customs, recipes, and treasured possessions that reflect our cultural heritage. Choose something that your family inherited from your ancestors and describe it in your notebook. Explain what that item or custom represents in your ethnic background.

LANGUAGE ARTS CONNECTION

The Hispanic children in this story are part of a bilingual education program in a U.S. school. They learn their school subjects partly in English and partly in Spanish, their native language.

Learning a second language is not easy. A common mistake that bilingual students tend to make is code switching—that is, combining their native language with English within a single phrase or sentence. For example, a Hispanic child might say *red corazón* instead of *corazón de roja* for "red heart."

READING CONNECTION

Predicting Using what you already know from a story to guess what will happen later is called predicting. Sometimes your prediction will be correct; sometimes what happens will be unexpected. Regardless of the actual outcome, predicting keeps you involved in the story.

You already know that cultural heritage plays a role in this story. As you read, look for clues that help you predict what may happen as the story progresses. As you make a prediction, jot it down in your notebook. Then read on to see what actually happens.

WHITE MICE

by Rubén Sálaz-Márquez

Mrs. Teubbes thrust her key into the knob, unlocked the door and swung it open. Her great bulk reacted against bending over to engage the stopper, but the motion was completed without undue strain for a woman her size. The classroom was pleasantly quiet as she walked to her desk and set down the papers she had graded last night. She pulled out another key, the smaller one for her desk drawer, unlocked it and deposited her purse within, shoved it shut and locked it once more. She glanced at the clock. Kids would start coming in after a spell. She sat at her desk and relaxed, as everything was ready for the coming day. *Two more days before Christmas vacation,* she thought. She would weather the storm of student anticipation. She was confident, and all she needed now was the students. Tomorrow she would meet some of the parents for the cultural day her aide, Mrs. Archunde, had set up. Now there was a gem. If Archunde had a college education, she would be a top teacher . . . *too,* she added quietly in her mind. These Hispanics, or Latins or Chicanos or whatever they were going by these days, had as much talent as anybody; they just didn't, well, apply themselves at the proper time or in gainful ways. There were exceptions, of course, nothing being one hundred percent, but Mrs. Archunde could be excellently qualified with a degree. Teubbes wondered why she didn't go to college now, for it was never too late. It wasn't that she couldn't speak English. She knew both languages and used them well. At least Teubbes thought

Archunde used Spanish well because she taught the Spanish component for all fourth graders in the school.

Thus far Mrs. Teubbes was enjoying the bilingual component, something new for her classroom, and she was picking up the language right along with the kids. Of course, the students already had a background in it, but the teachers could learn too. If the component would help the kids learn English better, then Teubbes was in favor of it. She had even attended the entire bilingual conference last month in an

Pleased with Herself (1989), Marjorie McDonald. Stevenson's Gallery, Corvallis, Oregon.

effort to learn firsthand how to combat code switching and maybe even cultural switching,[1] both of which her students were prone to. Her ardor cooled somewhat when she saw the conference was just a lark for a number of the participants. Some of them must have spent all their time at the lounge, for they weren't seen at any of the presentations. And she had seen some of them getting rather chummy. Well, no matter. You get out what you put in. But the real tragedy was that the *bilingual* conference had been conducted totally in English. Yes, after a few *Buenos días's* and such,

not a word was spoken in Spanish. Kathy Teubbes had gone prepared to make a herculean[2] effort to catch what would be said, but precious little turned up in Spanish. She still hadn't decided if she was relieved or disappointed, for it was her nature to take up new challenges, whether she conquered all of them or not. *After all, nobody's perfect.* But now she was quite certain the bilingual program was soft government money[3] being put to use until it ran out. If the language wasn't going to be used all through life, including bilingual conferences, it was just as well to teach the children English and forget about Spanish in school except as a transitional tool. If these were the facts of life, and the English bilingual conference proved they were, she didn't feel bad that she had never picked up much Spanish over the years. If Hispanic adults and intellectual leaders didn't use the language in conferences

---

1. **cultural switching:** changing back and forth between two sets of cultural beliefs as one thinks and acts.
2. **herculean** (hûr′kyə-lē′ən): of exceptional strength.
3. **soft government money:** government funds that are not budgeted for a specific purpose.

WORDS TO KNOW

component (kəm-pō′nənt) *n.* one part of a whole unit or system
prone (prōn) *adj.* having a tendency toward; inclined
ardor (är′dər) *n.* strong enthusiasm
transitional (trăn-zĭsh′ə-nəl) *adj.* passing from one state or stage to another

and whatever, they themselves were admitting Spanish isn't necessary in the good old U.S.A. *Why waste taxpayers' money?* Besides, mixing the two languages often trapped students in hilariously embarrassing code and cultural switching.

"Good morning, Mrs. Teubbes," said Ricardo as he bounced into the room.

"Good morning, Richard," replied the teacher as she came out of her reverie. Oh, that little imp had more energy than anyone, but the only thing he could do right was say good morning when he charged in ahead of everyone else. "Are you ready for another day of learning?"

Ricardo didn't answer. Instead he sat at his desk and looked intently at his teacher.

"Well?" she said.

"Two more days of school," he said, "and tomorrow is our cultural day, huh?"

"Yes, and I'm looking forward to it. We've never done that in this room."

"You like to eat, huh?" observed Ricardo as other students began to fill the room. That impish look was in his eyes, as usual. "I'll bring something good!"

"You like Mexican food?" asked Becky.

"Of course," said Mrs. Teubbes. "Now why don't you review your vocabulary words?" What children! Ah well, at least Richard wasn't vicious. *Of course, none of the children are,* she thought as they trooped into the room. She felt most of them had very good manners, actually, and were quite nice. They were followers more than leaders, but then followers were important too. She wished very sincerely these students were more interested in schoolwork, for the sake of their future.

"Good morning Mrs. Teubbes!" rang out a happy, feminine voice.

Well, good morning, America!" returned the teacher. Now there was a jewel if there ever was one. That Martinez girl was in a class by herself as far as Kathy Teubbes was concerned. Indeed, it could almost be said the teacher was in awe of America Martinez. She <u>scrutinized</u> the girl as she went over to the cages of gerbils and white mice even before putting down her books. How she loved those little animals! And when there were some to give away, America was sure to take them. The teacher often wondered what she did with them. They couldn't be made into hamburger. Teubbes had worked with such critters for several years, but down deep she had a revulsion for rodents as a species, and even the thought of "hamburger mice" almost turned her stomach. She wondered how the Martinez family could put up with them at home.

"Everybody made it through the night," said America as she went to her desk.

Mrs. Teubbes smiled at the girl. If the teacher were ever to adopt one of her students, it would be America Martinez. Not that she was underprivileged or anything like that, of course. She was always clean, well dressed, polite. Her skin was a bit on the olive side, but her jet black hair and pearly teeth went well with her complexion. But what impressed Teubbes the most was America's determined spirit. When she didn't understand something, she'd march right up to the teacher's desk and get help. And if she didn't get it right the next time, she'd come right back with another thoughtful question. She was good at language and had to work harder on her math, but she was usually equal to the task. Teubbes remembered once when she had been outside on recess duty, a couple of little nasties thought they were going to <u>intimidate</u> America. The two had each grabbed an arm,

231

but America broke loose, made a fist and whacked each one on the nose, causing them to bleed profusely. Later in the principal's office America was a picture of confidence and contentment. Lord! Most fourth graders would have been quaking in their little shoes.

"What would you do in my place?" the principal had asked.

"I'd send you back to class," America had replied matter-of-factly.

"What if those girls jump you again?"

"I'll bloody their noses again."

Heavens! Mrs. Teubbes now began to consider something she had been unable to define before. Something, perhaps bordering on the ineffable, *bothered* her about America. Was it the child's name? How could any parents name their daughter *America*? That was rather sacrilegious, wasn't it? She had heard children teasing "Miss America!" and "God Bless America!" on the playground. It never seemed to bother the little girl. Or maybe that's what disturbed Mrs. Teubbes: *nothing* seemed to bother America, such was her confidence and aplomb. Why, she could put many an eighteen-year-old to the blush. Somehow it just wasn't fair that a mere child, of a minority at that—

"*Buenos días, Señora Teubbes,*" repeated Mrs. Archunde.

"Oh, yes, *buenos días*, Magdalena. How are you today?"

"Fine, thank you. You seem to have been lost in thought."

"Not lost, just thinking. I'm looking forward to the cultural day tomorrow." Teubbes looked up at the wall clock just as the bell rang for classes to begin.

"You'll enjoy it," assured Archunde, "and unless I miss my guess, a number of parents will be here."

"Will America's be here, do you know?"

"We can ask her."

"Yes, of course," said Teubbes. "All right children, let's take out your mathematics workbooks." There was an audible groan from the class. "Come on, borrowing is not hard, and you have to learn it. How many of you worked on it at home and had your parents help you?" A couple of hands went up, including America's. "And what did your parents have to say about borrowing, America?"

"My Dad said it was what you did after you found a cosigner,"[4] replied the girl. Mrs. Archunde chuckled.

"Oh, I see," continued Mrs. Teubbes, "but that's not the kind of borrowing we mean, of course. Well, let's get busy. Richard, stay in your seat. Mrs. Archunde and I will walk around, then you come to the desk when you need help."

The students fell to working quickly, for Mrs. Teubbes believed in discipline and no one was allowed to clown it up. After a vigilant walk around the room, the teacher and her aide sat at their respective desks and tutored one-on-one. Mrs. Teubbes saw America look up with confusion wrinkled into her pretty face. "Come on up if you need help." The girl did. "Yes, dear?"

"Mrs. Teubbes, can you borrow from the dollar sign?"

Now it was the teacher who broke out

---

4. **cosigner:** a person who signs a loan along with another person, thus becoming responsible for the debt if the first signer fails to pay back the money.

laughing, everyone stopping what he or she had been doing and staring. "No, dear," said a chuckling Mrs. Teubbes. "The dollar sign just informs us we are dealing with dollars and cents. You can't borrow from it. Now let's take a look at your paper . . ." The problem was discovered and explained away.

After mathematics Mrs. Archunde drilled the class on vocabulary in both English and Spanish. She reviewed the old words and carefully introduced the new. ". . . and what do you buy when you go to the movies?"

"POPCORN!"

"Isn't it beautiful, children, to be able to use two languages?"

"And how do you say that in Spanish?"

"*Maíz,*"[5] said Caroline.

"Yes," encouraged Archunde, "that's part of it. Anybody know the rest?" No one did, so she told them: "*Palomitas de maíz.*"[6]

"Pigeon corn?" asked Martin.

"Yes," encouraged Archunde further, "and can anybody tell me why they call it that in Mexico?" She could tell the kids were trying hard to figure out the riddle, but no hands were up. "Now let's imagine as we think . . . the corn pops up and flies into the air, almost like little . . . white . . . pigeons."

"Ooooh!" chorused the class, impressed with the imagery.

"Yes, now let's review our vegetables quickly," said Archunde as she pointed to a chart on the wall. "Besides *maíz,* what do we have?"

"Cowcumbers!" said Martin.

Mrs. Teubbes almost interrupted to correct the code switching mistake which so many students were prone to make.

"Cucumbers," said Mrs. Archunde.

"My grandfather's are big!" explained Martin. Then to Mrs. Teubbes: "Remember those he sent you?"

"Yes, Martin." His grandfather, Mr. De La O, had sent her some very large cucumbers in September.

"He's coming tomorrow."

"Fine," said Archunde, "now let's get back to work." When all the vegetables were mentioned in English, they were reviewed in Spanish with equal gusto. "Isn't it beautiful, children, to be able to use two languages? Each one of you is worth two people if you learn both languages. Your lives will be that much richer. Now I want to teach you three new words. Maybe some of you know them; we'll see. What do you call a person who knows three languages?"

The children concentrated but couldn't come up with an answer.

"Trilingual," said Archunde, then she had everyone repeat it several times. She wrote it on the board and underlined the prefix. "Remember, *tri-* means 'three,' 'three.'" Most of the students wrote it down.

"Now who can tell me the word for a person who speaks *two* languages? You should know that one, children." But no one came up with it. "Bilingual!" said Archunde, then she repeated the procedure as before. "And don't forget: *bi-* means 'two.' Yes, I don't have to tell you to put it in your notebooks. Don't forget it over the Christmas vacation." Mrs. Teubbes walked up and down the rows verifying the notebook work.

---

5. *maíz* (mä-ēs′) *Spanish.*

6. *palomitas de maíz* (päl-ô-mē′täs dĕ mä-ēs′) *Spanish.*

"Now," said Archunde, "what is the word for a person who speaks just one language?" One hand instantly went up in the air. "America?"

"Gringo!" said the girl.

Archunde burst out laughing, but she controlled it quickly. "No, not quite," said the aide, who trembled mirthfully as she used to do as a young girl when she got the giggles in church. "The word I was looking for is *monolingual. Mono-* means 'one,' 'one,'" she said as she wrote it on the board.

Ricardo's hand went up. "Mrs. Archunde, what's gringo?" he asked mischievously.

Archunde felt like hitting him with a "cowcumber." She was momentarily at a loss for words.

"*Gringo,*" said Mrs. Teubbes, "is a word used to describe someone who is of American-English descent. It is not the nicest word to use."

"My grandmother uses it all the time and she's nice," said Ricardo.

"It depends on how you use it, how you say it," volunteered Archunde. "Technically it comes from the Spanish word *griego,*[7] which means 'Greek.' *Gringo* just means 'foreigner.' Now let's get back to our lesson so we can finish the details for the cultural day."

Other vocabulary words were introduced, written down, and drilled. When that was done, the aide reinforced the cultural unit from three days before. "All right, now let's see who can lead the class in a little Christmas carol. Who wants to do it?"

"In English or Spanish?" asked a student.

"Well, let me see, how should I do it?"

"I know," said Martin, "eenie, meenie, minie, moe."

"I like the way you taught it to us in Spanish," said America.

"All right, go ahead," encouraged the aide.

America got up from her desk and turned to face the class. She pointed to a different student with each syllable she uttered: "*Tela mela, teplatí, como sal que es para ti!*[8] Becky is it!" She sat down again.

Becky put on a <u>persevering</u> face, shrugged her shoulders a bit, and went up in front of the class. "But which one shall we sing?" she asked in mild protestation. Other students called out a number of carols.

"You pick it, dear," said Mrs. Archunde.

"Well, let's do 'Alarrú,' but you all have to sing!"

The class was enthusiastic as Archunde picked up her guitar and everyone joined voices with the Christmas lullaby:

No temas a Herodes
Que nada te ha de hacer;
Duérmete, Niño lindo,
No tienes que temer.

Alarrú, alamé,
Alarrú, alamé, mi Señor.[9]

The class finished the carol; contentment was expressed on the children's faces. They felt good about themselves, a sentiment the two professionals had labored strenuously to achieve.

"That was beautiful, children!" said Mrs. Teubbes. "I could listen to you all day. But let's take some time to review who is going to bring

---

7. *griego* (grē-ĕ′gô) *Spanish.*

8. *Tela mela, teplatí, como sal que es para ti!* (tĕ′lä mĕ′lä tĕ-plä-tē′ kô′mô säl kĕ ĕs pä′rä tē): a Spanish counting-out rhyme, similar to "One potato, two potato . . ."

9. *No temas . . . mi Señor Spanish:* Have no fear of Herod/Who has nothing to do with you;/Fall asleep, beautiful boy,/You have nothing to fear./Lullaby, lullay,/Lullaby, lullay, my Lord.

234

Empanadas [Turnovers] (1991), Carmen Lomas Garza. Gouache painting, 20" × 28". Collection of Romeo Montalvo, Brownsville, Texas. Copyright © 1991 Carmen Lomas Garza. Photo by Judy Reed.

what for tomorrow. I am so excited about our cultural day!" Quickly she wrote the students' names on the board, then gave the chalk to Mrs. Archunde to jot down the names of the foods, since she was more familiar with the spelling. When the task was completed, Mrs. Teubbes said, "Children, I'm looking forward to seeing your parents tomorrow, those who can come, and everything sounds so good I'm not even going to eat breakfast at home."

"That's okay; I'll bring you some *atole*,"[10] said Ricardo.

"Wonderful, Richard," Mrs. Teubbes sighed. One never knew what that boy was going to say.

"I'm a wonderful boy," admitted Ricardo as the bell sounded for recess. "I can hardly wait for tomorrow!"

---

10. *atole* (ä-tô′lĕ) *Spanish:* a Mexican drink made of cornmeal.

The following day no one realized how memorable the cultural day would be as the students got to class earlier than usual because of the food they brought. By the time the final bell rang to start the day, the food table was covered with all sorts of aromatic steaming crockpots, ovenware, and gaily painted dishes, which lent even more personality to the foods with which Mrs. Teubbes was becoming acquainted. Indeed, this experience would do a tremendous job of broadening her cultural perspectives, as well as her palate.

"Oh-oh, if it's no good, they'll throw us out for sure."

The children were remarkably well-behaved, especially with so much temptation at hand. Archunde put on a tape of Spanish-language Christmas carols to start the festivities. A choir of angels couldn't sound more heavenly, thought Mrs. Teubbes. She was glad she was able to make a contribution, for she had taken the time to go out and purchase the tape by José Feliciano, and afterward she would play it for everyone and maybe even lead them in his *"Feliz Navidad!"*[11]

Mrs. Teubbes saw Martin's grandfather, Mr. De La O, entering the room. Immediately she went to thank him for his gift from back in September. "I'm so glad you could come, Mr. De La Zero," she blurted as she shook the man's hand. "I wanted to express in person how much my family and I appreciated your thoughtfulness."

"Thank you, *señora,*" said the old gentleman, warmly receptive to the woman's intent. "I'm glad you enjoyed our little gift."

"We have a chair for you right over here," she said as she led him across the room.

Mrs. Archunde was mixing with everyone, but she went to America and her father when they walked into the room.

"I hope you won't throw us out for being fashionably late," said the man to Mrs. Archunde.

"Of course not," she replied.

"I brought the *pozole,*"[12] chirped America. "We even grew the corn that's in it."

"Oh-oh, if it's no good, they'll throw us out for sure," said the father, making Archunde smile. Little wonder America had such a sense of humor. "I'll put it right over here," he said as he placed the large pot on the last remaining space on the table.

"We were saving it for you," said Archunde.

"I guess we're ready to start," said Mrs. Teubbes. "Children, you all make a line on that side of the table, with your parents, and Mrs. Archunde and I will serve from this side if you need help." A second invitation was unnecessary, but everyone cooperated in an orderly fashion.

Mrs. Teubbes had not eaten breakfast, usually a very large meal for her, so she was quite hungry to begin with; and as she helped serve the different dishes, her mouth literally watered in expectation. She controlled herself by making pleasant comments on how good everything looked, but she could hardly wait to begin her own meal.

"Is this porridge or cement?" asked Denise as she looked at a white crockpot full of light blue *atole.*

---

11. *"Feliz Navidad!"* (fĕ-lēs′ nä-vē-däd′): the title of a popular song, from the Spanish for "Merry Christmas."

12. *pozole* (pô-sô′lĕ) *Spanish:* a Mexican stew.

palate (păl′ĭt) *n.* sense of taste

The people talked, music played, and when everyone had been through the line once, the two teachers finally served themselves. Mrs. Teubbes was not shy about sampling a little of everything, starting with the items familiar to her, devouring them in as dainty a fashion as possible. Then she began with the unfamiliar dishes, and this is where she got herself into a bit of difficulty. A *relleno*[13] had some hot chili in it, and the unsuspecting woman had to make a quick exit to the drinking fountain for some cold water. Undaunted, she returned to the food table and continued her adventures amid the happiness and jovial spirit which everyone shared. The good food, beautiful music, and happy people enriched the holiday season as nothing else could.

"Mrs. Teubbes, have you tasted my *pozole* yet?" asked America of her teacher.

"Your what?"

"This dish over here," said the girl, "the *pozole.*"

"No, dear," admitted Mrs. Teubbes, "but hand me a bowl and it will be next. I've never had such delicious food in my life!"

"Really?" said the smiling girl.

"Can you imagine that?" continued Mrs. Teubbes. "Of course, I grew up in a different part of the country. But they couldn't drag me away now." She took the bowl America handed to her and filled it generously. "Hmm, smells delicious." She was ever so slightly wary because of the chili relleno, but the woman was unable to discover anything potentially deleterious to her palate as she tasted a little. "Hmm, it's good." She looked at America, put a hand on her shoulder momentarily, and said, "You know, my dear, I've been wondering something for a long time . . . I mean, I have a question for you." She continued to eat the tasty *pozole.*

"I have always wondered, what do you do with all those little rodents you take home?"

"We put them to good use; we don't waste anything," replied America as she smiled.

"Heavens, this has such flavor!" said Mrs. Teubbes as she ate the *pozole.* "Quite unlike anything I've ever eaten. What do you call it again?"

After America told her, Mrs. Teubbes waxed rather poetic and said happily, "One thing is certain: this taste is not a waste! What is this that gives it such flavor?"

America couldn't see the bits of white pork meat the teacher was moving about with her spoon, so she assumed Mrs. Teubbes was referring to the white corn, for to her that was the best part of the *pozole.*

"Oh, *that's* the white *maíz!*" replied America.

Mrs. Teubbes's eyes opened wide as saucers, and an expression of terror swept into her face as she blurted: "WHITE MICE?!" She dropped the leprous bowl of *pozole,* clamped a hand over her mouth, and raced out of the room. ❖

---

13. *relleno* (rĕ-yĕ′nô) *Spanish:* stuffing; commonly refers to a chile relleno, or stuffed pepper.

RESPONDING
O P T I O N S

FROM PERSONAL RESPONSE *TO* CRITICAL ANALYSIS

REFLECT **1.** What was your reaction to the unexpected development on the cultural day? Did you predict what happened? Jot down your answer in your notebook and share it with a partner.

RETHINK **2.** What are the causes of the incident at the end of the story?
Consider
- Mrs. Teubbes's knowledge of Spanish
- America's knowledge of English
- Mrs. Teubbes's attitude toward Hispanics

3. A **stereotype** is an oversimplified mental picture of a person, a group, or an institution. How does Mrs. Teubbes stereotype Hispanics?

4. How do you think Mrs. Archunde and the students feel about Mrs. Teubbes as a teacher? Would you like Mrs. Teubbes for a teacher? Why or why not?

RELATE **5.** People have different opinions about the value of bilingual education. What do you think are the benefits and the drawbacks of this approach?

ANOTHER PATHWAY
Cooperative Learning
What do you think will happen when Mrs. Teubbes returns to the classroom? What might she say and do? What might the others say and do? With a group of classmates, dramatize the scene that might take place.

QUICKWRITES

1. How do you think America would have described her encounter with Mrs. Teubbes at the cultural day celebration? Rewrite this **incident** from America's point of view.

2. Imagine that you are a visitor to a foreign country. You have been handed a bowl of steaming hot food that, to you, is rather strange looking. Write a **narrative** that tells what you do next.

📁 *PORTFOLIO Save your writing. You may want to use it later as a springboard to a piece for your portfolio.*

LITERARY CONCEPTS

An unexpected twist in the plot at the end of a story can provide a **surprise ending.** For a surprise ending to be effective, it must be based on facts and clues provided earlier in the story. Find at least two facts or clues that lead up to the surprise ending in this story.

CONCEPT REVIEW: Theme The theme of a story is the message about life that the writer wants to share with the reader. What do you think is the theme of "White Mice"?

LITERARY LINKS

Compare and contrast Mrs. Teubbes in "White Mice" with Miss Bindle in "The Clown." Who do you think is the better teacher? Explain.

ALTERNATIVE ACTIVITIES

Prepare a homemade food that represents your ethnic background, and bring it to class for your classmates to sample. Tell them the name of the food, its ingredients, and the country it comes from.

Thai Chicken with Cellophane Noodles

6 ounces Thai noodles

1 pound chicken

2 tbsp. vegetable oil

1 cup sliced carrots

4 serrano chilis

2 cups chopped cabbage

1 cup sliced celery

3 green onions

1/3 cup soy sauce

2 tsp. grated lime peel

WORDS TO KNOW

Review the Words to Know at the bottom of the selection pages. Then, on your paper, revise each sentence by substituting a Word to Know for each boldfaced word or phrase.

1. Mrs. Teubbes showed an **enthusiasm** for pleasing her **taste buds.**

2. Mrs. Teubbes was **inclined** to show **great enjoyment** when eating.

3. She was **watchful** toward the children and **carefully studied** their every move.

4. Mrs. Teubbes's **determined** attitude could **frighten** the more timid students.

5. Mrs. Archunde had no doubts about the **part** of the curriculum that was meant to be an **intermediate** step from Spanish-speaking to English-speaking.

RUBÉN SÁLAZ-MÁRQUEZ

Rubén Sálaz-Márquez says that his inspiration for "White Mice" came from an anecdote he once heard: "A woman told me that her daughter had been asked to name her favorite food and the little girl answered, 'At my house, we like white maiz best of all.' The surprised questioner wanted to know how they cooked the mice—and whether they ate gray mice too!"

In addition to teaching for more than 20 years,

1935–

Sálaz-Márquez has written several books, including *Cosmic: The La Raza Sketchbook* and *Heartland: Stories of the Southwest.*

A lifelong resident of New Mexico, Sálaz-Márquez enjoys his home state's unique blend of Native American, Hispanic, and European-American cultures. "Living in New Mexico is a tremendous experience," he says, "because we have a long history of getting along without racial hatred."

PREVIEWING

The Bet
Anton Chekhov

PERSONAL CONNECTION

Whether to condemn a murderer to death or to life in prison is a question that has plagued societies for a long time. With your classmates, discuss arguments you have heard for and against capital punishment, or the death penalty. Use a chart like the one shown to organize your thoughts.

Capital Punishment	
Arguments For	**Arguments Against**

HISTORICAL CONNECTION

This story is about a bet made on the issue of capital punishment. Just as this issue is hotly debated in our country today, so was it a controversial issue in Russia in the late 1800s. At that time, Russia was going through a period of tremendous change. Peasants, artists, writers, and others were pressuring the czar, Nicholas II, to free the peasants from forced labor and military service, unfair taxes, and unjust treatment in courts. Among the leaders of this reform movement were the popular writers Leo Tolstoy, Maxim Gorky, and Anton Chekhov. As you read Chekhov's story, see if you can figure out where he stands on the issue of capital punishment.

Czar Nicholas II. UPI/Bettmann.

LASERLINKS
• HISTORICAL CONNECTION

Cause and Effect

Imagine that you are at a football game. Your team is only one yard away from the winning touchdown. The teams line up for the final play, and your fullback dives through the line and scores. Overjoyed fans run onto the field, cheering wildly.

Cause		Effect
touchdown is scored	→	fans run onto the field and cheer

In this situation, the touchdown is the reason why the fans run onto the field. In other words, the touchdown is the cause. The fans' running onto the field is the effect. A cause happens first in time; what follows is the effect.

Events in stories have a similar cause-and-effect relationship. However, in a story, an effect is not always described after its cause. The effect might be presented first, and you read on to discover the cause. Furthermore, an event might have multiple causes or multiple effects. Notice the several causes and one effect in the passage shown on the right:

To recognize causes and effects in all your reading, look for ways that events are connected. Mentally keep track of the order of events. The cause must precede the effect, even if you learn about them in a different order. Be aware, too, that an effect can become the cause of another effect. In addition, look for key words, such as *because, since,* and *therefore,* that point out cause-and-effect relationships.

As you read "The Bet," jot down causes and effects in a chart like the one below. For example, the bet is an effect; what is its cause?

You learn the **effect** first.

An unspeakable dread filled the heart of the murderer. His weapon had been badly damaged, and he had lost all contact with his accomplices. He felt cut off and isolated.

As you continue to read, several **causes** become apparent.

Cause		Effect
	→	A bet is made.

THE BET

by Anton Chekhov

It was a dark autumn night. The old banker was pacing from corner to corner of his study, recalling to his mind the party he gave in the autumn fifteen years ago. There were many clever people at the party and much interesting conversation. They talked among other things of capital punishment. The guests, among them not a few scholars and journalists, for the most part disapproved of capital punishment.

Portrait of Henri Matisse (1905), André Derain. Tate Gallery, London/Art Resource, New York. Copyright © 1996 Artists Rights Society (ARS), New York/ADAGP, Paris.

They found it obsolete as a means of punishment, unfitted to a Christian state and immoral. Some of them thought that capital punishment should be replaced universally by life imprisonment.

"I don't agree with you," said the host. "I myself have experienced neither capital punishment nor life imprisonment, but if one may judge a priori,[1] then in my opinion capital punishment is more moral and more humane than imprisonment. Execution kills instantly; life imprisonment kills by degrees. Who is the more humane executioner, one who kills you in a few seconds or one who draws the life out of you incessantly, for years?"

"They're both equally immoral," remarked one of the guests, "because their purpose is the same, to take away life. The state is not God. It has no right to take away that which it cannot give back, if it should so desire."

Among the company was a lawyer, a young man of about twenty-five. On being asked his opinion, he said:

"Capital punishment and life imprisonment are equally immoral; but if I were offered the choice between them, I would certainly choose the second. It's better to live somehow than not to live at all."

There ensued a lively discussion. The banker, who was then younger and more nervous, suddenly lost his temper, banged his fist on the table, and turning to the young lawyer, cried out:

"It's a lie. I bet you two millions you wouldn't stick in a cell even for five years."

"If you're serious," replied the lawyer, "then I bet I'll stay not five but fifteen."

"Fifteen! Done!" cried the banker. "Gentlemen, I stake two millions."

"Agreed. You stake two millions, I my freedom," said the lawyer.

So this wild, ridiculous bet came to pass. The banker, who at that time had too many millions to count, spoiled and capricious, was beside himself with rapture. During supper he said to the lawyer jokingly:

"Come to your senses, young man, before it's too late. Two millions are nothing to me, but you stand to lose three or four of the best years of your life. I say three or four, because you'll never stick it out any longer. Don't forget either, you unhappy man, that voluntary is much heavier than enforced imprisonment. The idea that you have the right to free yourself at any moment will poison the whole of your life in the cell. I pity you."

And now the banker, pacing from corner to corner, recalled all this and asked himself:

CLARIFY

Why do the banker and the lawyer make the bet?

"Why did I make this bet? What's the good? The lawyer loses fifteen years of his life and I throw away two millions. Will it convince people that capital punishment is worse or better than imprisonment for life? No, no! all stuff and rubbish. On my part, it was the caprice of a well-fed man; on the lawyer's, pure greed of gold."

He recollected further what happened after the evening party. It was decided that the lawyer must undergo his imprisonment under

---

1. **a priori** (ä′prē-ôr′ē): based on a theory rather than on experience.

WORDS TO KNOW

obsolete (ŏb′sə-lēt′) *adj.* out-of-date
immoral (ĭ-môr′əl) *adj.* contrary to what is considered to be correct behavior
humane (hyoo-mān′) *adj.* merciful; showing the best qualities of humans
incessantly (ĭn-sĕs′ənt-lē) *adv.* continually, without interruption
capricious (kə-prĭsh′əs) *adj.* unpredictable
rapture (răp′chər) *n.* a feeling of ecstasy; great joy

the strictest observation, in a garden wing of the banker's house. It was agreed that during the period he would be deprived of the right to cross the threshold, to see living people, to hear human voices, and to receive letters and newspapers. He was permitted to have a musical instrument, to read books, to write letters, to drink wine and smoke tobacco. By the agreement he could communicate, but only in silence, with the outside world through a little window specially constructed for this purpose. Everything necessary, books, music, wine, he could receive in any quantity by sending a note through the window. The agreement provided for all the minutest details, which made the confinement strictly solitary, and it obliged the lawyer to remain exactly fifteen years from twelve o'clock of November 14th, 1870, to twelve o'clock of November 14th, 1885. The least attempt on his part to violate the conditions, to escape if only for two minutes before the time, freed the banker from the obligation to pay him the two millions.

During the first year of imprisonment, the lawyer, as far as it was possible to judge from his short notes, suffered terribly from loneliness and boredom. From his wing day and night came the sound of the piano. He rejected wine and tobacco. "Wine," he wrote, "excites desires, and desires are the chief foes of a prisoner; besides, nothing is more boring than to drink good wine alone," and tobacco spoiled the air in his room. During the first year, the lawyer was sent books of a light character; novels with a complicated love interest, stories of crime and fantasy, comedies, and so on.

In the second year, the piano was heard no longer and the lawyer asked only for classics. In the fifth year, music was heard again, and the prisoner asked for wine. Those who watched him said that during the whole of

that year he was only eating, drinking, and lying on his bed. He yawned often and talked angrily to himself. Books he did not read. Sometimes at nights he would sit down to write. He would write for a long time and tear it all up in the morning. More than once he was heard to weep.

In the second half of the sixth year, the prisoner began zealously to study languages, philosophy, and history. He fell on these subjects so hungrily that the banker hardly had time to get books enough for him. In the space of four years about six hundred volumes were bought at his request. It was while that passion lasted that the banker received the following letter from the prisoner: "My dear jailer, I am writing these lines in six languages. Show them to experts. Let them read them. If they do not find one single mistake, I beg you to give orders to have a gun fired off in the garden. By the noise I shall know that my efforts have not been in vain. The geniuses of all ages and countries speak in different languages; but in them all burns the same flame. Oh, if you knew my heavenly happiness now that I can understand them!" The prisoner's desire was fulfilled. Two shots were fired in the garden by the banker's order.

Later on, after the tenth year, the lawyer sat immovable before his table and read only the New Testament. The banker found it strange that a man who in four years had mastered six hundred erudite[2] volumes, should have spent nearly a year in reading one book, easy to understand and by no means thick. The New Testament was then replaced by the history of religions and theology.

During the last two years of his confinement the prisoner read an extraordinary amount,

PREDICT

Will the lawyer stay for 15 years?

---

2. **erudite** (ĕr′yə-dīt′): scholarly.

quite <u>haphazardly</u>. Now he would apply himself to the natural sciences, then would read Byron[3] or Shakespeare. Notes used to come from him in which he asked to be sent at the same time a book on chemistry, a textbook of medicine, a novel, and some treatise on philosophy or theology. He read as though he were swimming in the sea among broken pieces of wreckage, and in his desire to save his life was eagerly grasping one piece after another.

The banker recalled all this, and thought:

"Tomorrow at twelve o'clock he receives his freedom. Under the agreement, I shall have to pay him two millions. If I pay, it's all over with me. I am ruined forever. . . ."

Fifteen years before he had too many millions to count, but now he was afraid to ask himself which he had more of, money or debts. Gambling on the stock exchange, risky speculation, and the recklessness of which he could not rid himself even in old age, had gradually brought his business to decay; and the fearless, self-confident, proud man of business had become an ordinary banker, trembling at every rise and fall in the market.

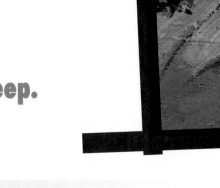

He yawned often and talked angrily to himself. . . . More than once he was heard to weep.

CLARIFY

Why might the banker be ruined?

"That cursed bet," murmured the old man clutching his head in despair. . . . "Why didn't the man die? He's only forty years old. He will take away my

---

3. **Byron:** George Gordon Byron (1788–1824), a leading English poet of the Romantic movement.

last penny, marry, enjoy life, gamble on the exchange, and I will look on like an envious beggar and hear the same words from him every day: 'I'm obliged to you for the happiness of my life. Let me help you.' No, it's too much! The only escape from bankruptcy and disgrace—is that the man should die."

The clock had just struck three. The banker was listening. In the house everyone was asleep, and one could hear only the frozen trees whining outside the windows. Trying to make no sound, he took out of his safe the key of the door which had not been opened

for fifteen years, put on his overcoat, and went out of the house. The garden was dark and cold. It was raining. A keen damp wind hovered howling over all the garden and gave the trees no rest. Though he strained his eyes, the banker could see neither the ground, nor the white statues, nor the garden wing, nor the trees. Approaching the place where the garden wing stood, he called the watchman twice. There was no answer. Evidently the watchman had taken shelter from the bad weather and was now asleep somewhere in the kitchen or the greenhouse.

"If I have the courage to fulfil my intention," thought the old man, "the suspicion will fall on the watchman first of all."

In the darkness he groped for the stairs and the door and entered the hall of the garden wing, then poked his way into a narrow passage and struck a match. Not a soul was there. Someone's bed, with no bedclothes on it, stood there, and an iron stove was dark in the corner. The seals on the door that led into the prisoner's room were unbroken.

When the match went out, the old man, trembling from agitation, peeped into the little window.

In the prisoner's room a candle was burning dim. The prisoner himself sat by the table. Only his back, the hair on his head, and his hands were visible. On the table, the two chairs, and on the carpet by the table, open books were strewn.

Five minutes passed and the prisoner never once stirred. Fifteen years' confinement had taught him to sit motionless. The banker tapped on the window with his finger, but the prisoner gave no movement in reply. Then the banker cautiously tore the seals from the door and put the key into the lock. The rusty lock gave a hoarse groan and the door creaked. The banker expected instantly to hear a cry of surprise and the sound of steps. Three minutes passed and it was as quiet behind the door as it had been before. He made up his mind to enter.

Before the table sat a man, unlike an ordinary human being. It was a skeleton, with tight-drawn skin, with a woman's long curly hair, and a shaggy beard. The color of his face was yellow, of an earthy shade; the cheeks were sunken, the back long and narrow, and the hand upon which he leaned his hairy head was so lean and skinny that it was painful to look upon. His hair was already silvering with grey, and no one who glanced at the senile emaciation[4] of the face would have believed that he was only forty years old. On the table, before his bent head, lay a sheet of paper on which something was written in a tiny hand.

"Poor devil," thought the banker, "he's asleep and probably seeing millions in his dreams. I have only to take and throw this half-dead thing on the bed, smother him a moment with the pillow, and the most careful examination will find no trace of unnatural death. But, first, let us read what he has written here."

The banker took the sheet from the table and read:

"Tomorrow at twelve o'clock midnight, I shall obtain my freedom and the right to mix with people. But before I leave this room and see the sun I think it necessary to say a few words to you. On my own clear conscience and before God who sees me, I declare to you that I despise freedom, life, health, and all that your books call the blessings of the world.

"For fifteen years I have diligently studied earthly life. True, I saw neither the earth nor the people, but in your books I drank fragrant wine, sang songs, hunted deer and wild boar in the forests, loved women . . . And beautiful women, like clouds ethereal,[5] created by the magic of your poets' genius, visited me by night and whispered to me wonderful tales, which made my head drunken. In your books I climbed the summits of Elbruz and Mont Blanc and saw from there how the sun rose in the morning, and in the evening overflowed the sky, the ocean and the mountain ridges with a purple gold. From there I saw how above me lightnings glimmered, cleaving the clouds; I saw green forests, fields, rivers, lakes, cities; I heard sirens[6] singing, and the playing of the pipes of Pan;[7] I touched the wings of beautiful devils who came flying to me to speak of God . . . In your books I cast myself into bottomless abysses,[8] worked miracles, burned cities to the ground, preached new religions, conquered whole countries . . .

"Your books gave me wisdom. All that unwearying human thought created in the centuries is compressed to a little lump in my skull. I know that I am more clever than you all.

"And I despise your books, despise all worldly blessings and wisdom. Everything is void, frail, visionary and delusive as a mirage. Though you be proud and wise and beautiful, yet will death wipe you from the face of the earth like the mice underground; and your posterity, your history, and the immortality of your men of genius will be as frozen slag, burnt down together with the terrestrial globe.

"You are mad, and gone the wrong way. You take lie for truth and ugliness for beauty. You would marvel if by certain conditions frogs and lizards should suddenly grow on apple and orange trees, instead of fruit, and if roses should begin to breathe the odor of a sweating horse. So do I marvel at you, who have bartered heaven for earth. I do not want to understand you.

"That I may show you in deed my contempt for that by which you live, I waive the two millions of which I once dreamed of as paradise, and which I now despise. That I may deprive myself of my right to them, I shall

---

4. **emaciation** (ĭ-mā′shē-ā′shən): abnormal thinness, usually caused by starvation.

5. **ethereal** (ĭ-thîr′ē-əl): delicate; heavenly.

6. **sirens**: from Greek mythology, sea goddesses whose sweet singing lured sailors to their deaths on rocky coasts.

7. **pipes of Pan**: Pan, the Greek god of woods, fields, and flocks, played a flutelike pipe instrument.

8. **abysses** (ə-bĭ′sĭz): deep gulfs, gorges, or chasms in the earth.

WORDS TO KNOW **posterity** (pŏ-stĕr′ĭ-tē) *n.* future generations

247

come out from here five minutes before the <u>stipulated</u> term, and thus shall violate the agreement."

When he had read, the banker put the sheet on the table, kissed the head of the

EVALUATE

What causes the lawyer's bitterness?

strange man, and began to weep. He went out of the wing. Never at any other time, not even after his terrible losses on the Exchange, had he felt such contempt for himself as now. Coming home, he lay down on his bed, but agitation and tears kept him long from sleep. . . .

The next morning the poor watchman came running to him and told him that they had seen the man who lived in the wing climbing through the window into the garden. He had gone to the gate and disappeared. With his servants the banker went instantly to the wing and established the escape of his prisoner. To avoid unnecessary rumors he took the paper with the <u>renunciation</u> from the table and, on his return, locked it in his safe. ❖

Gauguin's Armchair (1888), Vincent van Gogh. Van Gogh Museum, Amsterdam, the Netherlands. Art Resource/New York.

WORDS
TO
KNOW

stipulated (stĭp′yə-lā′tĭd) *adj.* arranged in an agreement **stipulate** *v.*
renunciation (rĭ-nŭn′sē-ā′shən) *n.* a declaration in which something is given up

248

RESPONDING
O P T I O N S

FROM **PERSONAL RESPONSE** TO **CRITICAL ANALYSIS**

REFLECT

1. Did you have stronger feelings about the banker or the lawyer? Jot down your thoughts in your notebook and share them with the class.

RETHINK

2. What do you think of the lawyer for walking away from the money?
   Consider
   • what he could have gained by not leaving early
   • the effects of long-term isolation on him

3. If the banker and the lawyer had foreseen the effects of this bet, do you think they would have agreed to it? Why or why not?

4. What do you think the bet proved? Explain your answer.

5. What does this story show about Chekhov's viewpoint on life imprisonment?

RELATE

6. After reading this story and considering your discussion with classmates for the Personal Connection on page 240, how do you think a murderer should be punished? Explain.

ANOTHER PATHWAY
Cooperative Learning

In a small group, discuss what the lawyer and the banker were like at the time the bet was made and after the 15 years had passed. Record the changes in these characters in a chart like the one below.

How the Characters Change		
	Lawyer	**Banker**
Before		
After		

QUICKWRITES

1. Write three **diary entries** the lawyer might have written—one during his first year of imprisonment, one during the middle years, and one near the end. Make sure your entries show changes in his personality and thinking.

2. Write at least three pieces of **graffiti** that the lawyer might have written on the walls of his room.

   📁 *PORTFOLIO Save your writing. You may want to use it later as a springboard to a piece for your portfolio.*

LITERARY CONCEPTS

A scene from an earlier time that interrupts the ongoing action in a story is called a **flashback.** Flashbacks provide information that helps readers understand a character's present situation. In "The Bet," the banker's recollection of a party he gave 15 years earlier is a flashback. Look for a second flashback the banker experiences. What does he recall in that flashback?

CONCEPT REVIEW: Climax You know that the climax is the most dramatic moment in a story, the point at which an important event, decision, or discovery takes place. What do you think is the climax of "The Bet"?

ALTERNATIVE ACTIVITIES

1. Sketch or paint a series of three **pictures** that the lawyer might have created at the beginning, the middle, and the end of his imprisonment. In planning your pictures, consider the lawyer's activities, thoughts, and feelings at those times.

2. With a small group of classmates, plan a **performance** of the scene in which the bet is made. You might want to expand the discussion about the death penalty with additional arguments for and against it. Act out the scene for your class.

3. Suppose that like the lawyer, you have agreed to imprisonment. What books would you most want to have with you—romance novels, mysteries, textbooks, poetry, science fiction? Make a **list** of titles and explain your choices.

LITERARY LINKS

When you read "A Mother in Mannville," you were asked to think about the difference between "alone" and "lonely." Compare and contrast Jerry's experience with the lawyer's experience in "The Bet." Were these two characters alone, lonely, or both? Explain your answer.

ACROSS THE CURRICULUM

 Social Studies Find out which states in the United States have a law that permits the use of capital punishment. If possible, use an encyclopedia program or an on-line computer service to start your research. Share your findings with your class.

 Mathematics If the lawyer had received two million dollars for his fifteen years, how much would he have earned per hour?

ART CONNECTION

Look at the portrait on page 242. What do you notice about the artist's style? If this artist painted a portrait of the lawyer at the end of the lawyer's 15 years of imprisonment, how might that portrait look different from this one?

Detail of *Portrait of Henri Matisse* (1905), André Derain. Tate Gallery, London/Art Resource, New York. Copyright © 1996 Artists Rights Society (ARS), New York/ADAGP, Paris.

EXERCISE A Review the Words to Know at the bottom of the selection pages. On your paper, write the word that is most closely related to each situation described below.

1. In some states, capital punishment is no longer used.
2. That judge is unpredictable in sentencing criminals.
3. The defendant felt thrilled when he was acquitted.
4. The corrupt politician stole government funds.
5. The judge laid down specific rules for the convict's parole.
6. A merciful judge treated the boy kindly.
7. The debaters argue on endlessly.
8. Both sides worry about future generations.
9. Is legalizing the death penalty a giving up of morality?
10. Could the death penalty be administered at random?

EXERCISE B Working in small groups, retell the plot of a popular movie using as many of the Words to Know as possible. Each student should provide a few sentences and try to use at least one of the words in each.

ANTON CHEKHOV

1860–1904

Anton Chekhov was the third of six children born to a peasant family in Taganrog, Russia, near the Black Sea. "Childhood was sheer suffering," he once said. "My father began my education, or, to put it more simply, began to beat me, before I reached the age of five."

When Chekhov was 15, his father's business failed, and Chekhov began to help support his family. He sold household goods and tutored younger students in Taganrog. In 1879 he entered medical school in Moscow. He later abandoned medicine for a career in writing.

Chekhov wrote for comic magazines before turning to longer and more serious stories and plays. His style of writing focuses on a character's mood rather than on action; Chekhov believed that writers should portray life as it really is and should raise questions about it. As a result of his masterful stories and plays, he became known as the father of the modern short story and of the modern play. Several decades after his death from tuberculosis, Chekhov's stories and plays were translated, and they continue to be popular throughout the world today.

OTHER WORKS *A Marriage Proposal*, "The Confession," "A Slander"

PREVIEWING

NONFICTION

from Once Upon a Time When We Were Colored
Clifton L. Taulbert

PERSONAL CONNECTION

Clifton L. Taulbert writes about an uncle he greatly admired in this autobiographical account of his childhood, which involves an unexpected encounter with racial discrimination. Share with the class any unexpected obstacles that you remember encountering in your life. These obstacles might be anything from discrimination to family crises, physical problems, or surprising disappointments.

HISTORICAL CONNECTION

The term *colored* in the title of this selection bluntly points to an earlier era in the United States when different standards and ideals governed people's lives. For example, segregation—the forced separation of races—was legal in the Mississippi of Taulbert's childhood, during the 1950s. However, laws passed by Congress in 1965 ended legal segregation.

The selection also reveals other aspects of this era that no longer exist. For example, the minstrel show described in this account is rarely, if ever, performed today. It was a traveling comic variety show featuring white performers who blackened their faces in order to appear African American.

WRITING CONNECTION

In this selection, Taulbert tells how he had been waiting to grow up enough to work with his uncle. Think about some things you have been waiting to be old enough or big enough to do. What obstacles are preventing you from doing them? Use a diagram, like the one below, to organize your thoughts.

Things I Have Been Waiting to Do		
Drive a car		
Too young		
Obstacles		

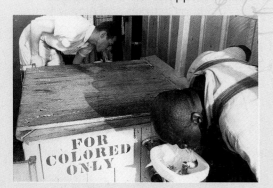

Segregated drinking fountain in use in the American South. The Bettmann Archive.

LASERLINKS
• *HISTORICAL CONNECTION*

FROM

ONCE UPON A TIME WHEN WE WERE COLORED

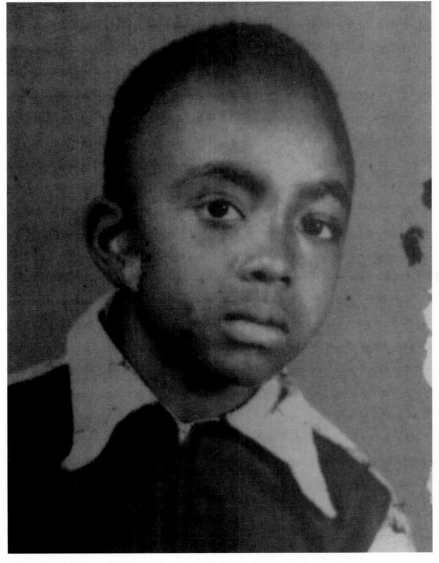

Courtesy, Council Oak Books.

by CLIFTON L. TAULBERT

urely if my Uncle Cleve were alive today, he'd find a reason to be a black Republican. He was short, neatly dressed, and conservative. Uncle Cleve came from Coldwater, Mississippi. I know very little about his early life with my great-aunt Willie, but I do recall his strong personality and the impact he had on my life growing up in Glen Allan.

I never heard him raise his voice. When he talked, he always talked politics and demonstrated a real business sense. Independence and nonconversance[1] were his most notable characteristics. I called him Uncle Cleve, Ma Ponk called him Bro. Cleve and every other colored person called him Mr. Cleve. The white community with which he had contact called him Mormon, his last name, their badge of respect.

Uncle Cleve, Mr. Cleve, Bro. Cleve, or Mormon—he was my first employer. From him, I learned a sense of responsibility that undergirds my approach today. He ran the only icehouse in town. Refrigerators were a rarity in the colored community and among the poor whites, and nearly all the small businesses used ice to keep their goods from spoiling. Only Mr. Cleve provided the ice needed in Glen Allan. Twice daily, we'd see him driving the red flatbed truck up and down the streets, announcing "The iceman is here." For years, I would run alongside the truck as Uncle Cleve stopped at each house and chipped his sales of fifteen or thirty pounds of ice. Occasionally someone would buy fifty pounds, but that was rare. He was always quick, responsive, and very polite—not given to extra conversation when waiting on his customer. His business made our lives better, and he was always received as a welcome sight.

Being an assistant to Mr. Cleve was viewed as a good job, and I couldn't wait until I was old enough to work with my cousin Joe, Uncle Cleve's son. Uncle Cleve had been training me by taking me with him to Hollandale, Mississippi, to buy ice from the ice factory. We would ride to Hollandale together, just the two of us. I recall the trip taking hours, but really it was very short. We'd drive down the road eating salami and crackers, and every once in a while he would talk to me about life.

"Yes, git you a good pattern and follow it. Always be early for work, and save fifty cents out of every dollar you make."

I didn't try to answer. I just sat in the cab of the truck and listened as he continued talking. All I wanted was the chance to show him that I could handle the big three-hundred-pound blocks of ice. If I could prove my ability to handle the big blocks, he would let me work at his icehouse.

Finally one Saturday, he gave me the chance. I must have been about twelve years old. Child-labor laws weren't in vogue in Glen Allan, and when you were strong enough to handle the job, nobody worried about how old you were. I could hardly sleep the Friday night before, although Ma Ponk had no problem getting me into bed on my little cot by the front windows.

"Boy, git to bed early, 'cause Bro. Cleve will leave you if you ain't ready to go when he comes by," Ma Ponk told me as she securely tucked me in bed.

Saturday morning didn't come soon enough. I found myself waking up nearly every hour, straining my eyes to see the hands on the clock. Finally I heard Ma Ponk's voice through the quilts. "Cliff, git up and git some food in you, 'cause you know Bro. Cleve ain't gonna stop."

---

1. **nonconversance** (nŏn′kən-vûr′səns): a term used here to describe Uncle Cleve's habit of saying very little.

WORDS TO KNOW

conservative (kən-sûr′və-tĭv) *adj.* traditional in style and manner
impact (ĭm′păkt′) *n.* a strong effect
responsive (rĭ-spŏn′sĭv) *adj.* quick to react or reply to another
vogue (vōg) *n.* style; fashion

No sooner had she spoken than I jumped from bed and ran to get the wash pan so I could wash up before eating my breakfast. The smell of hot oil sausages and grits[2] floated through the house, and I could hardly wait. How lucky could I be—a trip to Hollandale with Uncle Cleve, *and* my favorite breakfast. The food went fast, and I found myself ready and waiting when Uncle Cleve came by. True to form, he was a little early.

"Bye, Ma Ponk!" I yelled as I jumped from the porch to the ground.

Our trip was not unusual, but this time I would have the chance to show my uncle that I was big enough to help him with the business.

"Cleve, pull your truck in next," a colored man yelled as we pulled up to the Hollandale Icehouse.

Uncle Cleve let me out of the cab and told me to take the steps to the dock; he'd meet me there. He never made suggestions. You simply did what he told you, and quickly. After parking the truck so the bed would be against the dock, Uncle Cleve came around to the side where I was standing.

"OK, Cliff, we'll see if you can handle the big one."

As we walked into the icehouse, all I could see was a cold vapor rising from hundreds of blocks of ice. Each block weighed three hundred pounds. Standing inside the door, I felt the chill as Uncle Cleve took the giant ice hook off the wall.

"Cliff, pay attention." Uncle Cleve proceeded to show me how to put the ice hook securely into the block while using my knee as an anchor.

I watched and I watched and I watched. Finally, it was my turn. I walked over to a huge block of ice and carefully repeated what I had been shown many times. I securely hooked my ice, carefully placed my knee, and began to gently pull the block to the floor. Before I could get fearful, I had finished. The three-hundred-pound block of ice was on the floor, and I was pulling it out to the trucks.

"New helper you got, Mormon?" one of the white men asked.

"Yes, sir," Uncle Cleve nodded as he watched me load the truck for the very first time.

My ride home could not have been sweeter. Uncle Cleve stopped by a local store and bought me a large grape soda and a moon pie[3]—my reward. We didn't say much on the way back, but we both knew it had been a good day.

Many months later, nearing the end of the summer, Uncle Cleve promised to take me with him to Jackson as a gift for having done a good job for him. The day of our trip finally arrived. It started out as one of the happiest days of my life. My uncle was taking me to Jackson to the biggest tent show that had ever come our way. Ma Ponk got me all dressed up in my Sunday church clothes, combed my hair until my scalp was sore, and had me ready at least two hours early. Uncle Cleve was a slow driver, so we were going to leave in plenty of time to get to the seven o'clock grand opening.

I was ready at three o'clock and sitting out on the front steps waiting for the familiar sound of Uncle's 1947 green International truck that purred like a kitten. Ma Ponk and I were waiting, and there was absolutely no way

> **"OK, CLIFF, WE'LL SEE IF YOU CAN HANDLE THE BIG ONE."**

---

2. **grits:** short for *hominy grits,* a popular Southern breakfast dish made of coarsely ground dry corn.

3. **moon pie:** a chocolate-covered cookie that has a marshmallow filling sandwiched between two round graham crackers.

of missing Uncle Cleve. When the truck pulled up, I almost jumped out of my pants, but Uncle Cleve only smiled slightly as I ran around to the passenger's side and tucked myself firmly in, secure with the knowledge that tonight was going to be a really big night for me. Uncle Cleve was very confident, only telling me that he never messed with the small-town minstrel shows that came to Glen Allan to rob you blind. If he was going to waste his time and spend his money, it would be at something like the big show that we were going to in Jackson.

I know I counted every tree and rock between Glen Allan and Jackson, because Uncle drove so slowly. He never hurried about anything. Moving meticulously, like a well-greased snail, he'd get the work of two men done in half the time. His driving was the same, perfect execution of the rules, never speeding, just fast enough to beat running.

It was almost 150 miles to Jackson. Ma Ponk didn't even pack me a lunch, because Uncle Cleve had promised to buy my lunch. Packed lunches in greasy brown paper bags were for old church ladies, not the two of us.

Finally we reached Jackson. There were more bright lights than I had ever seen. This was a large city, not like Glen Allan. Uncle Cleve took the city in stride. After all, he had been to Memphis, and Jackson was just another city to him. To me, however, Jackson was the biggest and the brightest. It even had uniformed policemen directing the traffic, and I saw my first traffic jam.

I was so excited about being in a city I didn't realize we had gotten near the show grounds. There seemed to be hundreds of cars and people. But my uncle knew where we were going. He parked the truck and held my hand tightly as we followed the crowd. Finally we got to the main gate, where a big curly-headed white man reached down and took our tickets. We were ushered in with the crowds of other people to a tent that seemed big enough to cover the whole world.

White people were everywhere, laughing and talking and eating popcorn and pulling their children behind them, as we all headed toward the big tent.

It was so crowded in the tent and we were so far back that I could hardly see, but I remember when those gigantic curtains opened and I saw all those beautiful ladies in sequined stockings.[4] I could hardly sit still. I know I was too small to fully appreciate that beauty, but the glitter I understood. The music was loud all around us, and sweaty men were yelling and whistling; but my uncle just smiled slightly, ate one piece of popcorn at a time, and watched.

We couldn't have been there any more than twenty minutes when the usher came over to us and said, "I am sorry, but this ain't the night for niggers."[5]

My uncle's smile dropped from his face, and his warm eyes became cold as steel as he jerked me up and we walked out. We hadn't even seen half the show.

The long trip back was completely silent. I sat in the car, miserable, trying not to cry. I was too young to understand why this had happened to us, and my uncle would not explain. ❖

---

4. **sequined** (sē′kwĭnd) **stockings:** stockings decorated with small shiny disks.
5. **niggers:** derogatory slang term for African Americans. The word is considered to be extremely offensive.

WORDS TO KNOW

meticulously (mĭ-tĭk′yə-ləs-lē) *adv.* very carefully

RESPONDING
OPTIONS

FROM PERSONAL RESPONSE TO CRITICAL ANALYSIS

REFLECT
1. What questions does the selection raise in your mind? Jot them down in your notebook.

RETHINK
2. Why do you think Uncle Cleve chooses not to explain the discrimination he and Cliff encounter in Jackson?

3. Uncle Cleve seems able to handle certain obstacles in his life. How well does he handle the obstacle of racial discrimination at the tent show? Explain your answer.

4. How would you describe Uncle Cleve's personality?

5. Cliff is about 12 years old at the time of the incident, and yet he seems to have had little experience with racial prejudice. Do you think that is possible? Use as evidence examples from the account and from your own experience.

RELATE
6. The type of discrimination that Cliff and his uncle encounter is illegal today. However, discrimination still exists in a number of forms. Describe the kinds of discrimination you are aware of.

ANOTHER PATHWAY

Cliff shows many emotions, ranging from extreme happiness to misery. Make an "emotions graph." Plot at least three events on the horizontal line, and Cliff's emotions, from low to high, on the vertical line.

Events

QUICKWRITES

1. If Uncle Cleve had talked to Cliff about the incident in Jackson, what might he have said? How might Cliff have responded? Write the **dialogue** that you imagine might have occurred.

2. Uncle Cleve advises Cliff to get in the habit of being early for work and saving money. Write two **paragraphs** explaining the best and worst advice you have received.

📁 *PORTFOLIO Save your writing. You may want to use it later as a springboard to a piece for your portfolio.*

LITERARY CONCEPTS

This account is part of Taulbert's **autobiography,** or the true story of his life. Written from the first-person point of view, an autobiography provides insight into the writer's personality and development. Taulbert prefers to call his books "cultural biographies" because they reflect what it was like growing up African American before the civil rights movement. In this selection, how do Cliff's and his uncle's reactions reflect attitudes of the times? How might they react to the incident at the tent show if it happened today?

ALTERNATIVE ACTIVITIES

Draw a **map** of Mississippi that highlights the towns and cities mentioned in the selection: Coldwater, Glen Allan, Hollandale, and Jackson.

ACROSS THE CURRICULUM

Social Studies Taulbert suggests that no one in Glen Allan paid attention to child labor laws. Research the history of child labor laws in the United States. Share your findings.

THE WRITER'S STYLE

Taulbert writes dialogue using nonstandard English. **Nonstandard English** is a form of language that does not follow some of the standard rules of grammar. It shows how some people naturally talk and can lend an earthy, conversational style to writing. For example, Uncle Cleve says to Cliff, "Yes, git you a good pattern and follow it." He means, "Get yourself a good pattern and follow it." Go to page 254, and rewrite Ma Ponk's dialogue in standard English. What is the effect of your rewrite?

WORDS TO KNOW

Review the Words to Know at the bottom of the selection pages. Using the sample as a guide, create a word map containing at least six other related words for each of the five Words to Know.

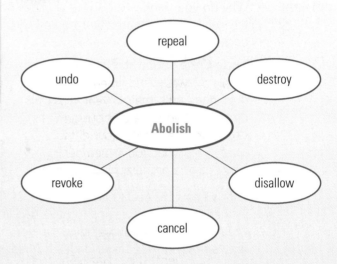

repeal

undo

destroy

Abolish

revoke

disallow

cancel

CLIFTON L. TAULBERT

1945–

Clifton L. Taulbert was raised in small-town Mississippi, where he graduated first in his high school class. He served in the U.S. Air Force and graduated from Oral Roberts University with a degree in sociology and history.

Of his childhood in segregated Mississippi he writes: "I would never want to return to forced segregation, but I also have a deeply felt sense that important values were conveyed to me in my colored childhood, values we're in danger of losing in our integrated world." The author expresses concern that his own children not lose these values: "Today my children are growing up in a world where 'color' is something that comes in a box of crayons. . . . I want my children to know of the life-style that gave them their father and their mother."

In 1993, for the second of his three autobiographical works, *The Last Train North*, Taulbert was nominated for a Pulitzer Prize and received a Mississippi Institute of Arts and Letters Award for Nonfiction. He shared the Mississippi honor with another writer and was the first African American to win the award.

OTHER WORKS *The Season Our Crops Came In*

NONFICTION

The Home Front: 1941–1945

Hazel Shelton Abernethy

PERSONAL CONNECTION

"I'll never forget what I was doing when . . ." Do these words remind you of a major event in your personal life or one that you heard about on the news? Can you picture the event? How did it affect you? Write down what you remember, using a chart or a creative organizer like the one shown here.

HISTORICAL CONNECTION

Like many others of her generation, Hazel Shelton Abernethy vividly remembers where she was and what she was doing on December 7, 1941. That was the day the Japanese bombed the U.S. naval base at Pearl Harbor, in Oahu, Hawaii. This attack caused the United States to enter World War II.

The impact of the war was keenly felt by the whole country. Almost immediately, men went overseas to fight, and many women took factory jobs helping to produce enormous numbers of ships, airplanes, tanks, and weapons. Products needed by the military were rationed, including metal, gasoline, and nylon. Read this account to find out other ways the war affected the lives of citizens at home.

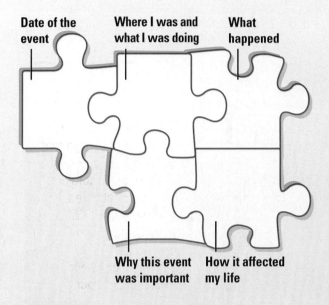

Date of the event
Where I was and what I was doing
What happened
Why this event was important
How it affected my life

READING CONNECTION

Questioning The process of raising questions while reading is called questioning. Good readers ask themselves questions in an effort to understand and think about what they're reading. Sometimes, but not always, their questions are answered later in the selection. As you read "Home Front," ask yourself questions and look for answers. For example, you might wonder why clothing was never rationed.

Honolulu Star-Bulletin 1st EXTRA

8 PAGES—HONOLULU, TERRITORY OF HAWAII, U. S. A., SUNDAY, DECEMBER 7, 1941—8 PAGES ★ PRICE FIVE CENTS

(Associated Press by Transpacific Telephone)

SAN FRANCISCO, Dec. 7.—President Roosevelt announced this morning that Japanese planes had attacked Manila and Pearl Harbor.

WAR!

OAHU BOMBED BY

JAPANESE PLANES

The H★me Fr★nt

1941–1945

BY HAZEL SHELTON ABERNETHY

I was fourteen years old and a sophomore at Nacogdoches High School on Sunday, December 7, 1941. Like all people old enough to have any memory of that day, I can tell you exactly where I was and what I was doing when I heard the news about Pearl Harbor. A group of friends and I had gone to the double-feature movie at the Stone Fort Theatre on the west side of the square. The movies were *Till We Meet Again* with George Brent and Merle Oberon and one of the "Maisie" movies with Ann Southern and Robert Sterling. When we came out of the theater, about 4:30, they were selling "extra" editions of the *Sentinel* that announced the Japanese attack. Most people were not completely sure at that time just where Pearl Harbor was, but our geographical knowledge widened significantly over the next few months.

On Monday, December 8, we gathered in the high school auditorium, the present-day middle school, and heard President Roosevelt ask for a declaration of war against Japan. When "The Star-Spangled Banner" was played, there were few dry eyes.

Almost immediately our lives began to change in response to the national war effort.

At school we had war-bond drives and scrap drives.[1] Tuesday was Stamp Day, and students

---

1. **war-bond drives and scrap drives:** nationwide campaigns to encourage U.S. citizens to buy government bonds and save recyclable materials to aid the war effort.

saved their pennies to buy savings stamps. The stamp books came in denominations of ten and twenty-five cents. When a student had bought $18.75 worth of stamps, he or she could purchase a savings bond that would mature in ten years at $25.00. There was competition between home rooms, and the room that sold the most stamps each week would receive some special recognition.

We had a scrap-metal drive that could have competed with any school in the country. The entire Mound Street campus was covered with metal scrap. High school students responded enthusiastically with discarded pots and pans, junked jalopies, an entire old bus "carcass," and parts of a locomotive. The drive lasted for six weeks and dominated our activities. This, too, was conducted as a home-room competition. We were in Miss Dora Grant's home room, and we won the prize—an entire page in the school annual.

At the government's request we began to save everything. Paper, tin cans, and bacon grease headed the list of vital "recyclables." We also learned to "make it do, wear it out, and do without." When clothing wore out completely, we saved everything salvageable. Buttons, snaps, and hooks and eyes were hoarded away. Silk stockings were a thing of the past, and nylons were a treasure rarely to be found, so we painted our legs with pancake makeup and drew a seam up the back with eyebrow pencil and prayed we wouldn't get caught out in the rain.

With the exception of shoes, clothing was never rationed, but there were shortages, espe-

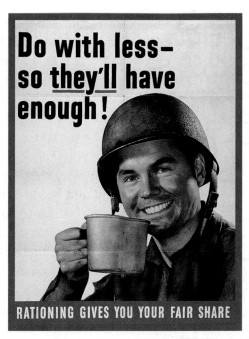

RATIONING GIVES YOU YOUR FAIR SHARE

Courtesy of the War Memorial Museum of Virginia.

cially of quality clothes. As wartime weddings increased, mothers of brides searched frantically for white satin or tulle.[2] My mother bought three pre-war evening dresses at the Episcopal Church rummage sale and constructed two semi-new formals for my freshman year in college. Shoe rationing allowed each person one pair of shoes for each season. This was particularly hard on families with young children whose growth was not seasonal, so there was pooling of shoe stamps among people according to need. Many a grandparent contributed his shoe stamp to a grandchild.

We worked for the Red Cross and rolled bandages and knitted socks and mufflers, and even Nacogdoches, with a population under 10,000, had a USO.[3] The high school and college girls acted as hostesses and gave dances there. It alternated as a youth center. The social clubs at the college went to Harmon Military Hospital in Longview and gave programs to entertain the recovering wounded. If they survived that entertainment, they were considered fit for active duty. We wrote letters, baked cookies to send to the boys in service, took strangers in uniform home for dinner, and never passed up a serviceman thumbing a ride on the highway. We followed the war news in the newspapers, radio, and newsreels with anxious hearts.

---

2. **tulle** (tool): a fine, stiff netting used for veils and gowns.

3. **USO**: United Service Organizations, volunteer-staffed groups offering recreational and other services to U.S. military personnel and their families.

Sometimes we would catch a glimpse of a loved one in a newsreel. Once we saw my cousin's face on the screen, and we came to the theater everytime the newsreel appeared. Who knew when or if we would see him again?

The real cost of the war was being brought sharply home by blue star banners, which were hung in the windows of businesses, schools, and homes. Each of these stars represented a hometown boy who was serving in the military. More and more gold stars began to appear on these banners. Gold stars represented the boys who would not come home again.

Our lives revolved around the comings and goings of our friends in the service. As my own group of friends began to leave in 1944, we developed almost a ritual of their leaving. We would give an all-day picnic for them at Fern Lake, and the night before they left we would have a family party for them. Our parents, brothers and sisters, and friends would all go with them to the station to see them off. The train to Houston left at two o'clock in the morning, and there were some emotional send-offs down at that old depot. We were lucky; all of those boys did come home.

The restrictions on transportation probably had the most immediate effect on the conduct of our daily lives. On January 1, 1942, an order was issued banning the production of civilian cars. The last civilian car rolled off the assembly line on February 10, 1942. A limit of five tires for each automobile was strictly enforced; garages and basements were checked for hoarding. Only retread tires could be purchased, and dire need had to be proved through many miles of red tape.

Gasoline rationing began on December 1, 1942, and the national speed limit was set at 35 miles an hour to conserve fuel. Stickers were placed on cars to show how much gas we were allowed to buy, and we were issued books of ration stamps to obtain our quota. Everyone with a car qualified for an A sticker, which allowed us to buy four gallons of gas a week, which was enough to drive about sixty miles a week. B and C stamps allowed more gas for salesmen, delivery men, essential war workers, and for carpools. About one-half the drivers in the country qualified for these stamps. E stamps were for doctors, emergency vehicles, ambulances, and Home Guard vehicles, and a T sticker for trucks approved unlimited gasoline mileage.

In 1943 all pleasure driving was banned—"Is this trip really necessary?"—and the use of public transportation greatly increased. A bus or train trip was never certain. Trains, especially, frequently were sidetracked for more essential uses. All public transportation was cramped and crowded.

In 1943, with SFA's[4] enrollment dipping dangerously low, the Board of Regents obtained a contract to establish the first WAAC school in the nation on our local campus. The Women's Army Auxiliary Corps

Collection of the National Archives.

---

4. **SFA:** Stephen F. Austin State University in Nacogdoches, Texas.

was on the SFA campus for about twelve months, and two thousand WACs were graduated there. My father, who was the basketball coach at SFA, was not happy. He said we were the only school in the Lone Star Conference who did not get some sort of military unit with men who could play basketball. The high school girls and college girls were not very happy either.

The last thing this community needed was more females injected into the population. When the high school class of 1944 entered SFA in the fall, there were about 25 or 30 men on campus out of a school population of around 300-350. It was bleak.

Food rationing came in gradually. There were periodical sugar and coffee shortages, and sugar was rationed in April of 1942. Food ration books were issued in May of 1942, one to each family member. Prices were frozen on sixty percent of all food items that same spring. As time went on, almost every item that we ate, wore, used, or lived in was subject to rationing or price controls.

Victory gardens[5] grew on almost every vacant lot. One of the best ones was on the corner of King and Raguet where the Raguet Apartments are now. Every family in the neighborhood took its turn tending to this garden. The Demonstration School children dug up the backyard of SFA President Dr. Birdwell's on the SFA Campus and had a flourishing garden. One summer a group of ladies in Central Heights canned vegetables for a nickel a can and no ration stamps if the customer furnished the vegetables. My mother and I used precious gasoline scouring the county for vegetables. They made a delicious soup mix at those kitchens, and my father said we still had some of those canned vegetables in our attic in the late 1950's.

There were several prisoner-of-war camps in the area. Prisoners worked primarily in the forest areas harvesting wood for the lumber companies. There were always rumors of escaped POW's at large but most of these internees did not want to escape. At the camp in Chireno one evening, two prisoners were missing, but when the truck went back to the work area, there they were.

They had been left behind, and they were waiting for the truck to return and take them to supper. Several years after the war some of these men returned to visit; they had very warm memories of their treatment here.

For three-and-a-half years our lives revolved around the comings and goings of our servicemen. After D-Day[6] and the rapid advance of the Allies toward Germany, we were sure the boys would be home to stay, maybe even by Christmas, but the German breakthrough that developed into the Battle of the Bulge[7] ended that hope. The American forces suffered 77,000 casualties, and that was the grimmest Christmas of the war. As the spring of 1945 arrived, our hopes for victory increased, and even the blow of President Roosevelt's death could not completely dim our optimism. When VE Day[8] came we rejoiced, but the total victory was a few months away.

In the early morning of August 14, 1945, we heard the civil defense siren sound, along with the fire trucks and all five of the mill whistles going full blast. People dressed and went down to the Square and just hugged each other. Just as on the day that began the war, there were

---

5. **victory gardens:** vegetable gardens cultivated during World War II to help relieve food shortages.

6. **D-Day:** June 6, 1944, the day Allied forces landed in western France.

7. **Battle of the Bulge:** a World War II battle that began in December 1944, when the German army advanced into Belgium, temporarily causing a bulge in the line of the Allied military forces.

8. **VE Day:** short for Victory in Europe Day, May 8, 1945, when Germany officially surrendered and the European phase of World War II ended.

extra editions of the *Sentinel* being distributed that said the war was over.

Since the military point system provided for a gradual demobilization,[9] the real impact of the returning veterans was not felt until 1946. On the campus of SFA, the change was dramatic. The enrollment jumped to one thousand that fall, and the ratio of men to women was over three to one. For those girls who had attended school while it was almost an all-girl campus, this was nothing short of miraculous. College life was what it was meant to be. Dances—with MEN, and stag lines, football games and MEN, normal college life and MEN. Life was wonderful! ❖

---

9. **point system . . . demobilization:** a system used to release U.S. military personnel from active duty after World War II, based on an accumulation of points awarded for time overseas, especially time in combat.

HISTORICAL INSIGHT

THE MILITARY DRAFT

In 1940, for the first time in U.S. history and just one year before the United States entered World War II, men were drafted for required military service in peacetime. As a result, the beginnings of a fighting force were in place when the Japanese attacked Pearl Harbor.

Passions ran high during the congressional debate over the peacetime draft. Six women dressed in widows' clothes kept a silent vigil at the Capitol. Two congressmen got into a fistfight over the issue. Despite the controversy, Congress finally passed the Selective Training and Service Act. The law required men between the ages of 21 and 35 to sign up for one year of service overseas.

The 16.5 million men who registered for the draft were given numbers between 1 and 9,000. Each of these numbers was placed in a capsule, which was put in a ten-gallon fishbowl. Blindfolded, Secretary of War Henry Stimson drew a capsule and handed it to President Franklin D. Roosevelt, who opened it and read "158." The lottery continued in this way until all of the numbers were drawn, establishing a selection order. All registered men holding the number 158 were the first to report.

American men have been drafted during wartime since the Revolutionary War. Today, the United States uses volunteer military forces; however, since 1980, all men have been required to register for the draft when they reach 18. In the event of an emergency, they may be required to serve in the armed forces.

Secretary of War Henry Stimson draws the first capsule in the draft lottery in October 1940.

RESPONDING
OPTIONS

FROM PERSONAL RESPONSE *TO* CRITICAL ANALYSIS

REFLECT **1.** What effect of World War II on the home front surprises you most? Why?

RETHINK **2.** If you had been living during World War II, what part of rationing would have been the most difficult adjustment for you? Explain your answer.

3. What effects do you think rationing had on civilians at home, other than forcing people to make do with less?

RELATE **4.** "Make it do, wear it out, and do without." How would environmentalists today view this World War II slogan? What

parallels do you see between what the U.S. government urged citizens to do during World War II and what modern environmentalists urge today's citizens to do? Present your response in the form of a print ad campaign for both the past and present.

ANOTHER PATHWAY

Cooperative Learning

Using the information in the selection, work in small groups to create a "How to Adjust" poster for citizens living in the United States during World War II. Visually portray what citizens could do to cope with shortages.

QUICKWRITES

1. Write a **paragraph** contrasting life in the United States during World War II with life as it is now.

2. Write a concise **encyclopedia entry** about rationing during World War II, using the information in the selection. Before beginning, refer to an encyclopedia to get a sense of style.

3. Create a **radio or television public service announcement** urging people to buy war bonds or save scrap metal. Explain the purpose of buying bonds or saving metal and tell how to do one or the other. Be sure to grab your listeners' attention.

📁 *PORTFOLIO Save your writing. You may want to use it later as a springboard to a piece for your portfolio.*

LITERARY CONCEPTS

A **memoir** is a first-person recollection of an experience. It relates the details of an event that the writer participated in or witnessed. Often, the writer describes the impact of the event on his or her personal life. How successfully do you think Abernethy conveys the impact of World War II on civilian life and on her personal life? Give evidence from the story to support your answer.

ALTERNATIVE ACTIVITIES

1. **Cooperative Learning** Assemble the unanswered questions that individuals in your group had when reading this selection. Divide up the task of doing **research** to answer those questions. Share both questions and answers with the rest of the class.

2. Interview a grandparent or another older person who lived during World War II, asking about his or her memories of the war overseas and of the home front. You might want to videotape or audiotape the **interview** or orally report what you learned to the class.

ACROSS THE CURRICULUM

Social Studies Abernethy mentions prisoner-of-war camps in the United States as well as three major military events of World War II—the Japanese attack on Pearl Harbor, D-Day, and the Battle of the Bulge. Research the details of one of these places or events. Share your research with the class.

D-Day assault by Americans on the northern coast of France.

WORDS TO KNOW

The root word of *rationing* is the Latin word *ratio.* Use a dictionary to find the meaning of *ratio;* then list as many other words as you can that have the same root. Show how those words reflect the meaning of *ratio.*

HAZEL SHELTON ABERNETHY

Hazel Shelton Abernethy is pleased to have received national recognition with the publication of "The Home Front: 1941–1945," as well as recognition from her family: "I have six wonderful grandchildren and being published increases my credibility and stature with them and the rest of the family!"

Abernethy sees herself not as a writer, but as a wife, mother, grandmother, college teacher, public speaker, actress, and—believe it or not—stagehand. She has spent her life in Nacogdoches, where she graduated from Stephen F. Austin University in 1948. That same year she married her high school sweetheart, a Navy man. "Twenty years and five children later," Abernethy went back to

1927–

SFA, where she received her master's degree in history and taught until 1992.

Abernethy is head of production for Nacogdoches Lamplite Community Theater. She also speaks on local history for the East Texas Historical Association and other groups.

For Abernethy, the greatest impact of World War II was hearing the news and then seeing her friends leave. This "crystallized for me what the world was about," she recalls. "As teenagers we were certainly influenced by the drama and romance and excitement of wartime. For most of us the war was the defining period of our lives. 'Before the war' and 'after the war' are standard introductions of our remembering."

POETRY

my enemy was dreaming
Norman Russell

Lost
Bruce Ignacio

PERSONAL CONNECTION

Have you ever thought that it would be more fun to live as your ancestors did? Would life be more exciting? Were the "good old days" really better?

Imagine yourself in the place of one of your ancestors. When and where would you be living? What problems would you face? What would be the pluses and minuses of your life? List them on a chart like the one shown here.

Time:_____	Place:_____
+ Pluses of that life	**– Minuses of that life**

HISTORICAL CONNECTION

The two poems you are about to read describe the thoughts and feelings of two Native Americans, one a warrior from the past, and the other a modern-day descendant. Early Native Americans faced situations and had to make decisions that affected not only their survival but also their status within their tribes.

Modern Native Americans have lifestyles that are very different from those of their ancestors. Yet they, like most other people, sometimes think that their ancestors' lives were better than theirs are. In "Lost," the speaker looks at the pluses and minuses of his life as opposed to his ancestors' lives.

READING CONNECTION

Free Verse These two poems are written in free verse, which is poetry that has no regular pattern of rhythm, rhyme, or line length. Such poetry is written in a conversational style. Therefore, read each poem the way you think the speaker would express his thoughts in a conversation.

Native Americans dance during a celebration at the Blackfeet Indian Reservation in Montana. Copyright © Pat and Tom Leeson/Photo Researchers.

MY ENEMY WAS DREAMING

by Norman Russell

The Branch (1993), Lee Teter. Copyright © 1993 Somerset House Publishing.

when i found my enemy sleeping
i stood over him and as still
as the owl at night
as the heron waiting fish
5 i raised my knife to kill him

then i saw my enemy was dreaming
his mouth made a little smile
his legs trembled

he made small sleep sounds
10 a happy dream was in his mind

only i will have this memory
i will show the others
only the horse of my enemy
i will not tell the others
15 i left my enemy dreaming his dream.

FROM PERSONAL RESPONSE *TO* CRITICAL ANALYSIS

REFLECT   **1.** Were you surprised by the speaker's actions in "my enemy was dreaming"? Why or why not?

RETHINK   **2.** Why does the speaker choose not to kill his enemy?

      3. What evidence in the poem suggests that the speaker has done something different from what is expected of him?

      4. Do you think the pluses of his decision outweigh its minuses? Explain your answer.

LOST

by Bruce Ignacio

Cheyenne in New Mexico (1993),
Malcolm Furlow. Courtesy of the artist.

I know not of my forefathers
nor of their beliefs
For I was brought up in the city.
Our home seemed smothered and surrounded
5 as were other homes on city sites.
When the rain came
I would slush my way to school
as though the street were a wading pool.
Those streets were always crowded.
10 I brushed by people with every step,
Covered my nose once in awhile,
Gasping against the smell of perspiration on humid days.
Lights flashed everywhere
until my head became a signal, flashing on and off.
15 Noise so unbearable
I wished the whole place would come to a standstill,
leaving only peace and quiet

And still, would I like this kind of life? . . .
The life of my forefathers
20 who wandered, not knowing where they were going,
but just moving, further and further
from where they had been,
To be in quiet,
to kind of be lost in their dreams and wishing,
25 as I have been to this day,
I awake.

RESPONDING
OPTIONS

FROM PERSONAL RESPONSE TO CRITICAL ANALYSIS

REFLECT   1. What might you say to the speaker in "Lost" if you met him? Share your ideas with a partner.

RETHINK   2. What "minuses" does the speaker find in modern life in the city?

3. What does he think are the "minuses" of the lives of his ancestors?

4. If the speaker were able to choose between the two lifestyles, which do you think he would pick?

RELATE   5. Whose life would you rather live, that of the first speaker or the second? Explain your choice.

ANOTHER PATHWAY

With a partner, act out a conversation the speakers of the two poems might have if they met. Include the subject of dreaming, and allow both speakers to comment on each other's lifestyle.

LITERARY CONCEPTS

The **mood** of a poem or story is the emotional effect it has on its reader. The sound and rhythm of the language, descriptive words, and figurative language all contribute to the mood in these two poems. Describe the mood of each poem. What details help to create that mood?

"my enemy was dreaming"
To me, the mood of the poem was

"Lost"
I found the mood to reflect

QUICKWRITES

1. Compose several different versions of the first **stanza** of "my enemy was dreaming." Use the poet's first line and replace the similes and lines 2 and 5. Keep the meaning of the stanza in your versions.

2. Choose the speaker in either poem and write a **character analysis** of him. Infer what you can about his personality through his words and actions.

📁 **PORTFOLIO** *Save your writing. You may want to use it later as a springboard to a piece for your portfolio.*

ALTERNATIVE ACTIVITIES

1. **Cooperative Learning** With a small group of classmates, do a **group reading** of either of the two poems. Work on the appropriate tone of voice for each part of the poem in order to reflect its mood. Perform the reading for your class.

2. Design your own **illustrations** for each of the poems. Focus on the poems' titles for your inspiration.

ACROSS THE CURRICULUM

Social Studies Use the library or an on-line computer service to find out about the modern-day descendants of a Native American group of your choosing. Investigate the lifestyle differences between the modern group and their ancestors. Explore where these Native Americans live today, and find out how they think their lives are better or worse than their ancestors.

NORMAN RUSSELL

Norman Russell (1921–) says he does not write his Native American poems because he is part Cherokee, but because he feels "there is much we might learn today from a re-examination of the Indian's respect for his environment." Russell is a part-time poet—his training and career are in teaching and biology. He has done research, written textbooks, and taught biology at several colleges and universities.

Russell has had six volumes of poetry published, and his poems have appeared in numerous magazines and anthologies.

OTHER WORKS *At the Zoo, Indian Thoughts: The Small Songs of God, Open the Flower*

BRUCE IGNACIO

A Native American of northern Ute ancestry, Bruce Ignacio was born in Fort Duchesne, Utah. From 1967 through 1970, he attended the Institute of American Indian Arts in Santa Fe, New Mexico, where he studied creative writing and jewelry making. He made jewelry for a living until 1985, when he became a carpenter. Ignacio now lives with his wife and three daughters on the Wampanoag Indian Reservation, Martha's Vineyard, Massachusetts. There, he makes jewelry and small carvings known as fetishes.

Magazine Photo

WRITING A FICTIONAL NARRATIVE

Have you ever finished reading a story or watching a movie and said to yourself, "That seemed so real!"? Some of the best fiction stories are based on struggles that real people experience. The stories in Unit Two, "Critical Adjustments," deal with such real-life issues.

GUIDED ASSIGNMENT
Write a Short Story The events of your life can inspire you to write your own short stories. You'll explore how to write a short fictional story in the next few pages.

These guys look like they're from outer space! A story about aliens would be fun.

Magazine Article

❶ Look for Inspiration

In a short story, writers explore an idea, event, or feeling that's important to them. Have you ever wondered how they get these ideas?

Getting Ideas from Experience Sometimes writers find inspiration in their own experiences. What are some of the most interesting situations you've faced in your life? Start a list of story ideas.

Getting Ideas from Reading Reading fiction, poetry, news articles, advertising, or even graffiti can give writers ideas for stories of their own. Reread a favorite story or poem and add story ideas to your list.

Finding the Story Good writers are observant and interested in the things they read and see. What story ideas do you see in these excerpts and pictures?

Maybe I can write a story about the photo and this article about twins.

Why Do You Act That Way?

Barbara Parker was 36 when she met her genetic double. Returning home from the chiropractor one afternoon, she found a neighbor at her door. "Remember you told me you were adopted and an only child?" the neighbor asked. "Well, your identical twin is in my living room."

There she was—Parker's unknown, unimagined twin. Separated from her at birth, Parker had never dreamed the woman existed. But there, unmistakably, were Parker's cheekbones, smile, curly brown hair—even, the neighbor gasped, Parker's gestures and her laugh.

"The instant I saw her, I believed yes, she was my twin," said Parker, a 45-year-old landscape designer and mother of two living in Canyon Country. "But shock became disbelief. I began grilling her: Who was our mother? When is our birthday?"

Janny Scott
from *Los Angeles Times*, April 18, 1992

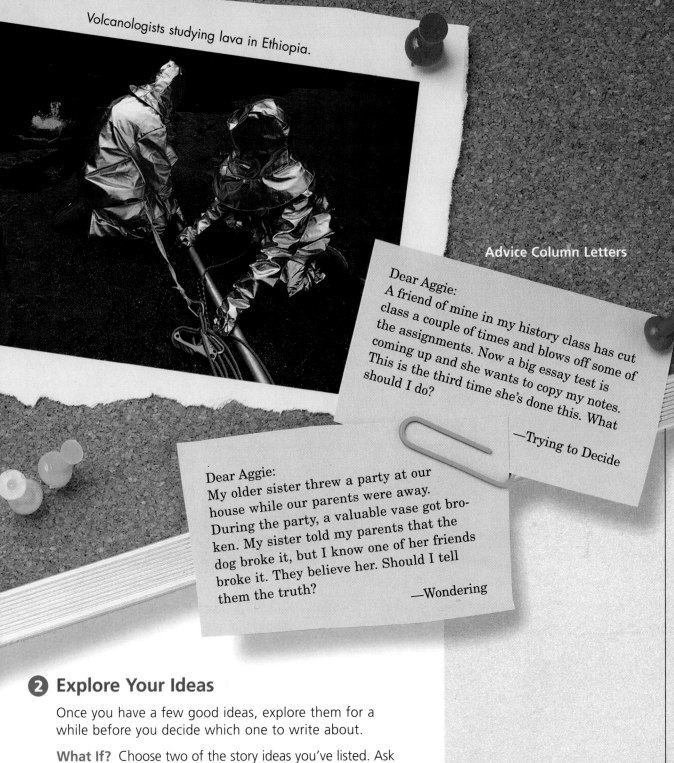

Volcanologists studying lava in Ethiopia.

Advice Column Letters

Dear Aggie:
A friend of mine in my history class has cut class a couple of times and blows off some of the assignments. Now a big essay test is coming up and she wants to copy my notes. This is the third time she's done this. What should I do?

—Trying to Decide

Dear Aggie:
My older sister threw a party at our house while our parents were away. During the party, a valuable vase got broken. My sister told my parents that the dog broke it, but I know one of her friends broke it. They believe her. Should I tell them the truth?

—Wondering

② Explore Your Ideas

Once you have a few good ideas, explore them for a while before you decide which one to write about.

What If? Choose two of the story ideas you've listed. Ask yourself "what if" questions to find possible story beginnings. For example, one student read the twins article, looked at the photo, and asked, "What if one twin was from outer space?"

LASERLINKS
• *WRITING SPRINGBOARD*

WRITING COACH

Working Out Your Ideas

Using Your Imagination Most of the work of writing occurs before you even set pen to paper. The more time you spend developing your ideas and mining your imagination, the more you'll have to work with when you begin to write.

① Choose a Topic

Look at the list of topic ideas you wrote earlier. Which one will you choose to write about? Write a brief explanation telling why you think this will make the best story.

② Think About Story Elements

A good story has a balance of several elements that can bring a conflict to life on the page. These are plot, setting, character, and conflict.

Plot A story's plot is the sequence of events that occur. Plot is the "what happens" of your story. The SkillBuilder at the right explains the different ways to order the events in your story.

Student's Planning Chart

Twin Story
Plot   story about
             twins who meet
             each other for
             the first time

Setting   my hometown

Character   boy my age and
             his twin

Conflict   maybe the twin
             could get the
             boy in trouble

Character Characters are the people in your story. Who will be the main characters in your story? What qualities will each character have?

Conflict Conflict is the central problem your characters face. What problems will your main character have to deal with?

Setting Setting is the "where" and "when" of your story. Will your story take place in the city? in the country? on another planet? Will your story take place in the 1800s? today? in the future?

③ Plan Your Story

Here are some suggestions to help you plan your story.

Sketch It Out Stories usually have a beginning, a middle, and an end. Making sketches of your ideas can help you to plan your setting and to order the details of your plot. Look at the drawings on the next page to see how one student planned his story.

Write Character Sketches Write brief descriptions, giving details about characters in your story. It might even help to draw sketches of each character.

④ Let the Story Unfold

These strategies may help you plan ways you can get your plot moving from the beginning to the end.

Take Time to Discover You won't know everything when you first start writing. Give yourself time to work through your ideas.

Plan the Conflict How will the main character try to resolve his or her problem?

Use Dialogue You can use dialogue to help move your plot along. For example: "Why did you break Steve's bike last week, Zolar?" Jakim asked. "Because I wanted you to get blamed for it," Zolar replied.

Show, Don't Tell Readers like to see things for themselves. Instead of telling them that a character is angry, why not let his actions show his anger?

Sketch a Story

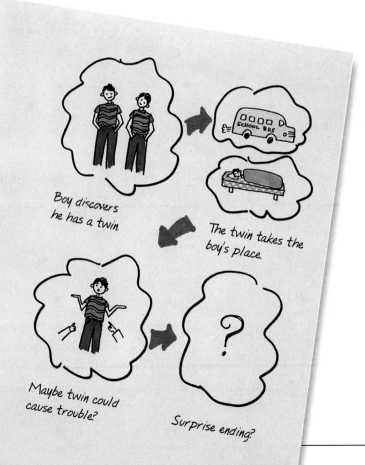

Boy discovers he has a twin.

The twin takes the boy's place.

Maybe twin could cause trouble?

Surprise ending?

Telling the Story

Telling It Your Way A story begins with the spark of
an idea and ends as a rich, descriptive journey through
the writer's mind. The next few pages will help you turn
your idea into a full-fledged story.

❶ Direct Your Draft

While you are writing, you can let the characters and situations
tell you what to say. Pretend you are watching a movie in your
head, and write down everything you see and hear.

Student's Draft

"You—you look just like me," Jakim said, as he
looked at Zolar.

"You look like me," Zolar corrected.

"Cool. Hmm. Maybe I can get out of taking the
history test on Friday. How are you at taking history
tests, Zolar?"

*Is this dialogue
interesting?
Would they
really say this?*

"I can't believe it!" Jakim screamed.

Zolar laughed an evil laugh. "Believe it. I'm really
from the planet Momax. I'm going to take over your
planet!" He walked away, laughing.

"I'll show that Zolar!" Jakim said. "We earthlings
aren't wimps!" He skated off.

He picked up speed, enjoying the crunch of dead
leaves beneath his skates. He felt like Jean-Claude van
Damme, Bruce Willis, Clint Eastwood, and Arnold
Schwarzenegger all rolled into one. Now, if only his
knees would stop shaking!

*How can I
resolve this
conflict?*

*Maybe I need
to add more
details.*

❷ Analyze Your Draft

Step back from the story. Asking yourself questions like these can help you evaluate your story ideas.

- Who will my readers be?
- How can I make the story flow more smoothly?
- Where are the characters and events leading me?
- What can I do to make my characters seem more real?
- What details can I add to help show the scene?
- Is it better to tell the story from the first-person point of view, with the narrator using the words *I, my,* and *me* to refer to himself or herself? Or should I use the third-person point of view, with the narrator using *he, she,* and *they* to describe what happens to all the characters?
- Should I present my story as a play? a comic strip? a story in a class booklet?

❸ Rework and Share

The following tips can help you rework your draft.

Descriptions You could describe a scene in several ways. Maybe you could start with sounds, then add smells and sights. It might be better to describe what's most important first, or to describe something in the order a movie camera might record it as the camera moves from one end to the other.

Sensory Details It's a good idea to involve your readers' eyes, ears, and nose by including sensory details. Look at the model on the previous page. The sentence "He picked up speed, enjoying the crunch of dead leaves beneath his skates" uses details of sight and sound to create a strong impression.

Dialogue Dialogue can be used to give information about the characters, show their personalities, and provide excitement and suspense in a scene. Try to make every line of dialogue add something to the story.

 PEER RESPONSE

Getting feedback from your peers will help you evaluate your story. Ask questions like the following:

- How did my story make you feel?
- What made you care about the characters?
- What was the most interesting part? the most boring part?

Polishing Your Story

Coming to the End It's time to take a look at your story with a fresh eye. Review your readers' responses and your own notes for your story. Use the feedback you received to make your story work.

Student's Final Draft

Double Trouble

"Why did I ever go on that stupid hike in the first place?" Jakim complained to his two goldfish. Blue and Sea swam in and out of their castle, not bothering to answer. "I wish I had never seen that Zolar!"

To think that he had once thought having a twin would be cool! But he had never dreamed that his twin would turn out to be a trouble-making alien from the planet Momax!

Jakim slipped two bottles of maple syrup into his jacket pocket. He was glad he had discovered that Zolar was allergic to maple syrup. He quickly put on his in-line skates and set off for Pointers Hill.

A slight breeze smelling of burning leaves carried him along. He felt like Jean-Claude van Damme, Bruce Willis, Clint Eastwood, and Arnold Schwarzenegger all rolled into one.

"I just wish my knees would stop shaking!" he thought.

He picked up speed, enjoying the crunch of dead leaves beneath his skates.

1 Revise and Edit

What do you like about your story? What needs to change?

- Consider comments made by your peers concerning the effect your story had on them. If there are comments you don't understand, ask reviewers to explain what they mean.
- Pretend you're the reader. Does the beginning of your story grab your attention? If not, go back and rethink it.
- Use the Standards for Evaluation and the Editing Checklist to be sure that the point of view in your story is consistently first person or third person.
- Read the excerpt of one student's draft to see how he used sensory details to make his descriptions vivid.

What do you feel, hear, taste, or smell through the character's senses?

How do the details support the plot?

This comic book shows another way of presenting your story.

2 Share Your Work

The format you use for your writing may depend on your audience and purpose for writing. You may decide on a more imaginative way to present your story. Below are some possibilities. What do you like best about each one?

PUBLISHING IDEAS

- You might turn your story into a play script. Include sound effects.
- A poem or ballad might also fit the mood of your story.
- You might choose to make a comic strip or comic book.
- You could use the story events to make a gameboard.

Standards for Evaluation

A short story
- has fully developed plot, character, and setting
- uses sensory details
- presents events in a clear order
- maintains a consistent point of view
- uses realistic dialogue

REFLECT & ASSESS

UNIT TWO: CRITICAL ADJUSTMENTS

As you read the selections in this unit, what did you discover about the adjustments that people make in their lives? What new insights did you gain into the causes and results of such changes? Use one or more of the options in each of the following sections to help you reflect on what you have learned.

REFLECTING ON THEME

OPTION 1 **Looking at Character** Think about the quotation that begins this unit: "There are two ways of meeting difficulties. You alter the difficulties or you alter yourself to meet them." Create a chart showing which of the two ways each major character in this unit chooses. Working with a partner, select one character from each column of your chart, and imagine a situation in which those two characters meet. Role-play a dialogue in which the characters discuss the quotation.

Alter the Difficulties	Alter Yourself

OPTION 2 **Learning a Lesson** Which selections in Unit Two do you think will cause you to alter

your own actions or attitudes in the future? Which have had little effect on you? Rank the selections in order of the impact they have had on you. Put the selection that has influenced you the most at the top; the selection that has influenced you the least should come last. Explain to a classmate the reasons for your rankings.

Self-Assessment: Now that you have seen several characters adjust to new circumstances, write a few short paragraphs in which you describe what you have learned about dealing with change. Outline any adjustments that you plan to make as a result of what you have learned, noting the titles of the selections that have influenced your decisions.

REVIEWING LITERARY CONCEPTS

OPTION 1 **Thinking About Point of View** Work with a partner, one of you listing the stories in this unit that are told from the first-person point of view and the other listing the stories that are told from the third-person point of view. Compare your lists, then discuss the following questions:

• Why do you think the author of each story chose the point of view that he or she used?

• How would each story be different if it were told from a different point of view?

OPTION 2 **Exploring Theme** As you know, a work's theme is a message about life that the work

conveys to the reader. Summarize in a phrase or two the theme of each selection you have read in this unit. Then look for ways of grouping the selections according to their themes—you might put selections together because they convey similar messages or because they convey opposite messages. In each case, say what the link is.

"Lost" | Link: the importance of one's ethnic heritage | "White Mice"

Self-Assessment: In your notebook, draw a step diagram like the one shown. After looking at the list of literary terms introduced in this unit, write each term in an appropriate place on the diagram. If you think you have a good knowledge of the term, write it on the top step. If you have little or no understanding of the term, write it on the bottom step. Then work with a small group of classmates to clarify the meanings of the terms you are least sure about.

allusion   surprise ending   memoir
setting   flashback   free verse
resolution   climax   mood
conflict   autobiography

PORTFOLIO BUILDING

- **QuickWrites** Look back at your work for the QuickWrites that asked you to write as a character from a selection. Choose the piece that you think best captures a character's personality and feelings about the changes in his or her life. Then write a note explaining why you think you were able to impersonate that character well. Add the piece and the note to your portfolio.

- **Writing About Literature** Earlier in this unit, you wrote an interpretive essay about one of the selections. Write a brief note about your essay. Do you feel now that your essay offers a reasonable interpretation? Did you find the assignment difficult? Why or why not? What would you do differently if you could do the assignment over? Decide whether to include your note in your portfolio.

- **Writing from Experience** Reread the fictional narrative you wrote earlier in this unit. Imagine that a student arts magazine wants to publish your story in the next issue. The editor wishes to include some background information about your story and your writing process. In a brief note, tell how you came to write the story, what steps you took to get it down on paper, and how successful you think it is.

- **Personal Choice** Look back through your records and evaluations of the activities you completed in this unit. Also look at the activities and writing you did on your own. Which of these pieces do you think best reflected the theme of this unit, "Critical Adjustments"? Write a note that explains the reasons for your choice, attach it to the piece, and add both to your portfolio.

Self-Assessment: Review the work you have added to your portfolio as you completed the first two units. Which pieces might you want to rework so that you can share them with a larger audience?

SETTING GOALS

As you completed the reading and writing activities in this section, you probably identified certain stories that you particularly liked. What kinds of stories would you like to read more of? What kinds of writing would you like to become more skillful at?

Prairie Fire (about 1953), Blackbear Bosin (Kiowa-Comanche people).
The Philbrook Museum of Art, Tulsa, Oklahoma.

Battle FOR CONTROL

When you get

to the end of your

rope, tie a knot

and hang on.

Franklin Delano Roosevelt
President of the United States
1933-1945

STRUGGLING FOR SURVIVAL

REFLECTING ON THEME

In order to get control of our lives, we sometimes have to "battle" other people, forces of nature, pressures of society, and even ourselves. Sometimes we have to struggle for our very lives. Use the activities on this page to explore the forms the struggle for survival can take.

Can you remember?

Difficult experiences often help people to mature. Think about an experience of yours that caused you to gain insight into yourself and the adult world. Design a chart that shows how your views or feelings changed as a result of the experience.

What went wrong?

Sometimes you can look back and laugh at events that were unpleasant, or even dangerous, at the time. Imagine that you are involved in a camping trip on which everything has gone haywire. Write a postcard, describing the trip.

What would you include?

Work with a small group to prepare an outline for a television documentary entitled "Teenage Survival Skills." Include advice on how teenagers can cope with the various demands placed upon them today.

How could you help?

Sometimes survival is a matter of adjusting to a new culture. If someone your age were immigrating to the United States from a country such as Vietnam or China, what problems might he or she face? Write a short guidebook designed to help immigrants adjust to life in the United States.

PREVIEWING

FICTION

Getting the Facts of Life
Paulette Childress White

PERSONAL CONNECTION

You probably know something about the welfare system, either from media reports or from personal experience. Welfare is government aid that provides needy people with regular financial help, and the future of the welfare system is a hotly debated issue. What attitudes does society have about the welfare system and people who receive welfare payments? Discuss what you know with your classmates.

SOCIAL STUDIES CONNECTION

In this story, 12-year-old Minerva learns about welfare at first hand. Welfare is not just a single U.S. government program but a group of programs funded by federal, state, and local governments. Assistance is based on need. Most cash payments come from a program called Aid to Families with Dependent Children (AFDC), which provides financial aid primarily to children and to their parents or the other adults who care for them. In 1994, AFDC distributed $22.5 billion to 14 million people, compared with $4 billion in 1974 and $8 billion in 1984.

Federal AFDC Benefits

(in billions of dollars)

READING CONNECTION

Character Changes Minerva changes as she gains insight into herself and the adult world by visiting a welfare office with her mother. As you read this story, look for signs of change in Minerva's attitude. When you finish reading, record the changes in a chart like the one shown here.

Minerva's Feelings	At the Beginning	At the End
About welfare		
About her mother		
About herself		

Getting the Facts of Life

The August morning was ripening into a day that promised to be a burner. By the time we'd walked three blocks, dark patches were showing beneath Momma's arms, and inside tennis shoes thick with white polish, my feet were wet against the cushions. I was beginning to regret how quickly I'd volunteered to go.

by
Paulette
Childress
White

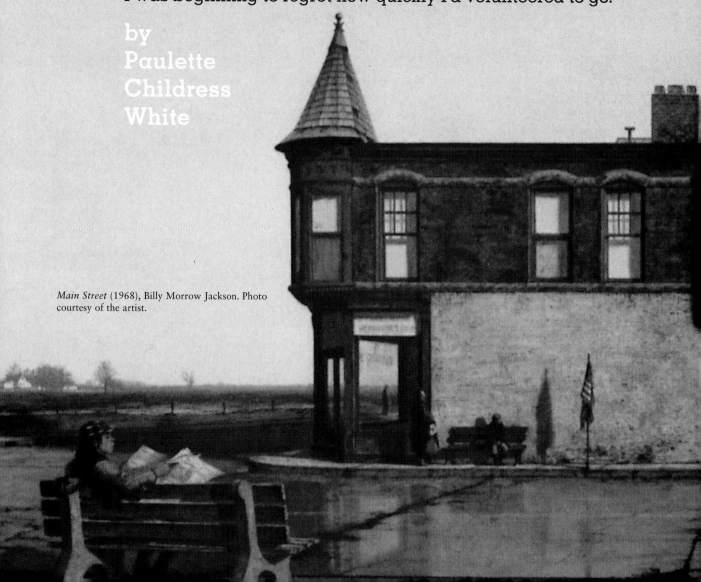

Main Street (1968), Billy Morrow Jackson. Photo courtesy of the artist.

"Dog. My feet are getting mushy," I complained.

"You should've wore socks," Momma said, without looking my way or slowing down.

I frowned. In 1961, nobody wore socks with tennis shoes. It was bare legs, Bermuda shorts[1] and a sleeveless blouse. Period.

Momma was chubby but she could really walk. She walked the same way she washed clothes—up-and-down, up-and-down until she was done. She didn't believe in taking breaks.

This was my first time going to the welfare office with Momma. After breakfast, before we'd had time to scatter, she corralled everyone old enough to consider and announced in her serious-business voice that someone was going to the welfare office with her this morning. Cries went up.

Junior had his papers to do. Stella was going swimming at the high school. Dennis was already pulling the *Free Press*[2] wagon across town every first Wednesday to get the surplus food—like that.

"You want clothes for school, don't you?" That landed. School opened in two weeks.

"I'll go," I said.

"Who's going to baby-sit if Minerva goes?" Momma asked.

Stella smiled and lifted her small golden nose. "I will," she said. "I'd rather baby-sit than do *that*."

That should have warned me. Anything that would make Stella offer to baby-sit had to be bad.

---

1. **Bermuda shorts:** short pants that end just above the knee.
2. ***Free Press:*** a daily newspaper published in Detroit, Michigan.

A small cheer probably went up among my younger brothers in the back rooms, where I was not too secretly known as "The Witch" because of the criminal licks I'd learned to give on my rise to power. I was twelve, third oldest under Junior and Stella, but I had long established myself as first in command among the kids. I was chief baby sitter, biscuit maker and broom wielder. Unlike Stella, who'd begun her development at ten, I still had my girl's body and wasn't anxious to have that changed. What would it mean but a loss of power? I liked things just the way they were. My interest in bras was even less than my interest in boys, and that was limited to keeping my brothers—who seemed destined for wildness—from taking over completely.

Even before we left, Stella had Little Stevie Wonder turned up on the radio in the living room, and suspicious jumping-bumping sounds were beginning in the back. They'll tear the house down, I thought, following Momma out the door.

We turned at Salliotte, the street that would take us straight up to Jefferson Avenue where the welfare office was. Momma's face was pinking in the heat, and I was huffing to keep up. From here, it was seven more blocks on the colored side, the railroad tracks, five blocks on the white side and there you were. We'd be cooked.

"Is the welfare office near the Harbor Show?" I asked. I knew the answer; I just wanted some talk.

"Across the street."

"Umm. Glad it's not way down Jefferson somewhere."

Nothing. Momma didn't talk much when she was outside. I knew that the reason she wanted one of us along when she had far to go was not for company but so she wouldn't have to walk by herself. I could understand that. To me, walking alone was like being naked or deformed—everyone seemed to look at you harder and longer. With Momma, the feeling was probably worse because you knew people were wondering if she were white, Indian maybe or really colored. Having one of us along, brown and clearly hers, probably helped define that. Still, it was like being a little parade, with Momma's pale skin and straight brown hair turning heads like the clang of cymbals. Especially on the colored side.

"Well," I said, "here we come to the bad part."

Momma gave a tiny laugh.

Most of Salliotte was a business street, with Old West-looking storefronts and some office places that never seemed to open. Ecorse, hinged onto southwest Detroit like a clothes closet, didn't seem to take itself seriously. There were lots of empty fields, some of which folks down the residential streets turned into vegetable gardens every summer. And there was this block where the Moonflower Hotel raised itself to three stories over the poolroom and Beaman's drugstore. Here, bad boys and drunks made their noise and did an occasional stabbing. Except for the cars that lined both sides of the block, only one side was busy—the other bordered a field of weeds. We walked on the safe side.

If you were a woman or a girl over twelve, walking this block—even on the safe side— could be painful. They usually hollered at you, and never mind what they said. Today, because it was hot and early, we made it by with only one weak *Hey baby* from a drunk sitting in the poolroom door.

"Hey baby yourself," I said, but not too loudly, pushing my flat chest out and stabbing my eyes in his direction.

"Minerva girl, you better watch your mouth with grown men like that," Momma said, her eyes catching me up in real warning, though I could see that she was holding down a smile.

"Well, he can't do nothing to me when I'm with you, can he?" I asked, striving to match the rise and fall of her black pumps.

> We had been on welfare for almost a year. I didn't have any strong feelings about it—my life went on pretty much the same.

She said nothing. She just walked on, churning away under a sun that clearly meant to melt us. From here to the tracks it was mostly gardens. It felt like the Dixie Peach I'd used to help water-wave my hair was sliding down with the sweat on my face, and my throat was tight with thirst. Boy, did I want a pop. I looked at the last little store before we crossed the tracks without bothering to ask.

Across the tracks, there were no stores and no gardens. It was shady, and the grass was June green. Perfect-looking houses sat in unfenced spaces far back from the street. We walked these five blocks without a word. We just looked and hurried to get through it. I was beginning to worry about the welfare office in earnest. A fool could see that in this part of Ecorse, things got serious.

We had been on welfare for almost a year. I didn't have any strong feelings about it—my life went on pretty much the same. It just meant watching the mail for a check instead of Daddy getting paid, and occasional visits from a social worker that I'd always managed to miss. For Momma and whoever went with her, it meant this walk to the office and whatever went on there that made everyone hate to go.

For Daddy, it seemed to bring the most change. For him, it meant staying away from home more than when he was working and a reason not to answer the phone.

At Jefferson, we turned left and there it was, halfway down the block. The Department of Social Services. I discovered some strong feelings. That fine name meant nothing. This was the welfare. The place for poor people. People who couldn't or wouldn't take care of themselves. Now I was going to face it, and suddenly I thought what I knew the others had thought, *What if I see someone I know?* I wanted to run back all those blocks to home.

I looked at Momma for comfort, but her face was closed and her mouth looked locked.

Inside, the place was gray. There were rows of long benches like church pews facing each other across a middle aisle that led to a central desk. Beyond the benches and the desk, four hallways led off to a maze of partitioned offices. In opposite corners, huge fans hung from the ceiling, humming from side to side, blowing the heavy air for a breeze.

Momma walked to the desk, answered some questions, was given a number and told to take a seat. I followed her through, trying not to see the waiting people—as though that would keep them from seeing me.

CONNECT

How would you feel if you were Minerva?

Gradually, as we waited, I took them all in. There was no one there that I knew, but somehow they all looked familiar. Or maybe I only thought they did, because when your eyes connected with someone's, they didn't quickly look away and they usually smiled. They were mostly women and children, and a few low-looking men. Some of them were white, which surprised me. I hadn't expected to see them in there.

Directly in front of the bench where we sat,

WORDS TO KNOW **partitioned** (pär-tǐsh′ənd) *adj.* divided by interior walls **partition** *v.*

a little girl with blond curls was trying to handle a bottle of Coke. Now and then, she'd manage to turn herself and the bottle around and watch me with big gray eyes that seemed to know quite well how badly I wanted a pop. I thought of asking Momma for fifteen cents so I could get one from the machine in the back, but I was afraid she'd still say no, so I just kept planning more and more convincing ways to ask. Besides, there was a water fountain near the door if I could make myself rise and walk to it.

We waited three hours. White ladies dressed like secretaries kept coming out to call numbers, and people on the benches would get up and follow down a hall. Then more people came in to replace them. I drank water from the fountain three times and was ready to put my feet up on the bench before us—the little girl with the Coke and her momma got called—by the time we heard Momma's number.

"You wait here," Momma said as I rose with her.

I sat down with a plop.

The lady with the number looked at me. Her face reminded me of the librarian's at Bunch school. Looked like she never cracked a smile. "Let her come," she said.

"She can wait here," Momma repeated, weakly.

"It's OK. She can come in. Come on," the lady insisted at me.

I hesitated, knowing that Momma's face was telling me to sit.

"Come on," the woman said.

Momma said nothing.

I got up and followed them into the maze. We came to a small room where there was a desk and three chairs. The woman sat behind the desk and we before it.

For a while, no one spoke. The woman studied a folder open before her, brows drawn together. On the wall behind her there was a calendar with one heavy black line drawn slantwise through each day of August, up to the twenty-first. That was today.

"Mrs. Blue, I have a notation here that Mr. Blue has not reported to the department on his efforts to obtain employment since the sixteenth of June. Before that, it was the tenth of April. You understand that department regulations require that he report monthly to this office, do you not?" Eyes brown as a wren's belly came up at Momma.

"Yes," Momma answered, sounding as small as I felt.

"Can you explain his failure to do so?"

Pause. "He's been looking. He says he's been looking."

"That may be. However, his failure to report those efforts here is my only concern."

Silence.

"We cannot continue with your case as it now stands if Mr. Blue refuses to comply with departmental regulations. He is still residing with the family, is he not?"

"Yes, he is. I've been reminding him to come in . . . he said he would."

"Well, he hasn't. Regulations are that any able-bodied man, head-of-household and receiving assistance, who neglects to report to this office any effort to obtain work for a period of sixty days or more is to be cut off for a minimum of three months, at which time he may reapply. As of this date, Mr. Blue is over sixty days delinquent, and officially, I am obliged to close the case and direct you to other sources of aid."

WORDS TO KNOW **comply** (kəm-plī′) v. to obey a rule or command
reside (rĭ-zīd′) v. to occupy a home

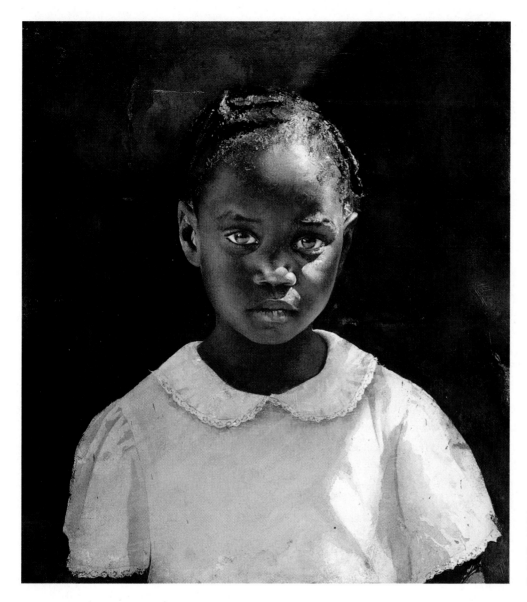

Pink Lace (1993),
Stephen Scott Young.
Photo courtesy of The
John H. Surovek Gallery,
Palm Beach, Florida.
Copyright © Stephen
Scott Young.

"What is that?"

"Aid to Dependent Children would be the only source available to you. Then, of course, you would not be eligible unless it was <u>verified</u> that Mr. Blue was no longer residing with the family."

Another silence. I stared into the gray steel front of the desk, everything stopped but my heart.

"Well, can you keep the case open until Monday? If he comes in by Monday?"

"According to my records, Mr. Blue failed to come in May, and such an agreement was made then. In all, we allowed him a period of seventy days. You must understand that what happens in such cases as this is not wholly my decision." She sighed and watched Momma with hopeless eyes, tapping the soft end of her

verify (vĕr′ə-fī′) *v.* to prove to be true by providing evidence

291

pencil on the papers before her. "Mrs. Blue, I will speak to my superiors on your behalf. I can allow you until Monday next . . . that's the"—she swung around to the calendar—"twenty-sixth of August, to get him in here."

"Thank you. He'll be in," Momma breathed. "Will I be able to get the clothing order today?"

> Then I heard our names and ages—all eight of them—being called off like items in a grocery list.

Hands and eyes searched in the folder for an answer before she cleared her throat and tilted her face at Momma. "We'll see what we can do," she said, finally.

My back touched the chair. Without turning my head, I moved my eyes down to Momma's dusty feet and wondered if she could still feel them; my own were numb. I felt bodyless—there was only my face, which wouldn't disappear, and behind it, one word pinging against another in a buzz that made no sense. At home, we'd have the house cleaned by now, and I'd be waiting for the daily appearance of my best friend, Bernadine, so we could comb each other's hair or talk about stuck-up Evelyn and Brenda. Maybe Bernadine was already there, and Stella was teaching her to dance the bop.

Then I heard our names and ages—all eight of them—being called off like items in a grocery list.

"Clifford, Junior, age fourteen." She waited.

"Yes."

"Born? Give me the month and year."

"October 1946," Momma answered, and I could hear in her voice that she'd been through these questions before.

"Stella, age thirteen."

"Yes."

"Born?"

"November 1947."

"Minerva, age twelve." She looked at me. "This is Minerva?"

"Yes."

No. I thought, no, this is not Minerva. You can write it down if you want to, but Minerva is not here.

"Born?"

"December 1948."

The woman went on down the list, sounding more and more like Momma should be sorry or ashamed, and Momma's answers grew fainter and fainter. So this was welfare. I wondered how many times Momma had had to do this. Once before? Three times? Every time?

More questions. How many in school? Six. Who needs shoes? Everybody.

"Everybody needs shoes? The youngest two?"

"Well, they don't go to school . . . but they walk."

My head came up to look at Momma and the woman. The woman's mouth was left open. Momma didn't blink.

The brown eyes went down. "Our allowances are based on the <u>median</u> costs for moderately priced clothing at Sears, Roebuck." She figured on paper as she spoke. "That will mean thirty-four dollars for children over ten . . . thirty dollars for children under ten. It comes to one hundred ninety-eight dollars. I can allow eight dollars for two additional pairs of shoes."

"Thank you."

WORDS TO KNOW   **median** (mē′dē-ən) *adj.* relating to the middle value in a series

"You will present your clothing order to a salesperson at the store, who will be happy to assist you in your selections. Please be practical, as further clothing requests will not be considered for a period of six months. In cases of necessity, however, requests for winter outerwear will be considered beginning November first."

Momma said nothing.

The woman rose and left the room.

For the first time, I shifted in the chair. Momma was looking into the calendar as though she could see through the pages to November first. Everybody needed a coat.

I'm never coming here again, I thought. If I do, I'll stay out front. Not coming back in here. Ever again.

CLARIFY

Why does Minerva have such strong feelings about the welfare office?

She came back and sat behind her desk. "Mrs. Blue, I must make it clear that, regardless of my feelings, I will be forced to close your case if your husband does not report to this office by Monday, the twenty-sixth. Do you understand?"

"Yes. Thank you. He'll come. I'll see to it."

"Very well." She held a paper out to Momma.

We stood. Momma reached over and took the slip of paper. I moved toward the door.

"Excuse me, Mrs. Blue, but are you pregnant?"

"What?"

"I asked if you were expecting another child."

"Oh. No, I'm not," Momma answered, biting down on her lips.

"Well, I'm sure you'll want to be careful about a thing like that in your present situation."

"Yes."

I looked quickly to Momma's loose white blouse. We'd never known when another baby was coming until it was almost there.

"I suppose that eight children are enough for anyone," the woman said, and for the first time her face broke into a smile.

Momma didn't answer that. Somehow, we left the room and found our way out onto the street. We stood for a moment as though lost. My eyes followed Momma's up to where the sun was burning high. It was still there, blazing white against a cloudless blue. Slowly, Momma put the clothing order into her purse and snapped it shut. She looked around as if uncertain which way to go. I led the way to the corner. We turned. We walked the first five blocks.

I was thinking about how stupid I'd been a year ago, when Daddy lost his job. I'd been happy.

"You-all better be thinking about moving to Indianapolis," he announced one day after work, looking like he didn't think much of it himself. He was a welder with the railroad company. He'd worked there for eleven years. But now, "Company's moving to Indianapolis," he said. "Gonna be gone by November. If I want to keep my job, we've got to move with it."

We didn't. Nobody wanted to move to Indianapolis—not even Daddy. Here, we had uncles, aunts and cousins on both sides. Friends. Everybody and everything we knew. Daddy could get another job. First came unemployment compensation.[3] Then came welfare. Thank goodness for welfare, we said, while we waited and waited for the job that hadn't yet come.

The problem was that Daddy couldn't take it. If something got repossessed[4] or somebody took sick or something was broken or another kid was coming, he'd carry on terribly until things got better—by which time things were always worse. He'd always been that way. So when the railroad left, he began to do everything wrong. Stayed out all hours. Drank and drank

---

3. **unemployment compensation:** a regular payment of money to an unemployed worker for a limited time.

4. **repossessed:** taken back by a seller because of the buyer's failure to make payment.

some more. When he was home, he was so grouchy we were afraid to squeak. Now when we saw him coming, we got lost. Even our friends ran for cover.

At the railroad tracks, we sped up. The tracks were as far across as a block was long. Silently, I counted the rails by the heat of the steel bars through my thin soles. On the other side, I felt something heavy rise up in my chest, and I knew that I wanted to cry. I wanted to cry or run or kiss the dusty ground. The little houses with their sun-scorched lawns and backyard gardens were mansions in my eyes. "Ohh, Ma . . . look at those collards!"

"Umm-humm," she agreed, and I knew that she saw it too.

"Wonder how they grew so big?"

"Cow dung, probably. Big Poppa used to put cow dung out to fertilize the vegetable plots, and everything just grew like crazy. We used to get tomatoes this big"—she circled with her hands—"and don't talk about squash or melons."

"I bet y'all ate like rich people. Bet y'all had everything you could want."

"We sure did," she said. "We never wanted for anything when it came to food. And when the cash crops were sold, we could get whatever else that was needed. We never wanted for a thing."

"What about the time you and cousin Emma threw out the supper peas?"

"Oh! Did I tell you about that?" she asked. Then she told it all over again. I didn't listen. I watched her face and guarded her smile with a smile of my own.

We walked together, step for step. The sun was still burning, but we forgot to mind it. We talked about an Alabama girlhood in a time and place I'd never know. We talked about the wringer washer[5] and how it could be fixed, because washing every day on a scrub board

was something Alabama could keep. We talked about how to get Daddy to the Department of Social Services.

Then we talked about having babies. She began to tell me things I'd never known, and the idea of womanhood blossomed in my mind like some kind of suffocating rose.

"Momma," I said, "I don't think I can be a woman."

> She began to tell me things I'd never known, and the idea of womanhood blossomed in my mind like some kind of suffocating rose.

"You can," she laughed, "and if you live, you will be. You gotta be some kind of woman."

"But it's hard," I said, "sometimes it must be hard."

"Umm-humm," she said, "sometimes it is hard."

When we got to the bad block, we crossed to Beaman's drugstore for two orange crushes. Then we walked right through the groups of men standing in the shadows of the poolroom and the Moonflower Hotel. Not one of them said a word to us. I supposed they could see in the way we walked that we weren't afraid. We'd been to the welfare office and back again. And the facts of life, fixed in our minds like the sun in the sky, were no burning mysteries. ❖

---

5. **wringer washer:** an old-fashioned washing machine in which laundry is pressed between rollers to remove water.

RESPONDING
OPTIONS

FROM PERSONAL RESPONSE TO CRITICAL ANALYSIS

REFLECT

1. What are your reactions to Minerva's experiences? Share your thoughts with the class.

RETHINK

2. Which change in Minerva do you think is the most important? Support your opinion with evidence from the story.

3. Evaluate the welfare worker's attitude toward Mrs. Blue. Do you think her attitude is justified? Why or why not?

4. Do you think that Minerva's father will report to the welfare office on the appointed day? Give reasons for your prediction.

5. In your opinion, is a trip to the welfare office, like that in the story, an appropriate or useful experience for a child? Why or why not?
   Consider
   • the conversation between Mrs. Blue and the welfare worker
   • Minerva's feelings about becoming an adult and her mother's response
   • what Minerva and her mother share on the walk home

6. How does the Blue family's experience relate to the unit theme, "Battle for Control"?

RELATE

7. Supporters of the welfare system say that financial assistance is a necessary "safety net" for families who are struggling to survive. Critics of the system claim that welfare discourages recipients from seeking employment. Consider your class's prereading discussion about society's attitudes toward welfare. What do you think about the welfare system now?

ANOTHER PATHWAY
Cooperative Learning

The action of this story can be divided into three or four scenes. With a group of classmates, stage a Readers Theater presentation of one of these scenes for the rest of the class.

QUICKWRITES

1. Compose a **poem** in which Minerva is the speaker. Write either about her reactions to the visit to the welfare office or about her thoughts on approaching adulthood.

2. Write a **character sketch** of one person in the story. Describe three of the character's prominent traits and explain how each is shown.

3. Near the end of the story, Minerva says that she and her mother "talked about how to get Daddy to the Department of Social Services." Write the **dialogue** that they might have had.

📁 *PORTFOLIO Save your writing. You may want to use it later as a springboard to a piece for your portfolio.*

Realistic fiction is imaginative writing set in the real, modern world. In such fiction, the characters act like real people, using ordinary human abilities to cope with problems and conflicts typical of modern life. In what ways is "Getting the Facts of Life" realistic? What conflicts do the characters face?

CONCEPT REVIEW: First-Person Point of View The author uses a first-person point of view in this story. Why do you think she chose Minerva rather than her mother to tell the story?

ALTERNATIVE ACTIVITIES

1. Think about the way this story made you feel. Then draw a **picture** or compose a **song** that reflects your feelings.

2. How might Minerva's mother have viewed the events of this story? With a classmate, act out a **telephone conversation** in which she discusses her trip with a friend.

3. Choose a classmate who disagrees with you on a topic related to the welfare system. Research the topic on your own. Then **debate** the topic with your classmate in front of your class.

ART CONNECTION

Look at the painting on pages 286–287. What mood does the painting evoke? How does the painter achieve that mood? Does the mood match that of the story? Explain your opinions.

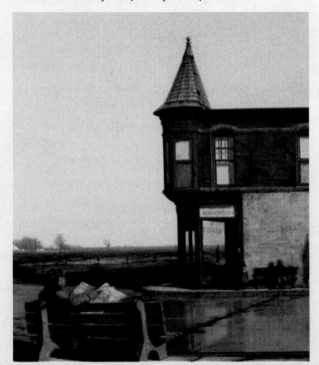

ACROSS THE CURRICULUM

Social Studies Each state decides who will receive money from Aid to Families with Dependent Children and how much each family will get. Contact your local AFDC office to learn how much a family of two unemployed adults and eight children, like the Blue family, would receive.

LITERARY LINKS

Compare and contrast the relationship between Minerva and her mother with that of Yollie and her mother in "Mother and Daughter" (page 203). How do circumstances affect each relationship?

Minerva and her mother

Yollie and her mother

WORDS TO KNOW

EXERCISE A Review the Words to Know at the bottom of the selection pages, and list them on your paper. Write the Word to Know that best completes the sentence.

1. In 1993, the average monthly AFDC payment to families ranged from $120 a month to $762. Eleven states gave benefits above the _____, or midpoint, of these two figures.

2. A government welfare office may be a large room with many _____ offices.

3. A welfare worker must ask questions in order to _____ that the recipient is still unemployed and qualifies for aid.

4. If a welfare recipient cannot _____ with the department's rules, the recipient may lose his or her benefits.

5. Public-housing programs allow needy families to _____ in low-cost rental apartments.

EXERCISE B For each of the five Words to Know, make a word map like the example shown.

Word Map	**Context Sentence** I never divulge a secret that a friend has entrusted to me.
Word divulge	**Association or Symbol**
Best Guess speak out	
One Good Sentence She will soon divulge the location of the treasure.	
Verified Definition to reveal; make public	

PAULETTE CHILDRESS WHITE

Like Minerva Blue, the 12-year-old narrator of "Getting the Facts of Life," Paulette Childress White grew up in Ecorse, Michigan, a town that was racially divided by railroad tracks. Now the mother of five grown children, White lives in Detroit with her husband. She is working on a doctorate in literature while teaching at Henry Ford Community College and Wayne State University.

1948–

White often writes about contemporary African-American women in an urban environment. She has written a collection of poetry entitled *The Watermelon Dress* and has contributed to such magazines as *Essence, Redbook,* and *Callaloo.* Short stories by her have appeared in the anthologies *Midnight Birds* and *Memory of Kin: Stories About Family by Black Writers,* from which "Getting the Facts of Life" was taken.

About her writing the author says, "I write from a sense of irony, because I want to make sense of my experience of life."

FICTION

Appetizer
Robert H. Abel

PERSONAL CONNECTION

Imagine that you are hiking in a beautiful, peaceful wilderness. Suddenly, you hear the heavy breathing of a wild animal that is creeping up behind you. Slowly you turn. The animal you see is the one you fear most. What animal is it? What will you do to survive? Jot down the ending of this story in your notebook. Then share it with your classmates.

SCIENCE CONNECTION

Perhaps the wild animal you fear most is a bear. If so, you have good reason. The size, strength, fierceness, and unpredictability of a bear make it a serious threat to the survival of anyone it encounters in the wild. The bear in this story, an Alaskan brown bear, is certainly no exception. The Alaskan brown bear is the largest carnivore, or meat eater, that lives on land. It can grow up to nine feet long, can weigh 1,800 pounds, and, when standing, can reach the rim of a basketball hoop. Found chiefly on the mainland of Alaska and on nearby islands, Alaskan brown bears dine on, among other things, the salmon in Alaska's rivers and coastal waters.

Like other species of bears, brown bears are usually peaceful animals, but if their safety, their cubs, or their homes are threatened, they will attack. Their powerful front paws and long, thick claws are dangerous weapons. As you read this story, see what happens when a fisherman encounters "Ms. Bear."

LASERLINKS
• *SCIENCE CONNECTION*
• *VISUAL VOCABULARY*

Evaluating

The skill of making judgments about people, things, and situations is the skill of evaluating. For instance, as you watch a movie, you automatically evaluate the actors, the filming, and the action. You might decide that you like or dislike certain characters. You might think that the story line is believable or that it is absolutely absurd. As the movie progresses and more information is presented to you, you probably make additional evaluations or change evaluations you made earlier. Later, when someone asks you whether you liked the movie, you base your overall evaluation on the criteria that are most important to you.

Fiction Evaluating a story is similar to evaluating a movie. As you read, you make judgments about the story's elements—its characters, setting, and plot. You might decide, for example, that one character is really smart and another is stupid or selfish. You might judge the setting to be confusing or clear, or the plot to be exciting or dull. You might consider the ending of the story touching or disappointing. All these individual judgments combine to form your evaluation of the story as a whole.

Poetry and Nonfiction You can evaluate the elements of poetry and nonfiction as well. When reading a poem, ask yourself such questions as, Can I picture the images? Does the sound of the poem appeal to me? Does the poem say anything important to me? For nonfiction, evaluate the work's organization. Decide how much of the work is opinion and how much is fact, and whether you agree with the writer's conclusions.

Author's Purpose Another aspect of a work to evaluate is how well the author has achieved his or her purpose. Keep in mind that authors write for four main reasons: to entertain, to inform, to express opinions, and to persuade. After you determine an author's main purpose in a work, evaluate how well he or she has achieved that purpose.

As you read "Appetizer," jot down your evaluations in your notebook as you find yourself making them. When you finish the story, determine what you think Robert H. Abel's main purpose for writing it was and how well he has achieved that purpose. Finally, evaluate the story as a whole on the basis of your evaluations of its individual elements. Give it a rating of one to five stars, with five stars being the best.

Appetizer

by Robert H. Abel

I'm fishing this beautiful stream in Alaska, catching salmon, char and steelhead, when this bear lumbers out of the woods and down to the stream bank. He fixes me with this half-amused, half-curious look which says: You are meat.

The bear's eyes are brown, and his shiny golden fur is standing up in spikes, which shows me he has been fishing, too, perhaps where the stream curves behind the peninsula of woods he has just trudged through. He's not making any sound I can hear over the rumble of the water in the softball-sized rocks, but his presence is very loud.

I say "his" presence because temporarily I am not interested in or able to <u>assess</u> the creature's sex. I am looking at a head that is bigger around than my steering wheel, a pair of paws, awash in river bubbles, that could cover half my windshield. I am glad that I am wearing polarized fishing glasses so the bear cannot see the little teardrops of fear that have crept into the corner of my eyes. To assure him/her I am not the least bit intimidated, I make another cast.

Immediately I tie into a fat Chinook.[1] The

---

1. **Chinook** (shĭ-nŏŏk′): Chinook salmon, a large fish of northern Pacific waters.

Copyright © Halstead Hannah.

splashing of the fish in the stream engages the bear's attention, but he/she registers this for the moment only by shifting his/her glance. I play the fish[2] smartly, and when it comes gliding in, tired, pink-sided, glittering and astonished, I pluck it out of the water by inserting a finger in its gill—something I normally wouldn't do in order not to injure the fish before I set it free, and I do exactly what you would do in the same situation—throw it to the bear.

The bear's eyes widen, and she—for I can see now, past her huge shoulder and powerful haunches, that she is a she—turns and pounces on the fish with such speed and nimbleness that I am numbed. There is no chance that I, in my insulated waders,[3] am going to outrun her, dodge her blows, escape her jaws. While she is occupied devouring the fish—I can hear

---

2. **play the fish:** keep the hooked fish on the line until it tires.
3. **waders:** a waterproof combination of trousers and boots, used for walking in water.

her teeth clacking together—I do what you or anyone else would do and cast again.

God answers my muttered prayer, and I am blessed with the strike of another fat salmon, like the others, on its way to spawning grounds upstream. I would like this fish to survive and release its eggs or sperm to perpetuate the salmon kingdom, but Ms. Bear has just licked her whiskers clean and has now moved knee-deep into the water and, to my consternation,[4] leans against me rather like a large and friendly dog, although her ears are at the level of my shoulder and her back is broader than that of any horse I have ever seen. Ms. Bear is intensely interested in the progress of the salmon toward us, and her head twists and twitches as the fish circles, darts, takes line away, shakes head, rolls over, leaps.

With a bear at your side, it is not the simplest thing to play a fish properly, but the presence of this huge animal, and especially her long snout, thick as my thigh, wonderfully concentrates the mind. She smells like the forest floor, like crushed moss and damp leaves, and she is as warm as a radiator back in my Massachusetts home, the thought of which floods me with a terrible nostalgia. Now I debate whether I should just drift the salmon in under the bear's nose and let her take it that way, but I'm afraid she will break off my fly and leader,[5] and right now that fly—a Doctor Wilson number eight—is saving my life. So, with much anxiety, I pretend to take charge and bring the fish in on the side away from the bear, gill and quickly unhook it, turn away from the bear and toss the fish behind me to the bank.

The bear wheels and clambers upon it at once, leaving a vortex of water pouring into the vacuum of the space she has left, which almost topples me. As her teeth snack away, I quickly and furtively regard my poor Doctor Wilson, which is fish-mauled now, bedraggled, almost unrecognizable. But the present emergency compels me to zing it out once again. I walk a few paces downstream, hoping the bear will remember an appointment or become distracted and I can sneak away.

But a few seconds later she is leaning against me again, raptly watching the stream for any sign of a salmon splash. My luck holds; another fish smacks the withered Wilson, flings sunlight and water in silver jets as it dances its last dance. I implore the salmon's forgiveness: something I had once read revealed that this is the way of all primitive hunters, to take the life reluctantly and to pray for the victim's return. I think my prayer is as urgent as that of any Mashpee or Yoruban, or Tlingit or early Celt,[6] for not only do I want the salmon to thrive forever, I want a superabundance of them now, right now, to save my neck. I have an idea this hungry bear, bereft of fish, would waste little time in conducting any prayer ceremonies before she turned me into the main course my salmon were just the appetizer for. When I take up this fish, the bear practically rips it from my hand and the sight of those teeth so close and the truly persuasive power of those muscled, pink-rimmed jaws cause a wave of fear in me so great that I nearly faint.

---

4. **consternation:** confusion; dismay.

5. **fly and leader:** a fishing lure made to look like an insect, and the part of the line to which it is attached.

6. **Mashpee or Yoruban** (yôr'ə-bən), **or Tlingit** (tlĭng'gĭt) **or early Celt:** member of an early people of North America, Africa, or Europe.

My vertigo[7] subsides as Ms. Bear munches and destroys the salmon with hearty shakes of her head, and I sneak a few more paces downstream, rapidly also with trembling fingers tie on a new Doctor Wilson, observing the utmost care (as you would, too) in making my knots. I cast and stride downstream, wishing I could just plunge into the crystalline water and bowl away like a log. My hope and plan is to wade my way back to the narrow trail a few hundred yards ahead and, when Ms. Bear loses interest or is somehow distracted, make a heroic dash for my camper. I think of the thermos of hot coffee on the front seat, the six-pack of beer in the cooler, the thin rubber mattress with the blue sleeping bag adorning it, warm wool socks in a bag hanging from a window crank, and almost burst into tears; these simple things, given the presence of Ms. Hungry Bear, seem so miraculous, so emblematic of the life I love to live. I promise the gods—American, Indian, African, Oriental—that if I survive, I will never complain again, not even if my teenage children leave the caps off the toothpaste tubes or their bicycles in the driveway at home.

"Oh, home," I think, and cast again.

Ms. Bear rejoins me. You may or may not believe me, and perhaps after all it was only my imagination worked up by terror, but two things happened which gave me a particle of hope. The first was that Ms. Bear actually belched—quite noisily and unapologetically, too, like a rude uncle at a Christmas dinner. She showed no signs of having committed any impropriety,[8] and yet it was clear to me that a belching bear is probably also a bear with a pretty-full belly. A few more salmon and perhaps Ms. Bear would wander off in search of a berry dessert.

Now the second thing she did, or that I imagined she did, was to begin—well, not *speaking* to me exactly, but *communicating* somehow. I know it sounds foolish, but if you were in my shoes—my waders, to be more precise—you might have learned bear talk pretty quickly, too. It's not as if the bear were speaking to me in complete sentences and English words such as "Get me another fish, pal, or you're on the menu," but in a much more indirect and subtle way, almost in the way a stream talks through its bubbling and burbling and rattling of rocks and gurgling along.

Believe me, I listened intently, more with my mind than with my ears, as if the bear were telepathizing[9] and—I know you're not going to believe this, but it's true, I am normally not what you would call an egomaniac with an inflated self-esteem such that I imagine that every bear which walks out of the woods falls in love with me—but I really did truly believe now that this Ms. Bear was expressing feelings of, well, *affection*. Really, I think she kinda liked me. True or not, the feeling made me less afraid. In fact, and I don't mean this in any erotic or perverse kind of way, but I had to admit, once my fear had passed, my feelings were kinda mutual. Like you might feel for an old pal of a dog. Or a favorite horse. I only wish she weren't such a big eater. I only wish she were not a carnivore, and I, carne.

---

7. **vertigo:** dizziness.
8. **impropriety** (ĭm′prə-prī′ĭ-tē): improper behavior.
9. **telepathizing:** communicating mentally, without speaking or gesturing.

Copyright © Bob Crofut.

Now she nudges me with her nose. "All right, all right," I say. "I'm doing the best I can."

Cast in the glide behind that big boulder, the bear telepathizes me. *There's a couple of whoppers in there.*

I do as I'm told and wham! The bear is right! Instantly I'm tied into a granddaddy Chinook, a really burly fellow who has no intention of lying down on anybody's platter beneath a blanket of lemon slices and scallion shoots, let alone make his last wiggle down a bear's gullet. Even the bear is excited and begins shifting weight from paw to paw, a little motion for her that nevertheless has big consequences for me as her body slams against my hip, then slams again.

Partly because I don't want to lose the fish, but partly also because I want to use the fish as an excuse to move closer to my getaway trail, I stumble downstream. This fish has my rod bent into an upside-down *U,* and I'm hoping my quick-tied knots are also strong enough to take this salmon's lurching and his intelligent, broadside swinging into the river current—a very smart fish! Ordinarily I might take a long time with a fish like this, baby it in, but now I'm putting on as much pressure as I dare. When the salmon flips into a little side pool, the bear takes matters into her own hands, clambers over the rocks, pounces, nabs the salmon smartly behind the head and lumbers immediately to the bank. My leader snaps at once, and while Ms. Bear attends to the destruction of the fish, I tie on another fly and make some shambling headway downstream.

Yes, I worry about the hook still in the fish, but only because I do not want this bear to be irritated by anything. I want her to be replete[10] and smug and doze off in the sun. I try to telepathize as much. Please, Bear, sleep.

Inevitably, the fishing slows down, but Ms. Bear does not seem to mind. Again she belches. Myself, I am getting quite a headache and know that I am fighting exhaustion. On a normal morning of humping along in waders over these slippery, softball-sized rocks, I would be tired in any case. The added emergency is foreclosing on my energy reserves. I even find myself getting a little angry, frustrated at least, and I marvel at the bear's persistence, her inexhaustible doggedness. And appetite. I catch fish; I toss them to her. At supermarket prices, I calculate she has eaten about six hundred dollars' worth of fish. The calculating gives me something to think about besides my fear.

At last I am immediately across from the opening to the trail which twines back through the woods to where my camper rests in the dapple shade of mighty pines. Still, five hundred yards separate me from this imagined haven. I entertain the notion perhaps someone else will come along and frighten the bear away, maybe someone with a dog or a gun, but I have already spent many days here without seeing another soul, and in fact have chosen to return here for that very reason. I have told myself for many years that I really do love nature, love being among the animals, am restored by wilderness adventure. Considering that right now I would like nothing better than to be nestled beside my wife in front of a blazing fire, this seems to be a sentiment in need of some revision.

---

10. **replete:** well-filled.

Copyright © Charles Reid.

Now, as if in answer to my <u>speculations</u>, the bear turns beside me, her rump pushing me into water deeper than I want to be in, where my footing is shaky, and she stares into the woods, ears forward. She has heard something I cannot hear, or smelled something I cannot smell, and while I labor back to shallower water and surer footing, I hope some backpackers or some bear-poaching Indians are about to appear and send Ms. Bear a-galloping away. Automatically, I continue casting, but I also cannot help glancing over my shoulder in hopes of seeing what Ms. Bear sees. And in a moment I do.

It is another bear.

Unconsciously, I release a low moan, but my voice is lost in the guttural warning of Ms. Bear to the trespasser. The new arrival answers with a defiant cough. He—I believe it is a he—can afford to be defiant because he is half again as large as my companion. His fur seems longer and coarser, and though its substance is as golden as that of the bear beside me, the tips are black, and this dark surface ripples and undulates over his massive frame. His nostrils are flared, and he is staring with <u>profound</u> concentration at me.

Now I am truly confused and afraid. Would it be better to catch another salmon or not? I surely cannot provide for two of these beasts and in any case Mister Bear does not seem the type to be distracted by or made friendly by any measly salmon tribute. His whole bearing—pardon the expression—tells me my intrusion into this bear world is a personal affront[11] to his bear honor. Only Ms. Bear stands between us and, after all, whose side is she really on? By bear standards, I am sure a rather regal and handsome fellow has made his appearance. Why should the fur-covered heart of furry Ms. Bear go out to me? How much love can a few hundred dollars' worth of salmon buy? Most likely, this couple even have a history, know and have known each other from other seasons, even though for the

---

11. **affront:** insult.

moment they prefer to pretend to regard each other as total strangers.

How disturbed I am is well illustrated by my next course of action. It is completely irrational, and I cannot account for it, or why it saved me—if indeed it did. I cranked in my line and laid my rod across some rocks, then began the arduous process of pulling myself out of my waders while trying to balance myself on those awkward rocks in that fast water. I tipped and swayed as I tugged at my boots, pushed my waders down, my arms in the foaming, frigid water, then the waders also filling, making it even more difficult to pull my feet free.

I emerged like a nymph from a cocoon, wet and trembling. The bears regarded me with clear stupefaction, as if one of them had casually stepped out of his or her fur. I drained what water I could from the waders, then dropped my fly rod into them and held them before me. The rocks were brutal on my feet, but I marched toward the trail opening, lifting and dropping first one, then the other leg of my waders as if I were operating a giant puppet. The water still in the waders gave each footfall an impressive authority, and

I was half thinking that, well, if the big one attacks, maybe he'll be fooled into chomping the waders first and I'll at least now be able to run. I did not relish the idea of pounding down the trail in my nearly bare feet, but it was a better way to argue with the bear than being sucked from my waders like a snail from its shell. Would you have done differently?

Who knows what the bears thought, but I tried to make myself look as much as possible like a camel or some other extreme and inedible form of four-footedness as I plodded along the trail. The bears looked at each other, then at me as I clomped by, the water in the waders making an odd gurgling sound, and me making an odd sound, too, on remembering just then how the Indians would, staring death in the eye, sing their death song. Having no such melody prepared, and never having been anything but a bathtub singer, I chanted forth the only song I ever committed to memory: "Jingle Bells."

Yes, "Jingle Bells," I sang, "jingle all the way," and I lifted first one, then the other wader leg and dropped it stomping down. "Oh what fun it is to ride in a one-horse open sleigh-ay!"

The exercise was to prove to me just how complicated and various is the nature of the bear. The male reared up, blotting out the sun, bellowed, then twisted on his haunches and crashed off into the woods. The female, head cocked in curiosity, followed at a slight distance, within what still might be called striking distance whether I was out of my waders or not. Truly, I did not appreciate her persistence. Hauling the waders half full of water before me was trying work, and the superfluous thought struck me: suppose someone sees me now, plumping along like this, singing "Jingle Bells," a bear in attendance? Vanity, obviously, never sleeps. But as long as the bear kept her distance, I saw no reason to change my modus operandi.[12]

When I came within about one hundred feet of my camper, its white cap gleaming like a remnant of spring snow and beckoning me, I risked everything, dropped the waders and sped for the cab. The bear broke into a trot, too, I was sure, because although I couldn't see her, had my sights locked on the gleaming handle to the pickup door, I sure enough could hear those big feet slapping the ground behind me in a heavy rhythm, a terrible and elemental beat that sang to me of my own frailty, fragile bones and tender flesh. I plunged on like a madman,

grabbed the camper door and hurled myself in.

I lay on the seat panting, curled like a child, shuddered when the bear slammed against the pickup's side. The bear pressed her nose to the window, then, curiously, unceremoniously licked the glass with her tongue. I know (and you know) she could have shattered the glass with a single blow, and I tried to imagine what I should do if indeed she <u>resorted</u> to this simple expedient. Fisherman that I am, I had nothing in the cab of the truck to defend myself with except a tire iron, and that not readily accessible behind the seat I was cowering on. My best defense, obviously, was to start the pickup and drive away.

Just as I sat up to the steering wheel and inserted the key, however, Ms. Bear slammed her big paws onto the hood and hoisted herself aboard. The pickup shuddered with the weight of her, and suddenly the windshield was full of her golden fur. I beeped the horn loud and long numerous times, but this had about the same effect as my singing, only caused her to shake her huge head, which vibrated the truck terribly. She stomped around on the hood and then lay down, back against the windshield, which now appeared to have been covered by a huge shag rug.

Could I believe my eyes?

No, I could not believe my eyes. My truck was being smothered in bear. In a moment I also could not believe my ears—Ms. Bear had decided the camper hood was the perfect place for a nap, and she was *snoring,* snoring profoundly, her body twitching like a cat's. Finally, she had responded to my advice and desires, but at the most inappropriate time. I was trapped. Blinded by bear body!

---

12. **modus operandi** (mō′dəs ŏp′ə-răn′dē): a way of doing something.

WORDS TO KNOW

superfluous (sŏŏ-pûr′flŏŏ-əs) *adj.* unnecessary; extra
resort (rĭ-zôrt′) *v.* (followed by *to*) to turn to

My exhaustion had been doubled by my sprint for the camper, and now that I was not in such a desperate panic, I felt the cold of the water that had soaked my clothes, and I began to tremble. It also crossed my mind that perhaps Mister Bear was still in the vicinity, and if Ms. Bear was not smart enough, or cruel enough, to smash my window to get at me, he just might be.

Therefore, I started the engine—which disturbed Ms. Bear not a whit—and rolled down the window enough to stick my head out and see down the rocky, limb-strewn trail. I figured a few jolts in those ruts and Ms. Bear would be off like a shot.

This proved a smug assumption. Ms. Bear did indeed awaken and bestir herself to a sitting position, a bit like an overgrown hood ornament, but quickly grew quite adept at balancing herself against the lurching and jolting of my truck, which, in fact, she seemed to enjoy. Just my luck, I growled, to find the first bear in Alaska who wanted a ride into town. I tried some quick braking and sharp-turn maneuvers I thought might send her tumbling off, but her bulk was so massive, her paws so artfully spread, that she was just too stable an entity. She wanted a ride, and there was nothing I could do about it.

When I came out of the woods to the gravel road known locally as the Dawson Artery, I had an inspiration. I didn't drive so fast that if Ms. Bear decided to clamber down, she would be hurt, but I did head for the main road which led to Buckville and the Buckville Cannery. Ms. Bear swayed happily along the whole ten miles to that intersection and seemed not to bat an eye when first one big logging truck, then another, plummeted by. I pulled out onto the highway, and for the safety of both of us—those logging trucks have dubious brakes, and their drivers get paid by the trip—I had to accelerate considerably.

I couldn't see much of Ms. Bear except her back and rump, as I had to concentrate on the road, some of which is pretty curvy in that coastal area, shadowed also by the giant pines. But from the attitude expressed by her posture, I'd say she was having a whale, or should I say a salmon, of a time. I saw a few cars and pickups veering out of the oncoming lane onto the shoulder as we swept by, but I didn't have time, really, to appreciate the astonishment of their drivers. In this way, my head out the window, Ms. Bear perched on the hood, I drove to the Buckville Cannery and turned into the long driveway.

Ms. Bear knew right away something good was ahead, for she rose on all fours now and stuck her nose straight out like a bird dog on a pheasant. Her legs quivered with nervous anticipation as we approached, and as soon as I came out of the trees into the parking area, she went over the front of the camper like someone plunging into a pool.

Don't tell me you would have done any differently. I stopped right there and watched Ms. Bear march down between the rows of cars and right up the truck ramp into the cannery itself. She was not the least bit intimidated by all the noise of the machines and the grinders and stampers in there, or the shouting of the workers.

Now the Buckville Cannery isn't that big—I imagine about two dozen people work there on any given day—and, since it is so remote, has no hurricane fence around it and no security guard. After all, what's anybody going to steal out of there besides a few cases of canned salmon or some bags of frozen fish parts that will soon become some company's cat food? The main building is up on a little hill, and conveyors run down from there to the docks where the salmon boats pull in—the sea is another half mile away—and unload their catch.

I would say that in about three minutes after Ms. Bear walked into the cannery, twenty of the twenty-four workers were climbing out down the conveyors, dropping from open windows, or charging out the doors. The other four just hadn't got wind of the event yet, but in a little while they came bounding out, too, one fellow pulling up his trousers as he ran. They all assembled on the semicircular drive before the main office and had a union meeting of some vigor.

Myself, I was too tired to participate, and in any case did not want to be held liable for the disturbance at the Buckville Cannery, and so I made a U-turn and drove on into Buckville itself, where I took a room above the Buckville Tavern and had a hot shower and a really nice nap. That night in the Tap and Lounge I got to hear many an excited story about the she-bear who freeloaded at the cannery for a couple of hours before she was driven off by blowing, ironically enough, the lunch whistle loud and long. I didn't think it was the right time or place to testify to my part in that historical event, and for once kept my mouth shut. You don't like trouble any more than I do, and I'm sure you would have done about the same. ❖

RESPONDING
OPTIONS

FROM *PERSONAL RESPONSE* TO CRITICAL ANALYSIS

REFLECT

1. How many stars did you give this story? Compare your evaluation with those of your classmates.

RETHINK

2. What do you think was the author's main purpose for writing this story? How well has he achieved that purpose?

3. What is your evaluation of the narrator as he struggles to survive?
   Consider
   - his response to the presence of "Ms. Bear"
   - his decision to leave "Ms. Bear" at the cannery
   - his decision to keep quiet about his adventure

4. The narrator repeatedly suggests that he is doing what you would do if you were in his situation. Do you agree with him? Why or why not?

5. In your opinion, is this story believable? Why or why not?

RELATE

6. What kinds of problems arise when wild animals venture into areas inhabited mostly by people or when people venture into areas inhabited mostly by wild animals? Discuss examples you've heard or read about.

ANOTHER PATHWAY

Create a comic strip that shows the events of this story. Before drawing, skim the story to plan how many frames you will need and what image each frame will show.

LITERARY CONCEPTS

The **tone** of a work of literature is an expression of the writer's attitude toward his or her subject. The tone might be admiring, joyful, humorous, sad, or angry. The tone of "Appetizer" is humorous—almost tongue-in-cheek. How does Abel achieve this tone?

LITERARY LINKS

Compare the narrator's situation in this story with that of the narrator in "Collecting Team" or the narrator in "The Inn of Lost Time." Evaluate which situation is the most threatening. Do the narrators have control over the outcome?

QUICKWRITES

1. Write a **news article** for a local paper about the bear's sudden appearance at the cannery. Answer the questions *who, what, when, where, why,* and *how* in your article.

2. When the narrator returns home, his wife will undoubtedly ask him about the damage to the truck. Write a **dialogue** that might take place between the narrator and his wife.

📁 *PORTFOLIO Save your writing. You may want to use it later as a springboard to a piece for your portfolio.*

ACROSS THE CURRICULUM

Science *Cooperative Learning* With a small group of classmates, gather additional information about the Alaskan brown bear—including its period of hibernation, its food, its behavior, and its relationship with humans. Using a desktop computer program if possible, create a pamphlet about the brown bear. Include drawings, maps, and copies of photographs.

ROBERT H. ABEL

1941–

Like the narrator of "Appetizer," Robert H. Abel is an avid fisherman, although he has competed for stream space with a bear only in his fiction. Abel recalls a happy small-town childhood in Ohio, where he was surrounded by relatives, including an uncle who taught him to fish. In elementary school he rewrote fairy tales "so the ending would turn out to my liking."

"I had my eyes on becoming a writer by the time I went to college," Abel says. After college, his work as a journalist and a college English teacher left him little time to write. Now, however, having settled in North Hadley, Massachusetts, he writes most of the time and teaches only occasionally.

Abel has published two volumes of short stories, one of which won the 1989 Flannery O'Connor Award for Short Fiction. He has also written a radio play, two novels, and many articles. Abel's work has appeared in several anthologies and literary magazines.

OTHER WORKS *Full-Tilt Boogie and Other Stories, Freedom Dues; or, A Gentleman's Progress in the New World*

Mother to Son
Langston Hughes

the lesson of the moth
Don Marquis

PERSONAL CONNECTION

How do you approach life? Use the scales shown here to illustrate your basic attitudes. On a sheet of paper, copy the words expressing opposing attitudes and the lines that connect them. Then place an X on each line to show where your attitude lies. For example, are you usually optimistic, expecting the best to happen, or pessimistic, bracing for the worst? Compare your attitude scales with those of a few classmates.

adventurous | **cheerful** | **optimistic** | **content**

cautious | **gloomy** | **pessimistic** | **dissatisfied**

LITERARY CONNECTION

In the poems you are about to read, Langston Hughes and Don Marquis make effective use of two very different speakers to express attitudes toward life. The speaker of Hughes's "Mother to Son" is a woman who has had a hard life. The poet presents her speech in her own dialect—a form of presentation he employed from the start of his career.

An insect is the speaker of much of Marquis's verse, including "the lesson of the moth." Marquis humorously insisted that his poems were written by a cockroach named archy. Unable to use the shift key, archy could type no capital letters, quotation marks, or question marks. Without these, and without other punctuation, the poem engagingly presents two contrasting philosophies of life.

WRITING CONNECTION

An **aphorism** is a short sentence that expresses a truth or a clever observation. Marquis uses an aphorism in his poem to present one attitude toward life—"come easy go easy." Write an aphorism that expresses one of your basic attitudes.

MOTHER to Son

by Langston Hughes

Well, son, I'll tell you:
Life for me ain't been no crystal stair.
It's had tacks in it,
And splinters,
5 And boards torn up,
And places with no carpet on the floor—
Bare.
But all the time
I'se been a-climbin' on,
10 And reachin' landin's,
And turnin' corners,
And sometimes goin' in the dark
Where there ain't been no light.
So boy, don't you turn back.
15 Don't you set down on the steps
'Cause you finds it's kinder hard.
Don't you fall now—
For I'se still goin', honey,
I'se still climbin',
20 And life for me ain't been no crystal stair.

Stairs, Provincetown (1920), Charles Demuth. Gouache and pencil on cardboard, 23½″ × 19½″ (59.7 × 49.5 cm). The Museum of Modern Art, New York. Gift of Abby Aldrich Rockefeller. Photograph Copyright © 1995 The Museum of Modern Art, New York.

to Son

FROM PERSONAL RESPONSE *TO* CRITICAL ANALYSIS

REFLECT   1. What is your first reaction to the mother in this poem? Write your thoughts in your notebook.

RETHINK   2. Do you agree with the advice the mother gives her son? Why or why not?

3. What does the mother suggest by the image of a "crystal staircase"? By contrast, what kind of staircase has her life been?
   Consider
   • what crystal (very clear, brilliant glass) brings to mind
   • the kind of life the mother has lived
   • how she has handled the obstacles in her life

the
lesson
of the
moth

by Don Marquis

i was talking to a moth
the other evening
he was trying to break into
an electric light bulb
5 and fry himself on the wires

why do you fellows
pull this stunt i asked him
because it is the conventional
thing for moths or why
10 if that had been an uncovered
candle instead of an electric
light bulb you would
now be a small unsightly cinder
have you no sense

15 plenty of it he answered
but at times we get tired
of using it
we get bored with the routine
and crave beauty
20 and excitement
fire is beautiful
and we know that if we get
too close it will kill us
but what does that matter
25 it is better to be happy

Candle, Eigg (1980), Winifred Nicholson.
58 × 43 cm, private collection. Photo by
John Webb. Copyright © The artist's family.

for a moment
and be burned up with beauty
than to live a long time
and be bored all the while
30 so we wad all our life up
into one little roll
and then we shoot the roll
that is what life is for
it is better to be a part of beauty
35 for one instant and then cease to
exist than to exist forever
and never be a part of beauty
our attitude toward life
is come easy go easy
40 we are like human beings
used to be before they became
too civilized to enjoy themselves

and before i could argue him
out of his philosophy
45 he went and immolated[1] himself
on a patent cigar lighter
i do not agree with him
myself i would rather have
half the happiness and twice
50 the longevity[2]

but at the same time i wish
there was something i wanted
as badly as he wanted to fry himself
archy

---

1. **immolated** (ĭm′ə-lā′tĭd): killed by burning.
2. **longevity** (lŏn-jĕv′ĭ-tē): length of life.

RESPONDING
OPTIONS

FROM PERSONAL RESPONSE TO CRITICAL ANALYSIS

REFLECT

1. Jot down several words that describe your reaction to "the lesson of the moth."

RETHINK

2. Do you think most people share the moth's attitude toward life? Why or why not?

Consider
- the opinions the moth expresses in lines 25–29 and 40–42
- archy's reaction in lines 51–53

3. Look again at the attitude scales you made for the Personal Connection on page 313. Are you more like archy or the moth? Explain your answer.

RELATE

4. In your opinion, would the moth have helpful advice about life to offer the mother in "Mother to Son"? Why or why not? Imagine the mother's encounter with the moth and illustrate it.

5. How does each of these poems relate to the theme of this part of Unit Three, "Struggling for Survival"? Are the speakers' struggles similar or different? Explain your answer.

ANOTHER PATHWAY
Cooperative Learning

With a small group of classmates, discuss which of these poems you consider to be more optimistic about life. Think about both the positive and the negative images in each poem, and draw pictures of them on poster board or the chalkboard. Also consider the speakers' attitudes.

QUICKWRITES

1. Using an extended metaphor, compose a **poem** titled "Father to Daughter"—or one that deals with some other relationship you would enjoy writing about. In the poem, one person should share his or her attitude toward life with another.

2. Select an organism—plant or animal—other than a cockroach, and write a poetic or prose **monologue** in which the organism teaches a lesson or expresses an attitude toward life.

📁 *PORTFOLIO Save your writing. You may want to use it later as a springboard to a piece for your portfolio.*

LITERARY CONCEPTS

As you have learned, a metaphor involves a comparison between two different things. When a metaphor is continued for several lines or throughout a poem, it is called an **extended metaphor.** In "Mother to Son," what is the extended metaphor for the mother's life? What images are used to develop the metaphor? How well do you think the metaphor works?

LANGSTON HUGHES

Langston Hughes was one of the first African Americans to earn his living solely from writing. Although he wrote novels, short stories, plays, song lyrics, newspaper columns, and radio scripts, he is best known for his poetry. Many of his poems reflect the speech patterns and jazz rhythms he heard on the streets of Harlem in New York City, where he lived as an adult.

1902–1967

Hughes had a lonely childhood, never receiving much support from his separated parents. For much of his youth, he lived like a nomad, moving from place to place. For a time, he lived with his grandmother, who introduced him to books.

After graduating from high school in Cleveland, Hughes spent a short and unhappy time in Mexico before enrolling at Columbia University in New York. He later dropped out and worked odd jobs. In Europe, he was robbed of everything he owned. When he returned to the United States, he began writing and eventually graduated from Lincoln University in Pennsylvania.

Hughes was "discovered" while working as a busboy. He left three of his poems at a table where the poet Vachel Lindsay was dining. Lindsay was impressed with the young poet's works and presented them at one of his own readings. Soon afterward, Hughes's writing career took off.

OTHER WORKS *Not Without Laughter, The Dream Keeper*

DON MARQUIS

One day "the biggest cockroach you ever saw" scampered across Don Marquis's desk at the offices of the *New York Sun,* giving Marquis the idea for a comic character—archy, the philosophical cockroach poet. Later, Marquis created mehitabel, a joyful, adventurous alley cat. Through such characters, Marquis expressed his views on life from 1912 to 1925 in his newspaper column, "Sun Dial." Of this column a well-known writer said, "Most of us didn't

1878–1937

consult the leading editorials to know what to think. The almost universal reflex, in New York at any rate, was 'Let's see what Don says about it.'"

Before becoming a prosperous writer, Marquis held a variety of jobs, including drugstore clerk, truck driver, poultry plucker, short-order cook, and teacher. Considered one of America's finest humorists, Marquis wrote novels, plays, short stories, poems, and essays.

NONFICTION

Von

"Von," a Vietnamese youth interviewed by Janet Bode

PERSONAL CONNECTION

Imagine that, like the boy in this story, you must flee your country because of political unrest and the dangers of war. Not only are you faced with the uncertainty of what lies ahead, but you can take only one person with you. What will you do? Share your thoughts with the class.

Vietnam Before Unification

HISTORICAL CONNECTION

From 1954 to 1975, Vietnam, a small country in Southeast Asia, was divided into Communist-ruled North Vietnam and non-Communist South Vietnam. The Communists, however, began to wage a war to establish communism in the South. During the 1960s and 1970s, the United States and the South Vietnamese army tried to stop them, but by 1975 the Communists had taken control of the whole of Vietnam.

Like many Vietnamese, Von and his father fled the brutality of the Communists in a crowded, unsafe boat. Such "boat people" risked illness, drowning, and pirate attacks on the South China Sea. Many died. Those who survived went to refugee camps in other Southeast Asian countries until they could be relocated.

READING CONNECTION

Predicting Good readers are active readers, gathering information as they read to predict the events in stories. In addition to predicting during reading, it is useful to begin making predictions before you read. Predict what problems emigrants like Von and his father might face as they leave their homeland, go on their journey, and try to adjust to a new country. Organize your ideas in a word web like the one shown here. Then, in your notebook, jot down predictions you make while you are reading the selection. After your reading, check to see whether your predictions were correct.

Leaving Their Homeland

During Their Journey

Predicted Problems of Emigrants

In Their New Country

VON

"Von," a Vietnamese youth as interviewed by Janet Bode

On April 30, 1975, Saigon, the capital of South Vietnam, fell, ending this stage of the tragedy that by then had cost 1.3 million Vietnamese and 56,000 American lives. Von is a survivor of that war and the devastating years that followed. Today when you see him— slim, handsome, with an optimistic and ready grin—it's hard to imagine what his eyes have seen. Over a series of days, we met in hours sandwiched between his busy schedule of school and work. He begins at his beginning.

Copyright © David Hartung/Gamma Liaison.

I was born in Saigon. My father was a navy officer for South Vietnam. He worked for the United States government. I have three brothers and three sisters. I am number four. I'm the only one who came to America with my father. My mother and the rest of them are still in Vietnam. Sometimes on Sundays after church, my father and I talk about our past memories, what brought us here and of the future. I decided that someday I would like to write of my family, and of him and me together. You are the first person I ever told my family's story. . . .

In 1972, when Von was four years old, the family moved to Da Nang in the central part of the country. Von's earliest memories of the war were of hiding and eating in bomb shelters while waiting for the daily bombing raids to end. When Saigon fell to the Communists in 1975, Von's father could have escaped to the United States, but he made his way back at great peril to rejoin his family. However, the Communists soon put Von's father in a "re-education center." At this center, actually a concentration camp, Von's father worked at hard labor from six in the morning until nine in the evening every day for three years, without breaks or vacations.

In the meantime, Von's family had to sell everything they owned in order to get enough money to buy food. For several years, Von could no longer go to school, but he continued to try to read on his own. When Von's father was finally released from the concentration camp in 1978, the government told him he must take only one child and work in the countryside. Von and his father were sent to a place near the border, where fierce battles

raged between Cambodia and Vietnam. "We were caught," Von says, "in the middle again."

One day they told my father, "You, tomorrow, because you were an officer, you must go and clean out the grenades." The Cambodians put grenades under the trees. They put boobytraps everywhere. In the morning when we went to the farms and started working, sometimes people blew up. They blew off their legs and their arms and often they get killed.

Of course my father didn't say "no" to them. He said, "When?" To me he said, "Oh, my God. I have to risk my life for this? NO! I can't take any more." My father, he could not sleep. He thought, it's my life. All this time I work to become a good man. I come back and for this? I will die for nothing? Should I leave or should I stay? If I stay, I will get killed. He kept what he planned a secret. He just said to me, "You and me, we're leaving. We must go back to your mother."

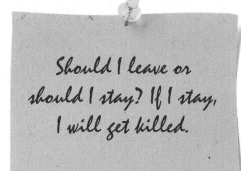

Should I leave or should I stay? If I stay, I will get killed.

At six o'clock in the morning, we were supposed to be in the mission at work. But at two o'clock at night, we left the house. They weren't strict with him anymore. They let him be free, because they knew him. They knew he'd been in a concentration camp. And they knew he was very good. They didn't think he would leave. It was dark out and I was afraid. Even in the countryside, they have security guards. We did not go on the road. We sneaked through the trees. Finally we got to a place where we could take a bus. We had little money left for the month, but I was so young, my father didn't have to pay for my bus ticket.

We got back to Saigon, but we could just see my mother for a few hours. It was too dangerous for everybody if we stayed. Too soon, he had to say to my mother, "I must leave you." To me he said, "I must take a younger son with me, you. I take you because you suffer so much. You have a feeling."

I always cared for my mother. I always helped her. My mother said to my father, "Von will be good." She was crying so much. She said, "This is right. This is the way we have to do it. You must leave me."

She said to me, "You take care of your father." And she told my father, "Take care of Von. Get him schooling." My brothers and sisters just looked at me. They were so sad. They knew we were leaving, even though my father didn't tell them. If he told them, they would say, "Why do you take Von? You don't love me?"

My mother said, "I love you." And we left.

At that time, many South Vietnamese people were trying to sneak out of the country. They were looking for navy men who knew how to row the boat, who knew how to get to Thailand. Do you know anything about the boat people? They make a boat and they sail and they try to get to freedom. My father was on the sea for almost twenty-five years. Some people learned this and they said to him, "We offer you a job. We make a fake ID for you and your son. We take care of a boat. We get food and you two can go with us."

My father said, "Okay." But somehow the Communists found out and took the boat and the money, too. He was afraid the government might be looking for him. "I must leave you," he told the people.

> She said to me, "You take care of your father." And she told my father, "Take care of Von."

My father found another connection. This time poor, poor people came to him. They could pay him no money, but they had a boat. For three months, my father prepared. He mended the motor. He bought a map, a compass. Then with the boat, my father and I sneaked out to the river. We were picking up people as we were going along. People here, people there, all poor, country people who wanted to escape to a better life.

There were fifty-two people in a twelve-foot-long boat. We could not move. I sat with my knees in my face. I could not lie down. There were a lot of men, and a few women. There were some kids, but most of the people were in their early twenties. I was maybe eleven or twelve.

We left on a rainy night. There were military police boats out in the sea looking for the escape boats, looking for the boat people. But with the rain, they went inside. We go and go and go. One night and the next day in the evening, we went all the way down the river to the sea because my father rowed so fast. We go and go and go. We were going to Indonesia. My father knew we shouldn't go to Thailand, because there were a lot of pirates. Most of the people who went to Thailand got killed. After four days we saw a blinking light! Oh, we thought, that's an American ship! We first saw the light around two in the morning, and by six we could see the boat.

The boat was all black. It was so big and it said "Thailand" on it. My father told me, "They are dangerous people." We were afraid they would attack us. They know the boat people often have money and gold. . . .We only had one gun, a shotgun. The people were saying, "What should we do? Shoot them?"

My father said, "No, we cannot. There are

so many of them. If we shoot at them, they will definitely kill us. It is better to let them rob us."

They came on board our little boat. They had knives and hammers. My father said, "Try to act cool." I was so scared I was shaking. Even everything they had, all their savings for their new lives. But after that the pirates gave us food. We were all very hungry people. They took us back to our boat. We were lucky. They didn't kill us. I guess they felt sorry for us.

Copyright © Patrick Bar/Gamma Liaison.

my feet were shaking. They ordered all the men to go onto their big ship. I was so small that one man took my hand, picked me up, and threw me to another man on their ship. It looked so far and the ship was rocking that I was afraid they would miss me and I would fall into the sea. They would not bother to save me.

The pirates went around our boat checking for gold. They asked for watches and rings and money and said, "If you lie, we'll throw you into the sea." Everybody gave them

We were back alone on the sea, and then we saw some more big, big ships. One was from Holland, another from Italy. They saw us and didn't stop! We lay there. We were so hot. Every time we saw a big ship we got so happy. They came so close that then we got afraid that we could get caught in their waves. My father always put a white flash, a message, and it said, "If you want to pick us up, we come close. If no, we stay away."

Some of the ships said, "Yes, we take you," and then when we came close, they tried to hit us to make us drown and die in the sea. My father knew they used that trick a lot. They didn't want us there, and if we died, nobody knew. So many people were coming out of Vietnam. Other countries didn't want to take any more. It's even worse today.

We go and go and go. In two weeks we saw a ship from Germany with a red cross on it. My father rowed, rowed, rowed, and he came very nicely right next to the ship. The Germans took us on board their ship. They gave us food, a shower, blankets. They told us to sleep. And they asked to speak to the captain of the boat. My father, he doesn't know German but he knows French, he went and spoke French to them. They said, "Tomorrow we will take you and your people to an island, to a refugee camp."

My father said, "Oh, thank you very much."

The first island they brought us to was one where nobody had lived. It was called Coocoo. The food was poison, the water polluted. And the mosquitoes! People had come there, cut down the trees, and built some houses. But it was dangerous for the people, and a lot of us were sick. Some of us died. They took us to the hospital at the refugee camp. They gave us injections.

After a month we had an interview from the United Nations. They called our names. My father said, "I worked for the United States government in South Vietnam." They took all the information down and then said, "Okay, we will call Washington, D.C. You must wait while we do that."

While we waited, my father worked for the chief commander in the refugee camp in Indonesia. I worked, too. The United Nations

had donated some money to build some more houses to make the camp bigger. I sought them out for a job. They said, "If you want to help the people, gather the wood so they can build the barracks."

I said, "Fine, fine, I volunteer."

Most of the people at the refugee camp were Vietnamese. Some of them had so sad stories, oh my. "In Thailand they stole my sister," one said. "My brother and my mother got killed because the boat sink," another said. But on the island, we all lived together in barracks, and life at that time was beautiful. Each day the United Nations gave every person a half cup of rice and a half cup of another food. The American Peace Corps[1] came there, too. We people built a school, and they tried to teach a little English. We stayed there for eight months, until one afternoon we heard our name called again. They told us, "You have a sponsor from the United States."

I thought, Oh wow! A new land! A new life! The United Nations had a special boat to Singapore. They take the refugees that are leaving to that city, we stay a week, and from there we take an airplane to Hong Kong and on to Alaska.

I thought, Oh wow! A new land! A new life!

I looked out the window of the airplane in Alaska and I was so surprised. I tell my father, "Rice! Rice! Rice is falling from the sky!" He explained to me what is snow. From there we went to California, where we stayed in a shelter for a week. The people said, "Enjoy this; soon you will be in your new home, Detroit, and there the weather is very cold."

---

1. **Peace Corps:** a volunteer organization set up by the U.S. government to help people in developing countries.

It was January when we came to Detroit. I said, "What a dirty city." There were a lot of newspapers flying in the air, and it was so cold. A lady met us at the airport and took us in a really strange and crazy hotel filled with new immigrants and mental people.[2] She said, "Here is fifty dollars. I'll see you in fifteen days." We never saw her again.

At night at the hotel, the people screamed loud. They banged on the walls. We had nothing to cook. We didn't know what to eat. We didn't know what is American food. My father went out to the corner store, and he got some coffee and a sandwich. Then he bought some soup and some rice to cook. He told me, "Stay inside." I said, "Why? American people very nice. They wouldn't hurt anybody." He told me, "Stay inside."

I think of South Vietnam. It is a beautiful country. I think of my mother and brothers and sisters and grandmother. I think new people to America are hungry for their countries. Governments can be so cruel.

After two, three weeks, we had a phone call, a Vietnamese voice. We were excited. There were no other Vietnamese in the hotel. He said, "You will meet your sponsor. It is a rabbi and his congregation. They have found a home for you. One of the ladies speaks French, so you can talk to them."

When we meet them, the lady asks me, "Von, do you drink milk?" I'm too big to drink milk. With Vietnamese, milk is only for a baby. It is too expensive to buy.

I think, this is strange. Why does she ask me this?

"How about soda?" she says.

"Oh, yes, I love soda."

"What kind of food do you eat? Hamburger?"

I tell her, "Oh, I love hamburger." I never eat hamburger, but I'd heard of it a lot.

So they took us to our home. It was in the basement, one bedroom and one living room. The Jewish people from the temple, everybody gave a little bit. We got a TV, two beds, some furniture, a table, cups and plates and cooking things. After that the lady and the rabbi took us to a supermarket. They said, "Von, take all the food you want."

I had never seen anything like this supermarket. The lady showed me the shopping cart and what to do. The first thing I grabbed was Coca-Cola. I knew that. And bread. Then I looked around and I didn't see anything to eat. It was all frozen. I'd never seen that in Vietnam. There we had all fresh fruit and vegetables. I got some cans of food. At the refugee camp, I saw those for the first time.

The lady said, "Do you like potato chips?"

I said, "What are potato chips?"

She bought some chicken for us. My father said, "I feel so bad. They brought us here and they had to take us shopping."

That afternoon, three more Jewish ladies came to the house. They showed us how to cook, how to make chicken, how to use the stove, where to put the milk and soda. They were so nice. I didn't understand a word they said, but I always smiled.

The next day they took me and my father shopping for clothes. I was so skinny and the pants were so big. They told my father and me, "You have to come to temple to meet the people." I got shoes, too. They said to my father, "Tomorrow, we will take Von to get a shot so you can put him in school."

"Oh, I love hamburger."
I never eat hamburger,
but I'd heard
of it a lot.

---

2. **mental people:** people suffering from mental illness.

They got my father a job as a typewriter repairman. He didn't know anything about that. He wanted to work on the ships, but they said to do that you must be a United States citizen. He said, "Okay."

I was very scared to start school after six years. I had to skip a lot of grades. Most of the students looked at me because the way I was dressing was strange. It was so cold, I wore everything I'd bought. I didn't know where anything was. I came late to every class. I was confused and I could not ask people. They told me in sign language, "Go to eat." I went into the cafeteria. There were hundreds of people.

A supervisor knew I was a new student. He took me to the head of the line to get a hamburger, and the other students got angry. "Why does that boy get to go first?" I told the supervisor, "I want to wait in the line. Please." He said, "Don't worry about it. Take the food."

On that day and on other days, when I had a hard problem to solve, or when I felt sad or confused, I always look back on my past. I say, "Wow, what happened in the past is even harder. This is nothing." Let's face it, this is easy here.

There were no Vietnamese kids at the school, and only one Chinese boy, but he became my best friend. After a while I got along with the other students. I met a very nice black boy. He thought I was Chinese and all Chinese know karate and kung fu. He said, "I like your country's movies." I told him, "I'm Vietnamese." But he didn't know what was Vietnamese. He took me home to meet his mother, and, wow, did they have a big TV. He said, "What do you want? Food?" "Yeah." He made food for me and we ate and drank soda. I didn't understand what I was seeing. I couldn't answer his questions, but we understood each other.

Later I invited him to my house. I was doing the laundry, but I didn't know how to do laundry here. In Vietnam we use a brush to scrub it, then take it outside and hang it in the wind. I washed it by hand in the bathtub and left it to dry. Two, three days, and it was not dry! The boy went, "Von, what is this? Why don't you bring it to a laundromat?" He didn't know my family never had even seen a washing machine.

Other kids did bring some trouble to me. They talked about the way my hair looked, my clothes. When they called me "Chinese," they did it to make fun of me. They didn't call me by name. They laughed because I could not speak well. I was really upset about it, but then again I thought, so what?

I took an art class and the teacher said, "You draw whatever you like." I drew a map of Vietnam, the boat I escaped in, my family, and all the blood. One of my drawings I put in my father's bedroom, and on it I wrote, "NO MORE WAR!!!"

I got along well with my teachers. The English teacher gave me vocabulary to learn, like *breakfast, dinner, orange juice*. I'd take it home and translate and study it. The pronunciation was hard for me, words like *brother*. I'd practice my English by recording my voice on a tape recorder. I'd read from a book, then play it back. I watched TV news a lot, CNN.[3]

Even though my father was working, the rabbi paid the rent, the telephone bill, the food, everything for six months! They took us to the temple and made a party to introduce us. They gave us a hat to wear, a yarmulke.[4]

---

3. **CNN:** the Cable News Network.
4. **yarmulke** (yär′məl-kə): a small brimless cap worn by some Jewish men and boys.

We still have it today. They knew it was my birthday. I had never had a birthday party in my life. They made a big cake, and they told me to hold it and blow out the candles. They told me to give a speech. I was only here two, three months. I didn't know anything. My father said, "Whatever people give you, you have to say 'Thank you.'" I said, "Thank you, thank you."

It was wonderful. They gave me the whole cake to take home. I ate it for one month! Every day after school, I cut one piece and ate it. The rabbi always called to see how we were. He said, "If you have any problem, we are here to help."

After six months, I said to my father and the rabbi, "Let me go look for a job." We don't want the temple to pay for us anymore.

The rabbi said, "We wouldn't recommend that you work. You better concentrate on school."

Without telling them, I looked. I saw a lot of students go to work, so I copied them. I started walking from my house. I went into a supermarket. I was interviewed by the manager, and he told me, "Sorry, you have an English problem. Study more and come back in six months." I went into many supermarkets that day, many small stores.

They didn't understand what I was talking about. I didn't understand what I was talking about. But I already knew the words for juice, milk, fruit, so that's why I was interested in those stores. I went home. I was so sad. I didn't want to bother my father. He was very busy, too, learning a new job and studying English in night school.

The next day after school, I went to look again. My school had a work-study program, and a teacher told me about a job at Burger King. I was interviewed and the boss knew that I had an English problem. I begged him, "I can do anything! I can take the cooking test, but I can't take the writing test. I don't know English." So he went check, check, check, like that, on the test and I passed. So my first job in America was to cook hamburgers. I took the frozen hamburger and put it inside the fire. That's all he wanted me to do.

But then I saw customers who didn't throw their food in the trash. I came out and I cleaned the tables. I saw someone had thrown sodas on the floor. I took a mop and cleaned it up. I wanted to show him that I could work. He gave me a uniform and said, "You start today."

I ran home and said to my father, "I must write a letter to the rabbi. I must say, 'Thank you for everything you've done for us. Someday when I have a good job, I will donate money to this temple to keep it forever. Now my father and I both work and won't need any more help.'"

My father said, "Oh, that is great."

The rabbi called my house. He said, "Von,

Copyright © Mark Lewis/Tony Stone Images.

we want to help you. We don't want anything from you. You've only been here a few months. Remember your schoolwork, but you do what you want." I sent my money to my mother.

My father and I have been here for a long time now, eight, nine years. For five years we have had all the papers in order to have my mother and my brothers and my sisters come here. We have sent a letter to the United States ambassador to Thailand. We have written to the United States representative at the United Nations. We contacted our congressman, and he wrote a letter. The congressman said, "Your family is qualified to come to the United States. They are at the top of the list." Still we wait and we wait and we wait. The Communist government doesn't want to give them visas.

This year on July 4th, my father and I became citizens of the United States. I'm a free man! I read the Constitution. We the people are all equal. Now no one can say, if the United States someday has a problem, "You have to go back to Vietnam." I love this country. This country is my country now. I never go back.

My brothers and sisters don't have the opportunities that I do. Today it is September, and I am starting university. I am a very lucky person. And when my family gets here and we are together again, we will make such a celebration! ❖

LITERARY INSIGHT

Foreign Student

BY BARBARA B. ROBINSON

In September she appeared
   row three, seat seven,
   heavy pleated skirt,
   plastic purse,
5   tidy note pad,
there she sat,
silent,
straight from Taipei,
and she bowed
10 when I entered the room.
A model student
I noticed,
every assignment complete,
on time, neat,
15 and she listened
when I talked.

But now it's May,
and Si Lan
is called Lani.
20 She strides in
with Lynne and Susan.
Her gear is crammed
into a macramé
shoulder sack.
25 And she chatters with Pete
during class
and
I'm glad.

WORDS TO KNOW	**ambassador** (ăm-băs′ə-dər) *n.* a country's chief diplomatic official in a foreign land
	visa (vē′zə) *n.* an official permission to leave or enter a country

329

RESPONDING
OPTIONS

FROM **PERSONAL RESPONSE** *TO* **CRITICAL ANALYSIS**

REFLECT **1.** What were your thoughts about Von as you read this selection? Jot down your thoughts in your notebook, and then share them with a partner.

RETHINK **2.** Which of Von's experiences do you think were the most difficult for him? Why?

3. Evaluate how well Von adjusts to life in the United States.
Consider
- his experience in the hotel during the first weeks
- his school experiences
- why he wants to work
- his attitude toward the United States

4. Review the predictions you made for the Reading Connection on page 319. What problem or problems faced by the emigrants in the selection were you unable to predict? Why do you think you were unable to do so?

RELATE **5.** Compare Von's adjustment to a new country with that of Lani in "Foreign Student" (page 329). If Von and Lani were to meet, what might they say to each other about their experiences?

6. In 1993, more than 1 million people immigrated to the United States. Like Von and his father, some of these immigrants were refugees. Should the United States accept all refugees? Explain your answer.

ANOTHER PATHWAY
Cooperative Learning
With a group of classmates, summarize Von's story orally and record the summary on audiotape. One person should recount the beginning, with the next student summarizing the next scene, and so on.

QUICKWRITES

1. What exactly does Von experience during one day and night on a refugee boat? Write a **journal entry** in which Von describes his feelings and experiences in more detail than the selection provides.

2. Write a **letter** Von might have written to the South Vietnamese government to persuade them to let the rest of his family emigrate from Vietnam to the United States.

📁 *PORTFOLIO Save your writing. You may want to use it later as a springboard to a piece for your portfolio.*

LITERARY CONCEPTS

One way to preserve people's stories—their history—is to let them "talk it." This is called **oral history.** Oral history includes personal reactions and factual recollections. In her introduction to the volume in which Von's story appears, Janet Bode wrote, "At times the sentence construction might seem a little awkward. The grammar might not always be perfect." Why do you think she chose not to correct Von's grammatical errors?

ALTERNATIVE ACTIVITIES

1. Create a **storyboard**—a series of sketches arranged in sequence—that depicts key events in the selection. Include a caption with each sketch, and share your work with the class.

2. Make a **collage** that portrays Von's experiences in Vietnam, on the boat, and in the United States.

CRITIC'S CORNER

Stephen Tremayne Johnson, a student reader, said about this selection, "I liked how much optimism Von had for his family, his future, and himself." Do you agree? If so, do you think Von is unusual in the optimism he feels? Explain your answer.

"VON"

"Von" (1968–), whose name was changed to protect his privacy and the safety of his family, was born in Saigon, South Vietnam. His father, an officer in the South Vietnamese army, studied in the United States before Von was born. When Von looked at his father's pictures of California, he secretly hoped, "Maybe someday I be there." As the selection explains, Von and his father eventually came to the United States and became citizens. Many years later, the rest of Von's family finally got permission to emigrate from Vietnam.

JANET BODE

1943–

Janet Bode has written a number of award-winning nonfiction books. Her experiences living in New York City inspired her with the idea for *New Kids on the Block: Oral Histories of Immigrant Teens,* from which "Von" was taken. According to her, "Walking by the diner, the stationery store, the market, the restaurant, and the deli, I pass a United Nations of recent immigrants to this country."

Many of Bode's books and articles explore problems facing today's teenagers, such as sibling rivalry, interracial and cross-cultural dating, and teenage pregnancy.

Bode says, "Women's issues are my primary concern, but I have a strong undercurrent of interest in all people regardless of gender."

OTHER WORKS *Different Worlds: Interracial and Cross-Cultural Dating, Truce: Ending the Sibling War, Beating the Odds: Stories of Unexpected Achievers*

PREVIEWING

DRAMA

The Hitchhiker
Lucille Fletcher

PERSONAL CONNECTION

What do you think makes a good horror story?
With your class, discuss the criteria for high-quality
horror—kinds of settings, types of characters, plot
elements, and other characteristics, such as sound
effects. Make a diagram like the one shown here
to record your ideas.

HISTORICAL CONNECTION

In the 1930s and 1940s, before television was a
part of daily life, families gathered around the radio
to listen to their favorite shows, such as *Fibber
McGee and Molly, The Green Hornet,* and *Suspense.* The vivid sounds of radio—voices, laughs,
screams, trains, creaking doors—helped create
pictures in listeners' imaginations.

   The sound effects in *The Hitchhiker,* which was
written for radio, helped the audience follow
Ronald Adams on his eerie coast-to-coast car
trip on Route 66. *The Hitchhiker* was originally
produced and narrated by 23-year-old Orson
Welles, who later became a well-known actor
and movie director.

A radio performer shows off items used to create sound effects for
a radio play in 1938.

WRITING CONNECTION

What role do you think a hitchhiker might play in a horror story? Write
your prediction in your notebook. After you have read the drama, decide
whether your prediction was accurate. If not, how did the hitchhiker's
role differ from the role you predicted?

LASERLINKS
• *HISTORICAL CONNECTION*

THE HITCHHIKER

by Lucille Fletcher

A Play for Radio

Cast of Characters:
Orson Welles
Ronald Adams
Adams's Mother
Voice of hitchhiker
Mechanic
Henry, a sleepy man
Woman's Voice (Henry's wife)
Girl
Operator
Long-distance Operator
Albuquerque Operator
New York Operator
Mrs. Whitney

Welles. Good evening, this is Orson Welles. (*Music in*)

Personally I've never met anybody who didn't like a good ghost story, but I know a lot of people who think there are a lot of people who don't like a good ghost story. For the benefit of these, at least, I go on record at the outset of this evening's entertainment with the sober <u>assurance</u> that although blood may be curdled on this program, none will be spilt. There's no shooting, knifing, throttling, axing, or poisoning here. No clanking chains, no cobwebs, no bony and/or hairy hands appearing from secret panels or, better yet, bedroom curtains. If it's any part of that dear old *phosphorescent*[1] foolishness that people who don't like ghost stories don't like, then again I promise you we haven't got it. What

we do have is a thriller. If it's half as good as we think it is, you can call it a shocker; and we present it proudly and without apologies. After all, a story doesn't have to appeal to the heart—it can also appeal to the spine. Sometimes you want your heart to be warmed—sometimes you want your spine to tingle. The tingling, it's to be hoped, will be quite audible as you listen tonight to *The Hitchhiker*—that's the name of our story, *The Hitchhiker*—

(*Sound: automobile wheels humming over concrete road*)
(*Music: something weird and shuddery*)

---

1. *phosphorescent* (fŏs′fə-rĕs′ənt): glowing with a cold light.

334

Hamptons Drive-In (1974), Howard Kanovitz. Photo courtesy of the artist.

Adams. I am in an auto camp on Route Sixty-six just west of Gallup, New Mexico. If I tell it, perhaps it will help me. It will keep me from going mad. But I must tell this quickly. I am not mad now. I feel perfectly well, except that I am running a slight temperature. My name is Ronald Adams. I am thirty-six years of age, unmarried, tall, dark, with a black mustache. I drive a 1940 Ford V-8, license number 6V-7989. I was born in Brooklyn. All this I know. I know that I am at this moment perfectly sane. That it is not I who have gone mad—but something else—something utterly beyond my control. But I must speak quickly. At any moment the link with life may break. This may be the last thing I ever tell on earth . . . the last night I ever see the stars. . . .

(Music in)

Adams. Six days ago I left Brooklyn to drive to California. . . .

Mother. Goodbye, Son. Good luck to you, my boy. . . .

Adams. Goodbye, Mother. Here—give me a kiss, and then I'll go. . . .

Mother. I'll come out with you to the car.

Adams. No. It's raining. Stay here at the door. Hey—what is this? Tears? I thought you promised me you wouldn't cry.

Mother. I know, dear. I'm sorry. But I—do hate to see you go.

Adams. I'll be back. I'll be on the coast only three months.

Mother. Oh—it isn't that. It's just—the trip. Ronald—I wish you weren't driving.

Adams. Oh—Mother. There you go again. People do it every day.

Mother. I know. But you'll be careful, won't you? Promise me you'll be extra careful.

Don't fall asleep—or drive fast—or pick up any strangers on the road. . . .

Adams. Lord, no. You'd think I was still seventeen to hear you talk—

Mother. And wire me as soon as you get to Hollywood, won't you, Son?

Adams. Of course I will. Now don't you worry. There isn't anything going to happen. It's just eight days of perfectly simple driving on smooth, decent, civilized roads, with a hot-dog or a hamburger stand every ten miles . . . . (fade)

(*Sound: auto hum*)

(*Music in*)

Adams. I was in excellent spirits. The drive ahead of me, even the loneliness, seemed like a <u>lark</u>. But I reckoned without him.

(*Music changes to something weird and empty.*)

Adams. Crossing Brooklyn Bridge that morning in the rain, I saw a man leaning against the cables. He seemed to be waiting for a lift. There were spots of fresh rain on his shoulders. He was carrying a cheap overnight bag in one hand. He was thin, <u>nondescript</u>, with a cap pulled down over his eyes. He stepped off the walk, and if I hadn't swerved, I'd have hit him.

(*Sound: terrific skidding*)

(*Music in*)

Adams. I would have forgotten him completely, except that just an hour later, while crossing the Pulaski Skyway over the Jersey flats, I saw him again. At least, he looked like the same person. He was standing now, with one thumb pointing west. I couldn't figure out how he'd got there, but I thought probably one of those fast trucks had picked him up, beaten me to the Skyway, and let him off. I didn't stop for him. Then—late that night, I saw him again.

(*Music changing*)

Adams. It was on the new Pennsylvania Turnpike between Harrisburg and Pittsburgh. It's 265 miles long, with a very high speed limit. I was just slowing down for one of the tunnels—when I saw him—standing under an arc light by the side of the road. I could see him quite distinctly. The bag, the cap, even the spots of fresh rain spattered over his shoulders. He hailed me this time. . . .

Voice (*very spooky and faint*). Hall-ooo. . . . (*echo as through tunnel*) Hall-ooo . . . !

Adams. I stepped on the gas like a shot. That's lonely country through the Alleghenies,[2] and I had no intention of stopping. Besides, the coincidence, or whatever it was, gave me the willies.[3] I stopped at the next gas station.

(*Sound: auto tires screeching to stop . . . horn honk*)

Mechanic. Yes, sir.

Adams. Fill her up.

Mechanic. Certainly, sir. Check your oil, sir?

Adams. No, thanks.

(*Sound: gas being put into car . . . bell tinkle, et cetera*)

Mechanic. Nice night, isn't it?

Adams. Yes. It—hasn't been raining here recently, has it?

Mechanic. Not a drop of rain all week.

Adams. I suppose that hasn't done your business any harm.

Mechanic. Oh—people drive through here all kinds of weather. Mostly business, you know.

---

2. **Alleghenies** (ăl′ĭ-gā′nēz): the Allegheny Mountains, a range extending from northern Pennsylvania to western Virginia.

3. **gave me the willies:** made me nervous.

WORDS
TO
KNOW

lark (lärk) *n.* a carefree adventure
nondescript (nŏn′dĭ-skrĭpt′) *adj.* lacking in distinctive qualities; drab

There aren't many pleasure cars out on the turnpike this season of the year.

Adams. I suppose not. (*casually*) What about hitchhikers?

Mechanic (*half laughing*). Hitchhikers *here*?

Adams. What's the matter? Don't you ever see any?

Mechanic. Not much. If we did, it'd be a sight for sore eyes.

Adams. Why?

Mechanic. A guy'd be a fool who started out to hitch rides on this road. Look at it. It's 265 miles long, there's practically no speed limit, and it's a straightaway. Now what car is going to stop to pick up a guy under these conditions? Would you stop?

Adams. No. (*slowly, with puzzled emphasis*) Then you've never seen anybody?

Mechanic. Nope. Mebbe they get the lift before the turnpike starts—I mean, you know, just before the toll house—but then it'd be a mighty long ride. Most cars wouldn't want to pick up a guy for that long a ride. And you know—this is pretty lonesome country here—mountains, and woods. . . . You ain't seen anybody like that, have you?

Adams. No. (*quickly*) Oh no, not at all. It was— just a—technical question.

Mechanic. I see. Well—that'll be just a dollar forty-nine—with the tax. . . . (*fade*)

(*Sound: auto hum up*)

(*Music changing*)

Adams. The thing gradually passed from my mind, as sheer coincidence. I had a good night's sleep in Pittsburgh. I did not think about the man all next day—until just outside of Zanesville, Ohio, I saw him again.

(*Music: dark, ominous note*)

Adams. It was a bright, sunshiny afternoon. The peaceful Ohio fields, brown with the autumn stubble, lay dreaming in the golden light. I was driving slowly, drinking it in, when the road suddenly ended in a detour. In front of the barrier, he was standing.

(*Music in*)

Adams. Let me explain about his appearance before I go on. I repeat. There was nothing sinister about him. He was as drab as a mud fence. Nor was his attitude menacing. He merely stood there, waiting, almost drooping a little, the cheap overnight bag in his hand. He looked as though he had been waiting there for hours. Then he looked up. He hailed me. He started to walk forward.

Voice (*far off*). Hall-ooo. . . . Hall-ooo. . . .

Adams. I had stopped the car, of course, for the detour. And for a few moments, I couldn't seem to find the new road. I knew he must be thinking that I had stopped for him.

Voice (*closer*). Hall-ooo. . . . Hallll . . . ooo. . . .

(*Sound: gears jamming . . . sound of motor turning over hard . . . nervous accelerator*)

Voice (*closer*). Halll . . . oooo. . . .

Adams (*panicky*). No. Not just now. Sorry. . . .

Voice (*closer*). Going to California?

(*Sound: starter starting . . . gears jamming*)

Adams (*as though sweating blood*). No. Not today. The other way. Going to New York. Sorry . . . sorry. . . .

(*Sound: Car starts with squeal of wheels on dirt . . . into auto hum.*)

(*Music in*)

Adams. After I got the car back onto the road again, I felt like a fool. Yet the thought of picking him up, of having him sit beside me,

WORDS TO KNOW
sinister (sĭn′ĭ-stər) *adj.* suggestive of evil or misfortune
menacing (mĕn′ĭ-sĭng) *adj.* threatening   **menace** *v.*

was somehow unbearable. Yet, at the same time, I felt, more than ever, unspeakably alone.

(*Sound: auto hum up*)

Adams. Hour after hour went by. The fields, the towns ticked off, one by one. The lights changed. I knew now that I was going to see him again. And though I dreaded the sight, I caught myself searching the side of the road, waiting for him to appear.

(*Sound: auto hum up . . . car screeches to a halt . . . impatient honk two or three times . . . door being unbolted*)

Sleepy man's voice. Yep? What is it? What do you want?

Adams (*breathless*). You sell sandwiches and pop here, don't you?

Voice (*cranky*). Yep. We do. In the daytime. But we're closed up now for the night.

Adams. I know. But—I was wondering if you could possibly let me have a cup of coffee—black coffee.

Voice. Not at this time of night, mister. My wife's the cook, and she's in bed. Mebbe farther down the road—at the Honeysuckle Rest. . . .

(*Sound: door squeaking on hinges as though being closed*)

Adams. No—no. Don't shut the door. (*shakily*) Listen—just a minute ago, there was a man standing here—right beside this stand—a suspicious looking man. . . .

Woman's voice (*from distance*). Hen-ry? Who is it, Henry?

Henry. It's nobuddy, Mother. Just a feller thinks he wants a cup of coffee. Go back into bed.

Adams. I don't mean to disturb you. But you see, I was driving along—when I just happened to look—and there he was. . . .

Henry. What was he doing?

Adams. Nothing. He ran off—when I stopped the car.

Henry. Then what of it? That's nothing to wake a man in the middle of his sleep about. (*sternly*) Young man, I've got a good mind to turn you over to the sheriff.

Adams. But—I—

Henry. You've been taking a nip; that's what you've been doing. And you haven't got anything better to do than to wake decent folk out of their hard-earned sleep. Get going. Go on.

Adams. But—he looked as though he were going to rob you.

Henry. I ain't got nothin' in this stand to lose. Now—on your way before I call out Sheriff Oakes. (*fade*)

(*Sound: auto hum up*)

Adams. I got into the car again and drove on slowly. I was beginning to hate the car. If I could have found a place to stop . . . to rest a little. But I was in the Ozark Mountains of Missouri now. The few resort places there were closed. Only an occasional log cabin, seemingly deserted, broke the monotony of the wild, wooded landscape. I had seen him at that roadside stand; I knew I would see him again—perhaps at the next turn of the road. I knew that when I saw him next, I would run him down. . . .

(*Sound: auto hum up*)

Adams. But I did not see him again until late next afternoon. . . .

(*Sound of railroad warning signal at crossroads*)

Adams. I had stopped the car at a sleepy little junction just across the border into Oklahoma—to let a train pass by—when he appeared, across the tracks, leaning against a telephone pole.

(*Sound: distant sound of train chugging . . . bell ringing steadily*)

Adams (*very tense*). It was a perfectly airless, dry day. The red clay of Oklahoma was baking under the southwestern sun. Yet there were spots of fresh rain on his shoulders. I couldn't stand that. Without thinking, blindly, I started the car across the tracks.

(*Sound: train chugging closer*)

Adams. He didn't even look up at me. He was staring at the ground. I stepped on the gas hard, veering the wheel sharply toward him. I could hear the train in the distance now, but I didn't care. Then something went wrong with the car. It stalled right on the tracks.

(*Sound: train chugging closer; above this, sound of car stalling*)

Adams. The train was coming closer. I could hear its bell ringing and the cry of its whistle. Still he stood there. And now—I knew that he was beckoning—beckoning me to my death.

(*Sound: Train chugging close. Whistle blows wildly. Then train rushes up and by with pistons going, et cetera.*)

Adams. Well—I frustrated him that time. The starter had worked at last. I managed to back up. But when the train passed, he was gone. I was all alone in the hot, dry afternoon.

(*Sound: Train retreating. Crickets begin to sing.*)
(*Music in*)

Adams. After that, I knew I had to do something. I didn't know who this man was or what he wanted of me. I only knew that from now on, I must not let myself be alone on the road for one moment.

(*Sound: auto hum up; slow down; stop; door opening*)

Adams. Hello, there. Like a ride?

Girl. What do you think? How far you going?

Adams. Amarillo . . . I'll take you to Amarillo.

Girl. Amarillo, Texas?

Adams. I'll drive you there.

Girl. Gee!

(*Sound: Door closes. Car starts.*)
(*Music in*)

Girl. Mind if I take off my shoes? My dogs[4] are killing me.

Adams. Go right ahead.

Girl. Gee, what a break this is. A swell car, a decent guy, and driving all the way to Amarillo. All I been getting so far is trucks.

Adams. Hitchhike much?

Girl. Sure. Only it's tough sometimes, in these great open spaces, to get the breaks.

Adams. I should think it would be. Though I'll bet if you get a good pickup in a fast car, you can get to places faster than—say, another person, in another car?

Girl. I don't get you.

Adams. Well, take me, for instance. Suppose I'm driving across the country, say, at a nice steady clip of about forty-five miles an hour. Couldn't a girl like you, just standing beside the road, waiting for lifts, beat me to town after town—provided she got picked up every time in a car doing from sixty-five to seventy miles an hour?

Girl. I dunno. Maybe she could and maybe she couldn't. What difference does it make?

Adams. Oh—no difference. It's just a—crazy idea I had sitting here in the car.

Girl (*laughing*). Imagine spending your time in a swell car thinking of things like that!

Adams. What would you do instead?

---

4. **dogs:** a slang term for feet.

Girl (*admiringly*). What would I do? If I was a good-looking fellow like yourself? Why—I'd just enjoy myself—every minute of the time. I'd sit back and relax, and if I saw a good-looking girl along the side of the road. . . . (*sharply*) Hey! Look out!

Adams (*breathlessly*). Did you see him too?

Girl. See who?

Adams. That man. Standing beside the barbed wire fence.

Girl. I didn't see—anybody. There wasn't nothing but a bunch of steers—and the barbed wire fence. What did you think you was doing? Trying to run into the barbed wire fence?

Adams. There was a man there, I tell you . . . a thin, gray man with an overnight bag in his hand. And I was trying to—run him down.

Girl. Run him down? You mean—kill him?

Adams. He's a sort of—phantom. I'm trying to get rid of him—or else prove that he's real. But (*desperately*) you say you didn't see him back there? You're sure?

Girl (*queerly*). I didn't see a soul. And as far as that's concerned, mister . . .

Adams. Watch for him the next time, then. Keep watching. Keep your eyes peeled on the road. He'll turn up again—maybe any minute now. (*excitedly*) There. Look there—

(*Sound: Auto sharply veering and skidding. Girl screams.*)

(*Sound: crash of car going into barbed wire fence; frightened lowing[5] of steer*)

Girl. How does this door work? I—I'm gettin' outta here.

Adams. Did you see him that time?

Girl (*sharply*). No. I didn't see him that time. And personally, mister, I don't expect never to see him. All I want to do is to go on living—and I don't see how I will very long, driving with you—

Adams. I'm sorry. I—I don't know what came over me. (*frightened*) Please—don't go. . . .

Girl. So if you'll excuse me, mister—

Adams. You can't go. Listen, how would you like to go to California? I'll drive you to California.

Girl. Seeing pink elephants all the way? No thanks.

Adams (*desperately*). I could get you a job there. You wouldn't have to be a waitress. I have friends there—my name is Ronald Adams—you can check up.

(*Sound: Door opens.*)

Girl. Uhn-huuh. Thanks just the same.

Adams. Listen. Please. For just one minute. Maybe you think I am half-cracked. But this man. You see, I've been seeing this man all the way across the country. He's been following me. And if you could only help me—stay with me—until I reach the coast—

Girl. You know what I think you need, big boy? Not a girl friend. Just a good dose of sleep. . . . There, I got it now.

(*Sound: Door opens . . . slams.*)

Adams. No. You can't go.

Girl (*screams*). Leave your hands offa me, do you hear! Leave your—

Adams. Come back here, please, come back.

(*Sound: struggle . . . slap . . . footsteps running away on gravel . . . lowing of steer*)

Adams. She ran from me as though I were a monster. A few minutes later, I saw a passing truck pick her up. I knew then that I was utterly alone.

(*Sound: lowing of steer up*)

Adams. I was in the heart of the great Texas

---

5. **lowing:** mooing.

Hilco (1989), Kit Boyce. Courtesy of the artist.

prairies. There wasn't a car on the road after the truck went by. I tried to figure out what to do, how to get hold of myself. If I could find a place to rest. Or even if I could sleep right here in the car for a few hours, along the side of the road. . . . I was getting my winter overcoat out of the back seat to use as a blanket (*hall-ooo*) when I saw him coming toward me (*hall-ooo*), emerging from the herd of moving steer. . . .

Voice. Hall-ooo. . . . Hall-oooo. . . .

(*Sound: auto starting violently . . . up to steady hum*)

(*Music in*)

Adams. I didn't wait for him to come any closer. Perhaps I should have spoken to him then, fought it out then and there. For now he began to be everywhere. Whenever I stopped, even for a moment—for gas, for oil, for a drink of pop, a cup of coffee, a sandwich—he was there.

(*Music faster*)

Adams. I saw him standing outside the auto camp in Amarillo that night when I dared to slow down. He was sitting near the drinking fountain in a little camping spot just inside the border of New Mexico.

(*Music faster*)

Adams. He was waiting for me outside the Navajo Reservation, where I stopped to check my tires. I saw him in Albuquerque,[6] where I bought twelve gallons of gas. . . . I was afraid now, afraid to stop. I began to drive faster and faster. I was in lunar landscape now—the great arid mesa country of

---

6. **Albuquerque** (ăl′bə-kûr′kē): a city in central New Mexico.

New Mexico. I drove through it with the indifference of a fly crawling over the face of the moon.

(*Music faster*)

Adams. But now he didn't even wait for me to stop. Unless I drove at eighty-five miles an hour over those endless roads—he waited for me at every other mile. I would see his figure, shadowless, flitting before me, still in its same attitude, over the cold and lifeless ground; flitting over dried-up rivers, over broken stones cast up by old glacial upheavals, flitting in the pure and cloudless air. . . .

(*Music strikes sinister note of finality.*)

Adams. I was beside myself when I finally reached Gallup, New Mexico, this morning. There is an auto camp here—cold, almost deserted at this time of year. I went inside and asked if there was a telephone. I had the feeling that if only I could speak to someone familiar, someone that I loved, I could pull myself together.

(*Sound: nickel put in slot*)

Operator. Number, please?

Adams. Long distance.

(*Sound: return of nickel; buzz.*)

Long-distance opr. This is long distance.

Adams. I'd like to put in a call to my home in Brooklyn, New York. I'm Ronald Adams. The number is Beechwood 2-0828.

Long-distance opr. Thank you. What is your number?

Adams. 312

Albuquerque opr. Albuquerque.

Long-distance opr. New York for Gallup. (*pause*)

New York opr. New York.

Long-distance opr. Gallup, New Mexico, calling Beechwood 2-0828. (*fade*)

Adams. I had read somewhere that love could banish demons. It was the middle of the morning. I knew Mother would be home. I pictured her, tall, white-haired, in her crisp house dress, going about her tasks. It would be enough, I thought, merely to hear the even calmness of her voice. . . .

Long-distance opr. Will you please deposit three dollars and eighty-five cents for the first three minutes? When you have deposited a dollar and a half, will you wait until I have collected the money?

(*Sound: clunk of six coins*)

Long-distance opr. All right, deposit another dollar and a half.

(*Sound: clunk of six coins*)

Long-distance opr. Will you please deposit the remaining eighty-five cents?

(*Sound: clunk of four coins*)

Long-distance opr. Ready with Brooklyn—go ahead, please.

Adams. Hello.

Mrs. Whitney. Mrs. Adams's residence.

Adams. Hello. Hello—Mother?

Mrs. Whitney (*very flat and rather proper . . . dumb, too, in a frizzy sort of way*). This is Mrs. Adams's residence. Who is it you wished to speak to, please?

Adams. Why—who's this?

Mrs. Whitney. This is Mrs. Whitney.

Adams. Mrs. Whitney? I don't know any Mrs. Whitney. Is this Beechwood 2-0828?

Mrs. Whitney. Yes.

Adams. Where's my mother? Where's Mrs. Adams?

Mrs. Whitney. Mrs. Adams is not at home. She is still in the hospital.

Adams. The hospital!

Mrs. Whitney. Yes. Who is this calling, please? Is it a member of the family?

Adams. What's she in the hospital for?

Mrs. Whitney. She's been prostrated[7] for five days. Nervous breakdown. But who is this calling?

Adams. Nervous breakdown? But—my mother was never nervous. . . .

Mrs. Whitney. It's all taken place since the death of her oldest son, Ronald.

Adams. Death of her oldest son, Ronald . . .? Hey—what is this? What number is this?

Mrs. Whitney. This is Beechwood 2-0828. It's all been very sudden. He was killed just six days ago in an automobile accident on the Brooklyn Bridge.

Operator (*breaking in*). Your three minutes are up, sir. (*silence*) Your three minutes are up, sir. (*pause*) Your three minutes are up, sir. (*fade*) Sir, your three minutes are up. Your three minutes are up, sir.

Adams (*in a strange voice*). And so, I am sitting here in this deserted auto camp in Gallup, New Mexico. I am trying to think. I am trying to get hold of myself. Otherwise, I shall go mad. . . . Outside it is night—the vast, soulless night of New Mexico. A million stars are in the sky. Ahead of me stretch a thousand miles of empty mesa, mountains, prairies—desert. Somewhere among them, he is waiting for me. Somewhere I shall know who he is, and who . . . I . . . am. . . .

(*Music up*) ❖

---

7. **prostrated:** in a state of mental collapse.

Route 66

Like Ronald Adams in *The Hitchhiker,* hundreds of thousands of travelers chose Route 66 to go west during the mid-twentieth century. Now part of history, Route 66 was one of America's most famous highways. Starting at Grant Park in Chicago, Illinois, it stretched 2,448 miles across two-thirds of the country and eight states to Los Angeles, California. Unlike today's interstate highways which bypass towns, Route 66 passed through the center of towns and became known as "The Main Street of America."

The idea for Route 66 grew out of a decision by the federal government in 1921 to develop a system of interconnected interstate routes. The resulting system included Route 66 as the main artery linking the East and the West. In the years that followed, this famous two-lane road was highly traveled by people moving west and tourists visiting spectacular sites, like the Grand Canyon. Lyrics from Bobby Troup's hit song of 1946 captured the excitement of the road:

If you ever plan to motor west
Travel my way, take the highway that's
  the best.
Get your kicks on Route Sixty-six! . . .

By the mid-1950s, despite the fact that the old highway was maintained and was divided into four lanes for long sections, it could not handle the growing traffic. Stretches of Route 66 were being replaced here and there to make way for new interstate highways. Even the popular television series of the early 1960s, *Route 66,* was not able to stop the road's death, and the last stretch of U.S. Highway 66 was bypassed by Interstate 40 in 1984 near Williams, Arizona.

RESPONDING OPTIONS

FROM PERSONAL RESPONSE TO CRITICAL ANALYSIS

REFLECT
1. If you were all alone, listening to this drama on the radio, how do you think you would feel? Explain your answer.

RETHINK
2. What do you think has happened to Adams? Give reasons for your answer.
   Consider
   - how he thinks the hitchhiker is a threat to his survival
   - whether he is dead
   - whether he is mad or insane
   - other possible explanations for his experiences

3. Who do you think the mysterious hitchhiker is? Use details from the play to support your answer.

4. Do you think *The Hitchhiker* is a good horror story? Why or why not?
   Consider
   - the criteria your class discussed for the Personal Connection on page 332
   - the statements and promises in Orson Welles's introduction
   - how it compares with more modern horror stories

RELATE
5. Horror stories have always fascinated readers and audiences of all ages. Why do you think these stories are so popular?

ANOTHER PATHWAY

Use tracing paper to copy the outline of the United States, then draw Adams's route on the map. At appropriate places along the route, write short sentences to describe the incidents that took place on his trip.

QUICKWRITES

1. The ending of this play leaves the audience hanging. Write an additional **scene** that will leave no questions in readers' minds.

2. How could Ronald Adams's drive to California have been different? Rewrite Welles's **introduction,** putting a different spin on the story or setting up the audience for an entirely different kind of horror story.

   📁 *PORTFOLIO Save your writing. You may want to use it later as a springboard to a piece for your portfolio.*

LITERARY CONCEPTS

Foreshadowing is a writer's hinting at a future event in a story. As this play progresses, Lucille Fletcher drops stronger and stronger hints that the innocent-looking fellow on the road will bring an end to Ronald Adams's story. Find some of these clues and connect them with what happens later.

ALTERNATIVE ACTIVITIES

Cooperative Learning With your classmates, produce *The Hitchhiker* as a radio play. Some students can play roles, while others can provide the necessary music and sound effects. Audiotape the performance for other classes to hear.

ACROSS THE CURRICULUM

Mathematics Use a current road map of the United States to calculate the mileage from Brooklyn, New York, to Los Angeles, California, using the most direct route that will take you through Gallup, New Mexico, and on to Los Angeles. Driving at 55 miles per hour, for 8 hours a day, how long would it take to reach Los Angeles?

WORDS TO KNOW

Review the Words to Know at the bottom of the selection pages. On your paper, create a word web like the one below for each vocabulary word.

LUCILLE FLETCHER

1912–

Lucille Fletcher was born in Brooklyn, New York, where Ronald Adams's frightening trip begins. A graduate of Vassar College, she married another writer, the novelist Douglass Wallop III. They lived on the eastern shore of Maryland's Chesapeake Bay until Wallop's death in 1985.

During the 1930s and 1940s, Fletcher kept radio audiences on the edge of their seats with her chilling mystery dramas. She is best known for her radio play *Sorry, Wrong Number,* a suspense classic. She wrote 20 plays for the radio series *Suspense* and scripts for the television series *Chrysler Theater* and *Lights Out.* Fletcher has also written several mystery novels—including *And Presumed Dead* and *Blindfold,* which were made into movies. Her first Broadway play, *Night Watch,* was produced in 1972 and later made into a movie starring Elizabeth Taylor.

OTHER WORKS *Mirror Image, Eighty Dollars to Stamford*

THE FLOOD

by Ralph Helfer

It was
raining that morning,

as usual. For weeks it had

been coming down—sometimes

heavily, with thunder and

lightning, and sometimes with

just a mist of light rain.

But it was always there,

and by now the blankets,

the beds, and the whole

house were constantly damp.

My career was at a peak. I'd spent twelve years struggling to get to the top, and I had finally made it. My life was pretty good. I had just completed the back-to-back shooting of *Daktari* and *Gentle Ben,* and I was living at our new ranch, Africa U.S.A., with 1500 wild animals and a crew of dedicated keepers and trainers.

The ranch was beautiful. Nestled at the bottom of Soledad Canyon, about thirty miles north of Los Angeles, the property snaked for a mile down the canyon beside the banks of the Santa Clarita stream. The highway wound above it on one side, the railroad track on the other.

As I left the rhinos, I noticed that I could no longer jump over the stream that ran beside their barn. I was starting to get a little concerned.

We'd had heavy rains before, and even a few floods, but nothing we couldn't handle. There was a flood-control dam above us, fifteen miles up the canyon, and we weren't too worried about the stream's overflowing. But just to make sure, we had asked the city's flood-control office to advise us. They checked their records for the biggest flood in the office's hundred-year history, and calculated that to handle one that size we would need a channel 100 feet wide, 12 feet deep, and 1 mile long. It cost us $100,000 and three months of hard work, but we built it. It was worth it to feel safe.

Toni and I had grabbed a few hours' sleep before leaving the house, which was located off the ranch up on a hill, and heading out into the rain again early this morning to make sure our animals were dry and safe.

On arriving at the compound, Toni went over to check on the "wild string," a group of lions, tigers, bears, and leopards that had been donated to us by people who never should have had them in the first place. Hopeless animal lovers that we were, we had taken them in, even though we knew that very few spoiled mature animals could ever be indoctrinated with affection training.

I checked at the office for messages, then headed for "Beverly Hills," our nickname for the area where our movie-star animals lived— Gentle Ben, Clarence the cross-eyed lion, Judy the chimp, Bullfrog the "talking" buffalo, Modoc the elephant, and many others. The rain had become a steady downpour by the time I arrived there. Everything seemed to be in order, so I went on to the rhinos. No problems there, either.

As I left the rhinos, I noticed that I could no longer jump over the stream that ran beside their barn. I was starting to get a little concerned. The sky was now opening up with a vengeance. I wrapped my poncho around me and continued my tour of inspection.

I was wondering how Toni was making out with the wild string, when Miguel, a Mexican keeper who had been with us for six years, arrived to care for the animals in the Beverly Hills section. He smiled his broad, gold-capped grin, then disappeared around a bend of the stream.

Then my head trainer, Frank Lamping, arrived. He told me that the earthen dam above us was about to go. To prevent the dam from bursting, the flood-control people were opening the floodgates to release the pressure. We were to watch out for some heavy water coming downstream.

The crew had all been working continuously from morning until night since the rains had

Copyright © Richard R. Hewett/Shooting Star.

begun, to make sure that the ranch was safe. Now we had to redouble our efforts.

I told Frank to check the stock area. A trainer yelled from the roadway above that he had the nursery section under control.

I found some pretty badly undermined cages in my area and set to work with a shovel to fill the erosion. I was looking down at my shovel, working hard, when I heard a noise. It was a low roar, and it was quickly becoming louder and closer. I remember just looking over my shoulder, and suddenly there it was—a wall of water carrying with it full-sized oak trees, sheds, branches. Down it came, crashing and exploding against the compound, uprooting cages, overturning buildings, trucks—anything in its way.

Instantly, everything was in chaos. Sheer panic broke out among the animals in the Beverly Hills section. Lions were roaring and hitting against the sides of their cages; bears were lunging against the bars; chimps were screaming. The water was starting to rock the cages. Some were already floating and were about to be swept downstream.

I didn't know what to do first! I raced for the cages but was thrown down by the weight of the water. Miguel came running over, yelling half in English and half in Spanish. I told him to grab a large coil of rope that was hanging in a tree nearby. I fastened it around me and, with Miguel holding the other end, I started out into the water. If I could just get to the cages, I could unlock them and set the animals free. At least then they could fend for themselves. It was their only chance. Otherwise, they would all drown in their cages.

The water was rushing past me furiously. I struggled through it to Gentle Ben's cage, fumbling for the key. "Don't *drop* it!" I mumbled to myself. The key turned, I threw open the door, and the great old bear landed right on top of me in his panic for freedom.

I grabbed Ben's heavy coat and hung on as his massive body carried me to a group of cages holding more than twenty animals. The water was now five or six feet deep. Cages were starting to come loose from their foundations; the animals were swimming inside them, fighting for breath. I let go of Ben and grabbed onto the steel bars of one of the cages. My heart sank as I saw Ben dog-paddling, trying to reach the embankment. He never did. I could just barely make out his form as he was carried through some rough white water and around a bend before he was lost from view.

One by one I released the animals—leopards, tigers, bears—talking as calmly as I could, even managing an occasional pat or kiss of farewell. I watched as they were carried away, swept along with the torrent of water. Some would come together for a moment and would then be whisked away, as though a giant hand had come up and shoved them. Some went under. I strained to see whether any of these came up again, but I couldn't tell.

My wonderful, beloved animals were all fighting for their lives. I felt sick and helpless.

To my right, about thirty feet out in the water and half submerged, was a large, heavy steel cage on wheels with a row of four compartments in it. I managed to get to it just as the force of the current started to move it. I began to open the compartments, one by one, but now the cage was moving faster downstream, carrying me with it. I looked back to the shore, at Miguel. He saw the problem, and with his end of the rope he threw a dally[1] around a large tree branch. We were running out of time. If the rope came to the end of its slack before I could get it off me and onto the cage, we would lose the cage. It was picking up

---

1. **threw a dally:** looped the rope around an immovable object to keep it from slipping.

speed, and the animals inside were roaring and barking in terror.

I decided to hold the cage myself, with the rope tied around my waist. There were two beautiful wolves in the last cage, Sheba and Rona. Toni and I had raised them since they were pups. I was at their door, fumbling with the lock, when the rope went taut. I thought it would cut me in half. I grabbed the steel bars with both hands, leaving the key in the lock, praying it wouldn't drop out. When I reached down once more to open the lock, the key fell into the water! I was stunned, frozen. I knew I had just signed those animals' death warrants. The water behind the cage was building up a wall of force. I held on as tightly as I could, but finally the cage was ripped out of my hands.

I fell backward into the churning water; when I surfaced, I could see the cage out in the mainstream, racing with the trees, bushes, and sides of buildings, heading on down the raging river. I looked for the last time at Sheba and Rona. They were looking at us quietly as if they knew, but their eyes begged for help. My tears joined the flood as my beloved friends were washed away.

By this time it had become clear to me what had happened. The floodgates on the dam had been opened, all right, but because the ground was already saturated with the thirty inches of rain that had fallen in the last few weeks, it wouldn't absorb any more. At the same time, the new storm had hit, pouring down another fourteen inches in just twenty-four hours. Together, these conditions had caused the flood.

It was a larger flood than any that had been recorded in the area in the last hundred years, and it was made worse because the water had been held up occasionally on its fifteen-mile journey down the canyon by debris in its path. When suddenly released, the water that had built up behind the naturally formed logjams doubled in force. By the time it reached us, huge waves had been built up: the water and debris came crashing down on us like a wall, then subsided, only to come crashing down again. We were to struggle through two days and nights of unbelievable havoc and terror, trying desperately to salvage what we could of the ranch.

At the same time, the new storm had hit, pouring down another fourteen inches in just twenty-four hours.

The storm grew worse. Heavy sheets of rain filled and overflowed our flood channel, undermining its sides until they caved in. By mid-morning the Santa Clarita had become a raging, murderous torrent, 150 feet wide and 15 feet deep, moving through Africa U.S.A. with the speed and force of an express train. In its fury it wiped out a two-lane highway, full-grown oak trees, generator buildings—everything. Our soundstage was in a full-sized building, 100 feet long by 50 feet wide, but the water just picked it up like a matchbox and carried it away downstream, end over end, rolling it like a toy and depositing it on a sand embankment a mile away. Electric wires flared brightly as the water hit them. We rushed for the main switch to the soundstage, shutting everything down for fear of someone being electrocuted. Everywhere, animals and people were in the water, swimming for safety.

We'd be half drowned, and then we'd make our way to the shore, cough and sputter, and go back into the water. You don't think at a time like that—you *do*.

My people risked their lives over and over again for the animals.

The waves next hit the elephant pens, hard. We moved the elephants out as the building collapsed and was carried downstream. Then the waves caught the camels' cage, pulling it into the water. One huge camel was turning over and over as he was swept along. (I thought at the time that somewhere, someday, if that animal drowned, some arche- ologist would dig up its bones

and say, "My God, there must have been camels in Los Angeles!")

We worked frenziedly. Bears, lions, and tigers were jumping out of their cages and immedi- ately being swept downstream. Others were hanging onto our legs and pulling us under, or we were hanging onto them and swimming for shore. I unlocked the cheetah's cage, and he sprang out over my head, right into the water, and was gone. Animals were everywhere.

I remember grabbing hold of a mature tiger as

he came out of his cage. He carried me on his back to temporary security on the opposite bank as smoothly as if we'd rehearsed it.

Another time I found myself being carried downstream with Zamba, Jr., who was caught in the same whirlpool that I was. I grabbed his mane, and together we swam for the safety of the shore. After resting a bit, I managed to get back to the main area, leaving the lion in as good a spot as any. At least for the moment he was safe.

As the storm rode on, the river was full of animals and people swimming together; there was no "kill" instinct in operation, only that of survival. Men were grabbing fistfuls of fur, clinging for life. A monkey grabbed a lion's tail, which allowed him to make it to safety.

Clarence the cross-eyed lion was in a state of panic. The river had surrounded him and was now flooding his cage. His trainer, Bob, waded across the water, put a chain on Clarence, took him out of his cage, and attempted to jump across the raging stream with him. But the lion wouldn't jump. The water was rising rapidly. Bob threw part of the chain to me. To gain some leverage, I grabbed a pipe that was running alongside a building. As we both pulled, Clarence finally jumped, and just then the pipe I was holding onto came loose. It turned out to be a "hot" electric conduit, for when Clarence leaped and the pipe came loose, we all got a tremendous electric shock! Fortunately, the pipe also pulled the wires loose, so the shock only lasted for an instant. Had it continued, it would certainly have killed us, as we were standing knee-deep in water.

We noticed a group of monkeys trapped in a small outcropping of dirt and debris in the middle of the river. Frank almost died trying to save them: he tied a rope around his waist and started across, but about halfway over he slipped and went under. We didn't know whether to pull on the rope or not. We finally saw him in midstream, trying to stay afloat. Whenever we pulled on the rope, he would go under. (We found out later that the rope had become tangled around his foot, and every time we yanked it we were pulling him under!) But he made it, thank God, and he was able to swim the animals to safety.

We were racing against time. The river was still rising, piling up roots and buildings and pushing them along in front, forming a wall of destruction. The shouts of half-drowned men and the screams of drowning animals filled the air, along with thunder and lightning and the ever-increasing downpour of rain.

Throughout the turmoil and strife one thing was crystal clear to me, and that is that without affection training, all would have been lost. It was extraordinary. As dangerous and frightening as the emergency was, these animals remained calm enough to let themselves be led to safety when it was possible for us to do so.

Imagine yourself in a raging storm, with buildings crashing alongside of you. You make your way to a cage that houses a lion or a tiger, and the animal immediately understands why you're there and is happy to see you. You open the door, put a leash on the animal, and you both jump out into the freezing, swirling water. Together, you're swept down the stream, hitting logs, rolling over and over, as you try to keep your arms around the animal. Together, you get up onto the safety of dry land. You dry off, give your animal a big hug, and then go back in for another one.

There was one big cage left in the back section containing a lion. This lion was a killer who had been fear trained rather than affection trained. We went out to him. The other lions were being saved because we could swim with them, but this fellow was too rough. I got to the cage and opened the door. A couple of my men threw ropes on the lion and pulled, trying to get him out of his potential grave—but he wouldn't come out. He was petrified! We pulled and struggled and fought to get him out of the cage, but we couldn't do it, and we finally had to let him go.

Then the "wild string" panicked, and in their hysteria they attacked their rescuers as if they were enemies. In the end, we had to resort to tranquilizer guns. We fired darts into each fear-trained animal, and as they succumbed to the medication, we held their bodies up above the water and carried them to safety. Tragically, there was not enough time to drag all of them to safety; several drowned in their drugged sleep before we could reach them.

> We eventually became stranded with some of the animals on an island—this was all that was left of Africa U.S.A.

The storm continued on into the night, and with the darkness came a nightmare of confusion. We worked on without sleep, sustained by coffee and desperation.

During that first night, it became clear that ancient Modoc, the elephant, the one-eyed wonder of the big top,[2] had by no means outlived her capacity for calmness and courage in the face of disaster. Modoc took over, understanding fully what was at stake and what was required of her. Animal after animal was saved as she labored at the water's edge, hauling their cages to safety on higher ground. When the current tore a cage free and washed it downstream, Modoc got a firmer grip on the rope with her trunk and, with the power of several bulldozers, steadily dragged the cage back to safety. Then a trainer would attach the rope to another endangered pen, and Modoc would resume her labors.

We eventually became stranded with some of the animals on an island—this was all that was left of Africa U.S.A., plus the area alongside the railroad track. When the dam had burst upstream, the wall of water that hit the ranch divided into two fast-moving rivers. As time passed, the rivers widened and deepened until they were impossible to cross. As dusk fell on the second day, we realized that we were cut off from the mainland. Since it was the highest ground on the ranch, the island in the center had become the haven for all the survivors. The office building, the vehicles, and about twenty cages were all well above the flooded zone and so were safe for the time being. The giraffes, some monkeys, and one lion were all housed in makeshift cages on the island. We all hoped the water would not rise any further.

Behind the office building ran a railroad track. By following the tracks for three miles, it would be possible to reach the highway. The problem would then be in crossing the torrent of water to get to the road.

I noticed that Bullfrog, our thousand-pound Indian buffalo, was gone. Buffalos are known to be excellent swimmers. Surely he could survive! I asked around to see whether anyone had seen him. No one had. Bullfrog's cage had been at the entrance to the ranch, because he always greeted visitors with a most unusual bellow that sounded exactly like the word "Hi." Now he was gone, too. Would it ever end? I felt weak. The temperature had dropped, and the wind had come up. The wind-chill factor was now thirty degrees below zero.

There's something horrible about tragedy that occurs in the dark. I could hear the water

---

2. **big top:** the main tent of a traveling circus.

running behind me, and every once in a while I'd hear a big timber go, or an animal cry, or a person shouting. It all seemed very unreal.

Throughout the night and all the next day the rain continued, and we worked on. Luckily, help came from everywhere. The highway, which we could no longer get to but which we could see, was lined with cars. Some people had successfully rigged up a bos'n chair[3] 50 feet in the air and were sending hot food and drink over to us, a distance of some 200 yards. Other people were walking three miles over the hills to bring supplies. Radio communication was set up by a citizens-band club. Gardner McKay, the actor and a true friend, put his Mercedes on the track, deflated the tires, and slowly drove down to help us. One elderly woman prepared ham and coffee and brought it in at two o'clock in the morning, only to find on her return that her car had been broken into and robbed!

Then a train engine came down the track to help (just an engine—no cars). Three girls from the affection-training school volunteered to rescue the snakes. The girls climbed onto the cowcatcher on the front of the engine. We then wrapped about thirty feet of pythons and boa constrictors around their shoulders and told them where to take the snakes once they were on the other side. (There was, of course, no more electricity in the reptile and nursery area, and unless we could get the reptiles to some heat, they would surely die.) Goats, aoudads, and llamas all rode in the coal bin behind the engine. I'll never forget the look on one girl's face as the engine pulled out and a python crawled through her hair.

By four the next morning, some twenty people had, by some method or another, made it over to our island to help. Some chose a dangerous way, tying ropes around their middles and entering the water slowly, with those on the island holding the other ends of the ropes. Then, with the current carrying them quickly downstream, they would look for a logjam or boulder to stop them so they could make their way to where we were.

I was having some coffee in the watchmen's trailer when the scream of an animal shattered the night. I dashed out to find a small group of people huddled together, trying to shine their flashlights on the animal who was out there in the dark, desperately struggling in the raging water. It had succeeded in swimming out of the turbulence in the middle of the stream, but the sides of the river were too slippery for it to get a foothold and climb to safety. In the dark, I couldn't make out which animal it was. Then I heard it: "Hi! Hi!" It was a call of desperation from Bullfrog, the buffalo, as he fought for his life. There was nothing we could do to help him, and his "Hi's" trailed down the dark, black abyss, fading as he was carried away around the bend.

Then Toni screamed at me in the dark, "Ralph, over here!" I fought my way through a maze of debris and water and burst into a clearing. There was Toni, holding a flashlight on—lo and behold—a big steel cage from Beverly Hills! It had been washed downstream and was lodged in the trunk of a toppled tree. It was still upright, but its back was facing us, and we couldn't see inside. We waded out to the cage. Toni kept calling, "Sheba, Rona, are you there? Please answer!" Our hearts were beating fast, and Toni was crying.

Hoping against hope that the wolves were still alive, we rounded the corner, half swimming, half falling. Then we eased up to the front of the cage and looked straight into two sets of the most beautiful eyes I'd ever seen. Rona and

---

3. **bos'n** (bō′sən) **chair:** a sling moved by an arrangement of ropes and pulleys, usually used to transfer people or materials from one ship to another or from a ship to shore.

Copyright © Richard R. Hewett/Shooting Star.

Sheba had survived! They practically jumped out of their skins when they saw us, as though to say, "Is it really *you*?" Toni had her key, and we unlocked the door. Both wolves fell all over us, knocking us into the water. They couldn't seem to stop licking our faces and whimpering. Thank God, at least *they* were safe!

The rain finally let up on the morning of the third day. The sun came out, and at last we had time to stop, look around, and assess the damage. It was devastating, and heartrending.

Most of the animals had been let out of their cages and had totally disappeared, including Judy, Clarence, Pajama Tops the zebra, and Raunchy, our star jaguar. We knew a few others had definitely drowned. Both rhinos were missing, and so were the hippos. Our beloved

Gentle Ben had been washed away, along with hundreds of other animals.

I was sitting there looking at the wreckage when somebody put a cup of hot chocolate in my hand. It was Toni. She stood before me, as exhausted as I was, clothes torn and wet, hair astray, cold and shivering. What a woman! Earlier, she had managed to make her way to the Africa U.S.A. nursery, where all of the baby animals were quartered. Without exception, the babies had all followed her to safety. Not one baby animal had been lost.

The hot liquid felt good going down. I stood up and hugged and kissed Toni, and arm in arm we walked. The sun was just topping the cottonwoods. The river had subsided. All was quiet, except for an occasional animal noise: a yelp, a growl, a snort. All of the animals were happy to see the sun, to feel its warmth.

Toni and I felt only the heavy, leaden feeling of loss. Ten years were, literally, down the drain. We had just signed a contract with Universal Studios to open our beautiful ranch to their tours; this would now be impossible. A million dollars was gone, maybe more. But what was far worse was the loss of some of our beloved animals.

We hiked to a ridge above the railroad track. Something caught my eye, and as we came near an outcrop of trees where we could have a better view, we looked over. There, on top of a nearby hill, we saw an incredible sight. Lying under the tree was Zamba, and at his feet, resting, were a multitude of animals. Deer, bears, tigers, llamas, all lying together peacefully. The animals must have fought their way clear of the treacherous waters and, together, climbed the hill, slept, and then dried off in the morning sun. They hadn't run away. In fact, they seemed to be waiting for our next move. It was as though God had caused the flood to make me realize how powerful affection training is, how deep it had gone. The lamb could truly lie down with the lion, without fear, and could do it by choice!

We called Zam over to us and smothered him with hugs and kisses. As we climbed down to the ranch, the other animals joined us. Camels, giraffes, eland—all came along as we wound our way down.

So many people were there at the ranch! We were once again connected with the rest of the world. Exhausted, wet, wonderful people—true animal lovers. They had come from everywhere. Some were employees, some friends, some strangers. All greeted us as we came down the hill. Their faces expressed hope and love. They cared . . . and it showed.

> The rain finally let up on the morning of the third day. The sun came out, and at last we had time to stop, look around, and assess the damage.

We took the animals one by one and fed, cleaned, and housed them as best we could.

"Ralph, come quickly!" screamed a voice. "He made it, he made it! *He's alive!*"

"Who, who?" I screamed, and was met by a resounding "Hi, Hi!" From around the corner came Bullfrog—disheveled and muddy, but alive!

"Hi, hi!"

Yes, *hi,* you big lovable . . . hi! hi!

We began searching for the animals that were still lost. The ranch was a network of people and animals working together on the massive cleanup effort. Animals were straining to pull big trucks out of the water and muck.

Bakery trucks were coming by with stale bread for the elephants. Farmers loaned us their skip loaders to round up the hippos and rhinos. (One hippo fell in love with the skip-loader bucket and coyly followed it home!) Charley and Madeline Franks, two loyal helpers, kept hot chili coming and must have dished out hundreds of meals. People from the Humane Society, Fish and Game, Animal Regulation, and the SPCA[4] all helped to comfort and tend the animals.

Everyone was busy constructing makeshift cages. The medical-lab trailer was pulled out of the mud. The nursery building and all of its kitchen storage area had been completely submerged, and some of it had been washed away. However, what could be salvaged was taken up to the island for immediate use.

> **Of 1500 other animals, only 9 had drowned. Five of these were animals that had not been affection trained.**

Outside the ranch, the animals began turning up everywhere. Elephants showed up in people's backyards. Eagles sat in the limbs of trees. Llamas and guanacos cruised the local restaurants and were seen in parking lots. There was no difficulty between animals and people.

We had had dozens of alligators, some weighing two hundred to three hundred pounds. The whole pen had been hit by the water; we lost most of them because the water was ice-cold, and it battered and beat them. For seven months afterward we'd read in the paper that the bodies of alligators were being found everywhere, up to forty-five miles away. There were helicopter and airplane photos of alligators

that had been killed, their bodies lying in the sand as the water subsided.

Of 1500 other animals, only 9 had drowned. Five of these were animals that had not been affection trained.

Only one animal remained lost and unaccounted for, and that was old Gentle Ben. I had last seen him being swept sideways down the river. We didn't have much hope for him.

I was starting to feel the full shock of everything that had happened. True, by some miracle most of the animals were safe, but other losses had been enormous. As the emergency lessened and mopping-up operations took over, I felt worse and worse. The shakes set in, and then I developed a high fever. The doctors said it was a walking pneumonia, and that rest, good food, and warmth were in order. But there were still too many things to do—now was not the time to stop. I did, however, need to find a place to sit down and relax for a while.

As I sat on a log, my body trembled with shock as well as illness. In looking over the debris, it seemed to me that everything I had worked for was gone. The emotional pain, the sheer physical exhaustion, and the pneumonia had overloaded me. I just couldn't handle any more. I had no more tears, no pain of any kind. I was numb. I sat in the middle of the chaos with an old blanket wrapped around me, unmoving, unable to give any more orders.

I had closed my eyes and was drifting off to sleep when something warm and wet on my face woke me up. I opened my eyes and saw Ben. *Gentle Ben had come home!!* I hugged him and cried like a big kid. I turned to get up to tell everyone, but I didn't have to. They

---

4. **SPCA:** Society for the Prevention of Cruelty to Animals.

were all there. Toni, joined by the rest, had brought him to me. He'd been found two miles down the canyon, mud-covered and a few pounds lighter, but safe! Tears were in everybody's eyes—and if you looked closely, it seemed that even old Ben had a few.

A beautiful rainbow arched its brilliant colors across the ravaged countryside, then was gone.

There was a time in my life when I felt I had reached the end of the rainbow. I had touched it, had dug my hand deep into its treasures of happiness and prosperity.

Suddenly, everything had changed. All that I had created was gone. I hadn't realized how vulnerable the world is, how delicate the balance of forces that sustain our existence.

I stood up and dusted off my jeans. In the distance I could see the sky clearing, and I knew that some day there would be another rainbow, its treasure awaiting. Until then, we had a job to do. We would need to start all over again. ❖

RALPH HELFER

Ralph Helfer (1931–) says that "blood, sweat, and tears" rebuilt his animal-rental business, the world's largest, after the devastating flood described in this selection from his book *The Beauty of the Beasts*. Whether it is a huge lion charging terrified campers, a python coiling around a screaming woman, or a half-ton grizzly frolicking with a woodsman, Helfer's animals have astounded film audiences around the world.

Many years ago, when Helfer was a Hollywood stuntman, he was attacked by an angry lion. As a result, he vowed to change the way that humans interacted with wild animals. During the three decades of Helfer's animal-training career, his animals collected 26 Patsy awards (the animal equivalent of the Oscar), and many of them became well-known personalities, including Clarence the cross-eyed lion, the bear Gentle Ben, Judy the Daktari chimpanzee, and the Mercury cougar.

No longer running the rental business, Helfer today spends most of his time in Africa, producing animal documentaries, writing books and magazine articles about wild animals, conducting safaris, lecturing, and working with conservation, ecology, and humane organizations to protect wild animals. He believes that his success in quieting the killer instinct in predators may help in the study of ways to control aggressiveness in humans and that his affection-training methods could be applied to the rearing of children. On an experimental basis, Helfer has taught delinquent teenagers to care for and train animals.

WRITING ABOUT LITERATURE

ASKING QUESTIONS

Every story you read creates its own unique world. Sometimes it's fun to go along with the story, enjoying the elaborate details and interesting scenes, but sometimes it's necessary to take a step back and ask some questions about the writing. Are the characters true to life? Are the details realistic? In these pages you will

- study methods authors use to elaborate on ideas
- write a critical response that questions a story
- question the effectiveness of a real-world setting

The Writer's Style: Elaboration Good writers make their work vivid by including details such as facts, incidents, examples, sensory details, and quotations.

Read the Literature

Notice the kinds of details these writers use to elaborate on their ideas.

Literature Models

Elaboration with Sensory Details
Sensory details help a reader "take part" in an experience. What details of smell, sight, and touch help you to "experience" the bear?

> With a bear at your side, it is not the simplest thing to play a fish properly, but the presence of this huge animal, and especially her long snout, thick as my thigh, wonderfully concentrates the mind. She smells like the forest floor, like crushed moss and damp leaves.
>
> Robert H. Abel, from "Appetizer"

Elaboration with Facts and Statistics
How does Helfer use facts and statistics to emphasize the power of the flood?

> The storm grew worse. Heavy sheets of rain filled and overflowed our flood channel, undermining its sides until they caved in. By mid-morning the Santa Clarita had become a raging, murderous torrent, 150 feet wide and 15 feet deep, moving through Africa U.S.A. with the speed and force of an express train. In its fury it wiped out a two-lane highway, full-grown oak trees, generator buildings—everything.
>
> Ralph Helfer, from "The Flood"

Connect to Science

Good newspaper and magazine writers often use examples, as in the paragraph below, to clarify their ideas and to add information. Examples bring specific meaning to a general statement.

Magazine Article

> What's so bad about UV? Those rays that fry your skin can also "sunburn" your eyes, causing temporary blindness. This condition is called "snow blindness" because it sometimes strikes skiers when strong rays bounce off the slopes into their eyes, "burning" the corneas (the outside layer of the eye). Fortunately, snow-blind eyes can usually repair themselves in a day or two.
>
> from "Sunglasses"
> *Zillions*, June/July 1995

Elaboration with Examples
What example is given in this article? What is the main idea that is explained?

Try Your Hand: Using Elaboration

1. **Find Examples of Elaboration** With a group, look through a science or history book to find examples of elaboration with examples, facts, and sensory details.

2. **Elaborate on a Main Idea** Choose one of the following ideas and write a paragraph elaborating on it:

   • When I arrived at home, I knew something was up.
   • I think it's best to walk away from an angry friend.

3. **Revise in Portfolio** Take a sentence from one of your finished papers and elaborate on it in three different ways, showing how elaboration can support ideas.

GRAMMAR FROM WRITING

Using Appositives
Elaboration can make a word or an idea more specific and easier to understand. One way to elaborate is to use an appositive noun or phrase.

An appositive noun or phrase explains one or more words in a sentence. Notice how the author Janet Bode uses an appositive in "Von" to add a detail about Saigon:

On April 30, 1975, Saigon, the capital of South Vietnam, fell.

APPLYING WHAT YOU'VE LEARNED
Rewrite the following sentences by elaborating with appositive nouns or phrases.

1. Von had never seen frozen vegetables before.
2. Ralph Helfer was living at Africa U.S.A.

Now try combining these pairs of sentences, using appositives.

1. The bear sat beside him as he fished. The bear was a huge animal.
2. The bear was friendly. This was a surprising trait.

GRAMMAR HANDBOOK

For more information on appositives, see the Grammar Handbook, pages 892–894.

Criticism

A good story is hard to put down. Writers who elaborate with well-chosen details can make you believe in people and places that never existed. Sometimes, however, a story isn't so believable. Something about the characters, plot, or setting makes you stop and question what you're reading. Critics, whether they are book reviewers or readers like you, often judge a story by how believable it is.

GUIDED ASSIGNMENT

Write a Critical Essay Evaluate the believability of a story you choose. Judge how well the author has crafted a believable character, setting, or plot, and elaborate on your opinions.

❶ Prewrite and Explore

Choose a story from this unit or one you have read outside of class. You can pick a story you liked or one you didn't believe. Remember that even fantastic creatures and settings can be believable if they make sense in the story's fictional world.

EXPLORING THE STORY ELEMENTS

Read the story a second time, writing down your reactions.

- Which story element do you believe or disbelieve the most?
- What details about the story element seem real? Which seem false?
- Why do you find these details easy or difficult to believe?

ORGANIZING YOUR IDEAS

Now that you've thought the story over, state your opinion about the believability of one story element. To convince readers that your criticism is fair, you will need to support your opinion with examples from the story. A chart like the one at the right can help organize your examples and ideas.

Student's Idea and Details Chart

"Appetizer" by Robert Abel

Opinion: Ms. Bear isn't believable

Reasons:
- Acts too friendly
- Not afraid enough

Examples:
- Leans against fisherman
- Nudges him with her nose
- Rides on camper
- Walks into cannery

② Write and Analyze a Discovery Draft

Freewriting can help you discover the reasons for your opinion. As you write, ask yourself these questions:

- What experiences have I had that cause me to believe or disbelieve the story element?
- How do my experiences or knowledge support or contradict details in the story?

Student's Discovery Draft

This is one way the bear is sort of believable.

The author thinks he's communicating with the bear. I believe that because I can tell when my cats want to be fed or want attention.

There's still something about the bear I don't believe. Would a big wild Alaskan bear be friendly to a human? Would it stand next to a man, waiting for him to catch a fish, and not attack him? It seems like the bear reasons all this out. Maybe that's what bothers me: the bear seems almost human.

I think I have my main point here: the bear acts too human to be believable.

③ Draft and Share

Use your discovery draft to write a more organized critical essay. Begin with an introduction that describes the story and states your main point. In the body of your essay, support your opinion with reasons and examples from the story. Finish with a conclusion summarizing your ideas. Have a classmate read your draft.

 PEER RESPONSE

- What reasons and examples do I give to support my opinion?
- Do you agree or disagree with my criticism? Why or why not?

 WRITER'S CRAFT

Creating Effective Paragraphs

Organizing your essay into paragraphs helps your readers focus on one main idea at a time. To create clear and interesting paragraphs, follow these guidelines:

- Begin a new paragraph each time you introduce a new idea.
- Try stating your new idea in a topic sentence.
- Elaborate on your idea with reasons or examples.
- Put ideas and examples in a logical order.
- Remove ideas or examples that do not support the main idea.

APPLYING WHAT YOU'VE LEARNED
Look at each paragraph in your essay to see if you have followed the guidelines above. If you need to revise a paragraph, you may want to focus on one guideline at a time.

 WRITING HANDBOOK

For more information on writing paragraphs, see the Writing Handbook, pages 827–829.

④ Revise and Edit

Now that you're ready to revise your draft, ask yourself if you have presented your response clearly. Read the story again. Do you still have the same opinion? After you finish your draft, read it over and reflect on how well you supported your ideas.

Student's Final Draft

In the story "Appetizer" Robert Abel describes an encounter between a bear and a fisherman. I think that the character of this bear is too human to be believable in the story. When the narrator talks with the bear, he seems to be communicating on a higher level than animals and humans can communicate. The bear is also much more friendly to humans than you would expect from a wild bear in Alaska.

Which sentence explains the main point of the essay?

How does the student use details from the story to show that the bear character is not believable?

When the bear stands right next to the narrator and nudges him with her nose, she communicates like my cat might when he wants attention. However, this is a wild bear! It's not believable that the bear would behave like a household pet. The narrator is convinced that the bear is expressing feelings of affection for him; later, as if to prove her love, she licks the window of his camper instead of smashing it and then won't leave. Unbelievable!

Standards for Evaluation

A critical essay
- has an introduction with a clearly stated criticism
- supports the criticism with appropriate examples
- has a logical organization that is easy to follow
- contains standard grammar and usage
- has a conclusion that clearly summarizes the evaluation

Grammar in Context

Complex Sentences When revising a critical essay, you can show the relationship between your ideas with complex sentences. A **complex sentence** contains an independent clause, which can stand alone as a sentence, and one or more subordinate clauses, which cannot stand alone.

A complex sentence can effectively show time or cause–and–effect relationships between your ideas. Use conjunctions such as *because, when, after, before, until, unless,* and *if* to connect your ideas.

> The bear was trying to communicate with the fisherman.
> *When*
> ∧The bear nudged him with her nose. ∧She was trying to tell him
> *If*
> something. ∧My dog does the same thing. ∧He wants to be fed.
> *After*
> ∧The bear told the narrator to fish behind a big boulder. ∧He
> landed a granddaddy fish.

In the example above, the short simple sentences are combined into complex sentences that clarify the relationships between the ideas.

Try Your Hand: Using Complex Sentences

Revise the following paragraph by making some of the simple sentences into complex sentences, using such conjunctions as *because, when, after, before, until, unless,* and *if.*

> Last Wednesday we had an exciting time at the cannery. A big bear came right through the truck ramp for a feast. We don't know how she got there. Most of us saw her coming and ran out. We knew we didn't stand a chance against her. We had a meeting out in front to decide what to do. Frank wanted to use his gun. We agreed that was not the answer. Marty suggested we all go home. The boss said no. Holly thought we should blow the lunch whistle. That finally drove the bear away. We spent the rest of the week cleaning up the mess and making repairs.

SkillBuilder

G→ GRAMMAR FROM WRITING

Using Commas with Subordinate Clauses

One way to add variety to your sentences is to vary the order of the clauses in your complex sentences. If the independent clause comes first, usually no comma is needed.

The bear takes matters into her own hands when the salmon flips into a little side pool.

However, if the subordinate clause comes first, a comma is used before the independent clause.

When the salmon flips into a little side pool, the bear takes matters into her own hands.

APPLYING WHAT YOU'VE LEARNED
Move the subordinate clause to the beginning of each complex sentence below, and punctuate the revised sentence correctly.

1. Ms. Bear seemed distracted after Mr. Bear stopped by.
2. Ms. Bear took a nap on the camper hood although I beeped the horn long and loud.
3. I stayed at the Buckville Tavern because I was still supposed to be on vacation.

 GRAMMAR HANDBOOK

For more help with commas, see pages 892–894 of the Grammar Handbook.

READING
THE WORLD

ELABORATE DETAILS

You've seen how writers use sensory details to make a story more believable to readers. Details can be used for a similar purpose in real life. This picture shows an imaginary setting that has been made to look real with elaborate details. How real does it seem to you?

View What imaginary setting is being created here? What details help to create the scene? What details do not fit? Is there anything that makes this place unbelievable?

Interpret Decide how effective you think this setting is. Write a critical paragraph, supporting your criticism with details from the photograph.

Discuss With a group, discuss what details you would add to or remove from the setting to make it more believable or interesting. What could affect your judgment here? Refer to the SkillBuilder at the right for help with establishing criteria for evaluation.

SkillBuilder

 CRITICAL THINKING

Establishing Criteria for Evaluation
As you evaluated the setting in this photograph, you used your own **criteria**, or standards, to make a judgment. Your standards probably depended on what you thought the setting should accomplish. Do you think it should inform visitors—or just entertain them?

Besides thinking about the purpose of the setting, you may also have thought about your own likes and dislikes. Do you enjoy places like this? Would your personal feelings make you judge the setting too easily or harshly?

You may have been unaware of what criteria you were using to evaluate the setting. Think about your criteria now.

APPLYING WHAT YOU'VE LEARNED
With a small group, write criteria for judging the effectiveness of each imaginary setting listed below. Afterwards, discuss reasons for similarities and differences between the criteria.

- a fantasy theme park
- a working colonial farm
- a haunted house
- the set of a realistic play

GOING TO EXTREMES

WHAT DO YOU THINK?

REFLECTING ON THEME

Have you ever battled for something you strongly believed in? If so, you know that emotions can become extreme. Use the activities on this page to explore some ways in which people go to extremes. Keep a record of your impressions. Compare them with the thoughts of the characters in Part 2.

To what extremes would you go?

Have you ever found yourself saying "I'd give anything to have that"? Design a questionnaire on which your classmates can identify three things they have wanted to have for a long time. Provide space for the student to record the extremes to which he or she would be willing to go to get each thing.

Thing Desired

1 _____

2 _____

3 _____

Would you

• use all your free time?

• spend all your savings?

• do something you didn't believe in?

What is worth dying for?

Sometimes people may be willing to put even their lives on the line. With your classmates, brainstorm names of people in history who were willing to sacrifice their lives to stand up for what they believed in. Pick several of these, and stage a debate about whether their actions were heroic or foolish.

How would you visualize a rock video?

Imagine that you are producing a music video for a rock group's new song, entitled "Going to Extremes." In your notebook, create a storyboard showing some of the images you might use to convey the theme of the song.

Looking Back

At the beginning of this unit, you thought about some different forms the struggle for survival can take. Did your ideas change as you read the selections in Part 1? What kinds of struggles for survival occur in the selections? What measures do the characters take in their battles for control? How successful are they? Discuss your answers to these questions with a partner.

PREVIEWING

FICTION

The Banana Tree
James Berry

PERSONAL CONNECTION

Each year powerful storms called hurricanes cause death and destruction in many parts of the world. What do you know about hurricanes? Have you ever been caught in one yourself? With a small group of classmates, use a word web like the one shown here to organize your knowledge of hurricanes.

SCIENCE CONNECTION

If you lived in Jamaica, the setting of "The Banana Tree," you would probably know a lot about hurricanes. Jamaica is an island nation in the Caribbean Sea. It is located in one of the three regions where most of the world's hurricanes occur.

Hurricanes develop from areas of low atmospheric pressure over warm ocean water. A hurricane produces torrents of rain and winds that swirl at up to 150 miles per hour around a calm spot in the center, called the eye. The eye is about 20 miles in diameter and travels 10 to 15 miles per hour. Picking up strength and speed as it moves, the hurricane may generate large waves that flood nearby coasts. As the hurricane moves over land, it brings heavy rain and strong winds, which cease as the eye passes.

Copyright © World Perspectives/Tony Stone Images.

READING CONNECTION

Understanding Dialect In describing the hurricane in this story, Mr. Bass says, "The storm's bad, chil'run. Really bad. But it'll blow off. It'll spen' itself out." Like most Jamaicans, Mr. Bass speaks in a dialect of English that incorporates words, pronunciations, and expressions from various African languages, Spanish, and French.

In the Jamaican dialect, the last letter of a word may be missing, as in *spen'* for *spend,* or a vowel sound may be changed, as in *chil'run* for *children.* Reading the dialogue in this story aloud may help you figure out the meanings of unfamiliar words.

LASERLINKS
• *SCIENCE CONNECTION*
• *CULTURAL CONNECTION*

369

THE BANANA TREE

by James Berry

In the hours the hurricane stayed, its presence made everybody older. It made Mr. Bass see that not only people and animals and certain valuables were of most importance to be saved.

From its very buildup the hurricane meant to show it was merciless, unstoppable, and, with its might, changed landscapes.

All day the Jamaican sun didn't come out. Then, ten minutes before, there was a swift shower of rain that raced by and was gone like some urgent messenger-rush of wind. And again everything went back to that quiet, that unnatural quiet. It was as if trees crouched quietly in fear. As if, too, birds knew they should shut up. A thick and low black cloud had covered the sky and shadowed everywhere, and made it seem like night was coming on. And the cloud deepened. Its deepening spread more and more over the full stretch of the sea.

The doom-laden afternoon had the atmosphere of Judgment Day[1] for everybody in all the districts about. Everybody knew the hour of disaster was near. Warnings printed in bold lettering had been put up at post offices, police stations, and schoolyard entrances and in clear view on shop walls in village squares.

Carrying children and belongings, people hurried in files and in scattered groups, headed for the big, strong, and safe community buildings. In Canerise Village, we headed for the schoolroom. Loaded with bags and cases, with bundles and lidded baskets, individuals carrying or leading an animal, parents shrieking for children to stay at their heels, we arrived there. And, looking around, anyone would think the whole of Canerise was here in this vast superbarn of a noisy chattering schoolroom.

With violent gusts and squalls the storm broke. Great rushes, huge bulky rushes, of wind struck the building in heavy, repeated thuds, shaking it over and over, and carrying on.

Families were huddled together on the floor. People sang, sitting on benches, desks, anywhere there was room. Some people knelt in loud prayer. Among the refugees' noises a goat bleated, a hen fluttered or cackled, a dog whined.

Mr. Jetro Bass was sitting on a soap box. His broad back leaned on the blackboard against the wall. Mrs. Imogene Bass, largely pregnant, looked a midget beside him. Their children were sitting on the floor. The eldest boy, Gustus, sat farthest from his father. Altogether, the children's heads made seven different levels of height around the parents. Mr. Bass forced a reassuring smile. His toothbrush mustache moved about a little as he said, "The storm's bad, chil'run. Really bad. But it'll blow off. It'll spen' itself out. It'll kill itself."

Except for Gustus's, all the faces of the children turned up with subdued fear and looked at their father as he spoke.

"Das true wha' Pappy say," Mrs. Bass said. "The good Lord won' gi' we more than we can bear."

Mr. Bass looked at Gustus. He stretched fully through the sitting children and put a lumpy, blistery hand—though a huge hand—on the boy's head, almost covering it. The boy's clear brown eyes looked straight and unblinkingly into his father's face. "Wha's the matter, bwoy?" his dad asked.

He shook his head. "Nothin', Pappy."

"Wha' mek you say nothin'? I sure somet'ing bodder you, Gustus. You not a bwoy who frighten easy. Is not the hurricane wha' bodder you? Tell Pappy."

"Is nothin'."

"You're a big bwoy now. Gustus—you nearly thirteen. You strong. You very useful fo' you

_____

1. **Judgment Day:** in traditional Christian belief, the day on which the world will end.

age. You good as mi right han'. I depen' on you. But this afternoon—earlier—in the rush, when we so well push to move befo' storm broke, you couldn' rememba a t'ing! Not one t'ing! Why so? Wha' on you mind? You harborin' t'ings from me, Gustus?"

Gustus opened his mouth to speak but closed it again. He knew his father was proud of how well he had grown. To strengthen him, he had always given him "last milk"[2] straight from the cow in the mornings. He was thankful. But to him his strength was only proven in the number of innings he could pitch for his cricket[3] team. The boy's lips trembled. What's the good of tellin', when Pappy don' like cricket. He only get vex an' say it's an evil game for idle hands! He twisted his head and looked away. "I'm harborin' nothin', Pappy."

"Gustus . . ."

> He knew his father was proud of how well he had grown.

At that moment a man called, "Mr. Bass!" He came up quickly. "Got a hymnbook, Mr. Bass? We want you to lead us singing."

The people were sitting with bowed heads, humming a song. As the repressed singing grew louder and louder, it sounded mournful in the room. Mr. Bass shuffled, looking around as if he wished to back out of the suggestion. But his rich voice and singing leadership were too famous. Mrs. Bass already had the hymnbook in her hand, and she pushed it at her husband. He took it and began turning the leaves as he moved toward the center of the room.

Immediately Mr. Bass was surrounded. He started with a resounding chant over the heads of everybody. "Abide wid me; fast fall the eventide. . . ." He joined the singing but broke off to recite the next line. "The darkness deepen; Lord, wid me, abide. . . ." Again, before the last long-drawn note faded from the deeply stirred voices, Mr. Bass intoned musically, "When odder helpers fail, and comfo'ts flee . . ."

In this manner he fired inspiration into the singing of hymn after hymn. The congregation swelled their throats, and their mixed voices filled the room, pleading to heaven from the depths of their hearts. But the wind outside mocked viciously. It screamed. It whistled. It smashed everywhere up.

Mrs. Bass had tightly closed her eyes, singing and swaying in the center of the children who nestled around her. But Gustus was by himself. He had his elbows on his knees and his hands blocking his ears. He had his own worries.

What's the good of Pappy asking all those questions when he treat him so bad? He's the only one in the family without a pair of shoes! Because he's a big boy, he don't need anyt'ing an' must do all the work. He can't stay at school in the evenings an' play cricket because there's work to do at home. He can't have no outings with the other children because he has no shoes. An' now when he was to sell his bunch of bananas an' buy shoes so he can go out with his cricket team, the hurricane is going to blow it down.

It was true: the root of the banana was his "navel string."[4] After his birth the umbilical cord[5] was dressed with castor oil and sprinkled with nutmeg and buried, with the banana tree

---

2. **last milk:** the last milk drawn from a cow; it has a greater fat content than first milk.

3. **cricket:** an English game somewhat akin to baseball.

4. **navel string:** the umbilical cord.

5. **umbilical** (ŭm-bĭl′ĭ-kəl) **cord:** the cord through which a fetus receives nourishment; a person's navel marks the place where it was attached.

Hurricane, Bahamas (1898), Winslow Homer. Watercolor and graphite on off-white woven paper,
14½″ × 21⅜″, The Metropolitan Museum of Art, Amelia B. Lazarus Fund, 1910 (10.228.7).

planted over it for him. When he was nine days old, the nana midwife[6] had taken him out into the open for the first time. She had held the infant proudly, and walked the twenty-five yards that separated the house from the kitchen, and at the back showed him his tree. "'Memba when you grow up," her toothless mouth had said, "it's you nable strings feedin' you tree, the same way it feed you from you mudder."

His shirt was fluttering from his back like a boat sail.

Refuse from the kitchen made the plant flourish out of all proportion. But the rich soil around it was loose. Each time the tree gave a shoot, the bunch would be too heavy for the soil to support; so it crashed to the ground, crushing the tender fruit. This time, determined that his banana must reach the market, Gustus had supported his tree with eight props. And as he watched it night and morning, it had become very close to him. Often he had seriously thought of moving his bed to its root.

Muffled cries, and the sound of blowing noses, now mixed with the singing. Delayed impact of the disaster was happening. Sobbing was everywhere. Quickly the atmosphere became sodden[7] with the wave of weeping outbursts. Mrs. Bass's pregnant belly heaved. Her younger children were upset and cried, "Mammy, Mammy, Mammy. . . ."

Realizing that his family, too, was overwhelmed by the surrounding calamity, Mr. Bass bustled over to them. Because their respect for him bordered on fear, his presence quieted all immediately. He looked around. "Where's Gustus! Imogene . . . where's Gustus!"

"He was 'ere, Pappy," she replied, drying her eyes. "I dohn know when he get up."

Briskly Mr. Bass began combing the schoolroom to find his boy. He asked; no one had seen Gustus. He called. There was no answer. He tottered, lifting his heavy boots over heads, fighting his way to the jalousie.[8] He opened it and his eyes gleamed up and down the road but saw nothing of the boy. In despair Mr. Bass gave one last thunderous shout: "Gustus!" Only the wind sneered.

By this time Gustus was halfway on the mile journey to their house. The lone figure in the raging wind and shin-deep road flood was tugging, snapping, and pitching branches out of his path. His shirt was fluttering from his back like a boat sail. And a leaf was fastened to his cheek. But the belligerent wind was

---

6. **nana midwife:** a woman who helps other women give birth and care for their newborn children.
7. **sodden:** soaked.
8. **jalousie** (jăl'ə-sē): a window covering having adjustable slats to let in light and air.

merciless. It bellowed into his ears and drummed a deafening commotion. As he grimaced and covered his ears, he was forcefully slapped against a coconut tree trunk that lay across the road.

When his eyes opened, his round face was turned up to a festered sky. Above the tormented trees a zinc sheet writhed, twisted, and somersaulted in the tempestuous flurry. Leaves of all shapes and sizes were whirling and diving like attackers around the zinc sheet. As Gustus turned to get up, a bullet drop of rain struck his temple. He shook his head, held grimly to the tree trunk, and struggled to his feet.

Where the road was clear, he edged along the bank. Once, when the wind staggered him, he recovered with his legs wide apart. Angrily he stretched out his hands with clenched fists and shouted, "I almos' hol' you that time . . . come solid like that again, an' we fight like man an' man!"

When Gustus approached the river he had to cross, it was flooded and blocked beyond recognition. Pressing his chest against the gritty road bank, the boy closed his weary eyes on the brink of the spating river. The wrecked footbridge had become the harboring fort for all the debris, branches, and monstrous tree trunks which the river swept along its course. The river was still swelling. More accumu-

lation arrived each moment, ramming and pressing the bridge. Under pressure it was cracking and shifting minutely toward a turbulent forty-foot fall.

Gustus had seen it! A feeling of dismay paralyzed him, reminding him of his foolish venture. He scraped his cheek on the bank looking back. But how can he go back? He has no strength to go back. His house is nearer than the school. An' Pappy will only strap him for nothin' . . . for nothin' . . . no shoes, nothin', when the hurricane is gone.

With trembling fingers he tied up the remnants of his shirt. He made a bold step and the wind half lifted him, ducking him in the muddy flood. He sank to his neck. Floating leaves, sticks, coconut husks, dead rat-bats, and all manner of feathered creatures and refuse surrounded him. Forest vines under the water entangled him. But he struggled desperately until he clung to the laden bridge and climbed up among leafless branches.

His legs were bruised and bore deep scratches, but steadily he moved up on the slimy pile. He felt like a man at sea, in the heart of a storm, going up the mast of a ship. He rested his feet on a smooth log that stuck to the water-splashed heap like a black torso. As he strained up for another grip, the torso came to life and leaped from under his feet. Swiftly sliding down, he grimly clutched some brambles.

WORDS TO KNOW	**grimace** (grĭm′ĭs) *v.* to make a facial expression that reflects pain
	debris (də-brē′) *n.* the scattered remains of something broken or destroyed
	turbulent (tûr′byə-lənt) *adj.* violently agitated or disturbed; disorderly
	torso (tôr′sō) *n.* the human body excluding the head and limbs; trunk

The urgency of getting across became more frightening, and he gritted his teeth and dug his toes into the debris, climbing with maddened determination. But a hard gust of wind slammed the wreck, pinning him like a motionless lizard. For a minute the boy was stuck there, panting, swelling his naked ribs.

He stirred again and reached the top. He was sliding over a breadfruit limb when a flutter startled him. As he looked and saw the clean-head crow and glassy-eyed owl close together, there was a powerful jolt. Gustus flung himself into the air and fell in the expanding water on the other side. When he surfaced, the river had dumped the entire wreckage into the gurgling gully. For once the wind helped. It blew him to land.

Gustus was in a daze when he reached his house. Mud and rotten leaves covered his head and face, and blood caked around a gash on his chin. He bent down, shielding himself behind a tree stump whose white heart was a needly splinter, murdered by the wind.

He could hardly recognize his yard. The terrorized trees that stood were writhing in turmoil. Their thatched house had collapsed like an open umbrella that was given a heavy blow. He looked the other way and whispered, "Is still there! That's a miracle. . . .That's a miracle."

Dodging the wind, he staggered from tree to tree until he got to his own tormented banana tree. Gustus hugged the tree. "My nable string!" he cried. "My nable string! I know you would stan' up to it, I know you would."

The bones of the tree's stalky leaves were broken, and the wind lifted them and harassed them. And over Gustus's head the heavy fruit swayed and swayed. The props held the tree, but they were squeaking and slipping. And around the plant the roots stretched and trembled, gradually surfacing under loose earth.

With the rags of his wet shirt flying off his back, Gustus was down busily on his knees, bracing, pushing, tightening the props. One by one he was adjusting them until a heavy rush of wind knocked him to the ground. A prop fell on him, but he scrambled to his feet and looked up at the thirteen-hand bunch of bananas. "My good tree," he bawled, "hol' you fruit. . . . Keep it to you heart like a mudder savin' her baby! Don't let the wicked wind t'row you to the groun' . . . even if it t'row me to the groun'. I will not leave you."

The terrorized trees that stood were writhing in turmoil.

But several attempts to replace the prop were futile. The force of the wind against his weight was too much for him. He thought of a rope to lash the tree to anything, but it was difficult to make his way into the kitchen, which, separate from the house, was still standing. The invisible hand of the wind tugged, pushed, and forcefully restrained him. He got down and crawled on his belly into the earth-floor kitchen. As he showed himself with the rope, the wind tossed him, like washing on the line, against his tree.

The boy was hurt! He looked crucified against the tree. The spike of the wind was slightly withdrawn. He fell, folded on the ground. He lay there unconscious. And the wind had no mercy for him. It shoved him, poked him, and molested his clothes like muddy newspaper against the tree.

As darkness began to move in rapidly, the wind grew more vicious and surged a mighty gust that struck the resisting kitchen. It was heaved to the ground in a rubbled pile. The brave wooden hut had been shielding the banana tree but in its death fall missed it by inches. The wind charged again and the soft tree gurgled—the fruit was torn from it and plunged to the ground.

The wind was less fierce when Mr. Bass and a searching party arrived with lanterns. Because the bridge was washed away, the hazardous roundabout journey had badly impeded them.

Talks about safety were mockery to the anxious father. Relentlessly he searched. In the darkness his great voice echoed everywhere, calling for his boy. He was wrenching and ripping through the house wreckage when suddenly he vaguely remembered how the boy had been fussing with the banana tree. Desperate, the man struggled from the ruins, flagging the lantern he carried.

The flickering light above his head showed Mr. Bass the forlorn and pitiful banana tree. There it stood, shivering and twitching like a propped-up man with lacerated throat and dismembered head. Half of the damaged fruit rested on Gustus. The father hesitated. But when he saw a feeble wink of the boy's eyelids, he flung himself to the ground. His bristly chin rubbed the child's face while his unsteady hand ran all over his body. "Mi bwoy!" he murmured. "Mi hurricane bwoy! The Good Lord save you. . . . Why you do this? Why you do this?"

"I did want buy mi shoes, Pappy. I . . . I can't go anywhere 'cause I have no shoes. . . . I didn' go to school outing at the factory. I didn' go to Government House. I didn' go to Ol' Fort in town."

Mr. Bass sank into the dirt and stripped himself of his heavy boots. He was about to lace them to the boy's feet when the onlooking men prevented him. He tied the boots together and threw them over his shoulder.

Gustus's broken arm was strapped to his side as they carried him away. Mr. Bass stroked his head and asked how he felt. Only then grief swelled inside him and he wept. ❖

LITERARY INSIGHT

The Hurricane

BY LUIS PALÉS MATOS

When the hurricane unfolds
Its fierce accordion of winds,
On the tip of its toes,
Agile dancer, it sweeps whirling
Over the carpeted surface of the sea
With the scattered branches of the palm.

RESPONDING
O P T I O N S

FROM PERSONAL RESPONSE TO CRITICAL ANALYSIS

REFLECT

1. Do you have stronger feelings about Gustus or about Mr. Bass? Why? Jot down your thoughts in your notebook.

RETHINK

2. Reread the last two paragraphs of the story. What do you think Mr. Bass is thinking and feeling after hearing Gustus's reasons for making the trip to the banana tree?

3. Do you think Gustus is courageous or foolish in trying to protect his tree? Explain your answer.

   Consider
   • what the tree means to him
   • what dangers he faces
   • how his decision might affect his relationship with his father

4. If you were in Gustus's situation, do you think you would go to the extremes he did to save the tree? Why or why not?

5. How would you describe the relationship between Gustus and his father? Give evidence to support your answer.

RELATE

6. Compare and contrast the image of a hurricane created by Palés Matos in "The Hurricane" (page 377) with the image created by Berry. Are the tones of the works the same, or are they different? Explain your answer.

7. Do you think the ways in which Gustus and his father interact are typical of most father-son relationships? Why or why not?

ANOTHER PATHWAY

Cooperative Learning

Imagine that you are a television reporter who has been assigned the task of interviewing Gustus and Mr. Bass after the hurricane. Prepare questions and answers for the interview. Then, with two classmates playing the roles of Gustus and Mr. Bass, present the interview to the class.

QUICKWRITES

1. Write a **dialogue** that might take place between Gustus and his father after Gustus's broken arm is treated.

2. Have you ever, like Gustus, wanted something badly but been unable or unwilling to ask for it? Write a **personal narrative** in which you describe the situation and what happened.

PORTFOLIO Save your writing. You may want to use it later as a springboard to a piece for your portfolio.

LITERARY CONCEPTS

The **protagonist** of a work of fiction is the story's main character—the one that arouses the most interest and sympathy in the reader. The protagonist usually struggles or competes against an **antagonist,** who might be another character, a force of nature or society, or a force within the protagonist. Identify the protagonist and the antagonist in "The Banana Tree." Does the personality of the protagonist change? If so, how?

ALTERNATIVE ACTIVITIES

Review the ways in which Berry personifies, or gives human qualities to, the hurricane. Then create a **drawing** or **painting** that shows the battle for control between the hurricane and Gustus. If you have a graphics program on your computer, here's a chance to use it.

ACROSS THE CURRICULUM

Geographical Connection The banana is an important food crop in many parts of the world. Find out which countries are the chief producers of bananas. What climate do they have?

WORDS TO KNOW

Review the Words to Know at the bottom of the selection pages. On your paper, draw the answer blanks that follow each clue below, then write the vocabulary word that fits the clue. Unscramble the letters in the boxes to make a word that relates to this story.

1. a trunk that is not used for storage __ __ __ __ ☐
2. a word that describes a raging river
   ☐ __ __ __ __ __ __ __ __
3. to show pain __ __ __ ☐ __ __ __
4. wreckage from an airplane crash __ __ __ ☐ __ __
5. the contents of a rubbish bin __ __ __ __ ☐ __

JAMES BERRY

1925–

"The Banana Tree" is from *A Thief in the Village and Other Stories,* a collection of stories that are "straight out of my own childhood and later observations," according to James Berry, who was born in Jamaica and emigrated to England in 1948. While working in the British school system, he noticed that there were few books about the experiences of children with African or Caribbean backgrounds. "No one has reported our stories, or the way we saw things," Berry has said. "It's the function of writers and poets to bring in the left-out side of the human family."

Berry's *A Thief in the Village and Other Stories* won the Grand Prix Smarties Prize in 1987 and was named a Coretta Scott King Award honor book in 1988. In these stories, Berry describes the harsh reality of Caribbean life and uses the Jamaican dialect to convey the authentic spirit and voice of the Caribbean culture.

Berry's Jamaican heritage has provided him with material for several of his other books. *Anancy-Spiderman* is a collection of retold West Indian folk tales, based on West African traditions, about a crafty man-spider. *When I Dance* contains poems that focus on the humor, struggles, injustice, and goodness of Jamaican teenage life.

OTHER WORKS *The Girls and Yanga Marshall, The Future-Telling Lady and Other Stories, Celebration Song*

FICTION

The Tell-Tale Heart
Edgar Allan Poe

PERSONAL CONNECTION

Some of the most frightening characters in movies originated in literature. Perhaps the most famous of these are Frankenstein's monster and Count Dracula. Though they may not have originated in literature, other movie creatures that draw on the traditions of literary horror include werewolves, King Kong, Godzilla, Freddy Krueger, and the Terminator. What kinds of horror characters scare you the most? What do they have in common? Lower the shades and turn down the lights as you discuss these questions with your classmates!

LITERARY CONNECTION

The best horror story writers are experts at scaring the wits out of us. Edgar Allan Poe was one of the first American authors to do this. Oddly enough, his work owes much to his own feverish dreams, to which he applied a rare talent for shaping believable tales. Poe's characters face mysterious forces both within and outside themselves. Underneath the bizarre and frightening details of his stories, Poe explored the conflict in the human soul.

Like Poe, today's master of horror, Stephen King, fully comprehends the frightening power of the unknown and the supernatural. Why do so many people love the horror stories of writers like Poe and King? As one critic put it, "There is no delight the equal of dread."

READING CONNECTION

Evaluating To enjoy "The Tell-Tale Heart" fully, keep your reading log handy as you read, and jot down answers to the questions inserted in the text. When you finish reading, evaluate the story's effectiveness as a horror story. Make judgments about the characters, the setting and mood, and the plot. How believable is the story? How horrifying is it?

Illustration of "The Raven"
The Bettman Archive

The Tell-Tale Heart

by Edgar Allan Poe

True!—nervous—very, very dreadfully nervous I had been and am! but why *will* you say that I am mad? The disease had sharpened my senses—not destroyed—not dulled them. Above all was the sense of hearing <u>acute</u>. I heard all things in the heaven and in the earth. I heard many things in hell. How, then, am I mad? Hearken! and observe how healthily—how calmly I can tell you the whole story.

It is impossible to say how first the idea entered my brain; but once <u>conceived</u>, it haunted me day and night. Object there was none. Passion there was none. I loved the old man. He had never wronged me. He had never given me insult. For his gold I had no desire. I think it was his eye! yes, it was this! He had the eye of a vulture—a pale blue eye, with a film over it. Whenever it fell upon me, my blood ran cold; and so by degrees—very gradually—I made up my mind to take the life of the old man, and thus rid myself of the eye forever.

Now this is the point. You fancy me mad. Madmen know nothing. But you should have seen *me*. You should have seen how wisely I proceeded—with what caution—with what foresight—with what dissimulation[1] I went to work!

I was never kinder to the old man than during the whole week before I killed him. And every night, about midnight, I turned the latch of his door and opened it—oh, so gently! And then, when I had made an opening sufficient for my head, I put in a dark lantern, all closed, closed, so that no light shone out, and then I thrust in my head. Oh, you would have laughed to see how cunningly I thrust it in! I moved it slowly—very, very slowly, so that I might not disturb the old man's sleep. It took me an hour to place my whole head within the opening so far that I could see him as he lay upon his bed. Ha!—would a madman have been so wise as this? And then, when my head was well in the room, I undid the lantern cautiously—oh, so cautiously—cautiously (for the hinges creaked)—I undid it just so much that a single thin ray fell upon the vulture eye. And this I did for seven long nights—every night just at midnight—but I found the eye always closed; and so it was impossible to do the work; for it was not the old man who <u>vexed</u> me, but his Evil Eye. And every morning, when the day broke, I went boldly into the chamber, and spoke courageously to him, calling him by name in a hearty tone, and inquiring how he had passed the night. So you see he would have been a very profound old man, indeed, to suspect that every night, just at twelve, I looked in upon him while he slept.

Upon the eighth night I was more than usually cautious in opening the door. A watch's minute hand moves more quickly than did mine. Never before that night had I *felt* the extent of my own powers—of my sagacity.[2] I could scarcely contain my feelings of triumph. To think that there I was, opening the door, little by little, and he not even to dream of my secret deeds or thoughts. I fairly chuckled at the idea; and perhaps he heard me; for he moved on the bed suddenly, as if startled. Now you may think that I drew back—but no. His room was as black as pitch with the thick darkness (for the shutters were close fastened, through fear of robbers), and so I knew that he could not see the opening of the door, and I kept pushing it on steadily, steadily.

I had my head in, and was about to open the lantern, when my thumb slipped upon the tin fastening, and the old man sprang up in the bed, crying out—"Who's there?"

I kept quite still and said nothing. For a whole hour I did not move a muscle, and in the meantime I did not hear him lie down. He was still sitting up in the bed listening—just as I have done, night after night, hearkening to the death watches[3] in the wall.

Presently I heard a slight groan, and I knew it was the groan of mortal terror. It was not a groan of pain or grief—oh, no!—it was the low, <u>stifled</u> sound that arises from the bottom of the soul when overcharged with awe. I

---

1. **dissimulation:** a hiding of one's true feelings.
2. **sagacity:** sound judgment; intelligence.
3. **death watches:** deathwatch beetles—wood-burrowing insects that make a tapping sound with their head.

WORDS
TO
KNOW

vex (věks) *v.* to disturb; annoy
stifled (stī'fəld) *adj.* smothered **stifle** *v.*

knew the sound well. Many a night, just at midnight, when all the world slept, it has welled up from my own bosom, deepening, with its dreadful echo, the terrors that distracted me. I say I knew it well. I knew what the old man felt, and pitied him, although I chuckled at heart. I knew that he had been lying awake ever since the first slight noise, when he had turned in the bed. His fears had been ever since growing upon him. He had been trying to fancy them causeless, but could not. He had been saying to himself—"It is nothing but the wind in the chimney—it is only a mouse crossing the floor," or "it is merely a cricket which has made a single chirp." Yes, he has been trying to comfort himself with these suppositions; but he had found all in vain. *All in vain;* because Death, in approaching him, had stalked with his black shadow before him, and enveloped the victim. And it was the mournful influence of the unperceived shadow that caused him to feel—although he neither saw nor heard—to *feel* the presence of my head within the room.

When I had waited a long time, very patiently, without hearing him lie down, I resolved to open a little—a very, very little crevice in the lantern. So I opened it—you cannot imagine how stealthily, stealthily—until, at length, a single dim ray, like the thread of the spider, shot from out the crevice and fell full upon the vulture eye.

It was open—wide, wide open—and I grew furious as I gazed upon it. I saw it with perfect distinctness—all a dull blue, with a hideous veil over it that chilled the very marrow in my bones; but I could see nothing else of the old man's face or person: for I had directed the ray as if by instinct, precisely upon the damned spot.

And now have I not told you that what you mistake for madness is but over-acuteness of

Presently I heard a slight groan, and I knew it was the groan of mortal terror.

Copyright © John Thompson.

the senses?—now, I say, there came to my ears a low, dull, quick sound, such as a watch makes when enveloped in cotton. I knew *that* sound well too. It was the beating of the old man's heart. It increased my fury, as the beating of a drum stimulates the soldier into courage.

But even yet I refrained and kept still. I scarcely breathed. I held the lantern motionless. I tried how steadily I could maintain the ray upon the eye. Meantime the hellish tattoo[4] of the heart increased. It grew quicker and quicker, and louder and louder every instant. The old man's terror *must* have been extreme! It grew louder, I say, louder every moment!—do you mark me well? I have told you that I am nervous: so I am. And now at the dead hour of the night, amid the dreadful silence of that old house, so strange a noise as this excited me to uncontrollable terror. Yet, for some minutes

longer I refrained and stood still. But the beating grew louder, louder! I thought the heart must burst. And now a new anxiety seized me—the sound would be heard by a neighbor! The old man's hour had come! With a loud yell, I threw open the lantern and leaped into the room. He shrieked once—once only. In an instant I dragged him to the floor, and pulled the heavy bed over him. I then smiled gaily, to find the deed so far done. But, for many minutes, the heart beat on with a muffled sound. This, however, did not vex me; it would not be heard through the wall. At length it ceased. The old man was dead. I removed the bed and examined the corpse. Yes, he was stone, stone dead. I placed my

---

4. **hellish tattoo:** awful drumming.

hand upon the heart and held it there many minutes. There was no pulsation. He was stone dead. His eye would trouble me no more.

If still you think me mad, you will think so no longer when I describe the wise precautions

PREDICT

Do you think he will be caught?

I took for the concealment of the body. The night waned,[5] and I worked hastily, but in silence. First of all I dismembered the corpse. I cut off the head and the arms and the legs.

I then took up three planks from the flooring of the chamber, and deposited all between the scantlings.[6] I then replaced the boards so cleverly, so cunningly, that no human eye—not even *his*—could have detected anything wrong. There was nothing to wash out—no stain of any kind—no blood-spot whatever. I had been too wary for that. A tub had caught all—ha! ha!

When I made an end of these labors, it was four o'clock—still dark as midnight. As the bell sounded the hour, there came a knocking at the street door. I went down to open it with a light heart,—for what had I *now* to fear? There entered three men, who introduced themselves, with perfect suavity,[7] as officers of the police. A shriek had been heard by a neighbor during the night: suspicion of foul play had been aroused; information had been lodged at the police office, and they (the officers) had been deputed to search the premises.

I smiled,—for *what* had I to fear? I bade the gentlemen welcome. The shriek, I said, was my own in a dream. The old man, I mentioned, was absent in the country. I took my visitors all over the house. I bade them search—search *well*. I led them, at length, to *his* chamber. I showed them his treasures, secure, undisturbed.

---

5. **waned:** approached its end.

6. **scantlings:** small wooden beams supporting the floor.

7. **suavity** (swäv′ĭ-tē): smooth courteousness.

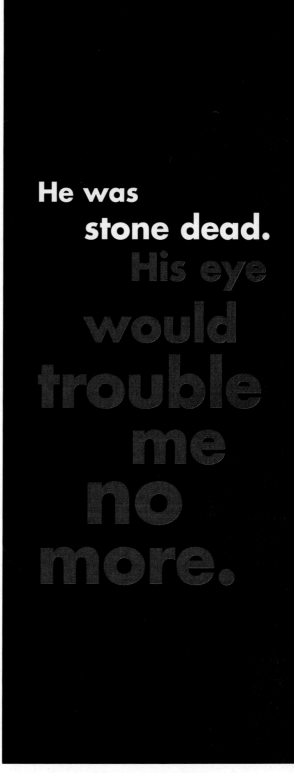

He was stone dead. His eye would trouble me no more.

In the enthusiasm of my confidence, I brought chairs into the room, and desired them *here* to rest from their fatigues, while I myself, in the wild audacity of my perfect triumph, placed my own seat upon the very spot beneath which reposed[8] the corpse of the victim.

The officers were satisfied. My *manner* had convinced them. I was singularly at ease. They sat, and while I answered cheerily, they chatted of familiar things. But, ere long, I felt myself getting pale and wished them gone. My head ached, and I fancied a ringing in my ears: but still they sat and still chatted. The ringing became more distinct:—it continued and became more distinct; I talked more freely to get rid of the feeling: but it continued and gained definitiveness—until, at length, I found that the noise was *not* within my ears.

No doubt I now grew *very* pale;—but I talked more fluently, and with a heightened voice. Yet the sound increased—and what could I do? It was *a low, dull, quick sound— much such a sound as a watch makes when enveloped in cotton.* I gasped for breath— and yet the officers heard it not. I talked more quickly—more vehemently; but the noise steadily increased. I arose and argued about trifles, in a high key and with violent gesticulations,[9] but the noise steadily increased.

Why *would* they not be gone? I paced the floor to and fro with heavy strides, as if excited to fury by the observations of the men—but the noise steadily increased. Oh God! what *could* I do? I foamed—I raved—I swore. I swung the chair upon which I had been sitting, and grated it upon the boards, but the noise arose over all and continually increased. It grew louder— louder—*louder!* And still the men chatted pleasantly, and smiled. Was it possible they heard not? Almighty God!—no, no! They heard!—they suspected!—they *knew!*—they were making a *mockery* of my horror!—this I thought, and this I think. But any thing was better than this agony! Any thing was more tolerable than this derision! I could bear those hypocritical smiles no longer! I felt that I must scream or die—and now—again!—hark! louder! louder!! *louder!*—

"Villains!" I shrieked, "dissemble[10] no more! I admit the deed!—tear up the planks—here, here! —it is the beating of his hideous heart!" ❖

CLARIFY

Why didn't the murderer keep quiet?

---

8. **reposed:** rested.
9. **gesticulations** (jĕ-stĭk′yə-lā′shənz): energetic gestures of the hands or arms.
10. **dissemble:** pretend.

WORDS TO KNOW	**audacity** (ô-dăs′ĭ-tē) *n.* shameless daring or boldness **vehemently** (vē′ə-mənt-lē) *adv.* with intense emotion **derision** (dĭ-rĭzh′ən) *n.* ridicule **hypocritical** (hĭp′ə-krĭt′ĭ-kəl) *adj.* false or deceptive, like a person who is pretending to be what he or she is not

RESPONDING
OPTIONS

FROM PERSONAL RESPONSE TO CRITICAL ANALYSIS

REFLECT

1. In your notebook, describe the part of this story that you found most memorable.

RETHINK

2. What are your impressions of the narrator?
   Consider
   - his insistence that he is sane
   - his obsession with the old man's eye
   - his care in planning the murder

3. Evaluate the narrator's behavior when he is with the police.

4. What do you think might have happened if the police had not come to the old man's house on the night of the murder?

5. How does this story relate to the theme "Going to Extremes"?

6. Consider your prereading discussion of horror characters and your evaluation of "The Tell-Tale Heart" as a horror story. How does Poe's tale measure up to your favorite horror stories?

RELATE

7. Under most systems of criminal law, an insane person cannot be found guilty of a crime. Defendants declared not guilty by reason of insanity are usually hospitalized until they are no longer considered mentally ill and dangerous. Do you think murderers should be able to use an insanity defense to avoid punishment? Explain your answer.

ANOTHER PATHWAY

Cooperative Learning

With a group of classmates, stage the narrator's trial for murder. Select a jury, a defense attorney, a prosecuting attorney, a judge, witnesses, and a defendant. All participants should use story details in presenting and judging the case.

QUICKWRITES

1. What if the police hadn't come? Write an alternative **ending** for the story, presenting what might have happened.

2. Consider how two different kinds of newspapers might report the murder in "The Tell-Tale Heart"—one a reputable daily newspaper that presents factual, objective reporting; the other a tabloid known for sensational stories. Write the **lead paragraph** of a murder report for each newspaper.

📁 *PORTFOLIO Save your writing. You may want to use it later as a springboard to a piece for your portfolio.*

LITERARY CONCEPTS

The **mood** of a literary work is the feeling or atmosphere that the writer creates for the reader. A story's events and setting and the way these are described all contribute to the mood of the story. One element of "The Tell-Tale Heart" that creates a mood of horror is the description of sounds, such as the victim's groan and the heartbeat. What other details in the story help produce its mood of horror?

LITERARY LINKS

Compare and contrast the narrators of "The Tell-Tale Heart" and "The Hitchhiker" (page 332). Consider their sanity and their personalities.

ALTERNATIVE ACTIVITIES

1. With a partner, make an **audiotape** of sound effects for several scenes in the story.

2. Imagine that you have been commissioned by a publisher to illustrate "The Tell-Tale Heart." Choose any memorable scene or image from the story (except one already illustrated in this book), and interpret it in a **painting** or **drawing**.

3. Draw **plans** for an amusement-park house of horrors called House of the Tell-Tale Heart. Include a description of the setting and the scares, thrills, and shocks visitors will experience as they make their way through the house.

ACROSS THE CURRICULUM

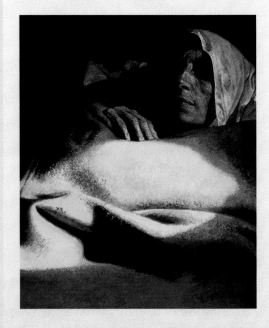

Science Find out about the physical effects of sudden fright. What happens to the heart and other parts of the body? Is it possible to become so agitated as to hear blood pounding loudly in one's ears?

ART CONNECTION

Refer to the illustration on page 384. Describe what you see. What aspects of the image do you think make it appropriate for this story? Now notice the artist's use of light and shadow. What does this element lend to the mood of the piece? Share your reaction with a partner.

EXERCISE A On your paper, write the letter of the word whose meaning is unrelated to the meanings of the other words in each set.

1. (a) destroyed, (b) wrecked, (c) conceived, (d) ruined

2. (a) insincere, (b) hypocritical, (c) truthful, (d) phony

3. (a) craving, (b) crevice, (c) crack, (d) cranny

4. (a) please, (b) vex, (c) gratify, (d) delight

5. (a) stifled, (b) muffled, (c) smothered, (d) heightened

EXERCISE B Review the Words to Know at the bottom of the selection pages. Then fill in each set of blanks below with the vocabulary word that relates to the sentence. Arrange the circled letters to name a character who sucks his victims' blood.

1. Many years ago the old man's eyesight was very sharp. ❏ __ ❏ __ __

2. The murderer treated his victim with cruel mockery. __ __ ❏ __ __ __ __ __

3. To commit an extreme act of violence requires great boldness. __ __ ❏ __ ❏ __ __ __

4. The thief entered the house as quietly and secretly as possible. __ __ __ ❏ __ __ __ __ __ __

5. The outraged witness strongly denounced the defendant. __ __ __ __ __ __ __ __ ❏ __

EDGAR ALLAN POE

1809–1849

More than a century after his death, Edgar Allan Poe remains one of the most popular of American writers. Poe was born in Boston, the son of traveling actors. The beginnings of his unhappy life were marked by his father's desertion of the family, followed by the death of his mother when he was two years old. The orphaned Poe was taken in by Mr. and Mrs. John Allan of Virginia, who gave him his middle name but never officially adopted him.

After being expelled from West Point, Poe sought work as a journalist. Although he received recognition for his biting literary reviews, money was scarce. Poverty intensified his despair over the lingering illness and eventual death of his beloved wife, Virginia, whom he had married 14 years earlier. During one of her bouts of illness, Poe wrote, "I became insane, with long intervals of horrible sanity." Deeply depressed, Poe often sought escape in alcohol. He died four days after being found on the streets of Baltimore, sick, delirious, and, in his doctor's words, "haggard, not to say bloated, and unwashed."

Poe was an innovator in the composition of the modern short story, and many critics also credit him with the invention of the detective story. His classic horror tales established his reputation as a master of the macabre. Poe also wrote haunting poetry, such as "The Raven" and "Annabel Lee."

OTHER WORKS "The Black Cat," *The Masque of the Red Death and Other Tales, The Pit and the Pendulum and Five Other Tales*

NONFICTION

Tsali of the Cherokees

Norah Roper

As told to Alice Marriott

PERSONAL CONNECTION

After the United States gained independence from England, and throughout the 1800s, the U.S. government repeatedly pushed Native Americans off their lands. What do you know about the government's treatment of Native Americans? Why might the government have wanted control of their lands? Why do you suppose it acted so forcefully? Discuss these questions with your classmates.

HISTORICAL CONNECTION

The Trail of Tears

The Cherokee are a Native American people whose original home was the southeastern United States. In 1838, the Georgia militia forced the Cherokee to leave their homes, because settlers wanted their land. Some Cherokee resisted and were killed. The rest were forced to march to what is now Oklahoma on a route that became known as the Trail of Tears.

READING CONNECTION

Contrast When you contrast groups of people, you look for differences. In this selection, the writer describes sharp cultural differences between the white settlers and a group of Cherokee. These differences in values help explain the conflict between the two groups. As you read, use a chart like the one shown here to note the groups' differences in attitude toward home and family, land, and gold.

	Cherokee	White Settlers
Home and Family		
Land		
Gold		

LASERLINKS
• *HISTORICAL CONNECTION*

Tsali
of the
Cherokees

by Norah Roper, as told to Alice Marriott

*In the time when their troubles began, the
ordinary Cherokees did not at first understand
that anything was really wrong.*

They knew that their tribal chiefs traveled back and forth to the white man's place called Washington more often than they used to do. They knew that when the chiefs came back from that place, there were quarrels in the tribal council.

Up in the hills and the back country, where the *Ani Keetoowah*—the true Cherokees—lived, word of the changes came more slowly than the changes themselves came to the valley Cherokees. Many of the hill people never left their farm lands, and those who did went only to the nearest trading post and back. Few travelers ever came into the uplands, where the mists of the Smokies[1] shut out the encroaching world.

So, when the news came that some of the chiefs of the Cherokees had touched the pen, and put their names or their marks on a paper, and agreed by doing so that this was no longer Cherokee country, the *Ani Keetoowah* could not believe what they heard. Surely, they said to each other, this news must be false. No Cherokee—not even a mixed-blood—would sign away his own and his people's lands. But that was what the chiefs had done.

Then the word came that the chiefs were even more divided among themselves and that not all of them had touched the pen. Some were not willing to move away to the new lands across the Mississippi and settle in the hills around Fort Gibson, Oklahoma.

---

1. **Smokies:** the Great Smoky Mountains (part of the Appalachian Mountain system) in North Carolina and Tennessee.

WORDS
TO
KNOW

encroaching (ĕn-krō′chĭng) *adj.* advancing gradually or sneakily **encroach** *v.*

391

"Perhaps we should hang on," the *Ani Keetoowah* said to one another. "Perhaps we will not have to go away after all." They waited and hoped, although they knew in their hearts that hope is the cruelest curse on mankind.

One of the leaders of the *Ani Keetoowah* was Tsali. The white men had trouble pronouncing his name, so they called him "Charley" or "Dutch." Tsali was a full blood, and so were his wife and their family. They were of the oldest *Keetoowah* Cherokee blood and would never have let themselves be shamed by having half-breed relatives.

Tsali and his four sons worked two hillsides and the valley between them, in the southern part of the hill country. Tsali and his wife and their youngest son lived in a log house at the head of the hollow. The others had their own homes, spread out along the hillsides. They grew corn and beans, a few English peas, squashes and pumpkins, tobacco and cotton, and even a little sugar cane and indigo.[2] Tsali's wife kept chickens in a fenced run[3] away from the house.

The women gathered wild hemp[4] and spun it; they spun the cotton, and the wool from their sheep. Then they wove the thread into cloth, and sometimes in winter when their few cattle and the sheep had been cared for and the chickens fed and there was not much else to do, the men helped at the looms[5] which they had built themselves. The women did all the cutting and the making of garments for the whole family.

Tsali and his family were not worldly rich, in the way that the chiefs and some of the Cherokees of the valley towns were rich. They had hardly seen white man's metal money in their lives. But Tsali's people never lacked for food, or good clothing, or safe shelter.

The missionaries seldom came into the uplands then. Tsali took his sons and their wives, and his own wife, to the great dance ground where the seven *Keetoowah* villages gathered each month at the time of the full moon. There they danced their prayers in time to the beating of the women's terrapin-shell[6] leg rattles, around and around the mound of packed white ashes on top of which bloomed the eternal fire that was the life of all the Cherokees.

The occasional missionaries fussed over the children. They gave them white men's names, so that by Tsali's time everyone had an Indian name and an English one. The Cherokees listened to the missionaries politely, for the missionaries were great gossips, and the Cherokees heard their news and ignored the rest of their words.

"You will have to go soon," said one white preacher to Tsali. "There's no hope this time. The lands have all been sold, and the Georgia troopers are moving in. You'll have to go west."

"We'll never leave," Tsali answered. "This is our land and we belong to it. Who could take it from us—who would want it? It's hard even for us to farm here, and we're used to hill farming. The white men wouldn't want to come here—they'll want the rich lands in the valleys, if the lowland people will give them up."

"They want these hills more than any other land," the missionary said. He sounded almost threatening. "Don't you see, you poor ignorant Indian? They are finding gold—gold, man, gold—downstream in the lower *Keetoowah* country. That means that the source of the gold is in the headwaters of the rivers that flow from here down into the valleys. I've seen gold dust in those streams myself."

---

2. **indigo:** a plant used to make blue dye.
3. **run:** an outdoor enclosed area for domestic animals.
4. **hemp:** a plant from which rope and coarse cloth are made.
5. **looms:** devices on which thread is woven into cloth.
6. **terrapin-shell:** turtle-shell.

"Gold?" asked Tsali. "You mean this yellow stuff?" And he took a buckskin pouch out of the pouch that hung from his sash, and opened it. At the sight of the yellow dust the pouch contained, the missionary seemed to go a little crazy.

"That's it!" he cried. "Where did you get it? How did you find it? You'll be rich if you can get more."

"We find it in the rivers, as you said," Tsali replied. "We gather what we need to take to the trader. I have this now because I am going down to the valley in a few days, to get my wife some ribbons to trim her new dress."

"Show me where you got it," the missionary begged. "We can all be rich. I'll protect you from the other white men, if you make me your partner."

"No, I think I'd better not," said Tsali thoughtfully. "My sons are my partners, as I was my father's. We do not need another partner, and, as long as we have our old squirrel guns, we do not need to be protected. Thank you, but you can go on. We are better off as we are."

The missionary coaxed and threatened, but Tsali stood firm. In the end, the white man went away, without any gold except a pinch that Tsali gave him, because the missionary seemed to value the yellow dust even more than the trader did.

Then it was time to go to the trading post. When Tsali came in the store, the trader said to him, "Well, Chief, glad to see you. I hear you're a rich man these days."

"I have always been a rich man," Tsali answered. "I have my family and we all have our good health. We have land to farm, houses to live in, food on our tables, and enough clothes. Most of all, we have the love in our hearts for each other and our friends. Indeed, you are right. We are very rich."

"That's one way of looking at it," said the trader, "but it isn't what I was thinking about. From what I hear, there's gold on your land. You've got a gold mine."

"A gold man?" repeated Tsali. "I never heard of a gold man."

"No!" shouted the trader. "A gold mine, I said. A place where you can go and pick up gold."

"Oh, that!" Tsali exclaimed. "Yes, we have some places like that on our land. Here's some of the yellow dust we find there."

And he opened the pouch to show the trader. The trader had seen pinches of Tsali's gold dust before, and taken it in trade, without saying much about it. Now he went as crazy as the missionary. "Don't tell anybody else about this, Charley," he whispered, leaning over the counter. "We'll just keep it to ourselves. I'll help you work it out, and I'll keep the other white men away. We'll all be rich."

"Thank you," said Tsali, "but I don't believe I want to be rich that way. I just want enough of this stuff to trade you for ribbons and sugar."

"Oh, all right," answered the trader sulkily, "have it your own way. But don't blame me if you're sorry afterwards."

"I won't blame anybody," said Tsali, and bought his ribbon.

A month later, when the Georgia militia[7] came riding up the valley to Tsali's house, the missionary and the trader were with them. The men all stopped in front of the house, and Tsali's wife came out into the dogtrot, the open-ended passage that divided the two halves of the house and made a cool breezeway where the family sat in warm weather. She spoke to the men.

---

7. **militia** (mə-lĭsh′ə): an army made up of ordinary citizens instead of professional soldiers.

"Won't you come in and sit down?"

"Where's the old man?" the militia captain asked.

"Why, he's working out in the fields," said Amanda. "Sit down and have a cool drink of water while I send the boy for him."

"Send the boy quickly," the captain ordered. "We'll wait in our saddles and not trouble to get down."

"All right, if you'd rather not," Amanda said. "Do you mind telling me why you're here?"

"We're here to put you off this place," said the captain. "Haven't you heard? This isn't Cherokee land any more; the chiefs signed it over to the government, and now it's open for settlement.

One or the other of these two gentlemen will probably claim it."

"They can't do that!" Amanda protested. "It's our land—nobody else's. The chiefs had no right to sign it away. My husband's father worked this place, and his father before him. This is our home. This is where we belong."

"No more," said the captain. "You belong in the removal camps down by the river, with the rest of the Indians. They're going to start shipping the Cherokees west tomorrow morning."

Amanda sat down on the bench in the dogtrot, with her legs trembling under her. "All of us?" she asked.

"Every one of you."

"Let me call my son and send him for his daddy," Amanda said.

"Hurry up!"

Amanda went into the house, calling to the boy, who was just fourteen and had been standing, listening, behind the door. She gave him his father's old squirrel gun, and he sneaked his own blowgun and darts and slid out the back of the house. Amanda went back to the dogtrot and sat and waited. She sat there and waited, while the missionary, the trader, and the captain quarreled about which of their wives should cook in her kitchen. She let them quarrel and hoped her men were all right.

Tsali and his older sons were working the overhill corn field, when the boy came panting up and told them what had happened.

"Is your mother all right?" Tsali asked.

"She was when I left," the boy answered.

"We'll hide in the woods till they're gone," Tsali told his older sons. "If they find us, they'll have to kill us to put us off this land."

"What about the women?" the oldest son asked.

"They'll be all right," Tsali answered. "Your mother's a quick-thinking woman; she'll take care of them. If we can hide in the caves by the river till dark, we'll go back then and get them."

They slipped away into the woods, downhill to the river, taking the boy with them, although he offered to go back and tell the white men he couldn't find his father.

All afternoon Amanda waited. Her daughters-in-law saw the strange men and horses in front of the big house and came to join her. At dusk, the captain gave up and ordered his men to make camp in the front yard. "We'll wait here until the men come back," he said.

With the white men camped all around the house, the women went into the kitchen and barred all the doors. It was a long time before the campfires made from the fence pickets ceased to blaze and began to <u>smolder</u>. It was a longer time until the women heard it—a scratch on the back door, so soft and so light that it would have embarrassed a mouse. Amanda slid back the bar, and Tsali and his sons slipped into the darkened room. There was just enough moonlight for them to make out each other's shapes.

"We came to get you," Tsali said. "Come quickly. Leave everything except your knives. Don't wait a minute."

Amanda and her daughters-in-law always wore their knives at their belts, so they were ready. One at a time, Tsali last, the whole family crept out of their home and escaped into the woods.

In the morning, when the white men stretched and scratched and woke, the *Ani Keetoowah* were gone.

It was spring, and the weather was warm, but the rain fell and soaked the Cherokees. They had brought no food, and they dared not fire a gun. One of the daughters-in-law was pregnant, and her time was close. Amanda was stiff and crippled with rheumatism.[8] They gathered wild greens, for it was too early for berries or plums, and the men and boy trapped small animals and birds in string snares the women made by pulling out their hair and twisting it.

Day by day, for four weeks, the starving family listened to white men beating through the woods. The Cherokees were tired and cold and hungry, but they were silent. They even began to hope that in time the white men would go away and the Indians would be safe.

---

8. **rheumatism** (roo′mə tĭz′əm): an inflammation and stiffness of the joints and muscles.

WORDS
TO
KNOW

smolder (smōl′dər) *v.* to burn with smoke but no flame

It was not to be. One trooper brought his dog, and the dog caught the human scent. So the dog, with his man behind him, came sniffing into the cave, and Tsali and his family were caught before the men could pick up their loaded guns.

The militiamen shouted, and other white men came thudding through the woods. They tied the Cherokee men's hands behind them and bound them all together along a rope. The militiamen pushed Tsali and his sons through the woods. The women followed, weeping.

At last they were back at their own house, but they would not have recognized it. The troopers had <u>plundered</u> the garden and trampled the plants they didn't eat. The door from the kitchen into the dogtrot hung <u>askew</u>, and the door to the main room had been wrenched off its hinges. Clothes and bedding lay in filthy piles around the yard. What the militiamen could not use, they ruined.

"Oh, my garden!" cried Amanda, and, when she saw the scattered feathers, "Oh, my little hens!"

"What are you going to do with us?" Tsali demanded.

"Take you down to the river. The last boat is loading today. There's still time to get you on it and out of here."

"I—will—not—go," Tsali said quietly. "You—nor you—nor you—nobody can make me go."

"Our orders are to take all the Cherokees. If any resist, shoot them."

"Shoot me, then!" cried Tsali. The captain raised his rifle.

"Stop!" Amanda screamed. She stepped over beside her husband. "If you shoot, shoot us both," she ordered. "Our lives have been one life since we were no older than our boy here. I don't want to go on living without my husband. And I cannot leave our home any more than he can. Shoot us both."

The four sons stepped forward. "We will die with our parents," the oldest one said. "Take our wives to the boat, if that is the only place where they can be safe, but we stay here." He turned to his wife and the other young women.

"That is my order as your husband," Tsali's son said. "You must go away to the west and make new lives for yourselves while you are still young enough to do so." The wives sobbed and held out their arms, but the husbands turned their backs on the women. "We will stay with our parents," all the young men said.

The young boy, too, stood with his brothers, beside his father. "Let this boy go," Tsali said to the white men. "He is so young. A man grows, and plants his seed, and his seed goes on. This is my seed. I planted it. My older sons and I have had our chances. They will leave children, and their names will never be forgotten. But this boy is too young. His seed has not ripened for planting yet. Let him go, to care for his sisters, on the way to the west."

"Very well," said the captain. "He can't do much harm if he does live." He turned to two militiamen. "Take the boy and the young women away," he ordered. "Keep them going till they come to the boats, and load them on board."

The young women and the boy, stunned and silenced, were driven down the road before they could say goodbye, nor would the troopers let them look back. Behind them, as they started on the long main road, they heard the sound of the shots. ❖

| WORDS TO KNOW | **plunder** (plŭn′dər) *v.* to take property by force
askew (ə-skyōō′) *adv.* crookedly |

The Trail of Tears

Although Tsali's family refused to leave the beautiful, fertile land that had been home to the Cherokee for over 1,000 years, most of the Cherokee did leave. In 1838, about 15,000 of them were forced to make a terrible 800-mile march westward to the so-called Indian Territory in what is now Oklahoma. One out of every four died along what came to be known as the Trail of Tears.

Back in the mid-1700s, the Cherokee had fought the colonists who were moving into their territory. By 1800, however, some Cherokee had begun to live among the colonists, and their economic and political structures began to mirror those of the white settlers. Some Cherokee owned large plantations and kept slaves. The tribe even established a republican form of government called the Cherokee Nation. But before long, white settlers demanded more Native American lands in Tennessee, Georgia, and Alabama for their own farms and plantations. The invention of the cotton gin (which made cotton farming more profitable) and the discovery of gold in Georgia made Cherokee land all the more desirable.

In 1830, a momentous event heralded the eventual doom of the Cherokee and other tribes. President Andrew Jackson signed the Indian Removal Act, requiring tribes east of the Mississippi to move west.

Trail of Tears, Jerome Tiger. Watercolor on paper. The Phillips Petroleum Collection, The Philbrook Museum of Art, Tulsa, Oklahoma.

The Cherokee resisted. Most stood their ground even when, in 1835, a small group of chiefs signed a new treaty with the government. They agreed to give up all remaining Cherokee lands, and many Cherokee left for the west. For those who would not give in, what followed was a tragic forced relocation.

Commanded to abandon homes, livestock, and ancestral burial grounds, the Cherokee were marched 800 miles through mud and manure. Many died during the 189-day journey.

RESPONDING OPTIONS

FROM PERSONAL RESPONSE TO CRITICAL ANALYSIS

REFLECT   1. What is your reaction to Tsali's fatal decision? Jot down your thoughts in your notebook, and share them with a partner.

RETHINK   2. Why do you think Tsali, his wife, and their four sons make the decision they do? Explain your answer.

Consider
- Tsali's and his family's feelings about the land
- the surviving son
- what happened to those who marched to Oklahoma

3. Review the chart you made for the Reading Connection on page 390. How do the cultural differences between the Cherokee and the white settlers explain the conflict between them?

4. The writer says that "hope is the cruelest curse on mankind." How does the selection support this view?

RELATE   5. In your opinion, should the Cherokee be compensated for the government's actions during the time of the Trail of Tears? If so, how? If not, why not?

ANOTHER PATHWAY

Imagine that you are Tsali's surviving son. Tell the story of your family's tragedy in a series of drawings. Share your illustrations with the class.

LITERARY CONCEPTS

An **author's purpose** is a writer's specific reason for writing. Authors write for four basic purposes: to entertain, to explain or inform, to express opinions, and to persuade readers to do or believe things. What purposes do you think Alice Marriott had in mind when she wrote this account? Which one seems most important to her? Explain your answer.

CONCEPT REVIEW: Oral History Recall that oral histories are stories passed by word of mouth from one generation to the next. How might the account of Tsali have been different if it had been researched and written up rather than told to a writer?

QUICKWRITES

1. In this selection, Tsali explains his conception of a rich man. Make two columns on a sheet of paper. List words and phrases describing Tsali's idea of wealth in one column and your own in the other. Then write a **paragraph** comparing Tsali's ideas with yours.

2. Write an **epitaph** for Tsali and his family. It can be a short prose inscription or a poem.

📁 *PORTFOLIO Save your writing. You may want to use it later as a springboard to a piece for your portfolio.*

ALTERNATIVE ACTIVITIES

1. *Cooperative Learning* With five class-mates, **role-play** a discussion among the following characters: the captain of the militia, a Cherokee chief who signed the government treaty, Tsali's youngest son, a Cherokee woman who survived the Trail of Tears, the missionary, and the trader. Have each character express his or her opinion about the statement "Tsali and his people should have obeyed the militia's orders."

2. Retell Tsali's story, including important de-tails and some of the dialogue from the selection. If possible, tape-record your **oral version** and share it with younger students.

ACROSS THE CURRICULUM

 Social Studies How many Cherokee escaped the Trail of Tears and remained in the Great Smoky Mountains of western North Carolina? What kind of lives did these people lead? Present your findings to the class in the form of a labeled visual display, using copies of old pictures.

WORDS TO KNOW

EXERCISE A Review the Words to Know at the bottom of the selection pages. Then, for each of the five words, create a word map like the one below.

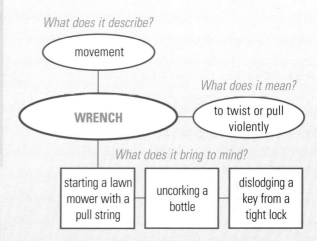

EXERCISE B Sketch or paint a series of five pictures that illustrate the meanings of the vocabulary words. Display them in your classroom.

ALICE MARRIOTT

While her grandfather was visiting the curator of Egyptology at Chicago's Field Museum, five-year-old Alice Marriott (1910–1992) wandered off by herself. To her delight, she found the museum's totem poles. This early interest in ancient cultures blossomed at the University of Oklahoma, where she became the first woman to receive a degree in anthropology. From Oklahoma she traveled to Oregon to study Native Americans: "We lived in tents, interviewed elderly Modoc Indians, and I fell completely and permanently in love with the desert country in general and Oregon in particular."

Marriott later returned to Oklahoma and became "one of the lucky few who worked with Plains Indians while the last of the buffalo hunters were still around." She wrote many books and articles on Native Americans, including "Tsali of the Chero-kees," which was told to her by Norah Roper, Tsali's granddaughter. "I am not interesting," claimed Marriott. "It is what I have done with where I have been that is."

OTHER WORKS *Maria, the Potter of San Ildefonso; The Ten Grandmothers; Hell on Horses and Women*

PREVIEWING

NONFICTION

Painful Memories of Dating
Dave Barry

PERSONAL CONNECTION

Think about the title of this selection. How could memories of dating be painful? If you knew that the selection was a humorous newspaper article and that the word *painful* referred to emotions, what might the title suggest to you? Discuss your ideas with your classmates. Use a word web like the one shown to record the class's ideas.

Painful Memories of Dating

MEDIA CONNECTION

Dave Barry writes a weekly humor column for the *Miami Herald.* Through syndication—sale for use by other news-papers—his articles appear in more than 150 papers, including some in foreign countries. Barry's humor depends on several ingredients: humorous references to current events, wild exaggerations of the truth, and irony (saying the opposite of what he means). In the article you are about to read, Barry combines all of these elements as he gives a boy named Eric some advice on dating.

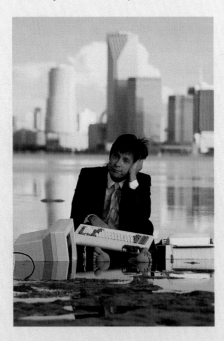

Dave Barry at work

READING CONNECTION

Hyperbole In this article, Barry claims that if a girl had refused his invitation for a date, he would have had to leave junior high school forever and "become a bark-eating hermit." Such extreme exaggeration, called hyperbole, helps make Barry's writing humorous. As you read, look for and jot down other examples of hyperbole.

Painful MEMORIES

OF DATING

BY DAVE BARRY

As a mature adult, I feel an obligation to help the younger generation, just as the mother fish guards her unhatched eggs, keeping her lonely vigil day after day, never leaving her post, not even to go to the bathroom, until her tiny babies emerge and she is able, at last, to eat them. "She may be your mom, but she's still a fish" is a wisdom nugget that I would pass along to any fish eggs reading this column.

But today I want to talk about dating. This subject was raised in a letter to me from a young person named Eric Knott, who writes:

"I have got a big problem. There's this girl in my English class who is really good-looking. However, I don't think she knows I exist. I want to ask her out, but I'm afraid she will say no, and I will be the freak of the week. What should I do?"

Eric, you have sent your question to the right mature adult, because as a young person, I spent a lot of time thinking about this very problem. Starting in about 8th grade, my time was divided as follows:

Academic Pursuits: 2 percent

Zits: 16 percent

Trying to Figure Out How to Ask Girls Out: 82 percent.

The most sensible way to ask a girl out is to walk directly up to her on foot and say, "So you want to go out or what?" I never did this. I knew, as Eric Knott knows, that there was always the possibility that the girl would say no, thereby leaving me with no viable option but to leave Harold C. Crittenden Junior High School forever and go into the

> Academic Pursuits:
> 2 percent
>
> Zits: 16 percent
>
> Trying to Figure Out How
> to Ask Girls Out:
> 82 percent.

woods and become a bark-eating hermit whose only companions would be the gentle and understanding woodland creatures.

"Hey, Zitface!" the woodland creatures would shriek in their cute little Chip 'n' Dale voices while raining acorns down up on my head. "You wanna *date?* Hahahahahaha."

So the first rule of dating is, Never risk direct contact with the girl in question. Your role model should be the nuclear submarine, gliding silently beneath the ocean surface, tracking an enemy target that does not even begin to suspect that the submarine would like to date it. I spent the vast majority of 1960 keeping a girl named Judy under surveillance, maintaining a minimum distance of 50 lockers to avoid the danger that I might somehow get into a conversation with her, which could have led to disaster.

Judy: Hi.

Me: Hi.

Judy: Just in case you have ever thought

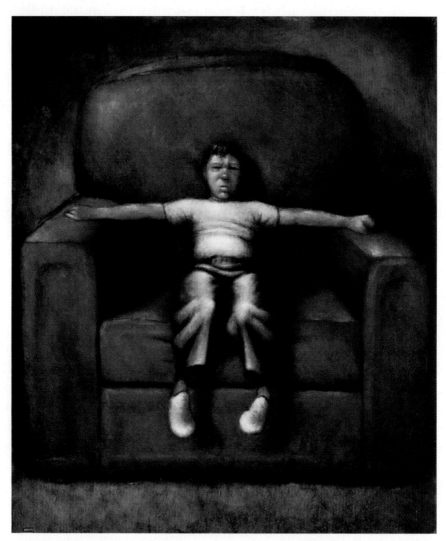

Copyright © David Shannon.

about having a date with me, the answer is no.

Woodland Creatures: Hahahahahaha.

The only problem with the nuclear-submarine technique is that it's difficult to get a date with a girl who has never, technically, been asked. This is why you need Phil Grant. Phil was a friend of mine who had the ability to talk to girls. It was a mysterious superhuman power he had, comparable to X-ray vision. So, after several thousand hours of intense discussion and planning with me, Phil approached a girl he knew named Nancy, who approached a girl named Sandy, who was a direct personal friend of Judy's and who passed the word back to Phil via Nancy that Judy would be willing to go on a date with me. This procedure protected me from direct humiliation, similar to the way President Reagan was protected from direct involvement in the Iran-Contra scandal[1] by a complex White House chain of command that at one point, investigators now believe, included his horse.

Thus it was that, finally, Judy and I went on an actual date, to see a movie in White Plains, N.Y. If I were to sum up the romantic ambience[2] of this date in four words, those words would be, "My mother was driving." This made for an extremely quiet drive, because my mother, realizing that her presence was hideously embarrassing, had to pretend she wasn't there. If it had been legal, I think she would have got out and sprinted alongside the car, steering through the window. Judy and I, sitting in the back seat about 75 feet apart, were also silent, unable to communicate without the assistance of Phil, Nancy and Sandy.

After what seemed like several years, we got to the movie theater, where my mother went off to sit in the Parents and Lepers Section. The movie was called *North to Alaska,* but I can tell you nothing else about it because I spent the whole time wondering whether it would be necessary to amputate my right arm, which was not getting any blood flow as a result of being perched for two hours like a petrified snake on the back of Judy's seat exactly one molecule away from physical contact.

So it was definitely a fun first date, featuring all the relaxed <u>spontaneity</u> of a real-estate closing,[3] and in later years I did regain some feeling in my arm. My point, Eric Knott, is that the key to successful dating is self-confidence. I bet that good-looking girl in your English class would *love* to go out with you. But *you* have to make the first move. So just do it! Pick up that phone! Call Phil Grant. ❖

> Judy: Just in case you have ever thought about having a date with me, the answer is no.

---

1. **Iran-Contra scandal:** a situation—uncovered in 1986, during the Reagan administration—in which U.S. government officials were suspected of improperly selling weapons to Iran to raise funds for Nicaraguan rebel forces.

2. **ambience** (ăm′bē-əns): the special atmosphere or mood created by an environment.

3. **real-estate closing:** a meeting at which the rights to land or a building are officially transferred from seller to buyer.

RESPONDING
O P T I O N S

FROM PERSONAL RESPONSE TO CRITICAL ANALYSIS

REFLECT   **1.** What was your reaction to Barry's experiences? Jot down your thoughts in your notebook.

RETHINK   **2.** Which parts of Barry's article seem realistic? Which parts seem exaggerated? Look back at the examples of hyperbole you jotted down for the Reading Connection on page 400.

         3. How does this article relate to the theme "Going to Extremes"?

         4. Reread the first paragraph of Barry's article. What does it reveal about what you can expect from the rest of the article?

         5. With a partner, present a humorous pantomime of Dave Barry's date.

RELATE   **6.** Some dating behaviors have changed since the 1960s, when Barry was a teenager. Judging from Barry's account and your own observations and experiences, what has changed and what has stayed the same?

ANOTHER PATHWAY
Cooperative Learning

With a small group of classmates, create a television situation-comedy episode entitled "Dave's First Date." Plan how you will portray the initial communication and the date itself. Also provide a satisfying conclusion to the episode. Act out the episode for the class.

QUICKWRITES

1. Imagine that you are Judy, the girl Barry writes about in this column. Write a **diary entry** describing your first date with Dave.

2. Write a quick draft of an **advice column,** responding as Dave Barry might to a request for advice about a problem that students your age face. Try to capture Dave Barry's humorous tone.

📁 *PORTFOLIO Save your writing. You may want to use it later as a springboard to a piece for your portfolio.*

LITERARY LINKS

Compare Dave Barry's description of his first date with Patrick McManus's description of the incident in Miss Bindle's math class (page 57). Which of the two descriptions do you think is more humorous? Why?

Dave Barry's First Date	Miss Bindle's Math Class

ALTERNATIVE ACTIVITIES

Cooperative Learning Produce a **how to video** about dating. First, decide whether you want to approach the subject seriously or humorously. Then start your video with tips on how to ask for a date. Afterwards, give pointers on how to have a successful date. Involve other students in your production by having them role-play various dating situations for your viewers.

DAVE BARRY

1947–

Born in Armonk, New York, Dave Barry was elected class clown by the Pleasantville High School class of 1965. Despite this honor, he did not immediately consider humor as a career. It was about 15 years later that he started writing freelance humor articles for a small newspaper—articles that soon were picked up by a few other papers, then by more. This widespread exposure of his work led to the offer of a job writing a humor column for the *Miami Herald,* the job he still holds today. In 1988, he won a Pulitzer Prize for his columns. "I always wanted to write when I was a kid," he says; "it just never occurred to me that you could have a job that didn't involve any actual work."

Barry has published 16 books, 2 of which became the basis of the CBS television series *Dave's World.* Often, while thinking about what he is going to write next, he plays a guitar that was once owned by Bruce Springsteen. Occasionally he plays in a "not very good" rock band at charitable functions.

Barry urges young people to write humor "even if it has no redeeming value." He says that thinking of jokes is easy; the hard part is saying it right: "I revise and revise and revise so my readers will feel and experience what is funny to me." **OTHER WORKS** *Dave Barry Is* Not *Making This Up, Dave Barry Talks Back, Dave Barry's Greatest Hits, Bad Habits*

POETRY

The Runaway
Robert Frost

Macavity: The Mystery Cat
T. S. Eliot

PERSONAL CONNECTION

Think about all of the animals you have observed—at home, in your neighborhood, on farms, at the zoo, and in the wild. Have you ever seen or heard about any animals that were out of control? How did they behave? Share your observations with the class.

CATS photo courtesy of The CATS Company.
Copyright 1991 Martha Swope.

LITERARY CONNECTION

You are about to read poems by two of the most famous 20th-century American poets, Robert Frost and T. S. Eliot. In these works, the poets write about unusual animal behavior: Frost focuses on a colt; Eliot, on a cat.

Robert Frost spent much of his life on a farm. He knew and loved the land and the farm animals. One critic has noted that Frost had no peer in his "ability to portray the local truth in nature." He could bring the actions of a colt so fully to life because he had not only observed horses but had handled them.

Similarly, Eliot was no mere observer of cats. He was a great fancier of felines, and was often photographed with his animals. Eliot was so captivated by these independent creatures that, in the 1930s, he was moved to compose for his godchildren and friends the poems that became *Old Possum's Book of Practical Cats*. In 1981, Andrew Lloyd Webber made Eliot's delightful and outrageous cats famous around the world when he adapted the poems for his stage musical *Cats*.

WRITING CONNECTION

As you read these poems, you may find that the colt and the cat seem to have personalities almost like those of people you know. Think about other animals whose behavior sometimes seems human—for example, you might know an angry dog or nervous parakeet. Write a short narrative illustrating the human-like personality traits of one or more of these animals.

The Runaway

by Robert Frost

Once when the snow of the year was beginning to fall,
We stopped by a mountain pasture to say, "Whose colt?"
A little Morgan[1] had one forefoot on the wall,
The other curled at his breast. He dipped his head
5 And snorted at us. And then he had to bolt.
We heard the miniature thunder where he fled,
And we saw him, or thought we saw him, dim and gray,
Like a shadow against the curtain of falling flakes.
"I think the little fellow's afraid of the snow.
10 He isn't winter-broken. It isn't play
With the little fellow at all. He's running away.
I doubt if even his mother could tell him, 'Sakes,
It's only weather.' He'd think she didn't know!
Where is his mother? He can't be out alone."
15 And now he comes again with clatter of stone,
And mounts the wall again with whited eyes
And all his tail that isn't hair up straight.
He shudders his coat as if to throw off flies.
"Whoever it is that leaves him out so late,
20 When other creatures have gone to stall and bin,
Ought to be told to come and take him in."

---

1. **Morgan:** a horse of a breed noted for strength, speed, and endurance.

FROM PERSONAL RESPONSE TO CRITICAL ANALYSIS

REFLECT   1. What are your feelings about the colt in this poem? Jot down your thoughts in your notebook.

RETHINK   2. Think about the human characteristics of the colt's behavior. How do its actions relate to the theme "Going to Extremes"?

3. Do you think Frost wants readers to learn a lesson about life from the colt's experience? Explain your answer.

Macavity: The Mystery Cat

By T.S. Eliot

Macavity's a Mystery Cat: he's called the Hidden Paw—
For he's the master criminal who can defy the Law.
He's the bafflement of Scotland Yard,[1] the Flying Squad's despair:[2]
For when they reach the scene of crime—*Macavity's not there!*

5   Macavity, Macavity, there's no one like Macavity,
He's broken every human law, he breaks the law of gravity.
His powers of levitation would make a fakir stare,
And when you reach the scene of crime—*Macavity's not there!*
You may seek him in the basement, you may look up in the air—
10 But I tell you once and once again, *Macavity's not there!*

---

1. **Scotland Yard:** the London police department, especially the detective bureau.
2. **the Flying Squad's despair:** a hopeless problem even for the special motorized emergency police unit in London.

Macavity's a ginger cat, he's very tall and thin;
You would know him if you saw him, for his eyes are sunken in.
His brow is deeply lined with thought, his head is highly domed;
His coat is dusty from neglect, his whiskers are uncombed.
15 He sways his head from side to side, with movements like a snake;
And when you think he's half asleep, he's always wide awake.

Macavity, Macavity, there's no one like Macavity,
For he's a fiend in feline shape, a monster of depravity.
You may meet him in a by-street, you may see him in the square—
20 But when a crime's discovered, then *Macavity's not there!*

He's outwardly respectable. (They say he cheats at cards.)
And his footprints are not found in any file of Scotland Yard's.
And when the larder's looted, or the jewel-case is rifled,
Or when the milk is missing, or another Peke's[3] been stifled,
25 Or the greenhouse glass is broken, and the trellis past repair—
Ay, there's the wonder of the thing! *Macavity's not there!*

And when the Foreign Office find a Treaty's gone astray,
Or the Admiralty lose some plans and drawings by the way,
There may be a scrap of paper in the hall or on the stair—
30 But it's useless to investigate—*Macavity's not there!*
And when the loss has been disclosed, the Secret Service say:
"It *must* have been Macavity!"—but he's a mile away.
You'll be sure to find him resting, or a-licking of his thumbs,
Or engaged in doing complicated long division sums.

35 Macavity, Macavity, there's no one like Macavity,
There never was a Cat of such deceitfulness and suavity.
He always has an alibi, and one or two to spare:
At whatever time the deed took place—MACAVITY WASN'T THERE!
And they say that all the Cats whose wicked deeds are widely
       known
40 (I might mention Mungojerrie, I might mention Griddlebone)
Are nothing more than agents for the Cat who all the time
Just controls their operations: the Napoleon[4] of Crime!

---

3. **Peke:** a Pekingese, a small dog with long hair.
4. **Napoleon** (nə-pō′lē-ən): emperor of the French, 1804–1814. As a military leader,
   Napoleon was powerful, clever, and seemingly unconquerable.

RESPONDING
O P T I O N S

FROM PERSONAL RESPONSE *TO* CRITICAL ANALYSIS

REFLECT   **1.** Are your feelings about Macavity in "Macavity: The Mystery Cat" different from your feelings about the runaway colt? Explain.

RETHINK   **2.** What kinds of crimes does Macavity commit? How does he resemble a human criminal?

         3. From what you know about cats, can you imagine a cat's behaving like Macavity? Give reasons for your answer.

RELATE   **4.** Compare and contrast the attitudes of these poems' speakers toward the animals they describe. Use details from the poems to support your conclusions.

         5. Compare and contrast the moods of the two poems.

ANOTHER PATHWAY

Plan a read-aloud of either "The Runaway" or "Macavity: The Mystery Cat" for your class. Study the punctuation in the poems and the techniques the poets use to convey particular sounds. You might want to tape practice readings to prepare for your performance.

LITERARY CONCEPTS

The pattern of rhymes in a poem is called the poem's **rhyme scheme.** A rhyme scheme can be described by assigning a different letter to each rhyming sound. Notice, for example, the rhyming words in these lines from "The Runaway":

Once when the snow of the year was beginning to fall,	A
We stopped by a mountain pasture to say, "Whose colt?"	B
A little Morgan had one forefoot on the wall,	A
The other curled at his breast. He dipped his head	C
And snorted at us. And then he had to bolt.	B

On a sheet of paper, write letters indicating the rhyme scheme of the first two stanzas of "Macavity: The Mystery Cat."

QUICKWRITES

1. Follow the example of Frost and Eliot by writing a **poem** about an animal that has human qualities. Use repetition and alliteration to create the sounds you want readers to hear.

2. If the colt and Macavity could talk, what would each say in response to the poem that has been written about him? Write either animal's reaction as a piece of **prose** or a **poem.**

     PORTFOLIO Save your writing. You may want to use it later as a springboard to a piece for your portfolio.

ROBERT FROST

1874–1963

Robert Frost, the most popular American poet of his time, nearly missed his calling. As a young adult, Frost married and worked at many odd jobs— mill hand, shoe salesman, farmer—to support his family. By the time he was 38, he was a discouraged man. His farm had failed, and he had suffered numerous rejections of his poetry. He decided to move his family to England and concentrate on writing.

Frost's work soon began to receive acclaim on both sides of the Atlantic, and he later returned to the United States. He is the only American poet to have won four Pulitzer Prizes, and in 1962 he was awarded a gold medal by Congress. Despite these honors, Frost endured much hardship. By 1940, three of his six children and his beloved wife were dead. Two infant daughters died from illness, and another daughter was committed to a psychiatric hospital, as was Frost's younger sister. His son committed suicide soon after the death of Frost's wife.

Most of Frost's poetry is inspired by rural life and emphasizes the individual's fight to retain an identity and the human struggle against natural forces.

OTHER WORKS *The Road Not Taken: A Selection of Robert Frost's Poems, Poems by Robert Frost: A Boy's Will and North of Boston*

T.S. ELIOT

1888–1965

Thomas Stearns Eliot ranks among the most important poets of the 20th century. Unlike "Macavity: The Mystery Cat," most of Eliot's poetry is written in a serious vein. His famous poem *The Waste Land,* considered by many critics to be the most influential poem of modern times, uses nontraditional techniques to portray a lack of faith and values in a world devastated by World War I.

Eliot was born in St. Louis, Missouri, and educated at Harvard University. Eliot studied at the graduate level in England, becoming a British subject in 1927. He began writing poetry during college and published his first major poem, "The Love Song of J. Alfred Prufrock," in 1915.

Eliot is also known for his plays, including *Murder in the Cathedral* and *The Cocktail Party,* and for his literary criticism. He worked as a literary editor and lectured at many colleges and universities in the United States and England. Eliot received numerous honors, including the 1948 Nobel Prize in literature.

OTHER WORKS *Selected Poems, The Waste Land and Other Poems*

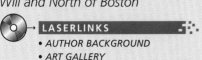

LASERLINKS
- *AUTHOR BACKGROUND*
- *ART GALLERY*

Student's Journal

WRITING TO EXPLAIN

If someone asked you to name the problems facing people you know, what would you say? As you have learned in Unit Three, "Battle for Control," problems come in all shapes and sizes. Some are easily solved, but others require the efforts of many people. How effective will you be at solving the problems you face?

GUIDED ASSIGNMENT

Write a Problem-Solution Essay In this lesson, you will have an opportunity to tackle a problem that is important to you. A problem-solution essay can help you evaluate a problem and find a positive solution.

Monday June 5
Today Sandra showed me this article from her school paper. She seemed really upset about what's going on at her school.

I think I'll write about the problem in the article Sandra gave me. This is a problem at my school too.

① Look Around You

As you read the excerpts and examine the chart on these pages, ask yourself questions about the problem described in each piece. Who is affected by the problem? Do you think there might be more than one point of view? Why should anyone care about the problem?

Reading the News Have you noticed in recent newspaper reports or news broadcasts problems such as those described on these pages? What were the problems? Why do you think they were in the news?

Chart

Taking a Poll Think about your own experiences. What would you say is the number one problem in your community? Why? You might take a poll of your classmates to see what they think the biggest problem is. Make a list of your findings.

WHeeL daNGer!

Each year there are approximately 1,000 bicycle-related deaths.

62% of those deaths involve head injuries.

38% other

Poll Shows Student Morale at a Record Low
by Lakisha Adams

The results are in on a poll conducted by the <u>Blue and Gold</u> newspaper. Seventy-five percent of the students at Palmer Middle School feel that morale is low. Students listed the new dress code, the football team's string of losses, and the decrease in school clubs as some of the issues bothering them.

"The students have been complaining more than usual these days," Principal Skinner remarked. "However, no one has offered any solutions."

Teenagers sing the blues: There's nothing legal to do

When the late singer Eddie Cochran wrote the 1950s song about teenagers of his day, he forever captured the frustrations youths face in dealing with parental authority.

The song's most memorable line: "There ain't no cure for the summertime blues," remains a rallying cry for today's highly mobile teens—struggling against boredom in the 1990s.

But recently, teenagers have begun clashing with another level of authority: suburban municipal officials armed with new laws.

And from Des Plaines to Palos Heights, these officials are taking aim at popular teen pastimes, everything from cruising in cars to gathering for teen dances.

"It's about time we got serious about certain kinds of activity that are a threat to the community," said Des Plaines Ald. Jean Higgason, outraged by large numbers of teens cruising the streets of her community.

"Gang members are infiltrating," Higgason added.

Ironically, some child behavior experts and teens say, wiping out these accessible and popular forms of activities leaves teens with fewer options for filling a critical need: healthy interaction with their peers.

Ray Quintanilla
from *Chicago Tribune*

❷ Write in Your Journal

Pick two or three of the problems you discovered. If you or a friend were involved in one of the situations, what would you do about it? Write your reactions.

Decision Point Choose a problem you want to write about. It can be one of the problems on these pages or one from your own life, but it should be something that's important to you.

LASERLINKS
• WRITING SPRINGBOARD
WRITING COACH

Exploring Solutions

Solutions That Work By now you've identified a problem that's important to you, one that you want to write about. The steps on these pages can help you explore possible solutions.

❶ Think About Possible Solutions

Think about the resources you would use to develop a solution to the problem. Two good resources are your own common sense and your friends' opinions. Another source is your school or neighborhood library. Try using the following strategies to explore solutions.

Research Sources

STUDY THE PROBLEM

Restate the situation in your own words. Make sure you understand all the issues involved.

BRAINSTORM IDEAS WITH FRIENDS

You might consider talking over the problem with some of your friends. Think about a time when you or someone you know experienced a similar problem. How did he or she solve that problem? Try brainstorming some additional solutions. The tips in the SkillBuilder on page 415 will help you and your friends work together to build a list of ideas.

RESEARCH POSSIBLE SOLUTIONS

Do you need to know more details about the problem? Sources such as your school newspaper, electronic bulletin boards, or daily newspapers can reveal ways people have solved problems similar to yours. You may even want to consult an expert. Use the advice in the Multimedia Handbook for additional research ideas. You might make a web like the one on the next page to keep track of your proposed solutions.

② Evaluate Your Ideas

Before you start your essay, you'll need to evaluate your ideas. How would you carry out each solution? What kinds of support would each require? Would any of your solutions create new problems?

Student's Solution Web

③ Pick Your Solution

Which solution seems most workable? Can you combine any of your solutions? Look at the web above that one student made for his report. After making this web, he combined some of the ideas to make one solution, which he wrote in his essay. What solution will you write about in your essay?

Writing Your Ideas

At the Starting Gate Now you're ready to put your ideas into draft form. As you write, you may find that your solution isn't working or that your problem isn't really a problem after all. Don't be afraid to go off in another direction, or even to start over.

① Write Your Rough Draft

As you draft your problem-solution essay, ask other people who are interested in the problem to help you develop your solution in more detail. Notice the peer comments in the student model below.

Student's Rough Draft with Peer Comments

Building School Spirit

Linda's Rough Draft

Problem: Low morale = No school spirit
Solution: Students need to get more involved.

I think it's important to ask the students what they want, first of all. If students are made to feel like they're a part of things, maybe morale would improve.

Maybe have students and teachers get together and talk about ways to develop more school spirit.

Sometimes kids may feel like they're not as important as the jocks or the cool kids. Maybe there should be more activities that everyone can get involved in, not just the jocks. Get the school paper involved and sponsor a school spirit contest.

NOTE: I NEED TO MENTION MORE ACTIVITIES. I THINK EXTRACURRICULAR ACTIVITIES ARE IMPORTANT, NOW THAT I THINK OF IT.

Peer Comments
Linda's Rough Draft

You need more examples of how to build school spirit, like wearing school colors or something.—R. G.

This would be a great speech for a rally. I agree about the extracurricular activities. —V. J.

---

❷ Shape Your Writing

As you rework your rough draft, consider the suggestions below to help you present your ideas clearly.

Writing Your Introduction Define or describe the problem, telling why it is a problem and who is affected. Look once more at the student model on the preceding page. How well does it describe the problem?

Making Your Draft Clear and Complete Include details to explain the problem and to support your proposed solution. The first student reviewer's note shows how important it is to use specific examples. Look back at your prewriting notes. Did you include everything you wanted to mention? The SkillBuilder at the right can help you elaborate on your ideas. For tips on organizing your problem-solution essay, see page 841 of the Writing Handbook.

Ending Your Essay Restate the problem and your proposed solution. Then look back at the notes you made during prewriting. What final thoughts can you give your readers?

❸ Evaluate Your Draft

Step back from your draft and look at it as if someone else had written it. Did you clearly state the problem? Do the solutions you proposed make sense? To evaluate the draft you wrote, ask yourself the following questions:

- How can I help the reader better understand the cause of the problem?
- Have I shown why the solution I proposed is a good one?
- Have I thought about the pros and cons of this solution?

 PEER RESPONSE

At this point, you may find it helpful to get comments from your peers, particularly the ones who gave you ideas for solutions. Peers can help you see points that you might have missed. Ask them questions like the following:

- How would you summarize the problem and the solution?
- What other solutions might I have overlooked?

SkillBuilder

 WRITER'S CRAFT

Elaborating on Ideas
To help readers understand your recommended solution, add specific details to what you have written. Use these suggestions:

- Add some statistics or other facts to back up your solution.
- Use incidents and examples. In the comments on the student model, the writer was reminded of how to build school spirit. The writer could mention these examples in her final draft.
- Use quotations from people who support the conclusions you have reached.

APPLYING WHAT YOU'VE LEARNED
Now go back and review the ideas you have written. Which ideas need more elaboration? For example, if you are writing about school spirit, what facts or statistics could you include to demonstrate the importance of your solutions?

RETHINK & EVALUATE

Preparing to Revise

1. What do you like best about the way you've stated the problem and its solution?
2. How will you use your peers' feedback to revise your essay?
3. How can you make the solution to your problem more convincing?

Finishing Your Essay

The Final Steps Now you're ready to take the next step: finalizing your essay. The next two pages will help you through the revision and publishing process. What type of format will you choose to show your readers how strongly you feel about the problem you're presenting?

Student's Speech Cards

① Revise and Edit Your Essay

Here are some suggestions to help you revise and improve your draft:

- Refer to the comments made by your peers to help you make sure your essay gives a clear explanation of the problem and the solution you're proposing.
- Use the Standards for Evaluation and the Editing Checklist to see whether your essay is complete. Is there anything you need to add to your essay?
- Check your conclusion to make sure you have summarized the problem and your solution.
- Look at how one student used examples to complete her draft.

How did the student use examples to explain her solution to the problem?

The problem of low student morale in our school seems to point to a lack of school spirit. In fact, a number of students don't even feel part of the school at all. According to my poll, some kids who aren't involved in sports feel they're not as important as the jocks or the top-of-the-class kids. One solution could be to have more extracurricular activities that everyone can get involved in. That way, all of us will feel like the school is really ours.

Perhaps the paper could sponsor a school spirit contest. Concerned students could form a committee and hand out questionnaires. We could then suggest school clubs that a wider variety of people could get involved in, and we could propose more school-related activities to promote unity. For example, one day we could all wear the school colors or dress like the school mascot. Maybe some students could make a banner for the school's lobby. If students get more involved, maybe more kids would start showing up for games too. The problem of low morale won't be solved until we all feel we have a say in what's going on at school.

How did the student incorporate the peer comments she received during the drafting stage?

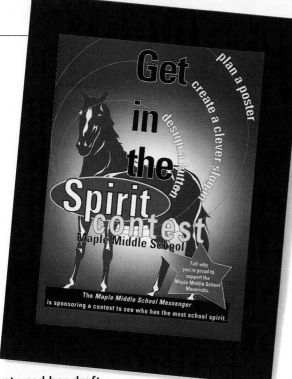

One student used her draft ideas in a speech illustrated by the poster above.

② Present Your Work

Think about a format that you think will fit your essay. If you want others to feel as strongly as you do about the problem you're discussing, you may choose a public format, such as a speech or a newspaper article.

PUBLISHING IDEAS

- Present your essay as a speech for a rally.
- Create an ad campaign that includes posters like the one above.
- Write an article for the school paper or a letter to your principal.

Standards for Evaluation

An effective problem-solution essay
- gives a clear and concise explanation of the problem and its significance
- presents a workable solution and includes details that explain and support it
- concludes by restating the problem and the solution

SkillBuilder

 GRAMMAR FROM WRITING

Using Direct Objects
One way to achieve clarity in an essay is to use direct objects properly. A direct object is a noun or pronoun that follows an action verb. It answers the question *whom* or *what*.

The students formed a committee.

Action Verb	Direct Object
formed	committee

GRAMMAR HANDBOOK

For more information on direct objects in sentences, see pages 876–877 of the Grammar Handbook.

Editing Checklist Ask yourself the following questions:

- Did I include examples to back up my solutions?
- Did I use direct objects correctly?
- Did I proofread my essay?

REFLECT & ASSESS

Evaluating Your Experience

1. How did you come up with the solution to the problem?
2. How could you use your problem-solving skills in other areas of your life?

PORTFOLIO Add your essay to your portfolio, along with a list of problem-solving tips you found helpful.

REFLECT & ASSESS

UNIT THREE: BATTLE FOR CONTROL

The characters in this unit battle for control in a variety of situations. Has reading about their struggles influenced your own thoughts about what is worth fighting for? Have you changed your mind about the extremes to which you would go in a conflict? To explore these questions, complete one or more of the options in each of the following sections.

REFLECTING ON THEME

OPTION 1 Reading from Within The characters in this unit would give very different answers to the question "What do you think is worth fighting for?" Jot down how you think the main character of each selection that you have read would respond to the question. Circle the response that most clearly reflects your own opinion, and write a journal entry explaining how you would answer the question.

OPTION 2 Connecting In which of this unit's selections do the characters face conflicts that remind you of experiences in your own life? For each case, write a few paragraphs explaining the similarities and differences between the two situations.

OPTION 3 Making Choices Get together with a few classmates and imagine that you are putting together a book called *Battle for Control,* intended to teach people how to deal with conflicts. Which of the selections in this unit would you choose to include in the book? Try to agree on a group list of four or five suitable selections, explaining the reasons for your choices.

REFLECT & ASSESS *Self-Assessment: Which selections in this unit have had the greatest impact on your own thoughts about dealing with conflict? Which might have the greatest influence on your behavior in the future? List the selection titles in order of the impact the selections have had on you. Next to each, jot down the lesson you have learned from the selection.*

REVIEWING LITERARY CONCEPTS

OPTION 1 Examining Protagonists and Antagonists After looking through the short stories in this unit, make a chart like the one shown, identifying the protagonist and the antagonist(s) in each story. Assign each protagonist a score, from 1 to 10, to indicate how successfully he or she battles for control, and note the reason for your score.

Story	Protagonist	Antagonist(s)	My Score	Reason
"The Banana Tree"	Gustus	the hurricane Gustus's father	5	Gustus does not stop the hurricane from destroying his tree, but he comes to understand his father better.

OPTION 2 **Identifying Mood** Remember that mood is a feeling or atmosphere that a writer creates for readers. Choose some selections (or parts of selections) that you think have clearly identifiable moods. For each one, jot down the word that best describes the mood. Compare your list of words with a classmate's.

Self-Assessment: Look over the following list of literary terms introduced in this unit. Write a one-sentence definition of each term, then use the Handbook of Reading Terms and Literary Concepts on page 812 to check your definitions.

realistic fiction	*oral history*
point of view	*foreshadowing*
tone	*author's purpose*
extended metaphor	*rhyme scheme*

PORTFOLIO BUILDING

- **QuickWrites** The QuickWrites in this unit asked you to write in a variety of forms, including poems, dialogues, diary entries, newspaper articles, and narratives. In which form was your writing most effective? Choose one or two good examples, and write a cover note for each piece, explaining what you like best about it. Then add the pieces and the notes to your portfolio.

- **Writing About Literature** Earlier in this unit, you evaluated the believability of one of the selections. Reread your critical essay, then evaluate it in a sentence or two. Did writing the essay teach you anything that you might bring to future reading?

- **Writing from Experience** Now that you've written a problem-solution essay, do you still feel strongly about the problem? Do you still think that your solution would work? Draft a letter to someone familiar with the problem. Discuss your proposed solution and your thoughts on the matter now. Decide whether to include your letter with your essay.

- **Personal Choice** Look back through your records and evaluations of all the activities you completed in this unit. Also look at activities and writing you have done on your own. In which

activity or writing assignment did you resolve a conflict in a way that you were especially pleased about? Write a paragraph explaining what went well, attach it to the work or evaluation, and include both in your portfolio.

Self-Assessment: Organize the work in your portfolio in a way that is not chronological. You could organize your work according to themes, types of activities, or successfulness. Consider the benefits of all of these options, and choose the one that suits you best.

SETTING GOALS

As you completed the reading and writing activities in this unit, you probably discovered topics that interest you—perhaps the history of the Cherokee people or the plight of immigrants to the United States. What kinds of further reading and what kinds of writing tasks might help you find out more about those topics? Record your thoughts in your notebook.

Facing the ENEMY

Kites rise highest

against the wind,

not with it.

Sir Winston Churchill
Prime minister of Great Britain during
World War II

Greed (1982), Carlos Almaraz. Oil on canvas, 34" × 44". Copyright © 1982 Carlos Almaraz. Courtesy of the Almaraz Estate.

SO MUCH AT STAKE

WHAT DO YOU THINK?

REFLECTING ON THEME

Have you ever faced up to an enemy? Maybe it wasn't a person, but some impersonal force, such as poverty or disease. In such a conflict, anything can be at stake—from your pride to your very survival. Use the activities on this page to explore what is at stake when people face different kinds of enemies.

How can you help?

Many people must confront poverty in their lives. How should we tackle this "enemy" in society? Working with two other students, create a list of practical suggestions for helping people in the community who do not have adequate food or shelter. Present your ideas in a booklet.

Whom would you choose?

Write a tribute praising someone who bravely faced an enemy such as illness, poverty, or injustice. Describe how the person's attitude or actions were an inspiration to others. What was at stake for him or her?

What is most important?

A person needs certain qualities to be able to face up to his or her enemies. Using the list provided, survey your classmates to find out the qualities they feel are most important. Have them grade the qualities on a scale of 1 to 10, with 10 being the most important. Report your findings in the form of a chart or a graph.

What is at stake?

In some jobs people must make vital decisions—decisions that sometimes are a matter of life or death. Pick a profession that you admire, in which the stakes are high. Draw a picture illustrating the profession. Show why the stakes are so high, and why you admire the profession.

Important Qualities	
caution	generosity
strength	helpfulness
honesty	reliability
intelligence	determination

FICTION

The Gift of the Magi
O. Henry

Special Gift Ideas

PERSONAL CONNECTION

Suppose you want to give a special gift to a person you love, but the gift is much more expensive than you can afford. How might you handle the situation? Record your thoughts in an idea map like the one shown here. Then share your ideas with the class.

HISTORICAL CONNECTION

In this story, O. Henry makes an allusion, or reference, to the Magi. According to Christian tradition, the Magi were three wise men or kings named Balthasar, Melchior, and Gaspar. They traveled from the east to Bethlehem, guided by a miraculous star, to present gifts of gold, frankincense, and myrrh to the infant Jesus.

Some scholars suggest that these gifts had both symbolic meanings and practical value. Gold symbolized love; frankincense, worship; and myrrh, sacrifice. Gold obviously had monetary value; frankincense and myrrh, both sweet-smelling tree resins, were burned as incense and used in medicines. Myrrh was also used in ancient times for embalming, or preserving, the bodies of the dead.

READING CONNECTION

In-Depth Reading How you read depends on what you are reading and why. Sometimes you can use skimming and scanning, or quick surface reading, to get information quickly. At other times you need to engage in in-depth reading, in which you slow down and really examine what is in front of you.

Some of O. Henry's vocabulary and references can be difficult to understand. Occasionally, you will need to reread a sentence to comprehend its full meaning. To help you keep track of the events in the selection, use your reading log to jot down answers to the questions inserted in the text. As you read, notice what the characters do to show their love through gifts.

The Three Magi (about A.D. 600–650), unknown artist. Sant' Apollinare Nuovo, Ravenna, Italy, Scala/Art Resource, New York.

LASERLINKS
- CULTURAL CONNECTION
- ART GALLERY

425

The GIFT of the MAGI

by O. Henry

One dollar and eighty-seven cents. That was all. And 60 cents of it was in pennies. Pennies saved one and two at a time by bulldozing the grocer and the vegetable man and the butcher until one's cheeks burned with the silent imputation of parsimony[1] that such close dealing implied. Three times Della counted it. One dollar and eighty-seven cents. And the next day would be Christmas.

There was clearly nothing to do but flop down on the shabby little couch and howl. So Della did it. Which <u>instigates</u> the moral reflection that life is made up of sobs, sniffles, and smiles, with sniffles <u>predominating</u>.

While the mistress of the home is gradually <u>subsiding</u> from the first stage to the second, take a look at the home. A furnished flat at $8 per week. It did not exactly beggar description, but it certainly had that word on the lookout for the mendicancy squad.[2]

In the vestibule below belonged to this flat a letterbox into which no letter would go and an electric button from which no mortal finger could coax a ring. Also appertaining[3] thereunto was a card bearing the name "Mr. James Dillingham Young."

CLARIFY

Why is Della crying?

The "Dillingham" had been flung to the breeze during a former period of prosperity when its possessor was being paid $30 per week. Now, when the income was shrunk to $20, the letters of "Dillingham" looked blurred, as though they were thinking seriously of contracting to a modest and unassuming D. But whenever Mr. James Dillingham Young came home and reached his flat above, he was called "Jim" and greatly hugged by Mrs. James Dillingham Young, already introduced to you as Della. Which is all very good.

Della finished her cry and attended to her cheeks with the powder rag. She stood by the window and looked out dully at a gray cat walking a gray fence in a gray backyard. Tomorrow would be Christmas Day, and she had only $1.87 with which to buy Jim a present. She had been saving every penny she could for months, with this result. Twenty dollars a week doesn't go far. Expenses had been greater than she had calculated. They always are. Only $1.87 to buy a present for Jim. Her Jim. Many a happy hour she had spent planning for something nice for him. Something fine and rare and sterling—something just a little bit near to being worthy of the honor of being owned by Jim.

There was a pier glass[4] between the windows of the room. Perhaps you have seen a pier glass in an $8 flat. A very thin and very <u>agile</u> person may, by observing his reflection in a rapid sequence of longitudinal strips, obtain a fairly accurate conception of his looks. Della, being slender, had mastered the art.

Suddenly she whirled from the window and stood before the glass. Her eyes were shining brilliantly, but her face had lost its color within twenty seconds. Rapidly she pulled down her hair and let it fall to its full length.

Now, there were two possessions of the James Dillingham Youngs in which they both

---

1. **imputation** (ĭm′pyŏŏ-tā′shən) **of parsimony** (pär′sə-mō′nē): suggestion of stinginess.
2. **mendicancy** (mĕn′dĭ-kən-sē) **squad:** a police unit assigned to arrest beggars. The author here is making a play on the word *beggar*, used earlier in the sentence to mean "make inadequate."
3. **appertaining** (ăp′ər-tā′nĭng): belonging as a part; attached.
4. **pier glass:** a narrow mirror set in a wall section between windows.

WORDS TO KNOW

instigate (ĭn′stĭ-gāt′) *v.* to stir up; provoke
predominating (prĭ-dŏm′ə-nā′tĭng) *adj.* most important or frequent **predominate** *v.*
subside (səb-sīd′) *v.* to sink down; settle
agile (ăj′əl) *adj.* able to move quickly and easily

took a mighty pride. One was Jim's gold watch that had been his father's and his grandfather's. The other was Della's hair. Had the Queen of Sheba[5] lived in the flat across the air shaft, Della would have let her hair hang out the window some day to dry and mocked at Her Majesty's jewels and gifts. Had King Solomon[6] been the janitor, with all his treasures piled up in the basement, Jim would have pulled out his watch every time he passed, just to see him pluck at his beard from envy.

So now Della's beautiful hair fell about her, rippling and shining like a <u>cascade</u> of brown waters. It reached below her knee and made itself almost a garment for her. And then she did it up again nervously and quickly. Once she faltered for a minute and stood still while a tear or two splashed on the worn red carpet.

On went her old brown jacket; on went her old brown hat. With a whirl of skirts and with the brilliant sparkle still in her eyes, she fluttered out the door and down the stairs to the street.

Where she stopped, the sign read "Mme. Sofronie. Hair Goods of All Kinds." One flight up Della ran and collected herself, panting, before Madame, large, too white, chilly, and hardly looking the "Sofronie."

"Will you buy my hair?" asked Della.

"I buy hair," said Madame. "Take yer hat off and let's have a sight at the looks of it."

Down rippled the brown cascade.

"Twenty dollars," said Madame, lifting the mass with a practiced hand.

"Give it to me quick," said Della.

Oh, and the next two hours tripped by on rosy wings. Forget the hashed metaphor. She was ransacking the stores for Jim's present.

She found it at last. It surely had been made for Jim and no one else. There was none other like it in any of the stores, and she had turned all of them inside out. It was a platinum fob chain[7] simple and chaste in design, properly proclaiming its value by substance alone and not by meretricious ornamentation[8]—as all good things should do. It was even worthy of The Watch. As soon as she saw it, she knew that it must be Jim's. It was like him. Quietness and value—the description applied to both. Twenty-one dollars they took from her for it, and she hurried home with the 87 cents. With that chain on his watch Jim might be properly anxious about the time in any company. Grand as the watch was, he sometimes looked at it on the sly on account of the old leather strap that he used in place of a chain.

When Della reached home, her intoxication gave way a little to <u>prudence</u> and reason. She got out her curling irons and lighted the gas and went to work repairing the ravages made by generosity added to love. Which is always a tremendous task, dear friends—a mammoth task.

Within forty minutes her head was covered with tiny, close-lying curls that made her look wonderfully like a truant schoolboy. She looked at her reflection in the mirror long, carefully, and critically.

> AS SOON AS SHE SAW IT, SHE KNEW THAT IT MUST BE JIM'S. IT WAS LIKE HIM.

---

5. **Queen of Sheba:** in the Bible, a rich Arabian queen.
6. **King Solomon:** a biblical king of Israel, known for his wisdom and wealth.
7. **fob chain:** a short chain for a pocket watch.
8. **meretricious** (mĕr´ĭ-trĭsh´əs) **ornamentation:** cheap, gaudy decoration.

WORDS TO KNOW

cascade (kă-skād´) *n.* a waterfall
prudence (prōōd´ns) *n.* the use of good judgment and common sense

Golden Fall (1940), Joseph Stella. Oil on canvas, 26" × 20", courtesy of Spanierman Gallery, New York.

"If Jim doesn't kill me," she said to herself, "before he takes a second look at me, he'll say I look like a Coney Island chorus girl. But what could I do—oh, what could I do with a dollar and eighty-seven cents!"

At 7 o'clock the coffee was made, and the frying pan was on the back of the stove hot and ready to cook the chops.

Jim was never late. Della doubled the fob chain in her hand and sat on the corner of the table near the door that he always entered. Then she heard his step on the stair away down on the first flight, and she turned white for just a moment. She had a habit of saying little silent prayers about the simplest everyday things, and now she whispered: "Please, God, make him think I am still pretty."

The door opened, and Jim stepped in and closed it. He looked thin and very serious. Poor fellow, he was only twenty-two—and to be burdened with a family! He needed a new overcoat, and he was without gloves.

Jim stopped inside the door, as immovable as a setter at the scent of a quail. His eyes were fixed upon Della, and there was an expression in them that she could not read, and it terrified her. It was not anger, nor surprise, nor disapproval, nor horror, nor any of the sentiments that she had been prepared for. He simply stared at her fixedly with that peculiar expression on his face.

CLARIFY

What is Jim's reaction to Della's hair?

Della wriggled off the table and went for him.

"Jim, darling," she cried, "don't look at me that way. I had my hair cut off and sold it because I couldn't have lived through Christmas without giving you a present. It'll grow again—you won't mind, will you? I just had to do it. My hair grows awfully fast. Say 'Merry Christmas!' Jim, and let's be happy. You don't know what a nice—what a beautiful, nice gift I've got for you."

"You've cut off your hair?" asked Jim, laboriously, as if he had not arrived at that patent fact yet even after the hardest mental labor.

"Cut it off and sold it," said Della. "Don't you like me just as well, anyhow? I'm me without my hair, ain't I?"

Jim looked about the room curiously.

"You say your hair is gone?" he said, with an air almost of idiocy.

"You needn't look for it," said Della. "It's sold, I tell you—sold and gone too. It's Christmas Eve, boy. Be good to me, for it went for you. Maybe the hairs of my head were numbered," she went on with a sudden serious sweetness, "but nobody could ever count my love for you. Shall I put the chops on, Jim?"

Out of his trance Jim seemed to quickly wake. He enfolded his Della. For ten seconds let us regard with discreet scrutiny[9] some inconsequential object in the other direction. Eight dollars a week or a million a year—what is the difference? A mathematician or a wit would give you the wrong answer. The magi brought valuable gifts, but that was not among them. This dark assertion will be illuminated later on.

Jim drew a package from his overcoat pocket and threw it upon the table.

"Don't make any mistake, Dell," he said, "about me. I don't think there's anything in the way of a haircut or a shave or a shampoo that could make me like my girl any less. But if you'll unwrap that package, you may see why you had me going awhile at first."

White fingers and nimble tore at the string

---

9. **scrutiny** (skroōt'n-ē): careful observation.

and paper. And then an ecstatic scream of joy, and then, alas! a quick feminine change to hysterical tears and wails, necessitating the immediate employment of all the comforting powers of the lord of the flat.

For there lay The Combs—the set of combs, side and back, that Della had worshiped for long in a Broadway window. Beautiful combs, pure tortoise shell, with jeweled rims—just the shade to wear in the beautiful vanished hair. They were expensive combs, she knew, and her heart had simply craved and yearned over them without the least hope of possession. And now, they were hers, but the tresses[10] that should have adorned the <u>coveted</u> adornments[11] were gone.

But she hugged them to her bosom, and at length she was able to look up with dim eyes and a smile and say, "My hair grows so fast, Jim!"

And then Della leaped up like a little singed cat and cried, "Oh, oh!"

Jim had not yet seen his beautiful present. She held it out to him eagerly upon her open palm. The dull, precious metal seemed to flash with a reflection of her bright and ardent spirit.

"Isn't it a dandy, Jim?" I hunted all over town to find it. You'll have to look at the time a hundred times a day now. Give me your watch. I want to see how it looks on it."

Instead of obeying, Jim tumbled down on the couch and put his hands under the back of his head and smiled.

"Dell," said he, "let's put our Christmas presents away and keep 'em a while. They're too nice to use just at present. I sold the watch to get the money to buy your combs. And now suppose you put the chops on."

The magi, as you know, were wise men—wonderfully wise men—who brought gifts to the Babe in the manger. They invented the art of giving Christmas gifts. Being wise, their gifts were no doubt wise ones, possibly bearing the privilege of exchange in case of duplication. And here I have lamely related to you the uneventful <u>chronicle</u> of two foolish children in a flat who most unwisely sacrificed for each other the greatest treasures of their house. But in a last word to the wise of these days let it be said that of all who give gifts these two were of the wisest. Of all who give and receive gifts, such as they are the wisest. Everywhere they are the wisest. They are the magi. ❖

"MY HAIR GROWS SO FAST, JIM!"

---

10. **tresses:** a woman's long, unbound hair.
11. **adornments:** things intended to beautify; ornaments.

431

RESPONDING
OPTIONS

FROM PERSONAL RESPONSE TO CRITICAL ANALYSIS

REFLECT **1.** What were your thoughts about Della and Jim? Write them down in your notebook, then share them with a partner.

RETHINK **2.** O. Henry sees Della and Jim as being both foolish and wise. How would you evaluate them?

3. What three words would you use to describe Della and Jim's relationship?

4. How does this story relate to the unit theme, "Facing the Enemy"? Who or what do you think is the enemy in the story? Explain your answer.

5. Do you think that people today would be willing to make such sacrifices to give gifts to those they love? Give reasons for your answer.

RELATE **6.** For most people, exchanging gifts is an experience very different from Della and Jim's. Work with a small group of classmates to examine people's attitudes toward giving and receiving gifts. In the discussion, recount some of your own experiences with gift giving.

ANOTHER PATHWAY
Cooperative Learning

With a small group of classmates, review the main events of the story. Then work together to create a collage that represents the key events. Your collage might modernize the story by showing how the events could happen in today's world.

QUICKWRITES

1. What might Jim be thinking when he notices Della's short hair? Write an **interior monologue** that expresses his thoughts.

2. Who do you think makes the greater sacrifice—Della or Jim? Write your opinion, and the reasons for it, in the form of a brief **paragraph.**

3. A gift that costs nothing can be the most valuable gift of all. Make a **list** of gifts that cost nothing. Share your list with the class.

📁 *PORTFOLIO Save your writing. You may want to use it later as a springboard to a piece for your portfolio.*

LITERARY CONCEPTS

Some works of literature burst on the scene, winning high praise and great popularity, only to be forgotten after a short time. Other works, like the stories of O. Henry, are read year after year by people around the world. Such enduring works are considered **classics.** Classics like "The Gift of the Magi" deal with emotions, behaviors, or truths that human beings of every age, race, and culture share. What aspects of this story do you think make it a classic?

THE WRITER'S STYLE

O. Henry is a master of the surprise ending. Were you surprised by Jim's sacrifice? Why or why not? Find clues in the story that foreshadow the surprise ending.

ALTERNATIVE ACTIVITIES

1. An example of a gift that costs nothing is a love song. As a gift to Della and Jim, compose a **love song** that captures the essence of their relationship.

2. "The Gift of the Magi" is a story of romantic love and mutual sacrifice. Create a **drawing, painting,** or **sculpture** that serves as a symbol of these romantic concepts and that could be used to illustrate the story.

WORDS TO KNOW

On your paper, write the letter of the word that is most *different* in meaning from the other words in the set. Use a dictionary if you need help.

1. (a) stop, (b) stir, (c) urge, (d) instigate
2. (a) predominating, (b) dominating, (c) ruling, (d) missing
3. (a) increase, (b) subside, (c) lessen, (d) decline
4. (a) history, (b) record, (c) chronicle, (d) prediction
5. (a) stream, (b) river, (c) brook, (d) cascade
6. (a) assertion, (b) declaration, (c) denial, (d) statement
7. (a) desired, (b) coveted, (c) craved, (d) unwanted
8. (a) carelessness, (b) caution, (c) prudence, (d) wisdom
9. (a) limber, (b) agile, (c) clumsy, (d) flexible
10. (a) important, (b) unnecessary, (c) inconsequential, (d) insignificant

O. HENRY

1862–1910

Using the pen name O. Henry, William Sydney Porter wrote nearly 300 short stories that brought him worldwide fame. During the two decades following his death, his short stories were more popular than those of any other American writer. Like his stories, his life was marked by surprises.

Born in Greensboro, North Carolina, Porter was raised by his grandmother and aunt after his mother's death. He left school at 16 to work in his uncle's drugstore. Later he moved to Texas and worked on a ranch there. At the age of 25, he married Athol Estes. After the birth of their child, they moved to Austin, Texas, where Porter became a bank clerk. Several years after leaving this position, he was suspected of having embezzled bank funds. Porter fled to Central America to avoid trial. When he returned to visit his dying wife, he was arrested, convicted, and jailed for three years. Throughout, he maintained his innocence.

It was in jail that Porter refined his short story style, writing stories based on his Western, Central American, and prison experiences.

OTHER WORKS *The Four Million, Heart of the West, The Gentle Grafter, Strictly Business, Whirligigs, Sixes and Sevens, Waifs and Strays,* "The Ransom of Red Chief," "A Retrieved Reformation," "Hearts and Hands"

POETRY

Speech to the Young
Speech to the Progress-Toward
Gwendolyn Brooks

A Man
Nina Cassian

PERSONAL CONNECTION

The poems you are about to read deal with the challenge of facing life's obstacles. What kinds of obstacles do people commonly encounter in their lives? What kinds of obstacles are extraordinarily difficult to overcome? To help you organize your thoughts, use a concept map like the one shown. Then share your ideas with the class. In your discussion, consider what gives people the courage to overcome obstacles.

LITERARY CONNECTION

Gwendolyn Brooks and Nina Cassian have both overcome obstacles in their lives. Much of Brooks's poetry draws on the painful experience of growing up African American in the early part of this century. She shows a keen awareness of the problems of color and justice in the United States. Though she examines despair and grief in her work, ultimately her attitude is positive.

While Brooks has struggled with the obstacle of racial discrimination, Nina Cassian, a Romanian, has faced political obstacles. Denounced by the Romanian government for failing to uphold Communist ideals in her work, she was forced to seek a new home in the United States in the 1980s.

WRITING CONNECTION

Think of a time in your life when a major obstacle stood in the way of something you wanted to do. How did you deal with it? Write a brief account of your experience. Then, as you read these poems, take note of the speakers' attitudes toward obstacles.

I remember that when I was nine I really wanted to play third base on my softball team . . .

Speech to the Young
Speech to the Progress-Toward
(Among them Nora and Henry III)

by Gwendolyn Brooks

Say to them,
say to the down-keepers,
the sun-slappers,
the self-soilers,
5 the harmony-hushers,
"Even if you are not ready for day
it cannot always be night."
You will be right.
For that is the hard home-run.

10 Live not for battles won.
Live not for the-end-of-the-song.
Live in the along.

Copyright © Nicholas Wilton.

FROM **PERSONAL RESPONSE** TO **CRITICAL ANALYSIS**

REFLECT **1.** What is your impression of the speaker's advice? Jot down your thoughts in your notebook.

RETHINK **2.** What do you think is the meaning of the last stanza of the poem?

3. What does the speaker think is at stake, or in danger of being lost, if young people do not follow the advice given in the poem?

4. What obstacles might make the speaker's advice difficult to follow?

5. What character trait is shared by the people mentioned in lines 2–5? Do you know people like these? Explain your answer.

A MAN

by Nina Cassian

Das Buch [The book] (1985), Anselm
Kiefer. Lead, steel and tin, 114" × 213½" ×
34", Los Angeles County Museum of Art,
Modern and Contemporary Art Council
Fund and Louise and Harold Held.

While fighting for his country, he lost an arm
and was suddenly afraid:
"From now on, I shall only be able to do things by halves.
I shall reap half a harvest.
5 I shall be able to play either the tune
or the accompaniment on the piano,
but never both parts together.
I shall be able to bang with only one fist
on doors, and worst of all
10 I shall only be able to half hold
my love close to me.
There will be things I cannot do at all,
applaud for example,
at shows where everyone applauds."

15 From that moment on, he set himself to do
everything with twice as much enthusiasm.
And where the arm had been torn away
a wing grew.

RESPONDING
O P T I O N S

FROM PERSONAL RESPONSE TO CRITICAL ANALYSIS

REFLECT **1.** What is your impression of the man described in "A Man"?

RETHINK **2.** Do you think that the man's reaction to his disability is common?
Consider
- his initial reaction in the first stanza
- how his attitude seems to have changed in the second stanza
- how you might react if the same thing happened to you

3. What do you think the poet means by "a wing grew"?

4. What does the man's decision reveal about the way in which he copes with obstacles?

RELATE **5.** Which poem—"Speech to the Young . . ." or "A Man"—has a more powerful message for you? Which seems more useful? Explain your choice.

6. Which poem do you consider more hopeful? Why?

ANOTHER PATHWAY

Think of a single image that conveys the messages of both poems. Then make an illustration of that image and think of an inspirational slogan to accompany your illustration. Write the slogan below the illustration.

LITERARY CONCEPTS

Alliteration is a repetition of consonant sounds at the beginnings of two or more words, as in "Peter Piper picked a peck of pickled peppers." Poets often use alliteration to emphasize words, to tie lines together, and to give their writing a musical quality. Find examples of alliteration in Brooks's poem. What words and ideas are emphasized by means of the alliteration?

She sells sea shells by the sea shore.

QUICKWRITES

1. Using either prose or poetry, write your own **speech** to the young, based on your own experiences. Offer advice about how to handle some obstacle they are likely to encounter.

2. Reread the words set in quotation marks in the first stanza of "A Man." Then write a similar **quotation** that reflects the man's new attitude in the second stanza.

📁 *PORTFOLIO Save your writing. You may want to use it later as a spring-board to a piece for your portfolio.*

ALTERNATIVE ACTIVITIES

1. Note the words and phrases that appeal to your senses of sight, sound, and touch in these two poems. Then work with a partner to choreograph a **dance** that is a visual interpretation of one of the poems. Perform your dance for the class.

2. Investigate poems having similar themes to the two you have just read. Select several to read on **audiotape,** and play your tape for the class.

ART CONNECTION

Look back to the photograph of the sculpture on page 436. First, think about what the artwork means to you simply as a piece of sculpture. Then, analyze the artwork as it relates to the poem "A Man."

If it were your job to illustrate the poem, describe what you might draw or paint. Discuss your ideas with a partner.

GWENDOLYN BROOKS

1917–

When Gwendolyn Brooks was young, both her parents encouraged her writing. Her father presented her with a writing desk, and her mother excused her from most household chores for the sake of her writing.

In her early poetry, Brooks wrote about the lives of ordinary African Americans, drawing on the experiences of her family and of the poor who lived around her in Chicago. In 1950, Brooks became the first African-American author to receive a Pulitzer Prize (for her collection of poetry *Annie Allen*). Later, she was the first black woman to serve as poetry consultant to the Library of Congress (1985–1986).

Brooks donates money to be given as prizes to winners of poetry contests. She has been Illinois's poet laureate since 1968.

OTHER WORKS *A Street in Bronzeville; Bronzeville Boys and Girls; The Bean Eaters; The Tiger Who Wore White Gloves, or What You Are You Are*

NINA CASSIAN

1924–

Born in Galati, Romania, Nina Cassian is one of Romania's notable poets of the 20th century. Her life, marked by poverty, political struggles, and exile, has not been easy.

At the age of 15, Cassian became a Communist, and her early volumes of poetry reflect her Communist beliefs. Many years later, however, she came to reject these political views.

In 1985, Cassian sought political asylum in the United States, and she has been teaching poetry at New York University ever since. In recent years, she has written five new volumes of poetry. In 1994, she was named a Literary Lion by the New York Public Library for her writing and literary activities.

OTHER WORKS *Call Yourself Alive?, Cheerleader for a Funeral, Life Sentences: Selected Poems*

PREVIEWING

NONFICTION and POETRY

from Lincoln: A Photobiography
Russell Freedman

O Captain! My Captain!
Walt Whitman

PERSONAL CONNECTION

Abraham Lincoln is one of the most famous of U.S. leaders and most respected of men. How much do you know about Abraham Lincoln the president and Abraham Lincoln the man? With a small group of classmates, discuss all that you know. Then share your knowledge with the entire class.

HISTORICAL CONNECTION

In 1863, as the Civil War raged, Walt Whitman wrote, "I have finally made up my mind that Mr. Lincoln has done as good as a human being could do—I still think him a pretty big President." Lincoln held the United States together, preserving the Union when powerful proslavery and antislavery forces risked tearing it apart. Little known when he first sought the presidency in 1860, Lincoln was elected with less than 40 percent of the popular vote. By the time of his inauguration, a number of Southern states had seceded and formed their own government. Six weeks later the Civil War began.

In 1864, after several important Union successes in the war, Lincoln was elected to a second term. A few weeks after his inauguration, the Confederacy surrendered, and Lincoln's focus became bringing the Southern states back into the nation through Reconstruction.

After Lincoln's death, Walt Whitman composed "O Captain! My Captain!" in memory of the president. Whitman had never been formally introduced to Lincoln, but during the war he had written, "I see the President almost every day, as I happen to live where he passes to or from his lodging out of town. . . . We have got so that we exchange bows, and very cordial ones."

WRITING CONNECTION

In your notebook, list questions you have about Abraham Lincoln as a man and as a president, and about his assassination. After you read these two selections, look back at your questions to see which have been answered and which you may want to answer by researching them on your own.

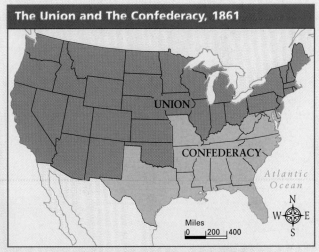

The Union and The Confederacy, 1861

UNION

CONFEDERACY

Atlantic Ocean

Miles
0   200   400

N W E S

LASERLINKS
• *HISTORICAL CONNECTION*

FROM

LINCOLN
A PHOTOBIOGRAPHY

by Russell Freedman

The president's friends were worried about his safety. They feared that rebel sympathizers would try to kidnap or kill him in a desperate attempt to save the Confederacy.

Lincoln had been living with rumors of <u>abduction</u> and assassination ever since he was first elected. Threatening letters arrived in the mail almost every day. He filed them away in a bulging envelope marked ASSASSINATION.

"I long ago made up my mind that if anyone wants to kill me, he will do it," he told a newspaper reporter. "If I wore a shirt of mail,[1] and kept myself surrounded by a bodyguard, it would be all the same. There are a thousand ways of getting at a man if it is desired that he should be killed."

Even so, his advisors insisted on taking precautions. Soldiers camped on the White House lawn, cavalry troops escorted Lincoln on his afternoon carriage rides, and plainclothes detectives served as his personal bodyguards. He complained about the protection, but he accepted it. Thoughts of death were certainly on his mind. More than once, he had been troubled by haunting dreams.

He told some friends about a dream he had early in April, just before the fall of Richmond.[2] In the dream, he was wandering through the halls of the White House. He could hear people sobbing, but as he went from room to room, he saw no one.

He kept on until he reached the East Room of the White House: "There I met with a sickening surprise. Before me was a . . . corpse wrapped in funeral vestments. Around it were stationed soldiers who were acting as guards; and there was a throng of people, some gazing mournfully upon the corpse, whose face was covered, others weeping pitifully. 'Who is dead in the White House?' I demanded of one of the soldiers. 'The President,' was his answer; 'he was killed by an assassin.' Then came a loud burst of grief from the crowd, which awoke me from my dream. I slept no more that night."

April 14, 1865, was Good Friday. Lee had surrendered just five days earlier, and Washington was in a festive mood. Lincoln arose early as usual, so he could work at his desk before breakfast. He was looking forward to the day's schedule. That afternoon he would tell his wife, "I never felt so happy in my life."

At eleven, he met with his cabinet. He had invited General Grant to attend the meeting as guest of honor. Most of the talk centered on the difficult problems of reconstruction in the conquered South. Lincoln emphasized again that he wanted no persecutions, "no bloody work." Enough blood had been shed. "There are men in Congress," he said, "who possess feelings of hate and <u>vindictiveness</u> in which I do not sympathize and cannot participate."

After lunch he returned to his office to review court-martial sentences.[3] He <u>revoked</u> the death sentence of a Confederate spy. And he pardoned a deserter, signing his name with the comment, "Well, I think this boy can do us more good above ground than under ground."

Late in the afternoon he went for a carriage ride with Mary. That evening they would attend the theater with another couple, but for the moment, they wanted some time to themselves.

---

1. **shirt of mail:** protective armor for the upper part of the body, made of small interlocking metal rings.
2. **the fall of Richmond:** the Union capture of Richmond, Virginia—the Confederate capital—in April 1865. This event assured the victory of the North in the Civil War.
3. **court-martial sentences:** punishments decided by military courts.

WORDS
TO
KNOW

abduction (ăb-dŭk′shən) *n.* kidnapping
vindictiveness (vĭn-dĭk′tĭv-nĭs) *n.* a desire for revenge
revoke (rĭ-vōk′) *v.* to withdraw or repeal

441

Courtesy of the Illinois State Historical Library.

The war had been hard on both of them. Since Willie's death, Mary had been plagued by depression and imaginary fears, and at times, Lincoln had feared for his wife's sanity. As their carriage rolled through the countryside, they talked hopefully of the years ahead. "We must both be more cheerful in the future," Lincoln said. "Between the war and the loss of our darling Willie, we have been very miserable."

After dinner, Lincoln and Mary left for Ford's Theater in the company of a young army major, Henry R. Rathbone, and his fiancee, Clara Harris. Arriving late, they were escorted up a winding stairway to the flag-draped presidential box overlooking the stage. The play had already started, but as Lincoln's party appeared in the box, the orchestra struck up "Hail to the Chief"[4] and the audience rose for a standing ovation. Lincoln smiled and bowed. He took his place in a rocking chair provided for him by the management and put on a pair of gold-rimmed eyeglasses he had mended with a string. Mary sat beside him, with Major

---

4. **"Hail to the Chief":** a patriotic song played at public appearances of the president of the United States since about 1828. The words, seldom heard, are from Sir Walter Scott's "The Boat Song"; James Sanderson wrote the music.

Rathbone and Miss Harris to their right.

The play was *Our American Cousin*, a popular comedy starring Laura Keene, who had already given a thousand performances in the leading role. Lincoln settled back and relaxed. He laughed heartily, turning now and then to whisper to his wife. Halfway through the play, he felt a chill and got up to drape his black overcoat across his shoulders.

During the third act, Mary reached over to take Lincoln's hand. She pressed closer to him. Behind them, the door to the presidential box was closed but not locked. Lincoln's bodyguard that evening, John Parker, had slipped away from his post outside the door to go downstairs and watch the play.

The audience had just burst into laughter when the door swung open. A shadowy figure stepped into the box, stretched out his arm, aimed a small derringer pistol at the back of Lincoln's head, and pulled the trigger. Lincoln's arm jerked up. He slumped forward in his chair as Mary reached out to catch him. Then she screamed.

Major Rathbone looked up to see a man standing with a smoking pistol in one hand and a hunting knife in the other. Rathbone lunged at the gunman, who yelled something and slashed Rathbone's arm to the bone. Then the <u>assailant</u> leaped from the box to the stage, twelve feet below. One of his boot spurs caught on the regimental flag draped over the box. As he crashed onto the stage, he broke the shinbone of his left leg.

The assailant struggled to his feet, faced the audience, and shouted the motto of the commonwealth of Virginia: *"Sic semper tyrannis"*—(Thus always to tyrants). The stunned and disbelieving audience recognized him as John Wilkes Booth, the well-known actor. What was going on? Was this part of the play?

Booth hobbled offstage and out the stage door, where a horse was saddled and waiting. Twelve days later he would be cornered by federal troops and shot in a Virginia barn.

The theater was in an uproar. People were shouting, standing on chairs, shoving for the exits, as Laura Keene cried out from the stage, "The president is shot! The president is shot!"

Two doctors rushed to the president's box. Lincoln had lost consciousness instantly. The bullet had entered his skull above his left ear, cut through his brain, and lodged behind his right eye. The doctors worked over him as Mary hovered beside them, sobbing hysterically. Finally, six soldiers carried the president out of the theater and across the fog-shrouded street to a boardinghouse, where a man with a lighted candle stood beckoning. He was placed on a four-poster bed in a narrow room off the hallway. The bed wasn't long enough for Lincoln. He had to be laid diagonally across its cornhusk mattress.

Five doctors worked over the president that night. Now and then he groaned, but it was obvious that he would not regain consciousness. The room filled with members of the cabinet, with congressmen and high government officials. Mary waited in the front parlor. "Bring Tad—he will speak to Tad—he loves him so," she cried. Tad had been attending another play that evening. Sobbing, "They killed my pa, they killed my pa," he was taken back to the White House to wait.

Robert Lincoln was summoned to join the hushed crowd around his father's bedside. Outside, cavalry patrols clattered down the street. Another assassin had just tried to murder Secretary of State William Seward. Everyone suspected that the attacks were part of a rebel <u>conspiracy</u> to murder several government officials and capture the city.

By dawn, a heavy rain was falling. Lincoln was still breathing faintly. Robert Lincoln surrendered to tears, then others in the room began to cry. At 7:22 A.M. on April 15, Lincoln died at the age of fifty-six. A doctor folded the president's hands across his chest. Gently he smoothed Lincoln's contracted face muscles, closed his eyelids, and drew a white sheet over his head. It was then that Secretary of War Edwin M. Stanton murmured, "Now he belongs to the ages."

The funeral was held in the East Room of the White House four days later, on April 19. Afterwards, the long funeral procession, led by a detachment of black troops, moved slowly up Pennsylvania Avenue to the muffled beat of drums and the tolling of church bells. When the procession reached the Capitol, Lincoln was carried inside to lie in state under the huge Capitol dome. The next day, thousands of people, black and white, soldiers and civilians, stood patiently in the rain, waiting to file past the open coffin.

On April 21, a funeral train set out on a sixteen-hundred-mile journey to Illinois, carrying Abraham Lincoln home to his final resting place in Springfield. The train followed the same route Lincoln had taken when he came to Washington as president-elect. It stopped at major cities along the way, so mourners could again file past the coffin. Where it did not stop, men and women with their children stood silently along the route to watch the train pass.

On the night of May 2, the train left Chicago and puffed its way southward through the rain across the Illinois prairie. People had built bonfires along the railroad tracks, and they stood outlined against the glowing red flames at every prairie village and country crossroads as the funeral train passed through.

At 9 A.M. it approached Springfield with its bell tolling. It steamed slowly through the business center and pulled up at the station, where regiments of soldiers and delegations of officials were waiting to meet it. Tens of thousands of people jammed the streets around the station and stood on nearby rooftops. A military band began to play a funeral dirge. All the bells of Springfield tolled. Guns fired a salute. And the crowd fell silent as the train came to a stop.

On the morning that Lincoln died, someone emptied the contents of his pockets and placed them in a box, which was wrapped in brown paper and tied with a string. Robert Lincoln passed the box on to his daughter, who presented it to the Library of Congress in 1937. Labeled "Do Not Open," it remained locked in a vault until 1976, when the string was untied and the paper unwrapped as the library staff looked on.

The morning he died, Lincoln had in his pockets a pair of small spectacles folded into a silver case; a small velvet eyeglass cleaner; a large linen handkerchief with *A. Lincoln* stitched in red; an ivory pocketknife trimmed with silver; and a brown leather wallet lined with purple silk. The wallet contained a Confederate five-dollar bill bearing the likeness of Jefferson Davis and eight newspaper clippings that Lincoln had cut out and saved. All the clippings praised him. As president, he had been denounced, ridiculed, and damned by a legion of critics. When he saw an article that complimented him, he often kept it.

One clipping found in Lincoln's wallet quotes the British reformer John Bright. Shortly before the presidential election of 1864, Bright wrote to the American newspaper publisher Horace Greeley and said:

"All those who believe that Slavery weakens America's power and tarnishes your good name throughout the world, and who regard the restoration of your Union as a thing to be desired . . . are heartily longing for the reelection of Mr. Lincoln. . . . they think they have observed in his career a grand simplicity of purpose and a patriotism which knows no change and does not falter." ❖

Abraham Lincoln lying in state.
Courtesy of the Illinois State Historical Library.

FROM **PERSONAL RESPONSE** TO **CRITICAL ANALYSIS**

REFLECT   **1.** Were you surprised by any aspect of this account of Lincoln's death? Write your thoughts in your notebook.

RETHINK   **2.** Lincoln had always believed that if anyone wanted to kill him, there was nothing he could do to prevent it. Do you think there is anything he could have done? Explain your answer.

3. From this account, what have you learned about the character of Lincoln, the man?

RELATE   **4.** Today, U.S. presidents are heavily protected when they appear in public. Consider what is good and what is bad about tight security for public figures. Should presidents be so heavily protected? Explain your opinion.

O Captain! My Captain!

by Walt Whitman

Decorative sculpture of Abraham Lincoln. Abby Aldrich Rockefeller Folk Art Center, Williamsburg, Virginia.

O Captain! my Captain! our fearful trip is done,
The ship has weather'd every rack,[1] the prize we sought is won,
The port is near, the bells I hear, the people all exulting,[2]
While follow eyes the steady keel, the vessel grim and daring;
5   But O heart! heart! heart!
     O the bleeding drops of red,
      Where on the deck my Captain lies,
      Fallen cold and dead.

O Captain! my Captain! rise up and hear the bells;
10 Rise up—for you the flag is flung—for you the bugle trills,
For you bouquets and ribbon'd wreaths—for you the shores a-crowding,
For you they call, the swaying mass, their eager faces turning;
     Here Captain! dear father!
      This arm beneath your head!
15   It is some dream that on the deck,
      You've fallen cold and dead.

My Captain does not answer, his lips are pale and still,
My father does not feel my arm, he has no pulse nor will,
The ship is anchor'd safe and sound, its voyage closed and done,
20 From fearful trip the victor ship comes in with object won:
     Exult O shores, and ring O bells!
      But I with mournful tread,
       Walk the deck my Captain lies,
       Fallen cold and dead.

---

1. **rack:** a battering, as by a storm.
2. **exulting:** rejoicing.

PRESIDENTIAL ASSASSINATIONS

Abraham Lincoln's assassination, the first murder of a president in the young history of the United States, shook the nation to its core, as can be seen in the excerpt from *Lincoln: A Photobiography* and in Whitman's grand poetic tribute. Over the next 36 years, the country was rocked by two more presidential assassinations—those of James A. Garfield and William McKinley. President Garfield was shot in the back by the evangelist Charles J. Guiteau as he walked through a train station in 1881. In 1901, at a public event in New York State, Leon Czolgosz gunned down William McKinley. The assassin seemed to be waiting to shake the president's hand but was hiding a pistol under what looked like an arm bandage.

It would be 62 years before another president—John F. Kennedy—would lose his life to an assassin. After a government investigation, it was determined that the alleged assassin, Lee Harvey Oswald, had acted alone. Some critics, however, believed that he had been part of a group that planned to murder Kennedy.

These tragedies are only part of the his-torical picture. There have also been numerous unsuccessful attempts on the lives of presidents. The first occurred in 1835, when Richard Lawrence shot two loaded pistols at Andrew Jackson from six feet away; miraculously, neither pistol released a bullet. Botched attempts were also made on the lives of Theodore Roosevelt, President-Elect Franklin D. Roosevelt, Harry S. Truman, Gerald R. Ford, and Ronald Reagan.

Who were these assassins? With the exception of Lincoln's assassin, the actor John Wilkes Booth, they were shy, ordinary people. Most had traumatic childhoods and a history of mental illness. They tended to be loners who nevertheless longed for fame. Most had an irrational dislike of the American way of life and of their victims' political views. Nearly all acted alone.

No one knows exactly how an assassination affects the country, but many historians insist that each killing of a significant U.S. political leader influences the course of U.S. history in a major way. For example, Reconstruction—the reorganization of the governments of the Southern states—might have been very different if Lincoln had lived.

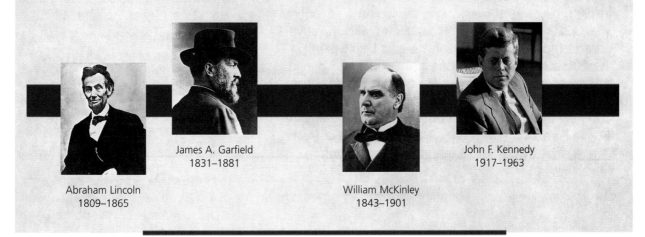

James A. Garfield
1831–1881

John F. Kennedy
1917–1963

Abraham Lincoln
1809–1865

William McKinley
1843–1901

RESPONDING
OPTIONS

FROM PERSONAL RESPONSE TO CRITICAL ANALYSIS

REFLECT **1.** What feeling does "O Captain! My Captain!" convey to you?

RETHINK **2.** In your opinion, how effective is Whitman's comparison of Lincoln's death to that of a ship's captain?

Consider
- what the ship represents
- the "fearful trip" the ship has completed
- how the crowd is reacting
- what is happening on deck

3. How does Whitman use contrasts to heighten the tragedy and irony of the captain's death?

RELATE **4.** Does the excerpt from *Lincoln: A Photobiography* or "O Captain! My Captain!" convey a greater sense of loss to you? Explain your answer.

5. Besides the loss of Lincoln himself, what were other consequences of his assassination? What do you think was the worst consequence of this tragedy?

ANOTHER PATHWAY
Cooperative Learning

Whitman chose to compare Lincoln to a ship's captain. With other students, think of two or three other metaphors for our country, its leader, the Civil War, and the leader's death. Together, try to write a poem that makes use of your metaphors.

LITERARY CONCEPTS

A **biography** is the true story of a person's life, told by someone else. If possible, a biographer usually tries to interview his or her subject. When the subject is no longer living, a biographer relies on letters, diaries, and any other available information. A biographer cannot help presenting his or her subject from a personal point of view—admiring, critical, or somewhere in between—but skilled biographers try to give as balanced an interpretation as they can.

Review the way in which Russell Freedman presents facts in his account of Lincoln. What is his point of view? Do you think he provides a balanced interpretation? Why or why not?

QUICKWRITES

1. Write a **letter** to President Lincoln in which you try to persuade him not to attend the play on April 14, 1865.

2. Write a **character sketch** of President Lincoln based only on what you can infer from the contents of his pockets at the time of his death.

3. Using "O Captain! My Captain!" as a model, write a **poem** about another loss.

📁 **PORTFOLIO** *Save your writing. You may want to use it later as a springboard to a piece for your portfolio.*

RUSSELL FREEDMAN

1929–

A story about Louis Braille, a blind boy who invented the Braille alphabet at the age of 16, inspired Russell Freedman to write his first book, *Teenagers Who Made History*. Since then he has written almost 40 nonfiction books for young people.

In his later books, Freedman has included photographs because of their ability to "reveal something that words alone can't express" and has returned to writing about people. "When I finish a book, like the one about Lincoln, I feel I know Lincoln better than my friends," he has said. Freedman is a three-time winner of the prestigious Newbery Medal.

OTHER WORKS *The Wright Brothers: How They Invented the Airplane, Eleanor Roosevelt: A Life of Discovery*

WALT WHITMAN

1819–1892

The poetry of Walt Whitman was praised by a few critics during his lifetime but denounced by many others. Abraham Lincoln reportedly read aloud from Whitman's *Leaves of Grass*, even though few bookstores carried it. Today Whitman is considered one of the greatest of American poets.

Born on Long Island, New York, Whitman quit school at the age of 11, working at various times as a printer, a teacher, a newspaper reporter, an editor, and a publisher.

Whitman's concern for others has recently been proved. In 1995, four volumes of Whitman's notes, which had been presumed stolen since the 1940s, resurfaced. The notebooks contain notes Whitman took while working as a nurse in a Union army hospital in Washington during the Civil War.

OTHER WORKS *Drum-Taps, Poems of Walt Whitman*

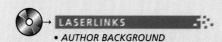

LASERLINKS

• AUTHOR BACKGROUND

NONFICTION

from Gifted Hands
Ben Carson, M.D., with Cecil Murphey

PERSONAL CONNECTION

Think about the responsibilities, the problems, the work schedule, the training, and the income of a doctor. What do you think would be satisfying about being a doctor? What would be difficult about it? Record your views in a chart like the one shown, then discuss them with the class.

Being a Doctor	
Satisfactions	**Difficulties**

SCIENCE CONNECTION

This selection describes the specialized work of Ben Carson, a leading pediatric neurosurgeon (pē′dē-ăt′rĭk nŏŏr′ō-sûr′jən)—a doctor who operates on the nervous system of children. Most of Dr. Carson's surgery involves the brain, the center of the nervous system.

Dr. Carson is the director of pediatric neurosurgery at Johns Hopkins Hospital in Baltimore, Maryland. Children requiring difficult brain surgery, like the removal of a tumor, are referred to Dr. Carson and other pediatric neurosurgeons by doctors who do not have specialized training in this type of surgery. Patients come to Johns Hopkins from all over the country and around the world.

Performing operations considered unthinkable a short time ago, Dr. Carson and his colleagues develop their own techniques for solving difficult medical problems. Sometimes these procedures work, and patients are cured; at other times the procedures fail. From these failures, the doctors often gain new knowledge that will benefit others.

READING CONNECTION

Specialized Vocabulary Medicine, like other specialized fields, has its own vocabulary. Some medical terms in this selection are defined in the Words to Know boxes and in footnotes. The meanings of others can be inferred from the context. The meaning of *metastasized* on page 456, for example, is suggested by the sentence clue "all over." Still others can be figured out from their word parts. For example in *chemotherapy* (page 455), *chemo-* refers to chemicals or drugs, and *therapy* means "treatment." As you read this account of a doctor's professional experiences, look for definitions and clues that will help you with the meanings of unfamiliar medical terms.

chemotherapy

chemical   treatment

LASERLINKS
• SCIENCE CONNECTION

f r o m

Gifted Hands

by Ben Carson, M.D., with Cecil Murphey

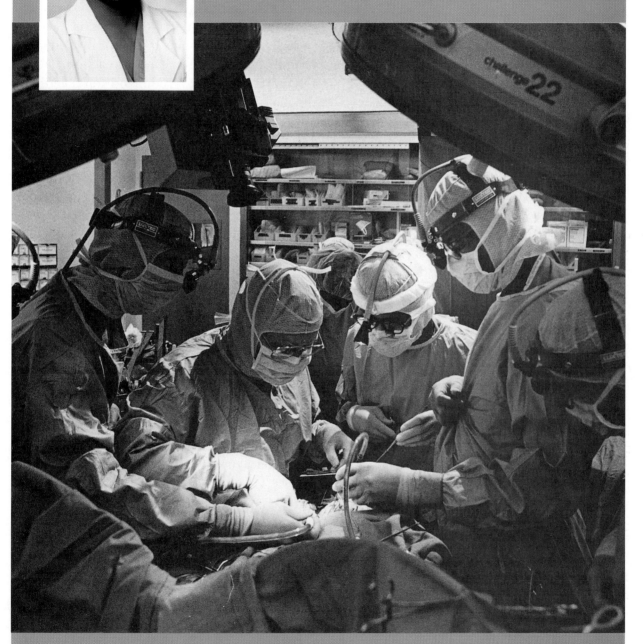

Courtesy of Johns Hopkins Children's Center.

Dr. Ben Carson is an outstanding neurosurgeon. He is famous for successfully performing many operations that others feared to try—such as, in 1987, when he and his team separated twin babies who were joined at the head. Time after time, people have credited him with performing miracles in the operating room on young patients who seemed to be facing certain death.

Three Special Children

The resident[1] flicked off his penlight and straightened up from the bedside of Bo-Bo Valentine. "Don't you think it's time to give up on this little girl?" he asked, nodding toward the 4-year-old child.

It was early Monday morning, and I was making rounds. When I came to Bo-Bo, the house officer explained her situation. "Just about the only thing she has left is pupilary response," he said. (That meant that her pupils still responded to light.) The light he shone in her eyes told him that pressure had built inside her head. The doctors had put Bo-Bo in a barbiturate coma[2] and given her hyperventilation[3] but still couldn't keep the pressures down.

Little Bo-Bo was another of the far-too-many children who run out into a street and are hit by a car. A Good Humor truck struck Bo-Bo. She'd lain in the ICU all weekend, comatose and with an intracranial pressure monitor in her skull. Her blood pressure gradually worsened, and she was losing what little function, purposeful movement, and response to stimuli she had.

Before answering the resident, I bent over Bo-Bo and lifted her eyelids. Her pupils were fixed and <u>dilated</u>. "I thought you told me the pupils were still working?" I said in astonishment.

"I did," he protested. "They were working just before you came in."

"You're telling me this just happened? That her eyes just now dilated?"

"They must have!"

"Four plus emergency," I called loudly but calmly. "We've got to do something right away!" I turned to the nurse standing behind me. "Call the operating room. We're on our way."

"Four plus emergency!" she called even louder and hurried down the corridor.

Although rare, a plus four—for dire emergency—<u>galvanizes</u> everyone into action. The OR[4] staff clears out a room and starts getting the instruments ready. They work with quiet efficiency, and they're quick. No one argues and no one has time to explain.

Two residents grabbed Bo-Bo's bed and half-ran down the hallway. Fortunately surgery hadn't started on the scheduled patient, so we bumped the case.

On my way to the operating room I ran into another neurosurgeon—senior to me and a man I highly respect because of his work with trauma accidents. While the staff was setting up, I explained to him what had happened and what I was going to do.

"Don't do it," he said, as he walked away from me. "You're wasting your time."

His attitude amazed me, but I didn't dwell on it. Bo-Bo Valentine was still alive. We had a chance—extremely small—but still a chance to save her life. I decided I would go ahead and do surgery anyway.

---

1. **resident:** a physician working at a hospital to receive specialized training in the care of patients.
2. **barbiturate coma** (bär-bĭch'ər-ĭt kō'mə): a deep unconsciousness produced by a drug that depresses the nervous system.
3. **hyperventilation** (hī'pər-věn'tl-ā'shən): a procedure that increases the rate of breathing, causing a loss of carbon dioxide in the blood and reducing blood pressure.
4. **OR:** an abbreviation of *operating room.*

WORDS TO KNOW

dilated (dī-lā'tĭd) *adj.* enlarged
galvanize (găl'və-nīz') *v.* to arouse; electrify

Bo-Bo was gently positioned on an "egg crate," a soft, flexible pad covering the operating table, and was covered with a pale green sheet. Within minutes the nurses and anesthesiologist had her ready for me to begin.

I did a craniectomy. First I opened her head and took off the front portion of her skull. The skull bone was put in a sterile solution. Then I opened up the covering of her brain—the dura.[5] Between the two halves of the brain is an area called the falx. By splitting the falx, the two halves could communicate together and equalize the pressure between her hemispheres. Using cadaveric dura (dura from a dead person), I sewed it over her brain. This gave her brain room to swell, then heal, and still held everything inside her skull in place. Once I covered the area, I closed the scalp. The surgery took about two hours.

Bo-Bo remained comatose for the next few days. It is heartbreaking to watch parents sit by the bedside of a comatose child, and I felt for them. I could only give them hope; I couldn't promise Bo-Bo's recovery. One morning I stopped by her bed and noted that her pupils were starting to work a little bit. I recall thinking, "Maybe something positive is starting to happen."

After two more days Bo-Bo started moving a little. Sometimes she stretched her legs or shifted her body as if trying to get more comfortable. Over the course of a week she grew alert and responsive. When it became apparent that she was going to recover, we took her back to surgery, and I replaced the portion of her skull that had been removed. Within six weeks Bo-Bo was once again, a normal 4-year-old girl—<u>vivacious</u>, bouncy, and cute.

This is another instance when I'm glad I didn't listen to a critic.

I've actually done one craniectomy since then. Again I encountered opposition.

In the summer of 1988, we had a similar situation except that Charles,* age 10, was in worse shape. He had been hit by a car.

When the head nurse told me that Charles's pupils had become fixed and dilated, that meant we had to take action. The clinic was especially busy that day, so I sent the senior resident to explain to the mother that, in my judgment, we ought to take Charles to the operating room immediately. We would remove a portion of his brain as a last-ditch effort to save his life. "It may not work," the resident told her, "but Dr. Carson thinks it's worth a try."

The poor mother was <u>distraught</u> and shocked. "Absolutely not," she cried. "I can't let you do it. You will not do that to my boy! Just let him die in peace. You're not going to be playing around with my kid."

"But this way we have a chance—"

"A chance? I want more than a chance." She kept shaking her head. "Let him go." Her response was reasonable. By then Charles wasn't responding to anything.

Only three days earlier we had regretfully told her that Charles's condition was so serious that he would probably not recover, and she should come to grips with the <u>inevitable</u> end. Then suddenly a man stood before her, urging her to give her consent to a <u>radical</u> procedure. The resident could give her no assurance that Charles would recover or even be better.

After the resident returned and repeated the

*For the sake of privacy, I have changed his name.

---

5. **dura** (dŏŏr′ə): the outermost and toughest of the three membranes covering the brain and spinal cord.

WORDS TO KNOW

vivacious (vǐ-vā′shəs) *adj.* full of life and spirit
distraught (dǐ-strôt′) *adj.* extremely agitated
inevitable (ǐn-ĕv′ǐ-tə-bəl) *adj.* impossible to avoid or prevent; certain
radical (răd′ǐ-kəl) *adj.* extreme

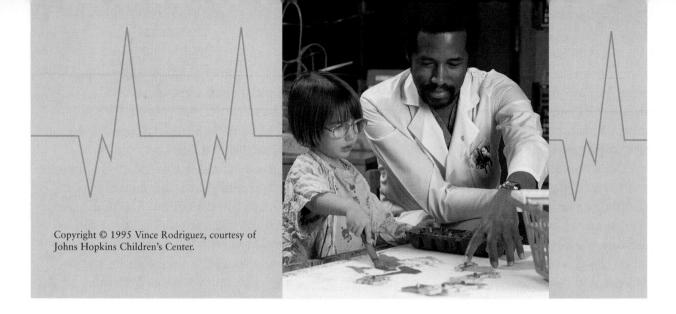

conversation, I went to see Charles's mother. I spent a long time explaining in detail that we weren't going to cut the boy in pieces. She still hesitated.

"Let me tell you about a similar situation we had here," I said. "She was a sweet little girl named Bo-Bo." When I finished I added, "Look, I don't know about this surgery. It may not work, but I don't see that we can give up in a situation where we still have even a glimmer of hope. Maybe it's the smallest chance of hope, but we can't just throw it away, can we? The worst thing that could happen is that Charles dies anyway."

Once she understood exactly what I would do, she said, "You mean there really is a chance? A possibility that Charles might live?"

"A chance, yes, if we do surgery. Without it, no chance whatsoever."

"In that case," she said, "of course I want you to try. I just didn't want you cutting him up when it didn't make any difference—"

Not defending ourselves that we don't do such things, I again emphasized that this was the only chance we could offer her. She signed the consent form immediately. We rushed the boy off to the operating room.

As with Bo-Bo, it involved removing a portion of the skull, cutting between the two halves of the brain, covering the swollen brain with cadaveric dura, and sewing the scalp back up.

As expected, Charles remained comatose afterward, and for a week nothing changed. More than one staff member said something to me like, "The ball game's over. We're wasting our time."

Someone presented Charles's case in our neurosurgical grand rounds. Neurosurgery grand rounds is a weekly conference attended by all neurosurgeons and residents to discuss interesting cases. Previously scheduled for an important surgery, I couldn't be present, but I was told what was said by several who had been in on the conference.

"What do you think?" the attending doctor asked one intern.

"Isn't this going a little bit beyond the call of duty?"

Another one said quite firmly. "I think it was a foolish thing to do."

Others agreed.

One of the attending neurosurgeons, familiar with the boy's condition, stated, "These types of situations never result in anything good."

Another said, "This patient has not yet recovered, and he's not going to recover. In my opinion, it's inappropriate to attempt a craniectomy."

Would they have been so vocal if I had been present? I'm not sure, yet they were speaking from their own conviction. And since seven days had passed with no change, their skepticism was understandable.

Maybe I'm just stubborn, or maybe I inwardly knew the boy still had a fighting chance. At any rate, I wasn't ready to give up.

On the eighth day a nurse noticed that Charles's eyelids were fluttering. It was the story of Bo-Bo all over again. Soon Charles started to talk, and before a month ended, we sent him to rehab.[6] He has made great strides ever since. In the long run, we believe he's going to be fine.

Bo-Bo won't have any seizures, but Charles may. His condition was more severe, he was older, and he didn't recover as quickly as Bo-Bo. Six months after the event (when I last had contact with the family), Charles had still not fully recovered, although he is active, walking and talking, and is developing a dynamic personality. Most of all, Charles's mother clearly is thankful to have her son alive.

Another case I don't think I'll ever forget involved Detroit-born Danielle. Five months old when I first saw her, she had been born with a tumor on her head that continued growing. By the time I saw Danielle, the tumor bulged out through the skull and was the same size as her head. The tumor had actually eroded the skin, and pus drained out of it.

Friends advised her mother, "Put your baby in an institution and let her die."

"No!" she said. "This is my child. My own flesh and blood."

Danielle's mother was doing the herculean task of taking care of her. Two or three times each day she changed Danielle's dressings, trying to keep the wounds clean.

Danielle's mother called my office because she had read an article about me in the *Ladies Home Journal* in which it stated that I frequently did surgeries that nobody else would touch. She talked to my physician's assistant, Carol James.

"Ben," Carol reported later that day, "I think this one is worth looking into."

After hearing the details, I agreed. "Have the mother send me the medical records and pictures."

> "This patient has not yet recovered, and he's not going to recover. In my opinion, it's inappropriate to attempt a craniectomy."

Less than a week later, I examined everything. I realized immediately that it was a dismal situation. The brain was abnormal, the tumor had spread all over the place, and we didn't know how the skin could be closed.

I called my friend Craig Dufresne, a superb plastic surgeon, and together we tried to figure out a way that we could remove the tumor and close the skull again. We also consulted Dr. Peter Phillips, one of our pediatric neuro-oncologists who specializes in treating kids with brain tumors.

Together we finally devised a way that we would actually get the tumor out. Then Dr. Dufresne would swing up muscle/skin flaps from the back and try to cover the head with them. Once that had healed, Doctors Peter Phillips and Lewis Strauss would come up with a chemotherapy program to kill any remaining malignant cells.

---

6. **rehab:** the hospital department where patients are sent for rehabilitation—therapy intended to restore full health.

WORDS TO KNOW

skepticism (skĕp'tĭ-sĭz'əm) *n.* a doubting or questioning attitude
dismal (dĭz'məl) *adj.* gloomy; depressing
malignant (mə-lĭg'nənt) *adj.* cancerous

455

We assumed it was going to be a tough case and would require a tremendous amount of time. We were right. The operation to remove the tumor and to sew in the muscle flaps took 19 hours. We had no concern about the time, only the results.

Dr. Dufresne and I tag-teamed the surgery. I needed almost half of the surgery hours to remove the tumor. Then Dufresne spent the next nine hours covering her skull with the muscular cutaneous skin flaps. He was able to get the skin closed over.

> "We know that you're a man of God, and that the Lord has all these things in His hands."

About halfway through the surgery, I said to Dufresne, "I think we're going to come out of this with our socks on."

He nodded, and I could tell he felt as confident as I did.

The surgery was successful. As we had anticipated, in the weeks following the removal of the tumor, Danielle had to go back to the operating room and have the flaps moved to take tension off certain areas and to improve blood circulation to the surgical site.

Initially, Danielle started to do well and responded like a normal infant. I could see the pleasure her parents took in the everyday motions of babyhood most parents can take for granted. Her tiny hand grasping one of their fingers. A little smile. Then Danielle turned the corner and started going in the wrong direction. First, she had a small respiratory problem, followed by gastrointestinal[7] problems. After we cleared them up, her kidneys reacted. We didn't know if these other problems were related to the tumor.

Doctors and nurses in the pediatric ICU worked around the clock trying to keep Danielle's lungs and kidneys going. They were just as involved as we were.

Finally all that could be done had been done, and she died. We did an autopsy, and we found that the tumor had metastasized all over her lungs, kidneys, and gastrointestinal tract. Our surgery for the tumor in her head was a little too late. Had we gotten to her a month earlier, before things had metastasized, we might have been able to save her.

Danielle's parents and grandparents had come from Michigan and stayed in Baltimore to be near her. During the weeks of waiting and hoping for her recovery they had been extremely dedicated, understanding, and encouraging to us in everything we tried. When she died, I marveled at their maturity.

"We want it to be clear that we don't harbor any grudges over anything you folks did here at Hopkins," Danielle's parents said.

"We've just been incredibly thankful," said the grandmother, "that you were willing to undertake a case that everyone else considered impossible anyway."

Especially I remember the words of Danielle's mother. In a voice that was barely audible, she choked back her own grief and said, "We know that you're a man of God, and that the Lord has all these things in His hands. We also believe we've done everything humanly possible to save our daughter. Despite this outcome, we'll always be grateful for everything that was done here."

I share Danielle's story because not all our cases are successful. I can count on my fingers the number of bad outcomes.

---

7. **gastrointestinal** (găs′trō-ĭn-tĕs′tə-nəl): involving the stomach and intestines.

WORDS
TO
KNOW

autopsy (ô′tŏp′sē) *n.* an examination of a dead person's body to determine the cause of death

RESPONDING
OPTIONS

FROM PERSONAL RESPONSE TO CRITICAL ANALYSIS

REFLECT

1. What is your impression of Dr. Carson and his work? Record your thoughts in your notebook.

RETHINK

2. Why do you think Dr. Carson accepts cases in which there seems to be little hope?
   Consider
   - his reasons for wanting to operate on Bo-Bo and Charles
   - the satisfaction and other personal benefits he gets from his work

3. Recall that the theme of this part of Unit Four is "So Much at Stake." Who or what is at stake in decisions of whether to operate on patients with little chance of survival?

RELATE

4. Examine Dr. Carson's presentation of other doctors' attitudes about the operations he describes. Do you feel the attitudes are presented fairly? Explain your opinion.

5. Difficult cases can force doctors to face heart-wrenching questions. What is your opinion about performing radical medical procedures in cases that seem hopeless?

ANOTHER PATHWAY

Imagine that you are part of a committee that will be nominating candidates for an Outstanding Physician of the Year Award. List the contributions to the medical profession that make Dr. Carson worthy of the award. Include examples from the selection.

Outstanding Physician of the Year

is hereby awarded to _____
on this, the ___th day of _____.

QUICKWRITES

1. Write a **letter to the editor** of your local newspaper, in which you either defend or oppose doctors who perform surgery in cases that appear to be hopeless.

2. Write a **diary entry** that one of the parents in this selection might have written after Dr. Carson performed surgery on his or her child.

📁 *PORTFOLIO Save your writing. You may want to use it later as a springboard to a piece for your portfolio.*

LITERARY CONCEPTS

An **autobiography,** like other kinds of nonfiction, usually contains both facts, or statements that can be proved, and opinions, or statements that express the writer's beliefs and cannot be proved. Because an autobiographer is writing about his or her own beliefs, he or she might state as a fact something that a reader might view as an opinion, such as "We had a chance to save her life." Look for apparent statements of fact in this selection. Which may really be opinions? How might someone else state a conflicting opinion?

CONCEPT REVIEW: Author's Purpose Authors write with specific purposes. What do you think was Ben Carson's purpose for writing about these three patients?

ALTERNATIVE ACTIVITIES

Cooperative Learning Imagine that a television series is being produced about the life of Dr. Ben Carson. With a small group of classmates, create a **sneak preview** of the first episode of the series by acting out a few events related to one of the three cases discussed in this selection. You may wish to videotape your sneak preview. Share your production with the class.

ACROSS THE CURRICULUM

Science Much brain research is being done currently, and the results of this research are reported in newspapers, magazines, and television programs. Use electronic resources or library resources to investigate one recent discovery about the brain, and then share your findings with the class.

WORDS TO KNOW

Review the Words to Know at the bottom of the selection pages, and list them on your paper. Then choose the best word to fill each blank in the following paragraph. Use each word only once.

The seriously ill boy __(1)__ the OR staff into action. One sign of his condition was his __(2)__ pupils. The patient's physicians had given a discouraging, __(3)__ medical report. Even the chief of surgery was showing great __(4)__. The boy had a __(5)__ tumor growing in his brain, and unless a __(6)__ operation was performed immediately, he would probably not survive.

As the staff prepared the boy for surgery, his __(7)__ parents stayed beside him. The surgeon thought that death was probably __(8)__. If the boy died, he thought, an __(9)__ would reveal the exact cause of death.

Miraculously, the operation was a success. In a few months, the little boy was his __(10)__ self once again.

BEN CARSON, M.D.

1951–

Ben Carson grew up poor in inner-city Detroit. When he began failing subjects in school as a young boy, his mother, Sonya Carson, gave him the inspiration and direction to make something of himself. She repeated to him over and over, "Bennie, you can do it. Don't stop believing that for one second." She turned off the television set and made her boys read two books a week. Not only did Ben's grades quickly improve; he began a path of increasing success. He graduated third in his high school class and won a scholarship to Yale University.

About the time he entered medical school, Carson realized he had "an unusual ability—a divine gift of extraordinary eye and hand coordination."

One of his most difficult cases required him to use his hands for 22 hours in order to separate conjoined twins who were attached at the back of the head. "I've adopted the philosophy that if somebody is going to die if we don't do something, we have nothing to lose by trying," he has said.

Carson, who has been profiled on ABC's *20/20,* struggles to balance his demanding career with the many other aspects of his full life. He devotes time to his wife, Candy, and their three sons as well as his church. He also enjoys giving inspirational talks to young African-American students all over the country.

LASERLINKS
• *AUTHOR BACKGROUND*

PREVIEWING

DRAMA

Survival
Alfred Brenner

PERSONAL CONNECTION

Television courtroom dramas are often popular. In the same way, major real-life trials are highly newsworthy and can keep Americans glued to their television sets for months at a time. Why do you suppose people are so fascinated with both real-life and fictitious legal battles? Do they fascinate you? Why or why not? As you read this drama, decide how much like a real court case you think it is.

SOCIAL STUDIES CONNECTION

Survival is based on a real court case tried 150 years ago. The legal terms used in it are the same as those used today. The **prosecution,** representing the United States, brings the criminal charge of **manslaughter**— murder without the intent of injury—against Holmes. It is the job of the prosecution to convince the jury that Holmes is guilty. Holmes—the **defendant** or **accused**—has an attorney who attempts to establish his innocence.

In a criminal trial, the attorneys on both sides make **opening statements.** Next, each side presents witnesses. The opposing attorney is allowed to **cross-examine** each witness in an attempt to find mistakes in the witness's testimony. Each side is also permitted to **object** to what the other side presents. The judge responds to an objection either by **overruling** it, allowing what has been presented to remain as part of the record, or by **sustaining** it, disallowing what has been said or shown.

The prosecution and the defense **rest** their cases when they have presented all of their evidence. Each may then choose to review the issues in a **summation** before the members of the jury make their decision.

READING CONNECTION

Reading a Teleplay Because *Survival* was written as a television play, the script includes a number of camera and film-editing directions. The chart below explains some key camera and film-editing terms used in the play.

Camera and Film-Editing Terminology	
Fade in/ fade out	A picture, with accompanying sounds, comes in slowly from black or goes out slowly to black.
Over	A picture or sound fades in over another picture or sound continuing in the background.
Pans away	The camera turns to show other characters or another part of the scene.
Cut to	A picture is abruptly replaced by another picture.
Dissolve to	A picture fades out at the same time that the next picture fades in.
Super (superimpose)	One picture is briefly shown on top of another one.
Hit film	One filmed sequence instantly replaces another.

LASERLINKS
- *READING CONNECTION*
- *VISUAL VOCABULARY*

Survival

by Alfred Brenner

CAST OF CHARACTERS

Narrator

David Holmes

Landlady

Policeman

Pat Askin

Armstrong

Clerk

Judge

Dallas

Frank Askin

Mary O'Brien

Thomas Able

Lorna Quinn

Steno

Captain Amos Tilton

Mrs. Reston

Foreman of the Jury

ACT ONE

Fade In:

A street in Philadelphia near the waterfront, 1842. A single street lamp drops a vague puddle of light on the cobbles. All we can see are the fronts of several buildings, some barrels, a coil of rope. David Holmes, a thick heavy-set seaman with hard obsessed eyes, about 30, carrying a seabag over his shoulder, is walking slowly along buildings.

Narrator. This story is based upon a real case. It was tried in the U.S. Circuit Court in the City of Philadelphia, on the 13th of April, 1842. It bears the title U.S. versus Holmes.

(Holmes halts abruptly at the door of a house over which hangs a sign:

The Jolly Rest

Rooms for Seamen

and Their Guests

He knocks on door. We hear footsteps within, a rusty lock turn; then door opens a crack and we see a landlady in nightdress, holding a candle, peering out suspiciously.)

Landlady (*looking him up and down*). Rent's two dollars a week . . . in advance. . . . (Holmes *reaches for his money bag, takes out several coins, drops them into her hand. She counts them quickly, glances up at him again.*) This way . . . (*He enters a vestibule, follows her a few steps to a door. She opens it, goes into a small* dingy *room containing a bolster bed, small table and chair. He steps in after her.*) You just come off ship? (*He nods.*) What's yer name?

Holmes (*throwing bag down, feeling bed*). Holmes . . .

Landlady (*scrutinizing him carefully*). Say, you ain't the one who brought in that longboat, saved all them women? (Holmes *glances at her swiftly, rigid, tense.*) Wait'll I tell Mrs. Brannigan I got a *hero* boardin' with me. . . .

Holmes (*leaping toward her, grabbing her throat, hissing*). You don't tell nobody who you got! Nobody! (*He slowly drops his hands. They stare at each other. An awkward silence. Suddenly she turns on her heel, leaves. He stands there, staring after her, exhausted. Abruptly he shakes it off, bends down beside his seabag, opens it, takes out several sheets of paper, pen, ink, goes to chest, sits down and begins to write. He writes slowly, painfully. There is no sound except the scratching of the pen. Camera pans away from him, moves slowly around the room.*)

Dissolve to: Holmes *slumped across desk, asleep. A partially addressed envelope is lying beside him. A shaft of sunlight lights up his face. It is morning. There is a knock on the door. His eyes open. He jerks up, suddenly awake, springs to his feet.*

Holmes. Who is it? (*Door opens. Two policemen, followed by landlady, enter.*)

First Policeman. David Holmes, we have a warrant for your arrest. . . . (*grabs Holmes' arm*)

Holmes (*jerks away rigidly*). Take your hands off me!

(He walks toward door erectly, almost proudly, exits. Policemen follow him out quickly. Landlady glances around room, notices something on the table. The letter Holmes wrote is still there. She picks up the envelope, looks at it.)

Cut to: Closeup of envelope. We read the name "Pat Askin" on it.

Dissolve to: Pat Askin, *an attractive girl in her*

ahead. We are able to distinguish the name, "William Brown," printed on the side of the craft near the bow.

Armstrong (*glancing at* Holmes). Exhibit A for the prosecution. (*He leads* Holmes *to defense table. They sit down.*) I tried to get a postponement. . . .

Holmes (*bristling*). Who said I wanted a postponement?

Armstrong. If I did everything you wanted, Holmes, there'd be a noose around your neck right now.

Holmes. I'm gonna plead guilty.

Armstrong. No!

Holmes (*defiantly*). I did everything they said I did! I'm not gonna deny it. Armstrong, you didn't have to come all the way down here from Boston to defend me. . . . Why did you?

Armstrong. I'm not sure. Maybe it's because I've never seen Philadelphia before. (*Pat Askin is coming down the aisle.*) Holmes, why don't you stop fighting me?

Holmes (*snapping*). I told you the facts—

Armstrong. I understand the facts! What I need to understand is you! (*But* Holmes *is not listening. He is staring out toward spectators.* Armstrong, *following his eyes, sees* Pat. *She takes a seat among six or seven girls in first row.*) What about Pat Askin?

Holmes (*turning on him angrily*). Listen, Armstrong! Why don't you let them sentence me and be done with it? (*The rapping of a gavel interrupts him.*)

Clerk (*calling out*). Oyez! Oyez![1] The United States Circuit Court, for the Third Eastern

20's standing somewhat nervously among a small knot of men and women outside a pair of paneled doors on which is printed:

U.S. Circuit Court for the
Third Eastern District
of Pennsylvania

A buzz of excited conversation rises from the men and women. Suddenly, Pat *sees someone. Her whole body stiffens. The others, following her eyes, turn, stare at* Holmes, *who had just arrived. Beside him is his attorney,* Armstrong, *a well-dressed man in his 40's holding a briefcase under his arm.* Holmes *catches sight of* Pat, *halts, tenses. But* Armstrong *quickly grabs his arm, pulls him through paneled doors, into courtroom.*

Cut to: Holmes *and* Armstrong *inside courtroom coming down the aisle. Suddenly* Holmes *stops, his eyes fixed rigidly on something just*

---

1. **Oyez! Oyez!** (ō′yĕs′ ō′yĕs′): "Hear ye, hear ye"; a call for silence and attention to open a court of law.

bristling (brĭs′lĭng) *adj.* acting in an angry and offended way **bristle** *v.*

District of Pennsylvania is now in session. The United States versus Holmes. Will everyone rise. (*Everyone rises.* Judge *enters, sits at bench. All are seated.*)

Judge. Is the accused ready for trial? (Armstrong *motions for* Holmes *to rise.*)

Holmes (*on his feet*). Yes, sir . . .

Clerk (*reading aloud from paper in his hands*). "In that David Holmes, ordinary seaman, on or about April 20, 1841, did commit manslaughter by unlawfully and feloniously[2] making an assault upon and casting Frank Askin, a passenger, from a longboat belonging to the merchant ship, the *William Brown,* into the Atlantic Ocean, by means of which Askin was suffocated and drowned. . . ." David Holmes, you have heard the charge against you: how say you, guilty or not guilty . . . ?

Holmes. (*A pause. He looks around hesitantly.*) I . . . Not guilty . . .

Pat (*crying out*). He's lying! I saw him! He . . . (Pat *leaps to her feet. She breaks,[3] sobbing. Several other girls move to her side quickly, hold and comfort her. Sounds of excited conversation . . . confusion in the courtroom.*)

Judge (*pounding the gavel*). Order! Order in the Court! (*Noise gradually ceases. He turns to prosecutor.*) Mr. Dallas, the United States District Attorney, will present the case for the people. . . .

Dallas (*rises, steps toward jury*). Gentlemen of the Jury, four months ago an American merchant ship, the *William Brown,* set sail from Liverpool, England. . . . (*His voice fades.*)

Dissolve to: Dallas *from a different angle, still addressing jury. His jacket is open now, and he is loosening his collar and mopping his brow. He has been talking for a while and is beginning to wind up his address . . .*

. . . Although the members of the crew and the mate have all disappeared and have still not been <u>apprehended</u>, fortunately there are a number of witnesses present who were on that longboat, who saw these horrible deeds with their own eyes . . . (*He turns toward women sitting in first row, who are watching, listening intently.*) . . . Why did Holmes do such a thing? I suggest, gentlemen, you will find the reason . . . the motive, if you will— in the character of the man himself. . . . (*We see* Holmes *sitting in his chair, his right hand clenched on the table. He is motionless, expressionless.* Armstrong *keeps glancing at him.*) A man who in a moment of panic exploded, and sent not only Frank Askin, but eleven of his fellow passengers to their death! (Dallas *turns, walks slowly back to his seat.* Judge *looks questioningly at* Armstrong. Armstrong *says something to* Holmes *who does not react. Finally he rises.*)

Armstrong. Your Honor, the defense will not address the jury at this time. (*He is seated.*)

Judge (*looks at him quizzically, then to* Dallas). Prosecution will proceed . . .

Clerk. Miss Pat Askin will take the stand . . . (Pat *crosses up aisle to stand.* Holmes *watches her intently.*) Raise your right hand—Do you solemnly swear that the testimony you are about to give will be the truth . . . the whole truth and nothing but the truth, so help you God?

Pat. I do. . . .

Clerk. State your name. . . .

---

2. **feloniously** (fə-lō′nē-əs-lē): in a manner that constitutes a felony—a serious crime that merits significant punishment, usually no less than one year in prison.

3. **breaks:** is overcome with emotion and unable to continue.

WORDS
TO
KNOW
apprehend (ăp′rĭ-hĕnd′) *v.* to take into custody; arrest

Pat. Patricia Askin. . . .

Dallas (*approaches*). You are the sister of Frank Askin who was thrown off a longboat and drowned in the Atlantic Ocean on April 20th of this year?

Pat. Yes. . . .

Dallas. Were you on the same longboat at that time?

Pat. I was. . . .

Dallas (*points to boat*). Is that the longboat?

Pat. Yes. . . .

Dallas. Miss Askin, did you see the defendant, David Holmes, forcibly throw your brother, Frank, out of *this* longboat and thus cause him to drown?

Pat. Yes . . . I did. . . . (*Murmuring, voices from courtroom.* Judge *bangs gavel.*)

Judge. Did I hear an objection, Mr. Armstrong?

Armstrong (*from far away*). What . . . ? No . . . Your Honor . . .

Judge (*to* Dallas). Proceed . . .

Dallas (*to* Pat). You and Frank were not the only passengers aboard the ship, the *William Brown*, were you, Miss Askin?

Pat. No . . . there were about thirty others emigrating with us. . . .

Dallas. Where were you coming from?

Pat. Ireland.

Dallas. Why did you decide to come to America?

Pat. Well . . . it was the famine . . . my father died. . . . Frank and I decided to sell our little plot and seek a better life in this country.

Dallas. Miss Askin, please tell the court what happened on the night of April 19th.

Pat. An iceberg hit the ship. . . .

Dallas. Would you describe the circumstances. . . .

Pat. Well, I was asleep when it happened. When I opened my eyes, everyone was in their nightclothes screaming . . . someone was yelling: "On deck! Into the boats!" We piled up the hatchway with the seas crashing down. Some climbed into the little jollyboat.[4] But most of us got into the longboat. . . . Soon after the two boats were lowered into the sea, the ship went down. . . .

Dallas. Miss Askin, I am now going to ask you to step down from the stand and get into the longboat, taking the exact position you were in that night. . . . (Dallas *begins to help her out of stand.*)

Judge. One moment—would the prosecutor please explain the purpose of his procedure?

Dallas. If it please the Court. It is necessary to indicate Miss Askin's position in the boat in order to show that she could see what was going on. . . .

Judge. You may proceed. . . . (Dallas *leads* Pat *to longboat, helps her inside.*)

Dallas. Is this where you were sitting?

Pat. Yes.

Dallas. What were you doing?

Pat. Bailing[5] . . .

Dallas (*over*). Bailing? There was water in the boat?

Pat. Oh, a great deal.

(*Super: Film, sound of sea, winds up.*)

Pat (*continued*). Besides, we had sprung a leak. . . . My clothes were soaked and I was exhausted. My brother was sitting in front of me. Then I saw Holmes. Beside him were two seamen. He had a terrible look as he faced my brother. (*We are in close, can almost see what* Pat *is describing.*) Frank asked him what was happening. For a moment there was no reply—

---

4. **jollyboat:** a ship's small boat, used for minor tasks.

5. **bailing:** removing water from a boat by repeatedly filling a container and emptying it over the side.

then Holmes took my brother by the shoulders and said, "It's your turn, Frank. You've got to go." (*There is a look of horror on* Frank's *face.*) Then they threw my brother over the side. (*She screams.*) Leave him be! Leave him be! (*We are in for a closeup of her face.*)

(*Sound of storm down and out. We hear nothing but* Pat's *sobbing. Lights come up on* Dallas *in courtroom.*)

Dallas. On that night, your brother as well as other male passengers were thrown over— Miss Askin, were any of the *crew* thrown overboard?

Pat. No.

Dallas. No further questions. (*begins to help her down*)

Armstrong (*rising*). You may remain where you are, Miss Askin. You just stated that none of the crew members were thrown overboard. Could you tell me why?

Pat. Well . . . they . . . Holmes said they were needed to row.

Armstrong. No more questions. (*He turns away. Court attendant helps* Pat *down.*)

Judge. Is that the extent of your cross-examination of this important witness, Mr. Armstrong?

Armstrong. Miss Askin will be called as a witness for the defense, Your Honor.

Judge. For the *defense?*

Armstrong. Yes, Your Honor. . . .

(*Judge stares at him, shrugs, turns toward clerk.*)

Clerk. Miss Mary O'Brien . . . (Mary *comes forward, glances angrily at* Holmes.)

(*He is gazing across at* Pat. Armstrong *notices the look on his face.*)

Dissolve to: Dallas *at stand.*

Dallas. Miss O'Brien, was Holmes in command of the longboat immediately after the ship went down?

Mary (*in stand*). No sir, John Widdows was— the first mate.

Dallas. Oh?

Mary. Holmes took over later. . . .

Dallas. Took over? Forcibly? Did he fight with the mate?

Mary. Not right away. But he started to argue with him. . . .

Dallas. What about, Miss O'Brien?

Mary. The direction we was to take. . . . The mate told Holmes to head west for land. . . . Holmes refused. He said our only chance was to head south where we might pick up a ship. . . . Well, sir, that's what we did—we went south. . . .

Dallas. Then Holmes actually took command.

Mary. All night long I heard this voice shoutin', cursin', threatenin'. . . . I tell you, I'm not a shrinkin' violet of a woman, but I was scared of him. . . . He's crazy!

Dallas. Crazy?

Mary. Yes, sir . . .

Dallas. Thank you, Miss O'Brien. . . . Your witness . . .

Armstrong (*rising*). How would you describe a man who was crazy, Miss O'Brien?

Mary. Well . . . out of his mind. . . . You know . . .

Armstrong. Would you say that a man who is crazy doesn't know what he's doing?

Mary. Yes, sir! That's it!

Armstrong. You mean Holmes didn't know what he was doing on that longboat?

Mary. I didn't say that. . . .

Armstrong. Well . . . You said he was crazy.

Mary. Well . . . He wasn't exactly crazy. . . . He . . .

Armstrong. No more questions. . . . (*He goes back to table. Camera stays on him and* Holmes.)

Clerk (*over, calling*). Thomas Able.

Dissolve to: Witness stand. Thomas Able, *a little wizened seaman, sitting there looking at* Dallas *who has just begun to question him.*

Dallas. Mr. Able, how long were you and Holmes members of the crew of the *William Brown?*

Able. Five years . . .

Dallas. At the time of the sinking, where did you go?

Able. In the jollyboat . . .

Dallas. When you heard what had happened aboard the longboat, were you surprised?

Able. No, sir . . . I wouldn't be surprised at anything Holmes did. . . . He's capable of anything. . . . He's like gunpowder, ready to explode at any time. . . .

Dallas. Had he ever done anything like that before?

Able. No, not exactly . . . but, well, he was proud. . . .

Dallas. Proud?

Able. Well, he always had to be the first one up on the crow's nest[6] . . . even during the worst weather. . . . I seen him hanging on to the top of the mizzenmast[7] once with the ship practically layin' over horizontal with the sea . . . and the mast all icy. . . . An' when he came down later, his hands all bloody, he didn't say one word . . . even when some of the men slapped his shoulder and told him he did a nice job. . . . He was crazy!

Dallas (*smiles*). Did you like him as a shipmate?

Able. Nobody likes him.

Dallas. Why not?

Able. Well, he was different. . . . Kept apart. . . . Never swapped a yarn. . . . On shore leave, he never joined us. . . . Never took a drink. . . . I don't trust a man who don't take a drink. . . . Not a seafarin' man . . .

Dallas. Thank you, Mr. Able . . . (*He returns to table.* Armstrong *approaches stand.*)

Armstrong. Tell me, Mr. Able, is Holmes a good seaman? In your opinion?

Able. Aye . . .

Armstrong. A brave man?

Able. Aye, I guess he's got courage, but it's stupid . . .

Armstrong (*sharply*). Would you just answer my questions, please! Now Mr. Able, in all the years that you knew the defendant, did he ever willfully harm anyone?

Able. Well . . . no. . . .

Armstrong. No further questions . . . (*He turns away.*)

Dallas. That's all, Mr. Able . . . (Able *steps down.*)

Clerk (*calling*). Miss Lorna Quinn . . . (Lorna *rises from among row of women. As she does, we see* Armstrong *at defense table making a few notes.* Holmes *glances at him.*)

Armstrong. That Tom Able reminds me of a man I once shipped with . . .

Holmes. What did *you* ever wanna go to sea for? It was a stupid thing to do.

Dissolve to: Lorna Quinn *on stand being questioned by* Dallas. *She is nervous.*

Dallas. . . . Do you actually mean, Miss Quinn, that on the night of April 20th, the night following the sinking of the *William Brown,* you heard the defendant order the crew to throw the male passengers overboard?

Lorna. I even saw it happen. . . . I saw Holmes and two of the crew go up to Riley and they

---

6. **crow's nest:** a small lookout platform near the top of a ship's mast (a tall pole rising from the deck and supporting the ship's sails).

7. **mizzenmast** (mĭz'ən-məst): the mast third from the front of a ship with three or more masts.

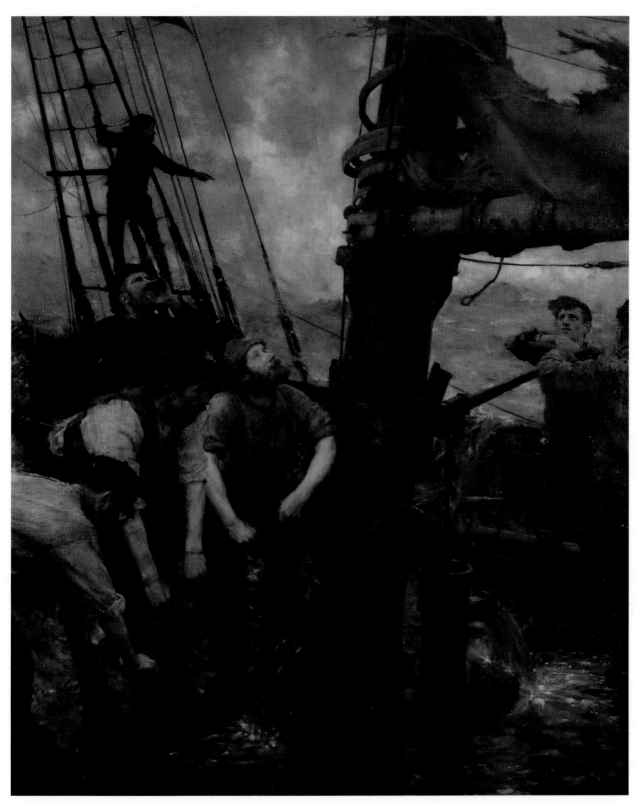

All Hands to the Pump (1888-1889), Henry Scott Tuke. Tate Gallery, London/Art Resource, New York.

told him to stand up . . . and when Riley stood up, they gave him a shove and he went right overboard. . . .

Dallas. How close were you to Riley when this happened?

Lorna. Well, no further than you are from me right now . . .

Dallas. Then what happened?

Lorna. Well, they threw over Duffy next, then Charlie Conlin. . . . Charlie offered Holmes five sovereigns[8] if he'd spare his life, but Holmes wouldn't even listen to him . . . and, well, this went on until every one of the men passengers except Ed McKenzie and Patrick Whelan, were thrown over. Holmes spared those two because their wives were aboard. . . .

Dallas. Are you able to tell the court—from your own observation—how many men were thrown overboard during that terrible night?

Lorna. Well, there was Riley, Duffy, Charlie Conlin, Frank Askin. . . . There were twelve. . . .

Dallas (*turning away swiftly*). Your witness . . .

Armstrong (*rises, approaches* Lorna). Miss Quinn, did you personally feel safer—when you saw that the boat had been lightened by those men?

Dallas. Objection!

Judge. You are placing the witness in an extremely delicate moral dilemma, Mr. Armstrong. . . .

Armstrong. If it please the Court, the defendant was faced with exactly the same moral dilemma.

Judge (*after a pause*). Objection overruled.

Armstrong. Miss Quinn, I asked you if you felt safer—more secure—when you saw that the

boat had been lightened by those. Remember, you're under oath.

Lorna (*almost in tears*). I . . . I . . . don't know. . . .

Armstrong. That's all, Miss Quinn. (*He returns to defense table. She steps down.* Dallas *comes forward.*)

Clerk. Miss Ann Flaherty . . .

Armstrong (*rising*). If the Court please, I understand the U.S. Prosecutor intends to call at least ten survivors as witnesses. . . .

Dallas. That's correct.

Armstrong. The defense <u>concedes</u> that the <u>testimony</u> of these witnesses will <u>corroborate</u> the testimony already heard. . . .

Judge. Mr. Armstrong, you're making a rather crucial concession. . . .

Armstrong. Your honor, the defense does not deny that Holmes was responsible for casting Frank Askin and other male passengers overboard. . . .

Judge (*taken aback*). Oh! (*He studies* Armstrong. *A silence.*) Mr. Armstrong, the Court understands you came all the way down from Boston to conduct this defense. . . .

Armstrong. That's correct, Your Honor. . . .

Judge. You attended college in Boston?

Armstrong. Harvard College, Your Honor.

Judge. Do you have any personal interest in this case, Mr. Armstrong?

Armstrong. Your Honor, the effect of <u>maritime</u> law is felt in Boston as well as in Philadelphia; on land as well as on sea. I believe

---

8. **sovereigns** (sŏv′ər-ĭnz): gold coins formerly used in Britain.

468

that this trial has meaning for all who travel on the sea—seamen and passengers. That is my personal interest.

Judge. The prosecution will proceed. . . . (Armstrong *is seated.*)

Clerk. Captain Amos Tilton . . . (Captain Tilton *lean, hard, tanned, in sea uniform, approaches.*)

Cut to: Armstrong *and* Holmes. Holmes *is tensely watching* Pat. *Then to* Pat.

Dissolve to: Witness stand. Dallas *is questioning the captain.*

Dallas. Captain Tilton, how long were you in command of the *William Brown?*

Captain. Eight years. . . .

Dallas. During her last voyage, how many had she on board?

Captain. A crew of 13 and 39 passengers. Scotch and Irish immigrants, as well as a heavy cargo. . . .

Dallas. What happened when she was hit by the iceberg?

Captain. Well, there was panic among the passengers, sir, but the crew with one exception handled themselves well. . . . The second mate, seven of the crew, two passengers and myself got into the small jollyboat, while the first mate, four seamen and thirty-seven passengers got into the longboat. We in the jollyboat were picked up six days later.

Dallas. How many male passengers were in the longboat?

Captain. Sixteen, sir . . .

Dallas. Captain, you just stated that you in the jollyboat were picked up six days later . . .

Captain. Yes, sir . . .

Dallas. During those six days conditions were extremely difficult. There was the same storm, the same unruly sea as that which the longboat encountered . . . and yet you brought your boat into safety with all aboard?

Captain. Yes, sir . . .

Dallas. Now Captain—had *you* instead of Holmes been in command of the longboat—would you have given the same order—in other words, would you have sacrificed the lives of any of the passengers, just to save your own life?

Armstrong. Objection!

Judge (*quickly*). Overruled! The court considers the captain an expert witness.

Dallas. Well, Captain? Would you have committed manslaughter?

Captain. I . . . no, sir. (*Uproar in court*)

Cut to: Holmes *and* Armstrong *for reaction. Both are deeply shaken. Uproar swells— Quick fade out.*

ACT TWO

Fade In:

The courtroom. No time lapse. Captain Tilton *is in the witness stand. Uproar continues.* Judge *is rapping for order.*

Dallas. Your witness.

Armstrong (*approaches stand*). Captain, in your testimony you stated that the crew with one exception handled themselves well. Please explain the exception.

Captain. John Widdows, first mate . . .

Armstrong (*surprised*). The first mate?

Captain. I would have taken him out of the longboat, but it was impossible due to the storm—the panic and all.

Armstrong. Why?

Shipwreck off Nantucket (1859–1860), William Bradford. Oil on canvas, 40" × 64", The Metropolitan Museum of Art, Purchase, John Osgood and Elizabeth Amis Cameron Blanchard Memorial Fund, Fosburgh Fund, Inc., Gift, and Maria DeWitt Jesup Fund, 1971 (1971.192). Copyright © 1995 The Metropolitan Museum of Art.

Captain. He was a coward.

Armstrong. And so Holmes took over. (Captain *looks down at his hands.*) Captain Tilton, how many people could the longboat normally hold?

Captain. She was built to hold twenty, sir. . . .

Armstrong. And how many were aboard?

Captain. Forty-two.

Armstrong. Captain Tilton, what was the condition of the longboat?

Captain. I felt she was in grave jeopardy, sir. . . .

Armstrong. Captain, based upon your experience, how did you estimate your chances of survival?

Captain. At the time? Not one chance in a hundred.

Armstrong. Were your estimates shared by your crew?

Captain. Yes, sir . . .

Armstrong. When the jollyboat and the longboat were lowered into the water, where did you assign Holmes?

Captain. To the jollyboat.

Armstrong (*surprised*). The jollyboat? How did he get into the longboat? Did you order him to go?

Captain. No, sir. . . . He volunteered. . . .

Armstrong. Do you mean he volunteered to go into the longboat, knowing that he was possibly going to his death?

Captain. Yes.

Armstrong. Do you know why Holmes volunteered?

Captain. No, sir. . . .

Armstrong. Did you have an opportunity to observe the defendant at the time the *William Brown* was hit by the iceberg?

Captain. Yes, sir. . . .

Armstrong. How did he act?

Captain. . . . His efforts to save the passengers were conspicuous, sir. Without him I'm sure more lives would have been lost. . . .

Armstrong. Captain, is it possible that Holmes volunteered to go into the longboat because he thought he could save the boat?

Dallas (*jumping up*). Objection! This is conjecture, suggestion. . . . It is not evidence. . . .

Judge. Sustained . . .

Armstrong. All right. . . . Captain, the longboat did survive . . . despite all the odds against her, and she was picked up eventually. . . . How do you account for this? Would you say it was due to Holmes' seamanship?

Captain. Well, Holmes is a fine seaman. It was very likely due to—

Armstrong (*quickly*). Due to the fact that the boat was lightened?

Dallas (*shouting*). Objection!

Armstrong. I am merely asking for the captain's expert opinion, Your Honor. It is crucial to this case to establish why this longboat stayed afloat.

Judge. It is a reasonable question. Objection overruled.

Armstrong. Captain, in your opinion, was the lightening of the longboat by approximately a ton important to its survival?

Captain. I cannot answer a question . . .

Judge. This is a court of law, not the deck of a ship. Answer the question!

Captain (*grudgingly*). Yes, it was possible. . . .

Armstrong. Thank you, Captain . . . (*He turns away.* Captain *starts to leave stand.*)

Dallas (*rising*). One moment, Captain . . . (Captain *remains in stand.*) Could the longboat have survived *without* Holmes? If he had *not* lightened the boat by throwing twelve human beings to their doom? Was there any chance at all, Captain?

Captain. There are always miracles, sir. . . .

Dallas (*vehement*). Would you answer my question, please! Yes, or no?

Captain. It was possible, sir. . . .

Dallas (*turning away*). No further questions! (Captain *rises, steps out of stand.*)

Judge (*with sarcasm*). Captain Tilton, you may leave the stand. . . . (Captain *hurries away.*)

Dallas. Prosecution rests. . . .

Judge. Is defense ready to present its case?

Armstrong (*rising*). Yes, Your Honor . . .

Judge. Proceed.

(Armstrong *nods to clerk.*)

Clerk (*calling out*). Mrs. Margaret Reston. . . . Please take the stand. . . .

(Mrs. Reston *rises, comes forward.*)

Cut to: Holmes *watching her tensely.*

Dissolve to: Witness stand.

Armstrong. You have a daughter, Mrs. Reston?

Mrs. Reston. Aye . . . Isabel. . . . She's 9 years old.

Armstrong. Mrs. Reston, would you please tell the Court what happened to your daughter on the night the *William Brown* was struck by the iceberg. . . .

Mrs. Reston. Well, she was left behind on the sinking ship. . . .

Armstrong. What did you do when you discovered this?

WORDS TO KNOW   **conjecture** (kən-jĕk′chər) *n.* a conclusion based on guesswork

Mrs. Reston. Well, I was like out of my mind. . . . I cried out for help. . . . And, praise God, one of the seamen, he climbed back on to the ship just as she was keeling over and rescued my daughter. Oh, I'll never forget it. That seaman didn't even know me, yet he risked his life.

Armstrong. Who was that seaman, Mrs. Reston?

Mrs. Reston. David Holmes . . .

Armstrong. Thank you, Mrs. Reston. Your witness.

Dallas. Mrs. Reston, I'm sure there was a great deal of bravery displayed. . . . The question is: Did he voluntarily and feloniously deprive a fellow creature of his life? . . . I therefore ask you: While you were on the longboat, did you see him cause any of the passengers to be thrown into the sea?

Mrs. Reston. I . . . I . . .

Dallas (*glowering*[9]). Well, Mrs. Reston . . . ?

Mrs. Reston. I . . . I . . . Please . . . Please don't ask me. . . . (*She sobs. Armstrong is on his feet.*)

Armstrong. Objection. Is it necessary to browbeat the witness, Your Honor?

Dallas. Your Honor, I would like to reserve the right to re-examine this witness later when she is more capable of answering questions.

Judge. Permission granted.

Dallas. No further questions. (*He turns away. Mrs. Reston comes down from stand.*)

Clerk (*calling out*). Miss Patricia Askin . . .

(*Pat rises nervously, comes forward, takes stand.*)

Armstrong. Miss Askin, when did you first meet the defendant?

Pat. On the *William Brown*. During the first week of the voyage.

Armstrong. Could you describe the circumstances?

Pat. My brother introduced us. . . .

Armstrong. Oh, he knew Holmes then?

Pat. Well, he met him aboard ship, too. . . .

Armstrong. Did he and Holmes see a lot of each other during the voyage?

Pat. Well, yes . . .

Armstrong. Your brother tilled the soil in Ireland, didn't he?

Pat. Yes. Farming was his whole life. His dream was to get to some land in America.

Armstrong. Looking back on it now, doesn't it seem unusual to you that your brother and Holmes should have struck up such a speedy acquaintanceship . . . considering the fact that Holmes is supposed to be such a difficult man to know, that he doesn't mix easily . . . and that *his* first love is the sea?

Pat. David Holmes' first love is *not* the sea. . . .

Armstrong. Oh, no, what is it then?

Pat. Farming. . . .

Armstrong. He told you that?

Pat. Yes. . . . All he wanted was to own a farm. . . .

Armstrong. No one else on board ship was aware of Holmes' attitude toward farming. You must have been quite intimate for him to confide in you like that. . . .

Dallas. Objection! I can see no purpose in this line of questioning, Your Honor. . . .

Armstrong. If it please the Court, I am attempting to show why Holmes volunteered to go into the longboat at the risk of his life. . . . I believe he had a good reason. . . . To understand it, however, it is necessary to understand his relationship with Pat and Frank Askin. . . .

Judge. Objection overruled.

---

9. **glowering** (glou′ər-ĭng): staring angrily.

Armstrong. How intimate with the defendant were you, Miss Askin?

Pat. Well, we used to talk a lot . . . that's all. . . .

Armstrong (*quickly*). You liked Holmes, didn't you?

Pat. I was blind. . . .

Armstrong (*sharply*). Were you in love with him?

Pat (*bursting out*). I didn't say that!

Armstrong. Were you?

Pat. Well . . . I . . . don't know. . . .

Armstrong. Was he in love with you?

Pat. I don't know! Ask him!

Armstrong. He thought a great deal of your brother, didn't he?

Pat. I . . . don't know. . . .

Armstrong. Didn't his actions indicate as much?

Pat. I don't know!

Armstrong. Miss Askin, during the ocean crossing, did you or your brother make any plans for the future in which the defendant was included?

Pat (*her voice low, broken*). I made plans, hundreds of them. . . . What good are they now?

Armstrong. Miss Askin, on the morning of April 21st, the morning after that terrible night in which your brother and the others were thrown overboard. . . . Did you think there was any chance of rescue?

Pat. No, I didn't care. . . .

Armstrong. Would you say that David Holmes—by his own exertions and at the risk of his own life—was responsible for saving that longboat?

Dallas (*jumping up*). Objection!

Judge. Sustained!

Armstrong (*turns away*). No further questions . . .

(Judge *looks at* Dallas. Dallas *shakes his head*.)

Judge. You may step down, Miss Askin. . . . (*She does*.)

Armstrong (*rises*). I call the accused. . . . (Holmes *stands*.)

Judge. Does the accused request that he be permitted to testify?

Holmes (*after a pause*). I do. . . .

Judge. You have the right to do so. . . . You also have the right not to take the stand. If you don't testify, that fact won't be held against you. If you do, you may be subjected to a rigorous cross-examination.

Holmes. I understand, Your Honor. . . . (Holmes *goes to stand*.)

Clerk. Raise your right hand. (*He does*.) Do you solemnly swear that the evidence you are about to give shall be the truth, the whole truth, and nothing but the truth, so help you God?

Holmes. I do. . . . (*He is seated*.)

Armstrong. David Holmes, how long have you been a seaman?

Holmes. Since I was fourteen . . .

Armstrong. Do you like the sea?

Holmes. I hate it!

Armstrong. Yet you have been a seaman all your life. Why?

Holmes. I had no other occupation . . . no money to buy a farm. . . .

Armstrong. Is that your ambition in life? To own a farm?

Holmes. Yes.

Armstrong. Have you ever worked on a farm?

Holmes. My father's farm . . .

Armstrong. Where was this?

Holmes. New York State. Near Albany.

Armstrong. Did you like the life, the work?

Holmes. For me it's the only life. . . .

Armstrong. Why did you leave? (*A long silence.* Holmes *doesn't answer.*) Did you hear my question?

Holmes (*to* Judge). Can I leave the stand?

Judge. Why?

Holmes. I'm not gonna answer these questions! (*Reaction from jury*)

Armstrong. May it please the Court, I beg for an opportunity to speak to my client. A brief delay. Two minutes.

Judge (*raps gavel*). There will be a two-minute pause in the proceedings.

Armstrong. (*To* Holmes. *Sotto voce.*[10] *Angry.*) If you leave the stand now, I walk out.

Holmes. Go ahead!

Armstrong. Holmes, what are you afraid of? A little rough questioning? Or maybe you threw Frank Askin overboard because you were frightened!

Holmes. No!

Armstrong. Well, prove it then! If not to me, to Pat. Answer the questions I ask you before the whole world. (*He walks away from stand.*)

Judge (*raps gavel*). Mr. Holmes, do you intend to submit to questioning, or do you wish to step down? (*There is a pause.* Holmes *looks across at* Armstrong.) You will not have another opportunity to change your mind. . . .

Holmes. I'll answer.

Armstrong. Your father had a farm. Why did you leave it?

Holmes. They took it away from my father.

Armstrong. Why did they take it away?

Holmes (*resisting*). I dunno! (*Then, after a silence, as* Armstrong *watches him, with great effort*) He owed money on it. . . . He never told anybody. . . . He was too proud. . . . When a man came to take it away, my father shot him dead. I saw it. . . . Then more men came and took my father, and they got a rope. . . . (*His voice chokes, remembering.*) I couldn't stand it . . . I ran away. . . .

Armstrong. Where did you go?

Holmes. New York City. . . .

Armstrong. What did you do there?

Holmes. I hung around the waterfront, slept in doorways. . . . One night some men came. They beat me unconscious. When I came to I was in the hold of a ship.

Armstrong. How old were you?

Holmes. Fourteen.

Armstrong. What happened on the ship? Did you become part of the crew?

Holmes. The mate sent me up on the mast the first day out. I couldn't stay there. I got dizzy . . . I fell. Musta been laying on the deck for hours. But them seamen—they just laughed. We were at sea eighteen months and they kept laughing at me. I couldn't do anything right. I hated them. (Holmes *is wound up, talking with difficulty, but getting it out of his system.* Armstrong *steps back, listens politely.*) I made up my mind then I'd show them. . . . It took me a year, two, three . . . I don't know how

---

10. **sotto voce** (sŏt′ō vō′chē): in soft tones, so as not to be overheard.

long. . . . I hated the sea, but I fought it. . . . I fought *them.* . . . I swore an oath to myself that I'd get my father's farm back. . . . Someday I'd return. . . . That's all I lived for. . . . I saved my money. . . .

Armstrong. What money?

Holmes. My pay . . .

Armstrong. What is your pay?

Holmes. Eleven dollars a month.

Armstrong. You mean you thought you could save enough out of that to buy back your father's farm?

Holmes (*triumphantly*). I did! The money is in a bank in New York City right now. . . .

Armstrong. How long did it take you to save that much money?

Holmes. Thirteen years.

Armstrong. Thirteen years? Is that why you never went ashore with your shipmates?

Holmes. I couldn't afford to.

Armstrong. Well, if you had all this money, why didn't you leave the sea?

Holmes. After this trip I was gonna quit.

Armstrong. David Holmes, during the last voyage of the *William Brown,* you became acquainted with Frank Askin. Explain the circumstances.

Holmes. Well . . . I heard some of the passengers one night. . . . I was on the lee'ard[11] watch. . . . Frank Askin was talking about farming. . . . He seemed to know what he was talking about, and he spoke like it really meant something to him. So I sought him out and <u>plied</u> him with questions.

Armstrong. You became friends?

Holmes. Yes. . . .

Armstrong. In the course of your friendship with him, did you often speak with his sister, Pat?

Holmes. Yes. . . .

Armstrong. What was your relationship with her?

Holmes. We got along. . . .

Armstrong. Is that all?

Holmes. We got along!

Armstrong. Did you ask her to marry you?

Holmes. No!

Armstrong. Did you *consider* asking her? (*As Holmes hesitates*) Did you?

Holmes. I considered a lot of things!

Armstrong (*reaches inside his jacket, takes out a letter, shows it to* Judge). Your honor, this has been recorded as Exhibit B for the defense. (*Turns to* Holmes) Have you ever seen this letter before? David Holmes, did you write this letter? Is this your signature? (*shows it to him*) It was given to me by Mrs. Althea Temple, landlady of the boarding house you stayed in on your first night ashore. It is addressed to Miss Pat Askin. Did you write this letter? (Holmes *nods—unable to speak.*) Please read it to the court. (*He hands it to him.*)

Holmes (*choked*). I didn't know what I was doing when I wrote it. . . . I . . .

Armstrong. I appreciate that. Please read it.

Holmes. (*Mumbling, hunched over. After a long pause, reading.*) "Dear Pat. I am going to ship out on the first vessel. I have some money. I want you to have it. Don't think of it as mine. Think of it as Frank's, that he left it for you. . . . Pat I want you to know that I

---

11. **lee'ard** (lo͞o′ərd): a contraction of *leeward,* referring to the side of the ship opposite to the direction from which the wind is blowing.

WORDS
TO
KNOW

ply (plī) *v.* to continue supplying or offering something to

Shipwreck, Robert L. Newman (1827–1912). Oil on canvas, 12" × 24½", New Britain Museum of American Art, Connecticut, Harriet Russell Stanley Fund (1949.13). Photo by E. Irving Blomstrann.

loved Frank, too. I know you hate me, but there was nothing else I could have done. . . . I don't know if he told you . . ." (Holmes *breaks.* Armstrong *takes letter, continues reading.*)

Armstrong. "I don't know if he told you, but we planned to farm together, as partners. . . . I had hoped you would be with us. . . . I am going to ship out on the first vessel. David Holmes . . ." (*Silence.* Holmes *is sitting there, his head bowed.* Armstrong *looks at him gently.*) Thank you, David. . . . Now can you tell the court why you volunteered to go into the longboat?

Holmes (*his voice low*). To save it. Everything I had was on that boat. (*Then crying out in anguish*) I *had* to save it! *And I did.* I did what I could! God, what else could I do? But I had to do it. I *had* to. *I loved them.*

Fade out.

ACT THREE

Fade In:

The courtroom. Holmes *still on stand.* Dallas, *having just completed his re-examination, returns to table.* Judge *looks across at* Armstrong *questioningly.*

Dallas. No further questions.

Armstrong. No re-examination. . . . Your Honor . . . the defense rests.

Judge. You may leave the stand, Mr. Holmes. (Holmes *steps down. There is a pause as* Judge *checks his notes, looks up.*) Gentlemen, are you ready for summation?

(*The* Foreman of the Jury *rises.*)

Foreman. Just a minute! Your Honor!

(*Commotion in the courtroom*)

Judge (*pounding gavel*). What is the cause of this outburst?

Foreman. There's been a mistake in some of the testimony.

Judge (*stern*). Mistake?

Foreman. Your Honor, maybe if you could have a portion of Captain Tilton's and Lorna Quinn's testimony that tells about the number of men thrown overboard . . .

Judge. (*Staring at foreman narrowly. After a long pause, to steno.*[12]) You may comply with the request. . . .

Steno. (*flipping through notes. Reads.*) "Question by Mr. Dallas to Miss Quinn: From your observation, are you able to tell the Court how many men were thrown overboard during that terrible night? Answer: well . . . there was Riley, Duffy, Charlie Conlin, Frank Askin. There were twelve."

Foreman (*quickly*). Now could you read the part where Captain Tilton tells how many men passengers were on the longboat.

Steno. (*Flipping through notes. Reads.*) "Question by Mr. Dallas: How many male passengers were in the longboat? Answer by Captain Tilton: Sixteen, sir . . ."

Foreman. There you are, sir! Since there were sixteen men passengers originally in the longboat, and twelve were thrown overboard, *four* must have survived. . . . But according to Miss Quinn's testimony, only *two* men passengers survived. She said they were not thrown overboard because their wives were present. Well, Your Honor, that leaves two men not accounted for. I'd like to know what happened to them!

Dallas (*rises*). If the Court please, both the defense and the prosecution are aware that two of the male passengers are not accounted for . . . the fact is, no one seems to know what happened to them . . . and it has no bearing on this case.

Judge. Gentlemen, the question you must decide involves only one point: is the defendant, David Holmes, guilty of the manslaughter of Frank Askin? Only Frank Askin. None other.

Foreman. But Your Honor! How can we come to a decision unless the evidence regarding those two men . . .

Judge. You're out of order, sir.

Voice. Your Honor! Your Honor! (*Everyone turns. We see* Mrs. Reston *extremely agitated, coming forward. Suddenly she halts, frightened at the judge's stern look.*) Excuse me, sir . . . I . . . Perhaps I can explain . . . I mean, about those two men . . .

Judge (*narrowly*). Do you know what happened to them?

Mrs. Reston. Yes . . . Yes . . . (*Reaction from the court*)

Armstrong (*rising*). Please the Court! I request that this witness be allowed to take the stand! I have no idea what she will say, but her evidence might have a bearing on this case. . . .

Judge. Any objection, Mr. Dallas?

Dallas. No objection.

Judge. Mrs. Reston, you may take the stand. . . .

Armstrong (*comes forward*). Now, Mrs. Reston, your testimony will bear directly upon the question which is disturbing the jury. . . . It will include nothing else. . . .

Mrs. Reston. Yes . . . (*glancing across at* Holmes *with difficulty*) I didn't say before; I didn't want to hurt anybody—I—but it is gnawing inside me, and I must get it out or I will never be able to look anyone in the face again. It is something I saw. . . .

Armstrong. What did you see?

Mrs. Reston. It was just before dawn (*hit film*)

---

12. **steno:** stenographer—a person who uses shorthand to record testimony during a trial. Today, court stenographers use a keyboard machine that prints shorthand symbols.

after that awful night. . . . I mean the night the men were cast over. The storm had quieted at that moment, and we were trying to rest when I noticed a movement beneath the canvas on the bottom of the boat . . . two of the men passengers were hidden. Their feet were sticking out. I realized that they had hidden during the night to escape being thrown over. Just then I saw that two of the seamen had also noticed them. They didn't know that I was watching. They bent down and struck and struck, and then they threw the two unconscious bodies overboard. . . . (*film out*) They didn't have to do it. There was no need for it any more. Yet they threw those men over anyway. . . . I sat there too frightened to say anything. (*She is sobbing.*)

Armstrong. Thank you, Mrs. Reston. (*He crosses to defense table, sits beside* Holmes.)

Holmes (*shocked deeply*). I didn't know. . . . I didn't know. . . .

Judge. Mr. Dallas . . . ?

Dallas (*rises*). No questions, Mrs. Reston. (*She leaves stand.*) Your Honor, I waive my right to final summation and would like to address the jury now.

Judge. Mr. Armstrong?

Armstrong. Agreed.

Dallas. Please the Court, Gentlemen of the Jury. The act just described by Mrs. Reston is murder—vicious, stupid, unreasonable killing for its own sake. Why did those seamen cast two human beings into the sea, when any necessity for such an act was clearly at an end? Because they had been ordered to kill and because once they started to kill, all sense of <u>morality</u> broke down. They couldn't stop. Who was responsible for it? The prisoner, David Holmes, for it was he alone who made the decision to take the lives of his fellow men! Did David Holmes have the right to issue such an order? Did he have the right to place himself above his fellow men and select those who should die and those who should live? Does any man have that right? Gentlemen, this case does not deal merely with the guilt or innocence of one man. In a sense we are all on that longboat, and at stake is a question of the most profound significance, a moral law. This law holds that *all* men's lives are sacred, of equal value . . . that in a crisis where some men have to die in order to save the rest, the decisions as to who will go cannot be left to the discretion of one man but must be decided upon equally by all concerned. . . . Gentlemen, David Holmes not only committed manslaughter but he broke the moral law upon which our democracy rests! Therefore you have no choice . . . but to find the defendant GUILTY! (*Uproar of crowd.* Judge *pounds gavel, courtroom becomes quiet. He looks towards* Armstrong. Armstrong *rises slowly now, approaches judge and jury.*)

Armstrong. Your Honor, Gentlemen of the Jury. As you sit here in this courtroom judging David Holmes . . . I ask you to look for one moment into your own hearts. What would *you* have done on the night of April 20th? A hundred leagues[13] from land . . . a boat filled with water . . . women screaming, knowing that at any moment all may perish. . . . What would you have done? Debated the moral law and the democratic process? Taken a ballot? As an experienced seaman, Holmes knew there was only one way to save the boat . . . a

---

13. **leagues** (lēgz): units of distance, each equal to 3 nautical miles or 4.8 kilometers.

WORDS TO KNOW **morality** (mə-răl′ĭ-tē) *n.* a set of ideas about right and wrong behavior terrible way. . . . Lighten it. And that is what he did. Considering the women and children first, he gave the order to cast over the male passengers . . . among them a man he loved and admired . . . a man in whom all his hopes for the future were placed—indeed, the very person he had come to save. Can you imagine the dreams which will torment him for the rest of his life? (*Quietly but with rising intensity*) Holmes acted out of duty, because it was his duty to save the boat, and out of love, because he believed human lives to be sacred. . . . And so he saved the majority of the passengers. (*He turns suddenly to face the witnesses.*) Look at them . . . would they be here today if it were not for Holmes? (*Turns swiftly to jury*) How can you declare him guilty?

Fade out.

Fade in slowly: Holmes *is standing before judge.*

Clerk. Gentlemen of the Jury, have you agreed upon a verdict?

Foreman. We have. . . .

Clerk. And how do you find, gentlemen?

Foreman. We find the defendant . . . *guilty.* (*We hear a gasp, a cry from spectators.*) But we recommend mercy. . . . (*We hear murmuring in courtroom.*)

Judge (*pounds gavel*). Order. (*Murmuring dies out.*) David Holmes, you have broken the basic moral law upon which our civilization rests. You have abrogated to your own hands a right which lies only in the people at large and in God himself. Although there are many circumstances of this case which are of a character to commend you to the admiration of this court and indeed to all humanity—the law demands punishment. In accordance with the jury's recommendation of mercy, I hereby sentence you, David Holmes, to six months in prison. Court dismissed! (*Noise in court.* Holmes *stands there swaying. Armstrong comes up to him, places his arm around his shoulder, leads him slowly down aisle toward doors in rear. As they reach doors,* Pat *approaches.*)

Pat (*choked, trembling*). David . . . I understand . . . (*They look at each other.*) Don't go back to sea. . . . (*Pause*) Buy the farm. . . .

Holmes (*inarticulate*). Yes . . .

(Armstrong *takes him off.* Pat *continues to watch until the two men have disappeared down the corridor. Her eyes are wet.*)

Slow fade.

RESPONDING
O P T I O N S

FROM **PERSONAL RESPONSE** TO **CRITICAL ANALYSIS**

REFLECT

1. What is your response to David Holmes? Record your thoughts in your notebook.

RETHINK

2. Do you agree or disagree with the jury's verdict? Explain your answer.
Consider
- what was at stake for the people on the longboat
- the prosecution's argument that one man cannot decide the fate of many
- whether Holmes's actions influenced the seamen to commit murder

3. What is your opinion of the sentence Holmes received? Explain your answer.

4. How would you characterize Holmes?
Consider
- his letter to Pat and his reluctance about the trial
- how he has lived his life and what his plans for the future are
- the motives for his actions on the longboat

5. What, if anything, do you think the women, children, and crew members on the longboat should have done when Holmes began throwing men overboard?

6. How realistic did you find this drama to be? Explain your opinion.

RELATE

7. The traditional, unwritten rule of the sea is that women and children should be protected first in times of crisis. What are your feelings about this rule?

ANOTHER PATHWAY

What are the characteristics of a successful courtroom drama? Think about this question and refer to your notes for the Personal Connection on page 459. Then write a review of *Survival* that might appear in a newspaper the day after it is broadcast on TV.

QUICKWRITES

1. Draft a short **essay** comparing and contrasting the trial in this drama with a trial you have heard about or watched recently.

2. Write an **alternative ending** for *Survival*, based on a different verdict.

3. Some real trials are shown on television as they happen. What do you think of this practice? Write a **paragraph** presenting the advantages and disadvantages of live courtroom broadcasts.

PORTFOLIO Save your writing. You may want to use it later as a springboard to a piece for your portfolio.

In addition to main characters, short stories and plays usually have a number of **minor characters** who interact with the main characters and with one another, moving the plot along and providing background for the story. Thomas Able and Captain Amos Tilton are among the minor characters in *Survival*. As witnesses, they provide different views of Holmes's personality. What do you learn about Holmes from Able? from the captain?

ALTERNATIVE ACTIVITIES

1. *Cooperative Learning* Work with a small group of classmates to present a **performance** of one scene from *Survival*. Each student can take on a different task in the production; some can be actors, while others can work as members of the crew. If you can, videotape the performance, following as closely as possible the camera directions given in the script. Present your performance to the class.

2. Create a **painting** that depicts the *William Brown* striking the iceberg. You may want to include the dramatic rescue attempt, showing the survivors in the jollyboat and the longboat.

LITERARY LINKS

Compare and contrast the murderer in "The Tell-Tale Heart" (page 380) with David Holmes. How are their motives and their behavior similar? Use a Venn diagram like the one shown to explore this and other questions: How are they different? Is one any more or less guilty than the other? Explain your answers.

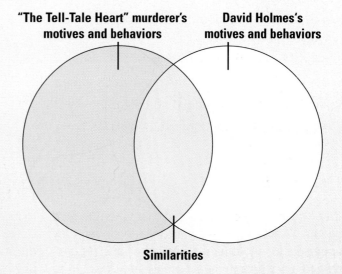

"The Tell-Tale Heart" murderer's motives and behaviors

David Holmes's motives and behaviors

Similarities

ACROSS THE CURRICULUM

History *Cooperative Learning* With a small group of classmates, research life on the sea in the 1840s. Each student can investigate a different question: What kinds of ships sailed the Atlantic Ocean? What were the crews' living conditions? What were their jobs? Present a group report to the class.

Science With a partner, discuss what you know about icebergs. How big do they get? In what seas are they most commonly found? Use references to check your information. Then, if you wish, work together to create an iceberg diorama.

Review the Words to Know at the bottom of the selection pages, and list them on your paper. Then choose the word most closely related to each of the following situations.

1. a person's being caught picking pockets in the ship's mess

2. a bystander's guessing the time when a crime was committed

3. goods' being imported by ship

4. the sailor's insisting that the mutiny was wrong

5. a defense attorney's admitting defeat

6. a ship cabin's falling into long neglect

7. a witness's describing the details of a murder in court

8. a cook's providing the ship's passengers with dish after dish of food

9. a prosecutor's finding another witness to the crime

10. a red-faced captain's responding to a rude seaman

ALFRED BRENNER

Alfred Brenner (1916–) has said that when he read Eugene O'Neill's seven sea plays as a teenager, they "appealed to his romantic and rebellious nature" and had a significant impact on his life. Deciding to become a playwright, he wasted no time. He wrote during high school and at the University of Wisconsin, and his first play was produced when he was only 21 years old.

Struggling to earn a living as a writer for the theater, Brenner turned in the 1950s to the exciting new medium of television, where he found success as a writer of television dramas. He sold scripts to *The Kraft Playhouse; The United States Steel Hour,* on which *Survival* was shown; and other major dramatic programs. When Brenner came across the story he tells in *Survival,* he was intrigued enough to locate the original trial transcript at the New York University Law Library. This drama is frequently produced in high schools and used in college philosophy classes to discuss moral issues.

In 1958, Brenner moved from the East to Hollywood, where there was a greater market for television and film scripts. It was not long before his script *Eddie* won an Emmy Award. Brenner has continued writing television and film scripts and stage plays and has published a handbook for screenwriters. He taught film writing at the University of California, Los Angeles, for almost 25 years. He encourages young people to be writers, saying, "It's a very exciting, very difficult, insecure but wonderful profession."

BATTLE BY THE BREADFRUIT TREE

by Theodore J. Waldeck

Smith and I were anxious to procure motion pictures of a herd of baboons. We had tried and tried, with no success whatever, though we saw many of these creatures.

Our camp was some miles from a little ravine through which a stream ran. Beyond the ravine was a plateau leading back to thick woods. The baboons, scores of them, came out of these woods with their young to play on the plateau, to drink from the stream, and to fight for the favors of the females. Often Smith and I watched them, tried to photograph them, but could never get close enough. The baboons enjoyed what we were doing. They thought it was a game of some sort.

Once we set up the camera at the edge of the plateau in order to take them when they came through the woods at dawn to greet the sun. We didn't even come close, for when the baboons saw us, they charged like a shrieking army of savages. They threw sticks and stones at us, and we fled as though the devil and all his imps were at our heels. A grown bull baboon could have torn either of us to shreds. We didn't even stop to take our camera. We felt sure that our camera would be a wreck when we returned, which could not be until the baboons had retired from the plateau. We went back then, to find it exactly as we had left it. They had not so much as touched it.

"We *must* get those pictures," said Smith, "and I think I know the answer. Those breadfruit trees[1] this side of the ravine. That big one, with the leafy top . . ."

"Yes?"

"We go there now and build a platform, up among the leaves, set up our camera, take blankets, a Thermos bottle filled with hot tea, and spend the night. Then, when they come out in the morning, we'll be looking right down on them."

I saw that he was right, and we set about it. The trekkers[2] got boards from the camp and carried them to the tree. Big limbs were cut off and lashed high among the leaves at the top of the breadfruit tree. Then the boards were laid across the limbs, the camera set up. We had supper, took our blankets, and went to the tree to spend an uncomfortable night; but however uncomfortable it might be, it would not matter if we got our pictures.

Night. We sat hunched up with our blankets over us listening to the sounds of the night. Now and again we dozed off. I'd have a cigarette; Smith would smoke a pipe. Then we'd waken. The wind blew steadily toward us from the plateau, which we could see dimly in the moonlight. The hours wore on.

Finally, animals began to greet the growing morning, though it would be some time, if they stuck to schedule, before the baboons appeared. I sat back on my blanket now—it was already warm enough to do without it—and watched the day break. I never tired of doing that. The sun comes up in a different way in Africa. First the leaves would be black. Then a grayish haze would outline their shapes. Then the gray would lighten into the green of the leaves. Then the sun itself would strike through, and morning would be with us, covering that part of Africa with a mixture of colors that ran through all the spectrum. Sunlight played upon colors like a mighty organist upon the keys, and the keys were everything the sunlight touched; when the dawn was come, it was music made visible. Not just the music that men played, but the music of Nature herself, with all the sounds that Nature used. A great sword of crimson was like a bloodcurdling scream you could not hear because you came before it sounded or after the sound had passed—and the sword struck deeply into the ravine and raised itself to slash across the plateau on which the baboons usually played. The green of the trees was light and like a touch of agony somehow— not the agony of pain, but the agony of an unexplainable kind of ecstasy. Far away and all around were the mounded hills, with the veldt[3] between them, and some of the hills wore caps of crimson or orange or gold, and some were still touched with the mystery of distance or the night that had not yet left them. Whatever color or combination of colors you cared to

---

1. **breadfruit trees:** tropical trees with seedless round fruit.
2. **trekkers:** people employed to carry equipment on an expedition.
3. **veldt** (vĕlt): an open grassland of southern Africa.

mention, you could find there. And they came out of the east in a magical rush, like paint of all colors flung across the world by a painter bigger than all the earth itself.

I sighed and drank it in. Smith was looking out through the leaves, watching for the baboons to appear. Then he nudged me, and I made an end, for the moment, of dreaming. I parted the leaves in utter silence, making sure that my lens was uncovered and aimed at the plateau, and looked through. The baboon herd had not come, but a single baboon and her baby. Smith had not actually seen her coming. One moment he had been watching, seeing nothing. Then he had blinked his eyes, and she was there. He signaled me to start the camera. I noted that the wind was toward us. I felt sure that the rest of the baboons would come, following this one. The mother baboon, while her baby played across the plateau behind her, came down to its edge to peer into the ravine, perhaps to dash down for a drink. I started the camera. It was almost silent but not quite. And with the first whirring sound, which we

ourselves could scarcely hear, though we were right beside it, the mother jumped up and looked around. Her ears had caught the little sound. She looked in all directions, twisting her head swiftly, and even in this her eyes kept darting to her young one. I stilled the whirring. We did not move or make a sound, even a whisper. She was so close we could see her nose wrinkling as she tried to get our scent. But the wind was toward us, and she got nothing. She even looked several times at the breadfruit tree that hid us.

I was about to start grinding again when a terrific squall came from the baby. It caught at my heart, that sound. I know it caught at the heart of Smith, too, for I could see it in his face. The mother baboon whirled around, so fast one could scarcely see the movement. The baby was jumping swiftly to the top of a rock, which was all too low to be of any use to him, as protection against the creature that was close behind him.

That creature was a hunting leopard, and it, like the baboon, had come so softly and silently that we had not seen it. It was simply there, a murderous streak behind the baby baboon. Did the female hesitate for a single moment? Not at all. If the leopard were a streak, so was the mother baboon. She shot toward that leopard and was in the air above him, reaching for his neck, while he was in midleap behind the baby, which now sat upon the rock and uttered doleful screams of terror.

The great cat instantly had his work cut out for him. For the baboon, by gripping his neck from behind, beyond reach of those talons, could break it. And that was what she tried, with hands and feet and killing incisors. But while I knew nothing of this fighting combination, the leopard must have, for he did what any cat would instinctively do in such a case. He spun to his back and reached for the baboon with all four of his brutally armed paws. One stroke across the abdomen of the baboon, and she would be killed outright. But she knew something of leopards.

Smith did not make a sound, nor did I. I don't think we even breathed.

Smith did not make a sound, nor did I. I don't think we even breathed. The great cat recovered himself as the baboon jumped free of the leopard and ran toward her baby. The leopard charged the baboon. The baboon waited until the last minute, shot into the air, allowed the cat to go under her, turned in the air, and dropped back for the killing hold on the back of the neck again.

She got some hair in her mouth, which she spat out disgustedly. The baby kept on squalling. As nearly as I could tell—though

I probably would not have heard even the trumpeting of elephants or the roaring of lions—there was no sound other than the screaming of the female baboon, the squalling of her baby, and the spitting and snarling of the leopard.

This time, when the leopard whirled to his back to dislodge the baboon, he managed to sink his claws into the baboon. I saw the blood spurt from the baboon's body, dyeing her fur. I knew that the smell of blood would drive the leopard mad, and it did. He would just as soon eat the meat of a grown baboon if he could not have the baby.

Both stood off for a second, regarding each other, to spit out fur and hair. Then the leopard charged once more. Again the baboon leaped high, started down, reaching for that neck. And this time, when she came down, the leopard had already turned, and she could not entirely avoid landing among those fearful talons. Even a baboon could not jump from a spot in midair. For a brief moment there was a terrific flurry of infighting, from which came the snarling of the leopard, the screaming of the she-baboon. Now we could see the leopard, now the baboon, the latter trying with all her strength and agility to escape a disemboweling stroke from one of the four feet of the killer. Then both were so mixed up, and fighting so much all over the plateau, that we could not distinguish them. We could tell they were together because they formed a ball of fighting fury, and the sounds of the two animals came out of the pinwheel of murderous action.

How long it lasted I do not know. To the she-baboon and her baby it must have seemed ages. It may have been seconds, even a minute. And then they were standing off, catching their breath, spitting out fur, regarding each other again. Both were tired. To my utter amazement the baboon was holding her own with the leopard. At that moment I would not have known which one had the edge, if either. For both were panting, weary, and stained with blood.

Neither gave ground. By common consent they stood for a few seconds, the baboon on her hind legs, the leopard crouching on all fours. Then the leopard charged. Again the baboon went into the air to let the leopard go under her. She knew better, at this stage of the game, than to run away or jump to either side. The leopard could overtake her if she ran, could turn instantly and follow her if she jumped to either side. So up and over was her only chance. Again she came down. But this time she was expecting the cat to whip upon his back and present his talons, and was ready. She twisted aside a little, and to the front, perhaps with some idea of reaching for the neck from the underside, now uppermost. The forepaws of the leopard lashed at her. The sun gleamed on the exposed talons and showed that they were red with baboon blood. I could see long weals[4] across the abdomen of the baboon. She had evaded those slashes at the last moment, each time. Feeling the talons' touch she had got away, just enough to escape disemboweling, not enough to escape deep, parallel gashes that reached inward for her life.

Now I began to see how the fight was going to go, though neither Smith nor I could have done anything about it because we were spellbound, rooted to our place in the breadfruit tree, watching something that few explorers had ever seen: a battle between a leopard and a baboon! And for the best reason in the world—the baboon to protect her baby.

But now the she-baboon was tiring. It was obvious in all her movements, though I knew and the leopard knew that as long as she stood upright and could see him, she was dynamite—fury incarnate,[5] capable of slaying if she got in the blows she wanted. So far she had not made it.

Now she panted more than the leopard did. She did not entirely evade his rushes, though she jumped over him as before. But she did not go as high or twist as quickly in the air. She couldn't. Her body was beginning to weigh too much for her tiring muscles. She was like an arm-weary prizefighter who has almost fought himself out. But her little eyes still glared defiance, her screaming still informed him that she was ready for more. Now there were other slashes upon her face, her head, her chest, and her abdomen—clear down even to her hands and feet. She was a bloody mess. But she never even thought of quitting. They drew apart once more, spitting fur. They glared at each other. Several times I saw the orange eyes of the leopard, and there was hell in them—the hell of hate and fury and thwarted hunger.

Now he charged before the baboon had rested enough. He was getting stronger, the baboon weaker. His second wind[6] came sooner perhaps, and he sorely needed it. Even yet the baboon could break his neck, given the one chance.

Again the baboon went into the air, came down, and was caught in the midst of those four paws. Again the battle raged, the two animals all mixed up together, all over the plateau. The little one squalled from his boulder, and there was despair in his voice. He cried hopeless encouragement to his mother. She heard, I knew she did, and tried to find some reserve with which to meet the attacks of the killer.

That last piece of infighting lasted almost too long. There was no relief from it, and the nerves of the two men who watched were strained to the breaking point, though neither was aware of

---

4. **weals:** ridges on the skin, produced by blows.

5. **incarnate** (ĭn-kär′nĭt): given form; in the flesh.

6. **second wind:** a burst of energy following a period of exhaustion.

it. How long they had held their breath they did not know.

The two beasts broke apart, and I saw instantly that the leopard had at last succeeded, managing the stroke he had been trying for since the battle began. He had raked deeply into the abdomen of the baboon. The result may be well imagined. The baboon drew off slowly and looked down at herself. What she saw told her the truth—that even if the leopard turned and ran away this minute, she was done.

But did she expect mercy? Death did not grant mercy in Africa—certainly not on this particular morning.

The baboon noted the direction of the leopard's glance. The great cat was crouched well back but facing the rock on which the baby squalled. He licked his chops, looked at the dying she-baboon, and growled, and it was as though he said:

"Not much time now. And when you are gone, nothing will keep me from getting him!"

As if the leopard had actually screamed those words, I got the thought which raced through his evil head. And the baboon got it too. For she turned slowly, like a dead thing walking, and moved to turn her back toward the rock, so that now the baby was almost over her head.

Then she looked at the leopard once more and screamed as though she answered: "Perhaps, but over my dead body!"

The leopard charged again, for the last time. It would be easy now. And as the she-baboon set herself against that last charge, the strangest, most nearly human cry I ever heard went keening[7] out across the veldt. It bounced against the breadfruit trees, dipped into the ravine; it went back through the forest whence the other baboons usually came to play and drink. It went out in all directions, that cry, across the plain. It rolled across the mounded hills. It was a cry that could never be forgotten by those that heard it.

And then, in the midst of the cry—like none she had uttered while the fight had been so fierce—the leopard struck her down. She sprawled, beaten to a pulp, at the base of the boulder, while that last cry of hers still moved across the veldt.

It was a cry that could never be forgotten by those that heard it.

And now, sure that the she-baboon was dead, the leopard backed away, crouched, lifted his eyes to the baby on the rock.

I came to life then, realizing for the first time what I was seeing. I couldn't have moved before. But now, somehow, my rifle was in my hands, at my shoulder, and I was getting the leopard in my sights. Why had I not done it before, saved the life of the mother? I'll never know. Certainly, and sincerely, I had not allowed the fight to continue simply in order to see which would win out. I had simply become a statue, possessing only eyes and ears.

I got the leopard in my sights as he crouched to spring. I had his head for a target. I'd get him before he moved, before he sprang. The baby—looking down, sorrow in his cries, with a knowledge of doom too—had nowhere to go. I tightened the trigger. And then . . .

On the instant, the leopard was blotted out, and for several seconds I could not understand what had happened, what the mother's last cry had meant. But now I did. For living baboons, leaping, screaming, had appeared out of nowhere. They came, the

---

7. **keening:** wailing.

whole herd of them, and the leopard was invisible in their midst. I did not even hear the leopard snarl and spit. I heard nothing save the baboons, saw nothing save the big blur of their bodies, over and around the spot where I had last seen the leopard.

How long that lasted I do not know. But when it was over, another she-baboon jumped to the rock, gathered up the baby, and was gone. After her trailed all the other baboons. Smith and I looked at each other, and if my face was as white and shocked as his, it was white and shocked indeed. Without a word, because we both understood, we slipped down from the tree, crossed the ravine, climbed its far side, crossed the plateau, looked down at the dead she-baboon, then looked away again. One mother had fought to the death for the life of her baby and had saved that life. We looked around for the leopard who had slain her. We couldn't find a piece of it as big as an average man's hand! So the baboons had rallied to the dying cry of the mother baboon.

We went slowly back to the tree, got our camera down, returned with it to our camp. Not until we were back did we realize that neither of us, from the beginning of that fight to its grim and savage end, had thought of the camera, much less touched it.

One of the greatest fights any explorer ever saw was unrecorded. ❖

THEODORE J. WALDECK

Theodore J. Waldeck (1894–) was just a child when both of his parents died. He and his sister were sent from their home in Brooklyn, New York, to live with their grandfather in Vienna, Austria. The grandfather was anxious to have his grandson become a doctor, but Waldeck was more interested in adventure.

When he was 18 years old, Waldeck accompanied a family friend, the Duke of Mecklenburg, on an African expedition. No sooner had they arrived at an African seaport than Waldeck became ill with a tropical fever. The Duke, unable to wait for his ailing friend, continued the expedition and left money for Waldeck to return home when he was fully recovered. However, when Waldeck was well again, he used the money to equip a safari and follow the expedition. "This foolhardy adventure luckily was the turning point in my life," Waldeck once said, "for I became convinced I wanted to be an explorer." Waldeck spent 18 years exploring Africa and leading expeditions. From these adventures came stories, including "Battle by the Breadfruit Tree," part of his book *On Safari*.

With his wife, writer Jo Besse McElveen Waldeck, Waldeck lived for many months among native tribes in the interior of British Guiana, South America (today called Guyana), making friends and learning their languages and customs.

OTHER WORKS *Lions on the Hunt, The White Panther*

SHOW HOW YOU FEEL

As you read the selections in Unit Four, "Facing the Enemy," were you excited? saddened? troubled? all of these? Good writing draws you into the world it depicts. Thoughtful reading allows you to make connections between your reading and your life. In this lesson you will

- see how writers *show* rather than *tell* information
- write a personal response to a piece of literature
- explore ways that people *show* reactions and feelings

Writer's Style: Show, Don't Tell Good writers don't just tell what happens or what something is like. They use details to show action, characters, or setting.

Read the Literature

These writers use details to show a place or character.

Literature Models

Showing a Place
Why are these details more effective than a simple statement telling you that the sunrise was magnificent?

Far away and all around were the mounded hills, with the veldt between them, and some of the hills wore caps of crimson or orange or gold, and some were still touched with the mystery of distance or the night that had not yet left them. Whatever color or combination of colors you cared to mention, you could find there. And they came out of the east in a magical rush, like paint of all colors flung across the world. . . .

Theodore Waldeck, from "Battle by the Breadfruit Tree"

Showing Character
What do Able's examples show about the man on the mast? Why would you see him less clearly if Able said nothing but "He was crazy!"

Able. Well, he always had to be the first one up on the crow's nest . . . even during the worst weather. . . . I seen him hanging on to the top of the mizzenmast once with the ship practically layin' over horizontal with the sea . . . and the mast all icy. . . . An' when he came down later, his hands all bloody, he didn't say one word . . . even when some of the men slapped his shoulder and told him he did a nice job. . . . He was crazy!

Alfred Brenner, from *Survival*

Connect to Life

Feature writers use details to show what real people, places, and events are like. Look at the feature article below. Think about how you respond to this description.

Magazine Article

Now he appears to float the remaining ball across the stage on top of his hands, as if he's nudging a soap bubble. It glides up over his fingertips and into his palm, runs back up one arm, across his chest and down the other arm. He peers at it, and it leaps onto his forehead. He sinks to the floor, puts his hands behind his head and casually crosses his feet, the ball still perched on his forehead. He looks like a man about to daydream beneath his personal moon.

Steve Kemper
from "The Magical Motion
of Michael Moschen"
Smithsonian, August 1995

Showing Action
How does the writer help you visualize what the juggler is doing?

Try Your Hand: Showing, Not Telling

1. **Show a Few Things** Rewrite these sentences so that they "show" rather than "tell" about a person, a place, or an event.

   - Herman was annoying.
   - The beach was beautiful.
   - My party was a disaster.

2. **It's Show Time** Write stage directions for the opening moments of a play set on a city sidewalk. The mood of the scene can be tense, lively, or peaceful. Tell how the main character should act as the play begins.

3. **Show Yourself** Complete the statement "I am . . ." with an adjective that describes part of your personality. Then write a paragraph that shows that part of your personality. Share your paragraph with a group of classmates and let them guess what adjective you used to describe yourself.

Personal Response

If a friend told you that a trip she'd taken was "weird," you might not know what she meant until she gave you the details. Describing your response to something you read is much like sharing your reaction to a real event. Details that show your readers why you responded as you did allow them to share your experience. These details could be from the story you read or from your own life.

GUIDED ASSIGNMENT

Write a Personal Response By writing a personal response you make a connection between the literature you read and your life and experiences. You support these thoughts and feelings with details from the selection.

Student's Prewriting Chart

CHARACTERS
"Battle by the Breadfruit Tree"

LEOPARD
Details
orange eyes
hungry   fierce
"hate"   hunter's instinct
"mad" killer   Impression

BABOONS
Details   Impression
mother
and baby   social, protective
mother attacks   seem more
attacker   like people

I feel like I'm supposed to care
about the baboons more because
they seem more human.

① Prewrite and Explore

Which piece of literature from Unit Four do you remember best? Which affected you the most when you read it? Choose a selection from this unit or one you have enjoyed on your own and had a strong reaction to.

REVIEWING THE LITERATURE

Look at any notes you took while you were first reading the selection. Read the selection again. Pay attention to what you are thinking or feeling as you read.

- What passages really get your attention? Why?
- What are your feelings about the characters, the events, and the writer's message?
- Is there anything in your own life that helps you to connect to this story in a unique way?

Remember that your reaction can be positive, negative, or anything else you want it to be. There is no wrong way to respond when you are writing about how you really feel.

CHOOSING A TOPIC

Try recording your reactions in a chart like the one at the left. When your chart is complete, decide what interests you the most about the literature and what you want to express to the reader about that topic.

② Write to Understand

Freewriting is one way to think more clearly about your topic before you begin drafting. You may not know where your reactions will take you until you write them down.

- How would you describe your overall reaction to the selection you've chosen? What reasons can you give?
- What life experiences have you had that affected the way you responded to this particular topic?
- What lessons, insights, or goals will you take with you?

Student's Freewriting

This writer makes it sound like the leopard is a horrible creature or something. Horrible creature? It's just an animal. When the leopard sees the baby baboon the writer says, "I got the thought which raced through his evil head." Waldeck, hungry is not the same as evil. It's like when Jimmy and I were fighting and the teacher assumed he was the "victim" just because I'm bigger than he is.

The writer makes the story more exciting by creating a good guy and a bad guy.

The weaker one can be wrong too, but the animal world doesn't have right or wrong.

③ Draft and Share

As you draft your response, think about how to organize your ideas.

- Begin with an introduction that identifies the work, tells what it's about, and explains the connections you saw.
- In the body, give reasons for your response. Include details that show why you reacted the way you did.
- Finish with a conclusion that summarizes your response.

 PEER RESPONSE

- How would you sum up my response?
- Which of the connections I made seem the most logical?

SkillBuilder

WRITER'S CRAFT

Achieving Sentence Variety

Varying the types of sentences you use as well as the way they begin will make your personal response more interesting to read. Try these sentence types.

- Simple sentences have one subject and one predicate.
  The leopard charged.
- Compound sentences consist of two or more simple sentences combined with a conjunction.
  The men ran, and they left the camera.
- Complex sentences contain one main clause and one or more subordinate clauses.
  Even after the baboon got tired, she still had the strength to yell.

Here are some ways to vary the beginning of your sentences.

- Use an adverb.
  ***Finally,** a single baboon and her baby appeared.*
- Use an *-ing* verb form.
  ***Spinning around,** the leopard reached for the baboon.*
- Use an adverbial clause.
  ***As they watched from the tree,** the men were spellbound.*

APPLYING WHAT YOU'VE LEARNED
Read over your draft and look for opportunities to vary your sentences.

④ Revise and Edit

Thoughtful reflection, colorful details, and clear organization make a personal response interesting to read. Consider the connections you have made between your life and this literature. Are they connections you were aware of at first reading? How did your feelings toward the story change as you were writing?

Student's Final Draft

The Big Guy Takes the Rap

"Battle by the Breadfruit Tree" is an exciting true story by Theodore Waldeck about a fight to the death between a leopard and a mother baboon. Waldeck and another wildlife photographer visit the African wilderness and watch the fight from a branch in a breadfruit tree. At first I rooted for the mother baboon to defeat the horrible leopard, just as Waldeck did. When I reread the story, though, I realized that turning the leopard into a villain isn't fair. The leopard is fighting for survival, too, just like the baboon.

What background information helps the reader understand this response? What sentences describe the student's response?

Waldeck made me feel for the mother baboon and her baby by describing the leopard as a cold-blooded murderer. He describes the leopard as "a murderous streak behind the baby baboon." However, that's just because the leopard is stronger and supposed to be a better hunter. As a kid who always gets blamed for starting fights because I am bigger than the other kids, I understand that it's not wrong to be strong. Also, these animals don't think about right and wrong.

What details from the story help you understand this student's response?

Standards for Evaluation

A personal response
- has an introduction that gives the title, author, and format of the literary work and introduces the response
- provides enough information about the literary work for the reader to understand the response
- gives reasons for the reaction and supports them with details
- draws an overall conclusion summarizing the response

Grammar in Context

Pronoun and Antecedent Agreement When revising your personal response, make sure that the pronouns you use agree with their antecedents. The **antecedent** of a pronoun is the noun (or other pronoun) that the pronoun is replacing.

> The baboons enjoyed what we were doing. They thought it was a game of some sort.

They is the pronoun that replaces *baboons*. *Baboons* is the pronoun's antecedent.

The pronoun must agree with its antecedent in number. If a pronoun's antecedent is singular, the pronoun must be singular. If the antecedent is plural, the pronoun must also be plural.

> Everyone can have their *(his or her)* own opinion, but when the writer says that the leopard was wrong because it was fierce, they're *(he's)* not looking at the facts. When the baboons came and attacked them *(it)*, they were fierce too.

Try Your Hand: Making Pronouns and Antecedents Agree

Fill in the blanks in each sentence with a pronoun that agrees with its antecedent.

1. When a leopard is hungry, _____ doesn't wonder whom to eat or if it is wrong to kill.
2. The men heard the baby baboon cry, and that's when _____ started thinking baboons were weak.
3. Would a hungry Waldeck feel guilty about eating a chicken, knowing _____ was not human?

For more information about pronoun and antecedent agreement, see page 876 of the Grammar Handbook.

SkillBuilder

G → GRAMMAR FROM WRITING

Using Indefinite Pronouns

Some indefinite pronouns are singular, others are plural, and a few may be either singular or plural. When you are trying to decide what verb form to use, you must first know whether the pronoun is singular or plural.

Singular	Plural
another	both
anybody	few
each	many
neither	several
someone	
Neither wants to give up.	*Both are tired and weak.*

Some, all, any, none, and *most* take a singular verb when they refer to a singular word.

All of my film is lost.

When they refer to a plural word or words, they need a plural verb.

All of the baboons are angry.

APPLYING WHAT YOU'VE LEARNED
Look over your draft to find the indefinite pronouns. Make sure indefinite pronoun subjects and verbs agree.

 GRAMMAR HANDBOOK

For more information on subject-verb agreement with indefinite pronouns, see page 865 of the Grammar Handbook.

SPEAKING WITHOUT WORDS

You know that you respond to what you read in very personal ways. However, do you ever think about how you respond to the people and situations around you? More importantly, do you ever think about exactly what you are responding to? Think about how you would respond if you were part of the event pictured here.

View Look at the scene on these pages. What is each person doing? How would you describe the expression on the dark-haired woman's face? How many other non-verbal signals can you find?

Interpret Decide what each gesture and expression might mean. Be as specific as possible. If you were in the audience, how do you think these signals would make you feel about this politician? How might they affect your reaction to what she said?

Discuss Compare your reactions to those of others in your group. If you were in the audience when this photograph was taken, what might this politician and her supporters want you to believe about her? How might her body language be meant to influence your opinion? Refer to the SkillBuilder at the right for help with understanding nonverbal cues.

SkillBuilder

 CRITICAL THINKING

Interpreting Nonverbal Cues

You may not know it, but you use many forms of nonverbal communication. The expression on your face and the ways you sit, stand, walk, and use your hands can communicate things about you and your message.

Body language sometimes is a truer reflection of someone's thoughts and feelings than words. Body language, however, can often be "read" in more than one way. Can you be sure that your reading is right? You need to be careful of the signals you interpret, as well as of the signals you send.

Some forms of nonverbal communication are standard signals, such as the thumbs-up sign and the V-for-victory sign that are shown here. What about other, less obvious forms of nonverbal communication?

APPLYING WHAT YOU'VE LEARNED

- Observe people in a situation such as a party or a presentation. What examples of nonverbal communication can you find? Are they consistent with each person's verbal communication?
- With a partner, list examples of nonverbal communication. Think of as many likely interpretations as possible. What might influence the ways the signals could be interpreted?

UNLIKELY HEROES

REFLECTING ON THEME

What does it take to act heroically? Sometimes the people who behave most admirably are the people you least expect. Use the activities on this page to consider what it takes to be a hero. Keep a record of your impressions. Later, you can compare them with the experiences of the characters in this part of Unit Four.

What is a hero?

Draw a picture of someone who is "the perfect hero" according to most movies and books. Try to make your drawing humorous, and use labels to point out what is heroic. Then draw the complete opposite— someone whom you would normally *never* expect to be the hero in a movie or book.

How would a hero handle it?

Think of a real-life crisis situation that would require a person to have self-control in order to survive—for example, a situation in which someone witnesses a bank robbery. Work together to create a skit, showing what might happen to someone who loses self-control and to someone who maintains it.

Looking back

At the beginning of this unit, you considered what is at stake when people confront their enemies. Did your ideas change as you read the selections in Part 1? Choose two of the selections and identify the enemies that they feature. What is at stake? How do the characters react? Jot down how you would have reacted under the same circumstances.

Whom would you feature?

History is full of people who rose to the occasion and became heroes. Imagine you are in charge of creating a calendar that features "unlikely heroes from history." Whom would you choose to be pictured each month? Work as a group to create a list of names and vote on your top 12 choices.

Selection

Enemies?

What is at stake?

Reaction

My reaction

FICTION

Playing for Keeps
Jack C. Haldeman II

PERSONAL CONNECTION

What do you know about UFO's—unidentified flying objects? Some people believe that UFO's may be spaceships from distant planets, but others think they have an earthly origin. Discuss with the class your thoughts about UFO's. Before you begin, you may wish to jot down some notes in a diagram like the one shown here.

SCIENCE CONNECTION

If you believe that UFO's come from outer space, you are not alone. According to a recent Gallup poll, almost half of all U.S. citizens are believers. Sightings of UFO's are nothing new, though. As long ago as A.D. 98, ancient Romans reported seeing a round burning shield flashing across the sky. Throughout the Middle Ages people told tales of strange objects and unexplained lights in the sky and on land. Today, UFO's are reported to have frightened animals, caused static on radios, and left marks on the ground when they landed.

In 1947, around the time of a great increase in the number of UFO reports, the U.S. Air Force began an investigation of UFO sightings. When the project ended in 1969, more than 12,000 reports had been studied. It was discovered that in over 90 percent of the cases the observers had actually seen Venus or other planets, bright stars, comets, meteors, strange cloud formations, artificial satellites, balloons, birds, or even insects.

WRITING CONNECTION

Imagine what might happen if space aliens were to invade and take control of the earth. How would they look? What would human life be like afterward? Let your imagination run wild, and write a brief account of such an invasion.

Playing for keeps

by Jack C. Haldeman II

Johnny Russell was playing in his backyard when the aliens landed. He was Tarzan in a land of giant ferns while they invaded Philadelphia, but had shifted over to Superman before Baltimore fell. Johnny was eight years old and easily bored. By the time his mother called him in for dinner, the aliens were all over Washington, D.C. Things were a mess. Ugly green monsters were everywhere. Lots of people were real upset, especially Johnny. They were having spinach for dinner.

Johnny hated spinach more than anything else in the world, except maybe brussels sprouts and creamed corn.

He made such a fuss at the table trying to slip the dog his spinach that his parents sent him to bed early. That was too bad, because there was a lot of neat stuff on television that night. Eight years old is just the right age for appreciating a good monster or two. Johnny slept through it all, dreaming that he was flying his tree house over the ocean in search of lost continents.

His parents, on the other hand, were totally <u>immersed</u> in aliens of the real sort. There was

no escaping them. Even the 24-hour sports network was full of monsters. Specials followed specials all night long. Bert and Sara stayed glued to the tube,[1] afraid they might miss something. It was an exciting time to watch television, even better than the time the dam burst at Fort Mudge. A good crisis brought out the best in the electronics media, no doubt about that.

They watched the national news for a while and then switched over to the local news. They even tuned in PBS and watched a panel of distinguished professors pointing sticks at an alien's picture. It was exciting. Sara made popcorn and Bert put another six pack of beer in the fridge.

"Don't you think we ought to wake up Johnny?" asked Sara, salting the popcorn.

Bert opened another beer. "No," he said. "We've got to teach him not to play with his food. A parent has certain obligations, you know." Bert had always been the strict one.

"But isn't that a little severe?" asked Sara.

---

1. **glued to the tube:** watching television attentively.

Einige Kreise [Several circles] (1926), Wassily Kandinsky. Oil on canvas, 55¼" × 55⅜", Solomon R. Guggenheim Museum, New York, gift of Solomon R. Guggenheim, 1941 (FN 41.283). Copyright © The Solomon R. Guggenheim Foundation, New York. Photo by David Heald.

"After all, he's very fond of hideous beasts."

"No," said Bert. "Remember what he did with the brussels sprouts?"

Sara turned pale. "I thought I'd never get it all out. The air conditioning hasn't worked right since."

"And the creamed corn?"

Sara shuddered at the memory of the bomb squad marching through their living room in knee-deep water. "You're right," she said, passing him the popcorn.

They settled back and watched the early news, the special news, the update news, the fast-break news, the late news, and the late-late news. In between, they watched the news in brief and the news in detail. They were

saturated with news and popcorn and all they got out of it was indigestion and no news at all. Nobody knew much of anything about the aliens except they were crawling all over the place and were meaner than junkyard dogs.

Their silver, cigar-shaped spaceships had simply appeared out of nowhere with a shimmering colorful splash of glitter not unlike the special effects of a once-popular TV show still in reruns. It was horrible. People fled in panic, especially when the monsters started coming out of the spaceships.

The aliens stood about eight feet tall with thick, stocky bodies. Their four arms had too many elbows and not enough fingers. Folds of wrinkled green skin covered their neckless teen heads, and their three unblinking eyes held what could only be interpreted as malice and contempt for the entire human race.

At first it was hoped that they might be a congenial star-roving race of beings, eager as puppy dogs to give mankind all sorts of marvelous inventions. These hopes were quickly dashed. The aliens seemed far more interested in vaporizing[2] people. Helicopters and airplanes that approached the hovering ships vanished in white-hot explosions. People who were foolish enough to make threatening gestures or stray too close went up in smoke. It made for good television footage, but did little to aid any kind of mutual understanding.

Mutual understanding, as a matter of fact, didn't seem to be the aliens' strong suit.[3] They just didn't appear to be interested. Some of the best minds on Earth had attempted to establish communication with the aliens. Some of the best minds on Earth had been vaporized, too. The aliens were obviously intelligent, but they didn't have much to say.

Bert and Sara were about ready to turn in, having watched the instant replay of the destruction of Washington for the fourth or fifth time. It was impressive, but not really all that great. The Japanese had done it better in that movie about the radioactive frog. Sara washed the popcorn bowls.

"I'll bet Johnny will be excited when he wakes up," she said. "Channel Four said they've even seen a couple aliens right here in town. Imagine that."

"I don't think we ought to tell the boy about them," said Bert. "At least not yet."

"For goodness sakes, honey. Why not?"

"The child has an active enough imagination as it is. There's no sense in getting him all riled up. Remember the time he thought he saw that UFO down by the river?"

Sara nearly dropped the bowl she was drying. That had been a near thing. Johnny had pulled every fire alarm in town, and only their friendship with the judge had kept their names out of the paper.

"Besides," said Bert. "What does a kid know about monsters? He's only eight years old."

Sara nodded. He was right, as always.

But Johnny wasn't completely fooled. When little Freddy Nabors didn't show up by twelve o'clock, he knew something was wrong. He and Freddy always messed around together on Saturday afternoon. Sometimes they went on dangerous secret missions, but usually they just played. By twelve-fifteen Johnny had decided a plague must have killed all the kids on Earth but him so he went out into the backyard to play.

He wasn't allowed to go out behind the garage, so naturally it was his favorite place. It was full of old lumber and rusty nails. Lumber was more fun to play with than

---

2. **vaporizing:** turning something solid into a gas; disintegrating.

3. **strong suit:** greatest talent; area of excellence.

WORDS TO KNOW
congenial (kən-jēn′yəl) *adj.* friendly

almost anything. Sometimes he built boats out of the scraps, and sometimes spaceships. Today he built a Grand Prix car.[4] It was low and sleek, faster than a bat. He pretended it was orange with black trim. Since he couldn't find any wheels, he used cinder blocks for racing tires.

Diving into the hairpin turn,[5] he had just passed Fangio and was gaining on Andretti[6] when he saw the monster. Johnny was not impressed. He'd seen better ones on television. Sticking his tongue out between his lips and making a rude noise, he downshifted with a raspberry[7] and pulled to the side of the road. After taking off his imaginary helmet and racing gloves, he got out of his fabricated car and stared at the alien. The alien stared back. Three eyes to two, the alien had an edge; but Johnny never flinched. The Lone Ranger[8] wouldn't have backed down, and neither would he.

In the distance Johnny could see one of their spaceships hovering over the river. It looked just like the one he'd seen before. He knew better than to head for the fire alarms this time, though. His father would tan his hide.

The alien grunted and pointed at his ship and then to himself. Johnny stood as firm as Wyatt Earp,[9] his jaw set like Montgomery Clift's, playing for keeps his body held with the stern proudness of John Wayne. He didn't nod, he didn't blink. He stared at the monster with Paul Newman's[10] baby-blue eyes, hard as ice. He wished he'd worn long pants, though. Shorts just didn't cut it when you were staring down a monster.

The alien started waving all its arms in the air, grunting like crazy. Johnny was frightened, but he didn't give an inch. He could have been Gary Cooper standing alone in the middle of a dusty street facing an angry mob with only the badge on his chest and the goodness in his heart to protect him. Johnny could almost hear the people scurrying for cover. The helmet and racing gloves were useless. He should have had his six-shooter.

The alien kicked at the dust, smoothing out an area between them. He bent over and Johnny hunkered down to join him. At least now he knew what to expect. They were about to talk, or *palaver*, as Slim Pickins[11] would say.

The alien picked up a stick and drew a large circle in the dirt. From a fold in his tunic he removed a small golden globe, which he placed precisely in the center. He pointed to the sun and then to the globe. Johnny nodded, his face as deadpan as if he was trying to fill an inside straight.[12]

The monster drew three concentric circles around the golden globe and placed another globe on the third circle. It was smaller than the first and covered with blue and white swirls. He patted the dirt, waved his arms in circles all around them and pointed to the globe. Johnny bit his lip. This was getting complicated.

The alien continued drawing circles in the dust and setting down the small globes. When he had finished, nine of them surrounded the

---

4. **Grand Prix** (grän′ prē′) **car:** a type of racing car used in an international series of road races over difficult courses.

5. **hairpin turn:** a U-shaped curve in a road.

6. **Fangio** (fän′jyō) . . . **Andretti** (ăn-drĕt′ē): Juan Manuel Fangio and Mario Andretti, famous racing-car drivers.

7. **raspberry:** a rude noise made by extending the tongue and exhaling so that the lips vibrate.

8. **Lone Ranger:** a fictional masked crime fighter of the Old West who was one of the great heroes of radio, television, and comics.

9. **Wyatt Earp:** a famous lawman of the American West in the late 19th century.

10. **Montgomery Clift . . . John Wayne . . . Paul Newman:** movie actors who have portrayed Western heroes.

11. **Gary Cooper . . . Slim Pickins:** movie actors who have appeared in Westerns.

12. **as deadpan . . . inside straight:** as without expression as the face of someone trying to bluff poker opponents.

larger yellow one. With a <u>flourish</u> he took one more from his tunic. This one was special; it was silver and seemed to glow with a light from within. He set it outside the farthest circle and pointed first to himself, then to the spaceship, and finally to the silver sphere.

Slowly he began rolling the sphere into the ring of circles. As he passed the outermost globe, he snarled and crushed it into the dirt beneath one of his massive thumbs. He continued rolling the silver sphere toward the center, snarling and crushing as he demolished each of the small globes. When he reached the third globe from the center, his lips drew back in a hideous sneer and he rose to his full height, towering over the crouching boy. The alien <u>gloated</u>, roaring with bone-chilling laughter as he crushed the small blue globe under his foot, grinding it into the dirt with a vengeance.[13]

This, at last, was something Johnny could understand. It was a challenge. Without rising, he reached around to his back pocket. It was still there, as he knew it would be. He'd won it from Freddy Nabors two years ago and he never went anywhere without it. It was his talisman, his good luck piece. It was also his weapon and had never let him down. He gritted his teeth and took it reassuringly in his hand. It was blue with milky white bands, a perfect agate.[14]

He dropped and took quick aim, <u>oblivious</u> to the ranting and raving of the alien. He'd been under pressure before, this was nothing new.

With a flick of his thumb the aggie sailed across the dust, crashing into the silver ball, sending it careening out of orbit into the yellow one. They both flew outside the circle.

He stood—as a man would stand after battle—and retrieved all the marbles. He held them high above his head.

"Keepsies,"[15] he said and slipped them into his pocket.

The alien backed away in horror, babbling wildly. With a shimmer and a pop, he disappeared. An instant later the spaceship vanished in a similar fashion, as did all the spaceships and all the aliens all over the world.

Johnny climbed back into his Grand Prix car and accelerated through the gears. He was nearly a lap behind by now and would have to do some fancy driving to catch up. Besides, his mother was fixing creamed corn tonight, and the boy who had saved the world had important things on his mind.

As he took the checkered flag he wondered how Conan[16] would have handled creamed corn. ❖

---

13. **with a vengeance:** with a great amount of force.

14. **agate** (ăg′ĭt): a playing marble made of a semiprecious stone.

15. **keepsies:** the marbles won from an opponent in a game of marbles.

16. **Conan:** the hero of a series of stories set in an imaginary prehistoric time; played by Arnold Schwarzenegger in the movie *Conan the Barbarian.*

RESPONDING
OPTIONS

FROM **PERSONAL RESPONSE** TO **CRITICAL ANALYSIS**

REFLECT 1. Do you find this story humorous? Why or why not? Write your thoughts in your notebook.

RETHINK 2. Why do you think Johnny is able to save the world when adults cannot?

Consider
  • what Johnny's parents say about him
  • his interest in television and movie heroes
  • the way he confronts the alien

3. Draw a picture illustrating Johnny's confrontation with the alien. Try to capture the humor of the story.

4. Do you think Johnny knows he is saving the world? On the basis of your answer, do you consider Johnny to be a hero? Explain your opinion.

RELATE 5. Because of their constant television viewing, the characters in this story can no longer tell the difference between entertainment and a real crisis. Do you think television has this effect in real life? Why or why not?

ANOTHER PATHWAY
Cooperative Learning

With a small group of classmates, discuss what aspects (if any) of this story are believable. In your discussion, compare the situations in the selection with the situations you made up for the Writing Connection on page 499.

QUICKWRITES

1. The aliens disappear from the face of the earth at the end of Johnny's "battle" with one of them. Write an **e-mail note** that the defeated alien might transmit to his home planet, telling what has happened.

2. Write one of two possible **epilogues** for this story: either describe what you think happens to the aliens and their spaceships, or predict what happens to Johnny after they leave.

3. What might have happened if Johnny had run away from the alien? Write an **alternative ending** based on this idea.

📁 *PORTFOLIO Save your writing. You may want to use it later as a springboard to a piece for your portfolio.*

LITERARY CONCEPTS

Science fiction is fiction that is based on real or possible scientific developments. It frequently presents an imaginary view into the future while still conveying writers' concerns about problems in present-day society. What makes "Playing for Keeps" a science fiction story? How is it similar to and different from other science fiction you've read? Give examples to support your answer.

CONCEPT REVIEW: Humor By treating Johnny's hatred of vegetables as seriously as the alien attack, the author makes light of the crisis and brings humor to "Playing for Keeps." Find another use of humor in the story.

ALTERNATIVE ACTIVITIES

With another student, rewrite one of the scenes in this story as a dramatic **script.** Present the scene to your classmates as a Readers Theater production.

ACROSS THE CURRICULUM

Science The alien uses small globes to show Johnny the arrangement of the planets in the solar system. Find out how the planets are arranged around the sun. Make a simple model that shows this arrangement and the relative sizes of the planets. Also, see if you can think of a fun phrase for remembering the order of the planets, like

"Mother Very Easily Makes Jelly Sandwiches Under No Protest."

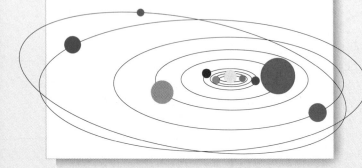

CRITIC'S CORNER

About the end of "Playing for Keeps," Beth Donaldson, a student reader, said, "I loved the way you knew exactly what the alien meant when he was diagramming the solar system, but Johnny didn't." It is often the case that readers of a work of literature know more than the characters in the work. As you read "Playing for Keeps," what else did you know that the characters didn't?

WORDS TO KNOW

Review the Words to Know at the bottom of the selection pages, and list them on your paper. Then choose the word that best fills each numbered blank in the following paragraph.

We were hoping that the aliens would be talkative and __(1)__ so that we could share ideas. Instead, the aliens were hostile. One alien showed his malice toward humans by waving with a __(2)__ the plans to invade our planet. It appeared, from the grin on its face, that the alien was beginning to __(3)__. The media recorded every stage of the crisis, causing the nation to be __(4)__ in the news of the alien attack. The aliens were so confident that they were __(5)__ to our successful efforts to kill their leaders.

JACK C. HALDEMAN II

Jack C. Haldeman II came to science fiction with a scientific background. He had worked as a research assistant and as a medical technician. Haldeman says, "I often draw on my scientific background as well as my sense of humor. Mostly I try to entertain, though I have been known to slip in a message or two.

Haldeman was first known for his stories about futuristic sports events, a rare theme in science fiction. "Louisville Slugger" describes a baseball game that decides the future of humankind. In

1941–

"The Thrill of Victory" and its sequel "The Agony of Defeat" a robotic football team, illegally programmed with the will to win, plays a championship game against genetically altered beings.

Occasionally, Haldeman collaborates with other science fiction writers, including his brother Joe. In addition to writing science fiction, Haldeman works at the University of Florida, doing research in the field of artificial intelligence. He lives in rural Florida.

OTHER WORKS "Thirty Love," *The Fall of Winter*

FICTION

The Dinner Party
Mona Gardner

PERSONAL CONNECTION

Copy the chart shown. Write predictions of what you think most females and most males would do in each situation. Then get together with a small group of classmates and compare predictions. Have female and male students responded differently? Discuss whether people have fixed ideas about male and female behavior.

Situation	Females	Males
1. Seeing a bleeding wound 2. Getting a flat tire 3. Seeing a rat or a snake		

HISTORICAL CONNECTION

India was under British control for nearly 200 years before gaining its independence in 1947. "The Dinner Party" takes place in British India, the part of the country ruled directly by the British government. Some of the attitudes held by the British people of the time would be considered backward today. Most British officials felt superior to their subjects and rarely socialized with Indians. In addition, most men viewed themselves as superior to women, and that attitude of male superiority becomes an issue in this story.

British India Before 1947

AFGHANISTAN
CHINA
PERSIA
New Delhi
BRITISH INDIA
Calcutta
Bombay
N W E S
Arabian Sea
Miles
0 300 600
CEYLON

READING CONNECTION

Stereotypes An oversimplified view of an entire group of people is known as a stereotype. Such sweeping statements as "That's what all police officers are like" and "That's how all rich people act" are based on stereotypes. As you read this story, look for the stereotype expressed by a guest at the dinner party, and see whether it proves to be accurate.

The Dinner Party

by Mona Gardner

Detail of *Dinner at Haddo House* (1884), Alfred Edward Emslie. National Portrait Gallery, London.

The country is India. A large dinner party is being given in an up-country station by a colonial official[1] and his wife. The guests are army officers and government attachés[2] and their wives, and an American naturalist.

At one side of the long table a spirited discussion springs up between a young girl and a colonel. The girl insists women have long outgrown the jumping-on-a-chair-at-sight-of-a-mouse era, that they are not as fluttery as their grandmothers. The colonel says they are, explaining that women haven't the actual nerve control of men. The other men at the table agree with him.

"A woman's unfailing reaction in any crisis," the colonel says, "is to scream. And while a man may feel like it, yet he has that ounce more of control than a woman has. And that last ounce is what counts!"

The American scientist does not join in the argument, but sits watching the faces of the other guests. As he looks, he sees a strange expression come over the face of the hostess. She is staring straight ahead, the muscles of her face contracting slightly. With a small gesture she summons the native boy standing behind her chair. She whispers to him. The boy's eyes widen: he turns quickly and leaves the room. No one else sees this, nor the boy when he puts a bowl of milk on the verandah[3] outside the glass doors.

The American comes to with a start. In India, milk in a bowl means only one thing. It is bait for a snake. He realizes there is a cobra in the room.

He looks up at the rafters—the likeliest place—and sees they are bare. Three corners of the room, which he can see by shifting only slightly, are empty. In the fourth corner a group of servants stand, waiting until the next course can be served. The American realizes there is only one place left—under the table.

His first impulse is to jump back and warn the others. But he knows the commotion will frighten the cobra and it will strike. He speaks quickly, the quality of his voice so arresting that it sobers everyone.

"I want to know just what control everyone at this table has. I will count three hundred—that's five minutes—and not one of you is to move a single muscle. The persons who move will forfeit 50 rupees.[4] Now! Ready!"

The 20 people sit like stone images while he counts. He is saying ". . . two hundred and eighty . . . " when, out of the corner of his eye, he sees the cobra emerge and make for the bowl of milk. Four or five screams ring out as he jumps to slam shut the verandah doors.

"You certainly were right, Colonel!" the host says. "A man has just shown us an example of real control."

"Just a minute," the American says, turning to his hostess, "there's one thing I'd like to know. Mrs. Wynnes, how did you know that cobra was in the room?"

A faint smile lights up the woman's face as she replies. "Because it was lying across my foot." ❖

---

1. **colonial official:** a person holding a position in the British government ruling India.
2. **attachés** (ăt´ə-shāz´): people who assist an ambassador.
3. **verandah:** a long porch, usually roofed, along the side of a building.
4. **rupees** (roō-pēz´): Indian units of money.

WORDS
TO
KNOW

naturalist (năch´ər-ə-lĭst) *n.* a person who studies living things by observing them directly

RESPONDING
OPTIONS

FROM PERSONAL RESPONSE TO CRITICAL ANALYSIS

REFLECT   1. What were your reactions to this story? Record them in your notebook.

RETHINK   2. In your opinion, who behaves heroically in this story? Is the hero an unlikely one in the context of the story's setting? Give reasons for your answers.

3. Review your predictions for the Personal Connection on page 507. How has this story affected your ideas about female and male reactions to tense situations?

4. Draw portraits of the characters in the story. Make sure their faces reflect their feelings and personalities.

RELATE   5. Do you think the incident presented in the story will change the colonel's stereotyped view of women? Explain your answer, using story details and your own experience.

ANOTHER PATHWAY
Cooperative Learning

With a group of classmates, discuss some of the other female characters you have read about in this book. Which characters, if faced with a crisis, might respond as Mrs. Wynnes does? How would the others respond? Present your ideas to the class in a chart.

LITERARY CONCEPTS

A writer creates **suspense** by keeping readers guessing about how a story will end. Early in "The Dinner Party," we learn something that most of the characters do not know—that there is a deadly snake loose in the room. We feel suspense as we begin to imagine all the things that could go wrong. How does the naturalist's challenge to the guests add to the suspense?

QUICKWRITES

1. What do you suppose Mrs. Wynnes is thinking as the cobra lies across her foot? Write Mrs. Wynnes's **interior monologue**—her train of thought—during these tense minutes.

2. Picture the look on the face of the colonel after Mrs. Wynnes tells the group about the cobra. What might the colonel say next? Write a **dialogue** between the colonel and Mrs. Wynnes that could be added to the end of the story.

📁 PORTFOLIO *Save your writing. You may want to use it later as a springboard to a piece for your portfolio.*

ACROSS THE CURRICULUM

Science A common image of the cobra is of the snake's being "charmed" by a man playing music. How is this possible, given that the cobra is one of the world's most dangerous snakes? Find out all you can about the cobra—why it is dangerous, where it lives, how large it grows, what it looks like, what it eats, and whether it can really be "charmed." Report your findings to the class. Include a picture of a cobra or your own drawing of one.

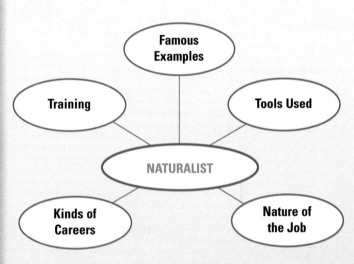

MONA GARDNER

During her childhood in Seattle, Washington, Mona Gardner (1900–1982) frequently visited Japan with her family. There she developed a life-long fascination with the Far East. She graduated from Stanford University in Stanford, California, in 1920. She began a career as a writer, specifically working as a journalist. She moved to Japan, covering the Far East as a correspondent for an American newspaper syndicate. Gardner wrote, "Twelve years of living with the Japanese has filled me with a life-long interest in these people and in their destiny in the East."

In the 1930s, she spent five months in China, reporting on that country's war with Japan. One of her three books, *The Menacing Sun,* tells of her travels in Indochina, the East Indies, and India.

FICTION

Flowers for Algernon
Daniel Keyes

PERSONAL CONNECTION

What if you woke up tomorrow and realized you had become a genius overnight? In your notebook or on a sheet of paper, answer the following questions:

- What would your initial reaction be?

- What drawbacks, if any, might there be to being a genius?

- How might your friends and members of your family respond to your intelligence?

SCIENCE CONNECTION

Imagine just taking a pill to help you with your math or history homework! What if you could simply swallow a tablet to become smarter? "Smart drugs" include a variety of food supplements and prescription drugs that some people think improve memory and increase concentration and intelligence. Some smart pills are medications that are used for treating mental disorders but which certain individuals have found to sharpen their minds. However, many doctors are skeptical of these effects.

Health-food stores and mail-order companies sell food supplements that they claim will make people feel younger and more energetic. Some health-food bars offer these supplements in "smart drinks" with names like Memory Fuel, Fast Blast, and Mind Mix.

Many scientists say that the only thing smart about these substances is the way they are pushed on the public. There is no scientific evidence—no recognized studies—to support the effectiveness of these drugs and supplements. Moreover, the Food and Drug Administration has not thoroughly tested many smart drugs for safety and effectiveness. Although legitimate drugs to restore lost memory and treat other mental disorders are under development, it will be many years before drugs that improve thinking ability are available to the public.

Inferences

An inference is a logical guess or conclusion based on facts. Making inferences is an important skill in reading nearly all categories of literature, including fiction, poetry, and nonfiction. By paying attention to what you read and applying what you know from your own experience, you can make inferences that go beyond what the words say.

You already know how to do this mental detective work. In the selections you have read thus far, you have picked up clues that helped you understand what was going on. You have made inferences about plots, settings, and characters' feelings and actions. For example, when you read that someone's face turns red, you might infer that the person is embarrassed or ashamed. If further reading does not support the inference, you discard it and make a different inference. You might discover that the red-faced character has, in fact, been mistreated and therefore infer that his or her red face is a sign of anger.

As you read "Flowers for Algernon," you will need to make many inferences. Because the story is presented as a series of progress reports written by the main character, Charlie, you will need to use the evidence in these reports to support your inferences. Look for clues in the spelling, punctuation, and style of Charlie's reports as well as in the events he writes about. Since in the beginning of the story Charlie is less intelligent than you, you will be able to make inferences by simply drawing on your own knowledge and experience. For example, you will know why Charlie's coworkers are laughing before he does.

Let the questions inserted at various points in the selection help you make inferences as you read. In addition, look for clues that can help you make inferences about Charlie's feelings about himself and others, his level of intelligence, and others' reactions to him. The inferences you make should change as the story moves forward. In your notebook, jot down notes to keep track of these changes. Use a chart similar to the one shown here, and you will have your own "progress report" for the story.

I can infer …	On the basis of Progress Reports from…				
	March 5–10	**March 15–29**	**April 3–30**	**May 15–June 4**	**June 5–July 28**
Charlie's feelings about himself					
Charlie's feelings about others					
Charlie's intelligence level					
Others' reactions to Charlie					

Flowers for Algernon

by Daniel Keyes

progris riport 1 — march 5 1965

Dr. Strauss says I shud rite down what I think and evrey thing that happins to me from now on. I dont know why but he says its importint so they will see if they will use me. I hope they use me. Miss Kinnian says maybe they can make me smart. I want to be smart. My name is Charlie Gordon. I am 37 years old and 2 weeks ago was my brithday. I have nuthing more to rite now so I will close for today.

progris riport 2—martch 6

I had a test today. I think I faled it. and I think that maybe now they wont use me. What happind is a nice young man was in the room and he had some white cards with ink spillled all over them. He sed Charlie what do you see on this card. I was very skared even tho I had my rabits foot in my pockit because when I was a kid I always faled tests in school and I spillled ink to.

I told him I saw a inkblot. He said yes and it made me feel good. I thot that was all but when I got up to go he stopped me. He said now sit down Charlie we are not thru yet. Then I dont remember so good but he wantid me to say what was in the ink. I dint see nuthing in the ink but he said there was picturs there other pepul saw some picturs. I coudnt see any picturs. I reely tryed to see. I held the card close up and then far away. Then I said if I had my glases I coud see better

I usally only ware my glases in the movies or TV but I said they are in the closit in the hall. I got them. Then I said let me see that card agen I bet Ill find it now.

I tryed hard but I still coudnt find the picturs I only saw the ink. I told him maybe I need new glases. He rote somthing down on a paper and I got skared of faling the test. I told him it was a very nice inkblot with littel points all around the eges. He looked very sad so that wasnt it. I said please let me try agen. Ill get it in a few minits becaus Im not so fast somtimes. Im a slow reeder too in Miss Kinnians class for slow adults but I'm trying very hard.

He gave me a chance with another card that had 2 kinds of ink spillled on it red and blue.

He was very nice and talked slow like Miss Kinnian does and he explaned it to me that it was a *raw shok*.[1] He said pepul see things in the ink. I said show me where. He said think. I told him I think a inkblot but that wasnt rite eather. He said what does it remind you— pretend somthing. I closd my eyes for a long time to pretend. I told him I pretned a fowntan pen with ink leeking all over a table cloth. Then he got up and went out.

I dont think I passd the *raw shok* test.

progris report 3—martch 7

Dr Strauss and Dr Nemur say it dont matter about the inkblots. I told them I dint spill the ink on the cards and I coudnt see anything in the ink. They said that maybe they will still use me. I said Miss Kinnian never gave me tests like that one only spelling and reading. They said Miss Kinnian told that I was her bestist pupil in the adult nite scool becaus I tryed the hardist and I reely wantid to lern. They said how come you went to the adult nite scool all by yourself Charlie. How did you find it. I said I askd pepul and sumbody told me whcre I shud go to lern to read and spell good. They said why did you want to. I told them becaus all my life I wantid to be smart and not dumb. But its very hard to be smart. They said you know it will probly be tempirery. I said yes. Miss Kinnian told me. I dont care if it herts.

Later I had more crazy tests today. The nice

---

1. **raw shok:** Charlie's way of writing *Rorschach* (rôr'shäk'), the name of a test used to analyze people's personalities on the basis of what they see in inkblot designs.

lady who gave it me told me the name and I asked her how do you spellit so I can rite it in my progris riport. THEMATIC APPERCEPTION TEST.[2] I dont know the frist 2 words but I know what *test* means. You got to pass it or you get bad marks. This test lookd easy becaus I coud see the picturs. Only this time she dint want me to tell her the picturs. That mixd me up. I said the man yesterday said I shoud tell him what I saw in the ink she said that dont make no difrence. She said make up storys about the pepul in the picturs.

I told her how can you tell storys about pepul you never met. I said why shud I make up lies. I never tell lies any more becaus I always get caut.

She told me this test and the other one the raw-shok was for getting personalty. I laffed so hard. I said how can you get that thing from inkblots and fotos. She got sore and put her picturs away. I dont care. It was sily. I gess I faled that test too.

Later some men in white coats took me to a difernt part of the hospitil and gave me a game to play. It was like a race with a white mouse. They called the mouse Algernon. Algernon was in a box with a lot of twists and turns like all kinds of walls and they gave me a pencil and a paper with lines and lots of boxes. On one side it said START and on the other end it said FINISH. They said it was *amazed*[3] and that Algernon and me had the same *amazed* to do. I dint see how we could have the same *amazed* if Algernon had a box and I had a paper but I dint say nothing. Anyway there wasnt time because the race started.

One of the men had a watch he was trying to hide so I woudnt see it so I tryed not to look and that made me nervus.

Anyway that test made me feel worser than all the others because they did it over 10 times with difernt *amazeds* and Algernon won every time. I dint know that mice were so smart.

Maybe thats because Algernon is a white mouse. Maybe white mice are smarter then other mice.

progris riport 4—Mar 8

Their going to use me! Im so exited I can hardly rite. Dr Nemur and Dr Strauss had a argament about it first. Dr Nemur was in the office when Dr Strauss brot me in. Dr Nemur was worried about using me but Dr Strauss told him Miss Kinnian rekemmended me the best from all the people who she was teaching. I like Miss Kinnian becaus shes a very smart teacher. And she said Charlie your going to have a second chance. If you volenteer for this experament you mite get smart. They dont know if it will be perminint but theirs a chance. Thats why I said ok even when I was scared because she said it was an operashun. She said dont be scared Charlie you done so much with so little I think you deserv it most of all.

So I got scaird when Dr Nemur and Dr Strauss argud about it. Dr Strauss said I had something that was very good. He said I had a good *motor-vation*.[4] I never even knew I had that. I felt proud when he said that not every body with an eye-q[5] of 68 had that thing. I dont know what it is or where I got it but he said Algernon had it too.

CLARIFY

Why does Charlie feel so excited?

---

2. **Thematic Apperception** (thĭ-măt′ĭk ăp′ər-sĕp′shən) **Test:** a test for analyzing people's personalities on the basis of the stories they make up about a series of pictures.

3. **amazed:** Charlie's way of writing *a maze.*

4. **motor-vation:** Charlie's way of writing *motivation,* a word referring to the inner drive that makes a person take a particular course of action.

5. **eye-q:** Charlie's way of writing *I.Q.* (an abbreviation of *intelligence quotient*). Based on the results of a standardized test, an I.Q. is a measurement of a person's mental ability relative to a normal level.

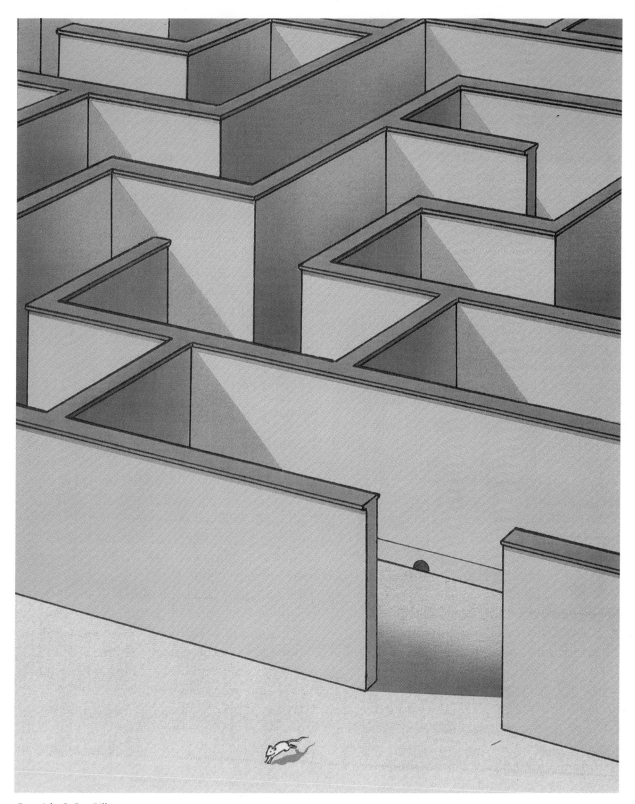

Algernons *motor-vation* is the cheese they put in his box. But it cant be that because I didnt eat any cheese this week.

Then he told Dr Nemur something I dint understand so while they were talking I wrote down some of the words.

He said Dr Nemur I know Charlie is not what you had in mind as the first of your new brede of intelek** (coudnt get the word) superman. But most people of his low ment** are host** and uncoop** they are usualy dull apath** and hard to reach. He has a good natcher hes intristed and eager to please.

Dr Nemur said remember he will be the first human beeng ever to have his intelijence trippled by surgicle meens.

Dr Strauss said exakly. Look at how well hes lerned to read and write for his low mentel age its as grate an acheve** as you and I lerning einstines therey of **vity[6] without help. That shows the intenss motor-vation. Its comparat** a tremen** achev** I say we use Charlie.

I dint get all the words and they were talking to fast but it sounded like Dr Strauss was on my side and like the other one wasnt.

Then Dr Nemur nodded he said all right maybe your right. We will use Charlie. When he said that I got so exited I jumped up and shook his hand for being so good to me. I told him thank you doc you wont be sorry for giving me a second chance. And I mean it like I told him. After the operashun Im gonna try to be smart. Im gonna try awful hard.

progris ript 5—Mar 10

Im skared. Lots of people who work here and the nurses and the people who gave me the tests came to bring me candy and wish me luck. I hope I have luck. I got my rabits foot and my lucky penny and my horse shoe. Only a black cat crossed me when I was comming to the hospitil. Dr Strauss says dont be superstitis

Charlie this is sience. Anyway Im keeping my rabits foot with me.

I asked Dr Strauss if Ill beat Algernon in the race after the operashun and he said maybe. If the operashun works Ill show that mouse I can be as smart as he is. Maybe smarter. Then Ill be abel to read better and spell the words good and know lots of things and be like other people. I want to be smart like other people. If it works perminint they will make everybody smart all over the wurld.

They dint give me anything to eat this morning. I dont know what that eating has to do with getting smart. Im very hungry and Dr Nemur took away my box of candy. That Dr Nemur is a grouch. Dr Strauss says I can have it back after the operashun. You cant eat befor a operashun . . .

Progress Report 6—Mar 15

PREDICT

What's going to happen to Charlie now?

The operashun dint hurt. He did it while I was sleeping. They took off the bandijis from my eyes and my head today so I can make a PROGRESS REPORT. Dr Nemur who looked at some of my other ones says I spell PROGRESS wrong and he told me how to spell it and REPORT too. I got to try and remember that.

I have a very bad memary for spelling. Dr Strauss says its ok to tell about all the things that happin to me but he says I shoud tell more about what I feel and what I think. When I told him I dont know how to think he said try. All the time when the bandijis were on my eyes I tryed to think. Nothing happened. I dont know what to think about. Maybe if I ask him he will tell me how I can think now that Im

---

6. **einstines therey of **vity:** Charlie's way of writing *Einstein's theory of relativity,* a reference to the scientific theory of space and time developed by Albert Einstein.

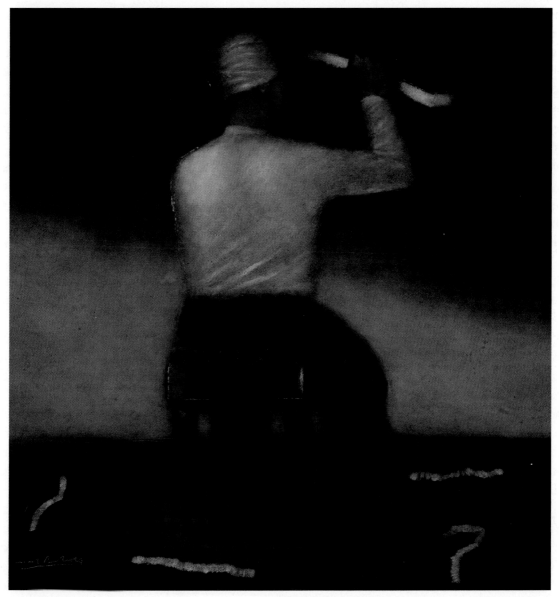

Copyright © Mark Penberthy.

suppose to get smart. What do smart people think about. Fancy things I suppose. I wish I knew some fancy things alredy.

Progress Report 7—mar 19

Nothing is happining. I had lots of tests and different kinds of races with Algernon. I hate that mouse. He always beats me. Dr Strauss said I got to play those games. And he said some time I got to take those tests over again.

Those inkblots are stupid. And those pictures are stupid too. I like to draw a picture of a man and a woman but I wont make up lies about people.

I got a headache from trying to think so much. I thot Dr Strauss was my frend but he dont help me. He dont tell me what to think or when Ill get smart. Miss Kinnian dint come to see me. I think writing these progress reports are stupid too.

Im going back to work at the factery. They said it was better I shud go back to work but I cant tell anyone what the operashun was for and I have to come to the hospitil for an hour evry night after work. They are gonna pay me mony every month for lerning to be smart.

Im glad Im going back to work because I miss my job and all my frends and all the fun we have there.

Dr Strauss says I shud keep writing things down but I dont have to do it every day just when I think of something or something speshul happins. He says dont get discoridged be-cause it takes time and it hap-pins slow. He says it took a long time with Algernon before he got 3 times smarter then he was before. Thats why Algernon beats me all the time because he had that operashun too. That makes me feel better. I coud probly do that *amazed* faster than a reglar mouse. Maybe some day Ill beat Algernon. Boy that would be something. So far Algernon looks like he mite be smart perminent.

Mar 25 (I dont have to write PROGRESS REPORT on top any more just when I hand it in once a week for Dr Nemur to read. I just have to put the date on. That saves time)

We had a lot of fun at the factery today. Joe Carp said hey look where Charlie had his operashun what did they do Charlie put some brains in. I was going to tell him but I remem-bered Dr Strauss said no. Then Frank Reilly said what did you do Charlie forget your key and open your door the hard way. That made me laff. Their really my friends and they like me.

Sometimes somebody will say hey look at Joe or Frank or George he really pulled a Charlie Gordon. I dont know why they say that but they always laff. This morning Amos Borg who is the 4 man at Donnegans used my name when he shouted at Ernie the office boy. Ernie lost a packige. He said Ernie for godsake what are you trying to be a Charlie Gordon. I dont understand why he said that. I never lost any packiges.

Mar 28 Dr Straus came to my room tonight to see why I dint come in like I was suppose to. I told him I dont like to race with Algernon any more. He said I dont have to for a while but I shud come in. He had a present for me only it wasnt a present but just for lend. I thot it was a little television but it wasnt. He said I got to turn it on when I go to sleep. I said your kidding why shud I turn it on when Im going to sleep. Who ever herd of a thing like that. But he said if I want to get smart I got to do what he says. I told him I dint think I was going to get smart and he put his hand on my sholder and said Charlie you dont know it yet but your getting smarter all the time. You wont notice for a while. I think he was just being nice to make me feel good be-cause I dont look any smarter.

Oh yes I almost for-got. I asked him when I can go back to the class at Miss Kinnians school. He said I wont go their. He said that soon Miss Kinnian will come to the hospitil to start and teach me speshul. I was mad at her for not comming to see me when I got the operashun but I like her so maybe we will be frends again.

Mar 29 That crazy TV kept me up all night. How can I sleep with something yelling crazy

> Maybe someday
> I'll beat Algernon.
> Boy that would be
> something.

CLARIFY

Why doesn't Charlie want to race with Algernon anymore?

things all night in my ears. And the nutty pictures. Wow. I dont know what it says when Im up so how am I going to know when Im sleeping.

Dr Strauss says its ok. He says my brains are lerning when I sleep and that will help me when Miss Kinnian starts my lessons in the hospitl (only I found out it isnt a hospitil its a labatory). I think its all crazy. If you can get smart when your sleeping why do people go to school. That thing I dont think will work. I use to watch the late show and the late late show on TV all the time and it never made me smart. Maybe you have to sleep while you watch it.

PROGRESS REPORT 9—April 3

Dr Strauss showed me how to keep the TV turned low so now I can sleep. I don't hear a thing. And I still dont understand what it says. A few times I play it over in the morning to find out what I lerned when I was sleeping and I dont think so. Miss Kinnian says Maybe its another langwidge or something. But most times it sounds american. It talks so fast faster than even Miss Gold who was my teacher in 6 grade and I remember she talked so fast I coudnt understand her.

I told Dr Strauss what good is it to get smart in my sleep. I want to be smart when Im awake. He says its the same thing and I have two minds. Theres the *subconscious* and the *conscious*[7] (thats how you spell it). And one dont tell the other one what its doing. They dont even talk to each other. Thats why I dream. And boy have I been having crazy dreams. Wow. Ever since that night TV. The late late late late late show.

I forgot to ask him if it was only me or if everybody had those two minds.

(I just looked up the word in the dictionary Dr Strauss gave me. The word is *subconscious. adj. Of the nature of mental operations yet not present in consciousness; as, subconscious conflict of desires.*) There's more but I still dont know what it means. This isnt a very good dictionary for dumb people like me.

Anyway the headache is from the party. My frends from the factery Joe Carp and Frank Reilly invited me to go with them to Muggsys Saloon for some drinks. I dont like to drink but they said we will have lots of fun. I had a good time.

Joe Carp said I shoud show the girls how I mop out the toilet in the factory and he got me a mop. I showed them and everyone laffed when I told that Mr Donnegan said I was the best janiter he ever had because I like my job and do it good and never come late or miss a day except for my operashun.

I said Miss Kinnian always said Charlie be proud of your job because you do it good.

Everybody laffed and we had a good time and they gave me lots of drinks and Joe said Charlie is a card when hes potted.[8] I dont know what that means but everybody likes me and we have fun. I cant wait to be smart like my best frends Joe Carp and Frank Reilly.

I dont remember how the party was over but I think I went out to buy a newspaper and coffe for Joe and Frank and when I came back there was no one their. I looked for them all over till late. Then I dont remember so good but I think I got sleepy or sick. A nice cop brot me back home. Thats what my landlady Mrs Flynn says.

But I got a headache and a big lump on my head and black and blue all over. I think maybe I fell but Joe Carp says it was the cop

---

7. **the subconscious** (sŭb-kŏn′shəs) **and the conscious** (kŏn′shəs): psychological terms for two kinds of mental activity. The subconscious consists of all a person's mental activity that he or she is not aware of, and the conscious is the mental activity of which the person is aware.

8. **Charlie is a card when hes potted:** Charlie is funny when he's drunk.

they beat up drunks some times. I don't think so. Miss Kinnian says cops are to help people. Anyway I got a bad headache and Im sick and hurt all over. I dont think Ill drink anymore.

April 6 I beat Algernon! I dint even know I beat him until Burt the tester told me. Then the second time I lost because I got so exited I fell off the chair before I finished. But after that I beat him 8 more times. I must be getting smart to beat a smart mouse like Algernon. But I dont *feel* smarter.

I wanted to race Algernon some more but Burt said thats enough for one day. They let me hold him for a minit. Hes not so bad. Hes soft like a ball of cotton. He blinks and when he opens his eyes their black and pink on the eges.

I said can I feed him because I felt bad to beat him and I wanted to be nice and make frends. Burt said no Algernon is a very specshul mouse with an operashun like mine, and he was the first of all the animals to stay smart so long. He told me Algernon is so smart that every day he has to solve a test to get his food. Its a thing like a lock on a door that changes every time Algernon goes in to eat so he has to lern something new to get his food. That made me sad because if he coudnt lern he woud be hungry.

I dont think its right to make you pass a test to eat. How woud Dr Nemur like it to have to pass a test every time he wants to eat. I think Ill be frends with Algernon.

April 9 Tonight after work Miss Kinnian was at the laboratory. She looked like she was glad to see me but scared. I told her dont worry Miss Kinnian Im not smart yet and she laffed. She said I have confidence in you Charlie the way you struggled so hard to read and right better than all the others. At werst you will have it for a littel wile and your doing somthing for sience.

We are reading a very hard book. I never read such a hard book before. Its called *Robinson Crusoe* about a man who gets merooned on a dessert Iland. Hes smart and figers out all kinds of things so he can have a house and food and hes a good swimmer. Only I feel sorry because hes all alone and has no frends. But I think their must be somebody else on the iland because theres a picture with his funny umbrella looking at footprints. I hope he gets a frend and not be lonly.

April 10 Miss Kinnian teaches me to spell better. She says look at a word and close your eyes and say it over and over until you remember. I have lots of truble with *through* that you say *threw* and *enough* and *tough* that you dont say *enew* and *tew*. You got to say *enuff* and *tuff*. Thats how I use to write it before I started to get smart. Im confused but Miss Kinnian says theres no reason in spelling.

Apr 14 Finished *Robinson Crusoe*. I want to find out more about what happens to him but Miss Kinnian says thats all there is. *Why*

Apr 15 Miss Kinnian says Im lerning fast. She read some of the Progress Reports and she looked at me kind of funny. She says Im a fine person and Ill show them all. I asked her why. She said never mind but I shoudnt feel bad if I find out that everybody isnt nice like I think. She said for a person who god gave so little to you done more then a lot of people with brains they never even used. I said all my frends are smart people but there good. They like me and they never did anything that wasnt nice. Then she got something in her eye and she had to run out to the ladys room.

CLARIFY

What is in Miss Kinnian's eye?

Apr 16 Today, I lerned, the *comma*, this is a comma (,) a period, with a tail, Miss Kinnian, says its importent, because, it makes writing, better, she said, somebody, coud lose, a lot of money, if a comma, isnt, in the, right place, I dont have, any money, and I dont see, how a comma, keeps you, from losing it,

But she says, everybody, uses commas, so Ill use, them too,

Apr 17 I used the comma wrong. Its punctuation. Miss Kinnian told me to look up long words in the dictionary to lern to spell them. I said whats the difference if you can read it anyway. She said its part of your education so now on Ill look up all the words Im not sure how to spell. It takes a long time to write that way but I think Im remembering. I only have to look up once and after that I get it right. Anyway thats how come I got the word *punctuation* right. (Its that way in the dictionary). Miss Kinnian says a period is punctuation too, and there are lots of other marks to lern. I told her I thot all the periods had to have tails but she said no.

You got to mix them up, she showed? me" how. to mix! them(up,. and now; I can! mix up all kinds" of punctuation, in! my writing? There, are lots! of rules? to lern; but Im gcttin'g them in my head.

One thing I? like about, Dear Miss Kinnian: (thats the way it goes in a business letter if I ever go into business) is she, always gives me' a reason" when—I ask. She's a gen'ius! I wish! I cou'd be smart" like, her;

(Punctuation, is; fun!)

April 18 What a dope I am! I didn't even understand what she was talking about. I read the grammar book last night and it explanes the whole thing. Then I saw it was the same way as Miss Kinnian was trying to tell me, but I didn't get it. I got up in the middle of the night, and the whole thing straightened out in my mind.

Miss Kinnian said that the TV working in my sleep helped out. She said I reached a plateau. Thats like the flat top of a hill.

After I figgered out how punctuation worked, I read over all my old Progress Reports from the beginning. Boy, did I have crazy spelling and punctuation! I told Miss Kinnian I ought to go over the pages and fix all the mistakes but she said, "No, Charlie, Dr. Nemur wants them just as they are. That's why he let you keep them after they were photostated, to see your own progress. You're coming along fast, Charlie."

That made me feel good. After the lesson I went down and played with Algernon. We don't race any more.

April 20 I feel sick inside. Not sick like for a doctor, but inside my chest it feels empty like getting punched and a heartburn at the same time.

I wasn't going to write about it, but I guess I got to, because its important. Today was the first time I ever stayed home from work.

Last night Joe Carp and Frank Reilly invited me to a party. There were lots of girls and some men from the factory. I remembered how sick I got last time I drank too much, so I told Joe I didn't want anything to drink. He gave me a plain coke instead. It tasted funny, but I thought it was just a bad taste in my mouth.

We had a lot of fun for a while. Joe said I should dance with Ellen and she would teach me the steps. I fell a few times and I couldn't understand why because no one else was dancing besides Ellen and me. And all the time I was tripping because somebody's foot was always sticking out.

"You're coming along fast, Charlie."

Then when I got up I saw the look on Joe's face and it gave me a funny feeling in my stomack. "He's a scream," one of the girls said. Everybody was laughing.

Frank said, "I ain't laughed so much since we sent him off for the newspaper that night at Muggsy's and ditched him."

"Look at him. His face is red."

"He's blushing. Charlie is blushing."

"Hey, Ellen, what'd you do to Charlie? I never saw him act like that before."

I didn't know what to do or where to turn. Everyone was looking at me and laughing and I felt naked. I wanted to hide myself. I ran out into the street and I threw up. Then I walked home. It's a funny thing I never knew that Joe and Frank and the others liked to have me around all the time to make fun of me.

Now I know what it means when they say "to pull a Charlie Gordon."

I'm ashamed.

PROGRESS REPORT 11

April 21 Still didn't go into the factory. I told Mrs. Flynn my landlady to call and tell Mr. Donnegan I was sick. Mrs. Flynn looks at me very funny lately like she's scared of me.

I think it's a good thing about finding out how everybody laughs at me. I thought about it a lot. It's because I'm so dumb and I don't even know when I'm doing something dumb. People think it's funny when a dumb person can't do things the same way they can.

Anyway, now I know I'm getting smarter every day. I know punctuation and I can spell good. I like to look up all the hard words in the dictionary and I remember them. I'm reading a lot now, and Miss Kinnian says I read very fast. Sometimes I even understand what I'm reading about, and it stays in my mind. There are times when I can close my eyes and think of a page and it all comes back like a picture.

Besides history, geography, and arithmetic, Miss Kinnian said I should start to learn a few foreign languages. Dr. Strauss gave me some more tapes to play while I sleep. I still don't understand how that conscious and unconscious mind works, but Dr. Strauss says not to worry yet. He asked me to promise that when I start learning college subjects next week I wouldn't read any books on psychology[9]—that is, until he gives me permission.

I feel a lot better today, but I guess I'm still a little angry that all the time people were laughing and making fun of me because I wasn't so smart. When I become intelligent like Dr. Strauss says, with three times my I.Q. of 68, then maybe I'll be like everyone else and people will like me and be friendly.

I'm not sure what an *I.Q.* is. Dr. Nemur said it was something that measured how intelligent you were—like a scale in the drugstore weighs pounds. But Dr. Strauss had a big arguement with him and said an I.Q. didn't weigh intelligence at all. He said an I.Q. showed how much intelligence you could get, like the numbers on the outside of a measuring cup. You still had to fill the cup up with stuff.

Then when I asked Burt, who gives me my intelligence tests and works with Algernon, he said that both of them were wrong (only I had to promise not to tell them he said so). Burt says that the I.Q. measures a lot of different things including some of the things you learned already, and it really isn't any good at all.

So I still don't know what I.Q. is except that mine is going to be over 200 soon. I didn't want to say anything, but I don't see how if they don't know *what* it is, or *where* it is—I don't see how they know *how much* of it you've got.

Dr. Nemur says I have to take a *Rorshach*

---

9. **psychology** (sī-kŏl′ə-jē): the study of mental processes and behavior.

Test tomorrow. I wonder what *that* is.

April 22 I found out what a *Rorshach* is. It's the test I took before the operation—the one with the inkblots on the pieces of cardboard. The man who gave me the test was the same one.

I was scared to death of those inkblots. I knew he was going to ask me to find the pictures and I knew I wouldn't be able to. I was thinking to myself, if only there was some way of knowing what kind of pictures were hidden there. Maybe there weren't any pictures at all. Maybe it was just a trick to see if I was dumb enough to look for something that wasn't there. Just thinking about that made me sore at him.

"All right, Charlie," he said, "you've seen these cards before, remember?"

"Of course I remember."

The way I said it, he knew I was angry, and he looked surprised. "Yes, of course. Now I want you to look at this one. What might this be? What do you see on this card? People see all sorts of things in these inkblots. Tell me what it might be for you—what it makes you think of."

I was shocked. That wasn't what I had expected him to say at all. "You mean there are no pictures hidden in those inkblots?"

He frowned and took off his glasses. "What?"

"Pictures. Hidden in the inkblots. Last time you told me that everyone could see them and you wanted me to find them too."

He explained to me that the last time he had used almost the exact same words he was using now. I didn't believe it, and I still have the suspicion that he misled me at the time just for the fun of it. Unless—I don't know any more—could I have been *that* feeble-minded?

We went through the cards slowly. One of them looked like a pair of bats tugging at something. Another one looked like two men fencing with swords. I imagined all sorts of things. I guess I got carried away. But I didn't trust him any more, and I kept turning them around and even looking on the back to see if there was anything there I was supposed to catch. While he was making his notes, I peeked out of the corner of my eye to read it. But it was all in code that looked like this:

WF+A DdF-Ad orig. WF–A SF+obj

The test still doesn't make sense to me. It seems to me that anyone could make up lies about things that they didn't really see. How could he know I wasn't making a fool of him by mentioning things that I didn't really imagine? Maybe I'll understand it when Dr. Strauss lets me read up on psychology.

So I still don't know what I.Q. is except that mine is going to be over 200 soon.

April 25 I figured out a new way to line up the machines in the factory, and Mr. Donnegan says it will save him ten thousand dollars a year in labor and increased production. He gave me a $25 bonus.

I wanted to take Joe Carp and Frank Reilly out to lunch to celebrate, but Joe said he had to buy some things for his wife, and Frank said he was meeting his cousin for lunch. I guess it'll take a little time for them to get used to the changes in me. Everybody seems to be frightened of me. When I went over to Amos Borg and tapped him on the shoulder, he jumped up in the air.

People don't talk to me much any more or kid around the way they used to. It makes the job kind of lonely.

April 27 I got up the nerve today to ask Miss Kinnian to have dinner with me tomorrow night to celebrate my bonus.

At first she wasn't sure it was right, but I asked Dr. Strauss and he said it was okay. Dr. Strauss and Dr. Nemur don't seem to be getting along so well. They're arguing all the time. This evening when I came in to ask Dr. Strauss about having dinner with Miss Kinnian, I heard them shouting. Dr. Nemur was saying that it was *his* experiment and *his* research, and Dr. Strauss was shouting back that he contributed just as much, because he found me through Miss Kinnian and he performed the operation. Dr. Strauss said that someday thousands of neurosurgeons[10] might be using his technique all over the world.

Dr. Nemur wanted to publish the results of the experiment at the end of this month. Dr. Strauss wanted to wait a while longer to be sure. Dr. Strauss said that Dr. Nemur was more interested in the Chair of Psychology at Princeton[11] than he was in the experiment. Dr. Nemur said that Dr. Strauss was nothing but an opportunist who was trying to ride to glory on *his* coattails.

When I left afterwards, I found myself trembling. I don't know why for sure, but it was as if I'd seen both men clearly for the first time. I remember hearing Burt say that Dr. Nemur had a shrew of a wife who was pushing him all the time to get things published so that he could become famous. Burt said that the dream of her life was to have a big shot husband.

CLARIFY

What does Charlie mean by this question?

Was Dr. Strauss really trying to ride on his coattails?

April 28 I don't understand why I never noticed how beautiful Miss Kinnian really is. She has brown eyes and feathery brown hair that comes to the top of her neck. She's only thirty-four! I think from the beginning I had the feeling that she was an unreachable genius—and very, very old. Now, every time I see her she grows younger and more lovely.

We had dinner and a long talk. When she said that I was coming along so fast that soon I'd be leaving her behind, I laughed.

"It's true, Charlie. You're already a better reader than I am. You can read a whole page at a glance while I can take in only a few lines at a time. And you remember every single thing you read. I'm lucky if I can recall the main thoughts and the general meaning."

"I don't feel intelligent. There are so many things I don't understand."

She took out a cigarette and I lit it for her. "You've got to be a *little* patient. You're accomplishing in days and weeks what it takes normal people to do in half a lifetime. That's what makes it so amazing. You're like a giant sponge now, soaking things in. Facts, figures, general knowledge. And soon you'll begin to connect them, too. You'll see how the different branches of learning are related. There are many levels, Charlie, like steps on a giant ladder that take you up higher and higher to see more and more of the world around you.

"I can see only a little bit of that, Charlie, and I won't go much higher than I am now, but you'll keep climbing up and up, and see more and more, and each step will open new worlds that you never even knew existed." She frowned. "I hope . . . I just hope to God—"

"What?"

---

10. **neurosurgeons** (nŏŏr´ō-sûr´jənz): doctors who perform operations on the brain and other parts of the nervous system.

11. **Chair of Psychology at Princeton:** the position of head of the Psychology Department at Princeton University.

WORDS TO KNOW

opportunist (ŏp´ər-tōō´nĭst) *n.* a person who takes advantage of any opportunity to achieve a goal, with little regard for moral principles

shrew (shrōō) *n.* a mean, nagging woman

Max Seabaugh/MAX.

"Never mind, Charles. I just hope I wasn't wrong to advise you to go into this in the first place."

I laughed. "How could that be? It worked, didn't it? Even Algernon is still smart."

We sat there silently for a while, and I knew what she was thinking about as she watched me toying with the chain of my rabbit's foot and my keys. I didn't want to think of that possibility any more than elderly people want to think of death. I *knew* that this was only the beginning. I knew what she meant about levels because I'd seen some of them already. The thought of leaving her behind made me sad.

I'm in love with Miss Kinnian.

PROGRESS REPORT 12
April 30 I've quit my job with Donnegan's Plastic Box Company. Mr. Donnegan insisted that it would be better for all concerned if I left. What did I do to make them hate me so?

The first I knew of it was when Mr. Donnegan showed me the petition. Eight hundred and forty names, everyone connected with the factory, except Fanny Girden. Scanning the list quickly, I saw at once that hers was the only missing name. All the rest demanded that I be fired.

Joe Carp and Frank Reilly wouldn't talk to me about it. No one else would either, except Fanny. She was one of the few people I'd known who set her mind to something and believed it no matter what the rest of the world proved, said, or did—and Fanny did not believe that I should have been fired. She had been against the petition on principle, and despite the pressure and threats she'd held out.

"Which don't mean to say," she remarked, "that I don't think there's something mighty strange about you, Charlie. Them changes. I don't know. You used to be a good, dependable, ordinary man—not too bright maybe, but honest. Who knows what you done to yourself to get so smart all of a sudden. Like everybody around here's been saying, Charlie, it's not right."

"But how can you say that, Fanny? What's wrong with a man becoming intelligent and wanting to acquire knowledge and understanding of the world around him?"

CLARIFY

Why has Mr. Donnegan asked Charlie to leave his job?

She stared down at her work, and I turned to leave. Without looking at me, she said: "It was evil when Eve listened to the snake and ate from the tree of knowledge. It was evil when she saw that she was naked. If not for that, none of us would ever have to grow old and sick and die.[12]"

Once again now I have the feeling of shame burning inside me. This intelligence has driven a wedge between me and all the people I once knew and loved. Before, they laughed at me and despised me for my ignorance and dullness; now, they hate me for my knowledge and understanding. What in God's name do they want of me?

They've driven me out of the factory. Now I'm more alone than ever before . . .

May 15 Dr. Strauss is very angry at me for not having written any progress reports in two weeks. He's justified because the lab is now paying me a regular salary. I told him I was too busy thinking and reading. When I pointed out that writing was such a slow process that it made me impatient with my poor handwriting, he suggested that I learn to type. It's much easier to write now because I can type nearly seventy-five words a minute. Dr. Strauss continually reminds me of the need to speak and write simply so that people will be able to understand me.

I'll try to review all the things that happened to me during the last two weeks. Algernon and I were presented to the American Psychological Association sitting in convention with the World Psychological Association last Tuesday. We created quite a <u>sensation</u>. Dr. Nemur and Dr. Strauss were proud of us.

I suspect that Dr. Nemur, who is sixty—ten years older than Dr. Strauss—finds it necessary to see <u>tangible</u> results of his work. Undoubtedly the result of pressure by Mrs. Nemur.

Contrary to my earlier impressions of him, I realize that Dr. Nemur is not at all a genius. He has a very good mind, but it struggles under the specter of self-doubt. He wants people to take him for a genius. Therefore, it is important for him to feel that his work is accepted by the world. I believe that Dr. Nemur was afraid of further delay because he worried that someone else might make a discovery along these lines and take the credit from him.

---

12. **It was evil . . . die:** a reference to the biblical story of Adam and Eve (Genesis 2–3). After they ate fruit from the tree of knowledge of good and evil, they were banished from the Garden of Eden, and they and their descendants became subject to illness and death.

WORDS TO KNOW

sensation (sĕn-sā′shən) *n.* a state of great interest and excitement
tangible (tăn′jə-bəl) *adj.* able to be seen or touched; material

Dr. Strauss, on the other hand, might be called a genius, although I feel that his areas of knowledge are too limited. He was educated in the tradition of narrow specialization; the broader aspects of background were neglected far more than necessary—even for a neurosurgeon.

I was shocked to learn that the only ancient languages he could read were Latin, Greek, and Hebrew and that he knows almost nothing of mathematics beyond the elementary levels of the calculus of variations.[13] When he admitted this to me, I found myself almost annoyed. It was as if he'd hidden this part of himself in order to deceive me, pretending—as do many people, I've discovered—to be what he is not. No one I've ever known is what he appears to be on the surface.

Dr. Nemur appears to be uncomfortable around me. Sometimes when I try to talk to him, he just looks at me strangely and turns away. I was angry at first when Dr. Strauss told me I was giving Dr. Nemur an inferiority complex.[14] I thought he was mocking me, and I'm oversensitive at being made fun of.

How was I to know that a highly respected psychoexperimentalist like Nemur was unacquainted with Hindustani[15] and Chinese? It's absurd when you consider the work that is being done in India and China today in the very field of his study.

I asked Dr. Strauss how Nemur could refute Rahajamati's attack on his method and results if Nemur couldn't even read them in the first place. That strange look on Dr. Strauss's face can mean only one of two things. Either he doesn't want to tell Nemur what they're saying in India, or else—and this worries me—Dr. Strauss doesn't know either. I must be careful to speak and write clearly and simply so that people won't laugh.

May 18 I am very disturbed. I saw Miss Kinnian last night for the first time in over a week. I tried to avoid all discussions of intellectual concepts and to keep the conversation on a simple, everyday level, but she just stared at me blankly and asked me what I meant about the mathematical variance equivalent in Dorbermann's Fifth Concerto.

When I tried to explain, she stopped me and laughed. I guess I got angry, but I suspect I'm approaching her on the wrong level. No matter what I try to discuss with her, I am unable to communicate. I must review Vrostadt's equations on levels of semantic progression. I find that I don't communicate with people much any more. Thank God for books and music and things I can think about. I am alone in my apartment at Mrs. Flynn's boarding house most of the time and seldom speak to anyone.

Contrary to my earlier impressions of him, I realize that Dr. Nemur is not at all a genius.

---

13. **calculus** (kăl′kyə-ləs) **of variations:** a branch of higher mathematics.

14. **inferiority complex:** a psychological condition involving feelings of personal worthlessness.

15. **Hindustani** (hĭn′dŏŏ-stä′nē): a group of languages used in India.

WORDS
TO
KNOW

specialization (spĕsh′ə-lĭ-zā′shən) *n.* a focus on a particular activity or area of study

absurd (əb-sûrd′) *adj.* ridiculously unreasonable

May 20 I would not have noticed the new dishwasher, a boy of about sixteen, at the corner diner where I take my evening meals if not for the incident of the broken dishes. They crashed to the floor, shattering and sending bits of white china under the tables. The boy stood there, dazed and frightened, holding the empty tray in his hand. The whistles and cat-calls from the customers (the cries of "Hey, there go the profits! . . ." *"Mazeltov! . . ."* and "Well, *he* didn't work here very long. . . ." which invariably seem to follow the breaking of glass or dishware in a public restaurant) all seemed to confuse him.

When the owner came to see what the excitement was about, the boy cowered as if he expected to be struck and threw up his arms as if to ward off the blow.

"All right! All right, you dope," shouted the owner, "don't just stand there! Get the broom and sweep that mess up. A broom . . . a broom, you idiot! It's in the kitchen. Sweep up all the pieces."

The boy saw that he was not going to be punished. His frightened expression disappeared, and he smiled and hummed as he came back with the broom to sweep the floor. A few of the rowdier customers kept up the remarks, amusing themselves at his expense.

"Here, sonny, over here there's a nice piece behind you. . . ."

"C'mon, do it again. . . ."

"He's not so dumb. It's easier to break 'em than to wash 'em. . . ."

As his vacant eyes moved across the crowd of amused onlookers, he slowly mirrored their smiles and finally broke into an uncertain grin at the joke which he obviously did not understand.

I felt sick inside as I looked at his dull, <u>vacuous</u> smile, the wide, bright eyes of a child, uncertain but eager to please. They were laughing at him because he was mentally retarded.

And I had been laughing at him too.

Suddenly, I was furious at myself and all those who were smirking at him. I jumped up and shouted, "Shut up! Leave him alone! It's not his fault he can't understand! He can't help what he is! But for God's sake . . . he's still a human being!"

The room grew silent. I cursed myself for losing control and creating a scene. I tried not to look at the boy as I paid my check and walked out without touching my food. I felt ashamed for both of us.

> I cursed myself for losing control and creating a scene.

How strange it is that people of honest feelings and sensibility, who would not take advantage of a man born without arms or legs or eyes—how such people think nothing of abusing a man born with low intelligence. It infuriated me to think that not too long ago, I, like this boy, had foolishly played the clown.

And I had almost forgotten.

I'd hidden the picture of the old Charlie Gordon from myself because now that I was intelligent, it was something that had to be pushed out of my mind. But today in looking at that boy, for the first time I saw what I had been. *I was just like him!*

Only a short time ago, I learned that people laughed at me. Now I can see that unknowingly I joined with them in laughing at myself. That hurts most of all.

I have often reread my progress reports and seen the illiteracy, the childish <u>naïveté</u>, the

vacuous (văk'yo͞o-əs) *adj.* showing a lack of intelligence or thought
naïveté (nä′ēv-tā′) *n.* a lack of sophistication; simplicity

mind of low intelligence peering from a dark room, through the keyhole, at the dazzling light outside. I see that even in my dullness I knew that I was inferior and that other people had something I lacked—something denied me. In my mental blindness, I thought that it was somehow connected with the ability to read and write, and I was sure that if I could get those skills I would automatically have intelligence too.

Even a feeble-minded man wants to be like other men.

A child may not know how to feed itself, or what to eat, yet it knows of hunger.

This, then, is what I was like. I never knew. Even with my gift of intellectual awareness, I never really knew.

This day was good for me. Seeing the past more clearly, I have decided to use my knowledge and skills to work in the field of increasing human intelligence levels. Who is better equipped for this work? Who else has lived in both worlds? These are my people. Let me use my gift to do something for them.

Tomorrow, I will discuss with Dr. Strauss the manner in which I can work in this area. I may be able to help him work out the problems of widespread use of the technique which was used on me. I have several good ideas of my own.

There is so much that might be done with this technique. If I could be made into a genius, what about thousands of others like myself? What fantastic levels might be achieved by using this technique on normal people? on *geniuses?*

There are so many doors to open. I am impatient to begin.

PROGRESS REPORT 13

May 23 It happened today. Algernon bit me. I visited the lab to see him, as I do occasionally, and when I took him out of his cage, he snapped at my hand. I put him back and watched him for a while. He was unusually disturbed and vicious.

May 24 Burt, who is in charge of the experimental animals, tells me that Algernon is changing. He is less cooperative; he refuses to run the maze any more; general motivation has decreased. And he hasn't been eating. Everyone is upset about what this may mean.

May 25 They've been feeding Algernon, who now refuses to work the shifting-lock problem. Everyone identifies me with Algernon. In a way we're both the first of our kind. They're all pretending that Algernon's behavior is not necessarily significant for me. But it's hard to hide the fact that some of the other animals who were used in this experiment are showing strange behavior.

Dr. Strauss and Dr. Nemur have asked me not to come to the lab any more. I know what they're thinking, but I can't accept it. I am going ahead with my plans to carry their research forward. With all due respect to both of these fine scientists, I am well aware of their limitations. If there is an answer, I'll have to find it out for myself. Suddenly, time has become very important to me.

May 29 I have been given a lab of my own and permission to go ahead with the research. I'm onto something. Working day and night. I've had a cot moved into the lab. Most of my writing time is spent on the notes which I keep in a separate folder, but from time to time I feel it necessary to put down my moods and my thoughts out of sheer habit.

I find the calculus of intelligence to be a fascinating study. Here is the place for the application of all the knowledge I have acquired. In a sense it's the problem I've been concerned with all my life.

May 31 Dr. Strauss thinks I'm working too hard. Dr. Nemur says I'm trying to cram a lifetime of research and thought into a few weeks. I know I should rest, but I'm driven on by something inside that won't let me stop. I've got to find the reason for the sharp <u>regression</u> in Algernon. I've got to know *if* and *when* it will happen to me.

June 4

LETTER TO DR. STRAUSS *(copy)*

Dear Dr. Strauss:

Under separate cover I am sending you a copy of my report entitled "The Algernon-Gordon Effect: A Study of Structure and Function of Increased Intelligence," which I would like to have you read and have published.

As you see, my experiments are completed. I have included in my report all of my formulae, as well as mathematical analysis in the appendix. Of course, these should be verified.

Because of its importance to both you and Dr. Nemur (and need I say to myself, too?) I have checked and rechecked my results a dozen times in the hope of finding an error. I am sorry to say the results must stand. Yet for the sake of science, I am grateful for the little bit that I here add to the knowledge of the function of the human mind and of the laws governing the artificial increase of human intelligence.

I recall your once saying to me that an experimental *failure* or the *disproving* of a theory was as important to the advancement of learning as a success would be. I know now that this is true. I am sorry, however, that my own contribution to the field must rest upon the ashes of the work of two men I regard so highly.

Yours truly,

Charles Gordon

encl.: rept.

June 5 I must not become emotional. The facts and the results of my experiments are

Copyright © Vivienne Flesher.

clear, and the more sensational aspects of my own rapid climb cannot obscure the fact that the tripling of intelligence by the surgical technique developed by Drs. Strauss and Nemur must be viewed as having little or no practical applicability (at the present time) to the increase of human intelligence.

As I review the records and data on Algernon, I see that although he is still in his physical infancy, he has regressed mentally. Motor activity[16] is <u>impaired</u>; there is a general reduction of glandular activity; there is an accelerated loss of coordination.

---

16. **motor activity:** movement produced by use of the muscles.

There are also strong indications of progressive amnesia.[17]

As will be seen by my report, these and other physical and mental deterioration syndromes can be predicted with statistically significant results by the application of my formula.

The surgical stimulus to which we were both subjected has resulted in an intensification and acceleration of all mental processes. The unforeseen development, which I have taken the liberty of calling the Algernon-Gordon effect, is the logical extension of the entire intelligence speedup. The hypothesis here proven may be described simply in the following terms: Artificially increased intelligence deteriorates at a rate of time directly proportional to the quantity of the increase.

I feel that this, in itself, is an important discovery.

As long as I am able to write, I will continue to record my thoughts in these progress reports. It is one of my few pleasures. However, by all indications, my own mental deterioration will be very rapid.

I have already begun to notice signs of emotional instability and forgetfulness, the first symptoms of the burnout.

June 10 Deterioration progressing. I have become absent-minded. Algernon died two days ago. Dissection shows my predictions were right. His brain had decreased in weight, and there was a general smoothing out of cerebral convolutions as well as a deepening and broadening of brain fissures.[18]

I guess the same thing is or will soon be happening to me. Now that it's definite, I don't want it to happen.

I put Algernon's body in a cheese box and buried him in the back yard. I cried.

June 15 Dr. Strauss came to see me again. I wouldn't open the door, and I told him to go away. I want to be left to myself. I have become touchy and irritable. I feel the darkness closing in. It's hard to throw off thoughts of suicide. I keep telling myself how important this introspective journal will be.

It's a strange sensation to pick up a book that you've read and enjoyed just a few months ago and discover that you don't remember it. I remembered how great I thought John Milton was, but when I picked up *Paradise Lost,* I couldn't understand it at all. I got so angry I threw the book across the room.

I've got to try to hold on to some of it. Some of the things I've learned. Oh, God, please don't take it all away.

June 19 Sometimes, at night, I go out for a walk. Last night I couldn't remember where I lived. A policeman took me home. I have the strange feeling that this has all happened to me before—a long time ago. I keep telling myself I'm the only person in the world who can describe what's happening to me.

June 21 Why can't I remember? I've got to fight. I lie in bed for days, and I don't know

---

17. **progressive amnesia** (ăm-nē′zhə): a steadily worsening loss of memory.

18. **cerebral convolutions** (sĕr′ə-brəl kŏn′və-lōō′shənz) . . . **brain fissures** (fĭsh′ərz): features of the brain. Cerebral convolutions are the ridges or folds on the brain's surface; fissures are grooves that divide the brain into lobes, or sections.

WORDS TO KNOW

syndrome (sĭn′drōm′) *n.* a group of symptoms that characterizes a disease or psychological disorder

statistically (stə-tĭs′tĭ-klē) *adv.* in terms of the principles used to analyze numerical data

hypothesis (hī-pŏth′ĭ-sĭs) *n.* a theory used as a basis for research

proportional (prə-pôr′shə-nəl) *adj.* having a constant relation in degree or number

introspective (ĭn′trə-spĕk′tĭv) *adj.* examining one's own thoughts, feelings, and sensations

Copyright © Joel Peter Johnson.

who or where I am. Then it all comes back to me in a flash. Fugues[19] of amnesia. Symptoms of senility—second childhood. I can watch them coming on. It's so cruelly logical. I learned so much and so fast. Now my mind is deteriorating rapidly. I won't let it happen. I'll fight it. I can't help thinking of the boy in the restaurant, the blank expression, the silly smile, the people laughing at him. No— please—not that again . . .

June 22 I'm forgetting things that I learned recently. It seems to be following the classic

---

19. **fugues** (fyo͞ogz): psychological states in which people seem to be acting consciously, although later they have no memory of the activity.

pattern—the last things learned are the first things forgotten. Or is that the pattern? I'd better look it up again . . .

I reread my paper on the Algernon-Gordon effect, and I get the strange feeling that it was written by someone else. There are parts I don't even understand.

Motor activity impaired. I keep tripping over things, and it becomes increasingly difficult to type.

June 23 I've given up using the typewriter completely. My coordination is bad. I feel that I'm moving slower and slower. Had a terrible shock today. I picked up a copy of an article I used in my research, Krueger's "Über psychische Ganzheit," to see if it would help me understand what I had done. First I thought there was something wrong with my eyes. Then I realized I could no longer read German. I tested myself in other languages. All gone.

June 30 A week since I dared to write again. It's slipping away like sand through my fingers. Most of the books I have are too hard for me now. I get angry with them because I know that I read and understood them just a few weeks ago.

I keep telling myself I must keep writing these reports so that somebody will know what is happening to me. But it gets harder to form the words and remember spellings. I have to look up even simple words in the dictionary now, and it makes me impatient with myself.

Dr. Strauss comes around almost every day, but I told him I wouldn't see or speak to anybody. He feels guilty. They all do. But I don't blame anyone. I knew what might happen. But how it hurts.

July 7 I don't know where the week went. Todays Sunday I know because I can see through my window people going to church. I think I stayed in bed all week but I remember Mrs. Flynn bringing food to me a few

times. I keep saying over and over Ive got to do something but then I forget or maybe its just easier not to do what I say Im going to do.

I think of my mother and father a lot these days. I found a picture of them with me taken at a beach. My father has a big ball under his arm and my mother is holding me by the hand. I dont remember them the way they are in the picture. All I remember is my father drunk most of the time and arguing with mom about money.

He never shaved much and he used to scratch my face when he hugged me. My mother said he died but Cousin Miltie said he heard his mom and dad say that my father ran away with another woman. When I asked my mother she slapped my face and said my father was dead. I dont think I ever found out which was true but I dont care much. (He said he was going to take me to see cows on a farm once but he never did. He never kept his promises . . .)

July 10 My landlady Mrs. Flynn is very worried about me. She says the way I lay around all day and dont do anything I remind her of her son before she threw him out of the house. She said she doesnt like loafers. If Im sick its one thing, but if Im a loafer thats another thing and she wont have it. I told her I think Im sick.

I try to read a little bit every day, mostly stories, but sometimes I have to read the same thing over and over again because I dont know what it means. And its hard to write. I know I should look up all the words in the dictionary but its so hard and Im so tired all the time.

Then I got the idea that I would only use the easy words instead of the long hard ones. That saves time. I put flowers on Algernons grave about once a week. Mrs Flynn thinks Im crazy to put flowers on a mouses grave but I told her that Algernon was special.

July 14 Its sunday again. I dont have

anything to do to keep me busy now because my television set is broke and I dont have any money to get it fixed. (I think I lost this months check from the lab. I dont remember)

I get awful headaches and asperin doesnt help me much. Mrs Flynn knows Im really sick and she feels very sorry for me. Shes a wonderful woman whenever someone is sick.

July 22 Mrs Flynn called a strange doctor to see me. She was afraid I was going to die. I told the doctor I wasnt too sick and that I only forget sometimes. He asked me did I have any friends or relatives and I said no I dont have any. I told him I had a friend called Algernon once but he was a mouse and we used to run races together. He looked at me kind of funny like he thought I was crazy.

He smiled when I told him I used to be a genius. He talked to me like I was a baby and he winked at Mrs Flynn. I got mad and chased him out because he was making fun of me the way they all used to.

July 24 I have no more money and Mrs Flynn says I got to go to work somewhere and pay the rent because I havent paid for over two months. I dont know any work but the job I used to have at Donnegans Plastic Box Company. I dont want to go back there because they all knew me when I was smart and maybe they'll laugh at me. But I dont know what else to do to get money.

July 25 I was looking at some of my old progress reports and its very funny but I cant read what I wrote. I can make out some of the words but they dont make sense.

Miss Kinnian came to the door but I said go away I dont want to see you. She cried and I cried too but I wouldnt let her in because I didnt want her to laugh at me. I told her I didn't like her any more. I told her I didnt

want to be smart any more. Thats not true. I still love her and I still want to be smart but I had to say that so shed go away. She gave Mrs. Flynn money to pay the rent. I dont want that. I got to get a job.

Please . . . please let me not forget how to read and write . . .

July 27 Mr. Donnegan was very nice when I came back and asked him for my old job of janitor. First he was very suspicious but I told him what happened to me then he looked very sad and put his hand on my shoulder and said Charlie Gordon you got guts.

Everybody looked at me when I came downstairs and started working in the toilet sweeping it out like I used to. I told myself Charlie if they make fun of you dont get sore because you remember their not so smart as you once thot they were. And besides they were once your friends and if they laughed at you that doesnt mean anything because they liked you too.

One of the new men who came to work there after I went away made a nasty crack he said hey Charlie I hear your a very smart fella a real quiz kid. Say something intelligent. I felt bad but Joe Carp came over and grabbed him by the shirt and said leave him alone you lousy cracker or Ill break your neck. I didnt expect Joe to take my part so I guess hes really my friend.

Later Frank Reilly came over and said Charlie if anybody bothers you or trys to take advantage you call me or Joe and we will set em straight. I said thanks Frank and I got choked up so I had to turn around and go into the supply room so he wouldnt see me cry. Its good to have friends.

July 28 I did a dumb thing today I forgot I wasnt in Miss Kinnians class at the adult

center any more like I use to be. I went in and sat down in my old seat in the back of the room and she looked at me funny and she said Charles. I dint remember she ever called me that before only Charlie so I said hello Miss Kinnian Im redy for my lesin today only I lost my reader that we was using. She startid to cry and run out of the room and everybody looked at me and I saw they wasnt the same pepul who use to be in my class.

Then all of a suddin I rememberd some things about the operashun and me getting smart and I said holy smoke I reely pulled a Charlie Gordon that time. I went away before she come back to the room.

Thats why Im going away from New York for good. I dont want to do nothing like that agen. I dont want Miss Kinnian to feel sorry for me. Evry body feels sorry at the factery and I dont want that eather so Im going someplace where nobody knows that Charlie Gordon was once a genus and now he cant even reed a book or rite good.

Im taking a cuple of books along and even if I cant reed them Ill practise hard and maybe I wont forget every thing I lerned. If I try reel hard maybe Ill be a littel bit smarter then I was before the operashun. I got my rabits foot and my luky penny and maybe they will help me.

If you ever reed this Miss Kinnian dont be sorry for me Im glad I got a second chanse to be smart becaus I lerned a lot of things that I never even new were in this world and Im grateful that I saw it all for a littel bit. I dont know why Im dumb agen or what I did wrong maybe its becaus I dint try hard enuff. But if I try and practis very hard maybe Ill get a littl smarter and know what all the words are. I remember a littel bit how nice I had a feeling with the blue book that has the torn cover when I red it. Thats why Im gonna keep trying to get smart so I can have that feeling agen. Its a good feeling to know things and be smart. I wish I had it rite now if I did I woud sit down and reed all the time. Anyway I bet Im the first dumb person in the world who ever found out somthing importent for sience. I remember I did somthing but I dont remember what. So I gess its like I did it for all the dumb pepul like me.

Goodbye Miss Kinnian and Dr. Strauss and evreybody. And P.S. please tell Dr Nemur not to be such a grouch when pepul laff at him and he woud have more frends. Its easy to make frends if you let pepul laff at you. Im going to have lots of frends where I go.

P.P.S. Please if you get a chanse put some flowers on Algernons grave in the bak yard. . . . ❖

P.P.S. Please if you get a chanse put some flowers on Algernons grave in the bak yard. . . .

CLARIFY

Why is Algernon special to Charlie?

RESPONDING
OPTIONS

FROM PERSONAL RESPONSE TO CRITICAL ANALYSIS

REFLECT

1. What is your reaction to Charlie's experiences? Write your thoughts in your notebook.

RETHINK

2. Do you think the doctors should have performed the operation on Charlie? Why or why not?

3. In your opinion, is Charlie a hero? Give reasons for your answer.

4. Refer to the chart you made for the Reading Connection on page 513, and decide which of the changes that Charlie goes through are most difficult for him. Explain your choices.

5. If Charlie were asked to participate in another experiment to increase his intelligence, do you think he would accept? Give reasons for your opinion.

   Consider
   - how he has felt about becoming intelligent
   - whether he is happier before or after becoming a genius
   - what, if anything, he has gained by the end of the story

6. What do you think might become of Charlie after he leaves New York?

RELATE

7. A patient gives "informed consent" to a medical procedure if his or her agreement is based on a thorough understanding of the risks and benefits involved. Do you think that when a patient cannot completely understand a procedure, doctors should make the decision for the patient? Weigh the possible benefits to the patient or to medical science against the rights of the patient.

ANOTHER PATHWAY

Cooperative Learning

Hold a debate about whether the operation should have been performed on Charlie. To review the events of the story and begin preparing for the debate, you might look over the chart you made for the Reading Connection on page 513.

QUICKWRITES

1. In his progress report of April 28, Charlie writes that he is in love with Miss Kinnian. If Miss Kinnian were also writing progress reports, what might she write about Charlie? Write her **entry** for that day.

2. Charlie says that he is leaving for a place where people won't feel sorry for him. He needs a job. Assume the identity of Mr. Donnegan, Charlie's boss, and write a **letter of recommendation** for Charlie.

3. Rewrite Charlie's **progress report** of "Martch 6," using correct spelling, punctuation, and grammar. When you have finished, compare your work with that of other students.

📁 *PORTFOLIO Save your writing. You may want to use it later as a springboard to a piece for your portfolio.*

LITERARY CONCEPTS

As you filled in the chart for the Reading Connection, you made inferences about dramatic changes in Charlie's personality and intelligence. An author can show **character development** through dialogue, through description, and in other ways. One way in which Daniel Keyes shows change in his main character is through the growth and decline of Charlie's ability to spell correctly. In what other ways does the author show Charlie changing?

ALTERNATIVE ACTIVITIES

1. ***Cooperative Learning*** With some classmates, watch a videotape of *Charly,* the film based on Keyes's novelization of "Flowers for Algernon." Then get together for a **discussion** in which you compare the film with the short story. Which do you like better? Does the film portray Charlie as you imagine him? What would you do differently if you were filming the story?

2. Research a topic related to this story, such as psychological testing or "smart drugs." Share your findings with the class in an **oral report.**

3. Investigate the controversy surrounding the question of animal experimentation. Find out about the arguments on both sides of the issue, and write a balanced **research paper** on the topic.

ACROSS THE CURRICULUM

Science After the operation, Charlie's ability to reason and solve problems develops dramatically. Find out what part of the brain is responsible for this ability and what other thinking functions it might control. Make a drawing of the brain and label that region.

Science Find an abstract—a summary, usually only one or two paragraphs long, of scientific research—in a scientific journal. Using it as a model, write a medical abstract describing the experiment in which Charlie was involved, including the hypothesis, the procedure, and the results.

ART CONNECTION

Look at the painting reproduced on page 537. What does this image mean to you? Take some time to examine the details of the work. How does it relate to the main character of the story?

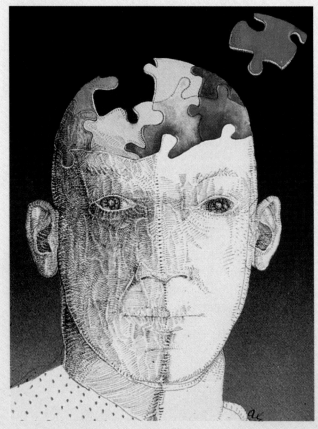

Copyright © Alan Cober/Stock Illustration Source.

On a separate sheet of paper, answer the following questions.

1. If a person calls you **vacuous,** are you being complimented or insulted? Why?
2. Is water **tangible** or not? Explain.
3. Who is probably more **introspective**—a poet or a doctor? Explain.
4. If eyeglasses **impair** your vision, are they good or bad for you?
5. Does an **opportunist** take chances? Why or why not?
6. Besides medicine, what other fields have areas of **specialization?**
7. Is a **hypothesis** true, false, or unproved?
8. Would a **shrew** be popular or unpopular? Why?
9. Who would be more likely to show **naïveté**—a child or an adult?
10. If a person proves an argument **statistically,** what is she using?
11. **Regression** suggests movement in what direction?
12. Which scientific discovery would cause a greater **sensation**—a cure for a foot disease or a cure for AIDS? Explain.
13. If a mouse's growth is directly **proportional** to the amount it eats, how will eating more affect its growth?
14. If someone thought that an idea of yours was **absurd,** would you be happy or sad? Explain.
15. What kind of professional would likely treat a **syndrome?**

DANIEL KEYES

1927–

After Daniel Keyes won a Hugo Award for "Flowers for Algernon" at the World Science Fiction Convention in 1959, he expanded the story into a novel. For the novel, he won a Nebula Award from the Science Fiction Writers of America in 1966. Even *Charly,* the feature film based on the novel, was a winner: Cliff Robertson was presented with an Academy Award in 1968 for his portrayal of Charlie in the movie. "Flowers for Algernon" has also been the basis for TV and stage plays (including a musical) produced in the United States, Canada, Britain, France, Poland, Australia, and Japan.

Given the subject matter of Keyes's famous story, it is not surprising that he majored in psychology at Brooklyn College. He says he is "fascinated by the complexities of the human mind." One of his novels—*The Minds of Billy Milligan,* based on the story of a real person—came about in an unusual way. Billy Milligan, who had 24 personalities, chose Keyes to write the book because several of his "selves" had read "Flowers for Algernon" and agreed that Keyes was the perfect author to tell their tale.

Born in Brooklyn, New York, Keyes joined the U.S. Maritime Service as a teenager, working as a ship's purser on oil tankers. After finishing college, he had jobs in publishing and in fashion photography, then became a teacher at the high school from which he had graduated. Since 1966, he has taught creative writing and American literature at Ohio University. Currently on extended leave in Boca Raton, Florida, he is writing full time.

PREVIEWING

POETRY

Paul Revere's Ride
Henry Wadsworth Longfellow

PERSONAL CONNECTION

In Paul Revere's time, people who showed strong support for, or risked their lives for, American independence were considered patriots. Whom would you consider to be a patriot today? Do you think patriotism is an old-fashioned idea, or is it a timeless concept—one that will never go out of fashion? How is patriotism shown today? Explore these questions, either alone or with a small group of classmates. Jot down your ideas in a chart like the one shown.

★ Patriotism: Outdated or Timeless? ★	
Modern Patriots	How Patriotism Is Shown Today

HISTORICAL CONNECTION

On the third Monday of each April, the city of Boston, Massachusetts, celebrates Patriots' Day to commemorate the battles of Lexington and Concord, which marked the beginning of the Revolutionary War. "Paul Revere's Ride" relates the dramatic events that took place on the night before these battles.

By 1775, many American colonists had grown rebellious toward their British rulers. The British decided to arrest the rebel leaders and to march on Concord to seize a stockpile of colonial weapons. The rebels did not know the route the British troops would take. On the night of April 18, Paul Revere nervously awaited the answer from a spy. He had agreed to ride out and warn the colonists of the British advance—and his ride that night would make him famous.

Map of Paul Revere's Ride

MASSACHUSETTS

Concord River
Concord

Sudbury River

Lexington

Mystic River

Boston Harbor

Middlesex County

Cambridge

Charles River

Boston

Miles
0   100   200

← Route of Paul Revere
← Route of British Forces
✕ Battle

READING CONNECTION

Summarizing "Paul Revere's Ride" tells the story of a patriot's daring mission. Summarizing the important ideas in the poem will help you understand and remember what you read. To summarize is to tell briefly in your own words the main ideas of a piece of writing, leaving out unimportant details. First read the poem without taking notes. Then go back and jot down the main ideas and important details in each stanza. Finally, use your notes to write a brief summary of Paul Revere's story.

Paul Revere's Ride

by Henry Wadsworth Longfellow

Listen, my children, and you shall hear
Of the midnight ride of Paul Revere,
On the eighteenth of April, in Seventy-five;
Hardly a man is now alive
5 Who remembers that famous day and year.

He said to his friend, "If the British march
By land or sea from the town to-night,
Hang a lantern aloft in the belfry arch[1]
Of the North Church tower as a signal light,—
10 One if by land, and two if by sea;
And I on the opposite shore will be,
Ready to ride and spread the alarm
Through every Middlesex[2] village and farm,
For the country folk to be up and to arm."

15 Then he said, "Good-night!" and with muffled oar
Silently rowed to the Charlestown shore,
Just as the moon rose over the bay,
Where swinging wide at her moorings[3] lay
The *Somerset,* British man-of-war;[4]
20 A phantom ship, with each mast and spar[5]
Across the moon like a prison bar,
And a huge black hulk, that was magnified
By its own reflection in the tide.

Meanwhile, his friend, through alley and street
25 Wanders and watches, with eager ears,
Till in the silence around him he hears
The muster of men at the barrack door,
The sound of arms, and the tramp of feet,

Midnight Ride of Paul Revere (1931),
Grant Wood. Oil on composition board,
30" × 40", The Metropolitan Museum
of Art, Arthur Hoppock Hearn Fund,
1950 (50.117). Copyright © 1996 Estate
of Grant Wood/Licensed by VAGA, New
York. Photo Copyright © 1988 The
Metropolitan Museum of Art.

---

1. **belfry** (bĕl′frē) **arch:** a curved opening in a bell tower.
2. **Middlesex:** a county of eastern Massachusetts, setting for the first battle of the Revolutionary War on April 19, 1775.
3. **moorings:** the place where a ship is docked.
4. **man-of-war:** warship.
5. **spar:** a pole supporting a ship's sail.

And the measured tread of the grenadiers,[6]
30 Marching down to their boats on the shore.

Then he climbed the tower of the Old North Church,
By the wooden stairs, with stealthy tread,[7]
To the belfry chamber overhead,
And startled the pigeons from their perch
35 On the somber[8] rafters, that round him made
Masses and moving shapes of shade,—
By the trembling ladder, steep and tall,
To the highest window in the wall,
Where he paused to listen and look down
40 A moment on the roofs of the town
And the moonlight flowing over all.

Beneath, in the churchyard, lay the dead,
In their night encampment on the hill,
Wrapped in silence so deep and still
45 That he could hear, like a sentinel's[9] tread,
The watchful night-wind, as it went
Creeping along from tent to tent,
And seeming to whisper, "All is well!"
A moment only he feels the spell
50 Of the place and the hour, and the secret dread
Of the lonely belfry and the dead;
For suddenly all his thoughts are bent
On a shadowy something far away,
Where the river widens to meet the bay,—
55 A line of black that bends and floats
On the rising tide like a bridge of boats.

Meanwhile, impatient to mount and ride,
Booted and spurred, with a heavy stride
On the opposite shore walked Paul Revere.
60 Now he patted his horse's side,
Now he gazed at the landscape far and near,
Then, impetuous,[10] stamped the earth,

---

6. **grenadiers** (grĕn´ə-dîrz´): foot soldiers.

7. **stealthy tread:** quiet footsteps.

8. **somber:** gloomy.

9. **sentinel's:** of a guard or sentry.

10. **impetuous** (ĭm-pĕch´ōō-əs): acting suddenly, on impulse.

And turned and tightened his saddle girth;[11]
But mostly he watched with eager search
65 The belfry tower of the Old North Church,
As it rose above the graves on the hill,
Lonely and spectral[12] and somber and still.
And lo! as he looks, on the belfry's height
A glimmer, and then a gleam of light!
70 He springs to the saddle, the bridle he turns,
But lingers and gazes, till full on his sight
A second lamp in the belfry burns.

A hurry of hoofs in a village street,
A shape in the moonlight, a bulk in the dark,
75 And beneath, from the pebbles, in passing, a spark
Struck out by a steed flying fearless and fleet;
That was all! And yet, through the gloom and the light,
The fate of a nation was riding that night;
And the spark struck out by that steed, in his flight,
80 Kindled the land into flame with its heat.
He has left the village and mounted the steep,
And beneath him, tranquil and broad and deep,
Is the Mystic,[13] meeting the ocean tides;
And under the alders[14] that skirt its edge,
85 Now soft on the sand, now loud on the ledge,
Is heard the tramp of his steed as he rides.

It was twelve by the village clock,
When he crossed the bridge into Medford town.
He heard the crowing of the cock,
90 And the barking of the farmer's dog,
And felt the damp of the river fog,
That rises after the sun goes down.

It was one by the village clock,
When he galloped into Lexington.
95 He saw the gilded weathercock
Swim in the moonlight as he passed,
And the meeting-house windows, blank and bare,
Gaze at him with a spectral glare,

---

11. **saddle girth:** the strap attaching a saddle to a horse's body.

12. **spectral:** ghostly.

13. **Mystic:** a short river flowing into Boston Harbor.

14. **alders:** trees of the birch family.

As if they already stood aghast[15]
100 At the bloody work they would look upon.

It was two by the village clock,
When he came to the bridge in Concord town.
He heard the bleating[16] of the flock,
And the twitter of birds among the trees,
105 And felt the breath of the morning breeze
Blowing over the meadow brown.
And one was safe and asleep in his bed
Who at the bridge would be first to fall,
Who that day would be lying dead,
110 Pierced by a British musket-ball.

You know the rest. In the books you have read
How the British Regulars[17] fired and fled,—
How the farmers gave them ball for ball,
From behind each fence and farmyard wall,
115 Chasing the redcoats down the lane,
Then crossing the fields to emerge again
Under the trees at the turn of the road,
And only pausing to fire and load.

So through the night rode Paul Revere;
120 And so through the night went his cry of alarm
To every Middlesex village and farm,—
A cry of defiance, and not of fear,
A voice in the darkness, a knock at the door,
And a word that shall echo forevermore!
125 For, borne on the night-wind of the Past,
Through all our history, to the last,
In the hour of darkness and peril[18] and need,
The people will waken and listen to hear
The hurrying hoof-beats of that steed,
130 And the midnight message of Paul Revere.

---

15. **aghast** (ə-găst′): terrified.
16. **bleating:** the crying of sheep.
17. **British Regulars:** members of Great Britain's standing army.
18. **peril:** danger.

Paul Revere: The Man

People living in the Boston of 1775 referred to Paul Revere as Bold Revere. His reputation was glowing; his contemporaries knew him to be sensible and even-tempered, living a life in which boldness and good sense were finely balanced. He was the best American silversmith of his time, and the scope of his patriotism extended far beyond his famous "midnight ride."

Born in Boston in 1735, Revere attended school until he was 13, when he began a long apprenticeship with his silversmith father. When Revere was 19, his father died, leaving the teenager in charge of the large family. At the age of 21, although he was against warfare in principle, he served briefly in the French and Indian War at Lake George, New York.

After returning to Boston, he married Sarah Orne and soon became the most accomplished silversmith in the New World, producing a greater variety of works than any other silversmith of his time. It was not long before he joined groups opposed to the British rule of the American colonies. He made frequent trips on horseback to Philadelphia, carrying secret information to revolutionary groups. Although these grueling, dangerous 11-day trips took him away from his work and his growing family, he eventually fathered 16 children—

Paul Revere (about 1768), John Singleton Copley. Oil on canvas, 35" × 28½", courtesy of Museum of Fine Arts, Boston, gift of Joseph W., William B., and Edward H. R. Revere (30.781). Copyright © 1995, all rights reserved.

8 with Sarah, who died in 1773, and 8 with his second wife, Rachel, whom he married later that year.

Revere aided in the dumping of British tea during the famous Boston Tea Party. He engraved political cartoons and patrolled the streets at night. For all of this, he was honored in a popular song as "Our . . . bold Revere, / With hands to do, and words to cheer / For liberty and laws . . ." By April 1775, however, the British knew about his activities. A marked man, he was ready to risk his life and all he had on a ride to warn his countrymen of the British advance.

After the Revolutionary War, Revere kept up his feverish pace. Eager to see the U.S. economy become independent of Europe's, he learned how to make hardware, parts for ships, and stoves. He was the first craftsman in the United States to make church bells, producing almost 400 of them. At the age of 65, still far from retirement, Revere opened the first mill for rolling copper sheets in the United States, risking $25,000 of his own money and borrowing another $10,000. Not long before his death in 1818, Revere worked with Robert Fulton, making copper for the boilers of the world's first successful steamboat.

RESPONDING OPTIONS

FROM PERSONAL RESPONSE TO CRITICAL ANALYSIS

REFLECT   1. Did anything in this account of Paul Revere's ride surprise you? Jot down your thoughts in your notebook.

RETHINK   2. Does Paul Revere match your concept of an unlikely hero? Why or why not?

3. Choose a stanza from "Paul Revere's Ride" that you think creates a strong mood. What feeling does the stanza call forth in you? In which lines do poetic devices—such as rhyme, rhythm, and figurative language—help to create the mood?

4. How does the effect of this poem differ from the effect a prose account of Revere's ride would have? Which form do you prefer for the telling of this story? Why?

RELATE   5. Look at the ideas about patriotism you recorded for the Personal Connection on page 542. If you had to name a present-day figure with the patriotic spirit of Paul Revere, whom would you choose? Explain your choice.

ANOTHER PATHWAY

Draw a series of cartoons showing the sequence of events on the night of April 18, 1775. To help you plan your drawings, refer to the notes and summary you made for the Reading Connection on page 542.

LITERARY CONCEPTS

"Paul Revere's Ride" is called a **narrative poem** because it tells a story, or narrative, in poetic form. Like a work of prose fiction, a narrative poem has a setting, a plot, and characters. What is the setting of this poem, and who are its main characters? How might you summarize the poem's plot in a single sentence?

QUICKWRITES

1. With a partner, choose a famous event in U.S. history. Then write a **narrative poem** about the event, imitating the style of "Paul Revere's Ride."

2. Turn the story of Paul Revere's ride into a **news article** that answers the important journalistic questions *who, what, when, where,* and *why.* Include a headline that conveys the drama and importance of the event.

📁 **PORTFOLIO** *Save your writing. You may want to use it later as a springboard to a piece for your portfolio.*

ALTERNATIVE ACTIVITIES

1. Plan a **dramatic reading** of "Paul Revere's Ride" or another of Longfellow's narrative poems. You may wish to work with a partner, reading passages alternately to the accompaniment of background music that reflects the mood of the poem. Perform the reading for your classmates.

2. A ballad is a narrative poem that is designed to be sung. Ballads are usually about ordinary people who have unusual adventures; they are often written in four-line stanzas with regular patterns of rhythm and rhyme. With a partner, compose a **ballad** about Paul Revere. Present a live or tape-recorded performance of it to the class.

LITERARY LINKS

Compare and contrast "Paul Revere's Ride" with "O Captain! My Captain!" For what purpose was each poem written? How are the subjects alike, and how are they different? How do the poets' uses of rhythm, rhyme, figures of speech (metaphors, similes, and personification), alliteration, and imagery compare?

ACROSS THE CURRICULUM

Social Studies Longfellow changed or omitted several key facts about Paul Revere's ride. Research what really happened that night, and report your findings to the class in a talk or a written narrative.

HENRY WADSWORTH LONGFELLOW

1807–1882

When Henry Wadsworth Longfellow was a senior at Bowdoin College, he wrote these words to his father: "I most eagerly aspire after future eminence in literature." Unlike many writers, Longfellow completely achieved his literary aspirations—he was to become the most popular American poet of his time.

Born in Portland, Maine, Longfellow left public school for private school when he was 5 because he was afraid of "rough boys." He was admitted to Bowdoin College at the age of 14 and had published nearly 40 poems by the time he graduated at 18. After his graduation, the skill he had shown in translating a Latin poem led the trustees of Bowdoin to offer him the unprecedented opportunity of becoming the first professor of modern languages there. He created his own texts in this new field and later accepted a professorship at Harvard.

Longfellow's personal life was marked by deep sadness. His first wife died from an illness after four years of marriage. "What a solitary, lonely being I am!" he wrote. Eight years later he married Frances Appleton, with whom he had six children. After 18 happy years, this marriage ended tragically with Frances's death from burns she received when her dress caught fire. Because Longfellow's face and hands had been badly burned while trying to save her, he was unable to attend her funeral, held on the anniversary of their wedding day. His life, Longfellow said, "crumbled away like sand."

OTHER WORKS *The Courtship of Miles Standish, Evangeline: A Tale of Acadia, The Song of Hiawatha,* "The Village Blacksmith," "The Children's Hour"

LASERLINKS
• *HISTORICAL CONNECTION*

NONFICTION

from Harriet Tubman: Conductor on the Underground Railroad

Ann Petry

PERSONAL CONNECTION

In the years immediately preceding the U.S. Civil War, about 4 million African Americans labored as slaves on Southern plantations. Each year, several thousand of these slaves would attempt to escape northward, and many succeeded. Those who were recaptured, however, might be beaten, maimed, or even killed. If you had been a slave at that time, would you have tried to escape? Why or why not? Write down your thoughts for class discussion.

HISTORICAL CONNECTION

The term *Underground Railroad*—referring not to a railroad but to a secret system of individuals who helped slaves escape to the North and to Canada—became popular after a slave named Tice Davids escaped from his Kentucky master in 1831. Davids's bewildered master said that his slave must have "gone off on an underground railroad."

The Underground Railroad had "stations" where fleeing slaves could get food and drink. The "commuter's ticket" was the password "A friend with friends." Most important, the railroad had "conductors" like Harriet Tubman, who helped escort the slaves to freedom. Conducting slaves to freedom became even more risky after the passage of the Fugitive Slave Law of 1850 made it a federal crime to assist a runaway slave.

READING CONNECTION

Motivation The reasons that move a person to act are his or her motivation. People can be motivated by such things as dedication, love, fear, and guilt. As you read this selection, think about what motivated Harriet Tubman to help so many slaves escape. Take note of her personality, her beliefs, and the circumstances she faced.

The Underground Railroad

LASERLINKS
• *HISTORICAL CONNECTION*

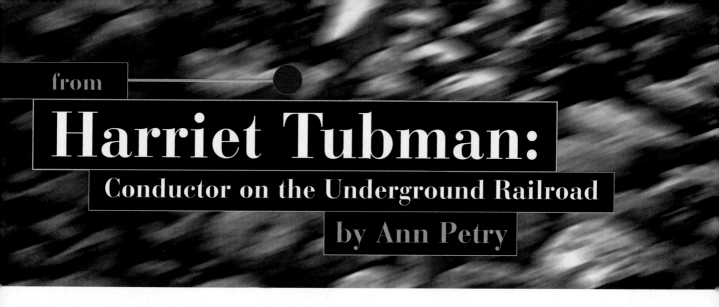

from
Harriet Tubman:
Conductor on the Underground Railroad
by Ann Petry

The Railroad Runs to Canada

ALONG THE EASTERN SHORE OF MARYLAND, IN DORCHESTER COUNTY, IN CAROLINE COUNTY, THE MASTERS KEPT HEARING WHISPERS ABOUT THE MAN NAMED MOSES, WHO WAS RUNNING OFF SLAVES. AT FIRST THEY DID NOT BELIEVE IN HIS EXISTENCE. THE STORIES ABOUT HIM WERE FANTASTIC, UNBELIEVABLE. YET THEY WATCHED FOR HIM. THEY OFFERED REWARDS FOR HIS CAPTURE.

They never saw him. Now and then they heard whispered rumors to the effect that he was in the neighborhood. The woods were searched. The roads were watched. There was never anything to indicate his whereabouts. But a few days afterward, a goodly number of slaves would be gone from the plantation. Neither the master nor the overseer had heard or seen anything unusual in the quarter.[1] Sometimes one or the other would vaguely remember having heard a whippoorwill call somewhere in the woods, close by, late at night. Though it was the wrong season for whippoorwills.

Sometimes the masters thought they had heard the cry of a hoot owl, repeated, and would remember having thought that the intervals between the low, moaning cry were wrong, that it had been repeated four times in succession instead of three. There was never anything more than that to suggest that all was not well in the quarter. Yet when morning came, they invariably discovered that a group of the finest slaves had taken to their heels.

Unfortunately, the discovery was almost always made on a Sunday. Thus a whole day was lost before the machinery of pursuit could be set in motion. The posters offering rewards for the fugitives could not be printed until Monday. The men who made a living hunting for runaway slaves were out of reach, off in the woods with their dogs and their guns, in pursuit of four-footed game, or they were in camp meetings saying their prayers with their wives and families beside them.

Harriet Tubman could have told them that there was far more involved in this matter of running off slaves than signaling the would-be runaways by imitating the call of a whippoorwill or a hoot owl, far more involved than a

---

1. **quarter:** the area in which slaves lived.

Forward (1967), Jacob Lawrence. Tempera on masonite, 23⅞" × 35¹⁵⁄₁₆", North Carolina Museum of Art, Raleigh, purchased with funds from the State of North Carolina.

matter of waiting for a clear night when the North Star was visible.

In December 1851, when she started out with the band of fugitives that she planned to take to Canada, she had been in the vicinity of the plantation for days, planning the trip, carefully selecting the slaves that she would take with her.

She had announced her arrival in the quarter by singing the forbidden spiritual—"Go down, Moses, 'way down to Egypt Land"[2]— singing it softly outside the door of a slave cabin late at night. The husky voice was beautiful even when it was barely more than a murmur <u>borne</u> on the wind.

Once she had made her presence known, word of her coming spread from cabin to cabin. The slaves whispered to each other, ear to mouth, mouth to ear, "Moses is here." "Moses has come." "Get ready. Moses is back again." The ones who had agreed to go north with her put ashcake and salt herring in an old bandanna, hastily tied it into a bundle, and then waited patiently for the signal that meant it was time to start.

There were eleven in this party, including one of her brothers and his wife. It was the largest group that she had ever conducted, but she was determined that more and more slaves should know what freedom was like.

---

2. **"Go down, Moses, 'way down to Egypt Land":** a line from a well-known African-American folk song about Moses leading the enslaved Israelites out of Egypt.

WORDS
TO
KNOW

borne (bôrn) *adj.* carried **bear** *v.*

She had to take them all the way to Canada. The Fugitive Slave Law[3] was no longer a great many incomprehensible words written down on the country's law books. The new law had become a reality. It was Thomas Sims, a boy, picked up on the streets of Boston at night and shipped back to Georgia. It was Jerry and Shadrach, arrested and jailed with no warning.

She had never been in Canada. The route beyond Philadelphia was strange to her. But she could not let the runaways who accompanied her know this. As they walked along, she told them stories of her own first flight; she kept painting vivid word pictures of what it would be like to be free.

But there were so many of them this time. She knew moments of doubt when she was half-afraid and kept looking back over her shoulder, imagining that she heard the sound of pursuit. They would certainly be pursued. Eleven of them. Eleven thousand dollars' worth of flesh and bone and muscle that belonged to Maryland planters. If they were caught, the eleven runaways would be whipped and sold south, but she—she would probably be hanged.

They tried to sleep during the day, but they never could wholly relax into sleep. She could tell by the positions they assumed, by their restless movements. And they walked at night. Their progress was slow. It took them three nights of walking to reach the first stop. She had told them about the place where they would stay, promising warmth and good food, holding these things out to them as an incentive to keep going.

When she knocked on the door of a farmhouse, a place where she and her parties of runaways had always been welcome, always been given shelter and plenty to eat, there was no answer. She knocked again, softly. A voice from within said, "Who is it?" There was fear in the voice.

She knew instantly from the sound of the voice that there was something wrong. She said, "A friend with friends," the password on the Underground Railroad.

The door opened, slowly. The man who stood in the doorway looked at her coldly, looked with unconcealed astonishment and fear at the eleven disheveled runaways who were standing near her. Then he shouted, "Too many, too many. It's not safe. My place was searched last week. It's not safe!" and slammed the door in her face.

She turned away from the house, frowning. She had promised her passengers food and rest and warmth, and instead of that there would be hunger and cold and more walking over the frozen ground. Somehow she would have to instill courage into these eleven people, most of them strangers, would have to feed them on hope and bright dreams of freedom instead of the fried pork and corn bread and milk she had promised them.

They stumbled along behind her, half-dead for sleep, and she urged them on, though she was as tired and as discouraged as they were. She had never been in Canada, but she kept painting wondrous word pictures of what it would be like. She managed to dispel their fear of pursuit so that they would not become hysterical, panic-stricken. Then she had to bring

---

3. **Fugitive Slave Law:** a law passed in 1850, allowing slave owners to recover escaped slaves even if they had reached free states.

WORDS	**disheveled** (dĭ-shĕv′əld) *adj.* messy; untidy
TO	**instill** (ĭn-stĭl′) *v.* to supply gradually
KNOW	**dispel** (dĭ-spĕl′) *v.* to drive away

some of the fear back so that they would stay awake and keep walking though they drooped with sleep.

Yet during the day, when they lay down deep in a thicket, they never really slept, because if a twig snapped or the wind sighed in the branches of a pine tree, they jumped to their feet, afraid of their own shadows, shivering and shaking. It was very cold, but they dared not make fires because someone would see the smoke and wonder about it.

She kept thinking, Eleven of them. Eleven thousand dollars' worth of slaves. And she had to take them all the way to Canada. Sometimes she told them about Thomas Garrett, in Wilmington. She said he was their friend even though he did not know them. He was the friend of all fugitives. He called them God's poor. He was a Quaker[4] and his speech was a little different from that of other people. His clothing was different, too. He wore the wide-brimmed hat that the Quakers wear.

She said that he had thick white hair, soft, almost like a baby's, and the kindest eyes she had ever seen. He was a big man and strong, but he had never used his strength to harm anyone, always to help people. He would give all of them a new pair of shoes. Everybody. He always did. Once they reached his house in Wilmington, they would be safe. He would see to it that they were.

She described the house where he lived, told them about the store where he sold shoes. She said he kept a pail of milk and a loaf of bread in the drawer of his desk so that he would have food ready at hand for any of God's poor who should suddenly appear before him, fainting with hunger. There was a hidden room in the store. A whole wall swung open, and behind it was a room where he could hide fugitives. On the wall there were shelves filled with small boxes—boxes of shoes—so that you would never guess that the wall actually opened.

While she talked, she kept watching them. They did not believe her. She could tell by their expressions. They were thinking, New shoes, Thomas Garrett, Quaker, Wilmington—what foolishness was this? Who knew if she told the truth? Where was she taking them anyway?

That night they reached the next stop—a farm that belonged to a German. She made the runaways take shelter behind trees at the edge of the fields before she knocked at the door. She hesitated before she approached the door, thinking, Suppose that he, too, should refuse shelter, suppose— Then she thought, Lord, I'm going to hold steady on to You, and You've got to see me through—and knocked softly.

She heard the familiar guttural voice say, "Who's there?"

She answered quickly, "A friend with friends."

He opened the door and greeted her warmly. "How many this time?" he asked.

"Eleven," she said and waited, doubting, wondering.

He said, "Good. Bring them in."

He and his wife fed them in the lamp-lit kitchen, their faces glowing as they offered food and more food, urging them to eat, saying there was plenty for everybody, have more milk, have more bread, have more meat.

They spent the night in the warm kitchen. They really slept, all that night and until dusk the next day. When they left, it was with reluctance. They had all been warm and safe and well-fed. It was hard to exchange the security offered by that clean, warm kitchen for the darkness and the cold of a December night.

---

4. **Quaker:** a member of a religious group known as the Society of Friends.

"Go On or Die"

Harriet had found it hard to leave the warmth and friendliness, too. But she urged them on. For a while, as they walked, they seemed to carry in them a measure of contentment; some of the serenity and the cleanliness of that big, warm kitchen lingered on inside them. But as they walked farther and farther away from the warmth and the light, the cold and the darkness entered into them. They fell silent, sullen, suspicious. She waited for the moment when some one of them would turn mutinous. It did not happen that night.

Two nights later she was aware that the feet behind her were moving slower and slower. She heard the irritability in their voices, knew that soon someone would refuse to go on.

She started talking about William Still and the Philadelphia Vigilance Committee.[5] No one commented. No one asked any questions. She told them the story of William and Ellen Craft and how they escaped from Georgia. Ellen was so fair that she looked as though she were white, and so she dressed up in a man's clothing, and she looked like a wealthy young planter. Her husband, William, who was dark, played the role of her slave. Thus they traveled from Macon, Georgia, to Philadelphia, riding on the trains, staying at the finest hotels. Ellen pretended to be very ill—her right arm was in a sling, and her right hand was bandaged, because she was supposed to have rheumatism. Thus she avoided having to sign the register at the hotels, for she could not read or write. They finally arrived safely in Philadelphia and then went on to Boston.

No one said anything. Not one of them seemed to have heard her.

She told them about Frederick Douglass,[6] the most famous of the escaped slaves, of his eloquence, of his magnificent appearance. Then she told them of her own first, vain effort at running away, evoking the memory of that miserable life she had led as a child, reliving it for a moment in the telling.

But they had been tired too long, hungry too long, afraid too long, footsore too long. One of them suddenly cried out in despair, "Let me go back. It is better to be a slave than to suffer like this in order to be free."

She carried a gun with her on these trips. She had never used it—except as a threat. Now as she aimed it, she experienced a feeling of guilt, remembering that time, years ago, when she had prayed for the death of Edward Brodas, the Master, and then not too long afterward had heard that great wailing cry that came from the throats of the field hands, and knew from the sound that the Master was dead.

One of the runaways said, again, "Let me go back. Let me go back," and stood still and then turned around and said, over his shoulder, "I am going back."

She lifted the gun, aimed it at the despairing slave. She said, "Go on with us or die." The husky, low-pitched voice was grim.

He hesitated for a moment, and then he joined the others. They started walking again. She tried to explain to them why none of them

---

5. **Philadelphia Vigilance Committee:** a fundraising organization set up before the Civil War to help slaves escaping from the South.

6. **Frederick Douglass:** an African-American leader of the 1800s who worked for the end of slavery in the United States.

WORDS TO KNOW	
sullen (sŭl'ən) *adj.* showing silent resentment; sulky
mutinous (myōōt'n-əs) *adj.* rebelling against a leader
eloquence (ĕl'ə-kwəns) *n.* an ability to speak forcefully and persuasively

could go back to the plantation. If a runaway returned, he would turn traitor; the master and the overseer would force him to turn traitor. The returned slave would disclose the stopping places, the hiding places, the corn stacks they had used with the full knowledge of the owner of the farm, the name of the German farmer who had fed them and sheltered them. These people who had risked their own security to help runaways would be ruined, fined, imprisoned.

She said, "We got to go free or die. And freedom's not bought with dust."

This time she told them about the long agony of the Middle Passage[7] on the old slave ships, about the black horror of the holds, about the chains and the whips. They too knew these stories. But she wanted to remind them of the long, hard way they had come, about the long, hard way they had yet to go. She told them about Thomas Sims, the boy picked up on the streets of Boston and sent back to Georgia. She said when they got him back to Savannah, got him in prison there, they whipped him until a doctor who was standing by watching said, "You will kill him if you strike him again!" His master said, "Let him die!"

Thus she forced them to go on. Sometimes she thought she had become nothing but a voice speaking in the darkness, cajoling, urging, threatening. Sometimes she told them things to make them laugh; sometimes she sang to them and heard the eleven voices behind her blending softly with hers, and then she knew that for the moment all was well with them.

She gave the impression of being a short, muscular, indomitable woman who could never be defeated. Yet at any moment she was liable to be seized by one of those curious fits of sleep,[8] which might last for a few minutes or for hours.

Even on this trip, she suddenly fell asleep in the woods. The runaways, ragged, dirty, hungry, cold, did not steal the gun, as they might have, and set off by themselves or turn back. They sat on the ground near her and waited patiently until she awakened. They had come to trust her implicitly, totally. They, too, had come to believe her repeated statement, "We got to go free or die." She was leading them into freedom, and so they waited until she was ready to go on.

Finally, they reached Thomas Garrett's house in Wilmington, Delaware. Just as Harriet had promised, Garrett gave them all new shoes and provided carriages to take them on to the next stop.

By slow stages they reached Philadelphia, where William Still hastily recorded their names and the plantations whence they had come and something of the life they had led in slavery. Then he carefully hid what he had written, for fear it might be discovered. In 1872 he published this record in book form and called it *The Underground Railroad*. In the foreword to his book he said: "While I knew the danger of keeping strict records, and while I did not then dream that in my day slavery would be blotted out, or that the time would come when I could publish these records, it used to afford me great satisfaction to take them down, fresh from the lips of

---

7. **Middle Passage:** the sea route along which African slaves were transported across the Atlantic Ocean to the Americas.

8. **curious fits of sleep:** mysterious spells of dizziness or unconsciousness experienced by Harriet Tubman.

| WORDS TO KNOW | **cajoling** (kə-jō′lĭng) *adj.* urging gently; coaxing **cajole** *v.* |
| | **indomitable** (ĭn-dŏm′ĭ-tə-bəl) *adj.* unable to be conquered |

Daybreak—A Time to Rest
(1967), Jacob Lawrence.
Tempera on hardboard, 30" ×
24", National Gallery of Art,
Washington, D.C., anonymous
gift. Copyright © Board of
Trustees, National Gallery of
Art, Washington, D.C.

fugitives on the way to freedom, and to
preserve them as they had given them."

William Still, who was familiar with all the
station stops on the Underground Railroad,
supplied Harriet with money and sent her and
her eleven fugitives on to Burlington, New Jersey.

Harriet felt safer now, though there were
danger spots ahead. But the biggest part of her
job was over. As they went farther and farther
north, it grew colder; she was aware of the
wind on the Jersey ferry and aware of the cold
damp in New York. From New York they
went on to Syracuse, where the temperature
was even lower.

In Syracuse she met the Reverend J. W.
Loguen, known as "Jarm" Loguen. This was
the beginning of a lifelong friendship. Both
Harriet and Jarm Loguen were to become
friends and supporters of Old John Brown.[9]

From Syracuse they went north again, into
a colder, snowier city—Rochester. Here they
almost certainly stayed with Frederick
Douglass, for he wrote in his autobiography:
"On one occasion I had eleven fugitives at

---

9. **Old John Brown:** an antislavery leader executed for
leading a raid on the federal arsenal at Harpers Ferry,
Virginia, in 1859.

the same time under my roof, and it was necessary for them to remain with me until I could collect sufficient money to get them to Canada. It was the largest number I ever had at any one time, and I had some difficulty in providing so many with food and shelter, but, as may well be imagined, they were not very <u>fastidious</u> in either direction, and were well content with very plain food, and a strip of carpet on the floor for a bed, or a place on the straw in the barn loft."

Late in December 1851, Harriet arrived in St. Catharines, Canada West (now Ontario), with the eleven fugitives. It had taken almost a month to complete this journey; most of the time had been spent getting out of Maryland.

That first winter in St. Catharines was a terrible one. Canada was a strange, frozen land, snow everywhere, ice everywhere, and a bone-biting cold the like of which none of them had ever experienced before. Harriet rented a small frame house in the town and set to work to make a home. The fugitives boarded with her. They worked in the forests, felling trees, and so did she. Sometimes she took other jobs, cooking or cleaning house for people in the town. She cheered on these newly arrived fugitives, working herself, finding work for them, praying for them, sometimes begging for them.

Often she found herself thinking of the beauty of Maryland, the mellowness of the soil, the richness of the plant life there. The climate itself made for an ease of living that could never be duplicated in this bleak, barren countryside.

In spite of the severe cold, the hard work, she came to love St. Catharines and the other towns and cities in Canada where black men lived. She discovered that freedom meant more than the right to change jobs at will, more than the right to keep the money that one earned. It was the right to vote and to sit on juries. It was the right to be elected to office. In Canada there were black men who were county officials and members of school boards. St. Catharines had a large colony of ex-slaves, and they owned their own homes, kept them neat and clean and in good repair. They lived in whatever part of town they chose and sent their children to the schools.

When spring came, she decided that she would make this small Canadian city her home—as much as any place could be said to be home to a woman who traveled from Canada to the Eastern Shore of Maryland as often as she did.

In the spring of 1852, she went back to Cape May, New Jersey. She spent the summer there, cooking in a hotel. That fall she returned, as usual, to Dorchester County and brought out nine more slaves, conducting them all the way to St. Catharines, in Canada West, to the bone-biting cold, the snow-covered forests—and freedom.

She continued to live in this fashion, spending the winter in Canada and the spring and summer working in Cape May, New Jersey, or in Philadelphia. She made two trips a year into slave territory, one in the fall and another in the spring. She now had a definite, crystallized purpose, and in carrying it out, her life fell into a pattern which remained unchanged for the next six years. ❖

WORDS TO KNOW   **fastidious** (fă-stĭd′ē-əs) *adj.* difficult to please

LETTER TO HARRIET TUBMAN

by Frederick Douglass

Rochester, August 29, 1868

Dear Harriet,

I am glad to know that the story of your eventful life has been written by a kindly lady, and that the same is soon to be published. You ask for what you do not need when you call upon me for a word of commendation. I need such words from you far more than you can need them from me, especially where your superior labors and devotion to the cause of the lately enslaved of our land are known as I know them. The difference between us is very marked. Most that I have done and suffered in the service of our cause has been in public, and I have received much encouragement at every step of the way. You, on the other hand, have labored in a private way. I have wrought in the day—you in the night. I have had the applause of the crowd and the satisfaction that comes of being approved by the multitude, while the most that you have done has been witnessed by a few trembling, scarred,

Frederick Douglass (1818–1895, abolitionist, statesman) (1856), unidentified photographer. Ambrotype, 4⁵⁄₁₆" × 3⅜", gift of an anonymous donor, National Portrait Gallery, Smithsonian Institution/Art Resource, New York.

and footsore bondmen and women, whom you have led out of the house of bondage, and whose heartfelt *"God Bless you"* has been your only reward. The midnight sky and the silent stars have been the witnesses of your devotion to freedom and of your heroism. Excepting John Brown—of sacred memory—I know of no one who has willingly encountered more perils and hardships to serve our enslaved people than you have. Much that you have done would seem improbable to those who do not know you as I know you. It is to me a great pleasure and a great privilege to bear testimony to your character and your works, and to say to those to whom you may come, that I regard you in every way truthful and trustworthy.

Your friend,
Frederick Douglass

RESPONDING
OPTIONS

FROM PERSONAL RESPONSE TO CRITICAL ANALYSIS

REFLECT 1. What impressed you most about Harriet Tubman? Write your thoughts in your notebook, then share them with a partner.

RETHINK 2. What do you think was Tubman's primary motivation for risking her life to help people realize their dream of freedom?

3. Do you think that if you had been a slave who decided to run away, you would have entrusted your life to Harriet Tubman? Explain your answer.
   Consider
   • Tubman's knowledge and experience
   • the risk of getting caught and punished
   • Tubman's threat "Go on with us or die"

RELATE 4. Review the Literary Insight selection on page 559. Do you agree or disagree with Frederick Douglass's evaluation of Harriet Tubman? Explain your opinion.

5. People who opened their homes to escaping slaves broke the Fugitive Slave Law. Do you think that breaking the law is justified in such cases? Why or why not?

ANOTHER PATHWAY

If you had been Harriet Tubman, what aspects of helping slaves to escape would have frightened you most? Why? Draw a sketch, based on details in the selection, to convey your answer. Compare and contrast your response with the responses of other students.

QUICKWRITES

1. Imagine that you are a slave escaping to freedom in Canada. Write a detailed **diary entry** describing one day of your journey.

2. Harriet Tubman helped many people escape from slavery. Think about a person who has helped you through a very difficult situation. Write a **description** of this person.

3. Imagine that you are one of the slaves whom Tubman has led safely to Canada. Write a **letter** to your former master in Maryland, telling him your thoughts now that you are free.

   📁 *PORTFOLIO Save your writing. You may want to use it later as a springboard to a piece for your portfolio.*

LITERARY CONCEPTS

A **biography** is a type of nonfiction in which a writer gives an account of someone else's life. Some biographies contain elements of fiction in addition to facts. This excerpt from *Harriet Tubman: Conductor on the Underground Railroad* contains dialogue, for example, as well as descriptions of some of Tubman's thoughts. The author clearly could not have known what was actually said and thought by Tubman, but she made an educated guess. What do the re-created thoughts and dialogue add to the biography? Support your opinion with examples from the selection.

ALTERNATIVE ACTIVITIES

Using a computer database or library resources, research slave memoirs. Then present an oral report, comparing what you have discovered in your research with what you have learned from this selection.

ACROSS THE CURRICULUM

Geography/Mathematics Imagine that you are leading slaves from Dorchester County, Maryland, to freedom in St. Catharines, Ontario, Canada. Do some research to find out what present-day trails and roads would be most suitable for the trip. Select your route and calculate how many miles a day you will have to travel to reach your destination in a month. Also decide on the safest places to stay along the way.

ANN PETRY

1912–

Ann Petry was born above her father's drugstore in Old Saybrook, Connecticut. As a child in one of only two African-American families in the small town, she heard family tales about her runaway-slave grandfather, and about her father, who had resisted a racial attack when he had opened his own pharmacy.

Despite her interest in writing as a career, Petry graduated from the Connecticut College of Pharmacy and went to work in the family store. There she listened to the stories of townspeople—people who would inspire some of the characters in her writing.

After she married, Petry moved to New York, where she worked as an ad salesperson, a reporter and editor for Harlem newspapers, a recreation spe-cialist at a Harlem elementary school, and an activist for racial justice and women's rights. During this time, a number of her short stories were printed in magazines. One of these attracted the attention of a major publishing company, from which she received a literary fellowship and encouragement to write a novel. The novel she wrote—*The Street*, a story of an African-American woman's struggle to survive in a hostile Harlem neighborhood—made Petry an overnight success. She was the first African-American female to write about problems African-American women face in the slums.

OTHER WORKS *Tituba of Salem Village, Legends of the Saints*

WRITING TO EXPLAIN

Think about the selections you've just read in Unit Four, "Facing the Enemy." Could you picture the fight of the mother baboon as you read the story? Could you hear the tolling of the bell on the funeral train as Lincoln was brought to Springfield? The rich details that are included in an eyewitness report can make you feel as if you were there.

GUIDED ASSIGNMENT

Write an Eyewitness Report This lesson will help you write your own eyewitness report of an event that captures the "you-are-there" excitement for readers.

Event Photos

① Look for the Story

Has anyone ever asked you to describe something you've seen? When you describe a scene or situation for a person who wasn't there, you're giving an eyewitness report. The following suggestions can help you explore topics for your own eyewitness report.

Writing About Past Events What events have you seen that you'd like to write about? You might have seen a live performance, such as a concert or a sports event, that grabbed your attention. Make a list of such events, in your journal. Then write a one-paragraph description of an event that you saw.

Hunting for the Story You may not realize it, but exciting events are happening all around you—at school and within your community. Is there an upcoming concert or sports event that you think might be exciting? Think of yourself as a reporter on the hunt for a story. Where can you go?

What kinds of information does each item give that the other items don't give?

Program of Events

Summer International Special Olympics Events (continued)	
Time	**Event**
10:00 A.M. 10:00 11:00	**Swimming** 50 m Freestyle 100 m Freestyle
10:00 A.M.	**Team Handball**
12:30 P.M.	**Powerlifting** Welterweight Heavyweight
1:00 P.M.	**Roller Skating**
1:30 P.M.	**Table Tennis**
2:00 P.M.	**Soccer**
2:30 P.M.	**Softball**
3:30 P.M.	**Volleyball**
(continued)	

The freestyle event was so exciting! It really ought to be written up

This girl was amazing! I should include her in my report.

This article doesn't sound exciting. I think I'll write my own version of the Special Olympics and send it in.

Article

Special Competition Results in Countless Winners

NEW HAVEN, Conn. The Special Olympics World Games ended Sunday, and almost everyone concerned was happy with the achievements—athletic and otherwise—over the last nine days.

There was almost endless competition for the 7,200 athletes, all mentally retarded and some physically disabled, from 140 nations. They made new friends from far-off nations. And they proved to themselves and to the public that mental retardation is not the end of a productive life, but just one more obstacle to be dealt with.

Frank Litsky
from *Chicago Tribune*

2 Analyze the Information

Take a look at the souvenir items on these pages. How could you use items like these to provide background information for your report?

LASERLINKS
• *WRITING SPRINGBOARD*

WRITING COACH

Uncovering the Story

At-the-Scene Reporting As a reporter, it's your job to find the story. What events can you find that you'd really like to share with others? You can use the suggestions on these two pages to record the details about your event.

❶ Choose Your Topic

Out of all of the events you have witnessed or plan to attend, is there one in particular that really grabs your attention? This might be a humorous event or one that you find powerful, tragic, or inspiring. You might try freewriting about the events you've seen to decide which event interests you the most.

❷ Look for a Focus

If the topic you chose seems broad, you may need to narrow your focus. What part of the event stands out? This could be the focus of your account. For example, one student attended the Special Olympics and wanted to write about what she saw. Since the topic of the Special Olympics is too broad, she decided to write about only one event.

❸ Record the Details

There are different ways to go about recording details about your topic. You might use one or all of the methods described on the next page.

Special Olympics
↳ 100 meter freestyle

Getting the Facts Your main goal is to help your readers watch the event through your eyes. Good reporters take careful notes and ask questions to get the facts for their stories. These questions begin with five w's and an h: *Who, What, When, Where, Why,* and *How.* You can use these kinds of questions to get the facts you need.

- Who participated in the event?
- What happened?
- When did the event take place?
- Where did the event take place?
- Why were these games established?
- How did the event end?

Using an Observation Chart Good reporters also are skilled observers. The SkillBuilder at the right will help you sharpen your observation skills to take in all the details of a scene. As you observe an event, you might make an observation chart similar to the one below, which one student made to record the details she witnessed.

Using Your Camera If you're planning to attend the event you'd like to write about, think about taking a camera or camcorder along. You might use it to help you record some of the excitement and to illustrate your final report.

Observation Chart

Sharing Your Experience

The Scene in Your Mind Remember how you felt after reading an exciting account of an event? What can you include in your draft to help your readers visualize the scene you witnessed? These pages will help you report on the experience for your readers.

① Draft and Discover

As you write your draft, try to keep the image of the scene in your mind. The details you use uncover bit by bit the photograph of the event in your mind. You might start by writing everything you remember about the event. Try to use details that will help your readers feel as if they were at the scene with you.

Student's Discovery Draft

The 100-meter freestyle swimming event at the Special Olympics was very exciting. Lots of people came to the race to support the competitors.

At the start of the race, many of the swimmers didn't look as if they would finish. But their family members and the cheering crowds didn't really seem to care whether anyone won a medal. They just wanted the swimmers to finish the race.

A family nearby was dressed all in blue sweatshirts that had the name "Alexis" stenciled in white lettering. They carried a big sign that read, "Go! Alexis" and cheered for a girl in Lane 1. She looked small and scared next to the others. When the race started, there was so much splashing, Alexis could barely be seen.

Alexis was in last place for a while. Then there were only five people ahead of her. Soon she had caught up with a girl in a red swimming cap. Finally it was over. Alexis came in second place, winning a silver medal.

> Maybe I should focus more on Alexis rather than on everyone there.

> I can use photos to make a slide presentation.

❷ Check Your Progress

Are there parts of the experience that you are having trouble capturing on paper? You might ask someone else who was there to help you recall some of the details. Snapshots, programs, ticket stubs, or other kinds of memorabilia from the event can also refresh your memory.

❸ Sharpen the Focus

Once you have evaluated your writing, you may decide that you need to change a few things as you fine-tune your draft. The following suggestions will help you rework your draft.

Add Colorful Details Good eyewitness reports keep readers' attention by relating facts in interesting ways. Dates, names, and even weather conditions can help make the event clearer for your readers, but by themselves these facts can be boring. The SkillBuilder at the right can help you describe incidents that will enliven your writing.

Show, Don't Tell As you write your draft, try using descriptions that show, rather than tell, what happened. In the student model, the sentence "The 100-meter freestyle swimming event at the Special Olympics was very exciting" is an example of telling. The writer could show the excitement with sentences such as "Alexis's arms moved like windmills. Soon she had passed another swimmer."

Add Some Dialogue Including portions of conversations can be more effective than writing several paragraphs of description. Is there an interesting quote from an official, a participant, or an observer that you can remember?

 PEER RESPONSE

You might ask peer reviewers to read your draft aloud and share their reactions to these questions:

- Which parts of my report did you have trouble "seeing"?
- What images or ideas do you recall most vividly?
- What emotions did you feel as you read my account?

Finishing Your Report

An Impression That Lasts Your eyewitness report can make a lasting impression on your readers. As you revise, consider using some or all of the following suggestions to polish your draft.

Student's Final Draft

A Race for Silver

3

by Regina Selkirk

There were plenty of tears and hugs at the 100-meter freestyle swimming event of the Special Olympics.

Many people were there to support the competitors and to pass out hugs. One family all wore blue sweatshirts with the name "Alexis" stenciled in white lettering. They carried a banner with the words, "Go! Alexis" and waved to a girl in Lane 1.

Alexis looked small and scared. When the race started, there was so much splashing that Alexis could barely be seen. Her dad pointed to her yellow cap bobbing above the water.

"Today, Alexis can forget about feeling different because she has Down syndrome," her dad said. "We just want her to have some fun today."

Alexis was in last place for a while, but soon there were only five people ahead of her. "Go, Alex!" her brother yelled. "You can do it!"

Alexis's arms moved like windmills. Soon she had passed another swimmer! Now only a girl in a white cap was ahead of her. Alexis was so close. Could she win a gold medal?

At the finish line, Alexis and the girl in a white cap seemed to reach the wall at the same time. The audience was silent as the judges tried to sort out who had won. The family in blue sweatshirts crossed their fingers. Finally the announcer said that the girl in the white cap had won. Even though Alexis didn't get the gold, her family was thrilled with her silver medal.

❶ Revise and Edit

Use the following tips as you revise your report.

- Add details to show the action rather than tell about it.
- Use the SkillBuilder on the right to help you vary your sentence lengths and create more interest.
- Consult the Standards for Evaluation and the Editing Checklist to be sure you have given readers enough information to understand the event and presented the details in a way that is easy to follow.
- Notice how the student's final draft at the left incorporates interesting details and dialogue.

How do the details this student used help you picture the scene?

What role do the quotations play in the report?

Script
Special Olympics 100-meter
Freestyle Race

Slide 1: Exterior of arena where
race is held

Cue music

V/O: There were plenty of tears
and hugs at the 100-meter
freestyle swimming event of the
Special Olympics.

Slide 2: Interior of arena

V/O: Many people were
there to support the
competitors and to
pass out hugs.

❷ Present Your Final Draft

If the topic you wrote about featured dramatic scenes or images, you might consider a more visual format for your final report. This student turned her report into a multimedia presentation describing her experience at the Special Olympics. This presentation included slides and a script. The student presented her report to various organizations. See the Multimedia Handbook for tips on accessing information on-line and for making a multimedia presentation.

PUBLISHING IDEAS

- You might send your report to a special-interest newsletter.
- You might share your report with special-interest groups on the World Wide Web.

Standards for Evaluation

An eyewitness report
- uses sensory details, dialogue, and action verbs to show what was observed, bringing the event to life
- has a clear focus
- provides readers with the information they need to understand the event
- presents details in a sensible order that is easy to follow

---

SkillBuilder

G → GRAMMAR FROM WRITING

Sentence Combining

One way to vary your sentence lengths and show clearer relationships among ideas is by combining two shorter sentences into one. For example:

Alexis was in last place for a while. Soon there were only five people ahead of her.

Alexis was in last place for a while, but soon there were only five people ahead of her.

GRAMMAR HANDBOOK

For more information on sentence combining, see page 860 in the Grammar Handbook.

Editing Checklist Review the following list as you revise your draft.

- Did you check for misspelled words?
- Did you vary your sentence lengths?
- Did you proofread your draft?

REFLECT & ASSESS

Evaluating the Experience

1. How did you choose the event that you wrote about?
2. How did you help the readers feel as if they were there?

📁 **PORTFOLIO** Add your report and any photographs you might have of the event to your portfolio.

REFLECT & ASSESS

UNIT FOUR: FACING THE ENEMY

Whom or what do you consider to be your enemies in life? How do you choose to deal with them? Perhaps the selections in Unit Four have influenced your thoughts on these questions. To explore them further, complete one or more of the options in each of the following sections.

REFLECTING ON THEME

OPTION 1 **Choosing Heroes** Look back through the selections in this unit, picking out two or three characters who you think act the most heroically. Create a "Heroes' Gallery" with drawings and brief character sketches of them.

OPTION 2 **Comparing and Contrasting** From this unit's selections, choose some situations that you found particularly interesting or gripping. How well do the characters handle those situations? How do you think you would react to the situations? Write a few paragraphs, comparing and contrasting the characters' actions with what you think yours would be.

OPTION 3 **Giving Advice** Prepare an outline of a speech entitled "How to Face Up to Your Enemy in Life." First decide who or what might be considered an enemy. Then, in offering your advice, draw on examples from the selections in this unit and from your personal experience.

Self-Assessment: Make a list of the most important things that you feel you must personally struggle against in life—perhaps school subjects that you find difficult or attitudes in society that you do not agree with. For each item on your list, make a note of any new ways of tackling them you have learned. Jot down the titles of any selections that have influenced your thinking.

REVIEWING LITERARY CONCEPTS

OPTION 1 **Contrasting Biography and Autobiography** What is the difference between biography and autobiography? What are the strengths and weaknesses of each form? Fill in a chart like the one shown. Then discuss with a partner your ideas about what information can be learned from each form that cannot be learned from the other.

Autobiography		Biography	
Strengths	**Weaknesses**	**Strengths**	**Weaknesses**

OPTION 2 **Examining Character Changes** Many of the characters in Unit Four change in some way. Select three or four characters that you think change in very important ways. Record each change in a chart like the one shown. Then identify the character who you think changes the most. Discuss your choice with a partner. If the two of you don't agree, try to persuade your partner.

Character: _____	
Beginning of the Story	**End of the Story**

Self-Assessment: With a small group of classmates, discuss how well you feel you understand the following literary terms introduced in this unit. On the basis of your discussion, divide the terms among the members of the group. Briefly explain to the group the meanings of the terms you have been assigned.

classic	*science fiction*
alliteration	*humor*
author's purpose	*suspense*
minor characters	*narrative poem*

PORTFOLIO BUILDING

- **QuickWrites** Look through the QuickWrites assignments that you completed in this unit. Choose one or two pieces that you would like to revise in the light of what you have learned since writing them. For each piece you choose, write a note saying what you would change, attach it to the piece, and add both to your portfolio.

- **Writing About Literature** In this unit, you wrote a personal response to one of the unit's stories or poems. Reread your personal response. How does it sound now? What, if anything, would you add to it or delete from it? Write a sentence or two explaining the subject of your response and the way you responded.

- **Writing from Experience** Earlier in this unit, you wrote an eyewitness report. Reread your report, pretending that you are reading it for the first time. What details stand out? Does the report cover the essential facts? In a note for your portfolio, tell whether you think your report is effective, giving reasons for your opinion.

- **Personal Choice** Look back through your records and evaluations of all the activities you completed in this unit, as well as any activities and writing you have done on your own. In which activity did you best express your own thoughts about facing enemies? Write a paragraph explaining what these thoughts are and how you were able to express them in the activity. Attach the paragraph to your record and add both to your portfolio.

Self-Assessment: Compare what you have added to your portfolio in Unit Four with the pieces you added in previous units. Can you see any progress in your work? In what areas? Jot down your thoughts in your notebook.

SETTING GOALS

As you completed the reading and writing activities in this unit, you may have identified certain writers whose work you would like to read more of. Write their names in your notebook, noting which of the titles listed in the Other Works section of their biographies sound interesting to you.

Personal
Discoveries

How I wish I could pigeon-hole

myself and neatly fix a label on!

But self-knowledge comes too late

and by the time I've known myself

I am no longer what I was.

Mabel Segun
Nigerian Poet

Detail of *Cross Cultural Dressing* (1993), Pacita Abad. Oil, fabric, and plastic buttons on stitched and padded canvas, 100″ × 136″, courtesy of the artist.

FINDING YOUR PLACE

REFLECTING ON THEME

What kind of person are you? Think about the things that shape who you are—your interests, your ethnicity, your family. Discovering more about yourself can help you find your place in the world. The activities on this page involve the kinds of personal discoveries that help people find their place.

Do you know them?

Our connections with family are often the strongest of all. But how well do you really know your family? Interview an older member of your family about an important event in their life that occurred when they were your age. Afterward, consider whether your impression of your relative has changed.

What would you miss?

Your country can have a great influence on your sense of identity. Imagine you and your family were leaving to live in another country. Create a collage, showing the things you would and would not miss about life in the United States.

What do you enjoy?

Your personal interests and hobbies say a lot about who you are. Pick something you are particularly interested in or enjoy doing. Share an aspect of this activity. If possible, try to show real examples: if you are interested in a certain kind of ethnic cookery, cook something and bring it to class for classmates to try; if you enjoy a particular kind of music, bring in a recording for them to sample.

Who are you?

Think about all the factors that shape who you are. Design a jigsaw puzzle with pieces that express your personality—your qualities, interests, and diversity. Make the shape and design reflect the factors you feel are most important in your life.

FICTION

Dancer
Vickie Sears

PERSONAL CONNECTION

In "Dancer," a young foster child of Native American descent must adjust to a new household and discover her place in the family. As you try to find your place in the world, how do you define yourself? Jot down what you think makes you the individual that you are. Use a word web, like the one started here, to help you organize your thoughts. Then share your ideas in a small group.

CULTURAL CONNECTION

In the Native American culture, ceremonial dances traditionally were performed to bring sun or rain, to ensure good hunting, to prepare for battle, and to get closer to nature. In many Native American communities today, a monthly dance called a powwow is a regular event. The powwow keeps the traditional culture alive. Dances such as the owl dance, the friendship dance, the circle dance, and the hoop dance are performed by Native Americans of all ages. For many of these Native Americans, this reminder of their ethnic heritage helps them to define themselves and often leads to the development of increased self-esteem and self-knowledge.

Native American dancer at an intertribal pow-wow in New Mexico. Copyright © 1992 Jonathan Meyers/FPG International Corp.

READING CONNECTION

Voice The first thing you may notice as you read this story is the narrator's voice. A Native American woman tells the story in her own distinctive way of speaking. She has an earthy, conversational style. Her language is often non-standard, as when she says, "I don't know nothing from that." Her descriptions are colorful; for example, she describes her foster child's nightmares as "real screamer dreams." As you read, be aware of the narrator's voice and how it makes her come alive on the page.

LASERLINKS
• CULTURAL CONNECTION

DANCER

BY VICKIE SEARS

TELL YOU JUST HOW IT

WAS WITH HER.

TOOK HER TO A DANCE

NOT LONG AFTER SHE

COME TO LIVE WITH US.

SMARTEST THING

I EVER DONE.

SEEMS LIKE SOME OLD

EAGLESPIRIT WOMAN SAW

HER LIVING DOWN HERE

AND CAME BACK JUST TO

BE WITH CLARISSA.

Five years old she was when she come to us. Some foster kids come with lots of stuff, but she came with everything she had in a paper bag. Some dresses that was too short. A pair of pants barely holding a crotch. A pile of ratty underwear and one new nightgown. Mine was her third foster home in as many months. The agency folks said she was *so-cio-path-ic*.[1] I don't know nothing from that. She just seemed like she was all full up with anger and scaredness like lots of the kids who come to me. Only she was a real loner. Not trusting nobody. But she ran just like any other kid, was quiet when needed. Smiled at all the right times. If you could get her to smile, that is. Didn't talk much, though.

Had these ferocious dreams, too. Real screamer dreams they were. Shake the soul right out of you. She'd be screaming and crying with her little body wriggling on the bed, her hair all matted up on her woody-colored face. One time I got her to tell me what she was seeing, and she told me how she was being chased by a man with a long knife what he was going to kill her with and nobody could hear her calling out for help. She didn't talk too much about them, but they was all bad like that one. Seemed the most fierce dreams I ever remember anybody ever having outside of a vision seek.[2] They said her tribe was Assiniboin,[3] but they weren't for certain. What was for sure was that she was a fine dark-eyed girl just meant for someone to scoop up for loving.

Took her to her first dance in September, like I said, not long after she came. It wasn't like I thought it would be a good thing to do. It was just that we was all going. Me, my own kids, some nieces and nephews and the other children who was living with us. The pow-wow was just part of what we done all the time. Every month. More often in the summer. But this was the regular first Friday night of the school year. We'd all gather up and go to the school. I was thinking on leaving her home with a sitter 'cause she'd tried to kill one of the cats a couple of days before. We'd had us a big talk and she was grounded, but, well, it seemed like she ought to be with us.

Harold, that's my oldest boy, he and the other kids was mad with her, but he decided to show her around anyhow. At the school he went through the gym telling people, "This here's my sister, Clarissa." Wasn't no fuss or anything. She was just another one of the kids. When they was done meeting folks, he put her on one of the bleachers near the drum and went to join the men. He was in that place where his voice cracks but was real proud to be drumming. Held his hand up to his ear even, some of the time. Anyhow, Clarissa was sitting there, not all that interested in the dance or drum, when Molly Graybull come out in her button dress. Her arms was all stretched out, and she was slipping around, <u>preening</u> on them spindles of legs that get skinnier with every year. She was well into her seventies, and I might as well admit, Molly had won herself a fair share of dance contests. So it wasn't no surprise how a little girl could get so <u>fixated</u> on Molly. Clarissa watched her move around-around-around. Then all the rest of the dancers

---

1. **so-cio-path-ic** (sō′sē-ə-păth′ĭk): spelled *sociopathic;* having a mental disorder that causes one to harm others, often violently.

2. **vision seek:** Native American rite in which a person in a dream or trancelike state receives guidance or powers.

3. **Assiniboin** (ə-sĭn′ə-boin′): Native American tribe of northeastern and north central Montana and parts of Canada.

Blackfoot Child, Charles La Monk. Oil on canvas, 16″ × 12″. Courtesy of Chuck La Monk, dedicated to Lauren La Monk.

after Molly. She sure took in a good eyeful. Fancy dance. Owl dance. Circle dance. Even a hoop dancer was visiting that night.[4] Everything weaving all slow, then fast. Around-around until that child couldn't see nothing else. Seemed like she was struck silent in the night, too. Never had no dreams at all. Well, not the hollering kind anyways.

Next day she was more quiet than usual, only I could see she was looking at her picture book and tapping the old one-two, one-two. Tapping her toes on the rug with the inside of her head going around and around. As quiet as she could be, she was.

A few days went on before she asks me, "When's there gonna be another dance?"

I tell her in three weeks. She just smiles and goes on outside, waiting on the older kids to come home from school.

The very next day she asks if she can listen to some singing. I give her the tape recorder and some of Joe Washington from up to the Lummi reservation and the Kicking Woman Singers. Clarissa, she takes them tapes and runs out back behind the chicken shed, staying out all afternoon. I wasn't worried none, though, 'cause I could hear the music the whole time. Matter of fact, it like to make me sick of them same songs come the end of three weeks. But that kid, she didn't get into no kind of mischief. Almost abnormal how good she was. Worried me some to see her so caught up but it seemed good too. The angry part of her slowed down so's she wasn't hitting the animals or chopping on herself with sticks like she was doing when she first come. She wasn't laughing much either, but she started playing with the other kids when they come home. Seemed like everybody was working hard to be better with each other.

Come March, Clarissa asks, "Can I dance?"

For sure, the best time for teaching is when a kid wants to listen, so we stood side to side with me doing some steps. She followed along fine. I put on a tape and started moving faster, and Clarissa just kept up all natural. I could tell she'd been practicing lots. She was doing real good.

SHE DIDN'T DANCE AGAIN THAT NIGHT, BUT I COULD SEE THERE WAS DREAMING COMING INTO HER EYES.

Comes the next powwow, which was outside on the track field, I braided Clarissa's hair. Did her up with some ermine and bead ties, then give her a purse to carry. It was all beaded with a rose and leaves. Used to be my aunt's. She held it right next to her side with her chin real high. She joined in a Circle dance. I could see she was watching her feet a little and looking how others do their steps, but mostly she was doing wonderful. When Molly Graybull showed up beside her, Clarissa took to a seat and stared. She didn't dance again that night, but I could see there was dreaming coming into her eyes. I saw that fire

---

4. **Fancy dance. Owl dance. Circle dance. Even a hoop dancer . . . that night:** references to traditional Native American dances—in order, a competitive dance for showing performers' best steps; an expressive dance honoring the sacredness of the owl; a social dance performed in a circle; a dance for a single male performer using hoops.

that said to practice. And she did. I heard her every day in her room. Finally bought her her very own tape recorder so's the rest of us could listen to music too.

Some months passed on. All the kids was getting bigger. Clarissa, she went into the first grade. Harvey went off to community college up in Seattle, and that left me with Ronnie being the oldest at home. Clarissa was keeping herself busy all the time going over to Molly Graybull's. She was coming home with Spider Woman stories and trickster tales.[5] One night she speaks up at supper and says, right clear and loud, "I'm an Assiniboin." Clear as it can be, she says it again. Don't nobody have to say nothing to something that proud said.

Next day I started working on a wing dress for Clarissa. She was going to be needing one for sure real soon.

Comes the first school-year powwow and everyone was putting on their best. I called for Clarissa to come to my room. I told her, "I think it's time you have something special for yourself." Then I held up the green satin and saw her eyes full up with glitter. She didn't say nothing. Only kisses me and runs off to her room.

Just as we're all getting out of the car, Clarissa whispered to me, "I'm gonna dance with Molly Graybull." I put my hand on her shoulder to say, "You just listen to your spirit. That's where your music is."

We all danced an Owl dance, a Friendship dance, and a couple of Circle dances. Things was feeling real warm and good, and then it was time for the women's traditional.[6] Clarissa joined the circle. She opened her arms to something nobody but her seemed to hear.

That's when I saw that old Eagle woman come down and slide right inside of Clarissa, scooping up that child. There Clarissa was, full up with music. All full with that old, old spirit, letting herself dance through Clarissa's feet. Then Molly Graybull come dancing alongside Clarissa, and they was both the same age. ❖

---

5. **Spider Woman stories and trickster tales:** Native American legends about Spider Woman's teachings and gift-giving and about mischievous heroes with magical powers.

6. **women's traditional:** slow Native American dance historically reserved for women.

CELEBRATION
BY ALONZO LOPEZ

I shall dance tonight.
When the dusk comes crawling,
There will be dancing
    and feasting.
5 I shall dance with the others
    in circles,
      in leaps,
        in stomps.
Laughter and talk
10   will weave into the night,
Among the fires
    of my people.
Games will be played
And I shall be
15   a part of it.

RESPONDING
OPTIONS

FROM PERSONAL RESPONSE *TO* CRITICAL ANALYSIS

REFLECT

1. What are you left wondering about as the story ends? Jot down your thoughts in your notebook.

RETHINK

2. How would you describe what happens to Clarissa on the dance floor at the end of the story?

3. Explain the influences you think help Clarissa to change and to find her place in the new community.
Consider
- her relationship with her foster mother
- the way the rest of the family treats her
- her reaction to Molly Graybull's dancing

4. Which character from the story had the greatest effect on you? Give reasons for your answer.

5. Clarissa's love of Native American dance amazes and delights those in her community. What do you predict for Clarissa's future?

RELATE

6. Clarissa proudly announces, "I'm an Assiniboin." Do you think that learning about your ethnic heritage helps you to define yourself? Why or why not?

7. Compare Clarissa's feelings about dancing at the powwow with the feelings about dancing expressed by the speaker in the Insight poem "Celebration," on page 580.

ANOTHER PATHWAY

When a child is placed in a foster home, a social worker is assigned to evaluate the care the child receives from the foster family. Imagine that you are Clarissa's social worker and that you are reporting back to your supervisor. Present an oral report to the class concerning Clarissa's progress.

QUICKWRITES

1. Some Native American tribes give each of their members a name that reflects the person's nature. For example, Molly's last name, Gray-bull, may suggest her importance in the tribe, her wisdom, and her leadership. Think of a tribal name for Clarissa or her foster mother that reflects some important quality or character trait. Write the **tribal name** and a brief **explanation** of why you chose it.

2. Assume the voice of Harold, the narrator's eldest son, and write a **paragraph** giving your impression of Clarissa.

📁 *PORTFOLIO Save your writing. You may want to use it later as a springboard to a piece for your portfolio.*

LITERARY CONCEPTS

In "Dancer," the foster mother, a main character, is the **narrator.** The reader sees the story through her eyes as she shares her thoughts and feelings about Clarissa. Think about how the foster mother's role as narrator affects what you learn about the events and people in the story. Who in "Dancer" do you feel you know best by the end? Why?

ALTERNATIVE ACTIVITIES

On your own or with a small group, find **music** to accompany a particular type of Native American dance. Bring the music to class and share it with your classmates. You also might tell them about the instruments used and about the history of the dance.

ACROSS THE CURRICULUM

 Social Studies *Cooperative Learning*
In a group, research the Assiniboin tribe, using an on-line computer service if possible. Present an exhibit to the class that includes a map showing where the Assiniboin now live; pictures and information about their history, culture, and traditions; and brief statements of what they are most known for and what traditions they still practice. You also may wish to recreate Assiniboin artifacts to include in your display.

Describe It	Compare It
squirming, not violently	moving like a snake, not a bat
Associate It	**Use It**
a person in pain	The boy was wriggling out of her arms.

VICKIE SEARS

Vickie Sears is part Cherokee, part Spanish, and part English. Like Clarissa, she was a foster child. Always feeling unwanted, she spent her years between 4 and 11 in an orphanage and various foster homes—all "pretty negative" experiences, she says. In her loneliness, she began to write and to dream of having "at least two big houses so I could have all of the children that no one wanted." Sears did not reach that goal, but over the years she did care for 32 Native American foster children. Now adults, all of these young people and their children—Sears's 117 "grandchildren"— gather for a reunion every four years.

1941–

After working her way through the University of San Francisco, Sears wrote for an anti–Vietnam War magazine, taught in a ghetto high school, worked on a tree farm, cleaned motels and welfare houses, wrote grants for the War on Poverty, did youth drug and alcohol counseling, and directed a tribal mental health program. Today, she is a therapist and writer in Seattle.

Sears writes short stories, poetry, and professional articles. She views her stories and poems as a "way to heal, as well as a way to create beauty."

OTHER WORKS *Simple Songs: Stories by Vickie Sears*

LASERLINKS
• *SOCIAL STUDIES CONNECTION*

PREVIEWING

The Moustache
Robert Cormier

PERSONAL CONNECTION

In this story, 17-year-old Mike learns about the plight of the elderly when he visits his grandmother in a nursing home. What do you know about the elderly and the problems they face? If you have ever visited a nursing home, what were your reactions? How do you feel about growing old? On a word web like the one shown here, jot down some of your images of and thoughts about the elderly and growing old.

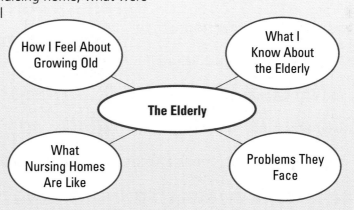

How I Feel About Growing Old — What I Know About the Elderly — The Elderly — What Nursing Homes Are Like — Problems They Face

SOCIAL STUDIES CONNECTION

Most elderly people in the United States live on their own or with their families. However, about 6 percent of the nation's elderly reside in nursing homes. An older person may decide to live in such a facility if he or she has health problems requiring constant medical attention. Such care is needed for many conditions that afflict the aged, including arteriosclerosis (är-tir´ē-ō-sklə-rō´sĭs)—commonly known as hardening of the arteries—a disease that affects the grandmother in this story.

Arteriosclerosis narrows the arteries and decreases blood flow to vital organs, such as the brain. It can cause strokes, which may result in dizziness, general weakness, slurred speech, and forgetfulness.

READING CONNECTION

Clarifying As you read "The Moustache," you may need to stop from time to time to clarify what you are reading. Recall that clarifying involves pausing occasionally for a quick review of what you understand so far and drawing conclusions about what is suggested but not stated directly. The questions that appear with this story will help you follow the motives of the characters and understand the theme. Use your reading log to record your responses to the questions inserted throughout the selection.

LASERLINKS
• *SOCIAL STUDIES CONNECTION*

583

The Moustache

by Robert Cormier

At the last minute Annie couldn't go. She was invaded by
one of those twenty-four-hour flu bugs that sent her to bed
with a fever, moaning about the fact that she'd also have

to break her date with Handsome
Harry Arnold that night. We call
him Handsome Harry because he's
actually handsome, but he's also a
nice guy, cool, and he doesn't treat

me like Annie's kid brother, which I am, but like a regular
person. Anyway, I had to go to Lawnrest alone that
afternoon. But first of all I had to stand inspection.

My mother lined me up against the wall. She stood there like a one-man firing squad, which is kind of funny because she's not like a man at all, she's very feminine, and we have this great relationship—I mean, I feel as if she really likes me. I realize that sounds strange, but I know guys whose mothers love them and cook special stuff for them and worry about them and all, but there's something missing in their relationship.

Anyway. She frowned and started the routine.

"That hair," she said. Then admitted: "Well, at least you combed it."

I sighed. I have discovered that it's better to sigh than argue.

"And that moustache." She shook her head. "I still say a seventeen-year-old has no business wearing a moustache."

"It's an experiment," I said. "I just wanted to see if I could grow one." To tell the truth, I had proved my point about being able to grow a decent moustache, but I also had learned to like it.

"It's costing you money, Mike," she said.

"I know, I know."

The money was a reference to the movies. The Downtown Cinema has a special Friday night offer—half-price admission for high school couples seventeen or younger. But the woman in the box office took one look at my moustache and charged me full price. Even when I showed her my driver's license. She charged full admission for Cindy's ticket, too, which left me practically broke and unable to take Cindy out for a hamburger with the crowd afterward. That didn't help matters, because Cindy has been getting impatient recently about things like the fact that I don't own my own car and have to concentrate on my studies if I want to win that college scholarship, for instance. Cindy wasn't exactly crazy about the moustache, either.

Now it was my mother's turn to sigh.

"Look," I said, to cheer her up. "I'm thinking about shaving it off." Even though I wasn't. Another discovery: You can build a way of life on postponement.

"Your grandmother probably won't even recognize you," she said. And I saw the shadow fall across her face.

Let me tell you what the visit to Lawnrest was all about. My grandmother is 73 years old. She is a resident—which is supposed to be a better word than *patient*—at the Lawnrest Nursing Home. She used to make the greatest turkey dressing in the world and was a nut about baseball and could even quote batting averages, for crying out loud. She always rooted for the losers. She was in love with the Mets until they started to win. Now she has arteriosclerosis, which the dictionary says is "a chronic disease characterized by abnormal thickening and hardening of the arterial walls." Which really means that she can't live at home anymore or even with us, and her memory has betrayed her as well as her body. She used to wander off and sometimes didn't recognize people. My mother visits her all the time, driving the thirty miles to Lawnrest almost every day. Because Annie was home for a semester break from college, we had decided to make a special Saturday visit. Now Annie was in bed, groaning theatrically—she's a drama major— but I told my mother I'd go, anyway. I hadn't seen my grandmother since she'd been admitted to Lawnrest. Besides, the place is located on the Southwest Turnpike, which meant I could barrel along in my father's new Le Mans. My ambition was to see the speedometer hit 75. Ordinarily, I used the old station wagon, which can barely stagger up to 50.

CONNECT

Have you ever known an elderly person with health problems similar to those described?

Frankly, I wasn't too crazy about visiting a nursing home. They reminded me of hospitals, and hospitals turn me off. I mean, the smell of ether[1] makes me nauseous, and I feel faint at the sight of blood. And as I approached Lawnrest—which is a terrible cemetery kind of name, to begin with—I was sorry I hadn't avoided the trip. Then I felt guilty about it. I'm loaded with guilt <u>complexes</u>. Like driving like a madman after promising my father to be careful. Like sitting in the parking lot, looking at the nursing home with dread and thinking how I'd rather be with Cindy. Then I thought of all the Christmas and birthday gifts my grandmother had given me, and I got out of the car, guilty, as usual.

Inside, I was surprised by the lack of hospital smell, although there was another odor or maybe the absence of an odor. The air was antiseptic, sterile. As if there was no atmosphere at all or I'd caught a cold suddenly and couldn't taste or smell.

A nurse at the reception desk gave me directions—my grandmother was in East Three. I made my way down the tiled corridor and was glad to see that the walls were painted with cheerful colors like yellow and pink. A wheelchair suddenly shot around a corner, self-propelled by an old man, white-haired and toothless, who cackled merrily as he barely missed me. I jumped aside—here I was, almost getting wiped out by a two-mile-an-hour wheelchair after doing seventy-five on the pike. As I walked through the corridors seeking East Three, I couldn't help glancing into the rooms, and it was like some kind of wax museum[2]—all these figures in various stances and attitudes, sitting in beds or chairs, standing at windows, as if they were frozen forever in these postures. To tell the truth, I began to hurry because I was getting depressed. Finally, I saw a beautiful girl approaching, dressed in white, a nurse or an attendant, and I was so happy to see someone young, someone walking and acting normally, that I gave her a wide smile and a big hello and must have looked like a kind of nut. Anyway, she looked right through me as if I were a window, which is about par for the course whenever I meet beautiful girls.

I finally found the room and saw my grandmother in bed. My grandmother looks like Ethel Barrymore.[3] I never knew who Ethel Barrymore was until I saw a terrific movie, *None But the Lonely Heart,* on TV, starring Ethel Barrymore and Cary Grant.[4] Both my grandmother and Ethel Barrymore have these great craggy faces like the side of a mountain and wonderful voices like syrup being poured. Slowly. She was propped up in bed, pillows puffed behind her. Her hair had been combed out and fell upon her shoulders. For some reason, this flowing hair gave her an almost girlish appearance, despite its whiteness.

She saw me and smiled. Her eyes lit up and her eyebrows arched and she reached out her hands to me in greeting. "Mike, Mike," she said. And I breathed a sigh of relief. This was one of her good days. My mother had warned me that she might not know who I was at first.

CLARIFY

Who is Mike referring to when he says, "these figures"?

---

1. **ether** (ē′thər): a chemical formerly used by surgeons as an anesthetic.
2. **wax museum:** a museum that displays wax statues of famous people.
3. **Ethel Barrymore** (1879–1959): U.S. stage and screen actress.
4. **Cary Grant** (1904–1986): U.S. movie star.

WORDS TO KNOW   **complex** (kŏm′plĕks′) *n.* an exaggerated concern or preoccupation

I took her hands in mine. They were fragile. I could actually feel her bones, and it seemed as if they would break if I pressed too hard. Her skin was smooth, almost slippery, as if the years had worn away all the roughness the way the wind wears away the surfaces of stones.

> "Mike, Mike, I didn't think you'd come," she said, so happy, and she was still Ethel Barrymore, that voice like a caress.

"Mike, Mike, I didn't think you'd come," she said, so happy, and she was still Ethel Barrymore, that voice like a caress. "I've been waiting all this time." Before I could reply, she looked away, out the window. "See the birds? I've been watching them at the feeder. I love to see them come. Even the blue jays. The blue jays are like hawks—they take the food that the small birds should have. But the small birds, the chickadees, watch the blue jays and at least learn where the feeder is."

She <u>lapsed</u> into silence, and I looked out the window. There was no feeder. No birds. There was only the parking lot and the sun glinting on car windshields.

She turned to me again, eyes bright. Radiant, really. Or was it a medicine brightness?

CLARIFY

What do you think is going on with Mike's grandmother?

"Ah, Mike. You look so grand, so grand. Is that a new coat?"

"Not really," I said. I'd been wearing my Uncle Jerry's old army-fatigue jacket for months, practically living in it, my mother said. But she insisted that I wear my raincoat for the visit. It was about a year old but looked new because I didn't wear it much. Nobody was wearing raincoats lately.

"You always loved clothes, didn't you, Mike?" she said.

I was beginning to feel uneasy because she regarded me with such intensity. Those bright eyes. I wondered—are old people in places like this so lonesome, so abandoned that they go wild when someone visits? Or was she so happy because she was suddenly <u>lucid</u> and everything was sharp and clear? My mother had described those moments when my grandmother suddenly emerged from the fog that so often obscured her mind.

I didn't know the answers, but it felt kind of spooky, getting such an emotional welcome from her.

"I remember the time you bought the new coat—the chesterfield,"[5] she said, looking away again, as if watching the birds that weren't there. "That lovely coat with the velvet collar. Black, it was. Stylish. Remember that, Mike? It was hard times, but you could never resist the glitter."

I was about to protest—I had never heard of a chesterfield, for crying out loud. But I stopped. Be patient with her, my mother had said. Humor her. Be gentle.

We were interrupted by an attendant who pushed a wheeled cart into the room. "Time for juices, dear," the woman said. She was the standard forty- or fifty-year-old woman: glasses, nothing hair, plump cheeks. Her manner was cheerful but a businesslike kind of cheerfulness. I'd hate to be called

---

5. **chesterfield:** an overcoat, usually with concealed buttons and a velvet collar.

WORDS
TO
KNOW

lapse (lăps) *v.* to drift or fall
lucid (lōō'sĭd) *adj.* mentally alert; clear-headed

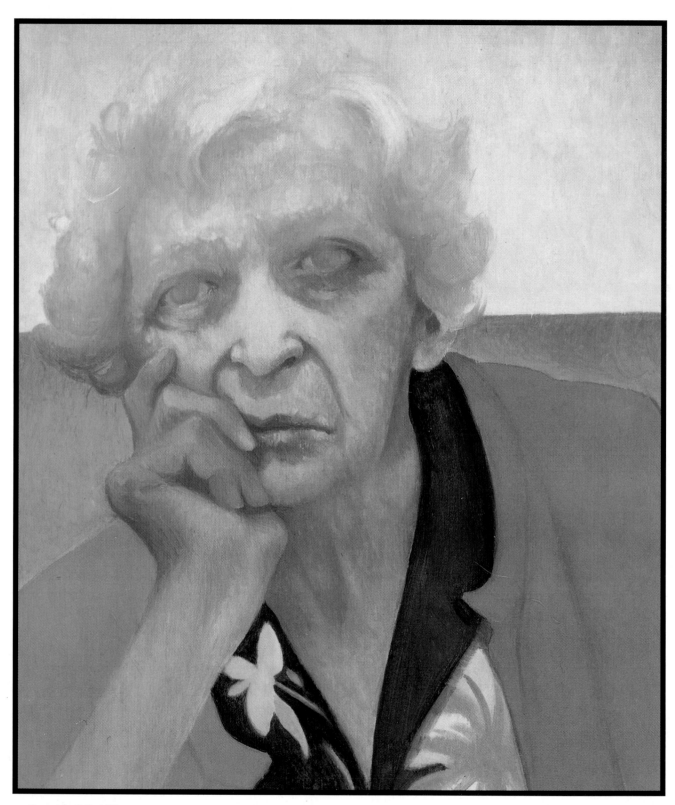

Copyright © Susi Kilgore.

"dear" by someone getting paid to do it. "Orange or grape or cranberry, dear? Cranberry is good for the bones, you know."

My grandmother ignored the interruption. She didn't even bother to answer, having turned away at the woman's arrival, as if angry about her appearance.

The woman looked at me and winked. A conspiratorial kind of wink. It was kind of horrible. I didn't think people winked like that anymore. In fact, I hadn't seen a wink in years.

"She doesn't care much for juices," the woman said, talking to me as if my grandmother weren't even there. "But she loves her coffee. With lots of cream and two lumps of sugar. But this is juice time, not coffee time." Addressing my grandmother again, she said, "Orange or grape or cranberry, dear?"

"Tell her I want no juices, Mike," my grandmother commanded regally, her eyes still watching invisible birds.

The woman smiled, patience like a label on her face. "That's all right, dear. I'll just leave some cranberry for you. Drink it at your leisure. It's good for the bones."

She wheeled herself out of the room. My grandmother was still absorbed in the view. Somewhere a toilet flushed. A wheelchair passed the doorway—probably that same old driver fleeing a hit-run accident. A television set exploded with sound somewhere, soap-opera voices filling the air. You can always tell soap-opera voices.

I turned back to find my grandmother staring at me. Her hands cupped her face, her index fingers curled around her cheeks like parenthesis marks.

"But you know, Mike, looking back, I think you were right," she said, continuing our conversation as if there had been no interruption. "You always said, 'It's the things of the spirit that count, Meg.' The spirit! And so you

> "You always said, 'It's the things of the spirit that count, Meg.' The spirit!"

bought the baby-grand piano—a baby grand in the middle of the Depression. A knock came on the door and it was the deliveryman. It took five of them to get it into the house." She leaned back, closing her eyes. "How I loved that piano, Mike. I was never that fine a player, but you loved to sit there in the parlor, on Sunday evenings, Ellie on your lap, listening to me play and sing." She hummed a bit, a fragment of melody I didn't recognize. Then she drifted into silence. Maybe she'd fallen asleep. My mother's name is Ellen, but everyone always calls her Ellie. "Take my hand, Mike," my grandmother said suddenly. Then I remembered—my grandfather's name was Michael. I had been named for him.

"Ah, Mike," she said, pressing my hands with all her feeble strength. "I thought I'd lost you forever. And here you are, back with me again. . . ."

Her expression scared me. I don't mean scared as if I were in danger but scared because of what could happen to her when she realized the mistake she had made. My mother always said I favored her side of the family. Thinking back to the pictures in the old family albums, I recalled my grandfather as tall and thin. Like me. But the resemblance ended there. He was thirty-five when he died, almost forty years ago. And he wore a moustache. I brought my hand to my face. I also wore a moustache now, of course.

CLARIFY

Who does Mike's grandmother think Mike is?

"I sit here these days, Mike," she said, her voice a lullaby, her hand still holding mine, "and I drift and dream. The days are fuzzy sometimes, merging together. Sometimes it's like I'm not here at all but somewhere else altogether. And I always think of you. Those years we had. Not enough years, Mike, not enough. . . ."

Her voice was so sad, so mournful that I made sounds of sympathy, not words exactly but the kind of soothings that mothers murmur to their children when they awaken from bad dreams.

"And I think of that terrible night, Mike, that terrible night. Have you ever really forgiven me for that night?"

"Listen . . ." I began. I wanted to say: "Nana, this is Mike your grandson, not Mike your husband."

"Sh . . . sh . . ." she whispered, placing a finger as long and cold as a candle against my lips. "Don't say anything. I've waited so long for this moment. To be here. With you. I wondered what I would say if suddenly you walked in that door like other people have done. I've thought and thought about it. And I finally made up my mind—I'd ask you to forgive me. I was too proud to ask before." Her fingers tried to mask her face. "But I'm not proud anymore, Mike." That great voice quivered and then grew strong again. "I hate you to see me this way—you always said I was beautiful. I didn't believe it. The Charity Ball when we led the grand march and you said I was the most beautiful girl there. . . ."

"Nana," I said. I couldn't keep up the pretense any longer, adding one more burden to my load of guilt, leading her on this way, playing a <u>pathetic</u> game of make-believe with an old woman clinging to memories. She didn't seem to hear me.

"But that other night, Mike. The terrible one. The terrible accusations I made. Even Ellie woke up and began to cry. I went to her and rocked her in my arms, and you came into the room and said I was wrong. You were whispering, an awful whisper, not wanting to upset little Ellie but wanting to make me see the truth. And I didn't answer you, Mike. I was too proud. I've even forgotten the name of the girl. I sit here wondering now—was it Laura or Evelyn? I can't remember. Later, I learned that you were telling the truth all the time, Mike. That I'd been wrong. . . ." Her eyes were brighter than ever as she looked at me now, but tear-bright, the tears gathering. "It was never the same after that night, was it, Mike? The glitter was gone. From you. From us. And then the accident . . . and I never had the chance to ask you to forgive me. . . ."

My grandmother. My poor, poor grandmother. Old people aren't supposed to have those kinds of memories. You see their pictures in the family albums, and that's what they are: pictures. They're not supposed to come to life. You drive out in your father's Le Mans doing seventy-five on the pike, and all you're doing is visiting an old lady in a nursing home. A duty call. And then you find out that she's a person. She's *somebody*. She's my grandmother, all right, but she's also herself. Like my own mother and father. They exist outside of their relationship to me. I was scared again. I wanted to get out of there.

"Mike, Mike," my grandmother said. "Say it, Mike."

I felt as if my cheeks would crack if I uttered a word.

"Say you forgive me, Mike. I've waited all these years. . . ."

I was surprised at how strong her fingers were.

"Say, '*I forgive you, Meg.*' "

I said it. My voice sounded funny, as if I were talking in a huge tunnel. "I forgive you, Meg."

Her eyes studied me. Her hands pressed mine. For the first time in my life, I saw love at work. Not movie love. Not Cindy's sparkling eyes when I tell her that we're going to the beach on a Sunday afternoon. But love like something alive and tender, asking nothing in return. She raised her face, and I knew what she wanted me to do. I bent and brushed my lips against her cheek. Her flesh was like a leaf in autumn, crisp and dry.

She closed her eyes and I stood up. The sun wasn't glinting on the cars any longer. Somebody had turned on another television set, and the voices were the show-off voices of the panel shows. At the same time you could still hear the soap-opera dialogue on the other television set.

I waited awhile. She seemed to be sleeping, her breathing <u>serene</u> and regular. I buttoned my raincoat. Suddenly she opened her eyes again and looked at me. Her eyes were still bright, but they merely stared at me. Without recognition or curiosity. Empty eyes. I smiled at her, but she didn't smile back. She made a kind of moaning sound and turned away on the bed, pulling the blankets around her.

I counted to twenty-five and then to fifty and did it all over again. I cleared my throat and coughed tentatively. She didn't move; she didn't respond. I wanted to say, "Nana, it's me." But I didn't. I thought of saying, "Meg, it's me." But I couldn't.

Finally I left. Just like that. I didn't say good-bye or anything. I stalked through the corridors, looking neither to the right nor the left, not caring whether that wild old man with the wheelchair ran me down or not.

> Her eyes studied me. Her hands pressed mine. For the first time in my life, I saw love at work.

On the Southwest Turnpike I did seventy-five—no, eighty—most of the way. I turned the radio up as loud as it could go. Rock music— anything to fill the air. When I got home, my mother was vacuuming the living-room rug. She shut off the cleaner, and the silence was deafening. "Well, how was your grandmother?" she asked.

I told her she was fine. I told her a lot of things. How great Nana looked and how she seemed happy and had called me Mike. I wanted to ask her—hey, Mom, you and Dad really love each other, don't you? I mean— there's nothing to forgive between you, is there? But I didn't.

Instead I went upstairs and took out the electric razor Annie had given me for Christmas and shaved off my moustache. ❖

RESPONDING
OPTIONS

FROM PERSONAL RESPONSE TO CRITICAL ANALYSIS

REFLECT   **1.** What aspect of the story did you find most moving? Record your thoughts in your notebook.

RETHINK   **2.** Why do you think Mike shaves off his moustache?

3. How do Mike's feelings about his grandmother change during the course of the story?

Consider

- Mike's guilt as he goes to the nursing home
- his feelings when his grandmother thinks he is her husband
- his thoughts when he returns home

4. If you were Mike, would you go along with your grandmother's fantasy about her husband? Why or why not?

5. What personal discovery does Mike make? Discuss your ideas with the class.

RELATE   **6.** When people like Mike's grandmother can no longer take care of themselves, what should they do? Some feel that the elderly should live with their children or grandchildren, whatever the costs. Others believe that the elderly receive better care in nursing homes and that the government should pay for nursing home care for patients who cannot afford it. What do you think?

ANOTHER PATHWAY
Cooperative Learning

Mike reveals different emotions in the story. Working in a group, identify these emotions. Imagine that your group represents all of the feelings that Mike expresses. Each student in the group can choose one emotion to act out. Classmates can try to guess the emotion that is being expressed.

QUICKWRITES

1. What do you suppose Mike is thinking about as he leaves the nursing home? Write an **interior monologue** expressing his thoughts.

2. Use evidence from the story to make inferences about Mike's grandmother. Then write a **character sketch** that reveals what she was like before and after her husband died. Be sure to include information about her outlook on life.

📁 **PORTFOLIO** *Save your writing. You may want to use it later as a springboard to a piece for your portfolio.*

LITERARY CONCEPTS

Sometimes a writer uses a concrete object—a **symbol**—to stand for an idea. For example, in "The Moustache," the piano symbolizes certain things about the grandfather—his generous spirit and his love of life. Similarly, Mike's moustache is a concrete object that symbolizes something about Mike. What do you think Mike's moustache might symbolize?

ALTERNATIVE ACTIVITIES

1. Create a **biographical sketch** by interviewing one of your older relatives or friends on audiotape or videotape. Request a photograph from his or her youth. Ask the person to tell you some stories about the picture. Play the interview for the class.

2. With a partner, look into the kinds of care provided for the elderly in your community. Then evaluate the availability and quality of care in your community. Present your findings in the form of a **chart.**

ACROSS THE CURRICULUM

Science Two diseases of the elderly are arteriosclerosis and Alzheimer's (älts′hī-mərz) disease. You know from this story some possible effects of arteriosclerosis. Research additional information about this disease as well as the causes and effects of Alzheimer's disease. Compare their causes and effects.

EXERCISE A Review the Words to Know at the bottom of the selection pages, and list them on your paper. Write the word that best completes each sentence.

1. Mike thought Lawnrest might be noisy, but it was really ____.

2. It had been a long time since Mike had seen his grandmother, and he had a strong guilt ____.

3. Mike wasn't sure whether his grandmother would be ____ enough to recognize him.

4. He wouldn't know what to do if she were to have a stroke and ____ into a coma.

5. When Mike saw his grandmother, he was struck by how frail and ____ she was.

EXERCISE B Choose the word *lucid, pathetic,* or *serene* and, with another student, create a collage that presents a visual representation of the word.

ROBERT CORMIER

Robert Cormier (1925–), who grew up during the Great Depression, says he was a "skinny kid living in a ghetto type of neighborhood wanting the world to know I existed." His childhood wish came true. Today, he is one of the country's best-known writers of adolescent fiction.

Several of Cormier's books, particularly *The Chocolate War,* have been considered controversial because of their complex themes. The author explains: "We're brought up to expect happy endings. . . . My books go against that: the hero doesn't always win, and sometimes you're not sure who the bad guy is."

Cormier's four children have provided ideas for his stories. "The Moustache" developed when his son, Peter, visited his grandmother in a nursing home. "He returned visibly moved, shaken," the author recalls. Cormier also looks to his ten grandchildren for story ideas.

Cormier's books have won many awards. In 1994, *We All Fall Down* was voted by the American Library Association as one of the best books for young adults written during the last 25 years. It also won a 1993–1994 young adult California Reader Medal, an award voted by teenagers.

OTHER WORKS *In the Middle of the Night, Tunes for Bears to Dance To, Other Bells for Us to Ring, Beyond the Chocolate War*

POETRY

The Other Pioneers
Roberto Félix Salazar

Saying Yes
Diana Chang

PERSONAL CONNECTION

We often identify one another with one-word labels, such as *jock, Democrat, brain,* and *nerd.* Sometimes people are labeled solely according to their ethnic heritage. Why do you think we label people in this manner rather than describe them in a way that shows their various qualities, interests, and talents? How might one-word labeling keep people from finding their place? Record your thoughts in your notebook, then discuss them with the class.

CULTURAL CONNECTION

Who are the people of the United States? Some say that the country's varied racial mix is like a salad bowl overflowing with a rich variety of ingredients that keep their individual flavors. However, many people in this country can claim several cultural backgrounds, or a mix of ethnic identities. It is possible for a single individual to have an ancestry that is Native American, Spanish, African, and Chinese combined.

Fifteen thousand years ago, people now called Native Americans migrated from Asia to North America, and some eventually reached the tip of South America. These pioneers explored the land and discovered valuable resources. When, a little more than 400 years ago, the first white settlers, the Spanish, arrived in the Southwest and in what is now Florida, Native Americans guided them.

Today, immigrants continue to pour into the United States. Almost 1 million arrived in 1992 alone, nearly one-third of them coming from Asia. These immigrants, like those who preceded them, have brought diverse cultural traditions to the United States.

READING CONNECTION

Contrasting Speakers You may recall that the voice that talks to the reader in poetry is called the speaker. As you read, compare and contrast the speakers in "The Other Pioneers" and "Saying Yes." Consider how each speaker identifies with his or her ethnic heritage. Use a chart, similar to the one shown, to record your ideas about each speaker.

Contrasting Speakers	
"The Other Pioneers"	**"Saying Yes"**

LASERLINKS
- *CULTURAL CONNECTION*
- *VISUAL VOCABULARY*

The Other Pioneers

by Roberto Félix Salazar

California Vaqueros, James Walker. Oil on canvas, 31" × 46". The Anschutz Collection, Denver.

Now I must write
Of those of mine who rode these plains
Long years before the Saxon[1] and the Irish came.
Of those who plowed the land and built the towns
5   And gave the towns soft-woven Spanish names.
Of those who moved across the Rio Grande
Toward the hiss of Texas snake and Indian yell.
Of men who from the earth made thick-walled homes
And from the earth raised churches to their God.
10   And of the wives who bore them sons
And smiled with knowing joy.

---

1. **Saxon** (săk′sən): English.

They saw the Texas sun rise golden-red with promised wealth
And saw the Texas sun sink golden yet, with wealth unspent.
"Here," they said. "Here to live and here to love."
15 "Here is the land for our sons and the sons of our sons."
And they sang the songs of ancient Spain
And they made new songs to fit new needs.
They cleared the brush and planted the corn
And saw green stalks turn black from lack of rain.
20 They roamed the plains behind the herds
And stood the Indian's cruel attacks.
There was dust and there was sweat.
And there were tears and the women prayed.

And the years moved on.
25 Those who were first placed in graves
Beside the broad mesquite and the tall nopal.[2]
Gentle mothers left their graces and their arts
And stalwart fathers pride and manly strength.
Salinas, de la Garza, Sánchez, García,
30 Uribe, Gonzálaz, Martinez, de León:
Such were the names of the fathers.
Salinas, de la Garza, Sánchez, García,
Uribe, Gonzálaz, Martinez, de León:
Such are the names of the sons.

---

2. **mesquite** (mĕ-skēt´) . . . **nopal** (nō-päl´): thorny tree or shrub common in the Southwestern United States and in northern Mexico; cactus with reddish flowers, found chiefly in Mexico.

FROM PERSONAL RESPONSE TO CRITICAL ANALYSIS

REFLECT   1. What lines or phrases from this poem linger the longest in your mind? Record your thoughts in your notebook.

RETHINK   2. What qualities do you think these pioneers display?

3. What do you think was the poet's purpose in writing this poem? Explain your answer.

4. What seems to be the speaker's attitude toward Native Americans and toward women? Give reasons for your answer.

RELATE   5. Do you think today's society encourages people to be proud of their ethnic identities? Why or why not? Discuss your thoughts with a partner.

Sa y i nYes g

by Diana Chang

"Are you Chinese?"
"Yes."

"American?"
"Yes."

5 "*Really* Chinese?"
"No . . . not quite."

"*Really* American?"
"Well, actually, you see . . ."

But I would rather say
10 yes

Not neither-nor,
not maybe,
but both, and not only

The homes I've had,
15 the ways I am

I'd rather say it
twice,
yes

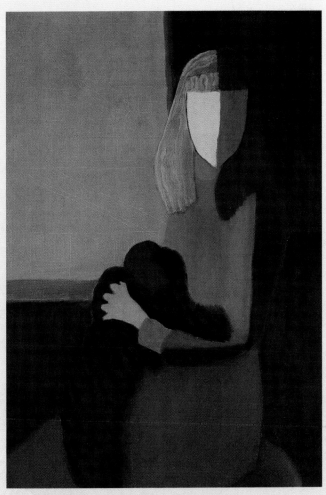

Seated Girl With Dog (1944), Milton Avery. Collection of Roy R.
Neuberger, New York. Copyright © 1996 Milton Avery Trust/Artists
Rights Society (ARS), New York.

RESPONDING
OPTIONS

FROM PERSONAL RESPONSE TO CRITICAL ANALYSIS

REFLECT 1. What is your impression of the main speaker in "Saying Yes"? Discuss your ideas with a classmate.

RETHINK 2. What idea is the main speaker trying to explain?

Consider
- the questions the speaker is asked
- how the answers change as the questions become more specific
- the meaning of lines 9–13
- the main speaker's conclusions

3. Who might be asking the questions in this poem, and why?

RELATE 4. How do the Chinese American and the Hispanics in the two poems identify themselves in relation to their ethnic heritage? Compare how they view themselves culturally. What ethnic label do you think each would choose?

5. Make an illustration that shows how each poem fits the theme "Finding Your Place."

ANOTHER PATHWAY

Imagine that the speakers in these two poems meet. What might they say to each other? With a partner, write their dialogue. Then act out the conversation for your class.

LITERARY CONCEPTS

Although the use of **dialogue** in poetry is certainly not unheard of, dialogue is used much less frequently in poems than in prose works. You may have noticed that both of the poems you just read contain dialogue. The first half of "Saying Yes" records conversation between the speaker and an unidentified person. In "The Other Pioneers," the pioneers' own words are added to the speaker's description of the pioneers' activities. What do you think the dialogue contributes to the meaning of each poem? Explain your answer.

QUICKWRITES

1. What qualities, interests, and ethnic heritage characterize you? Write a **poem** that conveys your identity.

2. Some people see the United States as a melting pot—a place in which immigrants of various nationalities and races are absorbed into one main culture. Other people see our nation as a salad bowl, with immigrants being part of one nation but retaining strong individual ethnic identities. Which of these concepts do you think the speaker of each poem would support? Why? Write a short **essay** that answers these questions.

📁 *PORTFOLIO Save your writing. You may want to use it later as a springboard to a piece for your portfolio.*

ALTERNATIVE ACTIVITIES

1. Choose a line from "The Other Pioneers" that might inspire a painting. Then create a **painting,** and share your results with the class.

2. Research some aspect of the history of Asian immigration to the United States. Then present your findings to the class in the form of a **posterboard display** containing photographs, drawings, charts, and graphs as well as brief descriptions of these graphics.

ROBERTO FÉLIX SALAZAR

Roberto Félix Salazar (1921–) is a Mexican-American poet. In "The Other Pioneers," Salazar celebrates his ethnic background and honors the contributions of his Spanish ancestors, who settled the Southwestern United States. Philip Ortego, a professor of Chicano Studies, explains that "The Other Pioneers" was written as a reminder that the early Southwestern pioneers had Spanish names and that many Americans today continue, with great pride, to call themselves by those names.

DIANA CHANG

Diana Chang, a contemporary Chinese-American poet, short story writer, and novelist, often writes about Asian-American identity. Her first novel, *The Frontiers of Love,* published in the 1960s, was criticized by some Asian Americans who said she should write about her own experiences in the United States, not about the experiences of Eurasians (people of mixed European and Asian descent) in China, where the novel is set. The novel has recently been republished and is considered a forerunner of literature about mixed-race people.

The daughter of a Chinese father and a Eurasian mother, Chang was born in the United States and today lives on Long Island, New York. She taught creative writing at Barnard College for ten years. Chang is also a painter, and her acrylics, pastels, and watercolors have been exhibited in both group and solo shows.

She adapted one of her stories, "Falling Free," into a radio play for public radio. About "Saying Yes," Chang remarks, "To my surprise, 'Saying Yes' has been reprinted very often. I can only suppose it's because it is sincere and simple."

• *CONTEMPORARY CONNECTION*

DRAMA

The Man Without a Country

Edward Everett Hale

Dramatized by Walter Hackett

PERSONAL CONNECTION

The central character in this play becomes separated from his American homeland, an important part of his personal identity. Imagine what it might be like to be forcibly separated from your homeland. How would you react? How might this affect your personal identity? Discuss your ideas with the class.

HISTORICAL CONNECTION

"The Man Without a Country" is a dramatized version of a story based on events in American history. The play spans 57 years of American history, beginning in 1805, during the presidency of Thomas Jefferson, and ending in 1862 with the presidency of Abraham Lincoln and the Civil War.

As the play opens, the reader meets real-life figure Aaron Burr, one of U.S. history's most controversial characters. The drama refers to Burr's plot to seize a portion of the United States and start a new country. Burr was in fact involved in such a plot in 1805. He was tried for treason but was later cleared of all charges for lack of evidence. The events of the life of the main character, Philip Nolan, as they are portrayed in the play, are largely fictitious. In reality, Nolan was a well-known horse trader of the American West. It has been written, but not confirmed, that in 1800, near the time of his death, he was preparing a military invasion of the very same land area targeted for seizure by Aaron Burr.

The time line shown here pinpoints other important events that occurred during the course of the play, some of which are referred to in the dialogue.

1800

Year	Event
1804	Lewis and Clark expedition begins
1812	War with Britain begins
1817	Erie Canal begun
1823	Monroe Doctrine
1825	Steam locomotive invented
1829	Andrew Jackson becomes president
1830	Indian Removal Act
1831	Nat Turner's Rebellion
1835	Seminole War begins
1849	California Gold Rush
1852	*Uncle Tom's Cabin* published
1857	Dred Scott case
1861	Lincoln becomes president/ Civil War begins

1865

Sequencing

When one thing follows another in chronological order, a sequence has been arranged. Events in fiction, nonfiction, and drama occur in a certain order, or sequence. One way to begin to make sense of a story or play is to pay attention to the sequence of events.

Sequencing can be particularly helpful when there is a long chronology of events or changes that the reader must keep track of. In some selections, events are arranged neatly and logically in sequence. In other selections, however, it is up to the reader to organize and make sense of the time order. Writers sometimes use time-order words or phrases to signal a sequence of events. These signal words and phrases include *first, next, then, now, this time,* and *before.*

Being aware of the correct sequence of events in a story or play can help readers explore the impact of events on the characters and determine how characters change. Understanding sequence also allows the reader to predict what might happen next. Refer to the guidelines presented here when you are examining the use of sequencing in a story.

In "The Man Without a Country," events involving Philip Nolan, the main character, occur rapidly, and the setting changes frequently. It will help you to understand what is happening if you keep track of the sequence of events in the plot as they relate to the time frame of the play. What happens first, next, and so on until the play comes to a conclusion? Notice how each event is affected by the event before it.

As you read "The Man Without a Country," make a time line of the play's dramatic events, adding to it the real events from the time line in the Historical Connection. To help you get started, refer to the time line begun for you here.

Strategies for Studying Sequencing

- Ask yourself the questions "What happened first?" and "What happened next?" If you like, keep notes in your notebook.

- Highlight passages in which an event is described.

- Make a list of any time-order words or phrases as they appear in the selection. These signal words help make the sequence clear.

- Use a sequence chart, similar to the one shown, to record information about each event in the selection.

| Event 1 | → | Event 2 | → | Event 3 |

1800

| 1804 | Lewis and Clark expedition begins |
| 1805 | Burr and Nolan meet at Fort Massac |

The Man Without a Country

a Country

BY EDWARD EVERETT HALE

DRAMATIZED BY WALTER HACKETT

CAST OF CHARACTERS

Voice 1

Voice 2

Narrator

Colonel

Aaron Burr, former Vice-President of the United States

Lieutenant Philip Nolan, junior officer drawn into Burr's plot

Prosecutor

Judge

Counsel

Defense

Thomas Jefferson

Captain Ethan Shaw

Lieutenant Mitchell

Guard

Officer 1

Officer 2

Captain Lane

Sailor

Officer 3

Dr. Bates

Lieutenant Harper

Captain Ben Rankin

Mrs. Anna Rutledge, a friend of Captain Rankin's

Navy Secretary

Doctor

(*Music: a strong Americana theme. Forte*[1] *and fade under.*)

Voice 1. I understand he's comin' aboard tomorrow. I've never seen him. I wonder what he looks like?

Voice 2. Who you talkin' about?

Voice 1. The Man Without a Country.

(*Music: forte briefly and under again.*)

Narrator. Fort Massac is a small yet strategic United States Army outpost that stands on the muddy banks of the lower Mississippi River. In this year of 1805, its officers and men are none too happy concerning their lonely detail. But on this particular day there is in evidence a more-than-average amount of excitement. A famous guest has come to visit them. At the evening mess[2] he sits in the place of honor, at the commanding officer's right. As the meal progresses the officers stare at the newcomer: Aaron Burr! Aaron Burr, former Vice-President of the United States, rabid Federalist, master politician, smooth-tongued orator; Aaron Burr, the man who had killed Alexander Hamilton[3] in a duel. (*Fading*) The Colonel turns to Burr and says.

(*Music out.*)

Colonel. Are you sure I can't get you to change your mind, Mr. Burr? You're welcome to remain here as long as you wish.

Burr. Thank you, Colonel, but I'm afraid I must be leaving within the next day or so.

Colonel. Pressing business, I imagine.

Burr. Yes, of a sort.

Officer (*away*). Mr. Burr, we had rather imag-

---

1. *Forte* (fôr′tā′): musical direction meaning "loud and forceful."
2. **mess:** meal served to soldiers eating together.
3. **Alexander Hamilton:** (1755?–1804) U.S. secretary of the treasury under President George Washington and long-time political enemy of Aaron Burr.

ined that this journey of yours was one of pleasure.

Burr. Suppose we call it a journey of observation. You see, gentlemen, my career has never allowed me to relax long enough to seek pleasure. By the way, I hope to talk more with some of you gentlemen before I leave.

Colonel. That is a pleasure all of us will look forward to, sir.

Burr. I hope so. And now if you will excuse me, (*fading*) I'll go to my quarters. I'm rather tired by my journey. (*a pause, then knock on door*)

Burr (*muffled tone*). Yes?

Nolan (*a young voice*). It's Lieutenant Nolan, sir. I have the tobacco you asked for this morning. (*sound of door opening and closing*)

Nolan. Here you are, sir, a pound of fine burley.

Burr. Thank you, er—

Nolan. Lieutenant Nolan.

Burr. First name?

Nolan. Philip, sir.

Burr. Thank you for the tobacco. (*pause*) Sit down.

Nolan. Thank you, Mr. Burr.

Burr. You haven't been in service too long, I take it.

Nolan. No, sir. Going on four years.

Burr. Like the Army?

Nolan (*slowly*). Why, yes, sir.

Burr. The pay of a junior officer isn't very much, eh?

Nolan. No, sir.

Burr. Ever get tired of this duty? (*beat*) Don't be afraid to speak up, Nolan. Remember I once was in the Army, too. I was very young when I enlisted. So I have an idea how you younger officers think.

Nolan (*hesitantly*). Well, Mr. Burr, to be frank . . .

(*He shoots it out.*) . . . to be very frank, life on a frontier post like this is just about the most boring existence in the world. (*beat*) Of course I wouldn't want the Colonel to hear me say that.

Burr (*laughs easily*). Of course you wouldn't.

Nolan. Then another thing—(*He hesitates.*)

Burr. Go on.

Nolan. I happen to be in debt. As you just said: an Army lieutenant's pay isn't very much.

Burr (*smoothly*). I'm sorry to hear that.

Nolan. I've been thinking of applying for a transfer.

Burr. Perhaps I could help you on that, Nolan.

Nolan (*eagerly*). Oh, if only you would, Mr. Burr—

Burr. It wouldn't mean you would be transferred to another post.

Nolan (*puzzled*). No?

Burr. No! It would mean a great chance for you. A chance for fame and position and money— a great deal of money.

Nolan. And where is this place, sir?

Burr. In a new country.

Nolan. A new country?

Burr. A new glorious empire. Nolan, there is a place for you in that empire. But before I tell you more, you must swear to say nothing to anyone. Understand—not a word! Will you swear it?

Nolan. Yes . . . I swear it.

(*Music: a theme of excitement. Forte and fade under for:*)

Voice (*reading rapidly*). "Washington, D.C., July 3, 1807. To all commanding officers of United States Army posts in the Mississippi River sector: You are hereby commanded to apprehend and secure the persons of Aaron

Burr, General James Wilkinson, and any other such conspirators guilty of attempting treason and plotting to seize a portion of these United States, on which to fashion a new country of their own. . . . Signed, John Clarke, Secretary of War."

(*Music up and out.*)

Prosecutor. To sum up my case as prosecution on this board of court-martial: Gentlemen, I accuse the defendant, Lieutenant Philip Nolan, of the crime of treason against the United States of America.

(*A buzz of voices. Sound of gavel on wood.*)

Judge. Silence! The prosecution will proceed.

Prosecutor. This man sitting here is guilty of actively <u>abetting</u> the most <u>odious</u> political plot in the entire history of our beloved country— and I am including the one another gentleman participated in—Mr. Benedict Arnold.[4]

Counsel. Objection.

Judge. Objection overruled.

Counsel. But, sir, I can present conclusive evidence that will prove that Philip Nolan—

(*Gavel rapped.*)

Prosecutor. There is not a bit of doubt that Philip Nolan knowingly entered into a secret and infamous agreement with Aaron Burr; an agreement to undermine the safety of his own native land. You have heard me question him concerning his dealings with Burr. And what has been his reply? That he is under oath to say nothing of what transpired between them.

Counsel. Objection.

Judge. Objection overruled.

Prosecutor. And why did this Judas[5] sell himself? The answer: for the empty promises of an egotistical dreamer, who promised him money and fame. That is why Philip Nolan sold his soul; that is why he broke the solemn oath of <u>fidelity</u> to country that he swore to abide by at the time of his enlistment.

Nolan (*away*). You're a liar.

(*gavel in sharply*)

Judge. I might warn the prisoner that any such further remarks might result in adversely swaying the members of this board of court-martial. The prosecution may proceed.

Prosecutor. I simply repeat what is obvious: Lieutenant Nolan should be adjudged guilty.

Judge. Has the defense anything to say?

Counsel. Sir, Lieutenant Nolan wishes to speak for himself.

Judge. Let *Mr.* Nolan proceed.

Nolan (*quietly*). For two days I have sat here and listened as the charges piled up against me. I have heard the prosecution deliberately distort every statement, every answer I gave.

Prosecutor. I object.

Judge. Sustained.

Nolan. I readily admit that I listened to Burr's offer to join him.

Prosecutor. Then why didn't you come forward and unmask him?

Nolan. Because I was under oath to say nothing.

Defense. I object. Lieutenant Nolan is not now being cross-examined. I request the court that he be allowed to finish uninterrupted.

---

4. **Mr. Benedict Arnold:** (1741–1801) American Revolutionary War general and, later, traitor to the United States. He plotted to surrender West Point to the British in exchange for money, but the plan was foiled.

5. **Judas** (jōō′dəs): person who betrays someone under the pretense of friendship; from *Judas Iscariot,* one of the 12 Apostles and the betrayer of Jesus.

WORDS TO KNOW	**abetting** (ə-bĕt′ĭng) *n.* encouraging or supporting an action or plan, especially one of wrongdoing **abet** *v.* **odious** (ō′dē-əs) *adj.* deserving hatred; disgusting **fidelity** (fĭ-dĕl′ĭ-tē) *n.* faithfulness to obligations or duties

Judge. Continue, Mr. Nolan.

Nolan. I swear that I rejected Burr's offer. (*beat*) I realize that military justice is of a necessity swift and sometimes unjust.

Prosecutor. Objection.

Judge. Sustained. The defendant will reword his line of reasoning.

Nolan. I realize that in any court of justice it is possible for an innocent man to be falsely accused of the wrongs done by others. (*His voice rises.*) For the past two weeks I have seen other officers—men actually guilty of the same crime I allegedly committed—go free. Free because this board wished to find them free.

(*Angry ad libs from members. Gavel.*)

Judge. Are you finished, Mr. Nolan?

Nolan. No! I know well what the verdict will be. I know I will be made an example of the fate in store for others.

Judge. Mr. Nolan, I believe it has been easily established that you have been unfaithful to your country, that you have committed against the United States—

Nolan (*angrily*). Damn the United States. I wish I may never hear of the United States again!

(*Music: angry theme up and out into sound of gavel on wood three times.*)

Judge. The prisoner will rise and face the board. (*beat*) Philip Nolan, hear the sentence of this board. The board of court-martial, subject to the approval of the President, decrees that you shall never again hear the name of the United States!

(*Music up and fade under.*)

Judge. Mr. Nolan is to be taken to New Orleans

America, Victoria & Albert, and Black Eagle off the Isle of Wight, 1851, Tim Thompson.
Oil on canvas, 20" × 40". Image used under license with T.F.R. Thompson.

and delivered to Lieutenant Mitchell, acting naval commander. You will request that no one will ever mention the United States to the prisoner while he is on board ship. Mr. Nolan is to be confined until further orders.

(*Music up briefly and under.*)

Jefferson. "Washington, D.C., October 28, 1807. To Secretary of Navy Crowninshield. Your deposition[6] relative to the case of Philip Nolan received and noted. You are hereby empowered to turn the prisoner over to Captain Ethan Shaw, commander of the *Nautilus,* now in New Orleans. Sincerely yours, your obedient servant, Thomas Jefferson, President of the United States."

(*Music up and out into distant sound of ship's bell striking six.*)

Shaw (*on fourth stroke*). Lieutenant Mitchell, I can't say I like this duty.

Mitchell. Sorry, Captain Shaw, but I'm just carrying out my orders.

Shaw. I understand. Go on and read the rest of the order.

Mitchell. "You will provide him with such quarters, rations, and clothing as would be proper for an officer of his late rank. The officers on board your ship will make arrangements agreeable to themselves regarding his society."

Shaw (*gloomily*). That is going to be a pleasant situation. Go on.

Mitchell. "He is to be exposed to no indignity of any kind, nor is he ever unnecessarily to be reminded that he is a prisoner. . . ."

Shaw. And I suppose that is going to be an easy order to obey.

---

6. **deposition** (dĕp′ə-zĭsh′ən): written testimony made by a witness under oath for use in court.

Mitchell. "But under no circumstances is Philip Nolan ever to hear of his country again, nor to see any information regarding it; and you will caution all your officers that these rules are not to be broken. It is the unswerving intention of the government that he shall never again see the country which he has disowned. Before the end of your cruise you will receive orders with regard to transferring the prisoner. Respectfully yours, W. Southard, assistant to the secretary of the Navy."

Shaw (*as though shrugging*). Well!—(*beat*) How does he take it?

Mitchell. I don't think he realizes what is going to happen.

Shaw. He'll soon learn. (*abruptly*) Where is he now?

Mitchell. Waiting outside, sir.

Shaw. Bring him in.

(*Chair scraping on floor. Hatch door slid open.*)

Shaw (*calling out*). Guard, bring the prisoner here.

Guard (*off*). Aye, sir. (*as an aside to* Nolan) Step lively, you.

Shaw. You can leave us now, Lieutenant Mitchell.

Mitchell. Thank you, sir.

(*Hatch slid closed.*)

Shaw. Well, Mr. Nolan, I suppose you're wondering quite a few things at the moment.

Nolan. I am.

Shaw. You're to be given quarters. You'll be fairly comfortable. The ship's commissary will supply anything you lack. Your meals will be served to you in your cabin.

Nolan. About my uniforms, the insignia has been removed.

Shaw. You are to be allowed to wear your uniforms minus all insignia.

Nolan. But—

Shaw. Orders.

Nolan. I see. (*pause*) Captain Shaw, exactly what is my position aboard your ship?

Shaw (*fumbling*). Why—why, er—(*quickly recovering himself*) You may consider your position as that of a guest—a slightly underprivileged guest.

Nolan. Am I to sail with you?

Shaw. Naturally.

Nolan. Where?

Shaw. Around the Horn, into the Pacific, and across to Tahiti.

Nolan. Tahiti? That's a long way from the United States.

Shaw. A very long way.

Nolan. How long are we to be gone?

Shaw. Two years!

(*Music: a dramatic theme. Forte and out.*)

Officer 1 (*lazily*). I sometimes wonder why I joined the Navy, rather than the Army. This idea of roaming the seven seas can be tiresome. When we get back to the States, I'm going to put in for shore duty.

Officer 2. I rather like it here in Tahiti. It's warm and peaceful, a nice lazy life.

Officer 1. It's been almost two years since I last saw my parents. In fact, it's been nine months since we sailed from New Orleans. A couple of nomads, you and I, men without a home.

Officer 2. Much better than being a man without a country.

Officer 1. What's that? Oh, yes. Poor Nolan! At times I feel sorry for him.

WORDS TO KNOW   **insignia** (ĭn-sĭg′nē-ə) *n.* a badge of rank or membership

608

Officer 2. Too bad he lost his head. Wonder if the government will ever <u>rescind</u> his sentence?

Officer 1. Hard to say.

Officer 2. It would have been a more merciful thing to have hanged him. Anything in place of being a floating derelict.[7]

Officer 1. (*He lowers his voice.*) Quiet! Here he comes now. Watch what you say.

Nolan. Good afternoon, gentlemen. Grand day, isn't it? (Officers *ad lib greetings.*) Mind if I join you?

Officer 1. Plenty of deck space.

Officer 2. Sit down.

Nolan (*sighs deeply*). Ahh! That sun feels good. Thought I would do a bit of reading. The surgeon passed on this old newspaper to me—an English newspaper.

Officer 2. You're a great reader, Mr. Nolan.

Nolan. Oh, yes. Helps pass away the time, you know. Keeps me in touch with what is taking place. (*pause*) Would you gentlemen tell me something?

Officer 1 (*cautiously*). Why . . . yes.

Nolan. I notice that these newspapers that are passed on to me have certain paragraphs cut out. For example, this one here.

(*Sound of newspaper being unfolded.*)

Nolan. Here! Now here is a story dealing with Napoleon's campaign, and just as it apparently starts to relate the policy of the United States toward The Little Corporal,[8] I discover that the rest of the account has been sheared out. Peculiar, isn't it? Er, could you tell me why?

Officer 1. No.

Officer 2. Hadn't noticed.

Nolan. Well, I guess it doesn't matter. By the way, what is the latest news from our country?

Officer 2. We have no news.

Nolan. But last night in the wardroom you were talking over the dispatches received from the States. As soon as I came in, you stopped. Why?

Officer 2. I wish you wouldn't ask, Mr. Nolan.

Nolan (*as though shrugging*). Very well. I realize you're not supposed to talk about the United States to me. I thought I could worm some information from you.

Officer 2. We're honor-bound not to discuss the matter with you.

Officer 1. You should understand.

Nolan (*dully*). Yes, I understand.

Officer 1. What about your parents, Mr. Nolan, or your relatives? Couldn't they—?

Nolan. My parents are dead. As for my relatives, they don't know, and I doubt if they'd help. (*a simple dignity*) Now, if you don't mind, I'll go to my quarters.

Officer 1. Nolan.

Nolan. Yes?

Officer 1. If I were in your position, I wouldn't show the courage you're displaying.

(*Music up dramatically and under.*)

Voice. "Belfast, Ireland, June 14, 1810. To Captain James Wyatt, U.S.S. *General Greene.*

---

7. **derelict:** poor, unemployed, friendless person with no home.

8. **Napoleon's campaign . . . The Little Corporal:** Napoleon I—originally Napoleon Bonaparte—emperor of France (1804–1814), was attempting to gain complete control of Europe at the time of the events described. He was called The Little Corporal because of his short stature and because of his courage during a battle in which he himself aimed the cannon, a risky task usually performed by a corporal.

WORDS TO KNOW   **rescind** (rĭ-sĭnd') *v.* to withdraw, repeal, or cancel

You will receive the person of Philip Nolan, who will accompany you on your voyage to the Straits of Gibraltar and through the Mediterranean."

(*Music up briefly and under.*)

Voice 2. "From the log of the U.S.S. *Enterprise.* November 11, 1814. Havana, Cuba. Today we took on fresh supplies for our cruise to the Far East. Also received as passenger Mr. Philip Nolan."

(*Music up and out into knock on door.*)

Lane. Enter.

(*Hatch slid open.*)

Sailor. Mr. Nolan, sir. He would like to speak with you.

Lane. Show him in.

Sailor. Aye, aye, sir. (*slightly away*) The captain will see you.

(*After a beat, hatch slid shut.*)

Lane. Yes, Mr. Nolan?

Nolan. Captain Lane, I have heard scuttlebutt[9] that we may engage the enemy at any moment.

Lane. That's no great secret. What about it?

Nolan. Well, Captain, I have heard you're a bit short-handed. I'm wondering if you can use me.

Lane (*surprised*). Hmmm?

Nolan. I know ship's routine well. Any detail would be welcome, sir, even that of a powder monkey.[10]

Lane. You mean you desire combat duty?

Nolan. Exactly, sir.

Lane (*not unkindly*). That's generous of you, Nolan, but I'm afraid it's impossible. Your position . . . my orders concerning you, they're very strict.

Nolan. Couldn't you forget them, just this once?

Lane. In the Navy you don't wink an eye at

orders. In fact, Mr. Nolan, when and if we do engage the enemy, I must ask that you go below and remain there until the action has stopped.

(*Music up briefly and out into voices singing a Christmas carol. They sing one chorus. As they stop:*)

Officer 3. A toast, gentlemen.

Voices. *"A toast."*

Officer 3. A toast to our ship, the mighty *Constitution.*

Voices. "Hear, hear." "A great fighting ship."

Officer 3. A toast. To this Christmas Day in the year of our Lord, 1821.

Voices. "Merry Christmas." "A great day."

Nolan. Gentlemen, may I propose a toast? (*There is an awkward pause.*)

Officer 3. Go ahead, Mr. Nolan.

Nolan. I propose a toast to the United States. (*another pause*)

Officer 3. Sorry, Mr. Nolan, but that toast will have to be drunk later, when you are not present.

(*Glass broken, as though dropped from Nolan's hand.*)

(*Music up dramatically and out.*)

Captain. Well, gentlemen, who would like to read next? Dr. Bates?

Bates. Thank you, Captain, but I'll remain just a ship's doctor.

Captain. Lieutenant Harper, how about you?

Harper. I'm not much of a hand at reading, but I'll try.

Captain. Try this. It's a new book of poems by

---

9. **scuttlebutt** (skŭt′l-bŭt′): slang for gossip or rumor.

10. **powder monkey:** slang for a person who carries or sets explosives.

that Scotsman, Walter Scott. Let me see. Ah, here's what seems to be a good poem: "The Lay of the Last Minstrel." Right here.

Harper (*He reads poorly.*).

"After due pause, they bade him tell

Why he, who touched the harp so well,

Should thus, with ill-rewarded toil,

Wander a poor and thankless soil,

When the most generous Southern Land

Would well requite his skillful hand . . ."

Nolan (*slightly away*). Stop! Stop!

Captain. What's wrong, Mr. Nolan?

Nolan. With all due respect to Lieutenant Harper, Captain, he's not doing justice to that poem.

(*A few surprised ad libs from others.*)

Harper. At least I thought I was reading intelligently.

Nolan. Perhaps! But with no feeling.

Captain. Are you an expert on Sir Walter Scott's works?

Nolan. As a matter of fact, I've never read this poem, but I do know enough to realize that it isn't being read the way it should.

Harper. Why don't you read it, Mr. Nolan?

Captain. You're at liberty to do so.

Nolan.

"The aged harper, howsoe'er

His friend, his harp, was dear,

Liked not to hear it, ranked so high

Above his flowing poesy:

Less liked he that still that scornful jeer

Misprized the land he loved so dear;

High was the sound as thus again

The bard resumed his minstrel strain.

Breathes there the man, with soul so dead,

(*a bit emotionally*)

Who never to himself hath said—

This is my own, my native land!

Whose heart hath ne'er within him burned

As home (*stumbling a bit*) his footsteps he hath turned

From wandering on a foreign strand?

If such there breathe, go, mark him well.

For him no minstrel raptures swell; (*His voice starts to break.*)

High though his titles, proud his name,

Boundless his wealth as wish can claim,

Despite these titles, power and pelf, (*He shouts.*) The wretch, concentred all in self . . ."

(*Book dropped to floor.*)

Nolan (*a beaten voice*). I . . . I guess I'm not such a fine reader, after all.

(*Music: a theme of motion. Forte and under for:*)

Voice 1 (*calling out, as though speaking through a speaking trumpet*). Hooo there, *Constellation.* Stand by to receive our longboat.

Voice 2 (*off in distance*). What have you for us? Any mail?

Voice 1. No mail. We are transferring Philip Nolan.

(*Music up and out.*)

Rankin. It's certainly a pleasure to have you aboard, Anna. Let me see, I haven't seen you in four—no, in five years.

Anna. As soon as I heard word at the Consulate that your ship was coming here, I said to myself: "I'll be the very first American to welcome Ben Rankin."

Rankin. And you kept your word. Your husband sent a message that he'd come aboard late this afternoon. You know, Anna, you don't seem to have aged one bit since I last saw you.

Anna. And I can return the compliment. Ben, you look just the same as you did thirty years ago. Yes, that's when we first met, thirty years ago in Charleston. You were just a plain midshipman then. And now look at you—a captain of a man-o-war.

Rankin. And here you are, married.

Anna. I'm a grandmother.

Rankin. How do you like Naples?

Anna. I like everything but the odors. (*Both laugh.*) You know, Ben, I haven't been home in seven years, not since 1840. (*Sighs*) Being wife to an American Consul isn't all sunshine. Right now, I'd give a pretty penny for one good whiff of Charleston Harbor.

Rankin (*suddenly*). Have you ever heard of Philip Nolan?

Anna. Nolan, Nolan!

Rankin. Perhaps you know him better under his other name . . . The Man Without a Country.

Anna. Don't tell me that he's—?

Rankin. Yes, I have him aboard.

Anna. When my husband was stationed at Marseilles[11]—which was six years back—the *Constellation* came in for repairs. Nolan was aboard, but I didn't see him.

(*Off in distance, some of the crew ad libbing.*)

Rankin. I've heard of him ever since I was a midshipman, but until fifteen months ago, I had never as much as laid eyes upon him.

Anna. He's become something of a legend.

Rankin. Practically a Navy tradition. Shifted from one ship to another. Poor man, he's the nearest thing to perpetual motion I have ever encountered.

Anna. Does he give you any trouble?

Rankin. No. I've heard that during the early days, he was quite aggressive, but he's lost all that. Getting fairly old. Must be around, oh,

I'd say at least sixty-five. Minds his own business and keeps pretty much to himself. (*He lowers his voice.*) Look! There he is walking toward us. Poor old devil!

Anna. I'm afraid I don't share your sympathy. In my opinion, Nolan deserves to suffer.

Nolan (*fading in*). Captain Rankin, sir.

Rankin. Yes, Mr. Nolan?

Nolan. The second officer wants to know if you have any instructions before the liberty party goes ashore.

Rankin. Anna, will you excuse me for several minutes?

Anna. Certainly.

Rankin. By the way, Anna, this is Mr. Nolan. Mr. Nolan this is Mrs. Rutledge.

Anna. Good afternoon.

Rankin (*fading*). Mr. Jenks, I wish to see you before you go ashore. Have a detail for you. (*Ad lib voices in background gradually die out.*)

Nolan. This is a nice day, don't you think, Mrs. Rutledge?

Anna (*coldly*). Quite comfortable.

Nolan. The last port we touched was Havre. Very interesting place. I wasn't allowed ashore, but I heard the crew talking. These foreign places are fine enough, but not like home. Mrs. Rutledge, what is the news from the United States?

Anna. I thought you were the man who once said he never wanted to hear that name again.

(*Music: a tragic theme up and out into clock striking five strokes.*)

Rankin. (*His voice has grown older. He speaks on the third stroke of the clock.*) Mr.

---

11. **Marseilles** (mär-sā′): France's oldest city, located in the southeast, on the Mediterranean Sea. Dramatic battles took place here in the late 1700s, during the French Revolution.

Old Willie—the Village Worthy (1886), James Guthrie. Oil on canvas, 60.8 cm × 50.8 cm. Glasgow Museums: Art Gallery and Museum, Kelvingrove, Scotland. Photo copyright © Glasgow Museums.

Secretary, it seems to me that you doubt the truth of my story. I assure you, sir, that I am speaking the truth.

Navy Secretary. I—I don't know what to think. I know your word is good, but hang it all, Rankin, the Navy Department's records show absolutely no trace of this man you speak of . . . this Philip Nolan.

Rankin. Naturally not, Mr. Secretary. Those records were destroyed by fire when the British seized Washington during the War of 1812.

Secretary. It all sounds like a fairy tale, like a nightmare.

Rankin. Whether you want to believe it or not, Philip Nolan was sentenced back in 1807, and this is 1859. Mind you, Mr. Secretary, for 52 years Philip Nolan has been shifted from one ship to another. For 52 years he has never set foot on American soil. For 52 years he has not heard the name of the United States even mentioned by anyone. For over a half-century this unfortunate derelict has experienced a living death.

Secretary. Captain Rankin, why do you concern yourself with this matter?

Rankin. Because I like Nolan. He has been committed to my care on two occasions, and each time I found him to be a kind, mild gentleman. (*pleadingly*) Mr. Secretary, won't you investigate his case? The man has only a few years of life ahead of him. Why not let him enjoy them?

Secretary. With the possibility of war with the South growing stronger this department hasn't time for such an investigation.

Rankin. Aren't you trying to tell me that you don't care to unearth any skeletons?

Secretary. An unfortunate choice of words, Captain. (*coldly*) Taking for granted there is such a man as Philip Nolan, he will have to remain an unknown; a legend, if you like.

Rankin (*casually*). Suppose the newspapers got hold of this story? The national election is only a year off.

Secretary (*significantly*). It is entirely within my power to depose you from your command. Then there is the Far East. That is a long voyage. (*fading*) You know how many days a voyage to Japan takes, do you not, Captain Rankin? Or don't you?

(*A pause, then telegraph buzzer sending message.*)

Voice 1. "Washington, D.C., January 12, 1860. To Captain Benjamin Rankin, Newport News, Virginia. . . . Prepare to sail on 27th for extended tour of Far East, including China and Japan. Detailed orders following."

(*Buzzer up briefly and under again.*)

Voice 2. "Shanghai, China, May 11, 1862. To Captain Benjamin Rankin, aboard U.S.S. *Levant*. . . . Captain Chalmers of the *Ohio* will deliver into your hands the person of Philip Nolan. From past contact with him, you will know how to receive and handle his case."

(*Music washes in over sound. Hold briefly and out.*)

Rankin (*low voice*). You think the end is in sight, doctor?

Doctor. He's liable to go off any minute.

Rankin. Suppose you leave me alone with him?

Doctor. Very well. (*slight fade*) If you need me, I'll be outside.

(*Hatch slid open, then closed.*)

Rankin. Philip. (*beat*) Philip, it's Rankin.

Nolan. Hello, Captain.

Rankin. Is there anything you wish?

Nolan. Just sit here and talk to me. (*beat*) I know I'm dying. Perhaps now you will tell me what I want to know.

Rankin. Anything you wish.

Nolan (*breathing heavily*). I want you to know that there is not a man on this ship—that there is not in America, God bless her!—a more loyal man than I. How like a wretched night's dream a boy's idea of personal fame or of separate sovereignty seems, when one looks back on it after such a life as mine.

Rankin (*after pause*). Now what would you like to hear?

Nolan. Is our country larger?

Rankin. A good many states have been added. Ohio, Kentucky, Michigan, Indiana, and Mississippi; and California and Texas and Oregon.

Nolan. What of America's progress?

Rankin. Our country has made tremendous strides. Her cotton manufacturing is the greatest in the world. We have made great improvements on the steam train.

Nolan. Steam train?

Rankin. Yes. A form of carriage propelled by steam. Then a Naval Academy has been established at Annapolis and a Military Academy at West Point in New York. A great piece of literature has been written by a woman named Stowe—*Uncle Tom's Cabin.*

Nolan. Are we at peace?

Rankin. There was a war with England.

Nolan. In 1812. I heard rumors of it at the time. I have also heard there is trouble between the North and the South. (*hastily*) No! Don't tell me. I prefer not to know. Who is our President now?

Rankin. A great man named Abraham Lincoln. He's from the state of Illinois, a man who worked his way up from the ranks.

Nolan. Good for him.

Rankin. The United States is fast growing into the greatest democracy in the world.

Nolan (*weakly*). Wonderful . . . wonderful news.

Rankin (*alarmed*). Philip, are you—?

Nolan. Better than I have ever been. You see that old flag against the wall?

Rankin. Yes.

Nolan. I want to be wrapped in it. You'll see to that?

Rankin. I promise.

Nolan. God bless you! (*His voice becomes weaker.*) On the table is a Bible.

Rankin. I have it.

Nolan. Open it. (*pause*) Now read what is written on the flyleaf.

Rankin (*slowly and with simple dignity*). "Bury me in the sea. It has been my home, and I love it. But will not someone set up a stone for my memory somewhere on my native soil, that my disgrace may not be more than I ought to bear? Say on it: 'In memory of Philip Nolan, Lieutenant in the Army of the United States. He loved his country as no other man has loved her; but no man deserved less at her hands.'"

(*Music up to curtain.*)

The End ❖

The Burial at Sea (1896), Sir Frank Brangwyn. Oil on canvas, 154.9 cm × 233.7 cm. Glasgow Museums: Art Gallery and Museum, Kelvingrove, Scotland. Photo copyright © Glasgow Museums.

AARON BURR: PORTRAIT OF A SLY MAN

Esther Burr described her one-year-old son, Aaron, as "a little dirty Noisy Boy . . . Sly and mischievous . . . not so good tempered . . . and requires a good Governor to bring him to terms." Her death six months later prevented her from seeing him grow up, but her words seem to predict the troublesome future of this controversial American.

During the Revolutionary War, Burr was praised for military actions but was never trusted by General George Washington. After the war, he became one of the nation's leading lawyers. He served New York as a state legislator and as its attorney general in 1789. In 1800, Burr ran for the presidency, but he lost to Thomas Jefferson in a run-off election and thereby became vice-president. Burr's longtime political enemy, Alexander Hamilton, used his influence to put Jefferson in office.

Burr's political career was shattered when, four years following his presidential defeat, he challenged Alexander Hamilton to a duel. For years, Burr had endured Hamilton's political opposition and harsh criticism. Burr's outrage peaked when Hamilton helped defeat Burr in the race for the governorship of New York. The duel took place at 7 a.m. on July 11, 1804, in Weehawken, New Jersey. Ten full paces were measured off. Each man fired one shot. Hamilton's bullet snapped a tree limb 12 feet above; Burr's bullet penetrated Hamilton's abdomen. Hamilton died at 2 p.m. the following day. Burr was indicted for murder but never tried.

Burr completed his term as vice-president and then turned to perhaps the strangest chapter in his life. It is alleged that for the next several years, he plotted radical schemes with James Wilkinson, a friend and general-in-chief of the U.S. Army, to rule Louisiana. It is also alleged that he conspired to take Spanish-owned Florida territory, Mexico, and the Southwest to form a new country. Burr was ultimately betrayed by Wilkinson, who arrested him. Burr was turned over to Supreme Court Chief Justice John Marshall and was charged with treason and misdemeanor.

On September 1, 1807, the jury acquitted Burr and his associates for lack of evidence. Certainly Burr was "sly and mischievous," but was he a traitor? You might want to read more about his alleged treason and decide for yourself. Scholars continue to debate the question.

RESPONDING
OPTIONS

FROM **PERSONAL RESPONSE** TO **CRITICAL ANALYSIS**

REFLECT

1. What is your first reaction to this play? Record your thoughts in your notebook.

RETHINK

2. In your opinion, is Nolan's punishment fair? Why or why not?
   Consider
   - how his outburst about his homeland must have affected the court
   - whether he is guilty of a crime
   - the length of his "sentence"
   - how he was treated by the officers and sailors at sea

3. List three of Nolan's character traits, and explain the circumstances in which each trait is revealed.

4. Why do you think Nolan becomes so upset when he reads Sir Walter Scott's poem?

RELATE

5. Does this drama seem real to you? Could something like what happened to Philip Nolan really occur? Explain.

6. Today, heads of state are sometimes banished from their countries when there is a change of government. How do you think these former leaders feel? Compare this kind of banishment with Nolan's punishment.

Ferdinand Marcos, former president of the Philippines, was forced to leave his country in 1986, after widespread protest against him.
Reuters/Bettmann.

ANOTHER PATHWAY
Cooperative Learning

Toward the end of the play, Captain Ben Rankin appeals to the Secretary of the Navy to investigate Nolan's case. With a group of students, plan a retrial of Nolan's case at the point in the play at which Rankin makes the appeal. Present the new trial with the rest of the class acting as jury.

QUICKWRITES

1. Imagine that Nolan insists on returning to the United States. Write the **letter** he might send to the President of the United States or the Secretary of the Navy asking to have his sentence revoked.

2. Write a **diary entry** for one of the days in the 55 years Nolan lives aboard ship. Use your imagination and clues from the play.

3. Compose a **poem** or **folksong** about the legend of Philip Nolan.

4. Nolan shows Rankin an epitaph he wants inscribed on a gravestone. Write another **epitaph** for Nolan, either from your point of view or from the point of view of someone who knew him at sea.

📁 *PORTFOLIO Save your writing. You may want to use it later as a springboard to a piece for your portfolio.*

LITERARY CONCEPTS

In a short story or play, the main character is usually the one who undergoes the most development and growth. A main character who changes dramatically is said to be a **dynamic character.** The minor characters in a story are often **static characters,** ones who change very little, if at all, as the plot unfolds. Identify the dynamic and static characters in "The Man Without a Country."

In a play, a **scene** is a section presenting events that occur in one place at one time. In a stage play, a curtain is drawn or a set is changed to indicate a change in scene. Such visual cues do not work with a radio play. How are scene changes indicated in "The Man Without a Country"?

LITERARY LINKS

Philip Nolan was imprisoned on a ship. The lawyer in "The Bet" (page 240) was imprisoned within the room of a house. Which situation do you think would be more difficult to endure, given all of the circumstances of each man's imprisonment? Give reasons for your answer.

ART CONNECTION

Look again at the artwork on pages 606–607. Examine the mood of the piece. What does it convey to you? Notice its content, scale, use of color, and any other elements that communicate the spirit or feeling of the painting. Would you have chosen a similar image to go with this selection? Why or why not?

ALTERNATIVE ACTIVITIES

1. Present a **dramatic reading** of several scenes in the play. Carefully select appropriate music to fit each scene and include this music in your presentation.

2. Create a **comic book** version of "The Man Without a Country." Follow the sequence of events in the plot. Use dialogue from the play or write your own, and then share your results with the class.

Objection!

Objection overruled.

ACROSS THE CURRICULUM

History During the time of Nolan's imprisonment, the number of states in the Union doubled. Find out which states entered the Union during the time frame of the play. Then, make two maps of the United States. The first should show the states and territories that existed before Nolan's imprisonment. The second should present the United States as it appeared at the time of Nolan's death. Indicate on the second map the date of each state's admittance to the Union. Display your results in the classroom.

EDWARD EVERETT HALE

Edward Everett Hale was minister of the South Congregational Church in Boston for 43 years, but he found time to write scores of stories, novels, nonfiction books, poems, songs, and ballads about history and adventure for both children and adults. Hale is known for writing stories about impossible situations that seem starkly real. His most famous story is "The Man Without a Country." First published anonymously during the Civil War, the story was written, Hale said, as a "sentiment of love to the nation."

A grandnephew of the Revolutionary War hero Nathan Hale, the author was born into a large family in Boston. He greatly admired his parents, who "made home the happiest place of all." He asked to go to school at the age of 2. By age 6, he could "rattle off about isosceles triangles"; a few years later, he and his sister "published" a magazine, produc-

1822–1909

ing, of course, only one copy per issue. When Hale was 13, he entered Harvard University only to find himself "thoroughly and completely homesick." After college, he taught at the Boston Latin School and studied theology on his own.

A believer in public service, Hale joined the Massachusetts Rifle Corps and the Sanitary Commission during the Civil War. He was a leader in several charitable organizations, including the New England Emigrant Aid Society and the Lend-a-Hand movement. He edited a monthly magazine, *Old and New,* for five years and traveled frequently in the United States and Europe, gathering material for his writing. Hale and his wife had two daughters and six sons. At 81, he was elected chaplain of the U.S. Senate, a post he kept until shortly before his death six years later.

OTHER WORKS *A New England Boyhood*

Think As I Think

by Stephen Crane

"Think as I think," said a man,

"Or you are abominably wicked;

You are a toad."

And after I had thought of it,

5   I said, "I will, then, be a toad."

Frog with Top Hat, Eyeglasses, and Cat-tail (1910), artist unknown. The Art Students League of New York. Photograph by Ariel Cortes.

STEPHEN CRANE

1871–1900

Although Stephen Crane was dead from tuberculosis by the time he was 28, he is considered one of America's most important writers. He was one of the first American writers to describe in fiction the harsh realities of life. He wrote six novels, more than 100 short stories, and two volumes of poetry.

Born in Newark, New Jersey, the youngest of 14 children, Crane left college to pursue a writing career. Upon reading that artists must experience hardship to be creative, he chose to live in New York City's slums. Out of this experience and his newspaper reporting on slum conditions came his first novel, which was considered so shocking for its time that no publisher would print it. Crane borrowed money to publish it himself. His second novel, *The Red Badge of Courage,* depicts the horrors of the Civil War. A huge success, the book's reputation has continued to the present day.

OTHER WORKS "A Man Said to the Universe," "A Mystery of Heroism"

The Choice

by Dorothy Parker

He'd have given me rolling lands,
   Houses of marble, and billowing farms,
Pearls, to trickle between my hands,
   Smoldering rubies, to circle my arms.
5 You—you'd only a lilting song,
   Only a melody, happy and high,
You were sudden and swift and strong,—
   Never a thought for another had I.

He'd have given me laces rare,
10 Dresses that glimmered with frosty sheen,
Shining ribbons to wrap my hair,
   Horses to draw me, as fine as a queen.
You—you'd only to whistle low,
   Gaily I followed wherever you led.
15 I took you, and I let him go,—
   Somebody ought to examine my head!

DOROTHY PARKER

A fiction writer and poet, Dorothy Parker is remembered for her ready wit. Readers have delighted in her ability to find humor even in tragedy—often her own. Her work frequently addresses such themes as lost love, women's issues, and racial oppression. Parker's poetry and fiction appeared in many magazines, including *The New Yorker,* to which she contributed for more than 30 years.

During the 1920s, Parker was known in New York City literary circles as a member of the Algon-

1893–1967

quin Round Table, a group of writers who met regularly at the Algonquin Hotel and became famous when their conversations were quoted in the press.

Parker's personal life was marked by depression. Her most lasting relationship was with her second husband, actor Alan Campbell. They wrote 16 screenplays together, including *A Star is Born,* which received an Academy Award nomination for best picture.

OTHER WORKS "Penelope," "Prayer for a New Mother"

Mountain Sunset—Southwest Series #181 (1994), Teruko Wilde. Oil on canvas, 44" × 50". Copyright © Teruko Wilde. Courtesy of Third Canyon Gallery, Denver. Photo courtesy of Leapingotis Fine Art Gallery, Vail, Colorado.

I Belong

by A. Whiterock

All that I see around me
   I am a part of.

I am the mountain, to stand
   with pride, strength, and faith.
5 I am the tree, to stand tall and straight,
   above all to be honest with myself,
   and to my brothers and my sisters.

I am the grass, to show kindness and love
   to all who surround me and
10 above all
   to love myself as well as others,
   to be more considerate of my
   brothers and my sisters.
To understand more clearly.

15 I am the fire, which is shared among my
   brothers and my sisters
   for survival.
   Sharing also comes from my four-legged
   relations who eat only enough
20 to survive
   and save some for us.

We use the fire to light our Sacred Pipe
   but only to share
   with our Grandfather.
25 No matter how small the flame
   it is still our life
   and we must care for and protect it.

We are the keepers of the fire
   We share this together.

There's This That I Like About Hockey, My Lad

by John Kieran

There's this that I like about hockey, my lad;
  It's a clattering, battering sport.
As a popular pastime it isn't half bad
  For chaps of the sturdier sort.
5 You step on the gas and you let in the clutch;
You start on a skate and come back on a crutch;
Your chance of surviving is really not much;
  It's something like storming a fort.

There's this that I like about hockey, my boy;
10   There's nothing about it that's tame.
The whistle is blown and the players deploy;
  They start in to maul and to maim.
There's a dash at the goal and a crash on the ice;
The left wing goes down when you've swatted him twice;
15 And your teeth by a stick are removed in a trice;
  It's really a rollicking game.

There's this that I like about hockey, old chap;
  I think you'll agree that I'm right;
Although you may get an occasional rap,
20   There's always good fun in the fight.
So toss in the puck, for the players are set;
Sing ho! for the dash on the enemy net;
And ho! for the smash as the challenge is met;
  And hey! for a glorious night!

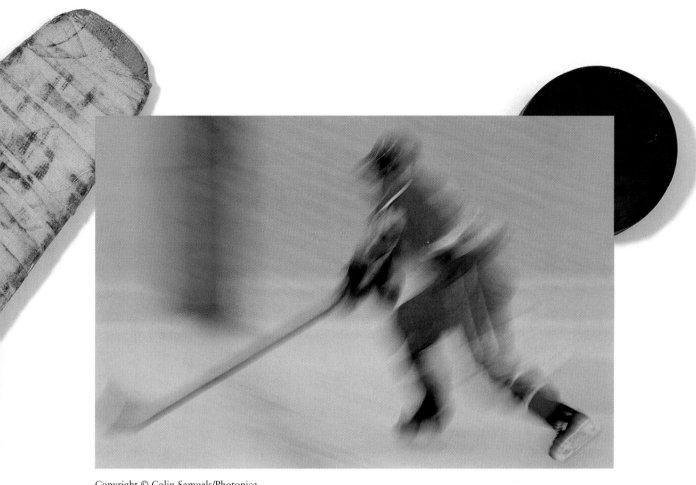

Copyright © Colin Samuels/Photonica.

JOHN KIERAN

1892–1981

By the time John Kieran became, in his 20s, a full-time sportswriter for the *New York Times,* he had graduated from Fordham University, served during World War I, taught in a country school, run a poultry business, and worked as a time-keeper for a sewer construction project.

Kieran covered sports for the *New York Times* from 1915 to 1943. In 1927, he became the first columnist to have a byline in the *Times.* In his long-running column, "Sports of the Times," he was known to use quotations from such ancient writers as Virgil or Plato in discussing the pitching style of a baseball player.

Kieran became known as "a walking encyclopedia" when, from 1938 to 1948, he was a panelist on the radio quiz show *Information, Please!* Kieran turned to ornithology and nature in his later years and wrote books about birds, flowers, and trees.

OTHER WORKS *The Story of the Olympic Games, 776 B.C.–1936 A.D.; A Natural History of New York City*

Rice and Rose Bowl Blues

I remember the day
Mama called me in from
the football game with brothers
and neighbor boys
5 in our front yard

said it was time
I learned to
wash rice for dinner

glancing out the window
10 I watched a pass interception
setting the other team up
on our 20

Pour some water
into the pot,
15 she said pleasantly,
turning on the tap
Rub the rice
between your hands,
pour out the clouds,
20 *fill it again*
(I secretly traced
an end run through
the grains in
between pourings)

by Diane Mei Lin Mark

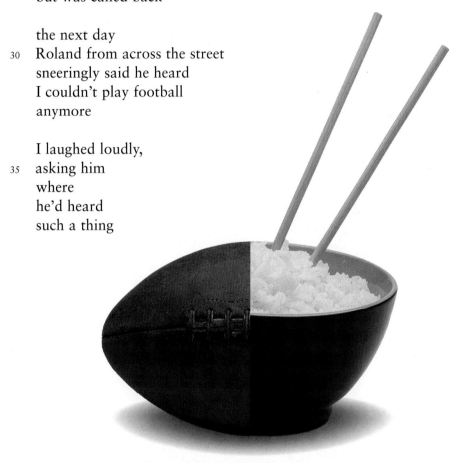

25 with the rice
settled into a simmer
I started out the door
but was called back

the next day
30 Roland from across the street
sneeringly said he heard
I couldn't play football
anymore

I laughed loudly,
35 asking him
where
he'd heard
such a thing

DIANE MEI LIN MARK

Diane Mei Lin Mark's academic pursuits and professional choices reflect her deep interest in Asian Americans. She completed her undergraduate work in English and Asian Studies at Mills College in California and then received a master's degree in American Studies from the University of Hawaii. Later, Mark studied filmmaking at New York University. She traveled and lived in Asia on a scholarship from the East-West Communication Institute.

Mark was a writer and an associate producer of *Pearls,* a documentary film series about Asian Americans that aired on public television. She co-produced the movie *Picture Bride.* Mark also has worked as a newspaper reporter and an oral history researcher.

OTHER WORKS "Suzie Wong Doesn't Live Here," "Liberation," "And The Old Folks Said"

THE SUM OF ITS PARTS

Poets are constantly tinkering with the elements of poetry—images, rhythm, sound, sentences, and meaning. Knowing more about these elements can help you understand the inner workings of a poem, its meaning, and the poet's intentions. In this lesson you will

- see how writers vary sentence structure and length
- identify and analyze the elements of a poem
- analyze the "poetry" of a building's design

Writer's Style: Sentence Variety Writers vary the structure, length, and beginnings of their sentences to add interest and impact to their writing.

Read the Literature

These writers keep the reader's interest by varying sentence structure and length.

Literature Models

Varying Structures
Notice the simple structure of the first sentence. How does the poet depart from that structure in the second sentence?

I shall dance tonight.
When the dusk comes crawling,
There will be dancing
   and feasting.

Alonzo Lopez
from "Celebration"

Varying Length
How do the short sentence and fragment reflect the character's action and attitude? What effect does the longest sentence have?

Finally I left. Just like that. I didn't say good-bye or anything. I stalked through the corridors, looking neither to the right nor the left, not caring whether that wild old man with the wheelchair ran me down or not.

Robert Cormier
from "The Moustache"

Connect to Life

Sentence variety also adds interest to nonfiction writing. This writer uses different sentence beginnings to spice up her description of a beach house.

Magazine Article

Home-made chaises fade to gentle turquoise in briny spray and hot sun. Beyond a kitchen-sill display, the sea pervades, as it does on all sides. Swimsuits dry in minutes on the porch rail. In the kitchen, tag-sale chairs and tables display signs of summer, from guests' tote bags to juicy melons.

Carol Prisant
from "Sun-soaked Beach House"
House Beautiful

Varying Sentence Openers

How does the author vary the way these sentences start?

Try Your Hand: Varying Sentences

1. **Make It Change** Write an alternate version of a paragraph you have read. This time, vary the sentence beginnings. You can change the structure of the sentences completely, but challenge yourself to keep the meaning the same.

2. **Make It Fast** Write a paragraph about one minute in an exciting game, using sentences that get increasingly long. Then write a paragraph in which the sentences get increasingly short. Does the action seem to get faster or slower?

3. **Make It Yours** Write a poem following the form of "Celebration" as closely as possible. For example, you could begin your poem with "I shall study tonight" and write about your evening plans.

GRAMMAR FROM WRITING

Using Adverb and Adjective Phrases

You can add details to your sentences by using adjective or adverb prepositional phrases. Beginning with a phrase once in a while can help vary your sentence structure. Look at the magazine article on this page. Two of the sentences begin with adverb phrases.

Beyond a kitchen-sill display, the sea pervades . . .

In the kitchen, tag-sale chairs and tables display . . .

These two phrases modify verbs to tell where the action is taking place. Putting them first gives the reader a nice break from the usual subject-verb construction.

APPLYING WHAT YOU'VE LEARNED

Try to make these sentences more interesting by adding adjective or adverb phrases.

1. I look forward to seeing my friends.
2. It seems as if the day will never end.
3. I'll call my friends and head for town.

 GRAMMAR HANDBOOK

For more about prepositional phrases, see page 902 of the Grammar Handbook.

Analysis

Poetry can communicate an enormous amount of meaning in very few words. Since every word counts, it is important to study each poetic element carefully to see how it works and what function it serves. Analyzing a poem is like taking apart an engine. It's sometimes easier to understand one piece, or element, at a time.

GUIDED ASSIGNMENT

Analyze a Poem Analyzing poetry means asking questions about how the writing works. It's like opening the poem up to look inside. Write an analysis of a poem, identifying the elements and explaining the use of each one.

❶ Prewrite and Explore

Before you can examine the use of different poetic elements, you have to discover which ones are present in the poem you choose.

FINDING A POEM TO ANALYZE

Look back at Unit Five. Which poem touched you? Which had an image or idea you really liked?

When you have decided on a poem, find a few elements or techniques you can analyze closely. Look at the list below to get some ideas. You may want to copy or retype the poem and write your notes directly on your copy, as shown here.

Elements of poetry

Form Analyze the way the poem looks—the lines and stanzas, the arrangement of words.

Sound Rhyme, rhythm, and repetition help the poet create emphasis and patterns in the poem.

Imagery Imagery involves words and phrases that appeal to the five senses. Look for images in the poem.

Figurative Language Identify examples of simile, metaphor, or personification in the poem.

Student's Marked Copy

Celebration
Alonzo Lopez

this is personification and alliteration

I shall (dance) tonight.
When the dusk comes crawling,
There will be (dancing)
    and feasting.
I shall (dance) with the others
    in circles,
    in leaps,
    in stomps.
Laughter and talk
    will weave into the night,
Among the fires ← *alliteration*
    of my people.
Games will be played
And I shall be
    a part of it.

this repeats

this helps me picture it— why did he break it up like this and make it slant?

why is this all in future tense?

❷ Write a Discovery Draft

Try to understand the poem by writing about it. As you write, ask yourself,

- What is the theme or meaning of this poem?
- How does each element contribute to that meaning?
- What was my response to the poem? Which elements affected my response?

Student's Discovery Draft

I'm pretty sure there's no rhyme in this poem, and there's no simile. There is repetition, though, and personification ("the dusk comes crawling"). There are some images I can talk about also.

Does the feast suggest an image? What are they eating?

Maybe this is supposed to make some kind of dance-like rhythm?

Forms of the word <u>dance</u> come up in the poem a few times. Why would he repeat it that way? It is probably just for emphasis. What about the repeated rhythm of "in circles, / in leaps, / in stomps"?

❸ Draft and Share

Before you draft, consider a few different ways to structure your analysis. You could list the elements one by one, explaining their significance in the poem. Another way would be to discuss the poem one line or idea at a time, dealing with the elements as they come up. Share your draft and use these questions to get feedback.

 PEER RESPONSE

- Which elements of the poem did I analyze?
- Did I explain how these elements work together?
- What part of my analysis could I explain more clearly?

Punctuating Poetry

Because poetry is a free form of expression, words and ideas often appear in unusual order. Writers try to punctuate their poems in a way that will help the reader understand the meaning. Commas and periods, for example, can help the reader find a change in ideas. If you are confused by a poem, it often helps to figure out where the sentences are.

Look at the poem "Celebration" by Alonzo Lopez. If you read each line by itself, the poem might not make as much sense as when you read the lines as continuous sentences. Line breaks don't always mean the end of an idea. They could signify a pause or a break in the rhythm.

APPLYING WHAT YOU'VE LEARNED
Find all the complete sentences in "Celebration." Write out each sentence in a notebook, and see if this helps you understand the poem.

Ⓖ GRAMMAR HANDBOOK

For more help with punctuation, see page 891 of the Grammar Handbook.

4 Revise and Edit

Before you write your final draft, go back and read the entire poem again to be sure you haven't gotten off track. When you are finished, reflect on the first time you read the poem. Now that you have taken apart the poem, reflect on how your analysis helped you understand the writing in new ways.

Student's Final Draft

Another technique used by Lopez is personification. When the speaker says, "When the dusk comes crawling," he is making the dusk seem human. Crawling is not a very pleasant or normal thing for dusk to do. When the speaker says "crawling," that sounds creepy and makes me think he wants to get away from the dusk. Otherwise why would he have chosen such a scary word? He sees the feast as a way to get away from the crawling dusk, by connecting with people.

The student explains Lopez's purpose by breaking down the poem and looking at one small piece.

Notice how the writer has identified the image and explained its purpose.

Image is an important part of this poem as well. Lopez says, "Laughter and talk / will weave into the night." I can almost see the laughter and talk coming out of the people and weaving themselves into the darkness. This is a very pretty image and it makes the night seem less frightening. I think what Lopez wants to do is weave some sort of protection by laughing and dancing. This will make the night seem good.

Standards for Evaluation

A poetry analysis
- identifies the author and title of the poem
- breaks the poem down into its parts and identifies the job of each part in the poem
- shows how the individual elements work together to create meaning
- includes a conclusion about the poet's choices

Grammar in Context

Verb Tense When you write your analysis, you will be using examples from the poem to illustrate your points. Sometimes it's difficult to get the verb tense right when you are working with a source. Here are two situations you'll run into. In both situations, it is proper to use present-tense verbs. Use present tense when

- quoting the writer:
  Lopez writes, "Games will be played."
- telling about an action:
  The speaker imagines the celebration.

>   *repeats*
> The way the speaker ~~repeated~~ "I shall dance" must
>   *expects*   *is*
> mean that he not only ~~expected~~ to dance but ~~was~~ looking
>   *says*
> forward to it. When he ~~said~~, "in circles, / in leaps, / in
>   *create*
> stomps," the lines ~~created~~ a rhythm I can follow. The
>   *is*
> speaker ~~was~~ practically dancing already!

Try Your Hand: Using Verb Tense Correctly

On a separate sheet of paper, revise the paragraph below, using the correct tense.

> The poet wrote, "in circles, / in leaps, / in stomps," putting one phrase on each line. By separating the phrases, he brought out their dancelike rhythm: move pause, move pause, move stop. The look of the lines stepping down the page suggested the motion of the dance the speaker pictured.

Using Verb Tense with Quotations

There are two ways to quote a selection in an analysis. One way is to write a direct quotation, in which you repeat the words of a passage exactly:

He says, "I shall dance."

The other way is to write an indirect quotation, in which you put a passage in your own words:

He says that he will dance.

The verb tense you use in explaining a direct or an indirect quote may differ from the tense of the quote itself. The quotes above are in future tense, but the explanatory expression (*He says*) is in present tense.

In the expressions that go with quotes for a selection, use present-tense verbs. That way, even if the tense of the quotes varies, your overall analysis will keep the same tense. Using one tense throughout the analysis will help make it easy to follow.

APPLYING WHAT YOU'VE LEARNED
Change the quotations below from direct to indirect, adjusting verb tense as needed.

1. The speaker says, "There will be dancing."
2. "Laughter and talk," writes Lopez, "will weave into the night."

BREAKING IT DOWN

Often you respond to something without thinking about your reasons. You like or dislike certain sights, people, even buildings—but why? What lies behind your reaction? Just as you analyze a poem by breaking it into pieces, you can analyze an object or a situation.

View How does this building strike you? What do you notice first? Take a closer look. What do you notice as you begin to study it?

Interpret What kind of building might this be? What do you think its purpose is? What words describe the building? dramatic? modern? traditional? What is it about the building that causes you to describe it in this way?

Discuss In a group, discuss your reactions to this building. Try to identify which elements of the building, such as size, shape, and setting, cause you to feel about it the way you do. Refer to the SkillBuilder for more tips on analysis.

 CRITICAL THINKING

Analyzing Parts of a Whole

Analysis is the process of breaking a subject into its parts in order to understand that subject more easily. For example, what did you do when you were asked to evaluate the building pictured on this page? You probably looked at each element of the building separately: its size, its design, the materials used to build it, and the setting, for example. The purpose can also be important. For instance, how does the fact that this building is the Rock and Roll Hall of Fame affect how you view it?

By breaking a subject into manageable parts and asking thoughtful questions, even a complicated subject can become much easier to understand.

APPLYING WHAT YOU'VE LEARNED
What else besides a poem or a building can you think of that you might analyze? Brainstorm with your group a list of possible subjects.

VITAL CONNECTIONS

WHAT DO Y?u THINK?

REFLECTING ON THEME

What have you learned from the key people in your life? Do you feel a strong connection to a particular person? Our links to people are vital to our personal development and happiness. Use the activities on this page to explore the connections that you feel to people around you.

What are the connections?

Who are the important people in your life—family, friends, teachers, acquaintances? Draw a diagram, with you in the middle, that shows all the important people in your life right now. Devise a way of showing what their link is with you and how important you consider it.

Meghan, my best friend

you

How did it affect you?

Have you ever had a discussion with a parent or a close relative about a difficult or serious issue? Did it change your relationship? In your notebook, write a diary entry describing the conversation and your feelings about the experience.

What made you proud?

POST CARD

address only this side

When were you really proud of a sibling or a friend? Was it because of something the person did, made, or said? Write a postcard to your sibling or friend explaining how you felt and why.

Looking back

At the beginning of this unit, you considered the ways in which people find a sense of identity. Having read the selections in Part 1, do you feel you have a better understanding of the different ways in which people discover what their place is in the world? Make a note of any ways in which the selections remind you of events in your own life or feelings you have experienced.

FICTION

Stop the Sun

Gary Paulsen

PERSONAL CONNECTION

How much do you know about the Vietnam War and about the problems of Vietnam veterans after the war? With a small group of classmates, or with the whole class, discuss what you already know about the Vietnam War and its veterans. Use a chart like the one started here to organize your ideas.

The Vietnam War	Vietnam Veterans
U.S. troops involved in 1960s and 1970s	no welcome-home parades

HISTORICAL CONNECTION

After entering the Vietnam War in 1965, the United States tried unsuccessfully to prevent North Vietnam from invading South Vietnam. Because of the conditions of this particular war, the morale and discipline of the U.S. soldier were worse, some say, than at any other time in U.S. history. By 1970, some military units were approaching collapse. Some men were refusing to engage in combat, and many were addicted to drugs—it was estimated that 10 to 15 percent of American troops were using heroin. In addition, there were reports of barracks thefts, other crimes, and racial strife.

How long does it take a man to get over his war experiences? According to the World War II hero Audie Murphy, one never does. Some Vietnam veterans still suffer from psychological problems stemming from the war. Sometimes referred to as the Vietnam syndrome, the symptoms include nervousness, anger, nightmares, and flashbacks to horrifying encounters on the battlefield.

READING CONNECTION

Connecting Recall that a reader's process of relating what happens in a story to his or her own experience or knowledge is called connecting. In "Stop the Sun," 13-year-old Terry has trouble communicating with his parents. He finds it particularly difficult to relate to his Vietnam veteran father, by whom he feels greatly embarrassed. As you read, see whether you connect with Terry's experiences. In a class discussion, compare and contrast how Terry relates to his parents with how you relate to yours. Also, to help you understand the story better as you read it, use your reading log to jot down answers to the questions inserted in the text.

The Vietnam Veterans Memorial in Washington, D.C. Copyright © Paul Merideth/Tony Stone Images.

STOP THE SUN

BY GARY PAULSEN

Terry Erickson was a tall boy, 13, starting to fill out with muscle but still a little awkward. He was on the edge of being a good athlete, which meant a lot to him. He felt it coming too slowly, though, and that bothered him.

But what bothered him even more was when his father's eyes went away.

Usually it happened when it didn't cause any particular trouble. Sometimes during a meal his father's fork would stop halfway to his mouth, just stop, and there would be a long pause while the eyes went away, far away.

After several minutes his mother would reach over and take the fork and put it gently down on his plate, and they would go back to eating—or try to go back to eating—normally.

They knew what caused it. When it first started, Terry had asked his mother in private what it was, what was causing the strange behavior.

"It's from the war," his mother had said. "The doctors at the veterans' hospital call it the Vietnam syndrome."

"Will it go away?"

"They don't know. Sometimes it goes away. Sometimes it doesn't. They are trying to help him."

"But what happened? What actually caused it?"

"I told you. Vietnam."

"But there had to be something," Terry persisted. "Something made him like that. Not just Vietnam. Billy's father was there, and he doesn't act that way."

"That's enough questions," his mother said sternly. "He doesn't talk about it, and I don't ask. Neither will you. Do you understand?"

"But, Mom."

"That's enough."

And he stopped pushing it. But it bothered him whenever it happened. When something bothered him, he liked to stay with it until he understood it, and he understood no part of this.

Words. His father had trouble, and they gave him words like Vietnam syndrome. He knew almost nothing of the war, and when he tried to find out about it, he kept hitting walls. Once he went to the school library and asked for anything they might have that could help him understand the war and how it affected his father. They gave him a dry history that described French involvement, Communist involvement, American involvement. But it told him nothing of the war. It was all numbers, cold numbers, and nothing of what had *happened*. There just didn't seem to be anything that could help him.

Another time he stayed after class and tried to talk to Mr. Carlson, who taught history. But some part of Terry was embarrassed. He didn't want to say why he wanted to know about Vietnam, so he couldn't be specific.

"What do you want to know about Vietnam, Terry?" Mr. Carlson had asked. "It was a big war."

Terry had looked at him, and something had started up in his mind, but he didn't let it out. He shrugged. "I just want to know what it was like. I know somebody who was in it."

"A friend?"

"Yessir. A good friend."

Mr. Carlson had studied him, looking into his eyes, but didn't ask any other questions. Instead he mentioned a couple of books Terry had not seen. They turned out to be pretty good. They told about how it felt to be in combat. Still, he couldn't make his father be one of the men he read about.

CONNECT

How do *you* respond when you cannot get answers to questions?

WORDS TO KNOW

persist (pər-sĭst′) *v.* to continue stubbornly
dry (drī) *adj.* direct and without emotion; matter-of-fact

And it may have gone on and on like that, with Terry never really knowing any more about it except that his father's eyes started going away more and more often. It might have just gone the rest of his life that way except for the shopping mall.

It was easily the most embarrassing thing that ever happened to him.

It started as a normal shopping trip. His father had to go to the hardware store, and he asked Terry to go along.

When they got to the mall they split up. His father went to the hardware store, Terry to a record store to look at albums.

Terry browsed so long that he was late meeting his father at the mall's front door. But his father wasn't there, and Terry looked out to the car to make sure it was still in the parking lot. It was, and he supposed his father had just gotten busy, so he waited.

Still his father didn't come, and he was about to go to the hardware store to find him, when he noticed the commotion. Or not a commotion so much as a sudden movement of people.

Later, he thought of it and couldn't remember when the feeling first came to him that there was something wrong. The people were moving toward the hardware store, and that might have been what made Terry suspicious.

There was a crowd blocking the entry to the store, and he couldn't see what they were looking at. Some of them were laughing small, nervous laughs that made no sense.

Terry squeezed through the crowd until he got near the front. At first he saw nothing unusual. There were still some people in front of him, so he pushed a crack between them. Then he saw it: His father was squirming along the floor on his stomach. He was crying, looking terrified, his breath coming in short,

hot pants like some kind of hurt animal.

It burned into Terry's mind, the picture of his father down on the floor. It burned in and in, and he wanted to walk away, but something made his feet move forward. He knelt next to his father and helped the owner of the store get him up on his feet. His father didn't speak at all but continued to make little whimpering sounds, and they led him back into the owner's office and put him in a chair. Then Terry called his mother and she came in a taxi to take them home. Waiting, Terry sat in a chair next to his father, looking at the floor, wanting only for the earth to open and let him drop in a deep hole. He wanted to disappear.

Words. They gave him words like Vietnam syndrome, and his father was crawling through a hardware store on his stomach.

When the embarrassment became so bad that he would cross the street when he saw his father coming, when it ate into him as he went to sleep, Terry realized he had to do something. He had to know this thing, had to understand what was wrong with his father.

When it came, it was simple enough at the start. It had taken some courage, more than Terry thought he could find. His father was sitting in the kitchen at the table and his mother had gone shopping.

PREDICT

What has happened to Terry's father?

Terry wanted it that way; he wanted his father alone. His mother seemed to try to protect him, as if his father could break.

Terry got a soda out of the refrigerator and popped it open. As an afterthought, he handed it to his father and got another for himself. Then he sat at the table.

His father smiled. "You look serious."

"Well . . ."

It went nowhere for a moment, and Terry was just about to drop it altogether. It may be the wrong time, he thought, but there might never be a better one. He tightened his back, took a sip of pop.

"I was wondering if we could talk about something, Dad," Terry said.

His father shrugged. "We already did the bit about girls. Some time ago, as I remember it."

"No. Not that." It was a standing joke between them. When his father finally got around to explaining things to him, they'd already covered it in school. "It's something else."

"Something pretty heavy, judging by your face."

"Yes."

"Well?"

I still can't do it, Terry thought. Things are bad, but maybe not as bad as they could get. I can still drop this thing.

"Vietnam," Terry blurted out. And he thought, there, it's out. It's out and gone.

"No!" his father said sharply. It was as if he had been struck a blow. A body blow.

"But, Dad."

"No. That's another part of my life. A bad part. A rotten part. It was before I met your mother, long before you. It has nothing to do with this family, nothing. No."

So, Terry thought, so I tried. But it wasn't over yet. It wasn't started yet.

"It just seems to bother you so much," Terry said, "and I thought if I could help or maybe understand it better . . ." His words ran until he <u>foundered</u>, until he could say no more. He looked at the table, then out the window. It was all wrong to bring it up, he thought. I blew it. I blew it all up. "I'm sorry."

But now his father didn't hear him. Now his father's eyes were gone again, and a shaft of something horrible went through Terry's heart as he thought he had done this thing to his father, caused his eyes to go away.

"You can't know," his father said after a time. "You can't know this thing."

Terry said nothing. He felt he had said too much.

"This thing that you want to know—there is so much of it that you cannot know it all, and to know only a part is . . . is too awful. I can't tell you. I can't tell anybody what it was really like."

It was more than he'd ever said about Vietnam, and his voice was breaking. Terry hated himself and felt he would hate himself until he was an old man. In one second he had caused such ruin. And all because he had been embarrassed. What difference did it make? Now he had done this, and he wanted to hide, to leave. But he sat, waiting, knowing that it wasn't done.

His father looked to him, through him, somewhere into and out of Terry. He wasn't in the kitchen anymore. He wasn't in the house. He was back in the green places, back in the hot places, the wet-hot places.

CLARIFY

If Terry's father is not "in the kitchen anymore," where is he?

"You think that because I act strange, that we can talk and it will be all right," his father said. "That we can talk and it will just go away. That's what you think, isn't it?"

Terry started to shake his head, but he knew it wasn't expected.

"That's what the shrinks say," his father continued. "The psychiatrists tell me that if I talk about it, the whole thing will go away. But they don't know. They weren't there. You weren't there. Nobody was there but me and some other dead people, and they can't talk because they couldn't stop the morning."

Terry pushed his soda can back and forth, looking down, frightened at what was happening. *The other dead people,* he'd said, as if he were dead as well. *Couldn't stop the morning.*

WORDS
TO
KNOW   **founder** (foun´dər) *v.* to get stuck; break down

"I don't understand, Dad."

"No. You don't." His voice hardened, then softened again, and broke at the edges. "But see, see how it was . . ." He trailed off, and Terry thought he was done. His father looked back down to the table, at the can of soda he hadn't touched, at the tablecloth, at his hands, which were folded, <u>inert</u> on the table.

"We were crossing a rice paddy in the dark," he said, and suddenly his voice flowed like a river breaking loose. "We were crossing the paddy, and it was dark, still dark, so black you couldn't see the end of your nose. There was a light rain, a mist, and I was thinking that during the next break I would whisper and tell Petey Kressler how nice the rain felt, but of course I didn't know there wouldn't be a Petey Kressler."

He took a deep, ragged breath. At that moment Terry felt his brain swirl, a kind of whirlpool pulling, and he felt the darkness and the light rain because it was in his father's eyes, in his voice.

"So we were crossing the paddy, and it was a straight sweep, and then we caught it. We began taking fire from three sides, automatic weapons, and everybody went down and tried to get low, but we couldn't. We couldn't get low enough. We could never get low enough, and you could hear the rounds hitting people. It was just a short time before they brought in the mortars,[1] and we should have moved, should have run, but nobody got up, and after a time nobody *could* get up. The fire just kept coming and coming, and then incoming mortars, and I heard screams as they hit, but there was nothing to do. Nothing to do."

"Dad?" Terry said. He thought, maybe I can stop him. Maybe I can stop him before . . .

before it gets to be too much. Before he breaks.

"Mortars," his father went on, "I hated mortars. You just heard them wump as they fired, and you didn't know where they would hit, and you always felt like they would hit your back. They swept back and forth with the mortars, and the automatic weapons kept coming in, and there was no radio, no way to call for artillery. Just the dark to hide in. So I crawled to the side and found Jackson, only he wasn't there, just part of his body, the top part, and I hid under it and waited, and waited, and waited.

"Finally the firing quit. But see, see how it was in the dark with nobody alive but me? I yelled once, but that brought fire again, so I shut up, and there was nothing, not even the screams."

His father cried, and Terry tried to understand, and he thought he could feel part of it. But it was so much, so much and so strange to him.

"You cannot know this," his father repeated. It was almost a <u>chant</u>. "You cannot know the fear. It was dark, and I was the only one left alive out of 54 men, all dead but me, and I knew that the Vietcong[2] were just waiting for light. When the dawn came, 'Charley'[3] would come out and finish everybody off, the way they always did. And I thought if I could stop the dawn, just stop the sun from coming up, I could make it."

Terry felt the fear, and he also felt the tears coming down his cheeks. His hand went out across the table, and he took his father's hand and held it. It was shaking.

---

1. **mortars:** small, portable cannons that fire explosive shells; also, the shells fired by such cannons.
2. **Vietcong:** Communist rebels fighting to overthrow the U.S.-supported South Vietnamese government.
3. **Charley:** a slang term used by U.S. soldiers to refer to the Vietcong.

Prometheus Under Fire (1984), Rupert Garcia. Pastel on paper, 29¾" × 84". Courtesy of the artist, Rena Bransten Gallery, San Francisco, and Galerie Claude Samuel, Paris. Copyright © 1995 Rupert Garcia.

"I mean I actually thought that if I could stop the sun from coming up, I could live. I made my brain work on that because it was all I had. Through the rest of the night in the rain in the paddy, I thought I could do it. I could stop the dawn." He took a deep breath. "But you can't, you know. You can't stop it from coming, and when I saw the gray light, I knew I was dead. It would just be minutes, and the light would be full, and I just settled under Jackson's body, and hid."

He stopped, and his face came down into his hands. Terry stood and went around the table to stand in back of him, his hands on his shoulders, rubbing gently.

"They didn't shoot me. They came, one of them poked Jackson's body and went on, and they left me. But I was dead. I'm still dead, don't you see? I died because I couldn't stop the sun. I died. Inside where I am—I died."

Terry was still in back of him, and he nodded, but he didn't see. Not that. He understood only that he didn't understand and that he would probably never know what it was really like, would probably never understand what had truly happened. And maybe his father would never be truly normal.

But Terry also knew that it didn't matter. He would try to understand, and the trying would have to be enough. He would try hard from now on, and he would not be embarrassed when his father's eyes went away. He would not be embarrassed no matter what his father did. Terry had knowledge now. Maybe not enough and maybe not all that he would need.

But it was a start. ❖

THE VIETNAM WAR

The Vietnam War, lasting from 1957 to 1975, was the longest, most unpopular war the United States ever fought in, and the first in which it did not meet its goals.

In 1954, Vietnam was divided into two nations, South Vietnam and Communist North Vietnam. When the North sought to take over the South, other nations, including the United States, feared Communist expansion and therefore intervened. Although more than 58,000 Americans lost their lives, today a Communist government rules a united Vietnam.

The U.S. role in the war became one of the most debated issues in the nation's history. Some saw it as a necessary battle in the global fight against Communism; others believed it to be morally wrong. Such opponents felt that other nations had no business interfering, much less risking the lives of their citizens, in the civil struggle of the Vietnamese.

Despite protests, the United States entered the war in 1965. While the United States set out to fight a mechanized war, North Vietnam fought a guerrilla war, relying on surprise attacks and hand-laid bombs in a strategy well suited to the jungle landscape. Some have said that the United States was woefully disadvantaged from the start because of the difficult Southeast Asian terrain and the Vietcong's intimate knowledge of it. Describing patrol duty, one soldier asked a friend to imagine walking through thick grass 8 to 15 feet high "while all around you are men possessing the latest automatic weapons who desperately want to kill you." To make matters worse, U.S. troops often could not distinguish between the enemy and the civilians for whom they were fighting: untold numbers of civilians were killed, and many of their villages were burned.

At home, mass antiwar protests hastened the American pullout. The returning soldiers received no ticker-tape parades and little thanks, and there was little national mourning for the dead. Nevertheless, many veterans were able to ease back into civilian life. Others, however—like Terry's father in "Stop the Sun"—were deeply scarred by their experiences and had to live with long-term emotional problems. Many are still wrestling with these problems today.

RESPONDING
O P T I O N S

FROM **PERSONAL RESPONSE** *TO* **CRITICAL ANALYSIS**

REFLECT **1.** Which character do you have the strongest response to—Terry or his father? Jot down your thoughts in your notebook, and share your writing with a partner.

RETHINK **2.** What personal discoveries do you think Terry has made by the end of the story? Explain your ideas.

Consider

- Terry's reaction to hearing his father's story
- the sense of hopelessness felt by his father
- whether Terry can really understand his father's experiences in Vietnam
- your own experiences with family discussions of difficult issues

3. For the Reading Connection on page 637, you were asked to connect Terry's experiences with your own. If you were in Terry's place, would you feel as embarrassed by your father as he does? Why or why not?

RELATE **4.** Do you agree or disagree with Terry's decision to ask his father about the war? Give reasons for your answer.

5. A number of Vietnam veterans feel that because they fought in an unpopular war, the public and the government have ignored their needs. How do you think the government should respond to these veterans?

ANOTHER PATHWAY
Cooperative Learning

What kind of card might Terry choose to give his father on Father's Day? With a small group of classmates, design and make a card that reflects Terry's new understanding of his father and of himself. Include a meaningful picture or design on the front and a personal message inside.

QUICKWRITES

1. Think back to an embarrassing moment in your life. Write a **diary entry** describing the incident.

2. Imagine you are starting a support group in which Vietnam veterans will gather to talk about their problems. Write an **advertisement** for the support group. Think of statements that might encourage troubled veterans like Terry's father to join the group.

3. Write a Veterans Day **poem** to honor Vietnam veterans. Before you begin, think about what you have learned about the Vietnam War and its veterans from this story. Share the poem with your class.

📂 **PORTFOLIO** *Save your writing. You may want to use it later as a springboard to a piece for your portfolio.*

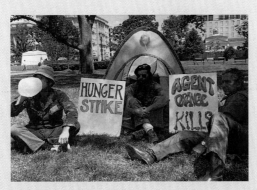

A hunger strike held near the White House by Vietnam veterans in 1981. UPI/Bettmann Newsphotos.

LITERARY CONCEPTS

Writers sometimes use **repetition,** a repeated use of certain words or phrases to emphasize important ideas or feelings. Paulsen uses repetition frequently in "Stop the Sun." On page 640, for example, the narrator says, "It burned into Terry's mind, the picture of his father down on the floor. It burned in and in. . . ." Find other examples of repeated words and phrases. What do you think the use of repetition adds to the story?

> **That's another part of my life.**
> **A bad part.**
> **A rotten part.**

CONCEPT REVIEW: Realistic Fiction "Stop the Sun" is realistic fiction, set in the modern, real world. You might recall that the characters in such fiction behave like real people as they deal with typical contemporary problems. Find details in the story that convey this kind of realism.

ART CONNECTION

Refer back to the illustration on page 643. What do you notice about the artist's style? Pay particular attention to the subject matter and use of color. Describe what you see. How might you connect this illustration to the war experiences described in the selection?

Detail of *Prometheus Under Fire* (1984), Rupert Garcia. Pastel on paper, 29¾″ × 84″. Courtesy of the artist, Rena Bransten Gallery, San Francisco, and Galerie Claude Samuel, Paris. Copyright © 1995 Rupert Garcia.

LITERARY LINKS

Terry in this story and Gustus in "The Banana Tree" (page 369) struggle in their relationships with their fathers. Compare and contrast the situations that lead to these struggles. Consider how the fathers and sons handle their conflicts and what personal discoveries are made.

ACROSS THE CURRICULUM

History The peak years of U.S. troop involvement in the Vietnam War were 1965–1969. Choose a particular day in this period, and at your library or via the Internet, locate a newspaper published on that day. Report to the class on what happened in the war on that day. You might try sketching the paper's front page to share with your classmates.

Science Many Vietnam veterans have, like Terry's father, suffered from "Vietnam syndrome" (also known as post-Vietnam stress syndrome). Research this syndrome—the symptoms that make it up, its effects, and the ways in which it is treated. If possible, interview a physician about the syndrome. Present your findings to the class.

ALTERNATIVE ACTIVITIES

1. If you were making a movie version of "Stop the Sun," what music would you use to convey the emotions of the story? Find or compose a piece of **music** that captures the mood of the father's memory of Vietnam. Play the music for the class.

2. Terry is deeply troubled whenever his father's eyes go "away, far away." Choose a scene in the story when this happens. With a partner, adopt the roles of father and son, study the emotions conveyed in the scene, and perform the scene as a **minidrama** for the class.

GARY PAULSEN

According to the National Council of Teachers of English, Gary Paulsen is one of the most important writers of young adult literature in the world. Paulsen has written 130 fiction and nonfiction books and more than 200 short stories and articles for adults and children. On a bet, he once wrote 11 short stories and articles in four days and sold them all.

Paulsen based his first book, *The Special War,* on interviews with Vietnam veterans. Many of his later works feature teenage characters who find self-awareness through challenging tests of survival in the wilderness. *Dogsong,* for example, is based on his own experience of competing in the Iditarod, a grueling 1,200-mile dogsled race across Alaska. Paulsen has received countless awards, including three prestigious Newbery Medals.

Life has not always been rewarding for the author, however. He spent an unhappy childhood living with

1939–

alcoholic parents and a series of relatives. According to Paulsen, "I was an 'army brat,' and it was a miserable life." In school, he says, "I was a geek, a nerd, a dweeb. . . . I was the last kid chosen for sports, barely got through high school, didn't have a girlfriend until I was in the army. I would skip school and go fishing or hunting." The one piece of advice he gives young people is to "read like a wolf eats. Read what they tell you not to read and read when they tell you not to. Read all the time."

Paulsen currently spends most of his time on his 44-foot sloop, which he plans to sail across the Pacific Ocean. When he is not on his boat, he lives in northern Minnesota or New Mexico.

OTHER WORKS *Dancing Carl, Hatchet, The Island, The Winter Room, The River,* the Culpepper Adventure Series, the Gary Paulsen World of Adventure Series

LASERLINKS
• *AUTHOR BACKGROUND*

FICTION

Raymond's Run
Toni Cade Bambara

PERSONAL CONNECTION

This story is about a young girl named Squeaky who has responsibility for her mentally disabled older brother. Imagine yourself in a situation like this. With your classmates, discuss what you think your relationship with your brother might be like and how you would handle the responsibility of caring for him. How would you react if someone made fun of him? If you in fact have a disabled brother or sister, describe your relationship with him or her.

SCIENCE CONNECTION

Squeaky's brother Raymond has a medical condition known as *hydrocephalus* (hī'drō-sĕf'ə-ləs), also called "water on the brain." The symptoms of this disorder include a swelling of the head caused by the excessive amount of fluid that collects in the skull. In the disorder's severest form, the excess fluid damages the brain and affects mental processes, as in Raymond's case.

Hydrocephalus may be caused by an infection, a tumor, a major head injury, or a malformation of the brain before birth. Childhood hydrocephalus is fairly rare, occurring in only about 1 of every 1,000 children. If detected early, hydrocephalus can be treated successfully with surgery.

READING CONNECTION

Analyzing The process of breaking something down into its elements and examining each element is called analyzing. Analyzing literature can be a valuable way of enhancing your understanding of it. To analyze the plot of a work of fiction, for example, you might divide the plot into an exposition, a series of complications, a climax, and a resolution.

In this story, you will read about Squeaky's relationships with her brother and the girls in her neighborhood. As you read, analyze the relationships by thinking of words that describe how Squeaky relates to each person. Jot the words down in a chart like the one shown, then discuss with the class how you would characterize Squeaky's relationships.

Analyzing Squeaky's Relationships	
Character	**Descriptive Words**
Raymond	
Gretchen	
Cynthia	
Mary Louise	
Rosie	

LASERLINKS
• *SCIENCE CONNECTION*

Raymond's Run

by Toni Cade Bambara

I don't have much work to do around the house like some girls. My mother does that. And I don't have to earn my pocket money by hustling; George runs errands for the big boys and sells Christmas cards. And anything else that's got to get done, my father does. All I have to do in life is mind my brother Raymond, which is enough.

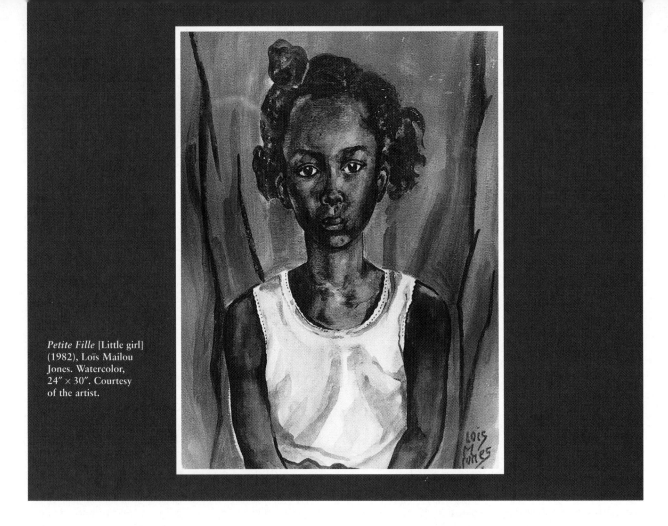

Petite Fille [Little girl] (1982), Loïs Mailou Jones. Watercolor, 24″ × 30″. Courtesy of the artist.

Sometimes I slip and say my little brother Raymond. But as any fool can see he's much bigger and he's older too. But a lot of people call him my little brother 'cause he needs looking after 'cause he's not quite right. And a lot of smart mouths got lots to say about that too, especially when George was minding him. But now, if anybody has anything to say to Raymond, anything to say about his big head,[1] they have to come by me. And I don't play the dozens[2] or believe in standing around with somebody in my face doing a lot of talking. I much rather just knock you down and take my chances even if I am a little girl with skinny arms and a squeaky voice, which is how I got the name Squeaky. And if things get too rough, I run. And as anybody can tell you, I'm the fastest thing on two feet. There is no track

meet that I don't win the first place medal. I use to win the twenty-yard dash when I was a little kid in kindergarten. Nowadays, it's the fifty-yard dash. And tomorrow I'm subject to run the quarter-meter relay all by myself and come in first, second, and third. The big kids call me Mercury[3] 'cause I'm the swiftest thing in the neighborhood. Everybody knows that—except two people who know better, my father and me. He can beat me to Amsterdam Avenue with me having a two-fire-hydrant head start and him running with his hands in his pockets

---

1. **big head:** enlarged skull (a result of Raymond's hydrocephalus).
2. **play the dozens:** exchange rhyming insults.
3. **Mercury:** in Roman mythology, the swift messenger of the gods.

and whistling. But that's private information. 'Cause can you imagine some thirty-five-year-old man stuffing himself into PAL shorts to race little kids? So as far as everyone's concerned, I'm the fastest and that goes for Gretchen, too, who has put out the tale that she is going to win the first-place medal this year. Ridiculous. In the second place, she's got short legs. In the third place, she's got freckles. In the first place, no one can beat me and that's all there is to it.

The big kids call me Mercury 'cause I'm the swiftest thing in the neighborhood.

I'm standing on the corner admiring the weather and about to take a stroll down Broadway so I can practice my breathing exercises, and I've got Raymond walking on the inside close to the buildings, 'cause he's subject to fits of fantasy and starts thinking he's a circus performer and that the curb is a tightrope strung high in the air. And sometimes after a rain he likes to step down off his tightrope right into the gutter and slosh around getting his shoes and cuffs wet. Then I get hit when I get home. Or sometimes if you don't watch him he'll dash across traffic to the island in the middle of Broadway and give the pigeons a fit. Then I have to go behind him apologizing to all the old people sitting around trying to get some sun and getting all upset with the pigeons fluttering around them, scattering their newspapers and upsetting the wax-paper lunches in their laps. So I keep Raymond on the inside of me, and he plays like he's driving a stagecoach

which is O.K. by me so long as he doesn't run me over or interrupt my breathing exercises, which I have to do on account of I'm serious about my running, and I don't care who knows it.

Now some people like to act like things come easy to them, won't let on that they practice. Not me. I'll high-prance down 34th Street like a rodeo pony to keep my knees strong even if it does get my mother uptight so that she walks ahead like she's not with me, don't know me, is all by herself on a shopping trip, and I am somebody else's crazy child. Now you take Cynthia Procter for instance. She's just the opposite. If there's a test tomorrow, she'll say something like, "Oh, I guess I'll play handball this afternoon and watch television tonight," just to let you know she ain't thinking about the test. Or like last week when she won the spelling bee for the millionth time, "A good thing you got 'receive,' Squeaky, 'cause I would have got it wrong. I completely forgot about the spelling bee." And she'll clutch the lace on her blouse like it was a narrow escape. Oh, brother. But of course when I pass her house on my early morning trots around the block, she is practicing the scales on the piano over and over and over and over. Then in music class she always lets herself get bumped around so she falls accidentally on purpose onto the piano stool and is so surprised to find herself sitting there that she decides just for fun to try out the ole keys. And what do you know—Chopin's waltzes[4] just spring out of her fingertips and she's the most surprised thing in the world. A regular prodigy. I could kill people like that. I stay up all night studying the words for the spelling

---

4. **Chopin's** (shō-pănz′) **waltzes:** works by the 19th-century pianist and composer Frédéric Chopin.

bee. And you can see me any time of day practicing running. I never walk if I can trot, and shame on Raymond if he can't keep up. But of course he does, 'cause if he hangs back someone's liable to walk up to him and get smart, or take his allowance from him, or ask him where he got that great big pumpkin head. People are so stupid sometimes.

I am not a strawberry. I do not dance on my toes. I run.

So I'm strolling down Broadway breathing out and breathing in on counts of seven, which is my lucky number, and here comes Gretchen and her sidekicks: Mary Louise, who used to be a friend of mine when she first moved to Harlem from Baltimore and got beat up by everybody till I took up for her on account of her mother and my mother used to sing in the same choir when they were young girls, but people ain't grateful, so now she hangs out with the new girl Gretchen and talks about me like a dog; and Rosie, who is as fat as I am skinny and has a big mouth where Raymond is concerned and is too stupid to know that there is not a big deal of difference between herself and Raymond and that she can't afford to throw stones. So they are steady coming up Broadway and I see right away that it's going to be one of those Dodge City scenes 'cause the street ain't that big and they're close to the buildings just as we are. First I think I'll step into the candy store and look over the new comics and let them pass. But that's chicken and I've got a reputation to consider. So then I think I'll just walk straight on through them or

over them if necessary. But as they get to me, they slow down. I'm ready to fight, 'cause like I said I don't feature a whole lot of chitchat, I much prefer to just knock you down right from the jump and save everybody a lotta precious time.

"You signing up for the May Day races?" smiles Mary Louise, only it's not a smile at all. A dumb question like that doesn't deserve an answer. Besides, there's just me and Gretchen standing there really, so no use wasting my breath talking to shadows.

"I don't think you're going to win this time," says Rosie, trying to signify with her hands on her hips all salty, completely forgetting that I have whupped her behind many times for less salt than that.

"I always win 'cause I'm the best," I say straight at Gretchen who is, as far as I'm concerned, the only one talking in this ventriloquist-dummy routine.[5] Gretchen smiles, but it's not a smile, and I'm thinking that girls never really smile at each other because they don't know how and don't want to know how and there's probably no one to teach us how, 'cause grown-up girls don't know either. Then they all look at Raymond who has just brought his mule team to a standstill. And they're about to see what trouble they can get into through him.

"What grade you in now, Raymond?"

"You got anything to say to my brother, you say it to me, Mary Louise Williams of Raggedy Town, Baltimore."

"What are you, his mother?" sasses Rosie.

"That's right, Fatso. And the next word out of anybody and I'll be their mother too." So they just stand there and Gretchen shifts from one leg to the other and so do they. Then Gretchen puts her hands on her hips and is

---

5. **ventriloquist-dummy routine:** Squeaky thinks that all the girls are speaking Gretchen's thoughts, like dummies being controlled by a ventriloquist.

about to say something with her freckle-face self but doesn't. Then she walks around me looking me up and down but keeps walking up Broadway, and her sidekicks follow her. So me and Raymond smile at each other and he says, "Gidyap," to his team and I continue with my breathing exercises, strolling down Broadway toward the ice man on 145th with not a care in the world 'cause I am Miss Quicksilver[6] herself.

I take my time getting to the park on May Day because the track meet is the last thing on the program. The biggest thing on the program is the May Pole dancing, which I can do without, thank you, even if my mother thinks it's a shame I don't take part and act like a girl for a change. You'd think my mother'd be grateful not to have to make me a white organdy dress with a big satin sash and buy me new white baby-doll shoes that can't be taken out of the box till the big day. You'd think she'd be glad her daughter ain't out there prancing around a May Pole getting the new clothes all dirty and sweaty and trying to act like a fairy or a flower or whatever you're supposed to be when you should be trying to be yourself, whatever that is, which is, as far as I am concerned, a poor Black girl who really can't afford to buy shoes and a new dress you only wear once a lifetime 'cause it won't fit next year.

I was once a strawberry in a Hansel and Gretel pageant when I was in nursery school and didn't have no better sense than to dance on tiptoe with my arms in a circle over my head doing umbrella steps and being a perfect fool just so my mother and father could come dressed up and clap. You'd think they'd know better than to encourage that kind of nonsense. I am not a strawberry. I do not dance on my toes. I run. That is what I am all about. So I always come late to the May Day program, just in time to get my number pinned on

and lay in the grass till they announce the fifty-yard dash.

I put Raymond in the little swings, which is a tight squeeze this year and will be impossible next year. Then I look around for Mr. Pearson, who pins the numbers on. I'm really looking for Gretchen, if you want to know the truth, but she's not around. The park is jam-packed. Parents in hats and corsages and breast-pocket handkerchiefs peeking up. Kids in white dresses and light-blue suits. The parkees[7] unfolding chairs and chasing the rowdy kids from Lenox[8] as if they had no right to be there. The big guys with their caps on backwards, leaning against the fence swirling the basketballs on the tips of their fingers, waiting for all these crazy people to clear out the park so they can play. Most of the kids in my class are carrying bass drums and glockenspiels[9] and flutes. You'd think they'd put in a few bongos or something for real like that.

Then here comes Mr. Pearson with his clipboard and his cards and pencils and whistles and safety pins and 50 million other things he's always dropping all over the place with his clumsy self. He sticks out in a crowd because he's on stilts. We used to call him Jack and the Beanstalk to get him mad. But I'm the only one that can outrun him and get away, and I'm too grown for that silliness now.

"Well, Squeaky," he says, checking my name off the list and handing me number seven and two pins. And I'm thinking he's got no right to call me Squeaky if I can't call him Beanstalk.

"Hazel Elizabeth Deborah Parker," I correct him and tell him to write it down on his board.

---

6. **Miss Quicksilver:** a reference to the speed with which quicksilver (the liquid metal mercury) flows.

7. **parkees:** park employees.

8. **Lenox:** a street in the Harlem section of New York City.

9. **glockenspiels** (glŏk′ən-spēlz′): musical instruments having tuned metal bars that are played with light hammers.

"Well, Hazel Elizabeth Deborah Parker, going to give someone else a break this year?" I squint at him real hard to see if he is seriously thinking I should lose the race on purpose just to give someone else a break. "Only six girls running this time," he continues, shaking his head sadly like it's my fault all of New York didn't turn out in sneakers. "That new girl should give you a run for your money." He looks around the park for Gretchen like a periscope in a submarine movie. "Wouldn't it be a nice gesture if you were . . . to ahhh . . ."

Grownups got a lot of nerve sometimes.

I give him such a look he couldn't finish putting that idea into words. Grownups got a lot of nerve sometimes. I pin number seven to myself and stomp away, I'm so burnt. And I go straight for the track and stretch out on the grass while the band winds up with "Oh, the Monkey Wrapped His Tail Around the Flag Pole," which my teacher calls by some other name. The man on the loudspeaker is calling everyone over to the track and I'm on my back looking at the sky, trying to pretend I'm in the country, but I can't, because even grass in the city feels hard as sidewalk, and there's just no pretending you are anywhere but in a "concrete jungle" as my grandfather says.

The twenty-yard dash takes all of the two minutes 'cause most of the little kids don't know no better than to run off the track or run the wrong way or run smack into the fence and fall down and cry. One little kid, though, has got the good sense to run straight for the white ribbon up ahead so he wins. Then the second-graders line up for the thirty-yard dash and I don't even bother to turn my head to watch 'cause Raphael Perez always wins. He wins before he even begins by psyching the runners, telling them they're going to trip on their shoelaces and fall on their faces or lose their shorts or something, which he doesn't really have to do since he is very fast, almost as fast as I am. After that is the forty-yard dash which I used to run when I was in first grade. Raymond is hollering from the swings 'cause he knows I'm about to do my thing 'cause the man on the loudspeaker has just announced the fifty-yard dash, although he might just as well be giving a recipe for angel food cake 'cause you can hardly make out what he's saying for the static. I get up and slip off my sweat-pants and then I see Gretchen standing at the starting line, kicking her legs out like a pro. Then as I get into place I see that ole Raymond is on line on the other side of the fence, bending down with his fingers on the ground just like he knew what he was doing. I was going to yell at him but then I didn't. It burns up your energy to holler.

Every time, just before I take off in a race, I always feel like I'm in a dream, the kind of dream you have when you're sick with fever and feel all hot and weightless. I dream I'm flying over a sandy beach in the early morning sun, kissing the leaves of the trees as I fly by. And there's always the smell of apples, just like in the country when I was little and used to think I was a choo-choo train, running through the fields of corn and chugging up the hill to the orchard. And all the time I'm dreaming this, I get lighter and lighter until I'm flying over the beach again, getting blown through the sky like a feather that weighs nothing at all. But once I spread my fingers in the dirt and crouch over the Get on Your Mark, the dream goes and I am solid again and am telling

Visa (1951), Stuart Davis. Oil on canvas, 40″ × 52″. The Museum of Modern Art, New York, gift of Mrs. Gertrud A. Mellon. Copyright ©1996 Estate of Stuart Davis/Licensed by VAGA, New York. Photograph copyright © 1995 The Museum of Modern Art, New York.

myself, Squeaky you must win, you must win, you are the fastest thing in the world, you can even beat your father up Amsterdam if you really try. And then I feel my weight coming back just behind my knees then down to my feet then into the earth and the pistol shot explodes in my blood and I am off and weightless again, flying past the other runners, my arms pumping up and down and the whole world is quiet except for the crunch as I zoom over the gravel in the track. I glance to my left and there is no one. To the right, a blurred Gretchen, who's got her chin jutting out as if it would win the race all by itself. And on the other side of the fence is Raymond with his arms down to his side and the palms tucked up behind him, running in his very own style, and it's the first time I ever saw that and I almost stop to watch my brother Raymond on his first run. But the white ribbon is bouncing toward me and I tear past it, racing into the distance till my feet with a mind of their own start digging up footfuls of dirt and brake me short. Then all the kids standing on the side pile on me, banging me on the back and slapping my head with their May Day programs, for I have won again and everybody on 151st Street can walk tall for another year.

"In first place . . ." the man on the loudspeaker is clear as a bell now. But then he pauses and the loudspeaker starts to whine. Then static. And I lean down to catch my breath and here comes Gretchen walking back, for she's overshot the finish line too, huffing and puffing with her hands on her hips taking it slow, breathing in steady time like a real pro and I sort of like her a little for the first time. "In first place . . ." and then three or four voices get all mixed up on the loudspeaker and I dig my sneaker into the grass and stare at Gretchen who's staring back, we both wondering just who did win. I can hear old Beanstalk arguing with the man on the loudspeaker and then a few others running their mouths about what the stopwatches say. Then I hear Raymond yanking at the fence to call me and I wave to shush him, but he keeps rattling the fence like a gorilla in a cage like in them gorilla movies, but then like a dancer or something he starts climbing up nice and easy but very fast. And it occurs to me, watching how smoothly he climbs hand over hand and remembering how he looked running with his arms down to his side and with the wind pulling his mouth back and his teeth showing and all, it occurred to me that Raymond would make a very fine runner. Doesn't he always keep up with me on my trots? And he surely knows how to breathe in counts of seven 'cause he's always doing it at the dinner table, which drives my brother George up the wall. And I'm smiling to beat the band 'cause if I've lost this race, or if me and Gretchen tied, or even if I've won, I can always retire as a runner and begin a whole new career as a coach with Raymond as my champion. After all, with a little more study I can beat Cynthia and her phony self at the spelling bee. And if I bugged my mother, I could get piano lessons and become a star. And I have a big rep as the baddest thing around. And I've got a roomful of ribbons and medals and awards. But what has Raymond got to call his own?

So I stand there with my new plans, laughing out loud by this time as Raymond jumps down from the fence and runs over with his teeth showing and his arms down to the side, which no one before him has quite mastered as a running style. And by the time he comes over I'm jumping up and down so glad to see him—my brother Raymond, a great runner in the family tradition. But of course everyone thinks I'm jumping up and down because the men on the loudspeaker have finally gotten themselves together and compared notes and are announcing, "In first place—Miss Hazel Elizabeth Deborah Parker." (Dig that.) "In second place —Miss Gretchen P. Lewis." And I look over at Gretchen, wondering what the "P." stands for. And I smile. 'Cause she's good, no doubt about it. Maybe she'd like to help me coach Raymond; she obviously is serious about running, as any fool can see. And she nods to congratulate me and then she smiles. And I smile. We stand there with this big smile of respect between us. It's about as real a smile as girls can do for each other, considering we don't practice real smiling every day, you know, 'cause maybe we too busy being flowers or fairies or strawberries instead of something honest and worthy of respect . . . you know . . . like being people. ❖

RESPONDING
O P T I O N S

FROM PERSONAL RESPONSE TO CRITICAL ANALYSIS

REFLECT 1. What were your strongest impressions of Squeaky? Jot your thoughts in your notebook, or make a drawing of Squeaky as you imagine her to be.

RETHINK 2. In what ways has Squeaky changed by the end of the story?

Consider
- her feelings about Raymond
- her view of her rival
- her view of herself

3. Think about Squeaky's vital connection with Raymond. Would Squeaky be a different person if Raymond were not her brother? Explain your answer.

4. Review your analysis of Squeaky's relationships for the Reading Connection on page 648. What does each of her relationships with the other girls reveal about her personality?

RELATE 5. What attitudes toward disabled people are presented in "Raymond's Run"? Do you think these attitudes are typical of the ways in which people respond to disabled individuals?

ANOTHER PATHWAY
Cooperative Learning
Think about the personal discovery with regard to Raymond that Squeaky has made by the end of the story. With a small group of classmates, brainstorm slogans that reflect this discovery. Then create an artistic presentation of each slogan and display the artwork in the classroom.

LITERARY CONCEPTS

Slang is a casual, informal form of language used more often in speaking than in writing. Slang terms may be new words, or they may be established words and phrases that have taken on new meanings. An example of slang in "Raymond's Run" is Squeaky's use of *uptight* to mean "tense" or "nervous."

Look back over the story for particularly colorful examples of slang, and read the examples aloud.

Then choose one passage containing slang and rewrite it in standard, formal English. Is the original better? Why or why not?

QUICKWRITES

1. Squeaky says, "I'm the fastest thing on two feet." What are *you* really good at? Write a **paragraph** that describes a skill that you feel very confident about.

2. Imagine that you are a sportswriter for your local newspaper. Write an **article** about Squeaky's May Day race. Be sure to cover the *who, what, when, where, why,* and *how* of the story. To add an element of human interest, you might mention Raymond's sideline run.

📁 *PORTFOLIO Save your writing. You may want to use it later as a springboard to a piece for your portfolio.*

ALTERNATIVE ACTIVITIES

With a partner, design a newspaper **advertisement** for a new business—Squeaky and Gretchen's coaching service. Think about what people you want to attract and what statements and images might persuade them to try the service.

> **Squeaky and Gretchen's**
> Coaching Service
> _____
> _____
> _____
> _____

ACROSS THE CURRICULUM

Physical Education Use library or Internet resources to research the Special Olympics. Try to find out who sponsors the competitions, where they are held, who competes, and what events are included. Report your findings to the class.

Mathematics Today, the distances of many running events are measured in meters rather than yards. Which is longer, Squeaky's 50-yard race or a 50-meter race? By how much? What is the length of a marathon in miles and yards? in kilometers?

LITERARY LINKS

Look back at the poem "A Man" on page 434. Both Raymond and the man in the poem have disabilities. Compare the feelings or attitudes about living with disabilities that are conveyed by the two works.

WORDS TO KNOW

Review the meaning of the word **prodigy** in the selection. Using the model as a guide, write the word vertically on your paper. Use each of the seven letters to form a word that you associate with a prodigy. (One has been done as an example.) Share your results with classmates.

```
S U P E R I O R
  R
  O
  D
  I
  G
  Y
```

TONI CADE BAMBARA

1939–1995

Toni Cade Bambara believed that authors "are everyday people who write stories that come out of their neighborhoods." Like the characters in "Raymond's Run" and in many of her other short stories, she grew up in New York City. She wrote about African Americans who show family pride and a strong sense of community. In 1981, she won the American Book Award for her novel *The Salt Eaters*.

Bambara said, "Temperamentally, I move toward the short story because I'm a sprinter rather than a long-distance runner. I cannot sustain characters over a long period of time. Walking around, frying eggs, being a mother, shopping—I cannot have those char-acters living in my house with me for more than a couple of weeks." Bambara credited her mother with having greatly influenced her work.

After attending college in New York City, Bambara studied theater and mime in Europe and dance and film in the United States. She planned recreational programs for the mentally ill and taught college English and African-American studies. During her later years she lived in Philadelphia, where she taught a writers' workshop, produced documentary videos, and was intensely involved in her community.

OTHER WORKS *Gorilla, My Love; The Seabirds Are Still Alive*

LASERLINKS
• *SPORTS CONNECTION*

PREVIEWING

FICTION

Keeping Time
Bill Meissner

PERSONAL CONNECTION

It is the dream of the narrator of this story to play on his high school's baseball team and eventually to become a major-league player. How do you feel about the team-sports program in your school? Consider the ways in which team sports are organized, the ways in which team members are selected, and the pros and cons of athletic competition in general. Record your thoughts in a chart like the one shown, then discuss your ideas with the class.

Team Sports in School	
Arguments For	Arguments Against

PHYSICAL EDUCATION CONNECTION

For some teenagers, participation in team sports is essential to a fulfilling school career. Many students get involved in sports just for the fun of it; others see organized athletics as a springboard to a career in professional sports. What many young people may not realize is that team sports can be a way to learn important life skills. Accomplished coaches teach discipline, competitiveness, teamwork, and the importance of excellence—qualities that can be applied in almost any field or endeavor.

Too often, however, teenage athletes are encouraged to set their sights on careers in professional sports only to find their dreams dashed. Professional athletics is among the most competitive of careers. Only about 1 out of every 100,000 students who participate in high school athletics goes on to play professionally. Reggie Williams, a former National Football League star, says, "As a society, we have an obsession with sports and put too much emphasis on professional sports and all that big money. That is too dangerous a carrot because the opportunities are too few."

WRITING CONNECTION

Write a description of one of your most important personal goals or dreams. Why is it important to you? How do you plan to attain it? Do you think your dream is likely to be realized?

Keeping

by Bill Meissner

Sometimes the human heart is the only clock in the world that keeps true time.

Coach John Brace, a pile of team jerseys on his arm, leaned rhythmically left, then right, like a pendulum between the two rows of wooden benches. As he walked down the aisle of that high school locker room, Coach tossed jerseys to the boys he'd chosen for the freshman baseball team after a day of tryouts. I sat in my gym shorts at the end of the bench, the varnished wood sticky and cool beneath my thighs, and though it wasn't cold in the room, shivers rushed outward from the middle of my spindly body like ripples from the center of a pond. I felt as though I'd been sitting on that bench all my life, waiting for that one moment. As Coach rocked closer, I remember watching the blue-and-gold jerseys fluttering, in slow motion, to the outstretched hands of each boy, and praying my hands would be next.

I had practiced tirelessly for that one day of tryouts—I knew it would be my first chance to make a real baseball team. Sometimes, alone in a field behind a warehouse, I bounced a ball off the brick wall and fielded grounders. Sometimes, dropping quarters into the slot, I'd swing and swing in a batting cage until my shoulder muscles ached. But more often than not, during the summer days of seventh and eighth grades, I practiced with my best friend, Steve Lyon, at the old West School field until our crew cuts[1] glistened with sweat. "Sheese, we're improving," Steve often mused afterward as we sat beneath the shade of a billowing elm. "There's no way we won't make the team, man."

One day, after our usual routine of batting practice, I was goofing around in the outfield with my ball cap on sideways; I jumped and shook my arms in the air and howled at the

---

1. **crew cuts:** hairstyles in which the hair is cut very close to the head (so called because rowers wore such a style).

WORDS TO KNOW

spindly (spĭnd′lē) *adj.* slender and long in a way that suggests weakness

Time

sky as Steve watched, laughing. In the middle of my act, Steve cut the laughter, then pointed subtly with his thumb and I looked behind me. My whole body went numb when I saw Coach Brace in his powder-blue car, watching me from the stoplight. Coach lifted one hand politely to wave to us as he drove off. Upset for the rest of that afternoon, I kept repeating to Steve how ridiculous I must have looked to the man who'd be our baseball coach next year. I knew Coach Brace was serious about baseball, and I cursed my luck that he'd driven by when I was acting stupid instead of when I was hitting a liner over third base or making one of my patented diving catches. I told Steve how I didn't look like a ballplayer but like some clowning kid who didn't care. "Don't worry," Steve assured me, "he'll never remember."

For Career Day in civics class that fall, leaning over my narrow-ruled paper, I scrawled an essay about how I planned to be a major league baseball player. Beneath the bright spotlight of my cone-shaped desk lamp, I wrote that I'd sign a pro baseball contract after high school, play a while in the minor leagues—maybe in nearby Madison or Wausau —then be called up to the majors. As I described each step of my career, the words flowed as easily as players running onto the field at the start of a game. To me, the logic and the progression of the essay seemed so simple, so undeniably true. When I was finished, I printed the title in tall, bold letters at the top: TOMORROW. At school the next morning, the civics teacher, Mrs. Griswald, handed the essay back to me, saying I had written it in pencil and I was supposed to write it in pen. Mrs. Griswald also jotted at the bottom of the essay, in red marker: *What if you* don't *make it???* As I recopied the essay that night with a black pen, I remember thinking to myself, *I'll make it. I will make it.*

In the locker room after freshman tryouts, we waited on the benches while Coach Brace unlocked the supply room. Somehow, nervous as I felt, I was still aware of the scents in the room: the smell of must[2] and the dank cement floor of the shower, the smell of leather where boys' palms had sweated into their gloves, the

---

2. **must:** staleness; mustiness.

WORDS
TO
KNOW

subtly (sŭt'lē) *adv.* in a way difficult to detect and not immediately obvious

661

faint odor of the damp, loamy April earth tracked in by our cleated shoes.

Coach reappeared with the jerseys and gave a brief speech. He was known throughout the high school and our town as a gentle man, and a great teacher, and he had a reputation for these inspirational speeches, but I was feeling too much anxiety to listen: All I could hear was the soft slapping of water dripping from the showerheads, a sound that seemed to grow louder until it nearly exploded in my ears. Then Coach stepped down the aisle, handing out the jerseys. He leaned left, then right, as if he were dancing a slow waltz.

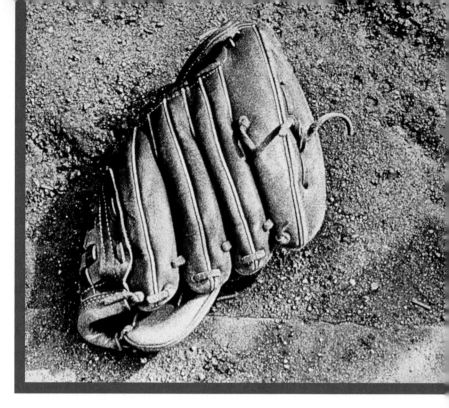

By the time Coach reached the end of the bench where Steve and I and a couple of other guys waited, only two jerseys were draped over his wrist. Coach hesitated a moment, tossed one jersey to Steve. Then he turned and tossed the second one to a boy who sat across from me.

With that tossed jersey, which I can still see now, a blue-and-gold blur floating softly in the air, the coach threw a young boy's dreams out a locker-room window, and they spiraled miles and miles to the hard ground.

I don't remember what Coach said after that. He might have been saying, "Boys, I'm really sorry," but the loud pain filling my skull blocked out his words.

Walking home with Steve, I couldn't help feeling an anger for Coach Brace, a kind of hatred growing steadily inside me, spreading to every artery and muscle and nerve. I'd never hated anyone before, but in my mind, Coach Brace became meaner and more vindictive by the second. I swore at him, I called him names, I did cruel imitations of his locker-room speeches.

"You got ripped off, man," Steve said, trying to make me feel better. "Plain and simple. You *deserve* to be on that team. You're better than *all* those guys who got jerseys."

I stopped in the middle of the sidewalk and glared at Steve. "Including you, I suppose."

Steve glanced down at the jersey folded on his duffel bag, then back at me. "Yeah," he said. "Including me."

His words didn't help. My world was changing at that moment; nothing could stop it from pivoting away from my future as a baseball player. Nothing could lighten the enormous disappointment that crushed me like a weight. I swore I'd never speak to Coach Brace again.

When we reached my front door, Steve uttered our usual farewell. "Tomorrow," he said.

"Yeah," I said feebly, unable to lift my gaze from the concrete. "Tomorrow."

After supper I pulled my civics class essay from my desk drawer, walked to the corner of the backyard, lit a match, and burned those pages one by one. I watched my looping words darken as the paper curled in on itself like a

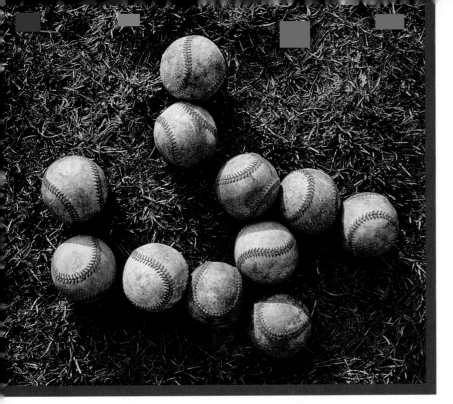

the cover on his science book. We both knew my being cut from the team created a kind of <u>chasm</u> between us, and neither of us was too comfortable talking about it. Then, before he turned, he gave me a quick grin, nodded, and said, "Tomorrow."

I nodded back as he hurried down the hall toward the locker room. Some afternoons I loitered in the empty hallway until the team took the field and began their warm-up exercises. Through the high, distorted glass of the second-story window, I watched the players wavering in the distance. As those four years passed, I decided it was a stupid, small idea of mine, anyway, to want to be a major leaguer. After all—what were my chances?

Twenty years later, when I returned to town for a high school reunion, someone said that Coach Brace had become seriously ill with cancer. The rumors circulated among my classmates that Coach, who had been our senior class advisor, would try to make it to the gathering that night, but everyone said he looked very bad, the illness eating away at him. Some of my classmates shook their heads and said his chances weren't good.

When Coach Brace walked into the reunion amid a flurry of handshakes and friendly calls from former students, his face looked as though the skin had collapsed inward onto the bone, and shadows, like dark gray bunting,[4]

fist. The ashes fell onto the worn spot in the dirt where home plate used to be.

I never tried out for the baseball team the next three years of high school, even though Steve said I should. I was too hurt, and just couldn't face Coach Brace for another tryout. Steve played well, a star third baseman during our four years of high school, and the team won the conference championship one year. After school on spring days, Steve stopped at his locker next to mine; he pulled his books out quickly, and I knew, as usual, he was headed to baseball practice.

"What's up tonight, buddy?" he asked me once after seventh period.

"Nothing," I shrugged, clicking my locker door shut, then opening it, then clicking it shut again.

"Man, I wish I had your free time," he said.

"I wish I had your practice," I replied.

Suddenly awkward in his untucked madras[3] shirt and white jeans, Steve pretended to adjust

---

3. **madras** (măd′rəs): a cotton cloth usually printed in a plaid or striped pattern (named for a city in India).

4. **bunting:** strips of cloth used as decorative drapery on festive occasions.

clung to the skin beneath his eyes. I turned toward him as he made his way through the crowd, and then, when the old hurt rose inside me, I turned away.

After the reunion dinner, Coach stepped to the microphone in the high school gym, his navy blue suit jacket seeming too large for him. During a short speech, he bowed his head slightly, lowered his voice, and told us the illness had been tough on him. "But I'm going to beat this thing," he said, raising his head. "I'm going to beat it. If baseball taught me one thing, it taught me not to give up."

After the speeches, Coach spotted me standing by the makeshift bar in the corner of the gym; he walked over and greeted me. We exchanged small talk for a few minutes, and while we talked, I couldn't stop that locker-room scene from replaying in my mind.

Then, out of nowhere, Coach said, "You always were a good ballplayer. I remember that. I remember seeing you and Steve Lyon practicing by the old West School." He toasted me with his plastic cup of punch. "You guys were always a great addition to my team," he said proudly.

To my team. I was stunned by those last words, and a sudden realization hit me: Coach Brace *never even remembered* cutting me from the team. That moment, which had meant so much to me, that moment I'd carried around for years inside my stomach like a huge, undissolved stone had simply disappeared from his mind. To him, I was just one of his former players who contributed to those conference championship teams. I thought about correcting him, telling him *No, I never played on your team. You cut me, remember?* Thought about telling how because of him, I went home that night and lay for hours in my unlit room, my future abruptly turned to ashes. Instead, I looked into Coach's eyes and what I saw there was the kindness I'd refused to acknowledge all those years. Then I began to visualize his illness—the cancer spreading its gray, deadly branches just beneath his skin.

"So," he said, erasing my vision, "do you still play ball?"

"Yeah," I replied. "Sometimes. With a few older guys, I mean."

He chuckled, grinned benignly. "That's the wonderful thing about baseball. You're never too old." He paused, then added solemnly, "When you've got baseball in your life, you're always a winner. Don't forget that."

His words reverberated in my head and I closed my eyes. I realized that these were the same words he'd spoken to us after the freshman tryouts in the locker room. I had the dizzying sensation that, without realizing it, I was walking on some wide, cyclical path, and I'd just passed a starting point again. I opened my eyes, and, for the first time, I understood those words. "I won't forget," I said.

Coach and I shook hands. Before he turned to leave, he caught me off guard by sliding his arm around me and giving me a hug. His frail hand clapped the back of my shoulder, and in those few seconds all the hurt feelings seemed to slide out of my body, rise through the blue and gold crepe paper wafting over our heads, drift through the ceiling of the high school gym, and evaporate into the endless night sky. My pain, which I'd always considered so enormous, suddenly seemed very small to me; I wondered how I could possibly have carried it for so long.

Later, as Coach walked toward the exit, I knew it might be the last time I'd ever see him. But then, I thought, maybe not. Maybe he'd be there, standing at the podium the next time we got together.

WORDS
TO
KNOW

benignly (bĭ-nīn′lē) *adv.* in a kind and gentle way

Tomorrow.

During the reunion, Steve and I talked for a while, but the evening passed too quickly, and we never got around to mentioning our ball-playing days. At one A.M. I said farewell to my classmates as we shuffled into the entryway of the gym. I glanced around to find Steve, but I couldn't spot him in the crowd.

Standing by the car with my wife, I heard a voice call to me from behind. "Hey, man," the voice said. "Wanna play some baseball?"

I turned to see Steve leaning against his car, mitt in one hand, beer in the other.

"You mean here?" I gasped. "Now?"

"Why not?"

I glanced at my wife, who smiled and nodded at me. Opening the car trunk, I pulled out my old glove.

Steve and I set down our cans of beer, slipped off our suit jackets, and draped them on posts at the edge of the parking lot. We stood beneath the glow of the full moon, awkward in our white shirts and ties, our waists a little thicker, our hair thinner and grayer, the cells inside our bodies subtly changing second by second. We tossed the ball across the open stretch of black asphalt. It wasn't the best playing surface, we agreed with a laugh as the soles of our shined shoes scuffed across it, but it would do for now. Though neither of us said it, Steve and I knew what each of us was thinking: Tomorrow we'd go to the old West School field, where we used to practice, and we'd play baseball. We'd slip into our worn spikes, torn T-shirts, and faded caps and play baseball. And if the field was gone, then we'd play in the place where it *used* to be. Tomorrow.

That night, in the <u>diffused</u> light, the ball seemed to flutter toward our outstretched gloves. I listened to the rhythmic beat of the ball in the leather pockets. The thought crossed my mind that you could keep time by a game of catch, this heartbeat, this throwing back and forth, back and forth, each swing of the arm like the sweep of a pendulum, each throw another year. It was then that I heard the honk of a horn, and in that instant, time stopped.

We turned to see Coach Brace, idling in his old powder-blue car, watching us from the far end of the lot, lifting his hand in a wave. ❖

RESPONDING
O P T I O N S

FROM PERSONAL RESPONSE TO CRITICAL ANALYSIS

REFLECT   1. What was your first impression of the narrator of this story? Jot down your thoughts in your notebook.

RETHINK   2. Compare the qualities of the narrator as an adult with his qualities as a teenager. In what ways does he remain the same? How does he change? Explain your answers.

Consider

- how he reacts when he does not make the baseball team
- what happens to his dream of playing professional baseball
- the personal discoveries he makes

3. Who do you think is to blame for the fact that the narrator's dream of playing professional baseball is not realized? Explain your opinion.

RELATE   4. What do you think the title of this story and the statement regarding the human heart at the beginning suggest about time, the nature of dreams, and the narrator's experience?

5. Consider the system in which coaches select members of school sports teams by trying out and handpicking athletes. Do you think the practice of cutting people from teams is fair? Do you think there might be a better selection method? As you discuss these questions with your classmates, give reasons for your answers.

ANOTHER PATHWAY
Cooperative Learning

In a small group, brainstorm what the narrator, both as a teenager and as an adult, might say directly to the coach. Write two scenes, and role-play them for the class. If possible, you may wish to record your performances on videotape.

QUICKWRITES

1. At the reunion, the coach says to the narrator, "When you've got baseball in your life, you're always a winner." Write a brief **paragraph** explaining what you think he means.

2. While speaking with the coach at the reunion, the narrator makes a personal discovery. Write a **pep talk** he might give to students about this discovery.

3. Write a **poem** about either the locker-room scene or the game of catch after the reunion. Try to capture the emotion of the scene in your poem.

📁 *PORTFOLIO Save your writing. You may want to use it later as a spring-board to a piece for your portfolio.*

LITERARY CONCEPTS

Some stories convey a **moral**—a lesson about human nature. For example, the well-known children's story "The Tortoise and the Hare" has as its moral "Slow and steady wins the race." In some stories, the moral is directly stated; in others, the reader must infer the moral from the words and actions. In your opinion, what is the moral of "Keeping Time"? Is it stated directly or indirectly?

ALTERNATIVE ACTIVITIES

On page 662, the narrator describes his anger at not being chosen for the team. Using information from the story and your imagination, create a piece of realistic or abstract **art**—a painting, montage, or collage—that represents his anger.

CRITIC'S CORNER

About "Keeping Time," our student-board reviewer Aaron Fitzstephens said, "It shows you that dreams don't always happen." In your opinion, does this statement express the moral of "Keeping Time"? Why or why not? How would you express the moral of the story?

WORDS TO KNOW

Review the Words to Know at the bottom of the selection pages. Then write the word that is most clearly related to each situation described below.

1. As the sun set behind the pitcher's mound, a soft glow replaced the harsh light of the blindingly sunny day.

2. Finding themselves on two different, brutally competitive teams, the two boys experienced a break in their long-time friendship.

3. Dumbfounded, the ballplayers watched the young deer wobble and collapse onto the field, steady itself on sticklike legs, fall, and right itself once again.

4. The players were happy that the mean-spirited coach was retiring and that his replacement treated them in a more pleasant way.

5. When he spied his girlfriend in the bleachers, the player tipped his cap to her so slightly that she did not notice.

BILL MEISSNER

"Keeping Time" is about the clash between dreams and reality and about forgiveness, says Bill Meissner (1948–). Like the narrator of the story, Meissner failed to make his freshman baseball team and held a grudge against his coach until they both met decades later at a reunion. Explains Meissner, "I had to switch gears quickly because my career goal was to be a major-league player." Unlike the narrator of the story, however, Meissner got back on his feet and forged ahead. He played American Legion baseball during high school. Today, he plays baseball informally with friends.

After graduating from the University of Wisconsin, Meissner received a master's degree in creative writing at the University of Massachusetts. For the last 20 years, he has taught at St. Cloud State University in Minnesota, where he is director of creative writing.

Meissner has published three volumes of poetry that draw on his childhood and adolescent experiences. "Keeping Time" is one of 30 short stories in his 1994 collection *Hitting into the Wind.* These stories use baseball themes to explore growing up and father-son relationships.

According to Meissner, "A story is like a pebble tossed into a still pond. The ripples hopefully reach out to touch the shoreline, the audience." He says he wants his writing "to touch the reader's personal experience."

PREVIEWING

NONFICTION

Power of the Powerless: A Brother's Lesson
Christopher de Vinck

PERSONAL CONNECTION

In this true story, Christopher de Vinck describes the valuable life lessons he learned from his severely disabled brother Oliver. His relationship with Oliver was a vital connection that deeply affected his life. Have you or anyone you know learned an important lesson from a physically or mentally disabled person? Write your thoughts in a diagram like the one shown. Then share your ideas with a small group of classmates.

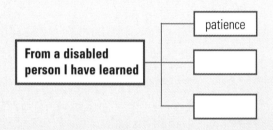

SCIENCE CONNECTION

Oliver was born with multiple birth defects. A birth defect can be a visible abnormality in the body's structure, such as a club-foot (a twisted or curled foot), or an internal defect, such as a hole in the heart. Although there are thousands of types of birth defects, they occur relatively infrequently. Only about two percent of newborn babies in the United States have a recognizable birth defect, and only half of them require treatment.

It has been established that some birth defects are inherited and others have environmental causes. Infants may inherit conditions resulting in defects, such as Down syndrome, from one or both parents.

A pregnant woman's exposure to tobacco smoke or to alcohol or poisonous substances, such as mercury in contaminated food, can also affect the development of a fetus. Such environmental causes have their greatest impact during the first three months of pregnancy. Early in her pregnancy, Oliver's mother was overcome by fumes that had a toxic effect on the child she was carrying.

WRITING CONNECTION

For the Personal Connection, you were asked to consider a disabled person from whom you or someone you know has learned valuable life lessons. Write a brief paragraph describing this person. If you do not know enough about the person to describe him or her, write what you imagine the person to be like.

POWER of the Powerless:

A Brother's Lesson

by Christopher de Vinck

I grew up in the house where my brother was on his back in his bed for almost 33 years, in the same corner of his room, under the same window, beside the same yellow walls. Oliver was blind, mute. His legs were twisted. He didn't have the strength to lift his head nor the intelligence to learn anything.

Today I am an English teacher, and each time I introduce my class to the play about Helen Keller, "The Miracle Worker," I tell my students about Oliver. One day, during my first year teaching, a boy in the last row raised his hand and said, "Oh, Mr. de Vinck. You mean he was a vegetable."

I stammered for a few seconds. My family and I fed Oliver. We changed his diapers, hung his clothes and bed linen on the basement line in winter, and spread them out white and clean on the lawn in the summer. I always liked to watch the grasshoppers jump on the pillowcases.

We bathed Oliver. Tickled his chest to make him laugh. Sometimes we left the radio on in his room. We pulled the shade down over his bed in the morning to keep the sun from burning his tender skin. We listened to him laugh as we watched television downstairs. We listened to him rock his arms up and down to make the bed squeak. We listened to him cough in the middle of the night.

"Well, I guess you could call him a

Sunroom (1980), Winifred Nicholson. Copyright © the artist's family.

vegetable. I called him Oliver, my brother. You would have liked him."

One October day in 1946, when my mother was pregnant with Oliver, her second son, she was overcome by fumes from a leaking coal-burning stove. My oldest brother was sleeping in his crib, which was quite high off the ground, so the gas didn't affect him. My father pulled them outside, where my mother revived quickly.

On April 20, 1947, Oliver was born. A healthy looking, plump, beautiful boy.

One afternoon, a few months later, my mother brought Oliver to a window. She held him there in the sun, the bright good sun, and there Oliver looked and looked directly into the sunlight, which was the first moment my mother realized that Oliver was blind. My parents, the true heroes of this story, learned, with the passing months, that blindness was only part of the problem. So they brought Oliver to Mt. Sinai Hospital in New York for tests to determine the extent of his condition.

The doctor said that he wanted to make it very clear to both my mother and father that there was absolutely nothing that could be done for Oliver. He didn't want my parents to grasp at false hope. "You could place him in an institution," he said. "But," my parents replied, "he is our son. We will take Oliver home of course." The good doctor answered, "Then take him home and love him."

Oliver grew to the size of a 10-year-old. He had a big chest, a large head. His hands and feet were those of a five-year-old, small and soft. We'd wrap a box of baby cereal for him at Christmas and place it under the tree; pat his head with a damp cloth in the middle of a July heat wave. His baptismal certificate hung on the wall above his head. A bishop came to the house and confirmed him.[1]

> I remember, too, my mother explaining to me that we were blessed with Oliver in ways that were not clear to her at first.

Even now, five years after his death from pneumonia on March 12, 1980, Oliver still remains the weakest, most helpless human being I ever met, and yet he was one of the most powerful human beings I ever met. He could do absolutely nothing except breathe, sleep, eat, and yet he was responsible for action, love, courage, insight. When I was small my mother would say, "Isn't it wonderful that you can see?" And once she said, "When you go to heaven, Oliver will run to you, embrace you, and the first thing he will say is 'Thank you.'" I remember, too, my mother explaining to me that we were blessed with Oliver in ways that were not clear to her at first.

So often parents are faced with a child who is severely retarded, but who is also hyperactive,[2] demanding or wild, who needs constant care. So many people have little

choice but to place their child in an institution. We were fortunate that Oliver didn't need us to be in his room all day. He never knew what his condition was. We were blessed with his presence, a true presence of peace.

When I was in my early 20s I met a girl and fell in love. After a few months I brought her home to meet my family. When my mother went to the kitchen to prepare dinner, I asked the girl, "Would you like to see Oliver?" for I had told her about my brother. "No," she answered.

Soon after, I met Roe, a lovely girl. She asked me the names of my brothers and sisters. She loved children. I thought she was wonderful. I brought her home after a few months to meet my family. Soon it was time for me to feed Oliver. I remember sheepishly asking Roe if she'd like to see him. "Sure," she said.

I sat at Oliver's bedside as Roe watched over my shoulder. I gave him his first spoonful, his second. "Can I do that?" Roe asked with ease, with freedom, with compassion, so I gave her the bowl and she fed Oliver one spoonful at a time.

The power of the powerless. Which girl would you marry? Today Roe and I have three children. ❖

---

1. **confirmed him:** performed the Christian ceremony admitting him into full membership in the church.

2. **hyperactive:** excessively active.

RESPONDING
OPTIONS

FROM PERSONAL RESPONSE TO CRITICAL ANALYSIS

REFLECT

1. What is your reaction to the author of this selection? Record your thoughts in your notebook.

RETHINK

2. De Vinck describes his brother Oliver as being "one of the most powerful human beings I ever met." How could such a helpless person be so powerful?

3. What is your opinion of the family's handling of Oliver's disability? Give reasons for your answer.

4. How would you express the lesson de Vinck learned from Oliver—and the lesson you have learned from de Vinck?

5. What do you think was the author's purpose in writing this account? Explain your answer.

RELATE

6. Oliver's parents felt strongly about caring for Oliver at home. Many families, however, feel unable to care for disabled children properly at home and choose to put them in institutions. Which choice do you think is appropriate? What factors might affect a family's decision? Why? Discuss your ideas with a partner.

ANOTHER PATHWAY
Cooperative Learning

Imagine that you are Oliver's brother and you want to keep a diary of key events, reactions, and feelings associated with Oliver's life. Work with a small group of classmates to create such a diary. Use details from the selection, but also use your imagination to fill in important events—for example, Oliver's first birthday.

QUICKWRITES

1. Suppose that Oliver had been able to communicate in writing. What might he have said to his brother? Write a **letter** he might have composed.

2. Imagine how Oliver's mother might have felt when she learned the extent of her baby's disabilities. Keeping in mind what you have learned about her character, record her feelings in the form of a **diary entry.**

📁 *PORTFOLIO Save your writing. You may want to use it later as a springboard to a piece for your portfolio.*

LITERARY LINKS

How does de Vinck's relationship with Oliver compare with Squeaky's relationship with Raymond in "Raymond's Run" (page 648). In what ways are the relationships alike? In what ways are they different? Compare the attitudes and the lessons conveyed in the two selections.

ALTERNATIVE ACTIVITIES

Cooperative Learning On page 671, de Vinck says that his brother was responsible for "action, love, courage, insight." Get together with three of your classmates, each choosing one of the words *action, love, courage,* and *insight.* Make an **illustration** or **design** to convey how your word applies to Oliver. Combine the group's work into one display, and share it with the class.

CRITIC'S CORNER

The student-board reviewer Theresa Ernst made the following comment about this selection: "I don't think many kids like to read about people who are disabled, but I think adults find it interesting because they understand disabilities better." Do you agree or disagree with this statement? Explain your opinion.

WORDS TO KNOW

WORDPLAY The word *sheepishly* in this selection (page 671) means "in an embarrassed or bashful way" and contains a reference to the behavior of sheep. With the class divided into two groups, brainstorm some other words that refer to animal-like characteristics, such as *mousy.* Then play a game of vocabulary charades, using the words you listed.

sheepishly

CHRISTOPHER DE VINCK

Christopher de Vinck (1951–) says that he began writing out of loneliness after a failed romantic relationship. He wrote poetry for ten years before the *Wall Street Journal* published his first essay in 1985. His second article, "Power of the Powerless: A Brother's Lesson," was also published that year by the *Journal.* Hundreds of readers, many with "Olivers" in their lives, responded strongly to de Vinck's work, phoning or writing letters to him. He eventually interviewed many of them for his book *The Power of the Powerless: A Brother's Legacy of Love.*

De Vinck has also published two collections of autobiographical essays and a novel for young people. He says that his prose style comes out of what he learned from writing poetry, which he continues to do. His essays are published in newspapers and magazines, including the *Reader's Digest.*

Since receiving degrees from Ramapo State College and Columbia University, de Vinck has juggled two careers—writing and teaching. He taught English for 16 years and is currently language arts supervisor for kindergarten through 12th grade in Wayne, New Jersey. He and his wife have three children.

After Oliver died, de Vinck's mother gave him Oliver's red dinner bowl. De Vinck keeps it in the room where he writes. He says, "If Oliver could make a contribution with such limited ability, we all can." To young people with disabled brothers or sisters, he offers this advice: "Just love them."

OTHER WORKS *Augusta and Trab*

PREVIEWING

POETRY

A Fairy Tale
Leroy V. Quintana

My Mother Really Knew
Wing Tek Lum

PERSONAL CONNECTION

Each of the two poems you are about to read focuses on the connection between a father and a child. Take a few minutes to think about father-child relationships. What words do you associate with a father's love? Use a diagram like the one started here to help organize your thoughts. Then share your ideas with a small group of classmates.

Words I Associate with a Father's Love — protective

CULTURAL CONNECTION

Children depend on their parents for love and the basic necessities of life. In traditional families, the mother runs the home and cares for the children, while the father makes the major family decisions. For many families in the United States and elsewhere, however, the traditional roles are changing.

More and more, parents are making decisions about their children together. Some fathers have even adopted the role of househusband, staying home with the children while their wives work. Today, the ways fathers love and care for their children are, in many cases, vastly different from what they were a century ago. Many fathers feel more comfortable about performing the more intimate tasks of parenting, such as diaper changing and toilet training.

WRITING CONNECTION

What is your idea of a good father? Use the words you listed for the Personal Connection to help you write a description of the qualities of a good father. Share your description with classmates.

A Good Father

BY LEROY V. QUINTANA

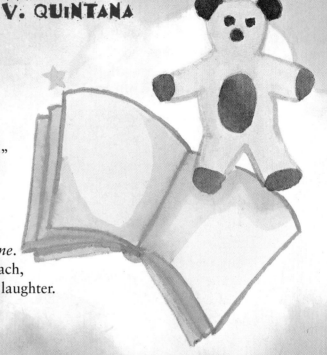

Bedtime. I tell stories, tales
of Robert Rattlesnake, Bennie Beaver,
Yolanda Panda Bear, Jerry Giraffe
and Danny the Dog.
5 And then it's Elisa's turn. She begins
"Once upanza time . . ."
"¡Panza!"[1] I say. "It's not upanza,
it's *once upon* a time. This is a panza,"
and grab her stomach, tickle her
10 until she can laugh no more.
"Once upanza time . . ."
"No No No No No!" I scream,
"It's *once upon* a time, not *upanza time*.
This is a panza," and I grab her stomach,
15 tickle her again until she's weak from laughter.
"Please tell me a real story," I plead,
"and please don't say panza."
"Once upanza time . . ." she begins.
"O.K.," I say, resigned. "You can say panza."
20 "Once upanza time . . .
there lived a panza
and it lived happily ever after.
Good night, Daddy."

---

1. **panza** (pän′sä) *Spanish:* belly.

FROM **PERSONAL RESPONSE** *TO* **CRITICAL ANALYSIS**

REFLECT   1. Think of a word or phrase that summarizes your reaction to this poem. Share it with your classmates.

2. How would you evaluate the parenting style of this father?

RETHINK   3. How would you characterize the relationship between the father and his daughter? *Consider*
- the father's parenting style
- the activity they are engaged in
- how they interact with each other

RELATE   4. Review the description of a good father you wrote for the Writing Connection on page 674. In your opinion, is the father in this poem a good father? Why or why not?

My Mother Really Knew

by *Wing Tek Lum*

My father was a tough cookie,
his friends still tell me with a smile.
He was hot-tempered
and had to have his own way,
5 but they loved him nonetheless,
and so did I.

I remember that
for maybe the first decade of my life
I had to kiss him every night
10 before I went to bed.

There was one time
he got into a big argument
with the rest of us at dinnertime,
and afterwards when he was in his study
15 I had to go to sleep
and refused to see him,
a chip off the old block.

But my mother and elder brothers
coaxed me to his door,
20 and I ran in
and pecked his cheek
without saying a word,
and went to bed
thinking of how unfair life was.

25 Love, my mother really knew,
was like these islands[1]
formed in part
by tidal waves and hurricanes
and the eruptions of volcanoes,
30 which suddenly appear
and just as suddenly go away.

---

1. **these islands:** the Hawaiian Islands.

RESPONDING OPTIONS

FROM PERSONAL RESPONSE TO CRITICAL ANALYSIS

REFLECT 1. What is your response to "My Mother Really Knew"? Record your reactions in your notebook.

RETHINK 2. What does the last stanza of the poem suggest about parent-child relationships?

3. The speaker of the poem is said to be "a chip off the old block." In what ways might the speaker be like the father? Explain your opinion.

4. What do you think the speaker's mother really knew?

RELATE 5. Recall that the mood of a work of literature is the emotional effect it has on the reader. Compare and contrast the moods of these two poems. What do the moods of the poems reveal about the children's feelings for their fathers?

6. How are the father-child relationships presented in the two poems alike, and how are they different? Use information from the poems to support your conclusions.

ANOTHER PATHWAY

A storyboard is a series of sketches arranged in sequence. Create a storyboard for one of the two poems, showing visually the sequence of events it presents. Label each sketch in the storyboard, then display it in the classroom.

QUICKWRITES

1. The mother in the poem "My Mother Really Knew" shows that she has wisdom about the love between parents and children, and it seems that the speaker benefits from her wisdom. Think of a time when someone showed wisdom that improved your understanding of a person or thing. Write a **paragraph** describing the situation, the nature of the wisdom, and the way it helped you.

2. Create a short **bedtime story** that expands on the story the little girl tells at the end of "A Fairy Tale."

📁 *PORTFOLIO Save your writing. You may want to use it later as a spring-board to a piece for your portfolio.*

LITERARY CONCEPTS

A writer's expression of his or her attitude toward a subject is called the writer's **tone.** A writer's tone might be described, for example, as angry, sad, humorous, or admiring. Think about the tones of the two poems and then compare them. Do you prefer one poem's tone to the other's? Explain your answer.

ALTERNATIVE ACTIVITIES

1. **Cooperative Learning** With a small group, compose a **lullaby** that the father in "A Fairy Tale" might sing to his daughter at bedtime. Keep in mind the kind of father that he appears to be. Then perform your lullaby for the class.

2. Create an **artistic representation** of the concept of love presented in the last stanza of "My Mother Really Knew." Use any medium or form you want—paint, pencil, collage, or clay, for example.

LEROY V. QUINTANA

1944–

Leroy Quintana is a descendant of the early Spanish settlers in what is now New Mexico. He grew up listening to traditional Mexican folk tales and stories of the Old West told by his grandparents, who raised him. "I have always," he has said, "enjoyed stories—I read comic books by the hundreds, went to the movies, and recited the stanzas in the back of the catechism [a book of religious instruction] religiously."

Drawing on folklore and his childhood experiences, Quintana's first volumes of poetry, *Hijo del Pueblo* and *Sangre*, describe village life in New Mexico. He has twice received the American Book Award for poetry from the Before Columbus Foundation.

Quintana began writing when he was a student at the University of New Mexico. He received graduate degrees in English from New Mexico State University and in counseling from Western New Mexico University. He currently teaches at San Diego Mesa College. His daughter Elisa, now an engineering student, is the girl featured in "A Fairy Tale."

OTHER WORKS *Interrogations, A History of Home*

WING TEK LUM

According to Wing Tek Lum (1946–), "My Mother Really Knew" is autobiographical. "My mother was a very good person," he says. "My father was more authoritarian—I respected him." Lum's mother died when he was 16 years old; his father, when the poet was 29. "The only way I can hold on to my relationship with them," he states, "is by thinking about them through my poetry."

"I slid into poetry as a hobby," explains Lum. "I am a slow reader and writer. Perhaps that stirred me into writing poetry, not prose. Poetry is like a snapshot, a slice of time. A prose writer sees many slices." Lum's Chinese-born mother and Hawaiian-born father made him aware, he says, of his Chinese roots while encouraging a strong identification with American culture.

An excellent mathematics and science student, Lum left his native Hawaii to study engineering at Brown University in Providence, Rhode Island. He then attended Union Theological Seminary in New York City and did social work in New York and Hong Kong before returning to Hawaii.

OTHER WORKS *Expounding the Doubtful Points*

POETRY

Sea-Fever	Mi Madre
John Masefield	Pat Mora

PERSONAL CONNECTION

The speakers of the poems you are about to read express their strong feelings for the natural world— specifically, the sea and the desert. To which of the two are you most drawn? What aspects of the desert and the sea appeal to you most? Jot down your thoughts in a word web like the one shown. Compare your ideas with those of your classmates.

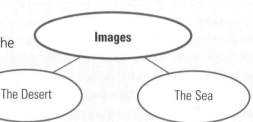

LITERARY CONNECTION

Elements of nature move some people to great emotion, compel the truly dedicated to live in the wilderness, and inspire creative expression. Nature has stirred some of our greatest writers. Henry David Thoreau, who in 1844 rejected creature comforts for a cabin in the woods, is among the most famous of America's poetic nature writers. Thoreau wrote, "I seek acquaintance with Nature—to know her moods and manners." His classic work *Walden* is a record of his experiment in living with nature.

In the early 20th century, several desert writers became popular. One of these was Mary Austin, who wrote lyrical sketches of the dry lands of the Southwest. Later, Joseph Wood Krutch, a resident of Arizona, wrote *The Desert Year* (1952) and *The Voice of the Desert* (1955). Also around that time, Anne Morrow Lindbergh described, in *Gift from the Sea,* her search of sea and sand to find "a new pattern of living."

In recent years, because of a heightened public concern with the environment, nature writing has become more popular. Thoreau's sentiment—"Give me the ocean, the desert, or the wilderness!"—probably means more to Americans today than it did 150 years ago.

READING CONNECTION

Symbol Recall that writers sometimes use concrete objects—people, places, or things—as symbols that stand for ideas or qualities. An eagle may be used to symbolize strength, for example, or a rose to stand for love. As you read these poems, think about how the poets make use of symbols.

Walden Pond in Massachusetts, site of Thoreau's cabin. Copyright © Doris De Witt/Tony Stone Images.

LASERLINKS
• *LITERARY CONNECTION*

679

Sea-Fever

I must go down to the seas again, to the lonely sea and the sky,
And all I ask is a tall ship and a star to steer her by,
And the wheel's kick and the wind's song and the white sail's
    shaking,
And a grey mist on the sea's face and a grey dawn breaking.

by John Masefield

5 I must go down to the seas again, for the call of the running tide
Is a wild call and a clear call that may not be denied;
And all I ask is a windy day with the white clouds flying,
And the flung spray and the blown spume[1] and the sea gulls crying.

I must go down to the seas again to the vagrant gypsy life,[2]
10 To the gull's way and the whale's way where the wind's like
    a whetted[3] knife;
And all I ask is a merry yarn from a laughing fellow-rover,
And quiet sleep and a sweet dream when the long trick's over.

---

1. **spume:** foam.
2. **vagrant gypsy life:** a carefree life of wandering from place to place.
3. **whetted:** sharpened.

FROM PERSONAL RESPONSE TO CRITICAL ANALYSIS

REFLECT 1. What is your impression of the speaker of this poem? Discuss your thoughts with the class.

RETHINK 2. Does the speaker ask for simple things or extravagant things? Explain your answer.

3. In the Reading Connection on page 679, you were asked to think about symbols. What do you think the sea symbolizes for the speaker? Give reasons for your answer.
   Consider
   • what the speaker asks of the sea
   • the description of the call of the tide
   • the kind of life the speaker yearns for

4. Explain what the title of the poem means to you.

Mi Madre[1]

BY PAT MORA

I say feed me.
She serves red prickly pear[2] on a spiked cactus.

I say tease me.
She sprinkles raindrops in my face on a sunny day.

5 I say frighten me.
She shouts thunder, flashes lightning.

I say comfort me.
She invites me to lay on her firm body.

I say heal me.
10 She gives me *manzanilla, orégano, dormilón.*[3]

I say caress me.
She strokes my skin with her warm breath.

I say make me beautiful.
She offers turquoise for my fingers, a pink blossom for my hair.

15 I say sing to me.
She chants lonely women's songs of femaleness.

I say teach me.
She endures: glaring heat
              numbing cold
20   frightening dryness.

She: the desert
She: strong mother.

---

1. **mi madre** (mē mä′drĕ) *Spanish:* my mother.
2. **prickly pear:** the pear-shaped edible fruit of a kind of cactus.
3. *manzanilla* (män-sä-nē′yä), *orégano* (ô-rĕ′gä-nô), *dormilón* (dôr-mē-lôn′) *Spanish:* sweet-smelling herbs that can be used to make home medicines.

RESPONDING
OPTIONS

FROM PERSONAL RESPONSE TO CRITICAL ANALYSIS

REFLECT
1. What feeling does "Mi Madre" leave you with? Write your thoughts in your notebook.

RETHINK
2. Why do you think the speaker calls the desert a mother?

3. Note the ways in which the maternal desert gives of herself. Describe some other ways—ones that the speaker does not mention.

RELATE
4. Compare and contrast the needs of the speakers of these two poems.

5. In your opinion, which speaker paints the most appealing or convincing picture of nature? Explain your choice.

ANOTHER PATHWAY
Cooperative Learning

What if "Mi Madre" were a poem about the sea? With a small group of classmates, reread the poem and brainstorm ways to turn the sentences beginning "She . . ." into statements about the sea. For example, your first stanza might read: "I say feed me. / She releases a scurrying crab on the shore."

LITERARY CONCEPTS

Words and phrases that appeal to readers' five senses are examples of **imagery.** Writers use imagery to convey how things look, feel, smell, sound, and taste. Note how the phrases "the lonely sea" and "red prickly pear on a spiked cactus" help you visualize the objects in these poems. Find other examples of imagery.

CONCEPT REVIEW: Elements of Poetry Make a chart, like the one shown, to analyze the elements of poetry in the poems. Record examples of each element and explain why you think the poet uses it.

Elements of Poetry		
Element	**Example**	**Why It Is Used**
Rhyme and rhythm Simile Repetition Alliteration Personification		

QUICKWRITES

1. The speaker of one of these poems has "sea fever." What in nature do you get feverish about? Perhaps you have Arctic fever or mountain fever! Write a **poem** about one of your favorite aspects of nature.

2. Create an **advertisement** for a seaside or desert vacation spot, using words, phrases, and lines from the appropriate poem.

📁 *PORTFOLIO Save your writing. You may want to use it later as a springboard to a piece for your portfolio.*

LITERARY LINKS

Like Masefield, Elinor Wylie wrote a poem about the sea—"Sea Lullaby" (page 131). Compare and contrast "Sea-Fever" with Wylie's poem. How are the poets' imagery and characterizations of the sea alike, and how are they different? What does the sea symbolize in each poem?

ALTERNATIVE ACTIVITIES

With a partner, choose appropriate **music** to accompany a reading of each poem. After each of you reads one of the poems with musical accompaniment, discuss which poem sounds best when set to music and why that poem sounds best.

JOHN MASEFIELD

1878–1967

As a teenager, John Masefield dreamed of becoming a writer. The adults who knew him had other ideas: "Put this writing-rubbish right out of your head," they would say, or, "Only clever people can be writers." They were undoubtedly surprised when Masefield was named poet laureate of England in 1930. Masefield published more than 30 volumes of poetry, 8 novels, 13 plays, and a number of short stories, biographies, and essays.

After the death of his parents, Masefield was raised in Ledbury, England, by his uncle. When he was 13, he ended his formal education by running away to the sea. For four years he traveled the world, working on ships. He eventually settled in New York City. There, he spent two years working on the waterfront and in a bakery, a stable, a saloon, and a rug mill. He also began to write.

Very unhappy and homesick, Masefield burned most of what he had written and returned to England, where he experimented with different writing styles and forms. "In verse, men must try for something of music and of painting; in prose, for something of drama and of portrait," Masefield once wrote. In 1902, he published his first collection of poems, *Salt-Water Poems and Ballads,* from which "Sea-Fever" is taken.

OTHER WORKS *Jim Davis*

PAT MORA

1942–

"I write," Pat Mora says, "in part, because Hispanic perspectives need to be part of our literary heritage. . . . I also write because I am fascinated by the pleasure and power of words." Mora's poetry, nonfiction, and short stories prove that she remains true to her words. In her work, she portrays the cultural diversity and visual beauty of the Southwest and the harmony that can exist between nature and human beings.

Mora has spent most of her life in El Paso, Texas, where she was born. (Her four grandparents had migrated from Mexico to El Paso to escape a revolution early in this century.) After receiving a master's degree from the University of Texas at El Paso, she pursued a career in teaching. She also for a time hosted a public-radio show called *Voices: The Mexican-American in Perspective.*

In 1986, Mora received a Kellogg National Fellowship to study ways of preserving cultures. She explains, "I am interested in how we save languages and traditions. What we have inside of our homes and our families is a treasure chest that we don't pay attention to." She urges young people to preserve their heritage by tape-recording their family's stories and finding out about the cultural treasures in their homes.

OTHER WORKS *Chants*

WRITING TO PERSUADE

In Unit Five, "Personal Discoveries," you read about individuals who faced opposition as they struggled to change people's minds. How often have you been in a similar situation? Were you as successful as you had hoped to be? In this lesson, you will learn how to persuade others, as well as to recognize when someone is trying to persuade you!

GUIDED ASSIGNMENT
Write a Persuasive Essay Write an essay persuading others to agree with you about an issue that you feel is important.

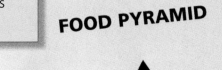

① Discuss the Issues

What situations are reflected in the items on these two pages? Have you heard any of these topics discussed on television or on the radio? Have you thought about any of these issues yourself?

Find the Message Write a summary of each of the topics presented here. Can you identify more than one side of each issue? How does the information each source presents help you understand the issues? What more would you want to know about each topic before forming an opinion?

Share the Message Compare your summaries with those of some of your classmates. In what ways are your summaries alike? How are they different?

② Choose an Issue

Make a list of other situations about which people disagree. Choose the issue you feel most strongly about. Write a paragraph briefly telling what the two sides of the issue are. What is your position?

Nutrition Chart
Leading doctors and scientists want the U.S. Department of Agriculture and the Department of Health and Human Services to revise the requirements for a balanced diet. They feel that people should eat more vegetables and less meat.

News Anchor: "Crowds gathered outside a stadium in Minneapolis today to protest sports teams' use of Native American names."

Personal Correspondence

Coach Bradley,
I'd like to try out for the football team this year. I love the game! I play football with my brothers and other kids in my neighborhood all the time.

Sincerely,
Carla Babrick

This is so wrong!
I think I'll write
about this.

 LINCOLN MIDDLE SCHOOL

Why shouldn't girls be allowed to try out for football?

Carla, thanks for your note. I'm sorry, but I think football is too dangerous for girls. Have you thought about trying out for the cheerleading squad?

— Coach Bradley

LASERLINKS
• WRITING SPRINGBOARD

WRITING COACH

WRITING FROM EXPERIENCE **685**

Building Your Case

Ways to Support Your Views Attorneys gather evidence to use in their clients' defense. Think of yourself as an attorney out to gather facts to defend your position on the issue you've chosen to argue in your persuasive essay. On these pages, you'll discover ways to add support to your argument.

1 List Your Views

Make a list of everything you know about the issue. Include any questions you might have. You can make an idea tree like the one below to list what you know and what you need to find out.

2 Look for Support

As you research your topic, consider including the following types of support.

Facts A fact is a statement that can be proved. Facts are important sources of support because they make your argument more persuasive.

Student's Idea Tree

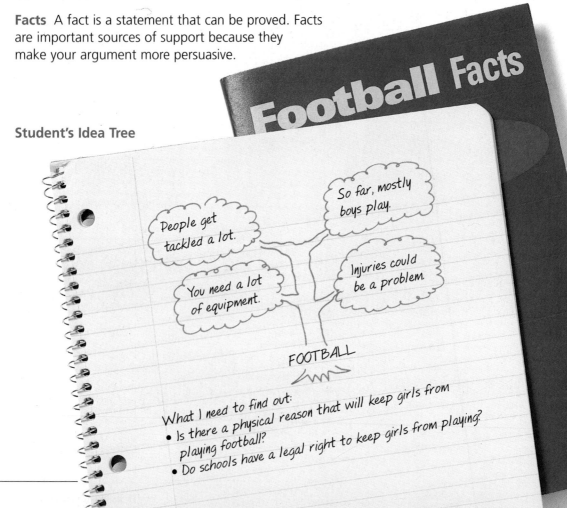

People get tackled a lot.

So far, mostly boys play.

You need a lot of equipment.

Injuries could be a problem.

FOOTBALL

What I need to find out:
- Is there a physical reason that will keep girls from playing football?
- Do schools have a legal right to keep girls from playing?

Opinions Opinions are personal feelings or beliefs. Therefore, they cannot be proved. However, opinions are important sources of support because they may summarize people's points of view. Opinions are also sometimes given by authorities in specific fields, such as doctors and professors.

Page 850 of the Multimedia Handbook offers tips on using on-line services to research facts, opinions, and opposing points of view. You can also do a computer search at your local library or use the card catalog to find books and articles on your subject. The SkillBuilder at the right will help you evaluate the sources you find.

❸ Identify Your Audience

Who is your audience? Decide how much they know about the issue. As you draft, and when you revise, make sure you've given your readers all the information they need to judge your argument.

❹ Explore Both Sides of the Issue

As you plan your essay, you'll need to consider both sides of the issue. You want to address opposing points of view effectively, as well as test your own reasons and support. A pro/con chart, such as the one below, can help you consider opposing viewpoints.

Student's Pro/Con Chart

THINK & PLAN

Reflecting on Your Ideas

1. How has your research affected the way you view the issues?
2. How will you use the information you gathered to write your essay?
3. How will your audience affect the way you write your essay?

Making Your Point

Your Views, Your Way Now that you've explored the issue, it's time to get your thoughts down on paper. State your case clearly and use strong support for your argument. Here are some suggestions to follow as you write.

❶ Draft and Discover

As you write your draft, use facts and statistics, examples and incidents, or graphic aids to elaborate on your ideas and support your position. For example, a student writing in favor of girls playing on the football team chose to use facts from sports doctors and other sports authorities to support her argument.

Student's Rough Draft

> ### Girls in the Huddle
>
> Is football a sport that only boys should be allowed to play? Should girls just stand on the sidelines and cheer? No way!
>
> Some people argue that football is not safe for girls, because boys are stronger. But that's stupid! Helmets, shoulder pads, and other equipment can shield a player from injury.

Maybe I could make this a speech for the school pep rally. I'll need to add more facts.

Loaded language in the second paragraph. -JB

Girls have the right to try out!

Is the point about equipment a strong enough argument in favor of girls playing football?

Madden, John. _The First Book of Football._

Anyone can play football.... If you're small and can run pretty fast, you can be a receiver, running back, or defensive back.

Quotation

② Analyze Your Draft

After letting your draft sit for a while, review it again. Have you addressed opposing views? Have any of your views changed? Decide whether the arguments in your rough draft are based mostly on fact or on emotional appeals.

③ Rework Your Draft

The following suggestions can help you present your views in a powerful way.

Writing Your Introduction You'll want to catch your readers' interest at the beginning, as you state your position on the issue. You could use a dramatic incident or a statistic to add interest to your introduction. The sentences that follow should support your position.

Organizing Your Ideas One way to organize your essay is to order the points you want to make from weakest to strongest. Mention your strongest point last, because that is the point that will stick with your reader. See the Writing Handbook, page 844, for more suggestions to help you organize your essay.

Drafting Your Conclusion In your conclusion, be sure to restate your position in some way. You might also consider leaving your readers with a challenging question. See the Writing Handbook for tips on writing conclusions.

 PEER RESPONSE

Peer reviewers can help you revise your draft. While you don't want to get into a debate over the issue, you do want to get their feedback on how well you present the issue. Ask a peer reviewer questions like these:

- How would you restate my position?
- Which ideas are strongest? weakest?
- Have I effectively addressed opposing arguments?
- Do you think my audience will be persuaded by my arguments? If not, how can I make my position stronger?

 SkillBuilder

✎→ WRITER'S CRAFT

Avoiding Loaded Language

The words you use can appeal to readers' emotions and can sway them to your point of view. **Connotation** is the feeling or thought that a particular word or phrase suggests. Which sentence below has a positive connotation? Which gives you a negative feeling?

The argument that girls can't play football is stupid.

The argument that girls can't play football isn't based on fact.

Emotional appeals usually contain very little information. Be sure to have good, solid support for your argument, rather than relying on loaded language.

APPLYING WHAT YOU'VE LEARNED
Change the adjective in the following sentence to make the connotation positive.

The coach's rash decision kept girls off the team.

RETHINK & EVALUATE

Preparing to Revise

1. What facts do you need to add to strengthen your argument?
2. How well did you present opposing viewpoints?

Finishing Your Essay

A Polished Draft Take time to consider your own suggestions and others' responses to your draft. The steps on these pages can help you clarify and strengthen your position.

1 Revise and Edit

Review the Standards for Evaluation, the Editing Checklist, and the following steps as you edit your draft.

- Review your position on the issue. Are there any points that need to be explained more clearly?
- Have you effectively used words with connotations?
- Have you ordered your points in a logical manner?
- Does your conclusion restate your position?

Student's Final Draft

Girls in the Huddle

Is football a sport for boys only? Should girls just stand on the sidelines and cheer? The answer is no. Here's why.

First of all, there is no physical reason why a girl should not play. According to John Madden in <u>The First Book of Football</u>, "Anyone can play football. . . . If you're small and can run pretty fast, you can be a receiver, running back, or defensive back." An article in the May 1995 <u>Sports Illustrated for Kids</u> proved Madden's point in an interview with a girl who became a starting quarterback on her school's football team. If girls love the game, why should they just be spectators?

Some football coaches have talked about an increased risk of injury for girls. This risk is not great, especially at the middle school level. In two books on sports injuries, doctors mentioned that most injuries don't occur until a player plays football in high school. Players may have to suffer sprains, bumps, or bruises, but nothing more serious.

Another reason that girls should be able to play is that they have a legal right to try out. Under Title IX, a 1972 law, schools getting federal aid cannot discriminate in sports on the basis of sex. That means girls can try out for football.

How did the student address opposing points of view?

How did the student use facts and opinions to support her argument?

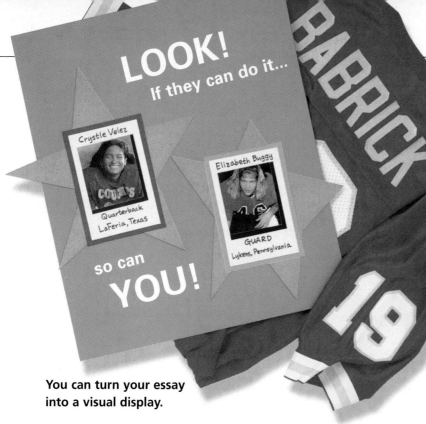

LOOK!
If they can do it...

Crystle Velez
COWBOYS
Quarterback
LaFeria, Texas

Elizabeth Buggy
GUARD
Lykens, Pennsylvania

so can
YOU!

You can turn your essay into a visual display.

❷ Show Your Work

The format you choose for your final essay can help you to make a strong impact on your readers. This student chose to create a visual display. You might also choose one of the publishing options below.

PUBLISHING IDEAS

- You might turn your essay into an article for your school newspaper or a letter to the editor of your community newspaper.
- A speech or petition might be a good format for persuading others about the issue.
- You might make a leaflet or brochure and use it as a teaching tool.

Standards for Evaluation
A persuasive essay • has a strong introduction • clearly states the issue and the writer's position • presents ideas logically and effectively • addresses opposing viewpoints • ends with a strong argument or summary or a call for action

SkillBuilder

 GRAMMAR FROM WRITING

Avoiding Double Negatives

Avoid using two negative words in one clause. Instead, use one negative word to express a negative idea.

Incorrect *Girls didn't have no chance to play football.*

Correct *Girls didn't have a chance to play football.*

GRAMMAR HANDBOOK

For more information on using negatives correctly, see page 880 of the Grammar Handbook.

Editing Checklist Check the following points as you finalize your draft.

- Did you effectively use words with connotations?
- Did you avoid using double negatives?
- Did you proofread for errors in verb agreement?

REFLECT & ASSESS

Evaluating Your Experience

1. What did you learn about yourself or your beliefs?
2. How did people react to the way you presented your views? What does that tell you about your writing?

📁 **PORTFOLIO** Include your essay and your research notes in your portfolio.

REFLECT & ASSESS

UNIT FIVE: PERSONAL DISCOVERIES

How do you view yourself in relation to others? Have you found your place in the world? These are the kinds of questions that arise for the characters in Unit Five. After reading the selections, are you better able to understand the search for personal identity? Choose one or more of the options in each section below to help you reflect on what you have learned.

REFLECTING ON THEME

OPTION 1 **Reading from Within** The characters in this unit are forced to examine who they are and how they fit in. Choose two characters—the one you think is the most successful in making discoveries about himself or herself, and the one you think is the least successful in making such discoveries. Then pretend that you are the most successful character and write a letter of advice to the least successful character, telling how he or she can achieve greater self-understanding.

OPTION 2 **Focusing on Poetry** Review the poetry that you read in this unit. Think about which poems best reflect for you the unit theme, "Personal Discoveries." Then make illustrations for the poems you have selected. Try to convey both the poems' subject matter and the theme of the unit.

OPTION 3 **Learning a Lesson** Which selections in this unit have had the greatest impact on the way you view yourself, both as an individual and in relation to others? Rate each selection on a scale of 1–10, according to the effect it has had on you. Discuss your ratings with a partner, explaining the reasoning behind them.

Self-Assessment: What is the best way to find your place in the world? What makes you who you are? What have you discovered about yourself? Write a few short paragraphs describing how you would answer these questions now. Then, using a different-colored pen, make notes in the margins, telling which selections have influenced your thoughts.

REVIEWING LITERARY CONCEPTS

OPTION 1 **Thinking About Symbols** Recall that a symbol is a person, a place, or an object that stands for something beyond itself—as a flag symbolizes a country, for example. Working with a small group of classmates, look back at the fiction, nonfiction, and poetry in this unit. After brainstorming a number of possibilities, select one symbol that stands for a major aspect of each selection. Make a chart like the one shown, drawing pictures of the symbols and explaining their meanings.

Selection	Symbol	Symbolic Meaning
"The Moustache"		stands for Mike's maturity, which increases with experience; stands for his grandfather

OPTION 2 **Stating Morals** Identify the selections in this unit from which you can infer a moral, or lesson. Write down each moral in a single sentence, then see if a partner can identify the selections that match the morals.

Self-Assessment: Make a chart like the one shown. Then, after looking at the following list of poetry terms discussed in this unit, write each term in one of the columns to show how well you think you understand it. Once you have targeted the terms you do not understand, find a partner who understands them well. Go back over the poetry in the unit together, reviewing the terms. Also try to help a student understand the terms of which you have a firm grasp.

dialogue in poetry   *simile*

imagery   *repetition*

rhyme   *alliteration*

rhythm   *personification*

My Knowledge of Poetry Concepts		
Understand Completely	**Understand Partially**	**Do Not Understand**

PORTFOLIO BUILDING

- **QuickWrites** Several of this unit's QuickWrites assignments asked you to construct paragraphs, make diary entries, and write poems. From your responses to each kind of assignment, choose one in which you notice an especially strong link to the unit theme, particularly with regard to relationships among loved ones. Write a cover note explaining why you feel good about your responses, then add them, along with the note, to your portfolio.

- **Writing About Literature** Earlier in this unit, you analyzed a poem. Reread the poem and your analysis now. Decide whether you still think your analysis is on target, and jot down a sentence explaining your opinion. Note how your analysis might help you read poetry in the future. You may wish to include your note in your portfolio.

- **Writing from Experience** As you think back on the persuasive essay you wrote in this unit, what part of the research and writing seems to have been the most challenging? What part was the most interesting? Why? What did you learn about understanding both sides of an issue before forming an opinion?

- **Personal Choice** Look back through the records and evaluations of all the activities you completed in this unit. In which activities or responses do you feel you offered a truly creative product or a clever solution to a problem? Write a paragraph giving a favorable critique of your work.

Self-Assessment: Compare the poems you have added to your portfolio for Unit Five with those that were already in your portfolio. Do you think you are becoming a better poet? If so, how? Write a note explaining how you feel you have developed as a poet. Attach it to the poetry in your portfolio.

SETTING GOALS

As you completed the reading and writing activities that focused on the poetry in this unit, you probably identified certain poems you liked. Which poets' works, or which kinds of poetry, would you like to read more of? What kinds of poems would you like to write yourself?

Across Time and Place

The Oral TRADITION

People can hear a story and

relate it to their own lives.

Stories can heal people.

Storytelling is a way for

people to find their power.

Olga Loya

Olga Loya is a Mexican American who grew up in East Los Angeles. She strives to keep the oral tradition alive through her storytelling.

STORYTELLERS PAST AND PRESENT

OLGA LOYA

A Present Day Storyteller Speaks

Many of Olga Loya's stories come out of her Mexican heritage as well as her own family history. She also shares tales from all over Latin America and from a variety of oral traditions around the world.

I've always told stories. My grandmother was a *curandera* (kōō-rän-dě′rä), a healer. When she died, her house was filled with flowers from all the people that came to say goodbye to her. She always told stories to get her point across to people and to help them. My father was also a storyteller. He was one of those people who would tell a story that lasted five minutes at first. Then the next time he told it, it would last ten minutes, then fifteen minutes, then twenty.

In 1980 I went to a storytelling conference. It was like a thunderbolt to my heart. I came home and said to my family, "I'm going to be a storyteller." At first I started telling stories from books. Within a year, I realized I had many stories within myself and within my own culture. Some of the first stories I told were from Mexico, because that is my heritage. As time passed, I began to realize that there were many stories within my own family. So now I tell a number of family stories as well as stories from Latin America and all over the world. Once I was invited by some Native Americans to come and tell stories to the elders of the tribe. They honored me by giving me permission to tell some of their stories, too.

There are many types of Latino stories. *Mitos* (mē′tôs), or myths, explain how things came to be. Myths are very powerful because they represent the heart of the culture. The *leyendas* (lě-yěn′däs), or legends, tell of people from times before. Legends are a way of connecting past and present. At one time in the past, the characters were believed to be real, but even now we can relate their lives to our own. There are also folk tales, *cuentos* (kwĕn′tôs). Many of these have animal characters. Sometimes these teach a lesson, sometimes they entertain, and often they do both. And there are *fábulas* (fä′bo͞o-läs), or fables, which always have a moral.

The themes of Latino stories are really universal ones such as honoring your parents, paying attention to how you deal with the land, and not going to extremes in behavior—keeping a balance is important. Another theme that often appears is that of death, but it is often treated in a playful way, which reflects the attitudes of the culture.

I'm always looking for stories that touch my heart. Those are the stories I want to tell, because those are the stories that people will want to listen to. Stories can help people communicate with each other. People can hear a story and relate it to their own lives. Stories can heal people. Storytelling is a way for people to find their power.

We are all storytellers. We all have stories that we carry with us, but some of us don't know we have them. We should be story detectives—find the stories that move us and tell them. Go to your parents and to other members of your family and ask them to tell stories. Take the time to find out your family's stories or they will not be passed on. If you don't have the stories to pass on to your children, the stories will die. They will not stay alive unless someone tells them.

Latin American folklore is a rich blend of Native American traditions and Spanish customs and values. This unique folklore continues to thrive in Hispanic communities throughout the United States.

An Ancient Storyteller
The Mexican-American grandmother of the turn of the century, highly respected in her close-knit extended family, often took responsibility for passing along family tales to her grandchildren.

This Mexican-American woman grew up in Texas. During her childhood, Texas was still a part of Mexico but fought for and won its independence in 1836.

Body language, including hand gestures, is effective in bringing a tale to life.

KEEPING THE PAST ALIVE

By giving voice to their cultural heritage, storytellers like Olga Loya keep the past alive. Even cultures that vanished centuries ago can be considered to live on as long as their tales are passed on to new listeners. These tales from cultures around the world make up what is called the oral tradition.

The stories in this unit are drawn from a wide range of regions, countries, and cultures in the Americas. The time line at the right illustrates this rich variety in the oral tradition. It shows what cultures the stories are associated with, along with a key event in each culture's history.

Besides being a celebration of varied cultures, the stories in this unit show the common elements that run through different types of folklore. These shared elements form a bridge linking tales from ancient civilizations with stories in the modern oral tradition. The chart below shows some of the common elements of folklore.

MYTHS
- *answer basic questions about the world*
- *are often considered truthful by their originators*

FOLK TALES
- *are told primarily for entertainment*
- *often feature human beings or humanlike animals*

COMMON ELEMENTS
- **keep the past alive**
- **teach lessons about human behavior**
- **reveal the values of the society**

FABLES
- *are short tales that illustrate morals*
- *frequently have characters that are animals*

LEGENDS
- *are often considered factual by those who tell them*
- *may have some basis in fact*
- *are usually set in the past*

ESKIMO
Otoonah 769

. . .

3000–1000 B.C. *Eskimos cross the Bering Sea from Siberia to North America.*

GUATEMALAN
The First Flute 791

. . .

A.D. 300–900 *The Mayan civilization flourishes in the Yucatán Peninsula.*

HAIDA
Raven and the Coming of Daylight 742

. . .

1000–1300 *The Northwest Coast is one of the most heavily populated areas in North America, with an estimated 129,000 inhabitants.*

LINKS TO UNIT ONE

Changing Perceptions

In the selections in Unit One, people and events are not always what they seem at first glance. With the benefit of experience, characters go beyond their initial perceptions and gain new insight and understanding. In the stories you are about to read, the characters' perceptions also change in the light of experience.

MEXICO

The Souls in Purgatory

retold by Guadalupe Baca-Vaughn

The first people to bring the Roman Catholic religion to Mexico were missionaries and priests from Spain who arrived in the 16th century. They converted millions of Native Americans to Catholicism, and the great majority of Mexicans now belong to the Roman Catholic Church. However, the ancient beliefs and traditions of the region did not disappear—many of them have been combined with Catholic beliefs. This blend of traditions is reflected in many Mexican customs and folk tales, including this tale of faith.

Paul Bunyan and the Winter of the Blue Snow

retold by Paul Robert Walker

In the 19th century, forests covered a much larger area of the United States than they do today. Chopping them down to clear farmland and to provide lumber was an immense task. It was almost certainly the lumberjacks of the northern woods who told the first tall tales about the greatest lumberjack of them all—Paul Bunyan. Tall tales are stories in which exaggerated characters perform incredible feats. This selection is based on several Bunyan tales, including ones told in the logging camps of Michigan.

The Girl in the Lavender Dress

retold by Maureen Scott

Urban legends are contemporary stories that are told repeatedly in many versions around the world. The people telling them usually claim the stories are true and that they actually happened to a relative or friend of a friend. In fact, urban legends simply represent modern-day folklore. Part of their appeal may be that they combine traditional fears—for example, the fear of ghosts—with more modern fears, such as the fear of random violence or of being stalked.

AS YOU READ . . .

See whether the stories remind you of any other tales from the same culture or other cultures.

Consider how the characters' thoughts and actions fit the theme "Changing Perceptions."

Notice how each story reflects various features of its culture.

Paul Bunyan and the Winter of the Blue Snow

retold by Paul Robert Walker

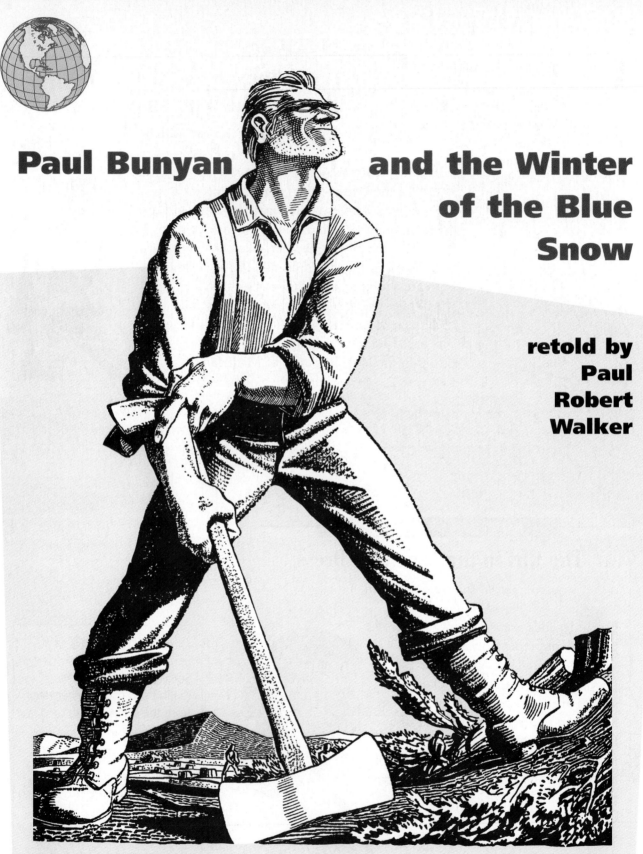

Illustration by Rockwell Kent. Courtesy of the Rockwell Kent Legacies.

Back in the Winter of the Blue Snow, the boys were logging the giant pines of the North Woods. It was a pretty big camp in those days, with a crew of 180 men. And every man was at least seven feet tall and weighed at least 350 pounds.

Joe Muffreau was too small to be a logger, being only six feet fourteen inches tall and weighing only 349 pounds and 53 ounces. But he was the fastest flapjack flipper in the North Woods, so they made him the camp cook.

One night, Joe looked out the window of the cook shack and saw something moving in the darkness. At first he thought it was a couple of pine trees coming in for dinner. But when it got closer, he realized it was a man—a big, big man with a bushy black beard, a red woolen cap, a plaid woolen shirt, and leather boots that were just about as tall as Joe Muffreau. Joe opened the door of the cook shack and smiled up at the stranger.

"You look mighty hungry," said Joe.

"I am," said the stranger. "My name's Paul Bunyan."

"Well, come on in and grab some grub."

Joe had a crew of twenty-two cookeys, and he put them all to work preparing dinner for the big lumberjack. After about three hours, it was all ready, and Paul sat down to have himself a little meal. He ate thirty-three pounds of beef, one whole venison, six hams, two bushels of fried potatoes, twelve four-pound loaves of bread, twelve dozen eggs, and 678 flapjacks topped off with six gallons of maple syrup, and he washed it all down with twenty-two gallons of coffee.

Illustration by Rockwell Kent. Courtesy of the Rockwell Kent Legacies.

When he was finished Paul said, "That'll tide me over. Now what about my ox?"

Joe looked out the window of the cook shack and squinted into the darkness. "What ox?" he asked. "All I see is a mountain covered with blue snow."

"That's no mountain—that's my ox," said Paul. "I call him Babe."

Joe looked out the window again. Sure enough, the mountain was really Babe, the Big Blue Ox. It was a reasonable mistake, because Babe was pretty big. Some folks say he measured fourteen ax handles between the eyes. Others say he measured forty-two and a half ax handles and a can of chewing tobacco. That just shows how people exaggerate. The truth is, Babe measured exactly seven ax handles between the eyes. . . . Of course, ax handles were a lot bigger in those days.

Joe had one of his boys show Paul and Babe to the stables. The stable boss let Babe eat as much as he wanted—which was a year's supply of hay for the entire camp. Then Paul and Babe kicked over a few hundred trees so they could lie down, and they went to sleep in the blue snow.

The next morning was crisp and clear and so cold that the thermometer outside Joe's cook shack froze at sixty below—it was perfect logging weather. After breakfast Paul and Babe went out with the lumberjacks to a section of tall pines. A section is a pretty big piece of land—640 acres—and the boys had been logging it all winter. It was slow, tedious work.

Why, some of those North Woods pines were so big that a two-man team could saw at one side of the trunk for three days before they'd run into another team sawing from the other side.

Of course, Paul didn't work with a partner, and he didn't work with a saw. He stepped right up to the biggest tree he could find, lifted his giant ax, and chopped that North Woods pine down with a single stroke—*Boom!* The sound exploded like thunder in the cold air. Then he stepped over to another tree and did it again—*Boom!* The other loggers stared in wide-eyed wonder. The way Paul was going, they'd be done with the whole section by lunchtime.

Then Paul did something that really surprised them. He set his giant ax on the ground, scratched his bushy black beard, and said, "Boys, I don't mind working hard, but there's gotta be a better method of logging. This is just too slow. First we chop down the trees; then we pull them over the skid roads to the river. It seems like double work." Paul scratched his beard some more, and all the boys could see his cleverality working away in his big brain.

After a few minutes Paul got a light in his eyes. He picked up Babe's leather harness and wrapped it around the whole section—all 640 acres. Then the Big Blue Ox dragged the land, pine trees and all, down to the river. Paul and the boys cut the timber just like they were shearing a sheep, and the logs fell right into the river. Of course, the river was frozen at the time, but this way they were all set for the spring thaw. After the logs were cut, Babe

Illustration by Rockwell Kent. Courtesy of the Rockwell Kent Legacies.

hauled the section back where it belonged, and Paul hitched him up to another one.

With Paul and Babe, the Winter of the Blue Snow turned out to be the biggest logging season in the history of the world. When the spring thaw came, there were one hundred million logs in the river. Paul and the boys floated them down nice and easy at first, but the snow kept melting, the river kept getting higher, the logs kept moving faster, and pretty soon it was out of control. Those hundred million logs started bumping and stopping and sliding and piling, and all of a sudden Paul and the boys had a logjam to beat all jams. The logs were piled two hundred feet high and backed up a mile upriver. Paul stood on the bank, scratching his bushy black beard. The boys could see his cleverality working pretty good. Finally Paul put Babe in the river and grabbed a shotgun. Then he peppered the Big Blue Ox with moose shot. Now, moose shot is good-sized ammunition, but Babe thought it was just a swarm of flies. He started swishing his tail around, stirring that river and stirring it some more, until pretty soon the whole dang river flowed backward and the logs came loose. Then Paul lifted Babe out of the water, and the logs floated downstream again.

Everything went pretty smoothly after that—until they got the logs to the sawmill. You see, Paul and the boys had so many logs, there weren't enough sawmills in the North Woods to buy them. Paul did a little checkin' around and discovered there was a big sawmill operator down near the Gulf of Mexico who was willing to buy all the logs they had. So the lumberjacks floated fifty million logs down the Mississippi River.

When the logs reached the Gulf of Mexico, the big sawmill operator refused to pay for them. Maybe he figured he was so far from the North Woods that he didn't have to worry about Paul Bunyan and the boys. But that's not the way Paul saw it. Paul never cared much about money—just logging—but a deal is a deal, and that fellow down on the Gulf of Mexico was cheating all the boys—and Babe, too. So Paul started scratching his beard and working his cleverality again. Then he got that light in his eyes, and the boys knew he had a plan.

Paul turned to Joe Muffreau and said, "Joe, I want you to bring me the biggest block of salt you can find."

"What about pepper?" asked Joe.

"No pepper," said Paul. "Just salt."

Joe sent his twenty-two cookeys back to the camp in an eight-horse flapjack wagon. When they came back, they were carrying a block of salt that was almost as big as Joe's cook shack. Paul picked it up in one hand and set it down in front of Babe, the Big Blue Ox. Well, Babe was always partial to salt, so he licked it and licked it until there was nothing left.

Of course, then Babe was pretty thirsty, so Paul led him over to the Mississippi River. Babe started drinking, and it must have tasted mighty good after that salt, because he just kept drinking and drinking until the water came all the way up from the Gulf of Mexico, with the fifty-million logs floating on the top.

Well, the sawmill operator paid right up after that. So Paul told Babe to stop drinking, and the Mississippi River flowed back down to the Gulf of Mexico, carrying the logs right with it. Paul split the profits with all the boys, including Babe. And that's what happened during the Winter of the Blue Snow. ❖

PAUL ROBERT WALKER

Paul Robert Walker (1953–) says he became a writer because "I was born this way. I delight in words, ideas, characters, and the stories they create. I'm fascinated with facts and the blurry line that separates them from—or turns them into—fiction." He admits he really became a writer because of his grandfather, a book called *The Swamp Fox,* and the Los Angeles Times.

Named after his Danish grandfather, who edited a Danish newspaper in the United States and was knighted by the King of Denmark for his writing, Walker thinks he inherited his grandfather's "writing genes." When, at the age of seven, Walker read *The Swamp Fox,* about Revolutionary War General Francis Marion, he discovered "the power of a good book." In 1986, he was hired to write articles for reference books. Although most of what he wrote was never published, Walker turned one of the articles into a full-length book about a baseball player. The book, *Pride of Puerto Rico: The Life of Roberto Clemente,* launched Walker's writing career.

Walker says it is a "totalaciously splendiferous" experience to read his stories to young people because it allows him not only to write but to teach and act.

OTHER WORKS *Big Men, Big Country; Bigfoot and Other Legendary Creatures*

THE SOULS

retold by Guadalupe Baca-Vaughn

Si es verdad, allá va, Si es mentira, queda urdida.[1]
(If it be true, so it is. If it be false, so be it.)

There was once an old lady who had raised a niece since she was a tiny baby. She had taught the girl to be good, obedient, and industrious, but the girl was very shy and timid and spent much time praying, especially to the Souls in Purgatory.[2]

As the girl grew older and very beautiful, the old woman began to worry that when she died her niece would be left all alone in the world, a world which her niece saw only through innocent eyes. The old lady prayed daily to all the saints in heaven for their <u>intercession</u> to Our Lord that he might send some good man who would fall in love with her niece and marry her; then she could die in peace.

As it happens, the old woman did chores for a *comadre*[3] who had a rooming house. Among her tenants there was a seemingly rich merchant who one day said that he would like to get married if he could find a nice, quiet girl who knew how to keep house and be a good wife and mother to his children when they came.

The old lady opened her ears and began to smile and scheme in her mind, for she could imagine her niece married to the nice gentleman. She told the merchant that he could find all that he was looking for in her niece, who was a jewel, a piece of gold, and so gifted that she could even catch birds while they were flying!

The gentleman became interested and said that he would like to meet the girl and would go to her house the next day.

The old woman ran home as fast as she could; she appeared to be flying. When she got home all out of breath, she called her niece and told her to straighten up the house and get herself ready for the next day, as there was a gentleman who would be calling. She told her to be sure to wash her hair and brush it until it shone like the sun and to put on her best dress, for in this meeting her future was at stake.

The poor timid girl was <u>dumbfounded</u>. She went to her room and knelt before her favorite *retablo*[4] of the Souls in Purgatory. "Please," she prayed, "don't let my aunt do something rash to embarrass us both."

The next day she obediently prepared herself for the meeting. When the merchant arrived, he asked her if she could spin. "Spin?" answered

1. *Si es verdad, allá va, / Si es mentira, queda urdida* (sē ĕs vĕr-däd′ ä-yä′ vä sē ĕs mĕn-tē′rä kĕ′dä o͞or-dē′dä) *Spanish.*
2. **Souls in Purgatory:** spirits of dead people in a place where they undergo temporary suffering to make up for their sins on Earth.
3. *comadre* (kô-mä′drĕ) *Spanish:* a female friend.
4. *retablo* (rĕ-tä′blô) *Spanish:* a wooden panel on which a religious picture is painted or carved.

WORDS TO KNOW

intercession (ĭn′tər-sĕsh′ən) *n.* the act of asking for something that will benefit someone else
dumbfounded (dŭm′foun′dĭd) *adj.* speechless with shock or amazement

IN PURGATORY

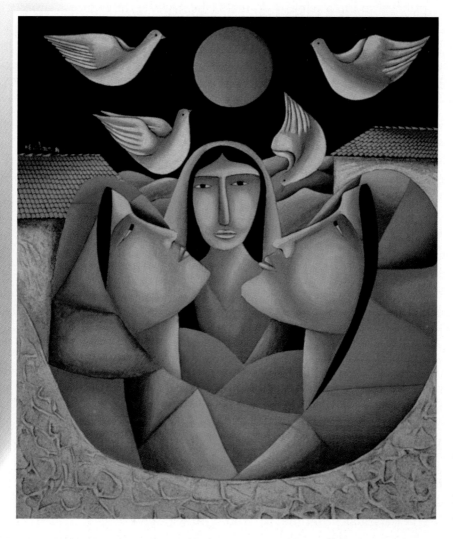

En busqueda de la paz
[In search of peace],
Alfredo Linares.

the old woman, while the poor embarrassed girl stood by with bowed head. "Spin! The hanks[5] disappear so fast you would think she was drinking them like water."

The merchant left three hanks of linen to be spun by the following day. "What have you done, *Tía?*"[6] the poor girl asked. "You know I can't spin!" "Don't sell yourself short," the old lady replied with twinkling eyes. "Where is your faith in God, the Souls in Purgatory? You

pray to them every day. They will help you. Just wait and see!" Sobbing, the girl ran to her room and knelt down beside her bed and began to pray, often raising her head to the *retablo* of the Souls in Purgatory which hung on the wall beside her bed. After she quieted down, she thought she heard a soft sound behind her. She

---

5. **hanks:** bundles of fibers that are spun into thread or yarn.
6. *tía* (tē′ä) *Spanish:* aunt.

turned and saw three beautiful ghosts dressed in white, smiling at her. "Do not be concerned," they said. "We will help you in gratitude for all the good you have done for us." Saying this, each one took a hank of linen and in a wink spun the linen into thread as fine as hair.

The following day when the merchant came, he was astonished to see the beautiful linen and was very pleased. "Didn't I tell you, sir?" said the old lady with pride and joy. The gentleman asked the girl if she could sew. Before the surprised girl could answer, the old aunt cried, "Sew? Of course she can sew. Her sewing is like ripe cherries in the mouth of a dragon." The merchant then left a piece of the finest linen to be made into three shirts. The poor girl cried bitterly, but her aunt told her not to worry, that her devotion to the Poor Souls would get her out of this one too, as they had shown how much they loved her on the previous day.

The three ghosts were waiting for the girl beside her bed when she went into her room, crying miserably. "Don't cry, little girl," they said. "We will help you again, for we know your aunt, and she knows what she is doing and why."

The ghosts went to work cutting and snipping and sewing. In a flash they had three beautiful shirts finished with the finest stitches and the tiniest seams.

The next morning when the gentleman came to see if the girl had finished the shirts, he could not believe his eyes. "They are lovely; they seem to have been made in heaven," he said.

This time the merchant left a vest of rare satin to be embroidered. He thought he would try this girl for the third and last time. The girl cried desperately and could not even reproach

"Wedding? Am I going to get married?"

her aunt. She had decided that she would not ask any more favors of the Souls. She went to her room and lay across the bed and cried and cried. When she finally sat up and dried her tears, she saw the three ghosts smiling at her. "We will help you again, but this time we have a condition, and that is that you will invite us to your wedding." "Wedding? Am I going to get married?" she asked in surprise. "Yes," they said, "and very soon."

The next day a very happy gentleman came for his vest, for he was sure that the lovely girl would have it ready for him. But he was not prepared for the beauty of the vest. The colors were vibrant and beautifully matched. The embroidery looked like a painting. It took his breath away. Without hesitation, he asked the old lady for her niece's hand in marriage. "For," he said, "this vest looks as if it was not touched by human hands but by angels!"

The old woman danced with joy and could hardly contain her happiness. She gave her consent at once. The merchant left to arrange for the wedding. Wringing her hands, the poor girl cried, "But *Tía,* what am I going to do when he finds out that I can't do any of those things?" "Don't worry, my *palomita,*[7] the Blessed Souls[8] will get you out of this trouble too. You wait and see!"

Almost at once the old woman went to her *comadre* to tell her the good news and to ask her to help get ready for the wedding. Soon everything was ready.

The poor girl did not know how to invite the Souls to her wedding. She timidly went and

---

7. *palomita* (pä-lô-mē′tä) *Spanish:* little dove.
8. **Blessed Souls:** the holy spirits of the dead.

WORDS TO KNOW

reproach (rĭ-prōch′) *v.* to criticize; blame

stood beside her bed and asked the *retablo* to come to her wedding.

The great day finally arrived. The girl looked beautiful in the gown which the merchant had brought as part of her *donas*.[9] Everyone in the village had been invited to the wedding.

During the fiesta when everyone was drinking *brindes*[10] to the bride and groom and the music was playing, three ugly hags came to the *sala*[11] and stood waiting for the groom to come and welcome them in. One of the hags had an arm that reached to the floor and dragged; the other arm was short. The second hag was bent almost double and had to turn her head sideways to look up. The third hag had bulging, bloodshot eyes like a lobster. "Jesús María," cried the groom. "Who are those ugly creatures?" "They are aunts of my father, whom I invited to my wedding," answered the bride, knowing quite well who they might be. The groom, being well-bred, went at once to greet the ugly hags. He took them to their seats and brought them refreshments. Very casually, he asked the first hag, "Tell me, señora, why is one of your arms so long and the other one short?" "My son," she answered, "my arms are like that because I spin so much."

The groom went to his wife and said, "Go at once and tell the servants to burn your spinning wheel, and never let me see a spinning wheel in my house; never let me see you spinning, ever!"

The groom went to the second hag and asked her why she was so humped over. "My son," she replied, "I am that way from embroidering on a frame so much." The groom went to his wife and whispered, "Burn your embroidery frame at once, and never let me see you embroider another thing."

Next, the groom went to the third hag and asked, "Why are your eyes so bloodshot and bulging?" "My son, it is because I sew so much and bend over while sewing." She had hardly finished speaking when the groom went to his wife and said, "Take your needles and thread and bury them. I never want to see you sewing, never! If I see you sewing, I will divorce you and send you far away, for the wise man learns from others' painful experiences."

Well—so the Souls, in spite of being holy, can also be rascals.

Colorín, colorado, ya mi cuento se ha acabado.[12]

(Scarlet or ruby red, my story has been said.) ❖

---

9. *donas* (dô′näs) *Spanish:* wedding presents a man gives to his bride.
10. *brindes* (brēn′dĕs) *Spanish:* drinks to someone's health or happiness; toasts.
11. *sala* (sä′lä) *Spanish:* a large room for entertaining.
12. *Colorín, colorado, ya mi cuento se ha acabado* (cô-lôr-ēn′ cô-lô-rä′dô yä mē kwēn′tô sĕ ä ä-kä-bä′dô) *Spanish.*

GUADALUPE BACA-VAUGHN

As a little girl, Guadalupe Baca-Vaughn (1905–) first heard "The Souls in Purgatory" from her aunt, "who told me the stories she heard as a child in Mexico." Baca-Vaughn was born in New Mexico, the birthplace of her father's family. Her mother's family was from California when it was still part of Mexico.

Baca-Vaughn was an interpreter and censor for the U.S. Government in El Paso, Texas, during World War II. She eventually returned to New Mexico. Over the next 35 years, she taught elementary and junior high school students.

After retiring, she received a grant to teach the history, culture, and stories of Northern New Mexico to children in local schools. Worried about people losing their cultural heritage, she says, "We should know what went before us."

The Girl in the Lavender Dress

retold by Maureen Scott

Copyright © Andrea Brooks

My grandmother was, I always believed, a truthful woman. She paid her taxes. She went to church. She considered the Lord's business as her own. When her children told lies, they soon saw the light of truth. They went to bed without any supper, the taste of soap still <u>pungent</u> on their tongues.

That's why the story that follows bothers me so much. It just *can't* be true. Of course, Grandma was 92 when she told it to me and her mind had started to fail. She might have really believed it. Who knows? Maybe you will, too.

I'll try to tell the story just the way she told it to me. She was in a nursing home then. It was late at night and the two of us were alone in the TV room. Grandma's eyelids hung low over her eyes. She worked her wrinkled jaw a few times and began:

It all happened about '42 or '43 [Grandma said]. It was during World War II. We didn't have much gas in those days. No one did. So whenever Herbert took the car somewhere, I tried to go along for the ride.

We lived in Vermont in those days. This time I'm thinking of, Herbert had some business in Claremont. That's in New Hampshire, just across the river. Well, seems Herbert had saved up the gas to go by car. About 25 miles. He said we could leave after work Friday. That night we'd have us a good restaurant meal. Maybe see a movie, too. Then we'd stay in a hotel and drive back the next day.

I don't remember the month, exactly. Sometime in the fall, 'cause it was cool. It was a misty night. I remember Herbert had to keep the wipers going. And it was after dusk when we first saw her. I know it was dark, 'cause I remember first seeing her in the lights ahead.

Neither Herbert nor I spoke. He slowed down, and the girl stopped walking. She just stood there on our side of the road. Not hitching, exactly, but she sure looked like she wanted a ride. It was a lonely road, and there weren't many cars.

First Herbert passed her, going real slow. Then he backed up to where she was. I rolled down my window. She was a pretty little thing, about eighteen or twenty. A round face and big round eyes. Brown hair, cut straight. The mist kind of made her face shine. But the funny thing was what she was wearing: only a thin lavender party dress. In that weather!

Well, I don't remember that anybody did any asking. I just opened the door and leaned forward. She climbed into the back seat, and Herbert started up again. Finally I asked her where she was going.

"Claremont." That was all she said at first. She had a light, breathless voice, like it took a whole lungful of air to say that one word.

"You're lucky," Herbert said. "We're going all the way."

The girl didn't reply. We rode on a little ways. I turned around once or twice, but the girl just smiled, sort of sadly. Anyhow, I didn't want to stare at her. But who was she, and why was she walking on a lonely road at night? I've never been the kind to pry into other people's business. So what I did then was, well, I'd taken off my sweater when the car got warm. I offered it to her, and she put it on.

The mist turned to light rain. Just before we got to the river, Herbert broke the silence. "Where are you going in Claremont, Miss?"

There was no reply.

"It's coming on to rain," Herbert said. "And we got time to deliver you."

"Oh," the girl breathed. "Could you *really*? That would be—that would be *nice*. To my parents' house. Corner of Bond and Mason."

"Claremont must be a nice place to grow up," I said, but again, there was no sound from the back of the car. You couldn't even hear her breathing. I just settled back into my seat and enjoyed the trip. We crossed the bridge, headed into town, and Herbert turned right onto Bond Street.

Back in the car, we sped away through the night.

We rode along, looking at the street signs. Mason was way out. There was only one house on the corner, on the opposite side. Herbert made a U-turn and stopped the car.

There was no one in the rear seat!

I looked at Herbert. He looked at me, his eyes popping. I pulled myself up so I could see the back floor. Nothing. Just a little wetness where her feet had been.

"Where'd she get out?" Herbert asked.

"At a stoplight?" I wondered. But we both knew it couldn't be. It was a two-door car, so we'd know it if a door opened. Both of us looked at the rear windows. They were closed, as they had been. Neither of us had felt a draft.

Yet there had to be some explanation. "Come," Herbert said. We hurried toward the house. It was a big square boxlike building. Lights were on in nearly every room. Splotches of brightness covered the wet lawn.

The door had a name on it: J. R. Bullard. It was opened by a long-faced man about fifty.

"Excuse me," Herbert said, "but there seems to be some mystery. You see, your daughter—"

"Daughter?" said the man. "Why, we don't have any daughter." A small woman, some years younger, now stood at his side.

"Well—" Herbert began.

"We *did* have a daughter," the woman said. "But Carol is deceased, you see. She was buried in Calhoun Cemetery four months ago."

Herbert gripped my arm. We both knew Calhoun Cemetery: it was on the Vermont side of the river. "Then who—?" Herbert wondered aloud. Suddenly he looked embarrassed. "Excuse us," he muttered. "It's all a—a mistake."

"Just a minute," I said. "Would you mind telling us what Carol looked like?"

The couple exchanged glances. If they were worried, it wasn't about Carol. It was about us. "A little on the short side," the woman said almost to herself. "A round face. Big round eyes. Dark, straight hair, cut in bangs."

Herbert's hand was a lobster claw on my elbow. We excused ourselves in a hurry. Back in the car, we sped away through the night. Then we drove around for a long time, looking. Across the bridge. Down every little road. Back into Claremont. Near every stoplight. Along Bond Street.

But we both knew the search was futile. There was only one answer. What we'd had in our car, sitting on the back seat and even talking, was the ghost of Carol Bullard. And the amazing thing was that we had proof. A ghost, you see, cannot cross water. That was why, when we came to the river, the ghost had only one choice: to disappear!

Grandma stopped talking, and I thought that was the end of her incredible story. But no—there was more:

And that isn't all [Grandma went on]. That night—the night that it happened—we were both pretty edgy. Didn't get much sleep, either. Not till the next morning did we think of my sweater. It had disappeared with the ghost.

That was a really good sweater, almost new. You see, we didn't have much money, and it was wartime. Clothes were hard to come by. But once in a while I'd blow a week's pay on something really nice, something that would last for years—like that sweater.

Now listen: it's like this. On the way home, we thought we'd swing around by Calhoun Cemetery. We wanted to find a certain gravestone, the one that would say "Carol Bullard" on it. So we did just that. It took a long time, but finally we found the new graves. And there, at last, was the stone. A small flat stone. Just "Carol Bullard" on it. No dates; nothing more. But next to the stone, neatly folded up, *was my sweater!*

True—or not? You decide. ❖

RESPONDING
OPTIONS

LITERATURE CONNECTION PROJECT 1

Plan a Storytelling Contest Organize a contest that involves the telling of tall tales and stories. Decide who will be organizers and judges, researchers, story writers, storytellers, and designers. Work in teams, and refer to the suggestions presented as you play your part in this project.

Organizers and Judges Decide on the rules of the contest. Include guidelines for judging the storytelling and any other elements that are significant to your contest planning. Assign a team of designers to create the awards that will be given to winners of the contest.

Researchers and Story Writers You can either find existing stories to retell or create your own stories. Keep in mind that tall tales include exaggeration, humor, and incredible feats. Your stories can be funny, strange, or both. Work from an outline or storyboards to create your story.

Storytellers Concentrate on telling the story effectively. Rehearse it several times. If you are using visual aids, practice handling them. Speak at a comfortable pitch, placing extra stress on important words. Let your enthusiasm show, and look people in the eye as if you were having a one-on-one conversation.

SOCIAL STUDIES CONNECTION PROJECT 2

Learn About the "Day of the Dead" Both the native peoples of Mexico and the conquering Roman Catholic Spaniards believed that the spirits of the dead return to Earth to visit the living. An important festival in Mexico today is El Día de los Muertos (ĕl dē'ä dĕ lôs mwĕr'tôs), which means "the Day of the Dead."

Find out about El Día de los Muertos. Research when the festival occurs, and why and how it is celebrated. Your research could include a visit to a museum that features Day of the Dead *ofrendas* (ô-frĕn'däs), or offerings to the dead.

Many Mexican and Mexican-American families celebrate the festival in their homes. Re-create some aspect of the festival in the form of paintings, drawings, or clay sculpture. You could even construct an *ofrenda*. Share your results with the class.

Day of the Dead Festival		
When	**Why**	**How**

Discover 16th-Century Mexico Find out about how the Spaniards conquered the Aztecs in the early 1500s in what is now south-central Mexico. Present your findings in the form of a television news broadcast with visual aids, perhaps including a historical map and time line. You could use an actual television news program as a model. If possible, a partner could videotape your report.

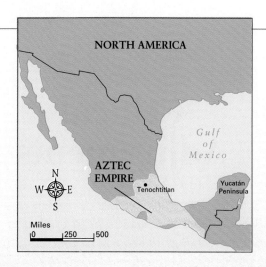

NORTH AMERICA

Gulf
of
Mexico

AZTEC
EMPIRE
• Tenochtitlan

Yucatán
Peninsula

N W E S

Miles
0   250   500

ACROSS CULTURES MINI-PROJECTS

Investigate Forest Conservation In the United States, the early settlers approached the nation's expansive forest land as though it would last forever, clearing land and felling more trees than they really needed. By 1891, a movement to save and manage the forests was underway. Find out about forest conservation from the 1890s to the present, and report your findings to the class. Present your statistics in the form of a graph.

Construct a *Retablo* The girl in "The Souls in Purgatory" prayed before a *retablo*. This painting of religious figures, often on wood, is one kind of *retablo*—a *retablo santo* (sän'tô). Today, another kind of *retablo*—a *retablo exvoto* (ĕs-vô'tô)—is far more common.

Use the library or Internet, or talk with a person of Mexican descent, to learn what is on a *retablo exvoto* and what it is used for. Then create one the girl might have made, or make one for yourself.

Compare and Contrast Tales There are more than 75 versions of the story "The Girl in the Lavender Dress." In the library, locate a version that is set in a different time or place. Use a Venn diagram, like the one shown, to compare and contrast the version you find in the library with the one in the book.

Version on page 710   Alternate version

MORE ABOUT THE CULTURES

- *Bold Journey: West with Lewis and Clark* by Charles Bohner
- *In This Proud Land: The Story of a Mexican-American Family* by Bernard Wolf
- *The United States in the Mexican War* by Don Lawson
- *Windmills, Bridges and Old Machines: Discovering Our Industrial Past* by David Weltzman

LINKS TO UNIT TWO

Critical Adjustments

In Unit Two, the selections explore decisive actions that the characters must take at critical moments—actions that may change the course of their lives forever. Similarly, in the tales you will read next, the characters find themselves in situations in which they must make crucial decisions and adjustments.

SOUTHEASTERN U.S.

Brer Possum's Dilemma

retold by Jackie Torrence

By the middle of the 19th century, slaves made up nearly one-third of the population of the Southern United States. Slavery flourished in the South, which was heavily dependent on cotton and tobacco plantations that required large numbers of workers. Slaves on these plantations came from a variety of African cultures. As they mingled traditions and swapped stories, they produced new kinds of folk tales and fables. Some of these African-American fables featured the "Brer" animals.

M'su Carencro and Mangeur de Poulet

retold by J. J. Reneaux

During the 1750s, the British and French were fighting for control of eastern North America in the French and Indian War. As part of the struggle, the British drove French settlers out of the colony of Acadia in eastern Canada. Many migrated to Louisiana. They brought with them their heritage of Acadian French culture and folk tales such as this one, which they gradually adapted to fit their new land. The Acadians eventually came to be known as Cajuns.

John Henry

traditional

Though he is now a part of American folklore, John Henry, an African American, was a real man. It was the early 1870s and railroads were changing the face of the United States. Henry was working on the Chesapeake and Ohio Railroad in West Virginia. His job was to dig railroad tunnels—work that required great strength. When a new invention—a steam drill—was brought to the railroad, Henry tested his strength by pitting himself against the machine, as this folk ballad tells.

Aunty Misery

retold by Judith Ortiz Cofer

Christopher Columbus claimed the island of Puerto Rico for Spain in 1493. Most Puerto Ricans are descended from Spanish settlers; others have African or Arawak (the island's original inhabitants) ancestry. These cultures blended over time to produce the island's rich folklore, with stories like the folk tale of Aunty Misery.

AS YOU READ . . .

Decide whether the tale explains a mystery or a challenge of life.

Determine whether it celebrates a human strength or pokes fun at a human weakness.

Decide what lesson it teaches.

JOHN HENRY

TRADITIONAL

When John Henry was a little boy,
Sitting upon his father's knee,
His father said, "Look here, my boy,
You must be a steel driving man[1] like me,
5   You must be a steel driving man like me."

John Henry went up on the mountain,
Just to drive himself some steel.
The rocks was so tall and John Henry so small,
He said lay down hammer and squeal,
10   He said lay down hammer and squeal.

John Henry had a little wife,
And the dress she wore was red;
The last thing before he died,
He said, "Be true to me when I'm dead,
15   Oh, be true to me when I'm dead."

John Henry's wife ask him for fifteen cents,
And he said he didn't have but a dime,
Said, "If you wait till the rising sun goes down,
I'll borrow it from the man in the mine,
20   I'll borrow it from the man in the mine."

John Henry started on the right-hand side,
And the steam drill started on the left.
He said, "Before I'd let that steam drill beat me down,
I'd hammer my fool self to death,
25   Oh, I'd hammer my fool self to death."

---

1. **steel driving man:** a person who used a ten-pound
   hammer to drive a steel drill into rock in order to make
   holes for explosives.

His Hammer in His Hand, Palmer C. Hayden (1890–1973). From the John Henry Series, Museum of African American Art, Los Angeles, Palmer C. Hayden Collection, gift of Miriam A. Hayden. Photo by Armando Solis.

The steam drill started at half-past six,
John Henry started the same time.
John Henry struck bottom at half-past eight,
And the steam drill didn't bottom till nine,
30 And the steam drill didn't bottom till nine.

John Henry said to his captain,
"A man, he ain't nothing but a man,
Before I'd let that steam drill beat me down,
I'd die with the hammer in my hand,
35 Oh, I'd die with the hammer in my hand."

John Henry said to his shaker,[2]
"Shaker, why don't you sing just a few more rounds?
And before the setting sun goes down,
You're gonna hear this hammer of mine sound,
40 You're gonna hear this hammer of mine sound."

---

2. **shaker:** the person who holds the steel drill for the steel
   driving man and shakes the drill to remove it from the rock.

John Henry hammered on the mountain,
He hammered till half-past three,
He said, "This big Bend Tunnel on the C. & O. road[3]
Is going to be the death of me,
45 Lord! is going to be the death of me."

John Henry had a little baby boy,
You could hold him in the palm of your hand.
The last words before he died,
"Son, you must be a steel driving man,
50 Son, you must be a steel driving man."

John Henry had a little woman,
And the dress she wore was red,
She went down the railroad track and never come back,
Said she was going where John Henry fell dead,
55 Said she was going where John Henry fell dead.

John Henry hammering on the mountain,
As the whistle blew for half-past two,
The last word I heard him say,
"Captain, I've hammered my insides in two,
60 Lord, I've hammered my insides in two."

---

3. **big Bend . . . road:** Construction work on the Big Bend
   Tunnel on the Chesapeake & Ohio Railroad in West
   Virginia took place from 1870 to 1873.

Brer Possum's Dilemma

retold by Jackie Torrence

Brer Possum, Barry Moser. From *Jump, Again!* by Van Dyke Parks, published by Harcourt Brace Jovanovich in 1987. Illustration Copyright © Barry Moser. Reprinted with permission from the artist.

Back in the days when the animals could talk, there lived ol' Brer[1] Possum. He was a fine feller. Why, he never liked to see no critters in trouble. He was always helpin' out, a-doin' somethin' for others.

Ever' night, ol' Brer Possum climbed into a persimmon tree, hung by his tail, and slept all night long. And each mornin', he climbed outa the tree and walked down the road to sun 'imself.

One mornin' as he walked, he come to a big hole in the middle of the road. Now, ol' Brer Possum was kind and gentle, but he was also nosey, so he went over to the hole and looked in. All at once, he stepped back, 'cause layin' in the bottom of that hole was ol' Brer Snake with a brick on his back.

Brer Possum said to 'imself, "I best git on outa here, 'cause ol' Brer Snake is mean and evil and low-down, and if I git to stayin' around 'im, he jist might git to bitin' me."

So Brer Possum went on down the road.

But Brer Snake had seen Brer Possum, and he commenced to callin' for 'im.

"Help me, Brer Possum."

Brer Possum stopped and turned around. He said to 'imself, "That's ol' Brer Snake a-callin' me. What do you reckon he wants?"

Well, ol' Brer Possum was kindhearted, so he went back down the road to the hole, stood at the edge, and looked down at Brer Snake.

"Was that you a-callin' me? What do you want?"

Brer Snake looked up and said, "I've been down here in this hole for a mighty long time with this brick on my back. Won't you help git it offa me?"

Brer Possum thought.

"Now listen here, Brer Snake. I knows you. You's mean and evil and low-down, and if'n I was to git down in that hole and git to liftin' that brick offa your back, you wouldn't do nothin' but bite me."

Ol' Brer Snake just hissed.

"Maybe not. Maybe not. Maaaaaaaybe not."

Brer Possum said, "I ain't sure 'bout you at all. I jist don't know. You're a-goin' to have to let me think about it."

So ol' Brer Possum thought—he thought high, and he thought low—and jist as he was thinkin', he looked up into a tree and saw a dead limb a-hangin' down. He climbed into the tree, broke off the limb, and with that ol' stick, pushed that brick offa Brer Snake's back. Then he took off down the road.

Brer Possum thought he was away from ol' Brer Snake, when all at once he heard somethin'.

"Help me, Brer Possum."

Brer Possum said, "Oh, no, that's him agin."

But bein' so kindhearted, Brer Possum turned around, went back to the hole, and stood at the edge.

"Brer Snake, was that you a-callin' me? What do you want now?"

Ol' Brer Snake looked up outa the hole and hissed.

"I've been down here for a mighty long time, and I've gotten a little weak, and the sides of this ol' hole are too slick for me to climb. Do you think you can lift me outa here?"

Brer Possum thought.

"Now, you jist wait a minute. If'n I was to git down into that hole and lift you outa there, you wouldn't do nothin' but bite me."

Brer Snake hissed.

"Maybe not. Maybe not. Maaaaaaaybe not."

Brer Possum said, "I jist don't know. You're a-goin' to have to give me time to think about this."

So ol' Brer Possum thought.

And as he thought, he jist happened to look down there in that hole and see that ol' dead limb. So he pushed the limb underneath ol' Brer Snake, and he lifted 'im outa the hole,

---

1. **Brer** *Southern dialect:* Brother.

way up into the air, and throwed 'im into the high grass.

Brer Possum took off a-runnin' down the road.

Well, he thought he was away from ol' Brer Snake when all at once he heard somethin'.

"Help me, Brer Possum."

Brer Possum thought, "That's him agin."

But bein' so kindhearted, he turned around, went back to the hole, and stood there a-lookin' for Brer Snake. Brer Snake crawled outa the high grass just as slow as he could, stretched 'imself out across the road, rared up, and looked at ol' Brer Possum.

Then he hissed. "I've been down there in that ol' hole for a mighty long time, and I've gotten a little cold 'cause the sun didn't shine. Do you think you could put me in your pocket and git me warm?"

Brer Possum said, "Now you listen here, Brer Snake. I knows you. You's mean and evil and low-down, and if'n I put you in my pocket, you wouldn't do nothin' but bite me."

Brer Snake hissed.

"Maybe not. Maybe not. Maaaaaaaybe not."

"No, sireee, Brer Snake. I knows you. I jist ain't a-goin' to do it."

But jist as Brer Possum was talkin' to Brer Snake, he happened to git a real good look at 'im. He was a-layin' there lookin' so pitiful, and Brer Possum's great big heart began to feel sorry for ol' Brer Snake.

"All right," said Brer Possum. "You must be cold. So jist this once I'm a-goin' to put you in my pocket."

So ol' Brer Snake coiled up jist as little as he could, and Brer Possum picked 'im up and put 'im in his pocket.

Brer Snake laid quiet and still—so quiet and still that Brer Possum even forgot that he was a-carryin' 'im around. But all of a sudden, Brer Snake commenced to crawlin' out, and he turned and faced Brer Possum and hissed.

"I'm a-goin' to bite you."

But Brer Possum said, "Now wait a minute. Why are you a-goin' to bite me? I done took that brick offa your back, I got you outa that hole, and I put you in my pocket to git you warm. Why are you a-goin' to bite me?"

Brer Snake hissed.

"You knowed I was a snake before you put me in your pocket."

And when you're mindin' your own business and you spot trouble, don't never trouble trouble 'til trouble troubles you. ❖

JACKIE TORRENCE

Growing up in North Carolina, Jackie Torrence loved hearing the stories told by her family, including her grandfather, who was the son of a slave. She first heard "Brer Possum's Dilemma" from her Aunt Mildred.

But it was not until a chance incident in 1972 that Torrence began her storytelling career at the library where she worked. She was asked to substitute for a storyteller. Soon she was captivating children and adults across the country, and she became known

1944–

as The Story Lady. Now Torrence spends most of the year away from her North Carolina home, telling folk tales and ghost stories and conducting workshops.

Torrence says, "I decided that I had a dream and I was either going to let it take me down or I was going to ride it and see where it goes. I'm still riding."

OTHER WORKS available on audiocassette: *Brer Rabbit Stories, Tales for Scary Times, Country Characters*

Aunty Misery

retold by Judith Ortiz Cofer

This is a story about an old, very old woman who lived alone in her little hut with no other company than a beautiful pear tree that grew at her door. She spent all her time taking care of her pear tree. But the neighborhood children drove the old woman crazy by stealing her fruit. They would climb her tree, shake its delicate limbs, and run away with armloads of golden pears, yelling insults at "Aunty Misery," as they called her.

One day, a pilgrim[1] stopped at the old woman's hut and asked her permission to spend the night under her roof. Aunty Misery saw that he had an honest face and bade the traveler come in. She fed him and made a bed for him in front of her hearth. In the morning while he was getting ready to leave, the stranger told her that he would show his gratitude for her hospitality by granting her one wish.

"There is only one thing that I desire," said Aunty Misery.

"Ask, and it shall be yours," replied the stranger, who was a sorcerer[2] in disguise.

"I wish that anyone who climbs up my pear tree should not be able to come back down until I permit it."

"Your wish is granted," said the stranger, touching the pear tree as he left Aunty Misery's house.

And so it happened that when the children came back to taunt[3] the old woman and to steal her fruit, she stood at her window watching them. Several of them shimmied up the trunk of the pear tree and immediately got stuck to it as

---

1. **pilgrim:** a wanderer; traveler.

2. **sorcerer:** a person who practices witchcraft or magic.

3. **taunt** (tônt): to make fun of in a mean way.

if with glue. She let them cry and beg her for a long time before she gave the tree permission to let them go, on the condition that they never again steal her fruit or bother her.

Time passed, and both Aunty Misery and her tree grew bent and gnarled with age. One day another traveler stopped at her door. This one looked suffocated and exhausted, so the old woman asked him what he wanted in her village. He answered her in a voice that was dry and hoarse, as if he had swallowed a desert: "I am Death, and I have come to take you with me."

Thinking fast, Aunty Misery said, "All right, but before I go I would like to pluck some pears from my beloved pear tree to remember how much pleasure it brought me in this life. But I am a very old woman and cannot climb to the tallest branches where the best fruit is; will you be so kind as to do it for me?"

With a heavy sigh like wind through a catacomb,[4] Death climbed the pear tree. Immediately he became stuck to it as if with glue. And no matter how much he cursed and threatened, Aunty Misery would not give the tree permission to release Death.

Many years passed, and there were no deaths in the world. The people who make their living from death began to protest loudly. The doctors claimed no one bothered to come in for examinations or treatments anymore, because they did not fear dying; the pharmacists' business suffered too, because medicines are, like magic potions, bought to prevent or postpone the inevitable; the priests and undertakers were unhappy with the situation also, for obvious reasons. There were also many old folks tired of life who wanted to pass on to the next world to rest from the miseries of this one.

Aunty Misery realized all this, and not wishing to be unfair, she made a deal with her prisoner, Death: if he promised not ever to come for her again, she would give him his freedom. He agreed. And that is why so long as the world is the world, Aunty Misery will always live. ❖

---

4. **catacomb** (kăt′ə-kōm′): an underground arrangement of tunnels or chambers, used as a burial place.

JUDITH ORTIZ COFER

As a child, Judith Ortiz Cofer grew up in two different worlds—she was born in Puerto Rico but moved to Paterson, New Jersey, as a young child. Where she lived depended on her father's U.S. Navy assignments—whenever he was at sea, she returned to Puerto Rico. Both worlds influenced her writing.

In Puerto Rico, she listened to her grandmother's stories in Spanish under a giant mango tree, surrounded by her extended family. It was there, Ortiz Cofer says, "that I first began to feel the power of words."

In New Jersey, she spent much time by herself, building up "an arsenal of [English] words by becom-

1952–

ing an insatiable reader of books." She also served as her mother's interpreter.

Ortiz Cofer left her two worlds to attend college in Georgia and then to teach. She has won such honors as the 1990 Pushcart Prize for Nonfiction and the 1994 O. Henry Award for outstanding American short stories.

In a 1992 article in *Glamour* magazine, Ortiz Cofer wrote, "With the stories I tell . . . I try to get my audience past the particulars of my skin color, my accent or my clothes."

OTHER WORKS *Silent Dancing: A Partial Remembrance of a Puerto Rican Childhood*

M'su Carencro and
Mangeur de Poulet

retold by J. J. Reneaux

Detail of *Buzzards' Roost* (1985),
Hubert Shuptrine. Copyright ©
1985 S. Hill Corporation, all rights
reserved, used with permission.

One day M'su Carencro,[1] the buzzard, was sitting on a fence post real patient-like, just waiting for something to drop dead so he could have his supper, when who should come flapping up but ol' Mangeur de Poulet,[2] the chicken hawk. Mangeur de Poulet calls out, "Hey, *ça va, mon padnat?*"[3]

M'su Carencro shook his head and sighed, "*Ça va mal!*[4] Not good at all! I am so hungry. I been waitin' for days for somethin' to drop dead so I can have my supper."

"What you talkin' 'bout?" says know-it-all Chicken Hawk. "If you're so hungry, why don'tcha get out there and hunt you some good fresh meat? You got eyes, you got wings, you got a beak. Go for it! You got to look out for Number One in this world, *mon ami.*"[5]

"*Non, non, non,*" says Buzzard, "you don't understand. I'm s'posed to wait for somethin' to drop dead before I eat it. It's my job. That's

---

1. ***M'su Carencro*** (mə-sŏŏ′ kä-răn-krô) *Cajun dialect:* Mr. Buzzard. *M'su* is a short form of *Monsieur* (mə-syœ′), the French word for "Mister."
2. ***Mangeur de Poulet*** (män-zhür′ də pŏŏ-lä′) *French:* The literal translation of this name is "Chicken Eater."
3. *ça va, mon padnat?* (sä vä′ môn päd-nä′) *French and Cajun dialect:* how's it going, partner?
4. ***Ça va mal!*** (sä-vä-mäl′) *French:* It's going badly!
5. *mon ami* (mô′ nä-mē′) *French:* my friend.

just the way *le Bon Dieu*[6] made me."

"*Le Bon Dieu? Aw, non!* Don't waste your breath talkin' 'bout the Good God," says Chicken Hawk. "Besides, *mon ami,* even if there is a God, what makes you think he cares whether you get your supper? You gotta do like me, look out fo' yourself. Here, let ol' Chicken Hawk show you how to do that thang."

With that, Mangeur de Poulet leaped into the air and started wildly flapping about in daring loop-the-loops and crazy figure eights, showing off like you've never seen. All of a sudden, he spied a juicy little rabbit right down there next to Buzzard's fence post.

"Aw, this'll show Buzzard," he thought. Chicken Hawk took dead aim, and down he zoomed after that rabbit, faster and faster. But Rabbit was smart-smart. She saw Chicken Hawk's shadow closing in on her, and she jumped down her hole just as the big showoff came zooming in. By this time, Chicken Hawk was speeding so fast that his brakes couldn't save him, and he slammed smack dab into that fence post! And down he dropped—thunk!—deader than the post itself, right at Buzzard's feet.

Buzzard looked down at that dead chicken hawk. Then he looked up to heaven. He grins real big and says, "*Merci beaucoup,*[7] *mon Grand Bon Dieu!* Good God Almighty, thank you!" Then he jumps down off the fence post, smacks his lips, and says, "Suppertime!" ❖

---

6. *le Bon Dieu* (lə bôɴ dyœ′) *French:* the Good Lord.
7. *merci beaucoup* (mĕr-sē′ bō-kōō′) *French:* thank you very much.

J. J. RENEAUX

J. J. Reneaux (1955–) is "mostly Cajun," with a little Choctaw Indian and Irish mixed in. She grew up in southern Louisiana in a storytelling family. Reneaux carefully researches her culture and draws on her own experiences to tell traditional and contemporary Cajun stories and other "down-home" Southern tales. She likes stories that bring people together. "As my Daddy says, 'We're all fishing out of the same bass boat.'"

About the traditional tales she tells, Reneaux says, "We are lost in a forest. Our ancestors' stories are the bread crumbs. They give us answers. They tell us who we are." She thinks that the tales also reflect the zest for life so central to Cajun culture. A talented guitar player, Reneaux combines music and stories in her performances. "For me, telling stories without music is like eating gumbo without hot sauce."

In addition to performing at schools, festivals, and clubs across the United States and Canada, Reneaux has told her award-winning Cajun stories on national television and radio. Before becoming a storyteller, she was a tree planter, a fry cook, a nurse's aide, a session singer and musician, and an oil-rig worker. Not surprisingly, she describes herself as "a graduate of the school of life."

OTHER WORKS *Haunted Bayou and other Cajun Ghost Stories;* available on audiocassette: *Cajun Folktales, Cajun Ghost Stories*

LITERATURE CONNECTION PROJECT 1

Adapt a Tale into a One-Act Play Working in groups, choose one of the tales you have just read, or pick another tale from one of the same cultures. For example, you could find and adapt another Brer story.

Assign tasks within your group—writers, actors, costumers, stage builders, and so on. Refer to these suggestions as you produce your play.

Writers Map out the plot in outline form or on storyboards. Use plays in this book as models for formatting the script.

Actors After learning your lines, work on expressing your character's personal qualities.

Stage Crew List the costumes and props you will need. If you are adapting an animal story, consider how to design costumes or make-up that represents the animals. If possible, find appropriate music from the story's culture to accompany the performance.

Stage all of the plays in a drama festival. If possible, you could videotape the festival for other students in your school.

SOCIAL STUDIES CONNECTION PROJECT 2

Create a Cajun Display "M'su Carencro and Mangeur de Poulet" is a folk tale from Louisiana's Cajun people. Research Cajun culture. Then create a display for your classroom showing your findings.

• Make a map with captions showing the native country of the Cajuns and how their ancestors came to settle in Louisiana. Include pictures of the Louisiana bayou.

• Explore other Cajun folk tales and music of the culture.

• You could select and include a passage from Henry Wadsworth Longfellow's poem "Evangeline," which is about the Cajuns' Louisiana migration.

• Investigate Cajun food and include some recipes in your display.

Explore the History of the Railroads The building of the railroads played a major role in the development of the United States in the 19th century. Research the history of the railroads. Use encyclopedias and computer databases to find out details.

• Create a map of the United States. Use one color to show railroads that existed in 1835, a few years after the first tracks were laid. Use another color to show railroads existing in 1875. With a third color, show the railroads that existed by the end of the century.

• Then record your key findings on a time line. Add drawings or pictures of the locomotives and of the machines used to build the railroads.

ACROSS CULTURES MINI-PROJECTS

Living Forever Imagine that you could live forever, like Aunty Misery. Make a word web showing your thoughts about the joys and sorrows of never dying.

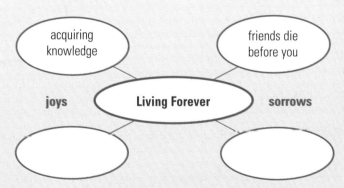

Ask an adult you know to do the same activity. Compare the similarities and differences between his or her word web and your own.

Compare Animal Tales Design a chart that indicates the similarities and differences between the two animal tales you have just read. Consider the purpose of each story, the animals' behavior, and how each story reflects its culture.

Research the Buzzard In the Cajun tale, M'su Carencro is referred to as the buzzard. In fact, the term "buzzard" is given to many species of birds around the world. Go to a library or use a computer database to find out about buzzards and their behavior. Which kind of bird do you think is featured in the story?

Write Morals The tale of Brer Possum ends with a moral—a lesson to be learned from the story. What lessons can be learned from the other stories? Write suitable morals for them.

MORE ABOUT THE CULTURES

• *America's Immigrants: Adventure in Eyewitness History* by Rhoda Hoff

• *The French and Indian Wars* by American Heritage

• *Railroads in the Days of Steam* by American Heritage

• *Slavery in America* by Robert Liston

PREVIEWING

Battle for Control

What battles for control does life present?
To what lengths should someone go in order to win?
Each of the tales in Unit Three explores a struggle for
control and considers the ways in which it affects the
characters' lives.

PACIFIC COAST

Raven and the Coming of Daylight

retold by Gail Robinson and Douglas Hill

The Haida (hī′də) were one of the Native American peoples who lived along the Pacific Northwest Coast. Resources in the area were plentiful, and the Haida developed an advanced society. This Haida myth is a trickster tale. Tricksters in folk tales are characters, often animals, who use cleverness to get what they want.

ECUADOR

The Five Eggs

retold by Frank Henius

Ecuador is a small South American country of great geographical variety. The mighty Andes mountains stand in stark contrast to the coastal lowlands in the west and the rain forests in the east. This geographical diversity and the mix of different traditions in Ecuador's history have contributed to its rich culture. The folk tale of "The Five Eggs" probably originated with the native mountain people, who had no written language.

Spotted Eagle and Black Crow

retold by Jenny Leading Cloud

The Oglala (ō-glä′lə), a Teton Sioux people living in what is now southwestern South Dakota, were famed hunters and warriors. When settlers overran their hunting lands in the 1860s, the Oglala, led by Chief Red Cloud, fought back with great pride and courage. This legend of two Oglala Sioux warriors demonstrates the high esteem in which bravery is held in the Sioux culture.

Pecos Bill

retold by Mary Pope Osborne

Before railroads reached Texas rangelands, trail drives were the best way of moving cattle to railroad stations for transport to markets in the East. Cowboys herded millions of longhorn cattle over dusty trails from the mid-1860s to the mid-1880s. Edward O'Reilly, inspired by stories of this rugged trail life and by tales of Paul Bunyan, wrote the first Pecos Bill tall tale in 1923. Other writers made more and more imaginative additions to O'Reilly's original tale.

AS YOU READ . . .

Decide who holds the power in these stories.

Notice who or what controls the fate of human beings.

Decide how each culture views conflict and power.

Pecos Bill

retold by Mary Pope Osborne

Copyright © Colin Poole.

Ask any coyote near the Pecos River in western Texas who was the best cowboy who ever lived, and he'll throw back his head and howl, "Ah-hooo!" If you didn't know already, that's coyote language for *Pecos Bill*.

When Pecos Bill was a little baby, he was as tough as a pine knot. He teethed on horseshoes instead of teething rings and played with grizzly bears instead of teddy bears. He could have grown up just fine in the untamed land of eastern Texas. But one day his pappy ran in from the fields, hollering, "Pack up, Ma! Neighbors movin' in fifty miles away! It's gettin' too crowded!"

Before sundown Bill's folks loaded their fifteen kids and all their belongings into their covered wagon and started west.

As they clattered across the desolate land of western Texas, the crushing heat nearly drove them all crazy. Baby Bill got so hot and cross that he began to wallop his big brothers. Pretty soon all fifteen kids were going at one another tooth and nail. Before they turned each other into catfish bait, Bill fell out of the wagon and landed *kerplop* on the sun-scorched desert.

The others were so busy fighting that they didn't even notice the baby was missing until it was too late to do anything about it.

Well, tough little Bill just sat there in the dirt, watching his family rattle off in a cloud of dust, until an old coyote walked over and sniffed him.

"Goo-goo!" Bill said.

Now it's an amazing coincidence, but "Goo-goo" happens to mean something similar to "Glad to meet you" in coyote language. Naturally the old coyote figured he'd come across one of his own kind. He gave Bill a big lick and picked him up by the scruff of the neck and carried him home to his den.

Bill soon discovered the coyote's kinfolk were about the wildest, roughest bunch you could imagine. Before he knew it, he was roaming the prairies with the pack. He howled at the moon, sniffed the brush, and chased lizards across the sand. He was having such a good time, scuttling about naked and dirty on all fours, that he completely forgot what it was like to be a human.

Pecos Bill's coyote days came to an end about seventeen years later. One evening as he was sniffing the sagebrush, a cowpoke came loping by on a big horse. "Hey, you!" he shouted. "What in the world are you?"

Bill sat on his haunches and stared at the feller.

"What *are* you?" asked the cowpoke again.

"Varmint," said Bill hoarsely, for he hadn't used his human voice in seventeen years.

"No, you ain't!"

"Yeah, I am. I got fleas, don't I?"

"Well, that don't mean nothing. A lot of Texans got fleas. The thing varmints got that you ain't got is a tail."

"Oh, yes. I do have a tail," said Pecos Bill.

"Lemme see it then," said the cowpoke.

Bill turned around to look at his rear end, and for the first time in his life he realized he didn't have a tail.

"Dang," he said. "But if I'm not a varmint, what am I?"

"You're a cowboy! So start acting like one!"

Bill just growled at the feller like any coyote worth his salt would. But deep down in his heart of hearts he knew the cowpoke was right. For the last seventeen years he'd had a sneaking suspicion that he was different from that pack of coyotes. For one thing, none of them seemed to smell quite as bad as he did.

So with a heavy heart he said good-bye to his four-legged friends and took off with the cowpoke for the nearest ranch.

Acting like a human wasn't all that easy for Pecos Bill. Even though he soon started dressing right, he never bothered to shave or comb his hair. He'd just throw some water on his face in the morning and go around the rest of the day looking like a wet dog. Ignorant cowpokes claimed Bill wasn't too smart. Some of the meaner ones liked to joke that he wore a ten-dollar hat on a five-cent head.

The truth was, Pecos Bill would soon prove to be one of the greatest cowboys who ever lived. He just needed to find the kind of folks who'd appreciate him. One night when he was licking his dinner plate, his ears perked up. A couple of ranch hands were going on about a gang of wild cowboys.

"Yep. Those fellas are more animal than human," one ranch hand was saying.

"Yep. Them's the toughest bunch I ever come across. Heck, they're so tough they can kick fire out of flint rock with their bare toes!"

"Yep. 'N' they like to bite nails in half for fun!"

"Who are these fellers?" asked Bill.

"The Hell's Gate Gang," said the ranch hand. "The mangiest, meanest, most low-down bunch of lowlife varmints that ever grew hair."

"Sounds like my kind of folks," said Bill, and before anyone could holler whoa, he jumped on his horse and took off for Hell's Gate Canyon.

Bill hadn't gone far when disaster struck. His horse stepped in a hole and broke its ankle.

"Dang!" said Bill as he stumbled up from the spill. He draped the lame critter around his neck and hurried on.

After he'd walked about a hundred more miles, Bill heard some mean rattling. Then a fifty-foot rattlesnake reared up its ugly head and stuck out its long, forked tongue, ready to fight.

"Knock it off, you scaly-hided fool. I'm in a hurry," Bill said.

The snake didn't give a spit for Bill's plans. He just rattled on.

Before the cussed varmint could strike, Bill had no choice but to knock him cross-eyed. "Hey, feller," he said, holding up the dazed snake. "I like your spunk. Come go with us." Then he wrapped the rattler around his arm and continued on his way.

After Bill had hiked another hundred miles with his horse around his neck and his snake around his arm, he heard a terrible growl. A huge mountain lion was crouching on a cliff, getting ready to leap on top of him.

"Don't jump, you mangy bobtailed fleabag!" Bill said.

Well, call any mountain lion a mangy bobtailed fleabag, and he'll jump on your back for sure. After this one leaped onto Bill, so much fur began to fly that it darkened the sky. Bill wrestled that mountain lion into a headlock, then squeezed him so tight that the big cat had to cry uncle.

When the embarrassed old critter started to slink off, Bill felt sorry for him. "Aw, c'mon, you big silly," he said. "You're more like me than most humans I meet."

He saddled up the cat, jumped on his back, and the four of them headed for the canyon, with the mountain lion screeching, the horse neighing, the rattler rattling, and Pecos Bill hollering a wild war whoop.

When the Hell's Gate Gang heard those noises coming from the prairie, they nearly fainted. They dropped their dinner plates, and their faces turned as white as bleached desert bones. Their knees knocked and their six-guns shook.

"Hey, there!" Bill said as he sidled up to their campfire, grinning. "Who's the boss around here?"

A nine-foot feller with ten pistols at his sides stepped forward and in a shaky voice said, "Stranger, I was. But from now on, it'll be you."

"Well, thanky, pardner," said Bill. "Get on with your dinner, boys. Don't let me interrupt."

Once Bill settled down with the Hell's Gate Gang, his true genius revealed itself. With his gang's help, he put together the biggest ranch in the Southwest. He used New Mexico as a corral and Arizona as a pasture. He invented tarantulas and scorpions as practical jokes. He also invented roping. Some say his rope was exactly as long as the equator; others argue it was two feet shorter.

The truth was, Pecos Bill would soon prove to be one of the greatest cowboys who ever lived.

Illustration by J. W. Stewart.

Things were going fine for Bill until Texas began to suffer the worst drought in its history. It was so dry that all the rivers turned as powdery as biscuit flour. The parched grass was catching fire everywhere. For a while Bill and his gang managed to lasso water from the Rio Grande. When that river dried up, they lassoed water from the Gulf of Mexico.

No matter what he did, though, Bill couldn't get enough water to stay ahead of the drought. All his horses and cows were starting to dry up and blow away like balls of tumbleweed. It was horrible.

Just when the end seemed near, the sky turned a deep shade of purple. From the distant mountains came a terrible roar. The cattle began to stampede, and a huge black funnel of a cyclone appeared, heading straight for Bill's ranch.

The rest of the Hell's Gate Gang shouted, "Help!" and ran.

But Pecos Bill wasn't scared in the least. "Yahoo!" he hollered, and he swung his lariat and lassoed that cyclone around its neck.

Bill held on tight as he got sucked up into the middle of the swirling cloud. He grabbed the cyclone by the ears and pulled himself onto her back. Then he let out a whoop and headed that twister across Texas.

The mighty cyclone bucked, arched, and screamed like a wild bronco. But Pecos Bill just held on with his legs and used his strong hands to wring the rain out of her wind. He wrung out rain that flooded Texas, New Mexico, and Arizona, until finally he slid off the shriveled-up funnel and fell into California. The earth sank about two hundred feet below sea level in the spot where Bill landed, creating the area known today as Death Valley.[1]

"There. That little waterin' should hold things for a while," he said, brushing himself off.

After his cyclone ride, no horse was too wild for Pecos Bill. He soon found a young colt that was as tough as a tiger and as crazy as a streak of lightning. He named the colt Widow Maker and raised him on barbed wire and dynamite. Whenever the two rode together, they back flipped and somersaulted all over Texas, loving every minute of it.

One day when Bill and Widow Maker were bouncing around the Pecos River, they came across an awesome sight: a wild-looking, red-haired woman riding on the back of the biggest catfish Bill had ever seen. The woman looked like she was having a ball, screeching, "Ride 'em, cowgirl!" as the catfish whipped her around in the air.

"What's your name?" Bill shouted.

"Slue-foot Sue! What's it to you?" she said. Then she war-whooped away over the windy water.

Thereafter all Pecos Bill could think of was Slue-foot Sue. He spent more and more time away from the Hell's Gate Gang as he wandered the barren cattle lands, looking for her. When he finally found her lonely little cabin, he was so love-struck he reverted to some of his old coyote ways. He sat on his haunches in the moonlight and began a-howling and ah-hooing.

Well, the good news was that Sue had a bit of coyote in her too, so she completely understood Bill's language. She stuck her head out her window and ah-hooed back to him that she loved him, too. Consequently Bill and Sue decided to get married.

On the day of the wedding Sue wore a beautiful white dress with a steel-spring bustle,

---

1. **Death Valley:** a desert area of California and Nevada, site of the Western Hemisphere's lowest point.

and Bill appeared in an elegant buckskin suit.

But after a lovely ceremony, a terrible catastrophe occurred. Slue-foot Sue got it into her head that she just had to have a ride on Bill's wild bronco, Widow Maker.

"You can't do that, honey," Bill said. "He won't let any human toss a leg over him but me."

"Don't worry," said Sue. "You know I can ride anything on four legs, not to mention what flies or swims."

Bill tried his best to talk Sue out of it, but she wouldn't listen. She was dying to buck on the back of that bronco. Wearing her white wedding dress with the bustle, she jumped on Widow Maker and kicked him with her spurs.

Well, that bronco didn't need any thorns in his side to start bucking to beat the band. He bounded up in the air with such amazing force that suddenly Sue was flying high into the Texas sky. She flew over plains and mesas, over canyons, deserts, and prairies. She flew so high that she looped over the new moon and fell back to earth.

But when Sue landed on her steel-spring bustle, she rebounded right back into the heavens! As she bounced back and forth between heaven and earth, Bill whirled his lariat above his head, then lassoed her. But instead of bringing Sue back down to earth, he got yanked into the night sky alongside her!

Together Pecos Bill and Slue-foot Sue bounced off the earth and went flying to the moon. And at that point Bill must have gotten some sort of foothold in a moon crater—because neither he nor Sue returned to earth. Not ever.

Folks figure those two must have dug their boot heels into some moon cheese and raised a pack of wild coyotes just like themselves. Texans'll tell you that every time you hear thunder rolling over the desolate land near the Pecos River, it's just Bill's family having a good laugh upstairs. When you hear a strange ah-hooing in the dark night, don't be fooled—that's the sound of Bill howling *on* the moon instead of *at* it. And when lights flash across the midnight sky, you can bet it's Bill and Sue riding the backs of some white-hot shooting stars. ❖

MARY POPE OSBORNE

When Mary Pope Osborne (1949–) was four, her father was in the army and was stationed in Austria along with his family. In her imagination, a nearby castle on a cliff became the home of Cinderella or Sleeping Beauty. She dreamed of worlds that she would later write about.

She studied drama, mythology, and religion at the University of North Carolina at Chapel Hill. After college, she traveled to faraway Eastern European and Asian countries, camping in a cave and riding in a rickety van.

One night, while attending the opening of a musical in Washington, D.C., she fell in love with Will Osborne, who was playing the role of Jesse James. Three years after their marriage, she wrote her first book, *Run, Run as Fast as You Can.* "Finally," Osborne says, "I knew exactly what I wanted to be when I grew up."

Since then, she has won many awards for her more than 25 books for children and young adults. "For years, I've been afraid of getting caught," says Osborne, "afraid that some day an authority figure will knock on my door and say, 'I think you're having too much fun here. Time to get serious and get a real job.'"

OTHER WORKS *Favorite Greek Myths; Haunted Waters; Best Wishes, Joe Brady; Mermaid Tales from Around the World*

The Five

retold by Frank Henius

In the fields near the city there lived two poor peasants named Juan and Juanica. They loved each other devotedly, but since they were very poor, they would sometimes go two or even three days without eating.

Once, after they had had nothing to eat for three days, Juanica asked her husband, "How long are we going to keep on living if we don't eat?"

"Don't worry," he said, "I will go to town today to see if I can manage to find money to buy five eggs for us to boil and eat."

Immediately he set out for town. On arrival, he stood on a corner to wait for a passerby from whom he could ask alms.[1] When he saw a man coming, he said to him, "Listen, my friend! Would you be good enough to give me four cents to buy an egg?" And the man, who was very charitable, gave him the four cents. That happened five times, and the peasant was fortunate enough not to have one of the five refuse him. When he had enough to buy the five eggs, he went on and bought them. And when he had bought them he returned home to tell his wife the good news.

When he reached home, he told his wife to boil the eggs at once, for he was so hungry he could eat a burro. When the eggs were all boiled, his wife said to him, "Juan, come eat your two eggs; I shall eat three because I cooked them."

But he immediately said no, that he was the one to have the three eggs and she should have only two. And he kept on by saying, "Three for me and two for you." But his wife was stubborn, maintaining that she was to have three and he two. And that went on and on.

After they had wasted a good deal of time talking, Juanica decided to tell Juan that if he did not give her the three eggs to eat, she would die. But he said to her, very indifferently, "All right, that makes no difference to me. Go ahead and die!"

So she fell to the ground as though dead. Then he began to weep, "Oh, my poor wife, I

---

1. **alms** (ämz): money given to the needy.

Eggs

loved her so. Oh, my poor wife!" And after he had wept until he was tired, he whispered in her ear, "Juanica, don't be so silly. I'll eat three and you two." But she answered, "No, I am going to eat three and you two, or else you can bury me." But he kept on weeping.

After he saw that his wife refused to come to life again, he decided to go and look for his best friend. But he had five friends, and when he reached their homes, he told them that he had come to ask them please to bury his wife, who had just died, and that he was counting on them, for he did not have a single cent to buy a casket. But his friends said not to worry, that they would see to that.

On his return home, he found her still playing dead. Then Juan burst into tears again, "Oh, Juanica, do not leave me alone, please!" And so that no one would see him, he slipped near where she lay to whisper in her ear, "I am going to eat three and you two." But she said no, that she was to eat the three and he the two. Then he said to her, "Take care, for we are going to bury you." And she replied, "That's nothing; bury me whenever you like."

After waiting a good while, they put her in the casket to carry her to the cemetery. And on the way, Juan kept on crying, "Oh, my poor wife, don't leave me!" And he made them stop the funeral procession, supposedly to kiss her, but really to tell her that he was going to eat three and she two. But her reply was always the same. When they reached the cemetery, they bore her to the edge of the grave dug to receive her. Then he went up to her and whispered in her ear, "Look, you are on the edge of the grave, and we are about to put you in it." Then, when she realized he was telling the truth, she sat up in the casket and said, "All right, then; you can eat all five of them."

So she got up out of the casket, and they both went home. But once they arrived there, Juanica set the five eggs on the table—and ate *three!* ❖

FRANK HENIUS

Not one to stay put, Frank Henius (1882–1955), born in Denmark, went to school in Germany, trained on a sailing ship, and immigrated to the United States.

Becoming a foreign trader and a trade counselor suited his adventurous spirit and frequently took him to South America during his 40-year career. He worked hard to open up United States trade relations with South America. Henius wrote three books on foreign trade, including *The ABC of Foreign Trade* in 1920. He also collected and published *Songs and Games of the Americas* and *Stories from the Americas* from which "The Five Eggs" is taken. These stories from twenty Central and South American countries were selected by Latin Americans as favorites of their children.

His wife, Gertruda, comments that "whenever there was a dispute, my husband was always for the underdog."

R A V E N
and the

Raven Opened the Box of Daylight (1970), Dale DeArmond. Woodblock. Courtesy of the Anchorage (Alaska) Museum of History and Art.

COMING OF DAYLIGHT

retold by Gail Robinson and Douglas Hill

When the earth was very young, it was dark and cold like a winter's night through all the year's seasons. Gull was the Custodian of Daylight, and he kept it locked tight in a cedar box beneath his wing. Being Custodian made Gull feel very important, and he was not going to lose his position by letting Daylight out of the box.

"He is too vain!" screeched Owl, at a meeting of the People upon Meeting Hill.

"We can never travel, in this darkness, to our half-homes in the south," cried Robin. Her breast was bleached of color for the lack of light.

"Even the dark mosses wither, and food is scarce," whimpered Rabbit.

"One person is like another because I cannot map his face," shouted Bear. "Enemies pretend to be friends to share my blanket and bowl."

"I cannot see my tail, to clean it of burrs," whined Fox.

So all the People complained of Gull's arrogance and thoughtless self-importance.

Then Squirrel turned to Raven and said, "Gull is your cousin. Perhaps he will listen to you. Perhaps you can tell him of your cold blood and your blunderings in the darkness and make him change his mind."

So it was settled that Raven should meet Gull on Meeting Hill the next day—or the next night, since without Daylight there was no difference between day and night.

Gull agreed to come to the meeting. But it

was clear, when he came, that he was not going to change his mind or listen to what Raven said. He had come only because it made him feel even more important to have Raven pleading with him.

"I was made Custodian of Daylight in the beginning of things," said Gull. "I am to keep Daylight safe. And I *will* keep it safe." And he curved his wing tighter round the cedar box.

Raven had run out of words to make Gull see the People's need for light. He thought angrily to himself, "I wish this Gull would step on a large thorn."

No sooner had he shaped this thought than Gull cried out, "Squee! My foot!"

"A thorn, Cousin?" asked Raven innocently. "Let me see—I will take it out for you."

But of course it was so dark that he could not see the thorn to remove it.

"I must have light to take out the thorn," said Raven.

"Light? Never!" said Gull.

"Then the thorn will remain."

Gull complained and hopped on one foot and wept, and he finally opened his cedar box a crack, so narrow that out glanced a shaft of light no brighter than a single star.

Raven put his hand to Gull's foot, then pretended not to see the thorn. Instead, he pushed it in deeper.

"Squee!" cried Gull. "My foot!"

"More light, more light!" shouted Raven.

Nootka raven spirit mask, northwest coast. The Philbrook Museum of Art, Tulsa, Oklahoma, Ellis Soper Collection.

And the lid of the box rose a further crack, so that light gleamed forth like a winter moon. Then Raven reached again for the thorn and pushed it even further into the soft flesh of Gull's foot.

"More light!" roared Raven.

"Squee, squee, squee!" screamed Gull, and in his pain he flung off the lid of the cedar box.

Like a molten fish the sun slithered from the box, and light and warmth blazed out over the world.

Nor was it ever to be recaptured, no matter how loudly or how sadly Gull called to it to return to its safe hiding place beneath his wing. ❖

GAIL ROBINSON

Gail Robinson (1935–) is a well-known Canadian poet and folklorist who heard firsthand many of the Native American tales she has recorded. Together with Douglas Hill, she published *Coyote the Trickster: Legends of the North American Indians,* which includes "Raven and the Coming of Daylight."

The publication of *Coyote the Trickster* coincided with the first appearance of Robinson's poems in book form. After a ten-year break from writing, she has put together a collection of short stories set in western Canada.

OTHER WORKS *Raven the Trickster*

DOUGLAS HILL

Douglas Hill (1935–) has published many books, including the first comprehensive history of western Canada. Influenced by his childhood heroes, Buck Rogers and Flash Gordon, he has written science fiction for young adults. "I was encouraged by the fact that television and films were creating a huge audience for space adventure, even in 1977 B.S.W. [Before *Star Wars*]."

OTHER WORKS *Master of Fiends; Blade of the Poisoner*

Spotted Eagle and Black Crow

retold by Jenny Leading Cloud

When the Eagle Spoke to Me (1979), Jerry Ingram (Choctaw).
Watercolor on paper, 18″× 24″, by permission of the artist.

This is a story of two warriors, of jealousy, and of eagles. This legend is supposed to have been a favorite of the great *Mahpiya Luta*—Chief Red Cloud of the Oglalas.

Many lifetimes ago, there lived two brave warriors. One was named *Wanblee Gleska*—Spotted Eagle. The other's name was *Kangi Sapa*—Black Crow. They were friends but, as it happened, they both loved the same girl, *Zintkala Luta Win*—Red Bird. She was beautiful, a fine tanner and quillworker,[1] and she liked Spotted Eagle best, which made Black Crow very jealous.

Black Crow went to his friend and said, "Let us, you and I, go on a war party against the Pahani. Let us get ourselves some fine horses and earn eagle feathers."[2] Spotted Eagle thought this a good idea. The two young men purified themselves in a sweat bath. They got out their war medicine[3] and their war shields. They painted their faces. They did all that warriors should do before a raid. Then they went against the Pahani.

Their raid was not a success. The Pahani were watchful. The young warriors got nowhere near the Pahani horse herd. Not only did they capture no ponies, but they even lost their own mounts, because while they were trying to creep up to their enemies' herd, the Pahani found their horses. The two young men had a hard time getting away on foot because the enemy were searching for them everywhere. At one time they had to hide themselves in a lake, under the water, breathing through long, hollow reeds which were sticking up above the surface. They were so clever at hiding themselves that the Pahani finally gave up searching for them.

The young men had to travel home on foot. It was a long way. Their moccasins were tattered, their feet bleeding. At last they came to a high cliff. "Let us go up there," said Black Crow, "and see whether the enemy is following us." They climbed up. They could see no one following them; but on a ledge far below them, halfway up the cliff, they spied a nest with two young eagles in it. "Let us at least get those eagles," Black Crow proposed. There was no way one could climb down the sheer rock wall, but Black Crow took his rawhide lariat, made a loop in it, put the rope around Spotted Eagle's chest under his armpits, and lowered him down. When his friend was on the ledge with the nest, Black Crow said to himself, "I will leave him there to die. I will come home alone, and then Red Bird will marry me." And he threw his end of the rawhide thong down and left without looking back and without listening to Spotted Eagle's cries of what had happened to the lariat and to Black Crow.

Spotted Eagle cried in vain. He got no answer, only silence. At last it dawned on him that his companion had betrayed him, that he had been left to die. The lariat was much too short for him to lower himself to the ground; there was an abyss of two hundred feet yawning beneath him. He was left with the two young eagles screeching at him, angered that this strange, two-legged creature had invaded their home.

Black Crow came back to his village. "Spotted Eagle died a warrior's death," he told

---

1. **tanner and quillworker:** a person who turns animal skins into leather and who weaves porcupine quills into decorations.

2. **earn eagle feathers:** to perform acts of bravery, for which a warrior was given eagle feathers to wear in his headdress.

3. **war medicine:** herbs, roots, and magical objects believed to provide protection during battle.

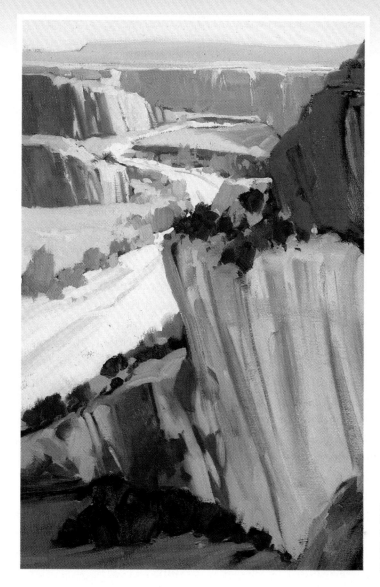

Up 'N' Down (1994),
Howard Carr. Oil on
canvas, 30″ × 24″, by
permission of the artist.
Photo by Bill McLemore
Photography.

the people. "The Pahani killed him." There
was loud wailing throughout the village
because everybody had liked Spotted Eagle.
Red Bird grieved more than the others. She
slashed her arms with a sharp knife and cut
her hair to make plain her sorrow to all. But
in the end she became Black Crow's wife,
because life must go on.

But Spotted Eagle did not die on his lonely
ledge. The eagles got used to him. The old
eagles brought plenty of food—rabbits, prairie
dogs, or sage hens—and Spotted Eagle shared
this raw meat with the two chicks. Maybe it

was the eagle medicine in his bundle which he
carried on his chest that made the eagles
accept him. Still, he had a very hard time on
that ledge. It was so narrow that when he
wanted to rest, he had to tie himself with the
rawhide thong to a little rock sticking out of
the cliff, for fear of falling off the ledge in his
sleep. In this way he spent a few very uncomfortable weeks; after all, he was a human
being and not a bird to whom such a crack in
the rock face is home.

At last the young eagles were big enough to
practice flying. "What will become of me

now?" thought the young warrior. "Once these fledglings have flown the nest for good, the old birds won't be bringing any more food up here." Then he had an inspiration. "Perhaps I will die. Very likely I will die. But I will try it. I will not just sit here and give up." He took his little pipe out of the medicine bundle and lifted it to the sky and prayed, "*Wakan Tanka, onshimala ye.* Great Spirit, pity me. You have created man and his cousin, the eagle. You have given me the eagle's name. I have decided to try to let the eagles carry me to the ground. Let the eagles help me, let me succeed."

He smoked and felt a surge of confidence. He grabbed hold of the legs of the two young eagles. "Brothers," he told them, "you have accepted me as one of your own. Now we will live together, or die together. *Hokahay.*" And he jumped off the ledge. He expected to be shattered on the ground below, but with a mighty flapping of wings the two young eagles broke his fall and all landed safely. Spotted Eagle said a prayer of thanks to the Ones Above. He thanked the eagles, telling them that one day he would be back with gifts and have a giveaway in their honor.

Spotted Eagle returned to his village. The excitement was great. He had been dead and had come back to life. Everybody asked him how it happened that he was not dead, but he would not tell them. "I escaped," he said, "and that is all." He saw his love married to his treacherous friend, but he bore it in silence. He was not one to bring enmity to his people, to set one family against the other. Besides, what happened could not be changed. Thus he accepted his fate.

A year or so later, a great war party of Pahani attacked his village. The enemy outnumbered them tenfold, and there was no chance of victory for Spotted Eagle's band. All the warriors could do was to fight a slow rear-guard action, which would give the helpless ones—the women, children, and old folks—a chance to escape across the river. Guarding their people this way, the few warriors at hand fought bravely, charging the enemy again and again, making them halt and regroup. Each time, the warriors retreated a little, taking up a new position on a hill or across a gully. In this way they could save their families.

Showing the greatest courage, exposing their bodies freely, were Spotted Eagle and Black Crow. In the end they alone faced the enemy. Then, suddenly, Black Crow's horse was hit by several arrows in succession and collapsed under him. "Brother, forgive me for what I have done," he cried to Spotted Eagle. "Let me jump up on your horse behind you."

Spotted Eagle answered, "You are a Fox. Pin yourself and fight. Then, if you survive, I will forgive you; and if you die, I will forgive you also."

What Spotted Eagle meant was this: Black Crow was a member of the Fox Warrior Society. The braves who belong to it sing this song:

> *I am a Fox.*
> *If there is anything daring,*
> *If there is anything dangerous to do,*
> *That is a task for me to perform.*
> *Let it be done by me.*

Foxes wear a long, trailing sash, decorated with quillwork, which reaches all the way to the ground even when the warrior is on horseback. In the midst of battle, a Fox will sometimes defy death by pinning his sash to the earth with a special wooden pin or with a knife or arrow. This means: I will stay here, rooted to this spot, facing my foes, until someone comes to release the pin, or until the enemies flee, or until I die.

Black Crow pinned his sash to the ground. There was no one to release him, and the enemy did not flee. Black Crow sang his death song. He was hit by lances and arrows and died a warrior's death. Many Pahani died with him.

Spotted Eagle had been the only one to see this. He finally joined his people, safe across the river. The Pahani had lost all taste to follow them there. "Your husband died well," Spotted Eagle told Red Bird. After some time had passed, Spotted Eagle married Red Bird. And much, much later he told his parents, and no one else, how Black Crow had betrayed him. "I forgive him now," he said, "because once he was my friend, and because he died like a warrior should, fighting for his people, and also because Red Bird and I are happy now."

After a long winter, when spring came again, Spotted Eagle told his wife, "I must go away for a few days to fulfill a promise. I must go alone." He rode off by himself to that cliff.

Again he stood at its foot, below the ledge where the eagles' nest had been. He pointed his sacred pipe to the four directions, down to Grandmother Earth and up to the Grandfather, letting the smoke ascend to the sky, calling out: "*Wanblee, misunkala.* Little eagle brothers, hear me."

High above him in the clouds appeared two black dots, circling. These were the eagles who had saved his life. They came at his call, their huge wings spread majestically, uttering a shrill cry of joy and recognition. Swooping down, they alighted at his feet. He stroked them with a feather fan, and thanked them many times, and fed them choice morsels of buffalo meat, and fastened small medicine bundles around their legs as a sign of friendship, and spread sacred tobacco offerings around the foot of the cliff. Thus he made a pact of friendship and brotherhood between *Wanblee Oyate*—the Eagle Nation—and his own people. After he had done all this, the stately birds soared up again into the sky, circling motionless, carried by the wind, disappearing into the clouds. Spotted Eagle turned his horse's head homeward, going happily back to Red Bird. ❖

JENNY LEADING CLOUD

Jenny Leading Cloud lived in White River, a little town on the Rosebud Sioux Reservation in South Dakota. There she was an outspoken advocate for the rights of Native Americans. As a result of an investigation by Jenny Leading Cloud, a wealthy white rancher was brought to trial, though not convicted, for the murder of her grandson.

1890?–1980?

She never wrote down the stories she heard but told them to her children and her grandchildren. "Spotted Eagle and Black Crow," one of her favorites, was first told by Chief Red Cloud of the Oglala Sioux.

RESPONDING
O P T I O N S

LITERATURE CONNECTION PROJECT 1

Prepare a Civil Trial Civil trials are designed to settle conflicts between individuals. Following official court procedure as much as possible, organize a civil trial that settles a dispute presented in one of the four stories. Conduct some research if necessary. Refer to the suggestions provided as you prepare for the trial.

Describe the Dispute and Assign Roles Working in a small group, read through the story and consider the dispute that you want to bring to trial. In a civil lawsuit, the plaintiff files a complaint, or suit, against another person or organization, called the defendant. Decide who will be the plaintiff and defendant.

Write Arguments
- Half of your group can brainstorm ideas to present the plaintiff's side of the argument in a statement of complaint. In this document, injuries or losses are declared.
- The other half of the group can brainstorm ideas to present the defendant's case. In response to the plaintiff's complaint, the defendant files a document called an answer, which gives the defendant's version of the facts of the case. Anticipate the other side's arguments and prepare counter-arguments.

Act Out Court Procedure Small groups can present their arguments to the class as a whole. Taking on the role of judge and jury, the class decides the outcome of each case.

SOCIAL STUDIES CONNECTION PROJECT 2

Create a Native American Time Line By the mid-1860s in the United States, white settlers were forcing their way onto Native American lands in great numbers. Once the transcontinental railroad was completed in 1869, the rush of settlers became a stampede. Like many of the Native Americans during this period, the Sioux suffered at the hands of the U.S. government. Create a sequencing time line like the one started to show the conflict between the Native Americans of the Great Plains and the federal government from 1851 to 1890. Begin your research at the library or use a computer database.

| Santee Sioux uprising 1851 | → | 1852 | → | |

Native Americans of the Great Plains
1851–1890

SCIENCE CONNECTION PROJECT 3

Construct an Eagle's Nest What is an eagle's nest really like? Find out what species of eagles inhabit the western plains where the Oglala Sioux lived. Then create a scientifically accurate, but much smaller, example of a typical eagle's nest. Use classroom materials to approximate the general look and feel of a real nest. Make a display that allows you to include information about the eagle's life cycle, what it eats, and the symbolism of this great bird.

ACROSS CULTURES MINI-PROJECTS

Create a Collage or Mobile From the cedar tree, which was central to the lives of the Haida people, houses, canoes, and other products were made. Find out what other items the Haida made from cedar. For what purposes is cedar most commonly used today? Create a collage or mobile that depicts cedar items from the early Haida and products used in the United States today.

Research Creation Myths Many cultures have myths describing the creation of some natural element or animal in nature, such as daylight or the butterfly. In a group, identify examples of these myths, share them with one another, and then compare them. What do these myths tell you about the values and beliefs of the societies that created them?

Investigate the People of Ecuador Use the library or the Internet to investigate the daily lives of Ecuador's rural people and its urban population. How do their lives differ? Which group makes up the largest percentage of the population? Present your findings in a classroom display.

Create Images of Paul Bunyan and Pecos Bill As a class, brainstorm similarities and differences between the legendary heroes Paul Bunyan and Pecos Bill. Then, use an art software program, if possible, or traditional art materials to create side-by-side images of these heroes. Label the images to highlight the similarities and differences between the two.

 MORE ABOUT THE CULTURES

- *Buffalo Hunt* by Russell Freedman
- *Cowboys of the Wild West* by Russell Freedman
- *Men of the Wild Frontier* by Bennet Wayne
- *The Way It Was—1876* by Suzanne Hilton

WRITING ABOUT
LITERATURE

STORIES ON STAGE

When you read a story, do you imagine that you can hear the characters speaking? Do you picture each event as it occurs? When you see a play, the characters really do speak, and you actually see what they are doing. The characters tell the story through their actions and words. In this lesson you will

- learn how writers use dialogue
- write a scene based on a legend you have read
- respond to and interpret a modern legend

Writer's Style: Using Dialogue Writers use dialogue to provide important information. In stories, dialogue often reveals character and advances the plot.

Read the Literature

How would you read these excerpts if you were speaking aloud?

Literature Models

Dialogue Advances the Plot
What important event is shown through this dialogue? Why is it important to the plot?

> "Hey, there!" Bill said as he sidled up to their campfire, grinning. "Who's the boss around here?"
> A nine-foot feller with ten pistols at his sides stepped forward and in a shaky voice said, "Stranger, I was. But from now on, it'll be you."
> "Well, thanky, pardner," said Bill.
>
> from "Pecos Bill," retold by Mary Pope Osborne

Dialogue Reveals Character
What type of a character is the chicken hawk? What type is the buzzard? Which one is the "good guy"?

> "What you talkin' 'bout?" says know-it-all Chicken Hawk. "If you're so hungry, why don'tcha get out there and hunt you some good fresh meat? You got eyes, you got wings, you got a beak. Go for it! You got to look out for Number One in this world, *mon ami*."
> "*Non, non, non*," says Buzzard, "you don't understand. I'm s'posed to wait for somethin' to drop dead before I eat it. It's my job. That's just the way *le Bon Dieu* made me."
>
> from "M'su Carencro and Mangeur de Poulet," retold by J. J. Reneaux

Connect to Life

Interviews give celebrities a chance to tell their own stories. In this segment Martina Navratilova and Steffi Graf interview each other about careers they would pick if they couldn't play tennis.

Interview

Navratilova. I think all tennis players want to be rock stars, personally. I could handle that. *[both laugh]* But for me, it would have been an athlete of some kind, because I like to move; I like to see the limits of my body while it's still capable of pushing the limits. I'll explore the limits of my mind later, when the body's not willing anymore. What about you, Steffi?

Graf. The thing is, I got into tennis so early, I didn't give much thought about what else I would have wanted to be. As a kid, I loved animals. I always wanted to be an animal doctor, like any kid. But I was kind of led into tennis. There was no other choice.

from "The Martina and Steffi Dream Team"
Interview magazine

Dialogue Presents Information
What information do you learn from this excerpt? What facts can you gather?

Try Your Hand: Writing Dialogue

1. **Where Are You?** Write a dialogue between two characters. Have them react to a setting without saying where they are. Can you describe the scene through dialogue only?

2. **One-liners** When you think about movies, you often remember certain lines that were especially funny, scary, or dramatic. Write down a couple of lines you remember, and ask yourself what those lines told you about the speaker.

3. **Spectator Sport** Write a few lines of dialogue in which two characters describe an action that they are witnessing. Then write a few lines of dialogue between the characters that are involved in the action directly. Which method is clearer?

SkillBuilder

G → GRAMMAR FROM WRITING

Using Commas in Quotations

When you are quoting a word, phrase, or clause from a story, use quotation marks to show that it is a quotation. If a comma directly follows a quotation, it is placed inside the quotation marks.

To Bill, the mountain lion was "a mangy bobtailed fleabag."

Osborne writes, "He teethed on horseshoes," but that is an exaggeration to make Bill seem tougher.

Never follow quotation marks with a comma.

APPLYING WHAT YOU'VE LEARNED
Put the quotation marks and commas into these sentences.

1. Bill says You can't do that but Slue-foot Sue wants to ride Widow Maker anyway.
2. Sue should have said I told you so but she was busy riding that horse to the moon.

 GRAMMAR HANDBOOK

For more help with using commas in quotations, see page 898 of the Grammar Handbook.

Creative Response

Folk tales present heroic figures, explain natural phenomena, or give moral lessons. Folk tales are also entertaining, but a folk tale survives when it explains or identifies an important belief or element of a community's culture. As the culture changes, the folk tales change or new ones are created that reflect new ideas. Modern writers sometimes bring folk tales to a new audience by turning them into plays.

GUIDED ASSIGNMENT

Write a Play Respond to a tale or legend by writing a scene for a play version of the story.

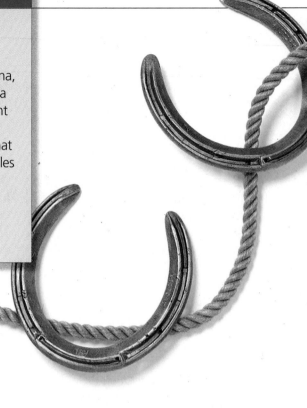

❶ Prewrite and Explore

You could respond to a folk tale by updating it for modern times, or you could simply change certain elements. You could even make up a story on your own that is specific to your community. Use questions such as these to brainstorm ideas:

- How could I update the story of Paul Bunyan and his amazing feats?
- If Nima-Cux were a politician's daughter today, what lesson might she be learning?
- Is there something in the natural world that I could explain by writing a legend?

❷ Plan Your Scene

Here are a few ideas to help you get started.

Characters Which characters will you use? Make a list of characters and describe them.

Plot What will happen in your scene? Decide on the events that will take place.

Setting At the beginning of your scene, you'll want to describe the setting in detail. Make a sketch of your stage set to help organize your thoughts.

Write a rough draft of your play that includes your main ideas.

Student's Sketch

Student's Plan

OLD CHARACTERS	NEW CHARACTERS
Pecos Bill	Bronco Betty
Slue-foot Sue	Buckskin Bob
Hell's Gate Gang	Texas Roping Team

Setting: *a pickup truck center stage, a fence against the back wall, two cow heads leaning over the fence.*

Plot: *Bronco Betty meets up with the Texas Roping Team and plans to lasso a factory and remove it from the desert.*

If I made this a rodeo, there would be different problems to tackle.

❸ Draft and Share

When you sit down to write your actual draft, think about everything that you need to express to your audience. Your dialogue and the characters' actions will get the story across. You'll have to think carefully about making every word and movement count.

- Write dialogue to advance the plot, develop characters, or provide information. Don't write dialogue just to fill in time. Think about every line you write.
- Use stage directions that show what the actors are doing. When you write a story, you might say "Bill punched the wall" to show that Bill is angry. In a play, you can't tell the audience that Bill is angry. His words and actions must show it.

Check the Grammar in Context on page 757 to help you format your scene. Try reading your play aloud with a couple of friends, and then ask them these questions.

 PEER RESPONSE

- Where did the action and dialogue sound the best?
- What do you think of my set?
- Which character did you like best? Why?

 SkillBuilder

SPEAKING & LISTENING

Giving a Performance
You may have a chance to produce your scene and act in it yourself. If so, you'll want to develop good performance skills such as those below so you can share your scene with friends.

- Speak loudly and clearly and project your voice. Looking at the floor or ceiling directs your voice away from your audience.
- Use gestures to emphasize your lines. Think about the character and what gestures he or she would use. Try to make physical motions as well as words describe the character.
- Exaggerate slightly when you are on stage. Remember that the audience is far away and won't necessarily catch every facial expression or line if you're too subtle.

APPLYING WHAT YOU'VE LEARNED
Get together with some friends and read one another's plays aloud. Critique yourself and your fellow actors, using the suggestions above as criteria.

4 Revise and Edit

As you continue to work on your scene, you'll probably notice a few things that you want to fix. The most important thing to work on is making sure your audience will be able to follow your story line. Consider producing your scene in class or with some friends, or recording it on video. How would you direct your scene?

Student's Script

Notice that the character descriptions are short.

Bronco Betty
A Scene for Six Players

Cast of Characters

Bronco Betty, who'd rope a comet if it were a challenge
Buckskin Bob, who owns a large ranch and a million cattle
Texas Roping Team, Betty's gang of wild rodeo girls

Scene 1

(pickup truck in the middle of the stage, cacti on floor, a fence at the back of the stage with two cow heads peering over)

Betty *(entering stage left).* What seems to be the trouble, rancher? You look perplexed, and I don't think it's just your cowlicks.

Bob. You know what the trouble is.

Betty. Do not. I just rode into town.

Bob. It's that factory. It spits out foul and smelly filth all over the valley and into my horses' and cows' food. I've never seen such trash. It would shame a rat!

Betty. What do they make at that factory? Besides filth?

What information is communicated through this dialogue?

Standards for Evaluation

An effective scene
- uses dialogue that enhances character and advances the plot
- includes stage directions that establish the setting, describe the action, and give clues to character
- presents a central problem or conflict
- is formatted clearly and accurately according to guidelines

Grammar in Context

Formatting a Script Writing a script is very different from writing a story. Here are a few key points to remember:

- Single-space character and setting descriptions. Double-space speakers' dialogue.
- Center the title of the scene on the page.
- Indent every line of the characters' speeches except the first line.
- Capitalize names of characters in setting descriptions and in dialogue tags.
- Use parentheses to set off your description of the setting at the beginning of the scene or to set off sections of action on stage without dialogue. Use parentheses to set off stage directions within the dialogue.
- Use a period after the character's name at the beginning of a line to show who is speaking. It is not necessary to use quotation marks in a play.

Here's an example of a line of dialogue that shows the correct capitalization, parentheses, and punctuation:

Betty (*motions wildly to the ropers*). Why, you folks are just the kind of maniacs I'm looking for!

The best way to figure out the correct format for a script is to look at a play that has been written correctly. Keep it handy so you can refer to it as you work.

Try Your Hand: Formatting a Script

Rework the draft of your play. Be sure that you have included enough stage direction so that the actors will know exactly what to do and how to say their lines. Use proper formatting to make sure that all of your directions are clear.

WRITER'S CRAFT

Showing Direct Address
When you read a play, it's important to know whom the characters are talking to. If someone screams "NO!" how is the reader or actor to know who is talking to whom? There are three ways to show direct address in scripts.

1. Make it obvious through content. Because of the words that are said, the reader can figure out who is hearing them.
   Bob. You're just a woman!
2. Have the character who is speaking say the other character's name in the dialogue, set off by commas.
   Betty. That's right, Bob.
3. Point out in the stage directions whom the actor should be looking at or talking to.
   Bob (*shakes finger at Betty*). You should know better!

APPLYING WHAT YOU'VE LEARNED
Write a few lines for a play in which Slue-foot Sue tells Pecos Bill to go bring in the horses and then tells her maid to cook dinner. Use all three ways of showing direct address.

Copyright © The Walt Disney Company, photo courtesy of Photofest.

Painting by an English artist (about 1616)

Still photo from an animated film (1995)

READING
THE WORLD

REAL OR IDEAL?

In this unit, you've seen how folklore and legends survive and change as a culture changes. Perhaps you responded creatively to one of these tales by updating it as a play. The adaptation of legends over time can take many forms, as the legend of Pocahontas illustrates.

View The images on these pages are all of the Native American princess Pocahontas. Jot down your initial reactions. Note how the images are like and unlike one another.

Interpret These different images came from different time periods. Why do you think these artists portrayed Pocahontas as they did? What kind of princess does each image show?

Discuss Share your reactions. Which image seems most real to you? most appealing? Why do you think Pocahontas inspired so many interpretations? Refer to the SkillBuilder at the right for help in evaluating these images.

SkillBuilder

 CRITICAL THINKING

Separating Fiction from Reality
When people tell "true" stories, they often tend to romanticize people and events. Romanticizing means making something seem much more interesting, more dramatic, or more beautiful than it actually is. Romanticizing can also be done to better reflect the values or culture of the times at which a story is told.

For example, some historians believe that Pocahontas was about 12 years old at the time she played the part of the sponsor in a ritual of adoption that was arranged by her father for political reasons. How does the romanticized version of the Pocahontas tale make her story seem more dramatic?

When you hear a story or look at an image, it is important to think about whether what you are seeing or hearing is real or an idealized version of the truth.

APPLYING WHAT YOU'VE LEARNED
Make a list of other stories or people that may have been romanticized. John Henry, Betsy Ross, and the cowhands of the Old West are some examples. Discuss how these stories were romanticized and why you think people tell these stories as they do. What are they trying to accomplish?

Engraving by an American artist (1800s)

LINKS TO UNIT FOUR

Facing the Enemy

Who or what is an enemy? A soldier with a rifle, an impersonal force such as poverty, or an attitude within our own hearts? The selections in Unit Four examine the ways in which people meet a wide range of enemies. Confronting an enemy is an important theme in folklore. The three tales you are about to read feature characters who must stand up to their own enemies.

PACIFIC COAST

Otoonah

retold by Robert D. San Souci (săn sōō-sē′)

The native peoples of Alaska arrived in North America between 3000 and 1000 B.C. Their way of life changed little until the arrival of European fur traders and whalers in the 1800s. In their bitter-cold world, they have lived by an unwritten rule: help one another to survive and find food. This legend tells how this rule was broken by one family of the Sugpiaq—the people who first settled Kodiak Island, off the coast of Alaska.

Racing the Great Bear

retold by Joseph Bruchac (broŏk′chäk′)

Centered in northern New York State, the Iroquois are not one Native American people but several. In 1570, tribes formed a confederacy known as the League of the Iroquois or the League of Five Nations. Later, the Iroquois became involved in four wars that took place between 1689 and 1763, in which the British and French battled for control of North America. The Iroquois sided with the British. The tribes excelled at warfare. As this legend shows, the Iroquois placed great importance on fighting skills.

The Woman in the Snow

retold by Patricia C. McKissack

Unlike legends from the distant past, this one comes out of a modern event—African Americans' struggle for civil rights. By the mid-1950s, several

rulings by the U.S. Supreme Court had already brought gains to the fight for equality. The events upon which this tale is based—the bus boycott in Montgomery, Alabama—focused the nation's attention on the boycott's leader, Martin Luther King, Jr. This legend reflects the struggle of King, and of all African Americans, for equal treatment.

AS YOU READ . . .

Notice the customs of each culture.

Decide what is considered to be good behavior and how it is rewarded.

Decide what traits are seen as negative.

Consider how other cultures value these positive and negative traits.

RACING THE GREAT BEAR

RETOLD BY JOSEPH BRUCHAC

NE ONENDJI. HEAR MY STORY, WHICH HAPPENED
LONG AGO. FOR MANY GENERATIONS, THE FIVE
NATIONS OF THE HAUDENOSAUNEE, THE PEOPLE
OF THE LONGHOUSE,[1] HAD BEEN AT WAR WITH
ONE ANOTHER.

No one could say how the wars began, but
each time a man of one nation was killed, his
relatives sought revenge in the blood feud, and
so the fighting continued. Then the Creator
took pity on his people and sent a messenger
of peace. The Peacemaker traveled from nation
to nation, convincing the people of the Five
Nations—the Mohawk, the Oneida, the
Onondaga, the Cayuga, and the Seneca—that
it was wrong for brothers to kill one another. It

---

1. **the Longhouse:** a large group dwelling used by some
   Native American groups, particularly the five tribes of
   the Iroquois Nation.

was not easy, but finally the nations agreed, and the Great Peace began. Most welcomed that peace, though there were some beings with bad hearts who wished to see the return of war.

One day, not long after the Great Peace had been established, some young men in a Seneca village decided they would pay a visit to the Onondaga people.

"It is safe now to walk the trail between our nations," the young men said. "We will return after the sun has risen and set seven times."

Then they set out. They walked toward the east until they were lost from sight in the hills. But many more than seven days passed, and those young men never returned. Now another group of young men left, wanting to find out where their friends had gone. They, too, did not return.

The people grew worried. Parties were sent out to look for the vanished young men, but no sign was found. And the searchers who went too far into the hills did not return, either.

The old chief of the village thought long and hard. He asked the clan mothers, those wise women whose job it was to choose the chiefs and give them good advice, what should be done.

"We must find someone brave enough to face whatever danger is out there," the clan mothers said.

So the old chief called the whole village to a council meeting. He held up a white strand of wampum beads[2] made from quahog[3] clamshells as he spoke.

"Hear me," he said. "I am of two minds about what has happened to our people. It may be that the Onondaga have broken the peace and captured them. It may be there is something with an evil mind that wishes to destroy this new peace and so has killed our people. Now someone must go and find out. Who is brave enough? Who will come and take this wampum from my hand?"

Many men were gathered in that council.

Some were known to speak of themselves as brave warriors. Still, though they muttered to one another, no man stepped forward to take the strand of wampum. The old chief began to walk about the circle, holding the wampum in front of each man in turn. But each man only lowered his eyes to the ground. No man lifted his hand to take the wampum.

Just outside the circle stood a boy who had not yet become a man. His parents were dead, and he lived with his grandmother in her old lodge at the edge of the village. His clothing was always torn and his face dirty because his grandmother was too old to care for him as a mother would. The other young men made fun of him, and as a joke they called him Swift Runner—even though no one had ever seen him run and it was thought that he was weak and lazy. All he ever seemed to do was play with his little dog or sit by the fire and listen when the old people were talking.

"Our chief has forgotten our greatest warrior," one of the young men said to another, tilting his head toward Swift Runner.

"Nyoh," the other young man said, laughing. "Yes. Why does he not offer the wampum to Swift Runner?"

The chief looked around the circle of men, and the laughing stopped. He walked out of the circle to the place where the small boy in torn clothes stood. He held out the wampum, and Swift Runner took it without hesitating.

"I accept this," Swift Runner said. "It is right that I be the one to face the danger. In the eyes of the people I am worthless, so if I do not return, it will not matter. I will leave when the sun rises tomorrow."

---

2. **wampum beads:** beads that are made from seashells and that were first used for ceremonial and historical purposes, and then also used as money.

3. **quahog** (kwô′hôg′): a type of clam with a hard, rounded shell.

Orion in December (1959), Charles E. Burchfield. Watercolor and pencil on paper, 39⅞″ × 32⅞″,
National Museum of American Art, gift of S. C. Johnson & Son, Inc., Smithsonian Institution,
Washington, D.C./Art Resource, New York.

When Swift Runner arrived home at his grandmother's lodge, the old woman was waiting for him.

"Grandson," she said, "I know what you have done. The people of this village no longer remember, but your father was a great warrior. Our family is a family that has power."

Then she reached up into the rafters and took down a heavy bow. It was blackened with smoke and seemed so thick that no man could bend it.

"If you can string this bow, Grandson," the old woman said, "you are ready to face whatever waits for you on the trail."

Swift Runner took the bow. It was as thick as a man's wrist, but he bent it with ease and strung it.

"Wah-hah!" said his grandmother. "You are the one I knew you would grow up to be. Now you must sleep. At dawn we will make you ready for your journey."

It was not easy for Swift Runner to sleep, but when he woke the next morning, he felt strong and clear-headed. His grandmother was sitting by the fire with a cap in her hand.

"This was your grandfather's cap," she said. "I have sewed four hummingbird feathers on it. It will make your feet more swift."

Swift Runner took the cap and placed it on his head.

His grandmother held up four pairs of moccasins. "Carry these tied to your waist. When one pair wears out, throw them aside and put on the next pair."

Swift Runner took the moccasins and tied them to his belt.

Next his grandmother picked up a small pouch. "In this pouch is cornmeal mixed with maple sugar," she said. "It is the only food you will need as you travel. It will give you strength when you eat it each evening."

Swift Runner took the pouch and hung it from his belt by the moccasins.

"The last thing I must give you," said the old woman, "is this advice. Pay close attention to your little dog. You have treated him well, and so he is your great friend. He is small, but his eyes and nose are keen. Keep him always in front of you. He will warn you of danger before it can strike you."

Then Swift Runner set out on his journey. His little dog stayed ahead of him, sniffing the air and sniffing the ground. By the time the sun was in the middle of the sky, they were far from the village. The trail passed through deep woods, and it seemed to the boy as if something was following them among the trees. But he could see nothing in the thick brush.

The trail curved toward the left, and the boy felt even more the presence of something watching. Suddenly his little dog ran into the brush at the side of the trail, barking loudly. There were the sounds of tree limbs breaking and heavy feet running. Then out of the forest came a Nyagwahe, a monster bear. Its great teeth were as long as a man's arm. It was twice as tall as a moose. Close at its heels was Swift Runner's little dog.

"I see you," Swift Runner shouted. "I am after you. You cannot escape me."

Swift Runner had learned those words by listening to the stories the old people told. They were the very words a monster bear speaks when it attacks, words that terrify anyone who hears them. On hearing those words, the great bear turned and fled from the boy.

"You cannot escape me," Swift Runner shouted again. Then he ran after the bear.

The Nyagwahe turned toward the east, with Swift Runner and his dog close behind. It left the trail and plowed through the thick forest, breaking down great trees and leaving a path of destruction like that of a whirlwind. It ran up the tallest hills and down through the swamps, but the boy and the dog stayed at its heels. They ran past a great cave in the rocks.

All around the cave were the bones of people the bear had caught and eaten.

"My relatives," Swift Runner called as he passed the cave, "I will not forget you. I am after the one who killed you. He will not escape me."

Throughout the day, the boy and his dog chased the great bear, growing closer bit by bit. At last, as the sun began to set, Swift Runner stopped at the head of a small valley and called his small dog to him.

"We will rest here for the night," the boy said. He took off his first pair of moccasins, whose soles were worn away to nothing. He threw them aside and put on a new pair. Swift Runner made a fire and sat beside it with his dog. Then he took out the pouch of cornmeal and maple sugar, sharing his food with his dog.

"Nothing will harm us," Swift Runner said. "Nothing can come close to our fire." He lay down and slept.

In the middle of the night, he was awakened by the growling of his dog. He sat up with his back to the fire and looked into the darkness. There, just outside the circle of light made by the flames, stood a dark figure that looked like a tall man. Its eyes glowed green.

"I am Nyagwahe," said the figure. "This is my human shape. Why do you pursue me?"

"You cannot escape me," Swift Runner said. "I chase you because you killed my people. I will not stop until I catch you and kill you."

The figure faded back into the darkness.

"You cannot escape me," Swift Runner said again. Then he patted his small dog and went to sleep.

As soon as the first light of the new day appeared, Swift Runner rose. He and his small dog took the trail. It was easy to follow the monster's path, for trees were uprooted and the earth torn by its great paws. They ran all through the morning. When the sun was in the middle of the sky, they reached the head of another valley. At the other end they saw the great bear running toward the east. Swift Runner pulled off his second pair of moccasins, whose soles were worn away to nothing. He put on his third pair and began to run again.

All through that day, they kept the Nyagwahe in sight, drawing closer bit by bit. When the

Kit Fox Society bow-lance, No Two Horns (Hunkpapa).
State Historical Society of North Dakota (SHSND 10491).

sun began to set, Swift Runner stopped to make camp. He took off the third pair of moccasins, whose soles were worn away to nothing, and put on the last pair.

"Tomorrow," he said to his small dog, "we will catch the monster and kill it." He reached for his pouch of cornmeal and maple sugar, but when he opened it, he found it filled with worms. The magic of the Nyagwahe had done this. Swift Runner poured out the pouch and said in a loud voice, "You have spoiled our food, but it will not stop me. I am on your trail. You cannot escape me."

That night, once again, he was awakened by the growling of his dog. A dark figure stood just outside the circle of light. It looked smaller than the night before, and the glow of its eyes was weak.

"I am Nyagwahe," the dark figure said. "Why do you pursue me?"

"You cannot escape me," Swift Runner said. "I am on your trail. You killed my people. You threatened the Great Peace. I will not rest until I catch you."

"Hear me," said the Nyagwahe. "I see your power is greater than mine. Do not kill me. When you catch me, take my great teeth. They are my power, and you can use them for healing. Spare my life, and I will go far to the north and never again bother the People of the Longhouse."

"You cannot escape me," Swift Runner said. "I am on your trail."

The dark figure faded back into the darkness, and Swift Runner sat for a long time, looking into the night.

At the first light of day, the boy and his dog took the trail. They had not gone far when they saw the Nyagwahe ahead of them. Its sides puffed in and out as it ran. The trail was beside a big lake with many alder trees close to the water. As the great bear ran past, the leaves were torn from the trees. Fast as the bear went, the boy and his dog came closer, bit by bit. At last, when the sun was in the middle of the sky, the giant bear could run no longer. It fell heavily to the earth, panting so hard that it stirred up clouds of dust.

Swift Runner unslung his grandfather's bow and notched an arrow to the sinewy string.

"Shoot for my heart," said the Nyagwahe. "Aim well. If you cannot kill me with one arrow, I will take your life."

"No," Swift Runner said. "I have listened to the stories of my elders. Your only weak spot is the sole of your foot. Hold up your foot and I will kill you."

The great bear shook with fear. "You have defeated me," it pleaded. "Spare my life and I will leave forever."

"You must give me your great teeth," Swift Runner said. "Then you must leave and never bother the People of the Longhouse again."

"I shall do as you say," said the Nyagwahe. "Take my great teeth."

Swift Runner lowered his bow. He stepped forward and pulled out the great bear's teeth. It rose to its feet and walked to the north, growing smaller as it went. It went over the hill and was gone.

Carrying the teeth of the Nyagwahe over his shoulder, Swift Runner turned back to the west, his dog at his side. He walked for three moons before he reached the place where the bones of his people were piled in front of the monster's empty cave. He collected those bones and walked around them four times. "Now," he said. "I must do something to make my people wake up." He went to a big hickory tree and began to push it over so that it would fall on the pile of bones.

"My people," he shouted, "get up quickly or this tree will land on you."

The bones of the people who had been killed all came together and jumped up, alive again and covered with flesh. They were filled with joy and gathered around Swift Runner.

"Great one," they said, "who are you?"

"I am Swift Runner," he said.

"How can that be?" one of the men said. "Swift Runner is a skinny little boy. You are a tall, strong man."

Swift Runner looked at himself and saw that it was so. He was taller than the tallest man, and his little dog was bigger than a wolf.

"I am Swift Runner," he said. "I was that boy, and I am the man you see before you."

Then Swift Runner led his people back to the village. He carried with him the teeth of the Nyagwahe, and those who saw what he carried rejoiced. The trails were safe again, and the Great Peace would not be broken. Swift Runner went to his grandmother's lodge and embraced her.

"Grandson," she said, "you are now the man I knew you would grow up to be. Remember to use your power to help the people."

So it was that Swift Runner ran with the great bear and won the race. Throughout his long life, he used the teeth of the Nyagwahe to heal the sick, and he worked always to keep the Great Peace.

Da neho. I am finished. ❖

JOSEPH BRUCHAC

Joseph Bruchac (1942–), whose ancestors include members of the Abenaki tribe, shares his extensive knowledge of Native American culture through his books, poetry, storytelling, and music.

Bruchac was raised by his grandparents in the foothills of the Adirondack Mountains. For years his grandfather denied that Bruchac had any Native American heritage because he did not want him to encounter prejudice. It was not until Bruchac was an adult that he uncovered the truth and began to appreciate the rich folklore of his Native American ancestors.

Bruchac has authored or co-authored more than 50 books. He states that one of the reasons he writes is "to share my insights into the beautiful and all too fragile world of human life and living things." In 1970, he and his wife founded the Greenfield Review Press, which publishes multicultural literature.

Bruchac has won many awards, including a Cherokee Nation Prose Award, and several National Endowment for the Arts grants. He writes "not to be a man apart, but to share."

OTHER WORKS *Dawn Land; Flying with the Eagle, Racing the Great Bear; The Girl Who Married the Moon* (with Gayle Ross); *Native American Stories*

OTOONAH

RETOLD BY ROBERT D. SAN SOUCI

A Man Cooking Fish as His Wife Softens Kamiks, unknown Inuit artist. Stonecut, 25″ × 39¼″. by permission of the Amway Environmental Foundation.

In those days of the past, there was an Eskimo family—the parents, two brothers, and a sister—who lived in a village near the ocean. Summer was nearly at an end, and bitter winter was coming soon. For one family, the hunting had been especially bad: they had found few edible plants and berries to store, and they had fewer fish and eggs to bury in the ground, where they wouldn't spoil.

One day, the brothers sent their younger sister to gather driftwood from the beach near the family's sod house. When she was gone, the older brother, Nanoona, said to his parents, "There is not enough food for five people. We must send our sister away. She is weak and does not hunt, yet she eats our food. Soon my brother and I will grow too weak to hunt. Then we will all starve."

Next the younger brother, Avraluk, said, "Four can live when five cannot. We will row our sister across the sea to one of the islands and leave her there."

Sadly, the parents agreed to this.

When the girl, Otoonah, returned with an armful of wood, her brothers told her what they had decided. *"Ahpah!* Father! *Ahkah!* Mother!" the wretched girl cried. But her parents turned away and would not look at her. Then her brothers put her in the family's large sealskin boat and rowed her to an island below the horizon. There they left her with only the poorest caribou hide that the family owned and flints to start a fire.

For a long time, she did nothing but sob. All the time she stared in the direction where the sun rises and imagined she could see traces of the mainland. Over and over she sang,

> Oh poor me!
> Oh unhappy daughter!
> So sad am I, so sad
> And so lonely!

Finally, when her hunger grew too much to bear, she gathered seaweed from the shore to eat. Then, piling up stones, she made herself a tiny hut. She wrapped herself in the skin at night. When she awoke, she ate more seaweed. But she grew weaker and weaker.

Then, one night, in her makeshift shelter of stones, an old man came to her in a dream. "Walk to the west until you find a broad, swift-flowing stream beside sweet berry bushes. Drink two times from the water, but do not drink again. And do not eat even one berry. But you will find there one other thing that you may take with you."

She awoke soon after this and walked for a long time over the stony ground until she found the broad, swift-flowing stream bordered with berry bushes.

Kneeling, she cupped her hands and drank. The first time she sipped the water, she felt her strength returning. The second time, she felt herself growing stronger still. Although she was still thirsty and hungry, she did as the old man in the dream had told her. She did not take a single drop more or taste a single ripe berry.

Looking across the current, she saw an *ulu*, a knife, with a carved ivory handle lying on a flat rock. With her newfound strength, she lifted a tree trunk and set it over the stream. Then she claimed the knife.

In the days that followed, she used the knife to make a bird spear, harpoon, and a bow and arrows for herself. She practiced throwing the spear and harpoon and shooting arrows until she became skilled at using these weapons.

At the same time, she explored the island and discovered that it was a plentiful hunting ground, with ptarmigans[1] and hares and seals that would sun themselves on the rocks. So she was able to provide plenty of food for herself. Then she made herself clothing, boots, and a cape of sealskin that she had scraped and stretched on the ground to dry. As the days grew cold, she even built a kayak.[2]

Sitting by herself in the warmth of her hut, over which she had packed dirt and which was filled with furs, she often dreamed of sailing home across the sea. She vowed to punish her brothers and her parents who had abandoned her so heartlessly.

Ice began to form on ponds and on the sea. Otoonah could no longer take her kayak out because the ice would pierce its skin cover. Snow fell and piled up against the hut; winds began to howl across the island. But she had plenty of dried seal meat and fish. Inside the shelter it was warm, lit by the yellow flame of a lamp that she had carved from soapstone. The wick was made of moss, and the basin was filled with oil from blubber that she had chewed to release the fuel. Several dried seal stomachs hung on the wall, holding more oil.

When the storms were at their worst and she was weathered in, the young woman sat on her bed platform covered with shrubs and skins and sang songs. Some she remembered her mother singing to her; some she made up:

---

1. **ptarmigans** (tär′mĭ-gənz): birds that are a basic part of the traditional Eskimo diet.
2. **kayak** (kī′ăk′): a watertight canoe completely covered with skins except for a small opening in the center.

Proud Hunter (1987), Pudlo Pudlat. Stonecut, 21½″ × 24″, by permission of the Amway Environmental Foundation.

happy songs about summer warmth, bitter songs about loneliness, or boastful songs that she would someday sing when she returned well-fed to mock her starving family.

The long Arctic night arrived. At noon, the sun—too weary to climb above the horizon— spread the thin light of false dawn over a world blanketed with snow and ice.

Now the young woman hunted seals by finding one of their breathing holes in the icebound sea. She would pile up blocks of snow and sit motionlessly. When she heard a seal snort, she would instantly plunge her harpoon straight down, haul the unhappy creature onto the ice, and finish it off.

In time, she recognized the promise of spring as the first rays of sunlight touched the highest peaks far inland. Although terrible cold still gripped the island, the coming of daylight made hunting easier. Soon the ice mass covering the sea began to break apart into smaller floes.[3]

One day, approaching her favorite hunting area, the young woman heard human voices. At first the sound alone startled her. She was even more astounded to discover that she knew those voices. Running forward, she met her brothers, who were just beaching their kayaks on the shore. At the sight of them, the young woman forgot all her thoughts of revenge.

The two men raised their harpoons at the sight of this strange person running toward them. But they lowered them when they heard her call out, "Nanoona! Avraluk! I am your sister. I am Otoonah!"

Hungry for the sound of human voices, she asked them many questions about her old home and her parents. But they merely shrugged and spoke a few words. They could only stare at the fine furs she wore and the glow of well-fed, good health in her face.

---

3. **floes** (flōz): sheets of floating ice.

Walrus Hunt (1986), Lucassie Tukaluk. Stonecut, 14½ ″ × 18″, by permission of the Amway Environmental Foundation.

"What man has given you so much food and such fine furs?" her older brother demanded.

"Your husband must give us a portion of what he has," said her younger brother, "since he has married our sister."

Angrily, she said, "No man has given me anything. What I have I have been given by the Old Woman of the Sea who let me take some of the seals and fish in her keeping."

"No woman is such a good hunter," said her older brother. Then they both laughed at her.

"If you are such a hunter," Nanoona continued, "I would challenge you to a hunt."

"And I," Avraluk added.

Angered by their laughter, the young woman said, "I accept your challenge."

They waited until she had launched her own kayak. Then they zigzagged swiftly amid the ice floes. Soon each was lost to the sight of the other.

For the young woman, the hunting was good. By the time she returned, she had two seals lashed to the narrow deck of her kayak. As she rowed with her single paddle which she held in the middle, dipping first right and then left, she sang a little song of thanksgiving to the Old Woman of the Sea.

Both her brothers returned much later, angry and empty-handed. She was already roasting some meat when they came to her hut. She invited them to share her food and spend the night. She did not mock them because she knew they were chewing on bitter defeat with every mouthful of meat—even as she was <u>savoring</u> her victory. When they had finished eating, they did not thank her. They sat apart and whispered together.

In the morning, she awoke and discovered that her brothers were gone. They had also stolen her ivory-handled *ulu* in the fish-skin pouch she had made for it, and most of her

WORDS TO KNOW   **savor** (sā′vər) *v.* to take great pleasure in furs and meat. Running to the shore, she saw the two of them far out to sea.

Angry at this second betrayal, she pursued them. She was stronger than either of them; and her boat was sturdier and swifter. Soon she overtook them. She shook her harpoon and cried, "Return what you have stolen, or I will gut your kayaks as I would a fish."

The two were cowards and quickly surrendered the stolen goods. Then the young woman laughed at *them*. To the shamefaced men, it sounded as though her laughter had been picked up by the roaring wind. Soon the sky itself was roaring with dark laughter, as a terrible storm arose.

The young woman, her goods safely tied down, paddled quickly back toward the island through a heavy sea. She called to her brothers to come back with her, but they ignored her. Stubbornly, they paddled on into the heart of the storm. Soon, she heard their calls for help as loud and <u>forlorn</u> as petrels'[4] cries. But although she turned around and tried to find them, they had vanished beneath the waves.

Barely escaping with her own life, she reached safe harbor. For a day and a night she huddled in her shelter, until the wind blew itself out.

When the storm subsided, the young woman took as much meat as she could carry. Then she rowed across to her old village. There she found her parents grieving for their lost sons and fearful that they would soon starve with no one to provide for them. Their grief turned to amazement when they saw Otoonah, her arms laden with food, coming up the beach toward them.

"*Punnick!* Daughter! Have you come home?" her father asked.

"I have come back because it is time for me to return," Otoonah said. "I will give you food from now on." So happy was she to be home that when she searched her heart, she found there no wish to hurt her parents any longer.

After this, she brought all her goods from the island and built herself a new hut, very close to the one in which her parents lived. She soon proved herself the best hunter in the village. Then she was sought by many men, each of whom wanted her to become his wife.

"NO MAN HAS GIVEN ME ANYTHING."

But she set her heart on one man, Apatasok. However, he alone would have no part of her because she insisted on taking a man's role in the hunt. "A woman is supposed to take care of the hunter," he said, "and watch out for his clothes. No more."

"Still, I am determined to have you for my husband," Otoonah said stubbornly.

"A girl does not take a husband of her own choosing. Her parents should seek a husband for her."

Then he walked away before she could argue any more.

---

4. **petrels':** belonging to a group of sea birds.

owever, the following winter, when they were hunting near each other on the edge of the frozen sea, Apatasok killed a seal. But while he was loading it on his sled, he discovered to his dismay that the scent of the kill had drawn a polar bear.

Quick-thinking Otoonah cut the traces[5] on her own sled dogs and sent them to harass the bear. Then, with a cry of encouragement to her fellow hunter, she charged behind them, brandishing her harpoon.

The bear fought the dogs with its paws and teeth. Two dogs were felled by crushing blows. But the beast could not move because the circling huskies would attack at every opening. The young man rushed forward, trying to spear the bear in its heart. But the bear turned sharply, its paw shattering the hunter's spear and tumbling the man into the snow. The angered bear turned toward the man to finish him off. But, at that instant, the young woman charged forward, putting all of her weight behind her harpoon. The weapon pierced the bear's heart, and it dropped on the spot.

When the young man got to his feet and stared at the young woman standing beside the slain creature, he began to laugh. But the woman recognized that he was laughing because he was still alive, and because here was an unlooked-for supply of meat, and because he saw the foolishness of his refusal to marry a woman who hunted as well as any man.

Soon she was laughing, too.

When they returned to the village, they were wed. And the polar bear meat provided a marriage feast for their families and neighbors. Afterwards, they became a familiar sight as they hunted together, paddling their kayaks side by side. ❖

---

5. **traces:** straps or chains connecting a harnessed animal to a vehicle.

ROBERT D. SAN SOUCI

"As far back as I can remember," says Robert San Souci (1946–), "I loved stories." He wrote his first "book," illustrated by his brother Daniel, when he was in second grade. Since then, he has written more than 50 books, several of which were illustrated by his brother.

San Souci's stories are set in such varied places as medieval Japan, Native American homelands, the Philippines, and the Bahamas. "I have always had a fascination with traveling to magical places. . . . I guess I'm the ultimate escapist."

He has won many awards, including ones from Parents' Choice, the American Library Association, and the Children's Book Council. *Cut From the Same Cloth: American Women in Myth, Legend, and Tall Tale,* from which "Otoonah" is taken, won a 1993 Aesop Prize from the American Folklore Society.

San Souci finds ideas in many places—from odd articles in newspapers, which he clips and saves in his "Weird File," and from just observing people in general. He has always had a love of folklore. In addition to writing books for young people, San Souci writes thrillers for adults.

A lifelong resident of the San Francisco area, San Souci worked at various jobs—teacher, book buyer, bookstore manager, copywriter, editor—before he was able to support himself through writing.

OTHER WORKS *Song of Sedna: An Eskimo (Inuit) Legend; Short and Shivery; More Short and Shivery: 30 More Terrifying Tales*

WORDS
TO
KNOW

brandishing (brăn′dĭsh-ĭng) *adj.* waving something (such as a weapon) in a threatening manner **brandish** *v.*

The Woman in the Snow

retold by Patricia C. McKissack

The year-long Montgomery, Alabama, bus boycott in 1955–56 was a <u>pivotal</u> event in the American civil rights movement. Blacks refused to ride the buses until their demand of fair and equal treatment for all fare-paying passengers was met. Today the right to sit anywhere on a public bus may seem a small victory over racism and discrimination. But that single issue changed the lives of African Americans everywhere. After the successful boycott in Montgomery, blacks in other cities challenged bus companies, demanding not only the right to sit wherever they chose but also employment opportunities for black bus drivers. Many cities had their own "bus" stories. Some are in history books, but this story is best enjoyed by the fireplace on the night of the first snowfall.

Grady Bishop had just been hired as a driver for Metro Bus Service. When he put on the gray uniform and boarded his bus, nothing mattered, not his obesity,[1] not his poor education, not growing up the eleventh child of the town drunk. Driving gave him power. And power mattered.

One cold November afternoon Grady clocked in for the three-to-eleven shift. "You've got Hall tonight," Billy, the route manager, said matter-of-factly.

"The Blackbird Express." Grady didn't care who knew about his nickname for the route. "Not again." He turned around, slapping his hat against his leg.

"Try the *Hall Street Express*," Billy corrected Grady, then hurried on, cutting their conversation short. "Snow's predicted. Try to keep on schedule, but if it gets too bad out there, forget it. Come on in."

Grady popped a fresh stick of gum into his mouth. "You're the boss. But tell me. How am I s'posed to stay on schedule? What do those people care about time?"

Most Metro drivers didn't like the Hall Street assignment in the best weather, because the road twisted and turned back on itself like

---

1. **obesity** (ō-bē'sĭ-tē): extreme fatness.

WORDS TO KNOW

pivotal (pĭv'ə-tl) *adj.* being of central importance

775

Illustration Copyright © 1992 Brian Pinkney. From *The Dark-Thirty* by Patricia McKissack, reprinted by permission of Alfred A. Knopf, Inc.

a retreating snake. When slick with ice and snow, it was even more hazardous. But Grady had his own reason for hating the route. The Hall Street Express serviced black domestics[2] who rode out to the fashionable west end in the mornings and back down to the lower east side in the evenings.

"You know I can't stand being a chauffeur for a bunch of colored maids and cooks," he groused.[3]

"Take it or leave it," Billy said, walking away in disgust.

Grady started to say something but thought better of it. He was still on probation,[4] lucky even to have a job, especially during such hard times.

Snow had already begun to fall when Grady pulled out of the garage at 3:01. It fell steadily all afternoon, creating a frosted wonderland on the manicured lawns that lined West Hall. But by nightfall the winding, twisting, and bending street was a driver's nightmare.

The temperature <u>plummeted</u>, too, adding a new challenge to the mounting snow. "Hurry up! Hurry up! I can't wait all day," Grady snapped at the boarding passengers. "Get to the back of the bus," he hustled them on impatiently. "You people know the rules."

The regulars recognized Grady, but except for a few muffled groans they paid their fares and rode in sullen silence out to the east side loop.

"Auntie! Now, just why are you taking your own good time getting off this bus?" Grady grumbled at the last passenger.

> **Snow had already begun to fall when Grady pulled out of the garage at 3:01.**

The woman struggled down the wet, slippery steps. At the bottom she looked over her shoulder. Her dark face held no clue of any emotion. "Auntie? Did you really call me *Auntie?*" she said, laughing sarcastically. "Well, well, well! I never knew my brother had a white son." And she hurried away, chuckling.

Grady's face flushed with surprise and anger. He shouted out the door, "Don't get uppity with me! Y'all know *Auntie* is what we call all you old colored women." Furious, he slammed the door against the bitter cold. He shook his head in disgust. "It's a waste of time trying to be nice," he told himself.

But one look out the window made Grady refocus his attention to a more immediate problem. The weather had worsened. He checked his watch. It was a little past nine. Remarkably, he was still on schedule, but that didn't matter. He had decided to close down the route and take the bus in.

That's when his headlights picked up the figure of a woman running in the snow, without a hat, gloves, or boots. Although she'd pulled a shawl over the lightweight jacket and flimsy dress she was wearing, her clothing offered very little protection against the elements. As she pressed forward against the driving snow and wind, Grady saw that the woman was very young, no more than twenty. And she was clutching something close to her body. What was it? Then Grady saw the baby, a small

---

2. **domestics:** household servants.

3. **groused:** complained.

4. **on probation:** working for a trial period before being permanently employed.

WORDS
TO
KNOW

plummet (plŭm′ĭt) *v.* to fall suddenly and steeply

777

bundle wrapped in a faded pink blanket.

"These people," Grady sighed, opening the door. The woman stumbled up the steps, escaping the wind that mercilessly ripped at her petite frame.

"Look here. I've closed down the route. I'm taking the bus in."

In big gulping sobs the woman laid her story before him. "I need help, please. My husband's gone to Memphis looking for work. Our baby's sick, real sick. She needs to get to the hospital. I know she'll die if I don't get help."

"Well, I got to go by the hospital on the way back to the garage. You can ride that far." Grady nodded for her to pay. The woman looked at the floor. "Well? Pay up and get on to the back of the bus so I can get out of here."

"I—I don't have the fare," she said, quickly adding, "but if you let me ride, I promise to bring it to you in the morning."

"Give an inch, y'all want a mile. You know the rules. No money, no ride!"

"Oh, please!" the young woman cried. "Feel her little head. It's so hot." She held out the baby to him. Grady recoiled.

Desperately the woman looked for something to bargain with. "Here," she said, taking off her wedding ring. "Take this. It's gold. But please don't make me get off this bus."

He opened the door. The winds howled savagely. "Please," the woman begged.

"Go on home, now. You young gals get hysterical over a little fever. Nothing. It'll be fine in the morning." As he shut the door the last sounds he heard were the mother's sobs, the baby's wail, and the moaning wind.

Grady dismissed the incident until the next morning, when he read that it had been a record snowfall. His eyes were drawn to a small article about a colored woman and child found frozen to death on Hall Street. No one seemed to know where the woman was going or why. No one but Grady.

"That gal should have done like I told her and gone on home," he said, turning to the comics.

*I*t was exactly one year later, on the anniversary of the record snowstorm, that Grady was assigned the Hall Street Express again. Just as before, a storm heaped several inches of snow onto the city in a matter of hours, making driving extremely hazardous.

By nightfall Grady decided to close the route. But just as he was making the turn-around at the east side loop, his headlight picked up a woman running in the snow—the same woman he'd seen the previous year. Death hadn't altered her desperation. Still holding on to the blanketed baby, the small-framed woman pathetically struggled to reach the bus.

Grady closed his eyes but couldn't keep them shut. She was still coming, but from where? The answer was too horrible to consider, so he chose to let his mind find a more reasonable explanation. From some dark corner of his childhood he heard his father's voice, slurred by alcohol, mocking him. *It ain't the same woman, dummy. You know how they all look alike!*

Grady remembered his father with bitterness and swore at the thought of him. This *was* the same woman, Grady argued with his father's memory, taking no comfort in being right. Grady watched the woman's movements breathlessly as she stepped out of the headlight beam and approached the door. She stood outside the door waiting . . . waiting.

The gray coldness of Fear slipped into the driver's seat. Grady sucked air into his lungs in big gulps, feeling out of control. Fear moved his foot to the gas pedal, careening[5] the bus out into oncoming traffic. Headlights. A truck. Fear made Grady hit the brakes. The back of the bus went into a sliding spin, slamming into a tree. Grady's stomach crushed against the steering wheel, rupturing his liver and spleen. *You've really done it now, lunkhead.* As he drifted into the final darkness, he heard a woman's sobs, a baby wailing—or was it just the wind?

Twenty-five years later, Ray Hammond, a war hero with two years of college, became the first black driver Metro hired. A lot of things had happened during those two and a half decades to pave the way for Ray's new job. The military had integrated its forces during the Korean War. In 1954 the Supreme Court had ruled that segregated schools were unequal. And one by one, unfair laws were being challenged by civil rights groups all over the South. Ray had watched the Montgomery bus boycott with interest, especially the boycott's leader, Dr. Martin Luther King, Jr.

Ray soon found out that progress on the day-to-day level can be painfully slow. Ray was given the Hall Street Express.

"The white drivers call my route the Blackbird Express," Ray told his wife. "I'm the first driver to be given that route as a permanent assignment. The others wouldn't take it."

"What more did you expect?" his wife answered, tying his bow tie. "Just do your best so it'll be easier for the ones who come behind you."

In November, Ray worked the three-to-eleven shift. "Snow's predicted," the route manager barked one afternoon. "Close it down if it gets bad out there, Ray."

The last shift on the Hall Street Express.

> No one seemed to know where the woman was going or why. No one but Grady.

Since he was a boy, Ray had heard the story of the haunting of that bus route. Every first snowfall, passengers and drivers testified that they'd seen the ghost of Eula Mae Daniels clutching her baby as she ran through the snow.

"Good luck with Eula Mae tonight," one of the drivers said, snickering.

"I didn't know white folk believed in haints,"[6] Ray shot back.

But parked at the east side loop, staring into the swirling snow mixed with ice, Ray felt tingly, as if he were dangerously close to an electrical charge. He'd just made up his mind to close down the route and head back to the garage when he saw her. Every hair on his head stood on end.

He wished her away, but she kept coming. He tried to think, but his thoughts were jumbled and confused. He wanted to look away, but curiosity fixed his gaze on the advancing horror.

Just as the old porch stories had described her, Eula Mae Daniels was a small-framed woman frozen forever in youth. "So young," Ray whispered. "Could be my Carolyn in a few more years." He watched as the ghost came around to the doors. She was out there, waiting in the cold. Ray heard the baby crying. "There but for the grace of God goes one of mine," he said, compassion overruling his fear. "Nobody deserves to be left out in this weather.

---

5. **careening:** causing to swerve or lean to one side while in motion.

6. **haints** *Southern dialect:* ghosts.

Ghost or not, she deserves better." And he swung open the doors.

The woman had form but no substance. Ray could see the snow falling *through* her. He pushed fear aside. "Come on, honey, get out of the cold," Ray said, waving her on board.

Eula Mae stood stony still, looking up at Ray with dark, questioning eyes. The driver understood. He'd seen that look before, not from a dead woman but from plenty of his passengers. "It's okay. I'm for real. Ray Hammond, the first Negro to drive for Metro. Come on, now, get on," he coaxed her gently.

Eula Mae moved soundlessly up the steps. She held the infant to her body. Ray couldn't remember ever feeling so cold, not even the Christmas he'd spent in a Korean foxhole. He'd seen so much death, but never anything like this.

The ghost mother <u>consoled</u> her crying baby. Then with her head bowed she told her story in quick bursts of sorrow, just as she had twenty-five years earlier. "My husband is in Memphis looking for work. Our baby is sick. She'll die if I don't get help."

"First off," said Ray. "Hold your head up. You got no cause for shame."

"I don't have any money," she said. "But if you let me ride, I promise to bring it to you tomorrow. I promise."

Ray sighed deeply. "The rule book says no money, no ride. But the book doesn't say a word about a personal loan." He took a handful of change out of his pocket, fished around for a dime, and dropped it into the pay box. "You're all paid up. Now, go sit yourself down while I try to get this bus back to town."

Eula Mae started to the back of the bus.

"No you don't," Ray stopped her. "You don't have to sit in the back anymore. You can sit right up front."

The ghost woman moved to a seat closer, but still not too close up front. The baby fretted. The young mother comforted her as best she could.

They rode in silence for a while. Ray checked in the rearview mirror every now and then. She gave no reflection, but when he looked over his shoulder, she was there, all right. "Nobody will ever believe this," he mumbled. "*I* don't believe it.

"Things have gotten much better since you've been . . . away," he said, wishing immediately that he hadn't opened his mouth. Still he couldn't—or wouldn't—stop talking.

"I owe this job to a little woman just about your size named Mrs. Rosa Parks. Down in Montgomery, Alabama, one day, Mrs. Parks refused to give up a seat she'd paid for just because she was a colored woman."

Eula Mae sat motionless. There was no way of telling if she had heard or not. Ray kept talking. "Well, they arrested her. So the colored people decided to boycott the buses. Nobody rode for over a year. Walked everywhere, formed car pools, or just didn't go, rather than ride a bus. The man who led the boycott was named Reverend King. Smart man. We're

> "It's okay. I'm for real. Ray Hammond, the first Negro to drive for Metro. Come on, now, get on."

sure to hear more about him in the future. . . . You still with me?" Ray looked around. Yes, she was there. The baby had quieted. It was much warmer on the bus now.

Slowly Ray inched along on the icy road, holding the bus steady, trying to keep the back wheels from racing out of control. "Where was I?" he continued. "Oh yeah, things changed after that Montgomery bus boycott. This job opened up. More changes are on the way. Get this: they got an Irish Catholic running for President. Now, what do you think of that?

About that time Ray pulled the bus over at Seventeenth Street. The lights at Gale Hospital sent a welcome message to those in need on such a frosty night. "This is it."

Eula Mae raised her head. "You're a kind man," she said. "Thank you."

Ray opened the door. The night air gusted up the steps and nipped at his ankles. Soundlessly, Eula Mae stepped off the bus with her baby.

"Excuse me," Ray called politely. "About the bus fare. No need for you to make a special trip . . . back. Consider it a gift."

He thought he saw Eula Mae Daniels smile as she vanished into the swirling snow, never to be seen again. ❖

PATRICIA C. MCKISSACK

Patricia C. McKissack (1944–) has written one award-winning book after another. Writing separately and together, she and her husband, Fredrick, have written more than 100 books for children and teenagers. Most are about the lives of African Americans and Native Americans—some famous, and others who are "left out of history books."

Their lives, McKissack says, were influenced by the civil rights movement of the 1960s, when "African Americans were really looking up, coming out of darkness, segregation, and discrimination, and doors were beginning to open—ever so slightly, but still opening."

Before becoming a full-time writer, McKissack taught eighth graders and college students, and edited children's books. When she found no biography of Paul Laurence Dunbar for her eighth graders, she wrote one herself. Among the many awards her books have won are three Coretta Scott King Awards and a Newbery Honor Award. She has also written radio and television scripts and an award-winning movie script.

McKissack was born in Smyrna, Tennessee. "We did not have television and I grew up sitting on the front porch listening to family and community stories," she says. She and her husband graduated from Tennessee State University. The McKissacks have three grown sons and live in St. Louis, Missouri.

OTHER WORKS *Christmas in the Big House— Christmas in the Quarters, Sojourner Truth: Ain't I a Woman?*

RESPONDING
OPTIONS

LITERATURE CONNECTION PROJECT 1

Create a Dust Jacket for a Book A dust jacket is a paper cover that protects a book and promotes the story to readers. Working in small groups, choose one of the stories you have just read. Imagine that the story is a book, and create a dust jacket for it. Decide who will create each component of the jacket. Refer to these suggestions as you carry out the project.

Cover Design and illustrate the front of the jacket. You could research the artwork of the story's culture and use elements of it in your design.

Back Select a short excerpt from the story that can go on the back of the jacket. Choose an excerpt that makes the reader want to find out more about the story.

Back Inside Flap Interview some classmates and write down their critical reactions to the story. Select three or four favorable quotations from these student reactions to put on the back inside flap.

Front Inside Flap Write a few paragraphs to go on the inside flap of the dust jacket. These should give an idea of what the story is about but not give the whole story away. The purpose of this text is to generate reader interest, so make it as engaging and exciting as possible.

SOCIAL STUDIES CONNECTION PROJECT 2

Design a Newspaper's Front Page The bus boycott in Montgomery, Alabama, in 1955–1956, marked a turning point in the civil rights movement in the United States.

Imagine you are a journalist. Working with a group of classmates, create the front page of a newspaper for the day the boycott ended. Use books or computer databases, if possible, to carry out your research. As you plan your articles for the page, investigate the parts played by Rosa Parks and Dr. Martin Luther King, Jr. Lay out your spread on a computer if possible.

SCIENCE CONNECTION PROJECT 3

Construct a Diorama of an Ecosystem
The story "Otoonah" comes from Kodiak Island, off the Alaskan coast. Find out more about this island's natural environment. Investigate the climate. What is the name of this kind of environment? Make a list of the animals and plants that live in it. Are they all mentioned in the story? How does this environment change from season to season? Create a diorama of this natural environment. Write a key that explains the different parts of the diorama and that gives extra information.

ACROSS CULTURES MINI-PROJECTS

Find the Enemy The enemy in these stories may be a real person or an animal, or it may be something less concrete, such as an attitude or situation. Who or what is the enemy in each story? Select a story from Unit Four that features an enemy similar to one you have just read about. Draw a picture that illustrates the similarities between the two.

Create an Iroquois Time Line Make a time line, like the one started here, showing the main events in the history of the Iroquois. Work with another student to select the dates you wish to feature.

The five tribes unite to form the League of the Iroquois.

1570

Compose a Song Discover who the Peacemaker referred to on the first page of "Racing the Great Bear" was. Then find out all you can about this person. Choose a style of music that you think is appropriate—pop, blues, ballad—and write a modern song about the Peacemaker. Share it with your class.

Compare Characters Compare and contrast Carol Bullard—the ghost in "The Girl in the Lavender Dress" (page 710)—and Eula Mae Daniels of "The Woman in the Snow." Begin by listing the qualities of each character. Then record their similarities and differences in a chart like the one shown.

Carol Bullard and Eula Mae Daniels	
Similarities	**Differences**

MORE ABOUT THE CULTURES

- *American Indians Today* by Judith Harlan
- *The Iroquois* by Barbara A. McCall
- *The Life and Words of Martin Luther King, Jr.* by Ira Peck
- *The Montgomery Bus Boycott, December, 1955* by Janet Stevenson

LINKS TO UNIT FIVE

Personal Discoveries

In Unit Five, painful as well as joyous experiences lead individuals to make discoveries about themselves. They gain a deeper insight into who they are and what they believe in. The characters in the tales you are about to read also follow their own paths to greater self-knowledge.

SOUTHEASTERN U.S.

Strawberries

retold by Gayle Ross

Up until the early 1800s, the Cherokee people lived and hunted in the southern Appalachian region, an area that included what is now part of North Carolina. These early Cherokee people believed their homeland was the center of the world. They pictured the earth as a floating island attached to the sky by four cords. In their mythology, the first man and the first woman were Kana'ti and Selu, who are featured in this myth.

No News

retold by Connie Regan-Blake and Barbara Freeman

"No News" is the kind of folk tale one hears, with subtle variations, across many cultures. Regan-Blake and Freeman first heard this story told about Down Easters, a term New Englanders sometimes use for people from Maine who are east of or downwind from Boston. These storytellers adapted the tale to their Southern culture.

The First Flute

*retold by
Dorothy Sharp Carter*

The Maya thrived in Guatemala—as well as in parts of what is now Mexico, Belize, El Salvador, and Honduras—between A.D. 250 and 900. Prospering in a difficult tropical forest ecosystem, the Maya built one of the most remarkable civilizations. "The First Flute" takes place during this period, long before the Spanish conquered the Maya in the 1500s.

AS YOU READ . . .

Think about what is fun about these tales.

Imagine their being repeated from generation to generation.

Consider the ways in which the characters have the ability to laugh at themselves.

Note how the cultures differ from each other and from your own.

STRAWBERRIES

RETOLD BY GAYLE ROSS

Long ago, in the very first days of the world, there lived the first man and the first woman. They lived together as husband and wife, and they loved one another dearly.

But one day, they quarreled. Although neither later could remember what the quarrel was about, the pain grew stronger with every word that was spoken, until finally, in anger and in grief, the woman left their home and began walking away—to the east, toward the rising sun.

The man sat alone in his house. But as time went by, he grew lonelier and lonelier. The anger left him, and all that remained was a terrible grief and despair, and he began to cry.

A spirit heard the man crying and took pity on him. The spirit said, "Man, why do you cry?"

The man said, "My wife has left me."

The spirit said, "Why did your woman leave?"

The man just hung his head and said nothing.

The spirit asked, "You quarreled with her?"

And the man nodded.

Strawberry Dance (1983), G. Peter Jemison (Seneca Nation, Heron Clan). Mixed media on handmade paper, 22″ × 30″, private collection, by permission of the artist.

"Would you quarrel with her again?" asked the spirit.

The man said, "No." He wanted only to live with his wife as they had lived before— in peace, in happiness, and in love.

"I have seen your woman," the spirit said. "She is walking to the east toward the rising sun."

The man followed his wife, but he could not overtake her. Everyone knows an angry woman walks fast.

Finally, the spirit said, "I'll go ahead and see if I can make her slow her steps." So the spirit found the woman walking, her footsteps fast and angry and her gaze fixed straight ahead. There was pain in her heart.

The spirit saw some huckleberry bushes growing along the trail, so with a wave of his hand, he made the bushes burst into bloom and ripen into fruit. But the woman's gaze remained fixed. She looked neither to the right nor to the left, and she didn't see the berries. Her footsteps didn't slow.

Again, the spirit waved his hand, and one

by one, all of the berries growing along the trail burst into bloom and ripened into fruit. But still, the woman's gaze remained fixed. She saw nothing but her anger and pain, and her footsteps didn't slow.

And again, the spirit waved his hand, and, one by one, the trees of the forest—the peach, the pear, the apple, the wild cherry—burst into bloom and ripened into fruit. But still, the woman's eyes remained fixed, and even still, she saw nothing but her anger and pain. And her footsteps didn't slow.

Then finally, the spirit thought, "I will create an entirely new fruit—one that grows very, very close to the ground so the woman must forget her anger and bend her head for a moment." So the spirit waved his hand, and a thick green carpet began to grow along the trail. Then the carpet became starred with tiny white flowers, and

each flower gradually ripened into a berry that was the color and shape of the human heart.

As the woman walked, she crushed the tiny berries, and the delicious aroma came up through her nose. She stopped and looked down, and she saw the berries. She picked one and ate it, and she discovered its taste was as sweet as love itself. So she began walking slowly, picking berries as she went, and as she leaned down to pick a berry, she saw her husband coming behind her.

The anger had gone from her heart, and all that remained was the love she had always known. So she stopped for him, and together, they picked and ate the berries. Finally, they returned to their home, where they lived out their days in peace, happiness, and love.

And that's how the world's very first strawberries brought peace between men and women in the world and why to this day they are called the berries of love. ❖

GAYLE ROSS

Gayle Ross says, "For me, being Cherokee is a true identification—a very real part of who I am." Ross is the great-great-great-granddaughter of John Ross, principal chief of the Cherokees before and during the Trail of Tears.

From her grandmother, Ross first heard the Cherokee stories she retells in books and to audiences across the country. "I don't want anyone to feel guilty about the Trail of Tears," she says. "Instead, I want us to learn from this tragic experience."

Ross left her studies in radio and television at the University of Texas to work in broadcasting, but

1951–

soon became dissatisfied. A trip to a storytelling festival changed her life. Ross quit her job and, with a partner, began performing as The Twelve Moons Storytellers throughout the United States.

Always looking for stories to tell, Ross may find "a piece of a story or a skeletal version" that she "fleshes out with accurate cultural context" and her imagination.

OTHER WORKS *How Rabbit Tricked Otter and Other Cherokee Trickster Stories, Second Best Stories at the National Storytelling Festival, The Girl Who Married the Moon* (with Joseph Bruchac)

No News

retold by Connie Regan-Blake and Barbara Freeman

Dorothy and Netti (1974), Alex Katz. Oil on canvas, 72″ × 96″, collection of the artist, courtesy of Marlborough Gallery, New York. Copyright © Alex Katz.

A certain Southern lady was returning home after recuperating in the mountains for three months. Her friend Georgeanne met her at the railway station.

"Georgeanne, has there been any news while I've been away?"

"Oh, no, there's no news."

"No news? Surely something has occurred in my absence. Why, I've been gone for nearly three months, and I'm anxious for any little bit of news you may have."

"Oh, now, since you mentioned it—'course it don't amount to much—but since you've been away, your dog died."

"My dog died? How did my dog die?"

"He ate some of the burnt horseflesh, and that's what killed the dog."

"Burnt horseflesh?"

"Well, after the fire cooled off, the dog ate some of the burnt horseflesh, and that's what killed the dog."

"Fire cooled off?"

"Well, the barn burned down, burned up all of the cows and horses, and when the fire cooled down, the dog ate some of the burnt horseflesh, and that's what killed the dog."

"My barn burned down? How did my barn burn down?"

"Oh, it was a spark from the house. Blew over, lit the roof of the barn, burned down the barn, burned up all the cows and horses, and when the fire cooled off, the dog ate some of the burnt horseflesh, and that's what killed the dog."

"A spark from the house?"

"Oh, yes, now that's completely burned down."

"But how did my house burn down?"

"It was the candle flame that lit the curtains, shot up the side of the wall, and burned down the house; a spark flew over on the roof of the barn, burned down the barn, burned up all of the cows and horses, and when the fire cooled off, the dog ate some of the burnt horseflesh, and that's what killed the dog."

"Candles? I don't even allow candles in my house. How did the candles get into my house?"

"Oh, they were around the coffin."

"Coffin? Who died?"

"Oh, now you needn't worry about that. Since you've been away, your mother-in-law died."

"Oh, my mother-in-law. What a pity. How did she die?"

"Well, some folks say that it was the shock of hearing that your husband had run away with the choir leader. But other than that, there ain't been no news." ❖

CONNIE REGAN-BLAKE AND BARBARA FREEMAN

Connie Regan-Blake (1947–) and Barbara Freeman (1944–) are Southern cousins. As children, they spent summers at an uncle's farm where they made up stories to tell. Little did they know at the time that they would travel together as adults telling stories for a living.

In 1971, they left their secure library jobs in Chattanooga, Tennessee, and began touring the country collecting and telling stories. Calling themselves The Folktellers, they developed a unique style of tandem storytelling in which they take turns delivering a line, but also pronounce lines in unison.

Regan-Blake and Freeman have been telling stories, many from Appalachia, for 20 years now. They have recorded audiotapes that have won awards from the American Library Association and *Parents' Choice* magazine. They have also produced videos.

The two women also perform solo. Regan-Blake tells tales accompanied by a chamber music trio; Freeman tells humorous mountain tales and true stories of Christian saints and martyrs.

THE FIRST FLUTE

retold by Dorothy Sharp Carter

During the glory of the Mayan[1] civilization, years before the coming of the Spanish, there lived a *cacique*[2] who had a beautiful daughter, the Princess Nima-Cux, whom he loved dearly.

Not only was Nima-Cux beautiful, she was possessed of talents. She could plait grass into fine baskets.

---

1. **Mayan** (mä′yən): belonging to the Maya, a Native American people of southern Mexico and northern Central America.
2. *cacique* (kə-sēk′): a Native American chief.

She could mold little animals out of clay—and you even knew exactly which animals they were supposed to be. The coati[3] had a long, ringed tail. The puma[4] had an open mouth showing sharp teeth. The tapir's[5] snout was definitely snoutish. The snake wound round and round and round—and if you unwound him, he reached from Nima-Cux's toes to her earlobes.

Above all, Nima-Cux could sing like a bird. Her voice tripped up and down the scale as easily as her feet tripped up and down the steps. The *cacique* sat back and counted his blessings. They all had to do with Nima-Cux, her beauty, her baskets, her clay work, and, especially, her voice.

As princesses should, Nima-Cux had everything she asked for—besides some things she hadn't thought of requesting. There were finely carved dolls, necklaces of rare shells, a cape of bright parrot feathers, an enormous garden filled with flowers and blossoming trees and singing birds and pet animals. No wonder Nima-Cux was happy.

Thus life flowed along contentedly for everyone in the household until Nima-Cux neared her sixteenth birthday. Suddenly she became sad and <u>melancholy</u>. Nothing made her happy. Then again, nothing made her unhappy. She just *was,* for no reason at all, she said.

Detail from *Aviary Triptych* (1992), Carol Cottone-Kolthoff. By permission of the artist. Copyright © 1992 Carol Cottone-Kolthoff.

The *cacique* was greatly <u>agitated</u>. He strode up and down the garden, wondering, wondering what would please Nima-Cux. Another doll? A bright fish? A golden plate for her breast-of-pheasant? But to whatever he proposed, Nima-Cux would only murmur politely, "No. But thank you, Papa."

The cook sent boys scampering up the tallest palm trees to bring back heart of palm for Nima-Cux's dinner.

Hunters were ordered into the jungle to capture monkeys. "Mind you, *funny* monkeys to entertain the princess. Not a sad one in the crowd—or off comes your head."

Maidens roamed the royal gardens gathering orchids to ornament the princess' bedchamber.

What happened? Nima-Cux would peer at the rare *palmito*[6] and moan softly, "I am not hungry."

She would stare at the monkeys cavorting[7] on the branches, while the royal household

---

3. **coati** (kō-ä′tē): a raccoonlike animal of the tropical Americas and the southwestern United States.
4. **puma** (pyo͞o′mə): a mountain lion.
5. **tapir's** (tā′pərz): belonging to a large, hoglike animal.
6. **palmito** (päl-mē′tô) *Spanish:* a bud of a palm tree, used as a food.
7. **cavorting** (kə-vôrt′ĭng): leaping about.

WORDS TO KNOW

melancholy (mĕl′ən-kŏl′ē) *adj.* depressed and gloomy
agitated (ăj′ĭ-tāt′ĭd) *adj.* emotionally excited or disturbed

screamed in amusement, and would whisper, "Yes, yes, very comical," and sigh deeply. The household would hush its laughter and echo her sighs.

The orchids went unnoticed until they dropped to the floor with a dry rustle.

Herb doctors came. Witch doctors came. Old hunched crones said to know the secrets of life came. They all said, "But she seems quite well and normal. A bit pale. A trifle listless. Perhaps a good tonic . . ."

Nima-Cux was annoyed enough to argue about the tonic. "That smelly stuff? I won't even taste it."

Finally a sorcerer somewhat wiser than the others spoke to the *cacique*. "After all, the princess is practically sixteen. Other girls her age are married. Find a good husband for the Princess Nima-Cux—and she will again shine radiant as a star."

The *cacique* shook his head. A *husband*? How could a mere husband bring her happiness if her own father could not? A poor suggestion. What were sorcerers coming to?

He peeked once more at Nima-Cux's dismal face—and in desperation sent messengers throughout his kingdom. The young man skillful enough to impress the princess and coax a smile to her lips would become her husband. In a week the first tournament would be held.

During the next week the roads were worn into holes by the thousands of footsteps.

Detail from *Aviary Triptych* (1992), Carol Cottone-Kolthoff. By permission of the artist. Copyright © 1992 Carol Cottone-Kolthoff.

Everyone in the kingdom hurried to the palace either to take part or to watch the take-parters (or is it takers-part?). Seats were constructed for the nobility. Those not so noble found a patch of thick grass, a loop of vine, or a high branch. The *cacique* and Nima-Cux sat on a canopied stand. The tournaments began.

The first contestant marched out, proud and arrogant in his gold tunic, attended by a troop of warriors. A handsome youth he was. Maidens fainted with joy at the sight of him. The rest of the contestants growled and trembled.

But Nima-Cux frowned and asked, "What can he *do*? Besides prance and preen, worse than any *quetzal*?"[8]

The *cacique* sighed and made a sign for the warrior to display his talents—if any. The soldiers stood before the young man and threw ears of corn into the air. With his bow and arrows the warrior shot kernels from the ears in regimental procession. One row, then the next and next until all the kernels were gone.

The spectators cheered and shouted with admiration. Such skill—and such elegance! Ayyyyyyy! The other contestants ground their teeth and sobbed.

---

8. *quetzal* (kĕt-säl′): a Central American bird with brilliant green and red feathers.

Nima-Cux yawned and asked politely, "May we see the second match, Papa? The first has taken up *so* much time."

The *cacique* sighed again and motioned for the tournament to continue.

The second competitor strode out as confident and proud as the first. He walked alone, bearing a large basket. When he set it down, out slithered a tremendous snake of a poisonous variety, its eyes glaring with malevolence.

The spectators gasped with horror. Maidens fainted with fear. The remaining rivals watched with relish.

The youth engaged the angry snake in combat, artfully evading its deadly fangs. The spectators held their breaths.

"How boring!" muttered Nima-Cux, staring into the distance.

"Really? Really, daughter? You don't like it?" asked the *cacique* with regret. (He was enjoying the contests immensely.)

He motioned for more action. The youth complied by squeezing the life from the snake. Then he bowed to the applause of the crowd. Or most of the crowd. Nima-Cux was already on her way to the palace and her couch with a headache.

For days the tournaments continued. The

Detail from *Aviary Triptych* (1992), Carol Cottone-Kolthoff. By permission of the artist. Copyright © 1992 Carol Cottone-Kolthoff.

most handsome and courageous of the Mayan youth competed with each other for the favor of Nima-Cux—favor that was nowhere to be seen. Certainly not on her lips, which remained clamped in a sulky line. Nor in her eyes, which gazed sadly at the competition without seeing it.

Finally the last contestant appeared, a merry boy wearing the tattered dress of a minstrel.[9] The spectators smiled. The other contestants laughed scornfully. With a quick bow to the princess, the boy began to sing. He sang of the lakes, the forests, the hills of the highlands. He sang of the crystal stars flashing from the dark river of night. He sang of love.

Not bad, not bad, nodded the *cacique*. Not, of course, to compare with Nima-Cux's singing. He glanced at his daughter. What astonishment! Her eyes resembled the crystal of the song. Her lips were open and curving—upward. She was smiling! The *cacique* sat back and pondered the puzzle of life and love.

"I like him, Papa. We can sing together. I will marry him. Only first, he must learn the song of each bird of the forest. Then he can teach me."

---

9. **minstrel** (mĭn′strəl): a singer or musician.

The minstrel was happy to oblige. He had *meant* it when he sang of love. At once he disappeared into the jungle.

Day after day he practiced, imitating this bird, then that one. But Guatemala is home to hundreds, thousands of birds. Some whistle a complicated tune. The minstrel began to despair of his task.

The god of the forest, after listening for days to the young minstrel's efforts, took pity on him. Also on the birds and other wild inhabitants of the woods—not to mention himself. He appeared before the minstrel, wearing a kindly smile.

"Perhaps I can help you," he offered. "It is a difficult exercise you are engaged in."

Severing a small limb from a tree, the god removed the pith and cut a series of holes in the tube. "Now attend carefully," he said. And he instructed the young man exactly how to blow into one end while moving his fingers over the holes. The notes of the birds tumbled out, clear and sweet.

With a torrent of thanks, the minstrel flew on his way, carrying the *chirimia*, or flute. Just in time. Nima-Cux, anxious that the chore she had assigned her lover had been impossible, was on the point of another decline. She received the youth with joy. Enchanted she was with the flute and its airs[10] . . . with the minstrel and his airs.

The two were married and lived long and happily in the palace of the *cacique*. And today the Indians of Guatemala will point to the *chirimia*, the most typical of native instruments, and tell you this is the way it came about. ❖

---

10. **airs:** melodies.

DOROTHY SHARP CARTER

Dorothy Sharp Carter (1921–) developed a strong affinity for Latin American folklore during her 11 years in South and Central America, where her husband worked as a United States foreign service officer.

When she returned to the United States, she entered a graduate program in library science at the University of Texas. One of her projects was collecting and translating Latin American folk tales. Impressed with her work, her professor sent the manuscript to a publisher. It was accepted, and *The Enchanted Orchard and Other Folktales of Central America*, from which "The First Flute" is taken, was published in 1973. Her stories have been published in the magazines *Travel, Nature, Highlights for Children,* and *Humpty Dumpty.*

She was born in Chicago and grew up in Galveston, Texas. Later, Carter went to Mills College in California and taught high school in California and Costa Rica, where she met her husband. They currently live in Texas, spending part of their time on a ranch on the Pedernales River, where they enjoy Texas wildlife.

OTHER WORKS *Greedy Mariani and Other Folktales of the Antilles; His Majesty, Queen Hatshepsut*

RESPONDING
OPTIONS

LITERATURE CONNECTION PROJECT 1

Make a Character "Report Card" Working in small groups, select a character from one of the selections you have just read. Prepare a "report card" to evaluate the character's personality, using the following guidelines.

The Character's Qualities Begin by deciding on the qualities you wish to evaluate—courage, kindness, greed, ingenuity, and so on.

The Grading Scale Then decide on the grades you will use to assess the character. You could use letters, numbers, or even symbols.

Group Debate and Class Report Within your group, discuss and debate each quality of the character. Assign a grade when your entire group is in agreement. Report your decision back to the class.

Report Card			
Character	**courage**	**kindness**	**ingenuity**
Nima-Cux			

MATHEMATICS CONNECTION PROJECT 2

Use the Mayan Number System The Maya developed a mathematical system based on the number 20, instead of 10 as in the decimal system we use. They used a dot to represent 1, a line for 5, and a shell or egg-shaped symbol for zero.

Given what you now know about the Mayan numerical system, identify the other Mayan numbers shown.

From the information provided thus far, figure out and write the Mayan numbers for 8, 16, and 80. Then working with a partner, see if you can figure out the Mayan number for 100.

SOCIAL STUDIES CONNECTION PROJECT 3

 Produce a Television Program Most of the remarkable accomplishments of the Maya have become understood only in this century as archaeologists study and continue to uncover Mayan ruins. In addition to developing a kind of picture writing, they made great advances in architecture, art, mathematics, and astronomy.

Use your school library to research Mayan accomplishments. If you have access to a computer, you could use an encyclopedia program or an on-line service to start your research. Visit a museum with Mayan artifacts if one is nearby. Then produce an educational television program using the following suggestions as a guide:

- Decide on the program's length.

- Write a script from your research, including a brief introduction that explains who the Maya were. You might also include information about their descendants today.

- Gather visual material, and rehearse the show to fit the time slot.

- Make a videotape of the program and show it to your class and other classes.

ACROSS CULTURES MINI-PROJECTS

Tell a Story Through Drawings Adapt one of the three stories to a present-day setting, and tell it through a series of drawings. Keep explanatory text to a minimum. You might want to create a comic strip, picture book, flipbook, or series of illustrations on wall-sized posterboard. Share your results with classmates.

Write a Letter of Advice Imagine you are training to be a counselor. Your assignment is to analyze the relationship of the couple in "Strawberries" or the couple in "No News." On the basis of your analysis of their behavior, write a letter of advice to the newly married couple in "The First Flute," suggesting how they might build a strong relationship.

Tell an Origin Myth Many cultures have origin myths similar to "Strawberries" and "The First Flute." Choose a nonliving thing in nature, an object such as a musical instrument, or a fruit or vegetable, and write an origin myth about it. Present your tale to the class.

Investigate Cherokee Beliefs and Customs All cultures have distinct beliefs and customs about marriage and family life. Cherokee women held great power, and families were matrilineal, tracing their descent through women instead of men. Find out more about Cherokee customs. Then form small discussion groups and compare and contrast traditional Cherokee beliefs to your own cultural standards.

 MORE ABOUT THE CULTURES

- *The Cherokees* by Elaine Landau

- *Indians of the Southeast: Then and Now* by Jesse Burt and Robert B. Ferguson

- *Lost Kingdoms of the Maya* by Gene S. Stuart and George E. Stuart

- *The Mysteries of the Ancient Maya* by Carolyn Meyer and C. Gallenkamp

WRITING A REPORT

In Unit Six, "Across Time and Place: The Oral Tradition," you read several stories from different cultures. New folklore continues to develop as stories, tales, and urban legends. Investigating and researching these stories can be fascinating.

GUIDED ASSIGNMENT
Write a Research Report In this lesson you will get a chance to research the culture of a story, folk tale, myth, fable, or urban legend. Then you'll write a report about your findings.

Company Disclaimer

① Look for a New Angle

What new and interesting facts can you discover about folklore?

Stories You've Read Which of the selections in the unit did you enjoy the most? Would you like to find out more about this type of story or the country it came from?

Cultural Connection Are there stories you've heard from your own culture or from that of a friend that you'd like to learn more about? Have you ever wondered about the stories represented in folk art, song, or dance?

Stories in the News The items on these pages represent some well-known urban legends. These stories describe scary or humorous experiences in urban settings. Usually they happened to "a friend of a friend." Have you heard similar stories? Make a list of such stories and any questions you might have about them.

To Our Customers

The widespread rumor that a customer discovered a rat in her bucket of Krispy Krunchy Chicken is false. Our standards for sanitation and proper food preparation procedures are among the highest in the industry. We regret the confusion this rumor has caused.

I've heard something similar to this. I thought the story was true when I heard it.

These incidents are variations of stories told throughout the United States and Canada. The stories are usually reported as fact. Why do you think these stories are so popular?

Letter

March 1

Dear Debbie,

Hey, girl, how are you?

I went camping last week, and my cousin told me a story that I keep thinking about. We were talking about bears, and she told me about a man and a woman who went camping with their baby and saw a bear. They wanted a picture of their kid with the bear, so they spread honey all over the kid's face and hands. The bear started to attack the kid, and the people barely escaped with their lives. Can you believe someone would actually do that? It made me nervous the rest of the trip. Do you think it's true?

Write me soon, or else!

Love,
Melvonne

Hey! Someone else told me this story too!

Comic Strip

Mother Goose and Grimm

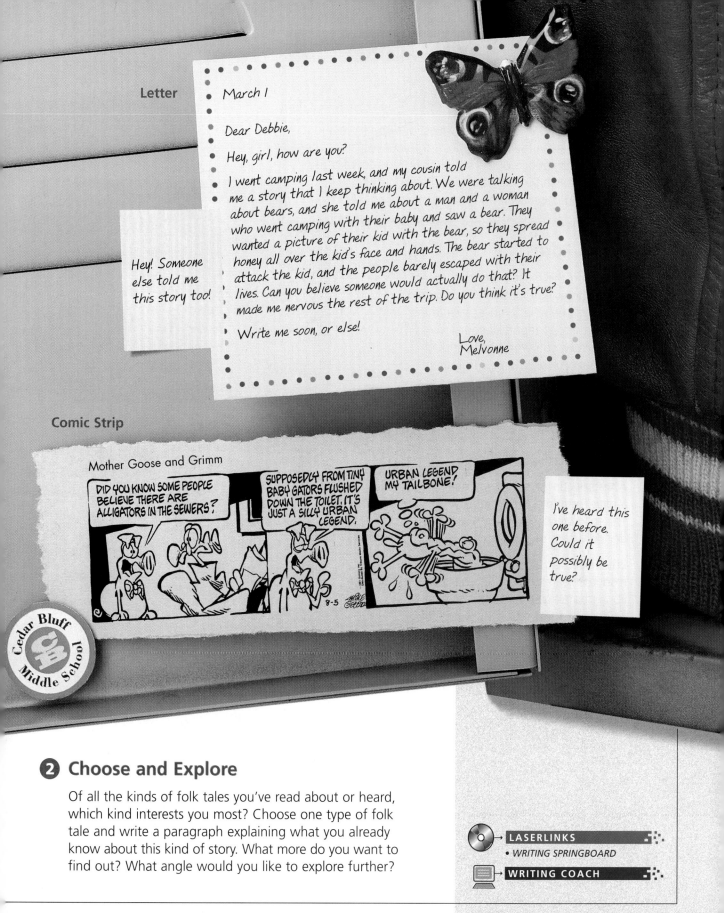

I've heard this one before. Could it possibly be true?

② Choose and Explore

Of all the kinds of folk tales you've read about or heard, which kind interests you most? Choose one type of folk tale and write a paragraph explaining what you already know about this kind of story. What more do you want to find out? What angle would you like to explore further?

LASERLINKS
• WRITING SPRINGBOARD

WRITING COACH

Researching Folklore

The Search for Answers The questions you have about your topic may be the starting point for your research. The kinds of information you want will point you toward the kinds of research sources you need. These pages will help you plan your research.

INFOTRAC

```
Infotrac        *Magazine Index Plus
(Backfile)
Heading         URBAN FOLKLORE

1.      Heard the one about the man-
eating squirrel? (coping with urban
legends) by Andre Henderson il v7
Governing July '94 p25 (1)

ABSTRACT / HEADINGS
```

❶ Find a Focus

Try to find the most interesting aspect of your topic. If your topic is too broad, you won't be able to cover everything about it in one report. If your topic is too narrow, you won't have enough information. Try writing a statement of controlling purpose, a one- or two-sentence description of what your report will be about.

❷ Plan Your Research

After selecting a focus, you need a plan for finding information. The following tips can help you decide where to go to find sources.

Library Hunt You can complete a resource search quickly by using a library database. List all the possible sources you find and group them by call numbers or location. Back copies of articles are kept on microfilm or microfiche. See the Multimedia Handbook, page 850, for information about on-line sources.

Expert Advice If you're looking for information on a culture or on another topic, you can look for newsletters or brochures written by groups or organizations associated with the culture or topic. You might also ask a librarian to help you find reference books, pamphlets, or other literature.

Source Cards

Encyclopedia

Dundes, Alan. "Folklore." The World Book
Encyclopedia. 1995 ed.

School Library   031
                        WOR
                        V.4

①

Brunvand, Jan Harold. The Vanishing Hitchhiker:
American Urban Legends and Their Meanings.
New York: Norton, 1981.

Public Library
                    3982
                    BRU

②

Book

Morris, Scot. "Paper Chase: Searching for
modern folklore on the office bulletin
board." OMNI. Apr. 1991: Vol. 13, No. 7.

Public Library

③

Magazine

③ Gather Information

Once you've found your sources, take some time to plan your fact-gathering process. Take the following steps to be as prepared as possible for writing your report.

Preview Sources Scan the tables of contents and indexes in the books and periodicals you've chosen. Do their contents seem to offer information that will help you? If not, you may need to choose another source.

Create Source Cards As you gather facts, you'll need to keep track of the sources you find. List the author's name and the publication information of each source on a separate index card. Be sure to number each card. This will help you stay organized when you take notes.

Take Notes The SkillBuilder on this page can help you take notes. Write information that you want to use on a note card. Paraphrase, or write in your own words, the main ideas and supporting details from the passage. This will help you avoid plagiarism, or using a person's words without giving him or her credit. Include the source number and indicate whether the information is a quote, a paraphrase, or general knowledge—a widely known fact that can be found in many sources.

Note Cards

SkillBuilder

  RESEARCH SKILLS

Taking Notes
Note taking is a helpful way to collect the information you find in sources. Here are some strategies for taking notes:

Paraphrase the main ideas of the material. Paraphrasing means using your own words to restate someone else's ideas. You still must credit the sources, however.

Quote a source directly if it states the idea in a particularly interesting way. Be sure to use quotation marks and to note that the information is a quote.

APPLYING WHAT YOU'VE LEARNED
Use your own words as you take notes, unless you plan to quote something exactly. In either case, credit your sources.

 WRITING HANDBOOK

For more information on note taking and research report writing, see page 846 of the Writing Handbook.

THINK & PLAN

Reflecting on Your Ideas

1. How has the research material you found helped you better understand your topic?
2. What aspect of your topic do you find the most interesting? Why?

Reporting the Facts

A Way with Words With organized notes and a clear idea of what your report is all about, you're already at the halfway point. Now you're ready to take the next step—writing your report.

Student's Outline and Draft

> Urban Legends
>
> Introduction—Urban legends are unusual, but somewhat believable, modern folk tales that are passed on from one person to another.
>
> I. Urban legends as part of folklore
>   A. Oral tradition of legends
>   B. Comparison with legends like Paul Bunyan
> II. Characteristics of urban folklore
>   A. Believability

> Some of the stories we hear about in conversations or in the news don't strike us as legends or folklore. Yet they are. The story of the alligator found in a city sewer is a good example of this kind of tale, which is called an urban legend. Urban legends are unusual tales that seem believable but usually are made up. "As with any folk legends, urban legends gain credibility from specific details of time and place or from references to source authorities" (Brunvand 3).
>   The story of the alligator in the sewers of New York was passed around in the 1960s. Many variations on the story exist. One mentions some kids who bought little alligators at Macy's department store. They got sick of the creatures after awhile and put them in a sewer.

Need to make thesis statement clearer so readers will know where this report is going. J.B.

Do you have any references for the alligator story? A.C.

① Organize Your Ideas

The suggestions below will help you organize your ideas before you begin drafting.

Write a Thesis Statement Use your statement of controlling purpose to write a thesis statement that describes the main idea of your report.

Make an Outline Divide your note cards into groups with similar headings. Use the main points from your note cards as the headings for an outline like the one on the left.

② Start Writing

As you draft, keep your note cards and outline handy to check quotes and other notes. Be sure to credit other people's ideas and information in parentheses as the student did on the left. Keep in mind that you will be making a Works Cited list that has all of the publication information. If your ideas change as you go along, feel free to adjust your outline.

③ Analyze Your Draft

What new questions about your topic came to mind as you were writing? You might want to do some additional research to answer them. Make a list of your questions. Where will you go to find answers?

④ Rework and Share

Try these suggestions for organizing and polishing your draft.

Write Your Introduction Try to write an opening paragraph that will draw your readers in. Remember, your first or second paragraph will probably develop around your thesis statement. You might open with an interesting anecdote or a hypothetical question. For more on writing introductions, see page 826 of the Writing Handbook.

Order Your Details Make sure that the ideas and details in your report flow logically. If you're researching the origin of a myth or a culture, for example, you might organize your details chronologically. If you're tracing the variations of a myth, you might compare and contrast the details of each variation.

Write a Conclusion End your report by summarizing your main points in the conclusion.

Credit Your Sources Double-check that you have credited any experts or authors you quote. The SkillBuilder on this page will help you credit sources properly.

 PEER RESPONSE

Peer feedback will help you know if your ideas are interesting and coherent. Ask a peer reviewer questions like these:

- What would you say is the main point of my report?
- Are there instances where you aren't sure that I used my own words? Explain.
- Have I organized my report in a way that is easy to follow?
- Is there a better word I can use to describe a particular idea?

Finishing Your Report

A Final Look When you revise your draft, keep your analysis and the peer comments in mind. The suggestions on these pages also can help you get your report into its final form.

Student's Final Report

Chan 1

Debbie Chan
Mr. Samuelson
5th Period English
11 March 1997

The Truth About Urban Legends

Do you believe that alligators roam the sewers of New York City? You've probably heard this story—or a version of it—and wondered whether it was true. Actually, it's an urban legend, an unusual tale that seems believable but usually is made up. Urban legends pop up in conversations on TV and in newspapers. People often hear these tales, wonder about them, and then pass them on to someone else as if they were true. Urban legends may not seem as literary as the folk tales and myths we've heard all our lives, but they are actually very similar. They have also become an accepted part of modern folklore.

One characteristic of urban legends is their believability. Jan Harold Brunvand, who teaches at the University of Utah, has studied many urban myths over the years. Brunvand writes, "As with any folk legends, urban legends gain credibility from specific details of time and place or from references to source authorities" (Brunvand 3). In other words, urban legends are believable because they contain so many realistic details.

① Revise and Edit

The Standards for Evaluation and the Editing Checklist will help you revise your research report. Here are other points to keep in mind.

- Use facts and statistics to elaborate on your points.
- Make sure you credited sources correctly.

② Prepare Your Final Copy

As you prepare your final copy, remember that your last step is to create a Works Cited list. The student model on the opposite page, as well as page 849 of the Writing Handbook, will help you.

Notice how the thesis statement sets up the main idea of the report.

How has the introduction changed since the rough draft?

Look at how one student incorporated quotes and examples in his research report.

Works Cited

Brunvand, Jan Harold. <u>The Vanishing Hitchhiker: American Urban Legends and Their Meanings</u>. New York: Norton, 1981.

Dundes, Alan. "Folklore." <u>The World Book Encyclopedia</u>. 1995 ed.

Morris, Scot. "Paper Chase: Searching for modern folklore on the office bulletin board." <u>OMNI</u> Apr. 1991: Vol. 13, No. 7.

Nicolini, Mary B. "Is There a FOAF in Your Future? Urban Folk Legends in Room 112." <u>English Journal</u> Dec. 1989: Vol. 78, No. 8.

" 'So there's this guy, see . . .'." <u>Maclean's</u> 2 Dec. 1991: Vol. 104, No. 48.

Standards for Evaluation

A research report
- has an interesting introduction that clearly states the topic and the purpose
- contains facts and details to support main ideas
- presents information in a logical order
- uses information from multiple sources
- gives credit for the ideas and facts of others
- ends with a strong conclusion
- includes a Works Cited list

REFLECT & ASSESS

UNIT SIX: THE ORAL TRADITION

The folklore in this unit is linked to the themes of the previous five units. Consider how you have analyzed those themes in Units One through Five. Has reading folklore in the oral tradition changed how you view the five themes? How? To explore these questions further, complete one or more of the options in each of the following sections.

REFLECTING ON THEME

OPTION 1 **Writing from Within** Look back at the works of art chosen to introduce each unit in this book. If you had to replace these works of art with pictures of scenes from Unit Six—scenes that reflect the unit themes—what scenes would you choose? Draw a picture or write a description of a scene for each unit.

OPTION 2 **Discussion** With a small group of classmates, consider how specific folklore selections might link to various unit themes. For example, "The Souls in Purgatory," which is here linked to the theme "Changing Perceptions," could also be connected to "Personal Discoveries" and "Critical Adjustments." Design a theme web to illustrate any connections your group sees. Do any of your new links seem stronger than the ones suggested in this unit? Present an oral report to the class, explaining how certain stories link to various themes.

OPTION 3 **Looking at Cultures** Get together with a group of classmates and discuss the cultures whose folklore you found especially interesting. Select two or three of the cultures and, for each one, jot down what you learned about it in this unit. Share your thoughts with the class in an oral report.

REFLECT & ASSESS *Self-Assessment: To what extent have this unit's selections changed how you understand the previous units' themes? For each theme, write a short paragraph explaining how your views of it have changed as a result of reading the folklore.*

REVIEWING LITERARY CONCEPTS

OPTION 1 **Looking at Values** Much folklore reveals the values of the society from which it comes. Choose three or four selections in which you think you can pinpoint certain values of a society most clearly. Then fill in a chart like the one shown. Review your chart with a classmate, discussing whether the values revealed are relevant to our own society.

Story	Values of Society Revealed
"Otoonah"	The need for people to cooperate

OPTION 2 **Examining Characterization** Many stories in the oral tradition feature animals. With a group of classmates, discuss the ways in which animals are portrayed in the stories in this unit. Consider the following questions:

- What personal qualities are the animals shown to have?
- How are the portrayals similar to and different from the portrayals of these animals in your own culture?
- Can you see any links with portrayals of animals in other folklore that you know?

Self-Assessment: Look at the following list of literary terms that relate to fiction. If you are uncertain about the meanings of any, look them up in the Handbook of Reading Terms and Literary Concepts on page 812. Then choose a tale from Unit Six that you particularly like, and write a few paragraphs in which you use the terms to analyze it.

characterization	*dialogue*
climax	*mood*
conflict	*plot*
description	*theme*

PORTFOLIO BUILDING

- **Mini-Project Writing** Look back at the writing you did for the mini-projects in this unit. Choose the piece that you think represents your best treatment of an element of folklore. (For example, you might be pleased with the morals you wrote for the Links to Unit Two.) Write a cover note explaining why you like that piece, then add the note and the piece to your portfolio.

- **Writing About Literature** By now you've responded to one of the unit's selections by writing a scene from a play. Write a review of your scene. Tell what the experience of writing it was like for you—what did you find challenging or enjoyable? Include your review in your portfolio.

- **Writing from Experience** Now that you've written a research report, explore your memory of the experience. Is the topic of folk tales easier or harder to research than other topics? In what ways? What methods did you use that you might employ in other research?

- **Personal Choice** Look back through the records and evaluations of all the activities you completed in this unit. In which of the major projects did you find your exploration of a culture or subject most

interesting? Make a brief note that explains your reaction, then add the note and the project evaluation to your portfolio.

Self-Assessment: Now is your chance to review all of the work in your portfolio. Decide on a final organization of what you have included, and write a brief table of contents to show where everything is and why you have included each piece of work.

SETTING GOALS

As you completed the reading and writing activities in this unit, you probably discovered folklore that especially interested you. What kinds of folklore—myths, folk tales, fables, and legends—would you like to read more of? Are there any cultures whose folklore you would like to explore further?

Student Resource Bank

Words to Know: Access Guide

A
abduction, 441
abetting, 605
abominably, 49
absurd, 529
abyss, 746
accommodation, 189
acute, 381
ad-libbing, 191
adulterate, 49
adversary, 168
agile, 427
agitated, 792
ajar, 19
ambassador, 329
appalling, 50
apprehend, 463
apt, 51
ardent, 48
ardor, 230
askew, 396
assailant, 443
assertion, 430
assess, 300
assurance 334
audacity, 386
autopsy, 456

B-C
benignly, 664
blithe, 111
blunt, 221
bonanza, 110
borne, 552
brandishing, 774
bristling, 462
bureaucrat, 35
burly, 305
cajoling, 556
capricious, 243
cascade, 428
catastrophic, 85
chant, 642
chasm, 663
chronicle, 431
clarity, 221
commence, 21
communion, 222
compensate, 95
competent, 188
complex, 586
comply, 290
component, 230
concede, 468

conceived, 381
congenial, 502
conjecture, 471
consequence, 187
conservative, 254
console, 780
conspiracy, 443
copious, 60
corroborate, 468
coveted, 431
cow, 168
crevice, 383

D
debris, 375
decrepit, 92
delusion, 98
derision, 386
desolate, 92
deter, 34
devastating, 50
diffused, 665
dilated, 452
dingy, 461
discreet, 196
disdainfully, 165
disheveled, 553
dismal, 455
dispel, 553
distraught, 453
diversion, 186
docile, 84
dry, 639
dubious, 309
dumbfounded, 706

E-F
eccentric, 190
ecologically, 111
ecstasy, 225
eloquence, 555
encroaching, 391
enmity, 748
evading, 794
excess, 32
fastidious, 558
fidelity, 605
fixated, 577
flourish, 504
forlorn, 773
founder, 641
furtively, 302
futile, 109

G-H
galvanize, 452
gilded, 95
gloat, 504
gnarled, 22
grimace, 375
gusto, 233
haphazardly, 245
hodgepodge, 113
homage, 163
humane, 243
hypocritical, 386
hypothesis, 533

I
immerse, 500
immoral, 243
impact, 254
impair, 532
impeccable, 164
impel, 223
implication, 100
imposing, 166
impromptu, 19
inadequate, 221
incessantly, 243
inconceivable, 34
incongruously, 151
inconsequential, 430
inconsistency, 102
incredulity, 38
indomitable, 556
inducing, 59
inert, 642
inevitable, 453
infested, 49
insignia, 608
insolence, 170
instigate, 427
instill, 553
instinctive, 222
inter, 157
intercession, 706
intimidate, 231
introspective, 533

J-M
judicious, 198
kindling, 221
lapse, 587
lark, 336
laudable, 50
lucid, 587
malevolent, 60

malice, 84
malignant, 455
maritime, 468
median, 292
melancholy, 792
menacing, 337
meticulously, 256
millennium, 151
mirth, 61
morality, 478
motivator, 59
mutinous, 555

N-O
naïveté, 530
naturalist, 509
nebulous, 113
nondescript, 336
nostalgia, 302
novice, 168
nuance, 60
oblivious, 504
obsolete, 243
odious, 605
ominous, 23
opportunist, 526

P
palate, 236
partitioned, 289
pathetic, 590
periphery, 151
persevering, 234
persist, 639
petite, 778
pivotal, 775
placid, 86
plummet, 777
plunder, 396
ply, 475
poignant, 92
posterity, 247
precarious, 194
predominating, 427
preening, 577
preliminaries, 114
preposterous, 110
prodigy, 651
profound, 306
prone, 230
proportional, 533
prudence, 428
psyche, 59
pungent, 711

Q-R

qualm, 103
radical, 453
rapt, 92
rapture, 243
rebuke, 190
recoil, 778
refuse, 374
regression, 532
reluctant, 100
remit, 101
renunciation, 248
repertoire, 53
repress, 109
reproach, 708
rescind, 609
reserve, 32
reside, 290
resignation, 38
resort, 308
responsive, 254
retribution, 169
revoke, 441
ricochet, 58

S

sabotaged, 113
sarcasm, 58
savor, 772
scrutinize, 231
sensation, 528
serene, 591
sheer, 746
shrew, 526
sinister, 337
skepticism, 455
smolder, 395
smug, 305
soberly, 50
specialization, 529
speculation, 306
spindly, 660
spontaneity, 403
statistically, 533
stealthily, 383
stifled, 382
stipulated, 248
subdued, 40
subside, 427
subtly, 661
sulkily, 393
sullen, 555
superfluous, 308
syndrome, 533

T

tangible, 528
tantalizing, 94
tentatively, 19
testimony, 468
torso, 375
transitional, 230
traumatic, 100
tuition, 34
turbulent, 375

U-Z

unrepentant, 33
unwary, 100
vacuous, 530
vain, 86
vault, 19
vehemently, 386
verdancy, 151
verify, 291
vex, 382
vigilant, 232
vindictiveness, 441
visa, 329
vivacious, 453
vogue, 254
writhe, 61
zealot, 164

Pronunciation Key

Symbol	Examples	Symbol	Examples	Symbol	Examples
ă	at, gas	m	man, seem	v	van, save
ā	ape, day	n	night, mitten	w	web, twice
ä	father, barn	ng	sing, anger	y	yard, lawyer
âr	fair, dare	ŏ	odd, not	z	zoo, reason
b	bell, table	ō	open, road, grow	zh	treasure, garage
ch	chin, lunch	ô	awful, bought, horse	ə	awake, even, pencil,
d	dig, bored	oi	coin, boy		pilot, focus
ĕ	egg, ten	ŏŏ	look, full	ər	perform, letter
ē	evil, see, meal	ōō	root, glue, through		
f	fall, laugh, phrase	ou	out, cow		**Sounds in Foreign Words**
g	gold, big	p	pig, cap	KH	*German* ich, auch;
h	hit, inhale	r	rose, star		*Scottish* loch
hw	white, everywhere	s	sit, face	N	*French* entre, bon, fin
ĭ	inch, fit	sh	she, mash	œ	*French* feu, cœur;
ī	idle, my, tried	t	tap, hopped		*German* schön
îr	dear, here	th	thing, with	ü	*French* utile, rue;
j	jar, gem, badge	*th*	then, other		*German* grün
k	keep, cat, luck	ŭ	up, nut		
l	load, rattle	ûr	fur, earn, bird, worm		

Stress Marks

ʹ   This mark indicates that the preceding syllable receives the primary stress. For example, in the word *language*, the first syllable is stressed: lăngʹgwĭj.

ʹ   This mark is used only in words in which more than one syllable is stressed. It indicates that the preceding syllable is stressed, but somewhat more weakly than the syllable receiving the primary stress. In the word *literature*, for example, the first syllable receives the primary stress, and the last syllable receives a weaker stress: lĭtʹər-ə-chŏŏrʹ.

Adapted from *The American Heritage Dictionary of the English Language, Third Edition*; Copyright © 1992 by Houghton Mifflin Company. Used with the permission of Houghton Mifflin Company.

Reading Terms
and Literary Concepts

Act An act is a major section of a play. Each act may be further divided into **scenes.** *Survival* has three acts.

Alliteration Alliteration is a repetition of consonant sounds at the beginning of words. Writers use alliteration for emphasis and to give their writing a musical quality. Note the repetition of the *s* sound in this line from "Macavity: The Mystery Cat":

> He sways his head from side to side, with movements like a snake

Allusion An allusion is a reference to a famous person, place, event, or work of literature. In "Playing for Keeps," the narrator makes an allusion to Wyatt Earp, a famous lawman of the American West, when he describes how Johnny stood up to the alien.

Analysis Analysis is a process of breaking something down into its elements so that they can be examined individually. In analyzing a poem, for example, one might consider such elements as form, rhyme, rhythm, figurative language, imagery, mood, and theme.

Anecdote An anecdote is a brief account of an interesting incident or event, usually intended to entertain or make a point. Dave Barry's humorous account of an early experience in "Painful Memories of Dating" can be considered an anecdote.

Antagonist In a story, an antagonist is a force working against the protagonist, or main character; it may be another character, society, a force of nature, or even a force within the main character. In "Getting the Facts of Life," poverty is an antagonist.

Aphorism An aphorism is a short statement that expresses a general observation about life in a clever or pointed way. The sentence at the beginning of "Keeping Time"—"Sometimes the human heart is the only clock in the world that keeps true time"—is an example of an aphorism.

Author's Purpose An author's purpose is his or her reason for creating a particular work. The purpose may be to entertain, to explain or inform, to express an opinion, or to persuade readers to do or believe something. An author may have more than one purpose for writing, but usually one is most important.

Autobiography An autobiography is a form of nonfiction in which a person tells the story of his or her own life. The excerpts from *Once Upon a Time When We Were Colored* and *Gifted Hands* are examples of autobiography.
See also **Memoir** *and* **Oral History.**

Biography A biography is the story of a person's life, written by someone else. The subjects of biographies are often famous people, as in the excerpts from *Lincoln: A Photobiography* and *Harriet Tubman: Conductor on the Underground Railroad.*

Cast of Characters In the script of a play, a cast of characters is a list of all the characters in the play, often in order of appearance. The list is usually found at the beginning of the script.

Cause and Effect Two events are related as cause and effect when one event brings about the other. The event that happens first is the cause; the one that follows is the effect. In "The Dinner Party," the placing of a bowl of milk on the verandah is the cause that produces a desired effect— the removal of the snake from the dining room.

Character A character is a person, an animal, or an imaginary creature that takes part in the action of a literary work. Generally, a work focuses on one or more **main characters. Minor characters** are less important characters who interact with the main characters and with one another, moving the plot along and providing background for the story.

Character Development Characters that grow or change during a story are said to undergo character development. A character that changes significantly is called a **dynamic character;** one that changes only a little or not at all is said to be a **static character.** Main characters often develop the most. In "Otoonah," for example, the title character is a dynamic character who changes dramatically during the course of the story.

Characterization Characterization consists of all the techniques writers use to create and develop characters. There are four basic methods of developing a character: (1) physical description of the character, (2) presentation of the character's thoughts, speech, and actions, (3) presentation of other characters' thoughts about, speech to, and actions toward the character, and (4) direct comments about the character's nature.

Clarifying The process of pausing occasionally while reading, to quickly review what one understands, is called clarifying. By clarifying as they read, good readers are able to draw conclusions about what is suggested but not stated directly.

Classic Classics are enduring works of literature that are read year after year by people around the world. They deal with emotions, behaviors, and truths that human beings of every age, race, and culture share. "The Gift of the Magi" is an example of a classic work of literature.

Climax In the plot of a story or play, the climax (or turning point) is the point of maximum interest. At the climax, the conflict is resolved and the outcome of the plot becomes clear. The climax of "Raymond's Run," for example, occurs when Squeaky wins the race. *See also* **Conflict** *and* **Plot.**

Comparison The process of identifying similarities is called comparison. In "Stop the Sun," for example, the father's terrified breathing is compared to the panting of "some kind of hurt animal."

Conflict Conflict is a struggle between opposing forces. In an **external conflict,** such as the battle between Gustus and the hurricane in "The Banana Tree," a character struggles against another person or some outside force. **Internal conflict,** on the other hand, is a struggle within a character. In "The Splendid Outcast," the narrator experiences inner conflict about what to do at the auction.

Connecting A reader's process of relating the content of a literary work to his or her own knowledge and experience is called connecting. In "The Moustache," for example, readers may connect with Mike's feelings as he interacts with his grandmother.

Context Clues Unfamiliar words are often surrounded by words or phrases—called context clues — that help readers understand their meaning. A context clue may be a definition, a synonym, an example, a comparison or contrast, or any other expression that enables readers to infer the word's meaning.

Contrast The process of pointing out differences between things is called contrast. In "Dancer," for example, the narrator contrasts Clarissa with other children when she says, "Some foster kids come with lots of stuff, but she came with everything she had in a paper bag."

Description A description is a picture, in words, of a scene, a character, or an object. Descriptions can be used to appeal to readers' senses or to provide detailed information about characters or events.

Dialect A dialect is a form of language that is spoken in a particular place or by a particular group of people. Dialects of a language may differ from one another in pronunciation, vocabulary, and grammar.

Some of the dialogue in *All Things Bright and Beautiful* features the dialect of Yorkshire, in the north of England.

Dialogue The words that characters speak aloud are called dialogue. In most literary works, dialogue is set off with quotation marks. In play scripts, however, each character's dialogue simply follows his or her name, without being indicated by quotation marks.

Drama A drama, or play, is a form of literature meant to be performed by actors before an audience. In drama, the characters' dialogue and actions tell the story.

Dynamic Character
See **Character Development.**

Essay An essay is a short work of nonfiction that deals with a single subject. A **formal essay** is highly organized, thoroughly researched, and serious in tone. **Informal essays** are lighter in tone and usually reflect their writers' feelings and personalities.

Evaluating Evaluating is the process of judging the worth of something or someone. A work of literature, or any of its elements, may be evaluated in terms of such criteria as entertainment, believability, originality, and emotional power.

Exaggeration An overstating of an idea is called exaggeration. For example, in "White Mice," one student exaggerates the consistency of the food in a pot by asking, "Is this porridge or cement?" Extreme exaggeration for the purpose of emphasis or humor is called **hyperbole.**

Exposition Exposition, which is usually found at the beginning of a story or play, serves to introduce the main characters, to describe the setting, and sometimes to establish the conflict. In "Spotted Eagle and Black Crow," for example, the first two paragraphs provide most of the exposition.
See also **Plot.**

Extended Metaphor
See **Metaphor.**

External Conflict
See **Conflict.**

Fable A fable is a brief tale that teaches a lesson about human nature. Many fables feature animals that act and speak like human beings, and many end with statements of their moral, or lesson. "Brer Possum's Dilemma" is an African-American fable.

Fact and Opinion A fact is a statement that can be proved. An opinion, in contrast, is a statement that reflects a writer's belief and cannot be proved. Much nonfiction contains both facts and opinions, and it is important for readers to distinguish between the two.

Fiction Fiction is prose writing that tells an imaginary story. The writer of a fictional work may invent all the events and characters in it or may base parts of the story on real people or events.
See also **Novel** *and* **Short Story.**

Figurative Language Writers use figurative language—expressions that are not literally true—to create fresh and original descriptions. For example, "The Banana Tree" contains a figurative description of Gustus's shirt "fluttering from his back like a boat sail."
See also **Metaphor, Personification,** *and* **Simile.**

First-Person Point of View
See **Point of View.**

Flashback In a literary work, a flashback is an interruption of the action to present events that took place at an earlier time. A flashback may provide information that helps readers understand a character's current situation. In "The Bet," for example, a flashback is used to present the banker's recollection of a party he gave 15 years earlier.

Folk Tale A folk tale is a simple story that has been passed from generation to generation by word of mouth. The characters in folk tales may be animals, people, or superhuman beings. Folk tales are told primarily to entertain rather than to explain something or teach a lesson. "The Five Eggs" is a folk tale from Ecuador.

Foreshadowing Foreshadowing occurs when a writer provides hints that suggest future events in a story. For example, in "The Inn of Lost Time" the folk tale about Urashima Taro anticipates elements in, and gives readers hints about, Zenta's story.

Form A literary work's form is its structure or organization. The form of a poem includes the arrangement of words and lines on the page. Some poems follow predictable patterns, with the same number of syllables in each line and the same number of lines in each stanza. Others, like "Foreign Student," have irregular forms. In some cases, a poem is given a form that reflects its content—as in "Mixed Singles," where the arrangement of words and lines suggests the movement of a tennis ball.

Frame Story Frame stories are stories that contain or connect other stories. For example, "The Inn of Lost Time" consists of a frame story containing two other stories.

Free Verse Poetry without regular patterns of rhyme and rhythm is called free verse. Some poets use free verse to capture the sounds and rhythms of ordinary speech. "Rice and Rose Bowl Blues" is an example of a poem written in free verse.

Generalization A generalization is a broad statement about an entire group, such as "Whales are larger than salmon." Not all generalizations are true. Some are too broad or not supported by sufficient evidence, like the statement "All eighth graders like yogurt."

Genre A type or category of literature is called a genre. There are four main literary genres: fiction, nonfiction, poetry, and drama.

Humor Humor is a quality that provokes laughter or amusement. Writers create humor through exaggeration, sarcasm, amusing descriptions, irony, and witty and insightful dialogue. "The Clown" is an example of a humorous work.

Hyperbole
See **Exaggeration.**

Idiom An idiom is an expression whose meaning is different from the sum of the meanings of its individual words. The expression "break her date" in "The Moustache" is an example of an idiom.

Imagery Imagery consists of words and phrases that appeal to readers' five senses. Writers use sensory details to help readers imagine how things look, feel, smell, sound, and taste. Note the imagery in this description of the bear in "Appetizer":

> She smells like the forest floor, like crushed moss and damp leaves, and she is as warm as a radiator back in my Massachusetts home, the thought of which floods me with a terrible nostalgia.

In-Depth Reading A reader who reads slowly and deliberately, carefully examining what he or she is reading, is engaging in in-depth reading. Works that contain specialized or challenging vocabulary—like "The Splendid Outcast"—usually require in-depth reading.

Inference An inference is a logical guess or conclusion based on evidence. By combining the information a writer provides with what they know from their own experience, readers can figure out more than the words say. For example, from James Herriot's handling of the bird's death in *All Things Bright and Beautiful,* readers can infer that he is willing to deceive the bird's owner in order to protect her feelings.

Informative Nonfiction
See **Nonfiction.**

Internal Conflict
See **Conflict.**

Irony Irony is a contrast between what is expected and what actually exists or happens. In "The Lie," for example, it is ironic that Dr. Remenzel, after lecturing Eli about not expecting special treatment, himself asks for Eli to be treated specially.

Legend A legend is a story handed down from the past about a specific person—usually someone of heroic accomplishments. Legends often have some basis in historical fact. "Spotted Eagle and Black Crow" is an Oglala legend.

Literary Nonfiction
See **Nonfiction.**

Lyric Poetry Lyric poetry is poetry that presents

the thoughts and feelings of a single speaker. "I Belong" is an example of a lyric poem.

Main Character
See **Character.**

Main Idea A main idea is a writer's principal message. It may be the central idea of an entire work or of a single paragraph. (The main idea of a paragraph is often stated in a **topic sentence.**) Usually, the term *main idea* is used in discussions of nonfiction.

Memoir A memoir is a first-person recollection of an experience or event. "The Home Front: 1941–1945" is an example of a memoir.

Metaphor A metaphor is a comparison of two things that have something in common. Unlike a simile, a metaphor does not contain an explicit word of comparison, such as *like, as,* or *resembles.* In "Moco Limping," for example, the reference to the dog's "stick of a leg" is a metaphor.

In an **extended metaphor,** two things are compared at some length and in several ways. The poem "Mother to Son" is based on an extended metaphor in which the course of the speaker's life is compared to a dark staircase.

Minor Character
See **Character.**

Mood A mood, or atmosphere, is a feeling that a literary work conveys to readers. In "The Woman in the Snow," for example, the description of the ghostly figure and her baby in the snow creates an ominous and heart-wrenching mood.

Moral A moral is a lesson that a story teaches. Morals are often stated directly at the end of fables—like the warning, in "Brer Possum's Dilemma," that one should not go looking for trouble.

Motivation A character's motivation is the reason why he or she acts, feels, or thinks a certain way. For example, Tsali in "Tsali of the Cherokees" is motivated by his Cherokee heritage and love of family.

Myth A myth is a traditional story, usually of unknown authorship, that answers basic questions

about the world. Myths attempt to explain such things as human nature, the origin of the world, mysteries of nature, and social customs. "Raven and the Coming of Daylight" is a Haida myth that explains how daylight came into the world.

Narrative Any writing that tells a story is a narrative. The events in a narrative may be real or imagined. Narratives dealing with real events include biographies and autobiographies. Fictional narratives include myths, short stories, novels, and narrative poems.

Narrative Poetry Poetry that tells a story is called narrative poetry. Like fiction, narrative poetry contains characters, settings, and plots. It may also contain such elements of poetry as rhyme, rhythm, imagery, and figurative language. "Paul Revere's Ride" is an example of a narrative poem.

Narrator A narrator is the teller of a story. See also **Point of View.**

Nonfiction Writing that tells about real people, places, and events is called nonfiction. **Literary nonfiction** is written to be read in much the same way as fiction. **Informative nonfiction** is written mainly to provide factual information. See also **Autobiography, Biography,** *and* **Essay.**

Nonstandard English Nonstandard English is English that does not follow some of the accepted standards of grammar and usage. It can be used to convey the way some people naturally talk, thus lending an authentic, conversational style to writing. For example, the story "Dancer" is narrated in nonstandard English:

> One night she speaks up at supper and says, right clear and loud, "I'm an Assiniboin." . . . Don't nobody have to say nothing to something that proud said.

Novel A novel is a work of fiction that is longer and more complex than a short story. In a novel, setting, plot, and characters are usually developed in great detail.

Oral History When people relate the stories of their lives by word of mouth, they are creating oral histories. These histories usually include both factual recollections and personal reactions. An oral history may be preserved in writing, like Janet Bode's account of the Vietnamese youth known as Von.

Personification The giving of human qualities to an animal, object, or idea is known as personification. In "The Hurricane," for example, the storm is personified as an "agile dancer" that whirls "on the tip of its toes."

Perspective
See **Point of View.**

Persuasion Persuasion is a type of writing that is meant to sway readers' feelings, beliefs, or actions. Persuasion normally appeals to both the mind and the emotions of readers.

Play
See **Drama.**

Plot A story's plot is the sequence of related events that make up the story; it includes all the action, everything that happens. Typically, a plot begins with **exposition** that introduces the characters and the conflict they face. **Complications** arise as the characters try to resolve the conflict. Eventually, the plot reaches a **climax,** the point of greatest interest or suspense. In the **resolution** that follows, loose ends are tied up and the story is brought to a close.

Poetry Poetry is a type of literature in which ideas and feelings are expressed in compact, imaginative, and musical language. Poets arrange words in ways designed to touch readers' senses, emotions, and minds. Most poems are written in lines, which may contain regular patterns of rhyme and rhythm. These lines may, in turn, be grouped in stanzas.

Point of View The perspective from which a story is told is called its point of view. When a story is told from the **first-person** point of view, the narrator is a character in the story and uses first-person pronouns, such as *I, me,* and *we.* This is the point of view used in "The Splendid Outcast," for example. In a story told from the **third-person** point of view, on the other hand, the narrator is not a character;

he or she uses third-person pronouns, such as *he, she,* and *it.* "The Banana Tree" is an example of a story told from the third-person point of view.

Predicting Using what you know to guess what may happen is called predicting. While reading stories, good readers gather information and combine it with prior knowledge to predict upcoming events. This process of predicting keeps the readers involved in what they are reading.

Prose Prose is the ordinary form of spoken and written language—that is, it is language that lacks the special features of poetry.

Protagonist In a story, a protagonist is a main character who is involved in the story's conflict. A story may have more than one protagonist—for example, Della and Jim are the protagonists of "The Gift of the Magi."

Questioning The process of raising questions while reading is called questioning. Good readers ask themselves questions in an effort to understand characters and events, looking for the answers as they continue to read.

Radio Play A drama written specifically to be heard and not seen is called a radio play. *The Hitchhiker* is an example of a radio play.

Realistic Fiction Realistic fiction is imaginative writing set in the real, modern world. The characters act like real people, using ordinary human abilities to cope with problems and conflicts typical of modern life. "The Treasure of Lemon Brown" is an example of realistic fiction.

Repetition Repetition is the use of any element of language—a sound, a word, a phrase, or a grammatical structure—more than once. Writers use repetition to stress important ideas and feelings and to create memorable sound effects, as in "Mi Madre," with its repetition of the words "I say."
See also **Alliteration** and **Rhyme.**

Resolution
See **Plot.**

Rhyme Rhyme is a repetition of sounds at the end

of words. Words rhyme when their accented vowels and all letters that follow have identical sounds. *Cat* and *bat* rhyme, as do *whether* and *feather.*

The most common form of rhyme in poetry is **end rhyme,** in which the rhyming words are at the end of lines. Rhyme that occurs within a line is called **internal rhyme.** These lines from "O Captain! My Captain!" show both end and internal rhyme:

> The ship is anchor'd safe and sound, its voyage closed and <u>done</u>,
> From fearful <u>trip</u> the victor <u>ship</u> comes in with object <u>won</u>

Rhyme Scheme The pattern of rhymes in a poem is the poem's rhyme scheme. A rhyme scheme can be described by using a different letter to represent each rhyming sound. In these lines from Dorothy Parker's "The Choice," words at the end of alternate lines rhyme:

> | He'd have given me rolling lands, | a |
> |---|---|
> | Houses of marble, and billowing farms, | b |
> | Pearls, to trickle between my hands, | a |
> | Smoldering rubies, to circle my arms. | b |

Rhythm Rhythm is a pattern of stressed and unstressed syllables in poetry. When the stressed syllables—the syllables that are emphasized—are arranged in a consistent pattern in a poem, the poem is said to have a regular beat. Note the rhythm in this line from "O Captain! My Captain!" (the mark ´ indicates a stressed syllable; the mark ˘, an unstressed syllable):

> The pórt ĭs néar, thĕ bélls Ĭ héar, thĕ péoplĕ áll ĕxúltĭng,

Scanning Scanning is the process of searching through writing for a particular fact or piece of information. When you scan, your eyes sweep across a page, looking for key words that may lead you to the information you want.

Scene In a play, a scene is a section presenting events that occur in one place at one time.

Science Fiction Science fiction is fiction based on real or imaginary scientific developments. It fre-quently presents an imaginative view into the future, as in "Collecting Team."

Sequencing Sequencing is a way of beginning to make sense of a story by paying attention to how the events are ordered chronologically. Understanding the sequence of events in a story allows readers to explore the impact of events on the characters and to predict what might happen next. A writer may use signal words—such as *first, next, then, now, this time,* and *before*—to indicate the sequence of events.

Setting The setting of a story, poem, or play is the time and place of the action. Sometimes the setting is clear and well-defined; at other times, it is left to readers' imagination. Elements of setting may include geographic location, historical period (past, present, or future), season, time of day, and the customs and manners of a society.

Short Story A short story is a brief work of fiction that can generally be read in one sitting. A short story usually focuses on one or two main characters who face a single problem or conflict.

Simile A simile is a comparison of two things that have some quality in common. In a simile, the comparison is expressed by means of a word such as *like, as,* or *resembles.* One of the similes in "Simile: Willow and Ginkgo" is "The ginkgo is leathery as an old bull."

Skimming Skimming is the process of reading quickly to find a main idea or to get an overview of a work or passage. It involves reading the title, the headings, the words in special type, and the first sentence of each paragraph, along with any charts, graphs, and time lines that accompany the writing.

Slang Slang is a casual, informal form of language used more often in speaking than in writing. Slang terms may be new words, or they may be established words and phrases that have taken on new meanings. In "The Treasure of Lemon Brown," for example, the slang term *bigheaded* is used to mean "smart."

Speaker In a poem, the speaker is the voice that

talks to the reader—like the narrator in a work of fiction. In some poems, such as "Saying Yes," the speaker expresses the feelings of the poet. In others, the speaker's attitude may not be the same as the poet's.

Specialized Vocabulary The words unique to a specific subject or profession make up a specialized vocabulary. The excerpt from *Gifted Hands,* for example, contains a number of terms drawn from the specialized vocabulary of the medical profession.

Stage Directions In the script of a play, the instructions to the actors, director, and stage crew are called stage directions. They may suggest scenery, lighting, music, sound effects, and ways for actors to move and speak. In this book, stage directions appear within parentheses and in italic type.

Stanza A group of lines within a poem is called a stanza. A stanza is like a paragraph in prose writing. "Sea Lullaby," for example, contains six stanzas.

Static Character
See **Character Development.**

Stereotype A stereotype is a broad generalization or oversimplified view that disregards individual differences. Stereotypes can lead to unfair judgments of people on the basis of race, ethnic background, or physical appearance.

Style A style is a manner of writing; it involves *how* something is said rather than *what* is said. The style of the poem "Mother to Son," for example, might be described as conversational—it reflects the speaker's usual, informal way of talking. Many elements contribute to style, including word choice, sentence length, tone, and figurative language.

Summarizing Summarizing is telling the main ideas of a piece of writing briefly in one's own words, omitting unimportant details.

Surprise Ending An unexpected twist in the plot at the end of a story is called a surprise ending. "White Mice" is an example of a story with a surprise ending.

Suspense Suspense is a feeling of growing ten-sion and excitement felt by a reader. Writers create suspense by raising questions in readers' minds about what might happen. For example, in "Battle by the Breadfruit Tree" a suspenseful moment occurs when the baboon fights to protect her baby from the leopard.

Symbol A symbol is a person, a place, an object, or an action that stands for something beyond itself. A flag, for example, may symbolize a state or country. The toad in "The Horned Toad" may be said to symbolize the need for personal freedom.

Teleplay A teleplay is a drama written specifically for television. In a teleplay, the stage directions usually include instructions for camera movements and editing. *Survival* is an example of a teleplay.

Theme A theme is a message about life or human nature that is communicated by a literary work. In many cases, readers must infer what the writer's message is. One way of figuring out a theme is to apply the lessons learned by the main characters to all people. For example, a theme of "The Lie" is that parents should avoid putting undue pressure on their children.

Third-Person Point of View
See **Point of View.**

Tone The tone of a work expresses the writer's attitude toward his or her subject. Words such as *angry, sad,* and *humorous* can be used to describe different tones. "Appetizer," for example, can be said to have a humorous tone.

Topic Sentence
See **Main Idea.**

Visualizing The process of forming a mental picture based on a written description is called visualizing. Good readers use the details supplied by writers to picture characters, settings, and events in their minds.

Voice An author's or narrator's voice is his or her distinctive style or manner of expression. It may reveal much about the author's or narrator's personality—as does the voice of Squeaky, the narrator of "Raymond's Run," for example.

The Writing Process

The writing process consists of four stages: prewriting, drafting, revising and editing, and publishing and reflecting. As the graphic to the right shows, these stages are not steps that you must complete in a set order. Rather, you may return to any one at any time in your writing process, using feedback from your readers along the way.

1.1 Prewriting

In the prewriting stage, you explore your ideas and discover what you want to write about.

Choosing a Topic

Ideas for writing can come from just about anywhere: experiences, memories, conversations, dreams, or imaginings. The following techniques can help you to generate ideas for writing and to choose a topic you care about.

Personal Techniques
Make a list of people, places, and activities that have had an effect on you.
Ask who, what, when, where, and why about an important event.
Ask what-if questions about everyday life.
Browse through magazines, newspapers, and on-line bulletin boards for ideas.

Sharing Techniques
With a group, brainstorm a topic by trying to come up with as many ideas as you can. Do not stop to evaluate your ideas for at least five minutes.
With a group, discuss a topic in depth, sharing your questions and ideas.

Writing Techniques
Use a word or picture as a starting point for freewriting.
Freewrite for a short time and then circle the ideas you would like to explore.
Pick a topic and list all the related ideas that occur to you.

Graphic Techniques
Create a time line of memorable events in your life.
Make a cluster diagram of subtopics related to a general topic.

Determining Your Purpose

At some time during your writing process, you need to consider your purpose, or general reason, for writing. Your purpose may be one of the following: to express yourself, to entertain, to inform, to explain, to describe, to analyze, or to persuade. To clarify your purpose, ask yourself questions like these:

- Why did I choose to write about my topic?
- What aspects of the topic mean the most to me?
- What do I want others to think or feel after they read my writing?

Identifying Your Audience

Knowing who will read your writing can help you clarify your purpose, focus your topic, and choose the details and tone that will best communicate your ideas. As you think about your readers, ask yourself questions like these:

- What does my audience already know about my topic?
- What will they be most interested in?
- What language is most appropriate for this audience?

1.2   Drafting

In the drafting stage, you put your ideas on paper and allow them to develop and change as you write.

There's no right or wrong way to draft. Sometimes you might be adventuresome and just dive right into your writing. At other times, you might draft slowly, planning carefully beforehand. You can combine aspects of these approaches to suit yourself and your writing projects.

LINK TO LITERATURE

Inspiration for your writing can come from everyday events. Robert Cormier got the idea for the short story "The Moustache," on page 583, from an actual experience his teenage son had while visiting his grandmother in a nursing home.

Describing the approach she used to draft stories like "Raymond's Run" on page 648, Toni Cade Bambara said, "I babble along, heading I think in one direction, only to discover myself tugged in another, or sometimes I'm absolutely snatched into an alley."

Discovery drafting is a good approach when you've gathered some information on your topic or have a rough idea for writing but are not quite sure how you feel about your subject or what exactly you want to say. You just plunge into your draft and let your ideas lead you where they will. After finishing a discovery draft, you may decide to start another draft, do more prewriting, or revise your first draft.

Planned drafting may work better for reports and other kinds of formal writing. Try thinking through a writing plan or making an outline before you begin drafting. Then, as you write, you can develop your ideas and fill in the details.

1.3 Using Peer Response

The suggestions and comments your peers or classmates make about your writing are called peer response.

Talking with peers about your writing can help you discover what you want to say or how well you have communicated your ideas. You can ask a peer reader for help at any point in the writing process. For example, your peers can help you develop a topic, narrow your focus, discover confusing passages, or organize your writing.

Questions for Your Peer Readers

You can help your peer readers provide you with the most useful kinds of feedback by following these guidelines:

- Tell readers where you are in the writing process. Are you still trying out ideas, or have you completed a draft?
- Ask questions that will help you get specific information about your writing. Open-ended questions that require more than yes-or-no answers are more likely to give you information you can use as you revise.
- Give your readers plenty of time to respond thoughtfully to your writing.
- Encourage your readers to be honest when they respond to your work. It's OK if you don't agree with them—you always get to decide which changes to make.

The chart on the following page explains different peer-response techniques you might use when you're ready to share your work with others.

Technique	When to Use It	Questions to Ask
Sharing	Use this when you are just exploring ideas or when you want to celebrate the completion of a piece of writing by sharing it with another person.	Will you please read or listen to my writing without criticizing it or making suggestions afterward?
Summarizing	Use this when you want to know if your main idea or goals are clear to readers.	What do you think I'm trying to say? What's my main idea?
Telling	Use this to find out which parts of your writing are affecting readers the way you want and which parts are confusing.	What did you think or feel as you read my words? Which passage were you reading when you had that response?
Replying	Use this when you want to get some new ideas to use in your writing.	What are your ideas about my topic? What do you think about what I have said in my piece?
Identifying	Use this when you want to identify the strengths and weaknesses of your writing.	Where do you like the wording, and where can it be improved? Does the organization make sense? What parts were confusing?

WRITING TIP

You may want to ask peer readers questions if their comments are not clear or helpful to you. For example, if a reader says, "This part is confusing," you can probe to find out why. Ask, "What are you confused about? What do you think might make this clearer?"

Tips for Being a Peer Reader

Remember these guidelines when you act as a peer reader:

- Respect the writer's feelings.
- Make sure you understand what kind of feedback the writer is looking for before you respond, and then limit your comments accordingly.
- Use "I" statements, such as "I like . . . ," "I think . . . ," or "It would help me if. . . ." Remember that your impressions and opinions may not be the same as someone else's.

1.4 Revising and Editing

In the revising and editing stage, you improve your draft, choose the words that best express your ideas, and proofread for mistakes in spelling, grammar, usage, and punctuation.

When you finish a draft, take a break before rereading it. The break will help you distance yourself from your writing and allow you to evaluate it more objectively. You may decide to make several drafts—in which you change direction or even start over—before you're ready to revise and polish a piece of writing.

WRITING TIP

For help identifying and correcting problems that are listed in the Proofreading Checklist, see the Grammar Handbook, pages 860–899.

The changes you make in your writing during this stage usually fall into three categories: revising for ideas, revising for form, and editing to correct mistakes. Use the questions and suggestions that follow to help you assess problems in your draft and determine what kinds of changes would improve it.

Revising for Ideas

- Have I discovered the main idea or focus of my writing? Have I expressed it clearly in my draft?
- Have I accomplished my purpose?
- Do my readers have all the information they need, or would adding more details help?
- Are any of my ideas unnecessary?

Revising for Form and Language

- Is my writing unified? Are all the ideas directly related to my main idea or focus?
- Is my writing organized well? Are the relationships among ideas clear?
- Is my writing coherent? Is the flow of sentences and paragraphs smooth and logical?

Editing to Improve Your Writing

When you are satisfied with your draft, proofread and edit it, correcting any mistakes you might have made in spelling, grammar, usage, and punctuation. You may want to proofread your writing several times, looking for different types of mistakes each time. The following checklist may help you proofread your work.

Proofreading Checklist	
Sentence Structure and Agreement	Are there any run-on sentences or sentence fragments? Do all verbs agree with their subjects? Do all pronouns agree with their antecedents? Are verb tenses correct and consistent?
Forms of Words	Do adverbs and adjectives modify the appropriate words? Are all forms of *be* and other irregular verbs used correctly? Are pronouns used correctly? Are comparative and superlative forms of adjectives correct?
Capitalization, Punctuation, and Spelling	Is any punctuation mark missing or not needed? Are all words spelled correctly? Are all proper nouns, all proper adjectives, and the first words of all sentences capitalized?

Use the proofreading symbols shown below to mark your draft with the changes that you need to make. See the Grammar Handbook for models that use these symbols.

Proofreading Symbols			
∧	Add letters or words.	/	Make a capital letter lowercase.
⊙	Add a period.	¶	Begin a new paragraph.
≡	Capitalize a letter.	– or ℐ	Take out letters or words.
⌒	Close up space.	∿	Switch the positions of letters, words, or punctuation marks.
∧	Add a comma.		

1.5   Publishing and Reflecting

After you've completed a writing project, consider sharing it with a wider audience—even when you've produced it for a class assignment. Reflecting on your writing process is another good way to bring closure to a writing project.

Creative Publishing Ideas

Following are some ideas for publishing and sharing your writing:

- Display your writing on a school bulletin board.
- Working with other students in your class, create an anthology, or a collection of stories, poems, plays, and other writing.
- Give a dramatic reading of your work for another class or group.
- Submit your writing to a local newspaper or a magazine that publishes student writing.
- Enter your piece in a writing contest.
- Go on-line with your writing by posting it on an electronic bulletin board or sending it to others via e-mail.
- Create a multimedia presentation and share it with classmates.

Reflecting on Your Writing

Think about your writing process and consider whether you'd like to add your writing to your portfolio. You might write yourself a note answering questions like these and attach it to your work:

- What did I learn about myself and my subject?
- Which parts of the writing process did I most and least enjoy?
- As I wrote, what was my biggest problem? How did I solve it?
- What did I learn that I can use the next time I write?

WRITING TIP

If you write a narrative for younger children, ask a grade school teacher if you may read it to his or her students. Afterward, you might ask the students to draw pictures of memorable scenes in your story.

Building Blocks of Good Writing

A good introduction catches your reader's interest and often presents the main idea of your writing. To introduce your writing effectively, try one of these methods.

Share a Fact

Beginning with an interesting fact can make your reader think, I'd like to learn more about that. In the example below, the surprising size of the items captures the reader's interest.

> A 45-foot-tall clothespin stands in front of Philadelphia's City Hall; a 74,000-pound flashlight stands beam-end down on the University of Nevada campus. These giant items are the work of artists Claes Oldenburg and Coosje van Bruggen, who prove that fine art can be fun.

Present a Description

A vivid description sets a mood and brings a scene to life for your reader. The contrasting details below paint a dramatic picture.

> On a July afternoon, fingers of cool water refreshed and pressed smooth the sizzling, footprinted sand of a beach dotted with rainbow-colored umbrellas. A week later, black, oily water stained the white sand and deposited dead fish and birds on the otherwise deserted shore.

Ask a Question

Beginning with a question can make your reader want to read on to find out the answer. Note how the introduction that follows invites the reader to learn more about a great sports achievement.

WRITING TIP

Writing an introduction does not need to be your first task when you begin a writing project. Instead, begin with any part of your piece that you feel ready to write. Once your ideas come into better focus, you'll probably get a good idea about how to introduce your piece.

> What did Baltimore Oriole Cal Ripken, Jr., do in 1995 that no other baseball player had ever done? He set a record for the most consecutive games played, breaking Lou Gehrig's record of 2,130 games. For more than 13 years, Ripken was motivated by his love of baseball and his desire to compete at the highest level.

Relate an Incident

An engaging story that includes sensory details or dialogue can help catch your reader's attention. After reading the anecdote below, your reader will want to find out more.

> Just when I think I know my mother, she proves me wrong. "I was engaged to another man when I met your father," she mentioned casually one day.

Use Dialogue

As you can see from the example above, quoting a person's words can be an effective beginning to a piece of writing. You can also write fictional dialogue to draw readers into your piece, as shown in the introduction below.

> "A little change?" asked a man bundled in old sweaters.
> "Sure," I responded, reaching inside my pockets.
> "You're a good kid," he said, as I walked away. "I hope you win the lottery someday."
> Unfortunately, a person stands a far greater chance of becoming homeless than of winning the lottery.

WRITING TIP

When writing dialogue, be sure to start a new paragraph every time the speaker changes, as in the example at the left. For help with punctuation and capitalization in quotations, see page 898 of the Grammar Handbook.

2.2 Paragraphs

A paragraph is made up of sentences that work together to develop an idea or accomplish a purpose. Whether or not a paragraph contains a topic sentence stating the main idea, it must have both unity and coherence.

LINK TO LITERATURE

Notice the strong topic sentence that begins the paragraph about the blue-star banners on page 262 of Hazel Shelton Abernethy's "The Home Front: 1941–1945."

Topic Sentences

A topic sentence makes the main idea or purpose of a paragraph clear to your reader. A topic sentence can appear anywhere in a paragraph, but when it is the first sentence, it can capture the reader's attention and clearly suggest what will follow.

> *The peregrine falcon, which was nearly extinct in the early 1970s, may soon be taken off the endangered-species list.* After World War II, ornithologists began noticing that falcon populations were declining. Finally, in the 1960s they learned that the pesticide DDT was poisoning the birds, causing them to lay thin-shelled eggs that broke in the nest or otherwise failed to hatch. Ever since DDT was banned in 1972, the falcons have been making a comeback. In the United States alone, there are now more than 1,200 pairs of peregrine falcons.

Unity

A paragraph has unity if every sentence in it supports the same main idea or purpose. One way to achieve unity in a paragraph is to state the main idea in a topic sentence and be sure that all the other sentences support that idea, as in the example above. You can create unity in a paragraph without using a topic sentence, however. Decide on a goal for your paragraph and make sure that each sentence supports that goal. Sentences should logically flow from one to the next, as shown in the narrative paragraph below.

WRITING TIP

When you revise your writing, be sure to delete any details that do not relate to the main idea of each paragraph. If a paragraph contains two main ideas, you may break it into two separate paragraphs.

> Maria approached her teacher shyly. "I didn't turn in the paper," she whispered. Ms. Williams, unaware of Maria's quiet presence, continued making red marks in her grade book. I'll say it just once more, Maria thought. At that moment, Ms. Williams glanced up to see her most bashful student wringing her hands and gazing at the floor.

Coherence

In a coherent paragraph, details are presented in a clear, sensible order. Notice that the following paragraph is coherent because the events of Pocahontas's life are related in chronological order.

> According to the English colonist John Smith, Pocahontas saved his life. A few years later, she was kidnapped by other colonists. While living with them, she fell in love with John Rolfe, and they were married. Later, Pocahontas, her husband, and their infant son traveled to England, where Pocahontas was introduced to the king.

2.3   Transitions

Transitions are words that show the connections between details, such as relationships in time and space, order of importance, causes and effects, and similarities or differences.

Chronological Order

Some transitions help to clarify the order in which events take place. To arrange details chronologically, as in the example below, use transitional words such as *first, second, always, then, next, later, soon, before, finally, after, earlier, afterward,* and *tomorrow.*

> It's easy to make a hummus sandwich. *First,* chop some tomatoes, onions, and lettuce. *Next,* heat the pita bread. *After* spreading hummus on the pita, add the vegetables and it's ready to eat.

Spatial Order

Transitional words and phrases such as *in front, behind, next to, nearest, lowest, above, below, underneath, on the left,* and *in the middle* can help show where items are located. The following example describes the arrangement of photos on a dresser.

> On my mother's dresser you can read the history of our family. *On the left,* a picture shows my parents' wedding. The picture *in the middle* is of my older brother as a baby, still toothless. The picture *on the right* shows all of us children in our fanciest clothes.

 LINK TO LITERATURE

Look at the anecdote about loading the ice truck on page 255 of the excerpt from *Once Upon a Time When We Were Colored.* Notice how Clifton Taulbert uses transitions to show the chronological order of events.

When you begin a sentence with a transition such as *most important, therefore, nevertheless, still,* or *instead,* set the transition off with a comma.

Degree

Transitions such as *mainly, strongest, weakest, first, second, most important, least important, worst,* and *best* show degree of importance or rank order of details, as in the model below.

> I look for several qualities in a friend. *Most important,* I like someone who shares my interests. *Second,* I want someone who can keep a secret. *Least important,* my new friend should get along with all my other friends.

Compare and Contrast

Words and phrases such as *similarly, likewise, also, like, as, neither . . . nor,* and *either . . . or* show similarity or likeness between details. *However, by contrast, yet, but, unlike, instead, whereas,* and *while* show contrast or difference. Note the use of both types of transitions in the model below.

> *Like* the lawyer in "The Bet," Jerry in "A Mother in Mannville" spent much of his time alone. *Both* characters experienced loneliness. *However,* as an orphan, Jerry never willingly chose to be alone, *whereas* the lawyer had agreed to his solitary confinement.

Cause and Effect

To show that details are linked in a cause-and-effect relationship, use transition words and phrases such as *since, because, thus, therefore, so, due to, for this reason,* and *as a result.* Transitions in the following example help readers understand the causes of the writer's attachment to an old notebook.

> My notebook might look tattered and worn, but I treasure it *because* Silvio gave it to me. He was my best friend, but he moved to New Jersey. *Since* the notebook is all I have to remember him by, I will never throw it away.

2.4 Elaboration

To develop the main idea of a paragraph or a longer piece, you need to provide elaboration, or details, so that your readers aren't left with unanswered questions.

Facts and Statistics

A fact is a statement that can be proved, while a statistic is a fact stated in numbers. As in the model below, the facts and statistics you use should strongly support the statements you make.

> The population is booming in cities in the Sunbelt. Between 1980 and 1990, 19 of the 20 fastest-growing U.S. cities were located in California, Arizona, Texas, Florida, and Nevada.

Sensory Details

By showing how something looks, sounds, smells, tastes, and feels, sensory details like the ones in the model below can help your readers more fully experience your subject.

> On the second day of the heat wave, the temperature hit a sweltering 106 degrees. Outside, the sun melted the soft tar of newly paved streets. Inside, people sipped sweet, cool lemonade and hovered around whirring old fans.

Incidents

Describing a brief incident can help to explain or develop an idea. The writer of the model below includes an incident to help make a point about safety.

> Pedestrians, like drivers, should follow certain rules of the road, such as looking both ways before crossing the street. I learned how dangerous it can be to break that rule when I was nearly hit by a driver who was traveling the wrong direction down a one-way street.

Look at the entry for April 20 in "Flowers for Algernon" on page 523. LINK TO LITERATURE

Look at the entry for April 20 in "Flowers for Algernon" on page 523. Notice how Daniel Keyes uses an example to develop his point that Charlie's new intelligence has driven a wedge between Charlie and all the people he once knew and loved.

Examples

The model below shows how using an example can help support or clarify an idea. A well-chosen example often can be more effective than a lengthy explanation.

> Fables frequently teach practical lessons. For example, in "Brer Possum's Dilemma," Brer Snake teaches Brer Possum to distrust a companion with an evil nature, despite the companion's reassurances that he's changed.

Quotations

Choose quotations that clearly support your points and be sure that you copy each quotation word for word. Remember to always credit the source.

> In his autobiography, *Once Upon a Time When We Were Colored*, Clifton Taulbert makes his readers feel the chill of the ice in the icehouse: "As we walked into the icehouse, all I could see was a cold vapor rising from hundreds of blocks of ice."

2.5 Description

Descriptive writing conveys images and impressions of a person, a place, an event, or a thing.

Descriptive writing appears almost everywhere, from reference books to poems. You might use a description to introduce a character in a narrative or to create a strong closing to a persuasive essay. Whatever your purpose and wherever you use description, the following guidelines for good descriptive writing will help you.

Include Plenty of Details

Vivid sensory details help the reader feel like an on-the-scene observer of the subject. The sensory details of the following scene appeal to the senses of sight, sound, smell, touch, and even taste.

Davis slouched at the table and gazed out the coffee shop window, his worn shirt soaked with perspiration. A fly began buzzing furiously against the torn window screen, so Davis took aim with a rolled-up newspaper. When an order of fried eggs and grits was served at the next table, his mouth watered and his stomach growled.

Organize Your Details

Details that are presented in a logical order help the reader form a mental picture of the subject. Descriptive details may be organized chronologically, spatially, by order of importance, or by order of impression, as in the model below.

The new teacher's towering height and her icy, blue eyes drew our attention immediately. As she strode firmly to the board, our gaze followed her nervously. Only when she finally spoke, in a tone that was warm and friendly, did we begin to relax.

Show, Don't Tell

Instead of just telling about a subject in a general way, provide details and quotations that expand and support what you want to say and that enable your readers to share your experience. The following example just tells and doesn't show.

It was a terrible day because I ruined my hair.

The paragraph below uses descriptive details to show what the writer experienced on this terrible day.

I began the day feeling daring and adventuresome, but by the time I went to sleep that night, I felt like crawling in a hole. It all started when, against my mother's better judgment, I tried to dye my hair blond. I wanted to look like the ravishing beauty on the front of the box. By the time I was through, my hair was the color of strained peas.

LINK TO LITERATURE

Try to use vivid, descriptive details to help your reader visualize the subject of your writing. Gary Soto's "Mother and Daughter," on page 203, uses a variety of descriptive details, each presented in order of impression.

Use Precise Language

To create a clear image in your reader's mind, use vivid and precise words. Instead of using general nouns, verbs, and adjectives (*boat, throw, sad*), use specific ones (*canoe, hurl, gloomy*). Notice what happens when vague, general words are replaced with precise words, as in the examples below.

> Joe was smiling.
> Joe was grinning from ear to ear.
>
> The tree fell to the ground.
> The old pine crashed to the forest floor.

2.6   Conclusions

A conclusion should leave readers with a strong final impression. Try any of these approaches for concluding a piece of writing.

Restate the Main Idea

Close by returning to your central idea and stating it in a new way. Link the beginning of your conclusion with the information you have presented, as the model below shows.

> It is therefore essential that environmental activists from countries around the world begin working together if our goal is to be achieved. Without international communication and cooperation, our individual efforts to improve the planet may not make a measurable difference.

Ask a Question

Try asking a question that sums up what you have said and gives readers something to think about. The following example from a piece of persuasive writing ends with a question that suggests a course of action.

> Therefore, since it takes many times more grain to feed animals than it takes to feed people, doesn't it make sense to reduce meat consumption?

Make a Recommendation

When you are writing to persuade, you can use your conclusion to tell readers what you want them to do. The conclusion below is from an essay on homelessness.

> Shawn, Maria, and José are all real children. The next time you see a homeless person, remember these children and what you can do to help.

End with the Last Event

If you're telling a story, you may end with the last thing that happens. Here, a story ends with an important moment of understanding.

> The room was mine—something I had wished for every time my sister and I had had a fight. But the prize I had dreamed about so long seemed completely hollow now.

Generalize About Your Information

The model below concludes by making a specific statement about the importance of the subject.

> The anecdotes in *Reflections on the Civil War* show the young volunteers' eagerness to fight as well as the painful consequences of battle. These stories communicate the senselessness of war in general—a powerful message for any age or time.

LINK TO LITERATURE

"The Gift of the Magi," on page 425, contains one of the most famous surprise endings in American literature. Notice how aptly this conclusion fits the story.

Narrative Writing

3

Narrative writing tells a story. If you write a story from your imagination, it is called a fictional narrative. A true story about actual events is called a nonfictional narrative.

Key Techniques of Narrative Writing

Writing Standards

Good narrative writing

▶ includes descriptive details and dialogue to develop the characters, setting, and plot

▶ has a clear beginning, middle, and end

▶ maintains a consistent tone and point of view

▶ uses language that is appropriate for the audience

▶ demonstrates the significance of the events or ideas

Define the Conflict

The conflict of a narrative is the problem that the main character faces. In the example below, the conflict is between the character and the Alaskan wilderness.

Example

When the temperature dropped and our tent wasn't enough to keep us warm, we weren't sure whether we should search for better shelter or go home.

Clearly Organize the Events

Choose the important events and explain them in an order that is easy to understand. In a fictional narrative, this series of events is the story's plot.

Example

- Jeff and I go winter camping to take photos.
- The temperature falls dangerously low.
- We decide not to leave but to look for better shelter.
- We find abandoned igloo and take shelter.
- We get photos the next day.

Depict Characters Vividly

Use vivid details to show your readers what your characters look like, what they say, and what they think.

Example

"I don't give up easily," I told Jeff. "If we quit now, I'll wonder later if we could have made it."

Organizing Narrative Writing

One way to organize a piece of narrative writing is to arrange the events in chronological order, as shown in Option 1 below.

Option 1

Focus on Events	**Example**
• Introduce characters and setting	Jeff and I went winter camping to take nature photos.
• Show event 1	The temperature dropped and it was too cold to stay in our tent. We had to decide whether to go home or stay and seek better shelter.
• Show event 2	We decided to stay and began seeking an abandoned igloo Jeff had heard about.
• End, perhaps showing the significance of the events	We found the igloo, took shelter from the cold, and were able to stay and get the photos the next day.

You may prefer to focus on characters, especially if a change in character—the way someone thinks, feels, or behaves—is important to the outcome of the story. In that case, try organizing your story according to Option 2. Try Option 3 if you plan to focus on a conflict that a character experiences within himself or herself or with society, nature, or another character.

Option 2

Focus on Character

- Introduce the main character

- Describe the conflict the character faces

- Relate the events and the changes the character goes through as a result of the conflict

- Present the final change or new understanding

Option 3

Focus on Conflict

- Present the characters and setting

- Introduce the conflict

- Describe the events that develop from the initial conflict

- Show the struggle of the main character with the conflict

- Resolve the conflict

Remember: Good narrative writing is organized logically, with clues to help the reader understand the order of events.

WRITING TIP

Introductions Try hooking your reader's interest by opening a story with an exciting event or some attention-grabbing dialogue. After your introduction, you may need to go back in time and relate the incidents that led up to the opening event.

LINK TO LITERATURE

Realistic dialogue is important for creating believable characters. What characters say in a story should sound like natural speech. Notice how Paulette Childress White uses contractions, slang expressions, and dialect in the conversation on page 294 of "Getting the Facts of Life."

4

Explanatory Writing

LINK TO LITERATURE

Explanatory writing techniques provide tools for exploring the issues presented by or in literature. The examples on the following pages examine Ralph Helfer's nonfiction narrative "The Flood," on page 347, and James Berry's fictional story about a hurricane, "The Banana Tree," on page 369.

Explanatory writing is writing that informs and explains. You can use it to explain how to cook spaghetti, to explore the origins of the universe, or even to compare pieces of literature.

Types of Explanatory Writing

Problem-Solution

Problem-solution writing examines a problem and proposes a solution to it.

Example
Ralph Helfer faces the ongoing problem of flooding on his wild-animal ranch.

Analysis

Analysis explains how something works, how it is defined, or what its parts are.

Example
Ralph Helfer faces physical, emotional, and intellectual challenges in the narrative "The Flood."

Compare and Contrast

Compare-and-contrast writing explores the similarities and differences between two or more subjects.

Example
Both Ralph Helfer and Gustus, a character from "The Banana Tree," face the challenges of natural disasters to save something they value.

Cause and Effect

Cause-and-effect writing explains why something happened, why certain conditions exist, or what resulted from an action or a condition.

Example
The flood's destruction leads Ralph Helfer to think and feel differently about his life.

4.1 Compare and Contrast

Compare-and-contrast writing explores the similarities and differences between two or more subjects.

Organizing Compare-and-Contrast Writing

When you compare and contrast subjects, you can organize your information in different ways. Two of your options are shown below.

Option 1

Feature by Feature

Feature 1
- Subject A
- Subject B

Feature 2
- Subject A
- Subject B

Example

Ralph Helfer and Gustus both face natural disasters to save something they value.

Ralph Helfer risks his life to save his trained animals from the flood waters.

Gustus risks his life to protect his banana tree from the hurricane.

Helfer values his animals for different reasons than Gustus does his banana tree.

Option 2

Subject by Subject

Subject A
- Feature 1
- Feature 2
- Feature 3

Subject B
- Feature 1
- Feature 2
- Feature 3

Example

Ralph Helfer risks his life to save his trained animals from the flood waters.

He acts bravely, crossing dangerous waters.

His motivation is love for his animals.

His solution is not completely effective.

Gustus risks his life to protect his banana tree.

He acts fearlessly, facing dangerous winds to prop up his tree.

His motivation is a desire to buy shoes.

His solution proves to be dangerous.

Writing Standards

Good compare-and-contrast writing

▶ clearly states the subjects being compared and shows how they are alike and different

▶ introduces the subjects in an interesting way and gives a reason for the comparison

▶ uses transitions to signal similarities and differences

▶ ends with a conclusion that explains the decision made or that provides a new understanding of the subjects compared

WRITING TIP

The goal of compare-and-contrast writing is to reveal something about the subjects that you wouldn't normally see. The example at left compares the challenges faced in a fictional account of a hurricane and a nonfiction narrative about a flood.

WRITING TIP

See page 829 of the Writing Handbook for information on using transitions in your compare-and-contrast writing.

WRITING TIP

You may want to include in your essay a diagram or chart that visually portrays the cause-and-effect relationship explained in your writing.

4.2   Cause and Effect

Cause-and-effect writing explains why something happened, why certain conditions exist, or what resulted from an action or a condition.

Organizing Cause-and-Effect Writing

Your organization will depend on your topic and purpose for writing. If your focus is on explaining the effects of an event such as the passage of a law, you might first state the cause and then explain the effects (Option 1). If you want to explain the causes of an event like the closing of a factory, you might first state the effect and then examine its causes (Option 2). Sometimes you'll want to describe a chain of cause-and-effect relationships (Option 3) to explore a topic such as the disappearance of tropical rain forests or the development of home computers.

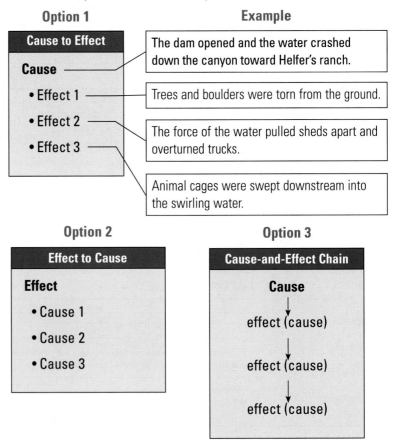

Remember: Don't assume that a cause-and-effect relationship exists simply because one event follows another. Be sure facts show that the effect couldn't have happened without the cause.

4.3 Problem-Solution

Problem-solution writing clearly states a problem, analyzes the problem, and proposes a solution to the problem.

Organizing Problem-Solution Writing

Your organization will depend on the goal of your problem-solution piece, your intended audience, and the specific problem you choose to address. The organizational methods outlined below are effective for different kinds of problem-solution writing.

Option 1

Simple Problem-Solution

Description of problem

Why it needs to be solved

Recommended solution

Explanation of solution

Conclusion

Example

Even with a drainage channel in place, Helfer's property is still vulnerable to flooding.

He knows the ranch will flood again sometime.

Helfer should develop a good evacuation plan to move the animals at the first sign of a flood.

He won't have to rely on uncertain safety measures, like the drainage channel, and he will have a routine in place to keep the animals safe.

Helfer should keep the safety measures but not rely on them, because nature is unpredictable.

Option 2

Deciding Between Solutions

Description of Problem

Solution A

• Pros

• Cons

Solution B

• Pros

• Cons

Recommendation

Example

Even with a drainage channel in place, Helfer's property is still vulnerable to flooding.

He can develop a plan to move the animals to safety at the first sign of a flood.

This way, Helfer can stay at his ranch.

However, Helfer will have to treat every potential flood as an emergency and evacuate the animals before the flooding is serious.

Helfer can move his ranch to a new location.

WRITING TIP

Anticipate possible objections to your solution. You can strengthen your arguments by responding to the objections in a clear, reasonable way.

4.4 Analysis

In an analysis you try to help your readers understand a subject by explaining how it works, how it is defined, or what its parts are.

The details you include will depend upon the kind of analysis you're writing.

- A **process analysis** should provide background information—such as definitions of terms and a list of needed equipment—and then explain each important step or stage in the process. For example, you might explain the steps to program a VCR or the stages in a plant's growth cycle.
- A **definition** should include the most important characteristics of the subject. To define a quality, such as honesty, you might include the characteristic of truthfulness.
- A **parts analysis** should describe each of the parts, groups, or types that make up the subject. For example, you might analyze the parts of the human brain, the groups affected by a new law, or the types of jazz music.

Organizing Your Analysis

Organize your details in a logical order appropriate for the kind of analysis you're writing. A process analysis is usually organized chronologically, with steps or stages in the order they occur.

Option 1	Example
Process Analysis	
Introduce topic	Carefully following flood evacuation procedures can save your life.
Background information	You need a battery-operated radio tuned to the radio station that provides emergency information.
Explain steps	
• Step 1	As soon as you sense danger, turn on the radio for evacuation instructions.
• Step 2	
• Step 3	Once the flood begins, leave before the water gets too deep to drive through.
	Finally, be sure to follow recommended escape routes.

You can organize the details in a definition or parts analysis in order of importance or impression. Characteristics in the following definition are organized from most to least obvious.

Option 2

Example

Definition	
Introduce term	Ralph Helfer is a hero in the narrative "The Flood."
General definition	Heroes are usually described as being strong and brave and having a noble purpose.
Explain qualities	Helfer shows heroic characteristics while battling a flood on his ranch.
• Quality 1	
• Quality 2	His strength of action and character is shown as he drags the caged animals from the flooded water.
• Quality 3	His bravery is shown as he faces the danger of the flood to save his animals.
	His noble purpose is shown by his goal of saving his animals from the flood.

In the following parts analysis, the challenge of battling a flood is broken down into three parts.

Option 3

Example

Parts Analysis	
Introduce subject	Ralph Helfer faces many demands in the narrative "The Flood."
Explain how subject can be broken into parts	His challenges are intellectual, physical, and emotional.
• Part 1	He faces the intellectual challenge of figuring out how to rescue the animals.
• Part 2	Helfer faces the physical challenges of the flood water, dragging animals to shore, and working for three days and nights.
• Part 3	He faces the emotional challenge of watching as some of his beloved animals are swept away.

WRITING TIP

Introductions You may want to begin with a vivid description of the subject to capture the reader's attention. For example, a description of people caught in a flood could introduce the analysis of flood evacuation procedures.

WRITING TIP

Conclusions Try ending an analysis by stating the importance of the subject to the reader. An analysis of Ralph Helfer's heroic qualities could end with a statement about his successful rescue effort.

5

Persuasive Writing

Persuasive writing allows you to use the power of language to inform and influence others.

Key Techniques of Persuasive Writing

Writing Standards

Good persuasive writing

▶ has a strong introduction

▶ clearly states the issue and the writer's position

▶ presents ideas logically

▶ answers opposing viewpoints

▶ ends with a strong argument or summary or a call for action

State Your Opinion

Taking a stand on an issue and clearly stating your opinion are essential to every piece of persuasive writing you do.

Example
Public tax dollars should continue to fund Green Park Zoo.

Know Your Audience

Knowing who will read your writing will help you decide what information you need to share and what tone you should use to communicate your message. In the example below, the writer has chosen a formal tone that is appropriate for a letter to a politician or for a newspaper editorial.

Example
In fact, an increase in funding will enable Green Park Zoo to expand its highly successful breeding program.

Support Your Opinion

Using reasons, examples, facts, statistics, and anecdotes to support your opinion will show your audience why you feel the way you do. Below, the writer uses an example to support her opinion.

Example
The zoo's breeding program concentrates on the conservation of endangered species such as orangutans.

Organizing Persuasive Writing

In persuasive writing, you need to gather information to support your opinions. Here are some ways you can organize that material to convince your audience.

Option 1

Reasons for Your Opinion
Your opinion
• Reason 1
• Reason 2
• Reason 3

Example

Public tax dollars should continue to fund Green Park Zoo.

This zoo enables scientists to learn more about the habits and diseases of animals.

The zoo educates city dwellers about nature.

Most important, the zoo breeds endangered species to protect them from extinction.

Depending on the purpose and form of your writing, you may want to show the weaknesses of other opinions as you explain the strength of your own. Two options for organizing writing that includes more than just your side of the issue are shown below.

Option 2

Why Your Opinion Is Stronger
Your opinion
• your reasons
Other opinion
• evidence refuting reasons for other opinion and showing strengths of your opinion

Option 3

Why Another Opinion Is Weaker
Other opinion
• reasons
Your opinion
• reasons supporting your opinion and pointing out the weaknesses of the other side

Remember: Effective persuasion often builds from the weakest argument to the strongest. Keep this in mind when you organize the reasons that support your opinion.

WRITING TIP

Introductions Start a persuasive piece with a question, a surprising fact, or an anecdote to capture your readers' interest and make them want to keep reading.

WRITING TIP

Conclusions The ending of a persuasive piece is often the part that sticks in a reader's mind. Your conclusion might summarize the two sides of an issue, restate your position, invite readers to make up their own minds, or call for some action.

6 Research Report Writing

In research report writing, you can find answers to questions about a topic you're interested in. Your writing organizes information from various sources and presents it to your readers as a unified and coherent whole.

Writing Standards

Good research report writing

▶ clearly states the purpose of the report in a thesis statement

▶ contains only accurate and relevant information

▶ documents sources correctly

▶ develops the topic logically

▶ reflects careful research on the topic

Key Techniques of Research Report Writing

Clarify Your Thesis

Your thesis statement explains to your readers the question your report will answer. In the example below, the thesis statement answers the question "How did Frederick Douglass draw support for the antislavery movement in a way that others could not?"

Example
Speaking and writing as a former slave, Frederick Douglass openly criticized racism in the United States and drew support for the antislavery movement.

Support Your Ideas

You need to support your ideas with details and facts from reliable sources. In the example below, the writer supports the claim that Douglass risked his freedom.

Example
Douglass wrote his autobiography at the risk of being arrested as a runaway slave. According to writer Richard Conniff, Douglass revealed his true identity because people doubted his stories about slavery.

Document Your Sources

You need to document, or credit, the sources where you found your information. In the example below, the writer quotes Douglass and documents the source.

Example
Douglass stated that the slaveholders tried to "disgust their slaves with freedom" so that the slaves would think they were better off in captivity (Douglass 85).

Finding and Evaluating Sources

Begin your research by looking for information on your topic in books, magazines, newspapers, and computer databases. In addition to using your library's card or computer catalog, look up your subject in indexes, such as the *Readers' Guide to Periodical Literature* or the *New York Times Index*. The bibliographies in books that you find during your research may also lead to additional sources. The following checklist will help you evaluate the reliability of the sources you find.

Checklist for Evaluating Your Sources	
Authoritative	Someone who has written several books or articles on your subject or whose work has been published in a well-respected newspaper or journal may be considered an authority.
Up-to-date	Check the publication dates to see if the source reflects the most current research on your subject.
Respected	In general, tabloid newspapers and popular-interest magazines are not reliable sources. If you have questions about whether you are using a respected source, ask your librarian.

Making Source Cards

For each source you find, record the bibliographic information on a separate index card. You will need this information to give credit to the sources you use in your paper. The samples at the right show how to make source cards for encyclopedia entries, magazine articles, and books. You will use the source number on each card to identify the notes you take during your research.

Taking Notes

As you find material that suits the purpose of your report, record each piece of information on a separate note card. You will probably use all three of the note-taking methods listed on the following page.

LINK TO LITERATURE

Your reading can inspire ideas for research topics. For example, after reading Frederick Douglass's letter to Harriet Tubman, on page 559, you may be interested in learning more about him. The research demonstrated in this part of the Writing Handbook was inspired by Douglass's statement "Most that I have done and suffered in the service of our cause has been in public."

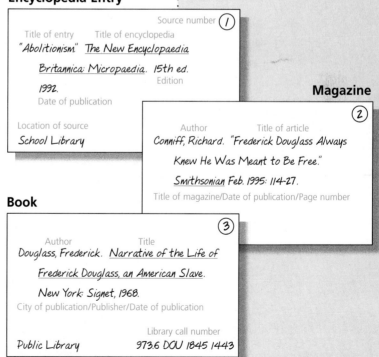

Encyclopedia Entry

Source number ①
Title of entry   Title of encyclopedia
"Abolitionism." The New Encyclopaedia
     Britannica: Micropaedia. 15th ed.
                                    Edition
     1992.
     Date of publication
Location of source
School Library

Magazine ②
        Author   Title of article
Conniff, Richard. "Frederick Douglass Always
     Knew He Was Meant to Be Free."
     Smithsonian Feb. 1995: 114-27.
     Title of magazine/Date of publication/Page number

Book ③
        Author   Title
Douglass, Frederick. Narrative of the Life of
     Frederick Douglass, an American Slave.
     New York: Signet, 1968.
     City of publication/Publisher/Date of publication
                          Library call number
Public Library   973.6 DOU 1845 1443

Douglass's lectures   Main idea   Source number ②

"What, to the American slave, is
your Fourth of July? . . . To him your
celebration is a sham." 115
                              Page number

Type of note
(Quotation)

- Paraphrase, or restate in your own words, the main ideas and supporting details from a passage.
- Summarize, or rephrase the original material in fewer words, trying to capture the key ideas.
- Quote, or copy the original text word for word, if you think the author's own words best clarify a particular point. Use quotation marks to signal the beginning and the end of the quotation.

Writing a Thesis Statement

A thesis statement in a research report defines the main idea, or overall purpose, of your report. A clear one-sentence answer to your main question will result in a good thesis statement.

Question: How did Frederick Douglass draw support for the antislavery movement in a way that others could not?

Thesis Statement: Speaking and writing as a former slave, Frederick Douglass openly criticized racism in the United States and drew support for the antislavery movement.

Making an Outline

To organize your report, group your note cards into main ideas and arrange them in a logical order. With your notes, make a topic outline, beginning with a shortened version of your thesis statement. Key ideas are listed after Roman numerals and sub-points are listed after uppercase letters and Arabic numerals, as in the following example.

WRITING TIP

Use the same form for items of the same rank in your outline. For example, if A is a noun, then B and C should be nouns.

Frederick Douglass: A Voice for Freedom
Introduction—Douglass's influence as a lecturer and writer
  I. Douglass's early life and background
    A. Enslavement
    B. Education
  II. Douglass's campaign against slavery
    A. Involvement with Massachusetts Anti-Slavery Society
      1. Treatment of slaves
      2. Criticism of Northern racism
    B. Publication of his autobiography
    C. Publication of the North Star, Douglass's newspaper
  III. Douglass's achievements in the antislavery movement

Documenting Your Sources

When you quote one of your sources or write in your own words information you have found in a source, you need to credit that source, using parenthetical documentation.

Guidelines for Parenthetical Documentation	
Work by One Author	Put the author's last name and the page reference in parentheses: **(Douglass 12)**. If you mention the author's name in the sentence, put only the page reference in parentheses: **(12)**.
Work by Two or Three Authors	Put the authors' last names and the page reference in parentheses: **(Meier and Rudwick 146)**.
Work by More Than Three Authors	Give the first author's last name followed by *et al.*, and the page reference: **(Ripley et al. 14)**.
Work with No Author Given	Give the title or a shortened version and the page reference: **("Abolitionism" 35)**.
One of Two or More Works by Same Author	Give the author's last name, the title or a shortened version, and the page reference: **(Conniff, "Frederick Douglass" 117)**.

WRITING TIP

Plagiarism Presenting someone else's writing or ideas as your own is plagiarism. To avoid plagiarism, you need to credit sources as noted at the left. However, if a piece of information is common knowledge—available in several sources—you do not need to credit the source. For an example of parenthetical documentation, see the report on page 804.

Creating a Works Cited Page

At the end of your research report, you need to include a Works Cited page. Any source that you have documented needs to be listed alphabetically by the author's last name. If there is no author, use the editor's last name or the title of the work. Note the guidelines for spacing and punctuation on the model page.

Student's last name   Page number

Center heading

1″

½″

Chan   14

Works Cited

"Abolitionism." Encyclopaedia Britannica: Micropaedia.

    15th ed. 1992.

├─1″─┤Conniff, Richard. "Frederick Douglass Always Knew He ├─1″─┤

    Was Meant to Be Free." Smithsonian Feb. 1995:

    114–27.

Douglass, Frederick. Narrative of the Life of Frederick

    Douglass, an American Slave. New York: Signet, 1968.

Meier, August, and Elliott Rudwick. From Plantation to

    Ghetto. 3rd ed. American Century Series. New York:

    Hill and Wang, 1976.

Indent additional lines ½″

Double-space between all lines

2 spaces after periods

1 Getting Information Electronically

Electronic resources provide you with a convenient and efficient way to gather information.

1.1 On-line Resources

When you use your computer to communicate with another computer or with another person using a computer, you are working "on-line." On-line resources include commercial information services and information available on the Internet.

Commercial Information Services

You can subscribe to various services that offer information such as the following:

- up-to-date news, weather, and sports reports
- access to encyclopedias, magazines, newspapers, dictionaries, almanacs, and databases (collections of information)
- electronic mail (e-mail) to and from other users
- forums, or ongoing electronic conversations among users interested in a particular topic

Internet

The Internet is a vast network of computers. News services, libraries, universities, researchers, organizations, and government agencies use the Internet to communicate and to distribute information. The Internet includes two key features:

- **World Wide Web,** which provides you with information on particular subjects and links you to related topics and resources (such as the linked Web pages shown at the left)
- **Electronic mail** (e-mail), which allows you to communicate with other e-mail users worldwide

1.2 CD-ROM

A CD-ROM (compact disc–read-only memory) stores data that may include text, sound, photographs, and video.

Almost any kind of information can be found on CD-ROMs, which you can purchase or you can use at the library, including

- encyclopedias, almanacs, and indexes
- other reference books on a variety of subjects
- news reports from newspapers, magazines, television, or radio
- museum art collections
- back issues of magazines
- literature collections

WHAT YOU'LL NEED

- To access on-line resources, you need a computer with a modem linked to a telephone line. Your school computer lab or resource center may be linked to the Internet or to a commercial information service.
- To use CD-ROMs, you need a computer system with a CD-ROM player.

1.3 Library Computer Services

Many libraries offer computerized catalogs and a variety of other electronic resources.

Computerized Catalogs

You may search for a book in a library by typing the title, author, subject, or key words into a computer terminal. When you find the book you're looking for, the screen will display the kind of information shown at right, including the book's call number and whether it is on the shelf or checked out of the library. When a particular work is not available, you may be able to search the catalogs of other libraries.

Other Electronic Resources

In addition to computerized catalogs, many libraries offer electronic versions of books or other reference materials. They may also have a variety of indexes on CD-ROM, which allow you to search for magazine or newspaper articles on any topic you choose. Ask your librarian for assistance in using these resources.

2 Word Processing

Many word-processing programs allow you to draft, revise, edit, and format your writing and to produce neat, professional-looking papers. They also allow you to share your writing with others.

2.1 Revising and Editing

Improving the quality of your writing becomes easier when you use a word-processing program to revise and edit.

Revising a Document

Most word-processing programs allow you to make the following kinds of changes:

- add or delete words
- move text from one location in your document to another
- undo a change you have made in the text
- save a document with a new name, allowing you to keep old drafts for reference
- view more than one document at a time, so you can copy text from one document and add it to another

Editing a Document

Many word-processing programs have the following features to help you catch errors and polish your writing:

- The **spell checker** automatically finds misspelled words and suggests possible corrections.
- The **grammar checker** spots possible grammatical errors and suggests ways you might correct them.
- The **thesaurus** suggests synonyms for a word you want to replace.
- The **dictionary** will give you the definitions of words so you can be sure you have used words correctly.
- The **search and replace** feature searches your whole document and corrects every occurrence of something you want to change, such as a misspelled name.

- Computer
- Word-processing program
- Printer

WRITING TIP

Even if you use a spell checker, you should still proofread your draft carefully to make sure you've used the right words. For example, you may have used *there* or *they're* when you meant to use *their*.

Format is the layout and appearance of your writing on the page. You may choose your formatting options before or after you write.

Formatting Type

You may want to make changes in the typeface, type size, and type style of the words in your document. For each of these, your word-processing program will most likely have several options to choose from. These options allow you to

- change the typeface to create a different look for the words in your document
- change the type size of the entire document or of just the headings of sections in the paper
- change the type style when necessary; for example, use italics or underline for the titles of books and magazines

Typeface	Size	Style
Geneva	7-point Times	*Italic*
Times	10-point Times	**Bold**
Chicago	12-point Times	<u>Underline</u>
`Courier`	14-point Times	

Formatting Pages

Not only can you change the way individual words look; you can also change the way they are arranged on the page. Some of the formatting decisions you make will depend on how you plan to use a printout of a draft or on the guidelines of an assignment.

- Set the line spacing, or the amount of space you need between lines of text. Double spacing is commonly used for final drafts.

Centered

Fall Dance Budget

The Fall Dance Committee is proposing the following budget for expenses. We need to get a final approval from the student council by Sept. 28 and from the advisers by Oct. 3.

Disc Jockey...............$350
Decorations..............$350
Refreshments..............$600
Total...........$1,300

Left-aligned

Right-aligned

- Set the margins, or the amount of white space around the edges of your text. A one-inch margin on all sides is commonly used for final drafts.
- Create a header for the top of the page or a footer for the bottom if you want to include such information as your name, the date, or the page number on every page.
- Determine the alignment of your text. The screen at the left shows your options.

TECHNOLOGY TIP

Some word-processing pro-
grams, such as the Writing
Coach software referred to in
this book, allow you to leave
notes for your peer readers in
the side column or in a separate text box. If you wish,
leave those areas blank so
your readers can write comments or questions.

**Computers allow you to share your writing electronically.
Send a copy of your work to someone via e-mail or put it
in someone's drop box if your computer is linked to other
computers on a network. Then use the feedback of your
peers to help you improve the quality of your writing.**

Peer Editing on a Computer

The writer and the reader can both benefit from the convenience
of peer editing "on screen," or at the computer.

- Be sure to save your current draft and then make a copy of it
  for each of your peer readers.
- You might have your peer readers enter their comments in a
  different typeface or type style from the one you used for your
  text.
- Ask each of your readers to include his or her initials in the
  file name.

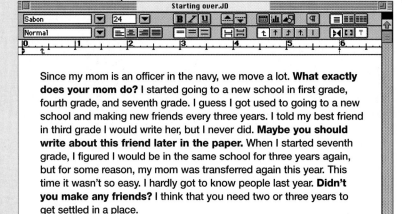

- If your computer
  allows you to
  open more than
  one file at a
  time, open each
  reviewer's file
  and refer to the
  files as you revise
  your draft.

Peer Editing on a Printout

Some peer readers prefer to respond to a draft on paper rather
than on the computer.

- Double- or triple-space your document so that your peer editor can make suggestions and changes between the lines.
- Leave extra-wide margins to give your readers room to note
  their reactions and questions as they read.
- Print out your draft and photocopy it if you want to share it
  with more than one reader.

Using Visuals

Tables, graphs, diagrams, and pictures often communicate information more effectively than words alone do. Many computer programs allow you to create visuals to use with written text.

3.1 When to Use Visuals

Use visuals in your work to illustrate complex concepts and processes or to make a page look more interesting.

Although you should not expect a visual to do all the work of written text, combining words and pictures or graphics can increase the understanding and enjoyment of your writing. Many computer programs allow you to create and insert graphs, tables, time lines, diagrams, and flow charts into your document. An art program allows you to create border designs for a title page or to draw an unusual character or setting for narrative or descriptive writing. You may also be able to add clip art, or premade pictures, to your document. Clip art can be used to illustrate an idea or concept in your writing or to make your writing more appealing for young readers.

3.2 Kinds of Visuals

The visuals you choose will depend on the type of information you want to present to your readers.

Tables

Tables allow you to arrange facts or numbers into rows and columns so that your reader can compare information more easily. In many word-processing programs, you can create a table by choosing the number of vertical columns and horizontal rows you need and then entering information in each box, as the illustration shows.

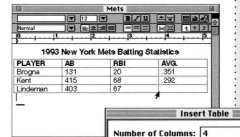

WHAT YOU'LL NEED

- A graphics program to create visuals
- Access to clip-art files from a CD-ROM, a computer disk, or an on-line service

TECHNOLOGY TIP

A spreadsheet program provides you with a preset table for your statistics and performs any necessary calculations.

Graphs and Charts

You can sometimes use a graph or chart to help communicate complex information in a clear visual image. For example, you could use a line graph to show how a trend changes over time, a bar graph like the one at the right to compare statistics from different years, or a pie chart to compare percentages. You might want to explore displaying data in more than one visual format before deciding which will work best for you.

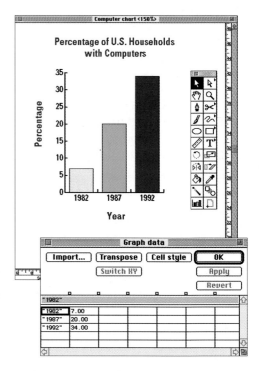

Other Visuals

Art and design programs allow you to create visuals for your writing. Many programs include the following features:

- drawing tools that allow you to draw, color, and shade pictures
- clip art that you can copy or change with drawing tools
- page borders that you can use to decorate title pages, invitations, or brochures
- text options that allow you to combine words with your illustrations
- tools for making geometric shapes in flow charts, time lines, and diagrams that show a process or sequence of events

Creating a Multimedia Presentation

4

A multimedia presentation is a combination of text, sound, and visuals such as photographs, videos, and animation. Your audience reads, hears, and sees your presentation at a computer, following different "paths" you create to lead the user through the information you have gathered.

4.1 Features of Multimedia Programs

To start planning your multimedia presentation, you need to know what options are available to you. You can combine sound, photos, videos, and animation to enhance any text you write about your topic.

Sound

Including sound in your presentation can help your audience understand information in your written text. For example, the user may be able to listen and learn from

- the pronunciation of an unfamiliar or foreign word
- a speech
- a recorded news interview
- a music selection
- a dramatic reading of a work of literature

Photos and Videos

Photographs and live-action videos can make your subject come alive for the user. Here are some examples:

- videotaped news coverage of a historical event
- videos of music, dance, or theater performances
- charts and diagrams
- photos of an artist's work
- photos or video of a geographical setting that is important to the written text

WHAT YOU'LL NEED

- Individual programs to create and edit the text, graphics, sound, and videos you will use
- A multimedia authoring program that allows you to combine these elements and create links between the screens

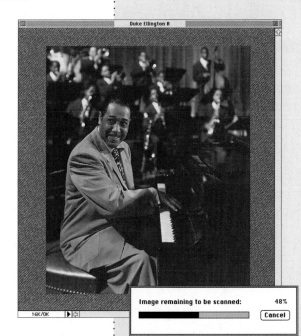

Animation

Many graphics programs allow you to add animation, or movement, to the visuals in your presentation. Animated figures add to the user's enjoyment and understanding of what you present. You can use animation to illustrate

- what happens in a story
- the steps in a process
- changes in a chart, graph, or diagram
- how your user can explore information in your presentation

4.2 Planning Your Presentation

To create a multimedia presentation, first choose your topic and decide what you want to include. Then plan how you want your user to move through your presentation.

Imagine that you are creating a multimedia presentation about the great jazz musician "Duke" Ellington. You know you want to include the following items:

- text about his influence on jazz
- a portrait of him
- a recording of him playing a song
- a photograph of him leading his band
- a videotape of his band in concert, audio included
- a recording of a radio interview with him
- text of interesting anecdotes from his concert tours

You can choose one of the following ways to organize your presentation:

- step by step with only one path, or order, in which the user can see and hear the information
- a branching path that allows users to make some choices about what they will see and hear, and in what order

A flow chart can help you figure out the path a user can take through your presentation. Each box in the flow chart on the following page represents something about Ellington for the user to read, see, or hear. The arrows on the flow chart show a branching path the user can follow.

Whenever boxes branch in more than one direction, it means that the user can choose which item to see or hear first.

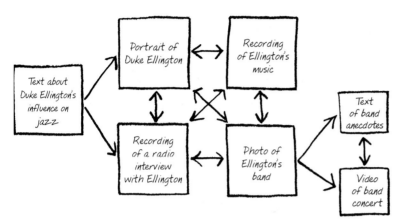

4.3 Guiding Your User

Your user will need directions to follow the path you have planned for your multimedia presentation.

Most multimedia authoring programs allow you to create screens that include text or audio directions that guide the user from one part of your presentation to the next. In the example below, the user can choose between several paths, and directions on the screen explain how to make the choice.

If you need help creating your multimedia presentation, ask your school's technology adviser. You may also be able to get help from your classmates or your software manual.

The user clicks on a button to select any of these options.

This screen shows the portrait of Ellington.

Navigational buttons can take the user back and forth, one screen at a time.

WRITING TIP

You usually need permission from the person or organization that owns the copyright on materials if you want to copy them. You do not need permission, however, if you are not making money from your presentation, if you use it only for educational purposes, and if you use only a small percentage of the original material.

Writing Complete Sentences

1.1 Sentence Fragments

A sentence fragment is a group of words that does not express a complete thought. It may be missing a subject, a predicate, or both. A sentence fragment makes you wonder *What is this about?* or *What happened?*

Missing Subject or Predicate

You can correct a sentence fragment by adding the missing subject or predicate to complete the thought.

Sound effects
∧Play an important part in a radio drama. The chug of
        signals danger   *The train whistle*
an oncoming train. A car engine stalls. ∧Blows frantically.

Phrase and Subordinate-Clause Fragments

When the fragment is a phrase or subordinate clause, you may join the fragment to an existing sentence.

In a radio drama, ⟋The music also stirs the listener's
emotions. As the music speeds up, ⟋The tension builds.
Suddenly, terror grips the listener, ⟋Because the music
has ended abruptly.

Rewrite this paragraph, correcting the sentence fragments.

1Like *The Hitchhiker*, the dramatization of *The War of the Worlds* was produced for radio by Orson Welles. **2**Reporting a Martian invasion of the United States. **3**Broadcast October 30, 1938. **4**An announcer interrupted the broadcast several times. **5**Said that it was just a play. **6**However, the story and the acting were so convincing that millions of Americans thought it was a real news report. **7**Terror struck. **8**Spreading quickly across the country. **9**Reports of panic-stricken people in the streets. **10**Welles later apologized to the nation. **11**The radio station also. **12**The Federal Communications Commission made new regulations after the broadcast. **13**To make sure a radio drama would never cause such panic again.

1.2   Run-On Sentences

A run-on sentence consists of two or more sentences written incorrectly as one. A run-on sentence occurs because the writer either used no end mark or used a comma instead of a period to end the first complete thought. A run-on sentence may confuse readers because it does not show where one thought ends and the next begins.

Forming Separate Sentences

One way to correct a run-on sentence is to form two separate sentences. Use a period or other end punctuation after the first sentence, and capitalize the first letter of the next sentence.

In "The Treasure of Lemon Brown" Lemon Brown lived in an abandoned building⊙ h̲e slept on a pile of rags. Homeless people have to live by their wits⊙ t̲hey don't have many other defenses against robbery and other dangers.

To correct run-on sentences, read them to yourself, noticing where you naturally pause between ideas. The pause usually indicates where you should place end punctuation.

Forming Compound Sentences

You can also correct a run-on sentence by rewriting it to form a compound sentence. One way to do this is by using a comma and a coordinating conjunction.

Never join simple sentences with a comma alone, or a run-on sentence will result. You need a comma followed by the conjunction *and, but,* or *or* to hold the sentences together.

> Lemon Brown was homeless, ^but^ he still had his treasure and his memories to comfort him.

You may use a semicolon to join two ideas that are closely related.

In addition, you can correct a run-on sentence by using a semicolon and a conjunctive adverb. Commonly used conjunctive adverbs are *however, therefore, nevertheless,* and *besides.*

> Lemon Brown had an interesting past,^ he had once been a famous blues singer. Homeless people are often ignored;^ *however,* ^Greg learned an important lesson by taking time to get to know Lemon Brown.

APPLY WHAT YOU'VE LEARNED

Rewrite this paragraph, correcting the run-on sentences.

[1]In "The Treasure of Lemon Brown" we learn a little about what it's like to be homeless, it's not the whole picture. [2]It has been estimated that 250,000 to 3 million homeless people are living in the United States today two-thirds of these people are children. [3]In fact, children are the fastest-growing segment of the homeless population their average age is three years old. [4]Many of these kids face other problems health is a particularly big concern. [5]In 1993 nearly half of the children in New York City's homeless shelters did not have up-to-date immunizations. [6]Education is another problem, homeless children are more likely to repeat a grade, and they are more likely to drop out or be placed in a special education program.

Making Subjects and Verbs Agree

2.1 Simple and Compound Subjects

A verb must agree in number with its subject. *Number* refers to whether a word is singular or plural. When a word refers to one thing, it is singular. When it refers to more than one thing, it is plural.

Agreement with Simple Subjects

Use a singular verb with a singular subject.

When the subject is a singular noun, you use the singular form of the verb. The present-tense singular form of a regular verb usually ends in *s* or *es*.

> In "Appetizer" a bear touch the narrator to show her
> affection.

Use a plural verb with a plural subject.

> These stories proves what I have always believed. Wild
> animals communicates with human beings.

Agreement with Compound Subjects

Use a plural verb with a compound subject whose parts are joined by *and*, regardless of the number of each part.

> The man and the bear develops a cautious friendship.

LINK TO LITERATURE

Notice the agreement of subjects with present-tense verbs on page 301 of "Appetizer" by Robert Abel. The present-tense verbs used by the narrator give the reader a sense of observing the action as it unfolds.

REVISING TIP

To find the subject of a sentence, first find the verb. Then ask *who* or *what* performs the action of the verb. Say the subject and the verb together to see if they agree.

When the parts of a compound subject are joined by *or* or *nor*, make the verb agree in number with the part that is closer to it.

> Neither the man nor the bear want [s] to hurt the other.
>
> However, the bear's appetite or her "gentle" nudges is [are] likely to endanger the man.

APPLY WHAT YOU'VE LEARNED

Write the correct form of the verb given in parentheses.

1. In "Appetizer" the narrator (encounter, encounters) some kind of Alaskan brown bear.
2. The Kodiak bear and the peninsula brown bear (live, lives) in Alaska.
3. Both bears (grow, grows) up to 9 feet long and 1,500 pounds in weight.
4. These bears (varies, vary) in color from yellowish to almost black.
5. Of the two kinds of brown bears, the grizzly (tends, tend) to be more dangerous.
6. In general, neither a mother bear nor her cubs willingly (approaches, approach) people.
7. However, if you're in the woods, either a grizzly or an Alaskan brown bear (represent, represents) danger.

2.2   Pronoun Subjects

When a pronoun is used as a subject, the verb must agree with it in number.

Agreement with Personal Pronouns

When the subject is a singular personal pronoun, use a singular verb. When the subject is a plural personal pronoun, use a plural verb.

Singular pronouns are *I, you, he, she,* and *it.* Plural pronouns are *we, you,* and *they.* With *I* and *you,* use the plural verb form.

> We disagrees about Philip Nolan in "The Man Without a Country." He claim [s] to be innocent, and he try [tries] to prove it. You believes the charges against him. I thinks Philip Nolan got an unfair trial.

When *he, she,* or *it* is the part of the subject closer to the verb in a compound subject containing *or* or *nor,* use a singular verb. When a pronoun is part of a compound subject containing *and,* use a plural verb.

> The judge appears to be prejudiced. Neither the prose-
> cutor nor he seem to have any doubt that Nolan is
> guilty of treason. The prosecutor and he wants Nolan
> to be convicted.

Agreement with Indefinite Pronouns

When the subject is a singular indefinite pronoun, use the singular form of the verb.

The following are singular indefinite pronouns: *another, either, nobody, nothing, anybody, everybody, somebody, no one, anyone, everyone, someone, one, anything, everything, something, each,* and *neither.*

> My friends sympathize with Nolan. Nobody believe his
> crime justifies his punishment. Someone know a story of
> a similar trial that had a happier ending than Nolan's
> trial had.

When the subject is a plural indefinite pronoun (*both, few, many,* or *several*), use the plural form of the verb.

> Few imagines being happy in Nolan's place, cut off
> from all news of his homeland. However, several hopes
> to live in another country someday.

The indefinite pronouns *some, all, any, none,* and *most* can be either singular or plural. When the pronoun refers to one thing, use a singular verb. When the pronoun refers to several things, use a plural verb.

In class we took a vote to see how many students agree with Nolan's punishment. Most thinks he was treated unfairly. Of all the evidence against Nolan, none seem to prove his guilt.

APPLY WHAT YOU'VE LEARNED

Choose the correct verb form from each pair.

1Among students of history, some (know, knows) of Aaron Burr. **2**Everybody (wonder, wonders) whether Burr really could have carried out his plot. **3**Many (believe, believes) that Burr even raised his own private army. **4**In the play Nolan and he (talk, talks) about starting a new country. **5**He (ask, asks) Nolan to help him. **6**They only (talk, talks) about Burr's plan; neither Nolan nor he (get, gets) the chance to take action because of their arrest. **7**We (know, knows) that after Burr is found guilty of treason, he and his grand plan (depart, departs) for Europe. **8**He spends much time in Europe. Most (pass, passes) in a search for foreign support for his plan. **9**Few (believe, believes) him when he (return, returns) five years later and (claim, claims) innocence of any wrongdoing. **10**I have read several stories about Aaron Burr. None (explain, explains) the reasons behind his foolish plans.

2.3 Common Agreement Problems

Several other situations can cause problems in subject-verb agreement.

Interrupting Words and Phrases

Be sure the verb agrees with its subject when words or phrases come between them.

Sometimes one or more words come between the subject and the verb. These interrupting words do not affect the number of the subject. The subject of a verb is never found in a prepositional phrase or an appositive, which may follow the subject and come before the verb.

> The images in the poem describes~~/~~hockey as a "battering sport." The poet, a masterful crafter of words, put you in the middle of the action.

(editing marks: "s" above "describes"; "s" inserted above "put")

Phrases beginning with *including, as well as, along with, such as,* and *in addition to* are not part of the subject.

> A hockey game, as well as other contact sports, often result in physical harm to the players. Even noncontact sports, such as baseball or basketball, ~~causes~~ injuries to players.

(editing marks: "s" above "result"; "cause" above "causes")

Inverted Sentences

When the subject comes after the verb, be sure the verb agrees with the subject in number.

A sentence in which the subject follows the verb is called an inverted sentence. Questions are usually in inverted form, as are sentences beginning with *here, there,* and *where.* (For example, Where are the <u>players</u>? There is a <u>game</u> today.)

> There ~~is~~ many references to fighting in the poem. Across the ice rushes the players to maul the enemy. Down go the left wing. Where in all this confusion ~~is~~ the referees?

(editing marks: "are" above "is"; "es" above "go"; "are" above "is")

> ### REVISING TIP
>
> Look carefully at words that come before the verb to find the subject. Remember that the subject may not be the noun or pronoun closest to the verb.

> ### REVISING TIP
>
> To check subject-verb agreement in inverted sentences, place the subject before the verb. For example, change *there are many references* to *many references are there.*

LINK TO LITERATURE

In "There's This That I Like About Hockey, My Lad" on page 624, notice how the poet repeats the use of inverted sentences starting with *There's* to add emphasis to his images and give the poem structure.

Singular Nouns with Plural Forms

Be sure to use a singular verb when the subject is a noun that is singular in meaning but appears to be plural.

Words like *mumps, news,* and *molasses* appear to be plural because they end in *-s.* However, these words are singular in meaning. Words ending in *ics* that refer to sciences or branches of study (*physics, mathematics, genetics, politics*) are also singular.

> The news about hockey games often sound_∧^s like the poem, with players bashing each other. Physics teach_∧^es that for every action, there is a reaction. Athletics often follow_∧^s this law.

Collective Nouns

Use a singular verb when the subject is a collective noun—such as *class, team, crowd,* or *flock*—that refers to a group acting as a unit. Use a plural verb when the collective noun refers to members of the group acting individually.

> Our hockey team play_∧^s hard. The majority of players agrees̶ with the poet's view.

Nouns of Time, Weight, or Measure

Use a singular verb with a subject that identifies a period of time, a weight, a measure, or a number.

> On average, nine-tenths of a game ~~are~~ *is* spent playing. By my calculations three to four hours ~~were~~ *was* the total penalty time that our team lost last season.

Titles

Use a singular verb when the subject is the title of a work of art, literature, or music, even though the title may contain plural words.

> Kiernan's poem could be describing our team, the Rams. "Battering Rams" sound^s like a better title than the one that the poet picked.

 REVISING TIP

The fact that a title is set off by quotation marks, italics, or underscoring helps to remind you that it is singular and takes a singular verb.

APPLY WHAT YOU'VE LEARNED

Write the correct form of each verb given in parentheses.

1. "There's This That I Like About Hockey, My Lad" (take, takes) a humorous look at the very serious subject of sports injuries.
2. The injuries of a hockey player often (come, comes) from fighting, but there (are, is) many sports injuries from too much exercise.
3. Among the most common sports injuries (are, is) soreness of the leg and back muscles.
4. My track team often (get, gets) cases of sore muscles.
5. Two to 24 hours (pass, passes) after your workout, and then the pain in your legs (start, starts).
6. The best treatment for sore muscles (are, is) rest and an ice pack.
7. Aerobics often (cause, causes) a muscle pull if the person doing the exercises (don't, doesn't) warm up first.
8. Our gym class always (do, does) stretching exercises before an aerobic workout to prevent muscle pulls.
9. Several injuries, including stiff neck and tennis elbow, often (have, has) plagued tennis players.
10. For your neck and elbow, there (are, is) an ice pack to bring relief.
11. *Women's Sports & Fitness* (have, has) many tips on sports injuries, and TV news also (give, gives) some information.
12. Among the best ways to prevent injuries (are, is) a slow start and a gradual cool down.

Using Nouns and Pronouns

3.1   Plural and Possessive Nouns

Nouns refer to people, places, things, and ideas. A noun is plural when it refers to more than one person, place, thing, or idea. Possessive nouns show who or what owns something.

Plural Nouns

Follow these guidelines to form noun plurals.

Nouns	To Form Plural	Examples
Most nouns	add -s	tree—trees
Most nouns that end in s, sh, ch, x, or z	add -es	dress—dresses brush—brushes
Most nouns that end in ay, ey, oy, or uy	add -s	essay—essays monkey—monkeys
Most nouns that end in a consonant and y	change y to i and add -es	story—stories duty—duties
Most nouns that end in o	add -s	photo—photos patio—patios cameo—cameos
Some nouns that end in a consonant and o	add -es	echo—echoes hero—heroes veto—vetoes
Most nouns that end in f or fe	change f to v and add -es or -s	leaf—leaves wife—wives but belief—beliefs

Some nouns have the same spelling in both singular and plural: *series, trout, sheep*. Some nouns have irregular plurals that don't follow any rule: *children, teeth*.

REVISING TIP

The plurals of many musical terms that end in *o* preceded by a consonant are formed by adding -*s*. These nouns include *pianos, solos,* and *sopranos*.

REVISING TIP

The dictionary usually lists the plural form of a noun if the plural is formed irregularly or if it might be formed in more than one way. Dictionary listings are especially helpful for nouns that end in *o, f,* and *fe*.

> "Getting the Facts of Life" looks at different varietys of [*ies*] power: the poweres [*o*] of money, of work, and of rules. In this story Minerva sees how heros [*e*]—her mother, in particular—can be forged in the struggle for survival, how lifes [*v*] can be changed by its outcome.

Possessive Nouns

Follow these guidelines to form possessive nouns.

Nouns	To Form Possessive	Examples
Singular nouns	add apostrophe and -*s*	girl—girl's
Plural nouns ending in *s*	add apostrophe	fields—fields' plays—plays'
Plural nouns not ending in *s*	add apostrophe and -*s*	men—men's oxen—oxen's

> Minerva could easily have quieted the childrens ruckus. Her sister Stellas approach was to turn up the radio and drown out the noise.

APPLY WHAT YOU'VE LEARNED

Write the correct noun given in parentheses.

1 "Getting the Facts of Life" explores change in a (families, family's) life. **2** Growing up is a change (childs, children) can't avoid. **3** In the Blue family, the (parent's, parents') (lives, lifes) change when they move from the rural South to Detroit. **4** (Changes', Changes) are not good for them. **5** The (fathers, father's) job is gone. **6** The (mothers, mother's) battles with the welfare system are endless. **7** Yet (citys, cities) have many attractions. **8** Shopping for (radios, radioes) and TV sets at stores whose (shelfs, shelves) are packed can be a child's dream. **9** Instead of working hard to grow (corn, corns), the family can go to the store and buy some.

3.2 Pronoun Forms

A personal pronoun is a pronoun that can be used in the first, second, or third person. A personal pronoun has three forms: the subject form, the object form, and the possessive form.

Subject Pronouns

Use the subject form of a pronoun when it is the subject of a sentence or the subject of a clause. *I, you, he, she, it, we,* and *they* are subject pronouns.

Using the correct pronoun form is seldom a problem when there is just one pronoun in a sentence. Problems can arise, however, when a noun and a pronoun, or two pronouns, are used in a compound subject or compound object. To see if you are using the correct pronoun form, read the sentence with only one pronoun.

> "The Flood" describes a disaster at Toni and Ralph Helfer's wild-animal ranch. Toni and him *he* had to think fast to save the animals.

Use the subject form of a pronoun when it is a predicate pronoun following a linking verb.

You often hear the object form used as a predicate pronoun in casual conversation (*It is her*). For this reason, the subject form may sound awkward to you, though it is preferred for more formal writing.

> As the waters rose, an elephant dragged the animals in cages to safety. There is no doubt about who was a hero. It was her. *she*

LINK TO LITERATURE

Notice how Ralph Helfer uses pronouns to avoid repetition of the same nouns and to link ideas in different sentences on page 348 of "The Flood."

REVISING TIP

To check the form of a predicate pronoun, see if the sentence still makes sense when the subject and the predicate pronoun are reversed. (*It was she. She was it.*)

Object Pronouns

Use the object form of a pronoun when it is the object of a sentence, the object of a clause, or the object of a preposition. *Me, you, him, her, it, us,* and *them* are object pronouns.

> Ralph grabbed a lion's mane. The flood water carried
> the lion and he^(*him*) to safety.

Possessive Pronouns

Never use an apostrophe in the possessive form of a pronoun. *My, mine, your, yours, his, her, hers, its, our, ours, their,* and *theirs* are possessive pronouns.

Writers often confuse the possessive pronouns *its, your,* and *their* with the contractions *it's, you're,* and *they're.* Remember that the pairs are spelled differently and have different meanings.

> By the time the flood had run it's^(*its*) course, nine animals
> had lost they're^(*their*) lives.

APPLY WHAT YOU'VE LEARNED

Write the correct pronoun form given in parentheses.

[1]After I read "The Flood" by Ralph Helfer, my family and (I, me) saw a museum display about the Johnstown flood of 1829. [2]The one most impressed by the display was (I, me). [3]The flood at the Helfers' ranch hit Ralph's wife, Toni, and (he, him) hard and killed nine animals of (their's, theirs). [4]However, between (they, them) and the people of Johnstown, I think the people of Johnstown suffered more. [5]Imagine many of the people in (you're, your) community losing (they're, their) homes. [6]In the Johnstown flood, an entire town and (it's, its) buildings were washed away. [7]More than 2,000 people from the town lost (its, their) lives. [8]Then a fire broke out and killed many of (they, them) who had survived the flood. [9]My dad promised to take my mother and (I, me) to see the site of the flood. [10](He, Him) and (I, me) agree that Ralph and Toni Helfer were lucky. [11]The flood left (they, them) and most of (they're, their) animals alive.

3.3 Pronoun Antecedents

An antecedent is the noun or pronoun to which a personal pronoun refers. The antecedent usually precedes the pronoun.

Pronoun and Antecedent Agreement

A pronoun must agree with its antecedent in
- number—singular or plural
- person—first, second, or third
- gender—masculine, feminine, or neuter

Use a singular pronoun to refer to a singular antecedent; use a plural pronoun to refer to a plural antecedent.

Do not allow interrupting words to determine the number of the personal pronoun.

> If Nima-Cux in "The First Flute" had explored one of her talents, she might have found that ~~they~~ *it* could have made her happy.

If the antecedent is a noun that could be either male or female, use *he or she* (*him or her, his or her*), or reword the sentence to avoid the need for a singular pronoun.

> Every other member of the household seemed to be content as ~~they~~ *he or she* worked for the cacique.
>
> Or
>
> ~~Every~~ other member*s* of the household seemed to be content as they worked for the cacique.

Be sure that the antecedent of a pronoun is clear.

In most cases, do not use a pronoun to refer to an entire idea or clause. Writing is much clearer if the exact reference is repeated.

Herb doctors, witch doctors, and old hunched crones
these people
came with different cures, but ~~they~~ did not help Nima-
All this failed effort   ∧
Cux at all. ~~This~~ shows that she should not have waited
          ∧
for someone else to make her happy. But then her father
                                    her father
found a young man to become Nima-Cux's husband; ~~he~~
                                                  ∧
finally made her happy.

⚠ REVISING TIP

To avoid vague pronoun reference, do not use *this* or *that* alone to start a clause. Instead, include a word that clarifies what *this* or *that* refers to—*this method, this grouping, that idea.*

Indefinite Pronouns as Antecedents

When a singular indefinite pronoun is the antecedent, use *he or she* (*him or her, his or her*), or rewrite the sentence to avoid the need for a singular pronoun.

Anybody can appreciate the beautiful music of the flute,
            him or her
which brings ~~them~~ so much pleasure.
            ∧
Or
All
~~Anybody~~ can appreciate the beautiful music of the flute,
   ∧
which brings them so much pleasure.

⚠ REVISING TIP

Avoid the indefinite use of *you* and *they.*

People could always

tell what animal

Nima-Cux molded.
The tribe members
~~In her tribe they~~ all
   ∧
knew she had talent.

Indefinite Pronouns					
Singular Indefinite Pronouns	another anybody anyone anything	each either	everybody everyone everything	neither nobody no one nothing one	somebody someone something
Plural Indefinite Pronouns	both	few	many	several	
Singular or Plural Indefinite Pronouns	all	any	most	none	some

REVISING TIP

In the first sentence of the example, *who* is the subject of the clause *who would be affected most*. In the second sentence, *whoever* is the subject of the sentence.

REVISING TIP

Whom should replace *who* in each sentence in the example:
To whom—object of the preposition
Whom do—direct object of the verb *do want*
Give whom—indirect object of *will give*

3.4 Pronoun Usage

The form that a pronoun takes is always determined by its function within its own clause or sentence.

Who and Whom

Use *who* or *whoever* as the subject of a clause or sentence.

> If things were rationed, as in "The Home Front: 1941–1945," whom would be affected most? Whomever needs the rationed items most should receive them first.

Use *whom* as the direct or indirect object of a verb or verbal and as the object of a preposition.

People often use *who* for *whom* when speaking informally. However, in written English the pronouns should be used correctly.

> The Rationing Boss might say, "To who should I issue these sports car stamps?" or "Who do I want behind the wheel of a dump truck?" or "I will give who the bicycle?"

In determining the correct pronoun form, ignore interrupters that come between the subject and the verb.

In the example that follows, *who* should replace *whom* because the pronoun is the subject of the clause "*Who* . . . deserves the 'hot' cars?"

> Whom̶ do you think deserves the "hot" cars?
>
> *who*

Pronouns in Contractions

Do not confuse the contractions *it's, they're, who's,* and *you're* with possessive pronouns that sound the same—*its, their, whose,* and *your*.

> *you're*
> When y̶o̶u̶r̶ talking about a big issue like rationing, you
> *who's*
> must consider w̶h̶o̶s̶e̶ affected.

Pronouns with Nouns

Determine the correct form of the pronoun in phrases such as *we girls* and *us boys* by saying the sentence without the noun.

> *we*
> I repeat, u̶s̶ girls need some of those vehicles!

APPLY WHAT YOU'VE LEARNED

Write the correct pronoun given in parentheses.

1. (Who, Whom), of all the people during World War II, would want to relive the times described in "The Home Front"?
2. (Who, Whom) remembers Hollywood's role on the home front?
3. No doubt the memory remains in those for (who, whom) movies like *Why We Fight* were the inspiration to enlist.
4. Consider all the people (whose, who's) lives changed after seeing such movies.
5. Hollywood produced movies for the U.S. government, praising (its, it's) allies.
6. Ask (whoever, whomever) you know has seen *Casablanca* whether he or she knows that this movie was meant to unite U.S. and French citizens.
7. When Hollywood went to war, (we, us) citizens went too.

4 Using Modifiers Effectively

4.1 Adjective or Adverb?

Use an adjective to modify a noun or a pronoun. Use an adverb to modify a verb, an adjective, or another adverb.

> In "The Lie" Eli's father slow̭ came to understand what was bothering Eli. He had been absolutḙ sure Eli was accepted at Whitehall, a privately̭ school for boys.

Use an adjective after a linking verb to describe the subject.

Remember that in addition to forms of the verb *be*, the following are linking verbs: *become, seem, appear, look, sound, feel, taste, grow,* and *smell*.

> Eli seemed sickly̭ when he knew his actions were about to be discovered. He felt sadly̭ that his parents might think differenṱ about him after hearing the truth.

REVISING TIP

Always determine first which word is being modified. For example, in the second sentence of the example, *sure* is the word being modified; since *sure* is an adjective, the modifier must be an adverb.

APPLY WHAT YOU'VE LEARNED

Write the correct modifier given in parentheses.

1. "The Lie" is a story by the (popular, popularly) author Kurt Vonnegut, Jr.
2. Even though his stories are often (humorous, humorously), they have (serious, seriously) important messages.
3. The messages in many of his stories are (simple, simply), like treat one another (kind, kindly).
4. Vonnegut's (sad, sadly) experiences as a soldier during World War II (particular, particularly) affected his outlook.
5. He was captured by the Germans and (prompt, promptly) imprisoned in Dresden.
6. Later, he saw the (beautiful, beautifully) city (complete, completely) destroyed by British and American bombs in 1945.
7. His stories show how people's (foolish, foolishly) actions can affect the world.

4.2 Comparisons and Negatives

Comparative and Superlative Adjectives

Use the comparative form of an adjective when comparing two things.

Comparative adjectives are formed by adding -*er* to short adjectives (*fierce—fiercer*) or by using the word *more* with longer adjectives (*unusual—more unusual*).

In the story "Otoonah," Otoonah's main challenges were finding food and shelter; she dealt with the easiest one first. Shelter was difficulter to find.

[handwritten corrections: "r" above "easiest"; "more" inserted before "difficulter"]

Use the superlative form when comparing three or more things.

Superlatives are formed by adding -*est* to short adjectives (*great—greatest*) or by using the word *most* with longer adjectives (*remarkable—most remarkable*).

Otoonah proved she was the successfulest hunter in her family. She found the larger number of animals.

[handwritten corrections: "most" inserted before "successfulest"; "st" above "larger"]

REVISING TIP

When comparing something with everything else of its kind, do not leave out the word *other*. (*Ilga is taller than any **other** girl in the class.*)

The comparative and superlative forms of some adjectives are irregular.

Adjective	Comparative	Superlative
good	better	best
bad	worse	worst
ill	worse	worst
little	less *or* lesser	least
much	more	most
many	more	most

Comparative and Superlative Adverbs

When comparing two actions, use a comparative adverb, formed by adding -er or the word *more*.

When attacking the young hunter, the polar bear moved
quickest and skillfuler than the man.

When comparing more than two actions, use a superlative adverb, formed by adding -est or the word *most*.

The songs Otoonah sang more enthusiastically were the
boastful ones.

Double Negatives

To avoid double negatives, use only one negative word in a clause. *Not, no, never, none*, and *nobody* are negatives.

Besides the compounds formed with *no*, the words *barely, hardly,* and *scarcely* also function as negative words.

Returning home, Otoonah didn't have no hard feelings
toward her parents. They couldn't hardly believe
Otoonah was alive.

APPLY WHAT YOU'VE LEARNED

Rewrite this paragraph, correcting mistakes in modifiers.

1One hundred years ago, the greater challenge facing Eskimos like those in the story "Otoonah" was finding enough food to feed a family during the harsh winters. **2**Compared to Eskimos today, a family like Otoonah's was worst off. **3**Hunting was more hard than it is today. **4**A handmade harpoon couldn't never match the rifle for ease of use and accuracy. **5**An Eskimo using a rifle hunted efficiently, while the Eskimo using a harpoon worked hardest. **6**Also, of the two methods of hunting, using a harpoon is most dangerous. **7**Of the two types of hunters, the one throwing the harpoon is likely to lose his balance and fall into the freezing waters.

4.3 Special Problems with Modifiers

Although the following terms are frequently misused in spoken English, they should be used correctly in written English.

Them and Those

Them is always a pronoun and never a modifier of a noun. Those is a pronoun when it stands alone. It is an adjective when followed by a noun.

In "The Other Pioneers" the poet honors ~~them~~ *those* settlers who plowed the land. He admires them for their strength and courage.

Bad and Badly

Always use *bad* as an adjective, whether before a noun or after a linking verb. *Badly* should generally be used to modify an action verb.

The settlers wanted so bad *ly* to be part of this country, but many times they felt bad~~ly~~ about leaving their homeland.

This, That, These, and Those

Whether used as adjectives or pronouns, *this* and *these* refer to people and things that are nearby, and *that* and *those* refer to people and things that are farther away.

Reading about "stalwart fathers" and "gentle mothers," I could tell the poet admires th*e*se hardworking people more than the*o*se wealthy enough to have a life of ease. More people plowed the land at ~~this~~ *that* long-ago time than do in ~~that~~ *this* day.

LINK TO LITERATURE

Notice how the writer of "The Other Pioneers," Roberto Félix Salazar, has used *those* throughout the first stanza to replace *ancestors*. Not only does *those* enhance the rhythm of the poem, but it also imparts a feeling of mystery and a sense of wider connection to the past.

REVISING TIP

Avoid the use of *here* with *this* and *these*; also, do not use *there* with *that* and *those*.

This ~~here~~ was a good movie. We hardly breathed as that ~~there~~ image appeared onscreen.

Good and Well

Good is always an adjective, never an adverb. Use well as either an adjective or an adverb, depending on the sentence.

When used as an adjective, *well* usually refers to a person's health. As an adverb, *well* modifies an action verb. In the expression "feeling good," *good* refers to being happy, comfortable, or pleased.

> When the weather was ~~well~~ _good_, the crops grew ~~good~~ _well_.
>
> The immigrants felt ~~well~~ _good_ about settling in a land that held so much promise for their children.

Few and Little, Fewer and Less

Few refers to numbers of things that can be counted; little refers to amounts. Fewer is used when comparing numbers of things; less is used when comparing amounts.

> Early settlers got ~~few~~ _little_ help from the government and ~~little~~ _few_ opportunities to rest. Who knows whether immigrants then had ~~less~~ _fewer_ problems than immigrants now?

APPLY WHAT YOU'VE LEARNED

Write the modifier from each pair that fits the meaning of the sentence.

[1] "The Other Pioneers" is written in English, but (those, this) poem actually honors early Spanish-speaking settlers of the southwestern United States. [2] At (that, this) time there were far (less, fewer) Spanish-speaking Americans than there are at (that, this) time. [3] (Less, Few) early immigrants could speak English (good, well). [4] (Few, Little) languages have escaped the influence of English words, and Spanish is no exception. [5] Whether you think this influence is (well, good) or (bad, badly), the Spanish language had (fewer, less) words when Spaniards first came to the Americas. [6] (Them, Those) explorers brought the speech of Castilla, a province in Spain, with them; however, (this, that) dialect had words added to it by the Spaniards who settled in America. [7] Spanish is a rich language: it adapts (good, well) to song lyrics.

Using Verbs Correctly

5.1   Verb Tenses and Forms

Verb tense shows the time of an action or condition. Writers sometimes cause confusion when they use different verb tenses in describing actions that occur at the same time.

Consistent Use of Tenses

When two or more actions occur at the same time or in a sequence, use the same verb tense to describe the actions.

> The narrator of "The Splendid Outcast" ~~goes~~ *went* to
> England, attended a horse auction, and ~~finds~~ *found* that the
> horse she wanted ~~is~~ *was* not the only outcast at the auction.

A shift in tense is necessary when two events occur at different times or out of sequence. The tenses of the verbs should clearly indicate that one action precedes the other.

> Each outcast was punished for things he ~~did~~ *had done* at some
> time in the past. Although the horse *had* killed a man and
> *had* injured others, the author still wanted him.

Tense	Verb Form
Present	walk/walks
Past	walked
Future	will walk
Present perfect	have/has walked
Past perfect	had walked
Future perfect	will/shall have walked

REVISING TIP

In telling a story, be careful not to shift tenses so often that the reader has difficulty keeping the sequence of events straight.

LINK TO LITERATURE

In "The Splendid Outcast" Beryl Markham uses the past tense to tell her story. However, notice on page 165 how she switches to the present tense for the flashback scene at the auction. Thus, she creates a sense of immediacy, a "you are there" feeling.

Past Tense and the Past Participle

The simple past form of a verb can always stand alone. Always use the past participles of the following irregular verbs when the verbs follow helping verbs.

Present	Past	Past Participle
be	was/were	(have, had) been
begin	began	(have, had) begun
break	broke	(have, had) broken
bring	brought	(have, had) brought
choose	chose	(have, had) chosen
come	came	(have, had) come
do	did	(have, had) done
drink	drank	(have, had) drunk
eat	ate	(have, had) eaten
fall	fell	(have, had) fallen
freeze	froze	(have, had) frozen
give	gave	(have, had) given
go	went	(have, had) gone
grow	grew	(have, had) grown
lose	lost	(have, had) lost

Although held firmly by two attendants, the horse
began
~~begun~~ to act up. He would have broke*n* away if the man
∧ *brought*
had not ~~brung~~ him under control.
∧

APPLY WHAT YOU'VE LEARNED

Write the correct verb for each sentence.

1. The setting of Beryl Markham's story "The Splendid Outcast" (was, is, will be) Newmarket, England.
2. Since the early 1600s, when James I (began, is beginning, begun) the racing tradition there, Newmarket (become, has became, has become) a center of horse racing.
3. In 1634—before he (losed, lost, will lose) his kingdom and his head in a civil war—Charles I offered a gold cup as the prize in a Newmarket race.
4. People (come, have came, have come) to the race every year since it (is starting, started, will have started).
5. Today, people (called, had called, call) horse racing the sport of kings.
6. Racing is now and probably (remained, remains, will remain) popular.

5.2　Commonly Confused Verbs

The following verb pairs are often confused.

Let and Leave

Let means "to allow or permit." Leave means "to depart" or "to allow something to remain where it is."

> *Let*
> ~~Leave~~ me tell you the tale of Pecos Bill. First, though,
> *leave*
> you must ~~let~~ behind your ideas of what is real.

Lie and Lay

Lie means "to rest in a flat position" or "to be in a certain place." Lay means "to put or place."

> When baby Bill fell off the family wagon, he didn't just
> *lie*
> ~~lay~~ there and scream. He met a coyote who carried him
> *laid*
> off and ~~lay~~ him down in its den.

REVISING TIP

If you're uncertain about which verb to use, check to see if the verb has an object. The verbs *lie, sit,* and *rise* never have objects.

Sit and Set

Sit means "to be in a seated position." Set means "to put or place."

> *sat*
> Bill just ~~set~~ in the dirt, not worrying. Bill always seemed
> *set*
> to ~~sit~~ his problems on a stump so they'd blow away.

Rise and Raise

Rise means "to move upward." Raise means "to move something upward."

> *rise*
> When Bill's horse couldn't ~~raise~~ after breaking his ankle,
> *raised*
> Bill just ~~rose~~ the horse in his arms and carried him.

Learn and Teach

Learn means "to gain knowledge or skill." *Teach* means "to help someone learn."

> It was strange how quickly the coyotes could ~~learn~~ ^teach^ Bill all their ways.

Here are the principal parts of these troublesome verb pairs.

Present	Past	Past Participle
let	let	(have, had) let
leave	left	(have, had) left
lie	lay	(have, had) lain
lay	laid	(have, had) laid
sit	sat	(have, had) sat
set	set	(have, had) set
rise	rose	(have, had) risen
raise	raised	(have, had) raised
learn	learned	(have, had) learned
teach	taught	(have, had) taught

APPLY WHAT YOU'VE LEARNED

Choose the correct verb from each pair of words.

1. Tall tales like "Pecos Bill" (rise, raise) many questions about the real life of cowboys.
2. The true life of cowboys (lies, lays) hidden from most Americans.
3. However, it's important to (set, sit) people straight and to (learn, teach) them the truth.
4. For example, if you (let, leave) people to their storybook understanding of the Old West, they'll never know that almost one-fourth of all cowboys were African American.
5. People should be (learned, taught) that almost another fourth of all cowboys were Mexican.
6. Today, more than ever, we must (rise, raise) people's awareness about who helped settle the West.

Correcting Capitalization

6.1 Proper Nouns and Adjectives

A common noun names a whole class of persons, places, things, or ideas. A proper noun names a particular person, place, thing, or idea. A proper adjective is an adjective formed from a proper noun. All proper nouns and proper adjectives are capitalized.

Names and Personal Titles

Capitalize the name and title of a person.

Also capitalize initials and abbreviations of titles. *Clarissa Harlowe Barton, C. H. Barton, Senator Charles Sumner,* and *Mr. Dred Scott* are capitalized correctly.

> Some of the young men whose Civil War experiences
>
> are described in *Reflections on the Civil War* idolized
>
> general robert e. lee.

Capitalize a word referring to a family relationship when it is used as someone's name (*Uncle Al*) but not when it is used to identify a person (*Jill's uncle*).

> Some soldiers called Lee uncle bobby, even though he
>
> wasn't their Uncle.

REVISING TIP

Do not capitalize personal titles used as common nouns. (*The **senator** spoke to us.*)

Languages, Nationalities, Religious Terms

Capitalize the names of languages and nationalities as well as religious names and terms.

Capitalize words referring to languages and nationalities, such as *Hindi, Sanskrit, Afrikaans, Korean, German,* and *Nigerian.* Capitalize religious names and terms, such as *God, Buddha, Bible,* and *Koran.*

> While young soldiers prayed for god's help in battle,
>
> Confederate diplomats sought french and british loans.

School Subjects

Capitalize the name of a specific school course (*Biology I, World History*). Do not capitalize a general reference to a school subject (*mathematics, history, music*).

> Most of the young soldiers had little knowledge of
>
> History. We studied the Civil War in u.s. history.

     REVISING TIP

Do not capitalize minor words in a proper noun that is made up of several words. (*University **of** Illinois*)

Organizations, Institutions

Capitalize the important words in the official names of organizations and institutions (*Congress, Duke University*).

Do not capitalize words that refer to kinds of organizations or institutions (*school, church, university*) or words that refer to specific organizations but are not their official names (*at the university*).

> Decisions made in the house of representatives cost
>
> many young soldiers their lives. The Government ran
>
> the war, but soldiers had to fight it.

Geographical Names, Events, Time Periods

Capitalize geographical names, as well as the names of events, historical periods and documents, holidays, and months and days, but not the names of seasons or directions.

Names	Examples
Continents	North America, Asia
Bodies of water	Atlantic Ocean, Ohio River, Lake Louise
Political units	China, Kentucky, Moscow
Sections of a country	New England, the Midwest
Public areas	Central Park, Civic Plaza
Roads and structures	Main Street, Aswan Dam, Acme Building
Historical events	Battle of Shiloh, Gettysburg Address
Documents	the Constitution, the Treaty of Ghent
Periods of history	Reconstruction, the Renaissance
Holidays	Christmas, Presidents' Day, Fourth of July
Months and days	June, Tuesday
Seasons	winter, spring
Directions	east, west

The civil war began at ft. sumter in the south on april 12, 1861. By the time the War ended in the Spring of 1865, it had raged across the united states from pennsylvania South to the gulf of mexico.

REVISING TIP

Don't capitalize a reference that does not use the full name of a place, event, or period. (*We went to Fort McHenry, but the* **fort** *was closed.*)

APPLY WHAT YOU'VE LEARNED

Write the correct forms of the words given in parentheses.

1. *Reflections on the Civil War* tells about the (Men, men) who fought in the Civil (War, war).
2. Both sides in the (War, war) lost twice as many men to disease as on the (Battlefield, battlefield).
3. Women served as nurses, set up hospitals, and organized relief for both (Union, union) and (Confederate, confederate) armies.
4. One such woman, (Clara, clara) Barton, went on to found the (American Red Cross, american red cross).
5. Barton also formed a (Bureau, bureau) that marked soldiers' graves at Andersonville (Cemetery, cemetery) in (Georgia, georgia).
6. Mary Rice Livermore formed the (United States Sanitary Commission, united states sanitary commission).
7. Union soldiers were aided by this (Commission, commission), whose members insisted on fresh food and (Sanitary, sanitary) hospitals.

Titles follow certain capitalization rules.

Books, Plays, Magazines, Newspapers, Films

Capitalize the first word, the last word, and all other important words in the title of a book, play or musical, magazine, newspaper, or film. Underline or italicize the title to set it off.

Within a title, don't capitalize articles, conjunctions, and prepositions of fewer than five letters.

> Perhaps Yollie in Gary Soto's "Mother and Daughter" might have thought reading the play <u>the merchant of Venice</u> would help her to prepare for college.

Poems, Stories, Articles

Capitalize the first word, the last word, and all other important words in the title of a poem, a story, or an article. Enclose the title in quotation marks.

> She might have enjoyed the poem "Dover beach." Writing a report about it, she might have come across the article "Matthew Arnold—poet and critic."

APPLY WHAT YOU'VE LEARNED

Rewrite this paragraph, correcting the punctuation and capitalization of titles.

1Like Yollie's mother in Gary Soto's story mother and daughter, I enjoy monster movies. **2**For me, a movie like the monster from the ocean floor is a true classic. **3**I used to learn about such movies in magazines like famous monsters of filmland. **4**Stephen King, author of the horror novels it, pet sematary, and the stand, supposedly read the magazine when he was growing up. **5**However, I find it hard to believe that someone who wrote a story as scary as the langoliers was inspired by the movie i was a teenage werewolf. **6**For me, Edgar Allan Poe's poem the raven is much scarier than the movie destroy all monsters, but the movie is more fun.

Correcting Punctuation

7

7.1   Compound Sentences

Punctuation helps organize longer sentences that have several clauses.

Commas in Compound Sentences

Use a comma before the conjunction that joins the clauses of a compound sentence.

In *Gifted Hands* Ben Carson describes his work as a neurosurgeon⸱and he retells his experiences with three young patients.

Semicolons in Compound Sentences

Use a semicolon between the clauses of a compound sentence when no conjunction is used. Use a semicolon before, and a comma after, a conjunctive adverb that joins the clauses of a compound sentence.

Conjunctive adverbs include *therefore, however, so, then, nevertheless, consequently,* and *besides.*

Two of his patients, Bo-Bo and Charles, live⸱however, one patient, Danielle, dies. Charles's condition left him very little chance at life⸱his doctors were at their wits' end.

LINK TO LITERATURE

Notice on pages 452–455 of *Gifted Hands* how Ben Carson uses compound and complex sentences to combine ideas and merge pieces of information in a way that shows their relation to one another.

REVISING TIP

Even when clauses are connected by a coordinating conjunction, you may use a semicolon between them if one or both clauses contain a comma. (*Two students, Joe and Jill, got perfect test scores;* **but** *Jill had a better overall average.*)

Rewrite these sentences, adding commas and semicolons where necessary.

1. Ben Carson wrote *Gifted Hands* as a factual record and he wanted to give hope to future patients.
2. Carson, a pediatric neurosurgeon, observed subtle changes in his patients his sharp eye often saved their lives.
3. Signs and symptoms of brain tumors include seizures and trouble speaking however these symptoms are sometimes absent.
4. Brain surgery is always major and the outcome cannot be guaranteed.
5. The bones of the human skull are fused in the adult but they are free to slide and overlap in babies during the birth process.
6. The adult skull is a solid case it began development as some 30 separate pieces of membrane and cartilage.

7.2   Elements Set Off in a Sentence

Most elements that are not essential to a sentence are set off by commas to highlight the main idea of the sentence.

Introductory Words

Use a comma to separate an introductory word or phrase from the rest of the sentence.

A single introductory prepositional phrase need not be set off with a comma. However, you should use a comma to set off more than one prepositional phrase.

In class, we read *Harriet Tubman: Conductor on the Underground Railroad.* For several chapters of the book, the author tells about how Harriet Tubman brought people out of slavery to safety in Canada. Clearly, she was an extraordinary woman.

In a complex sentence, set off an introductory subordinate clause with a comma.

> Although they were cold and afraid₍ᐱ₎Harriet and the
> fugitives struggled toward freedom in the North.
> Whenever they felt discouraged₍ᐱ₎Harriet kept them
> going.

Nouns of Address

Use commas to set off a name or noun in direct address.

> Perhaps Harriet said goodbye to their host in
> Wilmington with the words "Believe me₍ᐱ₎Thomas₍ᐱ₎
> we all thank you for the food and lodging."

Appositives

Use commas to set off some appositives.

When an appositive is necessary for the meaning of a sentence,
it is not set off with commas.

> That famous conductor,/Harriet,/told her exhausted
> travelers that Frederick Douglass₍ᐱ₎a famous escaped
> slave₍ᐱ₎had achieved great things once he gained freedom.

Unclear Elements

Use a comma to prevent misreading or misunderstanding.

> Despite all their trying₍ᐱ₎to cross the Canadian border
> seemed to be an impossible dream for most runaways.

REVISING TIP

Sometimes when a comma is
missing, parts of a sentence
can be grouped in more
than one way by a reader. A
comma separates the parts
so they can be read in only
one way.

Interrupters

Use commas to set off a word or a group of words that interrupts the flow of a sentence.

> Harriet tired as could be walked bravely forward and
> urged the fugitives to follow.

When a subordinate clause interrupts the main clause in a sentence, set it off with commas.

> Harriet though she was risking her own freedom,
> helped escaped slaves time and again. Thomas Garrett,
> because he wanted to help gave shelter and new shoes
> to the fugitives.

The words shown here are commonly used to begin subordinate clauses. When such words appear in introductory or interrupting clauses, the clauses need to be set off with one or more commas.

Words Often Used to Introduce Subordinate Clauses				
Subordinating Conjunctions	after although as as if as long as as though	because before if in order that provided since	so that than though till unless until	whatever when whenever where wherever while
Relative Pronouns	that	which	who whom	whose

Rewrite these sentences. Add commas where necessary.

1. Tell me Susan who was nicknamed Moses in *Harriet Tubman: Conductor on the Underground Railroad?*
2. Jim it was Harriet Tubman the one who led a group of escaping slaves.
3. Born a slave on a plantation in Maryland Tubman became very strong from her hard work.
4. In 1849 she escaped walking at night through strange territory.
5. She avoided capture and finally reached Pennsylvania a free state.
6. When she found work in Philadelphia William Still a leader in the Underground Railroad made her one of its conductors.
7. Tubman who was soon famous as an Underground Railroad conductor may have helped as many as 300 slaves escape.
8. After the Civil War ended she worked tirelessly to help African Americans now free from slavery to get an education and voting rights.

7.3 Elements in a Series

Commas should be used to separate three or more elements in a series and to separate adjectives preceding a noun.

Subjects, Verbs, Objects, and Other Elements

Use a comma after every item except the last in a series of three or more items.

The three or more items can be nouns, verbs, adjectives, adverbs, phrases, independent clauses, or other parts of a sentence.

> Theodore Waldeck's "Battle by the Breadfruit Tree" shows conflict involving a tribe of baboons‸a leopard‸ and a baby baboon.

Two or More Adjectives

In most sentences, use a comma after each, except the last, of two or more adjectives that precede a noun.

REVISING TIP

Note in the example that a comma followed by a conjunction precedes the last element in the series. That comma is always used.

If you can reverse the order of adjectives without changing the meaning or if you can use *and* between them, separate them with commas.

> The slashing͏ snarling͏ screaming baboon and leopard were locked in a fierce,͏ death struggle.

APPLY WHAT YOU'VE LEARNED

Rewrite each sentence, inserting commas where they are needed.

1. A baboon is a large powerful intelligent monkey.
2. It has a large head sharp teeth and a doglike muzzle.
3. There are five species of baboon; some have short stumpy tails, but others have long tails.
4. They all tend to eat eggs fruits grass insects leaves and roots.
5. Many farmers in Africa consider them pests because they destroy crops make lots of noise and are quite bold.
6. Their enormous teeth powerful limbs and habit of traveling in groups make them the kind of animal it is best not to cross.
7. When a member gives a doglike bark of alarm, the group responds by racing to the scene making lots of noise and attacking the predator.

7.4　Dates, Addresses, and Letters

Punctuation in dates, addresses, and letters makes information easy to understand.

Dates

Use a comma between the day of the month and the year. If the date falls in the middle of a sentence, use another comma after the year.

> Marjorie Kinnan Rawlings, who was born on August 8͏ 1896͏wrote "A Mother in Mannville." In this story she created the character of Jerry.

Addresses

Use a comma to separate the city and the state in an address. If the address falls in the middle of a sentence, use a comma after the state too.

> If the narrator had written to Jerry, the return address on her letters might have been Anchorage⋀Alaska⋀or Miami⋀Florida.

Parts of a Letter

Use a comma after the greeting and after the closing in a letter.

> Dear Jerry⋀
>
> I hope you like the roller skates in this package.
>
> Sincerely⋀
>
> The lady at the cabin

APPLY WHAT YOU'VE LEARNED

Rewrite the following sentences, correcting the comma errors.

1. The author Marjorie Kinnan Rawlings died on December 14 1953 after having lived in Florida for 25 years.
2. Previously, she had worked for the *Courier-Journal* in Louisville Kentucky.
3. Her first Florida residence was in Cross Creek Florida.
4. She moved to Hawthorn Florida when she decided to become a full-time novelist.
5. My grandmother wrote the following to the author after reading *The Yearling:*
   Dear Marjorie
   I think *The Yearling* should be a movie because it is a wonderful book.
   Sincerely
   Myrtle C. Beech
6. On September 14 1943 Grandma purchased Rawlings's cookbook *Cross Creek Cookery.*
7. Here is Grandma's next fan letter to Rawlings:
   Dear Marjorie
   My family loves your cookbook. Keep writing!
   Best wishes
   Myrtle
8. Grandma moved to Orlando Florida on June 14 1948 and always hoped to meet Rawlings somewhere.

Quotation marks let readers know exactly who said what. Incorrectly placed or missing quotation marks lead to misunderstanding.

Quotation Marks

Use quotation marks at the beginning and the end of direct quotations and to set off titles of short works.

> In class our group chose to analyze Robert Silverberg's "Collecting Team." Diego said, "Let's check out the author's use of dialogue."

Capitalize the first word of a direct quotation, especially of a piece of dialogue.

> Monica disagreed with the group, saying, "that's going to be too easy."

End Punctuation

Place periods inside quotation marks. Place question marks and exclamation points inside quotation marks if they belong to the quotation; place them outside if they do not belong to the quotation. Place semicolons outside quotation marks.

> Ira asked, "What do you suggest, Mieko?"
>
> Mieko said, "Let's discuss Silverberg's use of irony."
>
> Ira said, "I agree"; then he smiled.

REVISING TIP

If quoted words are from a written source and are not complete sentences, they can begin with a lowercase letter. (*Jefferson said that all people have a right to "life, liberty, and the pursuit of happiness."*)

Use a comma to end a quotation that is a complete sentence but is followed by explanatory words.

> "I'm in favor of Diego's idea‸" said Frank.

Divided Quotations

Capitalize the first word of the second part of a direct quotation if it begins a new sentence.

> "Let's vote on it," said Diego. "there are five of us, so majority rules."

Do not capitalize the first word of the second part of a divided quotation if it does not begin a new sentence.

> "I'll record the points of our discussion on the board," said Ira, "If we agree that's a good idea."

REVISING TIP

Should the first word of the second part of a divided quotation be capitalized? Imagine the quotation without the explanatory words. If a capital letter would not be used, then do not use one in the divided quotation.

APPLY WHAT YOU'VE LEARNED

Rewrite this paragraph, inserting quotation marks and other appropriate punctuation and correcting capitalization.

1 How can you go there. my sister said. zoos are just wrong. **2** What are you talking about? I replied. Do you think that animals live in harmony out in the wild? No way. It's eat or be eaten! **3** Why, if I were a gazelle, I concluded, I'd much rather be in a lion-free pen than out on the plains running for my life. **4** Well, she replied, let's say I lock you in your room for the next 50 years so that you won't get hit by a car. **5** That's ridiculous, I scoffed. **6** Oh, is it? she said. It's the same exact logic you used in your argument. We take risks every time we step outside, she continued, but that doesn't mean we're better off locked up. **7** She obviously had me there, but I refused to give in. **8** Oh, yeah? I said, just as our father called, Dinner's ready! interrupting my brilliant response.

Grammar Glossary

This glossary contains various terms you need to understand when you use the Grammar Handbook. Used as a reference source, this glossary will help you explore grammar concepts and how they relate to one another.

Adjective An adjective modifies, or describes, a noun or pronoun. (*fine* day, *poor* me)

A **predicate adjective** follows a linking verb and describes the subject. (I am *happy*.)

A **proper adjective** is formed from a proper noun. (*Spanish* rice)

The **comparative** form of an adjective compares two items. (*more elegant*, *stronger*)

The **superlative** form of an adjective compares three or more items. (*most alert*, *strongest*)

What Adjectives Tell	Examples
How many	*few* friends *many* painters
What kind	*new* techniques *older* buildings
Which one(s)	*this* painting *those* children

Adverb An adverb modifies a verb, an adjective, or another adverb. (Mieko jumped *quickly*.)

The **comparative** form of an adverb compares two actions. (*more slowly*, *sooner*)

The **superlative** form of an adverb compares three or more actions. (*most slowly*, *soonest*)

What Adverbs Tell	Examples
How	walk *carefully* skate *smoothly*
When	*Now* I see. *once* upon a time
Where	She went *out*. *here* in the forest
To what extent	I am *very* pleased. This is *quite* fine.

Agreement Sentence parts that correspond with one another are said to be in agreement.

In **pronoun-antecedent agreement**, a pronoun and the word it refers to are the same in number, gender, and person. (The *girl* lost *her* key. The *girls* lost *their* key.)

In **subject-verb agreement**, the subject and verb in a sentence are the same in number. (*I fly* home. He *flies* to Rio.)

Antecedent An antecedent is a noun or a pronoun to which a pronoun refers. (Because *Dan* practiced *his* backstroke, *he* improved.)

Appositive An appositive is a noun or phrase that explains one or more words in a sentence. (Julie, *a good student*, found algebra simple.)

Article Articles are the special adjectives *a, an,* and *the*. (*the* car, *a* bug, *an* apple)

A **definite article** (the word *the*) is used when a noun refers to a specific thing. (*the* boat)

An **indefinite article** indicates that a noun is not unique but is one of many of its kind. (*a* plate, *an* apple)

Clause A clause is a group of words that contains a verb and its subject. (*I wondered.*)

A **main (independent) clause** can stand by itself as a sentence.

A **subordinate (dependent) clause** does not express a complete thought and cannot stand by itself as a sentence.

Clause	Example
Main (independent)	The robot began operating
Subordinate (dependent)	before we were out of bed.

Collective noun. *See* **Noun.**

Common noun. *See* **Noun.**

Complete predicate The complete predicate of a sentence consists of the main verb plus any words that modify or complete the verb's meaning. (The sun *shimmered in the heat*.)

Complete subject The complete subject of a sentence consists of the simple subject plus any words that modify or describe the simple subject. (*The vast canyon* lay before us.)

Complex sentence A complex sentence contains one main clause and one or more subordinate clauses. (*When I get home, I will call you.*)

Compound sentence A compound sentence consists of two or more independent clauses. (*Sue will play, and the rest of us will cheer.*)

Compound sentence part A sentence element that consists of two or more subjects, verbs, or objects is compound. (*Jim* and *Jo* moved. Di *buys* and *sells* rings. Jan plays *soccer* and *tennis*.)

Conjunction A conjunction is a word that links other words or groups of words.

> A *coordinating conjunction* connects related words, groups of words, or sentences. (*and, but, or*)

> A *correlative conjunction* is one of a pair of conjunctions that work together to connect sentence parts. (*either . . . or, neither . . . nor*)

> A *subordinating conjunction* introduces a subordinate clause. (*unless, while, if*)

Conjunctive adverb A conjunctive adverb joins the clauses of a compound sentence. (*however, therefore, besides*)

Contraction A contraction is formed by joining two words and substituting an apostrophe for letters left out of one of the words. (*hasn't*)

Coordinating conjunction. *See* **Conjunction.**

Correlative conjunction. *See* **Conjunction.**

 D

Demonstrative pronoun. *See* **Pronoun.**

Dependent clause. *See* **Clause.**

Direct object A direct object receives the action of a verb. (Stanley hit the *ball*.)

Double negative A double negative is an incorrect use of two negative words when only one is needed. (It's so dark I *can't hardly* see.)

 E

End mark An end mark is any of the several punctuation marks that can end a sentence. See punctuation chart on page 903.

 F

Fragment. *See* **Sentence fragment.**

Future tense. *See* **Verb tense.**

 G

Gerund A gerund is a verbal that ends in *-ing* and functions as a noun. (*Hitting* a home run is easy.)

 H

Helping verb. *See* **Verb.**

 I

Indefinite pronoun. *See* **Pronoun.**

Independent clause. *See* **Clause.**

Indirect object An indirect object tells to or for whom (sometimes to or for what) something is done. (She told *Beth* a joke.)

Infinitive An infinitive is a verbal that begins with the word *to;* the two words create a phrase. (*to see*)

Intensive pronoun. *See* **Pronoun.**

Interjection An interjection is a word or phrase used to express strong feeling. (*Oh!*)

Interrogative pronoun. *See* **Pronoun.**

Inverted sentence An inverted sentence is one in which the subject comes after the verb. (*Where are my shoes? Here is the prize.*)

Irregular verb. *See* **Verb.**

 L

Linking verb. *See* **Verb.**

 M

Main clause. *See* **Clause.**

Modifier A modifier makes another word more precise; modifiers most often are adjectives or adverbs. (*sunny* day, scowled *grimly*)

 N

Noun A noun names a person, a place, a thing, or an idea. (*Don, home, plant, honor*)

> An *abstract noun* names an idea, a quality, or a feeling. (*truth*)

> A *collective noun* names a group of things. (*herd*)

> A *common noun* is the general name of a person, a place, a thing, or an idea. (*girl, mountain, snow, logic*)

> A *compound noun* contains two or more words. (*folklore, sidewalk, son-in-law*)

> A *noun of direct address* is the name of a person being directly spoken to. (*Sam*, will you do the dishes?)

> A *possessive noun* shows who or what owns something. (*Carl's* jacket, the *sun's* light)

A **predicate noun** follows a linking verb and renames the subject. (She is a good *friend*.)

A **proper noun** names a particular person, place, or thing. (*Drew Smith, Maine, Eiffel Tower*)

Number A word is **singular** in number if it refers to just one person, place, thing, idea, or action, and **plural** in number if it refers to more than one person, place, thing, idea, or action. (The words s*he, hat,* and *eats* are singular. The words *they, hats,* and *eat* are plural.)

Object of a preposition The object of a preposition is the noun or pronoun after the preposition. (We climbed over the *fence*.)

Object of a verb The object of a verb receives the action of a verb. (They moved *mountains*.)

Participle A participle is often used as part of a verb phrase. (had *danced*) It can also be used as a verbal that functions as an adjective. (the *shining* star)

The **present participle** is formed by adding *-ing* to the present tense of a verb. (*Skating* rapidly, we circled the rink.)

The **past participle** of a regular verb is formed by adding *-d* or *-ed* to the present tense. (*Astonished,* they opened the gift.) The past participle of irregular verbs does not follow this pattern.

Past tense. *See* **Verb tense.**

Perfect tenses. *See* **Verb tense.**

Person The person of a pronoun depends on the noun to which it refers.

A **first-person** pronoun refers to the person speaking. (*I* jumped.)

A **second-person** pronoun refers to the person spoken to. (*You* sat.)

A **third-person** pronoun refers to some other person(s) or thing(s) being spoken of. (*They* sang.)

Personal pronoun. *See* **Pronoun.**

Phrase A phrase is a group of related words that lacks both a subject and a verb. (*gracefully leaping*)

Possessive A noun or pronoun that is possessive shows ownership. (*Dean's* job, *her* sister)

Possessive noun. *See* **Noun.**

Possessive pronoun. *See* **Pronoun.**

Predicate The predicate of a sentence tells what the subject is or does. (The deer *ran away quickly.*)

Predicate adjective. *See* **Adjective.**

Predicate noun. *See* **Noun.**

Predicate pronoun. *See* **Pronoun.**

Preposition A preposition relates a word to another part of the sentence or to the sentence as a whole. (Carlos read *about* the book.)

Prepositional phrase A prepositional phrase consists of a preposition, its object, and the object's modifiers. (king *of the dark forest*)

Present tense. *See* **Verb tense.**

Pronoun A pronoun replaces a noun or another pronoun. Some pronouns allow a writer or speaker to avoid repeating a particular noun. Other pronouns let a writer show a situation in which some information is not known.

A **demonstrative pronoun** singles out one or more persons or things. (*this* boat)

An **indefinite pronoun** refers to an unknown or unidentified person or thing. (*Someone* called.)

An **intensive pronoun** emphasizes a noun or pronoun. (She *herself* performed the surgery.)

An **interrogative pronoun** asks a question. (*Who* took my wrench?)

A **personal pronoun** refers to the first, second, or third person. (*I* spoke. *You* heard. *He* won.)

A **possessive pronoun** shows ownership. (*Your* story is in the folder. Are these notes *his*?)

A **predicate pronoun** follows a linking verb and renames the subject. (The caller was *he*.)

A **reflexive pronoun** reflects an action back on the subject of the sentence. (Ed treated *himself* to a soda.)

A **relative pronoun** relates a subordinate clause to the word it modifies in the main clause. (We gave our reasons, *which* were very strong.)

Pronoun-antecedent agreement. *See* **Agreement.**

Pronoun forms

The **subject form of a pronoun** is used when the pronoun is the subject of a sentence or follows a linking verb as a predicate pronoun. (*He* subtracted. It is *she*.)

The **object form of a pronoun** is used when a personal pronoun is the direct or indirect object of a verb or the object of a preposition or verbal. (I gave *her* a clue. with *them*)

Proper adjective. *See* **Adjective.**

Proper noun. *See* **Noun.**

Punctuation Punctuation clarifies the structure of sentences. See punctuation chart on facing page.

Reflexive pronoun. *See* **Pronoun.**

Regular verb. *See* **Verb.**

Relative pronoun. *See* **Pronoun.**

Run-on sentence A run-on sentence consists of two or more sentences written incorrectly as one. (*I said OK Jim said no.*)

S

Sentence A sentence expresses a complete thought. The chart below shows the four kinds of sentences.

Kind of Sentence	Example
Declarative (statement)	They went home.
Exclamatory (strong feeling)	We won!
Imperative (request, command)	Let the dog out.
Interrogative (question)	Where is Ronnie?

Sentence fragment A sentence fragment is a group of words that is only part of a sentence. (*As I walked; Was coming to the door*)

Subject The subject is the part of a sentence that tells whom or what the sentence is about. (*Gene* drove.)

Subject-verb agreement. *See* **Agreement.**

Subordinate clause. *See* **Clause.**

 V

Verb A verb expresses an action, a condition, or a state of being. (*swim, is, seems*)

The subject of an ***active verb*** performs the action of a sentence. (Danielle *soared*.)

The subject of a ***passive verb*** receives the verb's action or expresses the result of action. (The story *was told*.)

A ***helping verb*** is used with the main verb; together they make up a verb phrase. (*has* gone)

A ***linking verb*** expresses a state of being or connects the subject with a word or words that describe the subject. (The ice *feels* cold.)

The past tense and past participle of a ***regular verb*** are formed by adding -*d* or -*ed*. (*sail, sailed*) An ***irregular verb*** does not follow this pattern. (*grow, grew, grown*)

Verb phrase A verb phrase consists of a main verb and one or more helping verbs. (*should have been working*)

Verb tense Verb tense shows the time of an action or a state of being. (*go, went, am, seemed*)

The ***present tense*** places an action or condition in the present. (We *walk* down the street.)

The ***past tense*** places an action or condition in the past. (They *left*.)

The ***future tense*** places an action or condition in the future. (They *will go*.)

The ***present perfect tense*** describes an action that was completed in an indefinite past time or that began in the past and continues in the present. (*has observed, have danced*)

The ***past perfect tense*** describes one action that happened before another action in the past. (*had wondered, had analyzed*)

The ***future perfect tense*** describes a future event that will be finished before another future action begins. (*will have fallen*)

Verbal A verbal is formed from a verb and acts as a noun, an adjective, or an adverb. *See* **Gerund; Infinitive; Participle.**

Punctuation	Uses	Examples
Apostrophe (')	Shows possession Forms contractions	John's bike Sara's car We'll go. The train's here.
Colon (:)	Introduces a list or long quotation	these games: tennis, golf, and soccer
Comma (,)	Separates ideas Separates modifiers Separates items in series	I went home, and I fed my iguana. The bored, restless children. She brought apples, pears, and grapes.
Exclamation point (!)	Ends an exclamatory sentence	Let's win this tournament!
Hyphen (-)	Joins words in some compound nouns	sister-in-law, great-grandfather
Period (.)	Ends a declarative sentence Indicates most abbreviations	We saw white-tailed deer and crows. lb. oz. St. Mr. Sept.
Question mark (?)	Ends an interrogative sentence	How are you?
Semicolon (;)	Joins some compound sentences Separates items in series that contain commas	I'm fine; my brother broke his leg. Edwina found a tiny, flat stone; a dark, fragile fossil; and a shiny, spiky seashell.

Index of Fine Art

Index of Skills

Literary Concepts

Reading and Critical Thinking Skills

Grammar, Usage, and Mechanics

Writing Skills, Modes, and Formats

order of events, 44, 275, 829
narrative, 837
paragraphs, 827–29
persuasive writing, 845
problem-solution writing, 841
statement of purpose, 800
theme, 124, 179
thesis statement, 847
topics, 799–800, 858–59
topic sentence, 45, 828
transitions for, 829–30
Paragraphs, 827–29
Paraphrasing, 801
Peer response, 77, 213, 226, 278, 363, 416, 417, 493, 567, 631, 684, 689, 691, 755, 822–23, 854
Persuasive writing, 844–45
advertisement, 65, 105, 645, 658
fund-raising letter, 201
letter of recommendation, 539
pep talk, 666
persuasive essay, 684–91
Prewriting, 76–77, 212, 272–75, 362, 414–15, 492, 564–65, 628–30, 686–87, 754, 800–1, 820–21
Problem-solution writing, 838, 841
Purpose, setting, 74, 76–77, 129, 136, 212, 272–74, 362, 414–15, 492, 562–64, 630, 684–87, 798–800, 821
Reflecting on writing, 139, 279, 419, 567, 569, 687, 805, 825
Research report writing, 846–49
Revising and editing, 54, 75, 76, 78, 88, 104, 136, 214, 238, 270, 277–78, 345, 364, 417–18, 480, 505, 567, 568, 690, 731, 756, 804–5, 823–25, 875. *See also* Word processing.
Standards for evaluation
analysis, 842
cause-and-effect writing, 840
compare-and-contrast writing, 839
creative response, 78
critical essay, 364
eyewitness report, 569
firsthand narrative, 139
interpretive essay, 214
narrative writing, 836
personal response, 494
persuasive writing, 691, 844
poetry analysis, 632
problem-solution writing, 419, 841
research report, 805, 846
scene, 756
short story, 279
Transitions, 829–30
Word processing, 852–56
Writing about literature
analyzing point of view, 74–75
asking questions about a story, 360–61
changing a story element, 76–79
character analysis, 270
character "report card," 796
character sketch, 27

comparing and contrasting characters, 64, 296, 388, 481, 645
comparing and contrasting poems, 125, 129, 134, 437
comparing and contrasting points of view, 74–75
comparing and contrasting selections, 159, 202, 239, 250, 311, 330, 448
critical essay, 360–65
finding a message, 210–11
interpreting the meaning, 212–15
literary analysis, 210–15
overview, 137
personal response, 27, 28, 41, 42, 54, 62, 104, 257, 266, 317, 318, 330, 490–95, 510
play, 752–57
poetry analysis, 127, 132, 176, 177, 268, 410, 598, 628–35
responding as character, 27, 28, 42, 62, 104, 249, 250, 257, 399, 404, 410, 432, 539, 560, 645
responding to characters, 27, 29, 41, 62, 63, 64, 88, 104–5, 120, 159, 200, 216, 270, 285, 295, 378, 387, 398, 407, 432, 457, 480, 539, 560, 666
responding to plot, 120, 173, 238, 345, 387, 548, 581, 592, 617
responding to speaker of poem, 125, 127, 132, 176, 268, 410, 598
responding to theme, 505
rewriting, 54, 76–79, 88, 104, 120, 137, 238, 506
Writing from experience
eyewitness report, 562–69
family history, 136–43
persuasive essay, 684–91
problem-solution essay, 412–19
research report, 798–805
short story, 272–79

Vocabulary Skills

Antonyms, 42, 89, 202, 313, 346
Colloquialisms, 55
Connotation, 28, 689
Context clues, 83, 106, 251, 297, 379, 388, 449, 458, 506, 593, 813
Definitions, 42, 56, 122, 160, 161, 331, 405, 433, 482, 541, 619, 647, 658, 669
Descriptive language, 491, 834
Dialect, 369, 813
Difficult words, 161
Figurative language, 124, 131, 317, 630. *See also* Similes.
Film terminology, 459
Idioms, 121
Legal terminology, 459
Loaded language, 689
Metaphors, 124, 317
Nonstandard English, 258, 816
Root words, 266
Similes, 124, 131, 134, 174, 561

Slang, 657, 819
Specialized vocabulary, 450, 819
Synonyms, 161, 202, 227, 239, 312, 346, 388
Vocabulary charades, 673
Word choice, 210

Research and Study Skills

Bibliography. *See* Works Cited list.
Dictionaries, 852, 870
Commercial information services, 850.
Copyrighted material, 859
Electronic mail, 850
Electronic resources
    CD-ROMs, 851
    library, 800, 851
    on-line, 850
Indexes, 801, 847
Internet, 850
Library research, 800, 847, 851
Note taking, 801, 847
On-line resources, *See* Electronic resources.
Outlining, 848
Plagiarism, avoiding, 801, 849
Research activities
    Alaskan brown bear, 312
    Asian immigration to United States, 599
    Assiniboin tribe, 582
    brain, 458, 540
    buzzards, 731
    Cajun culture, 731
    cobras, 511
    creation myths, 751
    Day of the Dead, 714
    eagle's nest, 751
    echoes, 65
    ecosystems, 121
    Ecuador, 751
    elderly, 593
    environmental problems, 175
    exchange rates, 201
    folklore, 798–805
    forest conservation, 715
    Great Britain in 19th century, 200, 201
    guided research assignment, 798–805
    horned toads, 160
    icebergs, 481
    islands, 64
    Japanese screen painting, 105
    Mayas, 797
    Mexican history, 714, 715
    Native Americans, 271, 797
    Paul Revere's ride, 549
    physiology of sudden fright, 388
    railroads, history of, 730
    scientific abstracts, 540

    solar system, 506
    Spanish words, 160
    Special Olympics, 658
    storytelling contest, 714
    survey/poll, 201
    unusual poems, 130
    U.S. roads, 561
    Vietnam syndrome, 646
    welfare system, 296
    World War II, 266
Source cards, 801–2, 847
Sources of information, 798–801, 847–48. *See also* Gathering information *under* Writing Skills, Modes, and Formats.
    documenting, 846, 849
    electronic, 850–51
    expert advice, 800
    library, 800, 847, 851
    news reports, 798, 850
    personal background, 798
    previewing, 801
    prior knowledge, 798–99
World Wide Web, 850
Works Cited list, 804–5, 849

Speaking, Listening, and Viewing

Cooperative learning. See Working in groups.
Creative response
    art, 106, 174, 250, 296, 331, 379, 399, 411, 424, 433, 481, 510, 599, 667, 673, 678, 715, 758–59, 797
    booklet, 130
    collage, 14, 574, 751
    comic book, 618
    dance, 438
    diorama, 121, 783
    drama. *See* Dramatic reading/presentation.
    dust jacket, 782
    graph/time line, 173
    guided written assignment, 74–79
    illustrations, 105, 130, 271
    map, 345
    mobile, 751
    montage, 227
    multimedia presentation, 857–59
    music/song, 27, 121, 296, 318, 433, 549, 647, 678, 783
    photographs, 857
    poster, 160
    posterboard display, 599
    Spanish match game, 160
    standards for evaluating, 78
    storyboard, 331, 368
Dramatic reading/presentation
    audiotape, 330, 399
    group reading, 271
    how-to videotape, 405
    The Man Without a Country, 618

Index of Titles and Authors

Acknowledgments *(continued)*

Henry Holt and Company, Inc.: "The Clown," from *Real Ponies Don't Go Oink!* by Patrick F. McManus; Copyright © 1974, 1981, 1985, 1989, 1990, 1991 by Patrick F. McManus. By permission of Henry Holt and Company, Inc.

Vivian Hixson: "The Apprentice," by Dorothy Canfield Fisher. By permission of Vivian Hixson, executor.

St. Martin's Press, Inc., and Harold Ober Associates, Inc.: Excerpt from *All Things Bright and Beautiful* by James Herriot; Copyright © 1973 and 1974 by James Herriot. By permission of St. Martin's Press, Inc., and Harold Ober Associates, Inc.

Ruth Cohen, Inc.: "The Inn of Lost Time" by Lensey Namioka, from *Short Stories by Outstanding Writers for Young Adults,* edited by Donald R. Gallo. By permission of Ruth Cohen, Inc. All rights reserved by the author.

Ralph M. Vicinanza, Ltd.: "Collecting Team," from *Explorers of Space: Eight Stories of Science Fiction* by Robert Silverberg; Copyright © 1975 by Headline Publications, Inc. By permission of Robert Silverberg, c/o Ralph M. Vicinanza, Ltd.

F. E. Albi: "Moco Limping" by David Nava Monreal, from *Sighs and Songs of Aztlan;* Copyright © 1975 by F. E. Albi and J. G. Nieto. Reprinted by permission of F. E. Albi, editor.

HarperCollins Publishers, Inc.: "Mixed Singles," from *Sports Pages* by Arnold Adoff; Copyright © 1986 by Arnold Adoff. By permission of HarperCollins Publishers, Inc.

Marian Reiner: "Simile: Willow and Ginkgo" from *A Sky Full of Poems* by Eve Merriam; Copyright © 1964, 1970, 1973 by Eve Merriam. By permission of Marian Reiner.

Alfred A. Knopf, Inc.: "Sea Lullaby," from *Collected Poems of Elinor Wylie* by Elinor Wylie; Copyright 1921 by Alfred A. Knopf, Inc., renewed by William Rose Benet 1949. Reprinted by permission of Alfred A. Knopf, Inc.

Unit Two

University of Nevada Press: "The Horned Toad" from *That Constant Coyote* by Gerald W. Haslam; Copyright © 1990 by the University of Nevada Press. By permission of the University of Nevada Press.

Chronicle Books: "In a Neighborhood in Los Angeles" from *Body in Flames* by Francisco X. Alarcón; Copyright © 1990. By permission of Chronicle Books.

Estate of Beryl Markham: "The Splendid Outcast" from *The Splendid Outcast: Beryl Markham's African Stories* by Beryl Markham. By permission of the Estate of Beryl Markham and Laurence Pollinger Ltd., London.

Harcourt Brace & Company: "We Alone" from *Horses Make a Landscape Look More Beautiful* by Alice Walker; Copyright © 1984 by Alice Walker. "Mother and Daughter," from *Baseball and Other Stories* by Gary Soto; Copyright © 1990 by Gary Soto. By permission of Harcourt Brace & Company.

The Wilderness Society: "Hard Questions" by Margaret Tsuda, from *The Living Wilderness*, Autumn, 1970; Copyright © 1970 by The Wilderness Society. By permission of the the Wilderness Society.

Naoshi Koriyama: "oil crisis," from *Selected Poems, 1954–1985* by Naoshi Koriyama; Copyright © 1989 by Naoshi Koriyama. By permission of the author.

Plays, Inc.: *The Million-Pound Bank Note* by Walter Hackett, adapted from a story by Mark Twain, from *Radio Plays for Young People,* edited by Walter Hackett; Copyright © 1950 by Plays, Inc. By permission of Plays, Inc., Publishers, 120 Boylston St., Boston, MA 02116 USA.

Atheneum Books for Young Readers: "A Mother in Mannville," from *When the Whippoorwill* by Marjorie Kinnan Rawlings; Copyright 1936, 1940 Marjorie Kinnan Rawlings; copyright renewed © 1964, 1968 by Norton Baskin. Reprinted with the permission of Atheneum Books for Young Readers, an imprint of Simon & Schuster Children's Publishing Division.

William Morrow & Company, Inc.: "The World Is Not a Pleasant Place to Be," from *My House* by Nikki Giovanni; Copyright © 1972 by Nikki Giovanni. By permission of William Morrow & Company, Inc.

Cosmic House, Inc.: "White Mice" by Rubén Sálaz-Márquez, from *Voces: An Anthology of Nuevo Mexicano Writers,* edited by Rudolfo A. Anaya. By permission of Mr. Sal Justin of Cosmic House, Inc., Alameda, N.M., on behalf of Mr. Sálaz-Márquez.

Council Oak Publishing, Inc.: Excerpt from *Once upon a Time When We Were Colored* by Clifton L. Taulbert; Copyright © 1989 by Clifton L. Taulbert. By permission of Council Oak Publishing, Tulsa, Oklahoma.

Hazel Shelton Abernethy: "Home Front," from *Nacogdoches Sampler* by Hazel Shelton Abernethy. By permission of the author.

Norman Russell: "my enemy was dreaming" by Normal Russell, from *The Dekalb Literary Arts Review,* Fall/Winter 1969; Copyright © 1969 by Norman Russell. By permission of Norman Russell.

South Dakota Review: "Lost" by Bruce Ignacio, from *South Dakota Review,* Summer 1969; Copyright © 1969 by the South Dakota Review. By permission of South Dakota Review, Vermillion, SD.

Range Road Music Inc., Quartet Music Inc., and Abilene Music Inc.: "What a Wonderful World" by Bob Thiele and George David Weiss; Copyright © 1967 by Range Road Music Inc. and Quartet Music Inc. Copyright renewed and assigned to Range Road Music Inc., Quartet Music Inc., and Abilene Music. Used by permission. All rights reserved.

Unit Three

Paulette Childress White: "Getting the Facts of Life" by Paulette Childress White, from *Memory of Kin, Stories About Family by Black Writers,* edited by Mary Ellen Washington. Reprinted by permission of the author.

University of Georgia Press: "Appetizer," from *Ghost Traps* by Robert H. Abel; Copyright © 1991 by Robert H. Abel. By permission of University of Georgia Press, Athens, GA.

Harold Ober Associates: "Mother to Son" from *Selected Poems of Langston Hughes* by Langston Hughes; Copyright © 1959 by Langston Hughes, renewed 1990 by George Houston Bass. Reprinted by permission of Harold Ober Associates, Inc.

Doubleday Books: "the lesson of the moth," from *archy and mehitabel* by Don Marquis; Copyright 1927, renewed 1933. By permission of Doubleday Books, a division of Bantam Doubleday Dell Publishing Group, Inc.

Franklin Watts, Inc.: "Von," from *New Kids on the Block: Oral Histories of Immigrant Teens* by Janet Bode; Copyright © 1989 by Janet Bode. By permission of Franklin Watts, Inc., New York.

National Council of Teachers of English: "Foreign Student," from *English Journal,* May 1976, by Barbara Robinson; Copyright © 1976 by the National

Council of Teachers of English. By permission of National Council of Teachers of English.

William Morris Agency, Inc.: "The Hitchhiker" by Lucille Fletcher, from *Radio's Best Plays;* Copyright 1947 by Lucille Fletcher. By permission of the William Morris Agency, Inc., on behalf of the author.

Putnam Publishing Group and Jeremy P. Tarcher, Inc.: Excerpt from *The Beauty of the Beasts* by Ralph Helfer; Copyright © 1990. By permission of Putnam Publishing Group, Inc., and Jeremy P. Tarcher, Inc.

Orchard Books: "The Banana Tree," from *A Thief in the Village and Other Stories* by James Berry; Copyright © 1988 by James Berry. By permission of Orchard Books, New York.

Anna Palés Matos: "The Hurricane" by Luis Palés Matos, translated by Alida Wright Malkus. By permission of Anna Palés Matos.

HarperCollins Publishers, Inc.: "Tsali of the Cherokees," from *American Indian Mythology* by Alice Marriot and Carol K. Rachlin; Copyright © 1968 by Alice Marriot and Carol K. Rachlin. By permission of HarperCollins Publishers, Inc.

Crown Publishers, Inc.: "Oh, he's a crude oper-a-tor," from *Dave Barry Is Not Making This Up* by Dave Barry; Copyright © 1992, renewed 1994 by Dave Barry. By permission of Crown Publishers, Inc., a division of Random House, Inc.

Henry Holt and Company, Inc.: "The Runaway," from *The Poetry of Robert Frost* by Robert Frost, edited by Edward Connery Lathem; Copyright 1951 by Robert Frost. Copyright 1923, renewed © 1969 by Henry Holt and Co., Inc. By permission of Henry Holt and Co., Inc. Reprinted by permission of Henry Holt and Company, Inc.

Harcourt Brace & Company and Faber and Faber Ltd.: "Macavity the Mystery Cat," from *Old Possum's Book of Practical Cats* by T. S. Eliot; Copyright 1939 by T. S. Eliot and renewed © 1967 by Esme Valerie Eliot, reprinted by permission of Harcourt Brace & Company and Faber and Faber Ltd.

Unit Four

Gwendolyn Brooks: "Speech to the Young / Speech to the Progress-Toward," by Gwendolyn Brooks; Copyright © 1991 by Third World Press, Chicago. By permission of the author.

Peter Owen Ltd., Publishers: "A Man" by Nina Cassian, from *The Other Voice: Twentieth-Century Women's Poetry in Translation.* By permission of Peter Owen Ltd., Publishers, London.

Houghton Mifflin Company: "Who Is Dead in the White House?" from *Lincoln: A Photobiography* by Russell Freedman; Copyright © 1987 by Russell Freedman. By permission of Clarion Books/Houghton Mifflin Company. All rights reserved.

Zondervan Publishing House: *Gifted Hands* by Ben Carson, M.D.; Copyright © 1990 by Riview & Harold® Publishing Association. By permission of Zondervan Publishing House.

Alfred Brenner: *Survival* by Alfred Brenner; Copyright © 1957 by Alfred Brenner. By permission of Alfred Brenner.

Viking Penguin: "Battle by the Breadfruit Tree," from *On Safari* by Theodore J. Waldeck; Copyright 1940 by Theodore J. Waldeck, renewed © 1968 by Jo Besse McElveen Waldeck. Reprinted by permission of Viking Penguin, a division of Penguin Books USA, Inc.

Jack C. Haldeman II: "Playing for Keeps" by Jack. C. Haldeman II, from *Isaac Asimov's Science Fiction Magazine,* Copyright © 1982 by Davis Publications. Reprinted by permission of the author.

Bill Berger Associates, Inc.: "The Dinner Party" by Mona Gardner, from *The Saturday Review;* Copyright 1942, renewed © 1970 by *The Saturday Review.* By permission of Bill Berger Associates, Inc.

Daniel Keyes: "Flowers for Algernon" by Daniel Keyes, from *Magazine of Fantasy and Science Fiction,* April 1959, Vol. 16 #4. By permission of the author.

Russell and Volkening, Inc.: Excerpt from *Harriet Tubman: Conductor on the Underground Railroad* by Ann Petry; Copyright 1955, renewed © 1983. By permission of Russell and Volkening, Inc.

Unit Five

Firebrand Books: "Dancer," from *Simple Songs* by Vickie Sears; Copyright © 1990 by Vickie Sears. By permission of Firebrand Books, Ithaca, New York.

T. D. Allen: "Celebration" by Alonzo Lopez, from *The Whispering Wind: Poetry by Young American Indians,* compiled by Terry D. Allen. Used by permission of T. D. Allen and the author.

Pantheon Books: "The Moustache," from *Eight Plus One* by Robert Cormier; Copyright © 1975 by Robert Cormier. By permission of Pantheon Books, a division of Random House, Inc.

Larry Trejo & Associates: "The Other Pioneers" by Roberto Félix Salazar, from *The LULAC National,* July 1939; Copyright 1939 by The LULAC National. By permission of Larry Trejo & Associates.

Diana Chang: "Saying Yes" by Diana Chang, from *Asian American Heritage: An Anthology of Prose and Poetry,* edited by David Hsin-fu Wand. By permission of the author.

Plays, Inc.: *The Man Without a Country* by Walter Hackett, based on a story by Edward Everett Hale, from *Radio Plays for Young People,* edited by Walter Hackett; Copyright © 1950 by Plays, Inc. By permission of Walter Hackett and Plays, Inc., Publishers, 120 Boylston St., Boston, MA 02116 U.S.A.

Viking Penguin: "The Choice," from *The Portable Dorothy Parker* by Dorothy Parker; Copyright 1926, copyright renewed 1954 by Dorothy Parker. By permission of Viking Penguin, a division of Penguin Books USA, Inc.

Indian Historian Press: "I Belong" by A. Whiterock, from *The Weewish Tree,* February 1978. Reprinted by permission of Indian Historian Press.

Scribner: "There's This That I Like About Hockey, My Lad," from *The American Sporting Scene* by John Kieran; Copyright 1941 by John Kieran and Joseph Golinkin, renewed © 1988 by John Kieran. By permission of Scribner, a division of Simon & Schuster, Inc.

Diane Mei Lin Mark: "Rice and Rose Bowl Blues," by Diane Mei Lin Mark from *Breaking Silence, An Anthology of Contemporary Asian American Poets,* edited by Joseph Bruchac. Reprinted by permission of Diane Mei Lin Mark.

Jennifer Flannery, Literary Representative: "Stop the Sun" by Gary Paulsen, from *Boys' Life,* January 1986; Copyright © 1986 by Gary Paulsen. By permission of Jennifer Flannery as literary representative of Gary Paulsen.

Random House, Inc.: "Raymond's Run," from *Gorilla, My Love* by Toni Cade Bambara; Copyright © 1971 by Toni Cade Bambara.
"Keeping Time," from *Hitting Into the Wind* by Bill Meissner; Copyright © 1994 by Bill Meissner.

Used by permission of Random House, Inc.

Wall Street Journal: "Power of the Powerless," by Christopher de Vinck from the *Wall Street Journal,* April 10, 1985; Copyright © 1985 by Dow Jones & Company, Inc. By permission of the Wall Street Journal. All rights reserved.

Leroy V. Quintana: "A Fairy Tale" by Leroy V. Quintana, from *Hispanics in the United States: An Anthology of Creative Literature,* edited by Gary D. Keller and Francisco Jiménez. By permission of Leroy V. Quintana.

Wing Tek Lum: "My Mother Really Knew," from *Expanding the Doubtful Points* by Wing Tek Lum. By permission of the author.

The Society of Authors: "Sea Fever," from *Poems* by John Masefield. By the permission of The Society of Authors as the literary representative of the Estate of John Masefield.

Arte Publico Press: "Mi Madre," from *Chants* by Pat Mora; Copyright © 1984 by Arte Publico Press—University of Houston. By permission of Arte Publico Press.

Unit Six

Harcourt Brace & Company: "Paul Bunyan and the Winter of the Blue Snow," from *Big Men, Big Country: A Collection of American Tall Tales* by Paul Robert Walker; Copyright © 1992 by Paul Robert Walker.
"The First Flute," from *The Enchanted Orchard and Other Folktales of Central America* by Dorothy Sharp Carter; Copyright © 1973 by Dorothy Sharp Carter. By permission of Harcourt Brace & Company.

Guadalupe Baca-Vaughn: "The Souls in Purgatory," by Guadalupe Baca-Vaughn, from *Voces: An Anthology of Nuevo Mexicano Writers,* edited by Rudolfo A. Anaya. By permission of Guadalupe Baca-Vaughn.

The Globe Book Company: "The Girl in the Lavender Dress," retold by Maureen Scott, from *The American Anthology;* Copyright © 1987. By permission of the Globe Book Company.

Jackie Torrence: "Brer Possum's Dilemma" as told by Jackie Torrence, from *Homespun-Tales from America's Favorite Storytellers* . Reprinted by permission of Jackie Torrence, The Story Lady.

Judith Ortiz Cofer: "Aunty Misery," by Judith Ortiz Cofer. By permission of the author.

August House Publishers, Inc.: "M'su Carenco and Mangeur de Poulet," from *Cajun Folktales* by J. J. Reneaux. By permission of August House Publishers, Inc.

Alfred A. Knopf, Inc.: "Pecos Bill," from *American Tall Tales* by Mary Pope Osborne. Text copyright © 1991 by Mary Pope Osborne. Reprinted by permission of Alfred A. Knopf, Inc.

Scribner: "The Five Eggs," from *Stories from the Americas* by Frank Henius; Copyright 1944 Charles Scribner's Sons; copyright renewed © 1972 Gertrude Henius. By the permission of Scribner, an imprint of Simon & Schuster, Inc.

Watson Little, Ltd.: "Raven and the Coming of Daylight," from *Coyote the Trickster: Legends of the North American Indians* by Gail Robinson and Douglas Hill, originally published by Chatto and Windus, Ltd. By permission of Watson Little, Ltd.

Random House, Inc.: "Spotted Eagle and Black Crow" by Jenny Leading Cloud, from *The Sound of Flutes and Other Indian Legends;* Text copyright © 1976 by Richard Erdoes and Alfonso Ortiz. By permission of Pantheon Books, a division of Random House, Inc.

Staniels Associates: "Racing the Great Bear," from *Flying with the Eagle,*

Racing the Great Bear: Stories from Native North America by Joseph Bruchac; Copyright © 1993 by Joseph Bruchac. By permission of Staniels Associates as agent for BridgeWater Books, an imprint of Troll Associates, Inc.

Philomel Books: "Otoonah," from *Cut from the Same Cloth: American Women of Myth, Legend, and Tall Tale* by Robert D. San Souci; Copyright © 1993 by Robert D. San Souci. Reprinted by permission of Philomel Books, an imprint of the Putnam Publishing Group.

Alfred A. Knopf, Inc.: "The Woman in the Snow," from *The Dark Thirty: Southern Tales of the Supernatural* by Patricia McKissack; Copyright © 1992 by Patricia McKissack. Reprinted by permission of Alfred A. Knopf, Inc.

Gayle Ross: "Strawberries," a traditional Cherokee story retold by Gayle Ross. By permission of the author.

The Folktellers: "No News," retold by Connie Regan-Blake and Barbara Freeman. By permission of the Folktellers.

The following sections were prepared by **Ligature, Inc., of Chicago, Illinois:** Learning the Language of Literature, Writing about Literature, Writing from Experience, Writing Handbook, Multimedia Handbook, and Grammar Handbook.

Art Credits

The editors have made every effort to trace the ownership of all copyrighted art and photography found in this book and to make full acknowledgment for their use.

Author Photographs and Portraits
42, 56, 73, 89, 174, 227, 318 *bottom,* 625 AP/Wide World Photos, Inc. 63 George Desaintrat. 106 Richard McNamee. 122, 506, 541 Jay Kay Klein. 135 *top,* 438 *left* Copyright © Layle Silbert. 135 *bottom,* 620–621, 683 *left* The Granger Collection, New York. 180 Jean Weisinger. 251 Itar Tass/Sovfoto. 312 University of Georgia Press. 318 *top,* 411 *right* National Portrait Gallery, Smithsonian Institution, Washington, D.C./Art Resource, New York. 346 By permission of the Vassar College Library. 389 The Edgar Allan Poe Museum of the Poe Foundation, Richmond, Virginia. 411 *left* National Archives. 433, 549 Stock Montage. 438 *left* Howard Simmons. 449 *left* Copyrighted © Chicago Tribune Company. All rights reserved, used with permission. 449 *right* Museum of the City of New York. 458 Johns Hopkins Children's Center, Office of Public Affairs. 582 Courtesy of Firebird Books. 599 Gordon Robotham. 619 Culver Pictures. 658 The Schomburg Center for Research in Black Culture, The New York Public Library, Astor, Lenox and Tilden Foundations. 683 *right,* 726 Courtesy of Arte Publico Press. 749 Courtesy of Richard Erdoes.

Commissioned Art and Photography
2 *top,* 212 *bottom,* 279, 416–418, 569, 684, 685 *bottom,* 686 *top,* 687, 690, 754 *bottom,* 804 Allan Landau.
4, 5, 74, 76, 78, 88, 91 *background,* 126, 132, 136–144, 210–214, 229, 231–232, 237, 272–275, 278, 284, 300, 303, 305, 308, 310, 312, 320–323, 324

background, 325–326, 328 *background*, 331, 360–365, 391, 394 *background*, 395, 412–415, 416 *bottom*, 419, 490–494, 506, 514, 520, 525, 530, 538, 563–566, 568, 572–573 *background*, 624–626, 628–632, 659, 686 *bottom*, 688, 691, 710–713, 730, 732 *right*, 740–741, 750–759, 782 *top and bottom*, 805 Sharon Hoogstraten.

109–110, 112, 117–118 Mr. Stobbs. 279 Josh Neufeld. 320–322, 326 Annmarie Burke. 333, 334–335 *background* Meighan Depke. 440, 442, 445 Sarah Figlio. 584 Susi Kilgore. 675–676 Lee Tracy.

Maps: 694–695, 698–701, 716–717, 732–733, 760–761, 784–785 John Sandford. 695–696 Gordon Lewis. 697 Richard Waldrep. Maps on all other Previewing pages and on all Responding pages: Robert Voights.

Miscellaneous Art Credits

x Detail of mountain landscape, Sesshu Toyo (1420–1506). Six-fold screen, ink and color on paper, 161.0 cm × 351.2 cm, Japan, Muromachi Period, courtesy of the Freer Gallery of Art, Smithsonian Institution, Washington, D.C. (58.5). **xiv** Copyright © David Shannon. **xxi, 784** *bottom* Detail of *Aviary Triptych* (1992), Carol Cottone-Kolthoff. By permission of the artist. Copyright © 1992 Carol Cottone-Kolthoff. **xxiv–1** *Moebius II*, M. C. Escher. Copyright © 1995 M. C. Escher/Cordon Art, Baarn, Holland, all rights reserved. **2** *center* Copyright © Peter Dean/Tony Stone Images; *bottom* Tass/Sovfoto. **3** *top* Copyright © Jim Ballard/Tony Stone Images; *top insets* Courtesy of Jim Ochsenreiter; *bottom* Copyright © Mark E. Gibson. **14** Copyright © 1990 Paul Barton/The Stock Market. **17** Copyright © David Young Wolff/Tony Stone Images. **18** Detail of *Midtown Sunset* (1981), Romare Bearden. Courtesy of the Estate of Romare Bearden. **31** *detail* Copyright © Fred Lynch. **45** Confederate cap worn during the Battle of Gettysburg. Private collection. From *Echoes of Glory: Arms & Equipment of the Confederacy*. Copyright © 1991 Time-Life Books Inc. Photo by Larry Sherer. **46, 550** Reproduced from the collections of the Library of Congress. **47** *top* Courtesy of the Bureau of State Office Buildings, Commonwealth of Massachusetts. Photo by Douglas Christian; *bottom* The Bettmann Archive. **49** Private Edwin Jennison. Reproduced from the collections of the Library of Congress. **50** Walter Miles Parker. Reproduced from the collections of the Library of Congress. **58** Copyright © David Calver. **65, 67, 70, 73** Copyright © Renee Lynn/Tony Stone Images. **80–81** Copyright © 1996 Joseph Gillette/Swanstock. **82** P. Degginer/H. Armstrong Roberts. **83** Copyright © Andy Sacks/Tony Stone Images. **84** ZEFA-U.K./H. Armstrong Roberts. **88** From *All Creatures Great and Small* by James Herriot. Copyright © 1972 James Herriot. Used by permission of Bantam Books, a division of Bantam Doubleday Dell Publishing Group, Inc. **90** Copyright © Dana Levy/Photo Researchers, Inc. **119** UPI/Bettmann. **126** *Fido*, Laura McDougall. Copyright © Laura McDougall. **128** Brent Bear/H. Armstrong Roberts. **131** *top* Copyright © Lefever/Grushow from Grant Heilman Photography, Inc.; *bottom* Copyright © S. W. Carter/Photo Researchers, Inc. **138** *top insets* Courtesy of Linda Washington. **146–147** *background*, **422–423** *background*, **595** *background*, **596, 627** *top*, **665, 681, 724** Copyright © 1995 PhotoDisc, Inc. **148** Photo Library International Ltd./Leo de Wys Inc. **150, 155** Detail of *A medio día/Pedacito de mi corazón* [At high noon/A little piece of my heart] (1986), Carmen Lomas Garza. Gouache on cotton rag paper, 28″ × 20″. Copyright © 1986 Carmen Lomas Garza. Photo by Wolfgang Dietze.

160 Copyright © Steven C. Wilson/Entheos. **161** Paramount Film Library.
175 Copyright © David Hiser/Tony Stone Images. **176–178** *detail* Copyright
© Roxana Villa/SIS. **183** Christie's Images. **203** *top* Detail of *Colombiane*
(1978), Fernando Botero. © 1995 Fernando Botero/Licensed by VAGA, New
York, courtesy of Marlborough Gallery, New York; *bottom* Detail of *Yucateca
Sentada* [Seated Yucatecan woman](1979), Alfredo Zalce. Acrylic on wood,
60 cm × 80 cm, courtesy of the Mexican Fine Arts Center Museum, Chicago.
216–217 Copyright © Bernie Boston. **218** Copyright © Kevin Schafer/Tony
Stone Images. **220** Detail of Autumn leaf (1991), Hilary Page. Watercolor,
courtesy of the artist. From page 28 of *Watercolor Right from the Start*,
Watson-Guptill 1992. **224** *background* Detail of Autumn leaves (1991),
Hilary Page. Watercolor, courtesy of the artist. From p. 28 of *Watercolor
Right from the Start*, Watson-Guptill 1992. **245, 247** Detail of *Portrait of
Henri Matisse* (1905), André Derain. Tate Gallery, London/Art Resource, New
York. Copyright © 1996 Artists Rights Society (ARS), New York/ADAGP,
Paris. **259** The Granger Collection, New York. **260** Photo by Douglas K.
Meyer. **264** The Bettmann Archive. **266** D-day assault by U.S. troops,
Normandy, France. UPI/Bettmann. **273** *top left* Bourseiller/Durieux/
HOA–QUI, Paris. **298** Copyright © Ron Sanford/Tony Stone Images.
313 Copyright © Deborah Davis/Photonica. **315** Detail of *Candle, Eigg*
(1980), Winifred Nicholson. 58 cm × 43 cm, private collection. Copyright ©
The artist's family. Photo by John Webb. **331** Photos by Nicole Nelson.
332 Copyright © FPG International Corp. **347, 351, 354, 357–358** Copyright
© Michael Orton/Tony Stone Images. **366–367** Copyright © Craig Aurness/
Westlight. **370** Phototone. **379** Copyright © 1989 Bildarchiv Okapia/Photo
Researchers, Inc. **380** *top left* Archive Photos; *top right* The Bettmann
Archive. **381** *detail* Copyright © John Thompson. **405** *top,* **574** Copyright ©
Don Smetzer/Tony Stone Images. **426** *comb* Copyright © Kei Muto/Photonica;
watch Copyright © Susumu Yasui/Photonica. **428** Copyright © Susumu
Yasui/Photonica. **431** Copyright © Kei Muto/Photonica. **447** *left, near left*
The Bettmann Archive; *right, near right* UPI/Bettmann. **451** Courtesy of Johns
Hopkins Children's Center. **483** Copyright © James P. Rowan/Tony Stone
Images. **490–494** Breadfruit leaves courtesy of The National Tropical
Botanical Garden, Lawai, Kauai, Hawaii, and the Missouri Botanical Garden,
St. Louis. **496–497** Reuters/Bettmann. **511** Copyright © Alan Smith/Tony
Stone Images. **550** Reproduced from the collections of the Library of
Congress. **562** *photos* Copyright © Rick Stewart/Allsport USA. **564** *bottom*
Copyright © Bob Thomas/Tony Stone Images. **566** *top* Copyright © Al
Bello/Allsport. **576** *background* Copyright © Gary Holscher/Tony Stone
Images; *top* Assiniboine, or Gros Ventre, moccasins (about 1890), unknown
Native American craftworker from Fort Belknap Reservation, Montana.
Buckskin, rawhide, glass, 26 cm wide, Detroit Institute of Arts, Richard and
Marion Pohrt Collection (cp-141). Photo Copyright © Dirk Bakker/Detroit
Institute of Arts. **579** Copyright © Gary Holscher/Tony Stone Images.
602–603, 606–607 *background* Copyright © J. A. Nemeth/Picturesque Inc.
616 Copyright © The Bettmann Archive. **618** *top* Copyright © 1995 Classic
PIO Partners; *bottom America, Victoria & Albert and Black Eagle off the Isle
of Wight, 1851,* Tim Thompson. Oil on canvas, 20″ × 40″. Image used under
license with T. F. R. Thompson. **634–635** Copyright © Timothy Hursley.
648 Copyright © Cathlyn Melloan/Tony Stone Images. **649, 651–652, 654**
Copyright © M. Yamazaki/Photonica. **662** Copyright © Takahisa

Ide/Photonica. **663** Copyright © Steven Edson/Photonica. **674** Copyright © 1991 Arthur Tilley/FPG International Corp. **685** *top* Courtesy Image Club Graphics, Inc. For a free catalog call: 1-800-661-9410; *top inset* Copyright © Eric Haase/Contact Press Images. **691** *left inset* Wyatt McSpadden; *right inset* Courtesy Elizabeth Buggy. **698** *top* Kayak with a sealskin vest, Greenland. The Greenland Museum, Werner Forman/Art Resource, New York; *middle* Ballplayer (about A.D. 600–900), unknown Mayan artist. Copyright © Lee Boltin; *bottom* Shaman rattle in the form of a crane with a figure representing a shaman on its back, Native American artist from Northwest Coast. Field Museum of Natural History, Chicago, Werner Forman/Art Resource, New York. **699** *top left* The Granger Collection, New York; *top right* The Bettmann Archive; *left, second from top* Detail from Codex Borbonicus (about A.D. 1200–1500), unknown Aztec artist. Bibliothèque du Palais Bourbon, Paris, Giraudon/Art Resource, New York; *left, second from bottom* Moccasins (1830), unknown Iroquois craftworker. Buckskin, wool, cotton, glass beads. The Detroit Institute of Arts, Founders Society Purchase with funds from Flint Ink Corporation (1988.32). Photo by Dirk Bakker. Photo Copyright © 1995 The Detroit Institute of Arts; *lower left* The Granger Collection, New York; *center, second from bottom* Copyright © L. Nelson/H. Armstrong Roberts; *center bottom* Red Cloud. The Bettmann Archive; *bottom right* H. Armstrong Roberts. **700** Detail of *En busqueda de la paz* [In search of peace], Alfredo Linares. **701** *top* Detail of Illustration by Rockwell Kent. Courtesy of the Rockwell Kent Legacies; *bottom* Detail Copyright © Andrea Brooks. **716** Detail of *Brer Possum*, Barry Moser. From *Jump, Again!* by Van Dyke Parks, published by Harcourt Brace Jovanovich in 1987. Illustration Copyright © Barry Moser. Reprinted with permission from the artist. **717** *top* Detail from *His Hammer in His Hand*, Palmer C. Hayden (1890–1973). From the John Henry Series, Museum of African American Art, Los Angeles, Palmer C. Hayden Collection, gift of Miriam A. Hayden. Photo by Armando Solis; *center* Detail of *Twilight* (1971), Hubert Shuptrine. Copyright © 1971, 1994 Hubert Shuptrine, all rights reserved. **728** *Buzzards' Roost* (1985), Hubert Shuptrine. Copyright © by S. Hill Corporation. All rights reserved. Used with permission. **732** *left* Nootka raven spirit mask, northwest coast. The Philbrook Museum of Art, Tulsa, Oklahoma, Ellis Soper Collection. **733** *top* Detail of *When the Eagle Spoke to Me* (1979), Jerry Ingram (Choctaw). Watercolor on paper, 18″ × 24″, by permission of the artist; *bottom* Detail Copyright © Colin Poole. **758** *top* Copyright © The Walt Disney Company, photo courtesy of Photofest; *bottom* Portrait of Pocahontas (after 1616), unknown artist, English School, after an engraving by Simon de Passe. National Portrait Gallery, Smithsonian Institution, Washington, D.C./Art Resource, New York. **759** *bottom* The Bettmann Archive. **760** *Proud Hunter* (1987), Pudlo Pudlat. Stonecut, 21 1/2″ × 24″, by permission of the Amway Environmental Foundation. **761** *bottom* Illustration Copyright © 1992 Brian Pinkney. From *The Dark-Thirty* by Patricia McKissack, reprinted by permission of Alfred A. Knopf, Inc.; **761** *top*, **762** From *The Spirit of Native America* by Anna Lee Walters. Copyright © 1989, published by Chronicle Books. **785** *top, Dorothy and Netti* (1974), Alex Katz. Oil on canvas, 72″ × 96″, collection of the artist, courtesy of Marlborough Gallery, New York. Copyright © Alex Katz; *bottom, Strawberry Dance* (1983), G. Peter Jemison (Seneca Nation, Heron Clan). Mixed media on handmade paper, 22″ × 30″, private collection, by permission of the artist. **791** Illustration from *La Ruta*

Maya: Yucatan, Guatemala and Belize—a travel survival kit (first edition) by Tom Brosnahan. By permission of Lonely Planet Publications. **799** Reprinted by permission of Tribune Media Services. **836** Copyright © Jeff Schultz/ Alaska Stock Images. **838** Copyright © Terry Farmer/Tony Stone Images. **844** Copyright © James P. Rowan/Tony Stone Images. **846** UPI/Bettmann. **850** *Vaquero* [Cowboy] (1980), Luis Jimenez. Copyright © Luis Jimenez. Homepage (http://www.nmaa.si.edu) Copyright © National Museum of American Art, Smithsonian Institution. Netscape, Netscape Navigator, and the Netscape Communications Corporation Logo are trademarks of Netscape Communications Corporation. **853–855** Screen shots reprinted with permission from Microsoft Corporation. **856** Used with express permission. Adobe and Adobe Illustrator are trademarks of Adobe Systems Incorporated. **857, 859** Photofest.

Teacher Review Panels *(continued)*

Bonnie Garrett, Davis Middle School, Compton School District

Sally Jackson, Madrona Middle School, Torrance Unified School District

Sharon Kerson, Los Angeles Center for Enriched Studies, Los Angeles Unified School District

Gail Kidd, Center Middle School, Azusa School District

Corey Lay, ESL Department Chairperson, Chester Nimitz Middle School, Los Angeles Unified School District

Myra LeBendig, Forshay Learning Center, Los Angeles Unified School District

Dan Manske, Elmhurst Middle School, Oakland Unified School District

Joe Olague, Language Arts Department Chairperson, Alder Middle School, Fontana School District

Pat Salo, 6th Grade Village Leader, Hidden Valley Middle School, Escondido Elementary School District

FLORIDA

Judi Briant, English Department Chairperson, Armwood High School, Hillsborough County School District

Beth Johnson, Polk County English Supervisor, Polk County School District

Sharon Johnston, Learning Resource Specialist, Evans High School, Orange County School District

Eileen Jones, English Department Chairperson, Spanish River High School, Palm Beach County School District

Jan McClure, Winter Park High School Orange County School District

Wanza Murray, English Department Chairperson (retired), Vero Beach Senior High School, Indian River City School District

Shirley Nichols, Language Arts Curriculum Specialist Supervisor, Marion County School District

Debbie Nostro, Ocoee Middle School, Orange County School District

Barbara Quinaz, Assistant Principal, Horace Mann Middle School, Dade County School District

OHIO

Joseph Bako, English Department Chairperson, Carl Shuler Middle School, Cleveland City School District

Deb Delisle, Language Arts Department Chairperson, Ballard Brady Middle School, Orange School District

Ellen Geisler, English/Language Arts Department Chairperson, Mentor Senior High School, Mentor School District

Dr. Mary Gove, English Department Chairperson, Shaw High School, East Cleveland School District

Loraine Hammack, Executive Teacher of the English Department, Beachwood High School, Beachwood City School District

Sue Nelson, Shaw High School, East Cleveland School District

Mary Jane Reed, English Department Chairperson, Solon High School, Solon City School District

Nancy Strauch, English Department Chairperson, Nordonia High School, Nordonia Hills City School District

Ruth Vukovich, Hubbard High School, Hubbard Exempted Village School District

TEXAS

Anita Arnold, English Department Chairperson, Thomas Jefferson High School, San Antonio Independent School District

Gilbert Barraza, J.M. Hanks High School, Ysleta School District

Sandi Capps, Dwight D. Eisenhower High School, Alding Independent School District

Judy Chapman, English Department Chairperson, Lawrence D. Bell High School, Hurst-Euless-Bedford School District

Pat Fox, Grapevine High School, Grapevine-Colley School District

LaVerne Johnson, McAllen Memorial High School, McAllen Independent School District

Donna Matsumura, W.H. Adamson High School, Dallas Independent School District

Ruby Mayes, Waltrip High School, Houston Independent School District

Mary McFarland, Amarillo High School, Amarillo Independent School District

Adrienne Thrasher, A.N. McCallum High School, Austin Independent School Distric

Manuscript Reviewers *(continued)*

Maryann Lyons, Literacy Specialist, Mentor teacher, San Francisco Unified School District, San Francisco, California

Karis MacDonnell, Ed.D., Dario Middle School, Miami, Florida

Bonnie J. Mansell, Downey Adult School, Downey, California

Martha Mitchell, Memorial Middle School, Orlando, Florida

Nancy Nachman, Landmark High School, Jacksonville, Florida

Karen Williams Perry, English Department Chairperson, Kennedy Jr. High School, Lisle, Illinois

Julia Pferdehirt, free-lance writer, former Special Education teacher, Middleton, Wisconsin

Phyllis Stewart Rude, English Department Head, Mears Jr./Sr. High School, Anchorage, Alaska

Leo Schubert, Bettendorf Middle School, Bettendorf, Iowa

Gertrude H. Vannoy, Curriculum Liaison Specialist, Gifted and Horizon teacher, Meany Middle School, Seattle, Washington

Richard Wagner, Language Arts Curriculum Coordinator, Paradise Valley School District, Phoenix, Arizona

Stephen J. Zadravec, Newmarket Jr./Sr. High School, Newmarket, New Hampshire